Bernd Engler & Oliver Scheiding (Eds.)

Key Concepts in American Cultural History: From the Colonial Period to the End of the 19th Century

2nd Edition

Key Concepts in American Cultural History

From the Colonial Period
to the End of the 19th Century

2nd Edition

Bernd Engler & Oliver Scheiding (Eds.)

wvt Wissenschaftlicher Verlag Trier

Key Concepts in American Cultural History:
From the Colonial Period to the End of the 19th Century / 2nd Edition
Bernd Engler / Oliver Scheiding (eds.):
Trier: WVT Wissenschaftlicher Verlag Trier, 2007
   ISBN 978-3-88476-975-1

Cover illustration: Benjamin Tanner, *America Guided by Wisdom:
An Allegorical Representation of the United States Denoting Their
Independence and Prosperity* (engraving after a drawing by
John J. Barralet, 1815). Courtesy Library of Congress.

Cover Design: Brigitta Disseldorf

© WVT Wissenschaftlicher Verlag Trier, 2007
ISBN 978-3-88476-975-1

Alle Rechte vorbehalten
Nachdruck oder Vervielfältigung nur mit
ausdrücklicher Genehmigung des Verlags

WVT Wissenschaftlicher Verlag Trier
Postfach 4005, D-54230 Trier
Bergstraße 27, D-54295 Trier
Tel. (0651) 41503, Fax (0651) 41504
Internet: http://www.wvttrier.de
E-Mail: wvt@wvttrier.de

TABLE OF CONTENTS

TO THE READER   XV

EARLY CONCEPTUALIZATIONS OF AMERICA   1

1. Hartmann Schedel: *Das Buch der Chroniken* (1493)   4
2. Anonymous: "Typus Cosmographicus Universalis" (1532)   5
3. Petrus Apianus: "Charta Cosmographica" (1544)   6
4. Abraham Ortelius: "Theatrum Orbis Terrarum" (1570)   7
5. Heinrich Bünting: "Die gantze Welt in ein Kleberblat" (1581)   8
6. Christopher Columbus: *Journal of the First Voyage to America* (1492-1493)   9
7. Richard Hakluyt the Younger: "On Westerne Discoveries" (1584)   10
8. Edward Hayes: "A Report of the Voyage and Successe Thereof" (1583)   12
9. Sir George Peckham: *A True Reporte of the Late Discoveries* (1583)   14
10. Thomas Hariot: *Briefe and True Report* (1588)   16
11. François van den Hoeye: "America" (early 17th century)   18
12. Edward Hayes and Christopher Carleill: "Concerning a Voyage" (1592)   19
13. Michael Drayton: "To the Virginian Voyage" (1606)   20
14. Alexander Whitaker: *Good Newes from Virginia* (1613)   21
15. John Smith: *A Description of New England* (1616)   23
16. John Cotton: *Gods Promise to His Plantation* (1630)   25
17. Robert Cushman: "On the Lawfulnesse of Removing out of England into the Parts of America" (1622)   27
18. Francis Higginson: *New-Englands Plantation* (1630)   29
19. Thomas Tillam: "Uppon the First Sight of New-England" (1638)   30
20. Samuel Sewall: *A Little before Break-a-Day* (1701)   31
21. George Berkeley: "On the Prospect of Planting Arts and Learning in America" (1752)   32

IMAGES OF NATIVE AMERICANS   33

22. John Mandeville: *Mandeville's Travels* (1356/1496)   36
23. Amerigo Vespucci: *Letter to Piero Soderini* (1504)   36
24. Johann Froschauer: *Dise figur anzaigt uns das volck und insel* (1505)   37
25. Michel Eyquem de Montaigne: "Of the Caniballes" (1562)   38
26. Bartholomew de Las Casas: "Destruction of the Indes" (1583)   41
27. Jan Sadeler the Elder: "America" (1581)   44
28. Philippe Galle: "America" (c. 1581-1600)   45

29. Levinus Hulsius: *Kurtze Wunderbare Beschreibung* (1599) — 46
30. Crispijn van de Passe the Elder: "America" (early 17th century) — 47
31. Jan van der Straet: "Discovery of America" (1589) — 48
32. William Bradford: "Of Plymouth Plantation" (1629-1646) — 49
33. Mary Rowlandson: *The Soveraignty & Goodness of God* (1682) — 50
34. Cotton Mather: "The Life of the Renowned John Eliot" (1702) — 52
35. Cotton Mather: "Troubles of the Churches of New-England" (1702) — 55
36. Philip Freneau: "The Indian Convert" (1797) — 58
37. Washington Irving: "Philip of Pokanoket" (1814) — 59

PURITANISM IN THE NEW WORLD — 63

38. George Goodwin: *Automachia, or The Self-Conflict of a Christian* (1607) — 67
39. Philip Pain: *Daily Meditations* (1666) — 69
40. Anne Bradstreet: "The Flesh and the Spirit" (after 1650) — 70
41. Edward Taylor: "Meditation 26" (1698) — 73
42. Thomas Shepard: "The Autobiography" (1649) — 74
43. Anne Bradstreet: "To My Dear Children" (1672?) — 77
44. Thomas Hooker: *The Application of Redemption* (1657) — 79
45. Cotton Mather: "A Confession of Faith" (1702) — 81
46. Samuel Mather: *The Figures or Types of the Old Testament* (1667/68) — 87
47. *Blazing Stars, Messengers of God's Wrath* (1759) — 89
48. Ichabod Wiswall: *A Judicious Observation of That Dreadful Comet* (1683) — 90
49. Washington Irving: "Philip of Pokanoket" (1814) — 93
50. Nathaniel Hawthorne: *The Scarlet Letter* (1850) — 93
51. Cotton Mather: *A Christian in His Personal Calling* (1701) — 94
52. *The New-England Primer* (1762) — 98
53. *An Exhortation to Young and Old to Be Cautious of Small Crime* (1773) — 99
54. *The Ladder of Fortune* (1875) — 100
55. *The Tree of Life – The Christian* (between 1835 and 1856) — 101

PROVIDENTIAL READINGS OF AMERICAN HISTORY — 103

56. "Wheel of Fortune" (13th Century) — 107
57. Walter Raleigh: *History of the World* (1614) — 108
58. William Bradford: "Of Plymouth Plantation" (1629-1646) — 109
59. John [?] Pond: "Letter to William Pond March 15, 1630/1" — 115
60. William Bradford: "Of Boston in New-England" (c. 1653/1657) — 116
61. William Bradford: "A Word to New-England" (after 1653) — 118
62. John Winthrop: "A Modell of Christian Charity" (1630) — 118

63. John Winthrop: "Speech on Liberty" (1645) — 122
64. Cotton Mather: "Nehemias Americanus: Life of John Winthrop" (1702) — 123
65. Michael Wigglesworth: "God's Controversy with New-England" (1662) — 128
66. John Higginson: *The Cause of God and His People in New-England* (1663) — 136
67. Urian Oakes: *The Soveraign Efficacy of Divine Providence* (1677) — 138
68. Increase Mather: *The Doctrine of Divine Providence* (1684) — 140
69. Mary Rowlandson: *The Sovereignty & Goodness of God* (1682) — 142
70. Cotton Mather: "General Introduction," *Magnalia Christi Americana* (1702) — 147
71. Cotton Mather: "Letter to John Richards" (1692) — 150
72. Increase Mather: *Cases of Conscience Concerning Evil Spirits* (1693) — 152
73. Cotton Mather: "The Life of Sir William Phips, Knt." (1702) — 155

MILLENNIALISM — 159

74. John Cotton: *The Churches Resurrection* (1642) — 163
75. Joseph Mede: "A Coniecture Concerning *Gog* and *Magog*" (1650) — 164
76. John Cotton: *Exposition upon the Thirteenth Chapter of the Revelation* (1655) — 166
77. Increase Mather: *The Mystery of Israel's Salvation* (1669) — 168
78. Increase Mather: *The Day of Trouble Is Near* (1673) — 170
79. Samuel Sewall: *Phænomena Quædam Apocalyptica* (1697) — 175
80. Nicholas Noyes: *New-Englands Duty* (1698) — 178
81. Cotton Mather: "Venisti tandem? Or Discoveries of America" (1702) — 182
82. Jonathan Edwards: *The Present Revival of Religion in New-England* (1742) — 184
83. Philip Freneau: *On the Rising Glory of America* (1772) — 186
84. Timothy Dwight: *America* (1780?) — 190
85. Samuel Sherwood: *The Church's Flight into the Wilderness* (1776) — 191
86. Samuel Hopkins: *A Treatise on the Millennium* (1793) — 195
87. George Richards: "Anniversary Ode on American Independence" (1788) — 199
88. Philip Freneau: "On the Emigration to America and Peopling the Western Country" (1795) — 201
89. David Humphreys: *The Future Glory of the United States of America* (1804) — 202
90. "The Earth Must Burn / And Christ Return" (1817) — 205

GREAT AWAKENING & ENLIGHTENMENT — 207

91. Gilbert Tennent: *Solemn Warning to the Secure World* (1735) — 210
92. Jonathan Edwards: *Sinners in the Hands of an Angry God* (1742) — 211
93. Jonathan Edwards: *A Faithful Narrative* (1736) — 216
94. Jonathan Edwards: "An Account of His Conversion" (c. 1739) — 217
95. Nathan Cole: "The Spiritual Travels of Nathan Cole" (1741-1765) — 221
96. Alexander Rider: *Camp Meeting* (c. 1829) — 224

97. Frances Trollope: *Domestic Manners of the Americans* (1832) — 225
98. Charles Chauncy: *Enthusiasm Described and Cautioned Against* (1742) — 228
99. Thomas Paine: "Predestination" (1809) — 233
100. Thomas Paine: "Of the Religion of Deism" (1804) — 234
101. Benjamin Franklin: "Letter to Ezra Stiles" (1790) — 236
102. Philip Freneau: "On the Universality of the God of Nature" (after 1797) — 236
103. Benjamin Franklin: "The Way to Wealth" (1757) — 237
104. Benjamin Franklin: *The Autobiography* (1771-1789) — 240
105. Cotton Mather: *Bonifacius* (1710) — 252
106. Mark Twain: "The Late Benjamin Franklin" (1907) — 254
107. Joel Barlow: *The Vision of Columbus* (1787) — 255

REVOLUTIONARY PERIOD — 259

108. John Locke: *An Essay on Civil Government* (1689/1690) — 262
109. Jonathan Mayhew: *A Discourse Concerning Unlimited Submission and Non-Resistance to the Higher Powers* (1750) — 264
110. Benjamin Franklin: "Join, or Die" (1754) — 268
111. James Otis: *The Rights of the British Colonies Asserted and Proved* (1764) — 268
112. Philoleutherus: *The Constitutional Courant* (1765) — 270
113. Philo Patriæ: *The Constitutional Courant* (1765) — 272
114. *Resolutions of the Stamp Act Congress, October 19, 1765* — 274
115. John Dickinson: *A New Song* (1768) — 275
116. Anthony Benezet: *Thoughts on the Nature of War* (1766) — 277
117. Benjamin Franklin: *Magna Britannia: Her Colonies Reduc'd* (1767) — 278
118. *The Massachusetts Spy* (1774) — 279
119. Samuel Adams: "The Rights of the Colonists" (1772) — 279
120. Benjamin Franklin: "Rules by Which a Great Empire May Be Reduced to a Small One" (1773) — 281
121. Paul Revere: *The Bloody Massacre in Boston* (1770) — 283
122. John Hancock: *An Oration* (1774) — 284
123. *The Bostonians Paying the Excise-man* (1774) — 287
124. Paul Revere: *The Able Doctor* (1774) — 288
125. Thomas Jefferson: *A Summary View of the Rights of British America* (1774) — 288
126. Samuel Williams: *Discourse on the Love of Our Country* (1774) — 290
127. "Preamble to the Massachusetts Articles of War" (1775) — 293
128. Jacob Duché: "The American Vine" (1775) — 294
129. "Proclamation by the Great and General Court of the Colony of Massachusetts Bay, January 23, 1776" — 297
130. Thomas Paine: *Common Sense* (1776) — 298
131. Thomas Jefferson: *The Declaration of Independence* (1776) — 303

132.	John Witherspoon: *Dominion of Providence over the Passions of Men* (1776)	304
133.	David Ramsay: "On the Advantages of American Independence" (1778)	306
134.	"America Triumphant and Britannia in Distress" (1782)	309

EARLY REPUBLIC 311

135.	Anonymous: "While Commerce Spreads Her Canvas" (1787)	314
136.	Aspasio: "Anniversary Ode, for July 4th, 1789"	315
137.	John James Barralet: *Apotheosis of Washington* (1802)	317
138.	John Warren: *An Oration, Delivered July 4th, 1783*	318
139.	Benjamin Rush: "Thoughts upon Education Proper in a Republic" (1786)	322
140.	Joel Barlow: *An Oration Delivered July 4th, 1787*	325
141.	Thomas Green Fessenden: "An Ode" (1798)	328
142.	Daniel Webster: *An Oration, Pronounced the 4th Day of July, 1800*	330
143.	Nathanael Emmons: "God Never Forsakes His People" (1800)	332
144.	Thomas Jefferson: "Inauguration Address" (1801)	338
145.	*The Altar of Gallic Despotism* (1800)	341
146.	*Mad Tom in a Rage* (1802)	342
147.	Thomas Green Fessenden: "Almighty Power: An Ode" (1806)	343
148.	John Howard Payne: "Ode on American Independence" (1807)	344
149.	John Quincy Adams: *An Oration Delivered at Plymouth* (1802)	345
150.	Benjamin Tanner: *America Guided by Wisdom* (1815)	350
151.	Hugh Swinton Legaré: *An Oration, Delivered on the Fourth of July, 1823*	351
152.	John Quincy Adams: "Inaugural Address" (1825)	354
153.	James Gates Percival: "Ode. For the 50th Anniversary of Independence"	356

EXPANSIONISM 359

154.	Jedidiah Morse: *The American Geography* (1789)	362
155.	William Linn: *The Blessings of America* (1791)	362
156.	Charles Paine: *An Oration, Pronounced July 4, 1801*	365
157.	Samuel Woodworth: "Columbia, the Pride of the World" (1820s)	367
158.	*California: The Cornucopia of the World* (1883)	368
159.	*Missouri Is Free!* (1880s)	369
160.	Henry David Thoreau: "Walking" (1862)	369
161.	Lewis Cass: "The Policy and Practice of the United States in Their Treatment of the Indians" (1827)	370
162.	Andrew Jackson: "Second Annual Message" (1830)	374
163.	John Marshall: "Cherokee Nation v. Georgia" (1831)	377
164.	Anonymous: "Oregon Territory" (1832)	379
165.	Lansford W. Hastings: *Emigrants' Guide to Oregon and California* (1845)	382

166. *Unanimous Declaration of Independence*, by the Delegates of the People of Texas (1836) — 382
167. William E. Channing: "A Letter on the Annexation of Texas" (1837) — 384
168. *Anti-Texas Meeting at Faneuil Hall!* (1838) — 385
169. John L. O'Sullivan: "The Great Nation of Futurity" (1839) — 386
170. Robert Charles Winthrop: "New England Society Address" (1839) — 387
171. John L. O'Sullivan: "Annexation" (1845) — 389
172. James K. Polk: "Inaugural Address" (1845) — 391
173. "Land of Liberty" (1847) — 395
174. William Gilpin: "Manifest Destiny" (1846) — 396
175. Anonymous: "The Popular Movement" (1845) — 397
176. John L. O'Sullivan: "The True Title" (1845) — 397
177. Thomas Hart Benton: *Speech on the Oregon Question* (1846) — 398
178. Anonymous: "The Destiny of the Country" (1847) — 400
179. Herman Melville: *White-Jacket* (1850) — 404
180. Anonymous: "Providence in American History" (1858) — 405
181. Walt Whitman: "Passage to India" (1871) — 408
182. John Gast: "American Progress" (1872/1874) — 410
183. Fanny F. Palmer: *Across the Continent* (1868) — 412
184. John Fiske: "Manifest Destiny" (1885) — 413
185. Frederick Jackson Turner: "The Significance of the Frontier" (1893) — 414
186. Frederick Jackson Turner: "The West and American Ideals" (1914) — 419
187. Frank Norris: "The Frontier Gone at Last" (1902) — 420

TRANSCENDENTALISM — 423

188. Rembrandt Peale: "The Beauties of Creation" (1800) — 426
189. Ralph Waldo Emerson: "The Rhodora" (1834/1839) — 427
190. Ralph Waldo Emerson: "Two Rivers" (1856/1858) — 427
191. Christopher Pearse Cranch: "Correspondences" (1841) — 428
192. Sampson Reed: *Observations on the Growth of the Mind* (1826) — 429
193. William Ellery Channing: "Likeness to God" (1828) — 431
194. Orestes A. Brownson: "Cousin's Philosophy" (1836) — 433
195. George Ripley: *Discourses on the Philosophy of Religion* (1836) — 437
196. Ralph Waldo Emerson: *Nature* (1836) — 440
197. Francis Bowen: "Transcendentalism" (1837) — 442
198. Ralph Waldo Emerson: "The American Scholar" (1837) — 444
199. Ralph Waldo Emerson: "Divinity School Address" (1838) — 446
200. Henry David Thoreau: *Walden* (1854) — 448
201. Margaret Fuller: *Summer on the Lakes* (1843) — 453
202. George Bancroft: "On the Progress of Civilization" (1838) — 459

203.	Ralph Waldo Emerson: "The Young American" (1844)	461
204.	Orestes A. Brownson: "The Laboring Classes" (1840)	462
205.	Amos Bronson Alcott: *Doctrine and Discipline of Human Culture* (1836)	464
206.	Robert Owen: *First Discourse on a New System of Society* (1825)	466
207.	George Ripley: "Letter to Ralph Waldo Emerson" (1840)	469
208.	George Ripley: "Advertisement" and "Introductory Notice" (1845)	470
209.	Ralph Waldo Emerson: "Life and Letters in New England" (1883)	472

WOMEN'S ROLES IN AMERICAN SOCIETY 475

210.	Anne Bradstreet: "An Epitaph on My Dear Mother (1643)	478
211.	Anne Bradstreet: "The Prologue" (1650)	478
212.	John Winthrop: *Journal* (1645)	480
213.	Milcah Martha [Hill] Moore: "The Female Patriots" (1768)	481
214.	Anonymous: "On Reading an Essay on Education" (1773)	482
215.	Abigail Adams: "Letter to John Adams" (1776)	483
216.	Benjamin Rush: *Thoughts upon Female Education* (1787)	483
217.	Judith Sargent Murray: "Thoughts upon Self-Complacency" (1784)	487
218.	Judith Sargent Murray: "On the Equality of the Sexes" (1790)	489
219.	Anonymous: "On Female Education" (1794)	493
220.	Anonymous: "Female Influence" (1795)	494
221.	Emma Willard: *A Plan for Female Education* (1819)	499
222.	*Keep within Your Compass* (c. 1785-1805)	503
223.	Catharine E. Beecher: *Improvements in Education* (1829)	504
224.	Thomas R. Dew: "Characteristic Differences between the Sexes" (1835)	505
225.	Jonathan F. Stearns: *Female Influence* (1837)	506
226.	Lydia Sigourney: *Letters to Mothers* (1838)	509
227.	Heman Humphrey: *Domestic Education* (1840)	510
228.	Lewis Jacob Cist: "Woman's Sphere" (1845)	512
229.	Anonymous: "Influence of Woman" (1840)	514
230.	Anonymous: "Pastoral Letter of the Massachusetts Congregationalist Clergy" (1837)	516
231.	Sarah Moore Grimké: "Province of Woman" (1837)	517
232.	Sarah Moore Grimké: "Social Intercourse of the Sexes" (1837)	519
233.	Angelina Emily Grimké: *Letters to Catherine E. Beecher* (1837)	520
234.	Anonymous: "Woman" (1841)	523
235.	Margaret Fuller: *Woman in the Nineteenth Century* (1844)	526
236.	Mrs. E. Little: "What Are the Rights of Woman?" (1847)	531
237.	*Declaration of Sentiments*, Seneca Falls Convention (1848)	531
238.	Theodore Parker: *A Sermon of the Public Function of Woman* (1853)	534
239.	Lucy Stone: "The Marriage of Lucy Stone under Protest" (1855)	537

xii   Key Concepts in American Cultural History

240.	*Age of Iron: Man as He Expects to Be* (1869)	539
241.	Catherine E. Beecher / Harriet Beecher Stowe: "The Christian Family" (1869)	539
242.	Sarah Grand: "The New Aspect of the Woman Question" (1894)	541
243.	Ouida: "The New Woman" (1894)	543
244.	Max O'Rell: "Petticoat Government" (1896)	545
245.	Rebecca L. Leeke: "The New Lady" (1896)	547
246.	John Paul MacCorrie: "The War of the Sexes" (1896)	548
247.	"New Woman" (1915)	551

SLAVERY   553

248.	*To Be Sold* (1769)	556
249.	Phillis Wheatley: "On Being Brought from Africa to America" (1786)	554
250.	William Byrd II: "Letter to John Perceval, Earl of Egmont" (1736)	555
251.	Thomas Jefferson: *Notes on the State of Virginia* (1788)	558
252.	John Woolman: *Considerations on Keeping Negroes* (1762)	561
253.	St. John De Crèvecœur: *Letters from an American Farmer* (1782)	564
254.	*Documents of the American Colonization Society* (1816/1817)	569
255.	David Walker: *Appeal to the Colored Citizens of the World* (1829)	572
256.	William Lloyd Garrison: "Truisms" (1831)	577
257.	George B. Cheever: *God's Hand in America* (1841)	579
258.	Albert Barnes: *An Inquiry into the Scriptural View of Slavery* (1846)	580
259.	Angelina E. Grimké: "Appeal to the Christian Women of the South" (1836)	583
260.	John C. Calhoun: "Slavery a Positive Good" (1837)	586
261.	Matthew Estes: *A Defence of Negro Slavery* (1846)	588
262.	*Am I Not a Man and a Brother?* (late 1830s)	591
263.	*Caution!! Colored People of Boston* (1851)	592
264.	George Fitzhugh: "Negro Slavery" (1854)	593
265.	Henry Highland Garnet: "Address to the Slaves of the United States of America" (1843)	595
266.	William Lloyd Garrison: "Universal Emancipation" (1831)	599
267.	William Lloyd Garrison: "Address to the Slaves of the United States" (1843)	600
268.	Frederick Douglass: *What to the Slave Is the Fourth of July?* (1852)	602
269.	William Lloyd Garrison: *No Compromise with Slavery* (1854)	609
270.	*Black and White Slaves: England* (c. 1841)	612
271.	*Black and White Slaves: America* (c. 1841)	613
272.	William J. Grayson: *The Hireling and the Slave* (1855)	614
273.	Theodore Parker: "Letter to Francis Jackson" (1859)	615

CIVIL WAR & RECONSTRUCTION — 619

274. Daniel Webster: "The Constitution and the Union Speech" (1850) — 622
275. *The Address of the People of South Carolina* (1860) — 624
276. Jefferson Davis: "First Inaugural Address" (1861) — 626
277. Abraham Lincoln: "First Inaugural Address" (1861) — 628
278. Abraham Lincoln: *Emancipation Proclamation* (1863) — 632
279. "The Promise of the Declaration of Independence Fulfilled" (1870) — 633
280. Abraham Lincoln: "Second Inaugural Address" (1865) — 634
281. Frederick Douglass: "What the Black Man Wants" (1865) — 635
282. Thomas Nast: "He Wants a Change, Too" (1876) — 638
283. *The Freedman's Bureau!* (1866) — 639
284. *The Two Platforms* (1866) — 640
285. "The Great Labor Question from a Southern Point of View" (1865) — 641
286. Thomas Nast: "Colored Rule in a Reconstructed (?) State" (1874) — 642
287. Frederick Douglass: "The Future of the Colored Race" (1886) — 643
288. E. Malcolm Argyle: "Report from Arkansas" (1892) — 644
289. Booker T. Washington: "The Atlanta Exposition Address" (1895) — 645
290. *The Dogwood Tree* (1908) — 648

GILDED AGE: PROBLEMS AT HOME AND ABROAD — 649

291. William M. Evarts: "Oration" (1876) — 652
292. *Leslie's Illustrated Historical Register of the Centennial Exposition* (1876) — 655
293. Henry W. Grady: "The New South" (1886) — 656
294. Charles L. Brace: *The Dangerous Classes of New York* (1872/1880) — 659
295. Edward Crapsey: "Prostitution" (1872) — 661
296. Josiah Strong: "Perils. – The City" (1885) — 664
297. Jacob A. Riis: *How the Other Half Lives* (1890) — 667
298. Henry George: *Progress and Poverty* (1879) — 669
299. William Graham Sumner: "The Challenge of Facts" (c. 1878-1882) — 675
300. James W. Buel: "The Rich" (1882) — 679
301. Thure de Thulstrup: "The Anarchist Riot in Chicago" (1886) — 681
302. *Constitution of the Knights of Labor* (1878) — 681
303. "To the Workingmen of America" (1883) — 682
304. John Most: *The Beast of Property* (1884) — 685
305. "The Commercial Vampire" (1898) — 688
306. August Spies: "Speech at Haymarket Trial" (1886) — 688
307. "The Bosses of the Senate" (1889) — 691
308. Andrew Carnegie: "Wealth" (1889) — 692
309. Mary Elizabeth Lease: "Monopoly Is the Master" (1890) — 696

310.	T. McCants Stewart: "Popular Discontent" (1891)	696
311.	Frederick Saunders / T. Bangs Thorpe: *The Progress and Prospects of America* (1855)	699
312.	Thomas Nast: "Uncle Sam's Thanksgiving Dinner" (1869)	701
313.	*Chinese Exclusion Act* (1882)	702
314.	Emma Lazarus: "The New Colossus" (1883)	702
315.	Josiah Strong: "Perils – Immigration" (1885)	703
316.	*The Magic Washer – The Chinese Must Go* (c. 1886)	705
317.	Carl Schurz: "Manifest Destiny" (1893)	706
318.	Josiah Strong: "The Anglo-Saxon and the World's Future" (1885)	709
319.	Albert Beveridge: "The March of the Flag" (1898)	710
320.	William Jennings Bryan: "Imperialism" (1900)	713
321.	Theodore Roosevelt: "Fourth Annual Message" (1904)	715
322.	Theodore Roosevelt: *The New Nationalism* (1910)	717

ABBREVIATIONS 721

INDEX 723

TO THE READER

> A dominant power may legitimate itself by *promoting* beliefs and values congenial to it; *naturalizing* and *universalizing* such beliefs so as to render them self-evident and apparently inevitable; *denigrating* ideas which might challenge it; *excluding* rival forms of thought, perhaps by some unspoken but systematic logic; and *obscuring* social reality in ways convenient to itself.
> (Terry Eagleton, *Ideology: An Introduction*, London: Verso, 1991, 5f.)

In recent years, numerous anthologies have been published in Early American Studies – among them Myra Jehlen's and Michael Warner's *The English Literatures of America, 1500-1800* (1997), Reiner Smolinski's *The Kingdom, the Power & the Glory: The Millennial Impulse in Early American Literature* (1998), Susan Castillo's and Ivy Schweitzer's *The Literatures of Colonial America* (2001), Carla Mulford's *Early American Writings* (2002), and David D. Hall's *Puritans in the New World* (2004) – all of them greatly broadening and enriching the student's awareness of the diversity of America's cultural development since colonial times. They seek to remap the field of American culture, either with a particular focus on the literary production of 'British America' (Jehlen/Warner), the proliferation of a prominent idea such as millennialism (Smolinski), the multiplicity of trans-national voices that shaped the cultures of the Americas from precolonial times to the late eighteenth century (Castillo/Schweitzer and Mulford), or the centrality of Puritanism for the formation of America (Hall). In comparison to the vast scope of texts and cultures which these collections explore in their attempts at revisioning earlier, more monolithic notions of American culture, this anthology pursues less 'expansive' intentions. It responds to a need to supply students in Europe and elsewhere with a less specialized, but nevertheless comprehensive, tool for investigating American culture. This need is clearly proven by the fact that a second edition became necessary within less than two years after its original publication in 2005.

Key Concepts in American Cultural History does not seek comprehensiveness by covering a vast array of texts and the diverse cultures they display, but aims at tracing some of the more pervasive ideas and concepts that shaped America from the early settlements to the end of the nineteenth century. Although many of the concepts that the texts of this anthology highlight have a defining power for the present, they do not capture the diversifications and many new trends of twentieth-century American culture. The editors are aware of the fact that this will require a further volume that they hope to see realized in the near future.

Given the fact that this anthology intends to trace prominent ideological concepts, it wishes to follow a twofold approach: It wants to focus on historical contexts that encompass central ideas and thoughts which are closely linked to particular epochs in American culture. It is also based on the observation that, in spite of its diversity, American culture is informed by a relatively limited set of ideas which were highly adaptable to new social and political situations. These ideas could thus be easily appropriated to individual and communal needs for orientation and sense-making in a world that changed dramatically as America developed from a colonial society to an industrialized world power. The fact that the number of those concepts that keep defining American culture is quite restricted has proven to be an enormous advantage in the formation of an 'American ideology,' as the constant re-articulation of these concepts and their ensuing 'visibility' in the public sphere led to a wide-spread identification with the beliefs and cultural norms they represented and propagated. The 'key concepts' that this anthology foregrounds – for instance the belief that America was singled out by divine providence as a model for the world – have been continuously rearranged in ever new configurations in order to explain current events and define political goals and agendas. Thus, to give just one example, the notion of America's particular mission was circulated in the late sixteenth century in English promotional texts, in which their authors advertized the 'New World' as a second Eden. Then it was transformed into the comforting ideology asserting the existence of a 'New Covenant' between God and his chosen people. In this way, it served as a means of moral sustenance in times of distress which resulted, for instance, from bad harvests, droughts, or other disasters as well as constant colonial and Indian warfare during the period of the early settlements. The same belief was then employed in the service of reform movements (both in terms of individual conversion and of communal utopias during the Great Awakening or the nineteenth century), but also made its appearance in the form of 'Manifest Destiny' in which it functioned as the principle justification for America's mid-nineteenth-century expansionism and later imperialism.

Similar continuities and transformations can be investigated in the shape of various other 'key concepts' which this anthology traces in its fourteen sections, for instance within the context of "Early Conceptualizations of America," "Images of Native Americans," "Providential Readings of American History," "Millennialism," or "Expansionism." Although these sections often highlight particular historical phases in the development of American society and its diverse cultures, they should not function as confining lenses and instruments of 'mental compartmentalization.' Instead, this anthology wants to encourage cross-segmental and diachronic readings that make the student aware of the continuities as well as discontinuities of ideological 'formations' which are incessantly 're-formed' in response to the changing functions they have to perform in order to promote, naturalize, and universalize beliefs by which cultures negotiate contesting interpretations of social reality.

The editors wish to thank all those who have made the publication of this anthology possible by their unfailing dedication: first of all, those who were willing to share their expertise and knowledge, and took part in this project by providing contributions and introductions to the sections – Melanie Fritsch, Dennis Hannemann, Charles T. Johnson, Frank Kelleter, Isabell Klaiber, Günter Leypoldt, Gesa Mackenthun, Frank Obenland, Margit Peterfy, Clemens Spahr, and Jan Stievermann –, then all those who invested their invaluable energy and proficiency in the process of editing and proof-reading the documents, and getting this anthology ready for publication – Lilian Chaitas, Christiane Goldkamp, Jonathan Majors, Eva-Maria Rettner, Caroline Reuter, Bettina Steiner, Christian Stindt, Maria Constanze Schwenk, and, once again, Melanie Fritsch, Frank Obenland, and Clemens Spahr.

Tübingen and Mainz
July 2007

Bernd Engler
Oliver Scheiding

Editorial policy

The texts collected in this anthology follow the editions quoted at the end of each document. According to our editorial principles, all texts have been reproduced in their earliest available print version without any modernization in spelling, punctuation, ligatures, etc., with the exception of a standardization of the frequently exchangeable use of "u" and "v" in seventeenth- and early eighteenth-century texts according to modern orthography, as well as the substitution of the "long s" ["ſ"] by a "round s" ["s"] and of the "ß" by a "double s" ["ss"].

In order to make the texts more accessible to the modern-day reader, we have standardized all idiosyncrasies of print that can be found in many seventeenth- and eighteenth-century texts, particularly on title pages. The printers' frequent mixing of two or even more display types such as bold, italics, spaced, gothic, etc., in one text is standardized in the following way: all capital letters were replaced by small capitals and gothic letters by italics; all italics and small capitals remained; spaced letters and boldface were eliminated.

Ongoing e-Text Project

The editors will supply additional documents on an electronic text website that complements the publication of this anthology (*http://www.amerikanistik.uni-mainz.de/key/*).

Copyright and other restrictions which apply to publication and other forms of distribution of images

The images reproduced in this publication are presented for educational and research purposes only. For those images that are not in the public domain, we have attempted to obtain permission from copyright holders or commercial stock image suppliers. The authors would be interested to hear from any copyright owners who are not properly identified.

Transmission or reproduction of protected items beyond that allowed by fair use requires the written permission of the copyright owners and may be subject to copyright fees and other legal restrictions.

EARLY CONCEPTUALIZATIONS OF AMERICA

Early conceptualizations of the 'New World' unfold a double process of inventing America and redefining Europe. The European encounter with the New World challenged many of the well established affirmations of previous writers about geography, religion, and history. The idea of a tri-partite world was deeply embedded in European thought. According to medieval cosmography, the world consisted of three continents: Europe, Asia, and Africa. This Christian division of the world mirrored the *orbis terrarum* already known to classical geographers, into which the new fourth continent and its people were difficult to assimilate. As sixteenth-century writers and mapmakers began to acknowledge the existence of a new continent to the West of Europe (cf. docs. 2-4), they were forced to find answers to three problems that the discovery of America had raised: First, America's geography had to be incorporated into Europe's mental image of the natural world. Second, the Native Americans had to be assigned a place among the peoples of mankind. Finally, America had to be integrated into Europe's conception of historical progress.

The liminal position of America, which resulted from the division of the world in three parts, can be seen in Heinrich Bünting's "Die gantze Welt in ein Kleberblat" (1581, doc. 5). Bünting's map builds the world around Jerusalem as the spiritual center of the earth. Excluding America, the map arranges the continents of Europe, Asia, and Africa, like the three leaves of a clover plant, around the Holy Land. Bünting's triple division of the world also exposes the distribution of power. The map advocates the leading role of the Catholic Church, and conceives of America in terms of Rome's global legacy. Bünting's map also suggests that Protestant nations like England play only a marginal role in both the history of salvation and the conquest of the New World.

Since the Middle Ages, geographical limits coincided with the boundaries of 'humanity.' Monstrous creatures with two heads, three arms and the like were supposed to inhabit those regions beyond known geographical boundaries. Hartmann Schedel's *Das Buch der Chroniken* (1493, doc. 1), published shortly after Columbus's discovery of the New World, unfolds the regional and geographical scattering of the sons of Noah that held a prominent place throughout the sixteenth and seventeenth centuries. The Bible maintains that the descendants of Noah peopled the three parts of the world. Europe belonged to the sons of Japheth, Africa to those of Ham, and Asia to the sons of Shem. Many illustrations of America that appeared in Europe depicted the New World as the land of cannibals and devilish fiends. As such, the people of America had no capacity for Christianity, and there was, therefore, never any possibility that they might achieve salvation.

Incorporating North America into the geographical views of the Protestant nations, English promoters of colonization drew a dividing line between the cannibals that inhabited 'America,' a name initially used to describe the southern regions of Spain's dominion in the New World, and the savages who occupied its northern portion. While the mental and social worlds of the cannibals were the outcome of the Devil's handiwork, the northern Indians were intelligible and would thus welcome the achievements of the English nation. Therefore, most English colonizers conceptualize the region of North America in terms of England's prominent role in the history of salvation. Carrying the light of the "True Church" into the vast regions of America implies that America has remained in darkness for such a long time since it was God's plan to open the continent for English expansion only at the beginning of the Reformation.

Among the European nations that considered the New World as a western extension of their imperial agendas, throughout most of the sixteenth century, Spain took the lead in both exploiting the land and converting the Indians. Not only Columbus's *Journal of the First Voyage to America* (doc. 6), but also François van den Hoeye's allegorical illustration of America (doc. 11) reveal the materialist motivations behind the Spanish conquest and settlement. Contrary to the Spanish colonization efforts overseas, England remained, however, a late-comer. Thus, the English promotional literature in this section draws attention to a strong anti-Spanish, pro-expansion lobby that began in the late sixteenth century when English privateers, merchants, and clergymen offered an alternative foreign policy much more dedicated to transatlantic conquest than the official views of Elizabeth, James I., and Charles I. Their tracts and pamphlets show that a militant Protestantism sustained English expansion throughout the seventeenth century.

At the intersection of the diverse colonizing projects and interests in late sixteenth-century England, was Richard Hakluyt the younger. In 1589, a year after the defeat of the Spanish Armada, he published his massive epic of English colonization, *The Principall Navigations, Voiages, and Discoveries of the English Nation*. Various promotional tracts and reports of exploration and settlement followed in subsequent years. Among these, was Thomas Hariot's *A Briefe and True Report of the New Found Land of Virginia* (1588, doc. 10), an eyewitness account of Sir Walter Raleigh's second voyage to Virginia, which included compelling descriptions of North Carolina Algonquian native culture. These accounts, as well as the accompanying maps and illustrations of the New World, marked the beginning of what historians have called the "imperial archive," a collection of documents and a fund of knowledge that influenced and propelled English expansion overseas.

The English propagandists of trade and settlement included in this section rearrange the triple division of the world as they move the spiritual center to the North. Since the sons of Japheth, as the sons of "true Religion," now occupy England, pamphlets like Hakluyt's *Discourse of Western Planting* (1584, doc. 7) proclaim the enlargement of Japheth in terms of England's extension to the West. English writers relocate the center of salvation by interpreting the discovery of America in light of the progressive course of Reformation history. In a co-authored pamphlet, Edward Hayes and Christopher Carleill unfold the westward course of civilization (doc. 12). They endow America with the vision of a Christianizing mission and cherish the idea of an empire in the west. As such, the woodlands and the inhabitants of North America finally enhanced the mental picture that Protestant England formed of America and inspired the colonial imagination of British America.

Thomas Hariot's report was the first published book about America by an English explorer. The pamphlet stirs the reader's fantasies of everything being "farre greater" in the New than in the Old World. While Hariot describes the geography, climate, vegetation, wildlife, and the manners of the "natural inhabitants" of Virginia, John Smith (doc. 15) turns the settlement of New England into a secular venture of exploration and appropriation of the land. His emphasizing of planting and building a plantation by "Gods blessing and his owne industrie" anticipates the rhetoric of opportunity that later characterizes the American Dream.

The religious writers that this section highlights – Alexander Whitaker, John Cotton, and Robert Cushman – expound on England's special role in the Atlantic world that had long been heralded by Richard Hakluyt and the apologists of English colonization overseas. Their promotional efforts involved the recovery of the newly discovered world and its inhabitants, from the influence of "Popish Spain," and the prevention of its being further corrupted by French Catholicism. Whitaker, who became known as the apostle of Virginia, was the first writer to advertise a belief in an English plantation assigned by God's providence (doc. 14). To promulgate the idea of a Puritan migration to the New World, eminent ministers such as John Cotton and Robert Cushman (cf. docs. 16 and 17) recalled the concept of improvement that had made an early appearance in Thomas More's *Utopia* (1516). More had stated that those who keep the land idle, forfeit legal possession of it. Conceptualizing America as a vast and empty space to be improved by Puritan settlers justified the possession of the land.

The three poems by Thomas Tillam, Samuel Sewall, and George Berkeley (docs. 19-21) that conclude this section contain an ironic twist on the exclusion of the New World from the history of salvation, since it becomes obvious that the fourth continent, once the devil's domain, now regenerates the Old World. The inclusion of America into eschatological schemes brings about the progressive conviction of America's manifest destiny. It is the West that turns into a field of futurity. Accordingly, ideas of progress and manifest destiny that have shaped conceptualizations of America during the colonial era as well as the revolutionary and early national periods, result from the rearticulation of Christian global designs during the sixteenth century.

Oliver Scheiding

1. Hartmann Schedel
Das Buch der Chroniken (1493)

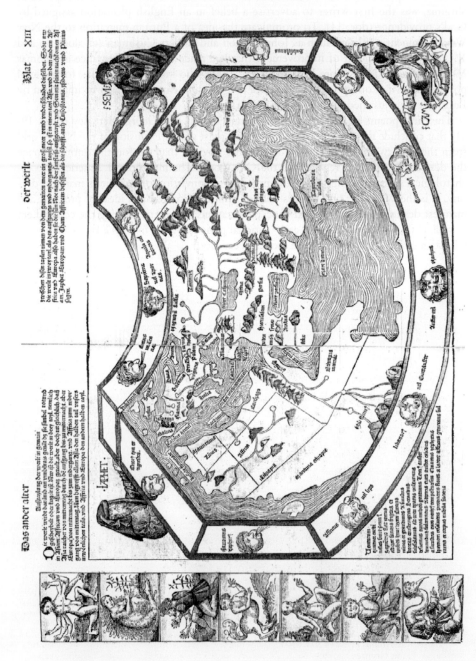

Source: Hartmann Schedel (1440-1514). *Das Buch der Chronicken und Geschichten (Liber Chronicarum)*. Nuremberg: Anton Koberger, 1493.

2. Anonymous
"Typus Cosmographicus Universalis" (1532)

Source: Anonymous [Sebastian Münster (1500?-1568)]. "Typus Cosmographicus Universalis." Woodcut in Simon Grynaeus' (1493-1541) *Novis Orbis Regionum ac Insularum Veteribus Incognitarum*. Basle: Johann Hervagius, 1555 [1532]. This oval map of the world was first published in 1532 as a supplement to the anthology of travel reports entitled *Novus Orbis* by Grynaeus and Johann Huttich, with a commentary by Sebastian Münster. The map is considered to be Münster's work.

3. Petrus Apianus
"Charta Cosmographica" (1544)

Source: Petrus Apianus (1495-1552). "Charta Cosmographica, cum Ventorum Propria Natura et Operatione." *Cosmographia Petri Apiani*. Antwerp: G. de Bonte, G. Coppens de Diest, 1544. The map was printed in Antwerp by R. Gemma Frisius together with Peter Apian's cosmography of 1524.

4. Abraham Ortelius
"Theatrum Orbis Terrarum" (1570)

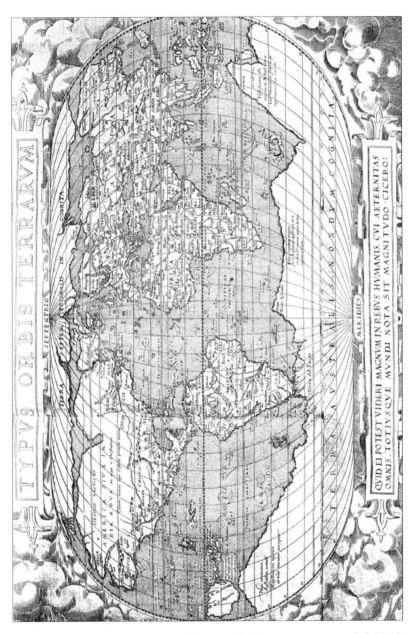

Source: Abraham Ortelius (1527-1598). "Theatrum Orbis Terrarum" (1570). Included in the 1st edition of Richard Hakluyt the Younger (1552-1616): *The Principal Navigations, Voyages, Traffiques & Discoveries of the English Nation, Made by Sea or Overland to the Remote & Farthest Distant Quarters of the Earth at Any Time Within the Compasse of These 1600 Yeares*. 2 vols. London 1598-1600, Vol. 1, n.p.

5. Heinrich Bünting
"Die gantze Welt in ein Kleberblat" (1581)

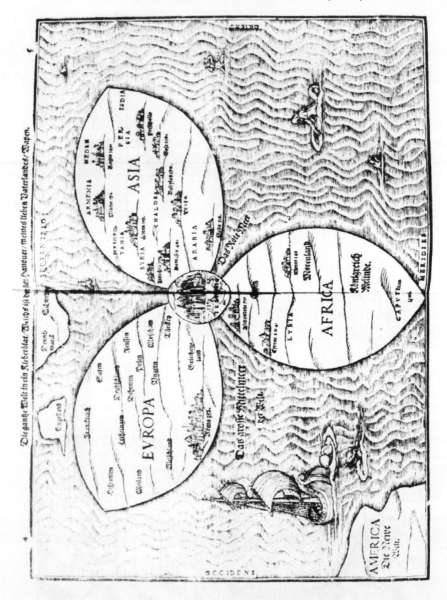

Source: Heinrich Bünting (1545-1606). "Die gantze Welt in ein Kleberblat" *Itinerarium Sacræ Scripturæ. Das ist Ein Reisebuch, Uber die gantze heilige Schrifft: in zwey Bücher getheilt. Das Erste Theil Begreifft alle Reisen der lieben Patriarchen Richter Könige Propheten Fürsten. Das Ander gehet auff das Newe Testament und zeiget an wie die Jungfraw Maria Joseph die Weisen aus Morgenlannd der Herr Jesus Christus und die lieben Apostel gereiset haben. Aus den glaubwirdigsten und fürnembsten Büchern zusamen gezogen und Geometrischerweise ausgerechnet*. Helmstedt: Jacobum Lucium Siebenbürger, 1581.

6. Christopher Columbus
Journal of the First Voyage to the New World (1492-1493)

Sunday 21 October
At the tenth hour I arrived here at this Cabo del Isleo[1] and anchored, and the caravels[2] [did] likewise; [...] for if the others already seen are very beautiful and green and fertile, this one is much more so and with large and very green groves of trees. Here there are some big lakes and over and around them the groves are marvelous. And here and in all of the island the groves are all green and the verdure like that in April in Andalusia. And the singing of the small birds [is so marvelous] that it seems that a man would never want to leave this place. And [there are] flocks of parrots that obscure the sun; and birds of so many kinds and sizes, and so different from ours, that it is a marvel. And also there are trees of a thousand kinds and all [with] their own kinds of fruit and all smell so that it is a marvel. I am the most sorrowful man in the world, not being acquainted with them. Because I am quite certain that all of them are things of value; and I am bringing samples of them, and likewise of the plants. [...] Later some of the men approached us, and one came up to us here. I gave him some bells and some small glass beads and he was very pleased and happy. And so that our friendship would increase and that something would be asked of them, I ordered that he be asked for water. And after I went on shipboard they soon came to the beach with their calabashes[3] full and were delighted to give it to us; and I ordered that they be given other trifling little strings of glass beads and they said that in the morning they would come around. I wanted to fill here all the water jars of the ship. Then, if weather permits, I will soon depart to go around this island until I have speech with this king and see if I can get from him the gold that I hear that he wears. [...]

Monday 22 October
All this night and today I stayed waiting [to see] if the king of this place or other persons would bring gold or something else of substance; and there came many of these people, like the others of the other islands, naked and painted, some of them with white, some with red, some with black, and so on in many fashions. They brought javelins and balls of cotton to barter, which they traded here with some sailors for pieces of broken glass cups and for pieces of clay bowls. Some of them were wearing pieces of gold hanging from their noses, and they willingly gave it for a bell of the sort [put] on the foot of a sparrow hawk and for small glass beads; but it is so little that it is nothing. For it is true that any little thing given to them, as well as our coming, they considered great marvels; and they believed that we had come from the heavens. [...]

Tuesday 23 October
I should like to leave today for the island of Cuba, which I believe must be Cipango[4] according to the indications that these people give of its size and wealth, and I will not delay here any longer [...]. And since one should go where there is large-scale commerce, I say that there is no reason to delay but [reason] to go forward and investigate much territory until we encounter a very profitable land [...].

---

[1] Island's cape.
[2] A small, light sailing ship.
[3] A type of pumpkin with a hard shell, suitable for transporting liquids.
[4] Japan.

Monday 12 November

[The Admiral, i.e. Columbus, left] to go to an island that the Indians he had with him strongly affirmed was called Baneque, where, as they said by means of signs, the people of it collected gold at night on the beach with lanterns, and afterward, with a hammer, they said that they would make bars of it. And in order to go to it, it was necessary to head east by south. [...] He said that the Sunday before, the eleventh of November, it had seemed to him that it might be well to capture some people of that river in order to take them to the king and queen so that they might learn our language and in order to know what there is in that land, and so that, returning, they might be interpreters for the Christians, and so that they would take on our customs and faith. Because I saw and recognize (says the Admiral) that these people have no religious beliefs, nor are they idolaters. They are very gentle and do not know what evil is; nor do they kill others, nor steal; and they are without weapons and so timid that a hundred of them flee from one of our men even if our men are teasing them. And they are credulous and aware that there is a God in heaven and convinced that we come from the heavens; and they say very quickly any prayer that we tell them to say, and they make the sign of the cross, †. So that Your Highnesses ought to resolve to make them Christians: for I believe that if you begin, in a short time you will end up having converted to our Holy Faith a multitude of peoples and acquiring large dominions and great riches and all of their peoples for Spain. Because without doubt there is in these lands a very great quantity of gold; for not without cause do these Indians that I bring with me say that there are in these islands places where they dig gold and wear it on their chests, on their ears, and on their arms, and on their legs; and they are very thick bracelets. And also there are stones, and there are precious pearls and infinite spicery. [...]

Source: Christopher Columbus (1451-1506). *The Diario of Christopher Columbus's First Voyage to America, 1492-1493: Abstracted by Fray Bartolomé de las Casas*. Transcribed and Translated into English, with Notes and a Concordance of the Spanish, by Oliver Dunn and James E. Kelley, Jr. Norman and London: University of Oklahoma Press, 1989, 105-111, 141-145.

7. Richard Hakluyt the Younger
"A Particuler Discourse Concerninge the Greate Necessitie and Manifolde Commodyties That Are Like to Growe to This Realme of Englande by the Westerne Discoveries Lately Attempted" (1584)

Cap. 1.
  That This westerne discoverie will be greately for thinlargemente of the gospell of Christe whereunto the Princes of the reformed Relligion are chefely bounde amongeste whome her Maiestie ys principall /

[...] It remayneth to be thoroughly weyed and considered by what meanes and by whome this moste godly and Christian worke may be performed, of inlarginge the glorious gospell of Christe, and reducinge of infinite multitudes of these simple people that are in errour into the righte and perfecte waye of their salvacion: [...] Then it is necessarie for the salvacion of those poore people which have sitten so longe in darkenes and in the shadowe of deathe that preachers shoulde be sente unto them: But by whome shoulde these preachers be sente? By them no doubte which have taken upon them the protection and defence of the Christian faithe: Nowe the Kinges and Queenes of England have the name of defendours of the faithe:[5] By which title I thincke they are not onely chardged to mayneteyne and patronize the faithe of Christe, but also to inlarge and advaunce the same [...]. Nowe yf they [the Spaniards] in their superstition by meanes of their plantinge in those partes have don so greate things in so shorte space, what may wee hope for in our true and syncere Relligion, proposinge unto our selves in this action not filthie lucre nor vaine ostentation as they in deede did, but principally the gayninge of the soules of millions of those wretched people, the reducinge of them from darkenes to lighte, from falshoodde to truthe, from dombe Idolls to the lyvinge god, from the depe pitt of hell to the highest heavens. [...] Even so wee whiles wee have soughte to goo into other Contries (I woulde I mighte say to preache the gospell) God by the frustratinge of our actions semeth to forbydd us to followe those courses, and the people of America crye oute unto us their nexte neighboures to comme and helpe them, and bringe unto them the gladd tidinges of the gospell. [...][6]

Cap. 11.
    That the Spaniardes have exercised moste outragious and more then Turkishe cruelties in all the west Indies, whereby they are every where there becomme moste odious unto them whoe woulde ioyne with us or any other moste willinglye to shake of their moste intollerable yoke, and have begonne to doo yt already in divers places where they were lordes heretofore /

    [...] As touchinge the mayne firme lande wee are certaine that our Spaniardes by their cruelties and cursed doinges have dispeopled and made desolate more then tenne Realmes greater then all Spaine comprisinge therein also Arragon and Portingale, and twise as moche or more lande then there is from Civill to Ierusalem, which are above a thousande leagues: which Realmes as yet unto this presente day remaine in a wildernes and utter desolation, havinge bene before time as well peopled as was possible /

    Wee are able to yelde a goodd and perfect accompte that there is within the space of 40 yeres by these said tyranies and develishe doinges of the Spaniardes don to deathe uniustly and tyranously more then xii millions of soules men women & children. [...]

    [...] And surely the more I thincke of the spanishe monarchie, the more me thinketh it is like the Empire of Alexander the greate, which grewe upp sooddenly and sooddenly upon his deathe was rente and dissolved for faulte of lauful yssue. [...]

Cap. 15.
    That spedie plantinge is divers fitt places is most necessarie upon these laste luckye westerne discoveries for feare of the danger of beinge prevented by other nations which have the like intention: with the order thereof and other reasons therewith all alleaged.

    [...] Contrarywise withoute this plantinge in due tyme wee shall never be able to have full knowledge of the language manners and custommes of the people of those Regions, neither shall wee be able throughly to knowe the riches and commodities of the Inlandes

---

[5] The manuscript here bears a marginal note: "The Prynces of England called the defendors of the faithe."
[6] Although in the first chapter of his manuscript, Hakluyt stresses the religious motivation for English colonization overseas, he also reveals the commercial interests most British explorers pursued. This is particularly evident in chapter 3, which is entitled: "That this westerne voyadge will yelde unto us all the commodities of Europe, Affrica, and Asia as farr as wee were wonte to travell, and supplye the wantes of all our decayed trades."

with many other secretes whereof as yet wee have but a small taste. And althoughe by other meanes wee mighte attaine to the knowledge therof, yet beinge not there fortified and strongly seated, the frenche that swarme with multitude of people, or other nations might secretly fortifie and settle themselves before us hearinge of the benefite that is to be reaped of that voyadge, and so wee should beate the bushe and other men take the birdes: wee shoulde be at the chardge and travell, and other men reape the gaine. [...]

Cap. 18.
That The Queene of Englandes Title to all the west Indies or at the leaste to as moche as is from Florida to the Circle articke is more lawfull and righte then the Spaniardes or any other christian Princes. /

[...] So to conclude whether wee beleve the Testimonie of Peter Martir and Ferdinandus Columbus[7] which affirme that Christopher Columbus discovered the firme firste in anno 1498, a greate and large tracte of the continente of the Indies was discovered by Gabot[8] and the englishe above twoo yeres before, To witt in the yere 1496 in the monethes of Iune and Iuly: [...] yet wee of England are the firste discoverers of the continent above a yere and more before them [...] which is above three yeres before the Spaniarde or any other for the kinges of Spaine had any sighte of any parte of the firme lande of the Indies [...].

> Source: Richard Hakluyt the Younger (1552-1616). *A Particuler Discourse Concerning the Greate Necessitie and Manifolde Commodyties That Are Like to Growe to This Realme of Englande by the Westerne Discoveries Lately Attempted, Written in the Yere 1584. by Richarde Hackluyt of Oxforde Known as Discourse of Western Planting.* Ed. David B. Quinn and Alison M. Quinn. London: Hakluyt Society, 1993, 8, 11, 52, 55-56, 60, 71-72, 88, 95-96.

8. Edward Hayes
"A Report of the Voyage and Successe Thereof" (1583)

[...] But most assuredly, the onely cause of religion hitherto hath kept backe, and will also bring forward at the time assigned by God, an effectuall and complet discovery and possession by Christians both of those ample countries and the riches within them, hitherto concealed: whereof notwithstanding God in his wisedome hath permitted to be revealed, from time to time, a certaine obscure and misty knowledge, by little and little, to allure the mindes of men that way [...] and thereby to prepare us unto a readiness for the execution of his will against the due time ordained, of calling thouse pagans unto Christianity.

In the meane while, it behoveth[9] every man of great calling, in whom is any instinct of inclination unto this attempt, to examine his owne motions: which if the same proceed of ambition or avarice, he may assure himselfe it commeth not of God, and therefore can

---

[7] Pedro Mártir De Anghiera (1457-1526) was a historian of Spanish explorations, who became a member of Emperor Charles V's Council of the Indies (1518). He collected documents from the various discoverers, including Christopher Columbus, and wrote *De Orbe Novo* in 1511 (published 1516). Ferdinand Columbus was Christopher Columbus' son. Ferdinand travelled on the fourth and final voyage to the New World in 1502 and compiled an account of that journey in which he defended his father's rights as vice-roy of the Indies.
[8] John Cabot (1450-1499; Giovanni Caboto) was a navigator who explored America in 1497 and 1498 in the name of Henry VII, and thus laid the groundwork for the later English claim to Canada.
[9] To behoof: to oblige.

not have confidence of Gods protection and assistance against the violence (els irresistable) both of sea, and infinite perils upon the land [...].

Otherwise, if his motives be derived from a vertuous & heroycall minde, preferring chiefly the honor of God, compassion of poore Infidels captived by the devill, tyrannizing in most wonderfull and dreadfull maner over theyr bodyes and soules: advancement of his honest and well disposed countreymen, willing to accompany him in such honourable actions: reliefe of sundry people within this realme distressed[10] [...].

And the same, who feeleth this inclination in himselfe, by all likelyhood, may hope, or rather confidently repose in the preordinance of God, that in this last age of the world (or likely never) the time is complet of receiving also these Gentils into his mercy: And that God will raise him an instrument to effect the same. It seeming probable by event of precedent attempts made by the Spanyardes and French sundry times: that the countryes lying North of *Florida*, God hath reserved the same to be reduced unto Christian civilitie by the English nation.

For not long after that Christopher Columbus had discovered the Islands and continent of the West Indies for Spaine, John and Sebastian Cabot made discovery also of the rest from *Florida* Northwards, to the behoofe of England.

And whensoever afterwards the Spanyards (very prosperous in all theyr Southerne discoveries) did attempt any thing into *Florida* and those regions inclining towards the North: they prooved most unhappy, and were at length discouraged utterly by the hard and lamentable successe of many both religious and valiant in armes, endevoring to bring those Northerly regions also under the Spanish iurisdiction: as if God had prescribed limits unto the Spanish nation which they might not exceed: as by theyr owne gests recorded may be aptly gathered.

The French, as they can pretend lesse title unto these Northerne parts then the Spanyard, [...] did but review that [land] before discovered by the English nation, usurping upon our right, and imposing names upon countryes, rivers, bayes, capes, or headlandes, as if they had beene the first finders of those coasts [...].

Then seeing the English nation onely hath right unto these countryes of America from the cape of *Florida* Northward by the privilege of first discovery, unto which Cabot was authorised by regall authority, & set forth by the expence of our late famous king Henry the seventh: Which right also seemeth strongly defended on our behalfe, by the powerfull hand of almighty God, withstanding the enterprises of other nations: It may greatly incourage us, upon so iust ground, as is our right, and upon so sacred an intent, as to plant religion, (our right and intent being meet foundations for the same:) to prosecute effectually unto a full possession of those so ample & pleasant countries apperteining unto the crowne of England: the same (as is to be coniectured by unfallible arguments of the worlds end approching) being now arrived unto the time by God prescribed of theyr vocation, if ever theyr calling unto the knowledge of God may be expected. Which also is very probable by the revolution and course of Gods word and religion, which from the beginning hath mooved from the East, towards, and at last unto the West, where it is like to end, unlesse the same begin againe where it did in the East, which were to expect a like world againe. But we are assured of the contrary by the prophesie of Christ, whereby we gather, that after his word preached throughout the world, shall be the end. And as the Gospell when it descended Westward beganne in the South, and afterward spred into the North of Europe: even so, as the same hath begunne in the South countries of America, no lesse hope may be gathered that it will also spred into the North. [...]

---

[10] "This realme distressed" refers to problems in England caused by overpopulation in the 1570s and 1580s.

Source: Edward Hayes (flourished 1580). "A Report of the Voyage and Successe Thereof, Attempted in the Yeere of Our Lord, 1583. By Sir Humfrey Gilbert Knight, with Other Gentlemen Assisting Him in That Action, Intended to Discover and to Plant Christian Inhabitants in Place Convenient, upon Those Large and Ample Countries Extended Northward from the Cape of Florida, Lying under the Very Temperate Climes, Esteemed Fertile and Rich in Minerals, yet Not in the Actuall Possession of Any Christian Prince, Written by M. Edward Haies Gentleman, and Principal Actor in the Same Voyage, Who Alone Continued unto the End, and by Gods Speciall Assistance Returned Home with His Retinue Safe and Entire." Richard Hakluyt. *The Principall Navigations Voiages and Discoveries of the English Nation.* London, 1589, reprint Cambridge: Hakluyt Society, 1965, 679-681.

9. Sir George Peckham
A True Reporte, of the Late Discoveries and Possession, Taken in the Right of the Crowne of Englande, of the New-found Landes: By That Valiaunt and Worthye Gentleman, Sir Humfrey Gilbert Knight.[11] *Wherein Is Also Breefely Sette Downe, Her Highnesse Lawfull Tytle Thereunto* (1583)

[1.] *The firste Chapiter, wherein the Argument of the Booke is Contayned*

[... A]nd that those Countries are at this day inhabited with Savages who have no knowledg of God. Is it not ther fore (I say) to be lamented, that these poore *Pagans*, so long living in ignoraunce and Idolatry, and in sorte, thirsting after christianitie, (as may appear by the relation of such as have travailed in those partes,) that our heartes are so hardned, that fewe or none can be found which wil put to theyr helping hands, and applie themselves to the relieving of the miserable and wretched estate of these sillie soules?

Whose Countrey dooth (as it were with arme advaunced) above the climats both of *Spayne* and *Fraunce*, stretche out it selfe towardes *England* onelie. In manner praying our ayde and helpe, as it is not onelie set foorth in *Mercators*[12] generall Mappe, but it is also founde to bee true by the discovery of our nation, and other straungers, who have often times travailed upon the same Coastes. [...]

[3.] *The third Chapter dooth shewe the lawfull tytle, which the Queenes most excellent Maiestie hath unto those Countries, which through the ayde of almightie God are mente to be inhabited.*

And it is very evident that the planting there shall in time right amplie enlarge her Maiesties Territories and Dominions (or I might rather say) restore her to her Highnesse auncient right and interest in those Countries, into the which a noble and woorthy personage, lyneally descended from the blood royall, borne in *Wales*, named *Madocke ap Owen Gwyneth*, departing from the coast of *England*, about the yeere of our Lord God 1170 arrived and there planted himselfe, and his Colonies, and afterward returned himselfe into *England*, leaving certaine of his people there, as appeareth in an aunci Welch Chronicle [...].

---

[11] English soldier and navigator who propagated overseas colonization. His poor leadership was responsible for the failure to establish the first permanent English colony in North America.
[12] Gerardus Mercator (1518-1594), famous Flemish mapmaker.

[6.] *The sixt Chapter, sheweth that the Traffique and Planting in those Countries, shall be unto the Savages themselves verie beneficiall and gainefull.*

Now to the end it may appeare, that this voiage is not undertaken altogether for the peculiar commoditie of our selves, and our Countrie, (as generallie other trades and iourneies be) it shall fall out in proofe, that the Savages shal heerby have iust cause to blesse the howre, when this enterprise was undertaken.

First and cheefly, in respect of the most happy and gladsome tidings of the most glorious Gospel of our Saviour Iesus Christ, whereby they may be brought from falsehood to truth, from darknes to lyght, from the hieway of death, to the path of life, from superstitious idolatry, to sincere christianity, from the devill to Christ, from hell to Heaven. And if in respect of all the commodities they can yeeld us (were they many moe) that they should but receyve this only benefite of christianity, they were more then fully recompenced.

But heerunto it may be obiected, that the Gospel must be freely preached, for such was the example of the Apostles, unto whom although the aucthorities and examples before alledged, of Emperors, Kings, and Princes, as wel before Christes time as since, might sufficiently satisfie: Yet for further aunswer, we may say with Saint *Paule. If we have sowen unto you heavenlie thinges, doo you thinke it much that we should reape your carnall thinges?* [1 Cor. 9.11] And withall, *The workman is worthy of his hier*. These heavenly tydings [...] farre exceed their earthly ritches. Moreover, if the other inferior worldlie, and temporall thinges, which they shall receive from us, be waied in equal balance, I assure my selfe, that by equall iudgement of any indifferent person, the benefites which they then receive, shall far surmount those which they shall depart withall unto us. And admitte that they had (as they have not) the knowledge to put theyr land to some use: Yet being brought from brutish ignoraunce, to civility and knowledge, and made them to understand how the tenth part of their land may be so manured and emploied, as it may yeeld more commodities to the necessary use of mans life, then the whole now dooth: What iust cause of complaint may they have? And in my private opinion, I doo verily think that God did create lande, to the end that it shold by Culture and husbandrie, yeeld things necessary for mans lyfe.

But this is not all the benefit which they shall receive by the christians, for, over & beside the knowledge how to tyl and dresse their grounds, they shalbe reduced from unseemly customes, to honest maners, from disordred riotous rowtes and companies, to a wel governed common wealth, & with all shalbe taught mecanicall occupations, artes, and lyberal Sciences: and which standeth them most upon, they shalbe defended from the cruelty of their tyrannicall & blood sucking neighbors, the *Canniballes*, wherby infinite number of their lives shalbe preserved. And lastly, by this meanes many of their poore innocent children shalbe preserved from the bloody knife of the sacrificer, a most horrible and detestable custome in the sight of God & man, now and ever heeretofore used amongst them. [...]

[7.] *The seaventh Chapter sheweth that the Planting there, is not a matter of such charge or diffycultie, as many would make it seeme to be.*

[...] Againe, this intended voiage for conquest, hath in lyke manner many other singular priviledges, wherewith Got hath as it were, with his holy hand blessed the same before all others. For after once we are departed the coast of *England*, we may passe straight way thether, without daunger of being driven into any the countries of our enimies, or doubtfull freends [...]. Also, the passadge is short, for we may go thither in thirty or forty daies at the most [...].

And may it not much encourage us to hope for good successe in the countrey of these Savages, beeing a naked kinde of people, voyde of the knowledge of the discipline of warre [...].

[...T]he sayd Coastes [...] dooth minister iust cause of incouragement to our countrymen, not to account it so harde and difficult athing for the subiectes of this noble Realme of Englande, to discover people plant and possesse the like goodly lands and rich Countries not farre from us, but neere adioyning and offering it selfe unto us [...].

Source: Sir George Peckham (?-1608). *A True Reporte, of the Late Discoveries and Possession, Taken in the Right of the Crowne of Englande, of the New-found Landes: By That Valiaunt and Worthye Gentleman, Sir Humfrey Gilbert Knight. Wherein Is Also Breefely Sette Downe, Her Highnesse Lawfull Tytle Thereunto, and the Great and Manifolde Commodities, That Is Likely to Grow Thereby, to the Whole Realme in Generall, and to the Adventurers in Particular. Together with the Easines and Shortnes of the Voyage.* London: I.C., 1583, n.p.

10. Thomas Hariot
A Briefe and True Report of the New Found Land of Virginia (1588)

The Conclusion.

Now I have as I hope made relation not of so fewe and smal things but that the countrey of men that are indifferent & wel disposed maie be sufficiently liked: If there were no more knowen then I have mentioned, which doubtlesse and in great reason is nothing to that which remaineth to bee discovered, neither the soile, nor commodities. As we have reason so to gather by the difference we found in our travails; for although all which I have before spoken of, have bin discovered & experimented not far from the sea coast where was our abode & most of our travailing: yet somtimes as we made our iourneies farther into the maine and countrey; we found the soyle to bee fatter; the trees greater and to growe thinner; the grounde more firme and deeper mould; more and larger champions; finer grasse and as good as ever we saw any in England; in some places rockie and farre more high and hillie ground; more plentie of their fruites; more abundance of beastes; the more inhabited with people, and of greater pollicie & larger dominions, with greater townes and houses.

Why may wee not then looke for in good hope from the inner parts of more and greater plentie, as well of other things, as of those which wee have alreadie discovered? Unto the Spaniardes happened the like in discovering the maine of the West Indies. The maine also of this countrey of *Virginia*, extending some wayes so many hundreds of leagues, as otherwise then by the relation of the inhabitants wee have most certaine knowledge of, where yet no Christian Prince hath any possession or dealing, cannot but yeeld many kinds of excellent commodities, which we in our discoverie have not yet seene.

What hope there is els to be gathered of the nature of the climate, being answerable to the Iland of *Iapan*, the land of *China*, *Persia*, *Iury*, the Ilandes of *Cyprus* and *Candy*, the South parts of *Greece*, *Italy*, and *Spaine*, and of many other notable and famous countreis, because I meane not to be tedious, I leave to your owne consideration.

Whereby also the excellent temperature of the ayre there at all seasons, much warmer then in England, and never so violently hot, as sometimes is under & between the Tropikes, or nere them; cannot bee unknowne unto you without farther relation.

For the holsomnesse thereof I neede to say but thus much: that for all the want of provision, as first of English victuall; excepting for twentie daies, wee lived only by drinking water and by the victuall of the countrey, of which some sorts were very straunge unto us, and might have bene thought to have altered our temperatures in such sort as to have brought us into some greevous and dangerous diseases: secondly the want of English meanes, for the taking of beastes, fishe, and foule, which by the helpe only of the inhabitants and their meanes, coulde not bee so suddenly and easily provided for us, nor in so great numbers & quantities, nor of that choise as otherwise might have bene to our better satisfaction and contentment. Some want also wee had of clothes. Furthermore, in all our travailes which were most speciall and often in the time of winter, our lodging was in the open aire upon the grounde. And yet I say for all this, there were but foure of our whole company (being one hundred and eight) that died all the yeere and that but at the latter ende thereof and upon none of the aforesaide causes. For all foure especially three were feeble, weake, and sickly persons before ever they came thither, and those that knewe them much marveyled that they lived so long beeing in that case, or had adventured to travaile.

Seeing therefore the ayre there is so temperate and holsome, the soyle so fertile and yeelding such commodities as I have before mentioned, the voyage also thither to and fro beeing sufficiently experimented, to bee perfourmed thrise a yeere with ease and at any season thereof: And the dealing of *Sir Walter Raleigh* so liberall in large giving and graunting lande there, as is alreadie knowen, with many helpes and furtherances els: (The least that hee hath graunted hath beene five hundred acres to a man onely for the adventure of his person): I hope there remaine no cause wherby the action should be misliked.

If that those which shall thither travaile to inhabite and plant bee but reasonably provided for the first yere as those are which were transported the last, and beeing there doe use but that diligence and care as is requisite, and as they may with ease: There is no doubt but for the time following they may have victuals that is excellent good and plentie enough; some more Englishe sortes of cattaile also hereafter, as some have bene before, and are there yet remaining, may and shall bee God willing thither transported: So likewise our kinde of fruites, rootes, and hearbes may bee there planted and sowed, as some have bene alreadie, and prove wel. And in short time also they may raise of those sortes of commodities which I have spoken of as shall both enrich them selves, as also others that shall deale with them.

And this is all the fruites of our labours, that I have thought necessary to advertise you of at this present: what els concerneth the nature and manners of the inhabitants of *Virginia*: The number with the particularities of the voyages thither made; and of the actions of such that have bene by *Sir Walter Raleigh* therein and there imployed, many worthy to bee remembred; as of the first discoverers of the Countrey: of our Generall for the time *Sir Richard Greinuile*; and after his departure, of our Governour there Master *Rafe Lane*; with divers other directed and imployed under theyr governement: Of the Captaynes and Masters of the voyages made since for transportation; of the Governour and assistants of those alredie transported, as of many persons, accidents, and thinges els, I have ready in a discourse by it self in maner of a Chronicle according to the course of times, and when time shall bee thought convenient shall be also published.

Thus referring my relation to your favourable constructions, expecting good successe of the action, from him which is to be acknowledged the authour and governour not only of this but of all things els, I take my leave of you, this moneth of *February*. 1588.

FINIS.

Source: Thomas Hariot (1560-1621). *A Briefe and True Report of the New Found Land of Virginia: Of the Commodities There Found and to Be Raysed, as Well Marchantable, as Others for Victuall, Building and Other Necessarie Uses for Those That Are and Shalbe the Planters There; and of the Nature and Manners of the Naturall Inhabitants: Discovered by the English Colony There Seated by Sir Richard Greinuile Knight in the Yeere 1585. Which Remained under the Government of Rafe Lane Esquier, One of Her Maiesties Equieres, During the Space of Twelve Monethes: At the Speciall Charge and Direction of the Honourable Sir Walter Raleigh Knight, Lord Warden of the Stanneries; Who Therein Hath Been Favoured and Authorised by Her Maiestie and Her Letters Patents: Directed to the Adventurers, Favourers, and Welweillers of the Action, for the Inhabitin and Planting There: By Thomas Hariot; Servant to the Abovenamed Sir Walter, a Member of the Colony, and there Imployed in Discovering*. London: R. Robinson, 1588, 31-33.

11. François van den Hoeye
"America" (early 17th century)

Source: François van den Hoeye (1591?-1636). "America." *The New Golden Land: European Images of America from the Discoveries to the Present Time*. Ed. Hugh Honour. New York: Pantheon, 1975, 90.

12. Edward Hayes and Christopher Carleill
"A Discourse Concerning a Voyage Intended for the Planting of Chrystyan Religion and People in the North West Regions of America"
(1592)

[2.] That our Churche & fayth shall receyve great advancement & propagation by perfourmance of thys Action.

Our adversaries have noted thys to be a veary great deffect in our Churche. that we have not Converted Infidells unto the fayth. And doe arrogat[e] unto theyr Romish churche, the Conversion of pagans (in the East & West Indes) as a singuler preheminence & propper marck of the trew churche. It shalbe therfo[re] a great honor & advancement unto our Churche: lyke as the same hath doone in the fyrst & primative state: So now agayn in thys latter are to travayll in sowyng the Seed of pure Religion in those exceeding large & popolus Nations lyeng to the Northwest of America and to sett them free from the Captivetie of the dyvell. Who houldeth them under miserable Idolatry & paganisme being nevertheles found a people docible & veary capable of Christianitie.

And lyke as the Portingalls & Spaniards have travaylled worthely in brynging many spatious Contries & kyngdoms in the East & west parts of the world into the fayth, yet not wythowt myxture of superstition & error wheareyn never the less they have prospered, bycause they preache Christ: Even so, thys la[rge] portion of America (greater than Europe) falleth into the lott of our Nation to be converted unto the fayth. Because God dyd fyrst discover the same unto us which in Scituation & temperature is nearest unto, and seme[th] to be reserved for us. No Nation havyng the power hytherto (according to theyr sondry[13] intents & attempts) to possess the same actually.

We must beleve by Chryst hys own prophesy that the gospell shalbe preached throughout the world: We may also beleve that the same shalbe carryed into these Northwest Regions of America, which are a veary great portion of the world and never yet preached unto.

Onto thys infallible prediction of Chryst, I wyll drawe a probable conjecture allso from the Revolution of Gods word, which hytherto hath moved Cyrcularly.

For lyke as the same begann in the East in paradice, And moved westwards in[to] Palestina, And at length into Europe. thear beginning in the East also proceded by South into the west, and spredd afterwards North: Even from Europe it hath contynewed hys Revolution west into America, wh[ile] it begann East: proceded South & west. And may happely more purely [be] preached also in the North by us. Unto which tyme (thys being the last of the last Age of the world:) we are now arryved. And therfore may ho[pe] by so muche the more, of our good success in thys Action now. Seing the last dayes are come upon us. And that now or never theyr conversion is to [be] expected.

Whearupon veary many zealouse men, are moved by the same Charitable Spyrit towards those paganish Americans. whearby holy men in elder tymes were styrred upp to the converting of us (in these North & than obscure regions of Europe) unto the Chrystyan fayth which we now enjoye by the same meanes. And withowt which we also had contynued Barbarouse unto thys daye.

Therfore doo desyer, Aswell for the saving of innumerable Soules amongst those Barbarians, As to supply that deffect in our churche (before noted by Our Adversar[ie])

---

[13] Different, various, individual.

to venter theyr Substance & persons in so honorable attempt as thys: to plant [or] to establish Religion in those remote lands. Which canot be doon without a habitation of Chrystians fyrst settled thear & Contynued. [...]

> Source: Edward Hayes & Christopher Carleill (both flourished in the 1580s). "A Discourse Concerning a Voyage Intended for the Planting of Chrystyan Religion and People in the North West Regions of America in Places Most Apt for the Constitution of Our Boddies, and the Spedy Advauncement of a State." *New American World: A Documentary History of North America to 1612*. 5 vols. Ed. David B. Quinn. Vol. 3: *English Plans for North America. The Roanoke Voyages. New England Ventures*. London: MacMillan Press, 1979, 158.

13. Michael Drayton
"To the Virginian Voyage" (1606)

You brave Heroique Minds,
Worthy your Countries Name,
   That Honour still pursue,
   Goe, and subdue,
Whilst loyt'ring Hinds[14]
Lurke here at home, with shame.

Britans, you stay too long,
Quickly aboord bestow you,
   And with a merry Gale
   Swell your stretch'd Sayle,
With Vowes as strong,
As the Winds that blow you. [...]

And cheerefully at Sea,
Successe you still intice,
   To get the Pearle and Gold,
   And ours to hold,
VIRGINIA,
Earth's onely Paradise.

Where Nature hath in store
Fowle, Venison, and Fish,
   And the fruitfull'st Soyle,
   Without your Toyle,
Three Harvests more,
All greater then your Wish. [...]

To whose, the golden Age[15]
Still Natures lawes doth give,
   No other Cares that tend,

---

[14] Those that stay behind idly.
[15] In Greek mythology, the first of a succession of four ages or races (Golden, Silver, Bronze, and Iron). The golden age is characterized by permanent feasting and merriment as well as an absence of aging, manual labor, and toil. Hesiod adds a fifth age, the Age (Race) of Heroes, between the Bronze and Iron Age. In the Age of Heroes, man lives in a 'restored' Golden Age existence in the Isles of the Blessed.

But Them to defend
From Winters age,
That long there doth not live. [...]

And in Regions farre
Such *Heroes* bring yee foorth,
   As those from whom We came,
   And plant Our name,
Under that Starre
Not knowne unto our North.

And as there Plenty growes
Of Lawrell every where,
   APOLLO'S Sacred tree,[16]
   You it may see,
A Poets Browes
To crowne, that may sing there.

Thy Voyages attend,
Industrious HACKLUIT,[17]
   Whose Reading shall inflame
   Men to seeke Fame,
And much commend
To after-Times thy Wit.

Source: Michael Drayton (1563-1631). "To the Virginian Voyage." *The Works of Michael Drayton*. 5 vols. Ed. J. William Hebel. Oxford: Basil Blackwell, 1961, Vol. 2, 363-364.

14. Alexander Whitaker
Good Newes from Virginia (1613)

[...] And now let me turne your eyes, my brethren of England, to behold the waters of *Virginia*: where you may behold a fit subiect for the exercise of your *Liberalitie* [...]. For it is evident that our wise God hath bestowed no gift upon any man, for their private use, but for the good of other men, whom God shall offer to their *Liberalitie*.

Wherefore, since God hath opened the doore of *Virginia*, to our countrey of England, wee are to thinke that God hath, as it were, by the word of mouth called us in, to bestow our severall *Charity* on them. [...]

[...] I have shut up many things in few words, and have alleadged this onely to prove unto us, that the finger of God hath been the onely true worker heere; that God first shewed us the place, God first called us hither, and here God by his speciall providence hath maintained us. Wherefore, by him let us be encouraged to lay our helping hands to this good work, (yea Gods works) with all the strength of our abilitie.

[... Let] the miserable condition of these naked slaves of the divell move you to compassion toward them. They acknowledge that there is a great good God, but know him not, having the eyes of their understanding as yet blinded: wherefore they serve the divell

---

[16] Laurel tree.
[17] British geographer who wrote *Principal Navigations, Voyages, and Discoveries of the English Nation* (1589); see doc. 7 in this collection.

for feare, after a most base manner, sacrificing sometimes (as I have heere heard) their owne Children to him. I have sent one Image of their god to the Counsell in *England*, which is painted upon one side of a toad-stoole, much like unto a deformed monster. Their Priests (whom the[y] call *Quiokosoughs*) are no other but such as our English Witches are. They live naked in bodie, as if their shame of their sinne deserved no covering: Their names are as naked as their bodie: they esteeme it a vertue to lie, deceive and steale as their master the divell teacheth them. Much more might be said of their miserable condition, but I refer the particular narration of these things to some other season. If this bee their life, what thinke you shall become of them after death? but to be partakers with the divell and his angels in hell for evermore. Wherefore my brethren, put on the bowels of compassion, and let the lamentable estate of these miserable people enter in your consideration: One God created us, they have reasonable soules and intellectuall faculties as well as wee; we all have *Adam* for our common parent: yea, by nature the condition of us both is all one, the servants of sinne and slaves of the divell. Oh remember (I beseech you) what was the state of *England* before the Gospell was preached in our Countrey? How much better were we then, and concerning our soules health, then these now are? Let the word of the Lord sound out that it may be heard in these parts; and let your faith which is toward God spread it selfe abroad, and shew forth the charitable fruits of it in these barren parts of the world: *And let him know that he which hath converted a sinner from going a stray out of his way, shall save a soule from death, and hide a multitude of sinnes*.[18]

But if any of us should misdoubt that this barbarous people is uncapable of such heavenly mysteries, let such men know that they are farre mistaken in the nature of these men, for besides the promise of God, which is without respect of persons, made as well to unwise men after the flesh, as to the wise, &c. let us not thinke that these men are so simple as some have supposed them: for they are of bodie lustie, strong, and very nimble: they are a very understanding generation, quicke of apprehension, suddaine in their dispatches, subtile in their dealings, exquisite in their inventions, and industrious in their labour. I suppose the world hath no better marke-men with their bow and arrowes then they be; they will kill birds flying, fishes swimming, and beasts running: they shoote also with mervailous strength, they shot one of our men being unarmed quite through the bodie, and nailed both his armes to his bodie with one arrow: one of their Children also, about the age of 12. or 13. yeares, killed a bird with his arrow in my sight. The service of their God is answerable to their life, being performed with great feare and attention, and many strange dumb shewes used in the same, stretching forth their limbes and straining their bodie, much like to the counterfeit women in *England* who faine themselves bewitched, or possessed of same evill spirit.

They stand in great awe of their *Quiokosoughs* or Priests, which are a generation of vipers even of Sathans owne brood. The manner of their life is much like to the popish Hermits of our age; for they live alone in the woods, in houses sequestred from the common course of men, neither may any man bee suffered to come into their house or to speake with them, but when this Priest doth call him. [...] At his command they make warre and peace, neither doe they any thing of moment without him. I will not bee teadious in these strange Narrations, when I have more perfectly entered into their secrets, you shall know all. Finally, there is a civill governement amongst them which they strictly observe, and shew thereby that the law of Nature dwelleth in them: for they have a rude

---

[18] Jas. 5.20 (*Geneva Bible*, 1587).

kinde of Common-wealth, and rough governement, wherein they both honour and obey their Kings, Parents, and Governours, both greater and lesse, they observe the limits of their owne possessions, and incroach not upon their neighbours dwellings. Murther is a capitall crime scarce heard of among them: adultery is most severely punished, and so are their other offences. These unnurtured grounds of reason in them, may serve to incourage us: to instruct them in the knowledge of the true God, the rewarder of all righteousnesse, not doubting but that he that was powerfull to save us by his word, when we were nothing, wil be mercifull also to these sonnes of *Adam* in his appointed time, in whom there bee remaining so many footsteps of Gods image. [...]

Source: Alexander Whitaker (1585-1617). *Good Newes from Virginia. Sent to the Counsell and Company of Virginia, Resident in England. From Alexander Whitaker, the Minister of Henrico in Virginia. Wherein Also Is a Narration of the Present State of That Countrey, and Our Colonies There. Perused and Published by Direction from That Counsell. And a Preface Prefixed of Some Matters Touching That Plantation, Very Requisite to be Made Knowne*. London: Felix Kyngston, 1613, 21, 23-27.

15. John Smith
A Description of New England (1616)

[...] All these and diverse other good things do heere, for want of use, still increase, & decrease with little diminution, whereby they growe to that abundance. You shall scarce finde any Baye, shallow shore, or Cove of sand, where you may not take many Clampes, or Lobsters, or both at your pleasure, and in many places lode your boat if you please; nor Iles where you finde not fruits, birds, crabs, and muskles, or all of them, for taking, at a lowe water. And in the harbors we frequented, a little boye might take [...] such delicate fish, at the ships sterne, more then sixe or tenne can eate in a daie; but with a casting-net, thousands when wee pleased [... There is] no River where there is not plentie of Sturgion, or Salmon, or both; all which are to be had in abundance observing but their seasons. But if a man will goe at Christmasse to gather Cherries in *Kent*, he may be deceived; though there be plentie in Summer: so, heere these plenties have each their seasons, as I have expressed. We for the most part had little but bread and vineger: and though the most part of Iuly when the fishing decaied they wrought all day, laie abroade in the Iles all night, and lived on what they found, yet were not sicke: But I would wish none put himself long to such plunges; except necessitie constraine it: yet worthy is that person to starve that heere cannot live; if he have sense, strength and health: for, there is no such penury[19] of these blessings in any place, but that a hundred men may, in one houre or two, make their provisions for a day: and hee that hath experience to mannage well these affaires, with fortie or thirtie honest industrious men, might well undertake (if they dwell in these parts) to subiect the Salvages, and feed daily two or three hundred men, with as good corne, fish, and flesh, as the earth hath of those kindes, and yet make that labor but their pleasure: provided that they have engins, that be proper for their purposes.

Who can desire more content, that hath small meanes;[20] or but only his merit to advance his fortune, then to tread, and plant that ground hee hath purchased by the hazard of his life? If he have but the taste of virtue, and magnanimitie, what to such a minde can bee more pleasant, then planting and building a foundation for his Posteritie, gotte from

---

[19] Scarcity, want.
[20] The text contains the following note on the margin: "A note for men that have great spirits, and smal meanes."

the rude earth, by Gods blessing & his owne industrie, without preiudice to any? If hee have any graine of faith or zeale in Religion, what can hee doe lesse hurtfull to any; or more agreeable to God, then to seeke to convert those poore Salvages to know Christ, and humanitie, whose labors with discretion will triple requite thy charge and paines? What so truely sutes with honour and honestie, as the discovering things unknowne? erecting Townes, peopling Countries, informing the ignorant, reforming things uniust, teaching virtue; & gaine to our Native mother-countrie a kingdom to attend her; finde imployment for those that are idle, because they know not what to doe: so farre from wronging any, as to cause Posteritie to remember thee; and remembring thee, ever honour that remembrance with praise? [...]

[...] Religion, above all things, should move us (especially the Clergie) if wee were religious, to shewe our faith by our workes; in converting those poore salvages, to the knowledge of God, seeing what paines the *Spanyards* take to bring them to their adulterated faith. Honor might move the Gentrie, the valiant, and industrious; and the hope and assurance of wealth, all; if wee were that we would seeme, and be accounted. Or be we so far inferior to other nations, or our spirits so far deiected, from our auncient predecessors, or our mindes so upon spoile, piracie, and such villany, as to serve the *Portugall*, *Spanyard*, *Dutch*, *French*, or *Turke* [...] rather then our God, our King, our Country, & our selves? excusing our idlenesse, and our base complaints; by want of imploiment; when heere is such choise of all sorts, and for all degrees, in the planting and discovering these North parts of *America*.

[...] But, to conclude, *Adam* and *Eve* did first beginne this innocent worke, To plant the earth to remaine to posteritie; but not without labour, trouble, & industrie. *Noe*, and his family, beganne againe the second plantation; and their seede as it still increased, hath still planted new Countries, and one countrie another: and so the world to that estate it is. But not without much hazard, travell, discontents, and many disasters. Had those worthie Fathers & their memorable off-spring not beene more diligent for us now in these Ages, then wee are to plant that yet unplanted, for the after livers: Had the seede of *Abraham*, our Saviour Christ, and his Apostles, exposed themselves to no more daungers to teach the Gospell, and the will of God then wee; Even wee our selves, had at this present beene as Salvage, and as miserable as the most barbarous Salvage yet uncivilized. [...] Then seeing we are not borne for our selves, but each to helpe other, and our abilities are much alike at the houre of our birth, and the minute of our death: Seeing our good deedes, or our badde, by faith in Christs merits, is all we have to carrie our soules to heaven, or hell: Seeing honour is our lives ambition; and our ambition after death, to have an honourable memorie of our life: and seeing by noe meanes wee would bee abated of

the dignities & glories of our
Predecessors; let us imitate
their vertues to bee
worthily their
successors.
FINIS.

Source: John Smith (1580-1631). *A Description of New England: Or the Observations, and Discoveries, of Captain Iohn Smith, (Admirall of That Country) in the North of America, in the Year of Our Lord 1614: With the Successe of Sixe Ships, That Went the Next Yeare 1615; and the Accidents Befell Him among the French Men of Warre: With the Proofe of the Present Benefit This Countrey Affoords: Whither This Present Yeare, 1616, Eight Voluntary Ships Are Gone to Make Further Tryall.* London: Humfrey Lownes, 1616, 30-32, 44-45, 59-61.

16. John Cotton
Gods Promise to His Plantation (1630)

2 Sam. 7.10.
Moreover I will appoint a place for my people Israel, *and I will plant them, that they may dwell in a place of their owne, and move no more.*

In the beginning of this chapter, we reade of *Davids* purpose to build God an house [...]. God refuseth *Davids* offer [... but] lest *David* should be discouraged with this [...] promiseth unto *David*, and his, for his sake [five blessings].

The first is in the 10. verse: *I will appoynt a place for my people Israel.* [...]

In this 10 verse is a double blessing promised:

First, the designment of a place for his people.

Secondly, a plantation of them in that place, from whence is promised a threefold blessing.

First, they shall dwell there like Free-holders in a place of their owne.

Secondly, hee promiseth them firme and durable possession, they shall move no more.

Thirdly, they shall have peaceable and quiet resting there, The sonnes of wickednesse shall afflict them no more: which is amplified by their former troubles, as before time.

From the appointment of a place for them, which is the first blessing, you may observe this note:

The placeing of a people in this or that Country is from the appointment of the Lord. [...]

Quest. Wherein doth this worke of God stand in appointing a place for a people?

Answ. First, when God espies or discovers a land for a people, as in *Ezek*. 20.6. he brought them into a land that he had espied for them: And that is, when either he gives them to discover it themselves, or heare of it discovered by others, and fitting them.

Secondly, after he hath espied it, when he carrieth them along to it, so that they plainly see a providence of God leading them from one Country to another: As in *Exod*. 19.4. *You have seene how I have borne you as on Eagles wings, and brought you unto my selfe*. So that though they met with many difficulties, yet hee carried them high above them all, like an eagle, flying over seas and rockes, and all hinderances.

Thirdly, when he makes roome for a people to dwell there, as in *Psal*. 80.9. *Thou preparedst roome for them.* [...]

Now God makes room for a people 3 wayes:

First, when he casts out the enemies of a people before them by lawfull warre with the inhabitants, which God calls them unto: as in *Psal*. 44.2. *Thou didst drive out the Heathen before them*. But this course of warring against others, and driving them out without provocation, depends upon speciall Commission from God, or else it is not imitable.

Secondly, when hee gives a forreigne people favour in the eyes of any native people to come and sit downe with them either by way of purchase, as *Abraham* did obtaine the field of *Machpelah*; or else when they give it in courtesie, as *Pharaoh* did the land of *Goshen* unto the Sons *of Iacob*.

Thirdly, when hee makes a Country though not altogether void of Inhabitants, yet void in that place where they reside. Where there is a vacant place, there is liberty for the sonnes of *Adam* or *Noah* to come and inhabite, though they neither buy it, nor ask their leaves. *Abraham* and *Isaac*, when they sojourned[21] amongst the *Philistins*, they did not

---

[21] The original text here adds the following explanatory note in the margin: "This soiourning was a constant residence there, as in a possession of their owne; although it bee called soiourning or dwelling as

buy that land to feede their cattle, because they said There is roome enough. And so did *Iacob* pitch his Tent by *Sechem*, *Gen.* 34.21. [...] but admitteth it as a Principle in Nature, That in a vacant soyle, hee that taketh possession of it, and bestoweth culture and husbandry upon it, his Right it is. And the ground of this is from the grand Charter given to *Adam* and his posterity in Paradise, *Gen.* 1.28. *Multiply, and replenish the earth, and subdue it.* If therefore any sonne of *Adam* come and finde a place empty, he hath liberty to come, and fill, and subdue the earth there. This Charter was renewed to *Noah*, *Gen.* 9.1. *Fulfill the earth and multiply:* So that it is free from that comon Grant, for any to take possession of vacant Countries. Indeed no Nation is to drive out another without speciall Commission from heaven, such as the *Israelites* had, unlesse the Natives do unjustly wrong them, and will not recompence the wrongs done in peaceable sort, & then they may right themselves by lawfull war, and subdue the Countrey unto themselves.

This placeing of people in this or that Country, is from Gods soveraignty over all the earth, and the inhabitants thereof: as in *Psal.* 24.1. *The earth is the Lords, and the fulnesse thereof.* [...] Therefore it is meete he should provide a place for all Nations to inhabit, and have all the earth replenished. Onely in the Text here is meant some more speciall appointment, because God tells them it by his owne mouth; he doth not so with other people, he doth not tell the children of *Seir*,[22] that hee hath appointed a place for them: that is, He gives them the land by promise; others take the land by his providence, but Gods people take the land by promise: And therefore the land of *Canaan* is called a land of promise. Which they discerne, first, by discerning themselves to be in Christ, in whom all the promises are yea, and amen.

[... It] is taken from the office God takes upon him, when he is our planter, hee becomes our husbandman; and *if hee plant us, who shall plucke us up? Isay* 27.1,2. *Iob* 34.29. When he giveth quiet, who can make trouble? If God be the Gardiner, who shall plucke up what hee sets downe? Every plantation that he hath not planted shall be plucked up, and what he hath planted shall surely be established. [...]

Use 1. To exhort all that are planted at home, or intend to plant abroad, to looke well to your plantation, as you desire that the sonnes of wickednesse may not afflict you at home, nor enemies abroad, looke that you be right planted, and then you neede not to feare, you are safe enough: God hath spoken it, I will plant them, and they shall not be moved, neither shall the sonnes of wickednesse afflict them any more.

Quest. What course would you have us take?

Answ. Have speciall care that you ever have the Ordinances planted amongst you, or else never looke for security. As soone as Gods Ordinances cease, your security ceaseth likewise; but if God plant his Ordinances among you, feare not, he will maintaine them. *Isay* 4.5.6: *Upon all their glory there shall be a defence*; that is, upon all Gods Ordinances: for so was the Arke called *the Glory of Israel*, 1 *Sam.* 4.22.

Secondly, have a care to be implanted into the Ordinances, that the word may be ingrafted into you, and you into it: If you take rooting in the Ordinances, grow up thereby, bring forth much fruite, continue and abide therein, then you are a vineyard of red wine, and the Lord will keepe you, *Isay* 27.2.3. that no sonnes of violence shall destroy you. Looke into all the stories whether divine or humane, and you shall never finde that God

---

strangers, because they neither had the soveraigne government of the whole Countrey in their owne hand, nor yet did incorporate them selves into the Commonwealth of the Natives, to submit themselves unto their government."

[22] A synonym for Edom, a land bordering ancient Israel. According to the Bible, the Edomites were descendants of Esau and closely related to the Israelites.

ever rooted out a people that had the Ordinances planted amongst them, and themselves planted into the Ordinances: never did God suffer such plants to be plucked up; on all their glory shall be a defence.

Thirdly, be not unmindfull of our *Ierusalem* at home, whether you leave us, or stay at home with us. [...]

Fourthly, goe forth, every man that goeth, with a publicke spirit, looking not on your owne things onely, but also on the things of others: *Phil.* 2.4. This care of universall helpfulnesse was the prosperity of the first Plantation of the Primitive Church: *Acts* 4.32.

Fifthly, have a tender care that you looke well to the plants that spring from you, that is, to your children, that they doe not degenerate as the Israelites did; after which they were vexed with afflictions on every hand. [...]

Sixthly, and lastly, offend not the poore Natives, but as you partake in their land, so make them partakers of your precious faith: as you reape their temporalls, so feede them with your spiritualls: winne them to the love of Christ, for whom Christ died. They never yet refused the Gospell, and therefore more hope they will now receive it. Who knoweth whether God have reared this whole Plantation for such an end?

Use 2. Secondly, for consolation to them that are planted by God in any place, that finde rooting and establishing from God, this is a cause of much encouragement unto you, that what hee hath planted he will maintaine, every plantation his right hand hath not planted shalbe rooted up, but his owne plantation shall prosper, & flourish. When he promiseth peace and safety, what enemie shall be able to make the promise of God of none effect? Neglect not walls, and bulwarkes, and fortifications for your owne defence; but

    ever let the Name of the Lord be your strong
     Tower; and the word of his Promise the
      Rocke of your Refuge. His word
       that made heaven and earth
       will not faile, till hea-
        ven and earth be
         no more.
         Amen.

        Finis.

Source: John Cotton (1584-1652). *Gods Promise to His Plantation. 2 Sam. 7.10. Moreover I Will Appoint a Place for My People Israel, and I Will Plant Them, That They May Dwell in a Place of Their Owne, and Move No More. As It Was Delivered in a Sermon, by Iohn Cotton, B.D. and Preacher of Gods Word in Boston.* London: William Jones, [2]1630, 1-6, 16-20.

17. Robert Cushman
"Reasons & Considerations Touching the Lawfulnesse of Removing out of England into the Parts of America" (1622)

Forasmuch as many exceptions are daily made against the going into, and inhabiting of foraigne desert places, to the hinderances of plantations abroad, and the increase of distractions at home: It is not amisse that some which have beene eare witnesses of the exceptions made, and are either Agents or Abettors of such removals and plantations; doe seeke to give content to the world, in all things that possibly they can. [...]

And being studious for brevitie, we must first consider, that whereas God of old did call and summon our Fathers by predictions, dreames, visions, and certaine illuminations to goe from their countries, places and habitations, to reside and dwell here or there, and to wander up and downe from citie to citie, and Land to Land, according to his will and pleasure. Now there is no such calling to be expected for any matter whatsoever, neither must any so much as imagine that there will now be any such thing. [...]

Neither is there any land or possession now, like unto the possession which the Iewes had in *Canaan*, being legally holy and appropriated unto a holy people the seed of *Abraham*, in which they dwelt securely, and had their daies prolonged, it being by an immediate voice said, that he (the Lord) gave it them as a land of rest after their wearie travels, and a type of *Eternall* rest in heaven, but now there is no land of that Sanctimonie, no land so appropriated; none typicall: much lesse any that can be said to be given of God to any nation as was *Canaan*, which they and their seed must dwell in, till God sendeth upon them sword or captivitie: but now we are all in all places strangers and Pilgrims, travellers and soiourners, most properly, having no dwelling but in this earthen Tabernacle;[23] our dwelling is but a wandring, and our abiding but as a fleeting, and in a word our home is no where, but in the heavens: in that house not made with hands, whose maker and builder is God, and to which all ascend that love the comming of our Lord Iesus.

Though then, there may be reasons to perswade a man to live in this or that land, yet there cannot be the same reasons which the Iewes had, but now as naturall, civill and Religious bands tie men, so they must be bound, and as good reasons for things terrene and heavenly appeare, so they must be led. And so here falleth in our question, how a man that is here borne and bred, and hath lived some yeares, may remove himselfe into another countrie.

I answer, a man must not respect only to live, and doe good to himselfe, but he should see where he can live to doe most good to others: for as one saith, *He whose living is but for himselfe, it is time he were dead*. Some men there are who of necessitie must here live, as being tied to duties either to Church, Commonwealth, houshold, kindred, &c. but others, and that many, who doe no good in none of those nor can doe none, as being not able, or not in favour, or as wanting opportunitie, and live as outcasts: nobodies, eiesores, eating but for themselves, teaching but themselves, and doing good to none, either in soule or body, and so passe over daies, yeares and moneths, yea so live and so die. Now such should lift up their eies and see whether there be not some other place and countrie to which they may goe to doe good [...].

[...] But some will say, what right have I to goe live in the heathens countrie?

Letting passe the ancient discoveries, contracts and agreements which our English men have long since made in those parts, together with the acknowledgement of the histories and Chronicles of other nations, who professe the land of *America* from the Cape *De Florida* unto the Bay of *Canado* [...] is proper to the King of England, yet letting that passe, lest I be thought to meddle further th[a]n it concerns me, or further th[a]n I have discerning: I will mention such things as are within my reach, knowledge, sight and practice, since I have travailed in these affaires.

And first seeing we daily pray for the conversion of the heathens, we must consider whether there be not some ordinary meanes, and course for us to take to convert them, or whether praier for them be only referred to Gods extraordinarie worke from heaven. Now it seemeth unto me that we ought also to endevour and use the meanes to convert them, and the meanes cannot be used unlesse we goe to them or they come to us: to us they cannot come, our land is full: to them we may goe, their land is emptie.

---

[23] Archaic: Dwelling place.

This then is a sufficient reason to prove our going thither to live, lawfull: their land is spacious and void, & there are few and doe but run over the grasse, as doe also the Foxes and wilde beasts: they are not industrious, neither have art, science, skill or facultie to use either the land or the commodities of it, but all spoiles, rots, and is marred for want of manuring, gathering, ordering, &c. [...]

It being then first a vast and emptie *Chaos:* Secondly acknowledged the right of our Soveraigne King: Thirdly, by a peaceable composition in part possessed of divers of his loving subiects, I see not who can doubt or call in question the lawfulnesse of inhabiting or dwelling there [...].

To conclude, without all partialitie, the present consumption which groweth upon us here, whilst the land groaneth under so many close-fisted and unmercifull men, being compared with the easinesse, plainnesse and plentifulnesse in living in those remote places, may quickly perswade any man to a liking of this course, and to practise a removal, which being done by honest, godly and industrious men, they shall there be right hartily welcome, but for other dissolute and prophane life, their roomes are better th[a]n their companies; for if here where the Gospell hath beene so long and plentifully taught, they are yet frequent in such vices as the Heathen would shame to speake of, what will they be when there is lesse restraint in word and deed? My onely sute[24] to all men is, that whether they live there or here, they would learne to use this world as they used it not, keeping faith and a good conscience, both with God and men, that when the day of account shall come, they may come forth as good and fruitfull servants, and freely be received, and enter into the ioy of their master.   R.C.

Finis.

Source: Robert Cushman (1577/78-1625). "Reasons & Considerations Touching the Lawfulnesse of Removing out of England into the Parts of America." *A Relation or Iournall of the Beginning and Proceedings of the English Plantation Setled at Plimoth in New England, by Certaine English Adventurers Both Merchants and Others. With Their Difficult Passage, Their Safe Arivall, Their Ioyfull Building of, and Comfortable Planting Themselves in the Now Well Defended Towne of New Plimoth. As Also a Relation of Foure Severall Discoveries Since Made by Some of the Same English Planters There Resident.* London, Printed for John Bellamie [1622], 65-69, 72.

18. Francis Higginson
New-Englands Plantation; or, a Short and True Description of the Commodities and Discommodities of That Countrey (1630)

Letting passe our Voyage by Sea, we will now begin our discourse on the shore of *New-England.* And because the life and wel-fare of everie Creature here below, and the commodiousnesse of the Countrey whereas such Creatures live, doth by the most wise ordering of Gods providence, depend next unto himselfe, upon the temperature and disposition of the foure Elements, Earth, Water, Aire and Fire [...]. Therefore I will indeavour to shew you what *New-England* is by the consideration of each of these apart, [...] both to tell you of the discommodities as well as of the commodities, though as the idle proverbe is, *Travellers may lye by authoritie,* and so may take too much sinfull libertie that way. [...] No verily: It becommeth not a Preacher of Truth to bee a Writer of Falshod in any degree: and therefore I have beene carefull to report nothing of *New-England* but what I have partly seene with mine owne Eyes [...].

---

[24] Petition, supplication, or entreaty.

First therefore of the Earth of *New-England* and all the app[u]rtenances[25] thereof: It is a Land of divers and sundry sorts all about *Masathulets* Bay, and at *Charles* River is as fat blacke Earth as can be seene any where: and in other places you have a clay soyle, in other gravell, in other sandy, as it is all about our Plantation at *Salem*, for so our Towne is now named, *Psal.* 76.2.[26]

The forme of the Earth here in the superficies of it is neither too flat in the plainnesse, nor too high in Hils, but partakes of both in a mediocritie, and fit for Pasture, or for Plow or Meddow ground, as Men please to employ it: though all the Countrey bee as it were a thicke Wood for the generall, yet in divers places there is much ground cleared by the *Indians*, and especially about the Plantation: and I am told that about three miles from us a Man may stand on a little hilly place and see divers thousands of acres of ground as good as need to be, and not a Tree in the same. It is thought here is good Clay to make Bricke and Tyles and Earthen-Pots as needs to bee. At this instant we are setting a Bricke-Kill on worke to make Brickes and Tiles for the building of our Houses. For Stone, here is plentie of Slates at the Ile of Slate in *Masathulets* Bay, and Lime-stone, Free-stone, and Smooth-stone, and Iron-stone, and Marble-stone also in such store, that we have great Rockes of it, and a Harbour hard by. Our Plantation is from thence called Marble-harbour. [...]

The fertilitie of the Soyle is to be admired at, as appeareth in the aboundance of Grasse that groweth everie where [...]: but it groweth verie wildly [...], because it never had been eaten with Cattle, nor mowed with a Sythe, and seldome trampled on by foot. [...]

[...T]he aboundant encrease of Corne proves this Countrey to bee a wonderment. [...] yea, *Iosephs* encrease in *Agypt* is out-script here with us.[27] [...]

Source: Francis Higginson (1586-1630). *New-Englands Plantation; or, a Short and True Description of the Commodities and Discommodities of That Countrey*. London: T. & R. Cotes, ²1630, n.p.

19. Thomas Tillam
"Uppon the First Sight of New-England June 29 1638"

>hayle holy-land wherin our holy lord
>hath planted his most true and holy word
>hayle happye people who have dispossest
>your selves of friends, and meanes, to find some rest
>for your poore wearied soules, opprest of late
>for Jesus-sake, with Envye, spight, and hate
>to yow that blessed promise truly's given
>of sure reward, which you'l receve in heaven
>methinks I heare the Lambe of God thus speake
>Come my deare little flocke, who for my sake
>have lefte your Country, dearest friends, and goods
>and hazarded your lives o'th raginge floods
>Posses this Country; free from all anoye

---

[25] A thing which naturally forms a subordinate part of a whole system; an accessory.
[26] Ps. 76.1f.: "In Judah *is* God known: / his name *is* great in Israel. // In Salem also is his tabernacle, / and his dwelling place in Zion."
[27] Cf. Gen. 47.

heare I'le bee with yow, heare yow shall Inioye
my sabbaths, sacraments, my minestrye
and ordinances in their puritye
but yet beware of Sathans wylye baites
hee lurkes amongs yow, Cunningly hee waites
to Catch yow from mee; live not then secure
but fight 'gainst sinne, and let your lives be pure
prepare to heare your sentence thus expressed
Come yee my servants of my father Blessed

Source: Thomas Tillam (?-after 1668). "Uppon the First Sight of New-England June 29 1638." *The First Century of New England.* Ed. Harold Jantz. Worcester, MA: Antiquarian Society, 1944, 115.

20. Samuel Sewall
Wednesday, January 1. 1701. A Little before Break-a-Day at Boston of the Massachusets

Once more! Our GOD, vouchsafe to Shine
Tame Thou the Rigour of our Clime.
Make haste with thy Impartial Light,
And terminate this long dark Night.

Let the transplanted *English* Vine
Spread further still: still call it Thine.
Prune[28] it with Skill: for yield it can
More Fruit to Thee the Husbandman.

Give the poor *Indians* Eyes to see
The Light of Life: and set them free;
That they Religion may profess,
Denying all Ungodliness.

From hard'ned *Jews* the Vail remove,
Let them their Martyr'd JESUS love;
And Homage unto Him afford,
Because He is their Rightful LORD.

So false Religions shall decay,
And Darkness fly before bright Day:
So Men shall GOD in CHRIST adore;
And worship Idols vain, no more.

So *Asia*, and *Africa*,
Europa, with *America*;
All Four, in Consort join'd, shall Sing
    New Songs of Praise to CHRIST our KING.

---

[28] To cut superfluous branches or twigs from a vine or tree, in order to promote fruitfulness.

Source: Samuel Sewall(1652-1730). *Wednesday January 1. 1701 A Little before Break-a-Day at Boston of the Massachusets.* Boston: Bartholomew Green & John Allen, 1701[Broadside].

21. George Berkeley, Bishop of Cloyne
"On the Prospect of Planting Arts and Learning in America" (1752)

>The Muse, disgusted at an Age and Clime,
>>Barren of every glorious Theme,
>In distant Lands now waits a better Time,
>>Producing Subjects worthy Fame:
>
>In happy Climes, where from the genial Sun
>>And virgin Earth such Scenes ensue,
>The Force of Art by Nature seems outdone,
>>And fancied Beauties by the true:
>
>In happy Climes the Seat of Innocence,
>>Where Nature guides and Virtue rules,
>Where Men shall not impose for Truth and Sense,
>>The Pedantry of Courts and Schools:
>
>There shall be sung another golden Age,
>>The rise of Empire and of Arts,
>The Good and Great inspiring epic Rage,
>>The wisest Heads and noblest Hearts.
>
>Not such as *Europe* breeds in her decay;
>>Such as she bred when fresh and young,
>When heav'nly Flame did animate her Clay,
>>By future Poets shall be sung.
>
>Westward the Course of Empire takes its Way;
>>The four first Acts already past,
>A fifth shall close the Drama with the Day;
>>Time's noblest Offspring is the last.

Source: George Berkeley (1685-1753). "Verses by the Author, on the Prospect of Planting Arts and Learning in America." *A Miscellany, Containing Several Tracts on Various Subjects. By the Bishop of Cloyne.* London: J. and R. Tonson and S. Draper, 1752, 186-187.

IMAGES OF NATIVE AMERICANS

While the discovery of America was already an enormous challenge to the European notion of the world, the need to come to terms, in one way or another, with an unexpected branch of humankind living on this new continent was to become an even more fundamental and enduring source of conflict. Since the cultures of the indigenous peoples of the Americas were oral ones, the records of their first encounters with the explorers were written from the perspective of the 'discoverers' and colonizers. The Europeans were convinced of their superiority in every respect, and they thus perceived the encounter generally as a problem of the Natives, in spite of the fact that they were the intruders. At the very beginning, the native population generally welcomed the strangers on their shores and seemed to yield to the claim that European civilization was of a higher order. Only when the colonizers began to approach the 'uncivilized' violently and destructively, did the natives realize that the technological advance of the Europeans did not imply moral superiority.

The earliest European visual and textual images of Native Americans were essentially influenced by European conceptions of primitivism which were rooted in the traditions of classical antiquity, on the one hand, and in Christian imagology on the other (cf. section "Early Conceptualizations of America"). The reported nakedness of America's inhabitants was, for example, represented in the iconographic traditions of classical and renaissance art, with "America" being an amazon-like woman featuring classical body proportions (docs. 27, 28, 30, 31). Fantastical and quasi-utopian accounts, such as John Mandeville's *Travels*, were highly influential in creating prototypical images of 'savages' (doc. 22). Mandeville's travelogue was originally written to serve as a guide for Christian pilgrims to the Holy Land, but it included descriptions of exotic settings in the Far East, mixing authentic geographical information with fanciful accounts of immeasurable riches, cities of gold, fountains of youth, gems growing on trees, and 'savages' without heads. The significance of Mandeville's *Travels* lies in the role it played for the collective imagination of European discoverers. As late as 1599, when Europeans had had a chance for more than a hundred years to collect first-hand information about America's native population, the printing presses still released publications presenting the "fabulous people" of new world without heads or with their eyes and mouths on their chests (doc. 29). Mandeville's account introduces also another recurring theme into the representation of Native Americans, in particular Native American women: their sexual promiscuity and their personal freedom, seemingly without attachment to family structures, as described by Amerigo Vespucci in an eye-witness account from 1504 (doc. 23). Although Vespucci seems to speak with the authority of real experience, it should not be forgotten that what he saw and what he thought he understood was related to his own culture. Thus he remarks mostly upon those things that astonish him because they deviate from his own experience. Communal structures that were not immediately visible (for example, matrilineal social arrangements) remained undisclosed to him – and to many other discoverers and colonizers claiming first-hand familiarity. As a direct and pernicious consequence of such half-knowledge arose the conviction that America's indigenous population was without morals, culture, and civilization; though human, only with the rudiments of humanity, and, consequently, in need of civilization by Christian Europe in the best case, facing brutal extinction in the worst.

The most disturbing news of the inhabitants of South and Middle America reaching Europe included the occurence of cannibalism (doc. 24). Current research confirms elements of related practices, but contrary to some of the early sensational accounts, which emphasized the beastly savagery of man-eating primitives, such customs are today seen as part of religious and cultural rituals. Interestingly enough, Michel de Montaigne held a similarly critical perspective in his essay "Of the Caniballes" (doc. 25) already in 1562. He relates and interprets authentic accounts of New World-'savages' and comes to the conclusion that "there is nothing in that nation, that is either barbarous or savage, unlesse men call that barbarisme which is not common to them." With his detailed description of Indian customs and habits, Montaigne challenges old conceptualizations and advocates the counter-image of the "noble savage." Montaigne's views of the "Caniballes" already entail the most important features of such a positive stereotype, and they also exhibit the function this concept later gained for many European thinkers: the virtues of the "barbarians" were listed in order to expose the shortcomings of their own civilization. Montaigne also takes care to emphasize the empirical foundation of his account; something that should long remain an important feature in the iconography of the Native Americans. Writers and audiences alike were aware of the danger of misinformation and the emphasis on the writer's credibility was to become a stock phrase in texts about Native Americans.

In spite of the insistence on the importance of first-hand experience, the conceptual frameworks, or, in other words, the lenses through which 'discoverers' and colonizers saw the natives of the Americas did not allow a disinterested view. Even such a compassionate and humane account as Bartholomew de Las Casas's "Brief Narration" about the atrocities commited by the Spaniards includes the stereotype of the savages as children (doc. 26). Las Casas's text is also an example of how Native Americans and their ordeal were functionalized in the power-politics between the Protestant (mainly English) and Catholic (mainly Spanish) colonial empires. The moral superiority that Protestants felt in the face of Catholic Spain's treatment of South American Indians led to the perpetuation of the so-called Black Legend, painting a gruesome and tyrannical image of Spain and its colonizing efforts. The ensuing conviction that Protestant civilization and missionizing would be both more peaceful and more reasonable, and thus also more successful, also influenced the religiously motivated settlers around William Bradford, the so-called Pilgrim Fathers, as well as later Puritans.

The Pilgrim Fathers were not the first to try to found permanent colonies on the North American continent, but their lasting success was partly due to a number of coincidences of which the most important was the fact that, shortly before the arrival of the pilgrims, the Indian coastal population had been ravaged by epidemics. Thus, when the Mayflower landed in America in 1620, the pilgrims found a "vacant land" with few inhabitants, who did not offer any serious resistance to the settlers. As William Bradford records in his "Of Plymouth Plantation," the Natives had a considerable, if not a crucial part in helping the colony to survive its first winter. But by 1637, when the more and more aggressive territorial expansion of the colonizers became an obvious threat to the survival of the native population, the relationship deteriorated between the English and especially the Pequot Indians. William Bradford describes the English attack on a Pequot village, mostly women and children, at Mystic River, Connecticut. This merciless assault was not an act of immediate self-defense, but part of a deliberate strategy, aiming both at the physical destruction and at the psychological annihilation of the enemy (doc. 32).

Mary Rowlandson's captivity narrative is an early example of a highly popular genre of the eighteenth and nineteenth centuries, both in the colonies and in England. In the frontier war between indigenous Americans and British intruders, the taking of hostages was a common practice, and if the captives were liberated, they often wrote about their experiences. Whereas most of these narratives were relatively crude fabrications, Rowlandson's account is remarkable for its literary and theological qualities. She describes her captivity and her captors in Biblical terms, as an "affliction," or trial, sent by God to test the firmness of her belief. Thus, her report is a gripping tale of an individual's survival among her adversaries, but also a spiritual autobiography, in which Native Americans were functionalized as God's tools, leading Rowlandson to a religious awakening (doc. 33). Later Cotton Mather, the Puritan divine and historian, interpreted the conflict with the Indians in even more systematically theological terms. Beside the violent frontier war between settlers and resisting Native Americans, the most bitter disappointment for the Puritans was, however, their failure to missionize the 'savages.' The Puritans' confidence in the supposedly obvious superiority of Christian civilization made them blind to the integrity of Indian culture. Thus they kept explaining Native American resistance as a conscious decision to turn towards the devil. Only at the end of the eighteenth century, under the influence of enlightenment thought and romanticism, did American writers begin to seriously challenge the more negative images of Native Americans that had been promulgated by Puritan historiographers throughout the colonial period (cf. docs. 36 and 37).

Margit Peterfy

22. John Mandeville
Mandeville's Travels (1356/1496)

[...] Fro this countre lii. iournes[1] is a countre that men call Lamory in that londe is greate hete and it is custome syth that men and women go all naked and they scorne theym that are clad. for they say that god made Adam and Eve al nakid and that men shulde have no shame of that that god made and they byleve in god that made Adam and Eve and all the worlde and there is no woman weddyd but women ar all comon there and they forsake no man. And they say that god commaunded to Adam and Eve and all that came of theym saynge.

Crescyte et multiplicamini et replete terram.[2]

That is for to say in englysshe wex and be multyplyed and fyll the erthe and no man may say there. Thys is my wyfe. Ne woman say. This is my husbond. And whan they have chyldren they gyve to whom they w[i]ll. of men that have delt with theym. Also the londe is alle com[mon] for that one man hathe in one yere another man hath it another yere. Also all the goodes and cornes[3] of the countre ar in comon for there is no thynge under lok[4] and as riche is one man as another. but they have an yll custume they ete gladlyer mans flesshe than other Theder[5] brynge marchauntes their children to sell and those that are fatte they ete theym. and the other kepe they tyll they be fatte and than are they eten. [...] But there is a great Ile that men call Iana. And the kynge of that countre hath under hym vii. kynges for he is full mighty In that Ile groweth all maner of spices more plenteuously than in other places [...]. The kynge of this londe hath a riche paleys:[6] and the best that is in the worlde for all the greces[7] in to his hall and chambers ben all of golde. another of sylver and all the walles ar covered and plated with golde and sylver.

Source: John Mandeville (flourished 1371). *Mandeville's Travels, editio princeps* [1st English edition] *by Richard Pynson*, 1496. Rpt. of *The Book of John Mandeville: An Edition of the Pynson Text*. Ed. Tamarah Kohanski. Tempe, AZ: Arizona Center for Medieval and Renaissance Studies, 2001, 55-56.

23. Amerigo Vespucci
Letter to Piero Soderini (1504)

[...] They [Indian women] are not very jealous, and are libidinous beyond measure, and the women far more than the men; for I refrain out of decency from telling you the trick which they play to satisfy their immoderate lust. They are very fertile women, and in their pregnancies avoid no toil. Their parturitions are so easy that one day after giving birth they go out everywhere, and especially to bathe in the rivers; and they are sound as fish. They are so heartless and cruel that, if they become angry with their husbands, they immediately resort to a trick whereby they kill the child within the womb, and a miscarriage is brought about, and for this reason they kill a great many

---

[1] A 52 days journey.
[2] Gen. 9.1; 9.7.
[3] The small hard seed or fruit of a plant, here fruits in general.
[4] Locked up.
[5] To or towards that place, thither.
[6] Palace.
[7] Steps or stairs (in a flight).

babies. They are women of pleasing person, very well proportioned, so that one does not see on their bodies any ill-formed feature or limb. And although they go about utterly naked, they are fleshy women, and that part of their privies which he who has not seen them would think to see is invisible; for they cover all with their thighs, save that part [for] which nature made no provision, and which is modestly speaking, the *mons veneris*. In short they are no more ashamed [of their shameful parts] than we are in displaying the nose and mouth. Only exceptionally will you see a woman with drooping breasts, or with belly shrunken through frequent parturition, or with other wrinkles; for all look as though they had never given birth. They showed themselves very desirous of copulating with us Christians. While among these people we did not learn that they had any religion. They can be termed neither Moors nor Jews; and they are worse than heathen; because we did not see that they offered any sacrifice, nor yet did they have [any] house of prayer. I deem their manner of life to be Epicurean.[8] [...]

Source: Amerigo Vespucci (1454-1512). *Letter to Piero Soderini, Gonfaloniere. The Year 1504*. Translated by George Tyler Northup. Princeton: Princeton University Press, 1916, 8-9.

24. Johann Froschauer
Dise figur anzaigt uns das volck und insel (1505)

Source: *Dise figur anzaigt uns das volck vnd insel die gefunden ist durch den cristenlichen künig zü Portigal oder von seinen underthonen. Die leüt sind also nackent hübsch. braun wolgestalt von leib. ir heübter halss. arm. scham. füss. frawen und mann ain wenig mit federn bedeckt. Auch haben die mann*

---

[8] Here used with the connotation of devoted to the pursuit of pleasure, luxurious, sensual, gluttonous.

in iren angesichten und brust vil edel gestain. Es hat auch nyemantz nichts sunder sind alle ding gemain. Und die mann habendt weyber welche in gefallen. es sey mütter. schwester. oder freündt. darjnn haben sy nit underschayd. Sy streyten auch mit ainander. Sy essen auch ainander selbs die erschlagen werden und hencken das selbig flisch in den rauch. Sy werden alt hundert vnd fünfftzig iar. Und haben kain regiment. Colored woodcut. Augsburg: Johann Froschauer, 1505. Single broadsheet, V, 2. *America: Early Maps of the New World.* Ed. Hans Wolff. Munich: Prestel, 1992, 29.

25. Michel Eyquem de Montaigne
"Of the Caniballes" (1562)

[...] I have had long time dwelling with me a man, who for the space of ten or twelve yeares had dwelt in that other world, which in our age was lately discovered in those parts where Villegaignon first landed, and surnamed Antartike France.[9] This discoverie of so infinit and vast a countrie, seemeth worthy great consideration. I wot not whether I can warrant my selfe, that some other be not discovered hereafter, sithence so many worthy men, and better learned than we are, have so many ages beene deceived in this. I feare me our eies be greater than our bellies, and that we have more curiositie than capacitie. We embrace all, but we fasten nothing but wind. [...]

[...] Now (to returne to my purpose) I finde (as farre as I have beene informed) there is nothing in that nation, that is either barbarous or savage, unlesse men call that barbarisme which is not common to them. As indeed, we have no other ayme of truth and reason, than the example and Idea of the opinions and customes of the countrie we live in. There is ever perfect religion, perfect policie, perfect and compleat use of all things. They are even savage, as we call those fruits wilde, which nature of her selfe, and of her ordinarie progresse hath produced: whereas indeed, they are those which our selves have altered by our artificiall devices, and diverted from their common order, we should rather terme savage. In those are the true and most profitable vertues, and naturall properties most lively and vigorous, which in these we have bastardized, applying them to the pleasure of our corrupted taste. And if notwithstanding, in divers fruits of those countries that were never tilled, we shall finde, that in respect of ours they are most excellent, and as delicate unto our taste; there is no reason, art should gaine the point of honour of our great and puissant mother Nature. We have so much by our inventions surcharged the beauties and riches of her workes, that we have altogether overchoaked her: yet where ever her puritie shineth, she makes our vaine and frivolous enterprises wonderfully ashamed.

> *Et veniunt hederæ sponte sua melius,*
> *Surgit et in solis formosior arbutus antris,*
> *Et volucres nulla dulcius arte canunt.* – PROPERT. i. *El.* ii. 10.
>
> Ivies spring better of their owne accord,
> Unhanted plots much fairer trees afford.
> Birds by no art much sweeter notes record.

[...] Those nations seeme therefore so barbarous unto me, because they have received very little fashion from humane wit, and are yet neere their originall naturalitie. The lawes of nature doe yet command them, which are but little bastardized by ours, and that with

---

[9] Island in Guanabara Bay, southeastern Brazil, where, in 1555, the French Huguenots under the explorer Nicolas Durand de Villegaignon established the colony of La France Antarctique.

such puritie, as I am sometimes grieved the knowledge of it came no sooner to light, at what time there were men, that better than we could have judged of it. [... For] me seemeth that what in those nations we see by experience, doth not only exceed all the pictures wherewith licentious Poesie hath proudly imbellished the golden age, and all her quaint inventions to faine[10] a happy condition of man, but also the conception and desire of Philosophy. They could not imagine a genuitie[11] so pure and simple, as we see it by experience; nor ever beleeve our societie might be maintained with so little art and humane combination. It is a nation, would I answer Plato,[12] that hath no kinde of traffike, no knowledge of Letters, no intelligence of numbers, no name of magistrat, nor of politike superioritie; no use of service, of riches or of povertie; no contracts, no successions, no partitions, no occupation but idle; no respect of kindred, but common, no apparell but naturall, no manuring of lands, no use of wine, corne, or mettle. The very words that import lying, falshood, treason, dissimulations, covetousnes, envie, detraction, and pardon, were never heard of amongst them. How dissonant would hee finde his imaginarie common-wealth from this perfection? [...]

Furthermore, they live in a country of so exceeding pleasant and temperate situation, that as my testimonies have told me, it is verie rare to see a sicke body amongst them; and they have further assured me they never saw any man there, either shaking with the palsie, toothlesse, with eies dropping, or crooked and stooping through age. They are seated alongst the sea-coast, encompassed toward the land with huge and steepie mountaines, having betweene both, a hundred leagues or thereabout of open and champaine ground. They have great abundance of fish and flesh, that have no resemblance at all with ours, and eat them without any sawces, or skill of Cookerie, but plaine boiled or broiled. The first man that brought a horse thither, although he had in many other voyages conversed with them, bred so great a horror in the land, that before they could take notice of him, they slew him with arrowes. [...] They beleeve their soules to be eternall, and those that have deserved well of their Gods, to be placed in that part of heaven where the Sunne riseth, and the cursed toward the West in opposition. [...] They warre against the nations, that lie beyond their mountaines, to which they go naked, having no other weapons than bowes, or woodden swords, sharpe at one end, as our broaches are. It is an admirable thing to see the constant resolution of their combats, which never end but by effusion of bloud and murther: for they know not what feare or rowts[13] are. Every Victor brings home the head of the enemie he hath slaine as a Trophey of his victorie, and fastneth the same at the entrance of his dwelling place. After they have long time used and entreated their prisoners well, and with all commodities they can devise, he that is the Master of them; sommoning a great assembly of his acquaintance; tieth a corde to one of the prisoners armes, by the end whereof he holds him fast, with some distance from him, for feare he might offend him, and giveth the other arme, bound in like manner, to the dearest friend he hath, and both in the presence of all the assembly kill him with swords: which done, they roast, and then eat him in common, and send some slices of him to such of their friends as are absent. It is not as some imagine, to nourish themselves with

---

[10] To pretend (obsolete).
[11] Simplicity (obsolete).
[12] Plato (427-348 BC) was one of the first writers to propagate the idea of a mythical Atlantis. In *Critias* (108e; 113e ff.) as well as in *Timaios* (25a-d) he tells us in great detail the story of a civilization with divine origins that lived on an island outside the columns of Hercules (usually interpreted as the Strait of Gibraltar).
[13] Disorderly retreat or flight.

it, [...] but to represent an extreme, and inexpiable[14] revenge. Which we prove thus; some of them perceiving the Portugales, who had confederated themselves with their adversaries, to use another kinde of death, when they tooke them prisoners; which was, to burie them up to the middle, and against the upper part of the body to shoot arrowes, and then being almost dead, to hang them up; they supposed, that these people of the other world (as they who had sowed the knowledge of many vices amongst their neighbours, and were much more cunning in all kindes of evils and mischiefe than they) under-tooke not this manner of revenge without cause, and that consequently it was more smartfull, and cruell than theirs, and thereupon began to leave their old fashion to follow this. I am not sorie we note the barbarous horror of such an action, but grieved, that prying so narrowly into their faults we are so blinded in ours. I thinke there is more barbarisme in eating men alive, than to feed upon them being dead; to mangle by tortures and torments a body full of lively sense, to roast him in peeces, to make dogges and swine to gnaw and teare him in mammockes[15] (as wee have not only read, but seene very lately, yea and in our owne memorie, not amongst ancient enemies, but our neighbours and fellow-citizens; and which is worse, under pretence of pietie and religion) than to roast and eat him after he is dead.

[...] We may then well call them barbarous, in regard of reasons rules, but not in respect of us that exceed them in all kinde of barbarisme. Their warres are noble and generous, and have as much excuse and beautie, as this humane infirmitie may admit: they ayme at nought so much, and have no other foundation amongst them, but the meere jelousie of vertue. They contend not for the gaining of new lands; for to this day they yet enjoy that naturall ubertie[16] and fruitfulnesse, which without labouring toyle, doth in such plenteous abundance furnish them with all necessary things, that they need not enlarge their limits. They are yet in that happy estate, as they desire no more, than what their naturall necessities direct them: whatsoever is beyond it, is to them superfluous.

[...] Three of that nation, ignorant how deare the knowledge of our corruptions will one day cost their repose, securitie, and happinesse, and how their ruine shall proceed from this commerce, which I imagine is already well advanced, (miserable as they are to have suffered themselves to be so cosoned[17] by a desire of new-fangled[18] novelties, and to have quit the calmenesse of their climate, to come and see ours) were at Roane[19] in the time of our late King Charles the ninth[20] [...].

Source: Michel Eyquem de Montaigne (1533-1592). "Of the Caniballes." *The Essays of Montaigne. Done into English by John Florio. Anno 1603*. London: David Nutt, 1892, 218, 221-227, 231.

---

[14] Of a feeling that cannot be appeased by expiation; implacable, irreconcilable.
[15] Shapeless piece, fragment, shred (archaic).
[16] Fertility, abundance.
[17] Cozen(ed): beguiled, cheated.
[18] Very fond of novelty or new things; easily carried away by whatever is new.
[19] Rouen, city in Normandy, France.
[20] Charles IX was king of France from 1560; he authorized the massacre of Protestants on St. Bartholomew's Day, Aug. 23-24, 1572, on the advice of his mother, Catherine de Medici.

26. Bartholomew de Las Casas
"A Briefe Narration of the Destruction of the Indes, by the Spanyardes" (1583)

The Indes were discovered the yeere one thousande, foure hundred, nientie two, and inhabited by the Spanish the yeere next after ensuing: so as it is about fourtie niene yeeres sithens that the Spaniards some of them went into those partes. And the first land that they entered to inhabite, was the great and most fertile Isle of Hispaniola,[21] which contayneth six hundreth leagues in compasse. There are other great and infinite Iles rounde about and in the confines on all sides: which wee have seen the most peopled, and the fullest of their owne native people, as any other countrey in the worlde may be. The firme lande[22] lying off from this Ilande two hundreth and fiftie leagues, and somewhat over at the most, contayneth in length on the seacoast more then tenne thousande leagues: which are alreadie discovered, and dayly be discovered more and more, all ful of people, as an Emmote[23] hill of Emmots. Insomuch, as by that which since, unto the yere the fourtieth and one hath beene discovered: It seemeth that God hath bestowed in that same countrey, the gulphe[24] or the greatest portion of mankinde.

God created all these innumerable multitudes in every sorte, very simple, without sutteltie, or craft, without malice, very obedient, and very faithfull to their naturall liege Lordes, and to the Spaniardes, whom they serve, very humble, very patient, very desirous of peace making, and peacefull, without brawles and struglings, without quarrelles, without strife, without rancour or hatred, by no meanes desirous of revengement.

They are also people very gentle, and very tender, and of an easie complexion, and which can sustayne no travell,[25] and doe die very soone of any disease whatsoever, in suche sorte as the very children of Princes and Noble men brought up amongst us, in all commodities, ease, and delicatenesse, are not more soft then those of that countrey: yea, although they bee the children of labourers. They are also very poore folke, which possesse litle, neither yet do so much as desire to have much worldly goodes, & therefore neither are they proud, ambitious, nor covetous. Their diet is such (as it seemeth) ye of the holy fathers in the desert, hath not been more scarse, nor more streight, nor lesse daintie, nor lesse sumptuous. Their appareling is commonly to goe naked: all save their shamefast partes alone covered. And when they be clothed, at the most, it is but of a mantell of bombacie[26] of an elle and a halfe, or a two elles of linnen square. Their lodging is upon a matte, and those which have the best: sleepe as it were upon a net fastened at the foure corners, which they call in the language of the Ile of Hispaniola, Hamasas.[27] They have their understanding very pure and quicke, being teachable and capable of all good learning, verye apt to receive our holy Catholique faith, and to be instructed in good and vertuous maners, having lesse encombrances[28] and disturbances to the atteyn-

---

[21] Formerly Española, second largest island of the West Indies. Columbus landed on the island in 1492 and named it La Isla Española. During Spanish colonial times it was commonly called Santo Domingo.
[22] Reference to the continent of South America.
[23] Ant.
[24] Figurative: Large portion that can be swallowed in an act of gulping.
[25] Work.
[26] Bombace: cotton fibre dressed for stuffing or padding garments; cotton-wadding.
[27] Hammock.
[28] Burden or impediment.

ing thereunto, then al the folke of the world besids, and are so enflamed, ardent, and importune to knowe and understand the matters of the faith after they have but begunne once to taste them, as likewise the exercise of the Sacraments of the Church, & the divine service: that in truth, the religious men have need of a singuler patience to support them. And to make an ende, I have heard many Spaniardes many times holde this as assured, and that whiche they could not deny, concerning the good nature which they sawe in them. Undoubtedly these folkes shoulde be the happiest in the worlde, if onely they knewe God.

Upon these lambes so meeke, so qualified & endewed of their maker and creator, as hath bin said, entred the Spanish incontinent as they knewe them, as wolves, as lions, & as tigres most cruel of long time famished: and have not done in those quarters these 40. yeres be past, neither yet doe at this present, ought els save teare them in peeces, kill them, martyre them, afflict them, torment them, & destroy them by straunge sortes of cruelties never neither seene, nor reade, nor hearde of the like (of the which some shall bee set downe hereafter) so farre foorth that of above three Millions of soules that were in the Ile of Hispaniola, and that we have seene, there are not nowe two hundreth natives of the countrey. The Isle of Cuba, the which is in length as farre as from Vallodolyd until Rome, is at this day as it were al wast. S. Johns ile,[29] and that of Iamayca both of them very great, very fertil, and very fayre: are desolate. Likewise the iles of Lucayos,[30] neere to the ile of Hispaniola, and of the north side unto that of Cuba, in number being above threescore Ilandes, together with those which they cal the iles of Geante, one with another, great and litle, whereof the very wurst is fertiler then the kings garden at Sevill,[31] and the countrey the healthsomest in the world: there were in these same iles more then five hundreth thousand soules, and at this day there is not one only creature. For they have bin all of them slayne, after that they had drawen them out from thence to labour in their minerals in the ile of Hispaniola, where there were no more left of the inbornes natives of that iland. A ship riding for the space of three yeeres betwixt all these ilands, to the ende, after the inning of this kinde of vintage, to gleane and cull the remainder of these folke (for there was a good Christian moved with pitie and compassion, to convert & win unto Christ such as might be found) there were not found but eleven persons whiche I saw: other iles more then thirtie nere to the ile of S. John have likewise bin dispeopled and marred. All these iles contayn above two thousand leagues of lande, and are all dispeopled and laide waste.

As touching the maine firme lande, wee are certaine that our Spaniardes, by their cruelties & cursed doings have dispeopled & made desolate more then ten realmes greater then all Spaine, comprising also therewith Aragon[32] and Portugall, and twise as much or more land then there is from Sevill to Jerusalem whiche are above a thousand leagues: whiche realmes as yet unto this present day remaine in a wildernes and utter desolation, having bin befor time as well peopled as was possible.

We are able to yeeld a good and certaine accompt,[33] that there is win ye space of ye said 40. yeeres, by those said tyranies & divlish doings of the Spaniards doen to death uniustly and tyrannously more then twelve Millions of soules, men, women, and children.

---

[29] St. John, one of the Virgin Islands.
[30] Bahamas, inhabited by the Lucayos before the arrival of the Europeans.
[31] Seville, Spain.
[32] Region of northeastern Spain.
[33] Account.

And I verilie do beleeve, and thinke not to mistake therein, that there are dead more then fifteene Millions of soules.

Those whiche have got them out of Spaine into that countrey, bearing them selves as Christians, have kept two generall and principall wayes to eradicate and abolishe from off the face of the earth those miserable nations: The one is their uniust, cruell, bloddie and tyrannicall warre. That other maner is, that they have slayne all those which coulde any kinde of wayes so muche as gaspe, breath, or thinke to set them selves at libertie, or but to withdrawe them selves from the tormentes whiche they endure, as are all the naturall Lordes, and the men of valour and courage. For commonly they suffer not in the warres to live any, save children and women: oppressing also afterwardes those very same with the most cruel, dreadful, and hainous thraldome[34] that ever hath been layde upon men or beastes. Unto these two kindes of tyranie diabolicall, may be reduced and sorted as it were the issues one under another to their head, all other their diverse and infinite maners of dooing which they keept to lay desolate, and roote out those folke without number.

The cause why the Spanishe have destroyed suche an infinite of soules, hath been onely, that they have helde it for their last scope and marke to gette golde, and to enriche them selves in a short tyme, and to mount at one leape to very high estates, in no wise agreeable to their persons: or, for to say in a word, the cause hereof hath been their avarice and ambition, whiche hath seased them the exceedingest in the worlde in consideration of those landes so happie and rich, and the people so humble, so patient, and so easie to be subdued. Whom they have never had any respect, or made any more accompt of (I speake the trueth of that whiche I have seene all the tyme that I was there conversant) I say not then of beastes (for woulde to GOD that they had entreated and esteemed them but as beastes:) but lesse then of the myre[35] of the streetes, and even as muche care is it that they have had of their lives and of their soules. And by this meanes have died so many Millions without faith and without sacramentes.

It is a certaine veritie, and that which also the tyrants them selves knowe right well and confesse, that the Indiens throughout all the Indes never brought any displeasure unto the Spaniardes: but rather that they reputed them as come from heaven, untill suche tyme as they, or their neighbours had received the first, sundrie wronges, being robbed, killed, forced, and tormented by them. [...]

Source: Bartolomew de las Casas (1474-1566). "A Briefe Narration of the Destruction of the Indes, by the Spanyardes." *The Spanish Colonie, or Briefe Chronicle of the Acts and Gestes of the Spaniardes in the West Indies, Called the Newe World, for the Space of xl. Yeeres: Written in the Castilian Tongue by the Reverend Bishop Bartholomew de las Casas or Casaus, a Friar of the Order of S. Dominicke: And Nowe First Translated into English, by M.M.S.* London: William Broome, 1583, n.p.

---

[34] Bondage, servitude, captivity.
[35] Mud, slimy soil.

27. Jan Sadeler the Elder "America" (1581)

Source: Jan Sadeler the Elder (1550?-1600?): "The Allegory of America" (1581). Copperplate engraving of Jan Sadeler after Dirk Barendz the Younger (1534-1592). Staatliche Graphische Sammlung Munich, 41232 D. *America: Early Maps of the New World.* Ed. Hans Wolff. Munich: Prestel, 1992, 38.

28. Philippe Galle
"America" (c. 1581-1600)

Source: Philippe Galle (1537-1612). "America" (ca. 1581-1600). *The New Golden Land: European Images of America from the Discoveries to the Present Time*. Ed. Hugh Honour. New York: Pantheon Books, 1975, 87.

29. Levinus Hulsius
Kurtze Wunderbare Beschreibung (1599)

Source: Levinus Hulsius (?-1606). *Kurtze Wunderbare Beschreibung Deß Goldreichen Königreichs Guiana in America oder newen Welt*. Nuremberg, 1599 [German translation of Sir Walter Raleigh's *The Discoverie of the Large Rich, and Bewtiful Empyre of Guiana*, 1596]. *America: Early Maps of the New World*. Ed. Hans Wolff. Munich: Prestel, 1992, 40.

30. Crispijn van de Passe the Elder
"America" (early 17th century)

Source: Crispijn van de Passe the Elder (1564-1637). "America." *The New Golden Land: European Images of America from the Discoveries to the Present Time*. Ed. Hugh Honour. New York: Pantheon, 1975, 88.

31. Jan van der Straet
"Discovery of America" (1589)

Source: Jan van der Straet (Stradanus; 1523-1605). "[Discovery of America: Vespucci Landing in America, 1589]." *Nova Reperta*. Amsterdam, 1600.

32. William Bradford
"Of Plymouth Plantation" (1629-1646)

In the mean time, the Pequents,[36] espetially in the winter before, sought to make peace with the Narigansets,[37] and used very pernicious arguments to move them therunto: as that the English were strangers and begane to overspred their countrie, and would deprive them therof in time, if they were suffered to grow and increse; and if the Narigansets did assist the English to subdue them, they did but make way for their owne overthrow, for if they were rooted out, the English would soone take occasion to subjugate them; and if they would harken to them, they should not neede to fear the strength of the English; for they would not come to open battle with them, but fire their houses, kill their katle, and lye in ambush for them as they went abroad upon their occasions; and all this they might easily doe without any or litle danger to them selves. The which course being held, they well saw the English could not long subsiste, but they would either be starved with hunger, or be forced to forsake the countrie; with many the like things; insomuch that the Narigansets were once wavering, and were halfe minded to have made peace with them, and joyned against the English. But againe when they considered, how much wrong they had received from the Pequents, and what an oppertunitie they now had by the help of the English to right them selves, revenge was so sweete unto them, as it prevailed above all the rest; so as they resolved to joyne with the English against them, and did. The Court here agreed forwith to send 50. men at their owne charg; and with as much speed as posiblie they could, gott them armed, and had made them ready under sufficiente leaders, and provided a barke to carrie them provisions and tend upon them for all occasions; buth when they were ready to march (with a supply from the Bay) they had word to stay, for the enimy was as good as vanquished, and their would be no neede.

I shall not take upon me exactly to describe their proceedings in these things, because I expecte it will be fully done by them selves, who best know the carrage and circumstances of things; I shall therfore but touch them in generall. From Connightecute[38] (who were most sencible of the hurt sustained, and the present danger), they sett out a partie of men, and an other partie mett them from the Bay, at the Narigansets, who were to joyne with them. The Narigansets were ernest to be gone before the English were well rested and refreshte, espetially some of them which came last. It should seeme their desire was to come upon the enemie sudenly, and undiscovered. Ther was a barke of this place, newly put in ther, which was come from Conightecutte, who did incourage them to lay hold of the Indeans forwardnes, and to shew as great forwardnes as they, for it would incorage them, and expedition might prove to their great advantage. So they went on, and so ordered their march, as the Indeans brought them to a forte of the enimies (in which most of their cheefe men were) before day. They approached the same with great silence, and surrounded it both with English and Indeans, that they might not breake out; and so assualted them with great courage, shooting amongst them, and entered the forte with all speed; and those that first entered found sharp resistance from the enimie, who both shott at and grapled with them; others rane into their howses, and brought out fire, and sett them on fire, which soone tooke in their matts, and,

---
[36] Pequot Indians: a group of Algonquian-speaking Indians who inhabited eastern Connecticut.
[37] Narragansetts: Algonquian-speaking Indian tribe that occupied most of what is now Rhode Island.
[38] Connecticut.

standing close togeather, with the wind, all was quickly on flame, and therby more were burnte to death then was otherwise slain; it burnte their bowstrings, and made them unservisable. Those that scaped the fire were slaine with the sword; some hewed to peeces, other rune throw with their rapiers, so as they were quickly dispatchte, and very few escaped. It was conceived they thus destroyed about 400. at this time. It was a fearfull sight to see them thus frying in the fyer, and the streams of blood quenching the same, and horrible was the stinck and sente ther of; but the victory seemed a sweete sacrifice,[39] and they gave the prays therof to God, who had wrought so wonderfuly for them, thus to inclose their enimis in their hands, and give them so speedy a victory over so proud and insulting an enimie. The Narigansett Indeans, all this while, stood round aboute, but aloofe from all danger, and left the whole execution to the English, except it were the stoping of any that broke away, insulting over their enimies in this their ruine and miserie, when they saw them dancing in the flames, calling them by a word in their owne language, signifing, O brave Pequents! which they used familierly among them selves in their own prayes, in songs of triumph after their victories. [...]

Source: William Bradford (1590-1657). *Bradford's History of Plymouth Plantation, 1606-1646.* Ed. William T. Davis. New York: Scribner's, 1908, 338-340.

33. Mary Rowlandson
The Soveraignty & Goodness of God, Together, with the Faithfulness of His Promises Displayed; Being a Narrative of the Captivity and Restauration of Mrs. Mary Rowlandson (1682)[40]

On the tenth of *February* 1675. Came the *Indians* with great numbers upon *Lancaster*[41]: Their first coming was about Sun-rising; hearing the noise of some Guns, we looked out; several Houses were burning, and the Smoke ascending to Heaven. There were five persons taken in one house, the Father, and the Mother and a sucking Child, they knockt on the head; the other two they took and carried away alive. The[re] were two others, who being out of their Garison[42] upon some occasion were set upon; one was knockt on the head, the other escaped: Another the[re] was who running along was shot and wounded, and fell down; he begged of them his life, promising them Money (as they told me) but they would not hearken to him but knockt him in head, and stript him naked, and split open his Bowels. Another seeing many of the *Indians* about his Barn, ventured and went out, but was quickly shot down. There were three others belonging to the same Garison who were killed; the *Indians* getting up upon the roof of the Barn, had advantage to shoot down upon them over their Fortification. Thus these murtherous wretches went on, burning, and destroying before them.

---

[39] Cf. Lev. 2.1-2.
[40] The title of the first English edition foregrounds the adventures among the Native Americans: *A True History of the Captivity & Restoration of Mrs. Mary Rowlandson, A Minister's Wife in New-England. Wherein Is Set Forth, the Cruel and Inhumane Usage She Underwent amongst the Heathens, for Eleven Weeks Time: And Her Deliverance from Them. Written by Her Own Hand, for Her Private Use: And Now Made Publick at the Earnest Desire of Some Friends, and for the Benefit of the Afflicted. Whereunto Is Annexed, a Sermon of the Possibility of God's Forsaking a People That Have Been Near and Dear to Him. Preached by Mr. Joseph Rowlandson, Husband to the Said Mrs. Rowlandson: It Being His Last Sermon.* London: Joseph Poole, 1682.
[41] Frontier town of approximately fifty families, some thirty miles west of Boston.
[42] One of six fortified houses in Lancaster; only the Rowlandson house fell to the Indians upon attack.

At length they came and beset our own house, and quickly it was the dolefullest day that ever mine eyes saw. The House stood upon the edge of a hill; some of the *Indians* got behind the hill, others into the Barn, and others behind any thing that could shelter them; from all which places they shot against the House, so that the Bullets seemed to fly like hail; and quickly they wounded one man among us, then another, and then a third, About two hours [... they fired the house] once and one ventured out and quenched [the fire], but they quickly fired it again, and that took. Now is that dreadfull hour come, that I have often heard of (in time of War, as it was the case of others) but now mine eyes see it. Some in our house were fighting for their lives, others wallowing in their blood, the House on fire over our heads, and the bloody Heathen ready to knock us on the head, if we stirred out: Now might we hear Mothers & Children crying out for themselves, and one another, *Lord, what shall we do?* Then I took my Children[43] (and one of my sisters, hers) to go forth and leave the house: but as soon as we came to the dore and appeared, the Indians shot so thick that the bulletts rattled against the House, as if one had taken an handfull of stones and threw them, so that we were fain to give back. We had six stout Dogs belonging to our Garrison, but none of them would stir, though another time, if any *Indian* had come to the door, they were ready to fly upon him and tear him down. The Lord hereby would make us the more to acknowledge his hand, and to see that our help is alwayes in him. But out we must go, the fire increasing, and coming along behind us, roaring, and the *Indians* gaping before us with their Guns, Spears and Hatchets to devour us. No sooner were we out of the House, but my Brother in Law (being before wounded, in defending the house, in or near the throat) fell down dead, wherat the *Indians* scornfully shouted, and hallowed, and were presently upon him, stripping off his cloaths, the bullets flying thick, one went through my side, and the same (as would seem) through the bowels and hand of my dear Child in my arms. One of my elder Sisters Children, named *William*, had then his Leg broken, which the *Indians* perceiving, they knockt him on head. Thus were we butchered by those merciless Heathen, standing amazed, with the blood running down to our heels. My eldest Sister being yet in the House, and seeing those wofull sights, the Infidels haling Mothers one way, and Children another, and some wallowing in their blood: and her elder Son telling her that her Son *William* was dead, and my self was wounded, she said, And, *Lord let me dy with them*; which was no sooner said, but she was struck with a Bullet, and fell down dead over the threshold. I hope she is reaping the fruit of her good labours, being faithfull to the service of God in her place. In her younger years she lay under much trouble upon spiritual accounts, till it pleased God to make that precious Scripture take hold of her heart, 2 *Cor.* 12. 9. *And he said unto me my Grace is sufficient for thee.* [...]

Oh the dolefull sight that now was to behold at this House! *Come, behold the works of the Lord, what dissolations*[44] *he has made in the Earth*. Of thirty seven persons who were in this one House, none escaped either present death, or a bitter captivity, save only one, who might say as he. Job 1.15. *And I only am escaped alone to tell the News.* There were twelve killed, some shot, some stab'd with their Spears, some knock'd down with their Hatchets. When we are in prosperity, Oh the little that we think of such dreadfull sights, and to see our dear Friends, and Relations ly bleeding out their heart-blood upon

---

[43] Rowlandson had three children. With the exception of her youngest daughter, who died within a week of wounds inflicted during the raid, her children were immediately separated from her during her captivity.
[44] In modern English: desolation.

the ground. There was one who was chopt into the head with a Hatchet, and stript naked, and yet was crawling up and down. It is a solemn sight to see so many Christians lying in their blood, some here, and some there, like a company of Sheep torn by Wolves. All of them stript naked by a company of hell-hounds, roaring, singing, ranting and insulting, as if they would have torn our very hearts out; yet the Lord by his Almighty power preserved a number of us from death, for there were twenty-four of us taken alive and carried Captive.

I had often before this said, that if the Indians *should come, I should chuse rather to be killed by them then taken alive* but when it came to the tryal my mind changed; their glittering weapons so daunted my spirit, that I chose rather to go along with those (as I may say) ravenous Beasts, then that moment to end my dayes; and that I may the better declare what happened to me during that grievous Captivity I shall particularly speak of the severall Removes we had up and down the Wilderness.

The first Remove

Now away we must go with those Barbarous Creatures, with our bodies wounded and bleeding, and our hearts no less than our bodies. About a mile we went that night, up upon a hill within sight of the Town where they intended to lodge. There was hard by a vacant house (deserted by the English before, for fear of the *Indians*) I asked them whither I might not lodge in the house that night? to which they answered, what will you love *English men* still? this was the dolefullest night that ever my eyes saw. Oh the roaring, and singing and danceing, and yelling of those black creatures in the night, which made the place a lively resemblance of hell. [...]

> Source: Mary Rowlandson (1637-1710/11). *The Sovereignty & Goodness of God, Together, with the Faithfulness of His Promises Displayed; Being a Narrative of the Captivity and Restauration of Mrs. Mary Rowlandson. Commended by Her, to All That Desires to Know the Lords Doings to, and Dealings with Her. Especially to Her Dear Children and Relations, The Second Addition Corrected and Amended. Written by Her Own Hand for Her Private Use, and Now Made Publick at the Earnest Desire of Some Friends, and for the Benefit of the Afflicted. Deut. 32.39, See now that I, even I am he, and there is no God with me: I kill and I make alive, I wound and I heal neither is there any can deliver out of my hand.* Cambridge, MA: Samuel Green, 1682, 1-6.

34. Cotton Mather
"The Triumphs of the Reformed Religion in America: Or, the Life of the Renowned John Eliot" (1702)

[...] The exemplary *Charity* of this excellent Person [the Indian missionary John Eliot ...] will not be seen in its due Lustres,[45] unless we make some Reflections upon several Circumstances which he beheld these forlorn *Indians* in. Know then, that these doleful Creatures are the veriest *Ruines of Mankind*, which are to be found any where upon the Face of the Earth. No such *Estates* are to be expected among them, as have been the *Baits* which the pretended *Converters* in other Countries have snapped at. One might see among them, what an *hard Master* the Devil is, to the most devoted of his *Vassals*! These abject Creatures, live in a Country full of *Mines*; we have already made entrance upon our *Iron*; and in the very Surface of the Ground among us, 'tis

---

[45] Radiant beauty or splendor.

thought there lies *Copper* enough to supply all this World; besides other Mines hereafter to be exposed; but our shiftless *Indians* were never Owners of so much as a *Knife*, till we come among them; their Name for an *English-man* was a *Knife-man*; Stone was instead of Metal for their *Tools*; and for their *Coins*, they have only little *Beads* with Holes in them to string them upon a *Bracelet* [...].

The[y] live in a Country, where *we* now have all the Conveniencies of human Life: But as for *them*, their *housing* is nothing but a few *Mats* ty'd about *Poles* fastened in the Earth, where a good *Fire* is their *Bed Clothes* in the coldest Seasons; their *Clothing* is but a Skin of a Beast, covering their *Hind-parts*, their *Fore-parts* having but a little Apron, where nature calls for Secrecy; their *Diet* has not a greater Dainty[46] than their *Nokehick*,[47] that is a spoonful of their *parch'd meal*, with a spoonful of *Water*, which will strengthen them to travel a Day together [...]. Their *Physick* is, excepting a few odd *Specificks*, which some of them Encounter certain Cases with, nothing hardly, but an *Hot-House* or a *Powaw*; their *Hot-House* is a little *Cave* about eight foot over, where after they have terribly heated it, a Crew of them go sit and sweat and smoke for an Hour together, and then immediately run into some very cold adjacent Brook, without the least Mischief to them; 'tis this way they recover themselves from some Diseases, particularly from the *French*; but in most of their dangerous Distempers, 'tis a *Powaw* that must be sent for; that is, a *Priest*, who has more Familiarity with Satan than his Neighbours; this Conjurer comes and Roars, and Howls, and uses Magical Ceremonies over the Sick Man, and will be well paid for it, when he has done; if this don't effect the Cure, the *Man's Time is come, and there's an end.*

They live in a Country full of the best *Ship-Timber* under Heaven: But never saw a *Ship*, till some came from *Europe* hither; and then they were scar'd out of their Wits, to see the *Monster* come sailing in, and spitting Fire with a mighty noise, out of her floating side [...].

Their way of living, is infinitely Barbarous: The Men are most abominably *slothful*; making their poor *Squaws*, or Wives, to plant and dress, and barn, and beat their Corn, and build their *Wigwams* for them; which perhaps may be the reason of their extraordinary Ease in Childbirth. In the mean time, their chief Employment, when they'll condescend unto any, is that of *Hunting*; wherein they'll go out some scores, if not Hundreds of them in a Company, driving all before them. [...]

Their Division of Time is by *Sleeps*, and *Moons*, and *Winters*; and by lodging abroad, they have somewhat observed the Motions of the *Stars*; among which it has been surprising unto me to find, that they have always call'd *Charles's Wain*[48] by the name of *Paukunnawaw*, or *The Bear*, which is the Name whereby *Europeans* also have distinguished it. Moreover, they have little, if any *Traditions* among them worthy of our Notice; and *Reading* and *Writing* is altogether unknown to them, tho' there is a Rock or two in the Country that has unaccountable Characters Engrav'd upon it. All the *Religion* they have amounts unto thus much; they believe, that there are many *Gods*, who made and own the several Nations of the World; of which a certain *Great God* in the South-West Regions of Heaven bears the greatest Figure. They believe, that every remarkable Creature has a peculiar *God* within it, or about it: There is with them, a *Sun God*, a *Moon God*, and the like; and they cannot conceive but that the Fire must be a

---

[46] Anything pleasing or delicious to the palate; a choice viand, a delicacy.
[47] Indian corn parched and pounded into meal.
[48] The asterism comprising the seven bright stars in Ursa Major; known also as The Plough.

kind of a *God*, inasmuch as a *Spark* of it will soon produce very strange effects. They believe that when any Good or Ill happens to them, there is the Favour or the Anger of a *God* expressed in it; and hence as in a Time of Calamity, they keep a *Dance*, or a Day of extravagant ridiculous Devotions to their God, so in a Time of Prosperity they likewise have *a Feast*, wherein they also make Presents one unto another. Finally, they believe, that their chief God *Kautantowit*,[49] made a Man and Woman of a *Stone*; which, upon Dislike, he broke to pieces, and made another Man and Woman of a *Tree*, which were the Fountains of all Mankind; and that we all have in us Immortal *Souls*, which if we were godly, shall go to a splendid Entertainment with *Kautantowit*, but otherwise must wander about in a restless Horror for ever. But if you say to them any thing of a *Resurrection*, they will reply upon you, *I shall never believe it*! And when they have any weighty Undertaking before them, 'tis an usual thing for them to have their Assemblies, wherein after the usage of some Diabolical *Rites*, a *Devil* appears unto them, to inform them and advise them about their Circumstances; and sometimes there are odd Events of their making these Applications to the *Devil*. For instance, 'tis particularly affirmed, That the *Indians* in their Wars with us, finding a sore Inconvenience by our *Dogs*, which would make a sad yelling if in the Night they scented the Approaches of them, they sacrificed a *Dog* to the Devil; after which no *English* Dog would bark at an *Indian* for divers Months ensuing. This was the miserable People, which our *Eliot* propounded unto himself, to teach and save! And he had a double Work incumbent on him; he was to make Men of them, [ere] he could hope to see them *Saints*; they must be *civilized* [ere] they could be *Christianized*; he could not [...] see any thing *Angelical* to bespeak his Labours for their Eternal Welfare, all among them was *Diabolical*. To think on raising a Number of these hideous Creatures, unto the *Elevations* of our Holy Religion, must argue more than common or little Sentiments in the Undertaker; but the Faith of an *Eliot* could encounter it!

I confess, that was one, I cannot call it so much *guess* as *wish*, wherein he was willing a little to indulge himself; and that was, *That our* Indians *are the Posterity of the dispersed and rejected* Israelites, *concerning whom our God has promised that they shall yet be saved, by the Deliverer coming to turn away Ungodliness from them*. He saw the *Indians* using many *Parables* in their Discourses; much given to anointing of their *Heads*; much delighted in *Dancing*, especially after Victories, computing their Times by *Nights* and *Months*; giving *Dowries* for Wives, and causing their Women to *dwell by themselves*, at certain Seasons, for secret Causes; and accustoming themselves to grievous *Mournings* and *Yellings* for the Dead; all which were usual things among the *Israelites*. [...] He also saw some learned Men, looking for the lost *Israelites* among the *Indians* in *America*, and counting that they had *thorow-good* Reasons for doing so. And a few small *Arguments*, or indeed but *Conjectures*, meeting with a favourable Disposition in the Hearer, will carry some Conviction with them; especially, if a Report of a *Menasseh ben Israel*[50] be to back them. [...]

The *First Step* which he judg'd necessary now to be taken by him, was to learn the *Indian* Language; for he saw them so stupid and senseless, that they would never do so

---

[49] Kitche Manitou or Kautantowit; chief Algonquin God, Great Spirit.
[50] Jewish leader (c. 1604-1657) who was brought up in Amsterdam. He established the first Hebrew press in Holland. In 1644 Menasseh met Antonio de Montesinos, who persuaded him that the North-American Indians were the descendants of the ten lost tribes of Israel. This gave a new impulse to Menassehs Messianic hopes. He became famous when, in 1650, an English version of the *Hope of Israel* appeared, in which he elaborated on his millennial ideas.

much as enquire after the Religion of the Strangers now come into their Country, much less would they so far imitate us, as to leave off their beastly way of living, that they might be Partakers of any Spiritual Advantage by us: Unless we could first address them in a *Language* of their own. [...]

> Source: Cotton Mather (1663-1728). "The Triumphs of the Reformed Religion in America: Or, the Life of the Renowned John Eliot; a Person Justly Famous in the Church of God; Not Only as an Eminent Christian, and an Excellent Minister among the English; but Also, as a Memorable Evangelist among the Indians of New-England. With Some Account Concerning the Late and Strange Success of the Gospel in Those Parts of the World, Which for Many Ages Have Lain Buried in Pagan Ignorance" [Third Part of Book III: "Polybius. The Third Book of the New English History: Containing the Lives of Many Reverend, Learned, and Holy Divines, (Arriving Such from Europe to America) by Whose Evangelical Ministry the Churches of New-England Have Been Illuminated"]. *Magnalia Christi Americana: Or, the Ecclesiastical History of New-England, from Its First Planting in the Year 1620. unto the Year of the Lord, 1698.* London: Thomas Parkhurst, 1702, 191-193.

35. Cotton Mather
"Arma Virosq; Cano: Or, the Troubles Which the Churches of New-England Have Undergone in the Wars, Which the People of that Country Have Had with the Indian Salvages" (1702)

§. 1. Two Colonies of Churches being *brought forth*, and a Third *conceived* within the Bounds of *New-England*, by the Year 1636. it was time for the *Devil* to take the *Alarum*,[51] and make some attempt in Opposition to the *Possession* which the Lord Jesus Christ was going to have of these *utmost Parts of the Earth*. These *Parts* were then covered with Nations of Barbarous *Indians* and Infidels, in whom the *Prince of the Power of the Air* did *Work as a Spirit*; nor could it be expected that Nations of Wretches, whose whole *Religion* was the most Explicit sort of *Devil-Worship*, should not be acted by the Devil to engage in some early and bloody Action, for the Extinction of a Plantation so contrary to his Interests, as that of *New-England* was. Of these Nations there was none more Fierce, more Warlike, more Potent, or of a greater *Terror* unto their Neighbours, than that of the PEQUOTS; but their being so much a *Terror* to their Neighbours, and especially to the *Narragansets* on the East-side of them, and the *Monhegins*[52] on the *West*, upon whom they had committed many Barbarous Outrages, produced such a *Division in the Kingdom of Satan* against it self, as was very serviceable to that of our Lord. In the Year 1634. these terrible *Salvages* killed one Captain *Stone*, and Captain *Norton*, with Six Men more, in a Bark sailing up *Connecticut* River, and then sunk her. In the Year 1635. a Bark sailing from the *Massachuset*-Bay to *Virginia*, being by a Tempest cast away at *Long-Island*, the same terrible Salvages killed several of the Shipwrack'd Englishmen. In the Year 1636. at *Block-Island* coming Aboard a Vessel to Trade, they Murdered the Master. And another coming that way, found that they had made themselves Masters of a Bark, which occasioned the sending of an Hundred and Twenty Soldiers thither, under the Command of Captain *Endicot*, Captain *Underhil*, and Captain *Turner*, by the Governour and Council at *Boston*, upon whom, at their Landing, the *Indians* violently shot, and so ran away

---

[51] A call to arms; a signal calling upon men to arm.
[52] Pequot, Narragansett and Monhegins Indians inhabited parts of what is now eastern Connecticut, Rhode Island, Massachusetts and Martha's Vineyard.

where no *English* could come at them.⁵³ Travelling further up to the *Pequot* Country, the *Pequots* refused, upon a Conference, to Surrender the Murderers Harboured among them which were then demanded; whereupon a Skirmish ensued, in which, after the Death of one of their Men, the *Indians* fled, but the *English* destroyed their *Corn* and their *Hutts*, and so returned.

Moreover, a Fort, with a Garrison of Twenty Men, being by some Agents that were sent over by the Lord *Say* and the Lord *Brook*, formed at the River's Mouth, (a place called *Say-Brook*) the *Piquots* after this lay sculking about that Fort almost continually; by which means divers of the *English* lost their Lives, and some that were seized by the *Indians* going up the River, were most horribly Tortured by them, and Roasted alive; and afterwards the *Tawnies*⁵⁴ would with Derision in the *English* hearing, imitate the doleful *Ejaculations* and *Invocations* of the poor Creatures that had perished under their cruel Tortures, and add infinite *Blasphemies* thereunto. Unto all which there was annexed the Slaughter of *Nine Men*, with the taking of *Two Maids*, by this horrid Enemy lying in Ambush for them as they went into the Fields at *Weatherfield*. So that the Infant Colonies of *New-England* finding themselves necessitated unto the *Crushing of Serpents*, while they were but yet in the *Cradle*, Unanimously resolved, that with the Assistance of Heaven they would root this *Nest of Serpents* out of the World. [...]

§. 2. When [the Pequots] perceived that they had made themselves to *stink* before the *New-English Israel*, they tried by all the Enchanting Insinuations that they could think upon, to reconcile themselves unto the other Nations of *Indians*, with whom they had been heretofore at Variance: Demonstrating to them how easie 'twould be for them, if they were *United*, quickly to extirpate the *English*, who if they were *Divided*, would from thence take their Advantage to Devour them one after another. But [...], in the beginning of *May*, 1637. *Connecticut*-Colony set out against these *Pequots* Ninety Men, under the Command of that Worthy Gentleman, Mr. *John Mason*,⁵⁵ whose Worth advanced him afterwards to be the *Deputy Governour* of the Colony; and these were accompanied with one *Uncas* an *Indian Sachem*, newly revolted from the *Pequots*. Captain *Underhil* also being with the Garrison at *Say-brook*, obtained leave to assist the Service now in Hand with *Nineteen* Men and himself, who was not the *Twentieth*, but as good as *Twenty* more. *Massachuset*-Colony were willing to do their part in this *Expedition*, with an *Army* [...] consisting of an Hundred and Sixty Men [...]. Captain *Mason* was by this time informed, that the *Pequots* had retired themselves into Two Impregnable Forts, whereof one was the Rendezvouz of *Sassacus*⁵⁶ the Chief Tyrant, and that fierce *Tyger*, at the very mention of whose Name the *Narragansets* trembled, saying, *He was all one a God, no Body could kill him*. The Council of War determined it necessary to *fall first* upon the Fort which they could *find first*; [...] and as they approached within a Rod of the Fort, a *Dog* Barking awaked another *Cerberus*, an *Indian* that stood Centinel, who immediately cried out, *Wannux, Wannux*, i.e. *English, English!* However, the Courageous Captains presently found a way to enter the Fort, and thereupon followed a Bloody Encounter, wherein

---

⁵³ Reference to a famous battle against the Long Island Indians in 1644, in which Captain Underhill attacked the Indian fort at Great Neck on Long Island, killing about 120 Indians.
⁵⁴ Name for the Wampanoag Indians common among early Puritan settlers.
⁵⁵ John Mason (1600-1672), conqueror of the Pequot Indians.
⁵⁶ Sassacus (perhaps the equivalent of *Sassakusu*, "he is wild, fierce"), last chief of the Pequot tribe; born near Groton, CT, about 1560, killed by the Mohawk in New York, June 1637; he was the successor of Wopigwooit, the first Pequot chief with whom the whites had come in contact. In 1634 Sassacus sent an emissary to the governor of the Massachusetts Bay colony to offer a treaty of friendship.

several of the *English* were wounded, and many of the *Indians* killed: But the *Wigwams* or Houses which filled the Fort consisting chiefly of Combustible *Mats*, we set Fire to them, and presently retiring out of the Fort, on every side surrounded it. The *Fire* by the Advantage of the Wind carried all before it; and such horrible Confusion overwhelmed the *Salvages*, that many of them were Broiled unto Death in the revenging Flames; many of them climbing to the Tops of the *Palizados*,[57] were a fair Mark for the Mortiferous Bullets there; and many of them that had the Resolution to issue forth, were Slain by the *English* that stood ready to bid 'em Welcome; nor were there more than *Two English* Men that lost their Lives in the *Heat* of this Action. It was on *Friday, May* 20. 1637. that this memorable Action was performed; and it was rendred the more memorable by *this*, that the very Night before what was now done, an Hundred and Fifty *Indians* were come from the other Fort unto this, with a purpose to go out with all speed unto the *Destruction* of some *English Town*; whereas they were now suddenly destroy'd themselves; and in a little more than *One Hour*, Five or Six Hundred of these Barbarians were dismissed from a World that was *Burdened* with them; not more than Seven or Eight Persons escaping of all that Multitude. [...]

§. 3. *Sampson* was not in much greater Distress by Thirst, after his Exploit upon the *Philistines*,[58] than our Friends the Day after this Exploit upon the *Pequots*; being distressed with the wants of a Thousand Necessaries, in the Country of an enraged and a numerous Enemy in the other Fort, from whence they expected that the mighty *Sassacus*, with all his Might, would pour forth upon them. Nevertheless, by the good Providence of God, their Pinaces,[59] with all other necessary Provision for 'em, arrived in the *Pequot* Harbour at the very nick of time, when they were most wishing for them; whither while our Forces were Marching, the Enemy came up, Three Hundred of them, from the other Fort, like *Bears bereaved of their Whelps*. They now continued a Bloody Fight for Six Miles together; in which the *Indians* meeting with much loss, notwithstanding their making a *Fort* of every *Swamp* in the way, were so discouraged, that for the present they gave over; but when they came to see the Ashes of their *Friends* mingled with the Ashes of the *Fort*, and the Bodies of so many of their Countrymen terribly *Barbikew'd*, where the *English* had been doing a good Mornings Work, they Howl'd, they Roar'd, they Stamp'd, they Tore their Hair; and though they did not *Swear*, [...] yet they *Curs'd*, and were the Pictures of so many *Devils* in Desparation. [...] Our Forces pursued the rest of the *Pequots* which way soever they could hear of them, and frequently had the Satisfaction of cutting them off by *Companies*: But among others, they met with one Crew which afforded them *Two Sachims*, both of which they Beheaded, and unto a Third they gave his Life, on Condition that he would effectually enquire after *Sassacus*, the Grand one of them all. This Wretch overlooking all National or Natural Obligations, proved faithful to his Employers; and in a few Days returning with Advice of the Place where *Sassacus* was Lodg'd, *Sassacus* from his withdraw, suspected the Matter, and so fled away with Twenty or Thirty of his Men to that People which are known by the Name of *Maqua*'s, a fierce Generation of *Man-Eaters*, for whom the Name of *Cannibal* or *Hannibal* [...] has been carried with them out of *Africa* into *America*; but these *Maqua's* being by the *Narragansets*, as was thought, hired thereunto, with a most *Indian Hospitality* cut 'em all to Pieces. By such Methods as these there was a quick period given to the *Pequot* War;

---

[57] Houses fortified with palisades.
[58] Cf. Judg. 15.18f.
[59] Pinnace: A small light vessel, generally two-masted.

and the few *Pequots* that survived, finding themselves a Prey to all the *other Indians*, who now prided themselves in presenting the *English* with as many *Pequot Heads* as they could [...]. But the rest of the *Indians*, who saw a little handful of Englishmen *Massacre* and *Captivate* seven Hundred of their Adversaries, and kill no less than Thirteen of their *Sachims* or little *Kings* in one short Expedition, such a *Terror from God* fell upon them, that after this the *Land rested from War for near Forty Years together*, even until the time when the Sins of the Land called for a *new Scourge*; and the *Indians* by being taught the Use of *Guns*, which hitherto they had not learnt, were more capable to be made the Instruments of inflicting it. The English Interest in *America* must at last with Bleeding Lamentations cry out,

Heu! Patior Telis, Vulnera facta meis.[60] [...]

Source: Cotton Mather (1663-1728). "Arma Virosque Cano: Or, The Troubles Which the Churches of New-England Have Undergone in the Wars, Which the People of That Country Have Had with the Indian Salvages" [Chapter VI of Book VII: "Ecclesiarum Prælia: or, A Book of the Wars of the Lord. The Seventh Book of the New English History: Relating the Afflictive Disturbances Which the Churches of New-England Have Suffered from Their Various Adversaries: And The Wonderful Methods and Mercies Whereby the Churches Have Been Delivered out of Their Difficulties"]. *Magnalia Christi Americana: Or, the Ecclesiastical History of New-England, from Its First Planting in the Year 1620. unto the Year of the Lord, 1698.* London: Thomas Parkhurst, 1702, 41-44.

36. Philip Freneau
"The Indian Convert" (1797)

An Indian, who lived at *Muskingum*,[61] remote,
Was teazed by a parson to join his dear flock,
To throw off his blanket and put on a coat,
And of grace and religion to lay in a stock.[62]

The Indian long slighted an offer so fair,
Preferring to preaching his fishing and fowling;
A *sermon* to him was a heart full of care,
And singing but little superior to howling.

At last by persuasion and constant harassing
Our Indian was brought to consent to be *good*;
He saw that the malice of *Satan* was pressing,
And the *means* to repel him not yet understood.

---

[60] Latin: "'Tis my own shaft that rankles in my wound."
[61] Reference to an Indian massacre. In March 1782, in one of their numerous expeditions into the Ohio country organized to subdue seemingly hostile Indians, the Pittsburgh militia killed some 96 peaceful christianized Moravian Indians living on the Muskingum River on the mere suspicion that they had acted as spies for the British colonial troops. Although the missionized Indians gave up their arms and surrendered to their alleged protectors, the militiamen brutally killed their captives. While bludgeoned and scalped, the Indians were singing hymns, suffering their martyrdom passively.
[62] Sarcastic reference to the willingness of many missionized Praying Indians to submit to missionary rule and regimens of punishment. Metaphorically speaking they accepted, being put in the stocks, an obsolete instrument of punishment, consisting of two planks set edgewise one over the other. The person to be punished was placed in a sitting posture with his ankles confined between the two planks, here symbolized by grace and religion.

Of heaven, one day, when the parson was speaking,
And painting the beautiful things of the place,
The *convert*, who something substantial was seeking,
Rose up, and confessed he had doubts in the case. –

Said he, *Master Minister*, this place that you talk of,
Of things for the stomach, pray what has it got;
Has it liquors in plenty? – if so I'll soon walk off
And put myself down in the heavenly spot.

You fool (said the preacher) no liquors are there!
The place I'm describing is most like our meeting,
Good people, all singing, with preaching and prayer;
They live upon these without eating or drinking.

But the doors are all locked against folks that are wicked:
And you, I am fearful, will never get there: –
A life of REPENTANCE must purchase the ticket,
And few of you, Indians, can buy it, I fear.

Farewell (said the Indian) I'm none of your mess;
On victuals, so airy, I faintish should feel,
I cannot consent to be lodged in a place
Where's there's nothing to eat and but little to steal.

Source: Philip Freneau (1752-1832). "The Indian Convert." *Poems of Freneau*. Ed. Harry Hayden Clark. New York: Harcourt, Brace & Co., 1929, 400-401.

37. Washington Irving
"Philip of Pokanoket: An Indian Memoir" (1814)

The following anecdotes, illustrative of Indian character, are gathered from various sources, that have every appearance of being authentic. It was thought needless to encumber the page with references.

It is to be regretted that those early writers, who treated of the discovery and settlement of our country, have not given us more frequent and candid accounts of the remarkable characters that flourished in savage life. The scanty anecdotes that have reached us are full of peculiarity and interest; they furnish us with nearer glimpses of human nature, and show what man is, in a comparatively primitive state, and what he owes to civilization. There is something of the charm of discovery, in happening upon these wild, unexplored tracts of human nature – in witnessing, as it were, the native growth of moral sentiment, and perceiving those generous and romantic qualities, which have been artificially wrought up by society, vegetating in spontaneous hardihood and rude magnificence.

In civilized life, where the happiness and almost existence of man depends so much upon public opinion, he is forever acting a part. The bold and peculiar traits of native character are refined away, or softened down by the levelling influence of what is termed good breeding, and he practises so many amiable deceptions, and assumes so many generous sentiments, for the purposes of popularity, that it is difficult to distinguish his real character from that which is acquired or affected. The Indian, on the contrary, free from the restraints and refinements of polished life, and living, in a great degree, solitary and independent, obeys the impulses of his inclination, or the dictates of his individual judgment, and thus the attributes of his nature, being freely indulged, grow singly great and striking. Society is like an artificial lawn, where every roughness is smoothed, every bramble eradicated, and the eye is delighted by the smiling verdure[63] of a velvet surface; he, however, who would study nature in its wildness and variety, must plunge into the forest, must explore the glen, must stem the torrent, and dare the precipice.

These reflections arose on casually looking through a volume of early provincial history, wherein are recorded, with great bitterness, the outrages of the Indians, and their wars with the settlers of New England. It is painful to perceive, even from those partial narratives, how the footsteps of civilization in this country may be traced in the blood of the original inhabitants; how easily the colonists were moved to hostility by the lust of conquest; how merciless and exterminating was their warfare. The imagination shrinks at the idea, how many intellectual beings were hunted from the earth; how many brave and noble hearts, of nature's sterling coinage, were broken down and trampled in the dust.

Such was the fate of PHILIP OF POKANOKET, an Indian warrior, whose name was once a terror throughout Massachusetts and Connecticut. He was the most distinguished of a number of cotemporary sachems, who reigned over the Pequods, the Narrhagansets, the Wampanoags,[64] and the other eastern tribes, at the time of the first settlement of New England – a band of native, untaught heroes, who made the most generous struggle of which human nature is capable; fighting to the last gasp for the deliverance of their country, without a hope of victory or a thought of renown; worthy of an age of poetry, and fit subjects for local story and romantic fiction, they have left scarcely any authentic traces on the page of history, but stalk, like gigantic shadows, in the dim twilight of tradition.

When the pilgrims, as they are termed, first took refuge on the shores of the new world from the persecutions of the old, they found themselves in the most gloomy and helpless situation. Few in number, and that number rapidly perishing away by sickness and hardships; surrounded by a howling wilderness and savage tribes; exposed to the rigours of an almost arctic winter, and the vicissitudes[65] of an ever shifting climate; their hearts were filled with the most gloomy forebodings, and nothing preserved them from sinking into utter despondency, but the strong excitement of religious enthusiasm. In this forlorn situation, they received from Massasoit, chief sagamore of the Wampanoags, the cheering rites of primitive hospitality. This powerful prince, who reigned over a great extent of country, came early in the spring, with a small retinue, to the new settlement of Plymouth; instead of taking advantage of the scanty numbers of the strangers, and expelling them from his territories, into which they had intruded, he entered into a solemn league of peace and amity, sold them a portion of the soil, and promised to secure to them the good will of his savage allies. Whatever may be said of Indian perfidy, it is certain that nothing appears to impeach the integrity and good faith of Massasoit. He continued a firm and generous friend of the white men, allowing them to extend and

---

[63] Lush greenness of flourishing vegetation.
[64] Pequot, Narragansett and Wampanoag Indians: Algonquian-speaking Indians who inhabited parts of what is now eastern Connecticut, Rhode Island, Massachusetts and Martha's Vineyard.
[65] Change, alteration, mutability.

strengthen themselves in the land, and betraying no jealousy at their increasing power and prosperity. Shortly before his death he came once more to New Plymouth, with his son Alexander, to renew the covenant of peace, and to secure it to his posterity. In his treaty he endeavoured to protect the religion of his forefathers from the zealous attacks of the missionaries; he stipulated that no further attempt should be made to draw off his people from their ancient faith; but finding the English obstinately opposed to any such condition, he mildly relinquished the demand. Almost the last act of his life was to bring his two sons, Alexander and Philip, to the residence of a principal settler, recommending mutual kindness and confidence, and entreating that the same love and amity which had existed between the white men and himself, might be continued afterwards with his children. The good old sachem died in peace [...].

His eldest son, Alexander, who succeeded him, soon incurred the hostilities of the settlers. [...]

[...] The successor of Alexander was Metamocet, or King Philip, as he was called by the settlers, on account of his lofty spirit and ambitious temper. The well known energy and enterprise of his character made him an object of great jealousy and apprehension, and he was accused of always cherishing a secret and implacable hostility towards the English. Such may very probably and very naturally have been the case. He considered them as originally mere intruders in the country, who were presuming upon indulgence, and extending an influence baneful[66] to savage life. He saw the whole race of his countrymen melting before them from the face of the earth; their territories slipping from their hands, and their tribes becoming feeble, scattered, and dependent. It may be said that the soil was originally purchased by the settlers; but who does not know the nature of Indian purchases? The nations were equally despoiled by the arts and the arms of the white men. The latter made thrifty bargains by their superior adroitness in traffic, and they gained vast accessions of territory by easily excited hostilities. An uncultivated savage is never a nice inquirer into the refinements of law, by which an injury may be legally inflicted. [...]

[...] There needs no better picture of [King Philip's] destitute and piteous situation than that furnished by the homely pen of the chronicler, who is unwarily enlisting the feelings of the reader in favour of the hapless warrior whom he reviles. "Philip," he says, "like a savage wild beast, having been hunted by the English forces through the woods above a hundred miles backward and forward, at last was driven to his own den upon Mount Hope,[67] where he retired with a few of his best friends, into a swamp, which proved but a prison to keep him fast till the messengers of death came by divine permission to execute vengeance upon him."

Even in this last refuge of desperation and despair a sullen grandeur seems to gather round his memory. We picture him to ourselves seated among his care-worn followers, brooding in silence over his blasted fortunes, and acquiring a savage sublimity from the wildness and dreariness of his lurking place. Defeated, but not dismayed – crushed to the earth, but not humiliated – he seemed to grow more haughty beneath disaster, and to receive a fierce satisfaction in draining the last dregs of bitterness. Little minds are tamed and subdued by misfortune; but great minds rise above it. The very idea of submission

---

[66] Destructive to well-being, pernicious, injurious.
[67] Reference to Mount Hope Miery Swamp, the site in Rhode Island where, on August 12, 1676, the Indian leader King Philip was shot by Alderman, an Indian who collaborated with the English soldiers. This place was called Mount Hope by the English as – after Philip's death – it designated a place of hope for the colonists.

awakened the fury of Philip, and he even smote to death one of his followers, who proposed an expedient of peace. The brother of the victim made his escape, and in revenge betrayed the retreat of his chieftain. A body of white men and Indians were immediately despatched to the swamp, where Philip lay crouched, glaring with fury and despair. Before he was aware of their approach they had began to surround him. In a little while he saw five of his trustiest followers laid dead at his feet; all resistance was vain; he rushed forth from his covert, and made a headlong attempt at escape, but was shot through the heart by a renegado Indian of his own nation.

Such is the scanty story of the brave, but unfortunate King Philip; persecuted while living, slandered and dishonoured when dead. If, however, we consider even the prejudiced anecdotes furnished us by his enemies, we may perceive in them traces of amiable and lofty character, sufficient to awaken sympathy for his fate, and respect for his memory. We find, amid all the harassing cares and ferocious passions of constant warfare, he was alive to the softer feelings of connubial love and paternal tenderness, and to the generous sentiment of friendship. [...] He was a patriot attached to his native soil – a prince true to his subjects, and indignant of their wrongs – a soldier, daring in battle, firm in adversity, patient of fatigue, of hunger, of every variety of bodily suffering, and ready to perish in the cause he had espoused. Proud of heart, and with an untameable love of natural liberty, he preferred to enjoy it among the beasts of the forests, or in the dismal and famished recesses of swamps and morasses, rather than bow his haughty spirit to submission, and live dependent and despised in the ease and luxury of the settlements. With heroic qualities, and bold achievements, that would have graced a civilized warrior, and rendered him the theme of the poet and the historian, he lived a wanderer and a fugitive in his native land, and went down, like a foundering bark, amid darkness and tempest – without an eye to weep his fall, or a friendly hand to record his struggle.

Source: Anonymous (i.e. Washington Irving, 1783-1859). "Philip of Pokanoket: An Indian Memoir." *The Analectic Magazine* 3 (June 1814), 502-505, 514-515.

PURITANISM IN THE NEW WORLD

As opposed to the settlers' self-understanding, the epithet 'Puritan' originally referred rather deprecatingly to those Protestants attempting to purify the Anglican church of Catholic elements. In 1534, King Henry VIII (r. 1509-47) had separated the Church of England from Rome, and his successor Edward VI (r. 1547-53) made every effort to propel the cause of Protestantism. During the subsequent reign of Mary Tudor, however, Catholicism was restored, and about 800 Protestant subjects were sent into exile. The stories of those who suffered the fate of being burnt at the stake were collected in John Foxe's *Book of Martyrs*, which, together with the Geneva Bible provided the fundament of Puritan self-conception. When Queen Elizabeth I. (r. 1558-1603) ascended the throne upon her sister's death in 1558, the Protestants' hopes that England would finally experience a dramatic shift toward a 'purer' church were raised. It was during this time that the term 'Puritan' was used for the first time, denoting those who demanded extensive church reform.

When it became perceptibly obvious that Elizabeth was more concerned with power politics rather than with a purification of the church, in the 1580s the Puritan church leader Robert Browne decided that the English government would never reform the church, and advocated separation from the Church of England. Despite the fact that with James I. (1603-1625) a Calvinist had ascended the throne, in 1609 a large number of separatists (often called Brownists) moved to Holland, which had the reputation of being one of the most liberal countries in Europe. The separatists believed that the Church of England was not a true church at all, and thus advocated an ecclesiastical enterprise which would cut off all relations to the old church. Nevertheless, Puritans did not find the amount of freedom that they had expected and in 1620 one hundred separatists with a charter under the title of the Plymouth Company set sail on the *Mayflower*. Intending to arrive at Virginia, they accidentally landed west of Cape Cod, where they founded Plymouth Colony. In 1630, one year after the charter had been issued by the Massachusetts Bay Company, a large group of Congregationalists under the leadership of John Winthrop followed the Separatist's example and embarked the *Arbella* to voyage to New England. The congregationalists harbored more moderate political and religious positions. For instance, they still hoped for a change in the English church, which they considered a true church. They wanted to bring about church reform by building a model community in the new world, a thought that was elaborated in John Winthrop's speech on the *Arbella*, "A Modell of Christian Charity" (1630), parts of which are reprinted in the next section.

The majority of the settlers arrived in the course of the Great Migration of the 1630s, branching out into Connecticut, New Haven – absorbed into Connecticut in 1665 –, and Rhode Island. Their motives were economic as well as religious. Upon their landing in what they considered a 'new' world, the Puritans had to face the challenge of accommodating their sense of providence with challenges from both the Old and the New World. A highly complex system of theology emerged from this constellation, a system which has always remained contested, as the various religious controversies with both dissenters in the New World and Christians in the Old World show. Even though theological conceptions had to be modified over the course of time, owing to external pressure and intrinsic theological contradictions pressing for solutions, certain elements can be identified as crucial in the Puritan's attempt to set up a purer church, a church of 'visible saints.'

Puritanism evolved out of the Calvinist tradition. Luther's tenet that salvation can be granted solely through faith (*sola fide*) was augmented by the theory that God allots grace through a covenant he has made with man. Covenant theory, which is summarized in Cotton Mather's "A Confession of Faith" (doc. 45), dealt with the relation between humankind and God. Originally, God had made a covenant of works with Adam and Eve. They were pledged eternal happiness if they lived according to the will of God. Succumbing to seduction, they ate the forbidden fruit, thereby committing the Original Sin which resulted in the total depravation of human faculties. In his unremitting love for humankind, however, God made a second covenant, a covenant of grace, through which the Elect were saved by Christ's sacrifice on the cross. In return for their faith they would receive saving grace through the authority of the Spirit. This approach stressed the fact that no one could earn his entry into heaven: Salvation was entirely dependent on God's grace. The fall of Adam was set up as the condition of all mankind, and thus the *New England Primer*'s entry for 'A' reads, "In Adam's Fall, / We sinned all" (doc. 52), a perception of mankind which can be traced through Edward Taylor's poetry (cf. doc. 41).

The basic beliefs underlying all conceptions of New England Puritanism can be found in the five tenets – sometimes captured in the acronym 'TULIP' – which John Calvin had laid down in his *Institutes of the Christian Religion* (1536). These dogmas further clarify the relation between God and man. They consist of firstly, the assumption of a complete corruption of human faculties due to the Original Sin (*T*otal depravity); secondly, the assumption that each individual was predestined to either salvation of damnation (*U*nconditional election); thirdly, the notion that only a limited number of persons – the Elect – were redeemed by Christ's sacrifice (*L*imited Atonement); fourthly, the fact that humans cannot refuse their being elected by God (*I*rresistible grace); and fifthly, the eternal righteousness and security of the Elected (*P*erseverance of the saints). Consequently, an understanding of God was beyond human capacities. Nevertheless, Puritans assumed a predestined course of history, whose divine origins could be detected in God's revelations. These revelations occasionally occurred in the form of direct divine revelations or wonders, and could furthermore be discerned in nature as well as, primarily, through exegesis of the Scripture. Yet human reason was corrupted to such an extent that in the final analysis humankind had to remain uncertain about their destination.

The gap that had been created by the Fall of Man could not be closed entirely by the reestablishment of the covenant of grace. If each individual's fate was predestined according to a providential scheme which was inaccessible to human intellect, and if exerting influence on one's fate through moral conduct or hard work was a futile effort in the covenant of grace, one ultimately had to raise the question why one should not surrender to total passivity. Puritans who regarded the principle of unconditional election problematic later developed a concept, which allowed them to put at least some emphasis on man's ability to work for salvation and find signs of God's grace in godly behavior and economic wealth.

Reacting toward both their historical origin as exiled people and to the uncertainties resulting from their theological position, the Puritans attempted to reach more solid ground by employing a dichotomy of doubt and reassurance, as enacted in Anne Bradstreet's "To My Dear Children" (doc. 43) and in George Goodwin's programmatically titled poem, "Automachia, or The Self-Conflict of a Christian" (doc. 38). Even those who were presumably predestined for heaven could not and were not allowed to be certain about their destiny, and thus had to retain a certain amount of doubt. If doubt ceased to exist, it was taken as a sign that someone was in fact not saved, but rather deluded into imagining salvation. Uncertainty was a sign of and necessary complement to certainty about sainthood. The same scheme was applied even to events in everyday life. Wars and droughts could be read as making sense in the larger context of God's providential design. As one's doubt would eventually be surrendered by one's salvation – if one were predestined – the allegedly random and incomprehensible events of New England history would eventually be rendered meaningful in God's plan.

Before the establishment of the New England colonies, it was incumbent on the individual to seek signs of his or her salvation since no one – besides God – could look into his or her heart. By 1640, after the Great Migration, which brought thousands of Puritans into the New World, the New Englanders had established a religious system, the so-called New England Way, which was supposed to provide evidence for the sainthood of applicants thus retaining the (alleged) purity of the church. This method aimed at collecting those individuals who had found signs of their salvation into a larger social group of visible saints. The demonstration of saving grace, which each applicant had to deliver before being admitted to the church, followed a plain pattern. The candidate described a struggle between faith and doubt, from which he emerged as a person of faith, yet never entirely sure about his fate. The church thus supplemented the concern for scriptural and ecclesiastical knowledge with a demonstration of signs of grace. The harsh requirements for church membership increasingly smacked of an attempt to establish a 'pure' church, an idea which ran counter to the notion of a fallen mankind. The path that New England Puritans followed led to such harsh restrictions that with growing alternative forms of religion and with declining numbers of church members it eventually resulted in a discussion about the extension of church membership in the synod of 1662.

But not only ecclesiastical debates dominated Puritan thought. Particular events had to be read in terms of God's providential plan. Thus confrontations with 'Indians,' challenges by non-conformist religious groups such as the Anabaptists or Antinomians, and draughts were interpreted as God's tests. New England Puritans even went so far as to read natural phenomena, such as meteors, as supernatural "messengers of God's Wrath," a perception of reality which retained its fascination until the times of Washington Irving and Nathaniel Hawthorne (docs. 47-50). Natural signs were supposed exhortations for the people of New England to remain true to the principles of the Puritan church. At a more fundamental level, these dangers had been present from the beginning on. In 1635, the Puritan clergy had to face the challenge of Roger Williams – the subsequent founder of the town of Providence – who in non-separatist Massachusetts proclaimed separatist congregations as the only true form of religious practice and also spoke out against the English policy to trade with land which he considered belonging to Native Americans. Anne Hutchinson, another dissident in terms of orthodoxy, threatened the entire hierarchical structure of the ministry by insisting that a covenant of grace made superfluous all forms of institutionalized piety. Roger Williams was banished from Massachusetts in 1635, Anne Hutchinson was expelled in 1637. Besides theological challenges, confrontations with Native Americans were present from the beginning on, as, for instance, in the Pequot War of 1636. In addition to challenges in the New World, Puritans could never be quite sure about Europe's political fate. All these instances put additional pressure on the New England clergy to maintain a coherent doctrine capable of incorporating the challenges provided by everyday life.

While accepting earthly matters as a necessary part of being, the emphasis was clearly put on the spiritual sphere. Even though the persona of Anne Bradstreet's "The Flesh and the Spirit" (doc. 40) for instance, acknowledges that flesh and spirit are "sisters," that is, that they are inevitably linked, spirit, after all, carries the day. Yet the stereotype of Puritans as totally ascetic individuals who directed their attention exclusively to Heaven does not hold true. Even though in the last analysis poetry remained a didactic means, poets such as Anne Bradstreet and Edward Taylor worked with highly elaborate images far from following the plain style principle propagated by Cotton Mather. If nature was created by God, then it was quite appropriate to describe nature in rather celebratory terms. This also pertained to human nature, and thus love between man and woman was seen as God's gift. All these ruminations were entertained in the light of an attempt to establish a colony which should promote mankind. The individual sought to lead an exemplary life, foregrounding a role model for all society; hence the emphasis on families as 'little commonwealths,' and town meetings as places of public discourse. Again, the sphere of the spirit also dominated the external world. Indian Wars and challenges from Europe were accepted as real threats. Within the larger scheme of God's providence, however, these seemingly arbitrary 'interruptions' of the Puritan experiment were contained within a coherent beyond.

As time proceeded, Puritan theology changed in numerous respects. Rather than merely seeing the great cause of Puritanism on a declining trajectory, it should be seen as a draft of theology and society trying to come to terms with both its intellectual and social European heritage and the circumstances encountered in the New World. The spiritual journey of the individual was always situated in and connected to its social context. Thus on the one hand, individual experience was transformed into communal experience, thereby attempting to work both individuals and society to a higher degree of purity; on the other hand, these experiences were exposed to social and political influences from both England and New England. Consequently, despite its coherent theological concept, Puritanism does not figure as an essential idea at the core of New England society but rather constitutes an ever-changing pious response to social and intellectual constellations.

Clemens Spahr

38. George Goodwin
Automachia, or The Self-Conflict of a Christian (1607)

Vertue I love, I leane to Vice: I blame
This wicked World, yet I embrace the fame
I clime to Heaven, I cleave to Earth: I both
Too-love my Selfe, and yet my Selfe I loath:
Peacelesse, I Peace pursue: In Civill Warre,
With, and against my Selfe, I ioine, I iarre:
I burne, I freeze: I fall downe, I stand fast:
Well-ill I fare; I glory, though disgrac't:
I die a-live: I triumph put to flight:
I feed on Cares: In Teares I take delight:
My slave (base-brave) I serve: I roame at large
In Libertie, yet lie in Gaolers[1] charge:
I strike, and stroake my selfe: I kyndly keen
Work mine own woe, rub my gal,[2] rouz my spleen:[3]
Oft in my sleepe, to see rare dreames, I dreame;
Waking, mine eye doth scarse discern a beame:
My minde's strange *Megrim*[4] whirling to and fro,
Now thrusts me hither, thither then doth throw:
In divers Factions I my Selfe divide;
And all I trie, and flie to every side:
What I but now desir'd, I now disdaine:
What late I weigh'd not, now I wish againe:
To-day, to-morrow; This, that; Now, anon:
All, nothing crave I (ever never-one).
  Dull Combatant, unready for the field,
Too-tardie take I after wounds my shield:
Still hurri'd head-long to unlawfull things,
Down-dragging Vice me downward easly dings:[5]
But sacred Vertue climes so hard and hie,
That hardly can I her steepe steps descrie.
Both Right and Wrong with me indifferent are:
My Lust is Law: what I desire, I dare: [...]
My minde's a Gulfe, whose gaping[6] nought can stuffe:
My hart a hell that never hath enough:
The more I have, I crave, and lesse content:
In store most poore, in plentie indigent:
For, of these Cates[7] how much soe'r I cramme,
It doth not stop my mouth, but stretch the same. [...]
I sink annoies, and drink the ioies of life.

---

[1] A keeper of a jail.
[2] Gall bladder, figurative use: to work oneself up into a bitterness of spirit.
[3] An abdominal organ once regarded as the seat of melancholy or violent ill-nature (obsolete).
[4] Headache, fancy, dizziness or vertigo (obsolete).
[5] To crush with a blow, smash (obsolete).
[6] A deep opening or chasm in the earth (obsolete).
[7] *Pl*. Provisions or victuals bought.

Dim Light, brim Night, Beames waving cloudy-cleer:
Unstable State, void Hope, vain Helpe, far-neer:
False-true Persuasion, Lawlesse Lawfulnesse:
Confused method; milde-wilde, Warlike Peace:
Disordered Order, Mournfull merriments:
Dark-day, wrong-way; dull, double-diligence:
Infamous Fame, know'n Error, skillesse Skill:
Mad Minde, rude Reason, an unwilling Will:
A healthy plague, a wealthy want, poore treasure:
A pleasing Torment, a tormenting Pleasure:
An odious Love, an ougly Beauty; base
Reproachfull Honour, a disgracefull Grace:
A fruitlesse Fruit, a drie dis-flowred Flower:
A feeble Force, a conquered Conquerour:
A sickly Health, dead Life, and restlesse Rest:
These are the Comforts of my Soule distrest.
  O how I like! dislike! desire! disdaine!
Repell! repeale! loath! and delight againe!
O what! whom! whether! (neither flesh nor fish)
How weary of, the same againe I wish!
I will, I nill; I nill, I will: my Minde
Persuading This, my Lust to That inclin'd:
My loose Affection (*Proteus*-like)[8] appeeres
In every forme: at-once it frownes and fleeres.[9]
Mine ill-good Will is vaine and variable:
My (*Hydra*)[10] Flesh buds Heads innumerable:
My Minde's a Maze, a Labyrinth my Reason:
Mine Eye (false Spie) the doore to Fancie's treason.
My rebell Sense (Self-soothing) still affects
What it should flie; what it should plie,[11] neglects.
My flitting Hope with Passion-stormes is tost
But now to Heav'n, anon to Hell almost.
Concording Discord kils me, and againe
Discording Concord doth my life maintaine.
My Selfe at-once I both displease and please:
Without my Selfe my Selfe I faine[12] would sease:
For, my too-much of Mee, mee much annoyes;
And my Selfe's Plentie my poore Selfe destroyes.
Who seeks mee in Mee, in mee shall not finde
Mee as my Selfe: *Hermaphrodite*,[13] in minde
I am at-once Male, Female, Neuter: yet
What e'r I am, I am not Mine (I weet):

---

[8] Proteus, sea god in Greek mythology who could assume whatever shape he wanted.
[9] To flear, to fleere: to look cheerfully, to smile, but also to sneer.
[10] Many-headed serpent that was slain by Hercules.
[11] To yield to s.th.; to submit, comply, consent to s.th. (obsolete).
[12] To be delighted or glad to do s.th.
[13] An organism having characteristics of both sexes.

I am not with my Selfe (as I conceive)
Wretch that I am; my Selfe my Selfe deceive:
Unto my Selfe, my Selfe my Selfe betray:
I from my Selfe banish my Selfe away:
My Selfe agree not with my Selfe a iot:[14]
Know not my Selfe; I have my Selfe forgot:
Against my Selfe my Selfe move iarres[15] uniust:
I trust my Selfe, and I my Selfe distrust:
My Selfe I follow, and my Selfe I flie:
Besides my Selfe, and in my Selfe am I:
My Selfe am not my Selfe, another Same:
Unlike my Selfe, and like my Selfe I am:
Selfe-fond, Selfe-furious: and thus, wayward Elfe,
I can not live with nor without my Selfe.

Source: George Goodwin (flourished 1607-1620). *Automachia, or the Self-Conflict of a Christian*. London: M. Bradwood, 1607, n.p.

39. Philip Pain
Daily Meditations: Or, Quotidian Preparations for, and Considerations of Death and Eternity (1666)

Meditat. 8.

Scarce do I pass a day, but that I hear
Some one or other's dead; and to my ear
Me thinks it is no news: but Oh! did I
Think deeply on it, what it is to dye,
    My Pulses all would bear, I should not be
    Drown'd in this Deluge of Security.

Meditat. 31.

We have no License from our God to waste
One day, one hour, one moment, that do haste
So swiftly from us in our sinful pleasures,
But rather to lay up for lasting treasures.
    Lord, Spare me yet a little, that I may
    Prepare for Death, and for the Judgement-day.

Meditat. 49.

In Heaven are eternal joyes; and sure
In that place there are Remedies to cure
Our here Sin-sick'ned Souls: but Oh shall I
Be made a Patient of this Remedy?
    Lord, I believe a Heaven there is; but this
    The Question is, *Shall I enjoy that bliss?*

---

[14] The very least or a very little part or amount; a whit.
[15] A vibration or tremulous movement resulting from concussion, *esp.* a movement of this kind running through the body or nerves; a thrill of the nerves, mind, or feelings caused by a physical shock (obsolete).

Meditat. 50.
In Hell are Torments, Torments without end;
And them I must endure, if that no friend
I have of Jesus. O my Soul, must I
Go from PAIN here, to Pain eternally?
  I know there is a Hell: Lord, grant that I
  May go from Earth to Heaven when I dye.

Source: Philip Pain (?-1668). *Daily Meditations: Or, Quotidian Preparations for, and Considerations of Death and Eternity. Begun July 19, 1666.* Cambridge: Marmaduke Johnson, 1668, 2, 8, 13.

40. Anne Bradstreet
"The Flesh and the Spirit"[16] (after 1650)

In secret place where once I stood
Close by the Banks of *Lacrim*[17] flood
I heard two sisters reason on
Things that are past, and things to come;
One flesh was call'd, who had her eye
On worldly wealth and vanity;
The other Spirit, who did rear
Her thoughts unto a higher sphere:
Sister, quoth Flesh, what liv'st thou on
Nothing but Meditation?
Doth Contemplation feed thee so
Regardlessly to let earth goe?
Can Speculation satisfy
Notion without Reality?
Dost dream of things beyond the Moon
And dost thou hope to dwell there soon?
Hast treasures there laid up in store
That all in th' world thou count'st but poor?
Art fancy sick or turn'd a Sot[18]
To catch at shadowes which are not?
Come, come, Ile shew unto thy sence,
Industry hath its recompence.

---

[16] Cf. Gal. 5.16-26: "This I say then, Walk in the Spirit, and ye shall not fulfil the lust of the flesh. For the flesh lusteth against the Spirit, and the Spirit against the flesh: and these are contrary the one to the other: so that ye cannot do the things that ye would. [...] Now the works of the flesh are manifest, which are these; Adultery, fornication, uncleanness, lasciviousness, idolatry, witchcraft, hatred, variance, emulations, wrath, strife, seditions, heresies, envyings, murders, drunkenness, revellings, and such like: of the which I tell you before, as I have also told you in time past, that they which do such things shall not inherit the kingdom of God. But the fruit of the Spirit is love, joy, peace, longsuffering, gentleness, goodness, faith, meekness, temperance [...]. Let us not be desirous of vain glory, provoking one another, envying one another."

[17] Lacrima (lat.): tear. Probably reference to Virgil's "lacrimæ rerum" (*Aeneid* I. 462): the sadness of life; tears shed for the sorrows of men.

[18] A foolish or stupid person.

What canst desire, but thou maist see
True substance in variety?
Dost honour like? acquire the same,
As some to their immortal fame:
And trophyes to thy name erect
Which wearing time shall ne're deject.
For riches dost thou long full sore?
Behold enough of precious store.
Earth hath more silver, pearls and gold,
Then eyes can see, or hands can hold.
Affect's thou pleasure? take thy fill,
Earth hath enough of what you will.
Then let not goe, what thou maist find,
For things unknown, only in mind.
Spir. Be still thou unregenerate part,
Disturb no more my setled heart,
For I have vow'd, (and so will doe)
Thee as a foe, still to pursue,
And combate with thee will and must,
Untill I see thee laid in th' dust.
Sisters we are, ye twins we be,
Yet deadly feud 'twixt thee and me;
For from one father are we not,
Thou by old Adam wast begot,
But my arise is from above,
Whence my dear father I do love.
Thou speak'st me fair, but hat'st me sore,
Thy flatt'ring shews Ile trust no more.
How oft thy slave, hast thou me made,
When I believ'd, what thou hast said,
And never had more cause of woe
Then when I did what thou bad'st doe.
Ile stop mine ears at these thy charms,
And count them for my deadly harms.
Thy sinfull pleasures I doe hate,
Thy riches are to me no bait,
Thine honours doe, nor will I love;
For my ambition lyes above.
My greatest honour it shall be
When I am victor over thee,
And triumph shall, with laurel head,
When thou my Captive shalt be led,
How I do live, thou need'st not scoff,
For I have meat thou know'st not off;
The hidden Manna[19] I doe eat,
The word of life it is my meat.

---

[19] The food sent by God to the Israelites in the wilderness; cf. Exod. 16.15.

My thoughts do yield me more content
Then can thy hours in pleasure spent;
Nor are they shadows which I catch,
Nor fancies vain at which I snatch,
But reach at things that are so high,
Beyond thy dull Capacity;
Eternal substance I do see,
With which inriched I would be:
Mine Eye doth pierce the heavens, and see
What is Invisible to thee.
My garments are not silk nor gold,
Nor such like trash which Earth doth hold,
But Royal Robes I shall have on,
More glorious then the glistring Sun;
My Crown not Diamonds, Pearls, and gold,
But such as Angels heads infold.
The City where I hope to dwell,[20]
There's none on Earth can parallel;
The stately Walls both high and strong,
Are made of pretious *Jasper* stone;
The Gates of Pearl, both rich and clear,
And Angels are for Porters there;
The Streets thereof transparent gold,
Such as no Eye did e're behold,
A Chrystal River there doth run,
Which doth proceed from the Lambs Throne:
Of Life, there are the waters sure,
Which shall remain for ever pure,
Nor Sun, nor Moon, they have no need,
For glory doth from God proceed:
No Candle there, nor yet Torch light,
For there shall be no darksome night.
From sickness and infirmity,
For evermore they shall be free,
Nor withering age shall e're come there,
But beauty shall be bright and clear;
This City pure is not for thee,
For things unclean there shall not be:
If I of Heaven may have my fill,
Take thou the world, and all that will.

Source: Anne Bradstreet (1612-1672). "The Flesh and the Spirit." *Several Poems Compiled with Great Variety of Wit and Learning, Full of Delight: Wherein Especially Is Contained a Compleat Discourse, and Description of the Four Elements, Constitutions, Ages of Man, Seasons of the Year, together with an Exact Epitome of the Three First Monarchyes, viz. the Assyrian, Persian, Grecian, and Beginning of the Romane Common-wealth to the End of Their Last King: With Diverse Other Pleasant & Serious Poems. By a Gentlewoman in New-England.* Boston: John Foster, 1678, 229-233.

---

[20] The ensuing description of the imaginary 'ideal' city follows the depiction of the heavenly city of the New Jerusalem in Rev. 21f.

41. Edward Taylor
"Meditation. 26. Heb. 9.13.14.
How much more shall the blood of Christ, &c." (1698)

26:4M 1698[21]

Unclean, Unclean:[22] My Lord, Undone, all vile,
    Yea all Defil'd: What shall thy servant doe?
Unfit for thee: not fit for holy soile,
    Nor for Communion of Saints below.
    A bag of botches,[23] Lump of Loathsomeness:
    Defild by Touch, by Issue: Leproast flesh.[24]

Thou wilt have all that enter do thy fold
    Pure, Cleane, and bright, Whiter than whitest Snow
Better refin'd than most refined Gold:
    I am not so: but fowle: What shall I doe?
    Shall thy Church Doors be shut, and shut out mee?
    Shall not Church-fellowship my portion bee?[25]

How can it be? Thy Churches do require
    Pure Holiness: I am all filth, alas!
Shall I defile them, tumbled thus in mire?
    Or they mee cleanse before I current pass?
    If thus they do, Where is the Niter[26] bright
    And sope they offer mee to wash me White?

The Brisk Red heifers Ashes,[27] when calcin'd,[28]
    Mixt all in running Water is too Weake
To wash away my Filth: The Dooves assign'd.
    Burnt, and sin Offerings[29] neer do the feate,
    But as they Emblemize the Fountain spring
    Thy Blood, my Lord, set ope to wash off Sin.[30]

Oh! richest Grace! Are thy Rich Veans[31] then tapt
    To ope this Holy Fountain (boundless Sea)

---

[21] June 26, 1698 (26th day of the 4th month of the year 1698; according to the Julian calendar).
[22] Lev. 13.44-46, instructing lepers to cry "Unclean, unclean." Lev. 13 and 14.1-32 record the priest's duty of identifying and ceremonially cleansing lepers.
[23] Swelling, tumor, ulcer.
[24] In *Upon the Types of the Old Testament* and corresponding meditations, Taylor refers to Old Testament classifications of uncleanness as resulting from touch, issue, leprosy, and moral impunity.
[25] In Sermons and Meditations 2.26-28, Taylor interprets purifications as prerequisites of church fellowship.
[26] Chile salpeter; here used allusively, with reference to the use of natron as a cleansing agent.
[27] Red heifer: In Jewish history, unblemished, never-before-yoked animal that was slaughtered and burned to restore ritual purity to those who had become unclean through contact with the dead. Cf. Num. 19.1-9: "And the Lord spake unto Moses and unto Aaron, saying [...] Speak unto the children of Israel, that they bring thee a red heifer without spot, wherein is no blemish, [...]. And Eleazar the priest shall take of her blood with his finger, and sprinkle of her blood directly before the tabernacle of the congregation seven times. And one shall burn the heifer in his sight [...]: it is a purification for sin."
[28] To purify.
[29] See Lev. 15; ceremonial cleansing from sin required the sacrifice of two turtledoves.
[30] Christ's sacrifice on the cross and the spilling of his blood are here regarded as the 'fountain' of his cleaning of man's sin and the source of salvation.
[31] A vein, a blood vessel.

For Sinners here to lavor off[32] (all Sapt
  With Sin) their Sins and Sinfulness away?
In this bright Chrystall Crimson Fountain flows
  What washeth whiter than, the Swan or Rose.

Oh! wash mee, Lord, in this Choice Fountain, White
  That I may enter, and not sully[33] here
Thy Church, whose floore is pav'de with Graces bright
  And hold Church fellowship with Saints most clear.
  My Voice all Sweet, with their melodious layes
Shall make Sweet Musick blossom'd with thy prais[e.]

Source: Edward Taylor (1642-1729). "Preparatory Meditations, Second Series, Meditation. 26." *Edward Taylor's God's Determinations and Preparatory Meditations: A Critical Edition*. Ed. Daniel Patterson. Kent, OH: Kent State UP, 2003, 253-254.

42. Thomas Shepard
"The Autobiography of Thomas Shepard" (1649)

To my deare son Thomas Shepard
with whom I leave these records
of gods great kindnes to him
not knowing that I shall
live to tell them my selfe
with my own mouth,
that so he may learne
to know & love
the great &
most high
god: the god of
his father:

In the yeare of the Lord 1634; Octob. 16. my selfe & family, with my first Son Thomas, committed our selves to the care of our god to keepe us on & to carry us over the mighty seas from old England to new England [...].

The reasons which swayed me to come to N.E.[34] were many; 1. I saw no call to any other place in old England nor way of subsistence in peace & comfort to me & my family; 2. diverse people in old England of my deare freends desired me to goe to N.E. there to live together & some went before & writ to me of providing a place for a company of us, on[e] of which was John Bridge;[35] & I saw diverse families of my Christian freends who were resolved thither to goe with me; 3. I saw the Lord depting from England where Mr Hooker & Mr Cotton were gone, & I saw the h[e]arts of most of the godly set & bent that way & I did thinke I should feele many miseries if I stayd behind, 4. my judgement was then convinced not only of the evill of Cæremonies but of

---

[32] To wash off, to bathe.
[33] To soil, to stain.
[34] New England.
[35] John Bridge, a deacon, was in New England as early as 1632, advocating emigration to America.

mixt communion & joyning with such in sacraments tho I ever judged it Lawfull to joyne with them in preaching, 5. I saw it my duty to desire the fruition[36] of all gods ordinances, which I could not enjoy in old England; 6. my deare wife did much long to see me setled there in peace & so put me on to it; 7. although it was true I should stay & suffer of Christ yet I saw no rule for it now the Lord had opened a doore of escape; otherwise I did incline much to stay & suffer especially after our sea stormes; 8. tho my ends were mixt & I looked much to my own quiet, yet the Lord let me see the glory of those Liberties in N[ew] England & made me purpose if ever I should come over to live among gods people as on[e] come out from the dead, to his prayse; tho since I have seene as the Lords godnes so my own exceeding weaknes to be as good as I thought to have bin: & although they did desire me to stay in the North & preach privatly, yet 1. I saw that this time could not be long without trouble from King Charles; 2. I saw no reason to spend my time privatly when I might possibly exercise my talent publikely in N.E. 3. I did hope my going over might make them to follow me. 4. I considered how sad a thing it would be for me to leave my wife & child, (if I should dy) in that rude place of the North where was nothing but barbarous wickednes generally & how sweet it would be to leave them among gods people tho poore; 5. my liberty in private was dayly threatned; & I thought it wisdom to depart before the Purseuants[37] came out for so I might depart with more peace, & lesse trouble & danger to me & my freends [...].

Now here the Lords woonderfull terrour & mercy to us did appear [...] & the Lord saw it good to chastise us for rushing onward too soone; & hazarding our selves in that manner & I had many feares & much darknes (I remember) overspread my soule, doubting of our way yet I say we could not now goe back: only I learnt from that time never to goe about a sad businesse in the darke, unles gods call within as well as that without be very strong & cleare & comfortable; so that in the yeare 1634, about the beginn[in]g of the winter, we set sayle from Harwich; & having gone some few leagues on to the sea; the wind stopt us that night & so we cast anchor in a dangerous place: & on the morning the wind grew feirce & rough agaynst us full, & dr[o]ve us toward the sands, but the vessel being laden too heavy at the head would not stir for all that which the seamen could doe, but dr[o]ve us full upon the sands, neare Harwich harbour; & the ship did grate[38] upon the sands, & was in great danger; but the Lord directed on[e] man to cut some cable or rope in the ship & so shee was turned about & was beaten quite backward toward Yarmouth, quite out of our way; but while the ship was in this great danger a woonderfull miraculous providence did appear to us; for on[e] of the seamen that he might save the vessel fell in, when it was in that danger & so was carryed out a mile or more from the ship; & given for dead & gone; the ship was then in such danger that none could attend to follow him; & when it was out of the danger it was a very great hazard to the lives of any that should take the ski[ff][39] to seeke to find him; yet it pleased the Lord that being discerned afar off floating upon the waters; 3 of the seamen adventured out upon the rough waters & at last about an houre after he fell into the sea (as we conjectured) they came & found him floating upon the waters, never able to swim, but supported by a divine hand all this while; when the men came to him they were glad to find him but concluded he was dead, & so got him into the ski[ff], & when he was there tumbled him down as on[e] dead; yet on[e] of them sayd to the rest

---

[36] Realization, enjoyment.
[37] Officers of the Church of England who had to enforce conformity.
[38] To scratch.
[39] A small sea-going boat, esp. one attached to a ship.

let us use what meanes we can if there be life to preserve it, & thereupon turned his head downward for the water to run out, & having done so, the fellow began to gaspe & breath then they applyed other meanes they had; & so he began at last to moove & then to speake, & by that time he came to the ship he was prety well & able to walke: & so the Lord shewed us his great power, whereupon a godly man in the ship then sayd; this mans danger & deliverance is a type of ours, for he did feare dangers were near unto us, & that yet the Lords power should be shewn in saving of us; for so indeed it was; for the wind did drive us quite backward out of our way & gave us no place to anchor at untill we came unto Yarmouth rodes; an open place at sea yet fit for anchorage [...].

At this time I cannot omit the goodness of god as to my selfe so to all the c[o]untry in delivering us from the Pekoat furies; these Indians were the stoutest proudest & most successefull in the[ir] wars of all the Indians; the[ir] cheefe Sachem was Sasakus, proud cruell unhappy & headstrong prince [... He] adventured to fall upon the English up the river at Wethersfeed where he slew 9 or 10 men women & children at unawares, & tooke two maids prisoners carrying them away captive to the Pekoat c[o]untry hereupon those upon the river [i.e. the English settlers] gathered about 70 men & sent them into Pekoat c[o]untry, to make that the seat of war, & to revenge the death of those innocents whom they barbarously & most unnaturally slew; these men marched two dayes & nights from the way of the Naraganset unto Pekoat; being guided by those Indians then the ancient enemies of the Pekoats they intended to assault Sasakus Fort but falling short of it the second night the providence of god guided them to another nearer, full of stout men & their best souldiers being as it were coopt up there to the number of 3 or 400 in all for the divine slaughter by the hand of the English; these therfore being all night making merry & singing the death of the English the next day, toward breake of the day being very heavy with sleepe the English drew neare within the sight of the fort, very weary with travayle & want of sleepe, at which time 500 Naragansets fled for feare & only 2 of the company stood to it to conduct them to the fort & the dore & entrance thereof; the English being come to it awakened the fort with a peale of muskets directed into the midst of the[ir] wigwams; & after this some undertaking to compasse the fort without some adventured into the fort upon the very faces of the enemy standing ready with the[ir] arrowes ready bent to shoot who ever should adventure; but the English casting by the[ir] peeces tooke the[ir] swoords in the[ir] hands (the Lord doubling the[ir] strength & courage) & fell upon the Indians where a hot fight continued about the space of an houre, at last by the direction of on[e]Captayne Mason the[ir] wigwams were set on fire which being dry & contiguous on[e] to another was most dreadfull to the Indians, some burning some bleeding to death by the swoord some resisting till they were cut off some flying were beat down by the men without untill the Lord had utterly consumed the whole company except 4 or 5 girles they tooke prisoners & dealt with them at Seabrooke as they dealt with ours at Wethersfeeld, & tis verily thought scarce on[e] man escaped unles on[e]or two to carry foorth tydings of the lamentable end of the[ir] fellowes; & of the English not on[e] man was kild but on[e] by the musket of an Englishman (as was conceived) some were wounded much but all recovered & restored agayne:

Thus the Lord having delivered the c[o]untry from war with Indians & Familists[40](who arose & fell together) he was pleased to direct the harts of the magistrates [...] to

---

[40] Religious community founded in Friesland in the 16th century by Hendrik Niclaes (1502?-1580?). The Family of Love, as his community was called, held the view that the divine spirit of love inspiring the

thinke of erecting a Schoole or Colledge, & that speedily to be a nursery of knowledge in these deserts & supply for posterity [...].

The Lord thus afflicting yet continud peace to the c[o]untry that amazing mercy when all England & Europe are in a flame the Lord hath set me & my children aside from the flames of the fires in Yorkshire & Northumberland whence if we had not bin delivered, I had bin in great afflictions & temptations, very weake & unfit to be tossed up & down & to beare violent p[ro]secution; the Lord therefore hath shewed his tenderness to me & mine in carrying me to a land of peace tho a place of tryall; where the Lord hath made the savage Indians who conspired the death of all the English by Miantinomo [...].

Source: Thomas Shepard (1605-1649). "The Autobiography of Thomas Shepard." *Publications of the Colonial Society of Massachusetts*. Vol. 27: *Transactions 1927-1930*. Boston: The Colonial Society of Massachusetts, 1932, 352, 375-378, 387-389, 391.

The text here presented is slightly modernized, using the following emendations: W^c > which; p > pro- [e.g. pvidence = providence], X^{stian} > Christian; w^t > with; frō > from; w^h > where; m^r > Mr.; fruitiō > fruition; X^t > Christ; o^r > our; m^c > much; w^tout > without; reasō > reason; upō > upon; w^n > when; wherever a colon was used for a full stop in Shepard's manuscript, it was replaced by the modern punctuation sign.

43. Anne Bradstreet
"To My Dear Children" (1672?)

This Book by Any yet unread,
I leave for you when I am dead,
That, being gone, here you may find
What was your liveing mother's mind.
Make use of what I leave in Love
And God shall blesse you from above.

A.B.

[...] Among all my experiences of God's gratious Dealings with me I have constantly observed this, that he hath never suffered me long to sitt loose from him, but by one affliction or other hath made me look home, and search what was amisse – so usually thus it hath been with me that I have no sooner felt my heart out of order, but I have expected correction for it, which most commonly hath been upon my own person, in sicknesse, weaknes, paines, sometimes on my soul, in Doubts and feares of God's displeasure, and my sincerity towards him, sometimes he hath smott a child with sicknes, sometimes chasstened by losses in estate, – and these Times (thro: his great mercy) have been the times of my greatest Getting and Advantage, yea I have found them the Times when the Lord hath manifested the most Love to me. Then have I gone to searching, and have said with David, Lord search me and try me, see what wayes of wickednes are in me, and lead me in the way everlasting: and seldome or never but I have found either some sin I lay under which God would have reformed, or some duty neglected which he would have performed. And by his help I have layd Vowes and Bonds upon my Soul to perform his righteous commands.

If at any time you are chastened of God, take it as thankfully and Joyfully as in greatest mercyes, for if yee bee his yee shall reap the greatest benefitt by it. It hath

---

community is superior to the teachings of the Bible and to liturgy. In 1560, Niclaes escaped to England. There his movement gained many adherents, although its emotionalism was criticized by the more orthodox. The sect died out in the 17th century, but strongly influenced similar radical groups.

been no small support to me in times of Darknes when the Almighty hath hid his face from me, that yet I have had abundance of sweetnes and refreshment after affliction, and more circumspection in my walking after I have been afflicted. I have been with God like an untoward child, that no longer then the rod has been on my back (or at least in sight) but I have been apt to forgett him and myself too. Before I was afflicted I went astray, but now I keep thy statutes.

I have had great experience of God's hearing my Prayers, and returning comfortable Answers to me, either in granting the Thing I prayed for, or else in satisfying my mind without it; and I have been confident it hath been from him, because I have found my heart through his goodnes enlarged in Thankfullnes to him.

I have often been perplexed that I have not found that constant Joy in my Pilgrimage and refreshing which I supposed most of the servants of God have; although he hath not left me altogether without the wittnes of his holy spirit, who hath oft given mee his word and sett to his Seal that it shall bee well with me. I have sometimes tasted of that hidden Manna that the world knowes not, [...] and have resolved with myself that against such a promis, such tasts of sweetnes, the Gates of Hell shall never prevail. Yet have I many Times sinkings and droopings, and not enjoyed that felicity that somtimes I have done. But when I have been in darknes and seen no light, yet have I desired to stay my self upon the Lord.

And, when I have been in sicknes and pain, I have thought if the Lord would but lift up the light of his Countenance upon me, altho: he ground me to powder, it would bee but light to me; yea, oft have I thought were it hell itself, and could there find the Love of God toward me, it would bee a Heaven. And, could I have been in Heaven without the Love of God, it would have been a Hell to me; for, in Truth, it is the absence and presence of God that makes Heaven or Hell.

Many times hath Satan troubled me concerning the verity of the scriptures, many times by Atheisme how I could know whether there was a God; I never saw any miracles to confirm me, and those which I read of how did I know but they were feigned. That there is a God my Reason would soon tell me by the wondrous workes that I see, the vast frame of the Heaven and the Earth, the order of all things, night and day, Summer and Winter, Spring and Autumne, the dayly providing for this great houshold upon the Earth, the preserving and directing of All to its proper end. The consideration of these things would with amazement certainly resolve me that there is an Eternall Being.

But how should I know he is such a God as I worship in Trinity, and such a Saviour as I rely upon? tho: this hath thousands of Times been suggested to mee, yet God hath helped me over. I have argued thus with myself. That there is a God I see. If ever this God hath revealed himself, it must bee in his word, and this must bee it or none. Have I not found that operation by it that no humane Invention can work upon the Soul? hath not Judgments befallen Diverse who have scorned and contemd it? [...]

The consideration of these things and many the like would soon turn me to my own Religion again.

But some new Troubles I have had since the world has been filled with Blasphemy, and Sectaries, and some who have been accounted sincere Christians have been carryed away with them, that somtimes I have said, Is there faith upon the earth? and I have not known what to think. But then I have remembered the words of Christ that so it must bee, and that, if it were possible, the very elect should bee deceived. Behold, saith our Saviour, I have told you before. That hath stayed my heart, and I can now say,

Return, O my Soul, to thy Rest, upon this Rock Christ Jesus will I build my faith; and, if I perish, I perish. But I know all the Powers of Hell shall never prevail against it. I know whom I have trusted, and whom I have bel[ie]ved, and that he is able to keep that I have committed to his charge.

Now to the King, Immortall, Eternall, and invisible, the only wise God, bee Honoure and Glory for ever and ever! Amen.

This was written in much sicknesse and weaknes, and is very weakly and imperfectly done; but, if you can pick any Benefitt out of it, it is the marke which I aimed at.

Source: Anne Bradstreet (1612-1672). "To My Dear Children." *The Works of Anne Bradstreet, in Prose and Verse*. Ed. John Harvard Ellis. Glouchester, MA: Peter Smith, 1962, 3, 5-10.

44. Thomas Hooker
The Application of Redemption by the Effectual Work of the Word, and the Spirit of Christ, for the Bringing Home of Lost Sinners to God (1657)

[...] A true sight of sin hath two Conditions attending upon it; or it appears in two things: We must see sin, 1. Cleerly. 2. Convictingly, what it is in it self, and what it is to us, not in the appearance and paint of it, but in the power of it; not to fadam[41] it in the notion and conceit only, but to see it with Application.

We must see it cleerly in its own Nature, its Native color and proper hue: It's not every slight conceit, not every general and cursorie, confused thought or careless consideration that will serve the turn, or do the work here, we are all sinners; it is my infirmity, I cannot help it; my weakness, I cannot be rid of it; no man lives without faults and follies, the best have their failings, *In many things we offend all*. But alas all this wind shakes no Corn, it costs more to see sin aright than a few words of course; It's one thing to say sin is thus and thus, another thing to see it to be such; we must look wis[e]ly and steddily upon our distempers, look sin in the face, and discern it to the full; the want whereof is the cause of our mistaking our estates, and not redressing of our hearts and waies [...].

Quest. But how shall we see cleerly the Nature of sin in his naked hue?

Answ. 1. This will be discovered, and may be conceived in the Particulars following. Look we at it: First, As it respects God. Secondly, As it concerns our selves. As it hath reference to God, the vileness of the nature of sin may thus appear.

It would dispossess God of that absolute Supremacy which is indeed his Prerogative Royal, and doth in a peculiar manner appertayn to him, as the Diamond of his Crown, and Diadem of his Deity [...].

Now herein lyes the unconceavable hainousness of the hellish nature of sin, it would justle[42] the Almighty out of the Throne of his Glorious Soveraignty, and indeed be above him. For the will of man being the chiefest of all his workmanship, all for his body, the body of the soul, the mind to attend upon the will, the will to attend upon God, and to make choyce of him, and his wil, that is next to him, and he onely above that: and that should have been his Throne and Temple or Chair of State, in which he would have Set his Soveraignty for ever. He did in an Especial manner intend to meet with man,

---

[41] To fathom; to get to the bottom of, dive into, penetrate, see through, thoroughly understand.
[42] To jostle, contend for a place, the best path, or the wall, by pushing another away from it; hence, to vie or struggle *with* some one *for* some advantage.

and to communicate himself to man in his righteous Law, as the rule of his Holy and righteous will, by which the will of *Adam* should have been ruled and guided to him, and made happie in him; and all Creatures should have served God in man, and been happy by or through him, serving of God being happy in him; But when the will went from under the government of his rule, by sin, *it would be above God, and be happy without him* [...].

Now by sin we justle the law out of its place, and the Lord out or his Glorious Soveraignty, pluck the Crown from his head, and the Scepter out of his hand, and we say and profess by our practice, there is not authority and power there to govern, nor wisdom to guide, nor good to content me, but I will be swayed by mine own wil and led by mine own deluded reason and satisfied with my own lusts.

[...] Thou that knowest and keepest thy pride and stubbornness and thy distempers, know assuredly thou dost justle God out of the Throne of his glorious Soveraignty and thou dost profess, Not Gods wil but thine own (which is above his) shall rule thee, thy carnal reason and the folly of thy mind, is above the wisdom of the Lord and that shal guide thee; to please thine own stubborn crooked pervers spirit, is a greater good than to please God and enjoy happines, for this more Contents, thee; That when thou considerest but thy Course, dost thou not wonder that the great and Terrible God doth not pash[43] such a poor insolent worm to pouder, and send thee packing to the pitt every moment. [...]

It smites at the Essence of the Almighty and the desire of the sinner, is not only that God should not be supream but that indeed he should *not be at all*, and therefore it would destroy the being of Jehovah. [...]

It crosseth the whol course of Providence, perverts the work of the Creature and defaceth the beautiful frame, and that sweet correspondence and orderly usefulness the Lord first implanted in the order of things; The Heavens deny their influence, the Earth her strength, the Corn her nourishment, thank sin for that. Weeds come instead of herbs [...], It crooks all things so as that none can straiten them, makes so many wants that none can supply them, *Eccles*. 1.15. This makes crooked Servants in a family no man can rule them, crooked inhabitants in towns, crooked members in Congregations, ther's no ordering nor joynting of them in that comly accord, and mutual subjection [...].

In regard of our selves, see we and consider nakedly the nature of sin, in Four particulars.

1. Its that which makes a separation between God and the soul, breaks that Union and Communion with God for which we were made, and in the enjoyment of which we should be blessed and happie [...].

2. It brings an incapability in regard of my self to receive good, and an impossibility in regard of God himself to work my spiritual good, while my sin Continues, and I Continue impenitent in it. [...] He that spils the Physick that should cure him, the meat that should nourish him, there is no remedy but he must needs dye, so that the Commission of sin makes not only a separation from God, but obstinate resistance and continuance in it, maintains an infinit and everlasting distance between God and the soul: So that so long as the sinful resistance of thy soul continues; God cannot vouchsafe the Comforting and guiding presence of his grace; because it's cross to the Covenant of Grace he hath made, which he will not deny, and his Oath which he will not alter. [...] Know, that by thy dayly continuance in sin, thou dost to the utmost of thy

---

[43] To break a thing into pieces.

power execute that Sentence upon thy soul: It's thy life, thy labor, the desire of thy heart, and thy dayly practice to depart away from the God of all Grace and Peace, and turn the Tomb-stone of everlasting destruction upon thine own soul.

3. It's the Cause which brings all other evils of punishment into the World, and without this they are not evil, but so far as sin is in them. The sting of a trouble, the poyson and malignity of a punishment and affliction, the evil of the evil of any judgment, it is the sin that brings it, or attends it [...].

[4.] It brings a Curse upon all our Comforts, blasts all our blessings, the best of all our endeavors, the use of all the choycest of all Gods Ordinances: it's so evil and vile, that it makes the use of all good things, and all the most glorious, both Ordinances and Improvements evil to us. [...]

Hence then it follows; *That sin is the greatest evil in the world, or indeed that can be.* For, That which separates the soul from God, that which brings all evils of punishment, and makes all evils truly evil, and spoils all good things to us, that must needs be the greatest evil, but this is the nature of sin, as hath already appeared.

But that which I will mainly press, is, Sin is only opposite to God, and cross as much as can be to that infinite goodness and holiness which is in his blessed Majesty [...].

Source: Thomas Hooker (1586-1647). *The Application of Redemption by the Effectual Work of the Word, and the Spirit of Christ, for the Bringing Home of Lost Sinners to God.* London: Peter Cole, 1657, 52-63.

45. Cotton Mather
"A Confession of Faith" (1702)

Chap. I.
Of the Holy Scriptures.

I. Although the Light of Nature, and the Works of Creation and Providence do so far manifest the Goodness, Wisdom and Power of God, as to leave Men inexcusable; yet are they not sufficient to give that knowledge of God and of his Will, which is necessary unto Salvation: Therefore it pleased the Lord, at sundry times, and in divers manners to reveal himself, and to declare that his Will unto his Church; and afterwards for the better Preserving and Propagating of the Truth, and for the more sure Establishment and Comfort of the Church against the Corruption of the Flesh, and the Malice of Satan, and of the World, to commit the same wholly to Writing: Which maketh the Holy Scripture to be most necessary; those former ways of God's revealing his Will unto his People being now ceased. [...]

VI. The whole Counsel of God concerning all things necessary for his own Glory, Man's Salvation, Faith and Life, is either expresly set down in Scripture, or by good and necessary Consequence may be deduced from Scripture; unto which nothing, at any time, is to be added, whether by new Revelations of the Spirit, or Traditions of Men. Nevertheless, we acknowledge the inward Illumination of the Spirit of God to be necessary for the saving understanding of such things as are revealed in the Word: And that there are some Circumstances concerning the Worship of God and Government of the Church, common to humane Actions and Societies, which are to be ordered by the Light of Nature and Christian Prudence, according to the general Rules of the Word, which are always to be observed.

VII. All things in Scripture, are not alike plain in themselves, nor alike clear unto all; yet those things which are necessary to be known, believed and observed for Salvation, are so clearly propounded and opened in some place of Scripture, or other, that not only the learned, but the unlearned, in a due use of the ordinary means, may attain unto a sufficient Understanding of them. [...]

CHAP. III.
Of God's Eternal Decree.

I. God from all Eternity did by the most Wise and Holy Counsel of his own Will, freely, and unchangeably ordain, whatsoever comes to pass; yet so, as thereby neither is God the Author of Sin, nor is Violence offered unto the Will of the Creatures, nor is the Liberty or Contingency of second Causes taken away, but rather established.

II. Although God knows whatsoever may or can come to pass upon all supposed Conditions, yet hath he not decreed any thing because he foresaw it, as future, or as that which would come to pass upon such Conditions.

III. By the Decree of God, for the manifestation of his Glory, some Men and Angels are predestinated unto everlasting Life, and others fore-ordained unto everlasting Death. [...]

VI. As God hath appointed the Elect unto Glory, so hath he by the eternal and most free Purpose of his Will, fore-ordained all the means thereunto: Wherefore they who are elected being fallen in *Adam*, are redeemed by Christ, are effectually called unto Faith in Christ by his Spirit working in due season, are justified, adopted, sanctified, and kept by his Power through Faith unto Salvation. [...]

CHAP. V.
Of Providence.

I. God the Great Creator of all things, doth uphold, direct, dispose and govern all Creatures, Actions and Things, from the greatest even to the least, by his most Wise and Holy Providence, according to his infallible Fore-knowledge, and the free and immutable Counsel of his own Will to the Praise of the Glory of his Wisdom, Power, Justice[,] Goodness and Mercy.

II. Although in relation to the Fore-knowledge and Decree of God, the First Cause, all things come to pass immutably and infallibly, yet by the same Providence he ordereth them to fall out, according to the Nature of Second Causes,[44] either necessarily, freely, or contingently.

III. God in his ordinary Providence, maketh use of means, yet is free to work without, above and against them at his Pleasure.

IV. The Almighty Power, unsearchable Wisdom, and the infinite Goodness of God, so far manifest themselves in his Providence, in that his determinate Counsel extendeth it self, even to the first Fall and all other Sins of Angels and Men, [...] yet so as the sinfulness thereof proceedeth only from the Creature, and not from God, who being most Holy and Righteous, neither is, nor can be the Author or Approver of Sin.

V. The most wise, righteous and gracious God doth oftentimes leave for a Season his own Children to manifold Temptations, and the Corruption of their own Hearts, to chastise them for their former Sins, or to discover unto them the hidden Strength of Corruption, and Deceitfulness of their Hearts, that they may be humbled, and to raise them to a more close and constant Dependance for their Support upon himself, and to

---

[44] While the term "First Cause" refers to God, the term "Second Causes" designates all effects that are brought about by man and his acts of volition.

make them more watchful against all future Occasions of Sin, and for sundry other just and holy Ends. [...]

Chap. VI.
Of the Fall of Man: Of Sin, and of the Punishment thereof.

I. God having made a Covenant of Works and Life thereupon, with our First Parents, and all their Posterity in them, they being seduced by the Subtilty and Temptation of Satan, did wilfully transgress the Law of their Creation, and break the Covenant, in eating the forbidden Fruit.

II. By this Sin, they and we in them, fell from Original Righteousness and Communion with God, and so became dead in Sin, and wholly defiled in all the Faculties and Parts of Soul and Body. [...]

IV. From this Original Corruption, whereby we are utterly indisposed, disabled and made opposite to all Good, and wholly inclined to all Evil, do proceed all actual Transgressions. [...]

Chap. VII.
Of God's Covenant with Man.

I. The Distance between God and the Creature is so great, that altho' reasonable Creatures do owe Obedience to him as their Creator, yet they could never have attained the Reward of Life, but by some voluntary Condescension on God's Part, which he hath been pleased to express by way of Covenant.

II. The first Covenant made with Man was a Covenant of Works, wherein Life was promised to *Adam*, and in him to his Posterity, upon Condition of Perfect and Personal Obedience.

III. Man by his Fall having made himself uncapable of Life by that Covenant, the Lord was pleased to make a Second, commonly call'd the Covenant of Grace; wherein he freely offereth unto Sinners Life and Salvation by Jesus Christ, requiring of them Faith in him, that they may be saved, and promising to give unto all those that are ordained unto Life, his Holy Spirit to make them willing and able to believe. [...]

Chap. VIII.
Of Christ the Mediator.

I. It pleased God in his Eternal Purpose, to chuse and ordain the Lord Jesus, his only begotten Son, according to a Covenant made between them both, to be the Mediator between God and Man [...], and to be by him, in time, redeemed, called, justified, sanctified and glorifyed. [...]

V. The Lord Jesus by his perfect Obedience, and Sacrifice of himself, which he, through the Eternal Spirit, once offered up unto God, hath fully satisfied the Justice of God, and purchased not only Reconciliation, but an everlasting Inheritance in the Kingdom of Heaven, for all those whom the Father hath given unto him.

VI. Altho' the *Work* of *Redemption* was not actually wrought by Christ, till after his Incarnation, yet the Virtue, Efficacy and Benefits thereof, were communicated unto the Elect in all Ages successively from the beginning of the World [...].

Chap. IX.
Of Free-Will.

I. God hath endued[45] the Will of Man with that Natural Liberty and Power of Acting upon Choice, that it is neither forced, nor, by any absolute Necessity of Nature, determined to do Good or Evil.

II. Man in his State of Innocency had Freedom and Power to Will and to Do that which was Good and well-pleasing to God; but yet mutably, so that he might fall from it.

III. Man by his Fall into a State of Sin, hath wholly lost all Ability of Will to any Spiritual Good, accompanying Salvation, so as a Natural Man being altogether averse from that Good, and dead in sin, is not able by his own strength to convert himself or to prepare himself thereunto.

IV. When God converts a Sinner, and translates him into the State of Grace, he freeth him from his natural Bondage under Sin, and by his Grace alone enables him freely to Will and to Do that which is Spiritually Good; yet so, as that, by reason of his remaining Corruption, he doth not perfectly nor only Will that which is Good, but doth that which is also Evil.

V. The Will of Man is made Perfectly and Immutably Free to Good alone, in the State of Glory only.

Chap. X.
Of Effectual Calling.

I. All those whom God hath prædestinated unto Life, and those only, he is pleased in his appointed and accepted Time effectually to call by his Word and Spirit, out of that State of Sin and Death, in which they are by Nature, to Grace and Salvation by Jesus Christ, inlightning their Minds Spiritually and Savingly to understand the Things of God, taking away their Heart of Stone, and giving unto them an Heart of Flesh, renewing their Wills, and by his Almighty Power determining them to that which is Good, and effectually drawing them to Jesus Christ: Yet so, as they come most Freely, being made willing by his Grace.

II. This effectual Call is of God's Free and Special Grace alone, not from any thing at all foreseen in Man, who is altogether Passive therein, until being quickned and renewed by the Holy Spirit, he is thereby enabled to answer this Call and to embrace the Grace offered and conveyed in it. [...]

Chap. XI.
Of Justification.

I. Those whom God effectually calleth, he also freely Justifieth, not by infusing Righteousness into them, but by pardoning their Sins, and by accounting and accepting their Persons, as Righteous, not for any thing wrought in them, or done by them, but for Christ's sake alone; nor by imputing Faith its self, the act of Believing, or any other Evangelical Obedience to them, as their Righteousness, but by imputing Christ's Active Obedience unto the whole Law, and Passive Obedience in his Sufferings and Death, for their whole and sole Righteousness, they receiving and resting on him and his Righteousness by Faith, which Faith they have not of themselves, it is the Gift of God.

II. Faith thus receiving and resting on Christ, and his Righteousness is the alone Instrument of Justification; yet it is not alone in the Person justified, but is ever accom-

---

[45] To 'invest' or endow with qualities.

panied with all other saving Graces, and is no dead Faith, but worketh by Love. [...]

V. God doth continue to forgive the Sins of those that are justified, and altho' they can never fall from the State of Justification, yet they may by their Sins fall under God's Fatherly Displeasure: And, in that Condition, they have not usually the Light of his Countenance restored unto them, until they humble themselves, confess their Sins, beg Pardon, and renew their Faith and Repentance. [...]

Chap. XII.

Of Adoption.

I. All those that are justified, God vouchsafeth in and for his only Son Jesus Christ to make Partakers of the Grace of Adoption, by which they are taken into the number and enjoy the Liberties and Priviledges of the Children of God, have his Name put upon them, receive the Spirit of Adoption, have Access to the Throne of Grace with Boldness, are enabled to cry *Abba Father*,[46] are pitied, protected, provided for, and chastned by him, as by a Father yet never cast off, but sealed to the Day of Redemption, and inherit the Promises, as Heirs of Everlasting Salvation.

Chap. XIII.

Of Sanctification.

I. They that are effectually called and regenerated being united to Christ, having a new Heart, and a new Spirit created in them, thro' the Virtue of Christ's Death and Resurrection, are also further Sanctified really and personally, through the same Virtue, by his Word and Spirit dwelling in them, the Dominion of the whole Body of Sin is destroy'd, and the several Lusts thereof are more and more weakned and mortified, and they more and more quickned and strengthened in all saving Graces, to the practice of all true Holiness, without which no Man shall see the Lord.

II. This Sanctification is throughout in the whole Man, yet imperfect in this Life; there abide still some Remnants of Corruption in every part, whence ariseth a continual and irreconcileable War, the Flesh lusting against the Spirit, and the Spirit against the Flesh.

III. In which War, altho' the remaining Corruption, for a time, may much prevail, yet thro' the continual supply of Strength from the sanctifying Spirit of Christ, the Regenerate part doth overcome, and so the Saints grow in Grace, perfecting Holiness in the fear of God. [...]

Chap. XV.

Of Repentance unto Life and Salvation.

I. Such of the Elect as are converted at riper Years, having sometime lived in the state of Nature, and therein served divers Lusts and Pleasures, God in their effectual Calling giveth them Repentance unto Life.

II. Whereas there is none that doth Good and sinneth not, and the best of Men may through the power and deceitfulness of their Corruptions dwelling in them, with the prevalency of Temptation, fall into great Sins and Provocations; God hath in the Covenant of Grace mercifully provided that Believers so sinning and falling be renewed, through Repentance unto Salvation. [...]

---

[46] Cf. Rom. 8.14-16: "For as many as are led by the Spirit of God, they are the sons of God. For ye have not received the spirit of bondage again to fear; but ye have received the Spirit of adoption, whereby we cry, Abba, Father. The Spirit itself beareth witness with our spirit, that we are the children of God [...]."

IV. As Repentance is to be continued through the whole Course of our Lives, upon the account of the Body of Death and the Motions thereof; so 'tis every Man's Duty to repent of his particular known Sins particularly.

V. Such is the Provision which God hath made, through Christ, in the Covenant of Grace, for the preservation of Believers unto Salvation, that altho' there is no sin so small, but it deserves Damnation; yet there is no sin so great, that it shall bring Damnation on them, who truly repent; which makes the constant preaching of Repentance necessary.

Chap. XVI.
Of Good Works.

I. Good works are only such as God hath commanded in his holy Word, and not such as, without the warrant thereof, are devised by Men out of blind Zeal, or upon any pretence of good Intentions. [...]

V. We cannot by our best Works merit Pardon of Sin, or eternal Life at the Hand of God, by reason of the great disproportion that is between them and the Glory to come, and the infinite distance that is between us and God, whom by them we can neither profit, nor satisfie for the Debt of our former Sins; but when we have done all we can, we have done but our Duty, and are unprofitable Servants: And because, as they are good they proceed from his Spirit, and as they are wrought by us, they are defiled and mixed with so much Weakness and Imperfection, that they cannot endure the Severity of God's Judgment. [...]

Chap. XVII.
Of the Perseverance of the Saints.

I. They whom God hath accepted in his Beloved, effectually called and sanctified by his Spirit, can neither totally nor finally fall away from the state of Grace, but shall certainly persevere therein to the End, and be eternally saved.

II. This Perseverance of the Saints depends not upon their own free will, but upon the immutability of the Decree of Election, from the free and unchangeable Love of God the Father upon the Efficacy of the Merit and Intercession[47] of Jesus Christ, and Union with him, the Oath of God, the abiding of his Spirit, and the Seed of God within them, and the Nature of the Covenant of Grace; from all which ariseth also the certainty and Infallibility thereof. [...]

Chap. XVIII.
Of the Assurance of Grace and Salvation.

I. Although Temporary Believers and other unregenerate Men may vainly deceive themselves with false Hopes, and carnal Presumptions of being in the Favour of God, and State of Salvation, which hope of theirs shall perish, yet such as truly believe in the Lord Jesus and love him in Sincerity, endeavouring to walk in good Conscience before him, may, in this Life, be certainly assured, that they are in the State of Grace, and may rejoyce in the Hope of the Glory of God, which Hope shall never make them ashamed.

II. This Certainty is not a bare conjectural and probable Perswasion, grounded upon a fallible Hope, but an infallible assurance of Faith, founded on the Blood and Righteousness of Christ, revealed in the Gospel; and also upon the inward Evidence of those

---

[47] The action of interceding, pleading, or praying on behalf of another.

Graces, unto which Promises are made, and on the immediate Witness of the Spirit, testifying our Adoption, and as a Fruit thereof, leaving the Heart more Humble and Holy.

III. This infallible Assurance doth not so belong to the Essence of Faith, but that a true Believer may wait long, and conflict with many Difficulties before he be Partaker of it; yet being enabled by the Spirit to know the Things which are freely given him of God, he may without extraordinary Revelation, in the right use of ordinary Means attain thereunto: And therefore it is the Duty of every one to give all diligence to make his Calling and Election sure, that thereby his Heart may be enlarged in Peace and Joy in the Holy Ghost, in Love and Thankfulness to God, and in Strength and Cheerfulness in the Duties of Obedience, the proper Fruits of this Assurance; so far is it from inclining Men to Looseness.

IV. True Believers may have the Assurance of their Salvation diverse ways shaken, diminish'd, and intermitted, as by Negligence in preserving of it, by falling into some special Sin, which woundeth the Conscience and grieveth the Spirit, by some sudden or vehement Temptation, by God's withdrawing the Light of his Countenance, suffering even such as fear him to walk in Darkness, and to have no Light, yet are they neither utterly destitute of that Seed of God, and Life of Faith, that Love of Christ and the Brethren, that Sincerity of Heart, and Conscience of Duty, out of which by the Operation of the Spirit, this Assurance may, in due time, be revived, and by the which, in the mean time, they are supported from utter Despair. [...]

Source: Cotton Mather (1663-1728). "A Confession of Faith; Owned, and Consented to, by the Elders and Messengers of the Churches, Assembled at Boston in New-England, May 12. 1680. Being the Second Session of That Synod." Book V: "CONTAINING the FAITH and the ORDER IN THE CHURCHES OF NEW-ENGLAND." *Magnalia Christi Americana: Or, the Ecclesiastical History of New-England, from Its First Planting in the Year 1620. unto the Year of the Lord, 1698.* London: Thomas Parkhurst, 1702, 5-13.

46. Samuel Mather
The Figures or Types of the Old Testament (1667/68)

Romans 5.14
—— Adam, *who was the Figure of Him that was to come.*

That the *Gospel was preached to* them under the *Old* Testament, as well as to us under the New; and that it was revealed to them in several *ways and manners* of Discovery; and in a *gradual way*, in several pieces and parcels, hath been formerly shewed. One signal Instance we gave of those divers ways and manners was this, *That the Gospel was preached to them of old by legal Types and Ceremonies.* Now concerning these (not to insist upon the *Analysis* of the Chapter) the Text gives you this Doctrine. [...]

There be three things included in this *Description*.

1. There is some *outward* or *sensible* thing, that represents some *other higher* thing.

2. There is the *thing represented* thereby, which is *good things to come*, which we call the *Antitype*.

3. There is the *work* of the *Type*, which is to *shadow forth* or represent these *future good things*.

1. There is in a *Type* some *outward or sensible* thing, that represents an higher spiritual thing, which may be called a *Sign* or a Resemblance, a *Pattern* or *Figure*, or the like. Here is the general Nature of a *Type*; it is *a Shadow*. It hath been the Goodness and

Wisdom of God in all times and ages, to teach Mankind *Heavenly* things by *Earthly*; spiritual and *invisible* Things, by outward and *visible*; as *Joh.* 3.12.

2. There is the *thing shadowed* or represented by the *Type*, And what is that? *Things to come*, faith the Apostle, *Col.* 2.17. and *good things to come*, Heb 10.1. The good things of the Gospel, *Christ and his Benefits; but the Body is of Christ*, as *Col.* 2.17. This we call the *Correlate*, or the *Antitype*; the other is the *Shadow*, this the *Substance*: The *Type* is the Shell, this the Kernel; the *Type* is the Letter, this the Spirit and Mystery of the *Type*. This we are still to look at, and to search into in every *Type*; we must look beyond the Shadow, to the Substance, to the Truth and Mystery of it: And this is Christ and the Gospel, as future, and hereafter to be exhibited. This may be called the *Prototype*, or the Pattern, out of which, and according to which the other is drawn; as Pictures from the Man, whose Visage they represent.

3. This Description holds forth the *Work* of the *Type*, which is to *shadow forth* the *Antitype*.

But what is this *shadowing*? And *how* do *Types* shadow?

It is a metaphorical expression. A Shadow represents the proportion of the Body, with its actions and motions; though it doth it but obscurely and darkly. So the Types had some dark resemblance of Christ and his Benefits, and did some way adumbrate and represent them, and hold them forth unto his People, to enlighten and inform their Understandings, and to strengthen and confirm their Faith in him: The *Types* had this Voice and Language; *Such* an One shall the *Messiah* be, He is *thus* to *act*, and *thus* to *suffer* for you.

Thus you have the Description of a Type. It is a *Shadow of good things to come*: Or if you would have it more at large, you may take it thus, *A Type is some outward or sensible thing ordained of God under the Old Testament, to represent and hold forth something of Christ in the New.* [...]

Here ariseth a Question. *How may we know when a thing is a Type, and that the Lord did ordain and design it to that end and use?*

The Answer is. We cannot safely judge of this but by the Scripture.

1. When there is express Scripture for it. As *Adam* here in the Text is called *a Type of him that was to come*: So the whole Ceremonial Law is said *to have a Shadow of the good things to come* under the Gospel, *Heb.* 10.1. The Buildings and holy Places of the earthly Temple are said to be *Figures of the true*, even of *Heaven it self, Heb.* 9.24. The Land of *Canaan*, *was a Figure of* the Country that *Abraham* and the Fathers fought for, it is said, *they desire a better Country, that is, an heavenly, Heb.* 11.16.

2. When there is a *permutation of Names* between the *Type* and the *Antitype*, this is a clear Indication of the Mind of God. As for instance, Christ is called *David, Ezek.* 34.23. and 37.24. *Hos.* 3.5. this shews that *David* was a Type of him, and Christ was the true *David*.

So Christ is called *Adam, the second Adam, Cor.* 15.45. [...]

3. When by comparing several Scriptures together, there does appear an *evident and manifest* Analogy *and parallel between Things under the Law, and things under the Gospel*, we may conclude, that such legal Dispensations were intended as *Types* of those Gospel Mysteries whose Image they bear. In such a case, *Res ipsa loquitur*. For the *Type* must be made like the *Antitype*, as the Apostle speaks of that illustrious Type *Melchisedec*, Hebr. 7.3. *he was made like unto the Son of God.*

As the Deliverance out of *Egypt* and *Babylon*, if we read the History thereof in the Old Testament, and compare it with the Prophesies in the New Testament, concerning the Churches Deliverance from Antichristian Bondage, we shall clearly see, that it was a Type thereof; there is such a resemblance, the one answers the other so remarkably. Hence Divines generally make *Samson* a Type of Christ, there is such a fair and full Analogy in sundry particulars of his Life and Death between him and Christ; So likewise *Joseph* is generally lookt upon as a Type of Christ; though there be no Scripture that doth expresly call him so: But if the History of *Joseph* in *Genesis* be compared with the History of Jesus Christ in the four Evangelists, the Analogy will be very clear and evident.

The *Old* Testament and the *New* should be compared together. The *Protasis* or Proposition of these sacred similitudes is in the Books of *Moses*, and in the Old Testament; but the *Apodosis* the Reddition or Application is to be found chiefly in the New.

Source: Samuel Mather (1621-1671). *The Figures or Types of the Old Testament, by Which Christ and the Heavenly Things of the Gospel Were Preached and Shadowed to the People of God of Old. Explain'd and Improv'd in Sundry Sermons.* London, Printed for Nathaniel Hillier, 1705 [1st ed. Dublin, 1683; the sermons were originally preached in 1667/1668], 51-55.

47. *Blazing Stars, Messengers of God's Wrath* (1759)

Blazing-Stars *Messengers of* GOD's *Wrath*: In a few serious and solemn Meditations upon the wonderful **COMET:** Which now appears in our Horizon, *April*, 1759: Together with a solemn Call to Sinners, and Counsel to Saints; how to behave themselves when GOD is in this wise speaking to them from Heaven.

Source: *Blazing-Stars, Messengers of God's Wrath: In a Few Serious and Solemn Meditations upon the Late Wonderful Comet: Which Now Appears in Our Horizon, April, 1759. Together with a Solemn Call to Sinners, and Counsel to Saints; How to Behave Themselves When God Is in This Wise Speaking to Them from Heaven*. Boston: R. Draper, 1759 [Broadside].

48. Ichabod Wiswall
A Judicious Observation of That Dreadful Comet Which Appeared on November 18, 1680, and Continued until the 10ᵗʰ of February Following (1681/1683)

Wherein is shewed the manifold Judgments that are like to attend upon most parts of the World

Nunquam futilibus excanduit ignibus Æther[48]

Heavens face such Comets ne're did stain,
But mortal Men felt grievous pain.

Heavens face with Flames was never fill'd,
But Sorrows great Mens hearts soon thrill'd.

Such Comets when Heav'ns face they cover,
Bespeak aloud that Changes hover. [...]

Silence all Flesh, your selves prepare
To read these Lines which written are
In Heavens large *folio*, with the hand
Of him that doth all things command.
My *Genius* moves me to declare,
And to relate what Changes are,
Like raging Waves of th' Ocean great,
Rouling themselves upon the seat
Of *Vesta*[49] now, whereon we dwell,
And must go hence to Heaven or Hell.
I'le not besmear my Paper with
Volatile Megrim-Fancies[50], sith[51]
The Eccho of approaching trouble
Upon us now doth daily double.
 My Muse grows solid,[52] and retires
From those chill-painted Fancy-Fires
Wherewith sometimes she lov'd to toy,
And therefore crys, *Pardon à moy*.[53]
A nobler Spark of heavenly heat,
Both Head and Heart doth actuate.
Heav'ns Sovereign doth unsheath his Sword,
Because Men do despise his Word,
Declar'd by them whom he hath sent
Into the World for that intent.

---

[48] Latin: "The heavens never grew so bright in vain."
[49] In Roman myth, the virgin goddess of the hearth.
[50] An illusion brought on by a headache.
[51] Archaic: since.
[52] Here: sober-minded.
[53] French: "Pardon me."

Heavens spangled Canopy above
Is neatly fill'd by th' hand of *Jove*,
With *Hyrogliphicks*, which contain
The certain draughts of Joy and Pain,
Which mortal Men must undergo:
He's wise who can forsee the Wo,
And timely shrowd himself from Harms,
Which usher'd are by loud Alarms.

Upon this eighteenth of *November*,
(God grant we all may it remember!)
A dreadful Comet did appear,
Enlightning all our Hemisphear. [...]
This Prodigy which blaz'd throughout
Earths vast Circumference, no doubt
Presages greater Change at hand,
Than hath yet vexed every Land.
Such Signals are *Preludium*
Of direful Changes that will come
Upon the Nations: on Men all,
'Cause Vices epidemical
Do now bear sway, are in their full:
Shew me the Land which you can cull,
Secur'd from Vice, to Vertue prone
And I'le engage they shall not moan
The dire effects of Wantonness. [...]
These flaming Lights which now appear,
Do shew the Judgment-Day draws near.
These sparkling Lights which flame and die,
Are Signs (tho small) the Judg draws nigh,
Who will appear with thundring Voice,
With Flames begirt, and hidden noise;
Tempestuous Storms of flaming Fire
Will seize the Earth, and Heavens higher.
Hee'l knead the Earth, and havock make
Of all wherein most pleasure take.
His Voice will roar, Nature will tremble
When Judgments shall themselves assemble
Like armed Troops, for to destroy
All those who did his Lambs anoy.
Heavens Firmament will melt like Lead,
And falling down, will scald the head
Of Wickedness. The Earth will burn,
And wrap them in its flaming Urn.
This Fire will Heavens purify;
Encircling Earth, it will descry
Close[54] Villany, and evil Men;
Then all shall be renew'd agen. [...]

---

[54] Hidden.

I'le give an hint, pray mind it well,
This Comet surely doth foretell
Light breaking forth from darkest Cell,
Strange Rays of Light which shall dispel
Traditions fond, and Practice too,
Tho not without a sad ado;
Mysterious Truths dark Riddles hide, [...]
Must all things hilter skilter run.
As if that we were quite undone?
– Such times draw nigh. –

Must Heathen Nations still combine
To ruine what is prov'd divine?
Shall Infidels boldly presume
God's holy People to consume?
Shall Hereticks be bold to vent
Such Fallaces as Churches rent?
Shall Truth be trodden to the Ground
By Policy of Hell profound?
Shall Antichrist his Wound now heal,
By trampling down the Common-weal?[55]
Shall Kings and Princes now fall down
Themselves and theirs to th' Triple Crown[56];
Basely prostrate, and willingly
Adore him who's in Villany
Doth cheat the World fallaciously,
Imposing on them cuningly?
Shall they their Swords and Spears cast down
At's Feet, and swear to guard his Crown,
Who is their Vassal, and no Prince,
As will appear when he goes hence? [...]
If any ask how this can be?
Let him anatomize these three:
I mean the *Pope*, the *Turk*, the *Devil*,
Grand Architects of all that's evil.
My Heart is cold, my Quill grows dry,
And must a while in silence lie. [...]

March 6. 1681

FINIS.

Source: Ichabod Wiswall (1637-1700). *A Judicious Observation of That Dreadful Comet Which Appeared on November 18, 1680, and Continued until the 10th of February Following, Wherein Is Shewed the Manifold Judgments That Are Like to Attend upon Most Parts of the World, Written by I.W. in New-England.* London: J. Darby, 1683. *Seventeenth-Century American Poetry.* Ed. Harrison T. Meserole, New York: Norton, 1968, 433-436, 442-445.

---

[55] Commonwealth, common well being.
[56] Papal tiara, crown.

49. Washington Irving
"Philip of Pokanoket: An Indian Memoir" (1814)

[...] In the early chronicles of these dark and melancholy times, we find symptoms of the diseased state of the public mind. The glooms of religious abstraction,[57] and the wildness of their situation among trackless forests and savage tribes, had disposed the colonists to superstitious fancies, and filled their imaginations with all the frightful chimeras of witchcraft, spectreology,[58] and omens. The troubles with Philip and his Indians, we are told, were preceded by a variety of those awful warnings that forerun great and public calamities. At one time the perfect form of an Indian bow appeared in the air at New Plymouth, which was looked upon by the inhabitants as a "prodigious apparition." At Hadley, Northampton, and other towns thereabouts, "was heard the report of a great piece of ordnance,[59] with a shaking of the earth and a considerable echo."[60] Others were alarmed on a still sunshine morning by the discharge of guns and muskets – bullets appeared to whistle past them, and the noise of drums resounded in the air, and seemed to pass away to the westward; others fancied the galloping of troops of horses over their heads; and certain monstrous births that took place about the time, filled the superstitious of some towns with doleful forebodings. These portentous noises may easily be ascribed to natural phenomena – to the uncouth sounds and echoes that will sometimes strike the ear amidst the profound stillness of woodland solitudes – to the casual rushing of a blast through the tree tops – the crash of falling wood or mouldering rocks – they may have startled some melancholy imagination – been exaggerated by the love for the marvellous, and listened to with that avidity with which we devour whatever is fearful and mysterious. The currency of their circulation, and the grave record made of them by one of the learned men of the day, are strongly characteristic of the times. [...]

Source: Anonymous (i.e Washington Irving, 1783-1859). "Philip of Pokanoket: An Indian Memoir." *The Analectic Magazine* 3 (June 1814), 507-508.

50. Nathaniel Hawthorne
The Scarlet Letter (1850)

[...] Nothing was more common, in those days, than to interpret all meteoric appearances, and other natural phenomena, that occurred with less regularity than the rise and set of sun and moon, as so many revelations from a supernatural source. [...] We doubt whether any marked event, for good or evil, ever befell New England, from its settlement down to Revolutionary times, of which the inhabitants had not been previously warned by some spectacle of this nature. Not seldom, it had been seen by multitudes. Oftener, however, its credibility rested on the faith of some lonely eyewitness, who beheld the wonder through the colored, magnifying, and distorting medium of his imagination, and shaped it more distinctly in his after-thought. It was, indeed, a majestic idea, that the destiny of nations should be revealed, in these awful hieroglyphics, on

---

[57] Here: vision, speculation.
[58] The science or study of apparitions, ghosts or phantoms.
[59] Cannon, artillery.
[60] Original footnote: "The Rev. Increase Mather's History."

the cope of heaven. A scroll so wide might not be deemed too expansive for Providence to write a people's doom upon. The belief was a favorite one with our forefathers, as betokening that their infant commonwealth was under a celestial guardianship of peculiar intimacy and strictness. But what shall we say, when an individual discovers a revelation, addressed to himself alone, on the same vast sheet of record! [...]

> Source: Nathaniel Hawthorne (1804-1864). *The Scarlet Letter*. Columbus: Ohio State UP, 1962, 154-155 [chap. XII].

51. Cotton Mather
A Christian in His Personal Calling (1701)

Gen. XLVII. 3.: What is your OCCUPATION?
[...] It was the *Question* that *Pharaoh* put unto the Sons of *Jacob*. And it implies, that every true *Israelite* should be able to give a good *Answer* unto such a *Question*. The *Question* which we are now to Discourse upon, is, How a *Christian*, may come to give a *Good Answer* unto that *Question*? or, How a Christian may come to give a *Good Account* of his *Occupation* & of his *Behaviour* in it?

There are *Two Callings* to be minded by *All Christians*. Every Christian hath a *General Calling*; Which is, to Serve the Lord Jesus Christ, and Save his own Soul, in the Services of *Religion*, that are incumbent on[61] all the Children of men. God hath *called* us, to *Believe* on His *Son*, and *Repent* of our *Sin*, and observe the Sacred Means of our *Communion* with Himself, and bear our *Testimony* to His *Truths* and *Wayes* in the World: And every man in the world, should herein conform to the Calls of that God, who *hath called us with this Holy Calling*. But then, every Christian hath also a *Personal Calling*; or, a certain *Particular Employment*, by which his *Usefulness*, in his Neighbourhood, is distinguished. God hath made man *a Sociable* Creature. We expect Benefits from *Humane Society*. It is but equal, that *Humane Society* should Receive Benefits from *Us*. We are Beneficial to *Humane Society* by the Works of that Special *Occupation*, in which we are to be employ'd, according to the Order of God.

A Christian, at his *Two Callings*, is a man in a Boat, Rowing for Heaven; the *House* which our Heavenly Father hath intended for us. If he mind but one of his *Callings*, be it which it will, he pulls the *Oar*, but on *one side* of the Boat, and will make but a poor dispatch to the Shoar of Eternal Blessedness.

It is not only necessary, That a Christian should follow his *General Calling*; it is of necessity, that he follow his *Personal Calling* too. The CASE therefore now before us, is, What is that Good Account, that a Christian should be able to give of his OCCUPATION? Or, *How should a Christian be Occupied in the Business of his Personal Calling, that he may give a Good Account of it*?

We will thus proceed in our Discourse upon it.

I. A Christian should be able to give this Account, *That he hath an Occupation*. Every Christian ordinarily should have a *Calling*. That is to say, There should be some *Special Business*, and some *Settled Business*, wherein a Christian should for the most part spend the most of his *Time*; and this, that so he may Glorify God, by doing of *Good* for *others*, and getting of *Good* for *himself*. It is enjoined upon Christians, I. Thes. 4.11.

---

[61] Imposed as a duty.

Do your own Business, that ye may walk honestly. 'Tis not *Honest*, nor *Christian*, that a *Christian* should have no *Business* to do. [...] And as a man is *Impious* towards God, if he be without *a Calling*, so he is *Unrighteous* towards his *Family*, towards his *Neighbourhood*, towards the *Commonwealth*, if he follow no *Calling* among them. Hence we read, 2 Thes. 3.11. they *Walk disorderly*, who *Work not at all*. Yea, A *Calling* is not only our *Duty*, but also our *Safety*. Men will ordinarily fall into horrible *Snares*, and infinite *Sins*, if they have not a *Calling*, to be their *preservative*. It is intimated, I Tim 5.13. They who *Learn to be Idle*, [a thing soon Learnt!] [sic] will soon Learn the *Things which they ought not*. Tho' it were part of the *Curse* brought in by *Sin*, *In the Sweat of thy Face thou shalt eat Bread*, the *Curse* is become a *Blessing*, and our *Sweat* has a tendency to keep us from abundance of *Sin*. Ordinarily no man does *Nothing*: If men have *nothing* to do, they'l soon do *Too much*, do what they *ought not*. The Temptations of the *Devil*, are best Resisted, by those that are least at *Liesure* [sic] to Receive them. An *Occupation* is an *Ordinance* of God for our safeguard against the *Temptations* of the Devil. A Bird on the *Wing* is not so soon catch'd by *the Hellish Fowler*.[62] A man is upon the *Wing*, when he is at the *Work*, which God hath set him to do.

There are *Gentlemen*, 'tis true, who live upon their *Means*; and some in their *Age* retire to eat the pleasant Fruit of the *Labour*, which they underwent in their *Youth*. But yet it well becomes the best *Gentlemen*, to Study some way of being *Serviceable* in the world, and Employ themselves in some good *Business*; [...]. *Idle Gentlemen* have done as much Hurt in the world, as *Idle Beggars*. And pardon me, if I say, any *Honest Mechanicks* really are more Honourable than *Idle* and Useless *men of Honour*. Every man ordinarily should be able to say, *I have something wherein I am Occupied for the Good of other men*.

Briefly; God hath placed us, as in a common *Hive*; Let there be no *Drone*[63] in the *Hive:* Every man is to take some fair way, that the whole *Hive* may fare the better for him. The Sin of *Sodom* was, *Abundance of Idleness*. All the Sins of *Sodom* will *abound*, where *Idleness* is countenanced. In some Cities and Countreys, there have been *Censors* of Manners, who severely punished, all that could not show, by what *Occupation* they Earn'd their *Bread*. [...]

II. But upon that Enquiry, *What is your Occupation?* a Christian should be able to give this further Account, *That he hath an Allowable Occupation, yea, an Agreeable Occupation; and that he Entred into it with a suitable Disposition*. [...] If our *Calling* be that whereby God will be *Offended*, it cannot be a *Calling* wherein we shall be our selves *Befriended*. What can any man be the better for a *Calling* that will bring him under the *Wrath* of God? But the *Wrath* of God will cleave to all the *Gain* gotten by a *Calling* that shall be Forbidden by the *Word* of God. The man and his Posterity will Gain but little, by a Calling whereto God hath not Called him. For our course of Life then, we must consult the Word of God, if we would not fall into a course of Sin. when we go to chuse our Occupation, we should say with him, Psal. 119 105. Thy Word is a Light unto my path. In the first place, Let this be taken for granted; except a Calling have a Tendency to the Happiness of Mankind, and except the Spiritual, or the Temporal Good of other men, be help'd forward by a Calling, a man may not meddle with it [...].

III. A Christian should be able to give a Good Account, not only, *What is his Occupation*, but also, *What he is in his Occupation*. It is not enough, That a Christian *have* an

---

[62] Satan; fowler: One who hunts wild birds, whether for sport or food, *esp*. with nets.
[63] A male bee, esp. a honeybee, that has no stinger, performs no work, and has the sole function of mating with the queen bee.

Occupation; but he must *mind* his *Occupation*, as it becomes a Christian. Well then, That a Christian may be able to give a *Good Account* of his *Occupation*, there are certain Vertues of Christianity, with which he is to follow it. Particularly,

1. A Christian should follow his *Occupation*, with *Industry*. It is a notable Hint, Rom. 12. 11. *Be not Slothful*[64] *in Business*, [...]. It seems a man *Slothful in Business*, is not a man *Serving the Lord*. By *Slothfulness* men bring upon themselves, What? but Poverty, but Misery, but all sorts of Confusion. How canst thou Snore on, O *Sluggard*, when there are so many loud Thunders in the Oracles of God, against *Sluggishness*, to awaken thee? Yea, a *David* himself, if he grow Slothful and Sleepy, he falls into the Crimes that are the astonishment of all Succeeding Ages. [...] Avoid all impertinent *Avocations*. Laudable *Recreations* may be used now and then: But, I beseech you, Let those *Recreations* be used for *Sawce*, but not for *Meat*. If *Recreations* go to incroach too far upon your *Business*, give to them that put off. [...] It may be, there are some, that neglect their *Occupation*, and squander away one *Hour*, and perhaps, one *Day*, after another, Drinking, and Gaming, & Smoking, & Fooling, at those Drinking *Houses*, that are so Sinful as to Entertain them. Unto you, O *Miserables*, I must address a Language like that of our Saviour; *Thou wicked and slothful person*, Reform thy ways, or thou art not far from *Outer Darkness*. Is it nothing to thee, that by much *Slothfulness*, thy Money, & Credit, and all is *Decaying*, and by the *Idleness of thy Hands*, thy *House* is coming to nothing? Is it nothing to thee, that thou art contracting the character of a *Vagabond*, and a *Prodigal?*[65] Dost thou not find the *Ale house*, to be the very Suburbs of *Hell*, and dost not thou carry about the Stings and Flames of *Hell* in thy Conscience, when thou comest home from that *Ale house?* [...]

II. A Christian should follow his *Occupation* with *Discretion*. We are told, Psal. 112.5. *A Good man, will guide his Affairs with Discretion*. [...]

III. A Christian should follow his *Occupation* with *Honesty*. It is required, Deut. 16. 20. *That which is altogether Just thou shalt follow, that thou mayst Live*. Truly, *Justice, Justice*, must be Exactly follow'd, in that *Calling*, by which we go to get our *Living*. A Christian in all his *Business*, ought so *altogether Justly* to do every thing, that he should be able to say with him, Act. 23.1. *Men and Brethren, I have lived in all Good Conscience*. A Christian should imitate his Lord; Of whom tis said, *He is Righteous in all His Wayes*. In your *Business*, you have Dealings with other Persons; but a certain Vein of *Honesty*, unspotted and Resolved *Honesty*, should run through all your *Dealings*. You aim at the getting of *Silver* and *Gold*, by your *Occupation*; but you should always act by that *Golden Rule*, Mat. 7.12. *All things whatsoever ye would, that men should do to you, do ye even so to them*. Shall I be more particular? I say then; Let a principle of *Honesty* in your *Occupation* cause you to speak the *Truth*, and nothing but the *Truth*, on all Occasions. We read, *A Righteous man hateth Lying*. And it is therefore the charge of God upon us, Eph 4.25 *Putting away Lying, speak the Truth every man with his Neighbour*. [...]

IV. A Christian should follow his *Occupation* with *Contentment*. It is written, I Cor 7 20. *Let every man abide in the same Calling, wherein he was called*. One thing in it, is, That a Christian should not be too ready to fall out with his *Calling*. It is the singular Favour of God, unto a man, That he can attend his *Occupation* with *Contentation* and *Satisfaction*. That one man has a Spirit formed & fitted for *One Occupation*, and an-

---

[64] Lazy, sluggish.
[65] One who spends his money extravagantly and wastefully; a spendthrift, waster.

other man for another, This is from the Operation of that God, who *forms the Spirit of man within him*. [...]

V. A Christian should with *Piety* follow his *Occupation*. The *Exhortation* to us, is That, I Cor. 7.24. *Brethren, Let every man, wherein he is called, therein Abide with God*. Oh, let every Christian *Walk* with *God*, when he *Works* at his *Calling*, and Act in his *Occupation* with an Eye to *God*, Act as under the Eye of *God*. Syrs, 'Tis a wondrous thing that I am going to say! A poor man, that minds the *Business* of his Calling, and weaves a Threed of *Holiness* into all his *Business*, may arrive to some of the highest Glories in Heaven at the last. The Ecclesiastical History of the Primitive Times, has left such a passage as this upon Record. One of the *Saints* in the Primitive Times, had many years Retired from the World, and Employ'd his whole Time in Devotion. He began to count himself an Heir unto an High place in Heaven, and wished he might know, who should be joined with him there. He had an Intimation from Heaven, to enquire for such a man in *Alexandria*, whom he should find an *Holier* man than himself. And who was this? It proved a poor *Shoe maker*, that work'd hard most of the day; but was very *Circumspect* in his Conversation, *Thankful* to God, *Honest* to man, *Patient* in his Afflictions, & *Constant* in his Prayers and Praises. This man, it seems, was to fit above a *Devout Hermit* in Heaven!

But now, these things call for your Attention.

First; Let not the *Business* of your *Personal Calling* swallow up the *Business* of your *General Calling*. [...] Much of thy *Business* lies in *Earthly Things*; but, Oh, Let not thy Fault be that of Theirs, Phil. 3 19 *Who mind Earthly Things*. Forget not, O *Mortal man*, That thou hast an *Immortal Soul* to be provided for. Let not that care, *What shall I Eat or Drink, and wherewithal shall I be Clothed?* make you forgetful of that care, *What shall I do to be Saved?* It may be said to many a man, who is drown'd in the Encumbrances of his *Occupation*; as Luk. 10.41,42. *Thou art careful and troubled about many Things; But one thing is Needful*. Thus, thou art careful to do the *Business*, that must be done for the Relief of thy *Bodily Wants*; It is well: Do it, Do it. But, thy *Soul*, thy *Soul*, the Salvation of thy *Soul*, an Acquaintance with *Christ*, and an Union with *Christ*, the only Saviour of thy *Soul*; This is the *One Thing* that is *Needful*. Be not so *Foolish* and *Unwise*, as to Neglect *That*, whatever thou doest! Oh, try and see if you don't upon Trial find, besides the vast *Blessings of Eternity*, the Fulfilment of that word, Mat. 6.33. *Seek first the Kingdom of God, & all these things shall be added unto you*. [...]

Source: Cotton Mather (1663-1728). *A Christian at His Calling: Two Brief Discourses. One Directing a Christian in His General Calling; Another Directing Him in His Personal Calling*. Boston: B. Green & J. Allen, 1701, 36-39, 41-44, 46-47, 49-50, 52, 56-57, 60-61, 64-67.

52. *The New-England Primer* (1762)

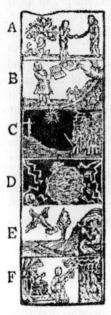

A	In ADAM's Fall, We finned all.		G	As runs the Glafs, Our Life doth pafs.
B	Heaven to find, The BIBLE mind.		H	My Book and Heart Muft never part.
C	CHRIST crucify'd, For Sinners dy'd.		J	*Job* feels the Rod, Yet blefses GOD.
D	The Deluge drown'd The Earth around.		K	Proud *Korah's* Troop Was fwallow'd up.
E	ELIJAH hid, By Ravens fed.		L	Lot fled to *Zoar*, Saw fiery Shower On *Sodom* pour.
F	The Judgment made *Felix* afraid.		M	*Moses* was he Who *Ifrael's* Hoft Led thro' the Sea.

N	*Noah* did view The old world & new.		T	Young *Timothy* Learnt Sin to fly.
O	Young *Obadias*, *David*, *Jofias*, All were pious.		V	*Vafhti* for Pride, Was fet afide.
P	*Peter* deny'd His Lord and cry'd.		W	Whales in the Sea, GOD's Voice obey.
Q	Queen *Efther* fues, And faves the *Jews*.		X	*Xerxes* did die, And fo muft I.
R	Young pious *Ruth*, Left all for Truth.		Y	While youth do chear Death may be near.
S	Young *Samuel* dear, The Lord did fear.		Z	*Zaccheus* he Did climb the Tree, Our Lord to fee.

Source: *The New-England Primer Improved. For the More Easy Attaining the True Reading of English. To Which Is Added, the Assembly of Divines, and Mr. Cotton's Catechism.* Boston: S. Adams, 1762.

53. *An Exhortation to Young and Old to Be Cautious of Small Crime* (1773)

An Exhortation to young and old to be cautious of small Crimes, lest they become habitual, and lead them before they are aware into those of the most heinous Nature. Occasioned by the unhappy Case of *Levi Ames,* Executed on *Boston*-Neck, *October* 21st, 1773, for the Crime of Burglary.

I.
BEWARE young People, look at me,
  Before it be too late,
And see Sin's End is Misery:
  Oh ! shun poor *Ames*'s Fate.

II.
I warn you all (beware betimes)
  With my now dying Breath,
To shun Theft, Burglaries, heinous Crimes;
  They bring untimely Death.

III.
Shun vain and idle Company;
  They'll lead you soon astray;
From ill-fam'd Houses ever flee,
  And keep yourselves away.

IV.
With honest Labor earn your Bread,
  While in your youthful Prime;
Nor come you near the Harlot's Bed,
  Nor idly waste your Time.

V.
Nor meddle with another's Wealth,
  In a defrauding Way:
A Curse is with what's got by stealth,
  Which makes your Life a Prey.

VI.
Shun Things that seem but little Sins,
  For they lead on to great;
From Sporting many Times begins
  Ill Blood, and poisonous Hate.

VII.
The Sabbath-Day do not prophane,
  By wickedness and Plays;
By needless Walking Streets or Lanes
  Upon such Holy days.

VIII.
To you that have the care of Youth,
  Parents and Masters too,
Teach them betimes to know the Truth,
  And Righteousness to do.

IX.
The dreadful Deed for which I die,
  Arose from small Beginning;
My Idleness brought poverty,
  And so I took to Stealing.

X.
Thus I went on in sinning fast,
  And tho' I'm young 'tis true,
I'm old in Sin, but catch't at last,
  And here receive my due.

XI.
Alas for my unhappy Fall,
  The Rigs that I have run!
Justice aloud for vengeance calls,
  Hang him for what he's done.

XII.
O may it have some good Effect,
  And warn each wicked one,
That they God's righteous Laws respect,
  And Sinful Courses Shun.

Source: *An Exhortation to Young and Old to Be Cautious of Small Crime, Lest They Become Habitual, and Lead Them Before They Are Aware into Those of the Most Heinous Nature. Occasioned by the Unhappy Case of Levi Ames, Executed on Boston-Neck, October 21st, 1773, for the Crime of Burglary* (Broadside).

54. *The Ladder of Fortune* (1875)

Source: Nathaniel Currier (1813-1888) and James Merritt Ives (1824-1895). *The Ladder of Fortune: Industry and Morality Bring Solid Rewards. Idle Schemes and Speculations Yield Poverty and Ruin*. New York, 1875.

55. *The Tree of Life – The Christian* (between 1835 and 1856)

Source: Nathaniel Currier (1813-1888). *The Tree of Life – The Christian: "Even so Every Good Tree Bringeth Forth Good Fruit" (Mat. VII. 17) "Wherefore by Their Fruits Shall Ye Know Them" (Mat. VII, 20)*. New York: N. Currier, between 1835 and 1856. [Fruits of Christian virtues from top/left to bottom/right: Perseverance, Contemplation, Heavenly Mindedness, Industry, Benevolence, Purity, Fidelity, Goodness, Gentleness, Justice, Truth, Mercy, Compassion, Fortitude, Peace, Prudence, Meekness, Chastity, Resignation, Joy, Temperance, Patience, Alms, Humility, Contrition, Fasting, Self Denial, Prayer].

PROVIDENTIAL READINGS OF AMERICAN HISTORY

Puritan readings of history were not merely concerned with chronicling past events; they rather interpreted these events in the light of present conditions and in the expectation of the heavenly Kingdom to come. The course of events was conceived as existing within a theological framework. The Puritans' interest was directed at detecting theologically meaningful hints in historical events. Divine providence was considered the sole determinant of the world's history, a salvational design which has arranged the world in a purposeful way. Since human beings were guilty of original sin, they were incapable of immediately perceiving and understanding divine truth. All they could do was to search for glimpses of God's supreme plan. Historical events, such as the reformation, could easily be read as fulfilling God's providential design. It proved more difficult, however, to incorporate the various failures and disappointments of history. This was done, for instance, by interpreting war as the struggle between the forces of good and evil, between God and Satan, or by reading droughts as signs of God's disapproval of his people's misbehavior. Thus Puritan historiography by overlaying history with a spiritual sphere made available a device for countering the fears and anxieties which resulted from conflicts with both Old and New World, a device which was exceedingly used and intensified as debates over theological positions, wars with Native Americans, and challenges from England increased.

The trust in providence, which resulted from this conception, is reflected in Increase Mather's ruminations on divine providence (cf. doc. 68). Since the wheel of providence moves the 'lower world,' human actions are predetermined. Even though things may look bleak – as they did, for instance, in the New England church in the latter part of the seventeenth century – it must be taken into consideration that these problems are contained in and controlled by a salvational design. This fundamental oscillation between the perception of an oftentimes brute reality and a higher, providential sphere was established as the guiding principle of Puritan historiography in what is considered the first formal history of Puritan New England, William Bradford's *Of Plymouth Plantation* (1629-46, doc. 58), which was not published, however, until 1856. Bradford diligently chronicles past events, albeit only those which carry relevance for the New England experiment. Yet, Bradford also attempts to write a universal history which seeks to lay bare the pattern of divine principles as manifested in historical events. History is thus imbued with a providential reading directed at justifying the New England enterprise in spite of its darker sides.

History as emanated from God is responsible for the Puritan's errand into what Bradford considers a wilderness – a position which regards America prior to the settlers' arrival as a pre-historic abode of 'savages.' Bradford describes both the Puritans' negative and their positive experiences in the Old and the New World as results of predestined history, results which can be understood in their full meaning only if situated within the larger providential context. Thus it is a sign of the predominance of God's will that despite hardships and enemies many of the Puritan settlers survived and settled in New England. Besides resulting from theological conceptions, this reading of history was also a reaction to what the Puritans experienced as hideous and hostile wilderness. As Bradford asks, "What could now sustaine them but the spirite of God and his grace?" As a consequence, despite the various setbacks in Europe and during the crossing of the Atlantic, the arrival in what was to become New England was considered a providential event, an interpretation which was to function as a narrative scheme structuring everyday social life, especially as daily experience came to contradict providential conceptions.

Even though Puritan historiography was strongly influenced by the perspective of the settlers' 'errand into the wilderness,' it must not be misunderstood as a complete break from the Old World. In "A Modell of Christian Charity" (1630, doc. 62), John Winthrop instructs his audience to join in building "a City upon a Hill," a term which must not be misunderstood as isolating America as the exclusive site of a New Jerusalem from the Old World. In fact, feeling that "the eies of all people are uppon us," the settlers set up a beacon which was to convince primarily England to imitate the Puritan's model society. In seeking a place for a theocratic civil government, especially the non-separatist New Englanders such as John Winthrop considered themselves as acting on behalf of England's reformation.

Besides the effort to justify and explain their voyage to a new world, Puritans were faced with various other hindrances. They were confronted with attacks from their mother country. The most prominent theological offensive was launched by Joseph Mede, who contended that America was not at all a New Jerusalem, but rather a place excluded from God's providential plan (cf. doc. 75 in the section "Millennialism"). Yet in New England challenges abounded as well. Other religious groups such as the Quakers and the Baptists questioned Puritanism's claim to be the sole true doctrine. Furthermore, Puritan orthodoxy was faced with the fact that church membership was declining – a problem to which they reacted by opening up church-membership ('half-way covenant') – as well as with an influx of merchants whose exemplary success allured more and more immigrants who sought commercial opportunities rather than religious fulfillment, a fact about which John Higginson ranted by insisting that New England had always been a place of religion, not of trade (cf. doc. 66). Finally, the Restoration in England raised its fundamental objection to the Puritans' readings of history. The New World beacon might have been there, yet the world was not paying attention to it. These external pressures on the Puritans led to the need to justify their enterprise.

Significantly, Michael Wigglesworth's admonishments concerning "God's Controversy with New-England" originate during a major drought. Experience is overlaid with a spiritual sphere that is capable of granting sense to a desperate situation. Mary Rowlandson's captivity narrative *The Soveraignty & Goodness of God* (doc. 69) is structured around the same pattern. The immediate experience of the captivity is perceived as disastrous and devoid of sense. Yet Rowlandson soon finds reasons for her captivity: she has disregarded God's tenets and thus comes to reinterpret her captivity as God's test of her faith. Reading the Bible, she becomes restored in a spiritual sense, and finally God answers her prayers. The captivity period has thus been a time for preparation. Rowlandson, however, is turned into a public figure or type. As the title shows, the topic of the narrative is not only her personal captivity and restoration, but rather the display of *The Soveraignty & Goodness of God* as it has occurred in history. This proceeding almost collapses the difference between individual and society, thus rendering autobiography and the writing of history as different instances of recording the same outpouring of providential design. The captivity narrative, in an exemplary manner, presents a way to deal with King Philip's War, which was – as an immediate experience – conceived as a devastating event. For New-England this war is what captivity was for Mary Rowlandson: a divine test of faith.

A further means of dealing with external pressures consisted in creating a genealogy which was to shift the New England experiment onto more solid ground. This constellation gave rise to 'jeremiads,' i.e. sermons and poems which served to remind and admonish the New England population to remain true to their faith. Exhortation had played an essential role as early as in Bradford's "Of Plymouth Plantation," in which he described what he considered signs of declension, that is, of a fall from the tradition of the fathers. Thus it is only consequent that it was Bradford himself who produced a number of important jeremiads. His "Of Boston in New-England" (doc. 60) and "A Word to New-Eingland [sic!]" (doc. 61) attempt to establish a genealogy of New England *patres* such as John Cotton and John Winthrop. Early New England history was thus evoked as a golden age, in which the colony was a place of freedom, free of corruption. The current historical situation of the colony was one of squalid excess, which, however, still contained some learned and wise men capable of continuing the father's model of Christianity. By connecting these current figures to the historical exempla of Cotton and Winthrop, they are mythologically charged with a spiritual content which remains palpable in and through history, even though the current state might look desolate.

The idea of history as the teacher of life is extended by Cotton Mather, who in his *Magnalia Christi Americana* (doc. 64) compares the New-England church fathers to the "Great Men of *Greece*, or of *Rome*" and, using typological concepts, even to Moses. Thus with Mather, the Puritan experiment, as it were, has come full circle. It continues the tradition already to be detected in the title page of Walter Raleigh's *The History of the World* (^{2}1617, doc. 57), which emblematically shows that history as *magistra vitae* carries in her hands the world. History, in turn, is watched and guided by the eye of God. The history of the world is controlled by *providentia*. Man, as a second cause, remains dependent on the first cause, i.e. on the workings of God's providence. Thus Mather stresses the importance not so much of man's deeds, but as man's actions as representative of *Magnalia Christi*, as the wondrous manifestation of divine power in America which need to be remembered and used as normative correctives to human behavior. Yet whereas Winthrop and Bradford had described and interpreted historical events which they had experienced themselves, Mather refers to the events of the first settlements in New England as he does to those of antiquity. The golden days of the Puritan fathers have passed. By depicting a glorious past, a depraved present, and an apocalyptic future, he seeks to adopt the people's word and deed to the course of providence. It is not God's plan, which has gone astray, but rather New England's conduct.

Yet, as social and historical contradictions grew more intense, it became increasingly more demanding to find a historiographical scheme which could fulfill the task of containing these conflicts in order to validate Winthrop's vision of New England theocracy. The notoriously infamous peak, in this respect, was reached with the Salem Witchcraft Trials. The witches, whose existence was doubted neither by the townsfolk nor by the clergy, were taken as yet another instance of Satan's attempt to fight God's plan. The devil was supposed to have organized a conspiracy against the divine kingdom.

Increase Mather thus pleads for the extirpation of witches from God's chosen people. In his *Magnalia Christi Americana*, Cotton Mather attempted to make sense of an event so charged with hysteria that Mather's providential reading becomes highly problematic. In the face of the drastic events in the latter half of the seventeenth century, it does not come as a surprise that this last major work of American historiography is concerned with reclaiming some of the past's glory for present America. In an intrepid effort to continue the tradition of John Winthrop and William Bradford, Mather seeks to detect once again the *"Golden Candlesticks"* which would illuminate the darkness. The darkness, however, was no longer solely referring to Native Americans and Europeans. It rather also comprised the pluralist tendencies which had emerged in New England, and which could no longer be contained within one theological model.

Clemens Spahr

56. "Wheel of Fortune" (13th Century)

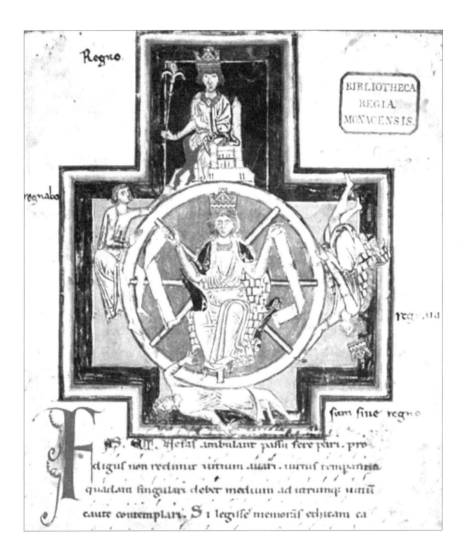

Source: "Wheel of Fortune." *Codex latinus Monacensis* (Clm) 4660. Bayerische Staatsbibliothek Munich, fol. 1ʳ (also known as *Carmina Burana*).

57. Walter Raleigh
History of the World (1614)

Source: Sir Walter Raleigh (1552-1618). *The History of the World*. London: William Stansby, 1617.[1]

---

[1] The title page of the original print was supplemented by a poem entitled "The Minde of the Front": "From Death, and darke Oblivion (neere the same) / The Mistresse of Mans life grave HISTORY, / Raising the World to good, or evill FAME, / Doth vindicate it to ETERNITY. // High PROVIDENCE would so: that nor the Good / Might be defrauded, nor the Great Secur'd, / both might know their waies are understood, / And the reward, and punishment assur'd. // This makes, that lighted by the beamy hand / of TRUTH, which searcheth the most hidden springs, / And guided by EXPERIENCE whose straight Wand, / Doth mete, whose Line doth sound the depth of things; // She chearefully supporteth what she reares: / Aissisted by no strengths, but are her owne. / Some note of which each varied Pillar beares, / By which, as proper titles, shee is knowne, // Times Witnesse, Herald of Antiquitie, / The Light of Truth, and Life of Memorie."

58. William Bradford
"Of Plymouth Plantation" (1629-1646)

1. Chapter [The Rise of Puritanism]

It is well knowne unto the godly and judicious, how ever since the first breaking out of the lighte of the gospell in our Honourable Nation of England, (which was the first of nations whom the Lord adorned ther with, afftter that grosse darknes of popery which had covered and overspred the Christian worled,) what warrs and oppossissions ever since, Satan hath raised, maintained, and continued against the Sainctes, from time to time, in one sorte or other. Some times by bloody death and cruell torments; other whiles imprisonments, banishments and other hard usages; as being loath his kingdom should goe downe, the trueth prevaile, and the churches of God reverte to their anciente puritie, and recover their primative order, libertie, and bewtie. But when he could not prevaile by these means, against the maine trueths of the gospell, but that they began to take rooting in many places, being watered with the blooud of the martires, and blessed from heaven with a gracious encrease; He then begane to take him to his anciente strategemes, used of old against the first Christians. That when by the bloody and barbarous persecutions of the Heathen Emperours, he could not stoppe and subuerte the course of the gospell, but that it speedily overspred, with a wounderfull celeritie the then best known parts of the world, He then begane to sow errours, heresies and wounderfull dissentions amongst the professours them selves, (working upon their pride and ambition, with other corrupte passions incidente to all mortall men, yea to the saints them selves in some measure,) by which wofull effects followed; as not only bitter contentions, and hartburnings, schismes, with other horrible confusions, but Satan tooke occasion and advantage therby to foyst in a number of vile ceremoneys, with many unprofftable cannons and decrees, which have since been as snares to many poore and peaceable souls even to this day. [...]

The like methode Satan hath seemed to hold in these later times [...].

[... When] as by the travell[2] and diligence of some godly and zealous preachers, and Gods blessing on their labours, as in other places of the land, so in the North parts, many became inlightened by the word of God, and had their ignorance and sins discovered unto them, and begane by his grace to reforme their lives, and make conscience of their wayes, the worke of God was no sooner manifest in them, but presently they were both scoffed and scorned by the prophane multitude, and the ministers urged with the yoak of subscription, or els must be silenced; and the poore people were so vexed with apparators, and pursuants,[3] and the comissarie courts,[4] as truly their affliction was not smale; which, notwithstanding, they bore sundrie years with much patience, till they were occasioned (by the continuance and encrease of these troubls, and other means which the Lord raised up in those days) to see further into things by the light of the word of God. How not only these base and beggerly ceremonies were unlawfull, but also that the lordly and tiranous power of the prelats ought not to be submitted unto; which thus, contrary to the freedome of the gospell, would load and burden mens consciences, and by their compulsive power make a prophane mixture of

---

[2] Travail, hard bodily and mental work.
[3] Officers of the Church of England who had to enforce conformity.
[4] County court.

persons and things in the worship of God. And that their offices and calings, courts and cannons, etc. were unlawfull and antichristian; being such as have no warrante in the word of God; but the same that were used in poperie, and still retained. [...]

But [...] they could not long continue in any peaceable condition, but were hunted and persecuted on every side, so as their former afflictions were but as flea-bitings in comparison of these which now came upon them. For some were taken and clapt up in prison, others had their houses besett and watcht night and day, and hardly escaped their hands; and the most were faine[5] to flie and leave their howses and habitations, and the means of their livelehood. Yet these and many other sharper things which afftterward befell them, were no other then they looked for, and therfore were the better prepared to bear them by the assistance of Gods grace and spirite. Yet seeing them selves thus molested, and that ther was no hope of their continuance ther, by a joynte consente they resolved to goe into the Low-Countries, wher they heard was freedome of Religion for all men; as also how sundrie from London, and other parts of the land, had been exiled and persecuted for the same cause, and were gone thither, and lived at Amsterdam, and in other places of the land. So afftter they had continued togeither aboute a year, and kept their meetings every Saboth in one place or other, exercising the worship of God amongst them selves, notwithstanding all the dilligence and malice of their adversaries, they seeing they could no longer continue in that condition, they resolved to get over into Holland as they could; which was in the year 1607. and 1608. [...]

The 4. Chap.
Showing the reasons and causes of [the Puritans'] remoovall [from Leyden].

After they had lived in this citie about some 11. or 12. years, [...] and sundrie of them were taken away by death, and many others begane to be well striken in years, the grave mistris Experience haveing taught them many things, those prudent governours with sundrie of the sagest members begane both deeply to apprehend their present dangers, and wisely to foresee the future, and thinke of timly remedy. In the agitation of their thoughts, and much discours of things hear aboute, at length they began to incline to this conclusion, of remoovall to some other place. Not out of any newfanglednes, or other such like giddie humor, by which men are oftentimes transported to their great hurt and danger, but for sundrie weightie and solid reasons; some of the cheefe of which I will hear breefly touch. And first, they saw and found by experience the hardnes of the place and countrie to be such, as few in comparison would come to them, and fewer that would bide it out, and continew with them. For many that came to them, and many more that desired to be with them, could not endure that great labor and hard fare, with other inconveniences which they underwent and were contented with. [... Yea], some preferred and chose the prisons in England, rather then this libertie in Holland, with these afflictions. But it was thought that if a better and easier place of living could be had, it would draw many, and take away these discouragments. Yea, their pastor would often say, that many of those who both wrote and preached now against them, if they were in a place wher they might have libertie and live comfortably, they would then practise as they did.

[...] They saw that though the people generally bore all these difficulties very cherfully, and with a resolute courage, being in the best and strength of their years, yet old

---

[5] Archaic: obliged, required.

age began to steale on many of them, (and their great and continuall labours, with other crosses and sorrows, hastened it before the time,) so as it was not only probably thought, but apparently seen, that within a few years more they would be in danger to scatter, by necessities pressing them, or sinke under their burdens, or both. And therfore according to the devine proverb, that a wise man seeth the plague when it cometh, and hideth him selfe, Pro. 22.3., so they like skillfull and beaten souldiers were fearfull either to be intrapped or surrounded by their enimies, so as they should neither be able to fight nor flie; And therfor thought it better to dislodge betimes to some place of better advantage and less danger, if any such could be found. Thirdly; as necessitie was a taskmaster over them, so they were forced to be such, not only to their servants, but in a sorte, to their dearest children; the which as it did not a litle wound the tender harts of many a loving father and mother, so it produced likwise sundrie sad and sorowful effects. [...] But that which was more lamentable, and of all sorowes most heavie to be borne, was that many of their children, by these occasions, and the great licentiousness of youth in that countrie, and the manifold temptations of the place, were drawne away by evill examples into extravagante and dangerous courses, getting the raines[6] off their neks, and departing from their parents. Some became souldiers, others tooke upon them farr viages by sea, and other some worse courses, tending to dissolutnes and the danger of their soules, to the great greefe of their parents and dishonour of God. So that they saw their posteritie would be in danger to degenerate and be corrupted.

Lastly, (and which was not least), a great hope and inward zeall they had of laying some good foundation, or at least to make some way therunto, for the propagating and advancing the gospell of the kingdom of Christ in those remote parts of the world; yea, though they should be but even as stepping-stones unto others for the performing of so great a work.

These, and some other like reasons, moved them to undertake this resolution of their removall; the which they afterward prosecuted with so great difficulties, as by the sequell will appeare.

The place they had thoughts on was some of those vast and unpeopled countries of America, which are frutfull and fitt for habitation, being devoyd of all civill inhabitants, wher ther are only salvage and brutish men, which range up and downe, litle otherwise then the wild beasts of the same. This proposition being made publike and coming to the scaning of all, it raised many variable opinions amongst men, and caused many fears and doubts amongst them selves. Some, from their reasons and hops conceived, laboured to stirr up and incourage the rest to undertake and prosecute the same; others, againe, out of their fears, objected against it, and sought to diverte from it, aledging many things, and those neither unreasonable nor unprobable; as that it was a great designe, and subjecte to many unconceivable perills and dangers; as, besids the casulties of the seas (which none can be freed from) the length of the vioage was such, as the weake bodys of women and other persons worne out with age and traville[7] (as many of them were) could never be able to endure. And yet if they should, the miseries of the land which they should be exposed unto, would be to hard to be borne; and lickly, some or all of them together, to consume and utterly to ruinate them. For ther they should be liable to famine, and nakednes, and the wante, in a maner, of all things. The

---

[6] Reins.
[7] Travail, work.

chang of aire, diate, and drinking of water, would infecte their bodies with sore sicknesses, and greevous diseases. And also those which should escape or overcome these difficulties, should yett be in continuall danger of the salvage people, who are cruell, barbarous, and most trecherous, being most furious in their rage, and merciles wher they overcome; not being contente only to kill, and take away life, but delight to tormente men in the most bloodie manner that may be; fleaing[8] some alive with the shells of fishes, cutting of[f] the members and joynts of others by peesmeale, and broiling on the coles, eate the collops of their flesh in their sight whilst they live; with other cruelties horrible to be related. [...]

It was answered, that all great and honourable actions are accompanied with great difficulties, and must be both enterprised and overcome with answerable courages. It was granted the dangers were great, but not desperate; the difficulties were many, but not invincible. For though their were many of them likly, yet they were not cartaine; it might be sundrie of the things feared might never befale; others by providente care and the use of good means, might in a great measure be prevented; and all of them, through the help of God, by fortitude and patience, might either be borne, or overcome. True it was, that such atempts were not to be made and undertaken without good ground and reason; not rashly or lightly as many have done for curiositie or hope of gaine, etc. But their condition was not ordinarie; their ends were good and honourable; their calling lawfull, and urgente; and therfore they might expecte the blessing of God in their proceding. Yea, though they should loose their lives in this action, yet might they have comforte in the same, and their endeavors would be honourable. They lived he[re] but as men in exile, and in a poore condition; and as great miseries might possibly befale them in this place, for the 12. years of truce were now out,[9] and ther was nothing but beating of drumes, and preparing for warr, the events wherof are allway uncertaine. The Spaniard might prove as cruell as the salvages of America, and the famine and pestelence as sore hear as ther, and their libertie less to looke out for remedie. After many other perticuler things answered and aledged on both sids, it was fully concluded by the major parte, to put this designe in execution, and to prosecute it by the best means they could. [...]

The 9. Chap.
Of their vioage, and how they passed the sea, and of their safe arrival at Cape Codd.

Sept^r: 6. These troubls being blowne over, and now all being compacte togeather in one shipe, they put to sea againe with a prosperus winde, which continued diverce days togeather, which was some incouragmente unto them; yet according to the usuall maner many were afflicted with seasicknes. And I may not omite hear a spetiall worke of Gods providence. Ther was a proud and very profane yonge man, one of the seamen, of a lustie, able body, which made him the more hauty; he would allway be contemning the poore people in their sicknes, and cursing them dayly with greevous execrations, and did not let to tell them, that he hoped to help to cast halfe of them over board before they came to their jurneys end, and to make mery with what they had; and if he were by any gently reproved, he would curse and swear most bitterly. But it plased God before they came halfe seas over, to smite this yong man with a greeveous

---

[8] To strip or pull off the skin.
[9] Reference to the Spanish rule in the Netherlands and the end of the truce in April 1621.

disease, of which he dyed in a desperate maner, and so was him selfe the first that was throwne overbord. Thus his curses light on his owne head; and it was an astonishmente to all his fellows, for they noted it to be the just hand of God upon him. [...]

[...] But to omite other things, (that I may be breefe,) after longe beating at sea they fell with that land which is called Cape Cod; the which being made and certainly knowne to be it, they were not a litle joyfull. After some deliberation [they ...] resolved to stande for the southward (the wind and weather being faire) to finde some place aboute Hudsons river for their habitation. But after they had sailed that course aboute halfe the day, they fell amongst deangerous shoulds and roring breakers, and they were so farr intangled ther with as they conceived them selves in great danger; and the wind shrinking upon them withall, they resolved to bear up againe for the Cape, and thought them selves hapy to gett out of those dangers before night overtooke them, as by Gods providence they did. And the next day they gott into the Cape-harbor wher they ridd in saftie. [...]

Being thus arived in a good harbor and brought safe to land, they fell upon their knees and blessed the God of heaven, who had brought them over the vast and furious ocean, and delivered them from all the periles and miseries therof, againe to set their feete on the firme and stable earth, their proper elemente. [...]

But hear I cannot but stay and make a pause, and stand half amased at this poore peoples presente condition; and so I thinke will the reader too, when he well considers the same. Being thus passed the vast ocean, and a sea of troubles before in their preparation (as may be remembered by that which wente before), they had now no freinds to wellcome them, nor inns to entertaine or refresh their weatherbeaten bodys, no houses or much less townes to repair too, to seeke for succoure. It is recorded in scripture[10] as a mercie to the apostle and his shipwraked company, that the barbarians shewed them no smale kindnes in refreshing them, but these savage barbarians, when they mette with them (as after will appeare) were readier to fill their sids full of arrows then otherwise. And for the season it was winter, and they that know the winters of that cuntrie know them to be sharp and violent, and subjecte to cruell and feirce stormes, deangerous to travill to known places, much more to serch an unknown coast. Besids, what could they see but a hidious and desolate wildernes, full of wild beasts and willd men? and what multituds ther might be of them they knew not. Nether could they, as it were, goe up to the tope of Pisgah,[11] to vew from this willdernes a more goodly cuntrie to feed their hops; for which way soever they turnd their eys (save upward to the heavens) they could have litle solace or content in respecte of any outward objects. For summer being done, all things stand upon them with a wetherbeaten face; and the whole countrie, full of woods and thickets, represented a wild and savage heiw.[12] If they looked behind them, ther was the mighty ocean which they had passed, and was now as a maine barr and goulfe to seperate them from all the civill parts of the world. [...] What could now sustaine them but the spirite of God and his grace? May not and ought not the children of these fathers rightly say: *Our faithers were Englishmen which came over this great ocean, and were ready to perish in this willdernes*;[13] *but they cried unto the Lord, and he heard their voyce, and looked on their adversitie, etc. Let them therfore praise the*

---

[10] Original footnote: "Act. 28."
[11] Mount Pisgah: after Yahweh had denied him entrance into Canaan, Moses climbed Mount Pisgah to look out over the land that he would not enter.
[12] Hue.
[13] Original footnote: "Deut. 26.5,7."

Lord, because he is good, and his mercies endure for ever.[14] *Yea, let them which have been redeemed of the Lord, shew how he hath delivered them from the hand of the oppressour. When they wandered in the deserte willdernes out of the way, and found no citie to dwell in, both hungrie, and thirstie, their sowle was overwhelmed in them. Let them confess before the Lord his loving kindnes, and his wonderfull works before the sons of men.* [...]

[Chapter Thirty-two][15]
Anno Dom: 1642. [Wickedness Breaks Forth]

Marvilous it may be to see and consider how some kind of wickednes did grow and breake forth here, in a land wher the same was so much witnesed against, and so narrowly looked unto, and severly punished when it was knowne; as in no place more, or so much, that I have known or heard of; insomuch as they have been somewhat censured, even by moderate and good men, for their severitie in punishments. And yet all this could not suppress the breaking out of sundrie notorious sins, [...] espetially drunkennes and unclainnes; not only incontinencie betweene persons unmaried, for which many both men and women have been punished sharply enough, but some maried persons allso. But that which is worse, even sodomie and bugerie,[16] (things fearfull to name,) have broak forth in this land, oftener then once. I say it may justly be marveled at, and cause us to fear and tremble at the consideration of our corrupte natures, which are so hardly bridled, subdued, and mortified; nay, cannot by any other means but the powerfull worke and grace of Gods spirite. But (besids this) one reason may be, that the Divell may carrie a greater spite against the churches of Christ and the gospell hear, by how much the more they indeaour to preserve holynes and puritie amongst them, and strictly punisheth the contrary when it ariseth either in church or comone wealth; that he might cast a blemishe and staine upon them in the eyes of [the] world, who use to be rash in judgmente. I would rather thinke thus, then that Satane hath more power in these heathen lands, as som have thought, then in more Christian nations, espetially over Gods servants in them.

2. An other reason may be, that it may be in this case as it is with waters when their streames are stopped or dammed up, when they gett passage they flow with more violence, and make more noys and disturbance, then when they are suffered to rune quietly in their owne chanels. So wikednes being here more stopped by strict laws, and the same more nerly looked unto, so as it cannot rune in a comone road of liberty as it would, and is inclined, it searches every wher, and at last breaks out wher it getts vente.

3. A third reason may be, hear (as I am verily perswaded) is not more evills in this kind, nor nothing nere so many by proportion, as in other places; but they are here more discoverd and seen, and made publick by due serch, inquisition, and due punishment; for the churches looke narrowly to their members, and the magistrats over all, more strictly then in other places. Besids, here the people are but few in comparison of other places, which are full and populous, and lye hid, as it were, in a wood or thickett, and many horrible evills by that means are never seen nor knowne; wheras hear, they are, as it were, brought into the light, and set in the plaine feeld, or rather on a hill, made conspicuous to the veiw of all. [...]

---

[14] Original footnote: "107 Psa.: v. 1, 2, 4, 5, 8."
[15] After chapter 10, the chapter count is not Bradford's, but an addendum of later editors.
[16] Unnatural intercourse of a human being with a beast, or of men with one another; sodomy. Also used of unnatural intercourse between a man and a woman.

[Chapter Thirty-three]
Anno Dom: 1643. [The Life and Death of Elder Brewster]

I am to begine this year whith that which was a mater of great saddnes and mourning unto them all. Aboute the 18. of Aprill dyed their Reve^d Elder, and my dear and loving friend, Mr. William Brewster; a man that had done and suffered much for the Lord Jesus and the gospells sake, and had bore his parte in well and woe with this poore persecuted church above 36. years in England, Holand, and in this wildernes, and done the Lord and them faithfull service in his place and calling. And notwithstanding the many troubles and sorrows he passed throw, the Lord upheld him to a great age. He was nere fourskore[17] years of age (if not all out) when he dyed. He had this blesing added by the Lord to all the rest, to dye in his bed, in peace, amongst the mids of his freinds [...].

[...] I cannot but here take occasion, not only to mention, but greatly to admire the marvelous providence of God, that notwithstanding the many changes and hardships that these people wente throwgh, and the many enemies they had and difficulties they mette with all, that so many of them should live to very olde age! It was not only this reve[rend] mans condition, (for one swallow maks no summer, as they say,) but many more of them did the like [...]. God, it seems, would have all men to behold and observe such mercies and works of his providence as these are towards his people, that they in like cases might be incouraged to depend upon God in their trials, and also blese his name when they see his goodnes towards others. [...]

Source: William Bradford (1590-1657). *Bradford's History of Plymouth Plantation (1606-1646)*. Ed. William T. Davis. New York: Scribner's, 1908, 23-24, 30, 32-33, 44-49, 92-97, 363-365, 375, 380-381.

59. John [?] Pond
"Letter to William Pond March 15, 1630/1"

Most loving and kind Father and Mother:

My humble duty remembered unto you, trusting in God you are in good health, [...] and my writing unto you is to let you understand what a country this new Eingland is where we live.

Here are but few eingeines [Indians], and a great sort of them died this winter. It was thought it was of the plague. They are a crafty people and they will cozen and cheat, and they are a subtle people [...]. They are proper men and clean-jointed men, and many of them go naked with a skin about their loins, but some of them get eingellische menes [Englishmen's] parell [apparel].

And the country is very rocky and hilly and some champion [open] ground, and the soil is very fleet [shallow], and here is some good ground and marsh ground [...]. Cattle thrive well here, but they give small store of milk. [...] Here is timber good store and acorns good store, and here is good store of fish, if we had boats to go eight or ten leagues to sea to fish in. Here are good store of wild fowl, but they are hard to come by. It is harder to get a shot than it is in ould eingland. And people here are subject to disease, for here have died of the scurvy and of the burning fever two hundred and odd,

---

[17] Eighty.

besides many layeth lame, and all Sudberey men[18] are dead but three and the women and some children. And provisions are here at a wonderful rate. [...] Father, though I be far distant from you, yet I pray you remember me as your child, and we do not know how long we may subsist, for we cannot live here without provisions from ould eingland. Therefore, I pray, do not put away your shopstuff, for I think that in the end if I live it must be my living, for we do not know how long this plantation will stand, for some of the merchants that did uphold it have turned off their men and have given it over. [...]

So, Father, I pray consider of my cause, for here will be but a very poor being and no being without, loving Father, your help with provisions from ould eingland. I had thought to have c[o]me home in this ship, for my provisions were almost all spent, but that I humbly thank you for your great love and kindness in sending me some provisions, or else I should and mine have been half famished, but now I will, if it please God that I have my health, I will plant what corn I can, and if provisions be no cheaper between this and Michaelmas[19] and that I do not hear from you what I was best to do, I purpose to come home at Michaelmas. [...]

from Walltur Toune in new eingland [no signature]
the 15 of March 1630[/1]

Source: John [?] Pond. "Letter to William Pond March 15, 1630/1." *Letters from New England: The Massachusetts Bay Colony, 1629-1638.* Ed. Everett Emerson. Amherst: University of Massachusetts Press, 1976, 64-66.

60. William Bradford
"Of Boston in New-England" (c. 1653/1657)

O boston though thow now art grown
to be a great & welthy towne
yet I have seen thee, a voyd place
Shrubs, and bushes, covering thy face

No – house, then in thee their were
nor such as gould and silk did weare
No drunkenness was then in thee
nor such excesse as now we see

We then drunke frely, of thy spring
without paying of any thing
We lodged frely, where we would
all things, were free, and nothing sould

and they that did thee first begine
had harts as free, and as willing
their pore frinds, for to entertaine
and neiver looked at sorded gaine

---

[18] People who emigrated from Sudbury, England, to Massachusetts.
[19] The feast of St. Michael, one of the quarter days in England; 29 September.

som thou hast had, whome I did know
that spent their selves to make thee grow
thy foundatyon they did lay
which doe remaine, unto this day

When thou wast weake; they did the nurce[20]
Or elce with thee it had been worce
they left thee not, but did defend
& succour thee, unto their end

Thou now art growne in wealth & store
doe not forget that thou wast pore
& lift not up thy selfe; in pride
from truth & Justice turne not aside

Remember thou a cotten[21] had
which made the harts of many glad
what he thee taught, bear thou in minde
its hard another such to find

a winthrop[22] once in thee was knowne
who unto thee, was as a crowne
Such orniments are very rare
yet thou enjoyed this blessed pare

But these are gone, their work is done
this day is past set is their sune
yet faithfull Willson, still remains
& learned Norten[23] doth take pains

live yee in peace; I could say more
oppresse yee not the weake & poore
the trade is all in your one hand
take heed thee doe not wrong the land

Least he that hath lift you; on high
when as the poore to him doe crye
doe throw you downe from your high state
& make you low, and desolate

Source: William Bradford (1588-1657). "Of Boston in New-England." Michael Gracen Runyan. *The Poetry of William Bradford: An Annotated Edition with Essays Introductory to the Poems.* Diss. University of California, Los Angeles, 1970, 217-219.

---

[20] In 1 Thess. 2.7 the model ministers of the gospel are described with a nurse metaphor: "But we were gentle among you, even as a nurse cherisheth her children."
[21] John Cotton (1585-1652), influential New England Puritan leader who served in the First Church of Boston as 'teacher,' whose prime function was the exposition of doctrines.
[22] John Winthrop (1588-1649), governor of the Massachusetts Bay Colony, chief figure among the Puritan founders of New England.
[23] John Wilson (1588-1667) and John Norton (1606-1663), ministers in Boston.

61. William Bradford
"A Word to New-Eingland" (after 1653)

O New-eingland thou canst not bost
thy formor glory thou hast lost
When Hooker winthrop, Cotton[24] dy'de
& many pretious ones besid
thy buety then it did decay
& still doth languish more a way
love truth goodmen mercy and grace
Wealth & the wourld have took their place
Thy open sinns none can them hide
Fraud, drunkenness, whordome & pride
the great oppressours, shall slay the poore
but Whimsie errours; they kille more
yet som thou hast which morne & weepe
& their garments unspoted keepe
Who seeke gods honour, to maintaine
that truth Religion may remaine
these doe Invite and sweetly call
each to other and say to all
Repent amend & turn to god
that we may prevent his sharp rod
yet time thou hast improve it well
that god's presence may with ye dwell

Source: William Bradford (1588-1657). "A Word to New-Eingland." Michael Gracen Runyan. *The Poetry of William Bradford: An Annotated Edition with Essays Introductory to the Poems*. Diss. University of California, Los Angeles, 1970, 216-217.

62. John Winthrop
"A Modell of Christian Charity" (1630)

Written
On Boarde the Arrabella,
On the Attlantick Ocean.
By the Honorable JOHN WINTHROP Esquire.

In His passage, (with the great Company of Religious people, of which Christian Tribes he was the Brave Leader and famous Governor;) from the Island of Great Brittaine, to New-England in the North America.
Anno 1630.

---

[24] Thomas Hooker (1586-1647), John Winthrop, and John Cotton were influential New England Puritan leaders in the late 16th and early 17th centuries.

CHRISTIAN CHARITIE.
A MODELL HEREOF.

God Almightie in his most holy and wise providence hath soe disposed of the Condicion of mankinde, as in all times some must be rich some poore, some highe and eminent in power and dignitie; others meane and in subieccion.

THE REASON HEREOF.

1. REAS. *First*, to hold conformity with the rest of his workes, being delighted to shewe forthe the glory of his wisdome in the variety and differ[e]nce of the Creatures, and the glory of his power, in ordering all these differences for the preservacion and good of the whole, and the glory of his greatnes that as it is the glory of princes to have many officers, soe this great King will have many Stewards counting himselfe more honoured in dispenceing his guifts to man by man, than if hee did it by his owne immediate hand.

2. REAS. *Secondly*, That he might have the more occasion to manifest the worke of his Spirit: first, upon the wicked in moderateing and restraineing them: soe that the riche and mighty should not eate upp the poore, nor the poore, and dispised rise upp against theire superiours, and shake off theire yoake; 2ly in the regenerate in exerciseing his graces in them, as in the greate ones, theire love, mercy, gentlenes, temperance &c., in the poore and inferiour sorte, theire faithe, patience, obedience &c.:

3. REAS. Thirdly, That every man might have need of other[s], and from hence they might be all knitt more nearly together in the Bond of brotherly affeccion: from hence it appears plainely that noe man is made more honourable than another or more wealthy &c., out of any perticuler and singular respect to himselfe but for the glory of his Creator and the Common good of the Creature, Man. [...] All men being thus (by divine providence) ranked into two sortes, riche and poore; under the first, are comprehended all such as are able to live comfortably by theire owne meanes duely improved; and all others are poore according to the former distribution. There are two rules whereby wee are to walke one towards another: JUSTICE and MERCY. [...]

The diffinition which the Scripture gives us of love is [that] this Love is the bond of perfection.[25] First, it is a bond, or a ligament. 2ly, it makes the worke perfect. There is noe body but consists of partes and that which knitts these partes together gives the body its perfeccion, because it makes eache parte soe contiguous to other as thereby they doe mutually participate with eache other, both in strengthe and infirmity in pleasure and paine, to instance in the most perfect of all bodies, Christ and his church make one body: the severall partes of this body considered aparte before they were united were as disproportionate and as much disordering as soe many contrary qualities or elements but when christ comes and by his spirit and love knitts all these partes to himselfe and each to other, it is become the most perfect and best proportioned body in the world [...].

It rests now to make some applicacion of this discourse [on Christian love] by the present designe which gave the occasion of writing of it. Herein are 4 things to be propounded: first the persons, 2ly, the worke, 3ly, the end, 4ly the meanes.

I. For the persons, wee are a Company professing our selves fellow members of Christ, In which respect onely though wee were absent from eache other many miles,

---

[25] Cf. Col. 3.14.

and had our imploymentes as farre distant, yet wee ought to account our selves knitt together by this bond of love, and live in the exercise of it, if wee would have comforte of our being in Christ [...].

2ly. for the worke wee have in hand, it is by a mutuall consent through a speciall overruleing providence, and a more then an ordinary approbation of the Churches of Christ to seeke out a place of Cohabitation and Consorteshipp under a due forme of Goverment both civill and ecclesiasticall. In such cases as this the care of the publique must oversway all private respects, by which not onely conscience,[26] but meare Civill pollicy doth binde us; for it is a true rule that perticuler estates cannott subsist in the ruine of the publique.

3ly. The end is to improve our lives to doe more service to the Lord the comforte and encrease of the body of christe whereof wee are members that our selves and posterity may be the better preserved from the Common corrupcions of this evill world to serve the Lord and worke out our Salvacion under the power and purity of his holy Ordinances.

4ly for the meanes whereby this must bee effected, they are 2fold, a Conformity with the worke and end wee aime at, these wee see are extraordinary, therefore wee must not content our selves with usuall ordinary meanes whatsoever wee did or ought to have done when wee lived in England, the same must wee doe and more allsoe where wee goe: That which the most in theire Churches mainteine as a truthe in profession onely, wee must bring into familiar and constant practise, as in this duty of love wee must love brotherly without dissimulation,[27] wee must love one another with a pure hearte fervently[28] wee must beare one anothers burthens,[29] we must not looke onely on our owne things, but allsoe on the things of our brethren [...].

[...] When God gives a speciall Commission he lookes to have it strickly observed in every Article, when hee gave Saule a Commission to destroy Amaleck hee indented with him upon certaine Articles and because hee failed in one of the least, [...] it lost him the kingdome, which should have beene his reward, if hee had observed his Commission:[30] Thus stands the cause betweene God and us, wee are entered into Covenant with him for this worke, wee have taken out a Commission, the Lord hath given us leave to drawe our owne Articles wee have professed to enterprise these Accions upon these and these ends, wee have hereupon besought him of favour and blessing: Now if the Lord shall please to heare us, and bring us in peace to the place wee desire, then hath hee ratified this Covenant and sealed our Commission, [and] will expect a strickt performance of the Articles contained in it, but if wee shall neglect the observacion of these Articles which are the ends wee have propounded, and dissembling with our God, shall fall to embrace this present world and prosecute our carnall intencions, seekeing greate things for our selves and our posterity, the Lord will surely breake out in wrathe against us be revenged of such a periured people and make us knowe the price of the breache of such a Covenant.

Now the onely way to avoyde this shipwracke and to provide for our posterity is to followe the Counsell of Micah, to doe Justly, to love mercy, to walke humbly with our

---

[26] The copyist wrote "consequence," above which a later hand has interlined "conscience."
[27] Rom. 12. 9-10.
[28] 1 Pet. 1.22.
[29] Gal. 6.2.
[30] 1 Sam. 15; 28.16-18.

God,[31] for this end, wee must be knitt together in this worke as one man, wee must entertaine each other in brotherly Affeccion, wee must be willing to abridge our selves of our superfluities, for the supply of others necessities, wee must uphold a familiar Commerce together in all meekenes, gentlenes, patience and liberallity, wee must delight in eache other, make others Condicions our owne, reioyce together, mourne together, labour, and suffer together, allwayes haveing before our eyes our Commission and Community in the worke, our Community as members of the same body, soe shall wee keepe the unitie of the spirit in the bond of peace,[32] the Lord will be our God and delight to dwell among us, as his owne people and will commaund a blessing upon us in all our wayes, soe that wee shall see much more of his wisdome power goodnes and truthe then formerly wee have beene acquainted with, wee shall finde that the God of Israell is among us, when tenn of us shall be able to resist a thousand of our enemies, when hee shall make us a prayse and glory, that men shall say of succeeding plantacions: the lord make it like that of New England: for wee must Consider that wee shall be as a Citty upon a Hill,[33] the eies of all people are uppon us; soe that if wee shall deale falsely with our god in this worke wee have undertaken and soe cause him to withdrawe his present help from us, wee shall be made a story and a by-word through the world, wee shall open the mouthes of enemies to speake evill of the wayes of god and all professours for Gods sake; wee shall shame the faces of many of gods worthy servants, and cause theire prayers to be turned into Cursses upon us till wee be consumed out of the good land whether wee are goeing: And to shutt upp this discourse with that exhortacion of Moses that faithfull servant of the Lord in his last farewell to Israell Deut. 30. Beloved there is now sett before us life, and good, deathe and evill in that wee are Commaunded this day to love the Lord our God, and to love one another to walke in his wayes and to keepe his Commaundements and his Ordinance, and his lawes, and the Articles of our Covenant with him that wee may live and be multiplyed, and that the Lord our God may blesse us in the land whether wee goe to possesse it: But if our heartes shall turne away soe that wee will not obey, but shall be seduced and worshipp other Gods our pleasures, and proffitts, and serve them; it is propounded unto us this day, wee shall surely perishe out of the good Land whether wee passe over this vast Sea to possesse it;

> Therefore lett us choose life,
> that wee, and our Seede,
> may live; by obeyeing his
> voyce, and cleaveing to him,
> for hee is our life, and
> our prosperity.[34]

Source: John Winthrop (1588-1649). "A Modell of Christian Charity. Written on Boarde the Arrabella, on the Attlantick Ocean. By the Honorable John Winthrop Esquire. In His Passage, (with the Great Company of Religious People, of Which Christian Tribes He Was the Brave Leader and Famous Governor); from the Island of Great Brittaine, to New-England in the North America. Anno 1630." *Winthrop Papers*. 5 vols. Vol. 2: *1623-1630*. Boston: Massachusetts Historical Society, 1931, 282-283, 288-289, 292-295.

---

[31] Mic. 6.8.
[32] Eph. 4.3.
[33] Matt. 5.14.
[34] Cf. Deut. 30.19-20.

63. John Winthrop
"Speech on Liberty" (1645)

[...] The great questions that have troubled the country, are about the authority of the magistrates and the liberty of the people. It is yourselves who have called us to this office, and being called by you, we have our authority from God, in way of an ordinance, such as hath the image of God eminently stamped upon it, the contempt and violation whereof hath been vindicated with examples of divine vengeance. I entreat you to consider, that when you choose magistrates, you take them from among yourselves, men subject to like passions as you are. Therefore when you see infirmities in us, you should reflect upon your own, and that would make you bear the more with us, and not be severe censurers of the failings of your magistrates, when you have continual experience of the like infirmities in yourselves and others. We account him a good servant, who breaks not his covenant. The covenant between you and us is the oath you have taken of us, which is to this purpose, that we shall govern you and judge your causes by the rules of God's laws and our own, according to our best skill. When you agree with a workman to build you a ship or house &c. he undertakes as well for his skill as for his faithfulness, for it is his profession, and you pay him for both. But when you call one to be a magistrate, he doth not profess nor undertake to have sufficient skill for that office, nor can you furnish him with gifts &c. therefore you must run the hazard of his skill and ability. But if he fail in faithfulness, which by his oath he is bound unto, that he must answer for. If it fall out that the case be clear to common apprehension, and the rule clear also, if he transgress here, the error is not in the skill, but in the evil of the will: it must be required of him. But if the cause be doubtful, or the rule doubtful, to men of such understanding and parts as your magistrates are, if your magistrates should err here, yourselves must bear it.

For the other point concerning liberty, I observe a great mistake in the country about that. There is a twofold liberty, natural (I mean as our nature is now corrupt) and civil or federal. The first is common to man with beasts and other creatures. By this, man, as he stands in relation to man simply, hath liberty to do what he lists; it is a liberty to evil as well as to good. This liberty is incompatible and inconsistent with authority, and cannot endure the least restraint of the most just authority. The exercise and maintaining of this liberty makes men grow more evil, and in time to be worse than brute beasts: omnes sumus licentia deteriores. This is that great enemy of truth and peace, that wild beast, which all the ordinances of God are bent against, to restrain and subdue it. The other kind of liberty I call civil or federal, it may also be termed moral, in reference to the covenant between God and man, in the moral law, and the politic covenants and constitutions, amongst men themselves. This liberty is the proper end and object of authority, and cannot subsist without it; and it is a liberty to that only which is good, just and honest. This liberty you are to stand for, with the hazard (not only of your goods, but) of your lives, if need be. Whatsoever crosseth this, is not authority, but a distemper thereof. This liberty is maintained and exercised in a way of subjection to authority; it is of the same kind of liberty wherewith Christ hath made us free. The woman's own choice makes such a man her husband; yet being so chosen, he is her lord, and she is to be subject to him, yet in a way of liberty, not of bondage; and a true wife accounts her subjection her honour and freedom, and would not think her condition safe and free, but in her subjection to her husband's authority. Such is the liberty of the church under the authority of Christ, her king and husband; his yoke is so easy and sweet to her as a bride's ornaments; and if through frowardness or wantonness &c. she shake it off, at any time, she is at no rest in her spirit, until she take it up again; and whether her lord smiles upon her, and embraceth her in his arms, or whether he frowns, or rebukes, or smites her, she apprehends the sweetness of his love in all, and is refreshed, supported and instructed by every such dispensation of his authority over her. On the other side, ye know who they are that complain of this yoke and say, let us break their bands &c. we will not have this man to rule over us. Even so, brethren, it will be between you and your magistrates. If you stand for your natural corrupt liberties, and will do what is good in your own eyes, you will not endure the least weight of authority, but will murmur, and oppose, and be always striving to shake off that yoke; but if you will be satisfied to enjoy such civil and lawful liberties, such as Christ allows you, then will you quietly and cheerfully submit unto that authority which is set over you, in all the administrations of it, for your good. Wherein, if we fail at any time, we hope we shall be willing (by God's assistance) to hearken to good advice from any of you, or in any other way of God; so shall your liberties be preserved, in upholding the honour and power of authority amongst you.

Source: John Winthrop (1588-1649). ["Speech on Liberty;" untitled speech given on the occasion of the inauguration of Thomas Dudley as Governor of the Massachusetts Bay Colony]. John Winthrop. *The History of New England, from 1630 to 1649*. 2 vols. Ed. James Savage. Boston: Thomas B. Wait & Son, 1826, Vol. 2, 228-230.

64. Cotton Mather
"Nehemias Americanus: The Life of John Winthrop, Esq, Governour of the Massachuset Colony" (1702)

Quicunq; Venti erunt, Ars nostra certe non aberit. Cicer.[35]

§. I. Let *Greece* boast of her patient *Lycurgus*,[36] the *Lawgiver*, by whom *Diligence*, *Temperance*, *Fortitude* and *Wit* were made the *Fashions* of a therefore Long-lasting and Renowned Commonwealth: Let *Rome* tell of her Devout *Numa*,[37] the *Lawgiver*, by whom the most Famous Commonwealth saw *Peace* Triumphing over extinguished *War*; and cruel *Plunders*, and *Murders* giving place to the more mollifying Exercises of his *Religion*. Our *New-England* shall tell and boast of her *Winthrop*, a *Lawgiver*, as patient as *Lycurgus*, but not admitting any of *his* Criminal Disorders; as Devout as *Numa*, but not liable to any of *his* Heathenish Madnesses; a *Governour* in whom the Excellencies of *Christianity* made a most improving Addition unto the *Virtues*, wherein even without *those* he would have made a *Parallel* for the Great Men of *Greece*, or of *Rome*, which the Pen of a *Plutarch*[38] has Eternized.

---

[35] Latin: "Whatever winds may blow, our art will surely never pass away;" Cicero *Epistulae ad Familiares* 12.25.5.
[36] According to tradition, the great reformer of the Spartan Constitution (7th century BC). His "criminal disorders" may refer to the war machine Lycurgus is said to have built or to the uprisings of wealthy citizens deprived by Lycurgus of their wealth.
[37] Numa Pompilius: legendary king of Rome after Romulus; his "heathenish madness" probably refers to his adherence to the doctrines of Pythagoras.
[38] Plutarch (46-after 119), Greek writer who wrote *Parallel Lives*, the biographies of eminent men in ancient Greece and Rome.

§. 2. A stock of *Heroes* by right should afford nothing but what is *Heroical*; and nothing but an extream Degeneracy would make any thing less to be expected from a Stock of *Winthrops*. Mr. *Adam Winthrop*, the Son of a Worthy Gentleman wearing the same Name, was himself a Worthy, a Discreet, and a Learned Gentleman, particularly Eminent for *Skill* in the *Law*, nor without Remark for *Love* to the *Gospel* [...]. This Mr. *Adam Winthrop* had a Son of the same Name also, and of the same Endowments and Imployments with his Father; and this Third *Adam Winthrop* was the Father of that Renowned *John Winthrop*, who was the Father of *New-England*, and the Founder *of a Colony*, which upon many Accounts, like *him* that Founded it, may challenge the *First Place* among the *English* Glories of *America*. Our *John Winthrop* thus Born at the Mansion-House of his Ancestors, at *Groton* in *Suffolk*, on *June* 12. 1587.[39] enjoyed afterwards an agreeable Education. [...]

§. 3. Being made, at the unusually early Age of *Eighteen*, a *Justice of Peace*, his Virtues began to fall under a more general Observation; and he not only so *Bound himself to the Behaviour* of a *Christian*, as to become Exemplary for a Conformity to the *Laws of Christianity* in his own Conversation, but also discovered a more than ordinary Measure of those Qualities, which adorn an *Officer of Humane Society*. His *Justice* was Impartial, and used the *Ballance* to weigh not the *Cash*, but the *Case* of those who were before him: *Prosopolatria*, he reckoned as bad as *Idololatria*:[40] His *Wisdom* did exquisitely Temper things according to the *Art of Governing*, which is a Business of more Contrivance than the *Seven Arts* of the *Schools*:[41] *Oyer* still went before *Terminer*[42] in all his Administrations: His *Courage* made him *Dare to do right*, and fitted him to stand among the *Lions*, that have sometimes been the *Supporters* of the Throne:[43] All which Virtues he rendred the more Illustrious, by *Emblazoning* them with the Constant *Liberality* and *Hospitality* of a *Gentleman*. This made him the *Terror* of the Wicked, and the *Delight* of the Sober, the *Envy* of the many, but the *Hope* of those who had any *Hopeful Design* in Hand for the Common Good of the Nation, and the Interests of Religion.

§. 4. Accordingly when the *Noble Design* of carrying a Colony of *Chosen People* into an *American* Wilderness, was by *some* Eminent Persons undertaken, *This* Eminent Person was, by the Consent of all, *Chosen* for the *Moses*, who must be the Leader of so great an Undertaking: And indeed nothing but a *Mosaic Spirit* could have carried him through the *Temptations*, to which either his *Farewel* to his *own Land*, or his *Travel* in a *Strange Land*, must needs expose a Gentleman of his *Education*. Wherefore having Sold a fair Estate of Six or Seven Hundred a Year, he Transported himself with the Effects of it into *New-England* in the Year 1630. where he spent it upon the Service of a famous Plantation founded and formed for the Seat of the most *Reformed Christianity*: And continued there, conflicting with *Temptations* of all sorts [...]. Those Persons were never concerned in a *New Plantation*, who know not that the unavoidable Difficulties of such a thing, will call for all the *Prudence* and *Patience* of a Mortal Man to Encounter therewithal; and they must be very insensible of the Influence, which the *Just Wrath* of Heaven has permitted the *Devils* to have upon *this World*, if they do not

---

[39] Should read January 12, 1583.
[40] The worship of men (*prosopolatria*) is tantamount to idolatry; literally *prosopolatria* means "faceworship."
[41] The trivium (grammar, rhetoric, logic) and the quadrivium (arithmetic, music, geometry, astronomy).
[42] Literally: "hearing" before "judging" – Winthrop was famous for listening to all sides of the argument before judging the case.
[43] Solomon's throne was supported by lions (1 Kings 10.19f., 2 Chron. 9.18f.); Daniel's faith saved him from the lions (Dan. 6.23).

think that the Difficulties of a *New-Plantation*, devoted unto the *Evangelical Worship* of our Lord Jesus Christ, must be yet more than Ordinary. How *Prudently*, how *Patiently*, and with how much Resignation to our Lord Jesus Christ, our brave *Winthrop* waded through these *Difficulties*, let Posterity Consider with Admiration. And know, that as the *Picture* of this their *Governour*, was, after his *Death*, hung up with Honour in the *State-House* of his Country, so the *Wisdom*, *Courage*, and Holy *Zeal* of his *Life*, were an Example well-worthy to be Copied by all that shall succeed in *Government*.

§. 5. Were he now to be consider'd only as a *Christian*, we might therein propose him as greatly Imitable. He was a very *Religious* Man; and as he strictly kept his *Heart*, so he kept his *House*, under the Laws of *Piety* [...]. But it is chiefly as a *Governour* that he is now to be consider'd. Being the *Governour* over the considerablest Part of *New-England*, he maintain'd the Figure and Honour of his Place with the Spirit of a true *Gentleman*; but yet with such obliging *Condescention* to the Circumstances of the Colony, that when a certain troublesome and malicious Calumniator,[44] well known in those Times, printed his Libellous *Nick-Names* upon the chief Persons here, the worst *Nick-Name* he could find for the Governour, was *John Temper well*[45] [...]. He was, indeed, a *Governour*, who had most exactly studied that Book, which pretending to Teach *Politicks*, did only contain *Three Leaves*, and but *One Word* in each of those Leaves, which Word was, MODERATION. Hence, though he were a Zealous Enemy to all *Vice*, yet his *Practice* was according to his *Judgment* thus expressed; *In the Infancy of Plantations, Justice should be administered with more Lenity than in a settled State; because People are more apt then to Transgress; partly out of Ignorance of new Laws and Orders, partly out of Oppression of Business, and other Straits.* [*LENTO GRADU*,[46]] *was the old Rule; and if the Strings of a new Instrument be wound up unto their height, they will quickly crack.* [...]

§. 6. But whilst he thus did as our *New-English Nehemiah*, the part of a *Ruler* in Managing the Publick Affairs of our *American Jerusalem*, when there were *Tobijahs* and *Sanballats*[47] enough to vex him, and give him the Experiment of *Luther*'s Observation, *Omnis qui regit, est tanquam signum, in quod omnia Jacula, Satan & Mundus dirigunt*;[48] he made himself still an exacter *Parallel* unto that Governour of *Israel*, by doing the part of a *Neighbour* among the distressed People of the *New-Plantation*. To teach them the Frugality necessary for those times, he abridged himself of a Thousand comfortable things, which he had allow'd himself elsewhere: His *Habit* was not that *soft Raiment*,[49] which would have been disagreeable to a *Wilderness*; his *Table* was not covered with the *Superfluities* that would have invited unto *Sensualities*: *Water* was commonly his *own Drink*, though he gave Wine to *others*. But at the same time his *Liberality* unto the Needy was even beyond measure Generous [...]. And for very many of the People, his *own good Works* were needful, and accordingly employed for the answering of his *Faith*. Indeed, for a while the Governour was the *Joseph*, unto whom the whole Body of

---

[44] Slanderer.
[45] Reference to Thomas Morton's slander of Winthrop in his *New-English Canaan* (London, 1637), part 4, chapter 23. Morton (c. 1590-c. 1647) was an adventurer and an Anglican who came into conflict with the Puritans on several occasions; the most famous of these was in 1628 at the settlement Morton founded at Mount Wollaston, or Merry Mount (now Quincy, MA).
[46] Latin: "By slow degrees."
[47] Sanballat, governor of Samaria, and Tobijah, a Persian official, opposed the rebuilding of the walls of Jerusalem and later tried to depose Nehemiah (Neh. 2, 4, 6).
[48] Latin: "All who rule are targets at which Satan and the world hurl their darts" (*Loci Communes*).
[49] Matt. 11.8; Luke 7.25.

the People repaired when their *Corn* failed them:[50] And he continued Relieving of them with his *open-handed Bounties*, as long as he had any Stock to do it with; and a lively *Faith* to *see* the return of the *Bread after many Days*, and not *Starve* in the Days that were to pass till that *return* should be *seen*, carried him chearfully through those Expences. Once it was observable, that on *Feb*. 5. 1630. when he was distributing the last Handful of *the Meal in the Barrel* unto a Poor Man distressed by the Wolf *at the Door*, at that Instant they spied a Ship arrived at the Harbour's Mouth Laden with *Provisions* for them all. Yea, the Governour sometimes made his own *private Purse* to be the *Publick*; not by *sucking* into it, but by *squeezing* out of it; for when the *Publick Treasure* had nothing in it, he did himself defray the Charges of the *Publick*. [...] 'Twas his Custom also to send some of his Family upon Errands, unto the Houses of the Poor about their *Meal time*, on purpose to *spy* whether they *wanted*; and if it were found that they *wanted*, he would make *that* the Opportunity of sending Supplies unto them. And there was one Passage of his *Charity* that was perhaps a little *unusual*: In an hard and long Winter, when *Wood* was very scarce at *Boston*, a man gave him a private *Information*, that a needy Person in the Neighbourhood stole *Wood* sometimes from *his* Pile; whereupon the Governour in a seeming Anger did reply, *Does he so? I'll take a Course with him*; go, *call that Man to me, I'll warrant you I'll cure him of Stealing!* When the Man came, the Governour considering that if he had Stoln, it was more out of *Necessity* than *Disposition*, said unto him, *Friend, It is a severe Winter, and I doubt you are but meanly provided for Wood; wherefore I would have you supply your self at my Wood-Pile till this cold Season be over*. And he then Merrily asked his Friends, *Whether he had not effectually cured this Man of Stealing his Wood?*

§. 7. [...] Great Attempts were sometimes made among the *Freemen*,[51] to get him left out from his Place in the *Government* upon little Pretences, lest by the too *frequent Choice* of One Man, the *Government* should cease to be by *Choice*; and with a particular aim at *him*, Sermons were Preached at the Anniversary Court of *Election*, to disswade the *Freemen* from chusing *One Man* Twice together. This was the Reward of his *extraordinary Serviceableness*! But when these Attempts *did* succeed, as they sometimes *did*, his Profound *Humility* appeared in that *Equality of Mind*, wherewith he applied himself cheerfully to serve the Country in whatever Station their *Votes* had allotted for him. [...]

§. 11. *Many were the Afflictions of this Righteous Man!* He lost much of his Estate in a Ship, and in an *House*, quickly after his coming to *New-England*, besides the Prodigious Expence of it in the Difficulties of his first coming hither. [...]

§. 12. [...] While he was yet Seven Years off of that which we call the *grand Climacterical*,[52] he felt the Approaches of his *Dissolution*; and [...] he then wrote this account of himself, *Age now comes upon me, and Infirmities therewithal, which makes me apprehend, that the time of my departure out of this World is not far off. However our times are all in the Lord's Hand, so as we need not trouble our Thoughts how long or short they may be, but how we may be found Faithful when we are called for.* But at last when *that* [70th] Year came, he took a *Cold* which turned into a *Feaver*, whereof he lay *Sick* about a Month, and in that *Sickness*, as it hath been observed, that there was allowed unto the *Serpent* the *bruising of the Heel*;[53] and accordingly at the *Heel* or the *Close* of our Lives

---

[50] Gen. 41.56.
[51] In early New England only male church-members could vote.
[52] I.e., he was 63 years old. The "grand climacterical" denotes the age of seventy.
[53] Gen. 3.15, the *protevangelium*, where God tells the snake – Satan, "that old serpent" (Rev. 12.9, 20.2) – that man "shall bruise thy head and thou shalt bruise his heel."

the *old Serpent* will be Nibbling more than ever in our Lives before; and when the Devil sees that we shall shortly be, *where the wicked cease from troubling*, that *wicked One* will *trouble* us more than ever; so this eminent Saint now underwent sharp Conflicts with the *Tempter*, whose *Wrath* grew *Great*, as the *Time* to exert it grew *Short*; and he was Buffetted with the Disconsolate Thoughts of Black and Sore *Desertions*, wherein he could use that sad Representation of his own Condition.

> *Nuper Eram Judex; Jam Judicor; Ante Tribunat,*
> *Subsistens paveo, Judicor ipse modo.*⁵⁴

But it was not long before those *Clouds* were Dispelled, and he enjoyed in his Holy Soul the *Great Consolations of God!* While he thus lay *Ripening* for Heaven' he did out of Obedience unto the *Ordinance* of our Lord, send for the *Elders of the Church* to *Pray* with him; yea, they and the whole Church *Fasted* as well as *Prayed* for him; and in that *Fast* the venerable *Cotton*⁵⁵ Preached on *Psal*. 35.13,14 [...] making this Application, "Upon this Occasion we are now to attend this Duty for a *Governour*, who has been to us as a *Friend* in his *Counsel* for all things, and *Help* for our *Bodies* by *Physick*, for our *Estates* by *Law*, and of whom there was no fear of his becoming an *Enemy*, like the *Friends of David:*⁵⁶ A *Governour* who has been unto us as a *Brother*; not usurping *Authority* over the Church; often speaking his *Advice*, and often contradicted, even by Young Men, and some of low degree; yet not replying, but offering Satisfaction also when any supposed Offences have arisen; a *Governour* who has been unto us as a *Mother*, Parent-like distributing his *Goods* to Brethren and Neighbours at his first coming; and *gently* bearing our *Infirmities* without taking notice of them."

Such a *Governour* after he had been more than *Ten* several times by the People chosen their *Governour*, was *New-England* now to lose; who having, like *Jacob*, first left his *Council* and *Blessing* with his Children gathered about his Bed side;⁵⁷ and, like *David, served his Generation by the Will of God,*⁵⁸ he *gave up the Ghost*, and *fell asleep on March 26. 1649*. Having, like the dying Emperour *Valentinian*,⁵⁹ this above all his other *Victories* for his Triumphs, *His overcoming of himself*.

The Words of *Josephus* about *Nehemiah*, the Governour of *Israel*, we will now use upon this Governour of *New-England*, as his

EPITAPH. [...]

VIR FUIT INDOLE BONUS, AC JUSTUS:
ET POPULARIUM GLORIÆ AMANTISSIMUS.
QUIBUS ETERNUM RELIQUIT MONUMENTUM,
Novanglorum MOENIA.⁶⁰

Source: Cotton Mather (1663-1728). "Nehemias Americanus: The Life of John Winthrop, Esq, Governour of the Massachuset Colony" [Chapter IV of Book II: "Ecclesiarum Clypei"]. *Magnalia Christi Americana: Or, the Ecclesiastical History of New-England, from Its First Planting in the Year 1620. unto the Year of Our Lord, 1698. In Seven Books*. London: Thomas Parkhurst, 1702, 8-10, 14-15.

---

⁵⁴ "Recently I was a judge, now I am judged; I tremble as I stand before the tribunal, to be judged myself."
⁵⁵ John Cotton (1584-1652), Cotton Mather's grandfather and namesake.
⁵⁶ David's appointed counsellors who joined with Absalom in his revolt against David (2 Sam. 16).
⁵⁷ Gen. 49.1-33.
⁵⁸ Acts 13.36.
⁵⁹ Christian emperor of Rome (321-375).
⁶⁰ "By nature he was a man good and just, and most zealous for the glory of his countrymen; he left behind for them an eternal memorial – the walls of New England." The Latin substitutes "New England" for the original Greek "Jerusalem." The passage from Josephus (c. 37-100) appears, in prose, in his *Antiquities of the Jews*, bk. 11, chap. 5. Citation in Greek deleted.

65. Michael Wigglesworth
"God's Controversy with New-England. Written in the Time of the Great Drought. Anno 1662. By a Lover of New-England's Prosperity"

Isaiah 5.4
What could have been done more to my vineyard,
that I have not done in it? wherefore, when I
looked that it should bring forth grapes,
brought it forth wilde grapes?

The Author's request unto the Reader.

Good christian Reader judge me not
   As too Censorious,
For pointing at those faults of thine
   Which are notorious.
For if those faults be none of thine
   I do not thee accuse:
But if they be, to hear thy faults
   Why shouldest thou refuse.

I blame not thee to spare my self:
   But first at home begin,
And judge my self, before that I
   Reproove anothers sin.
Nor is it I that thee reproove
   Let God himself be heard
Whose awfull providence's voice
   No man may disregard.

Quod Deus omnipotens regali voce minatur,
Quod tibi proclamant uno simul ore prophetae,
Quodq' ego cum lachrymis testor de numinis irâ,
Tu leve comentu ne ducas, Lector Amice.[61]

New-England planted, prospered, declining, threatned, punished.

Beyond the great Atlantick flood
   There is a region vast,
A country where no English foot
   In former ages past:
A waste and howling wilderness,
   Where none inhabited
But hellish fiends, and brutish men
   That Devils worshiped.

---

[61] Latin: "What God almighty warns you with a ruler's voice, / What the prophets proclaim unto you, crying in unison, / And what I with many tears testify concerning God's wrath, / Do not, Dear Reader, consider lightly."

This region was in darkness plac't
    Far off from heavens light,
Amidst the shaddows of grim death
    And of Eternal night.
For there the Sun of righteousness
    Had never made to shine
The light of his sweet countenance,
    And grace which is divine:

Until the time drew nigh wherein
    The glorious Lord of hostes
Was pleasd to lead his armies forth
    Into those forrein coastes.
At whose approach the darkness sad
    Soon vanished away,
And all the shaddows of the night
    Were turned to lightsome day.

The dark and dismal western woods
    (The Devils den whilere[62])
Beheld such glorious Gospel-shine,
    As none beheld more cleare.
Where sathan had his scepter sway'd
    For many generations,
The King of Kings set up his throne
    To rule amongst the nations.

The stubborn he in pieces brake,
    Like vessels made of clay:
And those that sought his peoples hurt
    He turned to decay.
Those curst Amalekites,[63] that first
    Lift up their hand on high
To fight against Gods Israel,
    Were ruin'd fearfully.

Thy terrours on the Heathen folk,
    O Great Jehovah, fell:
The fame of thy great acts, o Lord,
    Did all the nations quell.
Some hid themselves for fear of thee
    In forrests wide & great:
Some to thy people croutching came,
    For favour to entreat.

---

[62] A while before; some time ago.
[63] Ancient nomadic tribes described in the Old Testament as relentless enemies of Israel.

Some were desirous to be taught
  The knowledge of thy wayes,
And being taught, did soon accord
  Therein to spend their dayes.
Thus were the fierce and barbarous
  Brought to civility,
And those that liv'd like beasts (or worse)
  To live religiously.

O happiest of dayes wherein
  The blind received sight,
And those that had no eyes before
  Were made to see the light!
The wilderness hereat rejoyc't,
  The woods for joy did sing,
The vallys & the little hills
  Thy praises ecchoing.

Here was the hiding place, which thou,
  Jehovah, didst provide
For thy redeemed ones, and where
  Thou didst thy jewels hide
In per'lous times, and saddest dayes
  Of sack-cloth and of blood,
When th' overflowing scourge did pass
  Through Europe, like a flood.

While almost all the world beside
  Lay weltring in their gore:
We, only we, enjoyd such peace
  As none enjoyd before.
No forrein foeman did us fray,
  Nor threat'ned us with warrs:
We had no enemyes at home,
  Nor no domestick jarrs.

The Lord had made (such was his grace)
  For us a Covenant
Both with the men, and with the beasts,
  That in this desert haunt:
So that through places wilde and waste
  A single man, disarm'd,
Might journey many hundred miles,
  And not at all be harm'd.

Amidst the solitary woods
  Poor travellers might sleep
As free from danger as at home,
  Though no man watch did keep.

Thus were we priviledg'd with peace,
    Beyond what others were.
Truth, Mercy, Peace, with Righteousness,
    Took up their dwelling here.

Our Governour was of our selves,
    And all his Bretheren,
For wisdom and true piety,
    Select, & chosen men.
Who, Ruling in ye fear of God,
    The righteous cause maintained,
And all injurious violence,
    And wickedness, restrained.

Our temp'rall blessings did abound:
    But spirituall good things
Much more abounded, to the praise
    Of that great King of Kings.
Gods throne was here set up; here was
    His tabernacle pight:[64]
This was the place, and these the folk
    In whom he took delight.

Our morning starrs shone all day long:
    Their beams gave forth such light,
As did the noon-day sun abash,
    And's glory dazle quite.
Our day continued many yeers,
    And had no night at all:
Yea many thought the light would last,
    And be perpetuall.

Such, O New-England, was thy first,
    Such was thy best estate:
But, Loe! a strange and suddain change
    My courage did amate.[65]
The brightest of our morning starrs
    Did wholly disappeare:
And those that tarried behind
    With sack-cloth covered were.

Moreover, I beheld & saw
    Our welkin overkest,[66]
And dismal clouds for sun-shine late
    O'respread from East to West.

---

[64] Archaic: placed, set up.
[65] Archaic: was disheartened, was cast down.
[66] Sky overcast.

The air became tempestuous;
  The wilderness [be]gan quake:
And from above with awfull voice
  Th' Almighty thundring spake.

Are these the men that erst at my command
Forsook their ancient seats and native soile,
To follow me into a desert land,
Contemning all the travell and the toile,
  Whose love was such to purest ordinances
As made them set at nought their fair inheritances?

Are these the men that prized libertee
To walk with God according to their light,
To be as good as he would have them bee,
To serve and worship him with all their might,
  Before the pleasures which a fruitfull field,
And Country flowing-full of all good things, could yield?

Are these the folk whom from the brittish Iles,
Through the stern billows of the watry main,
I safely led so many thousand miles,
As if their journey had been through a plain?
  Whom having from all enemies protected,
And through so many deaths and dangers well directed,

I brought and planted on the Western-shore,
Where nought but bruits and salvage wights[67] did swarm
(Untaught, untrain'd, untam'd by Vertue's lore)
That sought their blood, yet could not do them harm?
  My fury's flaile them thresht, my fatall broom
Did sweep them hence, to make my people elbow-room.

Are these the men whose gates with peace I crown'd,
To whom for bulwarks I Salvation gave,
Whilst all things else with rattling tumults sound,
And mortall frayes send thousands to the grave:
  Whilest their own brethren bloody hands embrewed
In brothers blood, and fields with carcases bestrewed?

Is this the people blest with bounteous store,
By land and sea full richly clad and fed,
Whom plenty's self stands waiting still before,
And powreth out their cups well tempered?
  For whose dear sake an howling wildernes
I lately turned into a fruitfull paradeis? [...]

---

[67] Archaic: living being, creature.

If these be they, how is it that I find
In stead of holyness Carnality,
In stead of heavenly frames an Earthly mind,
For burning zeal luke-warm Indifferency,
For flaming Love, key-cold Dead-heartedness,
For temperance (in meat, and drink, and cloaths) excess?

Whence cometh it, that Pride, and Luxurie
Debate, Deceit, Contention and Strife,
False-dealing, Covetousness, Hypocrisie
(With such like Crimes) amongst them are so rife,
That one of them doth over-reach another?
And that an honest man can hardly trust his Brother?

How is it, that Security, and Sloth,
Amongst the best are Common to be found?
That grosser sinns, in stead of Graces growth,
Amongst the many more and more abound?
I hate dissembling shews of Holiness.
O practise as you talk, or never more profess.

Judge not, vain world, that all are hypocrites
That do profess more holiness then thou:
All foster not dissembling, guilefull sprites,
Nor love their lusts, though very many do.
Some sin through want of care and constant watch,
Some with the sick converse, till they the sickness catch.

Some, that maintain a reall root of grace,
Are overgrown with many noysome weeds,
Whose heart, that those no longer may take place,
The benefit of due correction needs.
And such as these however gone astray
I shall by stripes reduce into a better way.

Moreover some there be that still retain
Their ancient vigour and sincerity;
Whom both their own, and others sins, constrain
To sigh, and mourn, and weep, and wail, and cry:
And for their sakes I have forborn to powre
My wrath upon Revolters to this present houre.

To praying Saints I always have respect,
And tender love, and pittifull regard:
Nor will I now in any wise neglect
Their love and faithfull service to reward;
Although I deal with others for their folly,
And turn their mirth to tears that have been too too jolly.

For thinke not, O Backsliders, in your heart,
That I shall still your evil manners beare:
Your sinns me press as sheaves do load a cart;[68]
And therefore I will plague you for this geare.[69]
Except you seriously, and soon, repent,
Ile not delay your pain and heavy punishment. [...]

Now therefore hearken and encline your ear,
In judgement I will henceforth with you plead;
And if by that you will not learn to fear,
But still go on a sensuall life to lead:
I'le strike at once an All-Consuming stroke;
Nor cries nor tears shall then my fierce intent revoke.

Thus ceast his Dreadful-threatning voice
   The High & lofty-One.
The Heavens stood still Appal'd thereat;
   The Earth beneath did groane:
Soon after I beheld and saw
   A mortall dart come flying:
I lookt again, & quickly saw
   Some fainting, others dying.

The Heavens more began to lowre,
   The welkin Blacker grew:
And all things seemed to forebode
   Sad changes to ensew.
From that day forward hath the Lord
   Apparently contended
With us in Anger, and in Wrath;
   But we have not amended.

Our healthfull dayes are at an end,
   And sicknesses come on
From yeer to yeer, becaus our hearts
   Away from God are gone.
New-England, where for many yeers
   You scarcely heard a cough,
And where Physicians had no work,
   Now finds them work enough.
   [...]

Our fruitful seasons have been turnd
   Of late to barrenness,
Sometimes through great & parching drought,

---

[68] Cf. Amos 2.13 ("Behold, I am pressed under you, as a cart is pressed that is full of sheaves"); sheaf: a bundle of cut grain.
[69] Archaic: foolish behavior.

Sometimes through rain's excess.
Yea not the pastures & corn fields
    For want of rain do languish:
The cattell mourn, and hearts of men
    Are fill'd with fear and anguish.

The clouds are often gathered,
    As if we should have rain:
But for our great unworthiness
    Are scattered again.
We pray & fast, & make fair shewes,
    As if we meant to turn:
But whilest we turn not, God goes on
    Our fields & fruits to burn.

And burnt are all things in such sort,
    That nothing now appeares,
But what may wound our hearts with grief,
    And draw foorth floods of teares.
All things a famine do presage
    In that extremity,
As if both men, and also beasts,
    Should soon be done to dy.

This O New-England hast thou got
    By riot, and excess:
This hast thou brought upon thy self
    By pride and wantonness.
Thus must thy worldlyness be whipt.
    They, that too much do crave,
Provoke the Lord to take away
    Such blessings as they have.

We have been also threatened
    With worser things then these:
And God can bring them on us still,
    To morrow if he please.
For if his mercy be abus'd,
    Which holpe us at our need
And mov'd his heart to pitty us,
    We shall be plagu'd indeed.

Beware, O sinful-Land, beware;
    And do not think it strange
That sorer judgements are at hand,
    Unless thou quickly change.
Or God, or thou, must quickly change;
    Or else thou art undon:

> Wrath cannot cease, if sin remain,
> > Where judgement is begun.
>
> Ah dear New England! dearest land to me:
> Which unto God hast hitherto been dear,
> And mayst be still more dear than formerlie,
> If to his voice thou wilt incline thine ear.
>
> Consider wel & wisely what the rod,
> Wherewith thou art from yeer to yeer chastized,
> Instructeth thee: Repent, and turn to God,
> Who wil not have his nurture be despized.
>
> Thou still hast in thee many praying saints,
> Of great account, and precious with the Lord,
> Who dayly powre out unto him their plaints,
> And strive to please him both in deed and word.
>
> Cheer on, sweet souls, my heart is with you all,
> And shall be with you, maugre[70] Sathan's might:
> And whereso'ere this body be a Thrall,
> Still in New-England shall be my delight.

Source: Michael Wigglesworth (1631-1705). "God's Controversy with New-England. Written in the Time of the Great Drought. Anno 1662. By a Lover of New-England's Prosperity." *The Poems of Michael Wigglesworth*. Ed. Ronald A. Bosco. Lanham, MD: University Press of America, 1989, 87-97, 99-102.

66. John Higginson
The Cause of God and His People in New-England (1663)

I. Kings 8.57,58,59. *The Lord our GOD be with us, as He was with our Fathers, let him not leave us nor forsake us; That he may encline our hearts unto him, to walke in all his wayes, and to keep his Commandements, his Statutes and his Judgment, which he Commanded our Fathers. And let these my words wherewith I have made supplication before the Lord, be nigh unto the Lord our God day and night, that He maintain the cause of his Servant, and the cause of his people Israel at all times, as the matter shall require.* [...]

Doct. *The Lords gracious presence with his people inclining their hearts to keep his Commandements, and maintaining their cause; is a Sufficient means to Establish the welfare of such a people, even as their own hearts can wish.* [...]

[... In] the general the cause of God and his people amongst us is the *Cause of Religion*, I say the cause of Religion *i.e.* the profession and practize of the one true Religion to be in all things according to Gods Word. [...] To keep and seek for all the Commandements of God. To walk in his waies and to keep his Commandements which he Commanded our Fathers, as it is in the text: that every thing in Doctrine Worship and Disci-

---

[70] In spite of.

pline be conformed unto and regulated by the rule of the word. This is the Cause of God and his People in New-England in the Generall.

But that it may be more clearly understood, let me propound it more particularly [...] in the *Negative* what this cause is not [...].

It is
1. Not the getting of this Worlds good.
2. Not Separation from other Churches.
3. Not a toleration of all Religions.

1. *Not the getting of this Worlds good.* The cause we are speaking of, it never was, it is not now, the getting & increasing of this worlds good. Our Saviour Christ hath commanded, *seek first the Kingdome of God and the righteousness thereof, and all other things shall be added* Mat. 6,33. Accordingly when the Lord stirred up the spirits of so many of his people to come over into this wilderness, it was not for worldly wealth, or a better livelyhood here for the outward man: the generallity of the people that came over professed the contrary: nor had we any rationall grounds to expect such a thing in such a wilderness as this.

And though God hath blessed his poor people here with an addition of many earthly comforts, and there are [those] that have encreased here from small beginnings to great estates, that the Lord may call this whole generation to witness and say, *O generation see the word of the Lord, have I been a wilderness unto you? Jer.2.32.* O generation see! look upon your townes & fields, look upon your habitations & shops and ships, and behold your numerous posterity, and great encrease in the blessings of the Land & Sea, *have I been a wilderness unto you?* we must needs answer, *No Lord, thou hast been a gracious God, and exceeding good unto thy Servants, ever since we came into this wilderness, even in these earthly blessings, we live in a more plentifull & comfortable manner then ever we did expect,* But these are but additions, they are but additionall mercies, it was another thing and a better thing that we followed the Lord into the wilderness for.

My Fathers and Brethren, this is never to be forgotten, that *New-England is originally a plantation of Religion, not a plantation of Trade.* Let Merchants and such as are increasing *Cent per Cent* remember this, Let others that have come over since at several times understand this, that worldly gain was not the end and designe of the people of *New-England*, but *Religion*. And if any man amongst us make Religion as *twelve*, and the world as *thirteen*,[71] let such an one know he hath neither the spirit of a *true New-England man*, nor yet of a *sincere Christian.* [...]

Source: John Higginson (1616-1708). *The Cause of God and His People in New-England, as It Was Stated and Discussed in a Sermon Preached before the Honourable General Court of the Massachusets Colony, on the 27 Day of May 1663. Being the Day of Election at Boston.* Cambridge: Samuel Green, 1663, 1-2, 10-11.

---

[71] I.e., making religion less valuable than worldly affairs.

67. Urian Oakes
The Soveraign Efficacy of Divine Providence (1677)

[... The] Ablest men are often cross'd in their Designs, and defeated of their Ends and Hopes by [...] Intervening Accidents. Hence they deny the wise, overruling, all-disposing *Providence* of God; and make I know not what Imaginary blind *Fortune* the prædominant Deity in the World. [... But] we are not to understand that the Determination of Events is reduced and referred to meer *Chance & Fortune*, as the *Epicurean* Philosophers imagined: but that the Counsel and Providence of God disposes and orders out all Successes, or Frustrations of Second Causes,[72] casting in sometimes such unexpected Impediments and Obstructions, as defeat the Labours and hopes of men of greatest Sufficiency; which though they seem wholly casual and fortuitous Emergencies [...] yet they are governed by the secret Counsel and effctual Providence of God. The Summe is, that no man, how accomplish'd soever, is *Master of Events*, or absolute Determiner of the Issues of his *own* Actings and Endeavours: but the sovereign Counsel and the Providence of God orders TIME and CHANCE to be an effectual Furtherance, or Hindrance of the Designs of all men, as seems good in His sight. The Observation is

Doct. *That the Successes and Events of Undertakings and Affairs are not determined infallibly by the greatest Sufficiency of Men, or Second Causes; but by the Counsel and Providence of God ordering and governing Time and Chance according to his own good Pleasure.* [...]

[...] Though God is *able* to give Being to things in an immediate way, yet it is his *pleasure* in the course of his Providence to use Means, and to produce many things by the mediation and Agency of second Causes [...]. It is a good observation, that the Lord is pleased, not through any *defect of power* in Himself but out of *the abundance of his goodness* to communicate causal power and virtue to his Creatures, & to honour them with that Dignity that they may be his Instruments, by which He will produce these and those Effects: whereby He takes them, as it were, into partnership & fellowship with Himself in the way of his providential Efficiency, that they may be *Under-workers* to, yea *Co-workers* with Himself. [...]

Prop. 5. *Time and Chance which happens to men in the way of their Undertakings, is effectually ordered & governed by the Lord*. God is the Lord of Time, and Orderer, and Governour of all Contingencies.[73] Time and Chance that further or hinder the Designs of men, are under the Rule and Management of the Lord. His Counsel sets the *Times*, appoints the *Chances*; His Providence dispenses the *Times*, and frames the *Chances*, that befall men. The Lord hath in his own power the Dispensation of *Times*, Eph. 1.10. [...]

Prop. 6. *The great God hath the absolute and infallible Determination of the Successes and Events of all the Operations & Undertakings of created Agents & Second Causes, in his own Power.* [...]

1. *God is the Absolute First Cause, and Supream Lord of all*. Of Him, and to Him, and through Him are all Things, *Rom*. 11.36. He that understands any thing of God indeed, knows this to be a Truth. Here we might be large; as they that are acquainted with the Doctrine of *Creation* and *Providence*, in *Conservation* and *Gubernation*[74] of all

---

[72] While the term "First Cause" always refers to God, the term "Second Causes" designates all effects that are brought about by man and his acts of volition.
[73] A possible, but unlikely or unplanned event; something incidental.
[74] The act or fact of governing, or controlling.

Things, will readily apprehend: for here we might shew you, 1. That God is the absolute first Cause of all the causal power and virtue that is in Creatures. He gives them power to act, furnisheth them with a Sufficiency for their Operations. [...]

10. *That He renders the aptest means ineffectual, and the Undertakings of the most sufficient Agents unsuccessful, when He pleases.* He hath a Negative Voice[75] upon all the Counsels and Endeavours, and Active Power of the Creature. *He* can stop the Sun in its course, and cause it to withdraw its shining: *He* can give check to the Fire, that it shall not burn; & to the hungry Lions, that they shall not devour:[76] and *He* can order it so, that the men of might shall *sleep their sleep, and not find their Hands. He* can break the Ranks of the most orderly Souldiers, take away courage from the stoutest hearts, send a pannick Fear into a mighty Host, and defeat the Counsels of the wisest Leaders and Conducters. He can blow upon, and blast the likeliest Undertakings of the ablest Men. In a word: the Lord being the Absolute First Cause, and supream Governour of all his Creatures, and all their Actions; though He hath set an Order among his Creatures, this shall be the cause of that effect, &c. yet He himself is not tied to that Order; but Interrupts the course of it, when He pleases. The Lord reserves a Liberty to Himself to interpose, and to Umpire matters of Success and Event, contrary to the Law and common Rule of Second Causes. And though He ordinarily concurreth with Second Causes according to the Law given and Order set; yet sometimes there is in his Providence a Variation and Digression. Though He hath given Creatures power to act; and Man, to act as *a Cause by Counsel*, and hath furnished him with active Abilites; yet He hath not made any Creature *Master of Events*; but reserves the Disposal of Issues, and Events to Himself. Herein the absolute Soveraignty and Dominion of God appears. [...]

USE I. Of Instruction, in these Particulars.

[...] *The way of man is not in himself; it is not in man that walketh to direct his steps*, nor perform any thing that he purposeth, without divine Concurrence, or Permission. He hath not the Success of any of his actions in his own power; nor doth he know that any thing he doth shall prosper. One would wonder poor *dependent* man should be so *proud*! [...]

USE III. *A word of singular Incouragement to the dear People of God, that have an Interest in God through Jesus Christ, & walk with Him according to the Tenour of the Covenant of Grace.* All your Times, and Chances, and Changes are in *God's* Hands; and all that befalls you, is under *His* Management, and of *His* Ordering, and Disposal. [...] Though you are weak, and insufficient, in your selves, to do Duty, to walk with God in your course, to resist Temptations: yet [...] God can, and will prosper your sincere Endeavours, and give in suitable supplies of Strength and Grace [...]. Indeed you may at present have many *particular* Designs and Undertakings, and be frustrated and suffer disappointment therein: but then, it is *good* for you to be afflicted, crossed, disappointed; and Unsuccessfulness is *really best* for you, & most conducive to the prosperity of your Souls; & you shall be sure of good Success, so far as Infinite Wisdom sees it to be good for you. [...] This is matter of Comfort to the People of God in the worst Times; when it is with them as with *Jacob*, when he said, *All these Things are against me*, Gen. 42.36. when none on their Side, Refuge fails, and no Means appearing for them. And indeed the People of God in this Country have had great Experience of this. What Deliverances hath God commanded! [...] The Salvations of *New-England* have been most ap-

---

[75] Here: right to veto.
[76] Oakes here refers to the fiery furnace and the Lion's den episodes in Dan. 3.19-23 and 6.10-28.

parently by the Lord's Governing *Time*, and *Chance*. This or that *Chance* or *Occurrent* hath faln in the very Nick of Time to prevent Ruine. [...]

> Source: Urian Oakes (1631-1681). *The Soveraign Efficacy of Divine Providence; over Ruling and Omnipotently Disposing and Ordering All Humane Counsels and Affairs, Asserted, Demonstrated and Improved, in a Discourse Evincing, That (Not Any Arm of Flesh, but) the Right Hand of the Most High Is It, That Swayeth the Universal Scepter of This Lower World's Government. Oft Wheeling about the Prudentest Management of the Profoundest Plotts, of the Greatest on Earth; unto Such, Issues and Events, as Are Amazingly Contrary to All Humane Probabilities, and Cross to the Confident Expectation of Lookers on. As Delivered in a Sermon Preached in Cambridge, on Sept. 10. 1677. Being the Day of Artillery Election There*. Boston: Samuel Sewall, 1682, 3, 5-6, 14-16, 18-20, 23.

68. Increase Mather
The Doctrine of Divine Providence Opened and Applyed (1684)

The God of Heaven has an over-ruling hand of Providence
in whatever cometh to Pass in this world.

Ezek. 1. 26.

And above the firmament that was over their heads, was the likeness of a Throne as the appearance of a Sapphire stone, and upon the likeness of the Throne, was the likeness as the appearance of a man above upon it.

In this chapter we have the Prophet *Ezekiel* his vision concerning a wonderful *wheel*, whereby we are to understand the wheel of Providence. The changeable scene of affairs in this lower world, is fitly set forth by a similitude of that nature. [...]

Propos. 1. *The Lord in Heaven knows all that is done upon the Earth*. He knows all things long before their accomplishment. [...]

Propos. 2. *There is an holy Decree and Prædetermination in Heaven concerning all things which come to pass in the world*. He worketh all things after the counsel of his will. [...] Men often times take up Purposes and resolutions and all comes to nothing in the conclusion, because the most High had appointed otherwise. [...]

To make things depend chiefly upon the decrees and wills of man, is to place Man in the Throne and to dethrone him that sitteth in Heaven. We must therefore know, that all Events of Providence are the issues and executions of an Ancient, Eternal, Unchangeable decree of Heaven. [...]

The works of Divine Providence are great and wonderfull.
Revel. 15.3.
Great and marveilous are thy works. [...]

Quest. 1. *How does it appear that the works of divine Providence are great and wonderful?*

Answ. 1. In that they are *excellent works*. [...]

2. *In that many works of Providence are deep and incomprehensible*. [...]

3. *Sometimes there is a seeming contradiction in divine providence*. Hence in Ezek. 1.16. 'tis said *their appearance & their work was as it were a wheel in the middle of a wheel*. The providences of God seem to Interfere with one another sometimes. One providence seems to look this way, another providence seems to look that way quite contrary one to another. Hence these works are marveilous. Yea, and that which adds

to the wonderment, is, in that the works of God sometimes seem to run counter with his word: so that there is dark and amazing intricacie in the ways of providence. This is *a wheel within a wheel.* [...]

USE. *Here is matter of Encouragement to the Faith of God's People respecting the Present state of the Church.* Things look at this day with a dark and dismal face: Well but we have this to encourage us: there is a God whose works are great and marvellous.

Consider. 1. *God is able to deliver his People.* [...]

Consider. 2. *That the days are at hand wherein the Lord will do great and wonderful things.*

Consider. 3. *The great and wonderful things which God has done for his New-England People.* The truth is, that the setting up of Christ's Kingdom in this Part of the world, is one of the Wonders of divine providence, which this last age has seen. There was a wondrous hand of God in bringing so many of his People hither; that the hearts of those who dwelt in much remoteness from one another should be alike moved and inclined to venture themselves and theirs into a waste and howling Wilderness, that so they might build a Sanctuary for the Lords Name therein. And there was a wonderful providence of God seen in making way for the settlement of his People here. For he cast out the Heathen before them; first by the Plague, and after by the Small Pox, so as that thousands and thousands were swept away [...], who else would probably have bin instigated by Satan, so as to have hindred the planting of the Gospel and the establishment of the Kingdom of Christ in these remote corners of the earth. [...] Search the Records of Ancient times, and you will never find, that when God has Created a new Heaven and a new earth, all was layd utterly waste and desolate, whilest any of those whom God honoured to be the first foundation were living. Therefore be not faithless but believing. The Lord may afflict us because of our Backslidings which are many, but he will not destroy us. Call to mind the former Times. Has not God wrought wonderfully for us? Hath he not done so in the days of our Fathers, and in our days also? Has he not rebuked the Heathen, and that more than once for our sakes, yea and other enemies too? And is not our God as able to deliver us as ever. Our Fathers trusted in him, and He delivered them, yea they trusted in him and were not Confounded. And if their Children after them, shall trust in the God of their Fathers, will he suffer them to be Confounded? The Scripture speaks of Mountains being removed by Faith. My Brethren, a few of you may by secret actings of Faith
   in prayer make mountains to shake; you may cause mountains to come
    tumbling down, that the whole world shall *eccho* with the Lord
     sound of their fall. Therefore let us trust in the
      forever; even in that God *who alone*
       doeth wondrous
        Things.

Source: Increase Mather (1639-1723). *The Doctrine of Divine Providence Opened and Applyed: Also Sundry Sermons on Several Other Subjects.* Boston, 1684, 1, 3, 6, 8, 37, 41, 43, 53, 55-59.

69. Mary Rowlandson
The Sovereignty & Goodness of God, Together, with the Faithfulness of His Promises Displayed; Being a Narrative of the Captivity and Restauration of Mrs. Mary Rowlandson (1682)[77]

The second Remove.
But now, the next morning, I must turn my back upon the Town, and travel with them into the vast and desolate Wilderness, I knew not whither. It is not my tongue, or pen can express the sorrows of my heart, and bitterness of my spirit, that I had at this departure: but God was with me, in a wonderful manner, carrying me along, and bearing up my spirit, that it did not quite fail. One of the *Indians* carried my poor wounded Babe upon a horse, it went moaning all along, I shall dy, I shall dy. I went on foot after it, with sorrow that cannot be exprest. At length I took it off the horse, and carried it in my armes till my strength failed, and I fell down with it: Then they set me upon a horse with my wounded Child in my lap, and there being no furniture upon the horse back; as we were going down a steep hill, we both fell over the horses head, at which they like inhumane creatures laught, and rejoyced to see it, though I thought we should there have ended our dayes, as overcome with so many difficulties. But the Lord renewed my strength still, and carried me along, that I might see more of his Power; yea, so much that I could never have thought of, had I not experienced it.

After this it quickly began to snow, and when night came on, they stopt: and now down I must sit in the snow, by a little fire, and a few boughs behind me, with my sick Child in my lap; and calling much for water, being now (through the wound) fallen into a violent Fever. My own wound also growing so stiff, that I could scarce sit down or rise up; yet so it must be, that I must sit all this cold winter night upon the cold snowy ground, with my sick Child in my armes, looking that every hour would be the last of its life; and having no Christian friend near me, either to comfort or help me. *Oh, I may see the wonderfull power of God, that my Spirit did not utterly sink under my affliction: still the Lord upheld me with his gracious and mercifull Spirit, and we were both alive to see the light of the next morning.*

The third remove.
[...] The next day was the Sabbath: I then remembered how careless I had been of Gods holy time: how many Sabbaths I had lost and mispent, and how evily I had walked in Gods sight; which lay so close unto my spirit, that it was easie for me to see how righteous it was with God to cut off the thread of my life, and cast me out of his presence for ever. Yet the Lord still shewed mercy to me, and upheld me; and as he wounded me with one hand, so he healed me with the other. [...] About two houres in the night, my sweet Babe, like a Lambe departed this life, on *Feb. 18. 1675.* It being about *six yeares,*

---

[77] The title of the first English edition shows an interesting change in focus that foregrounds the adventures among the native Americans: *A True History of the Captivity & Restoration of Mrs. Mary Rowlandson, A Minister's Wife in New-England. Wherein Is Set Forth, The Cruel and Inhumane Usage She Underwent amongst the Heathens, for Eleven Weeks Time: And Her Deliverance from Them. Written by Her Own Hand, for Her Private Use: And Now Made Publick at the Earnest Desire of Some Friends, and for the Benefit of the Afflicted. Whereunto is Annexed, a Sermon of the Possibility of God's Forsaking a People That Have Been Near and Dear to Him. Preached by Mr. Joseph Rowlandson, Husband to the Said Mrs. Rowlandson: It Being His Last Sermon.* London: Joseph Poole, 1682.

and *five months* old. It was *nine dayes* from the first wounding, in this miserable condition, without any refreshing of one nature or other, except a little cold water. I cannot but take notice, how at another time I could not bear to be in the room where any dead person was, but now the case is changed; I must and could ly down by my dead Babe, side by side all the night after. I have thought since of the wonderfull goodness of God to me, in preserving me in the use of my reason and senses, in that distressed time, that I did not use wicked and violent means to end my own miserable life. In the morning, when they understood that my child was dead they sent for me home to my Masters Wigwam: (by my Master in this writing, must be understood *Quanopin*,[78] who was a *Saggamore*,[79] and married King *Phillips*[80] wives Sister; not that he first took me, but I was sold to him by another *Narrhaganset Indian*, who took me when first I came out of the Garison[81]). I went to take up my dead child in my arms to carry it with me, but they bid me let it alone: there was no resisting, but goe I must and leave it. [...] And as I was going along, my heart was even overwhelm'd with the thoughts of my condition, and that I should have Children, *and a Nation which* I *knew not ruled over them*. Whereupon I earnestly entreated the Lord, that he would consider my low estate, and shew me a token for good, and if it were his blessed will, some sign and hope of some relief. And indeed quickly the Lord answered, in some measure, my poor prayers: For as I was going up and down mourning and lamenting my condition, my Son came to me, and asked me how I did; I had not seen him before, since the destruction of the Town, and I knew not where he was, till I was informed by himself, that he was amongst a smaller percel of *Indians*, whose place was about six miles off [...]. I cannot but take notice of the wonderfull mercy of God to me in those afflictions, in sending me a Bible. One of the *Indians* that came from *Medfield* fight,[82] had brought some plunder, came to me, and asked me, if I would have a Bible, he had got one in his Basket, I was glad of it, and asked him, whether he thought the *Indians* would let me read? He answered, yes: So I took the Bible, and in that melancholy time, it came into my mind to read first the 28. *Chap.* of *Deut.*[83] which I did, and when I had read it, my dark heart wrought on this manner, *That there was no mercy for me, that the blessings were gone, and the curses come in their room, and that* I *had lost my opportunity*. But the Lord helped me still to go on reading till I came to *Chap.* 30 the seven first verses, where I found, *There was mercy promised again, if we would return to him by repentance; and though we were scattered from one end of the Earth to the other, yet the Lord would gather us together, and turn all those curses upon our Enemies.*[84] I do not desire to live to forget this Scripture, and what comfort it was to me. [...]

The fourth Remove.

[...] *Heart-aking thoughts here* I *had about my poor Children,*[85] *who were scattered up and down among the wild beasts of the forrest*: My head was light & dissey[86] (either through

---

[78] Husband of Weetamoo; Mrs. Rowlandson became her servant.
[79] A subordinate chief among the Algonquin Indians.
[80] Metacomet, called King Phillip by the English, was a chief of the Wampanoag Indians.
[81] A fortified place; permanently established military post.
[82] The attack on Medfield, MA, occurred on February 21, 1676.
[83] This chapter of Deuteronomy is concerned with blessings for obedience to God and curses for disobedience.
[84] Deut. 30.3: "[...] Then] the Lord thy God will turn thy captivity, and have compassion upon thee, and will return and gather thee from all the nations, whither the Lord thy God hath scattered thee."
[85] The author had just parted from her daughter, Mary, and from four little cousins.
[86] Dizzy.

hunger or hard lodging, or trouble or altogether) my knees feeble, my body raw by sitting double night and day, that I cannot express to man the affliction that lay upon my Spirit, but the Lord helped me at that time to express it to himself. I opened my Bible to read, and the Lord brought that precious Scripture to me, *Jer.* 31.16. *Thus saith the Lord, refrain thy voice from weeping, and thine eyes from tears, for thy work shall be rewarded, and they shall come again from the land of the Enemy.* This was a sweet Cordial to me, when I was ready to faint, many and many a time have I sat down, and weept sweetly over this Scripture. At this place we continued about four dayes.

The twentieth Remove.
[...] On *Tuesday morning* they called their *General* Court (as they call it) to consult and determine, whether I should go home or no: And they all as one man did seemingly consent to it, that I should go home; except *Philip*, who would not come among them.

But before I go any further, I would take leave to mention a few remarkable passages of providence, which I took special notice of in my afflicted time.

1. *Of the fair opportunity lost in the long March, a little after the* Fort-fight, *when our English Army was so numerous, and in pursuit of the* Enemy, *and so near as to take several and destroy them: and the* Enemy *in such distress for food, that our men might track them by their rooting in the earth for Ground-nuts, whilest they were flying for their lives.* I say, that then our Army should want Provision, and be forced to leave their pursuit and return homeward: and the very next week the *Enemy* came upon our *Town*, like Bears bereft of their whelps, or so many ravenous Wolves, rending us and our Lambs to death. But what shall I say? God seemed to leave his People to themselves, and order all things for his own holy ends. *Shal there be evil in the City and the Lord hath not done it?*[87] *They are not grieved for the affliction of* Joseph, *therefore shal they go Captive, with the first that go Captive.*[88] It is the Lords doing, and it should be marvelous in our eyes. [...]

3. *Which also I have hinted before, when the* English *Army with new supplies were sent forth to pursue after the enemy, & they understanding it: fled before them till they came to* Baquaug *River, where they forthwith went over safely: that that River should be impassable to the* English. I can but admire to see the wonderfull providence of God in preserving the heathen for farther affliction to our poor Countrey. They could go in great numbers over, but the *English* must stop: God had an over-ruling hand in all those things. [...]

5. *Another thing that I would observe is, the strange providence of God, in turning things about when the* Indians *was at the highest, and the* English *at the lowest*. I was with the Enemy eleven weeks and five dayes, and not one Week passed without the fury of the Enemy, and some desolation by fire and sword upon one place or other. They mourned (with their black faces) for their own losses; yet triumphed and rejoyced in their inhumane, and many times devilish cruelty to the *English*. They would boast much of their Victories [...].

When the Lord had brought his people to this, that they saw no help in any thing but himself: then he takes the quarrel into his own hand: and though they had made a pit, in their own imaginations, as deep as hell for the Christians that Summer, yet the Lord hurll'd them selves into it. And the Lord had not so many wayes before to preserve them, but now he hath as many to destroy them.

---

[87] Amos 3.6.
[88] Amos 6.6-7.

But to return again to my going home, where we may see a remarkable change of Providence: At first they were all against it, except my Husband would come for me; but afterwards they assented to it, and seemed much to rejoyce in it; some askt me to send them some Bread, others some Tobacco, others shaking me by the hand, offering me a Hood and Scarfe to ride in; not one moving hand or tongue against it. Thus hath the Lord answered my poor desire, and the many earnest requests of others put up unto God for me. In my travels an *Indian* came to me, and told me, if I were willing, he and his *Squaw* would run away, and go home along with me: I told him *No*: I was not willing to run away, but desired to wait Gods time, that I might go home quietly, and without fear. And now God hath granted me my desire. O the wonderfull power of God that I have seen, and the experience that I have had: I *have been in the midst of those roaring Lyons, and Salvage Bears, that feared neither God, nor Man, nor the Devil, by night and day, alone and in company: sleeping all sorts together, and yet not one of them ever offered me the least abuse of unchastity to me, in word or action.* Though some are ready to say, I speak it for my own credit; *But I speak it in the presence of God, and to his Glory.* Gods Power is as great now, and as sufficient to save, as when he preserved *Daniel* in the Lions Den; or the three Children in the fiery Furnace. I may well say as his Psal. 107.12 *Oh give thanks unto the Lord for he is good, for his mercy endureth for ever.*[89] Let the Redeemed of the Lord say so, whom he hath redeemed from the hand of the Enemy, especially that I should come away in the midst of so many hundreds of Enemies quietly and peacably, and not a Dog moving his tongue. So I took my leave of them, and in coming along my heart melted into tears, more then all the while I was with them, and I was almost swallowed up with the thoughts that ever I should go home again. About the Sun going down, Mr. *Hoar*, and my self, and the two *Indians* came to *Lancaster*, and a solemn sight it was to me. There had I lived many comfortable years amongst my Relations and Neighbours, and now not one *Christian* to be seen, nor one house left standing. We went on to a Farm house that was yet standing, where we lay all night: and a comfortable lodging we had, though nothing but straw to ly on. The Lord preserved us in safety that night, and raised us up again in the morning, and carried us along, that before noon, we came to *Concord*. Now was I full of joy, and yet not without sorrow: joy to see such a lovely sight, so many *Christians* together, and some of them my Neighbours: There I met with my Brother, and my Brother in Law, who asked me, if I knew where his Wife was? Poor heart! he had helped to bury her, and knew it not; she being shot down by the house was partly burnt: so that those who were at *Boston* at the desolation of the *Town*, and came back afterward, and buried the dead, did not know her. Yet I was not without sorrow, to think how many were looking and longing, and my own Children amongst the rest, to enjoy that deliverance that I had now received: and I did not know whither ever I should see them again. Being recruited with food and raiment, we went to *Boston* that day, where I met with my dear Husband, but the thoughts of our dear Children, one being dead, and the other we could not tell where, abated our comfort each to other. I was not before so much hem'd in with the merciless and cruel Heathen, but now as much with pittiful, tenderhearted and compassionate Christians. [...] About this time the Council had ordered a day of publick *Thanks-giving*: though I thought I had still cause of mourning, and being unsettled in our minds, we thought we would ride toward the *Eastward*, to see if we could hear any thing concerning our Children. And as we were riding along [God is the

---

[89] Ps. 118.1 and 118.29.

wise disposer of all things] between *Ipswich* and *Rowly* we met with Mr. *William Hubbard*, who told us that our Son *Joseph* was come in to Major *Waldrens*, and another with him, which was my Sisters Son. I asked him how he knew it? He said, the Major himself told him so. So along we went till we came to *Newbury*; and their Minister being absent, they desired my Husband to Preach the *Thanks giving* for them; but he was not willing to stay there that night, but would go over to *Salisbury*, to hear further, and come again in the morning; which he did, and Preached there that day. At night, when he had done, one came and told him that his Daughter was come in at *Providence*: Here was mercy on both hands. Now hath God fulfiled that precious Scripture which was such a comfort to me in my distressed condition. When my heart was ready to sink into the Earth [my Children being gone I could not tell whither] and my knees trembled under me, *And I was walking through the valley of the shadow of Death*:[90] Then the Lord brought, and now has fulfilled that reviving word unto me: Thus saith the Lord, *Refrain thy voice from weeping, and thine eyes from tears. [F]or thy Work shall be rewarded*, saith the Lord, *and they shall come again from the Land of the Enemy*.[91] [...]

I can remember the time, when I used to sleep quietly without workings in my thoughts, whole nights together, but now it is other wayes with me. When all are fast about me, and no eye open, but his who ever waketh, my thoughts are upon things past, upon the awfull dispensation of the Lord towards us; upon his wonderfull power and might, in carrying of us through so many difficulties, in returning us in safety, and suffering none to hurt us. I remember in the night season, how the other day I was in the midst of thousands of enemies, & nothing but death before me: It is then hard work to perswade my self, that ever I should be satisfied with bread again. But now we are fed with the finest of the Wheat, and, as I may say, *With honey out of the rock*: In stead of the Husk, we have the fatted Calf:[92] The thoughts of these things in the particulars of them, and of the love and goodness of God towards us, make it true of me, what *David* said of himself, Psal. 6.5. *I watered my Couch with my tears*. Oh! the wonderfull power of God that mine eyes have seen, affording matter enough for my thoughts to run in, that when others are sleeping mine eyes are weeping.

I have seen the extrem vanity of this World: One hour I have been in health, and wealth, wanting nothing: But the next hour in sickness and wounds, and death, having nothing but sorrow and affliction.

Before I knew what affliction meant, I was ready sometimes to wish for it. When I lived in prosperity; having the comforts of the World about me, my relations by me, my Heart chearfull: and taking little care for any thing; and yet seeing many, whom I preferred before my self, under many tryals and afflictions, in sickness, weakness, poverty, losses, crosses, and cares of the World, I should be sometimes jealous least I should have my portion in this life, and that Scripture would come to my mind, Heb. 12.6. *For whom the Lord loveth he chasteneth, and scourgeth every Son whom he receiveth*. But now I see the Lord had his time to scourge and chasten me. The portion of some is to have their afflictions by drops, now one drop and then another; but the dregs of the Cup, the Wine of astonishment, like a sweeping rain that leaveth no food, did the Lord prepare to be my portion / Affliction I wanted, and affliction I had, full measure (I thought) pressed down and running over: yet I see, when God calls a Person to any thing, and

---

[90] Ps. 23.4.
[91] Jer. 31.16.
[92] Luke 15.23.

through never so many difficulties, yet he is fully able to carry them through and make them see, and say they have been gainers thereby. And I hope I can say in some measure, As *David* did, *It is good for me that I have been afflicted.*[93] The Lord hath shewed me the vanity of these outward things. That they are the *Vanity of vanities, and vexation of spirit*; that they are but a shadow, a blast, a bubble, and things of no continuance. That we must rely on God himself, and our whole dependance must be upon him. If trouble from smaller matters begin to arise in me, I have something at hand to check my self with, and say, why am I troubled? It was but the other day that if *I* had had the world, I would have given it for my freedom, or to have been a Servant to a Christian. I have learned to look beyond present and smaller troubles, and to be quieted under them, as *Moses* said, *Exod.* 14.13. *Stand still and see the salvation of the Lord.*

Finis.

Source: Mary Rowlandson (1637-1710/11). *The Soveraignty & Goodness of God, Together, with the Faithfulness of His Promises Displayed; Being a Narrative of the Captivity and Restauration of Mrs. Mary Rowlandson. Commended by Her, to All That Desires to Know the Lords Doings to, and Dealings with Her. Especially to Her Dear Children and Relations, The Second Addition Corrected and Amended. Written by Her Own Hand for Her Private Use, and Now Made Publick at the Earnest Desire of Some Friends, and for the Benefit of the Afflicted. Deut. 32.39, See now that I, even I am he, and there is no God with me: I kill and I make alive, I wound and I heal neither is there any can deliver out of my hand.* Cambridge, MA: Samuel Green, 1682, 7-9, 11-17, 59-60, 62-68, 71-73.

70. Cotton Mather
"A General Introduction [to *Magnalia Christi Americana*]" (1702)

Dicam hoc propter utilitatem eorum qui Lecturi sunt hoc opus. Theodorit.[94]

§. 1. I WRITE the *Wonders* of the CHRISTIAN RELIGION, flying from the Depravations of *Europe*, to the *American Strand:* And, assisted by the Holy Author of that *Religion*, I do, with all Conscience of *Truth*, required therein by Him, who is the *Truth* it self, Report the *Wonderful Displays* of His Infinite Power, Wisdom, Goodness, and Faithfulness, wherewith His Divine Providence hath *Irradiated* an *Indian Wilderness*.

I Relate the *Considerable Matters*, that produced and attended the First Settlement of COLONIES, which have been Renowned for the Degree of REFORMATION, Professed and Attained by *Evangelical Churches*, erected in those *Ends of the Earth:* And a *Field* being thus prepared, I proceed unto a Relation of the *Considerable Matters* which have been acted thereupon.

I first introduce the *Actors*, that have, in a more exemplary manner served those *Colonies*; and give *Remarkable Occurrences*, in the exemplary LIVES of many *Magistrates*, and of more *Ministers*, who so *Lived*, as to leave unto Posterity, *Examples* worthy of *Everlasting Remembrance*.

I add hereunto, the *Notables* of the only *Protestant University*, that ever *shone* in that Hemisphere of the *New World*; with particular Instances of Criolians,[95] in our *Biography*, provoking the *whole World*, with vertuous Objects of Emulation.

---

[93] Ps. 119.71.
[94] Latin: "I say this for the benefit of those who are readers of this book." Theodoret was an early Church father, c. 393-458.
[95] Criolians or Creolians, an obsolete word for persons born or naturalized in America but of European race.

I introduce then, the *Actions* of a more Eminent Importance, that have signalized those *Colonies*; Whether the *Establishments*, directed by their *Synods*; with a Rich Variety of *Synodical* and *Ecclessiastical* Determinations; or, the *Disturbances*, with which they have been from all sorts of *Temptations* and *Enemies* Tempestuated; and the *Methods* by which they have still weathered out each *Horrible Tempest*.

And into the midst of these *Actions*, I interpose an entire *Book*, wherein there is, with all possible Veracity, a *Collection* made, of *Memorable Occurrences*, and amazing *Judgments* and *Mercies*, befalling many *particular Persons* among the People of *New-England*.

Let my Readers expect all that I have promised them, in this *Bill of Fair*; and it may be they will find themselves entertained with yet many other Passages, above and beyond their Expectation, deserving likewise a room in *History*: In all which, there will be nothing, but the *Author's* too mean way of preparing so great Entertainments, to Reproach the Invitation.

§. 2. The Reader will doubtless desire to know, what it was that

– *tot Volvere casus*
Insignes Pietate Viros, tot adire Labores,
Impulerit.[96]

And our *History* shall, on many fit Occasions which will be therein offered, endeavour, with all *Historical* Fidelity and Simplicity, and with as little Offence as may be, to satisfie him. [...]

§. 3. It is the History of these PROTESTANTS, that is here attempted: PROTESTANTS that highly honoured and affected *The Church of* ENGLAND, and humbly Petition to be a *Part* of it: But by the Mistake of a few powerful *Brethren*, driven to seek a place for the Exercise of the *Protestant Religion*, according to the Light of their Consciences, in the Desarts of *America*. And in this Attempt I have proposed, not only to preserve and secure the Interest of *Religion*, in the Churches of that little Country *NEW-ENGLAND*, so far as the Lord Jesus Christ may please to Bless it for that End, but also to offer unto the Churches of the *Reformation*, abroad in the World, some small *Memorials*, that may be serviceable unto the Designs of *Reformation*, whereto, I believe, they are quickly to be awakened. I am far from any such Boast, concerning these Churches, *That they have Need of Nothing*, I wish their *Works* were more *perfect before God*. Indeed, that which *Austin* called *The Perfection of Christians*, is like to be, until the Term for the *Antichristian Apostasie*[97] be expired, *The Perfection of Churches* too; *Ut Agnoscant se nunquam esse perfectas*.[98] Nevertheless, I perswade my self, that so *far as they have attained*, they have given *Great Examples* of the *Methods* and *Measures*, wherein an *Evangelical Reformation* is to be prosecuted, and of the *Qualifications* requisite in the Instruments that are to prosecute it, and of the *Difficulties* which may be most likely to obstruct it, and the most likely *Directions* and *Remedies* for those Obstructions. It may be, 'tis not possible for me to do a greater Service unto the Churches on the *Best Island* of the Universe, than to give a distinct Relation of those *Great Examples* which have been occurring among Churches of *Exiles*, that were driven out of that *Island*, into an horrible *Wilderness*, meerly for their being Well-willers unto the *Reformation*. When

---

[96] Latin: "Drove men eminent in piety to endure so many calamities and to undertake so many hardships." The quotation is slightly altered from Vergil's *Aeneid*, I, 9-11.
[97] Abandonment of one's religious beliefs.
[98] Latin: "That they may acknowledge themselves to be by no means perfect."

that Blessed Martyr *Constantine* was carried, with other Martyrs, in a *Dung-Cart*, unto the place of Execution, he pleasantly said, *Well, yet we are a precious Odour to God in Christ*. Tho' the *Reformed Churches* in the *American Regions*, have, by very Injurious Representations of their Brethren (all which they desire to Forget and Forgive!) been many times thrown into a *Dung-Cart*; yet, as they have been a *precious Odour to God in Christ*, so, I hope, they will be a *precious Odour* unto *His People*; and not only *Precious*, but *Useful* also, when the *History* of them shall come to be considered. A *Reformation of the Church* is coming on [...]. Thus I do not say, That the Churches of *New-England* are the most *Regular* that can be; yet I do say, and am sure, That they are very like unto those that were in the *First Ages* of Christianity. [...] In short, The *First Age* was the *Golden Age*: To return unto *That*, will make a Man a *Protestant*, and I may add, a *Puritan*. 'Tis possible, That our Lord Jesus Christ carried some Thousands of *Reformers* into the Retirements of an *American Desart*, on purpose, that, with an opportunity granted unto many of his Faithful Servants, to enjoy the precious *Liberty* of their *Ministry*, tho' in the midst of many *Temptations* all their days, He might there, To them first, and then *By* them, give a *Specimen* of many Good Things, which He would have His Churches elsewhere aspire and arise unto: And *This* being done, He knows not whether there be not *All done*, that *New-England* was planted for; and whether the Plantation may not, soon after this, *Come to Nothing*. Upon that Expression in the Sacred Scripture, *Cast the unprofitable Servant into Outer Darkness*, it hath been imagined by some, That the *Regiones Exteræ* of *America*, are the *Tenebræ Exteriores*,[99] which the *Unprofitable* are there condemned unto. No doubt, the Authors of those Ecclesiastical Impositions and Severities, which drove the English Christians into the *Dark Regions* of *America*, esteemed those *Christians* to be a very *unprofitable* sort of Creatures. But behold, ye *European* Churches, There are *Golden Candlesticks* [more than *twice Seven times Seven!*] in the midst of this *Outer Darkness*; Unto the *upright* Children of *Abraham*, here hath arisen *Light in Darkness*. And let us humbly speak it, it shall be *Profitable* for you to consider the *Light*, which from the midst of this *Outer Darkness*, is now to be Darted over unto the other side of the *Atlantick Ocean*. But we must therewithal ask your Prayers, that these *Golden Candlesticks* may not *quickly* be *Removed out of their place!* [100]

§. 4. But whether *New England* may *Live* any where else or no, it must *Live* in our *History!*

HISTORY, in general, hath had so many and mighty Commendations from the Pens of those Numberless Authors, who, from *Herodotus* to Howel,[101] have been the professed Writers of it, that a tenth part of them Transcribed, would be a Furniture for a *Polyanthea in Folio*.[102] We, that have neither liberty, nor occasion, to quote those Commendations of *History*, will content our selves with the Opinion of one who was not

---

[99] Reference to the prior formulation "*Outer Darkness*."
[100] Mather here refers to the numerous foundations of church communities in New England which seemed to fulfill the prophecies in St. John's Revelation (Rev. 1. 10-20): "I was in the Spirit on the Lord's day, and heard behind me a great voice, as of a trumpet, saying, I am Alpha and Omega, the first and the last: and, What thou seest, write in a book, and send *it* unto the seven churches which are in Asia [...]. And I turned to see the voice that spake with me [...]: Write the things which thou hast seen, and the things which are, and the things which shall be hereafter; the mystery of the seven stars which thou sawest in my right hand, and the seven golden candlesticks. The seven stars are the angels of the seven churches: and the seven candlesticks which thou sawest are the seven churches."
[101] William Howell (1631/32-1683), author of *An Institution of General History*, 1661.
[102] I.e., a large collection of select quotations, an anthology.

much of a *profess'd Historian*, expressed in that passage, whereto all Mankind subscribe, *Historia est Testis temporum, Nuntia vetustatis, Lux veritatis, vita memoriæ, magistra vitæ*.[103] But of all *History* it must be confessed, that the *Palm* is to be given unto *Church History*; wherein the *Dignity*, the *Suavity*, and the *Utility* of the *Subject* is transcendent. [...] And when I am thinking, what may be the Reason of this *Difference*, methinks it intimates unto us, That the *Church* wherein the Service of God is performed, is much more Precious than the *World*, which was indeed created for the Sake and Use of the *Church*. 'Tis very certain, that the greatest Entertainments must needs occur in the History of the *People*, whom the *Son* of God hath *Redeemed* and *Purified* unto himself, as a *Peculiar People*, and whom the *Spirit* of God, by *Supernatural Operations* upon their Minds, does cause to live like *Strangers* in *this World*, conforming themselves unto the *Truths* and *Rules* of his Holy Word, in Expectation of a *Kingdom*, whereto they shall be in another and a better *World* advanced. Such a *People* our Lord Jesus Christ hath procured and preserved in all Ages *visible*; and the Dispensations of his *wonderous Providence* towards this People (for, *O Lord, thou do'st lift them up, and cast them down!*) their Calamities, their Deliverances, the Dispositions which they have still discovered, and the considerable *Persons* and *Actions* found among them, cannot but afford Matters of *Admiration* and *Admonition*, above what any other Story can pretend unto [...].

Source: Cotton Mather (1663-1728). *Magnalia Christi Americana: Or, the Ecclesiastical History of New England, from Its First Planting in the Year 1620. unto the Year of Our Lord, 1698. In Seven Books*. London: Thomas Parkhurst, 1702, n.p.

71. Cotton Mather
"Letter to John Richards" (1692)

II. [...] I must humbly beg you that in the management of the affair in your most worthy hands, you do not lay more stress upon pure specter testimony than it will bear. When you are satisfied or have good, plain, legal evidence that the demons which molest our poor neighbors do indeed represent such and such people to the sufferers, tho' this be a presumption, yet I suppose you will not reckon it a conviction that the people so represented are witches to be immediately exterminated. It is very certain that the devils have sometimes represented the shapes of persons not only innocent, but also very virtuous, tho' I believe that the just God then ordinarily provides a way for the speedy vindication of the persons thus abused. Moreover, I do suspect that persons who have too much indulged themselves in malignant, envious, malicious ebullitions[104] of their souls, may unhappily expose themselves to the judgment of being represented by devils, of whom they never had any vision, and with whom they have much less written any covenant. I would say this: if upon the bare supposal of a poor creature's being represented by a specter, too great a progress be made by the authority in ruining a poor neighbor so represented, it may be that a door may be thereby opened for the devils to obtain from the courts in the invisible world a license to proceed unto

---

[103] "History is the witness of periods of time, the messenger of antiquity, the light of truth, the life of memory, the instructress of life." Cotton Mather here quotes Cicero (*De Oratore*, II, 9) but fails to preserve the original order.
[104] Here: sudden violent outpouring of emotions.

most hideous desolations upon the repute and repose of such as have yet been kept from the great transgression. If mankind have thus far once consented unto the credit of diabolical representations, the door is opened! [...]

III. Tho' 'tis probable that the devils may (tho' not often, yet sometimes) make most bloody invasions upon our exterior concerns, without any witchcrafts of our fellow creatures to empower them, and I do expect that as when our Lord was coming in His human nature among us, there was a more sensible annoyance of the destroyer upon our human nature than at other times, thus it will be just before our Lord's coming again in His human nature, when He will also dispossess the devils of their aerial region to make a New Heaven for His raised there. Nevertheless there is cause enough to think that it is a horrible witchcraft which hath given rise to the troubles wherewith Salem Village is at this day harassed; and the indefatigable pains that are used for the tracing [of] this witchcraft are to be thankfully accepted, and applauded among all this people of God.

IV. Albeit the business of this witchcraft be very much transacted upon the stage of imagination, yet we know that, as in treason there is an imagining which is a capital crime, and here also the business thus managed in imagination yet may not be called imaginary. The effects are dreadfully real. Our dear neighbors are most really tormented, really murdered, and really acquainted with hidden things, which are afterwards proved plainly to have been realities. [...]

V. To determine a matter so much in the dark as to know the guilty employers of the devils in this work of darkness, this is a work, this is a labor. Now first a credible confession of the guilty wretches is one of the most hopeful ways of coming at them, and I say a credible confession because even confession itself sometimes is not credible. But a person of a sagacity many times thirty furlongs less than yours, will easily perceive what confession may be credible, and what may be the result of only a delirious brain, or a discontented heart. All the difficulty is how to obtain this confession. For this I am far from urging the un-English method of torture, but instead thereof I propound these three things: first, who can tell but when the witches come upon their trials, they may be so forsaken, as to confess all. The Almighty God having heard the appeals of our cries to Heaven, may so thunder-strike their souls, as to make them show their deeds. [...] Secondly, I am ready to think that there is usually some expression or behavior whereto the devils do constantly oblige the witches, as a kind of sacrament, upon their least failure wherein the witches presently lose the thus forfeited assistances of the devils, and all comes out. Please then to observe, if you can find any one constant scheme of discourse or action, whereto the suspected seem religiously devoted, and (which may easily be done by the common policies of conversation) cause them to transgress that, a confession will probably then come on apace. Thirdly, whatever hath a tendency to put the witches into confusion is likely to bring them unto confession too. Here cross and swift questions have their use, but besides them, for my part, I should not be unwilling that an experiment be made whether accused parties can repeat the Lord's Prayer, or those other systems of Christianity which, it seems, the devils often make the witches unable to repeat without ridiculous depravations or amputations. [...]

VI. But what if no confession can be obtained; I say yet the case is far from desperate. For if there have been those words uttered by the witches, either by way of threatening, or of asking, or of bragging, which rationally demonstrate such a knowledge of the woeful circumstances attending the afflicted people, as could not be had without some diabolical communion, the proof of such words is enough to fix the guilt. [...]

VII. I begin to fear that the devils do more easily proselyte poor mortals into witchcraft than is commonly conceived. When a sinful child of man distempers himself with some exorbitant motions in his mind (and it is to be feared the murmuring phrensies of late prevailing in the country have this way exposed many to sore temptations) a devil then soon presents himself unto him, and he demands, Are you witches that I should go do this or that for you? If the man once comply, the devil hath him now in a most horrid snare, and by a permission from the just vengeance of God he visits the man with buffetings as well as allurements, till the forlorn man at first only for the sake of quietness, but at length out of improved wickedness, will commission the devil to do mischief as often as he requires it. And for this cause 'tis worth considering, whether there be a necessity always by extirpations by halter or fagot every wretched creature that shall be hooked into some degrees of witchcraft. What if some of the lesser criminals be only scourged with lesser punishments, and also put upon some solemn, open, public, and explicit renunciation of the devil? I am apt to think that the devils would then cease afflicting the neighborhood whom these wretches have stood them upon [...].

But I find my free thoughts thus freely laid before Your Honor, begin to have too much freedom in them. I shall now therefore add no more but my humble and most fervent prayers to the God who gives wisdom liberally, that you and your honorable brethren may be furnished from on high, with all that wisdom, as well as justice, which is requisite in the thorny affair before you. God will be with you. I am persuaded He will; and with that persuasion I subscribe myself,

Sir, Your very devoted servant,

C[otton] M[ather]

Source: Cotton Mather (1663-1728). "Letter to John Richards." *Selected Letters of Cotton Mather.* Ed. Kenneth Silverman. Baton Rouge, LA: Louisiana State UP, 1971, 36-40.

72. Increase Mather
Cases of Conscience Concerning Evil Spirits Personating Men (1693)

Christian Reader

So Odious and Abominable is the name of a Witch, to the Civilized, much more the Religious part of Mankind, that it is apt to grow up into a Scandal for any, so much as to enter some sober cautions against the over hasty suspecting, or too precipitant Judging of Persons on this account. [...]

That there are Devils and Witches, the Scripture asserts, and experience confirms[:] That they are common enemies of Mankind, and set upon mischief, is not to be doubted: That the Devil can (by Divine permission) and often doth vex men in Body and Estate, without the Instrumentality of Witches, is undeniable: That he often hath, and delights to have the Concurrence of Witches, and their consent in harming men, is consonant to his Native Malice to man, and too Lamentably exemplified: That Witches, when detected & convinced, ought to be exterminated and cut off, we have Gods warrant for. [...] *It is therefore exceeding necessary that in such a day as this men be informed what is evidence, and what is not.* [...] *There are not only Testimonies required by God, which are to be Credited according to the Rules given in His Word referring to witnesses: but there is also an Evidence supposed to be in the Testimony, which is throughly to be weighed, and if it do not infallibly prove the crime against the person accused, it ought not to determine him guilty of it; for so a righteous man may be Condemned unjustly. In the case of Witchcraft we know that the Devil is the immediate Agent in the Misch[ie]f done, the consent or compact of the Witch is the thing to be Demonstrated.*

Among many Arguments to evince this, that which is most under present debate, is that which refers to something Vulgarly,[105] *called* Spectre Evidence,[106] *and a certain sort of* Ordeal *or trial by the sight and touch. The Principal plea to justify the convictive evidence in these, is fetcht from the Consideration of the Wisdom and Righteousness of God in Governing the World, which they suppose would fail, if such things were permitted to befal an Innocent person: but it is certain, that too resolute conclusions drawn from hence, are bold usurpations upon spotless* Sovereignty; *and though, some things, if suffered to be common, would subvert this Government, and disband, yea ruine Humane society; yet God doth sometimes suffer such things to evene,*[107] *that we may thereby know how much we are beholden to Him, for thru restraint which he Layes upon the infernal Spirits, who would else reduce a World into a Chaos.* [...]

Cases of Conscience Concerning WITCHCRAFTS.

The First Case that I am desired to express my Judgement in, is this, *Whether it is not Possible for the Devil to impose on the Imaginations of Persons Bewitched, and to cause them to Believe that an Innocent, yea that a Pious person do[e]s torment them, when the Devil himself doth it, or whether Satan may not appear in the Shape of an Innocent and Pious, as well as of a Nocent and Wicked Person to Afflict such as suffer by Diabolical Molestations?*

The Answer to the Question must be Affirmative; Let the following Arguments be duely weighed in the Balance of the Sanctuary.[108] [...]

Argu. 1. There are several Scriptures from which we may infer the Possibility of what is Affirmed. [...]

[... T]hat evil Angels have sometimes appeared in the likeness of living absent persons is a thing abundantly confirmed by History. [...] A Man that is in one place cannot (Autoprosopos[109]) at the same time be in another. It remains then that such *spectres* are Prodigious & Supernatural, & not without Diabolical Operation. It has been Controverted among Learned men, whether innocent persons may not by the malice and deluding Power of the Devil be represented as present amongst witches at their dark Assemblies. The mentioned *Thyreus*[110] sayes that the Devil may and often does repre-

---

[105] Common, customary.
[106] Evidence produced by an apparition of a person. 'Spectre evidence' describes a witness's claim that the defendant's spectre or apparition had harassed him. No alibi could counter such an allegation.
[107] To come to pass, happen.
[108] To weigh or examine with the weights of the sanctuary; i.e., to test sth. by the standard of divine revelation. Also, to examine by an equal and just scale.
[109] Personally.
[110] Peter Thyraeus of Nuys (1546-1601), had concluded in *Divinarum Novi Testamenti, sive Christi Filii Dei, Novi testamenti mediatoris, apparitionum libris tres* (Cologne: Goswin Cholinus for Mater Cholinus, 1603) that the visible, audible, and tangible phenomena associated with hauntings are hallucinations caused by demons or spirits. The Divinarium is an essential piece in Thyraeus' studies in the appearances of angels and demons which were also propagated in *De Locis Infestis* and the *Libellus de Terrificationibus Nocturnisque Tumultibus*.

sent the Forms of innocent persons out of those Conventions, and that there is no Question to be made of it, but as to his natural Power and Art he is able to make their shapes appear amongst his own servants, but he supposeth the Providence of God will not suffer such an Injury to be done to an Innocent Person. [...]

Arg: 2. Because it is possible for the Devil in the Shape of an innocent person to do other mischiefs. [...]

[... Satan's] art is beyond what the wisest of men may pretend unto. He has perfect skill in Opticks, and can therefore cause that to be visible to one, which is not so to another; and things also to appear far otherwise then they are. He has likewise the Art of Limning[111] in the Perfection of it, and knows what may be done by Colours. [...] He searcheth into the Nature, Causes, and Reasons of things, whereby he is able to produce wonderful effects. So that if he does not form the Shape of an innocent person as afflicting others, it is not from want of either will or power. They that affirm that God never did nor ever will permit him thus to do, alledge that it is inconsistant with the Righteousness and Providence of God in Governing Humane Affairs thus to suffer men to be imposed on. [...]

Arg. 6. *Our own Experience has confirmed the Truth of what we affirm.*[...]

I have my self known several of whom I ought to think that they are now in Heaven, considering that they were of good Conversation, and reputed Pious by those that had the greatest Intimacy with them, of whom nevertheless, some complained that their Shapes appeared to them, and threatened them. Nor is this answered by saying, we do not know but those persons might be Witches. We are bound by the Rule of Charity to think otherwise. And they that censure any, meerly because such a sad Affliction as their being falsely represented by Satan, has befallen them, do not do as they would be done by. I bless the Lord, it was never the portion allotted to me, nor to any Relation of mine to be thus abused. But no man knoweth what may happen to him [...].

Postscript

The Design of the Preceeding *Dissertation*, is not to plead for Witchcrafts, or to appear as an Advocate for Witches. I have therefore written another Discourse, proving that there are such horrid Creatures as Witches in the World; and that they are to be extirpated and cut off from amongst the People of God, which *I* have Thoughts and inclinations in due time to Publish. And I am abundantly satisfied that there have been, and are still more cursed Witches in the Land. More then one or two of those now in Prison, have freely, and credibly acknowledged their Communion and Familiarity with the Spirits of Darkness, and have also declared unto me the Time and Occasion, with the particular circumstances of their Hellish Obligations and Abominations.

Nor is there designed any Reflection on those Worthy Persons who have been concerned in the late Proceedings at *Salem*. They are wise and good men, and have acted with all Fidelity according to their Light, and have out of tenderness declined the doing of some things, which in their own Judgments they were satisfied about. Having therefore so arduous a case before them, Pitty and Prayers rather than Censures are their due. On which Account I am glad that there is Published to the World (by my Son) a [report] of the *Trials* of some who were lately Executed, whereby I hope the thinking part of mankind will be satisfied, that there was more than that which is called *Spectre Evidence* for the Conviction of the persons Condemned. I was not my self present at

---

[111] Painting, coloring.

any of the Trials, excepting one, viz that of *George Burroughs*;[112] had I been one of his Judges, I could not have acquitted him. For several persons did upon Oath Testify, that they saw him do such things as no man that has not a Devil to be his Familiar could perform. And the Judges affirm that they have not Convicted any one meerly on the account of what *Spectres* have said, or of what has been Represented to the Eyes of Imagination of sick bewitched persons. If what is here exposed to publick view, may be a means to prevent it for the future, I shall not repent of my Labour in this Undertaking. I have been prevailed with so far as I am able to discern the Truth in their dark cases, to declare my Sentiments with the Arguments which are of weight with me, hoping that what is written may be of some use do discover the *Deeds of Satan*; and to prevent innocent ones having their Lives Endangered, or their Reputation Ruin'd, by being through the subtility and Power of the Devils, in consideration with the Ignorance and Weakness of men, involved amongst the guilty. It becomes those of my protection to be very tender in cases of Blood, and to imitate our Lord and Master, *Who came not to destroy the Lives of men, but to save them.* [...]

Source: Increase Mather (1639-1723). *Cases of Conscience Concerning Evil Spirits Personating Men, Witchcrafts, Infallible Proofs of Guilt in Such as Are Accused with That Crime. All Considered According to the Scriptures, History, Experience, and the Judgment of Many Learned Men.* Boston: Benjamin Harris, 1693, "Christian Reader," n.p., "Cases of Conscience" 1-2, 5, 11-12, 15, 33; "Postscript," n.p.

73. Cotton Mather
"Pietas in Patriam. Or, The Life of His Excellency Sir William Phips, Knt." (1702)

Reader, prepare to be entertained with as prodigious Matters as can be put into any History! And let him that writes the next *Thaumatographia Pneumatica*,[113] allow to these Prodigies the chief place among the Wonders.

[...] About the time of our Blessed Lord's coming to reside on Earth, we read of so many *possessed with Devils*, that it is commonly thought the *Number* of such miserable *Energumens*[114] was then encreased above what has been usual in other Ages [...].

Now the Arrival of Sir *William Phips*[115] to the Government of *New-England*, was at a time when [...] Scores of poor People had newly fallen under a prodigious *Possession of Devils*, which it was then generally thought had been by *Witchcrafts* introduced. It is

---

[112] George Burroughs, a Puritan minister born about 1650, who served in Salem Village, and later was accused as a ringleader of the Salem witches. He was executed during the trials and died in Salem on August 19, 1692.
[113] A writing dealing with the "wonders of the air." Cotton Mather's own *Wonders of the Invisible World* was thus a "Thaumatographia Pneumatica," and he uses this title for chapter 7 of Book VI of the *Magnalia*.
[114] One possessed by an evil spirit; a demoniac.
[115] William Phips was born on February 2, 1651 near Kennebec, Maine. Phips never attended school, but nevertheless he became captain of a cargo vessel that carried goods between New England and the West Indies. In 1687, an investor-backed expedition led by Phips recovered the treasure from sixteen Spanish ships that were lost at sea near the Bahamas in the early 1600s. As a result of his efforts, the king knighted Phips and appointed him the first Governor of Massachusetts. On May 14, 1692 Phips arrived in Boston and brought with him a new charter ending the 1684 English law banning colonies from self-government. During the Salem witchcraft trials Phips decided that spectral evidence and testimony would no longer suffice to convict suspects.

to be confessed and bewailed, that many Inhabitants of *New-England*, and Young People especially, had been led away with little *Sorceries*,[116] wherein they *did secretly those things that were not right against the Lord their God*; they would often cure Hurts with *Spells*, and practise detestable Conjurations with *Sieves*, and *Keys*, and *Pease*, and *Nails*, and *Horse-shoes*, and other Implements, to learn the things for which they had a forbidden and impious Curiosity. Wretched Books had stoln into the Land, wherein Fools were instructed how to become able Fortune-Tellers [...].

The *Devils* which had been so play'd withal, and, it may be, by some few Criminals more Explicitly engaged and imployed, now broke in upon the Country, after as astonishing a manner as was ever heard of. Some Scores of People, first about *Salem*, the Centre and First-Born of all the Towns in the Colony, and afterwards in several other places, were Arrested with many *Preternatural Vexations*[117] upon their Bodies, and a variety of cruel Torments, which were evidently inflicted from the *Dæmons*, of the *Invisible World*. The People that were *Infected* and *Infested* with such *Dæmons*, in a few Days time arrived unto such a *Refining Alteration* upon their Eyes, that they could see their Tormentors; they saw a *Devil* of a Little *Stature*, and of a Tawny *Colour*, attended still with *Spectres* that appeared in more Humane Circumstances.

These *Tormentors* tendred unto the afflicted a *Book*, requiring them to *Sign* it, or to *Touch* it at least, in token of their consenting to be Listed in the Service of the *Devil*; which they refusing to do, the *Spectres*[118] under the Command of that *Blackman*, as they called him, would apply themselves to Torture them with prodigious Molestations.

The afflicted Wretches were horribly *Distorted* and *Convulsed*; they were *Pinched Black and Blue*: *Pins* would be run every where in their Flesh; they would be *Scalded* until they had *Blisters* raised on them; and a Thousand other things before Hundreds of Witnesses were done unto them, evidently *Preternatural* [...].

Flashy People may *Burlesque* these Things, but when Hundreds of the most sober People in a Country, where they have as much *Mother-Wit* certainly as the rest of Mankind, know them to be *True*, nothing but the absurd and froward Spirit of *Sadducism*[119] can Question them. I have not yet mentioned so much as one Thing that will not be justified, if it be required by the *Oaths* of more considerate Persons than any that can ridicule these odd *Phænomena*.

But the worst part of this astonishing *Tragedy* is yet behind; wherein Sir *William Phips*, at last being dropt, as it were from the *Machin of Heaven*,[120] was an Instrument of easing the Distresses of the Land, now *so darkned by the Wrath of the Lord of Hosts*.[121] There were very worthy Men upon the Spot[122] where the *assault from Hell* was first made, who apprehended themselves call'd from the *God of Heaven*, to sift the business unto the bottom of it; and indeed, the continual *Impressions*, which the out-

---

[116] The practice of magic arts, witchcraft.
[117] The action of troubling or harassing caused by supernatural forces.
[118] An apparition or ghost, esp. one of a terrifying aspect.
[119] An epithet applied to disbelief in spirits of any kind.
[120] "Deus ex Machina," a proverb: "A God from the skies," used especially to indicate unexpected aid in an emergency.
[121] Cf. Isa. 9.19.
[122] Presumably the "Spot" was not only Salem and Salem Village but Massachusetts in general. Phips on May 29 appointed a Special Court of Oyer and Terminer, with Stoughton as chief justice, and John Richards, Nathaniel Saltonstall, Wait Winthrop, Bartholomew Gedney, Samuel Sewall, John Hathorne, and Peter Sergeant. Saltonstall disliked the methods of the judges and resigned. His place was filled by Jonathan Corwin, who, like Hathorne, gave no mercy to any suspected witch.

cries and the havocks of the *afflicted People* that lived nigh unto them caused on their Minds, gave no little Edge to this Apprehension.

The Persons were Men eminent for *Wisdom* and *Virtue*, and they went about their enquiry into the matter, as *driven* unto it by a *Conscience* of Duty to God and the World. They did in the first Place take it for granted, that there are *Witches*, or wicked Children of Men, who upon *Covenanting* with, and *Commissioning* of *Evil Spirits*, are attended by their Ministry to accomplish the things desired of them [...]. The Existence of such *Witches* was now taken for granted by those good Men, wherein so far the generality of reasonable Men have thought *they ran well*;[123] and they soon received the *Confessions* of some *accused* Persons to confirm them in it; but then they took one thing more for granted, wherein 'tis now as generally thought they *went out of the Way*.[124] The Afflicted People vehemently accused several Persons in several Places, that the *Spectres* which afflicted them, did exactly resemble *them* [...]. When many of the *accused* came upon their Examination, it was found, that the *Dæmons* then a thousand ways abusing of the poor *afflicted* People, had with a marvellous exactness *represented* them; yea, it was found, that many of the *accused* [...] would fall down and lye in a sort of a Swoon, wherein they would continue, whatever Hands were laid upon them, until the Hands of the *accused* came to touch them, and *then* they would revive immediately: And it was found, that various kinds of *natural Actions*, done by many of the *accused* in or to their own Bodies, as *Leaning, Bending, Turning* Awry, or *Squeezing* their Hands, or the like, were presently attended with the like things *preternaturally* done upon the Bodies of the *afflicted*, though they were so far asunder, that the *afflicted* could not at all observe the *accused*. [...]

Now many good Men took up an Opinion, That the *Providence* of God would not permit an *Innocent Person* to come under such a *Spectral Representation*; and that a concurrence of so many Circumstances would prove an *accused* Person to be in a *Confederacy* with the *Dæmons* thus afflicting of the Neighbours; they judged, that except these things might amount unto a *Conviction*, it would scarce be possible ever to *Convict* a *Witch*; and they had some *Philosophical Schemes* of *Witchcraft*, and of the Method and Manner wherein *Magical Poisons* operate, which further supported them in their Opinion.

Sundry of the *accused* Persons were brought unto their *Trial*, while this Opinion was yet prevailing in the Minds of the *Judges* and the *Juries*, and perhaps the most of the People in the Country, then mostly Suffering; and though against some of them that were Tried there came in so much *other Evidence* of their Diabolical Compacts, that some of the most *Judicious*, and yet *Vehement* Opposers of the Notions then in Vogue, publickly declared, *Had they themselves been on the Bench, they could not have Acquitted them*; nevertheless, divers were Condemned, against whom the *chief Evidence* was founded in the *Spectral Exhibitions*. [...]

On the other Part, there were many Persons of great Judgment, Piety and Experience, who from the beginning were very much dissatisfied at these Proceedings; they feared lest the *Devil* would get so far into the *Faith* of the People, that for the sake of many *Truths*, which they might find him telling of them, they would come at length to

---

[123] I.e., they were right.
[124] I.e., they followed the erroneous principle that when the specter of any man or woman of the community appeared to those afflicted, the individuals so represented were in all likelihood "in a *Confederacy*" with demons, and thus deserving of death. The two Mathers opposed judging any one guilty on the sole basis of "spectral evidence."

believe all his *Lies*, whereupon what a Desolation of *Names*, yea, and of *Lives* also, would ensue, a Man might without much *Witchcraft* be able to Prognosticate; and they feared, lest in such an extraordinary Descent of *Wicked Spirits* from their *High Places* upon us, there might such *Principles* be taken up, as, when put into *Practice*, would unavoidably cause the *Righteous to perish with the Wicked* [...].

And Sir *William Phips* arriving to his Government, after this *ensnaring horrible Storm* was begun, did consult the neighbouring Ministers of the Province, who made unto his Excellency and the Council a return, (drawn up at their desire by Mr. *Mather* the Younger, as I have been inform'd[125]) wherein they declared.

We judge, that in the Prosecution of these and all such Witchcrafts, *there is need of a very Critical and Exquisite Caution: Lest by too much Credulity for things received only upon the* Devil's Authority, *there be a Door opened for a long Train of miserable Consequences, and Satan get an Advantage over us; for* we should not be Ignorant of his Devices. [...]

Presumptions, *whereupon Persons may be committed, and much more* Convictions, *whereupon Persons may be condemned as guilty of* Witchcrafts, *ought certainly to be more considerable, than barely the* accused *Persons being represented by a* Spectre *to the afflicted: Inasmuch as it is an undoubted and a notorious Thing, that a* Dæmon *may, by God's Permission, appear even to ill Purposes in the shape of an* Innocent, *yea, and a Virtuous* Man: *Nor can we esteem* Alterations *made in the* Sufferers, *by a* look *or* touch *of the* accused, *to be an infallible Evidence of Guilt; but frequently liable to be abused by the Devil's* Legerdemains.[126]

Source: Cotton Mather (1663-1728). "Pietas in Patriam: The Life of His Excellency Sir William Phips, Knt. Late Captain General, and Governour in Chief of the Province of the Massachuset-Bay, New-England." *Magnalia Christi Americana: Or, the Ecclesiastical History of New England, from Its First Planting in the Year 1620. unto the Year of Our Lord, 1698. In Seven Books.* London: Thomas Parkhurst, 1702, Vol. I, Book II, 59-63.

---

[125] A further instance of Mather's pretense that he was not the author of the *Pietas*. Phips had consulted the "neighboring Ministers" for their opinion of the methods used by the court of Oyer and Terminer which he had established with the advice of the Council. Cotton Mather was one of the twelve ministers, and drew up *The Return of Several Ministers Consulted by His Excellency and the ... Council, Upon the Present Witchcrafts in Salem-Village*, dated at Boston, June 15, 1692, which was sent to the governor. There were eight sections in the *Return*, of which Mather below omits the first two and the eighth.
[126] Trickery; deception.

MILLENNIALISM

Based on a variety of biblical prophecies – most importantly on chapters 20 of The Book of Revelation –, millennialism denotes, in very broad theological terms, a belief that the apocalyptic destruction of the world, the end of history, and the Last Judgement are preceded by Christ's thousand-year reign on earth. During this period the earth would gradually or abruptly be transformed into a worldly paradise. As such, millennialism is in no way peculiar to the history of American Christianity, but dates back to the primitive churches of Asia Minor. While it had been rejected in its original radical form as a futuristic expectation by most church fathers (who favored a so-called preterite interpretation) and largely subdued as a heterodoxy by the medieval church, millennialism was revitalized in new forms by the Protestant reformation. It became one of the hallmarks of Calvinism that was generally fuelled by a strong apocalyptical spirituality.

Underlying the millennialist hopes of Protestants in general, and Calvinists in particular, was, on the one hand, the conviction that the reformation had set in motion the downfall of the Antichrist – identified as the Roman Catholic Church –, or the binding of the dragon mentioned in Revelation 20 as prerequisite to the rise of Christ's kingdom of earthly bliss. Such a millennialist reading of (church-)history, on the other hand, held out the promise to Protestants to play an instrumental part in God's providential plan, as well as to participate as members of a 'saintly community' in the manifestations of his glory on this side of heaven. Thus, when the Puritans were driven out of Old England under Bishop Laud after their ill-fated attempts to purify the Anglican Church and finally emigrated to New England, they not only retained the self-image of radical Calvinism as standard-bearer and spear-head of the reformation which had been halted, if not reversed in the mother-country [cf. the section on Puritanism]. They also brought with them its millennialist belief as well as the penchant for speculating about the when and where of Christ's Second Coming.

Theological discussions on millennialism – generating a plethora of learned books, tracts, pamphlets and sermons – centred around two central issues. First of all, clergymen endlessly split hairs over the intricacies of their 'millennium mathematics.' Drawing on a long exegetical tradition in Protestant Europe, virtually all American authors understood the cycles of visions in Revelation to constitute a progressive chronological sequence in which the apocalyptical seals, trumpets, vials, and woes could be synchronized with particular events of international history. Which events and dates should be matched with which biblical symbols was, however, a matter of enduring contention. As far as the selected documents are concerned, there is, generally speaking, a tendency to push back in time the anticipated date for the actual onset of the millennium; one reason for this obviously being the repeated frustrations of past calculations. While John Cotton, for instance, expected the 'advent' of the millennium in 1655, and his grandson Cotton Mather's computations pointed roughly at the early 1700s, Jonathan Edwards established the paradigm for most eighteenth-century interpreters when he argued that the latter-day glory would begin sometime around the year 2000. Secondly, exegetes struggled over the general mode of reading the scriptural prophecies.

On the one side, we find the 'literalists' who insisted that certain key-passages pertaining to Christ's Second Coming at the beginning of the millennium, to the resurrection of the saints, to the apocalyptic tribulations initiating the downfall of the Antichrist, and to the restoration of the Jewish tribes had to be read in a literal fashion as predicting very concrete events in the future. Despite their differences on certain questions, Increase and Cotton Mather (docs. 77, 78, 81) are in their own ways both representative of the 'literalists camp.' On the other side stood the 'allegorists' who suggested that these prophecies should rather be understood in a figurative sense. Most importantly, they did not think that Christ would suddenly appear in the body together with his raised saints at the beginning of the millennium. They rather envisioned the establishment of the millennial kingdom as a gradual process during which Christ's influence on earth would ever more strongly increase, and a rule of the saints would be established. An early representative of the 'allegorist camp' is John Cotton, whose *The Churches Resurrection* (1642, doc. 74) and *An Exposition* (1655, doc. 76) in many ways anticipate the even stronger allegorizing tendencies of the eighteenth-century texts in this collection. In accordance with their respective exegetical methods, these two camps – which would later develop into what is called pre- and postmillennialism – differed from each other in the degree to which they emphasized a supernatural interruption of worldly history before the Last Judgement, and the inevitability of cataclysmic events making way for the millennium.

Even though individual authors often were at odds with the mainstream, one can still detect some general trends in the historical development of millennialist beliefs in America between the 1630s and the early 1800s. Ignoring, for the present purpose, the danger of oversimplification, it might be said that between the first and the second half of the seventeenth century a shift occurred from a more optimistic to a more pessimistic keynote in American millennialism. If recent scholarship has refuted the much touted view that the first Puritan settlers were driven by the hope to establish a New Jerusalem on American soil, it still holds true that at least the leaders of the 1630s and 1640s such as John Winthrop, William Bradford, and John Cotton thought and acted within a millennialist horizon of expectation. Most of them understood it as their task and privilege to keep alive the millennial promise originally associated with the English reformation by setting up a model-community of primitive Christianity that would help to purge the mother country of its remaining Catholicism, thereby bringing it back on its providential course.

This conviction gave way to a sense of crisis amongst second- and third-generation clergymen when the hope for a radical ecclesiastical change in Old England abated during the (Catholic) Restoration, and the New England colonies themselves were seen as straying from their divinely ordained path. Thus, the texts from this period (docs. 78, 80, 81) dread the latter-days at least as much as they long for them, since their authors – including Increase and Cotton Mather – were no longer confident whether God would exempt their churches from the brunt of His wrath. A dramatic alteration in mood occurred when, during the so-called Great Awakening in the 1740s, waves of religious revival began to sweep the colonies which were perceived by Jonathan Edwards and his fellow New Light-ministers as tokens of God's coming kingdom.

In short terms, the revolutionary period obviously generated much public anxiety which often had apocalyptic overtones. Yet in the long run, the American Revolution did not reverse but strengthen the millennialist hopes generated in the second half of the eighteenth century, and indeed created a new confidence that, as Samuel Sherwood's *The Church's Flight into the Wilderness* (doc. 85) puts it already in 1776, there was doubtless a glorious future for America "in the womb of providence, which the present commotion thro' the nation and land may [...] be the means of bringing to pass." Confidence even turned into exuberant fantasies of America's future grandeur in many millennial texts written during the period of the Early Republic. The poems by Philip Freneau, Timothy Dwight, George Richards, and David Humphreys (docs. 83-84, 87-89) also demonstrate how the millennialist beliefs and hopes (which in colonial times were tied to a transatlantic, denominational sense of community) increasingly became attached to the idea of the American nation.

Speaking about the changing self-image of Americans leads to a second dimension of millennialism beyond its more narrow meaning as a concept of theology or church history. Recent scholarship has investigated millennialism as a rhetoric of 'community-building,' and emphasized its special significance for America. In very abstract terms, millennialist eschatology provides coherence to any community's understanding of its relationship with God and the world. It addresses the problems of the community's sufferings by offering a coherent 'cosmic narrative' based on a pattern of redemption through affliction. In more concrete terms, imagining and imaging oneself as God's chosen "fellowlabourers [sic] in the Gospel of Christ" (1 Thess. 2.3) working towards the advent of the millennium was an important means for the settlers to form a sense of a collective American identity – both in a denominational as well as in a regional and later on national sense. Their millennialist beliefs allowed them to transform all experienced calamities into the comforting assurance that this community was acting out a divinely preordained plan which would eventually lead towards a positive resolution.

Especially since the eighteenth century, the millennium also served as a screen on which evermore elaborate utopian visions were projected. This is most obvious in Samuel Hopkins' *A Treatise on the Millennium* (doc. 86) with its detailed and astonishingly technical descriptions of human progress during Christ's thousand-year reign. Conversely, ministers also employed millennialist rhetoric to castigate their congregations for their "backslidings." That millennialist rhetoric was often used in both ways at the same time, is most clearly illustrated by Increase Mather's *The Day of Trouble is Near* (doc. 78). With the onslaught of apocalyptic catastrophes pending, he warns the New England churches about the "great decay as to the power of godliness" amongst them, arguing "that if Christ hath a peculiar love unto them, then he will rebuke and chasten them [accordingly], as there shall be cause for it." Making use of a double-strategy that is characteristic of the Puritan Jeremiad, Mather therefore affirms the original self-image of Puritans as an elect people in the very act of warning his contemporaries about the consequences of not staying true to their millennial mission.

In both ways – as a means of affirmation and exhortation – millennialist rhetoric was constantly adapted by the clergy to the specific contexts of an ever-changing historical situation as well as to their specific power interests. Millennialist ministers were not only watching for the 'signs of the time' both at home and abroad which they sought to fit into their readings of the scriptures. With their millennialist interpretations, these influential public figures were simultaneously attempting to control public opinion on matters both ecclesiastical and temporal, and actively shape their society in political terms. John Cotton's texts, to pick an early example, respond to questions of state-power and church governance emerging from the English revolution. In identifying the Roman church with its intermixture of spiritual and temporal power as the apocalyptic beast, they argue "that all power that is on earth be limited, Church-power or other," and effectively promote a "Common-Wealth"-model based on a Congregationalist church-system. In a similar fashion, texts from the revolutionary period such as Samuel Sherwood's sermon (doc. 85) integrate the colonies' struggle for independence as well as "civil and religious liberties" into a millennialist framework.

Sherwood's demonization of Britain's "tyrannical and persecuting powers" as "the great red dragon" exemplifies that millennialist rhetoric simultaneously worked as a mechanism of community building by means of 'out-group'-formation. Within their referential framework of an apocalyptic battle between the forces of good and evil, the symbols from the prophetic scriptures held an enormous potential for polarization, and perfectly lent themselves for the construction of powerful enemy images. And because of their hermetic quality, such symbols as the various beasts from Daniel and the Book of Revelation, the dragon and the whore of Babylon could be applied to any historical situation, signifying external and/or internal, religious and/or political opponents. 'Naming the Antichrist' was thus a game which millennialist ministers played throughout the centuries, pointing their fingers at such different opponents as Catholics, Indians, Loyalists and radical Republicans.

Finally, it should be emphasized that millennialism is not only intimately related to almost all of the key-concepts documented and discussed in this volume. It connects these ideas to each other; for instance, millennialism fuses Puritan providentialism with the early conceptualizations of America into what Cotton Mather (doc. 81) aptly terms a *"Christianography."* Initially English theologians tended to exclude the New World from the history of salvation, and America was even seen as the location of the Anti-Christian forces of Gog and Magog by such prominent exegetes as Joseph Mede (doc. 75). In their millennialist tracts New England Puritans of the late seventeenth century argued against this exclusion (docs. 80 and 81) and occasionally, as in the case of Samuel Sewall (doc. 79), even attempted to turn tables on their English colleagues in arguing that the "aboriginal Natives of America" were in fact the lost tribes of Israel. Most of the colonial writers (and also many later ones for that matter) were, however, much too universalist in their conception of salvation history. Sewall's more cautious fellow-millennialist, such as Increase and Cotton Mather, at best dared to hope that the original New English congregations might have come closest in church history "to anticipate the State of the *New Jerusalem.*"

Contrary to a widely held opinion, the idea that America would play an exclusive part in the millennium, let alone the idea that it would be its centre, did not gain any prominence until the Great Awakening. And even then it remained highly controversial. While the rather scrupulous Jonathan Edwards in his *Some Thoughts* (1742, doc. 82) had allowed himself for a moment to hope that America might indeed be the starting-point of the millennium from where "the most glorious Renovation of the World" would spread, he later retreated from that optimistic assumption. True, the millennialist poems by Freneau, Richards, Dwight, and Humphreys do foresee a glorious future for America as the last great empire of history whose religious and social accomplishments would be instrumental in preparing the way for the millennium. Yet they still differentiate between the worldly nation-state as the "blissful prelude to Emanuel's reign" and the latter-day "new Jerusalem sent down from heav'n." It was not until the nineteenth century, when millennialism increasingly moved outside the strictly regulated discourse of professional theological exegesis, and became intermixed with a progressive philosophy of history as well as the idea of manifest destiny – another important example for the way millennialism interacted with other key-concepts – that the boundaries between Christ's kingdom on earth and America as a 'redeemer nation' were frequently dissolved.

Jan Stievermann

74. John Cotton
The Churches Resurrection, or the Opening of the Fift and Sixt Verses of the 20th Chapter of the Revelation[1] (1642)

[...] There is a double Resurrection: The word first implieth: The first Resurrection is of mens soules and bodies dead in sinne [...]. Now of this Resurrection there are two parts (which need to be attended to, or else some Scriptures will not be well cleared.) First, it is of particular persons [...]. Secondly, there is a first resurrection also of Churches when as they are recovered againe from their Apostatical[2] and dead estate in Idolatry and Superstition [...].

Now when hee saith, *blessed are they that have part in this first resurrection*, he doth not say there shall be a resurrection of churches, without reformation of the members also, for else they could not bee blessed [...].

But it implies, it shall be a resurrection of sincere members, or else it could not bee said those men are *blessed and holy that have part in the first resurrection*, if they had part only in outward reformation [...].

Use: For the use of this point, it is a strong warning to our Churches here [i.e. in New England], that we bee not deceived in our reformation, and deceived in our rules by which it is carryed, for I am cleere in that, and so I thinke are most of us, and it is our sinne if we be not. That our Reformation and rules of it are of God, neither do I doubt of the resurrection[3] of many choyce christians throughout the countrey. (the Lord increase their number.) But I am afraid there is more reformation th[a]n resurrection. Therefore it is a holy warning from Heaven to attend resurrection here also; here is a great reformation of Churches, I thinke I may speake it without vanity and vaine glory, and puffing up of the hearts of the sonnes of men, a greater face of reformation th[a]n in any churches are to bee found: But this first *Resurrection* in my text the first of these yeeres is not begun: For though it bee a very true observation which many Divines give, that Satans binding was graduall, and did not take his beginning at once [...]. Here is in the text, the third degree of Satans Satanicall power restrained before this thousand yeeres begin, And that will not be (my text is plaine) till Satan be cast into the bottomlesse pit, and the Romane Catholique Church damned from the face of churches also, and cast out: [...] if Antichrist[4] be not yet taken and Satan cast into the bottomles pit, then the thousand yeers are not yet begun, and so the first resurrection not begun.

Therfore let it be a serious warning to every one not to rest in Reformation and formes of it, and to blesse your selves in Church Membership, because to this day, this first Resurrection hath not taken its place, nor will not take his place till Antichrist be ruinated. This is a faire preparation, and I doubt not, there is a Resurrection of many precious soules throughout the Countrey, that abhorre Popery and the worship of the Beast[5] with a perfect hatred, and reigne with Christ in their hearts and Families, as

---

[1] Cf. Rev. 20.5f.: "But the rest of the dead lived not again until the thousand years were finished. This is the first resurrection. Blessed and holy is he that hath part in the first resurrection: on such the second death hath not power, but they shall be priests of God and of Christ, and shall reign with him a thousand years."
[2] Heretical.
[3] The rising again of the dead at the Last Judgement.
[4] The great antagonist expected by the early Church to cause chaos and corruption in the last days before the Second Coming.
[5] The doctrines, practices, and rituals of the Roman Catholic Church.

much as in them lyes. But if I should say there is a Resurrection in *New England* from resting in Pernis,[6] from resting in the World, and carnall selfe-love, and secret close haunts, (which God will search out) that I can say we are risen out of all our Oppression and Hypocrisie that the Name of the Lord Jesus might be exalted, and his Word Glorifyed, and rule in our houses and hearts; if I should say there is such a Resurrection, of which it is said, *blessed and holy are they that have part in it,* I should say more th[a]n I could justifie, or more th[a]n my text will give me leave to say [...].

Therefore let not *New England* be secure, and blesse our selves in our Resurrection, because we have our part in this Reformation: I cannot say, here is a Resurrection of Churches, such as the text speaks of, boild up to that consistence, which the Text speakes to, though I hope the Lord will bring us to it. [...]

> Source: John Cotton (1585-1652). *The Churches Resurrection, or the Opening of the Fift and Sixt Verses of the 20th Chapter of the Revelation. By That Learned and Reverend. Iohn Cotton, Teacher to the Church of Boston in New England, and There Corrected by His Own Hand.* London: R.O. & G.D. for Henry Overton, 1642, 8, 10, 19-22.

75. Joseph Mede
"A Coniecture Concerning *Gog* and *Magog* in the Revelation" (1650)

The Revelation is a book of the future estate of the Church of the Gentiles,[7] not of the Jews. For the Jews have prophesies sufficient touching their own condition in the old Testament, neither have they any wayes need of ours: their own abundantly being sufficient to decipher all the condition[s] of their nation, whether good or evil.

And that the scope of the Revelation aimeth at this, witness: First, the representation of the spectacle of the Revelation which, by four living creatures placed above the throne of God[8] toward so many coasts of heaven; sheweth the Church of Christ, containing within its pale, the Gentiles in the four quarters of the world; to wit, as the subject of all the Visions tending thereto. [...] Now if it be counted expedient that one people may represent another, so may also one kind of enemies represent others, that so the parable may every way agree with it self. Hence therefore Egypt and Babylon in the Revelation, are not the Babylon and Egypt of the Israelites, but the enemies of the Church of the Gentiles (which is figured in Israel) like that Babylon and Egypt. [...]

But from what kind of men this new enemy shal proceed, whether from the remains of those nations, which the deluge of fire at the first resurrection, did not overwhelm; or from those nations by profession Christians, who not taking it well that they should be excluded [from] the holy City, nor enjoy the like condition with her happy citizens, (Satan quickning their fewel of envy) shall endeavour to take it by force, it is not easie to determine; if we follow the latter, we shall be forced to no small inconveniences. I therefore approve of the first; namely, that this army shall come from those nations, which live in the Hemisp[h]ere opposite to us, whom the Best and most Great God in his secret judgement, for the most part shall not cherish with the light of his Gospel. But the circuit of our Hemisphere (which the Ocean encloseth within his compass, and which of old was esteemed the onely habitation of mankind, in which the first man was

---

[6] Pernicion: total destruction; perdition; ruin.
[7] Of or pertaining to all of the nations other than the Jewish.
[8] The four creatures represent the four gospels: eagle (John), lion (Matthew), ox (Mark), and man (Luke).

framed, and at the beginning Paradise planted, in which those foure great Empires[9] (the basis of the Prophecies) were founded, in the middle whereof Christ was incarnate, suffered and rose from the dead, in which alone the Apostles, and their disciples preached, in which the Church for so long [a] time sojourned, within whose limits that dispersion of the Jews throughout all nations is included and other Oracles of the Prophets are fulfilled): This universal Hemisphere (I say) of the Earth, and which onely is partaker of the promised instauration, shall become the camp of the Saints, and the seat of this blessed kingdome; but whatsoever nations are without this (in the places where the Ancients placed the seat of Hel[l]) shall be reserved to the last triumph of Christ, to be destroyed by fire from heaven, by his just (though to us unknown) judgement.

For while I more strictly examine the words of the context, I observe four things to be distinctly mentioned in them; 1. Of the beloved Citie.[10] 2. Of the Camp of the Saints.[11] 3. Of the breadth of the earth. 4. Of the nations, who coming from the foure corners of the world, went up in the compass thereof, to beleaguer the camp of the Saints.

Vers. 8. *Satan* (saith he) *shall go out to deceive the nations, which are in the foure quarters of the earth, Gog and Magog,*[12] *to gather them together to battel; the number of whom is as the sand of the sea.*

9. *And they went upon the breadth of the Earth, and compassed the Camp of the Saints about, and the beloved City, &c.*

The beloved City is New Jerusalem, which was to become the head Citie of that blessed kingdome. The Camp of the Saints, the Nations of those that are saved, which shall walk in the light thereof [...]. So here the nations (whom God shall adopt for a people to himself) shall dwell far and near about the new Jerusalem, the universall Temple of God, placed in the midst of our world, with its Kingly Priests.

The third, the breadth of the earth, is that whole extent of land, which the Ocean (which washeth with his waves the earth in the compasse thereof) boundeth out unto us with his circuit; in a word, it is the compasse of our Hemisphere, unto whose outmost limits the Oracles of the Prophets do testifie, that the kingdome of Christ shall be extended. *He shall have Dominion from sea to sea, and from the River unto the ends of the earth,* Psal. 72.8. *I have given thee for a light to the Gentiles that thou mayst be my salvation unto the end of the earth,* Esay 49.6. and other such like places, so that there cannot the least thing be thought of, touching the amplitude of this blessed kingdome, which the bounds of our world do not embrace within their circuit.

In this breadth of land, at the end of the thousand years, the nations are said to ascend, which are in the four corners of the earth, and the same to encompasse round the camp of the Saints there placed. By their ascension, I learn, that they come from another place abroad, so that they were seated, not within, but without this breadth of land: but by their sitting down round about, that they were so situated, that they might invade them not from this, or that coast onely, but from all parts of this land. And that

---

[9] Reference to the Babylonian, Persian, Grecian, and Roman empires.
[10] I.e., New Jerusalem.
[11] The elect to be resurrected at Christ's Second Coming.
[12] Gog and Magog, a great power, who according to the biblical prophecy will destroy Israel. Ezek. 38.2 describes Gog "of the land of Magog," who will lead a mighty host of nations to attack Israel. In Rev. 20.7f. it is Satan who summons Gog and Magog to battle. In later Jewish eschatology the war of Gog and Magog stood for the apocalyptic battle between the heathens and Israel, the prelude to the coming of the Messiah. The Roman historian Josephus identifies Magog with Scythia, but in antiquity this name was used to designate vaguely any northern population.

both which do appertain to the inhabitants of the land of *America*, both Northern and Southern, is unknown to none that understand Geography; for seeing they inhabit the Hemisphere opposite to us, they are so fitly situated that by directly passing the Ocean from their own coasts, they may easily encompasse round our world.

I hear (thou wilt say) a most wonderfull conspiracy of so many nations, so many people, distant so great a space one from the other, and who by crossing so vast a sea, must passe to our world; the world never saw the like expedition in any age, and therefore never likely to be enterprised, without the hope of some extraordinary benefit, which hath a mighty operation on the nature of man. But what shall we call that which will become so alluring a benefit? Surely, what other, but that they might [...] take into their possession a land of so blessed a soil and aire, and magnificent happiness, that they might live blessedly wherein, and [...] live again from the dead. Sathan certainly runneth his old course; for by the same craft he drove headlong to destruction the first parents of mankind, not likely to recede from the same proof of his diligence and wickednesse in this last end of the world.

And this is the summe of my opinion, which I submit to the judgement of learned men, and understanding those kind of mysteries.

One thing yet may I adde, if it be true which our *Fuller*[13] endeavoureth to prove by severall arguments, That the people of *America* are Colonies of the nation of *Magog*, by reason of the short passage through the Ocean, in those *Scythian* coasts[14] (otherwhere exceeding vast and large) there is no cause that any should make any contention more about the names of *Gog* and *Magog* [...].

Source: Joseph Mede (1586-1638). "A Coniecture Concerning *Gog* and *Magog* in the Revelation." *The Key of the Revelation, Searched and Demonstrated out of the Naturall and Proper Characters of the Visions. With a Comment Thereupon, According to the Rule of the Same Key, Published in Latine by the Profoundly Learned Mr. Joseph Mede [...]; Translated into English by Richard More [...]. The Second Edition in English, Whereunto is Added a Conjecture Concerning Gog and Magog by the Same Authour*. London: J.L., 1650, n.p.

76. John Cotton
An Exposition upon the Thirteenth Chapter of the Revelation (1655)

Revel. 13.1,2.
And I stood upon the sand of the Sea, and saw a Beast rise up out of the Sea, having seven heads, and tenne horns, and upon his horns ten Crowns, and upon his heads the name of blasphemy. [...]

Doct.: Come we now to gather one briefe note from the words:
The visible Catholicke Roman Church is in the esteem of the holy Ghost a monstrous Beast, that is the note. [...]

If God had made such a kinde of creature; a Leopard is no monster, nor a Beare, nor a Lyon: But if you make a Beast of all these, that will be a monster, that is contrary to the course of nature, cleare besides the ordinary course of naturall generation, that makes a thing monstrous, this then is the reason of the point.

Reason: A beast ingendred against the course of nature, that is a monster, especially if there be so many uncouth[15] shapes of which it is composed: And it is not so with this universall Catholick visible Church? [...]

---

[13] Nicolas Fuller (1557-1626), distinguished orientalist.
[14] The Scythians originally were a nomadic people who also settled into farming communities in Crimea.
[15] Unusual, uncommon, strange.

Use 1. It may first teach us the great and just reason which all Protestant Churches have to with-draw themselves from the fellowship of the Church of *Rome*, from the Catholick visible Roman Church [...]. Therefore I pray you consider, it is not time for the Lambs of Christ, and for all the Churches of Christ to flye off from this Monster, and to abandon them utterly, as having no part nor portion with such a beast as this? [...]

Revel. 13. 5,6.

And there was given unto him a mouth speaking great things, and blasphemies, and power was given unto him to continue forty and two moneths.
And he opened his mouth in blasphemies against God, to blaspheme his name, and his Tabernacle,[16] *and them that dwell in heaven.* [...]

Use 1. For the use of it, I might from hence first speak to this point; that it were therefore a necessary counsell to all Roman Catholicks, to consider diligently the grounds of the great priviledges of the visible Catholick Church, they stretch their authority beyond all degrees of Churches, beyond all Temporall States or particular Churches: Now necessary it were for them to reverse all the great things which are delivered, and which the Pope hath set open his mouth to speak, though they be delivered with never such fulnesse, and boldnesse, and plentitude of power: It behoves men to consider whether all these great words be not the words of a Beast, and blasphemies which the head of the Beast had taken upon him to utter [...].

Use 2. Secondly, This may serve to teach us the danger of allowing to any mortall man an inordinate[17] measure of power to speak great things, to allow to any man uncontrollableness of speech, you see the desperate danger of it: Let all the world learn to give mortall men no greater power th[a]n they are content they shall use, for use it they will [...]. And they that have liberty to speak great things, you will finde it to be true, they will speak great blasphemies. No man would think what desperate deceit and wickednesse there is in the hearts of men [...]. There is a straine in a mans heart that will sometime or other runne out to excesse, unlesse the Lord restraine it, but it is not good to venture it: It is necessary therefore, that all power that is on earth be limited, Church-power or other: If there be power given to speak great things, then look for great blasphemies, look for a licentious abuse of it. It is counted a matter of danger to the State to limit Prerogatives; but it is a further danger, not to have them limited: They will be like a Tempest, if they be not limited: A Prince himselfe cannot tell where hee will confine himselfe, nor can the people tell: But if he have liberty to speak great things, then he will make and unmake, say and unsay, and undertake such things as are neither for his owne honour, nor for the safety of the State. ☞Note:[18] It is therefore fit for every man to be studious of the bounds which the Lord hath set: and for the People, in whom fundamentally all power lyes, to give as much power as God in his word gives to men: And it is meet that Magistrates in the Common-wealth, and so Officers in Churches should desire to know the utmost bounds of their own power, and it is safe for both: All intrenchment upon the bounds which God hath not given, they are not enlargements, but burdens and snares; They will certainly lead the spirit of a man out of his way sooner or later.

[...] This transcendant power that he is able to carry all before him without controll; it is a strange power, he may say what he will, and doe what he will, for so many

---

[16] Archaic: Dwelling place of God.
[17] Unregulated, immoderate.
[18] The marker added to attract the reader's attention is printed on the margin of the text.

moneths, the time indeed is limited. So that it will be of this use to us, if we see men outrageous, and break bonds beyond measure in any common-weath or Church, our way is to see Gods hand in it, and to look up to him to muzzle that power [...].

> Source: John Cotton (1585-1652). *An Exposition upon the Thirteenth Chapter of the Revelation. By That Reverend and Eminent Servant of the Lord, Mr. John Cotton, Teacher to the Church at Boston in New-England. Taken from His Mouth in Short-writing, and Some Part of It Corrected by Himselfe Soon after the Preaching Thereof, and All of It since Viewed Over by a Friend to Him, and to the Truth; Wherein Some Mistakes Were Amended, but Nothing of the Sence Altered.* London: M.S. for Livewel Chapman, 1655, 1, 14, 16, 62, 70-72, 74.

77. Increase Mather
The Mystery of Israel's Salvation, Explained and Applyed: Or, a Discourse Concerning the General Conversion of the Israelitish Nation (1669)

[...] *I will shake the heaven*, saith God. Is not this come to pass? Are not the powers of heaven shaking? I am perswaded, that who ever liveth a while longer, will hear that the Stars are falling down from heaven, like untimely figs from a *shaken tree*.[19] *And the earth*; Is not this fulfilling also? Do you not feel an earthquake[20] at this day? Is not the Lord arising to shake terribly the earth? The *earth* is moved exceedingly, *the earth* reeleth to and fro, *the earth* is clean dissolved, the transgression thereof is heavy upon it, the windows from on high are open, and the foundations of *the earth* do shake. *And the Sea*; Is not this sign also fulfilling? what roarings have there been upon the Sea of late? Is not the day of the Lord upon the Ships of *Tarshish*?[21] How are men afraid to venture upon the Sea? because God is shaking not only the dry Land, but the Sea? *I will shake all Nations*; Is not this also fulfilling? God hath allarumed all the Nations, do you not hear the rushing of the Nations?[22] when were *all the Nations* in such a posture? *Europe, Asia, Africa, America*, all are in a tumult. The Lord hath allarm'd them all. Men know not where now to go; they cannot think of what Nation to transport themselves unto, but the *shaking of God* will take hold on them in that Nation. Now, these are signs, that he who is the *desire* of the Elect amongst *all Nations* will come ere long. Amen, even so, come, come, come Lord Jesus!

"Consider [...] That some of us are under special advantage to understand these mysterious truths *of God*;" That is to say, such of us as are in an exiled condition in this wilderness. Indeed some came hither upon worldly accounts, but others there are that

---
[19] Referring to Matt. 24.32-35: "Now learn a parable of the fig tree; When his branch is yet tender, and putteth forth leaves, ye know that summer *is* nigh: so likewise ye, when ye shall see all these things, know that it is near, *even* at the doors. Verily I say unto you, This generation shall not pass, till all these things be fulfilled. Heaven and earth shall pass away, but my words shall not pass away."
[20] According to Matt. 24.7, earthquakes in various places are a sign that would precede the coming of the Messiah.
[21] God appointed Jonah to go to Niniveh to preach against its wickedness. Jonah however, did not follow the Lord's command and travelled in the opposite direction to the city of Tarshish. When the Lord sent a terrible wind, Jonah realized his disobedience towards God's calling and let the sailors throw him into the sea. Mather might refer here to shipwrecks to demonstrate God's judgement on all people who are disobedient to him.
[22] Referring to Hag. 2.6f.: "For thus saith the Lord of hosts; Yet once, it is a little while, and I will shake the heavens, and the earth, and the sea, and the dry land; and I will shake all nations, and the Desire of all nations shall come: and I will fill this house with glory, saith the Lord of hosts."

came into this wilderness purely upon spiritual accounts; (yea, and that continue here upon no other account) that so they might bear witness not only against the Name of the Beast,[23] and against his character, but also against his Number [... and] against all humane inventions in the worship of God [...]. God hath led us into a wilderness, and surely it was not because the Lord hated us, but because he loved us, that he brought us hither into this *Jeshimon*.[24] Who knoweth but that he may send down his spirit upon us here, if we continue faithful before him?[25] [...]

"*Consider* [...] Prayer may be a means to hasten the coming of this glorious day of *Israels* salvation." Would we not have *Sion*[26] to be delivered, and that speedily? pour forth earnest and continual prayer, and it will hasten the birth of *Sion*, that even a Nation shall be born in one day. It is prayer that sets the wheels of divine providence a going; It is prayer that turns the world upside down. Therefore you may observe, that seldom doth any great alteration of the state and face of things come to pass in the world, but the Lord first sends down a spirit of prayer into the hearts of his Saints, "and that shaketh heaven and earth in pieces in a short time." Observe then (my friends, and brethren, beloved in the Lord) and be awakened this day, I say, observe, that when the prayers of Saints ascend before the Throne of God, with the incense of the merits and intercession of the Lord Jesus, there followeth upon it *thundrings, voices, lightnings, and an earthquake, Rev.* 8.4,5. [...] Oh then pray as for your lives *all manner of prayer*, even publick prayer, family prayer[,] secret prayer; and in all stir up your selves to call upon the Lord, and say, "awake, awake, O arm of the Lord as in the days of old; awake, as in the years of ancient generations, that *Sion* may return with singing, and everlasting joy upon her head." [...] if the Lord stir up the hearts of his poor servants to favour the dust of *Sion*, and to shew it by earnest prayer before him at all times, surely the day will not be long before the Lord appear in glory to build up *Sion*, for he will have regard to the prayer of the destitute, and he will not despise their prayer. Know ye this, you servants of the Lord, to your everlasting encouragement. *But thou O Lord how long! how long! how long!*

FINIS.

Source: Increase Mather (1639-1723). *The Mystery of Israel's Salvation, Explained and Applyed: Or, a Discourse Concerning the General Conversion of the Israelitish Nation. Wherin Is Shewed, 1. That the Twelve Tribes Shall Be Saved. 2. When This Is to Be Expected. 3. Why This Must Be. 4. What Kind of Salvation the Tribes of Israel Shall Partake of (viz.) a Glorious, Wonderful, Spiritual, Temporal Salvation. Being the Substance of Several Sermons Preached.* London: John Allen, 1669, 162-164, 180-181.

---

[23] The "name of the beast" refers to Satan.
[24] Reference to Num. 21.20; wilderness.
[25] A reference to God's dealing with the nation of Israel: Num. 32.13: "The Lord's anger burned against Israel and he made them wander in the desert for forty years, until the whole generation of those who had done evil in his sight was gone."
[26] Zion is the New Jerusalem. After King David's death, his son Solomon took over Zion, which is also called "the city of David" or Jerusalem. Solomon built a glorious Temple and the city became the capital of the kingdom of Judah. When Judah turned away from God, God let the Babylonians destroy the Temple and lead Judah into exile. Years later, God let Judah return and Jerusalem and the temple were rebuild by prophets such as Nehemiah, Esra and others. Christians are called to "come unto mount Zion, and unto the city of the living God, the heavenly Jerusalem, and to an innumerable company of angels," where they will one day live eternally (Heb. 12.22). Mather here encourages Christians to pray for that day to come.

78. Increase Mather
The Day of Trouble is Near. Two Sermons Wherein Is Shewed, What Are the Signs of a Day of Trouble Being Near. And Particularly, What Reason There Is for New-England to Expect a Day of Trouble. Also What Is to Be Done, That We May Escape These Things Which Shall Come to Pass (1673)

Christian Reader,
It is a known Observation, verified by Experience, as well as grounded upon Scripture-Prediction, That sinfull Security is the great Disease of the last Times, whereunto those Churches are especially obnoxious,[27] *that have escaped the grosser Pollutions of the World and Antichrist,*[28] *and do enjoy Rest, and Peace, and Freedome from hard Bondage. Who sees not (that sees any thing) that the Security of this Age is very great? And may we not rationally fear that many of the Wise, as well as the Foolish Virgins*[29] *in this Land of Rest, and Quietness, and Fulness of Spiritual Enjoyments, are slumbering and sleeping? Consult we the Sacred Oracle, and we shall readily be informed, that one great Reason of the prevailing of this Distemper, is, because we put far from us the evil day, Amos 6.1,3.*[30] *Banishing the Thoughts of* a day of Trouble, *is both the Cause and Effect of carnal ease in Sion. How seasonable then is this practicall, solid, succinct, and comprehensive Discourse, which here offers it self to thy view, wherein the Reverend and Judicious Author demonstrates with much strength and evidence (yea, I say, gives not onely* Probable Indications, *but Scriptural and* Rational Demonstrations, *according to the Common Law of Divine Dispensations) that* a day of Trouble is near to *New England? Many are the solemn Warnings that the Lord hath given of a day of Trouble hastning upon us.* The Lion hath roared, and the Trumpet hath been blown;[31] And shall not the people be afraid? [...] *Though there are many Reasons to conceive (as the worthy Author of these Sermons intimates) that God will not make an utter End of us; yet we have cause enough to conclude, that* He will not leave us altogether unpunished. [...]
Thy servant for Christ's sake.
Urian Oakes.

---

[27] Exposed, or open *to* something actually or possibly harmful; the usual sense before the 19th century.
[28] The great antagonist expected by the early Church to cause chaos and corruption in the last days before the Second Coming.
[29] Reference to the Parable of the Wise and Foolish Virgins, Matt. 25.1-13: "Then shall the kingdom of heaven be likened unto ten virgins, which took their lamps, and went forth to meet the bridegroom. And five of them were wise, and five *were* foolish. They that *were* foolish took their lamps, and took no oil with them: but the wise took oil in their vessels with their lamps. While the bridegroom tarried, they all slumbered and slept. And at midnight there was a cry made, Behold, the bridegroom cometh; go ye out to meet him. Then all those virgins arose, and trimmed their lamps. And the foolish said unto the wise, Give us of your oil; for our lamps are gone out. But the wise answered, saying, *Not so;* lest there be not enough for us and you: but go ye rather to them that sell, and buy for yourselves. And while they went to buy, the bridegroom came; and they that were ready went in with him to the marriage: and the door was shut. Afterward came also the other virgins, saying, Lord, Lord, open to us. But he answered and said, Verily I say unto you, I know you not. Watch therefore; for ye know neither the day nor the hour wherein the Son of man cometh."
[30] "Woe to them that are at ease in Zion, and trust in the mountain of Samaria, which are named chief of the nations, to whom the house of Israel came! Pass ye unto Calneh, and see; and from thence go ye to Hamath the great: then go down to Gath of the Philistines: be they better than these kingdoms? or their border greater than your border? Ye that put far away the evil day, and cause the seat of violence to come near [...]".
[31] Reference to Judgement Day as described in the Book of Revelation.

[...] USE III. If God doth sometimes bring dayes of trouble upon his own people, here then is matter of solemn Awakening unto us; *It concerns us well to consider, whether there be not a day of trouble near unto us.* For Awakening here, I shall mention some things, which look awfully upon us. Some *Arguments* let us here take notice of, which seem to speak as if *a day of trouble* were *near unto us,* yea and *not the sounding again of the Mountains.*

1. (To begin with that which is most general) *There is a day of trouble coming upon all the World*; and such trouble too, as the like hath not been: for I am perswaded that Scripture is yet to be fulfilled, even that *Dan.* 12.1. where it is said, *There shall be a time of trouble, such as never was since there was a Nation, to that same time.* We are in expectation of glorious times, wherein Peace and Prosperity shall run down like a River, and like a mighty stream over all the earth; but immediately before those dayes, there will be such horrible Combustions[32] and Confusions, as the like never was. It is said, *Psal.* 46.9. *He maketh Wars to cease unto the end of the earth*: but the words immediately foregoing are, *Come, behold the works of the Lord, what desolations he hath made in the earth.* Before the dayes come, wherein the Nations shall learn war no more, O what desolations will the Lord make in the earth? [...]

2. *Our eyes see, and our ears hear of the beginnings of sorrows.* That which Christ spake with immediate reference to the troubles preceding the destruction of the *Jewish* Church and State, may be applied to the troubles of the last times, the former being a Type of the latter, *Matt.* 24.6,7,8. *And ye shall hear of wars, and rumours of wars, see that you be not troubled, for all these things must come to pass, but the end is not yet: for Nation shall rise against Nation, and Kingdome against Kingdome, and there shall be Famines, and Pestilences, and Earthquakes in divers places: All these are the beginnings of sorrows.* What do we hear of at this day, but Wars, and rumours of Wars? and Nation rising up against Nation, and Kingdome against Kingdome?[33] Now if these are the beginnings of sorrows, what, and where, and when will the end be? There's an overflowing scourge[34] breaking in upon the world, even a Judgement, that will not keep within ordinary banks or bounds, but shall pass over into many Lands. And how far will it go? where will the Tayle of this Storm fall at last, do we think? How if it should fall upon *America?* Will not some drops at least light upon *New-England?* We may speak in the words of the Prophet in my Text, and say, *The morning is come,* The day of trouble begins to dawn upon the world. Alas for this day, it is great, there is none like it. It is then high time for us to awake out of sleep.

3. To come nearer home; *The fatal Strokes which have been amongst us speak ominously.* Is not that a plain Scripture, *Isa.* 57.1. *The righteous is taken away from the evil to come?* The Lord hath been taking away many righteous ones from the midst of us; yea righteous ones, that should have stood in the gap, now when the waters of many Troubles are breaking in upon us, whereby he hath *made a way to his anger,* Psal. 78.50. How many Magistrates, and Ministers especially, hath the Lord bereaved us of? When Kings call home their Ambassadors, it's a sign they will proclaim War. God hath called home many of his Ambassadors of late,[35] and that's a sign that War is determined in Heaven against

---

[32] A conflagration, fire (obsolete).
[33] Increase Mather might here refer to the growing tensions between the British and the French who, with the help of Native American allies, tried to enforce their claims on Western territories.
[34] Whip or lash, here used figuratively: a thing or person that is an instrument of divine chastisement (cf. *Scourge of God = flagellum Dei*).
[35] Mather refers here to the deaths of first generation Puritans such as John Winthrop († 1649), Thomas Shepard († 1649), John Cotton († 1652), William Bradford († 1657), John Norton († 1663), John Wilson († 1667), John Davenport († 1670), Richard Bellingham († 1673).

us. [...] And I would not pass by in silence, the observable Providence of God, who hath so ordered, that many Ancient Christians have been taken away of late, as it were together. I have made some Enquiry about that matter, and finde it to be a general observation, That in many Plantations round about, in one or two years time, a great number of aged Christians have been hid in their graves. [...]

4. *There are manifold transgressions, and mighty sins amongst us.* And here if I should leave off speaking, and we should all of us joyn together in weeping and lamenting, it would be the best course that could be taken. Brethren, what shall I say? As to *matters of Religion*, things are not as should be. There is a great decay as to the power of godliness amongst us. Professors are many of them of a loose, carnal, ungirt Conversation. We can now see little difference between Church-members and other men, as to their discourses, or their spirits, or their walking, or their garb, but Professors of Religion *fashion themselves according to the world*. And what *Pride* is there? Spiritual Pride, in Parts and common Gifts of the Spirit, and in Spiritual Priviledges; yea carnal, shameful, foolish Pride, in Apparel, Fashions, and the like. Whence is all that rising up, and disobedience in Inferiours towards Superiours, in Families in Churches, and in the Commonwealth, but from the unmortified Pride which is in the hearts of the sons and daughters of men? And is there not Oppression amongst us? Are there no biting Usurers in *New-England*? Are there not those that grinde the faces of the poor? [...] *O this World! this World!* undoeth many a man, that thinks he shall go to Heaven when he dieth. And in this respect our Land is full of Idolatry. What is like to come on us? Alas! we have changed our Interest. The Interest of *New-England* was Religion, which did distinguish us from other *English Plantations*, they were built upon a Worldly design, but we upon a Religious design, when – as now we begin to spouse a Worldly Interest, and so to chuse a new God, therefore no wonder that War is like to be in the gates. I cannot but admire the Providence of God, that he should threaten to punish us with a generation of men that are notorious for that sin of Worldliness, as if the Lord would make us see what our great sin is, in the Instruments of our trouble. [...] And as for the *Children of the Covenant*, as the Scripture calls them, are not they lamentably neglected? Me-thinks it is a very solemn Providence, that the Lord should seem at this day to be *numbering many of the Rising Generation for the Sword*; as if the Lord should say, I will bring a Sword to avenge the quarrel of a *neglected Covenant*. Churches have not so performed Covenant-duties towards their Children, as should have been; and especially, the Rising Generation have many of them broken the Covenant themselves, in that they do not endeavour to come up to that which their solemn Vow in Baptism doth engage them to before the Lord, even *to know and serve the Lord God of their Fathers.*[36] Yet again, *How unfruitfull have we been under precious Means of Grace?* How hath the Lord been disappointed in his righteous and reasonable Expecta-

---

[36] Mather refers to the new policy of the "Half-Way Covenant" that was adopted by many congregations in the early 1660s. As the first generation of Puritans began to die in the mid-17th century, the Congregational churches faced a membership crisis. Full Church membership and thus full participation in the political decisions of the communities had been limited to the "Visible Saints" – those who after a public affirmation of their faith had been accepted into membership by a vote of the congregation. The churches had also provided a limited form of membership, which allowed people to be baptized, but prevented them from partaking in Communion or voting on church matters. If they could later convince the congregation of their conversion, they would be advanced to full membership. In 1662, several congregations approved the "Half-Way Covenant," designed to liberalize membership rules. Henceforth, children of church members could be baptized and, with evidence of a conversion experience, aspire to full membership. This compromise was, however, accepted only by some New England congregations. The "Half-Way Covenant" provoked much controversy and resulted in the secession of parts of the congregations that formed new independent settlements.

tions concerning us? We have not in this our day known the things that do belong unto our peace, and therefore now things look as if the dayes of our peace were ended. [...]

5. *Signs have appeared in Heaven and Earth, presaging sad Mutations to be at hand.* By *Signs*, I mean *Prodigies*, which the Scripture calls Signs. It is a celebrated Saying, *That God never brings great Judgements upon any place, but he first giveth Warning of it, by some portentous Signs.* So did the Lord deal by *Egypt* in the dayes of old: and so it was with *Jerusalem*, a few years before the *Roman* destruction. [...] Moreover, we have all seen and felt *Blazing Stars, Earthquakes, Prodigious Thunders, and Lightnings, and Tempests*. We may here make use of that Scripture, which though it have a spirituall meaning, yet some good Interpreters do not reject a literal Sense of the words, *Isa. 29.6. And thou shalt be visited of the Lord of Hosts with Thunder, and with Earthquake, and great noise, with storm, and tempest, and the flame of devouring fire.* Hath it not been so with us? We have been visited with great noise, and with the devouring flame, that is, with terrible Thunders and Lightnings, and with *Earthquakes*, which are often a Prognostick of *State-quakes*, yea and *Heart-quakes*, not far off; and with Storms and Tempests, and that too upon Lords-dayes, in a very dismall manner. Now let us not be of those, that regard not the work of the Lord, nor the operation of his hands.

6. *There is a black Cloud over our heads, which begins to drop upon us.* Providence hath so ordered, that our Enemies are come near, and may we not then think that trouble is near? The Lord hath been whetting his glittering Sword a long time; we have heard a noise, and a dismall din hath been in our ears, but now the Sword seems to be facing and marching directly towards us: yea, we see *Jerusalem* compassed about with Enemies. [...]

7. *Without doubt the Lord Jesus hath a peculiar respect unto this place, and for this people.* This is *Immanuels Land*. Christ by a wonderful Providence hath dispossessed Satan, who reigned securely in these Ends of the Earth, for Ages the Lord knoweth how many, and here the Lord hath caused as it were *New Jerusalem* to come down from Heaven; He dwels in this place: therefore we may conclude that he will scourge us for our backslidings. So doth he say, *Rev. 3.19. As many as I love, I rebuke and chasten.* It is not onely true concerning particular persons, but as to Churches, (those words were spoken to a Church) that if Christ hath a peculiar love unto them, then he will rebuke and chasten them, as there shall be cause for it. Indeed we may therefore hope that the Lord will not destroy us. Through the grace of Christ, I am not at all afraid of that. The Lord will not as yet destroy this place: Our Fathers have built Sanctuaries for his Name therein, and therefore he will not destroy us. The Planting of these Heavens, and the laying the Foundations of this Earth, is one of the Wonders of this last Age. As *Moses* said, *Ask now of the dayes that are past, ask from one side of Heaven to the other, hath God essayed to go and take him a Nation out of the midst of a Nation?* Deut. 4.32,34. God hath culled out a people, even out of all parts of a Nation, which he hath also had a great favour towards, and hath brought them by a mighty hand, and an out-stretched arm, over a greater then the Red Sea, and here hath he planted them, and hath caused them to grow up as it were into a little Nation: And shall we think that all this is to destroy them within forty or fifty years? Destruction shall not as yet be. Nevertheless, the Lord may greatly afflict us, and bring us very low. [...]

These things then are enough to awaken us out of our Security. [...]

USE IV. I conclude with a word of Exhortation. *Let us carry our selves as doth become those that have a day of trouble near unto them; yea, so as that we may prevent the troubles which seem to be near.* [...]

2. *It becometh us in such a day as this, to be a very Heavenly people.* [...]

3. *We should be a Believing people.* [...]

4. *It concerns us in this day of trouble to be a Reforming people.* Let us *amend our wayes and our doings, and the Lord will cause us to dwell in this place, Jer.7.3.* Certainly we need Reformation. Where is the old *New-England Spirit,* that once was amongst us? Where is our first love? Where is our Zeal for God, especially in matters respecting the first Table, which once was our glory? What is become of that life and power of godliness, that hath been in this place? Now if the Lord help us to reform whatever is amiss, he will still do us good, notwithstanding all our sins, which have provoked him, and caused him to frown upon us. We have a plain text for this, Jer. 18.7,8. *At what instant I shall speak concerning a Nation, and concerning a Kingdome, to pluck up, and to pull down, and to destroy it; if that Nation against whom I have pronounced, turn from their evil, then will I repent of the evil which I thought to do unto them.*

5. *It concerns us and becomes us,* now that trouble is near, *to be a United people:* otherwise our Enemies will say, that we are under a penal Infatuation. [...]

6. *We should be a Praying people, Psal.* 50.15. *Call upon me in the day of trouble.* Thus *David,* Psal. 22.11. *Be not far from me, for trouble is near.* In a time when trouble was near, he doth betake himself to God by Faith and Prayer. What people under Heaven have ever had more encouragement unto Prayer, then we have had? Know it Enemies to your terrour; Know it all the World, That the Lords poor *New-England-People,* have ever found him to be a *God that heareth Prayer:* and therefore let's be at that work still. And truly, there is as much need now as ever. We may even say, as sometimes that blessed Martyr did, *Pray, pray, pray, never more need then now.* Alas, that we are no oftener in such a solemn manner, as at this day before the Lord! We may here allude to that which is spoken, *Rev.* 8. we there reade that there was *silence in Heaven half an hour,* and then followeth *an Earthquake.* It's sad to consider, that there hath been so great a silence in Heaven amongst us: I have thought on it with some grief of heart, that there hath not been so much Fasting and Praying in *New-England* of late years, as sometimes formerly, though never so much need as now. Who knoweth, but the Lord may bring these troubles within our sight, that so we may seek him early, yea that so the Spirit of Prayer may be awakened amongst us? There are some that cannot pray, all unregenerate sinners are destitute of the Spirit of Prayer; many poor miserable Souls, that keep their Prayers and Tears till such time as they will do them no good. But I know that there are many, Scores, Hundreds here this day, that have an Interest in Heaven, and know how to improve it. Why then, up and be doing. If thou hast but one Tear in thy eyes, if thou hast but one Prayer in thy heart, spend it now. And let us remember the words of the Lord Jesus, *Luke* 21.36. *Watch ye therefore, and pray alwayes, that ye may be counted worthy to escape all these things which shall come to pass.*

FINIS.

Source: Increase Mather (1639-1723). *The Day of Trouble Is Near. Two Sermons Wherein Is Shewed, What Are the Signs of a Day of Trouble Being Near. And Particularly, What Reason There Is for New-England to Expect a Day of Trouble. Also What Is to Be Done, That We May Escape These Things Which Shall Come to Pass. Preached the 11th Day of the 12th Moneth, 1673. Being a Day of Humiliation in One of the Churches in Boston.* Cambridge: Marmaduke Johnson, 1674, n.p. ["Christian Reader ..."], 19-31.

79. Samuel Sewall
Phænomena Quædam Apocalyptica, Ad Aspectum Novi Orbis Configurata. Or, Some Few Lines towards a Description of the New Heaven as It Makes to Those Who Stand upon the New Earth (1697)

To the Honorable William Stoughton Esq.
Lieut. Governour and Commander in Chief, in and over His Majesties Province of the Massachusetts Bay in New England.

[...] *I have endeavoured to prove that* America's *Name is to be seen fairly Recorded in the Scriptures; particularly, in the Book of* Psalms, *in* Daniel, *and the* Revelation. *That* Euphrates *may be distinguished from the Sea, and from other Rivers, it ought to be limited to some proper Place; for which place, I propound the New World: as being so far from deserving the Nick names of* Gog *and* Magog; *that it stands fair for being made the Seat of the Divine Metropolis.* [...] *Another thing that seemeth probable to me, is, that the* New-English *Planters were the Forerunners of the Kings of the East; and as the Morning Star, giving certain Intelligence that the Sun of Righteousness will quickly rise and Shine with Illustrious Grace and Favour, upon this despised Hemisphere. If some Accommodations seem novel and harsh at the first view; yet I suppose, I have Mr.* Mede's *Indulgence for the producing them* [...].[37]

Some Few Lines towards a Description of the New Heaven

Not to begin to be; and so not to be limited by the concernments of *Time*, and *Place*; is the Prerogative of GOD alone. But as it is the Priviledge of Creatures, that GOD has given them a beginning: so to deny their *actions*; or *them*, the respect they bear to *Place*, and *successive duration*, is, under a pretence of Promotion, to take away their very Being. Yet notwithstanding, some Things have had this to glory of; that they have been time out of mind; and their Continuance refuses to be measured by the memory of Man. Whereas *New-England*, and *Boston* of the *Massachusets* have this to make mention of; that they can tell their Age; and account it their Honour to have their Birth, and Parentage kept in everlasting Remembrance. And in very deed, the Families, and Churches which first ventured to follow Christ thorow the *Atlantick* Ocean, into a strange Land, full of wild men, were so Religious; their End so Holy; their Selfdenyal in pursuing of it, so Extraordinary; that I can't but hope that the Plantation has thereby gaind a very strong Crasis; and that it will not be of one or two, or three Centuries only; but very long lasting. Some who peremptorily conclude that *Asia* must afford situation for *New-Jerusalem*, are of the mind, when that divine City comes to be built, the Commodities of it will be so inviting as will drain disconsolate *America* of all its Christian Inhabitants, as not able to brook so remote a distance from the beloved City. But if *Asia* should be again thus highly favored, and the eldest daughter be still made the darling; yet 'tis known there will be a River, *the Streams whereof shall make glad the City of God*. The Correspondence, and Commerce of the little cities, and villages in the three Kingdoms, and Plantations, do make LONDON glad. And so it will be with *New Jerusalem: the Nations of them which are saved, shall walk in the light of it: and the Kings of the Earth do bring their glory and honour into it.* New-Jerusalem will not straiten, and enfeeble; but wonderfully dilate, and invigorate Christianity in the several Quarters of

---

[37] Samuel Sewall here distinctly marks his treatise as a reply to and refutation of Joseph Mede's seminal exegesis of the Book of Revelation in his *Key of the Revelation* (1650; Latin version 1627) in which America was dismissed from the history of salvation as the site of Gog and Magog.

the World; in *Asia*, in *Africa*, in *Europe*, and in *America*. And one that has been born, or but liv'd in *America*, between thirty, and fourty years; it may be pardonable for him to ask, Why may not that be the place of New Jerusalem? Problematical Questions do circulate; and this was set up by Dr. *Twisse* above threescore years ago;[38] the newness of it in its return after so co[n]siderable a space of time, will, I hope, render it gratefull; or at least, will procure leave for one, with a little alteration, to enquire, Why may not *New-Spain* be the place of *New Jerusalem?* Its being part of the New World, one would think, carries with it no contradiction thereunto. Places are usually called new from the newness of their situation; and not from their being built anew; as *New-Spain*, *New-England*, *New-London*. For certain, If Mr. *Eliot*'s Opinion prove true; *viz.* that the aboriginal Natives of *America* are of *Jacob*'s Posterity, part of the long since captivated Ten Tribes; and that their Brethren the *Jews* shall come unto them: the dispute will quickly be at an end. [...] Mr. *Eliot* was wont to say The *New-English* Churches are a preface to the New Heavens: and if so, I hope the preface and Book will be bound up together, and this *Mexican* Continent shall comprehend them both. [...] Who can tell but that Christ may in this manner expose the lewd fondness of the Unholy War, and happily umpire the Difference about the holiness of Places by causing New Jerusalem to come down from God out of Heaven, upon that Earth wherein Satan, for many Ages, has peaceably possessed an entire, and far more large empire than any where else in the whole world besides? No body doubts but that our Saviour *can* enter into this strong man's house, bind him, and spoil his goods: Let us wait till He revive us by saying, I am *willing*. If I mistake not we have a warrant sufficient enough to encourage us unto a perseverance in hoping, and waiting upon God for this Salvation.

Ask of me, and I shall give thee the heathen for thine inheritance, and the Uttermost *parts of the earth for thy possession.*

Of all the parts of the world, which do from this Charter, entitle themselves to the Government of Christ, *America*'s plea, in my opinion, is the strongest. For when once *Christopher Columbus* had added this *fourth* to the other *three* parts of the foreknown World; they who sailed farther Westward, arriv'd but where they had been before. The Globe now failed of offering any thing New to the adventurous Travailer: Or however, it could not afford another new World. And probably, the consideration of *America*'s being *the Beginning of the* East, *and the End of the West*; was that which moved *Columbus* to call some part of it by the Name of *Alpha* and *Omega*. Now if the *Last ADAM* did give Order for the engraving of his own Name upon this *last Earth*: 'twill draw with it great Consequences; even such as will, in time, bring the poor *Americans* out of their Graves, and make them live. [...]

Dan. 11. 45. *And he shall plant the tabernacles of his palace between the seas in the glorious holy Mountain; yet he shall come to his end, and none shall help him.*

The complexion of this portion of Scripture is such, as constrains me to imagin, that the place designed by the Holy Spirit, is no other than *America*. Every word almost, has an emphasis carrying in it, to me, the perswasion of this sence. They who remove from one Land to another, there to dwell; that settlement of theirs is call'd a Plantation. Especially, when a Land, before rude and unfurnish'd, is by the New-comers replenished with usefull Arts, Vegetables, Animals. Thus when in the year 1492. *Christopher Columbus* had opened the way, the *Spaniards* planted themselves in the spatious Regions of *America*; and, too much, planted Antichristianisme in the room of Heathenisme. [...]

---

[38] Joseph Mede, *The Key of the Revelation*, Epist. 42, 979.

[...] The first and most, so far as I know, that hath given countenance to this Bill of Exclusion;[39] is the Conjecture of the Learned and Pious Mr. *Mede*. And therefore it may not be amiss to take a View of that Chapter entituled, DE GOGO & MAGOGO in Apocalypsi Conjectura. lib. 3. p. 713. Altho the Author be incomparably more than my Match; yet [...] Love to my Country; and the Advantage, as I apprehend, on my side, do prompt me to the Undertaking. Dr. *Twisse* in a Letter to Mr. *Joseph Mede*, dated *Ap*. 6. 1635. mentions his having written to my Lord *Say* touching his Counsels for advancing the Plantations of the *West*, and telling him, that his Lordship little thought that they tended to promote the Kingdom of *Gog* and *Magog*. My Lord in his Answer to the Doctor, gave a touch only thereupon; which was this, That surely, the *Americans* were not *Gog* and *Magog*. The Dr. writ more largely of this Subject in his next Letter. Upon this his Lordship wrote a large Letter Opposing the Conceipt of *Gog*, and *Magog*; tho the *Millennium* of Christ's Kingdom were granted [...].

[...] Dr. *Twisse* his Answer to this Letter [to Mr. Mede], bears date the 2d of *March* next following [1635]; out of which I have transcribed the Paragraph that chiefly concerns the *Conjecture*; which is as followeth; *N*OW, *I beseech you, let me know what your Opinion is of our* English *Plantations in the* New-World. *Heretofore I have wondered in my thoughts at the Providence of God concerning that World, not discovered till this Old World of ours is almost at an end: and then no footsteps found of the knowledge of the True God; much less of Christ. And then considering our* English *Plantations of late, and the Opinion of many grave Divines, concerning the Gospel's fleeting Westward: somtimes I have had such thoughts; Why may not that be the Place of NEW JERUSALEM? But you have handsomly and fully cleared me from such odd conceits. But what? I pray, shall our* English *there, degenerate and joyn themselves with* Gog *and* Magog? *We have heard lately divers ways, that our people there, have no hope of the Conversion of the Natives. And the very Week after I received your last Letter, I saw a Letter written from* New-England, *discoursing of an impossibility of subsisting there; and seems to prefer the Confession of God's Truth in any condition here in* Old England, *rather than run over to enjoy their liberty there; yea and that the Gospel is like to be more dear in* New England, *than in* Old: *and lastly, unless they be exceeding carefull, and God wonderfully mercifull; they are like to lose that life and zeal for God and his Truth, in* New England, *which they enjoyed in* Old; *as whereof they have already wofull experience, and many there feel it to their smart.* [...]

It may be hoped that Christ will be so far from quitting what He hath already got in *New England*; that He will sooner enlarge his Dominion, by bringing on a glorious Reformation in *New Spain*; and so making the New World deserve the significant Name of *Columbina* [...].

First Thoughts are sometimes the best. The Doctor had once very high Thoughts of the Gospels Enterance into *America*; which put him upon saying, Why may not that be the place of *New-Jerusalem?* And it is not altogether inconsiderable, that Mr. *Medes Clavis* was first printed in the Year, 1627. which was a notable means to revive the Thinking and Speaking of *New Jerusalem*. And this was the Year wherein the Design for planting of the Gospel in *New England*, began to be ripened. For in the Year 1628. the first Town in the *Massachusets* Bay, was begun by Mr. *John Endecott*,[40] and was called

---

[39] Sewall here deals with the concept held by many exegetes of apocalyptic prophesies that most European nations as well as the greater part of Asia, Africa, and all America must be "*Extra Ecclesiam*," i.e., excluded from the history of salvation.
[40] The following note was appended in the margins of the original text: *This was a singular Honour prepard by God for him. And when He was chosen Deputy-Gov five times & fifteen times Governour: He very honorably discharged the Trust reposed in him; & put off those Robes, & his Life together*; March 15. 1664, 65.

SALEM; which may give occasion to hope, that GOD intendeth to write upon these Churches the Name of *New Jerusalem:* They shall be near of Kin to, and shall much resemble that City of GOD.

> Source: Samuel Sewall (1652-1730). *Phænomena Quædam Apocalyptica, Ad Aspectum Novi Orbis Configurata. Or, Some Few Lines towards a Description of the New Heaven as It Makes to Those Who Stand upon the New Earth.* Boston: Bartholomew Green and John Allen, 1697, 1-5, 27, 49-51.

80. Nicholas Noyes
New-Englands Duty and Interest, to Be an Habitation of Justice, and Mountain of Holiness. [...] with Something Relating to the Restaurations, Reformations and Benedictions, Promised to the Church and World in the Latter Dayes; with Grounds of Hope, That America in General, & New-England in Particular, May Have a Part Therein (1698)

JERE. 31.23.
Thus saith the Lord of Hosts, the God of Israel, *as yet they shall use this Speech in the Land of* Judah, *and in the Cities thereof, when I shall bring again their Captivity, The Lord bless thee, O Habitation of Justice, and Mountain of Holiness.*

We are here presented with a comfortable Vision in the Prophesies of *Jeremiah*, the man who for the most part was filled with bitterness, and had his Pen dipped in waters of Gall, that like a *Comet* foretold the fates of Kings and Kingdoms, that denounced Sword, Famine, Pestilence, Captivity, and such like Judgments against *Judah*, for their Apostacy, Impiety, Iniquity, Impenitency, and Incorrigibleness, and made the Cup of Divine Fury to go round among the Nations, he hath now and then a little sweetning put into his mouth, for his own and the Churches Consolation [...].

[...] *God was in Christ reconciling the World unto himself, not imputing to them their trespasses*; and some of the Blessings promised, were the manifestation of the New Covenant, the Gathering and Enlarging the Catholick Church, writing the Law in the heart &c. which the Apostle to the Hebrews refers to Gospel times. *Heb.* 8.10. 11.12. And the whole by way of *Analogy* and just accommod[a]tion may be referred to Kingdoms, Countries & Places, Nations professing the Christian Religion; thus the New Testament teacheth us to interpret, accommodate and apply to our selves, Texts of the Old Testament. See Rom. 15.4. *For whatsoever things were written aforetime were written for our Learning, that we through patience and comfort of the Scriptures might have hope.* So 1 Co. 10.11. *Now all these things hapned unto them for ensamples, and are written for our instruction on whom the ends of the world are come.* So also 2 Tim. 3.16. *All Scripture is given by inspiration of God, and is profitable for Doctrine, for Reproof, for Correction, for Instruction in righteousness.* Thus having shewed how this text that nextly concerned the Jews comes to affect us, and concern these last ages of the professing world: I shall only for further Explication of the Text, shew what intended by Justice, what by a Habitation of Justice, and then what by Holiness, and what by a Mountain of Holiness; and then proceed to give you the Doctrines. [...]

Q. What [is] intended by a Mountain of Holiness?

A. As it respects *Jerusalem*, it meaneth that it should regain its ancient purity, and be as renowned for *Holiness* as ever it was; that had not only been beautiful for its *Situation*, but for its *Sanctification* wherein not only *Holy men* had dwelt, but the *Holy God*; [...]. When it is applyed to Christian Countries, it means that they should abound in holiness, and excel other places therein, as much as *Judea* did other lands, and *Jerusalem* did other Cities in the day that they were *Holiness to the Lord*. So you have the meaning of the Text, & its words & phrases, both in the literal sence as it nextly concern'd the Jews, and also in its *Analogical sense*, as it concerns Christians of all Kingdoms and Plantations to the end of the world. We come now to the Doctrines that result from the Text thus explained, which are three. The first from the doctrinal hints in the Text: the second from the historical hints: the third from the Text as it is a Prophecy.

DOCT. *I. That it is the duty of all People or Places professing the Christian Religion, to abound and excel in Holiness and Righteousness: or to be an Habitation of Righteousness, and Mountain of Holiness.*

DOCT. II. *That such People and Places as profess the Christian Religion, may expect to be Happy or Miserable, according as it goeth with them, as to Holiness and Righteousness.*

DOCT. III. *That although Places that have been Habitations of Righteousness and Mountains of Holiness, should become very degenerate, and for their Sin be made very desolate; yet there is ground of hope that God will again Restore, Reform and Bless them.*

The first DOCTRINE Confirm'd by Reasons. [...]

1. The first Planters of the Israelitish Vineyard, or the first Plants therein, were *a noble Vine, a right Seed*. Jer. 2.21. The twelve *Patriarchs*, were all Godly, and God led them like a flock by the hand of *Moses* and *Aaron*. *Israel* was Holiness to the Lord. So the first Undertakers, Planters; the Foundation men of *New England* were *Holiness to the Lord*; though not *universally*, yet *generally* so; This Land was planted with *choice Vines*; Men Eminent in Piety, and Vertue; that Served God and their Generation, according to the Will of God.

2. The great End for which Israel went into the Wilderness, and the Land of *Canaan*, was that they might Worship God according to his own *Institution* with more *purity*, and *less peril*, than they could do in the Countrey where they were. Exod. 8.1. *Let my people go that they may Serve me*. Exod. 8.27. *We will go three days Journey into the Wilderness, and Sacrifice to the Lord our God, as He shall command us*. [...] Even so was the Design of our Predecessors in coming more than three days Journey, *viz*. three thousand miles into this Wilderness, that they might Serve God with pure Worship according to his own Institution, without offence to others; and with more liberty and safety to themselves, than at that time could be had in their own Countrey. The World knows, that our Predecessors did not leave their Native Soil, that *dulce solum Patriam*,[41] for better Accommodations in wordly respects; they did not come into the *Wilderness* for *Worldliness*; but for *Godliness* sake: and that the first Rulers & Teachers, and Churches had the Glory of God, and the liberty and purity of his Worship in their Eye. And their Memory will be precious in Ages to come [...].

3. As the *Israelites* underwent many hazards & hardships in that Enterprize, and had special assistance, preservation, provision and protection from the good Providence of God, that was very peculiar about them for good: So did the first Comers into *New-England* run many great risks, and grapple with many difficulties; both of Sea and Land (too many to enumerate) in all which, the good Providence of God was very circum-

---

[41] Latin: "Only one's homeland is sweet."

spect about them, in sending suitable and seasonable succours and supplies. *They cried to the Lord in their troubles, and he saved them out of their distresses*; as the brief Histories of *New-Englands* Affairs show.

4. As God made room for the *Israelitish* Vine, and caused it to take root, and spread and flourish, *so that its boughs went to the Sea, and its branches by the rivers, its Shade covered hills*. Whilst Religion and Righteousness flourisht among them, they were both numerous and prosperous. And so it was in *New England* in a good degree, God blessed them and caused them to multiply greatly. No Out going of the *English* Nation, for the time, can compare with it.

5. As there grew declension and degeneration among that people, notwithstanding all God had done for them, and notwithstanding all done for maintaining and transmitting pure Religion to succeeding Generations: so hath it befallen *New-England*. [...]

6. As they chang'd their ways from Good to Evil, and walkt contrary to God; so God chang'd his ways, from ways of Mercy, to ways of Affliction; and walkt contrary to them. And as was threatned, *did them evil after that he had done them good*. So hath it also been with us. As for our Degeneracy, it is too *palpable* to be denied; and too *gross* to be excused. It calls for *Lamentation*, *Humiliation*, and *Reformation*, rather than proof and demonstration; though that also be needful enough in order to the former. [...]

[... N]otwithstanding the present bad circumstances of *America*, I know no reason to conclude this Continent shall not partake of the *Goodness of God in the latter days*; [42] nor why the *Sun of Righteousness* may not go round the Earth, as the Sun in the Firmament doth go round Heaven. No Scripture asserts the *contrary*: but many seem to favour the *Affirmative*. I suppose that Christ is not called the *Sun of Righteousness*, meerly because of his *Light*, and *Heat*, and *quickening vivisick Influences*, but also because of his *Circuition* or *Circuit* round the World, by the Preaching of the Gospel; and his expanding and extending his saving Virtue to those that *Sit in darkness, and in the Region and shadow of Death*. [...] Methinks men should not be hasty to Reprobat a Fourth Part of the World, without Express Order from Heaven. I know not how it came to pass, that Conjectures about *America* have been so various, strange and uncomfortable; as to its Rise, State, and final Destiny. *Burnet* M.D.[43] affirms that the *Americans*, in their Progenitors, came not out of the Ark; that their Progenitors descended not from *Noah*. And indeed they are beholden to him, that he let them descend from *Adam*; and did not bring them out of the Slime, as he doth *Gog* and *Magog*. But it is enough to reply to this, that it is not only *Unscriptural*, but also *Antiscriptural*. A late Annotator on the Bible (who is otherwise a very worthy man; but I think, misses it in this) in his Preface to the New Testament, in the separate Edition, alloweth the *Americans* to be descended of *Noah*; but by *Cham*: and thence gathers that they shall not be gathered into the Church. [...] Certainly it is not reasonable to draw so hard a Conclusion on such a Text, that admits of such and so many various Interpretations: Seeing it tends to discourage all Endeavours for the Conversion of the *Indians*; and so may greatly prejudice the Souls of Millions of Men, and hinder the inlargement of the Kingdom of Christ. [...] Nor can I, possibly, otherwise understand Christ's Commission to his Apostles, and their Successors in the Ministry. *Mark* 16.15. *Go ye into All*

---

[42] Pertaining to the end of the world and Christ's Second Coming.
[43] Thomas Burnet (1635-1715), English divine who published his famous *Telluris Theoria Sacra* in 1681 (engl. translation: *Sacred Theory of the Earth*, 1729). This work contains a theory of the earth's structure in which he attempts to reconcile the Biblical account of creation, paradise and the deluge with scientific principles.

the World, and Preach the Gospel to Every Creature. Matt. 28. 19,20. *Go ye therefore, and teach All Nations &c and lo, I am with you alway[s] unto the End of the World;* Which seemeth as plain as words can make it, that whatsoever Nation, or Nations shall be discovered to the End of the World, they are to be *Evangelized*, and *Baptised*. [...]

Others have *conjectured* that *America* will be the head Quarters of *Gog* and *Magog*; and that it will be *Hell* it self. This is worse and worse still! But may be something alleviated by an opposite *Conjecture*. For there are Others that ask why it may not be the *New Jerusalem*, or a part of it? and this *New World* that is Under the Eastern Earth, be the *New Heaven*, and *New Earth*. These Opinions are as wide from one another, as Heaven is from Hell. I count it sufficient to set them one against the other; without saying which is widest from the Truth. Only, Who of an *American* (though only so *Natione, non gente*) had not much rather (if it may stand with the Counsel of God) that it should be the *New Jerusalem*, than the *Old Tophet*.[44] Known unto God are all his Works from the beginning of the World: And He that made this *New World*, knoweth *why* He made it, and what to do with it; though men do not. It is certain, Antichrist boasted in his *American* ΕΥΡΗΚΑ,[45] and Conquest, when he began to be routed in *Europe*, by the Reformation. And who can blame him to provide a *New World* against [the loss of] his *Old One*. But the Son of GOD followed him at the heels, and took Possession of *America* for Himself. And this Province, so far as I know, is the very *Turf* and *Twig*.[46] He took Possession by; as to the Reformation and Conversion of the *Natives*, and gathering of them into Churches. And I am not without Hope, but that He will hold his Possession; not only to the end of *this* World, but to the end of *the* World: if there be a difference; as there may be for ought I know to the contrary. [...]

Now as for *New England*, if the *First Planters* of it had dream'd that the very Situation or Climate of this Land had been crime enough to make men *aliens from the Covenants of promise*; they would not have Sold their *European Birthright*, for a mess of *American Pottage*.[47] For ought I can see to the contrary, our *Declensions* are the *worst Omen* and *Objection* against us; and *Reformation* would be the best *Answer* to them: and Hope and Prayer are powerful helps and inducements to it. [...] yet there is Scripture ground to hope, that after God had vindicated his Holiness by sore punishments on us, God would again *restore, reform* and *bless New-England*; and have a name, and a praise to himself, in the *Wilderness*, of the *Posterity of his People*. [...]

Finally, be ye *followers of God as dear Children*, in Holiness, Righteousness and Charity. *Love as Brethren*, yea *as holy Brethren partakers of the Heavenly Calling; Love one another; Care for one another, and the things each of other; Admonish one another, Exhort one another, Forgive one another, Pray for one another.* Let all Ranks and Orders of men seek the Increase and Advancement of *Holiness* and *Righteousness*;
    and mourn for, and turn from, and seek the pardon of all our *Unholiness*
    and *Unrighteousness*, and that through the plentiful Effusion of the
        Holy Spirit; *the Skyes may as it were pour down, and Shower
           down Holiness and Righteousness*; that this Land may
                be an Habitation of Righteousness
                      and Mountain of
                          Holiness.

---

[44] Place near Jerusalem associated with the worship of Molech. Tophet became a name for hell.
[45] Eureka: "I have found it;" a discovery justifying self-congratulation.
[46] A piece of sod cut from the turf of an estate as a token or symbol of possession.
[47] A dish or soup composed of vegetables; often used to refer to primitive peoples' soup.

Source: Nicholas Noyes (1647-1717). *New-Englands Duty and Interest, to Be an Habitation of Justice, and Mountain of Holiness. Containing Doctrine, Caution & Comfort with Something Relating to the Restaurations, Reformations and Benedictions, Promised to the Church and World in the Latter Dayes; with Grounds of Hope, That America in General, & New-England in Particular, May Have a Part Therein. Preached to the General Assembly of the Province of the Massachusetts-Bay, at the Anniversary Election. May, 25. 1698*. Boston: Bartholomew Green and John Allen, 1698, 1-2, 6-7, 9-10, 45-48, 68-72, 74-77, 87-88.

81. Cotton Mather
"Venisti tandem? Or Discoveries of America, Tending to, and Ending in, Discoveries of New-England" (1702)

CHAP. I.

Venisti tandem? [Hast thou come at last] *Or Discoveries of* AMERICA, *tending to, and ending in, Discoveries of* NEW-ENGLAND.

[...] §. 2. If the *Wicked One in whom the whole World lyeth*, were *he*, who like a *Dragon*, keeping a Guard upon the spacious and mighty *Orchards* of *America*, could have such a *Fascination* upon the Thoughts of Mankind, that neither this *Ballancing half* of the Globe should be considered in *Europe* till a little more than two Hundred Years ago [...]; yet the over-ruling *Providence* of the *great God* is to be acknowledged, as well in the *Concealing* of *America* for so long a time, as in the *Discovering* of it, when the fulness of Time was come for the Discovery: For we may count *America* to have been concealed, while Mankind in the other *Hemisphere* had lost all Acquaintance with it, if we may conclude it had any from the Words of *Diodorus Siculus*,[48] That *Phœnecians* were by great Storms driven off the Coast of *Africa*, far *Westward* [...] *for many Days together*, and at last fell in with an Island of prodigious Magnitude;[49] or from the Words of *Plato*, that beyond the Pillars of *Hercules*[50] there was an Island in the *Atlantick Ocean* [...] *larger than* Africa *and* Asia *put together*: Nor should it pass without Remark, that *Three* most memorable things which have born a very great Aspect upon *Humane Affairs*, did near the same time, namely at the Conclusion of the *Fifteenth*, and the beginning of the *Sixteenth Century*, arise unto the World: The First was the *Resurrection of Literature*; the Second was the opening of *America*; the Third was the *Reformation* of *Religion*. But, as probably, the *Devil* seducing the first Inhabitants of *America* into it, therein aimed at the having of them and their Posterity out of the sound of the *Silver Trumpets* of the *Gospel*, then to be heard through the *Roman Empire*; if the *Devil* had any Expectation, that by the Peopling of *America*, he should utterly deprive any *Europeans* of the Two Benefits, *Literature* and *Religion*, which dawned upon the miserable World, one just *before*, t'other just *after*, the first famed *Navigation* hither, 'tis to be hop'd he will be disappointed of that Expectation. The *Church* of God must no longer be wrapp'd up in *Strabo's* Cloak:[51] *Geography* must now find work for a *Christianog-*

---

[48] Greek historian, the author of a universal history, *Bibliotheca historica*.
[49] The reference probably is to the mythical Atlantis.
[50] Rock of Gibraltar.
[51] Strabo, Greek geographer and historian whose *Geography* is the only extant work covering the whole range of peoples and countries known to both Greeks and Romans during the reign of Augustus (27 BC–14 AD). Strabo believed that it would be possible to sail around the globe from Spain to India. The reference to Strabo's cloak implies that the Greek geographer imagined the habitable portion of the earth as an island in the shape of a military cloak.

raphy in Regions far enough beyond the Bounds wherein the *Church* of God had thro' all former Ages been circumscribed. [...]

This at last is the Spot of *Earth*, which the God of Heaven *Spied out* for the Seat of such *Evangelical*, and *Ecclesiastical*, and very remarkable Transactions, as require to be made an *History*; here 'twas that our Blessed *Jesus* intended a *Resting-place*, must I say? Or only an *Hiding-place* for those *Reformed* CHURCHES, which have given him a little Accomplishment of his Eternal Father's Promise unto him; to be, we hope, yet further accomplished, *of having the utmost Parts of the Earth for his Possession?*

§. 7. The Learned *Joseph Mede*[52] conjectures that the *American Hemisphere* will escape the *Conflagration*[53] of the *Earth*, which we expect at the descent of our Lord JESUS CHRIST from *Heaven*: And that the People here will not have a share in the Blessedness which the *Renovated World* shall enjoy, during the *Thousand Years* of *Holy Rest* promised unto the Church of God: And that the Inhabitants of these Regions, who were Originally *Scytheans*,[54] and therein a notable fulfilment of the Prophecy, about the *Enlargement of* Japhet,[55] will be the *Gog* and *Magog*[56] whom the *Devil* will seduce to Invade the *New-Jerusalem*, with an Envious Hope to gain the *Angelical Circumstances* of the People there. All this is but Conjecture; and it may be 'twill appear unto some as little probable, as that of the later *Pierre Poiret* in his *L'Oeconomy Divine*,[57] that by *Gog* and *Magog* are meant the *Devils* and the *Damned*, which he thinks will be let loose at the end of the *Thousand Years*, to make a furious, but a fruitless Attempt on the glorified Saints of the *New-Jerusalem*. However, I am going to give unto the *Christian Reader* an *History* of *some feeble Attempts* made in the *American Hemisphere* to anticipate the State of the *New-Jerusalem*, as far as the unavoidable *Vanity* of *Humane Affairs*, and *Influence* of *Satan* upon them would allow of it; and of *many worthy Persons*, whose Posterity, if they make a *Squadron* in the *Fleets* of *Gog* and *Magog*, will be *Apostates*[58] deserving a Room, and a Doom with the *Legions* of the *Grand Apostate*, that will deceive the Nations to that *Mysterious Enterprize*.

Source: Cotton Mather (1663-1728). "Book I, Chap. I. Venisti tandem? Or Discoveries of America, Tending to, and Ending in, Discoveries of New-England." *Magnalia Christi Americana: Or, the Ecclesiastical History of New England, from Its First Planting in the Year 1620. unto the Year of Our Lord, 1698. In Seven Books.* London: Thomas Parkhurst, 1702, 2, 4-5.

---

[52] 17th-century Anglican biblical scholar, who was the pioneer in millennialism and wrote an extensive exegesis of the Book of Revelation (*The Key of Revelation*, Latin version 1627, English translation 1650). Ignoring the allegorical interpretation long associated with the book, Mead took a fresh look at the text of Revelation. He concluded that the Scriptures held the promise of a literal Kingdom of God.
[53] Burning up.
[54] The Scythians set themselves up as rulers of an empire stretching from west Persia through Syria and Judaea to the borders of Egypt.
[55] Japheth, Noah's three sons, Shem, Ham, and Japheth were the ancestors of three of the races of mankind. Japhet stands for the people of Europe.
[56] Gog, in the Bible, a hostile power that is ruled by Satan and will manifest itself immediately before the end of the world (Rev. 20). In the biblical passage in Revelation and in other Christian and Jewish apocalyptic literature, Gog is joined by a second hostile force, Magog; but elsewhere (Ezek. 38; Gen. 10.2) Magog is apparently the place of Gog's origin.
[57] Dutch mystic (1646-1719) who in his *L' oeconomie divine, ou systéme universel et démontré des oeuvres & de desseins de dieu envers les hommes* (Amsterdam: Wetstein, 1687) propounded the view that God deals with his people on earth under seven dispensations (or economies) between creation and the end of the Millennium.
[58] A person unfaithful to religious principles or creed, or to moral allegiance; renegade, infidel, rebel.

82. Jonathan Edwards
Some Thoughts Concerning the Present Revival of Religion in New-England (1742)

[...] 'Tis not unlikely that this Work of God's Spirit, that is so extraordinary and wonderful, is the dawning, or, at least, a Prelude of that glorious Work of God, so often foretold in Scripture, which in the Progress and Issue of it, shall renew the World of Mankind. If we consider how long since, the Things foretold, as what should preceed this great Event, have been accomplished; and how long this Event has been expected by the Church of God, and thought to be nigh by the most eminent Men of God in the Church; and withal consider what the State of Things now is, and has for a considerable Time been, in the Church God, and World of Mankind, we can't reasonably think otherwise, than that the Beginning of this great Work of God must be near. And there are many Things that make it probable that this Work will begin in *America*. 'Tis signified that it shall begin in some very remote Part of the World, that the rest of the World have no Communication with but by Navigation, in Isai. 60.9. *Surely the Isles shall wait for me, and the Ships of* Tarshish[59] *first, to bring my Sons from far*. It is exceeding manifest that this Chapter is a Prophecy of the Prosperity of the Church, in its most glorious State on Earth, in the latter Days; and I can't think that any Thing else can be here intended but *America* by the Isles that are far off, from whence the First-born Sons of that glorious Day shall be brought. [...] And what is chiefly intended is not the *British* Isles, nor any Isles near the other Continent; for they are spoken of as at a great Distance from that Part of the World where the Church had 'till then been. This Prophecy therefore seems plainly to point out *America*, as the first Fruits of that glorious Day.

GOD has made as it were two Worlds here below, The old and the new, (according to the Names they are now called by,) two great habitable Continents, far separated one from the other; The latter is but newly discover'd, it was formerly wholly unknown, from Age to Age, and is as it were now but newly created: It has been, 'till of late, wholly the Possession of *Satan*, the Church of GOD having never been in it, as it has been in the other Continent, from the beginning of the World. This new World is probably now discovered, that the new and most glorious State of GOD'S Church on Earth might commence there; That GOD might in it begin a new World in a spiritual Respect, when he creates the *new Heavens* and *new Earth*.

GOD has already put that Honour upon the other Continent, that CHRIST was born there literally, and there made the *Purchase of Redemption*: So, as Providence observes a Kind of equal Distribution of Things, 'tis not unlikely that the great spiritual Birth of CHRIST, and the most glorious *Application of Redemption* is to begin in this: [...].

The old Continent has been the Source and Original of Mankind, in several Respects. The first Parents of Mankind dwelt there; and there dwelt *Noah* and his Sons; and there the second *Adam* was born, and was crucified and rose again: and 'tis probable that, in some Measure to balance these Things, the most glorious Renovation of

---

[59] Tarshish, a Sanscrit or Aryan word, meaning "sea coast." The question as to the locality of Tarshish has given rise to various interpretations. Some think there was a Tarshish in the East, on the Indian coast, some argue that Carthage or a Phoenician port in Spain was the place so named. It was to this port that Jonah's ship was about to sail from Joppa. It appears, however, that the name was also used without reference to any locality. "Ships of Tarshish" could thus be an expression denoting ships intended for a long voyage.

the World shall originate from the new Continent, and the Church of GOD in that Respect be from hence. [...]

And 'tis worthy to be noted that *America* was discovered about the Time of the Reformation, or but little before: Which Reformation was the first Thing that GOD did towards the glorious Renovation of the World, after it had sunk into the Depths of Darkness and Ruin, under the great Antichristian Apostacy.[60] So that as soon as this new World is (as it were) created, and stands forth in View, GOD presently goes about doing some great Thing to make Way for the Introduction of the Churches Latter-Day Glory, that is to have its first Seat in, and is to take its Rise from that new World.

[...] When GOD is about to turn the Earth into a Paradi[s]e, he don't begin his Work where there is some good Growth already, but in a Wilderness, where nothing grows, and nothing is to be seen but dry Sand and barren Rocks; that the Light may shine out of Darkness, and the World be replenished from Emptiness, and the Earth watered by Springs from a droughty Desart [...].

I observed before, that when GOD is about to do some great Work for his Church, his Manner is to begin at the lower End; so when he is about to renew the whole habitual Earth, 'tis probable that he will begin in this utmost, meanest, youngest and weakest Part of it, where the Church of GOD has been planted last of all; and so the First shall be the last and the Last first [...].

And if we may suppose that this glorious Work of God shall begin in any Part of *America*, I think, if we consider the Circumstances of the Settlement of *New-England*, it must needs appear the most likely of all *American* Colonies, to be the Place whence this Work shall principally take [its] Rise.

And if these Things are so, it gives us more abundant Reason to hope that what is now seen in *America*, and especially in *New-England*, may prove the Dawn of that glorious Day: And the very uncommon & wonderful Circumstances and Events of this Work, seem to me strongly to argue that God intends it as the Beginning or Forerunner of some Thing vastly great. [...]

Source: Jonathan Edwards (1703-1758). *Some Thoughts Concerning the Present Revival of Religion in New-England, and the Way in Which It Ought to Be Acknowledged and Promoted: Humbly Offered to the Publick, in a Treatise on That Subject: In Five Parts; Part I. Shewing That the Work That Has of Late Been Going on in This Land, Is a Glorious Work of God. Part II. Shewing the Obligations That All Are Under, to Acknowlege [sic], Rejoice in and Promote This Work, and the Great Danger of the Contrary. Part III. Shewing in Many Instances, Wherein the Subjects, or Zealous Promoters, of This Work Have Been Injuriously Blamed. Part IV. Shewing What Things Are to Be Corrected or Avoided, in Promoting This Work, or in Our Behaviour under It. Part V. Shewing Positively What Ought to Be Done to Promote This Work.* Boston: S. Kneeland and T. Green, 1742, 96-98, 100-102, 104.

---

[60] Abandonment of one's belief.

83. Philip Freneau
A Poem, on the Rising Glory of America (1772)

[...] ACASTO.
  This is a land where the more noble light
Of holy revelation beams, the star
Which rose from Judah lights our skies, we feel
Its influence as once did Palestine
And Gentile lands, where now the ruthless Turk
Wrapt up in darkness sleeps dull life away.
Here many holy messengers of peace
As burning lamps have given light to men.
To thee, O Whitefield![61] favourite of Heav'n,
The muse would pay the tribute of a tear.
Laid in the dust thy eloquence no more
Shall charm the list'ning soul, no more
Thy bold imagination paint the scenes
Of woe and horror in the shades below;
Or glory radiant in the fields above;
No more thy charity relieve the poor;
Let Georgia mourn, let all her orphans weep. [...]

          EUGENIO.
  For him we found the melancholy lyre,
The lyre responsive to each distant sigh;
No grief like that which mourns departing souls
Of holy, just and venerable men,
Whom pitying Heav'n sends from their native skies
To light our way and bring us nearer God.
But come Leander since we know the past
And present glory of this empire wide,
What hinders to pervade with searching eye
The mystic scenes of dark futurity?
Say shall we ask what empires yet must rise
What kingdoms pow'rs and states where now are seen
But dreary wastes and awful solitude,
Where melancholy sits with eye forlorn
And hopes the day when Britain's sons shall spread
Dominion to the north and south and west
Far from th' Atlantic to Pacific shores?
A glorious theme, but how shall mortals dare
To pierce the mysteries of future days,
And scenes unravel only known to fate.

---

[61] Reference to George Whitefield who was born in Gloucester in 1714 and appointed minister at Savannah, Georgia, in 1738. He returned to England but decided to go back to Georgia where he made extensive preaching tours during the Great Awakening. Whitefield made the last of his seven evangelistic visits to America in 1769; he died near Boston in 1770.

ACASTO.
This might we do if warm'd by that bright coal
Snatch'd from the altar of seraphic fire,
Which touch'd Isaiah's lips,[62] or if the spirit
Of Jeremy and Amos, prophets old,
Should fire the breast; but yet I call the muse
And what we can will do. I see, I see
A thousand kingdoms rais'd, cities and men
Num'rous as sand upon the ocean shore;
Th' Ohio then shall glide by many a town
Of note: and where the Missisippi stream
By forests shaded now runs weeping on
Nations shall grow and states not less in fame
Than Greece and Rome of old: we too shall boast
Our Alexanders, Pompeys, heroes, kings
That in the womb of time yet dormant lye
Waiting the joyful hour for life and light.
O snatch us hence, ye muses! to those days
When, through the veil of dark antiquity,
Our sons shall hear of us as things remote,
That blossom'd in the morn of days, alas!
How could I weep that we were born so soon,
In the beginning of more happy times!
But yet perhaps our fame shall last unhurt.
The sons of science nobly scorn to die
Immortal virtue this denies, the muse
Forbids the men to slumber in the grave
Who well deserve the praise that virtue gives.

EUGENIO.
'Tis true no human eye can penetrate
The veil obscure, and in fair light disclos'd
Behold the scenes of dark futurity;
Yet if we reason from the course of things,
And downward trace the vestiges of time,
The mind prophetic grows and pierces far
Thro' ages yet unborn. We saw the states
And mighty empires of the East arise
In swift succession from the Assyrian
To Macedon and Rome; to Britain thence
Dominion drove her car, she stretch'd her reign
O'er many isles, wide seas, and peopled lands.
Now in the West a continent appears;

---

[62] Cf. Isa. 6.5-8, reporting Isaiah's calling as a prophet: "Then said I, Woe *is* me! for I am undone; because I *am* a man of unclean lips, and I dwell in the midst of a people of unclean lips: for mine eyes have seen the King, the Lord of hosts. Then flew one of the seraphim unto me, having a live coal in his hand, *which* he had taken with the tongs from off the altar: and he laid *it* upon my mouth, and said, Lo, this hath touched thy lips; and thine iniquity is taken away, and thy sin purged. Also I heard the voice of the Lord, saying, Whom shall I send, and who will go for us? Then said I, Here *am* I; send me."

A newer world now opens to her view;
She hastens onward to th' Americ shores
And bids a scene of recent wonders rise.
New states new empires and a line of kings,
High rais'd in glory, cities, palaces
Fair domes on each long bay, sea, shore or stream
Circling the hills now rear their lofty heads. [...]
To mighty nations shall the people grow
Which cultivate the banks of many a flood,
In chrystal currents poured from the hills
Apalachia nam'd, to lave the lands
Of California, Georgia, and the plains
Stretch'd out from thence far to the burning Line [...].

LEANDER.
And here fair freedom shall forever reign.
I see a train, a glorious train appear,
Of Patriots plac'd in equal fame with those
Who nobly fell for Athens or for Rome.
The sons of Boston resolute and brave
The firm supporters of our injur'd rights,
Shall lose their splendours in the brighter beams
Of patriots fam'd and heroes yet unborn.

ACASTO.
'Tis but the morning of the world with us
And Science yet but sheds her orient rays.
I see the age the happy age roll on
Bright with the splendours of her mid-day beams,
I see a Homer and a Milton rise
In all the pomp and majesty of song,
Which gives immortal vigour to the deeds
Atchiev'd by Heroes in the fields of fame. [...]

LEANDER.
From Alleghany[63] in thick groves imbrown'd,
Sweet music breathing thro' the shades of night
Steals on my ear, they sing the origin
Of those fair lights which gild the firmament;
From whence the gale that murmurs in the pines;
Why flows the stream down from the mountains brow
And rolls the ocean lower than the land.
They sing the final destiny of things,
The great result of all our labours here,
The last day's glory, and the world renew'd.
Such are their themes for in these happier days
The bard enraptur'd scorns ignoble strains,

---

[63] Mountainous eastern part of the Allegheny Plateau in the Appalachian Mountains.

Fair science smiling and full truth revealed,
The world at peace, and all her tumults o'er,
The blissful prelude to Emanuel's reign.[64]

EUGENIO.
  And when a train of rolling years are past,
(So sang the exil'd seer in Patmos isle,)[65]
A new Jerusalem sent down from heav'n
Shall grace our happy earth, perhaps this land,
Whose virgin bosom shall then receive, tho' late,
Myriads of saints with their almighty king,
To live and reign on earth a thousand years
Thence call'd Millennium. Paradise a new
Shall flourish, by no second Adam lost.
No dang'rous tree or deathful fruit shall grow,
No tempting serpent to allure the soul,
From native innocence; a Canaan here
Another Canaan shall excel the old
And from fairer Pisgah's top be seen,[66]
No thistle here or briar or thorn shall spring
Earth's curse before: the lion and the lamb
In mutual friendship link'd shall browse the shrub,
And tim'rous deer with rabid tygers stray
O'er mead or lofty hill or grassy plain.
Another Jordan's stream shall glide along
And Siloah's[67] brook in circling eddies flow,
Groves shall adorn their verdant banks, on which
The happy people free from second death
Shall find secure repose; no fierce disease
No fevers, slow consumption, direful plague
Death's ancient ministers, again renew
Perpetual war with man: Fair fruits shall bloom
Fair to the eye, sweet to the taste, is such
Divine inhabitants could need the taste
Of elemental food, amid the joys
Fit for a heav'nly nature. Music's charms
Shall swell the lofty soul and harmony
Triumphant reign; thro' ev'ry grove shall sound
The cymbal and the lyre, joys too divine
For fallen man to know. Such days the world
And such America thou first shall have
When ages yet to come have run their round
And future years of bliss alone remain.

---

[64] Jesus Christ; cf. Isa. 7.14.
[65] Reference to the visionary St. John who wrote the Book of Revelation on the island of Patmos; cf. Rev. 1.9.
[66] After Moses had renewed the Sinai Covenant with the survivors of the wanderings in the desert, he climbed Mount Pisgah to look over the 'promised' land.
[67] Shiloh, generally understood as denoting the Messiah, "the peaceful one," as the word signifies (Gen. 49.10). Shiloh, also a place of rest, a city of Ephraim. Here the tabernacle was set up after the Conquest.

ACASTO.
> This is thy praise America thy pow'r
> Thou best of climes by science visited
> By freedom blest and richly stor'd with all
> The luxuries of life. Hail happy land
> The seat of empire the abode of kings,
> The final stage where time shall introduce
> Renowned characters, and glorious works
> Of high invention and of wond'rous art,
> Which not the ravages of time shall waste
> Till he himself has run his long career;
> Till all those glorious orbs of light on high
> The rolling wonders that surround the ball,
> Drop from their spheres extinguish'd and consum'd;
> When final ruin with her fiery car
> Rides o'er creation, and all nature's works
> Are lost in chaos and the womb of night.
>
> FINIS.

Source: Philip Freneau (1752-1832). *A Poem, on the Rising Glory of America; Being an Exercise Delivered at the Public Commencement at Nassau-Hall, September 25, 1771*. Philadelphia: Joseph Crukshank, 1772, 19-27. The text of the poem is attributed to Henry H. Brackenridge (1748-1816) as joint-author, as it was recited by him at their graduation from the College of New Jersey.

84. Timothy Dwight
America, or, a Poem on the Settlement of the British Colonies; Addressed to the Friends of Freedom, and Their Country (1780?)

> [...] O Land supremely blest! to thee tis given
> To taste the choicest joys of bounteous heaven;
> Thy rising Glory shall expand its rays,
> And lands and times unknown rehearse thine endless praise. [...]
> "Hail Land of light and joy! thy power shall grow
> Far as the seas, which round thy regions flow;
> Through earth's wide realms thy glory shall extend,
> And savage nations at thy scepter bend. [...]
> Earth's richest realms their treasures shall unfold,
> And op'ning mountains yield the flaming gold;
> Round thy broad fields more glorious ROMES arise,
> With pomp and splendour bright'ning all the skies;
> EUROPE and ASIA with surprise behold
> Thy temples starr'd with gems and roof'd with gold. [...]
> "Then, then an heavenly kingdom shall descend,
> And Light and Glory through the world extend;
> Th' Almighty Saviour his great power display
> From rising morning to the setting day;
> Love reign triumphant, Fraud and Malice cease,

And every region smile in endless peace:
Till the last trump[68] the slumbering dead inspire,
Shake the wide heavens, and set the world on fire;
Thron'd on a flaming cloud, with brightness crown'd,
The Judge descend, and angels shine around,
The mountains melt, the moon and stars decay,
The sun grow dim, and Nature roll away;
GOD'S happy children mount to worlds above,
Drink streams of purest joy and taste immortal love."

Source: Timothy Dwight (1752-1817). *America, or, a Poem on the Settlement of the British Colonies: Addressed to the Friends of Freedom, and Their Country by a Gentleman Educated at Yale-College*. New Haven: T. and S. Green, 1780?, 9, 11-12.

85. Samuel Sherwood
The Church's Flight into the Wilderness: An Address on the Times, Containing Some Very Interesting and Important Observations on Scripture Prophecies: Shewing, That Sundry of Them Plainly Relate to Great-Britain, and the American Colonies; and Are Fulfilling in the Present Day. Delivered on a Public Occasion, January 17, 1776

[...] 3. Since these prophecies and predictions, relating to the trials and sufferings, the wars and conflicts of the church with her anti-christian enemies and adversaries, may be justly taken in such a large, extensive sense and latitude; we may rationally conclude that many of them have reference to the state of Christ's church, in this American quarter of the globe; and will sooner or later, have their fulfilment and accomplishment among us. The providences of God in first planting his church in this, then howling wilderness, and in delivering and preserving of it to this day, are in a manner unequalled, and marvelous; and are reckoned among the most glorious events that are to be found in history, in these latter ages of the world. And there are doubtless yet more glorious events in the womb of providence, which the present commotion[69] thro' the nation and land may (however unlikely in the view of some) be the means of bringing to pass. There is no part of this terraqueous globe better fitted and furnished in all essential articles and advantages, to make a great and flourishing empire; no part of the earth, where learning, religion, and liberty have flourished more for the time. And as to the rapid increase of its inhabitants, and swift population, it cannot be paralleled in all history. There is no part of the world where its inhabitants, through such a large extent of territory, are under such bonds and obligations, from self-interest, to keep in the strictest union and harmony together. They have every motive and inducement to this, that can well be conceived of. And this union, by the blessing of Heaven, is become as general, perfect and complete, as could well be expected in such a corrupt disordered world as this in which we live.

---

[68] Trumpet; the reference here is to the description of the resurrection of the saints during the Last Judgement in 1 Cor. 15.51f.: "Behold, I show you a mystery; We shall not all sleep, but we shall all be changed, in a moment, in the twinkling of an eye, at the last trump: for the trumpet shall sound, and the dead shall be raised incorruptible, and we shall be changed."

[69] Public disorder, tumult, sedition, insurrection; here reference to the pre-revolutionary disturbances of public order.

These United Colonies have arisen to such a height as to become the object of public attention thro' all Europe, and of envy to the mother from whence they derived; whose unprovoked attack upon them in such a furious hostile manner, threatening their entire ruin, is an event that will make such a black and dark period in history, and does so deeply affect, not only the liberty of the church here in the wilderness, but the protestant cause in general, thro' the christian world, and is big with such consequences of glory or terror, that we may conjecture at least, without a spirit of vanity and enthusiasm, that some of those prophecies of St. John[70] may, not unaptly, be applied to our case, and receive their fulfilment in such providences as are passing over us.

I do not mean to undertake a nice, exact calculation of the periods pointed out in this prophetic book; nor to range thro' the history of the world for events to find their accomplishment. I am of opinion, that the church of Christ in every age, may find something in this book applicable to her case and circumstances; and all such passages that are so, may lawfully be applied and improved by us accordingly. There are many cases which happen, that bear a near likeness and resemblance to each other, and which the same prophecy may well suit, in the most material parts of it. It has pleased that God who exercises a universal providence over all things, so to dispose and order events, that the calamities and afflictions of the church, in some measure, run parallel one to another; and all the former efforts of that tyrannical persecuting power, called the *beast*, may be the types and figures, as it were, of his last and general effort against the faithful witnesses of Christ, and the true members of his church. [...]

[...] Hence, as the trials and sufferings of the Christian church were parallel in some measure, with those of the Jewish, and there is a great similarity and likeness in the manner of God's dealings with the one to the other; it must be evident, that expositors have been mistaken, when they represent this flight of the woman into the wilderness, as denoting the church's going into greater peril, danger and affliction, where she was to be more violently distressed and persecuted, for a long time. The word WILDERNESS might possibly suggest to their delicate, but inattentive minds, this frightful and shocking idea. It is true, our fathers had the difficulties of an uncultivated wilderness to encounter; but it soon, by the blessing of Heaven on their labour and industry, became a pleasant field or garden, and has been made to blossom like the rose. The passage, in its most natural, genuine construction, contains as full and absolute a promise of this land, to the Christian church, as ever was made to the Jewish, of the land of Canaan.[71] It is, in an appropriated sense, "her place;" where she is nourished, from the face of the serpent. And the dealings of God in his providence, in bringing his church from a state of oppression and persecution, into this good land, are very parallel and similar to his dealings with the Israelites, in delivering them from the tyrannical power of the haughty, cruel monarch of Egypt, and conducting them to the good land of promise in

---

[70] Sherwood refers to Rev. 12.14-17, in which the flight of the woman (true church) into the wilderness and her temptations by Satan are described: "And to the woman were given two wings of a great eagle, that she might fly into the wilderness, into her place, where she is nourished for a time, and times, and half a time, from the face of the serpent. And the serpent cast out of his mouth water as a flood after the woman, that he might cause her to be carried away of the flood. And the earth helped the woman, and the earth opened her mouth, and swallowed up the flood which the dragon cast out of his mouth. And the dragon was wroth with the woman, and went to make war with the remnant of her seed, which keep the commandments of God, and have the testimony of Jesus Christ."

[71] When the Israelites were oppressed by the Egyptians with forced labor, God promised Moses to lead his people into Canaan, "a good and large land", "a land flowing with milk and honey" (cf. Exod. 3.8).

Canaan. Thus, they that wait on the Lord, shall renew their strength; they shall mount up with wings, as eagles; they shall run, and not be weary, they shall walk and not faint.

Thus the church, in this difficult, distressed season, whenever it happened, was supported and carried, as it were, on eagles wings, to a distant remote wilderness, for safety and protection. And what period or event is there in all the history of her trials and persecutions, which these expressions more exactly describe, and to which they can be applied with more truth and propriety, than to the flight of our fore-fathers into this then howling wilderness, which was a land not sown nor occupied by any ruling power on earth, except by savages and wild beasts? It is an indisputable fact, that the cruel hand of oppression, tyranny and persecution drove them out from their pleasant seats and habitations, in the land of their nativity; and that the purest principles of religion and liberty, led them to make the bold adventure across the wide Atlantic ocean; for which they surely needed the two wings of the great eagle, to speed their flight, and to shelter and cover them from danger, while seeking a safe retreat from the relentless fury and shocking cruelty of the persecuting dragon; and a secure abode for unadulterated christianity, liberty and peace. It is remarked by the inspired penman of this prophecy, and is worthy of notice, that when the woman fled into the wilderness, she came INTO HER PLACE. This American quarter of the globe seemed to be reserved in providence, as a fixed and settled habitation for God's church, where she might have property of her own, and the right of rule and government, so as not to be controul'd and oppress'd in her civil and religious liberties, by the tyrannical and persecuting powers of the earth, represented by the great red dragon. The church never before this, had *prime occupancy*, or first possession of any part of this terraqueous globe, in any great extent of territory. In all countries and kingdoms wherever Christianity had been planted, before its introduction into this American wilderness, the ruling powers in possession of the property, and right of jurisdiction and dominion, were in opposition to this benevolent institution; and the church had to make her way through the greatest possible difficulties and dangers. [...] When that God, to whom the earth belongs, and the fulness thereof, brought his church into this wilderness, as on eagles wings, by his kind, protecting providence, he gave this good land to her, to be her own lot and inheritance for ever. He planted her as a pleasant and choice vine; and drove out the Heathen before her. He has tenderly nourished and cherished her in her infant state, and protected and preserved her amidst innumerable dangers. He has done wonders in his providence for our fathers, and for us their sinful posterity: They, and we have many a time, stood still, and seen the salvation of the Lord. The woman, the church of Christ, has such a gift and grant from Heaven, of this part of God's world, for the quiet enjoyment of her liberties and privileges, civil and religious, that no power on earth can have any right to invade, much less to dispossess her of them. And every attempt of this kind to oppress and enslave her, must be absolutely unrighteous, and a gross violation of justice and truth. He that has all power in heaven and on earth, who will soon destroy the man of sin, and all his confederate powers, by the spirit of his mouth, and brightness of his coming, declares in this prophecy, that the "woman" shall be nourished and preserved in her place here described, "from the face of the serpent." The serpent spoken of, is the great dragon, called the Devil and Satan; the chief directing agent in all the dark plots of tyranny, persecution and oppression; [...]

[...] And from the commotions that began to be raised among them therefor, should this civil war continue, it is highly probable, that within the term of another year, it may flame forth from the very bowels of the kingdom, where it seems to be already kindling up, and where our brethren, which keep the commandments of God, will unavoidably be distressed. But in the issue hereof, it is to be hoped, that the dragon will be wholly consumed and destroyed; that the seat and foundation of all tyranny, persecution and oppression, may be for ever demolished; that the horns, whether civil or ecclesiastical, may be knocked off from the beast, and his head receive a deadly wound, and his jaws be effectually broken; that peace, liberty and righteousness might universally prevail; that salvation and strength might come to Zion;[72] and the kingdom of our God, and the power of his Christ might be established to all the ends of the earth.

IMPROVEMENT.

1. We learn from what has been said, the true cause, as well as the deplorable effects of all dissentions and violent commotions amidst the Christian states and kingdoms of the world; which, like terrible earthquakes, to which they are compared, often shake them from the centre, and convulse them to death and ruin. If we trace them up to their time, source, and origin, we shall presently find, by the help of scripture-light, they all proceed from the inveterate envy and malice which the dragon has against the woman, and the war and contest he is carrying on against her, and her seed. This is plainly held forth in these prophecies of St. John, and is the grand subject of them. It has, from the beginning, been the constant aim and design of the dragon, sometimes called the beast, and the serpent, satan, and the devil, to erect a scheme of absolute despotism and tyranny on earth, and involve all mankind in slavery and bondage; and so prevent their having that liberty and freedom which the Son of God came from heaven to procure for, and bestow on them; that he might keep them in a state of servile subjection to himself. He has been, and still is the chief counsellor and directing agent in all the dark plots of oppression and persecution against God's church, to effect her destruction; that his own wicked scheme of tyranny might have a full establishment on earth, and bear down all before it. And it is truly marvellous what success he has been permitted to have in accomplishing this malignant design: How, not only men of lower abilities and less discernment have been deluded and infatuated by him; but many kings and chief rulers in church and state, of whom better things might have been expected. Such, after they have been made drunk with the intoxicating wine of his fornication and whoredom, have been his chief instruments in this cruel and bloody work. They are of such dark complexion in their counsels, and pursuing such black designs, that they are represented as "ascending out of the bottomless pit, to make war against the faithful witnesses and servants of Jesus Christ, and to kill them." And who can count up the numbers that have been slain by them? Rivers of blood have been shed, at one time and another, in this terrible war and conflict which the tyrannical, persecuting powers of the earth have been instigated by Satan, to carry on against the church of Christ. [...]

[...] Now, the administration seems here described, that has for a number of years, been so grievous and distressing to these colonies in America, claiming an absolute power and authority to make laws, binding in all cases whatever, without check or controul from any; which has proceeded in the exercise of this despotic, arbitrary power, to deprive one of them, of their most essential and chartered privileges; sent over fleets and armies to enforce their cruel, tyrannical edicts, which have involved us in all the calamities and horrors of a civil war; which have destroyed many useful lives,

---

[72] Name of one of the hills of Jerusalem, on which the city of David was built, and which became the center of Jewish life and worship; in biblical use: The house of God; also the Israelites and their religious system, the Christian Church, heaven as the final home of believers.

burnt two of our flourishing towns, captured many of our vessels that fell in their way, prohibited and destroyed our fishery and trade, forbidding us to buy or sell, and taken in a hostile manner, in a way of piracy and robbery, our interest and property, and threaten us with general destruction, for no other reason than that we will not surrender our liberties, properties and privileges, and become abject vassals and slaves to despotic and arbitrary power. I say, the administration seems described, and appears to have many of the features, and much of the temper and character of the image of the beast which the apostle represents, which had two horns like a lamb, and spoke as a dragon. And the language of our pusillanimous foes, and even their adherents amongst us, seems plainly predicted, Rev. xiii.4. "Who is like unto the beast? Who is able to make war with him." [...]

Source: Samuel Sherwood (1730-1783). *The Church's Flight into the Wilderness: An Address on the Times. Containing Some Very Interesting and Important Observations on Scripture Prophecies: Shewing, That Sundry of Them Plainly Relate to Great-Britain, and the American Colonies; and Are Fulfilling in the Present Day. Delivered on a Public Occasion, January 17, 1776.* New-York: S. Loudon, 1776, 17-19, 22-26, 38-40, 42-43.

86. Samuel Hopkins
A Treatise on the Millennium (1793)

Section II
In which it is considered, in what the Millennium will consist, and what will be the peculiar happiness and glory of that day, according to Scripture.

There have been, and still are, very different opinions, respecting the Millennium, and the events which will take place in that day; which are grounded chiefly on the six first verses in the twentieth chapter of the Revelation[73] [...].

Some have supposed, that this passage is to be taken literally, as importing that at that time, Jesus Christ will come in his human nature, from heaven to earth; and set his kingdom up here, and reign visibly, and personally, and with distinguished glory on earth. And that the bodies of the martyrs, and other eminent christians, will then be raised from the dead, in which they shall live and reign with Christ here on earth, a thousand years. And some suppose, that all the saints, the true friends to God and Christ, who have lived before that time, will then be raised from the dead, and live on earth perfectly holy, during this thousand years. And this they suppose, is meant by the first resurrection. Those who agree in general in this notion of the Millennium, differ with respect to many circumstances, which it is needless to mention here.

Others have understood this paragraph of scripture, in a figurative sense. That by this reign of Christ on earth, is not meant his coming from heaven to earth, in his hu-

---

[73] Rev. 20.1-6: "And I saw an angel come down from heaven, having the key of the bottomless pit and a great chain in his hand. And he laid hold on the dragon, that old serpent, which is the Devil, and Satan, and bound him a thousand years, and cast him into the bottomless pit, and shut him up, and set a seal upon him, that he should deceive the nations no more, till the thousand years should be fulfilled: and after that he must be loosed a little season. And I saw thrones, and they sat upon them, and judgment was given unto them: and *I saw* the souls of them that were beheaded for the witness of Jesus, and for the word of God, and which had not worshipped the beast, neither his image, neither had received *his* mark upon their foreheads, or in their hands; and they lived and reigned with Christ a thousand years. But the rest of the dead lived not again until the thousand years were finished. This *is* the first resurrection. Blessed and holy *is* he that hath part in the first resurrection: on such the second death hath no power, but they shall be priests of God and of Christ, and shall reign with him a thousand years."

man, visible nature; but his taking to himself his power, and utterly overthrowing the kingdom of satan, and setting up his own kingdom in all the world [...]. And they suppose, that this revival of the truths and cause of Christ, by the numerous inhabitants of the earth, rising up to a new and holy life, and filling the world with holiness and happiness, is that which is here called the *first resurrection*, in distinction from the second, which will consist in the resurrection of the body; whereas this is a spiritual resurrection; a resurrection of the truths and cause of Christ, which had been in a great degree, dead and lost; and a resurrection of the souls of men, by the renovation of the Holy Ghost.

That this important passage of scripture, is to be understood in the figurative sense, last mentioned, is very probable, if not certain. [...]

In the Millennium, there will be a spiritual resurrection, a resurrection of the souls of the whole church on earth, and in heaven. All nations will be converted, and the world will be filled with spiritual life, as it never was before; and this will be a general resurrection of the souls of men. [...] And this will be a most remarkable resurrection of the church on earth from a low, dark, afflicted state, to a state of great life and joy. It will be multiplied to an exceeding great army, which will cover the face of the earth. And heaven will in a sense and degree, come down to earth; the spirit of the martyrs, and of all the just made perfect, will now revive and appear on earth, in their numerous successors, and the joy of those in heaven will be greatly increased. [...]

The way is now prepared, to consider and show more particularly, in what the happiness and glory of the Millennium will consist; and what particular circumstances will attend the church at that day: What is revealed concerning this by express prophecies, and what is implied in them, or may be deduced as consequences from what is expressly declared. It will be no wonder if some mistakes should be made on this point; but it is hoped if there should be any, they will not be very hurtful: And it is apprehended that the greatest error will be in falling short, and not coming up to the reality, in the description of the happiness and glory of that day; for doubtless, our ideas of these, when raised to the highest of which we are at present capable, fall vastly short of the truth. There is good reason to conclude, however, that the church, and christians, will not be perfectly holy in that day; but that every one will be attended with a degree of sinful imperfection, while in the body, however great may be his attainments and advantages in knowledge and holiness. [...]

The following things will take place in the Millennium in an eminent degree, as they never did before; which may be mentioned as generals, including many particulars, some of which will be afterwards suggested.

I. That will be a time of eminent holiness, when it shall be acted out by all, in a high degree, in all the branches of it, so as to appear in its true beauty, and the happy effects of it. This will be the peculiar glory, and the source of the happiness of the Millennium. [...]

II. There will be a great increase of light and knowledge to a degree vastly beyond what has been before. This is indeed implied in the great degree of holiness, which has been mentioned. For knowledge, mental light, and holiness, are inseparably connected; and are, in some respects, the same. Holiness is true light and discerning, so far as it depends upon a right taste, and consists in it; and it is a thirst after every kind and degree of useful knowledge; and this desire and thirst for knowledge, will be great and strong, in proportion to the degree of holiness exercised: And forms the mind to constant attention, and to make swift advances in understanding and knowledge; and becomes a strong guard against mistakes, error and delusion. Therefore, a time of eminent holiness, must be a time of proportionably great light and knowledge. [...] And a happy foundation will be laid for great advances in knowledge and usefulness to the end of life. [... Children] shall then make such early progress in knowledge, and in religion, and in all excellent and useful attainments, that they shall equal, if not surpass, the highest attainments in these things, of the oldest men who have lived in former ages.

They will then have every desirable advantage and opportunity to get knowledge. They will all be engaged in the same pursuit, and give all the aid and assistance to each other, in their power. – They will all have sufficient leisure to pursue and acquire learning of every kind, that will be beneficial to themselves and to society; especially knowledge of divinity. And great advances will be made in all arts and sciences, and in every useful branch of knowledge, which tends to promote the spiritual and eternal good of men, or their convenience and comfort in this life.

III. It will be a time of universal peace, love and general and cordial friendship. War and all strife and contention shall then cease, and be succeeded by mutual love, friendship and benificence. Those lusts of men, which originate in self love, or selfishness, which produce all the wars and strifes among men, shall be subdued and mortified, and yield to that disinterested benevolence, that heavenly wisdom, which is peaceable, gentle and easy to be intreated. This will effectually put an end to war, as the scripture teaches. "And he shall judge among the nations, and shall rebuke many people: And they shall beat their swords into plowshares, and their spears into pruning hooks: Nation shall not lift up sword against nation, neither shall they learn war any more. And my people shall dwell in a peaceable habitation, and in sure dwellings, and in quiet resting places." The whole world of mankind will be united as one family, wisely seeking the good of each other, in the exercise of the most sweet love and friendship, founded upon the best and everlasting principles. "The meek shall inherit the earth, and shall delight themselves in the abundance of peace." [...]

IV. In that day, men will not only be united in peace and love, as brethren; but will agree in sentiments, respecting the doctrines and truth contained in the Bible, and the religious institutions and practice, which are there prescribed. [...]

It has been often said by some professing christians, and is a sentiment which appears to be spreading at this day, That difference in religious sentiments, and in attendance on the institutions of the gospel, and modes of worship, is attended with no inconvenience, but is rather desirable, and advantageous; and by this variety, christianity is rendered more agreeable and beautiful. That it is impossible that all men, whose capacities and genius are so different and various, and their minds, and way of thinking and conception are naturally so far from being alike, should ever be brought to think alike, and embrace the same religious sentiments. That this difference in man's belief and sentiment cannot be criminal; for men are no more obliged to think alike, than they are to look alike, and have the same bodily features and stature. All the union that is required, or that can take place, is that of kind affection, love and charity.

[...] The natural faculties of the mind, of perception and understanding or reason, considered as separate from the inclination or will, do not lead, and have no tendency in themselves, to judge wrong, or contrary to the truth of things. [...]

[... In] the Millennium, which will be a greater image of heaven than ever was before on earth, holiness, light and knowledge, will rise so high, that the former errors in principle and practice will subside, and there will be a great and general union in the belief and practice of the truth, contained in divine revelation. [...]

Those of every denomination will doubtless expect, that the doctrines they hold, and their mode of worship and discipline, and practice, with respect to the institutions and ordinances of Christ, will be then established as agreeable to the truth; and all others will be given up; and all men will freely conform to them. But the most, and perhaps all, will be much disappointed in this expectation; especially with regard to the different modes of worship, and practises relating to discipline, and the ordinances of the gospel. When the church comes to be built up in that day, and put on her beautiful garments, it will doubtless be different from any thing which now takes place; and what church and particular denomination is now nearest the truth, and the church which will exist at that time, must be left to be decided by the event. [...]

V. The Millennium will be a time of great enjoyment, happiness and universal joy. [...]

There are many other things and circumstances which will take place in that day, which are implied in what has now been observed, or may be inferred from it, and from the scripture, by which the advantages, happiness and glory of the Millennium will be promoted; some of which will be mentioned in the following particulars:

I. All outward worldly circumstances will then be agreeable and prosperous, and there will be for all, a sufficiency and fulness of every thing needed for the body, and for the comfort and convenience of every one. [...]

[...] There will then be no war to impoverish, lay waste and destroy. This has been a vast expense and scourge to mankind in all ages, by which poverty and distress have been spread among all nations; and the fruits of the earth, produced and stored by the hard labour of man, have been devoured, and worse than lost. Then there will be no unrighteous persons, who shall be disposed to invade the rights and property of others, or deprive them of what justly belongs to them; but every one shall securely sit under his own vine, and fig tree; and there shall be none to make him afraid. [...]

And at that time, the art of husbandry will be greatly advanced, and men will have skill to cultivate and manure the earth, in a much better and more easy way, than ever before; so that the same land will then produce much more than it does now, twenty, thirty, sixty, and perhaps an hundred fold more. And that which is now esteemed barren, and not capable of producing any thing, by cultivation, will then yield much more, for the sustenance of man and beast, than that which is most productive now: So that a very little spot will then produce more of the necessaries and comforts of life, than large tracts of land do now. And in this way, the curse which has hitherto been upon the ground, for the rebellion of man, will be in a great measure removed.

There will also doubtless, be great improvement and advances made in all those mechanic arts, by which the earth will be subdued and cultivated [...]. There may be inventions and arts of this kind, which are beyond our present conception. And if they could be now known by any one, and he could tell what they will be, they would be thought by most, to be utterly incredible and impossible; as those inventions and arts, which are now known and familiar to us, would have appeared to those who lived before they were found out and took place. [...]

When all these things are considered, which have now been suggested, and others which will naturally occur to them who attend to this subject, it will appear evident, that in the days of the Millennium, there will be a fulness and plenty of all the necessaries and conveniences of life, to render all much more easy and comfortable, in their worldly circumstances and enjoyments, than ever before, and with much less labour and toil: And that it will not be then necessary for any men or women to spend all, or the greatest part of their time in labour, in order to procure a living, and enjoy all the comforts and desirable conveniences of life. It will not be necessary for each one, to labour more than two or three hours in a day, and not more than will conduce to the health and vigour of the body. And the rest of their time, they will be disposed to spend in reading and conversation, and in all those exercises which are necessary and proper, in order to improve their minds, and make progress in knowledge; especially in the knowledge of divinity: And in studying the scriptures, and in private and social and public worship, and attending on public instruction, &c. [...]

And there will be then such benevolence and fervent charity in every heart, that if any one shall be reduced to a state of want by some casuality, or by inability to provide for himself, he will have all the relief and assistance that he could desire; and there will be such a mutual care and assistance of each other, that all worldly things will be in a great degree, and in the best manner common; so as not to be withheld from any who may want them; and they will take great delight in ministering to others and serving them, whenever, and in whatever ways, there shall be opportunity to do it. [...]

Source: Samuel Hopkins (1721-1803). *A Treatise on the Millennium. Showing from Scripture Prophecy, That It Is Yet to Come; When It Will Come; in What It Will Consist; and the Events Which Are First to Take Place, Introductory to It.* Boston: Isaiah Thomas and Ebenezer T. Andrews, 1793, 42-44, 52, 55-63, 65, 69-73.

87. George Richards
"Anniversary Ode on American Independence, for the Fourth of July, 1788"[74]

Tune, "In a mouldering cave," &c.

IN the regions of bliss, where the Majesty reigns,
 Ten thousand bright Seraphim[75] shone;
Wing'd for flight they all stand, harps of gold in each hand,
 When a voice issu'd mild from the throne.

"Ye pow'rs and dominions! bright guardians of realms!
 Whose sway[76] Europe's sons have rever'd;
Eastern monarchs no more your aid shall implore;
 To the WEST all your cares be transferr'd.

That *Vine* which from Egypt to Canaan[77] I brought,
 With an out-strech'd, omnipotent arm,

---

[74] The poem was originally printed in the pamphlet publication of Jonathan Mitchel Sewall's *An Oration Delivered at Portsmouth, New Hampshire, on the Fourth of July, 1788.* It gained a wide audience, however, when it was read during the Boston celebration in 1793. Richards later included it in his *The Declaration of Independence. A Poem Accompanied by Odes, Songs, etc. Adapted to the Day* (Boston, 1793), 22f. An account of the Boston reading can be found in the *Columbian Centinel* on July 3, 1793 and July 6, 1793 respectively.
[75] In the Old Testament, seraphim appear as six-winged angels serving as God's throne guardians. The seraphim are the highest-ranking celestial beings in the hierarchy of angels.
[76] Archaic: dominion, power, rule.
[77] Cf. Ps. 80.8-9, 13-15 ["A Prayer for Restoration"]: "Thou hast brought a vine out of Egypt: thou hast cast out the heathen, and planted it. Thou preparedst *room* before it, and didst cause it to take deep root, and it filled the land. [...] The boar out of the wood doth waste it, and the wild beast of the field doth devour it. Return, we beseech thee, O God of hosts: look down from heaven, and behold, and visit this vine; and the vineyard which thy right hand hath planted [...]."

In AMERICA's soil, from Britannia's bleak isle,
    Shall flourish - and brave ev'ry storm.

In vain *Persecution* her wheel[78] shall prepare,
    The tyrant his scourge lift on high;
The wheel shall be broke, the scourge and the yoke
    All shatter'd in pieces shall lie!

T' accomplish my pleasure, a HERO I'll raise,
    Unrivall'd in counsel and might,
Like the PROPHET of old, wise, patient, and bold,
    Resistless as JOSHUA[79] in fight.

See the plains of Columbia with banners o'erspread!
    Hark! the roar of the battle's begun!
Like a son of the skies, when proud rebels arise,
    He drives the dire hurricane on!

Him, terrors, nor treasons, nor dangers, shall daunt,
    'Till his country, from bondage restor'd,
Independent and free, all her greatness shall see,
    Due alone to his conquering sword.

When the thunder is o'er, and fair Peace spreads her wing,
    The chief still refulgent shall beam,
Presiding at helm, framing laws for the realm,
    In *peace*, as in *war*, still supreme!

Then the bright golden-age shall triumphant return,
    Millenium's new paradise bloom;
While from earth's distant end, their high state to attend,
    All nations, with transport, shall come.

Hail, AMERICA, hail! the glory of lands!
    To thee those high honours are given,
Thy STARS still shall blaze, 'till the moon veil her rays,
    And the sun lose his path-way in heav'n.

Source: George Richards (1755?-1814). "Anniversary Ode on American Independence, for the Fourth of July, 1788." Jonathan Mitchel Sewall. *An Oration Delivered at Portsmouth, New Hampshire, on the Fourth of July, 1788, Being the Anniversary of American Independence*. Portsmouth, NH: George Jerry Osborne, 1788, 21-23.

---

[78] In this context, the wheel represents British jurisdiction upon the former colonies. From the Middle Ages through the early 18th century, large wooden wheels were used as a legal means to perform executions.

[79] The leader of the Israelite tribes after the death of Moses, who conquered Canaan and distributed its lands to the 12 tribes.

88. Philip Freneau
"On the Emigration to America and Peopling the Western Country" (1795)

TO western woods, and lonely plains,
Palemon[80] from the crowd departs,
Where nature's wildest genius reigns,
To tame the soil, and plant the arts –
What wonders there shall freedom show
What mighty *States* successive grow!

From Europe's proud, despotic shores
Hither the stranger takes his way,
And in our new found world explores
A happier soil, a milder sway,[81]
Where no proud despot holds him down,
No slaves insult him with a crown,

What charming scenes attract the eye,
On wild Ohio's savage stream!
Here Nature reigns, whose works outvie
The boldest pattern art can frame;
Here ages past have roll'd away,
And forests bloom'd – but to decay.

From these fair plains, these rural seats,
So long conceal'd, so lately known,
The unsocial Indian far retreats,
To make some other clime his own,
Where other streams, less pleasing, flow,
And darker forests round him grow.

Great Sire of floods![82] whose varied wave
Through climes and countries takes its way,
To whom creating Nature gave
Ten thousand streams to swell thy sway!
No longer shall *they* useless prove,
Nor idly through the forests rove;

Nor longer shall thy princely flood
From distant lakes be swell'd in vain,
Nor longer through a darksome wood
Advance, unnotic'd, to the main,
Far other ends the heavens decree –
And commerce plans new freights for thee.

---
[80] In Greek mythology, a god of the sea, usually represented riding a dolphin and held to be powerful in saving from shipwreck.
[81] Archaic: dominion, power, rule.
[82] Mississippi River.

While virtue warms the generous breast,
Here heaven-born freedom shall reside,
Nor shall the voice of war molest,
Nor Europe's all-aspiring pride –
Here Reason shall new laws devise,
And order from confusion rise.

Forsaking kings and regal state,
With all their pomp and fancied bliss.
The traveller owns, convinc'd though late,
No realm so free, so blest as this –
The *east* is half to slaves consign'd,
Where kings and priests enchain the mind.

O come the time, and haste the day,
When man shall man no longer crush,
When Reason shall enforce her sway,
Nor these fair regions raise our blush,
Where still the *African* complains,
And mourns his yet unbroken chains.

Far brighter scenes a future age,
The muse predicts, these States shall hail,
Whose genius[83] shall the world engage,
Whose deeds shall over death prevail,
And happier systems bring to view
Than all the eastern sages knew.

Source: Philip Freneau (1752-1832). "On the Emigration to America and Peopling the Western Country." *Poems, Written between the Years 1768 & 1794*. Monmouth, NJ: The Press of the Author, 1795, 276-277.

89. David Humphreys
A Poem on the Future Glory of the United States of America (1804)

ADVERTISEMENT.

AMERICA, after having been concealed for so many ages from the rest of the world, was probably discovered, in the maturity of time, to become the theatre for displaying the illustrious designs of Providence, in its dispensations to the human race. These States arose from the condition of colonies to that of an independent nation, at an epocha, and under circumstances singularly favourable for improvement. Previous to our revolution, though refinements and luxuries had made but little progress, useful education had been cultivated with care, valuable inventions had been multiplied, and arts and sciences were in a flourishing state. In giving a scope to the exertion of their faculties, the inhabitants of the United States had, perhaps, fewer obstacles to impede their pro-

---

[83] The quasi-mythologic personification of something immaterial (e.g. of a virtue, a nation), esp. as portrayed in painting or sculpture. Hence an embodied type of some abstract idea. With reference to a nation: distinctive character, or spirit.

ficiency than the people of any other country. There existed among them no privileged orders, no predominant religion, no discouragement to industry, and no exclusion from office. Wide was the field that was opened before them for the range of the human mind. They possessed the advantage of having in view the whole history of mankind, to warn them against the dangers, and to save them from the calamities to which other nations had been exposed. The examples of the wise, the brave, and the good were not wanting to awaken their emulation. They had an opportunity of profiting in every thing, by the experience of all who had preceded them.

Since the conclusion of our revolutionary war, the extraordinary prosperity of the United States has surpassed the most sanguine expectation. If the past is to furnish any criterion for forming a judgment of the future, we are undoubtedly destined, as a nation, to advance with large and rapid strides towards the summit of national aggrandisement. Fully persuaded of the magnitude of the blessings which await us there, the writer wishes to impress the same conviction on the minds of his fellow citizens. Because, he thinks, a confidence in the future felicity and glory of their country will operate usefully in nourishing principles and producing actions sublime and splendid as their destinies. He doubts not then that he shall be pardoned by his countrymen for thus venturing to explore for them the *field of futurity* [...].

A POEM ON THE FUTURE GLORY OF THE *UNITED STATES OF AMERICA*

RISE now, my soul! intelligence refin'd!
Ethereal efflux of th' eternal mind!
Rise, in immortal youth and vigour fresh,
Expand thy vision unobscur'd by flesh;
On rapture's plume, with boundless flight, explore
Our prospect opening and our bliss in store!
What though our state, in untried prime, appears
A freighted vessel on the flood of years;
Though unknown perils, tempests, foes and shelves
Surround, and factions rise amidst ourselves;
Though worlds combin'd, or adverse fates annoy,
What but disunion can our bliss destroy?
Though many a dubious day and dismal scene,
Ere our probation cease, must intervene;
Beyond these glooms what brighter days appear,
Where dawns on mortals heav'n's millennial year!
In western wilds what scenes of grandeur rise,
As unborn ages crowd upon my eyes!
A better æra claims its destin'd birth,
And heav'n descending dwells with man on earth. [...]

Why turns th' horizon red? the dawn is near:
Infants of light, ye harbingers[84] appear;
With ten-fold brightness gild the happier age,
And light the actors o'er a broader stage!

---

[84] Forerunner, someone who prepares the way.

This drama closing – ere th' approaching end,
See heav'n's perennial year to earth descend.
Then wake, Columbians! fav'rites of the skies,
Awake to glory, and to rapture rise!
Behold the dawn of your ascending fame
Illume the nations with a purer flame;
Progressive splendours spread o'er ev'ry clime!
Then wrapt in visions of unfolding time,
Pierce midnight clouds that hide his dark abyss,
And see, in embryo, scenes of future bliss!
See days, and months, and years, there roll in night,
While age succeeding age ascends to light;
Till your blest offspring, countless as the stars,
In open ocean quench the torch of wars:
With God-like aim, in one firm union bind
The common good and int'rest of mankind;
Unbar the gates of commerce for their race,
And build the gen'ral peace on freedom's broadest base.

Source: David Humphreys (1752-1818). "A Poem on the Future Glory of the United States of America." *The Miscellaneous Works of David Humphreys*. New York: T. & J. Swords, 1804, 47-48, 51, 65.

90. "The Earth Must Burn / And Christ Return" (1817)

Source: "The Earth Must Burn / And Christ Return." Jonathan Fisher (1768-1847). *The Youth's Primer: Containing a Series of Short Verses in Alphabetical Order*. Boston: Samuel T. Armstrong, 1817.

GREAT AWAKENING & ENLIGHTENMENT

There is no better example for the power of ideas in human history than the period usually referred to as the Enlightenment. This blanket term covers a whole set of interconnected, yet frequently competing intellectual revolutions that fundamentally transformed the Western world in the so-called Age of Reason. The socio-political, economic, cultural, and psychological changes that we routinely associate with the modern age are all but inconceivable without preceding changes in the ways European and American intellectuals thought and wrote about their world in the seventeenth and eighteenth centuries.

Cultural historians nowadays tend to minimize the innovative potential of philosophical ideas by pointing to the various modes in which human thought is determined by prior forces, such as language, desire, or economy. But this notion itself is derived from eighteenth-century thinking, in particular from the investigations by Enlightenment philosophers into the conditions and limits of human reason. Surprisingly, then, the Enlightenment's concept of reason takes its departure from the recognition of man's rational imperfection. In his *Essay Concerning Human Understanding* (1689/1700), John Locke, for instance, claims that every human being is born a *tabula rasa*, without innate or divinely infused ideas about the world. Instead, Locke explains, human beings acquire knowledge by purely *empirical* means: we know only what we can see, hear, taste, or touch with our own senses. Perception precedes knowledge, and there is no true knowledge of things we cannot perceive.

Locke's seemingly simple model launched a momentous paradigm shift in all major fields of human inquiry in the eighteenth century, from theology and philosophy to biology and law. The British colonies in North America experienced the full impact of this shift mainly on the ideological battleground of religion, during the so-called Great Awakening of the 1730s and 1740s. Not an 'enlightened' movement itself, the Great Awakening brought into sharp focus Locke's belief in the epistemological priority of the senses. In wave after wave of revivalist fervor, originally set in motion by the travels of British itinerant preacher George Whitefield through the thirteen colonies, the Great Awakening replaced the older Puritan belief in ministerial guidance and strenuous "preparation" (cf. doc. 44) with the evangelical doctrines of immediate grace and sensuous rebirth. Thus, revivalists such as George Whitefield, Gilbert Tennent (cf. doc. 91), and (to a lesser degree) Jonathan Edwards (cf. docs. 92-94) held that God's grace touches the believer suddenly and without mediators – in one supremely intimate moment of spiritual conversion. The evangelical vocabulary, with its strong emphasis on radical sensual transformation – awakening, revival, rebirth, regeneration –, attests to the Lockean sources of this new "religion of the heart."

Many historians have argued that the Great Awakening provided the mental and cultural foundations for the American Revolution three decades later. Ideologically, both movements have little in common. In terms of its socio-cultural reverberations, however, the Great Awakening can indeed be seen as preparing for the revolt of 1776, as well as for later cultural upheavals, such as the sentimental reform literatures of the nineteenth century. As a movement that emphasized a heartfelt sense of faith over the institutional authority of clergy or scripture, the Great Awakening drew numerous people from the lower classes and from marginalized groups into Protestant churches and sects, staking out for the first time a space of legitimate public speech for women, African Americans, and Native Americans. In addition, the Great Awakening democratized American religion by weakening the influence of the established denominations (Congregational Puritanism in New England, Quakerism in Pennsylvania, Anglicanism in the South) in favor of a highly diversified and pluralistic religious landscape. Altogether, about 150 new denominations came into existence in the wake of the revival; some evangelical churches (Presbyterianism, Baptism, Methodism) transformed into principal religious forces in North America. Last but not least, as the first truly common experience of all thirteen colonies, the Great Awakening inaugurated a trans-colonial public sphere in all of British America, which the secular elites of the American Revolution would profitably put to political use in the 1760s and 1770s.

Among these secular revolutionaries, no one formulated the logical consequences of Locke's empiricism in a more radical manner than Thomas Paine (cf. docs. 99-100). Like the Protestant revivalists of the pre-revolutionary era, Paine insisted on the epistemological priority of the human senses. His conclusions, however, were opposed to the evangelical doctrine of immediate grace. With his penetrating and frequently scornful critique of "revealed religion" (i.e. of all religious systems supposedly communicated to humanity through divine and holy scriptures), Paine became a leading American advocate of the religious philosophy of deism. Also known as "freethinkers," the deists believed that there is a God who created the universe as a perfect and fully rational mechanism. Hence, the deists claimed, this creator-God is in no need of intervening in his creation with miracles or spectacular communications, such as Christ's sacrifice, but can safely withdraw from the world. With this thought, enlightened religion at last dismisses Christianity, because Christian discourse is inextricably rooted in the narrative of God's active and constant care for his creation. Deism attempts to replace this narrative of divine incarnation with a narrative of scientific progress, claiming that the only way to know God is to study the laws of his creation, i.e. to study the empirical laws of nature. Thus, deism is a "natural religion" in the sense that it identifies the activities of the natural sciences as a form of religious worship. For Paine, the legitimate source of human knowledge is no longer the Bible, nor the scholastic wisdom of dead philosophers. The only legitimate source of human knowledge is nature.

Most American revolutionaries toyed with deism in the 1760s and 1770s; many experienced its intellectual radicalism as a liberating force. In his *Autobiography* (cf. doc. 104), Benjamin Franklin, for instance, admits to a youthful infatuation with "natural religion." Even the *Declaration of Independence*, drafted by Thomas Jefferson, shows the influence of deist vocabulary in Jefferson's talk about the "Creator" (rather than "God") who endowed all men with inalienable (i.e. natural) rights, as well as in Jefferson's reference to "the laws of nature and of nature's God" (cf. doc. 131). But deism was never a dominant strain within the American Enlightenment. The continued cultural authority of American Calvinism did much to tone down the more radical varieties of Enlightenment thought after the American Revolution. In the 1790s, then, when the French Revolution sent its shock waves over the United States, deism became a favorite object of paranoid scenarios and fears of conspiracy. Thomas Paine, whose pamphlet *Common Sense* (cf. doc. 130) in 1776 had introduced a new and thoroughly modern tone into the previously accommodating rhetoric of the American rebels, thirty years later had to bear the full brunt of this political sea-change. Much maligned as a radical atheist after the publication of his deist manifesto *The Age of Reason* (1794), he spent the last years of his life as *persona non grata* in America, and died almost forgotten in 1809.

While deism failed to establish itself as the new creed of a secular nation, revolutionary America produced other, stunningly original and successful syntheses of modern Enlightenment thought and religious faith. One of the most intriguing authors in this regard is

Charles Chauncy, who in the 1740s became increasingly concerned about the religious excesses of the Great Awakening (cf. doc. 98). Equally committed to his traditional Protestant beliefs as to the Lockean promises of progress and natural reason, Chauncy diagnosed a socio-psychological mass hysteria, complaining that the revival's enthusiasm (i.e. belief in the immediate communication between God and believer) and antinomianism (i.e. self-authorized opposition to established law) imperiled the stability and legitimacy of the New England commonwealth. As minister of the First Church of Boston, he considered himself a bastion against the opposing threats of evangelism and deism alike. The result of this dual struggle was an increasing interest in the social utility of religion, culminating in Benjamin Franklin's statement that the doctrine of deism "tho' it might be true, was not very useful."[1] Years later, under the impression of the American Revolution, Chauncy and Franklin, each in his own way, developed thoroughly pragmatic conceptions of religion which valued the social utility of faith higher than its dogmatic substance. This surprising solution to the problem of reason and spirituality prepared the way for the specifically American ideal of (trans-)denominationalism which regards all (Christian) churches as legitimate expressions of faith, deserving of equal esteem and independence, as long as they stay within their own sphere and do not interfere in public affairs. That such tolerance fulfilled a civic service was clear to those who drafted the American Constitution in 1787. Avoiding both the fervor of evangelism and the skepticism of the radical Enlightenment, without abandoning either, the Federalists opted for a maximum extension and diversification of the religious landscape, hoping that the existence of an abundant number of local sects and churches would prevent any one of them from establishing a monopoly, while each single creed would instill in its members that sense of civic commitment necessary for a pluralistic republic to flourish. It is a small step from this functional understanding of faith to some of the more contemporary forms of American civil religion.

Frank Kelleter

---

[1] Cf. *Benjamin Franklin's Autobiography*. Ed. J.A. Leo Lemay and P.M. Zall. New York: Norton, 1986, 46.

91. Gilbert Tennent
Solemn Warning to the Secure World (1735)

[...] Awake to Righteousness and sin not: for some have not the Knowledge of God: I speak this to your Shame. I *Cor.* 15. 34. And especially knowing the Time, that now it is high Time to awake out of Sleep. *But I can't in Regard of you add the Apostle's Reason, Rom. 13. 11. For now is your Salvation nearer than when ye believed. No Brethren! I am oblig'd in* Faithfulness *to* God, *and* Love *to you, to tell that inasmuch as you did not, and now do not* believe, *that your* Damnation *is nearer than when ye first* heard *the* Gospel *of* Christ, *and* Salvation *by his* Blood; *because of your* unbelieving Obstinacy *and* presumptuous Security.

Awake, Awake Sinners, stand up and look where you are hastning, least you drink of the Hand of the Lord, the Dregs[2] of the Cup of his Fury; the Cup of trembling, and wring them out, *Isai.* 51. 17. Awake ye Drunkards, *and* weep and howl, *Joel* 1. 5. *For what can ye expect (so continuing) but to drink of that* Cup of Trembling *I but now mention'd.*

Awake ye prophane Swearers, *and remember ye will not get a* drop of Water to cool your cursing cursed Tongues in Hell,[3] *when they and you shall* flame *in the* broad burning Lake, *Luke* 16. 24. God has said he will not hold you Guiltless, that take his Name in vain, *Exod* 20. 7.

Awake *ye* unclean Adulterers, *and* Whoremongers,[4] *and remember that without a speedy Repentance, your dismal* abode *shall be ever with* unclean Devils, *the* Soul *of a God shall be* aveng'd *upon you, Jer.* 5. 8, 29.

Awake ye Sabbath-Breakers, *and* reform; *or* God *will* break *you upon the* Wheels *of his* Vengeance, *and* torture *you eternally upon the* Rack[5] *of his* Justice, *Nehem.* 13. 16,17,18.

And let all other sorts of prophane Sinners *be entreated to* awake *out of* Sleep *and consider their* Danger. [...]

Awake ye secure Moralists, *and* lifeless, sapless Formalists, *who are Strangers to the* Power *of experimental* Religion: *Remember your* shadowy Appearances, *can't* deceive *the* Rein trying God, *Gal.* 6. 7. [...]

Awake *every of you that are yet in a* Christless unconvinced State! *Are you not asham'd to sleep all the Day in Sloth, while some are trembling, troubled and distress'd about their Souls, who are not greater Sinners than your selves?* [...]

Source: Gilbert Tennent (1703-1764). *Solemn Warning to the Secure World, from the God of Terrible Majesty. Or, the Presumptuous Sinner Detected, His Pleas Consider'd, and His Doom Display'd. Being an Essay, in Which the Strong Proneness of Mankind to Entertain a False Confidence Is Proved; the Causes & Foundations of This Delusion Open'd and Consider'd in a Great Variety of Particulars; the Folly, Sinfulness and Dangerous Consequences of Such a Presumptuous Hope Expos'd, and Directions Propos'd How to Obtain that Scriptural and Rational Hope, Which Maketh Not Ashamed. In a Discourse from Deut. xxix. 19, 20, 21.* Boston: S. Kneeland and T. Green, 1735, viii-ix, xi.

---

[2] Sediments contained in a liquid.
[3] Jesus tells the story of a rich man and a beggar, named Lazarus. When both men died, the rich man was tormented in the flames of hell. He cried out to God for mercy, asking God to send Lazarus, so that Lazarus may dip the tip of his finger into water and cool the rich man's tongue.
[4] Men who associate with prostitutes.
[5] Instrument of torture on which the victim's body was stretched.

92. Jonathan Edwards
Sinners in the Hands of an Angry God. A Sermon Preached at Enfield, July 8th 1741. At a Time of Great Awakenings (1742)

DEUT. XXXII. 35. – *Their Foot shall slide in due Time.*[6]
In this Verse is threatned the Vengeance of God on the wicked unbelieving Israelites, that were God's visible People, and lived under Means of Grace; and that, notwithstanding all God's wonderful Works that he had wrought towards that People, yet remained, as is expressed, *ver.* 28. void of Counsel, having no Understanding in them; and that, under all the Cultivations of Heaven, brought forth bitter and poisonous Fruit; as in the two Verses next preceding the Text.[7]

The Expression that I have chosen for my Text, *Their foot shall slide in due Time*; seems to imply the following Things, relating to the Punishment and Destruction that these wicked Israelites were exposed to.

1. That they were *always* exposed to Destruction, as one that stands or walks in slippery Places is always exposed to fall. This is implied in the Manner of their Destruction's coming upon them, being represented by their Foot's sliding. The same is express'd, Psal. 73.18. *Surely thou didst set them in slippery Places; thou castedst them down into Destruction.*

2. It implies that they were always exposed to *sudden* unexpected Destruction. As he that walks in slippery Places is every Moment liable to fall; he can't foresee one Moment whether he shall stand or fall the next; and when he does fall, he falls at once, without Warning. Which is also expressed in that, Psal. 73.18,19: *Surely thou didst set them in slippery Places; thou castedst them down into Destruction. How are they brought into Desolation as in a Moment?* [...]

The Observation from the Words that I would now insist upon is this,
> *There is nothing that keeps wicked Men, at any one*
> *Moment, out of Hell, but the meer Pleasure of* GOD.

By the meer Pleasure of God, I mean his sovereign Pleasure, his arbitrary Will, restrained by no Obligation, hinder'd by no manner of Difficulty, any more than if nothing else but God's meer Will had in the least Degree, or in any Respect whatsoever, any Hand in the Preservation of wicked Men one Moment.

The Truth of this Observation may appear by the following Considerations.

1. There is no Want of *Power* in God to cast wicked men into Hell at any Moment. Mens Hands can't be strong when God rises up: The strongest have no Power to resist him, nor can any deliver out of his Hands.

He is not only able to cast wicked Men into Hell, but he can most *easily* do it. [...] There is no Fortress that is any Defence from the Power of God. Tho' Hand join in Hand, and vast Multitudes of God's Enemies combine and associate themselves, they are easily broken in Pieces: They are as great Heaps of light Chaff[8] before the Whirlwind; or large Quantities of dry Stubble before devouring Flames. We find it easy to tread on and crush a Worm that we see crawling on the Earth; so 'tis easy for us to cut or singe a slender Thread that any

---

[6] God speaking to the Israelites through the prophet Moses. An expression of God's anger towards the Israelites who have turned their back on God.
[7] Deut. 32.32-33: "For their vine *is* of the vine of Sodom, / and the fields of Gomorrah: / their grapes *are* grapes of gall, / their clusters *are* bitter: / their wine *is* the poison of dragons, / and the cruel venom of asps."
[8] Finely cut straw or hay.

Thing hangs by; thus easy is it for God, when he pleases to cast his Enemies down to Hell. What are we, that we should think to stand before him, at whose Rebuke the Earth trembles, and before whom the Rocks are thrown down?

2. They *deserve* to be cast into Hell; so that divine Justice never stands in the Way, it makes no Objection against God's using his Power at any Moment to destroy them. Yea, on the contrary, Justice calls aloud for an infinite Punishment of their Sins. [...]

4. They are now the Objects of that very *same* Anger & Wrath of God that is expressed in the Torments of Hell: and the Reason why they don't go down to Hell at each Moment, is not because God, in whose Power they are, is not then very angry with them; as angry as he is with many of those miserable Creatures that he is now tormenting in Hell, and do there feel and bear the fierceness of his Wrath. Yea God is a great deal more angry with great Numbers that are now on Earth, yea doubtless with many that are now in this Congregation, that it may be are at Ease and Quiet, than he is with many of those who are now in the Flames of Hell. [...]

5. The *Devil* stands ready to fall upon them and seize them as his own, at what Moment God shall permit him. They belong to him; he has their Souls in his Possession, and under his Dominion. The Scripture represents them as his *Goods*, [...]. The Devils watch them; they are ever by them, at their right Hand; they stand waiting for them, like greedy hungry Lions that see their Prey, and expect to have it, but are for the present kept back; if God should withdraw his Hand, by which they are restrained, they would in one Moment fly upon their poor Souls. The old Serpent is gaping for them; Hell opens its Mouth wide to receive them; and if God should permit it, they would be hastily swallowed up and lost.

6. There are in the Souls of wicked Men those hellish *Principles* reigning, that would presently kindle and flame out into Hell Fire, if it were not for God's Restraints. There is laid in the very Nature of carnal Men a Foundation for the Torments of Hell: There are those corrupt Principles, in reigning Power in them, and in full Possession of them, that are Seeds of Hell Fire. These Principles are active and powerful, and exceeding violent in their Nature, and if it were not for the restraining Hand of God upon them, they would soon break out, they would flame out after the same Manner as the same Corruptions, the same Enmity does in the Hearts of damned Souls, and would beget the same Torments in 'em as they do in them. [...]

7. [...] God has so many different unsearchable Ways of taking wicked Men out of the World and sending 'em to Hell, that there is nothing to make it appear that God had need to be at the Expen[s]e of a Miracle, or go out of the ordinary Course of his Providence, to destroy any wicked Man, at any Moment. [...]

10. God has laid himself under *no Obligation* by any Promise to keep any natural Man out of Hell one Moment. God certainly has made no Promises either of eternal Life, or of any Deliverance or Preservation from eternal Death, but what are contained in the Covenant of Grace,[9] the Promises that are given in Christ, in whom all the Promises are Yea and Amen. But surely they have no Interest in the Promises of the Covenant of Grace that are not the Children of the Covenant, and that don't believe in any of the Promises of the Covenant, and have no Interest in the *Mediator* of the Covenant. [...]

So that thus it is, that natural Men are held in the Hand of God over the Pit of Hell; they have deserved the fiery Pit, and are already sentenced to it; and God is dreadfully provoked,

---

[9] The promise of the covenant of grace is eternal life in fellowship with God.

his Anger is as great towards them as to those that are actually suffering the Executions of the fierceness of his Wrath in Hell, and they have done nothing in the least to appease or abate that Anger, neither is God in the least bound by any Promise to hold 'em up one moment; the Devil is waiting for them, Hell is gaping for them, the Flames gather and flash about them, and would fain lay hold on them, and swallow them up; the Fire pent up[10] in their own Hearts is struggling to break out; and they have no Interest in any Mediator, there are no Means within Reach that can be any Security to them. In short, they have no Refuge, nothing to take hold of, all that preserves them every moment is the meer arbitrary Will, and uncovenanted unobliged Forbearance of an incensed[11] God.

APPLICATION.

The USE may be of *Awakening* unconverted Persons in this Congregation. This that you have heard is the Case of every one of you that are out of Christ. *That World of Misery, that Lake of burning Brimstone*[12] *is extended abroad under you. There is the dreadful Pit of the glowing Flames of the Wrath of God; there is Hell's wide gaping Mouth open; and you have nothing to stand upon, nor any Thing to take hold of: there is nothing between you and Hell but the Air; 'tis only the Power and meer Pleasure of God that holds you up.*

You probably are not sensible of this; you find you are kept out of Hell, but don't see the Hand of God in it, but look at other Things, as the good State of your bodily Constitution, your Care of your own Life, and the Means you use for your own Preservation. But indeed these Things are nothing; if God should withdraw his Hand, they would avail no more to keep you from falling, than the thin Air to hold up a Person that is suspended in it.

Your Wickedness makes you as it were heavy as Lead, and to tend downwards with great Weight and Pressure towards Hell; and if God should let you go, you would immediately sink and swiftly descend & plunge into the bottomless Gulf, and your healthy Constitution, and your own Care and Prudence, and best Contrivance,[13] and all your Righteousness, would have no more Influence to uphold you and keep you out of Hell, than a Spider's Web would have to stop a falling Rock. Were it not that so is the sovereign Pleasure of God, the Earth would not bear you one Moment; for you are a Burden to it; the Creation groans with you; the Creature is made Subject to the Bondage of your Corruption, not willingly; the Sun don't willingly shine upon you to give you Light to serve Sin and Satan; the Earth don't willingly yield her Increase to satisfy your Lusts; nor is it willingly a Stage for your Wickedness to be acted upon; the Air don't willingly serve you for Breath to maintain the Flame of Life in your Vitals, while you spend your Life in the Service of God's Enemies. God's Creatures are Good, and were made for Men to serve God with, and don't willingly subserve to any other Purpose, and groan when they are abused to Purposes so directly contrary to their Nature and End. And the World would spue you out, were it not for the sovereign Hand of him who hath subjected it in Hope. There are black Clouds of God's

---

[10] Shut up, confined, repressed.
[11] Inflamed with wrath, made angry, enraged.
[12] Formerly the common vernacular name for sulphur. Now used chiefly when referring to its inflammable character, and to the biblical use in Gen. 19.24 ("Then the Lord rained upon Sodom and upon Gomorrah brimstone and fire from the Lord out of heaven") or in Rev. 19.20 ("And the beast was taken, and with him the false prophet that wrought miracles before him, with which he deceived them that had received the mark of the beast, and them that worshipped his image. These both were cast alive into a lake of fire burning with brimstone").
[13] The action of inventing or making with thought and skill; invention.

Wrath now hanging directly over your Heads, full of the dreadful Storm, and big with Thunder; and were it not for the restraining Hand of God it would immediately burst forth upon you. The sovereign Pleasure of God for the present stays his rough Wind; otherwise it would come with Fury, and your Destruction would come like a Whirlwind, and you would be like the Chaff of the Summer threshing Floor.

The Wrath of God is like great Waters that are dammed for the present; they increase more and more, & rise higher and higher, till an Outlet is given, and the longer the Stream is stop'd, the more rapid and mighty is it's Course, when once it is let loose. 'Tis true, that Judgment against your evil Works has not been executed hitherto; the Floods of God's Vengeance have been with-held; but your Guilt in the mean Time is constantly increasing, and you are every Day treasuring up more Wrath; the Waters are continually rising and waxing more and more mighty; and there is nothing but the meer Pleasure of God that holds the Waters back that are unwilling to be stopped, and press hard to go forward; if God should only withdraw his Hand from the Flood-Gate, it would immediately fly open, and the fiery Floods of the Fierceness and Wrath of God would rush forth with inconceivable Fury, and would come upon you with omnipotent Power; and if your Strength were ten thousand Times greater than it is, yea ten thousand Times greater than the Strength of the stoutest, sturdiest Devil in Hell, it would be nothing to withstand or endure it.

The Bow of God's Wrath is bent, and the Arrow made ready on the String, and Justice bends the Arrow at your Heart, and strains the Bow, and it is nothing but the meer Pleasure of God, and that of an angry God, without any Promise or Obligation at all, that keeps the Arrow one Moment from being made drunk with your Blood. [...]

The God that holds you over the Pit of Hell, much as one holds a Spider, or some loathsome[14] Insect, over the Fire, abhors you, and is dreadfully provoked; his Wrath towards you burns like Fire; he looks upon you as worthy of nothing else, but to be cast into the Fire; he is of purer Eyes than to bear to have you in his Sight; you are ten thousand Times so abominable in his Eyes as the most hateful venomous Serpent is in ours. You have offended him infinitely more than ever a stubborn Rebel did his Prince: and yet 'tis nothing but his Hand that holds you from falling into the Fire every Moment: 'Tis to be ascribed to nothing else, that you did not go to Hell the last Night; that you was suffer'd to awake again in this World, after you closed your Eyes to sleep: and there is no other Reason to be given why you have not dropped into Hell since you arose in the Morning, but that God's Hand has held you up: There is no other Reason to be given why you han't gone to Hell since you have sat here in the House of God, provoking his pure Eyes by your sinful wicked Manner of attending his solemn Worship: Yea, there is nothing else that is to be given as a Reason why you don't this very Moment drop down into Hell.

O Sinner! Consider the fearful Danger you are in: 'Tis a great Furnace of Wrath, a wide and bottomless Pit, full of the Fire of Wrath, that you are held over in the Hand of that God, whose Wrath is provoked and incensed as much against you as against many of the Damned in Hell: You hang by a slender Thread, with the Flames of divine Wrath flashing about it, and ready every Moment to singe it, and burn it asunder; and you have no Interest in any Mediator, and nothing to lay hold of to save yourself, nothing to keep off the Flames of Wrath, nothing of your own, nothing that you ever have done, nothing that you can do, to induce God to spare you one Moment. [...]

---

[14] Exciting disgust or loathing, sickening.

Consider this, you that are here present, that yet remain in an unregenerate State. That God will execute the fierceness of his Anger, implies that he will inflict Wrath without any Pity [...].

How dreadful is the State of those that are daily and hourly in Danger of this great Wrath, and infinite Misery! But this is the dismal Case of every Soul in this Congregation, that has not been born again, however moral and strict, sober and religious they may otherwise be. Oh that you would consider it, whether you be Young or Old. There is Reason to think, that there are many in this Congregation now hearing this Discourse, that will actually be the Subjects of this very Misery to all Eternity. We know not who they are, or in what Seats they sit, or what Thoughts they now have: it may be they are now at Ease, and hear all these Things without much Disturbance, and are now flattering themselves that they are not the Persons, promising themselves that they shall escape. If we knew that there was one Person, and but one, in the whole Congregation that was to be the Subject of this Misery, what an awful Thing would it be to think of! If we knew who it was, what an awful Sight would it be to see such a Person! How might all the rest of the Congregation lift up a lamentable and bitter Cry over him! But alass! instead of one, how many is it likely will remember this Discourse in Hell? [...]

Are there not many here that have lived *long* in the World, that are not to this Day born again, and so are Aliens from the Common-wealth of Israel, and have done nothing ever since they have lived, but treasure up Wrath against the Day of Wrath? Oh Sirs, your Case in an especial Manner is extreamly dangerous; your Guilt and Hardness of Heart is extreamly great. Don't you see how generally Persons of your Years are pass'd over and left, in the present remarkable & wonderful Dispensation of God's Mercy? You had need to consider your selves, and wake throughly out of Sleep; you cannot bear the Fierceness and Wrath of the infinite GOD.

And you that are *young Men*, and *young Women*, will you neglect this precious Season that you now enjoy, when so many others of your Age are renouncing all youthful Vanities, and flocking to CHRIST? You especially have now an extraordinary Opportunity; but if you neglect it, it will soon be with you as it is with those Persons that spent away all the precious Days of Youth in Sin, and are now come to such a dreadful pass in blindness and hardness.

And you *Children* that are unconverted, don't you know that you are going down to Hell, to bear the dreadful Wrath of that God that is now angry with you every Day, and every Night? Will you be content to be the Children of the Devil, when so many other Children in the Land are converted, and are become the holy and happy Children of the King of Kings? [...]

Therefore let every one that is out of CHRIST, now awake and fly from the Wrath to come. The Wrath of almighty GOD is now undoubtedly hanging over [a] great Part of this Congregation: Let every one fly out of *Sodom: Haste and escape for your Lives, look not behind you, escape to the Mountain, least you be consumed.*[15]

FINIS.

---

[15] According to Gen. 18.20, Abraham's nephew Lot, and Lot's family, were safely led out of Sodom shortly before the destruction of Sodom and Gomorrah. As soon as they had left the city, they were told by one of the men who led them: "Escape for thy life; look not behind thee, neither stay thou in all the plain; escape to the mountain, lest thou be consumed" (Gen. 19.17).

Source: Jonathan Edwards (1703-1758). *Sinners in the Hands of an Angry God: A Sermon Preached at Enfield, July 8th 1741. At a Time of Great Awakenings; and Attended with Remarkable Impressions on Many of the Hearers*. Boston: S. Kneeland and T. Green, 1742, 3-9, 11-16, 18, 22-25.

93. Jonathan Edwards
A Faithful Narrative of the Surprising Work of God in the Conversion of Many Hundred Souls (1736)

[...] Persons are often revived out of their dead and dark frames by religious Conversation: while they are talking of divine things, *or ever* they are *aware*, their *Souls* are carried away into holy Exercises with abundant Pleasure. And oftentimes, while they are relating their past Experiences to their Christian Brethren, they have a fresh sense of them revived, and the same Experiences in a Degree again renewed. [...]

Many in the Country have entertain'd a mean Thought of this great Work that there has been amongst us, from what they have heard of *Impressions* that have been made on Persons *Imaginations*. But there have been exceeding great Misrepresentations, and innumerable false Reports concerning that Matter. 'Tis not, that I know of, the Profession or Opinion of any one Person in the Town, that any weight is to be laid on any thing seen with the bodily Eyes: I know the contrary to be a receiv'd and established Principle amongst us. I cannot say that there have been no Instances of Persons that have been ready to give too much heed to vain and useless *Imaginations*; but they have been easily corrected, and I conclude it will not be wondered at, that a Congregation should need a Guide in such Cases, to assist them in distinguishing *Wheat* from *Chaff*. But such *Impressions* on the Imagination as have been more usual, seem to me, to be plainly no other, than what is to be expected in human Nature in such Circumstances, and what is the natural Result of the strong Exercise of the Mind, and Impressions on the Heart.

I do not suppose that they themselves imagined that they saw any thing with their bodily Eyes; but only have had within them *Ideas* strongly impress'd, and as it were, lively Pictures in their Minds: As for instance, some when in great Terrors, through fear of Hell, have had lively Ideas of a dreadful Furnace. Some, when their Hearts have been strongly impress'd, and their affections greatly moved with a sense of the Beauty and Excellency of *Christ*, it has wrought on their Imaginations so, that together with a sense of his glorious spiritual Perfections, there has arisen in the Mind an *Idea* of one of glorious Majesty, and of a sweet and a gracious Aspect: So some when they have been greatly affected with *Christ's* Death, have at the same time a lively *Idea* of *Christ* hanging upon the Cross, and of his Blood running from his Wounds; which things won't be wondred at by them that have observed how strong Affections about temporal Matters will excite lively *Ideas* and Pictures of different things in the Mind. [...]

There have indeed been some few Instances of *Impressions* on Persons *Imaginations*, that have been something mysterious to me, and I have been at a loss about them; for tho' it has been exceeding evident to me by many things that appear'd in them, both then (when they related them) and afterwards, that they indeed had a great sense of the spiritual Excellency of Divine Things accompanying them; yet I have not been able well to satisfy myself, whether their imaginary *Ideas* have been more than could naturally arise from their spiritual Sense of things. However, I have used the utmost Caution in such Cases; great Care has been taken both in publick and in private to teach Persons the difference between what is *spiritual* and what is merely *imaginary*. I have often warned Persons not to lay the stress of their Hope on any *Ideas* of any outward Glory, or any external thing whatsoever, and have met with no Opposition in such Instructions. But 'tis not strange if some weaker Persons, in giving an account of their Experiences, have not so prudently distinguished between the spiritual and imaginary Part; which some that have not been well affected to Religion, might take advantage of. [...]

'Tis easily perceived by the foregoing Account that 'tis very much the Practice of the People here, to converse freely one with another of their spiritual Experiences, which is a thing that many have been disgusted at. But however our People *may have*, in some respects, gone to extremes in it, yet 'tis doubtless a Practice that the Circumstances of this Town, and neighbouring Towns, has naturally led them into. [...] And it has been a Practice which, in the general, has been attended with many good Effects, and what God has greatly blessed amongst us: But it must be confest, there may have been some ill Consequences of it; which yet are rather to be laid to the indiscreet Management of it, than to the Practice it self; and none can wonder, if among such a multitude some fail of exercising so much Prudence in choosing the time, manner, and occasion of such Discourse, as is desireable. [...]

Source: Jonathan Edwards (1703-1758). *A Faithful Narrative of the Surprising Work of God in the Conversion of Many Hundred Souls in Northampton, and the Neighbouring Towns and Villages of the County of Hampshire, in the Province of the Massachusetts-Bay in New-England. In a Letter to the Reverend Dr. Benjamin Colman, of Boston.* [...] 3rd ed. Boston: S. Kneeland and T. Green, 1738, 52-56. Republished in Jonathan Edwards, *Discourses on Various Important Subjects, Nearly Concerning the Great Affair of the Soul's Eternal Salvation: Viz. I. Justification by Faith Alone. II. Pressing into the Kingdom of God. III. Ruth's Resolution. IV. The Justice of God in the Damnation of Sinners. V. The Excellency of Jesus Christ: Delivered at Northampton, Chiefly at the Time of the Late Wonderful Pouring out of the Spirit of God There.* Boston: S. Kneeland and T. Green, 1738.

94. Jonathan Edwards
"An Account of His Conversion, Experiences, and Religious Exercises, Given by Himself" (c. 1739)

I had a variety of Concerns and Exercises about my Soul from my Childhood; but had two more remarkable Seasons of Awakening, before I met with that Change, by which I was brought to those new Dispositions, and that new Sense of Things, that I have since had. The first Time was when I was a Boy, some Years before I went to College, at a Time of remarkable Awakening in my Father's Congregation. I was then very much affected for many Months, and concerned about the Things of Religion, and my Soul's Salvation; and was abundant in Duties. I used to pray five times a Day in secret, and to spend much Time in religious Talk with other Boys; and used to meet with them to pray together. I experienced I know not what Kind of Delight in Religion. My Mind was much engaged in it, and had much self-righteous Pleasure; and it was my Delight to abound in religious Duties. I, with some of my School-mates joined together, and built a Booth in a Swamp, in a very secret and retired Place, for a place of Prayer. And besides, I had particular secret Places of my own in the Woods, where I used to retire by my self; and used to be from time to time much affected. My Affections seemed to be lively and easily moved, and I seemed to be in my Element, when engaged in religious Duties. And I am ready to think, many are deceived with such Affections, and such a kind of Delight, as I then had in Religion, and mistake it for Grace.

But in process of Time, my Convictions and Affections wore off; and I entirely lost all those Affections and Delights, and left off secret Prayer, at least as to any constant Performance of it; and returned like a Dog to his Vomit, and went on in Ways of Sin.

Indeed, I was at some Times very uneasy, especially towards the latter Part of the Time of my being at College. 'Till it pleas'd GOD, in my last Year at College, at a Time when I was in the midst of many uneasy Thoughts about the State of my Soul, to seize me with a Pleurisy;[16] in which he brought me nigh to the Grave, and shook me over the Pit of Hell.

But yet, it was not long after my Recovery, before I fell again into my old Ways of Sin. But God would not suffer me to go on with any Quietness; but I had great and violent inward Struggles: 'till after many Conflicts with wicked Inclinations, and repeated Resolutions, and Bonds that I laid my self under by a kind of Vows to God, I was brought wholly to break off all former wicked Ways, and all Ways of known outward Sin; and to apply my self to seek my Salvation, and practice the Duties of Religion: But without that kind of Affection and Delight, that I had formerly experienced. My Concern now wrought more by inward Struggles and Conflicts, and Self-reflections. I made seeking my Salvation the main Business of my Life. But yet it seems to me, I sought after a miserable manner: Which has made me some times since to question, whether ever it issued in that which was saving; being ready to doubt, whether such miserable seeking was ever succeeded. But yet I was brought to seek Salvation, in a manner that I never was before. I felt a Spirit to part with all Things in the World, for an Interest in Christ. My Concern continued and prevailed, with many exercising Things and inward Struggles; but yet it never seemed to be proper to express my Concern that I had, by the Name of Terror.

From my Childhood up, my Mind had been wont to be full of Objections against the Doctrine of GOD's Sovereignty, in choosing whom he would to eternal Life, and rejecting whom he pleased; leaving them eternally to perish, and be everlastingly tormented in Hell. It used to appear like a horrible Doctrine to me. But I remember the Time very well, when I seemed to be convinced, and fully satisfied, as to this Sovereignty of God, and his Justice in thus eternally disposing of Men, according to his sovereign Pleasure. But never could give an Account, how, or by what Means, I was thus convinced; not in the least imagining, in the Time of it, nor a long Time after, that there was any extraordinary Influence of God's Spirit in it: but only that now I saw further, and my Reason apprehended the Justice and Reasonableness of it. However, my Mind rested in it; and it put an end to all those Cavils[17] and Objections, that had 'till then abode with me, all the preceding part of my Life. And there has been a wonderful Alteration in my Mind, with respect to the Doctrine of God's Sovereignty, from that Day to this; so that I scarce ever have found so much as the rising of an Objection against God's Sovereignty, in the most absolute Sense, in shewing Mercy on whom he will shew Mercy, and hardening and eternally damning whom he will. [...] But I have often times since that first Conviction, had quite another Kind of Sense of God's Sovereignty, than I had then. I have often since, not only had a Conviction, but a *delightful* Conviction. The Doctrine of God's Sovereignty has very often appeared, an exceeding pleasant, bright and sweet Doctrine to me: and absolute Sovereignty is what I love to ascribe to God. But my first Conviction was not with this.

---

[16] Inflammation of the pleura and lungs.
[17] Unnecessary and trivial objections.

The first that I remember that ever I found any thing of that Sort of inward, sweet Delight in GOD and divine Things, that I have lived much in since, was on reading those Words, I *Tim.* 1.17. "Now unto the King eternal, immortal, invisible, the only wise GOD, be Honor and Glory for ever and ever, Amen." As I read the Words, there came into my Soul, and was as it were diffused thro' it, a Sense of the Glory of the Divine Being; a new Sense, quite different from any Thing I ever experienced before. Never any Words of Scripture seemed to me as these Words did. I thought with my self, how excellent a Being that was; and how happy I should be, if I might enjoy that GOD, and be wrapt up to GOD in Heaven, and be as it were swallowed up in Him. I kept saying, and as it were singing over these Words of Scripture to my self; and went to Prayer, to pray to GOD that I might enjoy him; and prayed in a manner quite different from what I used to do; with a new sort of Affection. But it never came into my Thought, that there was any thing spiritual, or of a saving Nature in this.

From about that Time, I began to have a new Kind of Apprehensions and Ideas of Christ, and the Work of Redemption, and the glorious Way of Salvation by him. I had an inward, sweet Sense of these Things, that at times came into my Heart; and my Soul was led away in pleasant Views and Contemplations of them. And my Mind was greatly engaged, to spend my Time in reading and meditating on Christ; and the Beauty and Excellency of his Person, and the lovely Way of Salvation, by free Grace in him. [... And I] found, from Time to Time, an inward Sweetness, that used, as it were, to carry me away in my Contemplations; in what I know not how to express otherwise, than by a calm, sweet Abstraction of Soul from all the Concerns o[f] this World; and a kind of Vision, or fix'd Ideas and Imaginations, of being alone in the Mountains, or some solitary Wilderness, far from all Mankind, sweetly conversing with Christ, and wrapt and swallowed up in GOD. The Sense I had of divine Things, would often of a sudden as it were, kindle up a sweet burning in my Heart; an ardor of my Soul, that I know not how to express.

Not long after I first began to experience these Things, I gave an Account to my Father, of some Things that had pass'd in my Mind. I was pretty much affected by the Discourse we had together. And when the Discourse was ended, I walked abroad alone, in a solitary Place in my Father's Pasture, for Contemplation. And as I was walking there, and looked up on the Sky and Clouds; there came into my Mind, a sweet Sense of the glorious Majesty and Grace of GOD, that I know not how to express. I seemed to see them both in a sweet Conjunction: Majesty and Meekness join'd together: it was a sweet and gentle, and holy Majesty; and also a majestick Meekness; an awful Sweetness; a high, and great, and holy Gentleness.

After this my Sense of divine Things gradually increased, and became more and more lively, and had more of that inward Sweetness. The Appearance of every thing was altered: there seem'd to be, as it were, a calm, sweet Cast, or Appearance of divine Glory, in almost every Thing. God's Excellency, his Wisdom, his Purity and Love, seemed to appear in every Thing; in the Sun, Moon and Stars; in the Clouds, and blue Sky; in the Grass, Flowers, Trees; in the Water, and all Nature; which used greatly to fix my Mind. I often used to sit & view the Moon, for a long time; and so in the Day time, spent much time in viewing the Clouds & Sky, to behold the sweet Glory of GOD in these Things: in the mean Time, singing forth with a low Voice, my Contemplations of the Creator & Redeemer. [...]

I had then, and at other Times, the greatest Delight in the holy Scriptures, of any Book whatsoever. Oftentimes in reading it, every Word seemed to touch my Heart. I felt an Harmony between something in my Heart, and those sweet and powerful Words. I seem'd often to see so much Light, exhibited by every Sentence, and such a refreshing ravishing[18] Food communicated, that I could not get along in reading. Used often-times to dwell long on one Sentence, to see the Wonders contained in it; and yet almost every Sentence seemed to be full of Wonders. [...]

Since I came to this Town,[19] I have often had sweet Complacency[20] in GOD, in Views of his glorious Perfections, and the Excellency of Jesus Christ. GOD has appeared to me, a glorious and lovely Being, chiefly on the account of his Holiness. The Holiness of GOD has always appeared to me the most lovely of all his Attributes. The Doctrines of God's absolute Sovereignty, and free Grace, in shewing Mercy to whom he would shew Mercy; and Man's absolute Dependance on the Operations of God's Holy Spirit, have very often appeared to me as sweet and glorious Doctrines. These Doctrines have been much my Delight. GOD's Sovereignty has ever appeared to me, as great Part of his Glory. It has often been sweet to me to go to GOD, and adore Him as a sovereign GOD, and ask sovereign Mercy of him. [...]

I have often since I lived in this Town, had very affecting Views of my own Sinfulness and Vileness;[21] very frequently so as to hold me in a kind of loud Weeping, sometimes for a considerable time together: so that I have often been forced to shut my self up. I have had a vastly greater Sense of my own Wickedness, and the Badness of my Heart, since my Conversion, than ever I had before. It has often appeared to me, that if GOD should mark Iniquity[22] against me, I should appear the very worst of all Mankind; of all that have been since the beginning of the World to this time: and that I should have by far the lowest Place in Hell. When others that have come to talk with me about their Soul Concerns, have expressed the Sense they have had of their own Wickedness, by saying that it seem'd to them, that they were as bad as the Devil himself; I thought their Expressions seemed exceeding faint and feeble, to represent my Wickedness. I thought I should wonder, that they should content themselves with such Expressions as these, if I had any Reason to imagine, that their Sin bore any Proportion to mine. It seemed to me, I should wonder at my self, if I should express *my* Wickedness in such feeble Terms as they did.

My Wickedness, as I am in my self, has long appear'd to me perfectly ineffable, and infinitely swallowing up all Thought and Imagination; like an infinite Deluge, or infinite Mountains over my Head. I know not how to express better, what my Sins appear to me to be, than by heaping Infinite upon Infinite, and multiplying Infinite by Infinite. I go about very often, for this many Years, with these Expressions in my Mind, and in my Mouth, "Infinite upon Infinite. Infinite upon Infinite!" When I look into my Heart, and take a view of my Wickedness, it looks like an Abyss infinitely deeper than Hell. And it appears to me, that were it not for free Grace, exalted and raised up to the infinite Height of all the fulness and glory of the great JEHOVAH, and the Arm of his Power and Grace stretched forth, in all the Majesty of his Power, and in all the Glory of his Sovereignty; I should appear sunk down in my Sins infinitely below Hell it self, far beyond Sight of every Thing, but the piercing Eye of God's Grace, that can pierce even down to such a Depth, and to the bottom of such an Abyss. [...]

---

[18] Exciting ecstasy.
[19] Northampton, Massachusetts.
[20] Self-satisfaction accompanied by unawareness of actual dangers or deficiencies.
[21] Moral depravity.
[22] Gross injustice.

I have vastly a greater Sense, of my universal, exceeding Dependence on God's Grace and Strength, and meer good Pleasure, of late, than I used formerly to have; and have experienced more of an Abhorrence of my own Righteousness. The Thought of any Comfort or Joy, arising in me, on any Consideration, or Reflection on my own Amiableness, or any of my Performances or Experiences, or any Goodness of Heart or Life, is nauseous and detestable to me. And yet I am greatly afflicted with a proud and self-righteous Spirit; much more sensibly, than I used to be formerly. I see that Serpent rising and putting forth it's Head, continually, every where, all around me. [...]

Source: Samuel Hopkins (1721-1803). *The Life and Character of the Late Reverend Mr. Jonathan Edwards, President of the College at New-Jersey. Together with a Number of His Sermons on Various Important Subjects.* Boston: S. Kneeland, 1765, 23-27, 31, 33, 36-38 [Hopkins was the first to print the piece that has become known as the "Personal Narrative;" he entitled it "An Account of His Conversion, Experiences, and Religious Exercises, Given by Himself"].

95. Nathan Cole
"The Spiritual Travels of Nathan Cole" (1741-1765)

I was born Feb 15th 1711 and born again octo 1741 –
When I was young I had very early Convictions; but after I grew up I was an Arminian[23] untill I was *near* 30 years of age; I intended to be saved by my own works such as prayers and good deeds. [...]

[Conversion Crisis]
I began to think I was not Elected, and that God made some for heaven and me for hell. And I thought God was not Just in so doing, I thought I did not stand on even Ground with others, if as I thought; I was made to be damned; My heart then rose against God exceedingly, for his making me for hell; Now this distress lasted Almost two years: – Poor – Me – Miserable me. – It pleased God to bring on my Convictions more and more, and I was loaded with the guilt of Sin, I saw I was undone for ever; I carried Such a weight of Sin in my breast or mind, that it seemed to me as if I should sink into the ground every step; and I kept all to my self as much as I could; I went month after month mourning and begging for mercy, I tryed every way I could think to help my self but all ways failed: – Poor me it took away *most* all my Comfort of eating, drinking, Sleeping, or working. Hell fire was most always in my mind; and I have hundreds of times put my fingers into my pipe when I have been smoking to feel how fire felt: And to see how my Body could bear to lye in Hell fire for ever and ever. Now my countenance was sad so that others took notice of it.

Sometimes I had some secret hope in the mercy of God; that some time or other he would have mercy on me; And so I took some hopes, and thought I would do all that I could do, and remove all things out of the way that might possibly be an hindrance; and I thought I must go to my Honoured Father and Mother and ask their forgiveness for every thing I had done amiss toward them in all my life: if they had any thing against me [... T]hey said they had not any thing against me, and both fell aweeping like Children for Joy to see me so concerned for my Soul.

---

[23] Arminianism is the belief that God has given man the free choice to accept or reject him. Calvinists considered Arminianism heretical.

Now when I went away I made great Resolutions that I would forsake every thing that was Sinfull; And do to my uttermost every thing that was good; And at once I felt a calm in my mind, and I had no desire to any thing that was sin as I thought; But here the Devil thought to Catch me on a false hope, for I began to think that I was converted, for I thought I felt a real Change in me. But God in his mercy did not leave me here to perish; but in the space of ten days I was made to see that I was yet in the Gall of bitterness; my Convictions came on again more smart than ever – poor me – Oh then I long'd to be in the Condition of some good Man.

There was then a very Mortal disease in the land, the fever and bloody flux; and I was possest with a notion that if I had it I should die and goe right to hell, but I presently had it and very hard too: then my heart rose against God again for making me for hell, when he might as well have made me for heaven; or not made me at all: – Poor me – Oh that I could be a Dog or a toad or any Creature but Man: I thought that would be a happy Change for they had no Souls and I had.[24] Oh what will become of me was the language of my mind; for now I was worse than ever, my heart was as hard as a Stone: my Eyes were dry, once I could weep for my Self but now cannot shed one tear; I was as it were in the very mouth of hell. The very flashes of hell fire were in my Mind; Eternity before me, and my time short here. Now when all ways failed me then I longed to be annihilated; or to have my Soul die with my body; but that way failed too. Hell fire hell fire ran Swift in my mind and my distemper grew harder and harder upon me, and my nature was just wore out – Poor me – poor Soul.

One night [… when my Father and Mother] came into the house Mother seem'd to bring heaven into the house; but there was no heaven for me: She said Oh Nathan will you despair of the mercy of God, do not for a thousand of worlds, don't despair of the mercy of God, for he can have mercy at the very last gasp; I told her there was no mercy for me, I was going right down to hell, for I cannot feel grieved for my self, I can't relent, I can't weep for my self, I cannot shed one tear for my Sins; I am a gone Creature: Oh Nathan says she I have been so my self that I could not shed one tear if I might have had all the world for it; And the next moment I could cry as freely for Joy as ever I could for any thing in the world: Oh said she I know how you feel now, O if God should Shine into your Soul now it would almost take away your life, it would almost part soul and body; I beg of you not to despair of the mercy of God. I told her I could not bear to hear her talk so; for I cannot pray, my heart is as hard as a stone, do be gone, let me alone: do go home; you cannot do me any good, I am past all help of men or means, either for soul or Body, and after some time I perswaded them to go away; and there I lay all night in such a Condition untill sometime the next day with pining thoughts in my mind that my Soul might die with my Body.

And there came some body in with a great Arm full of dry wood and laid it on the fire, *and went out* and it burnt up very briskly as I lay on my Bed with my face toward the fire looking on, with these thoughts in my mind, Oh that I might creep into that fire and lye there and burn to death and die for ever Soul and Body; Oh that God would suffer it – Oh that God would suffer it. – Poor Soul.

---

[24] Cf. John Bunyan: "Now again I blessed the condition of the Dogge and Toad, […] yea, gladly would I have been in the condition of Dog or Horse, for I knew they had no Soul to perish under the everlasting weights of Hell for sin, as mine was like to do." *Grace Abounding to the Chief of Sinners*. Ed. Roger Sharrock. Oxford: Clarendon Press, 1962, 33.

And while these thoughts were in my mind God appeared unto me and made me Skringe:[25] before whose face the heavens and the earth fled away; and I was Shrinked into nothing; I knew not whether I was in the body or out,[26] I seemed to hang in open Air before God, and he seemed to Speak to me in an angry and Sovereign way what won't you trust your Soul with God; My heart answered O yes, yes, yes; before I could stir my tongue or lips, And then He seemed to speak again, and say, may not God make one Vessel to honour and an other to dishonour and not let you know it;[27] My heart answered again O yes yes before I cou'd stir my tongue or lips. Now while my Soul was viewing God, my fleshly part was working imaginations and saw many things which I will omitt to tell at this time.

When God appeared to me every thing vanished and was gone in the twinkling of an Eye, as quick as [a] flash of lightning; But when God disappeared or in some measure withdrew, every thing was in its place again and I was on my Bed. My heart was broken; my burden was fallen of[f] my mind; I was set free, my distress was gone, and I was filled with a pineing desire to see Christs own words in the bible; and I got up off my bed being alone; And by the help of Chairs I got along to the window where my bible was and I opened it and the first place I saw was the 15th Chap: John – on Christs own words and they spake to my very heart and every doubt and scruple that rose in my heart about the truth of Gods word was took right off; and I saw the whole train of Scriptures all in a Connection, and I believe I felt just as the Apostles felt the truth of the word when they writ it, every leaf line and letter smiled in my face; I got the bible up under my Chin and hugged it; it was sweet and lovely; the word was nigh me in my hand, then I began to pray and to praise God. [...]

Now I saw that I must Suffer as well as do for Christ, now I saw that I must forsake all and follow Christ;[28] now I saw with new eyes; all things became new, A new God; new thoughts and new heart; Now I began to hope I should be converted some time or other, for I was sure that God had done some great thing for my soul; I knew that God had subdued my stubborn heart: I knew my heart would never rise so against God as it had done; here I saw in the aforesaid 15 Chap: of John where I opened the bible first that Christ says to his disciples if ye love me keep my Commandments and then says he this is my Commandment that ye love one another. Oh I thought I could die [a] thousand deaths for Christ, I thought I could have been trodden under foot of man, be mocked or any thing for Christ – Glory be to God. [...]

Source: Nathan Cole (1711-1783). "The Spiritual Travels of Nathan Cole." Ed. Michael J. Crawford. *William and Mary Quarterly* 33 (January 1976), 92, 94-97.

---

[25] To flinch, cower.
[26] Cf. 2 Cor. 12.3: "I knew a man in Christ above fourteen years ago, (whether in the body, I cannot tell; or whether out of the body, I cannot tell: God knoweth;) such a one caught up to the third heaven."
[27] Rom. 9.21.
[28] Luke 18.22.

96. Alexander Rider
Camp Meeting (c. 1829)

Source: Alexander Rider (flourished 1810-1834). *Camp Meeting* (Kennedy & Lucas lithograph after A. Rider, c. 1829). Courtesy Library of Congress.

97. Frances Trollope
Domestic Manners of the Americans (1832)

[...] We had not been many months in Cincinnati when our curiosity was excited by hearing the "revival" talked of by every one we met throughout the town. "The revival will be very full" – "We shall be constantly engaged during the revival" – were the phrases we constantly heard repeated, and for a long time without in the least comprehending what was meant; but at length I learned that the un-national church of America required to be roused, at regular intervals, to greater energy and exertion. At these seasons the most enthusiastic of the clergy travel the country, and enter the cities and towns by scores, or by hundreds, as the accommodation of the place may admit, and for a week or fortnight, or, if the population be large, for a month; they preach all day, and often for a considerable portion of the night, in the various churches and chapels of the place. This is called a revival.

I took considerable pains to obtain information on this subject; but in detailing what I learned I fear that it is probable I shall be accused of exaggeration; all I can do is cautiously to avoid deserving it. The subject is highly interesting, and it would be a fault of no trifling nature to treat it with levity.

These itinerant clergymen are of all persuasions, I believe, except the Episcopalian, Catholic, Unitarian, and Quaker. I heard of Presbyterians of all varieties; of Baptists of I know not how many divisions; and of Methodists of more denominations than I can remember; whose innumerable shades of varying belief it would require much time to explain, and more to comprehend. They enter all the cities, towns, and villages of the Union in succession; I could not learn with sufficient certainty to repeat, what the interval generally is between their visits. These itinerants are, for the most part, lodged in the houses of their respective followers, and every evening that is not spent in the churches and meeting-houses, is devoted to what would be called parties by others, but which they designate as prayer-meetings. Here they eat, drink, pray, sing, hear confessions, and make converts. To these meetings I never got invited, and therefore I have nothing but hearsay evidence to offer, but my information comes from an eyewitness, and one on whom I believe I may depend. If one-half of what I heard may be believed, these social prayer-meetings are by no means the most curious, or the least important part of the business.

It is impossible not to smile at the close resemblance to be traced between the feelings of a first-rate Presbyterian or Methodist lady, fortunate enough to have secured a favourite itinerant for her meeting, and those of a first rate London blue,[29] equally blest in the presence of a fashionable poet. There is a strong family likeness among us all the world over.

The best rooms, the best dresses, the choicest refreshments solemnize the meeting. While the party is assembling, the load-star[30] of the hour is occupied in whispering conversations with the guests as they arrive. They are called brothers and sisters, and the greetings are very affectionate. When the room is full, the company, of whom a vast majority is always women, are invited, entreated, and coaxed to confess before their brothers and sisters all their thoughts, faults, and follies.

These confessions are strange scenes; the more they confess, the more invariably are they encouraged and caressed. When this is over, they all kneel, and the itinerant prays

---

[29] Usually reference to a particular color of fine cloth; here, old and aristocratic family.
[30] A 'guiding star'; that on which one's attention or hopes are fixed.

extempore. They then eat and drink; and then they sing hymns, pray, exhort, sing, and pray again, till the excitement reaches a very high pitch indeed. These scenes are going on at some house or other every evening during the revival, nay, at many at the same time, for the churches and meeting-houses cannot give occupation to half the itinerants, though they are all open throughout the day, and till a late hour in the night, and the officiating ministers succeed each other in the occupation of them.

It was at the principal of the Presbyterian churches that I was twice witness to scenes that made me shudder; in describing one I describe both, and every one; the same thing is constantly repeated.

It was in the middle of summer, but the service we were recommended to attend did not begin till it was dark. The church was well lighted, and crowded almost to suffocation. On entering we found three priests standing side by side, in a sort of tribune, placed where the altar usually is, handsomely fitted up with crimson curtains, and elevated about as high as our pulpits. We took our places in a pew close to the rail which surrounded it.

The priest who stood in the middle was praying; the prayer was extravagantly vehement, and offensively familiar in expression; when this ended, a hymn was sung, and then another priest took the centre place, and preached. The sermon had considerable eloquence, but of a frightful kind. The preacher described, with ghastly minuteness, the last feeble fainting moments of human life, and then the gradual progress of decay after death, which he followed through every process up to the last loathsome stage of decomposition. Suddenly changing his tone, which had been that of sober accurate description, into the shrill voice of horror, he bent forward his head, as if to gaze on some object beneath the pulpit. And as Rebecca made known to Ivanhoe[31] what she saw through the window, so the preacher made known to us what he saw in the pit that seemed to open before him. The device was certainly a happy one for giving effect to his description of hell. No image that fire, flame, brimstone, molten lead, or red-hot pincers could supply; with flesh, nerves, and sinews quivering under them, was omitted. The perspiration ran in streams from the face of the preacher; his eyes rolled, his lips were covered with foam, and every feature had the deep expression of horror it would have borne had he in truth been gazing at the scene he described. The acting was excellent. At length he gave a languishing look to his supporters on each side, as if to express his feeble state, and then sat down, and wiped the drops of agony from his brow.

The other two priests arose, and began to sing a hymn. It was some seconds before the congregation could join as usual; every up-turned face looked pale and horror-struck. When the singing ended, another took the centre place, and began in a sort of coaxing, affectionate tone, to ask the congregation if what their dear brother had spoken had reached their hearts? Whether they would avoid the hell he had made them see? "Come, then!" he continued, stretching out his arms towards them, "come to us, and tell us so, and we will make you see Jesus, the dear gentle Jesus, who shall save you from it. But you must come to him! You must not be ashamed to come to him! This night you shall tell him that you are not ashamed of him; we will make way for you; we will clear the bench for anxious sinners to sit upon. Come, then! come to the anxious bench, and we will show you Jesus! Come! Come! Come!"

---

[31] In Sir Walter Scott's *Ivanhoe* (chap. 29), the hero wants to watch a battle from the window, but is too weak to rise from his bed. Rebecca, the heroine of the novel, stands at the window and describes what she sees.

Again a hymn was sung, and while it continued, one of the three was employed in clearing one or two long benches that went across the rail, sending the people back to the lower part of the church. The singing ceased, and again the people were invited, and exhorted not to be ashamed of Jesus, but to put themselves upon "the anxious benches," and lay their heads on his bosom. "Once more we will sing," he concluded, "that we may give you time." And again they sung a hymn.

And now in every part of the church a movement was perceptible, slight at first, but by degrees becoming more decided. Young girls arose, and sat down, and rose again; and then the pews opened, and several came tottering out, their hands clasped, their heads hanging on their bosoms, and every limb trembling, and still the hymn went on; but as the poor creatures approached the rail their sobs and groans became audible. They seated themselves on the "anxious benches;" the hymn ceased, and two of the three priests walked down from the tribune, and going, one to the right, and the other to the left, began whispering to the poor tremblers seated there. These whispers were inaudible to us, but the sobs and groans increased to a frightful excess. Young creatures, with features pale and distorted, fell on their knees on the pavement, and soon sunk forward on their faces; the most violent cries and shrieks followed, while from time to time a voice was heard in convulsive accents, exclaiming, "O Lord!" "O Lord Jesus!" "Help me, Jesus!" and the like.

Meanwhile the two priests continued to walk among them; they repeatedly mounted on the benches, and trumpet-mouthed proclaimed to the whole congregation "the tidings of salvation," and then from every corner of the building arose in reply, short, sharp cries of "Amen!" "Glory!" "Amen!" while the prostrate penitents continued to receive whispered comfortings, and from time to time a mystic caress. More than once I saw a young neck encircled by a reverend arm. Violent hysterics and convulsions seized many of them, and when the tumult was at the highest, the priest who remained above again gave out a hymn, as if to drown it.

It was a frightful sight to behold innocent young creatures, in the gay morning of existence, thus seized upon, horror-struck, and rendered feeble and enervated for ever. One young girl, apparently not more than fourteen, was supported in the arms of another, some years older; her face was pale as death; her eyes wide open, and perfectly devoid of meaning; her chin and bosom wet with slaver; she had every appearance of idiotism. I saw a priest approach her; he took her delicate hands, "Jesus is with her! Bless the Lord!" he said, and passed on.

Did the men of America value their women as men ought to value their wives and daughters, would such scenes be permitted among them?

It is hardly necessary to say that all who obeyed the call to place themselves on the "anxious benches" were women, and by far the greater number, very young women. The congregation was, in general, extremely well dressed, and the smartest and most fashionable ladies of the town were there; during the whole revival the churches and meetinghouses were every day crowded with well-dressed people.

It is thus the ladies of Cincinnati amuse themselves; to attend the theatre is forbidden; to play cards is unlawful; but they work hard in their families, and must have some relaxation. For myself, I confess that I think the coarsest comedy ever written would be a less detestable exhibition for the eyes of youth and innocence than such a scene.

Source: Frances Milton Trollope (1780-1863). *Domestic Manners of the Americans*. London and New York: Whittaker, Treacher, 1832, 76-80.

98. Charles Chauncy
Enthusiasm Described and Cautioned Against (1742)

I COR. XIV. xxxvii.
If any Man among you think himself to be a PROPHET, *or* SPIRITUAL, *let him acknowledge that the Things that I write unto you are the Commandments of the* LORD.

Many things were amiss in the *Church* of *Corinth*, when *Paul* wrote this Epistle to them. There were envyings, strife and divisions among them, on account of their ministers. Some cried up one, others another: one said, I am of PAUL, another I am of APPOLLOS. They had form'd themselves into parties, and each party so admired the teacher they followed, as to reflect unjust contempt on the other.

Nor was this their only fault. A spirit of pride prevailed exceedingly among them. They were conceited of their gifts, and too generally dispos'd to make an ostentatious shew of them. From this vain glorious temper proceeded the forwardness of those that had the *gift* of *tongues*, to speak in languages which others did not understand, to the disturbance, rather than edification of the church: And from the same principle it arose, that they spake not by turns, but several at once, in the same place of worship, to the introducing such confusion, that they were in danger of being tho't mad.

Nor were they without some pretence to justify these disorders. Their great plea was, that in these things they were guided by the Spirit, acted under his immediate influence and direction. This seems plainly insinuated in the words I have read to you. *If any man think himself to be a prophet, or spiritual, let him acknowledge that the things that I write unto you are the commandments of the Lord.* As if the apostle had said, you may imagine your selves to be *spiritual* men, to be under a divine afflatus[32] in what you do; but 'tis all imagination, meer pretence, unless you pay a due regard to the *commandments* I have here *wrote to you*; receiving them not as the *word of man*, *but of* GOD. Make trial of your spiritual pretences by this rule: If you can submit to it, and will order your conduct by it, well; otherwise you only cheat yourselves, while you think yourselves to be *spiritual* men, or *prophets:* You are nothing better than *Enthusiasts*;[33] your being acted by the SPIRIT, immediately guided and influenced by him, is meer pretence; you have no good reason to believe any such thing.

From the words thus explained, I shall take occasion to discourse to you upon the following Particulars.
I. I shall give you some account of *Enthusiasm*, in its *nature* and *influence*.
II. Point you to a rule by which you may judge of persons, whether they are under the influence of *Enthusiasm*.
III. Say what may be proper to guard you against this unhappy turn of mind.
The whole will then be follow'd with some suitable Application.
I. I am in the first place, to give you some account of *Enthusiasm*. And as this is a thing much talk'd of at present, more perhaps than at any other time that has pass'd over us, it will not be tho't unseasonable, if I take some pains to let you into a true understanding of it.

---
[32] The miraculous communication of supernatural knowledge; hence an over-mastering impulse, inspiration.
[33] Member of a Christian group (the Society of Friends) that stresses the guidance of the Holy Spirit and limits the influence of the ordained ministry. The name, originally derisive, refers to the fact that many Friends showed physical signs of religious emotion in their meetings. Enthusiasts were often attacked on grounds of their alleged frenzy in Englightenment dicourses; cf. Shaftesbury, *Letter Concerning Enthusiasm* (1708).

The word, from it's Etymology, carries in it a good meaning, as signifying *inspiration from* GOD: in which sense, the prophets under the old testament, and the apostles under the new, might properly be called *Enthusiasts*. For they were under a divine influence, spake as moved by the HOLY GHOST, and did such things as can be accounted for in no way, but by recurring to an immediate extraordinary power, present with them.

But the word is more commonly used in a bad sense, as intending an *imaginary*, not a *real* inspiration: according to which sense, the *Enthusiast* is one, who has a conceit of himself as a person favoured with the extraordinary presence of the *Deity*. He mistakes the workings of his own passions for divine communications, and fancies himself immediately inspired by the SPIRIT of GOD, when all the while, he is under no other influence than that of an over-heated imagination.

The cause of this *enthusiasm* is a bad temperament of the blood and spirits; 'tis properly a disease, a sort of madness: And there are few; perhaps, none at all, but are subject to it; tho' none are so much in danger of it as those, in whom *melancholy* is the prevailing ingredient in their constitution.[34] In these it often reigns; and sometimes to so great a degree, that they are really beside themselves, acting as truly by the blind impetus of a wild fancy, as tho' they had neither reason nor understanding.

And various are the ways in which their *enthusiasm* discovers itself.

Sometimes, it may be seen in their countenance. A certain wildness is discernable in their general look and air; especially when their imaginations are mov'd and fired.

Sometimes, it strangely loosens their tongues, and gives them such an energy, as well as fluency and volubility in speaking, as they themselves, by their utmost efforts, can't so much as imitate, when they are not under the enthusiastick influence.

Sometimes, it affects their bodies, throws them into convulsions and distortions, into quakings and tremblings. This was formerly common among the people called *Quakers*. I was myself, when a Lad, an eye-witness to such violent agitations and foamings, in a boisterous female speaker, as I could not behold but with surprize and wonder.

Sometimes, it will unaccountably mix itself with their conduct, and give it such a tincture of that which is freakish or furious, as none can have an idea of, but those who have seen the behaviour of a person in a phrenzy.

Sometimes, it appears in their imaginary peculiar intimacy with heaven. They are, in their own opinion, the special favourites of GOD, have more familiar converse with him than other good men, and receive immediate, extraordinary communications from him. The tho'ts, which suddenly rise up in their minds, they take for suggestions of the SPIRIT; their very fancies are divine illuminations; nor are they strongly inclin'd to any thing, but 'tis an impulse from GOD, a plain revelation of his will.

And what extravagances, in this temper of mind, are they not capable of, and under the specious pretext too of paying obedience to the authority of GOD? Many have fancied themselves acting by immediate warrant from heaven, while they have been committing the most undoubted wickedness. There is indeed scarce any thing so wild, either in *speculation* or *practice*, but they have given into it: They have, in many instances, been blasphemers of GOD, and open disturbers of the peace of the world.

---

[34] Refers to the humoral body. Man is a considered to be in the proper condition or constitution only if the four humors (blood, phlegm, choler, and melancholy) are balanced.

But in nothing does the *enthusiasm* of these persons discover it self more, than in the disregard they express to the Dictates of *reason*. They are above the force of argument, beyond conviction from a calm and sober address to their understandings. As for them, they are distinguish'd persons; GOD himself speaks inwardly and immediately to their souls. "They see the light infused into their understandings, and cannot be mistaken; 'tis clear and visible there, like the light of bright sunshine; shews it self and needs no other proof but its own evidence. They feel the hand of GOD moving them within, and the impulses of his SPIRIT; and cannot be mistaken in what they feel. Thus they support themselves, and are sure reason hath nothing to do with what they see and feel. What they have a sensible experience of, admits no doubt, needs no probation."[35] And in vain will you endeavour to convince such persons of any mistakes they are fallen into. They are certainly in the right, and know themselves to be so. They have the SPIRIT opening their understandings and revealing the truth to them. They believe only as he has taught them: and to suspect they are in the wrong is to do dishonour to the SPIRIT; 'tis to oppose his dictates, to set up their own wisdom in opposition to his, and shut their eyes against that light with which he has shined into their souls. They are not therefore capable of being argued with; you had as good reason with the wind.

And as the natural consequence of their being thus sure of every thing, they are not only infinitely stiff and tenacious, but impatient of contradiction, censorious and uncharitable: they encourage a good opinion of none but such as are in their way of thinking and speaking. Those, to be sure, who venture to debate with them about their errors and mistakes, their weaknesses and indiscretions, run the hazard of being stigmatiz'd by them as poor unconverted wretches, without the SPIRIT, under the government of carnal reason, enemies to GOD and religion, and in the broad way to hell. [...]

This is the nature of *Enthusiasm*, and this its operation, in a less or greater degree, in all who are under the influence of it. 'Tis a kind of religious Phrenzy, and evidently discovers it self to be so, whenever it rises to any great height.

And much to be pitied are the persons who are seized with it. Our compassion commonly works towards those, who, while under distraction, fondly imagine themselves to be Kings and Emperors: And the like pity is really due to those, who, under the power of *enthusiasm*, fancy themselves to be *prophets*; *inspired of* GOD, and *immediately called* and *commissioned by him to deliver his messages to the world:* And tho' they should run into disorders, and act in a manner that cannot but be condemned, they should notwithstanding be treated with tenderness and lenity; and the rather, because they don't commonly act so much under the influence of a *bad mind*, as a *deluded imagination*. And who more worthy of christian pity than those, who, under the notion of serving GOD and the interest of religion, are filled with zeal, and exert themselves to the utmost, while all the time they are hurting and wounding the very cause they take so much pains to advance. 'Tis really a pitiable case: And tho' the honesty of their intentions won't legitimate their bad actions, yet it very much alleviates their guilt: We should think as favourably of them as may be, and be dispos'd to judge with mercy, as we would hope to obtain mercy.

But I come [to]

II. In the second place, to point you to a *rule* by which you may judge of persons, whether they are *enthusiasts*, meer pretenders to the immediate guidance and influence of

---

[35] Cf. John Locke, *An Essay Concerning Human Understanding*, Book IV, Chapter 19.

the SPIRIT. And this is, in general, *a regard to the bible, an acknowledgement that the things therein contained are the commandments of* GOD. This is the rule in the text. And 'tis an infallible rule of tryal in this matter: We need not fear judging amiss, while we keep closely to it.

'Tis true, it wont certainly follow, that a man, pretending to be a *prophet*, or *spiritual*, really is so, if he owns the *bible*, and receives the truths therein revealed as the mind of GOD: But the conclusion, on the other hand, is clear and certain; if he pretends to be conducted by the SPIRIT, and disregards the scripture, pays no due reverence to *the things there delivered as the commandments of GOD*, he is a meer pretender, be his pretences ever so bold and confident, or made with ever so much seeming seriousness, gravity, or solemnity.

And the reason of this is obvious; viz that the things contained in the scripture were wrote by holy men as they were moved by the HOLY GHOST: they were received from GOD, and committed to writing under his immediate, extraordinary influence and guidance. And the divine, ever-blessed SPIRIT is consistent with himself. He cannot be suppos'd to be the author of any *private* revelations that are contradictory to the *public standing* ones, which he has preserved in the world to this day. This would be to set the SPIRIT of truth at variance with himself; than which a greater reproach can't be cast upon him. 'Tis therefore as true, that those are *enthusiastical*, who pretend to the SPIRIT, and at the same time express a disregard to the scripture, as that the SPIRIT is the great revealer of the things therein declared to us. [...]

'Tis not therefore the pretence of being moved by the *SPIRIT*, that will justify *private christians* in quitting their own proper station, to act in that which belongs to another. Such a practice as this naturally tends to destroy that order, GOD has constituted in the church, and may be followed with mischiefs greater than we may be aware of.

'Tis indeed a powerful argument with many, in favour of these persons, their pretending to *impulses*, and a call from GOD; together with their insatiable thirst to do good to souls. And 'tis owing to such pretences as these, that encouragement has been given to the rise of such numbers of *lay-exhorters* and *teachers*, in one place and another, all over the land. But if 'tis one of the things wrote by the apostle as the *commandment of* GOD, that there should be *officers* in the church, an *order of men* to whom it should belong, as their *proper, stated work*, to exhort and teach, this cannot be the business of others: And if any who think themselves to be *spiritual*, are under *impressions* to take upon them *this ministry*, they may have reason to suspect, whether their *impulses* are any other than the workings of their own imaginations: And instead of being under any divine extraordinary influence, there are just grounds of fear, whether they are not acted from the vanity of their minds: Especially, if they are but beginners in religion; men of weak minds, babes in understanding: as is most commonly the case. The apostle speaks of *novices*, as in danger of being *lifted up with pride, and falling into the condemnation of the devil*: And it is a seasonable caution to this kind of persons. They should study themselves more, and they will see less reason to think their disposition to exhort and teach to be from the SPIRIT OF GOD. And indeed, if the SPIRIT has bid men to *abide in their own callings*, 'tis not conceivable he should influence them to *leave their callings*: And if he has set a mark of disgrace upon *busy-bodies in other men's matters*, 'tis impossible he should put men upon *wandring about from house to house, speaking the things they ought not*.

And it deserves particular consideration, whether the suffering, much more the encouraging WOMEN, yea, GIRLS to speak in the assemblies for religious worship, is not a plain breach of that *commandment of the* LORD, wherein it is said, *Let your* WOMEN *keep silence in the churches; for it is not permitted to them to speak – It is a shame for* WOMEN *to speak in the church*. After such an express constitution, designedly made to restrain WOMEN from speaking in the church, with what face can such a practice be pleaded for? They may pretend, they are moved by the SPIRIT and such a tho't of themselves may be encouraged by others; but if the apostle *spake by the* SPIRIT, when he delivered *this commandment*, they can't *act by the* SPIRIT when they break it. 'Tis a plain case, these FEMALE EXHORTERS are condemned by the apostle; and if 'tis the *commandment of the* LORD, that they should not speak, they are *spiritual* only in their own tho'ts, while they attempt to do so. [...]

III. The third thing, which is to caution you against giving way to *enthusiastic impressions*. And here much might be said,

I might warn you from the *dishonour* it reflects upon the SPIRIT of GOD. And perhaps none have more reproach'd the blessed SPIRIT, than men pretending to be under his extraordinary guidance and direction. The veryest fancies, the vainest imaginations, the strongest delusions, they have father'd on him. There is scarce any absurdity in *principle*, or irregularity in *practice*, but he has been made the patron of it. – And what a stone of stumbling has the wildness of *Enthusiasm* been to multitudes in the world? What prejudices have been hereby excited in their minds against the very being of the SPIRIT? What temptations have been thrown in their way to dispute his OFFICE as the SANCTIFYER and COMFORTER of GOD'S people? And how have they been over-come to disown HIS WORK, when it has been really wro't in the hearts of men?

I might also warn you from the damage it has done in the world. No greater mischiefs have arisen from any quarter. It is indeed the genuine source of infinite evil. POPERY it self han't been the mother of more and greater blasphemies and abominations. It has made strong attempts to destroy all property, to make all things common, *wives* as well as *goods*. – It has promoted faction and contention; filled the church oftentimes with confusion, and the state sometimes with general disorder. – It has, by its pretended spiritual interpretations, made void the most undoubted laws of GOD. It has laid aside the *gospel sacraments* as weak and carnal things; yea, this *superior light within* has, in the opinion of thousands, render'd the *bible* a *useless dead letter*. – It has made men fancy themselves to be *prophets* and *apostles*; yea, some have taken themselves to be CHRIST JESUS; yea, the blessed GOD himself. It has, in one word, been a pest to the church in all ages, as great an enemy to real and solid religion, as perhaps the grossest *infidelity*.[36]

Source: Charles Chauncy (1705-1787). *Enthusiasm Described and Cautioned Against: A Sermon Preach'd at the Old Brick Meetinghouse in Boston, the Lord's Day after Commencement, 1742*. Boston: J. Draper, 1742, 1-8, 10, 12-15.

---

[36] Explanation in the original text: "Undoubted instances of these, and many other things of a like nature, are well known to such as are, in any measure, acquainted with the *history* of the *church*."

99. Thomas Paine
"Predestination: Remarks on Romans, IX, 18-21[37] Addressed to the Ministers of the Calvinistic Church" (1809)

But the [comparison between God and a potter as well as between man and the potter's clay as mentioned by Paul in Romans, 9,18-21, does not work] with man, either in this world or the next. [Man] is a being sensible of misery as well as of happiness, and therefore Paul argues like an unfeeling idiot when he compares man to clay on a potter's wheel, or to vessels made therefrom: and with respect to God, it is an offense to His attributes of justice, goodness and wisdom to suppose that He would treat the choicest work of creation like inanimate and insensible clay. If Paul believed that God made man after His own image, he dishonors it by making that image and a brickbat[38] to be alike.

The absurd and impious doctrine of predestination, a doctrine destructive of morals, would never have been thought of had it not been for some stupid passages in the Bible, which priestcraft at first, and ignorance since, have imposed upon mankind as revelation.

Nonsense ought to be treated as nonsense wherever it be found; and had this been done in the rational manner it ought to be done, instead of intimating and mincing[39] the matter, as has been too much the case, the nonsense and false doctrine of the Bible, with all the aid that priestcraft can give, could never have stood their ground against the divine reason that God has given to man.

Doctor Franklin gives a remarkable instance of the truth of this in an account of his life, written by himself. He was in London at the time of which he speaks. "Some volumes," says he, "against Deism, fell into my hands. They were said to be the substance of sermons preached at Boyle's lectures."

"It happened that they produced on me an effect precisely the reverse of what was intended by the writers; for the arguments of the Deists, which were cited in order to be refuted, appeared to me more forcible than the refutation itself. In a word I soon became a perfect Deist."[40] –

All America, and more than all America, knows Franklin. His life was devoted to the good and improvement of man. Let, then, those who profess a different creed, imitate his virtues, and excel him if they can.

Source: Thomas Paine (1737-1809). "Predestination: Remarks on Romans, IX, 18-21 – Addressed to the Ministers of the Calvinistic Church." *The Complete Writings of Thomas Paine*. 2 vols. Ed. Philip S. Foner. New York: Citadel, 1945, Vol. 2, 896-897. This address was published in the form of an article in London; it was probably written by Paine shortly before his death in 1809.

---

[37] "Therefore hath he [God] mercy on whom he will *have mercy*, and whom he will he hardeneth. Thou wilt say then unto me, Why doth he yet find fault? For who hath resisted his will? Nay but, O man, who art thou that repliest against God? Shall the thing formed say to him that formed *it*, Why hast thou made me thus? Hath not the potter power over the clay, of the same lump to make one vessel unto honor, and another unto dishonor?"

[38] A piece or fragment of a brick.

[39] To cut up or grind into very small pieces; in extended use, to subdivide minutely.

[40] Original reference in the text to "New York edition of Franklin's Life, page 93."

100. Thomas Paine
"Of the Religion of Deism Compared with the Christian Religion, and the Superiority of the Former over the Latter" (1804)

Every person of whatever religious denomination he may be is a DEIST in the first article of his Creed. Deism from the latin word DEUS, God, is the belief of a God, and this belief is the first article of every man's creed.

[... When] the divine gift of reason begins to expand itself in the mind and calls man to reflection, he then reads and contemplates God in his works and not in books pretending to be revelation. The Creation is the bible of a true believer in God. Every thing in this vast volume inspires him with sublime ideas of the Creator. The little and paltry, and often obscene, tales of the bible sink into wretchedness when put in comparison with this mighty work. [...]

There is a happiness in Deism, when rightly understood, that is not to be found in any other system of religion. All other systems have something in them that either shock our reason or are repugnant[41] to it, and man, if he thinks at all, must stifle his reason in order to force himself to believe them. But in Deism our reason and our belief become happily united. The wonderful structure of the universe and every thing we behold in the system of creation prove to us, far better than books can do, the existence of a God, and at the same time proclaim his attributes. It is by the exercise of our reason that we are enabled to contemplate God in his works and imitate him in his ways. When we see his care and goodness extended over all his creatures, it teaches us our duty toward each other, while it calls forth our gratitude to him. It is by forgetting God in his works, and running after the books of pretended revelation that man has wandered from the strait path of duty and happiness, and become by turns the victim of doubt and the dupe of delusion.

Except in the first article in the Christian creed, that of believing in God, there is not an article in it but fills the mind with doubt as to the truth of it the instant man begins to think. Now every article in a creed that is necessary to the happiness and salvation of man ought to be as evident to the reason and comprehension of man as the first article is, for God has not given us reason for the purpose of confounding us, but that we should use it for our own happiness and his glory.

[...] When we see a watch we have as positive evidence of the existence of a watch-maker as if we saw him; and in like manner the creation is evidence to our reason and our senses of the existence of a Creator. But there is nothing in the works of God that is evidence that he begat a son, nor any thing in the system of creation that corroborates such an idea, and therefore we are not authorised in believing it. [...] The four books called the Evangelists, Matthew, Mark, Luke, and John, which give, or pretend to give, the birth, sayings, life, preaching, and death of Jesus Christ, make no mention of what is called the fall of man, nor is the name of Adam to be found in any of those books, which it certainly would be if the writers of them believed that Jesus was begotten, born, and died for the purpose of redeeming mankind from the sin which Adam had brought into the world. Jesus never speaks of Adam himself, of the Garden of Eden, nor of what is called the fall of man. [...]

---

[41] Repulsive; arousing disgust or aversion.

But the church of Rome having set up its new religion which it called Christianity, and invented the creed which it named the apostles creed, in which it calls Jesus the *only son of God, conceived by the Holy Ghost, and born of the Virgin Mary*, [...] it then manufactured the allegories in the book of Genesis into fact, and the allegorical tree of life and tree of knowledge into real trees, contrary to the belief of the first christians, and for which there is not the least authority in any of the books of the New Testament, for in none of them is there any mention made of such place as the Garden of Eden, nor of any thing that is said to have happened there. [...] As priest-craft was always the enemy of knowledge, because priest-craft supports itself by keeping people in delusion and ignorance, it was consistent with its policy to make the acquisition of knowledge a real sin.

[...] Reason is the forbidden tree of priest-craft, and may serve to explain the allegory of the forbidden tree of knowledge, for we may reasonably suppose the allegory had some meaning and application at the time it was invented. [...] The dogma of the redemption is the fable of priest-craft invented since the time the New Testament was compiled, and the agreeable delusion of it suited with the depravity of immoral livers. When men are taught to ascribe all their crimes and vices to the temptations of the Devil, and to believe that Jesus, by his death, rubs all off and pays their passage to heaven gratis, they become as careless in morals as a spendthrift would be of money, were he told that his father had engaged to pay off all his scores.

It is a doctrine, not only dangerous to morals in this world, but to our happiness in the next world, because it holds out such a cheap, easy, and lazy way of getting to heaven as has a tendency to induce men to hug the delusion of it to their own injury.

But there are times when men have serious thoughts, and it is at such times when they begin to think, that they begin to doubt the truth of the Christian Religion, and well they may, for it is too fanciful and too full of conjecture, inconsistency, improbability, and irrationality, to afford consolation to the thoughtful man. [...]

He may believe that Jesus was crucified, because many others were crucified, but who is to prove he was crucified *for the sins of the world?* This article has no evidence not even in the New Testament; and if it had, where is the proof that the New Testament, in relating things neither probable nor proveable, is to be believed as true? When an article in a creed does not admit of proof nor of probability the salvo[42] is to call it revelation; But this is only putting one difficulty in the place of another, for it is as impossible to prove a thing to be revelation as it is to prove that Mary was gotten with child by the Holy Ghost.

Here it is that the religion of Deism is superior to the Christian religion. It is free from all those invented and torturing articles that shock our reason or injure our humanity, and with which the Christian religion abounds. Its creed is pure and sublimely simple. It believes in God and there it rests. It honours reason as the choicest gift of God to man, and the faculty by which he is enabled to contemplate the power, wisdom, and goodness of the Creator displayed in the creation; and reposing itself on his protection, both here and hereafter, it avoids all presumptuous beliefs, and rejects, as the fabulous inventions of men, all books pretending to revelation. T. P.

Source: Thomas Paine (1737-1809). "Of the Religion of Deism Compared with the Christian Religion, and the Superiority of the Former over the Latter." *Prospect; or, View of the Moral World*, June 30, 1804, 235-239, and July 7, 1804, 243-247.

---

[42] A solution, explanation, an answer to an objection (obsolete).

101. Benjamin Franklin
"To Ezra Stiles" (1790)

REVEREND AND DEAR SIR, Philadª, March 9. 1790.

[...] You desire to know something of my Religion. It is the first time I have been questioned upon it. But I cannot take your Curiosity amiss, and shall endeavour in a few Words to gratify it. Here is my Creed. I believe in one God, Creator of the Universe. That he governs it by his Providence. That he ought to be worshipped. That the most acceptable Service we render to him is doing good to his other Children. That the soul of Man is immortal, and will be treated with Justice in another Life respecting its Conduct in this. These I take to be the fundamental Principles of all sound Religion, and I regard them as you do in whatever Sect I meet with them.

As to Jesus of Nazareth, my Opinion of whom you particularly desire, I think the System of Morals and his Religion, as he left them to us, the best the World ever saw or is likely to see; but I apprehend it has received various corrupting Changes, and I have, with most of the present Dissenters in England, some Doubts as to his Divinity; tho' it is a question I do not dogmatize upon, having never studied it, and think it needless to busy myself with it now, when I expect soon an Opportunity of knowing the Truth with less Trouble. I see no harm, however, in its being believed, if that Belief has the good Consequence, as probably it has, of making his Doctrines more respected and better observed; especially as I do not perceive, that the Supreme takes it amiss, by distinguishing the Unbelievers in his Government of the World with any peculiar Marks of his Displeasure.

I shall only add, respecting myself, that, having experienced the Goodness of that Being in conducting me prosperously thro' a long life, I have no doubt of its Continuance in the next, though without the smallest Conceit of meriting such Goodness. My Sentiments on this Head you will see in the Copy of an old Letter enclosed, which I wrote in answer to one from a zealous Religionist, whom I had relieved in a paralytic case by electricity, and who, being afraid I should grow proud upon it, sent me his serious though rather impertinent Caution. I send you also the Copy of another Letter, which will shew something of my Disposition relating to Religion. With great and sincere Esteem and Affection, I am, Your obliged old Friend and most obedient humble Servant. [...]

Source: Benjamin Franklin (1706-1790). "To Ezra Stiles". *Benjamin Franklin: Writings*. New York: Literary Classics of the United States, 1987, 1179-1180.

102. Philip Freneau
"On the Universality and Other Attributes of the God of Nature" (after 1797)

All that we see, about, abroad,
What is it all, but nature's God?
In meaner works discover'd here
No less than in the starry sphere.

In seas, on earth, this God is seen;
All that exist, upon him lean;

He lives in all, and never stray'd
A moment from the works he made:

His system fix'd on general laws
Bespeaks a wise creating cause;
Impartially he rules mankind,
And all that on this globe we find.

Unchanged in all that seems to change,
Unbounded space is his great range;
To one vast purpose always true,
No time, with him, is old or new.

In all the attributes divine
Unlimited perfections shine;
In these enwrapt, in these complete,
All virtues in that centre meet.

This power who doth all powers transcend,
To all intelligence a friend,
Exists, the *greatest and the best*[43]
Throughout all worlds, to make them blest.

All that he did he first approved
He all things into *being* loved;
O'er all he made he still presides,
For them in life, or death provides.

Source: Philip Freneau (1752-1832). "On the Universality and Other Attributes of the God of Nature." *A Collection of Poems, on American Affairs, and a Variety of Other Subjects, Chiefly Moral and Political; Written between the Year 1797 and the Present Time, in Two Volumes.* Vol. 1. New York: David Longworth, 1815, 99-100.

103. Benjamin Franklin
"The Way to Wealth" – Preface to *Poor Richard Improved* (1757)

Courteous Reader,

I have heard that nothing gives an Author so great Pleasure, as to find his Works respectfully quoted by other learned Authors. This Pleasure I have seldom enjoyed; for tho' I have been, if I may say it without Vanity, an *eminent Author* of Almanacks annually now a full Quarter of a Century [...].

Judge then how much I must have been gratified by an Incident I am going to relate to you. I stopt my Horse lately where a great Number of People were collected at a Vendue of Merchant Goods. The Hour of Sale not being come, they were conversing on the Badness of the Times, and one of the Company call'd to a plain clean old Man, with

---

[43] Original footnote: "— Jupiter, optimus, maximus. — CICERO."

white Locks, *Pray, Father Abraham, what think you of the Times? Won't these heavy Taxes quite ruin the Country? How shall we be ever able to pay them? What would you advise us to?* – Father Abraham stood up, and reply'd, If you'd have my Advice, I'll give it you in short, for a *Word to the Wise is enough*, and *many Words won't fill a Bushel*, as Poor Richard says. They join'd in desiring him to speak his Mind, and gathering round him, he proceeded as follows;[44]

"Friends, says he, and Neighbours, the Taxes are indeed very heavy, and if those laid on by the Government were the only Ones we had to pay, we might more easily discharge them; but we have many others, and much more grievous to some of us. We are taxed twice as much by our *Idleness*, three times as much by our *Pride*, and four times as much by our *Folly*, and from these Taxes the Commissioners cannot ease or deliver us by allowing an Abatement. However let us hearken to good Advice, and something may be done for us; *God helps them that help themselves*, as Poor Richard says, in his Almanack of 1733.

It would be thought a hard Government that should tax its People one tenth Part of their *Time*, to be employed in its Service. But *Idleness* taxes many of us much more, if we reckon all that is spent in absolute *Sloth*, or doing of nothing, with that which is spent in idle Employments or Amusements, that amount to nothing. *Sloth*, by bringing on Diseases, absolutely shortens Life. *Sloth, like Rust, consumes faster than Labour wears, while the used Key is always bright*, as Poor Richard says. But *dost thou love Life, then do not squander Time, for that's the Stuff Life is made of*, as Poor Richard says. How much more than is necessary do we spend in Sleep! forgetting that *The sleeping Fox catches no Poultry*, and that *there will be sleeping enough in the Grave*, as Poor Richard says. If Time be of all Things the most precious, *wasting Time* must be, as Poor Richard says, *the greatest Prodigality*, since, as he elsewhere tells us, *Lost Time is never found again*; and what we call *Time-enough, always proves little enough*: Let us then be up and be doing, and doing to the Purpose; so by Diligence shall we do more with less Perplexity. *Sloth makes all Things difficult, but Industry all easy*, as Poor Richard says; and *He that riseth late, must trot all Day, and shall scarce overtake his Business at Night*. While *Laziness travels so slowly, that Poverty soon overtakes him*, as we read in Poor Richard, who adds, *Drive thy Business, let not that drive thee*; and *Early to Bed, and early to rise, makes a Man healthy, wealthy and wise*.

So what signifies *wishing* and *hoping* for better Times. We may make these Times better if we bestir ourselves. *Industry need not wish*, as Poor Richard says, and *He that lives upon Hope will die fasting. There are no Gains, without Pains*; then *Help Hands, for I have no Lands*, or if I have, they are smartly taxed. And, as Poor Richard likewise observes, *He that hath a Trade hath an Estate*, and *He that hath a Calling hath an Office of Profit and Honour*; but then the *Trade* must be worked at, and the *Calling* well followed, or neither the *Estate*, nor the *Office*, will enable us to pay our Taxes. [...] Work while it is called To-day, for you know not how much you may be hindered To-morrow, which makes Poor Richard say, *One To-day is worth two To-morrows*; and farther, *Have you somewhat to do To-morrow, do it To-day*. If you were a Servant, would you not be ashamed that a good Master should catch you idle? Are you then your own Master, *be ashamed to catch yourself idle*, as Poor Dick says. When there is so much to be done for yourself, your Family, your Country, and your gracious King, be up by Peep of Day; *Let not the Sun look down*

---

[44] Father Abraham's speech consists of a careful arrangement of approximately one hundred of the aphorisms and maxims contained in the earlier *Poor Richard* almanacs. No almanac is ignored, but in many cases Franklin reworked the maxims by changing phrases.

and say, Inglorious here he lies. Handle your Tools without Mittens; remember that *the Cat in Gloves catches no Mice,* as Poor Richard says. 'Tis true there is much to be done, and perhaps you are weak handed, but stick to it steadily, and you will see great Effects, for *constant Dropping wears away Stones,* and by *Diligence and Patience the Mouse ate in two the Cable;* and *little Strokes fell great Oaks,* as Poor Richard says in his Almanack, the Year I cannot just now remember.

Methinks I hear some of you say, *Must a Man afford himself no Leisure?* I will tell thee, my Friend, what Poor Richard says, *Employ thy Time well if thou meanest to gain Leisure;* and, *since thou art not sure of a Minute, throw not away an Hour.* Leisure, is Time for doing something useful; this Leisure the diligent Man will obtain, but the lazy Man never; so that, as Poor Richard says, a *Life of Leisure and a Life of Laziness are two Things.* Do you imagine that Sloth will afford you more Comfort than Labour? No, for as Poor Richard says, *Trouble springs from Idleness, and grievous Toil from needless Ease. Many without Labour, would live by their* WITS *only, but they break for want of Stock.* Whereas Industry gives Comfort, and Plenty, and Respect [...].

And again, *Pride is as loud a Beggar as Want, and a great deal more saucy.* When you have bought one fine Thing you must buy ten more, that your Appearance may be all of a Piece; but Poor Dick says, *'Tis easier to* suppress *the first Desire, than to* satisfy *all that follow it.* And 'tis as truly Folly for the Poor to ape the Rich, as for the Frog to swell, in order to equal the Ox.

Great Estates may venture more,
But little Boats should keep near Shore.

'Tis however a Folly soon punished; for *Pride that dines on Vanity sups on Contempt,* as Poor Richard says. And in another Place, *Pride breakfasted with Plenty, dined with Poverty, and supped with Infamy.* [...]

And now to conclude, *Experience keeps a dear School, but Fools will learn in no other, and scarce in that;* for it is true, *we may give Advice, but we cannot give Conduct,* as Poor Richard says: However, remember this, *They that won't be counselled, can't be helped,* as Poor Richard says: And farther, That *if you will not hear Reason, she'll surely rap your Knuckles.*

Thus the old Gentleman ended his Harangue. The People heard it, and approved the Doctrine, and immediately practised the contrary, just as if it had been a common Sermon; for the Vendue opened, and they began to buy extravagantly, notwithstanding all his Cautions, and their own Fear of Taxes. I found the good Man had thoroughly studied my Almanacks, and digested all I had dropt on those Topicks during the Course of Five-and-twenty Years. The frequent Mention he made of me must have tired any one else, but my Vanity was wonderfully delighted with it, though I was conscious that not a tenth Part of the Wisdom was my own which he ascribed to me, but rather the *Gleanings* I had made of the Sense of all Ages and Nations. However, I resolved to be the better for the Echo of it; and though I had at first determined to buy Stuff for a new Coat, I went away resolved to wear my old One a little longer. *Reader,* if thou wilt do the same, thy Profit will be as great as mine. I am, as ever, Thine to serve thee, RICHARD SAUNDERS.
July 7, 1757.

Source: Franklin, Benjamin (1706-1790). "The Way to Wealth or Poor Richard Improved." *The Papers of Benjamin Franklin.* 32 vols. Vol. 7: *October 1, 1756, through March 31, 1758.* Ed. Leonard W. Labaree. New Haven and London: Yale University Press, 1963, 340-343, 347, 349-350.

104. Benjamin Franklin
The Autobiography (1771-1789)

Part One

Twyford, at the Bishop of St Asaph's 1771.
Dear Son,

I have ever had a Pleasure in obtaining any little Anecdotes of my Ancestors. You may remember the Enquiries I made among the Remains of my Relations when you were with me in England; and the Journey I took for that purpose. Now imagining it may be equally agreable to you to know the Circumstances of *my* Life, many of which you are yet unacquainted with; and expecting a Weeks uninterrupted Leisure in my present Country Retirement, I sit down to write them for you. To which I have besides some other Inducements. Having emerg'd from the Poverty & Obscurity in which I was born & bred, to a State of Affluence & some Degree of Reputation in the World, and having gone so far thro' Life with a considerable Share of Felicity, the conducing Means I made use of, which, with the Blessing of God, so well succeeded, my Posterity may like to know, as they may find some of them suitable to their own Situations, & therefore fit to be imitated. – That Felicity, when I reflected on it, has induc'd me sometimes to say, that were it offer'd to my Choice, I should have no Objection to a Repetition of the same Life from its Beginning, only asking the Advantage Authors have in a second Edition to correct some Faults of the first. So would I if I might, besides correcting the Faults, change some sinister Accidents & Events of it for others more favourable, but tho' this were deny'd, I should still accept the Offer. However, since such a Repetition is not to be expected, the Thing most like living one's Life over again, seems to be a *Recollection* of that Life; and to make that Recollection as durable as possible, the putting it down in Writing. – Hereby, too, I shall indulge the Inclination so natural in old Men, to be talking of themselves and their own past Actions, and I shall indulge it, without being troublesome to others who thro' respect to Age might think themselves oblig'd to give me a Hearing, since this may be read or not as any one pleases. And lastly, (I may as well confess it, since my Denial of it will be believ'd by no body) perhaps I shall a good deal gratify my own *Vanity*. Indeed I scarce ever heard or saw the introductory Words, *Without Vanity I may say*, &c. but some vain thing immediately follow'd. Most People dislike Vanity in others whatever Share they have of it themselves, but I give it fair Quarter wherever I meet with it, being persuaded that it is often productive of Good to the Possessor & to others that are within his Sphere of Action: And therefore in many Cases it would not be quite absurd if a Man were to thank God for his Vanity among the other Comforts of Life. –

And now I speak of thanking God, I desire with all Humility to acknowledge, that I owe the mention'd Happiness of my past Life to his kind Providence, which led me to the Means I us'd & gave them Success. – My Belief of This, induces me to *hope*, tho' I must not *presume*, that the same Goodness will still be exercis'd towards me in continuing that Happiness, or in enabling me to bear a fatal Reverso, which I may experience as others have done, the Complexion of my future Fortune being known to him only: and in whose Power it is to bless to us even our Afflictions. [...]

[...] At Ten Years old, I was taken home to assist my Father in his Business, which was that of a Tallow Chandler and Sope-Boiler. A Business he was not bred to, but had assumed on his Arrival in New England & on finding his Dying Trade would not maintain his Family, being in little Request. Accordingly I was employed in cutting Wick for the

Candles, filling the Dipping Mold, & the Molds for cast Candles, attending the Shop, going of Errands, &c. – I dislik'd the Trade and had a strong Inclination for the Sea; but my Father declar'd against it; however, living near the Water, I was much in and about it, learnt early to swim well, & to manage Boats, and when in a Boat or Canoe with other Boys I was commonly allow'd to govern, especially in any case of Difficulty; and upon other Occasions I was generally a Leader among the Boys, and sometimes led them into Scrapes, of which I will mention one Instance, as it shows an early projecting public Spirit, tho' not then justly conducted. There was a Salt Marsh that bounded part of the Mill Pond, on the Edge of which at Highwater, we us'd to stand to fish for Minews.[45] By much Trampling, we had made it a mere Quagmire.[46] My Proposal was to build a Wharf there fit for us to stand upon, and I show'd my Comrades a large Heap of Stones which were intended for a new House near the Marsh, and which would very well suit our Purpose. Accordingly in the Evening when the Workmen were gone, I assembled a Number of my Playfellows, and working with them diligently like so many Emmets,[47] sometimes two or three to a Stone, we brought them all away and built our little Wharff. – The next Morning the Workmen were surpriz'd at Missing the Stones; which were found in our Wharff; Enquiry was made after the Removers; we were discovered & complain'd of; several of us were corrected by our Fathers; and tho' I pleaded the Usefulness of the Work, mine convinc'd me that nothing was useful which was not honest. –

I think you may like to know something of [my father's] Person & Character. [... H]is great Excellence lay in a sound Understanding, and solid Judgment in prudential Matters, both in private & publick Affairs. In the latter indeed he was never employed, the numerous Family he had to educate & the Straitness of his Circumstances, keeping him close to his Trade, but I remember well his being frequently visited by leading People, who consulted him for his Opinion on Affairs of the Town or of the Church he belong'd to & show'd a good deal of Respect for his Judgment and Advice. He was also much consulted by private Persons about their Affairs when any Difficulty occur'd, & frequently chosen an Arbitrator between contending Parties. – At his Table he lik'd to have as often as he could, some sensible Friend or Neighbour, to converse with, and always took care to start some ingenious or useful Topic for Discourse, which might tend to improve the Minds of his Children. By this means he turn'd our Attention to what was good, just, & prudent in the Conduct of Life [...].

From a Child I was fond of Reading, and all the little Money that came into my Hands was ever laid out in Books. Pleas'd with the Pilgrim's Progress,[48] my first Collection was of John Bunyan's Works, in separate little Volumes. I afterwards sold them to enable me to buy R. Burton's Historical Collections;[49] they were small Chapmen's Books and cheap, 40 or 50 in all. – My Father's little Library consisted chiefly of Books in polemic Divinity, most of which I read, and have since often regretted, that at a time when I had such a Thirst for Knowledge, more proper Books had not fallen in my Way, since it was now resolv'd I should not be a Clergyman. Plutarch's Lives[50] there was, in which I read

---

[45] Various small, usually freshwater fish.
[46] A piece of wet and boggy ground.
[47] Ants.
[48] John Bunyan's (1628-1688) famous allegory about the journey of Everyman, named Christian, to salvation.
[49] Richard Burton was the pseudonym for Nathaniel Crouch (1632?-1725?), a pupularizer of British history.
[50] Plutarch's (46-after 119) biographies of 46 noted Greek and Roman figures.

abundantly, and I still think that time spent to great Advantage. There was also a Book of Defoe's called an Essay on Projects[51] and another of Dr Mather's call'd Essays to do Good,[52] which perhaps gave me a Turn of Thinking that had an Influence on some of the principal future Events of my Life.

This Bookish Inclination at length determin'd my Father to make me a Printer, tho' he had already one Son, (James) of that Profession. In 1717 my Brother James return'd from England with a Press & Letters to set up his Business in Boston. [...]

When about 16 Years of Age, I happen'd to meet with a Book written by one Tryon,[53] recommending a Vegetable Diet. I determined to go into it. My Brother being yet unmarried, did not keep House, but boarded himself & his Apprentices in another Family. My refusing to eat Flesh occasioned an Inconveniency, and I was frequently chid for my singularity. I made my self acquainted with Tryon's Manner of preparing some of his Dishes, such as Boiling Potatoes, or Rice, making Hasty Pudding, & a few others, and then propos'd to my Brother, that if he would give me Weekly half the Money he paid for my Board, I would board my self. He instantly agreed to it, and I presently found that I could save half what he paid me. This was an additional Fund for buying Books: But I had another Advantage in it. My Brother and the rest going from the Printing House to their Meals, I remain'd there alone, and dispatching presently my light Repast, (which often was no more than a Bisket or a Slice of Bread, a Handful of Raisins or a Tart from the Pastry Cook's, and a Glass of Water) had the rest of the Time till their Return, for Study, in which I made the greater Progress from that greater Clearness of Head & quicker Apprehension which usually attend Temperance in Eating & Drinking. [...]

While I was intent on improving my Language, I met with an English Grammar (I think it was Greenwood's)[54] at the End of which there were two little Sketches of the Arts of Rhetoric and Logic, the latter finishing with a Specimen of a Dispute in the Socratic Method. And soon after I procur'd Xenophon's Memorable Things of Socrates,[55] wherein there are many Instances of the same Method. I was charm'd with it, adopted it, dropt my abrupt Contradiction, and positive Argumentation, and put on the humble Enquirer & Doubter. And being then, from reading Shaftsbury & Collins,[56] become a real Doubter in many Points of our Religious Doctrine, I found this Method safest for my self & very embarassing to those against whom I used it, therefore I took a Delight in it, practis'd it continually & grew very artful & expert in drawing People even of superior Knowledge into Concessions the Consequences of which they did not foresee, entangling them in Difficulties out of which they could not extricate themselves, and so obtaining Victories that neither my self nor my Cause always deserved. – I continu'd this Method some few Years, but gradually left it, retaining only the Habit of expressing my self in Terms of modest Diffidence, never using when I advance any thing that may possibly be disputed, the Words, *Certainly*, *undoubtedly*, or any others that give the Air of

---

[51] Daniel Defoe's (1660-1731) *Essay Upon Projects* (1697).
[52] Reference to Cotton Mather's essay *Bonifacius: An Essay upon the Good That is to be Devised and Designed, by Those Who Desire to Answer the Great End of Life, and to Do Good while They Live* (1710); cf. doc. 105 in this collection.
[53] Thomas Tryon (1634-1703), *The Way to Health, Long Life and Happiness, or A Discourse of Temperance* (1683).
[54] James Greenwood (?-1737), *An Essay towards a Practical English Grammar* (1711).
[55] Xenophon, *The Memorable Things of Socrates*, transl. by Edward Bysshe (1712).
[56] Anthony Ashley Cooper, 3rd Earl of Shaftesbury (1671-1713), a religious skeptic; Anthony Collins (1676-1729), a deist.

Positiveness to an Opinion; but rather say, *I conceive*, or *I apprehend* a Thing to be so or so, *It appears to me*, or *I should think it so or so for such & such Reasons*, or *I imagine* it to be so, or *it is so if I am not mistaken*. – This Habit I believe has been of great Advantage to me, when I have had occasion to inculcate my Opinions & persuade Men into Measures that I have been from time to time engag'd in promoting. – And as the chief Ends of Conversation are to *inform*, or to be *informed*, to *please* or to *persuade*, I wish well meaning sensible Men would not lessen their Power of doing Good by a Positive assuming Manner that seldom fails to disgust, tends to create Opposition, and to defeat every one of those Purposes for which Speech was given us, to wit, giving or receiving Information, or Pleasure: For If you would *inform*, a positive dogmatical Manner in advancing your Sentiments, may provoke Contradiction & prevent a candid Attention. If you wish Information & Improvement from the Knowledge of others and yet at the same time express your self as firmly fix'd in your present Opinions, modest sensible Men, who do not love Disputation, will probably leave you undisturb'd in the Possession of your Error; and by such a Manner you can seldom hope to recommend your self in *pleasing* your Hearers, or to persuade those whose Concurrence you desire. [...]

My Brother had in 1720 or 21, begun to print a Newspaper. It was the second that appear'd in America, & was called *The New England Courant*. The only one before it, was *the Boston News Letter*. I remember his being dissuaded by some of his Friends from the Undertaking, as not likely to succeed, one Newspaper being in their Judgment enough for America. – At this time 1771 there are not less than five & twenty. – He went on however with the Undertaking, and after having work'd in composing the Types & printing off the Sheets I was employ'd to carry the Papers thro' the Streets to the Customers. – He had some ingenious Men among his Friends who amus'd themselves by writing little Pieces for this Paper, which gain'd it Credit, & made it more in Demand; and these Gentlemen often visited us. – Hearing their Conversations, and their Accounts of the Approbation their Papers were receiv'd with, I was excited to try my Hand among them. But being still a Boy, & suspecting that my Brother would object to printing any Thing of mine in his Paper if he knew it to be mine, I contriv'd to disguise my Hand, & writing an anonymous Paper I put it in at Night under the Door of the Printing House. It was found in the Morning & communicated to his Writing Friends when they call'd in as Usual. They read it, commented on it in my Hearing, and I had the exquisite Pleasure, of finding it met with their Approbation, and that in their different Guesses at the Author none were named but Men of some Character among us for Learning & Ingenuity. – I suppose now that I was rather lucky in my Judges: And that perhaps they were not really so very good ones as I then esteem'd them. Encourag'd however by this, I wrote and convey'd in the same Way to the Press several more Papers, which were equally approv'd, and I kept my Secret till my small Fund of Sense for such Performances was pretty well exhausted, & then I discovered it; when I began to be considered a little more by my Brother's Acquaintance, and in a manner that did not quite please him, as he thought, probably with reason, that it tended to make me too vain. And perhaps this might be one Occasion of the Differences that we began to have about this Time. Tho' a Brother, he considered himself as my Master, & me as his Apprentice; and accordingly expected the same Services from me as he would from another; while I thought he demean'd me too much in some he requir'd of me, who from a Brother expected more Indulgence. Our Disputes were often brought before our Father, and I fancy I was either generally in the right, or else a better Pleader, because the Judgment was generally in my favour: But my

Brother was passionate & had often beaten me, which I took extreamly amiss;[57] and thinking my Apprenticeship very tedious, I was continually wishing for some Opportunity of shortening it, which at length offered in a manner unexpected.[58] [...]

Before I enter upon my public Appearance in Business, it may be well to let you know the then State of my Mind, with regard to my Principles and Morals, that you may see how far those influenc'd the future Events of my Life. My Parent's had early given me religious Impressions, and brought me through my Childhood piously in the Dissenting Way.[59] But I was scarce 15 when, after doubting by turns of several Points as I found them disputed in the different Books I read, I began to doubt of Revelation it self. Some Books against Deism[60] fell into my Hands; they were said to be the Substance of Sermons preached at Boyle's Lectures.[61] It happened that they wrought an Effect on me quite contrary to what was intended by them: For the Arguments of the Deists which were quoted to be refuted, appeared to me much Stronger than the Refutations. In short I soon became a thorough Deist. [...]

And from the Attributes of God, his infinite Wisdom, Goodness & Power concluded that nothing could possibly be wrong in the World, & that Vice & Virtue were empty Distinctions, no such Things existing: appear'd now not so clever a Performance as I once thought it; and I doubted whether some Error had not insinuated itself unperceiv'd, into my Argument, so as to infect all that follow'd, as is common in metaphysical Reasonings. – I grew convinc'd that *Truth, Sincerity & Integrity* in Dealings between Man & Man, were of the utmost Importance to the Felicity of Life, and I form'd written Resolutions, (which still remain in my Journal Book) to practise them ever while I lived. Revelation had indeed no weight with me as such; but I entertain'd an Opinion, that tho' certain Actions might not be bad *because* they were forbidden by it, or good *because* it commanded them; yet probably those Actions might be forbidden *because* they were bad for us, or commanded *because* they were beneficial to us, in their own Natures, all the Circumstances of things considered. And this Persuasion, with the kind hand of Providence, or some guardian Angel, or accidental favourable Circumstances & Situations, or all together, preserved me (thro' this dangerous Time of Youth & the hazardous Situations I was sometimes in among Strangers, remote from the Eye & Advice of my Father,) without any *wilful* gross Immorality or Injustice that might have been expected from my Want of Religion. – I say *wilful*, because the Instances I have mentioned, had something of *Necessity* in them, from my Youth, Inexperience, & the Knavery of others. – I had therefore a tolerable Character to begin the World with, I valued it properly, & determin'd to preserve it. [...]

I should have mention'd before, that in the Autumn of the preceding Year, I had form'd most of my ingenious Acquaintance into a Club, for mutual Improvement, which we call'd the Junto. We met on Friday Evenings. The Rules I drew up, requir'd that every Member in his Turn should produce one or more Queries on any Point of Morals, Poli-

---

[57] Original footnote: "I fancy his harsh & tyrannical Treatment of me, might be a means of impressing me with that Aversion to arbitrary Power that has stuck to me thro' my whole Life."
[58] In the following, Franklin leaves his brother's print shop in Boston and tries to set up his own business in Philadelphia.
[59] Franklin refers to the liberal religious creeds of those who 'dissent' from religious orthodoxy.
[60] Belief in the existence of a Supreme Being as the source of the universe; deists rejected revelation and the supernatural doctrines of Christianity.
[61] Robert Boyle (1627-1691), defended Christianity against skepticism in a series of lectures.

tics or Natural Philosophy, to be discuss'd by the Company, and once in three Months produce and read an Essay of his own Writing on any Subject he pleased. [...] And the Club continu'd almost as long [as 40 years] and was the best School of Philosophy, Morals & Politics that then existed in the Province; for our Queries which were read the Week preceding their Discussion, put us on reading with Attention upon the several Subjects, that we might speak more to the purpose: and here too we acquired better Habits of Conversation, every thing being studied in our Rules which might prevent our disgusting each other. [...]

Mem°.

Thus far was written with the Intention express'd in the Beginning and therefore contains several little family Anecdotes of no Importance to others. What follows was written many Years after in compliance with the Advice contain'd in these Letters, and accordingly intended for the Publick. The Affairs of the Revolution occasion'd the Interruption.

Part Two
Letter from Mr. Abel James, with Notes of my Life, (received in Paris.)

My dear & honored Friend. [...]

The Influence Writings under that Class [of autobiography] have on the Minds of Youth is very great, and has no where appeared so plain as in our public Friends' Journals. It almost insensibly leads the Youth into the Resolution of endeavouring to become as good and as eminent as the Journalist. Should thine for Instance when published, and I think it could not fail of it, lead the Youth to equal the Industry & Temperance of thy early Youth, what a Blessing with that Class would such a Work be. I know of no Character living nor many of them put together, who has so much in his Power as Thyself to promote a greater Spirit of Industry & early Attention to Business, Frugality and Temperance with the American Youth. Not that I think the Work would have no other Merit & Use in the World, far from it, but the first is of such vast Importance, that I know nothing that can equal it.

———

The foregoing letter and the minutes accompanying it being shewn to a friend, I received from him the following:

LETTER FROM MR. BENJAMIN VAUGHAN.

Paris, January 31, 1783.

MY DEAREST SIR,

When I had read over your sheets of minutes of the principal incidents of your life, recovered for you by your Quaker acquaintance; I told you I would send you a letter expressing my reasons why I thought it would be useful to complete and publish it as he desired. Various concerns have for some time past prevented this letter being written, and I do not know whether it was worth any expectation: happening to be at leisure however at present, I shall by writing at least interest and instruct myself; but as the terms I am inclined to use may tend to offend a person of your manners, I shall only tell you how I would address any other person, who was as good and as great as yourself, but less diffident. I would say to him, Sir, I *solicit* the history of your life from the following motives.

Your history is so remarkable, that if you do not give it, somebody else will certainly give it; and perhaps so as nearly to do as much harm, as your own management of the thing might do good.

It will moreover present a table of the internal circumstances of your country, which will very much tend to invite to it settlers of virtuous and manly minds. And considering the eagerness with which such information is sought by them, and the extent of your reputation, I do not know of a more efficacious advertisement than your Biography would give.

All that has happened to you is also connected with the detail of the manners and situation of *a rising* people; and in this respect I do not think that the writings of Caesar and Tacitus can be more interesting to a true judge of human nature and society.

But these, Sir, are small reasons in my opinion, compared with the chance which your life will give for the forming of future great men; and in conjunction with your *Art of Virtue*, (which you design to publish) of improving the features of private character, and consequently of aiding all happiness both public and domestic.

The two works I allude to, Sir, will in particular give a noble rule and example of *self-education*. School and other education constantly proceed upon false principles, and shew a clumsy apparatus pointed at a false mark; but your apparatus is simple, and the mark a true one; and while parents and young persons are left destitute of other just means of estimating and becoming prepared for a reasonable course in life, your discovery that the thing is in many a man's private power, will be invaluable!

Influence upon the private character late in life, is not only an influence late in life, but a weak influence. It is in *youth* that we plant our chief habits and prejudices; it is in youth that we take our party as to profession, pursuits, and matrimony. In youth therefore the turn is given; in youth the education even of the next generation is given; in youth the private and public character is determined; and the term of life extending but from youth to age, life ought to begin well from youth; and more especially *before* we take our party as to our principal objects.

But your Biography will not merely teach self-education, but the education of *a wise man*; and the wisest man will receive lights and improve his progress, by seeing detailed the conduct of another wise man. And why are weaker men to be deprived of such helps, when we see our race has been blundering on in the dark, almost without a guide in this particular, from the farthest trace of time. Shew then, Sir, how much is to be done, *both to sons and fathers*; and invite all wise men to become like yourself; and other men to become wise.

When we see how cruel statesmen and warriors can be to the humble race, and how absurd distinguished men can be to their acquaintance, it will be instructive to observe the instances multiply of pacific acquiescing manners; and to find how compatible it is to be great and *domestic*; enviable and yet *good-humoured*.

The little private incidents which you will also have to relate, will have considerable use, as we want above all things, *rules of prudence in ordinary affairs*; and it will be curious to see how you have acted in these. It will be so far a sort of key to life, and explain many things that all men ought to have once explained to them, to give them a chance of becoming wise by foresight.

The nearest thing to having experience of one's own, is to have other people's affairs brought before us in a shape that is interesting; this is sure to happen from your pen. Your affairs and management will have an air of simplicity or importance that will not fail to strike; and I am convinced you have conducted them with as much originality as if you had been conducting discussions in politics or philosophy; and what more worthy of experiments and system, (its importance and its errors considered) than human life! [...]

Besides all this, the immense revolution of the present period, will necessarily turn our attention towards the author of it; and when virtuous principles have been pretended in it, it will be highly important to shew that such have really influenced; and, as your own character will be the principal one to receive a scrutiny, it is proper (even for its effects upon your vast and rising country, as well as upon England and upon Europe), that it should stand respectable and eternal. For the furtherance of human happiness, I have always maintained that it is necessary to prove that man is not even at present a vicious and detestable animal; and still more to prove that good management may greatly amend him; and it is for much the same reason, that I am anxious to see the opinion established, that there are fair characters existing among the individuals of the race; [...].

             Signed BENJ. VAUGHAN.

Continuation of the Account of my Life.
Begun at Passy 1784

It is some time since I receiv'd the above Letters, but I have been too busy till now to think of complying with the Request they contain. It might too be much better done if I were at home among my Papers, which would aid my Memory, & help to ascertain Dates. But my Return being uncertain, and having just now a little Leisure, I will endeavour to recollect & write what I can; If I live to get home, it may there be corrected and improv'd. [...]

I had been religiously educated as a Presbyterian; and tho' some of the Dogmas of that Persuasion, such as the Eternal Decrees of God, Election, Reprobation,[62] &c. appear'd to me unintelligible, others doubtful, & I early absented myself from the Public Assemblies of the Sect, Sunday being my Studying-Day, I never was without some religious Principles; I never doubted, for instance, the Existance of the Deity, that he made the World, & govern'd it by his Providence; that the most acceptable Service of God was the doing Good to Man; that our Souls are immortal; and that all Crime will be punished & Virtue rewarded either here or hereafter; these I esteem'd the Essentials of every Religion, and being to be found in all the Religions we had in our Country I respected them all, tho' with different degrees of Respect as I found them more or less mix'd with other Articles which without any Tendency to inspire, promote or confirm Morality, serv'd principally to divide us & make us unfriendly to one another. [...]

It was about this time that I conceiv'd the bold and arduous Project of arriving at moral Perfection. I wish'd to live without committing any Fault at any time; I would conquer all that either Natural Inclination, Custom, or Company might lead me into. As I knew, or thought I knew, what was right and wrong, I did not see why I might not *always* do the one and avoid the other. But I soon found I had undertaken a Task of more Difficulty than I had imagined: While my Care was employ'd in guarding against one Fault, I was often surpriz'd by another. Habit took the Advantage of Inattention. Inclination was sometimes too strong for Reason. I concluded at length, that the mere speculative Conviction that it was our Interest to be compleatly virtuous, was not sufficient to prevent our Slipping, and that the contrary Habits must be broken and good Ones ac-

---

[62] Rejection by God; being ordained to eternal misery.

quired and established, before we can have any Dependance on a steady uniform Rectitude of Conduct. For this purpose I therefore contriv'd the following Method. –

In the various Enumerations of the moral Virtues I had met with in my Reading, I found the Catalogue more or less numerous, as different Writers included more or fewer Ideas under the same Name. Temperance, for Example, was by some confin'd to Eating & Drinking, while by others it was extended to mean the moderating every other Pleasure, Appetite, Inclination or Passion, bodily or mental, even to our Avarice & Ambition. I propos'd to myself, for the sake of Clearness, to use rather more Names with fewer Ideas annex'd to each, than a few Names with more Ideas; and I included under Thirteen Names of Virtues all that at that time occurr'd to me as necessary or desirable, and annex'd to each a short Precept, which fully express'd the Extent I gave to its Meaning. –

These Names of Virtues with their Precepts were

1. TEMPERANCE.
   Eat not to Dullness
   Drink not to Elevation.
2. SILENCE.
   Speak not but what may benefit others or your self. Avoid trifling Conversation.
3. ORDER.
   Let all your Things have their Places. Let each Part of your Business have its Time.
4. RESOLUTION.
   Resolve to perform what you ought. Perform without fail what you resolve.
5. FRUGALITY.
   Make no Expence but to do good to others or yourself: i.e. Waste nothing.
6. INDUSTRY.
   Lose no Time. – Be always employ'd in something useful. – Cut off all unnecessary Actions. –
7. SINCERITY.
   Use no hurtful Deceit.
   Think innocently and justly; and, if you speak; speak accordingly.
8. JUSTICE.
   Wrong none, by doing Injuries or omitting the Benefits that are your Duty.
9. MODERATION.
   Avoid Extreams. Forbear resenting Injuries so much as you think they deserve.
10. CLEANLINESS
    Tolerate no Uncleanness in Body, Cloaths or Habitation. –
11. TRANQUILITY
    Be not disturbed at Trifles, or at Accidents common or unavoidable.
12. CHASTITY.
    Rarely use Venery[63] but for Health or Offspring; Never to Dulness, Weakness, or the Injury of your own or another's Peace or Reputation. –
13. HUMILITY.
    Imitate Jesus and Socrates. –

My intention being to acquire the *Habitude* of all these Virtues, I judg'd it would be well not to distract my Attention by attempting the whole at once, but to fix it on one of them at a time, and when I should be Master of that, then to proceed to another, and so on till I should have gone thro' the thirteen. And as the previous Acquisition of some might facilitate the Acquisition of certain others, I arrang'd them with that View as they stand above.

---

[63] The pursuit of sexual pleasure; indulgence of sexual desire.

Temperance first, as it tends to procure that Coolness & Clearness of Head, which is so necessary where constant Vigilance was to be kept up, and Guard maintained, against the unremitting Attraction of ancient Habits, and the Force of perpetual Temptations. This being acquir'd & establish'd, *Silence* would be more easy, and my Desire being to gain Knowledge at the same time that I improv'd in Virtue, and considering that in Conversation it was obtain'd rather by the Use of the Ears than of the Tongue, & therefore wishing to break a Habit I was getting into of Prattling, Punning & Joking, which only made me acceptable to trifling Company, I gave *Silence* the second Place. This, and the next, *Order*, I expected would allow me more Time for attending to my Project and my Studies; RESOLUTION once become habitual, would keep me firm in my Endeavours to obtain all the subsequent Virtues; *Frugality* & *Industry*, by freeing me from my remaining Debt, & producing Affluence & Independance would make more easy the Practice of *Sincerity* and *Justice*, &c. &c.. Conceiving then that agreeable to the Advice of Pythagoras in his Golden Verses,[64] daily Examination would be necessary, I contriv'd the following Method for conducting that Examination.

I made a little Book in which I allotted a Page for each of the Virtues. I rul'd each Page with red Ink so as to have seven Columns, one for each Day of the Week, marking each Column with a Letter for the Day. I cross'd these Columns with thirteen red Lines, marking the Beginning of each Line with the first Letter of one of the Virtues, on which Line & in its proper Column I might mark by a little black Spot every Fault I found upon Examination, to have been committed respecting that Virtue upon that Day.

Form of the Pages

Temperance.							
Eat not to Dulness.							
Drink not to Elevation.							
	S	M	T	W	T	F	S
T							
S	••	•		•		•	
O	•	•	•		•	•	•
R			•		•		
F		•		•			
I			•	•			
S							
J							
M							
Cl							
T							
Ch							
H							

I determined to give a Week's strict Attention to each of the Virtues successively. Thus in the first Week my great Guard was to avoid every the least Offence against Temperance, leaving the other Virtues to their ordinary Chance, only marking every Evening the Faults of the Day. Thus if in the first Week I could keep my first Line marked T clear of Spots, I suppos'd the Habit of that Virtue so much strengthen'd and its opposite weaken'd, that I might venture extending my Attention to include the next, and for the

---

[64] In a footnote, Franklin quotes extensively from Pytagoras' poems.

following Week keep both Lines clear of Spots. Proceeding thus to the last, I could go thro' a Course compleat in Thirteen Weeks, and four Courses in a Year. [...]
This my little Book had for its Motto these Lines from *Addison's Cato*;[65]

> Here will I hold: If there is a Pow'r above us,
> (And that there is, all Nature cries aloud
> Thro' all her Works) he must delight in Virtue,
> And that which he delights in must be happy. [...]

Another from the Proverbs of Solomon speaking of Wisdom or Virtue;

> Length of Days is in her right hand, and in her Left Hand Riches and Honours;
> Her Ways are Ways of Pleasantness, and all her Paths are Peace. III, 16, 17.

And conceiving God to be the Fountain of Wisdom, I thought it right and necessary to solicit his Assistance for obtaining it; to this End I form'd the following little Prayer, which was prefix'd to my Tables of Examination; for daily Use.

> *O Powerful Goodness! bountiful Father! merciful Guide! Increase in me that Wisdom which discovers my truest Interests; Strengthen my Resolutions to perform what that Wisdom dictates. Accept my kind Offices to thy other Children, as the only Return in my Power for thy continual Favours to me.*

I us'd also sometimes a little Prayer which I took from *Thomson's* Poems.[66] viz

> *Father of Light and Life, thou Good supreme,*
> *O teach me what is good, teach me thy self!*
> *Save me from Folly, Vanity and Vice,*
> *From every low Pursuit, and fill my Soul*
> *With Knowledge, conscious Peace, & Virtue pure,*
> *Sacred, substantial, neverfading Bliss!*

The Precept of *Order* requiring that *every Part of my Business should have its allotted Time*, one Page in my little Book contain'd the following Scheme of Employment for the Twenty-four Hours of a natural Day,

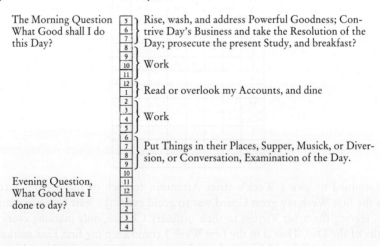

---

[65] Joseph Addison (1672-1719), *Cato: A Tragedy* (1713), V,i,15-18.
[66] James Thomson (1700-1748), *The Seasons*, "Winter" (1726), ll. 218-223.

I enter'd upon the Execution of this Plan for Self Examination, and continu'd it with occasional Intermissions for some time. I was surpriz'd to find myself so much fuller of Faults than I had imagined, but I had the Satisfaction of seeing them diminish. [...] In Truth I found myself incorrigible with respect to *Order*; and now I am grown old, and my Memory bad, I feel very sensibly the want of it. But on the whole, tho' I never arrived at the Perfection I had been so ambitious of obtaining, but fell far short of it, yet I was by the Endeavour made a better and a happier Man than I otherwise should have been, if I had not attempted it; As those who aim at perfect Writing by imitating the engraved Copies, tho' they never reach the wish'd for Excellence of those Copies, their Hand is mended by the Endeavour, and is tolerable while it continues fair & legible. –

And it may be well my Posterity should be informed, that to this little Artifice, with the Blessing of God, their Ancestor ow'd the constant Felicity of his Life down to his 79th Year in which this is written. What Reverses may attend the Remainder is in the Hand of Providence: But if they arrive the Reflection on past Happiness enjoy'd ought to help his Bearing them with more Resignation. To *Temperance* he ascribes his long-continu'd Health, & what is still left to him of a good Constitution. To *Industry* and *Frugality* the early Easiness of his Circumstances, & Acquisition of his Fortune, with all that Knowledge which enabled him to be an useful Citizen, and obtain'd for him some Degree of Reputation among the Learned. To *Sincerity* & *Justice* the Confidence of his Country, and the honourable Employs it conferr'd upon him. And to the joint Influence of the whole Mass of the Virtues, even in their imperfect State he was able to acquire them, all that Evenness of Temper, & that Chearfulness in Conversation which makes his Company still sought for, & agreable even to his younger Acquaintance. I hope therefore that some of my Descendants may follow the Example & reap the Benefit. –

It will be remark'd that, tho' my Scheme was not wholly without Religion there was in it no Mark of any of the distinguishing Tenets of any particular Sect. – I had purposely avoided them; for being fully persuaded of the Utility and Excellency of my Method, and that it might be serviceable to People in all Religions, and intending some time or other to publish it, I would not have any thing in it that should prejudice any one of any Sect against it. – I purposed writing a little Comment on each Virtue, in which I would have shown the Advantages of possessing it, & the Mischiefs attending its opposite Vice; and I should have called my Book the ART *of Virtue*, because it would have shown the *Means & Manner* of obtaining Virtue; which would have distinguish'd it from the mere Exhortation to be good, that does not instruct & indicate the Means; but is like the Apostle's Man of verbal Charity, who only, without showing to the Naked & the Hungry *how* or where they might get Cloaths or Victuals, exhorted them to be fed & clothed. *James* II, 15, 16. –

But it so happened that my Intention of writing & publishing this Comment was never fulfilled. [...]

In this Piece it was my Design to explain and enforce this Doctrine, that vicious Actions are not hurtful because they are forbidden, but forbidden because they are hurtful, the Nature of Man alone consider'd: That it was therefore every ones Interest to be virtuous, who wish'd to be happy even in this World. And I should from this Circumstance, there being always in the World a Number of rich Merchants, Nobility, States and Princes, who have need of honest Instruments for the Management of their Affairs, and such being so rare, have endeavoured to convince young Persons, that no Qualities were so likely to make a poor Man's Fortune as those of Probity & Integrity.

My List of Virtues contain'd at first but twelve: But a Quaker Friend having kindly inform'd me that I was generally thought proud; that my Pride show'd itself frequently in Conversation; that I was not content with being in the right when discussing any Point, but was overbearing & rather insolent; of which he convinc'd me by mentioning several Instances; – I determined endeavouring to cure myself if I could of this Vice or Folly among the rest, and I added *Humility* to my List, giving an extensive Meaning to the Word. – I cannot boast of much Success in acquiring the *Reality* of this Virtue; but I had a good deal with regard to the *Appearance* of it. – I made it a Rule to forbear all direct Contradiction to the Sentiments of others, and all positive Assertion of my own. [...] When another asserted something that I thought an Error, I deny'd my self the Pleasure of contradicting him abruptly, and of showing immediately some Absurdity in his Proposition; and in answering I began by observing that in certain Cases or Circumstances his Opinion would be right, but that in the present case there *appear'd* or *seem'd* to me some Difference, &c. I soon found the Advantage of this Change in my Manners. The Conversations I engag'd in went on more pleasantly. The modest way in which I propos'd my Opinions, procur'd them a readier Reception and less Contradiction; I had less Mortification when I was found to be in the wrong, and I more easily prevail'd with others to give up their Mistakes & join with me when I happen'd to be in the right. And this Mode, which I at first put on, with some violence to natural Inclination, became at length so easy & so habitual to me, that perhaps for these Fifty Years past no one has ever heard a dogmatical Expression escape me. And to this Habit (after my Character of Integrity) I think it principally owing, that I had early so much Weight with my Fellow Citizens, when I proposed new Institutions, or Alterations in the old; and so much Influence in public Councils when I became a Member. For I was but a bad Speaker, never eloquent, subject to much Hesitation in my choice of Words, hardly correct in Language, and yet I generally carried my Points. –

In reality there is perhaps no one of our natural Passions so hard to subdue as *Pride*. Disguise it, struggle with it, beat it down, stifle it, mortify it as much as one pleases, it is still alive, and will every now and then peep out and show itself. You will see it perhaps often in this History. For even if I could conceive that I had compleatly overcome it, I should probably be proud of my Humility. –

Thus far written at Passy 1784

Source: Benjamin Franklin (1706-1790). *The Autobiography*. *Writings*. New York: Viking, 1987, 1307-1308, 1313-1315, 1317, 1320-1324, 1358-1362, 1372-1376, 1378-1379, 1382-1394.

105. Cotton Mather
Bonifacius: An Essay upon the Good (1710)

§ 21. *Reforming-Societies*, or *Societies for the Suppression of Disorders*, have begun to grow somewhat into Fashion; and it is one of the best *Omens* that the World has upon it. *Behold, how great a Matter a little* of this Heavenly *Fire* may Kindle! Five or Six Gentlemen in *London*, began with an Heroic Resolution, & Association, to Encounter the Torrent of Wickedness, which was carrying all before it in the Nation. More were soon added unto them; and tho' they met with great Opposition, from *Wicked Spirits*, and these *Incarnate* as well as *Invisible*, and some in *High Places* too, yet they proceeded with a most honourable and invincible Courage. Their *Success*, if not proportionable to their

Courage, yet was far from *Contemptible*. In the *Punishments* inflicted on them who transgressed the Laws of *Good Morality*, there were soon offered many Thousands of *Sacrifices*, unto the Holiness of GOD. Hundreds of *Houses* which were the *Chambers* of Hell, and the *Scandals* of Earth, were soon Extinguished. There was a Remarkable Check soon given to raging *Profanity*; and the *Lords-Day* was not openly and horribly Profaned as formerly. And among other *Essays to Do Good*, they Scattered Thousands of *Good Books*, that had a Tendency to Reform the Evil Manners of the People. It was not long before this Excellent Example was followed in other parts of the *British* Empire. Vertuous men of diverse Qualities and Perswasions, became the Members of the *Societies*: Persons High and Low, Con and Non-con,[67] United; the Union became Formidable to the Kingdom of Darkness. The Report of the *Societies* flew over the Seas; the Pattern was follow'd in other Country's; Men of Wisdom in Remote Parts of *Europe* have made their joyful Remark upon them, *That they cause Unspeakable Good, & annunciate a more illustrious State of the Church of God, which is to be Expected* [...].

[The Report of the Societies] is enough to make way for the PROPOSAL;

That a Fit Number in a Neighbourhood, whose Hearts God has touched with a *Zeal to Do Good*, would Combine into a *Society*, to meet, when & where they shall agree; and Consider that Case, *What are the* Disorders *that we may see Rising among us? And what may be done, either by ourselves immediately, or by others thro' our Advice, to Suppress those Disorders?* That they would obtain if they can, the Presence of a *Minister* with them; and every time they meet, have a *Prayer* wherein the Glorious Lord shall be call'd upon, to Bless the Design, Direct and Prosper it. That they would also have a *Justice of Peace*, if it may be, to be a Member of the Society. [...] That they do with as *Modest* and *Silent* a Conduct as may be, carry on all their Undertakings. [...]

I will finish the PROPOSAL, by Reciting the *Points of Consideration* which the SOCIETIES may have Read unto them from time to time at their Meetings, with a due *Pause* upon each of them [...].

I. Is there any *Remarkable Disorder* in the Place, that requires our Endeavour for the Suppression of it? And in what Good, Fair, likely way, may we Endeavour it?

II. Is there any *Particular Person*, whose *Disorderly Behaviours* may be so Scandalous & so Notorious, that we may do well to send unto the said Person our Charitable *Admonitions?* Or, Are there any *Contending Persons*, whom we should Admonish, to Quench their *Contentions?* [...]

VI. Can any further Methods be devised, that *Ignorance* and *Wickedness* may be more chased from our People in general? And that *Household-Piety* in Particular, may flourish among them? [...]

Source: Cotton Mather (1663-1728). *Bonifacius: An Essay upon the Good, That Is to Be Devised and Designed, by Those Who Desire to Answer the Great End of Life, and to Do Good While They Live. A Book Offered, First, in General, unto All Christians, in a Personal Capacity, or in a Relative. Then More Particularly, unto Ministers, unto Physicians, unto Lawyers, unto Scholemasters [sic], unto Wealthy Gentlemen, unto Several Sorts of Officers, unto Churches, and unto All Societies of a Religious Character and Intention. With Humble Proposals, of Unexceptionable Methods, to Do Good in the World.* Boston: B. Green, 1710, 167-168, 171-172.

---

[67] Reference to conformist members of the Church of England and non-conformist denominations.

106. Mark Twain
"The Late Benjamin Franklin" (1907)

[Never put off till to-morrow what you can do day after to-morrow just as well. – B.F.]

This party was one of those persons whom they call Philosophers. He was twins, being born simultaneously in two different houses in the city of Boston. [...] The subject of this memoir was of a vicious disposition, and early prostituted his talents to the invention of maxims and aphorisms calculated to inflict suffering upon the rising generation of all subsequent ages. His simplest acts, also, were contrived with a view to their being held up for the emulation of boys forever – boys who might otherwise have been happy. It was in this spirit that he became the son of a soap-boiler; and probably for no other reason than that the efforts of all future boys who tried to be anything might be looked upon with suspicion unless they were the sons of soap-boilers. With a malevolence which is without parallel in history, he would work all day and then sit up nights and let on to be studying algebra by the light of a smouldering fire, so that all other boys might have to do that also or else have Benjamin Franklin thrown up to them. Not satisfied with these proceedings, he had a fashion of living wholly on bread and water, and studying astronomy at meal time – a thing which has brought affliction to millions of boys since, whose fathers had read Franklin's pernicious biography.

His maxims were full of animosity toward boys. Nowadays a boy cannot follow out a single natural instinct without tumbling over some of those everlasting aphorisms and hearing from Franklin on the spot. [...] If he does a virtuous action, he never gets anything for it, because "Virtue is its own reward." And that boy is hounded to death and robbed of his natural rest, because Franklin said once in one of his inspired flights of malignity –

> Early to bed and early to rise
> Make a man healthy and wealthy and wise.

As if it were any object to a boy to be healthy and wealthy and wise on such terms. The sorrow that that maxim has cost me through my parents' experimenting on me with it, tongue cannot tell. The legitimate result is my present state of general debility, indigence, and mental aberration. My parents used to have me up before nine o'clock in the morning, sometimes, when I was a boy. If they had let me take my natural rest, where would I have been now? Keeping store, no doubt, and respected by all. [...]

Source: Mark Twain (1835-1910). "The Late Benjamin Franklin." *The Galaxy: A Magazine of Entertaining Reading* 10.1 (July 1907), 138-139.

107. Joel Barlow
The Vision of Columbus (1787)

ARGUMENT.
Condition and soliloquy of Columbus. Appearance and speech of the Angel. They ascend the Mount of Vision. Continent of America draws into view, and is described by the mountains, rivers, lakes, soil, temperature and some of the natural productions.

BOOK I.

LONG had the Sage,[68] the first who dared to brave
The unknown dangers of the western wave,
Who taught mankind where future empires lay
In these fair confines of descending day,
With cares o'erwhelm'd, in life's distressing gloom,
Wish'd from a thankless world a peaceful tomb;
While kings and nations, envious of his name,
Enjoy'd his toils and triumph'd o'er his fame,
And gave the chief, from promised empire hurl'd,
Chains for a crown, a prison for a world.
Now night and silence held their lonely reign,
The half-orb'd moon declining to the main;
Descending clouds, o'er varying ether driven,
Obscured the stars and shut the eye from heaven;
Cold mists through opening grates the cell invade,
And deathlike terrors haunt the midnight shade;
When from a visionary, short repose,
That raised new cares and temper'd keener woes,
Columbus woke, and to the walls address'd
The deep-felt sorrows of his manly breast.
 Here lies the purchase, here the wretched spoil,
Of painful years and persevering toil:
For these dread walks, this hideous haunt of pain,
I traced new regions o'er the pathless main,
Dared all the dangers of the dreary wave,
Hung o'er its clefts and topp'd the surging grave,
Saw billowy seas, in swelling mountains roll,
And bursting thunders rock the reddening pole,
Death rear his front in every dreadful form,
Gape from beneath and blacken in the storm;
Till, tost far onward to the skirts of day,
Where milder suns dispens'd a smiling ray,
Through brighter skies my happier sails descry'd
The golden banks that bound the western tide,

---

[68] A man of profound wisdom; one of those persons of ancient history or legend traditionally famous as the wisest of mankind; here the reference is to Columbus.

And gave the admiring world that bounteous shore
Their wealth to nations and to kings their power. [...]
    Thus mourn'd the hapless chief; a thundering sound
Roll'd round the shuddering walls and shook the ground;
O'er all the dome, where solemn arches bend,
The roofs unfold and streams of light descend;
The growing splendor fill'd the astonish'd room,
And gales etherial breathed a glad perfume;
Mild in the midst a radiant seraph shone,
Robed in the vestments of the rising sun;
Tall rose his stature, youth's primeval grace
Moved o'er his limbs and brighten'd in his face,
His closing wings, in golden plumage drest,
With gentle sweep came folding o'er his breast,
His locks in rolling ringlets glittering hung,
And sounds melodious moved his heavenly tongue.
    Rise, trembling Chief, to scenes of rapture, rise,
This voice awaits thee from the approving skies;
Thy just complaints, in heavenly audience known,
Call mild compassion from the indulgent throne;
Let grief no more awake the piteous strain,
Nor think thy piety or toils are vain.
Tho' faithless men thy injured worth despise,
Depress all virtue and insult the skies,
Yet look thro' nature, Heaven's own conduct trace,
What power divine sustains the unthankful race!
From that great Source, that life-inspiring Soul,
Suns drew their light and systems learn'd to roll,
Time walk'd the silent round, and life began,
And God's fair image stamp'd the mind of man
Down the long vale, where rolling years descend,
To thy own days, behold his care extend;
From one eternal Spring, what love proceeds!
Smiles in the seraph, in the Saviour bleeds,
Shines through all worlds, that fill the bounds of space,
And lives immortal in thy favour'd race.
Yet no return the almighty Power can know,
From earth to heaven no just reward can flow,
Men spread their wants, the all-bounteous hand supplies,
And gives the joys that mortals dare despise.
In these dark vales where blinded faction sways,
Wealth pride and conquest claim the palm of praise,
Aw'd into slaves, while groping millions groan,
And blood-stain'd steps lead upwards to a throne.
    Far other wreaths thy virtuous temples claim,
Far nobler honours build thy sacred name,
Thine be the joys the immortal mind that grace

Pleas'd with the toils, that bless thy kindred race.
Now raise thy ravish'd soul to scenes more bright,
The glorious fruits ascending on thy sight;
For, wing'd with speed, from brighter worlds I came,
To sooth thy grief and show thy distant fame.

    As that great Seer, whose animating rod
Taught Israel's sons the wonder-working God,
Who led, thro' dreary wastes, the murmuring band
To the fair confines of the promised land,
Oppress'd with years, from Pisgah's[69] beauteous height,
O'er boundless regions cast the raptured sight;
The joys of unborn nations warm'd his breast,
Repaid his toils and sooth'd his soul to rest;
Thus, o'er thy subject wave, shalt thou behold
Far happier realms their future charms unfold,
In nobler pomp another Pisgah rise,
Beneath whose foot thine own Canäan lies;
There, rapt in vision, hail the distant clime,
And taste the blessings of remotest time.

Source: Joel Barlow (1754-1812). *The Vision of Columbus: A Poem in Nine Books*. Hartford: Hudson and Goodwin, 1787, 25f., 28-30.

---

[69] Mount Pisgah: after Yahweh had denied him entrance into Canaan, Moses climbed Mount Pisgah to look out over the land that he would not enter.

REVOLUTIONARY PERIOD

> Revolutions are not made; they come. A revolution is as natural a growth as an oak. It comes out of the past. Its foundations are laid far back. (Wendell Phillips, "Public Opinion," *Speeches, Lectures, and Letters*, Boston: Lee and Shepard, 1872, 36)

Considering the fact that 'metaphors of naturalization' have often been used as facile means of legitimizing political developments that did not at all reflect a 'natural' course of events, but depended on the machinations of powerful individuals or interest groups, the reader might have every reason to be skeptical of Wendell Phillips' somewhat naïve projection of notions of natural processes onto history. Phillips is right, however, in the assumption that revolutions are not at all events that come unexpectedly. As the history of the American Revolution may well illustrate, their "foundations are laid far back," usually at a time when no one had yet intended to pursue policies that might eventually lead to a revolution.

Historians tend to locate the origin of the American Revolution in the imprudent tax policy of the British Parliament after the French and Indian War (1754-1763), and they are certainly right in seeing a direct correspondence between the various acts of Parliament[1] and the rise of a rebellious spirit in the British Colonies. They misjudge, however, the long-term political and ideological 'innovations' and changes in political mentality it took to transform a spirit of occasional resistance to single acts of British 'oppression' (such as the revocation of the Massachusetts Charter in 1684) into a spirit of rebellion that would not even shrink back from declaring independence and thus risking a war with a far superior military power. Indeed, many documents and pamphlets of the revolutionary period display traces of a long debate over the prerogatives and rights of rulers, a debate that dates back to the Glorious Revolution (1688) and, in particular, the Bill of Rights (1689) which restricted the right of the monarch to suspend laws, keep a standing army, or levy taxes without due involvement of Parliament. Although the Bill of Rights was not legally binding in the colonies, it very much influenced the political attitudes of the colonists toward their king and all political authority. Moreover, the overthrow of James II had set a precedent for a justifiable revolution against a monarch, and it encouraged revolutionary American patriots to follow suit, especially as they succeeded in constructing numerous parallels between the tyrannous regimes of James II and George III. The various references to the "long train of abuses" with which George III had allegedly tried to suppress and "enslave" his American subjects (see, e.g., docs. 122, 125, 131) bear witness to justifications of acts of rebellion as they were propagated during the Glorious Revolution.

Many of the documents of the American Revolution also give testimony to the extraordinary influence John Locke's political philosophy had on the formation of a revolu-

---

[1] Cf., for instance, the Royal Proclamation (1763, forbidding land grants and settlements west of the Appalachian Mountains), the Revenue Act (or Sugar Act, 1764, enforcing already existing taxation of sugar), the Currency Act (1764, forbidding the issuing of colonial paper currency), the Stamp Act (1765, enforcing tax stamps to be fixed to all printed matter and legal documents), the Quartering Act (1765, requiring the colonists to supply British troops with provisions and quarters), the Townshend Acts (1767, suspending the 'rebellious' New York Assembly, or, much later, the Boston Port Act (1774, closing the harbor of Boston for an indefinite time until the tea destroyed during the Boston Tea Party in 1773 was paid for).

tionary spirit in America. In his *Two Treatises on Government* (1690), the English philosopher had convincingly defended the deposition of James I: while the *First Treatise* refuted theories of the divine right of kings, the *Second Treatise* (cf. doc. 108) developed Locke's contract theory of government, which would eventually be evoked again and again in pro-revolutionary tracts and pamphlets of the late 1760s and the 1770s. Most of these later texts – in particular James Otis' *The Rights of the British Colonies Asserted and Proved* (doc. 111), Samuel Adams' "The Rights of the Colonists" (doc. 119), Thomas Jefferson's *A Summary View of the Rights of British America* (doc. 125), the "Preamble to the Massachusetts Articles of War" (doc. 127), and the *Declaration of Independence* (doc. 131) – make explicit reference to Locke's theory that people are endowed with certain 'natural' (and thus inalienable) rights – i.e. the rights to life, liberty, and property –, and that people also have the right to change their government once their chosen rulers violate these rights in a systematic way. Furthermore, as political power structures and government in the American colonies often originated in contractual arrangements (cf. the Mayflower Compact, the Cambridge Agreement, or the Fundamental Orders of Connecticut), the colonists could be easily convinced that John Locke's description of man's decision to enter into a social contract was a correct rendering of the system of government their ancestors had deliberately chosen when establishing their settlements in the New World. In this respect, any ruler – the colonial Governors as well as the King himself – was but his peoples' "chief servant" who had to fulfill the task of safeguarding their rights and pursuit of happiness against the infringements of potential external and internal adversaries.

The pervasive influence of Locke's civil contract theory cannot only be gathered, however, from documents that were written in the context of the colonists' revolutionary opposition to British violations of their 'natural rights.' As Jonathan Mayhew's *Discourse Concerning Unlimited Submission and Non-Resistance to the Higher Powers* (1750, doc. 109) demonstrates, Locke's theories of government were *en vogue* much earlier and were also adopted by relatively conservative ministers in Boston. Blending quotations from the Bible with Locke's concepts, Mayhew reminded colonial rulers of the fact that their vested authority only rested on their ability to promote the well-being of their respective communities. "Common tyrants and oppressors," he self-consciously asserted, "[were] not entitled to obedience from their subjects." Moreover, Mayhew also introduced another new argumentative strategy into the political rhetoric that would later dominate the pamphlets of the revolutionaries. Adopting enlightenment concepts to his own agendas, Mayhew claimed validity for his arguments by pointing out that they were based on principles of common sense and universal reason. He thus anticipated the strategy that Thomas Paine employed twenty-six years later in *Common Sense* (1776, doc. 130), probably the most widely circulated and also the most influential text of the pre-revolutionary period.

As some of the early documents included in this section of *Key Concepts* prove (cf. docs. 109 and 111), opposition to British policies was already well under way before the Stamp Act crisis of 1765 and the outbreak of mob actions that forced most royal tax collectors and stamp distributors to resign. But it was occurrences such as the Stamp Act Riots and later, in 1770, the Boston Massacre, which fuelled patriotic fervor and finally led to a significant political mobilization of the masses. Long before the War of Independence was waged on the battlefields, pamphleteers and contributors to colonial journals like *The Boston Gazette*, *The Massachusetts Spy* (cf. doc. 118), or *The Constitutional Courant* (cf. docs. 112-113) waged a war of letters and of vitriolic political cartoons. While Benjamin Franklin still used the weapons of wit and sophisticated satire (cf. doc. 120; see also 117), most later pamphleteers used cruder tools of attacking their political opponents, be they British crown agents or American-born supporters of the loyalist cause (cf. esp. docs. 123 and 124). Thus Boston patriots such as the engraver Paul Revere or the prominent merchant and politician John Hancock did not hesitate to level their assaults on the British and their adherents in the wake of the Boston Massacre. Both Revere's engraving of 1770 (doc. 121) and Hancock's *Boston Massacre Oration* of 1774 aroused anti-British sentiments by 'transforming' the occurrences – British soldiers shooting at an incensed mob and killing several Bostonians, possibly in self-defense – into narratives of the slaughter of innocent and peaceful citizens by blood-thirsty 'fiends.' While Revere and Hancock also served their cause by establishing a genealogy of 'freedom-fighters' who died for the sake of liberty, other patriots created powerful icons of national identity that translated the antagonism between Britain and America into an easily accessible pictorial language. The rattlesnake emblem bearing the inscription "Join, or Die" (doc. 110), which Benjamin Franklin had designed in 1754 in order to exhort the colonies to join their forces against the enemy during the French and Indian War, was re-employed by patriots as an apt means of summoning their supporters to join the cause of liberty. Soon, the rattlesnake (representing the thirteen colonies) was found fiercely opposing the British griffin on the front page of the *Massachusetts Spy* (cf. doc. 118) or on the flags of the American revolutionary army.

Although the intensifying political antagonisms of the revolutionary period obviously caused the rise of a more aggressive kind of political rhetoric, numerous writers and orators – primarily ministers – proposed more conciliatory stands or campaigned for a policy of moral regeneration that shifted the focus from the political arena to the private sphere. Becoming aware of the danger of losing their authority in the course of an imminent revolution, prominent public leaders like Samuel Williams, Jacob Duché, or John Witherspoon tried to regain the initiative by insisting on the importance of the patriots' submission to the designs of divine providence. Drawing on the tradition of the Puritan jeremiad, they lamented the present state of public affairs, interpreted the political 'calamities' as a sign of god's displeasure with his "chosen people," and suggested measures of moral regeneration as the only means of reaching either reconciliation with the mother country or independence (cf. docs. 126, 128, 132). Only with a common commitment to public virtue was America destined to overcome its "present difficulties" and fulfill its mission of being a beacon of freedom to the rest of the world (cf. esp. docs. 126 and 133). But employing the rhetorical strategies of the American jeremiad, Samuel Williams, David Ramsay and many others did not only succeed in mustering courage in the face of adversity, they also prepared the ground for the extraordinary success of the concept of a "virtuous republic" in post-revolutionary America. Moreover, in anticipating America's glorious future, they also established a powerful formula that directly correlated freedom with progress, and instilled a sense of exceptionalism and mission that was to define American politics throughout the nineteenth and twentieth centuries.

Bernd Engler

108. John Locke
"An Essay Concerning the True Original, Extent, and End of Civil Government" (1689/1690)

CHAP. I

[...] 3. *Political Power* then I take to be *a Right* of making Laws with Penalties of Death, and consequently all less Penalties, for the Regulating and Preserving of Property, and of employing the force of the Community, in the Execution of such Laws, and in the defence of the Common-wealth from Foreign Injury, and all this only for the Publick Good.

CHAP. II
Of the State of Nature.

4. To understand Political Power right, and derive it from its Original, we must consider what State all Men are naturally in, and that is, a *State of perfect Freedom* to order their Actions, and dispose of their Possessions, and Persons as they think fit, within the bounds of the Law of Nature, without asking leave, or depending upon the Will of any other Man.

A *State* also *of Equality*, wherein all the Power and Jurisdiction is reciprocal, no one having more than another: there being nothing more evident, than that Creatures of the same species and rank promiscuously born to all the same advantages of Nature, and the use of the same faculties, should also be equal one amongst another without Subordination or Subjection, unless the Lord and Master of them all, should by any manifest Declaration of his Will set one above another, and confer on him by an evident and clear appointment an undoubted Right to Dominion and Sovereignty. [...]

6. But though this be a *State of Liberty*, yet it is *not a State of Licence*, though Man in that State have an uncontroleable Liberty, to dispose of his Person or Possessions, yet he has not Liberty to destroy himself, or so much as any Creature in his Possession, but where some nobler use, than its bare Preservation calls for it. The *State of Nature* has a Law of Nature to govern it, which obliges every one: And Reason, which is that Law, teaches all Mankind, who will but consult it, that being all equal and independent, no one ought to harm another in his Life, Health, Liberty, or Possessions. For Men being all the Workmanship of one Omnipotent, and infinitely wise Maker; All the Servants of one Sovereign Master, sent into the World by his order and about his business, they are his Property, whose Workmanship they are, made to last during his, not one anothers Pleasure. And being furnished with like Faculties, sharing all in one Community of Nature, there cannot be supposed any such *Subordination* among us, that may Authorize us to destroy one another, as if we were made for one anothers uses, as the inferior ranks of Creatures are for ours. Every one as he is *bound to preserve himself*, and not to quit his Station wilfully; so by the like reason when his own Preservation comes not in competition, ought he, as much as he can, *to preserve the rest of Mankind*, and may not unless it be to do Justice on an Offender, take away, or impair the life, or what tends to the Preservation of the Life, the Liberty, Health, Limb or Goods of another. [...]

13. To this strange Doctrine, *viz.*, That *in the State of Nature every one has the Executive Power* of the Law of Nature, I doubt not but it will be objected, That it is unreasonable for Men to be Judges in their own Cases, that Self-love will make Men partial to themselves and their Friends. And, on the other side, that Ill Nature, Passion and Revenge will carry them too far in punishing others. And hence nothing but Confusion and

Disorder will follow, and that therefore God hath certainly appointed Government to restrain the partiality and violence of Men. I easily grant, that *Civil Government* is the proper Remedy for the Inconveniences of the State of Nature, which must certainly be Great, where Men may be Judges in their own Case, since 'tis easy to be imagined, that he who was so unjust as to do his Brother an Injury, will scarce be so just as to condemn himself for it: But I shall desire those who make this Objection, to remember that *Absolute Monarchs* are but Men, and if Government is to be the Remedy of those Evils, which necessarily follow from Mens being Judges in their own Cases, and the State of Nature is therefore not to be endured, I desire to know what kind of Government that is, and how much better it is than the State of Nature, where one Man commanding a multitude, has the Liberty to be Judge in his own Case, and may do to all his Subjects whatever he pleases, without the least liberty to anyone to question or control those who Execute his Pleasure? And in whatsoever he doth, whether led by Reason, Mistake, or Passion, must be submitted to? Much better it is in the State of Nature wherein Men are not bound to submit to the unjust will of another. And if he that judges, judges amiss in his own, or any other Case, he is answerable for it to the rest of Mankind.

Chap. IX.
Of the Ends of Political Society and Government.

123. If Man in the State of Nature be so free, as has been said; If he be absolute Lord of his own Person and Possessions, equal to the greatest, and subject to no Body, why will he part with his Freedom? Why will he give up this Empire, and subject himself to the Dominion and Controul of any other Power? To which 'tis obvious to Answer, that though in the state of Nature he hath such a right, yet the Enjoyment of it is very uncertain, and constantly exposed to the Invasion of others. For all being Kings as much as he, every Man his Equal, and the greater part no strict Observers of Equity and Justice, the enjoyment of the property he has in this state is very unsafe, very unsecure. This makes him willing to quit a Condition, which however free, is full of fears and continual dangers: And 'tis not without reason, that he seeks out, and is willing to joyn in Society with others who are already united, or have a mind to unite for the mutual *Preservation* of their Lives, Liberties and Estates, which I call by the general Name, *Property*.

124. The great and *chief end* therefore, of Mens uniting into Commonwealths, and putting themselves under Government, *is the Preservation of their Property*. [...]

Chap. XVIII.
Of Tyranny.

199. As Usurpation is the exercise of Power, which another hath a Right to; so *Tyranny* is *the exercise of Power beyond Right*, which no Body can have a Right to. And this is making use of the Power any one has in his hands; not for the good of those, who are under it, but for his own private separate Advantage. [...]

Chap. XIX.
Of the Dissolution of Government.

222. The Reason why Men enter into Society, is the preservation of their Property; and the end why they chuse and authorize a Legislative, is, that there may be Laws made, and Rules set as Guards and Fences to the Properties of all the Members of the Society, to limit the Power, and moderate the Dominion of every Part and Member of the Society. For since it can never be supposed to be the Will of the Society, that the Legislative should have a

Power to destroy that, which every one designs to secure, by entering into Society, and for which the People submitted themselves to the Legislators of their own making; whenever the *Legislators endeavour to take away, and destroy the Property of the People*, or to reduce them to Slavery under Arbitrary Power, they put themselves into a state of War with the People, who are thereupon absolved from any farther Obedience, and are left to the common Refuge, which God hath provided for all Men, against Force and Violence. Whensoever therefore the *Legislative* shall transgress this fundamental Rule of Society; and either by Ambition, Fear, Folly or Corruption, *endeavour to grasp* themselves, *or put into the hands of any other an Absolute Power* over the Lives, Liberties, and Estates of the People; By this breach of Trust they *forfeit the Power*, the People had put into their hands, for quite contrary ends, and it devolves to the People, who have a Right to resume their original Liberty, and, by the Establishment of a new Legislative (such as they shall think fit) provide for their own Safety and Security, which is the end for which they are in Society. [...]

243. To conclude, The *Power that every individual gave the Society*, when he entered into it, can never revert to the Individuals again, as long as the Society lasts, but will always remain in the Community; because without this, there can be no Community, no Common-wealth, which is contrary to the original Agreement: So also when the Society hath placed the Legislative in any Assembly of Men, to continue in them and their Successors, with Direction and Authority for providing such Successors, *the Legislative can never revert to the People* whilst that Government lasts: Because having provided a Legislative with Power to continue for ever, they have given up their Political Power to the Legislative, and cannot resume it. But if they have set Limits to the Duration of their Legislative, and made this Supreme Power in any Person, or Assembly, only temporary: Or else when by the Miscarriages of those in Authority, it is forfeited; upon the Forfeiture of their Rulers, or at the Determination of the Time set, *it reverts to the Society*, and the People have a Right to act as Supreme, and continue the Legislative in themselves, or erect a new Form, or under the old form place it in new hands, as they think good.

FINIS.

Source: John Locke (1632-1704). "An Essay Concerning the True Original, Extent, and End of Civil Government" [1689/1690]. *Two Treatises of Government*. Ed. Peter Laslett. Cambridge: Cambridge University Press, 1963, 286-287, 293-294, 368-369, 416-417, 430-431, 445-446. Locke's essay is also known and often published as "The Second Treatise of Government."

109. Jonathan Mayhew
A Discourse Concerning Unlimited Submission and Non-Resistance to the Higher Powers (1750)

ROM. XIII. 1.-8.

1. *Let every soul be subject unto the higher powers. For there is no power but of God: the powers that be, are ordained of God.*
2. *Whosoever therefore resisteth the power, resisteth the ordinance[2] of God: and they that resist, shall receive to themselves damnation.*
3. *For rulers are not a terror to good works, but to the evil. Wilt thou then not be afraid of the power? do that which is good, and thou shalt have praise of the same:*

---

[2] An authoritative command or order.

4. *For he is the minister of God to thee for good. But if thou do that which is evil, be afraid; for he beareth not the sword in vain: for he is the minister of God, a revenger to execute wrath upon him that doth evil.*
5. *Wherefore ye must needs be subject, not only for wrath, but also for conscience sake.*
6. *For this cause pay you tribute also: for they are God's ministers, attending continually upon this very thing.*
7. *Render therefore to all their dues: tribute to whom tribute is due; custom, to whom custom; fear, to whom fear; honour, to whom honour.*

It is evident that the affair of civil government may properly fall under a *moral* and *religious* consideration, at least so far forth as it relates to the general nature and end of magistracy, and to the grounds and extent of that submission which persons of a private character, ought to yield to those who are vested with authority. This must be allowed by all who acknowledge the divine original of christianity. For although there be a sense, and a very plain and important sense, in which Christ's *kingdom is not of this world*; his inspired apostles have, nevertheless, laid down some general principles concerning the office of civil rulers, and the duty of subjects, together with the reason and obligation of that duty. And from hence it follows, that it is proper for all who acknowledge the authority of Jesus Christ, and the inspiration of his apostles, to endeavour to understand what is in fact the doctrine which they have delivered concerning this matter.

It is the duty of *christian* magistrates to inform themselves what it is which their religion teaches concerning the nature and design of their office. And it is equally the duty of all *christian* people to inform themselves what it is which their religion teaches concerning that subjection which they owe to *the higher powers*. It is for these reasons that I have attempted to examine into the scripture-account of this matter, in order to lay it before you with the same *freedom* which I constantly use with relation to other doctrines and precepts of christianity; not doubting but you will *judge* upon every thing offered to your consideration, with the same spirit of *freedom* and *liberty* with which it is *spoken*.

The passage read, is the most full and express of any in the new testament, relating to rulers and subjects: And therefore I thought it proper to ground upon it, what I had to propose to you with reference to the authority of the civil magistrate, and the subjection which is due to him. [... St. Paul's doctrine[3]] may be summed up in the following observations; viz.:

That the end of magistracy is the good of civil society, *as such*:

That civil rulers, *as such*, are the ordinance and ministers of God; it being by his permission and providence that any bear rule; and agreeable to his will, that there should be *some persons* vested with authority in society, for the well-being of it:

That which is here said concerning civil rulers, extends to all of them in common: it relates indifferently to monarchical, republican and aristocratical government; and to all other forms which truly answer the sole end of government, the happiness of society; and to all the different degrees of authority in any particular state; to inferior officers no less than to the supreme:

That disobedience to civil rulers in the due exercise of their authority, is not merely a *political sin*, but an heinous[4] *offense against God* and *religion*:

---

[3] Cf. Rom. 13.1-7, quoted at the beginning of Mayhew's *Discourse*.
[4] Hateful, odious, highly criminal or wicked.

That the true ground and reason of our obligation to be subject to the *higher powers*, is the usefulness of magistracy (when properly exercised) to human society, and its subserviency to the general welfare:

That obedience to civil rulers is here equally required under all forms of government, which answer the sole end of all government, the good of society; and to every degree of authority in any state, whether supreme or subordinate: [...].

[...] It is blasphemy to call tyrants and oppressors, *God's ministers*. They are more properly *the messengers of satan to buffet us*. No rulers are properly God's ministers, but such as are *just, ruling in the fear of God*. [...]

[...] But how does this argument conclude for paying taxes to such princes as are continually endeavoring to ruin the public? And especially when such payment would facilitate and promote this wicked design! *Render therefore to all their dues; tribute, to whom tribute is due; custom, to whom custom; fear, to whom fear; honor, to whom honor*. Here the apostle sums up what he had been saying concerning the duty of subjects to rulers. And his argument stands thus – "Since magistrates who execute their office well, are common benefactors to society; and may, in that respect, be properly stiled the *ministers and ordinance of God*; and since they are constantly employed in the service of the public; it becomes you to pay them tribute and custom; and to reverence, honor, and submit to, them in the execution of their respective offices." This is apparently good reasoning. But does this argument conclude for the duty of paying tribute, custom, reverence, honor and obedience, to such persons as (although they bear the title of rulers) use all their power to hurt and injure the public? such as are not *God's ministers*, but *satan's?* such as do not take care of, and attend upon, the public interest, but their own, to the ruin of the public? that is, in short, to such as have no natural and just claim at all to tribute, custom, reverence, honor and obedience? [...]

Thus, upon a careful review of the apostle's reasoning in this passage, it appears that his arguments to enforce submission, are of such a nature, as to conclude only in favor of submission *to such rulers as he himself describes*; i.e. such as rule for the good of society, which is the only end of their institution. Common tyrants, and public oppressors, are not intitled to obedience from their subjects by virtue of any thing here laid down by the inspired apostle.

I now add, farther, that the apostle's argument is so far from proving it to be the duty of people to obey, and submit to, such rulers as act in contradiction to the public good, and so to the design of their office, that it proves *the direct contrary*. For, please to observe, that if the end of all civil government, be the good of society; if this be the thing that is aimed at in constituting civil rulers, and if the motive and argument for submission to government, be taken from the apparent usefulness of civil authority; it follows, that when no such good end can be answered by submission, there remains no argument or motive to enforce it; if instead of this good end's being brought about by submission, a *contrary end* is brought about, and the ruin and misery of society effected by it, here is a plain and positive reason against submission in all such cases, should they ever happen. And therefore, in such cases, a regard to the public welfare, ought to make us with-hold from our rulers, that obedience and subjection which it would, otherwise, be our duty to render to them. [...]

If we calmly consider the nature of the thing itself, nothing can well be imagined more directly contrary to common sense, than to suppose that *millions* of people should be subjected to the arbitrary, precarious pleasure of *one single man*, (who has *naturally* no superiority over them in point of authority) so that their estates, and every thing that is valuable in life, and even their lives also, shall be absolutely at his disposal, if he happens to be wanton and capricious enough to demand them. What unprejudiced man can think, that God made ALL to be thus subservient to the lawless pleasure and phrenzy of ONE, so that it shall always be a sin to resist him! Nothing but the most plain and express revelation from heaven could make a sober impartial man believe such a monstrous, unaccountable doctrine, and, indeed, the thing itself, appears so shocking – so out of all *proportion*, that it may be questioned, whether all the *miracles* that ever were wrought, could make it credible, that this doctrine *really* came from God. [...]

A people, really oppressed to a great degree by their sovereign, cannot well be insensible when they are so oppressed. And such a people (if I may allude to an ancient *fable*) have, like the *hesperian* fruit, a DRAGON for their *protector* and *guardian*:[5] nor would they have any reason to mourn, if some HERCULES should appear to dispatch him – For a nation thus abused to arise unanimously, and to resist their prince, even to the dethroning him, is not criminal; but a reasonable way of vindicating their liberties and just rights; it is making use of the means, and the only means, which God has put into their power, for mutual and self-defense. And it would be highly criminal in them, not to make use of this means. It would be stupid tameness, and unaccountable folly, for whole nations to suffer *one* unreasonable, ambitious and cruel man, to wanton and riot in their misery. And in such a case it would, of the two, be more rational to suppose, that they did NOT *resist*, than that they who did, would *receive to themselves damnation*. [...]

To conclude: Let us all learn to be *free*, and to be *loyal*. Let us not profess ourselves vassals to the lawless pleasure of any man on earth. But let us remember, at the same time, government is *sacred*, and not to be *trifled* with. It is our happiness to live under the government of a PRINCE who is satisfied with ruling according to law; as every other *good prince* will – We enjoy under his administration all the liberty that is proper and expedient for us. It becomes us, therefore, to be contented, and dutiful subjects. Let us prize our freedom; but not *use our liberty for a cloke of maliciousness*. There are men who strike at *liberty* under the term *licentiousness*. There are others who aim at *popularity* under the disguise of *patriotism*. Be aware of both. *Extremes* are dangerous. There is at present amongst us, perhaps, more danger of the *latter*, than of the *former*. For which reason I would exhort you to pay all due Regard to the government over us; to the KING and all in authority; and to *lead a quiet and peaceable life*. – And while I am speaking of loyalty to our *earthly Prince*, suffer me just to put you in mind to be loyal also to the supreme RULER of the universe, *by whom kings reign, and princes decree justice* (Prov. 8:15). To which king eternal immortal, invisible, even to the ONLY WISE GOD, be all honor and praise, DOMINION and thanksgiving, through JESUS CHRIST our LORD. AMEN.
Finis.

Source: Jonathan Mayhew (1720-1766). *A Discourse Concerning Unlimited Submission and Non-Resistance to the Higher Powers, with Some Reflections on the Resistance Made to King Charles I. and on the Anniversary of His Death: In Which the Mysterious Doctrine of That Prince's Saintship and Martyrdom Is Unriddled: The Substance of Which Was Delivered in a Sermon Preached in the West Meeting-House in Boston the Lord's-Day after the 30th of January, 1749/50*. Boston: D. Fowle and D. Gookin, 1750, 1-3, 10-11, 24, 27-29, 34-35, 38-40, 54-55.

---

[5] The Dragon, in astronomy, a constellation of the northern hemisphere; the Greeks had many fables concerning this constellation, for instance the story of Heracles who killed the dragon guarding the Hesperian fruit. Hera then transferred the dragon to heaven as a reward for its services.

110. Benjamin Franklin
"Join, or Die" (1754)

Source: Benjamin Franklin (1706-1790). "Join, or Die." *The Pennsylvania Gazette*, May 9, 1754. Courtesy Library of Congress.

111. James Otis
The Rights of the British Colonies Asserted and Proved (1764)

Introduction.
Of the Origin of Government

[...] Let no Man think I am about to commence [to be an] advocate for *despotism*, because I affirm that government is founded on the necessity of our natures; and that an original supreme Sovereign, absolute, and uncontroulable, *earthly* power *must* exist in and preside over every society; from whose final decisions there can be no appeal but directly to Heaven. It is therefore *originally* and *ultimately* in the people. I say this supreme absolute power is *originally* and *ultimately* in the people; and they never did in fact *freely*, nor can they *rightfully* make an absolute, unlimited renunciation of this divine right.[6] It is ever in the nature of the thing given in *trust*, and on a condition, the performance of which no mortal can dispence with; namely, that the person or persons on whom the sovereignty is confer'd by the people, shall *incessantly* consult *their* good. Tyranny of all kinds is to be abhor'd, whether it be in the hands of one, or of the few, or of the many. – And tho' "in the last age a generation of men sprung up that would flatter Princes with an opinion that *they* have a *divine right* to absolute power"; yet "slavery is so vile and miserable an estate of man and so directly opposite to the generous temper and courage of our nation, that 'tis hard to be conceived that an *englishman*, much less a *gentleman*, should plead for it."[7] Especially at a time when the finest writers of the most polite nations on the continent of

---

[6] Original footnote: "The power of GOD almighty is the only power that can properly and strictly be called supreme and absolute. In the order of nature immediately under him comes the power of a simple *democracy* or the power of the whole over the whole. Subordinate to both these, are all other political powers, from that of the French Monarque, to a petty constable."
[7] Original footnote: "Mr. Locke."

Europe, are enraptured with the beauties of the civil constitution of *Great-Britain*; and envy her, no less for the *freedom* of her sons, than for her immense *wealth* and *military* glory.

But let the *origin* of government be placed where it may, the *end* of it is manifestly the good of *the whole*. *Salus populi suprema lex esto*,[8] is of the law of nature, and part of that grand charter given the human race, (tho' too many of them are afraid to assert it,) by the only monarch in the universe, who has a clear and indisputable right to *absolute* power; because he is the *only* ONE who is *omniscient* as well as *omnipotent*.

It is evidently contrary to the first principles of reason, that supreme *unlimited* power should be in the hands of *one* man. It is the greatest "*idolatry*, begotten by *flattery*, on the body of *pride*," that could induce one to think that a *single mortal* should be able to hold so great a power, if ever so well inclined. Hence the origin of *deifying* princes: It was from the trick of gulling the vulgar into a belief that their tyrants were *omniscient*; and that it was therefore right, that they should be considered as *omnipotent*. Hence the *Dii majorum et minorum gentium*;[9] the great, the monarchical, the little, Provincial subordinate and subaltern gods, demi-gods, and semidemi-gods, ancient and modern. Thus deities of all kinds were multiplied and increased in *abundance*; for every devil incarnate, who could enslave a people, acquired a title to *divinity*; and thus the "rabble of the skies" was made up of locusts and caterpillars; lions, tygers and harpies; and other devourers translated from plaguing the earth![10]

The *end* of government being the *good* of mankind, points out its great duties: It is above all things to provide for the security, the quiet, and happy enjoyment of life, liberty, and property. There is no one act which a government can have a *right* to make, that does not tend to the advancement of the security, tranquility and prosperity of the people. If life, liberty and property could be enjoyed in as great perfection in *solitude*, as in *society*, there would be no need of government. But the experience of ages has proved that such is the nature of man, a weak, imperfect being; that the valuable ends of life cannot be obtained, without the union and assistance of many. Hence 'tis clear that men cannot live apart or independent of each other: In solitude men would perish; and yet they cannot live together without contests. These contests require some arbitrator to determine them. The necessity of a common, indifferent and impartial judge, makes all men seek one; tho' few find him in the *sovereign power*, of their respective states or any where else in *subordination* to it.

Government is founded *immediately* on the necessities of human nature, and *ultimately* on the will of God, the author of nature; who has not left it to men in general to choose, whether they will be members of society or not, but at the hazard of their senses if not of their lives. Yet it is left to every man as he comes of age to chuse *what society* he will continue to belong to. Nay if one has a mind to turn *Hermit*, and after he has been born, nursed, and brought up in the arms of society, and acquired the habits and passions of social life, is willing to run the risque of starving alone, which is generally most unavoidable in a state of hermitage, who shall hinder him? I know of no human law, founded on the law of *nature*, to restrain him from separating himself from all the spe-

---

[8] Latin: "The well-being of the people is the supreme law."
[9] Otis here makes a common distinction between the major and the minor gods.
[10] Original footnote: "Kingcraft and Priestcraft have fell out so often, that 'tis a wonder this grand and ancient alliance is not broken off for ever. Happy for mankind will it be, when such a separation shall take place."

cies, if he can find it in his heart to leave them; unless it should be said, it is against the great law of *self-preservation:* But of this every man will think himself *his own judge.* [...]

The same law of nature and of reason is equally obligatory [i]n a *democracy,* an *aristocracy,* and a *monarchy*: Whenever the administrators, in any of those forms, deviate from truth, justice and equity, they verge towards tyranny, and are to be opposed; and if they prove incorrigible, they will be *deposed* by the people, if the people are not rendered too abject. Deposing the administrators of a *simple democracy* may sound oddly, but it is done every day, and in almost every vote. A. B. & C. for example, make a *democracy*. Today A & B are for so vile a measure as a standing army. To morrow B & C vote it out. This is as really deposing the former administrators, as setting up and making a new king is deposing the old one. *Democracy* in the one case, and *monarchy* in the other, still remain; all that is done is to change the administration.

The first principle and great end of government being to provide for the best good of all the people, this can be done only by a supreme legislative and executive ultimately in the people, or whole community, where GOD has placed it; but the inconveniencies, not to say impossibility, attending the consultations and operations of a large body of people, have made it necessary to transfer the power of the whole to a *few*: This necessity gave rise to deputation, proxy or a right of representation.

Source: James Otis (1725-1783). *The Rights of the British Colonies Asserted and Proved*. Boston: Edes and Gill, 1764, 9-11,13.

112. Philoleutherus (Pseudonym) Article in *The Constitutional Courant* (1765)

At a time when our dearest privileges are torn from us, and the foundation of all our liberty subverted, every one who has the least spark of love to his country, must feel the deepest anxiety about our approaching fate. The hearts of all who have a just value for freedom, must burn within them, when they see the chains of abject slavery just ready to be riveted about our necks. It has been undeniably demonstrated, by the various authors who have dared to assert the cause of these injured colonies, that no Englishman can be taxed, agreeable to the known principles of our constitution, but by his own consent, given either by himself or his representatives, – that these colonies are not in any sense at all represented in the British parliament, – that the first adventurers into these uncultivated desarts, were, in every colony, either by royal charters, or royal concessions, in the most express terms possible, assured, that all their rights and privileges as British subjects, should be preserved to them unimpaired, – that these original concessions have been repeatedly allowed by the crown, and have never been controverted till this *memorable period*. The arguments by which these points have been established beyond all dispute, I need not repeat; their evidence is such as must flash conviction into the minds of all but the vile minions[11] of tyranny and arbitrary power. The tremendous conclusion, therefore, forces itself upon us, that the public faith of the nation, in which, till now, we thought we might securely confide, is violated, and we robbed of our dearest rights by the late law erecting *a stamp-office* among us.

---

[11] Here: slave, underling.

What then is to be done? Shall we sit down quietly, while the yoke of slavery is wreathing about our necks? He that is stupid enough to plead for this, deserves to be a *slave*. Shall we not hope still that some resource is left us in the royal care and benevolence? We have the happiness to be governed by one of the best of kings, who is our common father, and must be supposed to be under no temptations to sacrifice the rights of one part of his subjects to the caprice of another. [...]

Let none censure these free thoughts as treasonable: I know they will be called so by those who would gladly transform these flourishing colonies into the howling seats of thraldom[12] and wretchedness; but the sentiments of such miscreants[13] are little to be regarded. We cherish the most unfeigned loyalty to our rightful sovereign; we have a high veneration for the British parliament; we consider them as the most august assembly on earth; but the wisest of kings may be misled; some persons they must trust for the information they receive; those persons are generally such, whose interest it is to represent all things to them in false lights; so that it is rather to be admired that they are not oftener misled than they are. Parliaments also are liable to mistakes, yea, sometimes fall into capital errors, and frame laws the most oppressive to the subject, yea, sometimes take such steps, which, if persisted in, would soon unhinge the whole constitution. Our histories bear innumerable attestations to the truth of this. It cannot be treason to point out such mistakes and the consequences of them, yea to set them in the most glaring light, to alarm the subject. By acting on this principle, our ancestors have transmitted to us our privileges inviolated; let us therefore prosecute the same glorious plan. Let the British parliament be treated with all possible respect, while they treat us as fellow-subjects; but if they transgress the bounds prescribed them by the constitution, if they usurp a jurisdiction, to which they have no right; if they infringe our liberties, and pursue such measures as will infallibly end in a Turkish despotism; if they violate public faith, and destroy our confidence in the royal promises, let us boldly deny all such usurped jurisdiction [...]. We abhor slavery, and detest the remotest aiders and abettors[14] of our bondage: but native Americans, who are diabolical enough to help forward our ruin, we execrate as the worst of parricides.[15] Parricides! 'tis too soft a term: Murder your fathers, rip up the bowels of your mothers, dash the infants you have begotten against the stones, and be blameless; – but enslave your country! entail vassalage,[16] that worst of all human miseries, that sum of all wretchedness, on millions! This, this is guilt, this calls for heaven's fiercest vengeance. But rouse, rouse my countrymen, let the villain that is hardy enough to persist, do it at his peril. Shew them we have resentment no less keen than our Eastern brethren; will you tamely suffer the execution of a law that reduces you to the vile condition of slaves, and is abhorred by all the genuine sons of liberty? Let the wretch that sleeps now, be branded as an enemy to his country.

PHILOLEUTHERUS.

Source: Philoleutherus. *The Constitutional Courant: Containing Matters Interesting to Liberty, and No Wise Repugnant to Loyalty* 1 (Sept. 21, 1765), 1-2.

---

[12] The state of being in bondage, captivity.
[13] Depraved, villainous, wicked person.
[14] Supporter, advocate.
[15] One who murders his father (or either parent).
[16] Subjection, subordination, servitude.

113. Philo Patriæ (Pseudonym)
Article in *The Constitutional Courant* (1765)

The late violences committed in the Eastern colonies, in resentment and opposition to the Stamp Act, and all its contrivers and abettors; whether they proceeded from the misguided zeal of those who had a strong sensibility of the injury done their country by that act, or from the villainous cunning of those who took the opportunity of the public discontent, to promote and increase the tumult, in order to perpetrate the most atrocious crimes; in either case, the true lovers of liberty and their country, who detest and abhor the Stamp Act from principle, and a certain knowledge of their rights, violated by that act, are far from countenancing, or being pleased with these violences; on the contrary, they hear of them with concern and sorrow, not only as they must necessarily involve many innocent persons in distress, who had no share in the guilt that excited the public resentment; but also as they injure a good cause, and check the spirit of opposition to an act illegally obtruded upon us, to deprive us of our most sacred rights, and change our freedom to slavery, by a legislature who have no lawful authority over us. The terrible effects of those popular tumults, are likely to startle men who have been accustomed to venerate and obey lawful authority, and who delight in peace and order; and to make them doubt the justice of the cause attended with such direful consequences. But the guilt of all these violences is most justly chargeable upon the authors and abettors of the Stamp Act. They who endeavour to destroy the foundations of the English constitution, and break thro' the fence of the laws, in order to let in a torrent of tyranny and oppression upon their fellow-subjects, ought not to be surprized if they are overwhelmed in it themselves. [...] If they become arbitrary, and use their power against the people who give it; can they suppose that the people, in their turn, will not exert their inherent power against their oppressors, and be as arbitrary as they? [...] For the moment we submit to pay this tax, as to lawful authority, that moment we commence as errant slaves as any in Turkey, the fence of our liberty and property is broken down, and the foundation of the English constitution, with respect to us, is utterly destroyed. Let us not flatter ourselves, that we shall be happier, or treated with more lenity than our fellow slaves in Turkey: human nature is the same every where, and unlimited power is as much to be dreaded among us, as it is in the most barbarous nations upon earth: It is slavery that hath made them barbarous, and the same cause will have the same effect upon us. The inhabitants of Greece, Rome, and Constantinople, were once free and happy, and the liberal arts and sciences flourished among them; but slavery has spread ignorance, barbarism and misery over those once delightful regions, where the people are sunk into a stupid insensibility of their condition, and the spirit of liberty, after being depressed above a thousand years, seems now to be lost irrecoverably. It is better to die in defence of our rights, than to leave such a state as this to the generations that succeed us.

It cannot be possible that our sovereign, or any of our English fellow-subjects, who understand and value their own rights, can be displeased with us for asserting ours. Do we claim any but what are as clear as the noon day? Have we not by nature a right to liberty and property; as Englishmen, by laws and charters, in terms as plain as words can express? Is it not a fundamental principle of the English constitution, that no man shall be bound but by laws of his own making, nor taxed but by his own consent, given by representatives of his own choosing? And have we not a right to have all our causes tried by our peers, that is by juries, men of our own rank, indifferently chosen, and to whom we have no reasonable objection; – and does not the Stamp Act, in the most flagrant manner, violate all these rights, our liberty, our property, and trials by juries? Our liberty, in being subjected to laws that we had no share in making; our property, in being taxed without our own consent, in a parliament where we never had either the choice of a person to represent us, nor any that were qualified for the office, or interested in our welfare; and in our trials by juries, because an informer or prosecutor has it in his choice, whether to try the matter in a court of common law, or a court of admiralty: – and as these courts are immediately under the influence of the crown, and the act allows no appeal from them, except to a court of vice-admiralty, which is of the same kind, we have reason to think these courts will be as arbitrary and as oppressive as ever the high commission and star chamber courts were: And as this act gives them jurisdiction over matters that have no relation to navigation or sea affairs, they may, with equal propriety, have jurisdiction in cases of life and death. This is a real representation of the slavish state we are reduced to by the Stamp Act, if we ever suffer it to take place among us. It is easy to see that the ministry design to alter and overturn the English constitution, and have invented a number of expedients to break thro' the restraints that the laws lay upon arbitrary dispositions, and are labouring to become despotic and uncontroulable. [...]

Let none falsely insinuate, that this spirit of opposition to the Stamp Act, which prevails throughout the British dominions in America, has in it the least tincture of rebellion against lawful authority, or disloyalty to our king. Whoever brings such charges against us, is a slanderer and a villain. We have the highest degree of veneration for the laws and constitution of England; they are our birth-right and inheritance, and we would defend them with our lives. We have the most affectionate loyalty to our rightful sovereign George the third,[17] and his royal house, and we are ready to risk our lives and fortunes in his and their defence. We have the highest respect and reverence for the British parliament, which we believe to be the most august and respectable body of men upon earth, and we desire that all their rights, privileges and honors may forever be preserved to them, and to every rank and order of men in the kingdom of Great-Britain, whose welfare, prosperity, and honor we sincerely wish, and should rejoice in. We consider ourselves as one people with them, and glory in the relation between us; and we desire our connection may forever continue, as it is our best security against foreign invaders, and as we may reciprocally promote the welfare and strength of each other. Such are our sentiments and affections towards our mother country. But, at the same time, we cannot yield up to her, or to any power on earth, our inherent and most valuable rights and privileges. If she would strip us of all the advantages derived to us from the English constitution, why should we desire to continue our connection? We might as well belong to France, or any other power; none could offer a greater injury to our rights and liberties than is offered by the Stamp Act. If we have delivered our sentiments of the parliament with greater freedom than they are usually mentioned with, let it be considered that it is only when they have taken upon them to deprive us of our rights, which are not under their jurisdiction: If any then take offence at the freedom with which they are treated, let them blush at the occasion given for it. Such an alarming attempt upon British liberty was never made before, nor I hope ever will again. – We have been told from England, that the Stamp Act passed without so much debate or consideration, as sometimes arose upon the most trifling bills that are brought before the house! If it had been well debated and

---

[17] George III (1738-1820), King of Great Britain and Ireland 1760-1820.

considered, surely it never could have passed; it must astonish all concern'd in it, when they come to consider it, that ever it did pass at all, and it will doubtless be repealed as soon as ever the nature of it is fully understood. – Mean while let us never, for one moment, acknowledge that it is binding upon us, nor pay one farthing in obedience to it, for it was made by a power, that, by the fundamental laws that both they and we acknowledge, hath no jurisdiction over us.

As the ministry under whose influence this act was made, are, we have reason to hope, by this time discarded and out of place, no other I suppose will ever be found that will approve it: and it may be worth the serious consideration of those who would officiously endeavour to enslave their countrymen to enforce it, whether they will not be more likely to receive the frowns than the smiles of their superiors, for their activity in so odious an office. For if this act takes place and is established, it may be depended upon, that liberty in Great Britain will not long survive its extinction in America.

PHILO PATRIÆ.

Source: Philo Patriæ. *The Constitutional Courant: Containing Matters Interesting to Liberty, and No Wise Repugnant to Loyalty* 1 (Sept, 21, 1765), 2.

114. *Resolutions of the Stamp Act Congress, October 19, 1765*

The members of this Congress, sincerely devoted, with the warmest sentiments of affection and duty to His Majesty's Person and Government, inviolably attached to the present happy establishment of the Protestant succession, and with minds deeply impressed by a sense of the present and impending misfortunes of the British colonies on this continent; having considered as maturely as time will permit the circumstances of the said colonies, esteem it our indispensable duty to make the following declarations of our humble opinion, respecting the most essential rights and liberties of the colonists, and of the grievances under which they labour, by reason of several late Acts of Parliament.

I. That His Majesty's subjects in these colonies, owe the same allegiance to the Crown of Great-Britain, that is owing from his subjects born within the realm, and all due subordination to that august body the Parliament of Great-Britain.

II. That His Majesty's liege subjects in these colonies, are entitled to all the inherent rights and liberties of his natural born subjects within the kingdom of Great-Britain.

III. That it is inseparably essential to the freedom of a people, and the undoubted right of Englishmen, that no taxes be imposed on them, but with their own consent, given personally, or by their representatives.

IV. That the people of these colonies are not, and from their local circumstances cannot be, represented in the House of Commons in Great-Britain.

V. That the only representatives of the people of these colonies, are persons chosen therein by themselves, and that no taxes ever have been, or can be constitutionally imposed on them, but by their respective legislatures.

VI. That all supplies to the Crown, being free gifts of the people, it is unreasonable and inconsistent with the principles and spirit of the British Constitution, for the people of Great-Britain to grant to His Majesty the property of the colonists.

VII. That trial by jury is the inherent and invaluable right of every British subject in these colonies.

VIII. That the late Act of Parliament, entitled *An Act for granting and applying certain Stamp Duties, and other Duties, in the British colonies and plantations in America, etc.*, by imposing taxes on the inhabitants of these colonies, and the said Act, and several other Acts, by extending the jurisdiction of the courts of Admiralty beyond its ancient limits, have a manifest tendency to subvert the rights and liberties of the colonists.

IX. That the duties imposed by several late Acts of Parliament, from the peculiar circumstances of these colonies, will be extremely burthensome and grievous; and from the scarcity of specie, the payment of them absolutely impracticable.

X. That as the profits of the trade of these colonies ultimately center in Great-Britain, to pay for the manufactures which they are obliged to take from thence, they eventually contribute very largely to all supplies granted there to the Crown.

XI. That the restrictions imposed by several late Acts of Parliament, on the trade of these colonies, will render them unable to purchase the manufactures of Great-Britain.

XII. That the increase, prosperity, and happiness of these colonies, depend on the full and free enjoyments of their rights and liberties, and an intercourse with Great-Britain mutually affectionate and advantageous.

XIII. That it is the right of the British subjects in these colonies, to petition the King or either House of Parliament.

Lastly, That it is the indispensable duty of these colonies, to the best of sovereigns, to the mother country, and to themselves, to endeavour by a loyal and dutiful address to his Majesty, and humble applications to both Houses of Parliament, to procure the repeal of the Act for granting and applying certain stamp duties, of all clauses of any other Acts of Parliament, whereby the jurisdiction of the Admiralty is extended as aforesaid, and of the other late Acts for the restriction of American commerce.

Source: *Resolutions of the Stamp Act Congress, October 19, 1765*. Reprinted in *Great Issues in American History: From Settlement to Revolution, 1584-1776*. Ed. Clarence L. Ver Steeg and Richard Hofstadter. New York: Vintage, 1969, 404-406.

115. John Dickinson
A New Song (1768)

To the Tune of "Hearts of Oak, &c."

Come join Hand in Hand, brave AMERICANS all,
And rouse your bold Hearts at fair LIBERTY'S Call;
No *tyrannous Acts*, shall suppress your *just Claim*,
Or stain with *Dishonor* AMERICA'S Name –
  In FREEDOM we're BORN, and in FREEDOM we'll LIVE;
    Our Purses are ready,
    Steady, Friends, Steady,
  Not as SLAVES, but as FREEMEN our Money we'll give.

Our worthy *Forefathers* – let's give them a Cheer –
To *Climates unknown* did courageously steer;
Thro' *Oceans* to *Deserts* for *Freedom* they came,

And dying bequeath'd us their *Freedom* and *Fame* –
In FREEDOM we're BORN, &c.

Their generous Bosoms all Dangers despis'd,
So *highly*, so *wisely*, their BIRTH-RIGHTS they priz'd;
We'll keep what they gave, we will piously keep,
Nor frustrate their Toils on the Land and the Deep.
In FREEDOM we're BORN, &c.

The TREE their own Hands had to LIBERTY rear'd,[18]
They liv'd to behold growing strong and rever'd;[19]
With Transport then cry'd, "Now our Wishes we gain,
For our Children shall gather the Fruits of our Pain."
In FREEDOM we're BORN, &c.

Swarms of PLACEMEN[20] and PENSIONERS soon will appear,
Like Locusts deforming the Charms of the Year;
Suns vainly will rise, Showers vainly descend,
If *we* are to *drudge*[21] *for* what *others* shall *spend*.
In FREEDOM we're BORN, &c.

Then join Hand in Hand brave AMERICANS all,
By *uniting* We stand, by *dividing* We fall;
IN SO RIGHTEOUS A CAUSE let us hope to succeed,
For Heaven approves of each generous Deed –
In FREEDOM we're BORN, &c.

All Ages shall speak with *Amaze* and *Applause*,
Of the *Courage* we'll shew IN SUPPORT OF OUR LAWS.
To DIE we can *bear* – but. to SERVE we *disdain* –
For SHAME is to *Freemen* more dreadful than PAIN –
In FREEDOM we're BORN, &c.

This Bumper I crown for our SOVEREIGN'S Health,
And this for BRITANNIA'S Glory and Wealth:
That Wealth, and that Glory immortal may be,
If *She* is but *just* – and *We* are but *Free* –
In FREEDOM we're BORN, &c.

Source: John Dickinson (1732-1808). *A New Song*. Philadelphia: David Hall & William Sellers, 1768.

---

[18] Raise upright.
[19] Regarded with awe and devotion.
[20] Men who have a political appointment in the government. Original footnote placed in front of "Swarms": "The *Ministry* have already begun to give away in PENSIONS *the Money* THEY have *lately* taken out of OUR Pockets WITHOUT OUR CONSENT."
[21] To work hard or slavishly; to toil at laborious and distasteful work.

116. Anthony Benezet
Thoughts on the Nature of War (1766)

[...] But the true Christian Spirit being almost departed from the earth, true Christian knowledge, as its inseparable companion, is departed with it, and men seem to be gone back again to their old animal life: and tho', in speculation and idea, they profess an assent to the truths of Revelation; yet, in heart and practice, they are too apt to consider the course of all things as connected only with temporal good and evil, and themselves as the center and circumference, the first cause and the last end of all; ascribing to human understanding designs which only Infinite Wisdom can form, and to human power events which Omnipotence only can produce. [...]

If the Christian, however, recollects himself, he will find War to be a sad consequence of the apostasy[22] and fall of man; when he was abandoned to the fury of his own lusts and passions, as the natural and penal effect of breaking loose from the Divine Government, the fundamental law of which is LOVE – "*Thou shalt love the* LORD *thy* GOD *with all thy heart, with all thy soul, with all thy mind, and with all thy strength; and thy* FELLOW-CREATURE, *as thyself.*"[23]

[... T]he consequences of War, when impartially examined, will be found big, not only with outward and temporal distress, but with an evil that extends where in the darkness and tumult of human passions it is neither expected nor conceived to reach. That property is confounded, scattered, and destroyed; that laws are trampled under foot, government despised, and the ties of all civil and domestic order broken into pieces; that fruitful countries are made deserts, and stately cities a heap of ruins; that matrons and virgins are violated; and neither the innocence of unoffending infancy, nor the impotence of decrepit age, a protection from the rage and thirst for blood – is but the mortal progeny of this teeming womb of mischief. The worst is still behind – and tho' remote from those senses and passions that are exercised only by present good and evil, and, therefore, not the object of common concern; must yet, upon the least recollection, impress with horror every mind that believes there is a Righteous God, and a state of retribution that is to last for ever. But what must the Christian feel? – he, who knows that the fall of man is a fall from meekness, purity, and love, into sensuality, pride, and wrath; that the Son of God became incarnate, and suffered, and died, to restore that first life of meekness, purity, and love; and that for those, in whom the restoration of that life is not begun in the present state, the Son of God incarnate has, it is to be dreaded, suffered and died in vain – what, I say, must he feel for those immortal spirits, that, in the earliest dawn of their day of purification, are by hundreds and thousands driven into eternity, in the bitterness of enmity and wrath – some inflamed with drunkenness; some fired with lust; and all stained with blood? In those direful conflicts, which are maintained with so much rage, that when the Vanquished at last retreats with the loss of TWENTY-THOUSAND HUMAN BEINGS, the Victor finds he has purchased some little advantage at the expence of MORE THAN HALF THAT NUMBER – Heaven and earth! what a possibility is here of a sacrifice made to *the prince of darkness*, the first and chief apostate! who rejoices in beholding men, thro' the abuse of those benefits which undeserved Mercy has conferred upon them, transformed into enmity and hatred of God and their brethren; forsaken by God, and destroying one

---

[22] Abandonment or renunciation of one's religious faith or moral allegiance.
[23] Luke 10.27.

another: and thus hastening once more into his horrid society; that having been accomplices in his rebellion: they may become partakers of his misery and torment.

Now, if the man of valour, whom consenting nations have dignified with the title of HERO, and the man devoted to the world, are asked, from whence this immortal mischief, that may thus extend its influence into the regions of eternity, can proceed; what must they answer? – indeed, what can they answer, but that it is engendered by the love of human glory – as vain a phantom as ever play'd before a madman's eye! by the lust of dominion; the avarice of wealth; and the infamous ambition of being dreaded as the conquerors and tyrants of mankind? Heaven preserve Britain from these "*earthly, sensual, develish*" motives – so repugnant to the generous, compassionate, and forgiving temper, with which Redeeming Mercy has blest it, in union with the purer beams of heavenly light; that light which is intended to remove all the darkness of human corruption, and transform selfish, sensual, proud, and malignant spirits, into Angels of patience, humility, meekness, purity, and love; the "*children and heirs of God, the brethren and joint heirs of Christ!*" [...]

Source: Anthony Benezet (1713-1784). *Thoughts on the Nature of War, and Its Repugnancy to the Christian Life: Extracted from a Sermon, on the 29th November, 1759; Being the Day of Public Thanksgiving for the Successes Obtained in the Late War* [...]. Philadelphia: Henry Miller, 1766, 4-9.

117. Benjamin Franklin
Magna Britannia: Her Colonies Reduc'd (1767)

Source: Benjamin Franklin (1706-1790). *Magna Britannia: Her Colonies Reduce'd* (1767). Courtesy Library Company of Philadelphia.

118. *The Massachusetts Spy* (1774)

Source: *The Massachusetts Spy; or, Thomas's Boston Journal*, Vol. 4, No. 179, July 7, 1774. Courtesy Library of Congress.

119. Samuel Adams "The Rights of the Colonists" (1772)

1st. Natural Rights of the Colonists as Men. –

Among the Natural Rights of the Colonists are these First. a Right to *Life*; Secondly to *Liberty*; thirdly to *Property*; together with the Right to support and defend them in the best manner they can – Those are evident Branches of, rather than deductions from the Duty of Self Preservation, commonly called the first Law of Nature –

All Men have a Right to remain in a State of Nature as long as they please: And in case of into[l]erable Oppression, Civil or Religious, to leave the Society they belong to, and enter into another. –

When Men enter into Society, it is by voluntary consent; and they have a right to demand and insist upon the performance of such conditions, And previous limitations as form an equitable[24] *original compact.* –

Every natural Right not expressly given up or from the nature of a Social Compact necessarily ceded remains. –

All positive and civil laws, should conform as far as possible, to the Law of natural reason and equity. –

As neither reason requires, nor relig[i]on permits the contrary, every Man living in or out of a state of civil society, has a right peaceably and quietly to worship God according to the dictates of his conscience. –

"Just and true liberty, equal and impartial liberty" in matters spiritual and temporal, is a thing that all Men are clearly entitled to, by the eternal and immutable laws Of God and nature, as well as by the law of Nations, & all well grounded municipal laws, which must have their foundation in the former. – [...]

---

[24] Just and impartial.

The natural liberty of Men by entring into society is abridg'd or restrained so far only as is necessary for the Great end of Society[,] the best good of the whole –

In the state of nature, every man is under God, Judge and sole Judge, of his own rights and the injuries done him: By entering into society, he agrees to an Arbiter or indifferent Judge between him and his neighbours; but he no more renounces his original right, than by taking a cause out of the ordinary course of law, and leaving the decision to Referees or indifferent Arbitrations. [...]

"The natural liberty of man is to be free from any superior power on earth, and not to be under the will or legislative authority of man; but only to have the law of nature for his rule." –

[...] Governors have no right to seek what they please; by this, instead of being content with the station assigned them, that of honourable servants of the society, they would soon become Absolute masters, Despots, and Tyrants. [...]

3^d. *The Rights of the Colonists as Subjects*

A Common Wealth or state is a body politick or civil society of men, united together to promote their mutual safety and prosperity, by means of their union.[25]

The *absolute Rights* of Englishmen, and all freemen in or out of Civil society, are principally, *personal security personal liberty* and *private property*.

All Persons born in the British American Colonies are by the laws of God and nature, and by the Common law of England, *exclusive of all charters from the Crown*,[26] well Entitled, and by the Acts of the British Parliament are declared to be entitled to all the natural essential, inherent & insep[a]rable Rights Liberties and Privileges of Subjects born in Great Britain, or within the Realm. Among those Rights are the following; which no m[a]n or body of men, consistently with their own rights as men and citizens or members of society, can for themselves give up or take away from others.

First, "The first fundamental positive law of all Commonwealths or States, is the establishing the legislative power; as the first fundamental *natural* law also, which is to govern even the legislative power itself, is the preservation of the Society."[27]

Secondly, The Legislative has no right to absolute arbitrary power over the lives and fortunes of the people: Nor can mortals assume a prerogative, not only too high for men, but for Angels; and therefore reserved for the exercise of the *Deity* alone. – [...]

Thirdly, The supreme power cannot Justly take from any man, any part of his property without his consent, in person or by his Representative. –

These are some of the first principles of natural law & Justice, and the great Barriers of all free states, and of the British Constitution in particular. It is utterly irreconcil[a]ble to these principles, and to many other fundamental maxims of the common law, common sense and reason, that a British house of commons, should have a right, at pleasure, to give and grant the property of the Colonists. [...]

Source: Samuel Adams (1722-1803). "The Right of the Colonists as Men, as Christians, and as Subjects" [dated November 20, 1772]. *The Writings of Samuel Adams*. 4 vols. Ed. Harry Alonzo Cushing. Vol. 2: *1770-1773*. New York, 1968, 351-354, 356-357.

---

[25] Original footnote: "See Lock [sic] and Vatel [sic];" reference to John Locke and Emerich de Vattel (1714-1767), the Swiss philosopher and jurist who authored the influential 1758 treatise *The Law of Nations or Principles of the Law of Nature*.

[26] A written grant from the sovereign power of a country conferring certain rights and privileges on a person, a corporation, or the people: A royal charter exempted the Massachusetts colony from direct interference by the Crown.

[27] Original footnote: "Locke on Government. Salus Populi Suprema Lex esto – ."

120. Benjamin Franklin
"Rules by Which a Great Empire May Be Reduced to a Small One" (1773)

For the Public Advertiser.
RULES *by which a* GREAT EMPIRE *may be reduced to a* SMALL ONE. [Presented privately to a *late Minister*[28], when he entered upon his Administration; and now first published.]
An ancient Sage valued himself upon this, that tho' he could not fiddle, he knew how to make a *great City* of a *little one*.[29] The Science that I, a modern Simpleton, am about to communicate is the very reverse.

I address myself to all Ministers who have the Management of extensive Dominions, which from their very Greatness are become troublesome to govern, because the Multiplicity of their Affairs leaves no Time for *fiddling*.

I. In the first Place, Gentlemen, you are to consider, that a great Empire, like a great Cake, is most easily diminished at the Edges. Turn your Attention therefore first to your remotest Provinces; that as you get rid of them, the next may follow in Order.

II. That the Possibility of this Separation may always exist, take special Care the Provinces are never incorporated with the Mother Country, that they do not enjoy the same common Rights, the same Privileges in Commerce, and that they are governed by *severer* Laws, all of *your enacting*, without allowing them any Share in the Choice of the Legislators. By carefully making and preserving such Distinctions, you will (to keep to my Simile of the Cake) act like a wise Gingerbread Baker, who, to facilitate a Division, cuts his Dough half through in those Places, where, when bak'd, he would have it *broken to Pieces*. [...]

IV. However peaceably your Colonies have submitted to your Government, shewn their Affection to your Interest, and patiently borne their Grievances, you are to *suppose* them always inclined to revolt, and treat them accordingly. Quarter Troops among them, who by their Insolence may *provoke* the rising of Mobs, and by their Bullets and Bayonets *suppress* them. By this Means, like the Husband who uses his Wife ill *from Suspicion*, you may in Time convert your *Suspicions* into *Realities*.

V. Remote Provinces must have *Governors*, and *Judges*, to represent the Royal Person, and execute every where the delegated Parts of his Office and Authority. You Ministers know, that much of the Strength of Government depends on the *Opinion* of the People; and much of that Opinion on the Choice of Rulers placed immediately over them. If you send them wise and good Men for Governors, who study the Interest of the Colonists, and advance their Prosperity, they will think their King wise and good, and that he wishes the Welfare of his Subjects. If you send them learned and upright Men for judges, they will think him a Lover of Justice. This may attach your Provinces more to his Government. You are therefore to be careful who you recommend for those Offices. If you can find Prodigals who have ruined their Fortunes, broken Gamesters or Stock-Jobbers, these may do well as *Governors*; for they will probably be rapacious, and provoke the People by their Extortions. [...]

VIII. If when you are engaged in War, your Colonies should vie in liberal Aids of Men and Money against the common Enemy, upon your simple Requisition, and give far be-

---

[28] Reference to the 1st Earl of Hillsborough (1718-1793), British politician and secretary of state for the colonies from 1768 to 1772.
[29] The sage was Themistocles. Franklin's wording follows *Plutarch's Lives*, 6 vols., London, 1770, Vol. 1, 281.

yond their Abilities, reflect, that a Penny taken from them by your Power is more honourable to you than a Pound presented by their Benevolence. Despise therefore their voluntary Grants, and resolve to harrass them with novel Taxes. They will probably complain to your Parliaments that they are taxed by a Body in which they have no Representative, and that this is contrary to common Right. They will petition for Redress. Let the Parliaments flout their Claims, reject their Petitions, refuse even to suffer the reading of them, and treat the Petitioners with the utmost Contempt. Nothing can have a better Effect, in producing the Alienation proposed; for though many can forgive Injuries, *none ever forgave Contempt*. [...]

XVI. If you are told of Discontents in your Colonies, never believe that they are general, or that you have given Occasion for them; therefore do not think of applying any Remedy, or of changing any offensive Measure. Redress no Grievance, lest they should be encouraged to demand the Redress of some other Grievance. Grant no Request that is just and reasonable, lest they should make another that is unreasonable. Take all your Informations of the State of the Colonies from your Governors and Officers in Enmity with them. Encourage and reward these *Leasing-makers*;[30] secrete their lying Accusations lest they should be confuted; but act upon them as the clearest Evidence, and believe nothing you hear from the Friends of the People. Suppose all *their* Complaints to be invented and promoted by a few factious Demagogues, whom if you could catch and hang, all would be quiet. Catch and hang a few of them accordingly; and the *Blood of the Martyrs* shall *work Miracles* in favour of your Purpose. [...]

XX. Lastly, Invest the General of your Army in the Provinces with great and unconstitutional Powers, and free him from the Controul of even your own Civil Governors. Let him have Troops enow under his Command, with all the Fortresses in his Possession; and who knows but (like some provincial Generals in the Roman Empire, and encouraged by the universal Discontent you have produced) he may take it into his Head to set up for himself. If he should, and you have carefully practised these few *excellent Rules* of mine, take my Word for it, all the Provinces will immediately join him, and you will that Day (if you have not done it sooner) get rid of the Trouble of governing them, and all the *Plagues* attending their *Commerce* and Connection from thenceforth and for ever.

Q.E.D.

Source: Benjamin Franklin (1706-1790). "Rules by Which a Great Empire May Be Reduced to a Small One." *The Papers of Benjamin Franklin*. 32 vols. Vol. 20. *January 1 through December 31, 1773*. Ed. William B. Willcox. New Haven and London: Yale University Press, 1976, 391-394, 397-399.

---

[30] Liars, a phrase derived from Scottish law.

121. Paul Revere
The Bloody Massacre Perpetrated in King Street, Boston, on March 5, 1770

Source: Paul Revere (1734-1818). *The Bloody Massacre Perpetrated in King Street, Boston, on March 5, 1770* (engraving 1770). Courtesy Library of Congress. Inscription: "Unhappy BOSTON! see thy Sons deplore, / Thy hallowed Walks besmear'd with guiltless Gore: / While faithless P—n [i.e. Captain Thomas Preston] and his savage Bands, / With murd'rous Rancour stretch their bloody Hands; / Like fierce Barbarians grinning o'er their Prey; / Approve the Carnage and enjoy the Day. // If scalding drops from Rage from Anguish Wrung, / If speechless Sorrows lab'ring for a Tongue, / Or if a weeping World can ought appease / The plaintive Ghosts of Victims such as these; / The Patriot's copious Tears for each are shed, / A glorious Tribute which embalms the Dead. // But know, FATE summons to that awful Goal, / Where JUSTICE strips the Murd'rer of his Soul: / Should venal C—ts [i.e. British Crown Courts] the scandal of the Land, / Snatch the relentless Villain from her Hand, / Keen Execrations on this Plate inscrib'd, / Shall reach a JUDGE who never can be brib'd."

122. John Hancock
An Oration; Delivered March 5, 1774

MEN, BRETHREN, FATHERS AND FELLOW COUNTRYMEN!

The attentive gravity, the venerable appearance of this crouded audience, the dignity which I behold in the countenances of so many in this great Assembly, the solemnity of the occasion upon which we have met together, join'd to a consideration of the part I am to take in the important business of this day, fill me with an awe hitherto unknown; and heighten the sense which I have ever had, of my unworthiness to fill this sacred desk; but, allur'd by the call of some of my respected fellow-citizens, with whose request it is always my greatest pleasure to comply, I almost forgot my want of ability to perform what they required. In this situation, I find my only support, in assuring myself that a generous people will not severely censure what they know was well intended, though it's want of merit, should prevent their being able to applaud it. And I pray, that my sincere attachment to the interest of my country, and hearty detestation of every design formed against her liberties, may be admitted as some apology for my appearance in this place.

I have always from my earliest youth, rejoiced in the felicity of my Fellow-men, and have ever consider'd it as the indispensible duty of every member of society to promote, as far as in him lies, the prosperity of every individual, but especially of the community to which he belongs; and also, as a faithful subject of the state, to use his utmost endeavours to detect, and having detected, strenuously to oppose every traiterous plot which its enemies may devise for its destruction. Security to the persons and properties of the governed, is so obviously the design and end of civil government, that to attempt a logical proof of it, would be like burning tapers at noon day, to assist the sun in enlightening the world; and it cannot be either virtuous or honorable, to attempt to support a government, of which this is not the great and principal basis; and it is to the last degree vicious and infamous to attempt to support a government which manifestly tends to render the persons and properties of the governed insecure. Some boast of being *friends to government*; I am a friend to *righteous* government, to a government founded upon the principles of reason and justice; but I glory in publickly avowing my eternal enmity to tyranny. Is the present system which the British administration have adopted for the government of the colonies, a righteous government? Or is it tyranny? – Here suffer me to ask (and would to Heaven there could be an answer) What tenderness? What regard, respect or consideration has *Great-Britain* shewn in their late transactions for the security of the persons or properties of the inhabitants of the colonies? or rather, What have they omitted doing to destroy that security? They have declared that they have, ever had, and of right ought ever to have, full power to make laws of sufficient validity to bind the colonies in all cases whatever: They have exercised this pretended right by imposing a tax upon us without our consent; and lest we should shew some reluctance at parting with our property, her fleets and armies are sent to inforce their mad pretensions. The town of Boston, ever faithful to the British Crown, has been invested by a British fleet: The troops of George the Third have cross'd the wide atlantick, not to engage an enemy, but to assist a band of TRAITORS in trampling on the rights and liberties of his most loyal subjects in America, – those rights and liberties which as a father he ought ever to regard, and as a King he is bound in honour to defend from violations, even at the risque of his own life.

Let not the history of the illustrious house of Brunswick inform posterity, that a King descended from that glorious monarch George the second,[31] once sent his British subjects to conquer and enslave his subjects in America; but be perpetual infamy entail'd upon that villain who dared to advise his Master to such execrable measures; for it was easy to foresee the consequences which so naturally followed upon sending troops into America, to enforce obedience to acts of the British parliament, which neither God nor man ever empowered them to make. It was reasonable to expect that troops who knew the errand they were sent upon, would treat the people whom they were to subjugate, with a cruelty and haughtiness, which too often buries the honorable character of a *soldier*, in the disgraceful name of an *unfeeling ruffian*. The troops upon their first arrival took possession of our Senate House, and pointed their cannon against the Judgment-hall, and even continued them there whilst the Supreme Court of Judicature for this Province was actually sitting to decide upon the lives and fortunes of the King's subjects. [...] But this was not all: As though they thought it not enough to violate our civil Rights, they endeavoured to deprive us of the enjoyment of our religious privileges, to vitiate our morals, and thereby render us deserving of destruction. Hence the rude din of arms which broke in upon your solemn devotions in your temples, on that day hallowed by Heaven, and set apart by God himself for his peculiar worship. Hence, impious oaths and blasphemies so often tortur'd your unaccustomed ear. Hence, all the arts which idleness and luxury could invent, were used, to betray our youth of one sex into extravagance and effeminacy, and of the other to infamy and ruin; and did they not succeed but too well? Did not a reverence for religion sensibly decay? Did not our infants almost learn to lisp out curses before they knew their horrid import? Did not our youth forget they were Americans, and regardless of the admonitions of the wise and aged, servilely copy from their tyrants those vices which finally must overthrow the empire of Great-Britain? And must I be compelled to acknowledge, that even the noblest, fairest part of all the lower creation did not entirely escape the cursed snare? [...]

But I forbear, and come reluctantly to the transactions of that dismal night, when in such quick succession we felt the extremes of grief, astonishment and rage; when Heaven in anger, for a dreadful moment, suffer'd Hell to take the reins; when Satan with his chosen band open'd the sluices of New-England's blood, and sacrilegiously polluted our land with the dead bodies of her guiltless sons. Let this sad tale of death never be told without a tear; let not the heaving bosom cease to burn with a manly indignation at the barbarous story, thro' the long tracts of future time: Let every parent tell the shameful story to his listening children till tears of pity glisten in their eyes, and boiling passion shakes their tender frames; and whilst the anniversary of that ill-fated night is kept a jubilee in the grim court of pandæmonium,[32] let all America join in one common prayer to Heaven, that the inhuman, unprovok'd murders of the Fifth of March 1770, planned by Hillsborough,[33] and a knot of treacherous knaves in Boston, and executed by the cruel hand of Preston[34] and his sanguinary coadjutors, may ever stand on history without a parallel. [...]

---

[31] George II (George Augustus, 1683-1760) was King of Great Britain and Ireland, Duke of Brunswick-Lüneburg (r. 1727-1760).
[32] Capital of hell in Milton's *Paradise Lost*.
[33] England's Secretary of State for the Colonies.
[34] The British troop's captain; he was tried for murder but eventually acquitted.

Patriotism is ever united with humanity and compassion. This noble affection which impels us to sacrifice every thing dear, even life itself, to our country, involves in it a common sympathy and tenderness for every citizen, and must ever have a *particular feeling* for one who suffers in a public cause. Thoroughly persuaded of this, I need not add a word to engage your compassion and bounty towards a fellow citizen, who with long protracted anguish falls a victim to the relentless rage of our common enemies. [...]

Surely you never will tamely suffer this country to be a den of thieves. Remember, my friends, from whom you sprang – Let not a meanness of spirit, unknown to those whom you boast of as your Fathers, excite a thought to the dishonour of your mothers. I conjure you by all that is dear, by all that is honourable, by all that is sacred, not only that ye pray, but that you act; that, if necessary, ye fight, and even die for the prosperity of our Jerusalem. Break in sunder, with noble disdain, the bonds with which the Philistines have bound you. [...]

[...] I thank God, that America abounds in men who are superior to all temptation, whom nothing can divert from a steady pursuit of the interest of their country; who are at once it's ornament and safe-guard. [...] From them, let us, my friends, take example; from them let us catch the divine enthusiasm; and feel, each for himself, the God-like pleasure of diffusing happiness on all around us; of delivering the oppressed from the iron grasp of tyranny; of changing the hoarse complaints and bitter moans of wretched slaves, into those cheerful songs, which freedom and contentment must inspire. [...]

I have most animating confidence that the present noble struggle for liberty, will terminate gloriously for America. And let us play the man for our God, and for the cities of our God; while we are using the means in our power, let us humbly commit our righteous cause to the great Lord of the universe, who loveth righteousness and hateth iniquity. – And having secured the approbation of our hearts, by a faithful and unwearied discharge of our duty to our country, let us joyfully leave her important concerns in the hands of HIM who raiseth up and putteth down the empires and kingdoms of the world as HE pleases; and with cheerful submission to HIS sovereign will, devoutly say,

"*Although the Fig-Tree shall not Blossom, neither shall Fruit be in the Vines; the Labour of the Olive shall fail, and the Fields shall yield no Meat; the Flock shall be cut off from the Fold, and there shall be no Herd in the Stalls: Yet we will rejoice in the* LORD, *we will joy in the* GOD *of our Salvation.*"[35]

Source: John Hancock (1737-1793). *An Oration; Delivered March 5, 1774: At the Request of the Inhabitants of the Town of Boston: To Commemorate the Bloody Tragedy of the Fifth of March 1770*. Boston: Edes and Gill, ²1774, 5-10, 12, 18-20.

---

[35] Hab. 3.16-17.

123. *The Bostonians Paying the Excise-man* (1774)

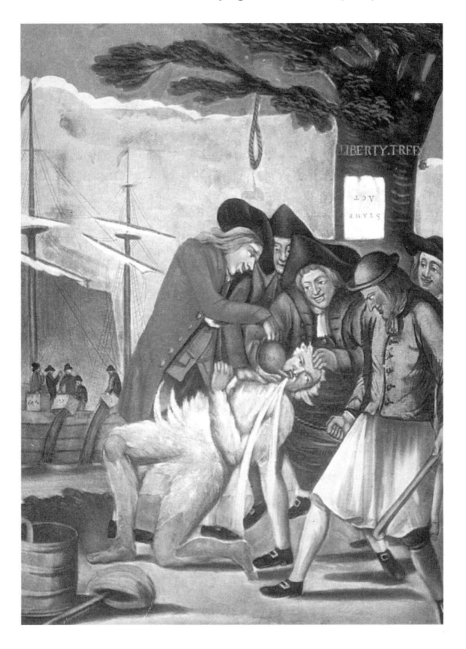

Source: *The Bostonians Paying the Excise-man, or Tarring & Feathering* (engraving attributed to Philip Dawe, London, 1774). Courtesy Library of Congress.

124. Paul Revere
The Able Doctor (1774)

Source: Paul Revere (1734-1818). *The Able Doctor, or America Swallowing the Bitter Draught.* (engraving 1774). Courtesy Library of Congress.

125. Thomas Jefferson
A Summary View of the Rights of British America (1774)

Resolved, that it be an instruction to the said deputies, when assembled in general congress[36] with the deputies from the other states of British America, to propose to the said congress that an humble and dutiful address be presented to his Majesty,[37] begging leave to lay before him, as Chief Magistrate of the British empire, the united complaints of his Majesty's subjects in America; complaints which are excited by many unwarrantable encroachments and usurpations, attempted to be made by the Legislature of one part of the empire, upon those rights which God and the laws have given equally and independently to all. To represent to his Majesty that these his states have often individually made humble application to his imperial throne to obtain, through its intervention, some redress[38]

---

[36] Reference to the First Continental Congress which convened in Philadelphia's Carpenters Hall on September 5, 1774. The members of Continental Congress acted for the people of the 13 colonies.
[37] King George III, king of Great Britain from 1760-1820.
[38] A reparation or compensation for a wrong.

of their injured rights, to none of which was ever even an answer condescended; humbly to hope that this their joint address, penned in the language of truth, and divested of those expressions of servility which would persuade his Majesty that we are asking favours, and not rights, shall obtain from his Majesty a more respectful acceptance. And this his Majesty will think we have reason to expect when he reflects that he is no more than the chief officer of the people, appointed by the laws, and circumscribed with definitive powers, to assist in working the great machine of government, erected for their use, and consequently subject to their superintendance. And in order that these our rights, as well as the invasions of them, may be laid more fully before his Majesty, to take a view of them from the origin and first settlement of these countries.

To remind him that our ancestors, before their emigration to America, were the free inhabitants of the British dominions in Europe, and possessed a right which nature has given to all men, of departing from the country in which chance, not choice, has placed them, of going in quest of new habitations, and of there establishing new societies, under such laws and regulations as to them shall seem most likely to promote public happiness. [...] America was conquered, and her settlements made, and firmly established, at the expence of individuals, and not of the British public. Their own blood was spilt in acquiring lands for their settlement, their own fortunes expended in making that settlement effectual; for themselves they fought, for themselves they conquered, and for themselves alone they have right to hold. Not a shilling was ever issued from the public treasures of his Majesty, or his ancestors, for their assistance, till of very late times, after the colonies had become established on a firm and permanent footing. [...] We do not, however, mean to under-rate those aids, which to us were doubtless valuable, on whatever principles granted; but we would shew that they cannot give a title to that authority which the British Parliament would arrogate over us, and that they may amply be repaid by our giving to the inhabitant of Great-Britain such exclusive privileges in trade as may be advantageous to them, and at the same time not too restrictive to ourselves. [...]

[...] The true ground on which we declare these acts void is, that the British parliament has no right to exercise authority over us.

That these exercises of usurped power have not been confined to instances alone, in which themselves were interested, but they have also intermeddled with the regulation of the internal affairs of the colonies. [...]

[...] Scarcely have our minds been able to emerge from the astonishment into which one stroke of parliamentary thunder has involved us, before another more heavy, and more alarming, is fallen on us. Single acts of tyranny may be ascribed to the accidental opinion of a day; but a series of oppressions begun at a distinguished period, and pursued, unalterably through every change of ministers, too plainly prove a deliberate and systematical plan of reducing us to slavery. [...]

To render these proceedings [i.e. the British military occupation of American territory] still more criminal against our laws, instead of subjecting the military to the civil powers, his majesty has expressly made the civil subordinate to the military. But can his majesty thus put down all law under his feet? Can he erect a power superior to that which erected himself? He has done it indeed by force, but let him remember that force cannot give right.

That these are our grievances, which we have thus laid before his majesty, with that freedom of language and sentiment which becomes a free people claiming their rights, as derived from the laws of nature, and not as the gift of their chief magistrate: Let those flatter who fear, it is not an American art. To give praise which is not due might be well from the venal, but would ill beseem those who are asserting the rights of human nature. They know, and will therefore say, that kings are the servants, not the proprietors of the people. Open your breast, sire, to liberal and expanded thought. Let not the name of George the third be a blot in the page of history. You are surrounded by British counsellors, but remember that they are parties. You have no ministers for American affairs, because you have none taken from among us, nor amenable to the laws on which they are to give you advice. It behoves you, therefore, to think and to act for yourself and your people. The great principles of right and wrong are legible to every reader; to pursue them requires not the aid of many counsellors. The whole art of government consists in the art of being honest. Only aim to do your duty, and mankind will give you credit where you fail. No longer persevere in sacrificing the rights of one part of the empire to the inordinate desires of another; but deal out to all equal and impartial right. Let no act be passed by any one legislature which may infringe on the rights and liberties of another. This is the important post in which fortune has placed you, holding the balance of a great, if a well poised empire. This, sire, is the advice of your great American council, on the observance of which may perhaps depend your felicity and future fame, and the preservation of that harmony which alone can continue both to Great Britain and America the reciprocal advantages of their connection. It is neither our wish nor our interest to separate from her. We are willing, on our part, to sacrifice every thing which reason can ask to the restoration of that tranquillity for which all must wish. [... Let it not] be proposed that our properties within our own territories shall be taxed or regulated by any power on earth but our own. The God who gave us life gave us liberty at the same time; the hand of force may destroy, but cannot disjoin them. This, sire, is our last, our determined resolution; and that you will be pleased to interpose with that efficacy which your earnest endeavours may ensure to procure redress of these our great grievances, to quiet the minds of your subjects in British America, against any apprehensions of future encroachment, to establish fraternal love and harmony through the whole empire, and that these may continue to the latest ages of time, is the fervent prayer of all British America!

Source: Thomas Jefferson (1743-1826). *A Summary View of the Rights of British America. Set Forth in Some Resolutions Intended for the Inspection of the Present Delegates of the People of Virginia. Now in Convention. By a Native, and Member of the House of Burgesses*. Philadelphia: John Dunlap, 1774 [originally printed in Williamsburg, 1774], 5-7, 10-11, 21-23.

126. Samuel Williams
Discourse on the Love of Our Country (1774)

Psalm CXXXVII. 5,6.

If I forget thee, O Jerusalem, let my right hand forget her cunning. If I do not remember thee, let my tongue cleave to the roof of my mouth; if I prefer not Jerusalem above my chief joy.

The wise and benevolent Author of nature has made the human race capable of continual advances towards a state of perfection and happiness. All those religious institutions which God has appointed among mankind, are evidently designed and adapted to promote this end. And this is what human wisdom has been aiming at by the various methods of education, instruction, laws, and government. To a virtuous mind, nothing can yield a more rational or benevolent pleasure, than to see this great design taking place, in the increase and progress of human happiness: To all the friends of mankind, such views and prospects cannot but prove one of their chief joys. [...]

We have but few principles from which we can argue with certainty, what will be the state of mankind in future ages. But if we may judge of the designs of providence, by the number and power of the causes that are already at work, we shall be lead to think that the perfection and happiness of mankind is to be carried further in America, than it has ever yet been in any place. [...]

[... But] the situation in which we are placed, the time when our political state began, the improvements we are receiving from the ancient countries, with the general operation of things among ourselves, indicate strong tendencies towards a state of greater perfection and happiness than mankind has yet seen.

Thus many and powerful causes are already at work, which if we may judge from the common methods of providence, are leading the way to a more perfect and happy state. The prospect and probability is, that things will operate this way in America, for many centuries yet to come. Our present difficulties may retard the event; but they cannot finally defeat the tendencies and preparations of nature and providence: Tendencies and preparations which will naturally operate to increase the perfection and happiness of mankind; and of consequence to attach us to that country, in which alone we can look for such a state.

What has been said on the Love of our country, will naturally turn our thoughts to the present unhappy and critical state of the North-American colonies. Amidst all the pleasure a benevolent mind must receive from the growth, progress, and general tendency of the colonies; the unhappy disputes we are engaged in with our mother-country, seem to cast a shade over all other prospects. Both countries were long happily united in mutual affection, friendship, and confidence. We looked upon her as a wise and tender parent: And she regarded us as her friends and children. [...] But instead of our former peace and friendship, what fears, murmurs, and unusual commotions now prevail from one end of the *American* continent to the other? From what *Innovations* these disputes and difficulties began, or to what a dangerous height late measures have carried them, no one need to be informed. We seem to be on the eve of some great and unusual events: Events, which it is not improbable, may form a new æra, and give a new turn to human affairs. The state of both countries is critical and dangerous to the last degree. A few more alarming measures on either side, and all public confidence will cease. While both countries are preparing to proceed, may Heaven interpose, and prevent the sword from engaging in that which ignorance and folly first began! – The cause of *America* seems indeed to be much the better cause. It is not the cause of a mob, of a party, or a faction that *America* means to plead. May these things to which some have been unhappily driven, but which are unnatural productions in this country, cease forever from among us. Nor is it the cause of independency that we have in view. It is the cause of *Self-Defence*, of *Public Faith*, and of the *Liberties of Mankind*, that America is engaged in. [...] To oppose Britain by force and violence, is an extreme to which all wise and good men among us, most ardently pray we may never be forced. But to give up to her the management of taxes, is to give up all that we have. Dreadful extremes! May the wise and good on both sides, instead of increasing the difficulty, join to find out some happy expedient for restoring such mutual justice, friendship and union, as shall leave this country free, and set that at the head of human affairs for many ages yet to come.

The subject we have been considering, should lead us to shew our love to our country, in every way in which we can promote its good. It is not the business of the pulpit to determine measures of state, or to invade the office or power of civil rulers; but to inculcate that public and private virtue which is agreeable to the laws of God, and adapted to promote the interest and welfare of mankind. – The surest way we can take to promote the good of our county, is to attend to this. It should lead us to repent of all the vice, wickedness, and moral evils that are among us. It is our interest to renounce whatever is contrary to the rules of religion, to purity of morals, and the prosperity of the state. It is our duty to reform every kind of extravagance, superfluity, and unnecessary expence. It would be our wisdom to put on the most strict frugality, œconomy, and self-denial, in all unnecessary articles of food, raiment,[39] convenience and pleasure. – Such virtue will naturally tend to promote the good of our country. And this is what the united councils and voice of America now call us to. If therefore, my brethren, you have any value for your own interest, any feeling for the love of your country, or any regard for the generations that are to come; if you are *Americans* any more than by name, if you have the spirit, or desire to have the privileges of *Free-men*, you must now vigorously exert yourselves in this way, for the interest and welfare of your country.

In the present singular situation of this province, it may not be unseasonable to caution you against loosing your regard to good laws and government. It is an unhappy necessity which forces our attention so much to matters of state. But while we see every thing in a state of disorder and confusion around us, it is of the last importance that we keep up a steady regard to the rules of righteousness, of personal and social virtue. Now is the time, my brethren, when our enemies expect that we shall run wild and mad, for want of something to guide us. The extremes of power, and the wanton abuse of liberty, you may assure yourselves will always end alike, in absolute tyranny at last. – God give you firmness to adhere to your liberties, with prudence and discretion at the same time, to maintain quiet and peaceable lives in all godliness and honesty. Government is a wise, a necessary, and a sacred thing. And while you see it abused by men of high, and of low degree; instead of wishing to be free from its necessary restraints, let us be looking to the Ruler of all nations to put us again upon a good foundation, that duty and interest may both lead us to be subject to the ordinances of man. [...]

And while we are thus anxious for the welfare of our country, let us praise God's holy name for the blessings we yet enjoy in it. These, amidst all our gloomy prospects, are neither few nor small things. We yet enjoy the means of grace, and the rights of conscience. [...] Such a spirit of benevolence has been shewn towards that part of this province which is suffering the vengeance of power, as was not to be expected among mankind. And what must be ascribed to the influence of heaven, the very measures that were designed to divide, have proved the means of establishing a firm and solid union among the colonies. To all these mercies we may add, the life of our sovereign Lord the King has been preserved: To his family and throne, it is our duty and interest to bear a steady allegiance; and in whose royal favour and protection, we hope this country will find peace, safety and happiness, for many ages yet to come. For these and all other mercies, let us return sincere thanks to almighty God; whose providence has always appeared for our help and protection, in all the difficulties we have passed through. – One way, my brethren, in which we should express our gratitude to God for his mercies, should be by un-

---

[39] Clothing.

feigned repentance for all our past sins: And this, with prayer and supplication, is the proper way to seek his favour for the time to come. Let us return then to the Almighty, that he may build us up. Let us return to that sober sense of piety and religion, which animated and encouraged our Fathers in that noblest enterprize of public virtue, laying the foundation of these colonies. Then shall we have reason to expect that heaven and earth will once more join to remove our difficulties and fears, and to make us a free, a grateful, and a happy people. To this then, repentance and reformation, we are now called by all that is holy in religion, by all that is important to our country, and by all that is valuable to mankind. And may God arise and have mercy upon Zion: May the time to favour her, yea, may the set time now come.

Source: Samuel Williams (1743-1817). *A Discourse on the Love of Our Country; Delivered on a Day of Thanksgiving, December 15, 1774.* Salem: Samuel and Ebenezer Hall, 1775, 5, 22, 25-29.

127. "Preamble to the Massachusetts Articles of War" (1775)

Whereas the lust of power, which of old oppressed, persecuted, and exiled our pious and virtuous ancestors from their fair possessions in Britain, now pursues with tenfold severity us, their guiltless children, who are unjustly and wickedly charged with licentiousness, sedition, treason, and rebellion, and being deeply impressed with a sense of the almost incredible fatigues and hardships our venerable progenitors encountered, who fled from oppression for the sake of civil and religious liberty for themselves and their offspring, and began a settlement here on bare creation, at their own expense; and having seriously considered the duty we owe to God, to the memory of such invincible worthies, to the King, to Great Britain, our country, ourselves, and posterity, do think it our indispensable duty, by all lawful ways and means in our power, to recover, maintain, defend, and preserve the free exercise of all those civil and religious rights and liberties for which many of our forefathers fought, bled, and died, and to hand them down entire for the free enjoyment of the latest posterity [...];

And whereas the great law of self-preservation may suddenly require our raising and keeping an army of observation and defense in order to prevent or repel any further attempts to enforce the late cruel and oppressive acts of the British Parliament,[40] which are evidently designed to subject us and the whole continent to the most ignominious slavery; *and whereas* in case of raising and keeping such an army it will be necessary that the officers and soldiers in the same be fully acquainted with their duty, and that the articles, rules, and regulations thereof be made as plain as possible; and having great confidence in the honor and public virtue of the inhabitants of this colony that they will readily obey the officers chosen by themselves, and will cheerfully do their duty when known, without any such severe articles and rules (except in capital cases), and cruel punishments as are usually practised in standing armies; and will submit to all such rules and regulations as are founded in reason, honor, and virtue – :

It is therefore resolved, that the following articles, rules, and regulations for the army that may be raised for the defense and security of our lives, liberties, and estates be, and

---

[40] Reference to acts passed by British Parliament, e.g. Revenue (Sugar) Act (1764), Stamp Act (1765), Declaratory Act (1766), Townshend Duties Act (1767), Tea Act (1773), Coercive Acts (1774).

hereby are, earnestly recommended to be strictly adhered to by all officers, soldiers, and others concerned, as they regard their own honor and the public good.

Source: "Preamble to the Massachusetts Articles of War" (April 5, 1775). *The Revolutionary Years*. Ed. Mortimer J. Adler. Chicago et al.: Encyclopædia Britannica, 1976, 125-126.

128. Jacob Duché
The American Vine[41] (1775)

[...] I. Great and astonishing have been the blessings of Providence, by which these American colonies have been distinguished from their very first settlements to the present period. They have indeed been a VINEYARD PLANTED BY THE LORD'S RIGHT HAND. And though some gloomy scenes have now and then shaded the brightness of the prospect, yet even these have greatly contributed to their prosperity and enlargement.

If we look back a little into the annals of America, we shall find, that this very spot, on which our large and populous city now stands, was, less than a century ago, a wild uncultivated desart. The arts and customs of civilized life were here unknown. Nought else was visible, but the sad effects of ignorance, superstition and idolatry. The untutor'd savage roamed the wood, like a beast of prey, stranger to the comforts and advantages of mental culture, involved in Pagan darkness, with scarcely one ray of heavenly truth to irradiate the gloom of nature.

Such was the dark and dreary prospect, when Providence conducted our Forefathers to this new world. He took the tender slip from the PARENT VINE. HE CAST OUT THE HEATHEN AND PLANTED IT. THE HILLS WERE SOON COVER'D WITH THE SHADOW OF IT [...]. THE WILDERNESS AND SOLITARY PLACE WERE MADE GLAD, AND THE DESART REJOICED AND BLOSSOMED LIKE THE ROSE.

Our sober Ancestors brought over with them, not only the several useful arts and improvements, of which the natives were ignorant, but a treasure of infinitely greater value, even the charter of TEMPORAL FREEDOM, and the records of ETERNAL TRUTH. The banners of CHRISTIAN and BRITISH Liberty were at once unfolded, and these remote parts of the earth were thereby added to the MESSIAH'S kingdom.

Numberless, indeed, were the toils, difficulties, and dangers, to which the first founders of these colonies, as well as their successors were exposed, before they arrived at their present height of opulence and splendor. So remarkable, however, were the interpositions of Providence, that the most inattentive mind must have frequently discerned them.

Scarcely is there recorded in the annals of history a more rapid series of successes of every kind in the settlement and population of any country on the globe. Whilst favoured with the nurturing care and protection of the mother country, whose fleets and armies, in conjunction with our own, have ever been faithfully and successfully employed in our defence, our common enemies have looked with astonishment and envy upon our rising glory, nor have dared for years to interrupt a repose, purchased, under the smiles of Heaven, by virtue, industry, and British and American valour.

---

[41] According to John 15, Jesus is the vine and his children are the branches. The promise is that whoever remains in Christ will also bear fruit. Grapes, therefore, are a sign for a spiritually fruitful life, as well as a sign for union and fellowship with Christ.

And happy, my dear brethren, should we still remain, if the parent would be satisfied with such returns from the children, as filial duty would always prompt them to pay, and not exact such an illegal and unrighteous tribute, as by weakening and distressing them, must in the end weaken and distress the parent too.

Here then our present calamities commence. Our MORNING JOYS are past – and a NIGHT of HEAVINESS succeeds – The HEDGES OF LIBERTY, by which we hoped our VINEYARD was secured, ARE BROKEN DOWN, and THEY THAT PASS BY THE WAY, ARE seeking to PLUCK OUR GRAPES.

'Tis not indeed THE WILD BOAR OUT OF THE WOOD, OR THE WILD BEAST OF THE FIELD, that are ready to WASTE AND DEVOUR IT. 'Tis not now a foreign enemy, or the savages of our own wilderness, that have made the cruel and unrighteous assault – But it is even, thou, BRITAIN, that with merciless and unhallowed hands, wouldst cut down and destroy this BRANCH of thine own VINE, the very BRANCH, which Providence HATH MADE STRONG even FOR THYSELF!

II. Injured and oppressed as we are, unmeriting the harsh and rigorous treatment, which we have received from such an unexpected quarter, let us, however, look up to an higher cause for the awful infliction; and whilst we are faithfully persevering in the defence of our TEMPORAL RIGHTS, let us humble ourselves before God, lay our hands upon our hearts, and seriously and impartially enquire, what returns we have made to Heaven for its past favours, and whether its present chastisements[42] have not been drawn down upon us by a gross neglect of our SPIRITUAL PRIVILEGES. [...]

Have we been careful to check that overweening fondness of gaiety and pleasure, which frequently discovers itself in the dispositions of our children? – to check it did I say – yea, to endeavour to root it out of their hearts, and plant and nourish in its room the love of GOD and of goodness? [...]

Alas! my brethren, have we not rather been so far carried away by the stream of prosperity, as to be forgetful of the source from whence it was derived? So elevated by the prospect, which peace and a successful commerce have opened to us, as to neglect those impressions of goodness, which former afflictions had left upon our hearts? Have not luxury and vice, the common attendants of wealth and grandeur, too soon made their appearance amongst us, and begun to spread a dangerous infection through our hitherto healthy and thriving state? Amid the hurry and tumult of the passions, hath not conscience fallen asleep? Hath not a false security gained ground? And a worldly spirit too generally prevailed?

And is it not for this, that the ALMIGHTY hath bared his arm against us? – Is it not for this, that he now speaks to us in thunder? [...]

III. But wherewithal, my dear brethren, SHALL WE COME BEFORE THE LORD, AND BOW OURSELVES BEFORE THE HIGH GOD? With what sacrifice shall we approach his altar? With what language, or by what conduct shall we invite him to return?

THE SACRIFICE OF GOD IS A BROKEN SPIRIT: A BROKEN AND A CONTRITE HEART, O GOD, THOU WILT NOT DESPISE. PRAYER AND SUPPLICATION, is a language, which he will not refuse to hear: And REPENTANCE and REFORMATION of life, through the redeeming power of his EVER-BLESSED SON, is the only conduct, that will reinstate us in his favour.

Let us adore, then, the divine wisdom and goodness, for putting it into the hearts of that Honourable Assembly, now entrusted with the great cause of American Liberty, to

---

[42] Corrective or disciplinary punishment, correction.

call upon the whole people, whom they represent, in the most solemn and affectionate manner, to join in deprecating[43] the Divine displeasure, by one general act of religious humiliation. Heaven be praised, that they have hereby shewn their attention and zeal for our eternal as well as temporal welfare.

Go on, ye chosen band of Christian Patriots! Testify to the world, by your example as well as by your counsels, that ye are equally the foes of VICE and of SLAVERY – Banish the Syren[44] LUXURY, with all her train of fascinating pleasures, idle dissipation,[45] and expensive amusements from our borders. Call upon honest industry, sober frugality, simplicity of manners, plain hospitality and christian benevolence to throw down the usurpers, and take possession of their seats. Recommend every species of reformation, that will have a tendency to promote the glory of GOD, the interest of the Gospel of JESUS, and all those private and public virtues, upon the basis of which alone, the superstructure of true Liberty can be erected. [...]

We cannot expect, my dear brethren, that the GOD OF HOSTS WILL RETURN, LOOK DOWN FROM HEAVEN, AND BEHOLD AND VISIT OUR VINE; that he will cause his sun to shine, and his refreshing dews and rains to [descend] upon it, unless we are careful to cultivate and improve the soil, and to root out every useless noxious weed, that will impede its growth. By neglecting this, we shall be in danger of incurring the dreadful sentence denounced against the barren fig-tree, CUT IT DOWN: WHY CUMBERETH[46] IT THE GROUND?

But whilst I am recommending in general those essential branches of a true reformation, piety and gratitude to GOD, repentance and humiliation for past neglects, together with the revival of every private and public virtue, which can adorn and dignify the citizen and the christian, let me not forget to remind you, at this awful season in particular, of the great gospel duty of CHARITY, which will ever prompt us to sympathize with the distresses, and to relieve the wants of our brethren. [...]

If our hearts and hands are employed in such deeds of beneficence and love, OUR LIGHT SHALL BREAK FORTH AS THE MORNING, AND OUR HEALTH SHALL SPRING FORTH SPEEDILY: OUR RIGHTEOUSNESS SHALL GO BEFORE US: THE GLORY OF THE LORD SHALL BE OUR REAR-WARD.

In a word, if we would wish THE GOD OF HOSTS TO RETURN, TO LOOK DOWN FROM HEAVEN AND BEHOLD AND VISIT our American VINE,[47] we must be prepared to meet him by such heavenly tempers and dispositions, as alone can testify our vital union and communion with him. Happy, if we find him a reconciled GOD in CHRIST JESUS! Thrice happy, if our faith has fixed us to the ROCK OF AGES! Then indeed the rude winds may blow, the billows of public or private adversity may rise and rage: But we shall stand collected and secure, like the stately cedars of the mountain, amid the general storm.

FINIS.

Source: Jacob Duché (1737-1798). *The American Vine: A Sermon, Preached in Christ-Church, Philadelphia, before the Honourable Continental Congress, July 20th, 1775. Being the Day Recommended by Them for a General Fast throughout the United English Colonies of America.* Philadelphia: J. Humphreys, 1775, 16-30, 33-34.

---

[43] Praying for deliverance from; seeking to avert by prayer.
[44] An imaginary species of serpent; one of several fabulous monsters, part woman, part bird, who lured sailors to destruction by their singing.
[45] Wasteful consumption of means or faculties.
[46] To occupy obstructively; to block up.
[47] Referring to Ps. 80.14 in which the nation of Israel cries out: "Return to us, O God Almighty! Look down from heaven and see! Watch over this vine."

129. "Proclamation by the Great and General Court of the Colony of Massachusetts Bay, January 23, 1776"

As the happiness of the people is the sole end of government, so the consent of the people is the only foundation of it, in reason, morality, and the natural fitness of things. And, therefore, every act of government, every exercise of sovereignty against or without the consent of the people is injustice, usurpation, and tyranny.

It is a maxim that in every government there must exist, somewhere, a supreme, sovereign, absolute, and uncontrollable power; but this power resides always in the body of the people; and it never was, or can be delegated to one man, or a few; the great Creator has never given to men a right to vest others with authority over them, unlimited either in duration or degree.

When kings, ministers, governors, or legislators, therefore, instead of exercising the powers entrusted with them, according to the principles, forms and proportions stated by the constitution, and established by the original compact, prostitute those powers to the purposes of oppression – to subvert, instead of supporting a free constitution; to destroy, instead of preserving the lives, liberties and properties of the people – they are no longer to be deemed magistrates vested with a sacred character, but become public enemies, and ought to be resisted.

The administration of Great Britain, despising equally the justice, humanity, and magnanimity of their ancestors, and the rights, liberties, and courage of *Americans*, have, for a course of years, labored to establish a sovereignty in America, not founded in the consent of the people but in the mere will of persons, a thousand leagues from us, whom we know not, and have endeavored to establish this sovereignty over us, against our consent, in all cases whatsoever. [...]

No effectual resistance to the system of tyranny prepared for us could be made without either instant recourse to arms or a temporary suspension of the ordinary powers of government and tribunals of justice. To the last of which evils, in hope of a speedy reconciliation with Great Britain, upon equitable terms, the Congress advised us to submit: – And mankind has seen a phenomenon, without example in the political world, a large and populous colony, subsisting in great decency and order, for more than a year, under such a suspension of government.

But as our enemies have proceeded to such barbarous extremities, commencing hostilities upon the good people of this colony, and with unprecedented malice exerting their power to spread the calamities of fire, sword, and famine through the land, and no reasonable prospect remains of a speedy reconciliation with Great Britain, the Congress have resolved: "That no obedience being due to the act of Parliament for altering the charter of the colony of Massachusetts Bay, nor to a governor or lieutenant governor, who will not observe the directions of, but endeavor to subvert the charter, the governor and lieutenant governor of that colony are to be considered as absent, and their offices vacant." [...]

In pursuance of which advice, the good people of this colony have chosen a full and free representation of themselves, who, being convened in assembly, have elected a Council; who, as the executive branch of government, have constituted necessary officers through the colony. The present generation, therefore, may be congratulated on the acquisition of a form of government more immediately, in all its branches, under the influence and control of the people; and therefore more free and happy than was enjoyed by their ancestors. But as a government so popular can be supported only by universal knowledge and virtue in the body of the people, it is the duty of all ranks to promote the means of education, for the rising generation, as well as true religion, purity of manners, and integrity of life among all orders and degrees. [...]

That piety and virtue, which alone can secure the freedom of any people, may be encouraged, and vice and immorality suppressed, the Great and General Court have thought fit to issue this proclamation, commanding and enjoining it upon the good people of this colony, that they lead sober, religious, and peaceable lives, avoiding all blasphemies, contempt of the Holy Scriptures, and of the Lord's Day, and all other crimes and misdemeanors, all debauchery, profaneness, corruption, venality,[48] all riotous and tumultuous proceedings, and all immoralities whatsoever; and that they decently and reverently attend the public worship of God, at all times acknowledging with gratitude His merciful interposition in their behalf, devoutly confiding in Him, as the God of armies, by whose favor and protection alone they may hope for success in their present conflict.

Source: "Proclamation by the Great and General Court of the Colony of Massachusetts Bay, January 23, 1776." *The Revolutionary Years*. Ed. Mortimer J. Adler. Chicago et al.: Encyclopædia Britannica, 1976, 145-147.

130. Thomas Paine
Common Sense: Addressed to the Inhabitants of America (1776)

THOUGHTS, *on the present* STATE *of* AMERICAN AFFAIRS.
In the following pages I offer nothing more than simple facts, plain arguments, and common sense: and have no other preliminaries to settle with the Reader, than that he will divest himself of prejudice and prepossession, and suffer his reason and his feelings to determine for themselves: that he will put *on* or rather that he will not put *off* the true character of a man, and generously enlarge his views beyond the present day.

Volumes have been written on the subject of the struggle between England and America. Men of all ranks have embarked in the controversy, from different motives, and with various designs; but all have been ineffectual, and the period of debate is closed. Arms as the last resource decide the contest: the appeal was the choice of the King, and the Continent has accepted the challenge. [...]

The Sun never shined on a cause of greater worth. 'Tis not the affair of a City, a County, a Province, or a Kingdom; but of a Continent – of at least one eight[h] part of the habitable Globe. 'Tis not the concern of a day, a year, or an age; posterity are virtually involved in the contest, and will be more or less affected even to the end of time by the proceedings now. Now is the seed time of Continental union, faith, and honour. The least fracture now, will be like a name engraved with the point of a pin on the tender rind of a young oak; the wound will enlarge with the tree, and posterity read it in full grown characters.

By referring the matter from argument to arms, a new æra for politics is struck – a new method of thinking hath arisen. All plans, proposals, &c. prior to the 19th of April, *i.e.* to the commencement of hostilities, are like the almanacks of the last year; which tho proper then, are superceded and useless now. [...]

---
[48] Being open to bribery and corruption.

As much hath been said of the advantages of reconciliation, which like an agreeable dream, hath passed away and left us as we were, it is but right, that we should examine the contrary side of the argument, and enquire into some of the many material injuries which these Colonies sustain, and always will sustain, by being connected with, and dependant on Great Britain. To examine that connection and dependance on the principles of nature and common sense, to see what we have to trust to if separated, and what we are to expect if dependent.

I have heard it asserted by some, that as America has flourished under her former connection with Great Britain, that the same connection is necessary towards her future happiness and will always have the same effect – Nothing can be more fallacious than this kind of argument: – we may as well assert that because a child hath thrived upon milk, that it is never to have meat, or that the first twenty years of our lives is to become a precedent for the next twenty. But even this is admitting more than is true, for I answer, roundly, that America would have flourished as much, and probably much more had no European power taken any notice of her. The commerce by which she hath enriched herself are the necessaries of life, and will always have a market while eating is the custom of Europe.

But she has protected us say some. That she hath engrossed us is true, and defended the Continent at our expence as well as her own is admitted; and she would have defended Turkey from the same motive viz. the sake of trade and dominion.

Alas! we have been long led away by ancient prejudices and made large sacrifices to superstition. We have boasted the protection of Great Britain, without considering, that her motive was *interest* not *attachment*; that she did not protect us from *our enemies* on *our account*, but from *her enemies* on *her own account*, from those who had no quarrel with us on any *other account*, and who will always be our enemies on the *same account*. Let Britain wave her pretensions[49] to the continent, or the continent throw off the dependance, and we should be at peace with France and Spain, were they at war with Britain. [...]

But Britain is the parent country says some. Then the more shame upon her conduct. Even brutes do not devour their young, nor savages make war upon their families; wherefore the assertion if true, turns to her reproach; but it happens not to be true, or only partly so, and the phrase, *parent* or *mother country*, hath been jesuitically adopted by the King and his parasites, with a low papistical[50] design of gaining an unfair bias on the credulous weakness of our minds. Europe and not England is the parent country of America. This new World hath been the asylum for the persecuted lovers of civil and religious liberty from *every part* of Europe. Hither have they fled, not from the tender embraces of the mother, but from the cruelty of the monster; and it is so far true of England, that the same tyranny which drove the first emigrants from home, pursues their descendants still.

In this extensive quarter of the Globe, we forget the narrow limits of three hundred and sixty miles (the extent of England) and carry our friendship on a larger scale; we claim brotherhood with every European Christian, and triumph in the generosity of the sentiment.

[...] Not one third of the inhabitants, even of this province, are of English descent. Wherefore, I reprobate[51] the phrase of parent or mother country applied to England only, as being false, selfish, narrow and ungenerous.

---

[49] A rightful or justifiable claim.
[50] Pertaining, or adhering to the Church of Rome and its doctrines, ceremonies, and traditions; popish; usually hostile or opprobrious.
[51] To condemn strongly as unworthy, unacceptable, or evil.

But admitting, that we were all of English descent, what does it amount to? Nothing. Britain being now an open enemy, extinguishes every other name and title: and to say that reconciliation is our duty, is truly farcical. The first king of England, of the present line (William the Conqueror) was a Frenchman, and half the Peers of England are descendants from the same country; wherefore, by the same method of reasoning, England ought to be governed by France. [...]

I challenge the warmest advocate for reconciliation, to shew, a single advantage that this Continent can reap, by being connected with Great Britain. I repeat the challenge, not a single advantage is derived. Our corn will fetch its price in any market in Europe, and our imported goods must be paid for buy them where we will.

But the injuries and disadvantages we sustain by that connection, are without number, and our duty to mankind at large, as well as to ourselves, instruct us to renounce the alliance: Because any submission to, or dependance on Great Britain, tends directly to involve this Continent in European wars and quarrels. As Europe is our market for trade, we ought to form no political connection with any part of it. 'Tis the true interest of America, to steer clear of European contentions, which she never can do, while by her dependance on Britain, she is made the make-weight in the scale of British politics.

Europe is too thickly planted with Kingdoms, to be long at peace, and whenever a war breaks out between England and any foreign power, the trade of America goes to ruin, *because, of her connection with Britain*. The next war may not turn out like the last, and should it not, the advocates for reconciliation now, will be wishing for separation then, because neutrality in that case, would be a safer convoy than a man of war.[52] Every thing that is right or reasonable pleads for separation. The blood of the slain, the weeping voice of nature cries, 'TIS TIME TO PART. Even the distance at which the Almighty hath placed England and America, is a strong and natural proof, that the authority of the one over the other, was never the design of Heaven. The time likewise at which the Continent was discovered, adds weight to the argument, and the manner in which it was peopled encreases the force of it. – The Reformation was preceded by the discovery of America; As if the Almighty graciously meant to open a sanctuary to the persecuted in future years, when home should afford neither friendship nor safety.

The authority of Great Britain over this Continent is a form of government which sooner or later must have an end: And a serious mind can draw no true pleasure by looking forward, under the painful and positive conviction, that what he calls "the present constitution," is merely temporary. As parents, we can have no joy, knowing that *this government* is not sufficiently lasting to ensure any thing which we may bequeath to posterity: And by a plain method of argument, as we are running the next generation into debt, we ought to do the work of it, otherwise we use them meanly and pitifully. In order to discover the line of our duty rightly, we should take our children in our hand, and fix our station a few years farther into life; that eminence will present a prospect, which a few present fears and prejudices conceal from our sight.

Though I would carefully avoid giving unnecessary offence, yet I am inclined to believe, that all those who espouse[53] the doctrine of reconciliation, may be included within the following descriptions. Interested men who are not to be trusted, weak men who *cannot* see, prejudiced men who *will not* see, and a certain set of moderate men who think better of

---

[52] A ship equipped for warfare, belonging to the recognized navy of a country.
[53] To attach oneself to; to adopt, embrace a doctrine, opinion, etc.

the European world than it deserves; and this last class, by an ill judged deliberation, will be the cause of more calamities to this continent, than all the other three. [...]

Men of passive tempers look somewhat lightly over the offences of Britain, and still hoping for the best are apt to call out. *"Come, come, we shall be friends again for all this."* But examine the passions and feelings of mankind: Bring the doctrine of reconciliation to the touchstone of nature, and then tell me, whether you can hereafter love, honour, and faithfully serve the power that hath carried fire and sword into your land? [I]f you cannot do all these, then are you only deceiving yourselves, and by your delay bringing ruin upon posterity. Your future connection with Britain whom you can neither love nor honour, will be forced and unnatural, and being formed only on the plan of present convenience, will in a little time, fall into a relapse more wretched than the first. But if you say, you can still pass the violations over, then I ask, Hath your house been burnt? Hath your property been destroyed before your face? Are your wife and children destitute of a bed to lie on, or bread to live on? Have you lost a parent or a child by their hands, and yourself the ruined and wretched survivor? If you have not, then are you not a judge of those who have. But if you have, and still can shake hands with the murderers, then are you unworthy the name of husband, father, friend, or lover, and whatever may be your rank or title in life, you have the heart of a coward, and the spirit of a sycophant.[54]

This is not inflaming or exaggerating matters, but trying them by those feelings and affections which nature justifies, and without which, we should be incapable of discharging the social duties of life, or enjoying the felicities of it. I mean not to exhibit horror for the purpose of provoking revenge, but to awaken us from fatal and unmanly slumbers, that we may pursue determinately some fixed object. [...]

'Tis repugnant[55] to reason, to the universal order of things, to all examples from former ages, to suppose, that this continent can long remain subject to any external power. The most sanguine in Britain doth not think so. The utmost stretch of human wisdom cannot at this time, compass a plan, short of separation, which can promise the continent even a year's security. Reconciliation is *now* a fallacious dream. Nature hath deserted the connection, and Art cannot supply her place. For as Milton wisely expresses "never can true reconcilement grow where wounds of deadly hate have pierced so deep."[56]

Every quiet method for peace hath been ineffectual. Our prayers have been rejected with disdain; and hath tended to convince us that nothing flatters vanity or confirms obstinacy in Kings more than repeated petitioning – and nothing hath contributed more, than that very measure, to make the Kings of Europe absolute. [...] Wherefore, since nothing but blows will do, for God's sake let us come to a final separation, and not leave the next generation to be cutting throats under the violated unmeaning names of parent and child. [...]

Small islands not capable of protecting themselves, are the proper objects for government to take under their care; but there is something very absurd, in supposing a Continent to be perpetually governed by an island. In no instance hath nature made the satellite larger than its primary planet, and as England and America with respect to each other reverses the common order of nature, it is evident they belong to different systems. England to Europe: America to itself.

I am not induced by motives of pride, party, or resentment to espouse the doctrine of Separation and independance; I am clearly, positively, and conscientiously persuaded that

---

[54] Servile self-seeking flatterer.
[55] Repulsive; arousing disgust or aversion.
[56] John Milton, *Paradise Lost* (1667), Book IV, ll. 98-99.

'tis the true interest of this continent to be so; that every thing short of *that* is mere patchwork, that it can afford no lasting felicity, – that it is leaving the sword to our children, and shrinking back at a time, when, a little more, a little farther, would have rendered this continent the glory of the earth. [...]

A government of our own is our natural right: and when a man seriously reflects on the precariousness of human affairs, he will become convinced, that it is infinitely wiser and safer, to form a constitution of our own, in a cool deliberate manner, while we have it in our power, than to trust such an interesting event to time and chance. If we omit it now, some Massanello[57] may hereafter arise, who laying hold of popular disquietudes, may collect together the desperate and the discontented, and by assuming to themselves the powers of government, may sweep away the liberties of the Continent like a deluge. Should the government of America return again into the hands of Britain, the tottering situation of things will be a temptation for some desperate adventurer to try his fortune; and in such a case, what relief can Britain give? Ere she could hear the news, the fatal bu[s]iness might be done; and ourselves suffering like the wretched Britons under the oppression of the Conqueror. Ye that oppose independance now, ye know not what ye do. ye are opening a door to eternal tyranny, by keeping vacant the seat of government. There are thousands, and tens of thousands, who would think it glorious to expel from the Continent, that barbarous and hellish power, which have stirred up the Indians and the Negroes to destroy us; the cruelty hath a double guilt, it is dealing brutally by us, and treacherously by them.

To talk of friendship with those in whom our reason forbids us to have faith, and our affections wounded thro' a thousand pores instruct us to detest, is madness and folly. Every day wears out the little remains of kindred between us and them, and can there be any reason to hope, that as the relationship expires, the affection will encrease, or that we shall agree better, when we have ten times more and greater concerns to quarrel over than ever?

Ye that tell us of harmony and reconciliation, can ye restore to us the time that is past? Can ye give to prostitution its former innocence? Neither can ye reconcile Britain and America. The last cord is now broken, the people of England are presenting addresses against us. There are injuries which nature cannot forgive; she would cease to be nature if she did. As well can the lover forgive the ravisher[58] of his mistress, as the Continent forgive the murders of Britain. The Almighty hath implanted in us these unextinguishable feelings for good and wise purposes. They are the Guardians of his Image in our hearts. They distinguish us from the herd of common animals. The social compact would dissolve, and justice be extirpated [from] the earth, or have only a casual existence were we callous to the touches of affection. The robber and the murderer would often escape unpunished, did not the injuries which our tempers sustain, provoke us into justice.

O ye that love mankind! Ye that dare oppose not only the tyranny, but the tyrant, stand forth! Every spot of the old world is over-run with oppression. Freedom hath been hunted round the Globe. Asia and Africa have long expelled her. – Europe regards her like a stranger, and England hath given her warning to depart. O! receive the fugitive, and prepare in time an asylum for mankind. [...]

---

[57] Thomas Anello, otherwise Massanello, a fisherman of Naples, who, after spiriting up his countrymen in the public market place, against the oppression of the Spaniards, to whom the place was then subject, prompted them to revolt, and in the space of a day became King (original footnote).
[58] Person who rapes someone.

Source: Thomas Paine (1737-1807). *Common Sense: Addressed to the Inhabitants of America, on the Following Interesting Subjects. I. Of the Origin and Design of Government in General, with Concise Remarks on the English Constitution. II. Of Monarchy and Hereditary Succession. III. Thoughts on the Present State of American Affairs. IV. Of the Present Ability of America, with Some Miscellaneous Reflections.* Philadelphia: R. Bell, 1776, 29-45, 58-60.

131. Thomas Jefferson
The Declaration of Independence (1776)

A Declaration by the Representatives of the United States of America, in *General* Congress assembled.[59]

When, in the course of human events, it becomes necessary for one people to dissolve the political bands which have connected them with another, and to assume among the powers of the earth the separate and equal station to which the laws of nature and of nature's God entitle them, a decent respect to the opinions of mankind requires that they should declare the causes which impel them to the separation.

We hold these truths to be self evident: that all men are created equal; that they are endowed by their creator with certain inalienable rights; that among these are life, liberty, and the pursuit of happiness; that to secure these rights, governments are instituted among men, deriving their just powers from the consent of the governed; that whenever any form of government bec[o]mes destructive of these ends, it is the right of the people to alter or to abolish it, and to institute new government, laying its foundation on such principles, and organizing its powers in such form, as to them shall seem most likely to effect their safety and happiness. Prudence, indeed, will dictate that governments long established should not be changed for light and transient causes; and accordingly all experience hath shown that mankind are more disposed to suffer while evils are sufferable, than to right themselves by abolishing the forms to which they are accustomed. But when a long train of abuses and usurpations, pursuing invariably the same object, evinces a design to reduce them under absolute despotism, it is their right, it is their duty to throw off such government, and to provide new guards for their future security. Such has been the patient sufferance of these colonies; and such is now the necessity which constrains them to alter their former systems of government. The history of the present king of Great Britain is a history of repeated injuries and usurpations, all having in direct object the establishment of an absolute tyranny over these states. To prove this, let facts be submitted to a candid world.

He has refused his assent to laws the most wholesome and necessary for the public good.

He has forbidden his governors to pass laws of immediate and pressing importance [...].

He has abdicated government here by declaring us out of his protection, and waging war against us.

He has plundered our seas, ravaged our coasts, burnt our towns, and destroyed the lives of our people.

He is at this time transporting large armies of foreign mercenaries to complete the works of death, desolation and tyranny already begun with circumstances of cruelty and

---

[59] The text reproduced here is not Jefferson's original draft, but the version with alterations that was finally adopted by the members of Congress.

perfidy scarcely paralleled in the most barbarous ages, and totally unworthy the head of a civilized nation. [...]

In every stage of these oppressions we have petitioned for redress in the most humble terms: our repeated petitions have been answered only by repeated injuries.

A prince whose character is thus marked by every act which may define a tyrant is unfit to be the ruler of a free people. [...]

We, therefore, the representatives of the United States of America in General Congress assembled, appealing to the supreme judge of the world for the rectitude of our intentions, do in the name, and by the authority of the good people of these colonies, solemnly publish and declare, that these united colonies are, and of right ought to be free and independent states; that they are absolved from all allegiance to the British crown, and that all political connection between them and the state of Great Britain is, and ought to be, totally dissolved; and that as free and independent states, they have full power to levy war, conclude peace, contract alliances, establish commerce, and to do all other acts and things which independent states may of right do.

And for the support of this declaration, with a firm reliance on the protection of divine providence, we mutually pledge to each other our lives, our fortunes, and our sacred honor.

Source: Thomas Jefferson (1743-1826). "The Declaration of Independence as Adopted by Congress in Congress, July 4, 1776." *The Writings of Thomas Jefferson: Being His Autobiography, Correspondence, Reports, Messages, Addresses, and Other Writings, Official and Private*. 9 vols. Ed. H.A. Washington, New York: Taylor & Maury, 1853, Vol. 1, 19-26.

132. John Witherspoon
The Dominion of Providence over the Passions of Men (1776)

The truth, then, asserted in this text, which I propose to illustrate and improve, is, – *That all the disorderly passions of men, whether exposing the innocent to private injury, or whether they are the arrows of divine judgment in public calamity, shall, in the end, be to the praise of God*: Or, to apply it more particularly to the present state of the American Colonies, and the plague of war, – *The ambition of mistaken princes, the cunning and cruelty of oppressive and corrupt ministers, and even the inhumanity of brutal soldiers, however dreadful, shall finally promote the glory of God, and in the meantime, while the storm continues, his mercy and kindness shall appear in prescribing bounds to their rage and fury.*

[...] Both nations in general, and private persons are apt to grow remiss and lax in a time of prosperity and seeming security, but when their earthly comforts are endangered or withdrawn, it lays them under a kind of necessity to seek for something better in their place. Men must have comfort from one quarter or another. When earthly things are in a pleasing and promising condition, too many are apt to *find their rest*, and be satisfied with them as their only portion. But when the vanity and passing nature of all created comfort is discovered, they are compelled to look for something more durable as well as valuable. What therefore can be more to the praise of God, than that when a whole people have forgotten their resting place, when they have abused their privileges, and despised their mercies, they should by distress and suffering be made to *hearken to the rod*, and return to their duty.

There is an inexpressible depth and variety in the judgments of God, as in all his other works, but we may lay down this as a certain principle, that if there were no sin, there could be no suffering. Therefore they are certainly for the correction of sin, or for the trial, illustration, and perfecting of the grace and virtue of his own people. [...]

[...] Can you have a clearer view of the sinfulness of your nature, than when the rod of the oppressor is lifted up, and when you see men putting on the habit of the warrior, and collecting on every hand the weapons of hostility and instruments of death? I do not blame your ardour in preparing for the resolute defence of your temporal rights. But consider I beseech you, the truly infinite importance of the salvation of your souls. Is it of much moment whether you and your children shall be rich or poor, at liberty or in bonds? Is it of much moment whether this beautiful country shall increase in fruitfulness from year to year being cultivated by active industry, and possessed by independent freemen, or the scanty produce of the neglected fields shall be eaten up by hungry publicans, while the timid owner trembles at the tax gatherers approach? And is it of less moment my brethren, whether you shall be the heirs of glory, or the heirs of hell? Is your state on earth for a few fleeting years of so much moment? And is it of less moment, what shall be your state through endless ages? Have you assembled together willingly to hear what shall be said on public affairs, and to join in imploring the blessing of God on the councils and arms of the united colonies, and can you be unconcerned, what shall become of you for ever, when all the monuments of human greatness shall be laid in ashes, for *the earth* itself *and all the works that are therein shall be burnt up*. [...]

While we give praise to God the supreme disposer of all events, for his interposition in our behalf, let us guard against the dangerous error of trusting in, or boasting of an *arm of flesh*. [...] If I am not mistaken, not only the holy scriptures in general, and the truths of the glorious gospel in particular, but the whole course of providence seems intended to abase the pride of man, and lay the vain-glorious in the dust. How many instances does history furnish us with of those who after exulting over, and despising their enemies, were signally and shamefully defeated.[60] [...]

[...] From what has been said you may learn what encouragement you have to put your trust in God, and hope for his assistance in the present important conflict. He is the Lord of hosts, great in might, and strong in battle. Whoever hath his countenance and approbation, shall have the best at last. I do not mean to speak prophetically, but agreeably to the analogy of faith, and the principles of God's moral government. Some have observed that true religion, and in her train dominion, riches, literature, and arts, have taken their course in a slow and gradual manner, from east to west since the earth was settled after the flood, and from thence forbode the future glory of America. I leave this as a matter rather of conjecture than certainty, but observe, that if your cause is just, – if your principles are pure, – and if your conduct is prudent, you need fear the multitude of opposing hosts.

If your cause is just – you may look with confidence to the Lord and intreat him to plead it as his own. You are all my witnesses, that this is the first time of my introducing any political subject into the pulpit. At this season however, it is not only lawful but necessary, and I willingly embrace the opportunity of declaring my opinion without any hesitation, that the cause in which America is now in arms, is the cause of justice, of liberty, and of human nature. So far as we have hitherto proceeded, I am satisfied that the confederacy of the colonies, has not been the effect of pride, resentment, or sedition, but

---

[60] Original footnote: "There is no story better known in British history, than that of the French army the night preceding the battle of Agincourt, played at dice for English prisoners before they took them and the next day were taken by them."

of a deep and general conviction, that our civil and religious liberties, and consequently in a great measure the temporal and eternal happiness of us and our posterity depended on the issue. The knowledge of God and his truths have from the beginning of the world been chiefly, if not entirely confined to these parts of the earth, where some degree of liberty and political justice were to be seen, and great were the difficulties with which they had to struggle from the imperfection of human society, and the unjust decisions of usurped authority. There is not a single instance in history in which civil liberty was lost, and religious liberty preserved entire. If therefore we yield up our temporal property, we at the same time deliver the conscience into bondage. [...]

> Source: John Witherspoon (1722-1794). *The Dominion of Providence over the Passions of Men: A Sermon Preached at Princeton, on the 17th of May, 1776. Being the General Fast Appointed by the Congress through the United Colonies*. Philadelphia: R. Aitken, 1776, 5-6, 17-19, 29-31, 35-36, 39-41.

133. David Ramsay
"An Oration on the Advantages of American Independence" (1778)

Friends and fellow citizens,

We are now celebrating the anniversary of our emancipation from British tyranny; an event that will constitute an illustrious æra in the history of the world, and which promises an extension of all those blessings to our country, for which we would choose to live, or dare to die.

Our present form of government is every way preferable to the royal one we have lately renounced. It is much more favourable to purity of morals, and better calculated to promote all our important interests. Honesty, plain-dealing, and simple manners, were never made the patterns of courtly behaviour. Artificial manners always prevail in kingly governments; and royal courts are reservoirs, from whence insincerity, hypocrisy, dissimulation, pride, luxury, and extravagance, deluge and overwhelm the body of the people. On the other hand, republics are favourable to truth, sincerity, frugality, industry, and simplicity of manners. Equality, the life and soul of Commonwealths, cuts off all pretensions to preferment, but those which arise from extraordinary merit: Whereas in royal governments, he that can best please his superiors, by the low arts of fawning[61] and adulation,[62] is most likely to obtain favour.

It was the interest of Great-Britain to encourage our dissipation and extravagance, for the two-fold purpose of *increasing the sale of her manufacturers*, and of *perpetuating our subordination*. In vain we sought to check the growth of luxury, by sumptuary laws;[63] every wholesome restraint of this kind was sure to meet with the royal negative: While the whole force of example was employed to induce us to copy the dissipated manners of the country from which we sprung. If therefore, we had continued dependent, our frugality, industry, and simplicity of manners, would have been lost in an imitation of British extravagance, idleness, and false refinements. [...]

The times in which we live, and the governments we have lately adopted, all conspire to fan the sparks of genius in every breast, and kindle them into flame. When like chil-

---

[61] Servile flattery or homage.
[62] Exaggerated and hypocritical praise
[63] Laws regulating expenditure, esp. restraining excess in food, etc.

dren, we were under the guardianship of a foreign power, our limited attention was naturally engrossed by agriculture, or directed to the low pursuit of wealth. In this state, the powers of the soul, benumbed with ease and indolence, sunk us into sloth and effeminacy. Hardships, dangers, and proper opportunities; give scope to active virtues, and rouse the mind to such vigorous exertions, as command the admiration of an applauding world. Rome, when she filled the earth with the terror of her arms, sometimes called her Generals from the plough: In like manner, the great want of proper persons to fill high stations, has drawn from obscurity many illustrious characters, which will dazzle the world with the splendor of their names. [...]

We are the first people in the world, who have had it in their power to choose their own form of government. Constitutions were forced on all other nations, by the will of their conquerors; or they were formed by accident, caprice, or the over-bearing influence of prevailing parties or particular persons: But, happily for us, the bands of British government were dissolved at a time when no rank above that of freemen existed among us, and when we were in a capacity to choose for ourselves among the various forms of government, and to adopt that which best suited our country and people. Our deliberations on this occasion, were not directed by the over-grown authority of a conquering general, or the ambition of an aspiring nobility, but by the pole star of public good, inducing us to prefer those forms that would most effectually secure the greatest portion of political happiness to the greatest number of people. We had the example of all ages for our instruction, and many among us were well acquainted with the causes of prosperity and misery in other governments. [...]

Our Independence will naturally tend to fill our country with inhabitants. Where life, liberty, and property, are well secured, and where land is easily and cheaply obtained, the natural increase of people will much exceed all European calculations. Add to this, the inhabitants of the Old World becoming acquainted with our excellent forms of government, will emigrate by thousands. In their native lands, the hard-earned fruits of uninterrupted labour, are scarcely equal to a scanty supply of their natural wants; and this pittance is held on a very precarious tenure: While our soil may be cheaply purchased, and will abundantly repay the toil of the husbandman, whose property no rapacious landlord dare invade. Happy America! whose extent of territory westward, is sufficient to accommodate with land, thousands and millions of the virtuous peasants, who now groan beneath tyranny and oppression in three quarters of the globe. Who would remain in Europe, a dependent on the will of an imperious landlord, when a few years industry can make him an independent American freeholder?

Such will be the fruits of our glorious revolution, that in a little time, gay fields adorned with the yellow robes of ripening harvest, will smile in the remotest depths of our western frontiers, where impassable forests now frown over the uncultivated earth. The face of our interior country will be changed from a barren wilderness, into the hospitable abodes of peace and plenty. Cities too will rise majestick to the view, on those very spots which are now howled over by savage beasts and more savage men. [...]

It is difficult to compute the number of advantages arising from our present glorious struggle; harder still, perhaps impossible, precisely to ascertain their extent. It has attracted the attention of all Europe to the nature of civil liberty, and the rights of the people. Our constitutions, pregnant with the seeds of liberty and happiness, have been translated into a variety of languages, and spread far and wide. Who can tell what great events, now concealed in the womb of time, may be brought into existence by the nations of the Old World emulating our successful efforts in the cause of liberty? The thrones of tyranny and despotism will totter,[64] when their subjects shall learn and know, by our example, that the happiness of the people is the end and object of all lawful government. The wondering world has beheld the smiles of Heaven on the numerous sons of America resolving to die or be free: Perhaps this noble example, like a wide-spreading conflagration may catch from breast to breast, and extend from nation to nation, till tyranny and oppression are utterly extirpated from the face of the earth.

The tyrants and landlords of the Old World, who hold a great part of their fellow men in bondage because of their dependence for land, will be obliged to relax of their arbitrary treatment, when they find that America is an asylum for freemen from all quarters of the globe. They will be cautious of adding to the oppressions of their poor subjects and tenants, lest they should force them to abandon their country for the enjoyment of the sweets of American Liberty. In this view of the ma[t]ter, I am confident that the cause of America is the cause of Human Nature, and that it will extend its influence to thousands who will never see it, and procure them a mitigation of the cruelties and oppressions imposed by their arbitrary task-masters. [...]

Ever since the flood, true religion, literature, arts, empire, and riches, have taken a flow and gradual course from east to west, and are now about fixing their long and favourite abode in this new western world. Our sun of political happiness is already risen, and hath lifted his head over the mountains, illuminating our hemisphere with liberty, light, and polished life. Our Independence will redeem one quarter of the globe from tyranny and oppression, and consecrate it the chosen seat of truth, justice, freedom, learning and religion. We are laying the foundation of happiness for countless millions. Generations yet unborn will bless us for the blood-bought inheritance, we are about to bequeath them. Oh happy times! Oh glorious days! Oh kind, indulgent, bountiful Providence, that we live in this highly favoured period, and have the honour of helping forward these great events, and of suffering in a cause of such infinite importance!

Source: David Ramsay (1749-1815). "An Oration on the Advantages of American Independence: Spoken before a Public Assembly of the Inhabitants of Charlestown in South-Carolina, on the Second Anniversary of That Glorious Æra." *The United States Magazine* (January-March 1779), 22-24, 57, 101-103, 106.

---

[64] To stagger, to walk or move with unsteady steps.

134. "America Triumphant and Britannia in Distress" (1782)[65]

Source: "America Triumphant and Britannia in Distress." Abraham Weatherwise (Pseudonym). *Weatherwise's Town and Country Almanack, for the Year of Our Lord, 1782. Calculated for the Meridian of Boston, New-England* [...]. Boston: Nathaniel Coverly and Robert Hodge, 1781, 1.

---

[65] The illustration that introduces the Weatherwise's 1782-Almanck is followed by the following explanation: "I. America sitting on that quarter of the globe with the Flag of the United States displayed over her head; holding in one hand the Olive branch, inviting the ships of all nations to partake of her commerce; and in the other hand supporting the Cap of Liberty. II. Fame proclaiming the joyful news to all the world. III. Britannia weeping at the loss of the trade of America, attended with an evil genius. IV. The British flag struck, on her strong Fortresses. V. French, Spanish, Dutch shipping in the harbours of America. VI. A view of New York, wherein is exhibited the Tra[i]tor Arnold, taken with remorse for selling his country, and Judas like hanging himself.

EARLY REPUBLIC

The importance of the Early Republic for an understanding of American culture derives from the fact that it is the very era during which Americans for the first time addressed and negotiated the problem of a collective national identity. Although the temporal boundaries of the period vary among historians, the era commonly referred to as the 'Early Republic' or the 'Early National Period' roughly comprises the first five decades of U. S. history, which extend from the end of the Revolutionary War (1783) to the presidency of John Quincy Adams (1825-1829). Viewed from a historical perspective, the Early Republic has often been described as intermediate in character, since it is framed by the two major political caesurae of early American history, the Revolution and the Civil War. For that reason, the Early Republic has at times remained somewhat on the margins of critical interest.

Yet the coming-of-age of the United States as a nation is marked by a number of political, social, economic, and cultural transformations that shaped the Americans' self-perception significantly for future generations. After the ratification of the Federal Constitution in 1788, the United States witnessed the birth of a two-party system. A decade of embittered partisan politics terminated in what Thomas Jefferson retrospectively dubbed "the revolution of 1800," when the Republicans succeeded the Federalists to the presidency. Although the United States' first president, George Washington, hoped in his Farewell Address that America would not interfere with European politics, the United States had to endure two confrontations with foreign powers, the 'Quasi-War' with France and the War of 1812 against Great Britain, before it entered a period of domestic tranquility and President Monroe formally declared the United States' political neutrality in 1823. With immigration continually on the rise, the American population grew from four to ten million between 1790 and 1820. Along went the commercial boom of America's overseas trade, which brought wealth and prosperity to American citizens and gradually transformed the United States into an entrepreneurial, market-oriented society. At the same time, the United States enlarged its territory to the west by admitting new states to the union and, most crucially, by purchasing French Louisiana in 1803. In cultural terms, the ever-increasing number of newspapers and periodicals published in the United States as well as the appearance of a new literary genre, the American novel, created a vast bourgeois readership and turned the land of settlers into what some scholars have termed a genuine 'republic of letters.'

The textual genres that reflect the social and political dynamics of the Early Republic most prominently are political orations and festive poetry. Primarily written for public occasions, such early examples of popular literature reached comparatively wide audiences since they were first performed, and afterwards printed in pamphlets or newspapers. Both genres proved to be well-suited platforms for conceptualizing American citizens as members of one national community. The need for articulating ideas of national coherence arose from the simultaneous existence of countless regional, ethnic, political, and religious identities which at different stages tended to fragmentize American society into ideologically conflicting groups and thus to subvert the republican project of a sovereign United States.

After the continental army had won the Revolutionary War against the British, political orators of the 1780s were chiefly concerned with the problem of republican fragility. Both ancient and modern history provided ample evidence for the fast and seemingly inevitable decline of republican states. Believing that the successful progression of a republic largely depended on a virtuous citizenry, authors like John Warren and Benjamin Rush (docs. 138, 139) argued for a disinterested patriotism that subjected the individual's concern to the common good. As numerous others who realized that the Articles of Confederation could not provide a basis for a national politics, Joel Barlow in his Fourth of July oration (doc. 140) supported the idea of resting the American republic on a strong federal government, without which the Revolution would remain unfinished and which was hoped to function as an unprecedented tool that would establish republican continuity.

The years that followed the ratification of the Constitution saw the gradual emergence of what scholars have termed an American civil religion, which denotes a set of practices and symbols which have been instrumental in shaping a unique form of nationalism. The three earliest of the United States' national symbols, which have served their unifying function till the present day, were the Declaration of Independence, the Constitution, and George Washington. Independence Day soon became the major national holiday, which was celebrated in a highly ritualistic fashion, whereas the Constitution was praised as the culmination of Enlightenment thought and as the very document enshrining equality, liberty, and justice. George Washington was venerated as the nation's savior and lawgiver. Addressed as an American Cincinnatus and Moses in laudatory texts, the revolutionary hero was transfigured into America's foremost icon and has ever since remained a favorite theme in the visual arts of the United States, which around the turn of the century had a strong bearing of neoclassicism (see docs. 137, 150).

Both political orations and Fourth of July odes were integrated into the early rites of an American civil religion, which marked the beginning of an elaborate commemorative culture in the United States. The texts of both genres display a rhetoric of consensus, by which the authors attempted to mask the social reality of regional difference and ideological conflict. One rhetorical strategy consisted in recapitulating the Revolutionary struggle for independence. By doing so, the authors took a first step in sketching out a normative narrative of national history. The major protagonists of this narrative were the political founders and the generals who fought the war against Britain. Some texts, like the odes of Aspasio and George Richards (docs. 136, 87), focus on the role of Washington as a paternal savior of the country. Other writers, like Thomas Fessenden in his 1798 ode (doc. 141), which echoes the Federalists' fear of French imperialism, and Hugh Legaré in his Fourth of July oration (doc. 151), which reflects the economic optimism of the 1820s, transformed America's revolutionary figures into a catalogue of national heroes, which heightened a sense of collective identity. Still others, like John Quincy Adams in his oration commemorating the forefathers' landing at Plymouth (doc. 149), projected the republican ideology back to the first settlers and thus sought to legitimize the United States' progressive impulse into the territories of Native Americans. In addition to venerating their national ancestors, writers of the Early Republic relied on allegorical figures for creating a sense of community. Most often, such allegories were female. Artists visualized a woman in a long white gown with her head covered by a helmet (see doc. 150), while authors addressed her as either Columbia or the goddess of Liberty, as the texts of Aspasio and Daniel Webster demonstrate in an exemplary fashion (docs. 136, 142).

Another concept that figures prominently in the occasional literature of the Early Republic reveals itself in the imaginary renderings of America's exceptional role in secular history. The authors boosted America's historical significance by transposing the United States into the progressive concept of a *translatio imperii* and by identifying post-revolutionary America with the onset of a golden age of prosperity. Adopted from Biblical history, the idea of *translatio imperii* implies that the worldly dominion moves from east to west. Other than the writers of the Revolutionary period, who merely prophesied America's future glory, political authors of the Early Republic like Hugh Legaré and John Quincy Adams (see docs. 149, 151, 152) read the United States' economic and territorial growth as evidence for the actual completion of the westward course of empire. In his Thanksgiving sermon preached in the controversy-ridden year 1800 (doc. 143), Nathanael Emmons seeks to appease the conflicting groups within American society by arguing that the transfer of empire from Europe to America is well under way. With multiple references to God's election of the American nation, Emmons' sermon reads as an early example of justifying the United States' role as a prospective political world power. Another exemplary text that displays both a rhetoric of consensus and a conviction of America's historical exceptionalism is Thomas Jefferson's widely read First Inaugural Address of 1801 (doc. 144), which was delivered in the new capital Washington, D. C., and reprinted all over the nation. It sought to terminate the long-winding ideological battle that had been fought between Federalists and Republicans, a battle during which Jefferson himself figured as a prominent target for polemical attacks (see docs. 145, 146). Famous not only for its reconciling statement that all Americans are both Republicans and Federalists, Jefferson's address vividly demonstrates the conflation of Enlightenment ideas, a firm belief in economic progress, and the application of a providential vocabulary in a context of secular history.

Dennis Hannemann

135. Anonymous
"While Commerce Spreads Her Canvas O'er the Main" (1787)

Source: Anonymous. "While Commerce Spreads Her Canvas O'er the Main" (178). Courtesy Library of Congress. The print shows Columbia with two children being welcomed by Minerva, the goddess of war and wisdom. The inscription added to the image reads: "While Commerce spreads her canvass o'er the main, / And Agriculture ploughs the grateful plain / Minerva aids Columbia's rising race / With arms to triumph and with arts to grace."

136. Aspasio [Pseudonym]
"Anniversary Ode, for July 4th, 1789"

TUNE – "COLUMBIA."

Let laureats[1] endeavor their monarchs to praise,
And celebrate princes in bombastic lays;[2]
Let kingdoms and empires implicitly fall
And deify tyrants and despots extol,
Let orient nations, where slavery e'er reigns,
To sultans pay homage, benumb'd with their chains;
While Freedom, blest goddess, expell'd from their shores,
Their stupor and blindness, and folly deplores.
Thus, exil'd those regions, the seraph[3] has flown
And left the dull myriads in shackles to groan;
While Europe invites her, she skims o'er the main,[4]
And in this new Empire commences her reign.
Hail heaven born Freedom, of virtue the spring!
Hail bright Independence! thy birth-day we sing;
Unfold all thy graces, thy brilliance display,
Enrapture our souls and inspirit our lay.

What time the proud Briton, with conquest elate,
Our charters infring'd and invaded our state;
Consign'd us to slavery, the mansion of woe,
And vainly predestin'd our final o'erthrow:
'Twas thou, O Columbia![5] thy CHIEFTAIN[6] arouse,
Who, aided by Heaven, defeated our foes;
Caus'd the tumults and horrors of combat to cease,
And rais'd us to freedom, to glory and peace.
No more the dread clangors of battle shall roar;
No longer each field be incrimson'd with gore;
But peace, smiling cherub, transcendently gay,
Her heart-cheering prospects and glories display.
To day let the trumpet of liberty sound;
Let sorrow be banish'd; let gladness abound;

---

[1] Poet laureate; distinguished poet, worthy of the Muses' crown.
[2] A narrative poem; a ballad.
[3] Seraph (sg.), seraphim (pl.); In the Old Testament, the seraphim appear as six-winged celestial beings who serve as guardians to God's throne. The highest-ranking among angels, the seraphim are sometimes called the burning ones and are hence depicted in red colors symbolizing fire.
[4] Poetic: the open sea.
[5] The most prominent female personification of America. Derived from Christopher Columbus, the term was first used allegorically by the African American poetess Phillis Wheatley in 1775. Serving as a major icon for American identity formation, Columbia was commonly depicted as a Caucasian female dressed in a white, toga-like gown.
[6] I.e., George Washington (1732-1799), who served as commander-in-chief of the Continental Army (1775-1783). Washington was inaugurated as the first president of the United States on April 30, 1789.

Let grateful sensations in each breast arise,
And tuneful hosannas ascend to the skies.

Awake fair Columbia, thou child of the skies;
Awake to importance; to virtue arise;
On pinions of genius and industry soar;
The fountains of science and wisdom explore.
See rich agriculture exult o'er the land,
And new manufactures, fast rising, expand;
While nature propitious luxuriantly smiles;
Mechanics and farmers rejoice in their toils.

See hills, plains and vallies invested with grain,
Which, wantonly[7] waving, resembles the main;[8]
See verdant savannas and landscapes display,
Where steeds, herds and lambkins promiscuously stray;
See forests majestic their branches extend;
See gardens and orchards rich fruitage portend:
Hence gladness and plenty exults o'er the plain,
And commerce triumphant glides over the main.
Hail Source of all being! Hail Essence divine!
Thou Fountain of goodness! Columbia combine;
On Virtue's firm basis sublime may she rise;
"Extend with the main and dissolve with the skies."
May righteousness triumph; may union prevail,
And justice impartial exhibit her scale;
May discord and slavery be banish'd [from] our shore,
And liberty bless us till time be no more.
                                        ASPASIO.

Source: Aspasio [Pseudonym]. "Anniversary Ode, for July 4th, 1789." *The Christian's, Scholar's, and Farmer's Magazine* 1 (1789), 518-519.

---

[7] Here: Profuse in growth, luxuriant.
[8] Poetic: the open sea.

137. John James Barralet:
Apotheosis of Washington (1802)

Source: John James Barralet (c. 1747-1815). *Apotheosis of Washington* [Engraving and etching, 1800-1802]. Philadelphia: Simon Chaudron and John J. Barralet, 1802. Initial advertisement: "The subject General Washington raised from the tomb, by the spiritual and temporal Genius – assisted by Immortality. At his feet America weeping over his Armour, holding the staff surmounted by the Cap of Liberty, emblematical of his mild administration, on the opposite side, an Indian crouched in surly sorrow. In the third ground the mental virtues, Faith, Hope, and Charity [...] (*Aurora*, December 19, 1800)." Courtesy Library of Congress.

138. John Warren
An Oration, Delivered July 4th, 1783

FATHERS, BRETHREN, AND FELLOW-CITIZENS!
To mark with accuracy and precision, the principles from which the great and important transactions on the theatre of the political world originate, is an ind[i]spensable duty, not only of legislators, but of every subject of a free State; fraught with the most instructive lessons on the passions that actuate[9] the human breast, the inquiry is amply adapted to the purpose of regulating the social concerns of life.

The laws and penalties by which subjects are compelled to promote the general interests of a community, should ever be instituted with a special reference to these principles, and the greatest perfection of human government consists in the judiciousness of this application.

The constitution or frame of government in a republican State, is circumscribed by Barriers, which the ambitious or designing cannot easily remove, without giving the alarm to those whose priviledges might be infringed by the innovation; but that the principle of administration may be grossly corrupted, that the people may be abused, and enslaved under the best of constitutions, is a truth to which the annals of the world may be adduced to bear a melancholy attestation.

So silently have the advances of arbit[r]ary power been made, that a community has often been upon the verge of misery and servitude, whilst all was calm and tranquil in the State.

To revert to first principles is so essentially requ[i]site to public happiness and safety, that Polybius[10] has laid it down as an incontrovertible axiom, that every State must decline more or less rapidly, in proportion as she recedes from the principles on which she was founded.[11]

That virtue is the true principle of republican governments[12] has been sufficiently proved by the ablest writers on the subject, and, that whereas other forms of government may be supported without her, yet that in this she is absolutely necessary to their existence.

A general prevalence of that love for our country which teaches us to esteem it glorious to die in her defence, is the only means of perpetuating the enjoyment of that liberty and security, for the support of which all government was originally intended.

Laws and punishments are but the ensigns of human depravity, to render them as few as the public safety will admit, is the study of every wise, humane legislature.[13] The happy influences of this noble passion, by precluding the necessity of a multiplicity of Laws will free a People from those spectacles of misery and horror, which the penalties annexed to the breach of them must inevitably create.

The contempt of dangers, and of death, when liberty was the purchase, has been the means of elevating to the highest pitch of glory, those famed Republics of antiquity, which later ages have considered as the models of political perfection; instructed from early infancy to deem themselves the property of the State, they were ever ready to sacri-

---

[9] To stir up, arouse, or excite (obsolete).
[10] Greek statesman and historian of the 2nd century BC, who wrote of the rise of Rome to world prominence.
[11] Original footnote: "Polyb. Hist. Lib. 6, 6[2]8."
[12] Original footnote: "Aristotle thinks there is not any one virtue belonging to the subjects of a despotic government."
[13] Original footnote: "A multiplicity of rigorous penal laws is not only incompatible with the liberty of a free state, but even repugnant to human nature. Montesquieu."

fice their concerns to her interests; "dear to us (says the eloquent Cicero) dear to us are our Parents, dear are our Children, our Neighbours and Associates, but above all things, dear is our Country;"[14] the Injuries that are done to an individual are limited, those to a community may involve millions in destruction. [...]

From *public spirit* proceeds almost every other virtue. The man who willingly would die to save his Country, would surely sacrifice his fortune and possessions, to secure her peace and happiness. The noble examples of frugality which were exhibited in the conduct of the Spartan governors, who began the reformation of the state, by delivering up their own private property, to convince the citizens that their intentions were sincere, is a proof how much it may be made to triumph over avarice and selfishness.

The Thebans, under the matchless Epaminondas,[15] when they were deserted by their allies, and reduced to the greatest extremities, were by the wise example of their general, and frequent skirmishes with the enemy, inspired with a spirit of enterprize and bravery, which at length enabled them to vanquish thrice their number of Lacedemonian troops,[16] and having slain their general, to march in hostile array to the very gates of Sparta.[17]

These are the principles which have more or less animated the subjects of every state, that has arrived to any considerable degree of opulence and grandeur, and it is of the greatest use to observe how others have gradually crept into governments, and suppressed, or eradicated the public virtue of a people.

Alas! to what amounts the summit of all human greatness! Sparta, the nurse of heroes and legislators, Athens, the seat of arts and sciences, Carthage[18] the mart of all the trading nations, and even Rome, the haughty mistress of the world, have all long since been level'd with the dust! of all the states and cities of the globe that have experienced the like catastrophe, scarce can we mention one that has not met her ruin, in a forgetfulness of those *fundamental principles* on which her happiness depended.

So nearly is the most prosperous condition of a people, allied to decay and ruin, that even this flattering appearance conceals the seeds, that finally must produce her destruction.[19]

The object of public virtue, is to secure the liberties of the community, a security of liberty admits of every man's pursuing, without molestation, the measures most likely to increase his ease, and to place him in a state of independent affluence, nothing is more conducive to these ends than a free and unlimited commerce, the encouragement of which is undoubtedly the duty of the Commonwealth, and the feelings of humanity are, in a general sense, highly interested in the prosecution of it. [...]

That we may learn wisdom by the misfortunes of others, that by tracing the operation of those causes which have proved ruinous to so many states and kingdoms, we may escape the rocks and quicksands on which they have been shipwreck'd, it may be useful to take a cursory retrospect of the motives and opinions, which have effected the dis-

---

[14] Original footnote: "Cicero de Officiis."
[15] Theban statesman who, by defeating a Spartan army at Leuktra, 371 BC, was largely responsible for breaking the dominance of Sparta and for altering permanently the balance of power among the Greek states.
[16] Lacedaemon is the historical name for Sparta.
[17] Reputedly founded in the 9th century BC with a rigid oligarchic constitution, the state of Sparta for centuries retained in times of war two kings as lifetime co-rulers. In time of peace, power was held by a Senate of 30 members. From the 5th century, Sparta devoted itself to war and diplomacy, deliberately neglecting the arts, philosophy, and literature, and forged the most powerful army standing in Greece.
[18] City of antiquity, founded on the north coast of Africa by the Phoenicians of Tyre in 814 BC.
[19] Original footnote: "It was the victory over the Persians, obtained in the straits of Thalamis, that corrupted the Republic of Athens, and the defeat of the Athenians, ruined the Republic of Syracuse. Montesquieu's Spirit of Laws, Vol.I, 163."

memberment of a very large and valuable part of the British dominions, and thereby deprived them of a principal source of strength and greatness; under a constitution which has ever been the boast of Englishmen, we have seen a most shameful prostitution of wealth to the purposes of bribery and corruption, with a view still farther to augment that opulence of individuals, which when exorbitant, must always be injurious to the common interest.[20]

We have seen the members of a House of Commons, which was once the bulwark of the nation, and the palladium[21] of Liberty, availing themselves of the meanest artifices for securing a seat, because it enabled them to gratify their favorite passions; and shame to human nature! We have seen a people, once famed for honesty and temperance, intoxicated at the gambols[22] of an election, and stupidly selling their suffrages for representatives in Parliament! [...]

Religious tyranny had forced from the unnatural bosom of a parent, a race of hardy sons, who chose rather to dwell in the deserts of America with the savage natives, than in the splendid habitations of *more* savage men.

Scarcely had these persecuted fugitives breathed from the fatigues of a dangerous voyage, when behold the cruel hand of power stretched over the atlantic to distress them in their new possessions! Having found a rude uncultivated soil, inadequate to the supply of the conveniences of life, they attempted those arts of which they stood immediately in need[23]; a prohibition of the manufactures necessary to cloath them in these then inhospitable wilds was early threatned, and though they were afterwards permitted, yet it was under the most humiliating restrictions[24].

From a principle of avarice and the most unjustifiable partiality in prejudice of these infant settlements, all commercial communication between them was forbidden, the importation of mercantile articles was laid under the heaviest restraints, none were to be freighted, not even the produce of foreign countries, from any other than British ports, and all exportations were finally to terminate in Britain. [...]

The mild voice of supplication and petition had in vain assailed the royal ear, the blood of your fellow-countrymen was wantonly shed on the memorable plains of *Lexington*,[25] you flew to arms and made *your last appeal to Heaven*.

Never did an enthusiastic ardor in the cause of an injured country blaze forth with such resistless fury, never did patriotic virtue shine out with such transcendent lustre, as on that solemn day! scarcely was there to be seen a peasant through the land "whose bosom beat not in his country's cause." Angels must have delighted in the fight! A wide extended country, roused into action at the first flash of arms, and pouring forth her thousands of virtuous yeomen[26] to avenge the blood of their slaughtered brethren on the

---

[20] Original footnote: "The great increase of our commerce after the peace of Utrecht, brought in a vast accession of wealth; and that wealth revived, and gradually diffused that luxury through the whole nation, which had laid dormant during the warlike reigns of William and Ann; to this universal luxury, and to this only, we must impute the amazing progress of corruption which seized the very vitals of our constitution. Montague on Republics, 376."
[21] Anything on which the safety of a nation, institution, etc. is believed to depend; a protecting institution.
[22] Frolic, merrymaking.
[23] Original footnote: "Vide Abbe Raynal's history of British settlements, Vol. II."
[24] Original footnote: "It ever was, and ever would have been the policy of Great Britain, had this country continued under her government, as much as possible to suppress our manufactures. [...]"
[25] The Battles of Lexington and Concord (1775) confirmed the alienation between the majority of colonists and the mother country, and it roused 16,000 New Englanders to join forces.
[26] A man holding a small landed estate; a countryman of respectable standing; one who cultivates his own land.

unprincipled aggressors! Quickly they fled from merited destruction, and fleeing, shed their blood, an immolation[27] to the beloved manes of those who fell the early martyrs to this glorious cause; you then convinced *deluded* Britons, that bravery was not the growth of any one *peculiar* spot or soil[28].

The enterprize 'tis true was bold and daring! The nations of the world stood still, astonished at the desperate blow! The brave alone are capable of noble actions; Defenceless, and unfurnished with the means of war, you placed your confidence in that God of armies who approves the struggles of the oppressed, and relying on the honest feelings of the heart for your success, you ventured to contend with veteran armies, and to defy the formidable power of a nation accustomed to success and conquest.

Your Guardian Genius patronized your cause, presided in your counsels, inspired you with intrepidity[29] and wisdom, and mysteriously infatuated the British chiefs; protected in the days of weakness and of danger, by the concealment of your real wants, the boasted wisdom of your crafty foe was baffled and confounded.

Through all the various fortunes of the field, you persevered with an undaunted front, and whilst your coasts were swarming with fleets, full freighted with the choicest legions of the enemy, a force that would have stiffened with dispair a less determined people, you dared to pass the irrevocable decree, that forever cut asunder the ties that bound you to a cruel parent, assumed your rank amongst the nations of the world, and instituted a new Epoch in the annals of your country; with solemn oaths, you pledged your sacred honor, to die united in defence of your much injured rights, or live in virtuous possession of *peace*, of *liberty* and *safety*. – The generations yet unborn shall read with rapture that distinguished page, whereon in capitals shall stand recorded, the important transaction of that day, and celebrate to the latest ages of this republic, the anniversary of that resolution of the American Congress, which gave the rights of sovereignty and independence to these United States. [...]

At length, ye favoured Sons of freedom, THE GLORIOUS WORK IS DONE[30]! Heralds of Peace proclaim the joyful tidings! Let the remotest corners of the globe resound with acclamations of applause, 'till even the inanimate creation shall join the concert, and dance to more sublime than *Orphean*[31] strains! Genius of liberty rejoice, for Heaven has opened a new asylum to your long persecuted sons! Rejoice ye inhabitants of this chosen land! Let songs of joy dwell long upon your thankful tongues, and notes of gratitude to Heaven be raised on ten thousand strings, 'till angels catch the sound, and echo back, *Peace and good will to men!* Had I a thousand tongues, and all the eloquence of Cicero or Demosthenes,[32] too feeble were my accents, too small my energy for this *transporting* theme! [...]

Had conquest crowned the efforts of our enemies, numbers of our *worthy patriots*, had *now* been bleeding under the vindictive hand of a successful foe, and *we* perhaps in mines or dungeons, been dragging out a life of wretchedness, and weeping in silence, over the

---

[27] A sacrificial victim, a sacrifice.
[28] Original footnote: "Nothing more strikingly demonstrates the folly of the commander, than his *really* undervaluing the prowess of the enemy. Fabius thought highly of the abilities of Hannibal and made his dispositions accordingly."
[29] The quality of being fearless and courageous.
[30] Original footnote: "Vide last paragraph of the Oration, delivered *March* 5th, 1775, on the anniversary of the *Boston* massacre."
[31] Orpheus was an ancient Greek legendary hero endowed with superhuman musical skills.
[32] Athenian statesman (384-322 BC), recognized as the greatest of ancient Greek orators, who roused Athens to oppose Philip of Macedon and, later, his son Alexander the Great.

memory of *those*, to whom were justly due, the applause and gratitude of every friend to liberty and virtue.

What a contrast to this frightful picture does the joyfulness of the occasion which has this day assembled us together, exhibit to our view! Many of these illustrious freemen now meet us here, and mingle tears of joy and gratitude with ours! [...]

Transported from a distant clime, less friendly to its nurture, you have planted here the *stately Tree of Liberty*, and lived to see it flourish! But whilst you pluck the fruit from the bending branches, remember that *its roots were watered with your blood!* Remember the price at which you purchased it, "nor barter liberty for gold."

Go search the vaults, where lay enshrined the relicks of your martyred fellow-citizens, and from their dust receive a lesson on the value of your freedom! When virtue fails, when luxury and corruption shall undermine the pillars of the state, and threaten a total loss of liberty and patriotism, then solemnly repair to those *sacred repositories* of the dead, and if you *can*, return and sport away your rights.

When you forget the value of your freedom, read over the history that recounts the wounds from which your country bled; peruse the picture which brings back to your imaginations, in the lively colours of undisguised truth, the wild, distracted feelings of your hearts! – But if your happy lot has been not to have felt the pangs of a convulsive separation from *friend* or *kindred*, learn them of *those that have*. [...]

If to latest ages we retain the *spirit* which gave our INDEPENDENCE birth; if taught by the fatal evils that have subverted so many *mighty states*, we learn to sacrifice our dearest interests in our country's cause, enjoin upon our children *a solemn veneration*[33] *for her laws*, as next to adoration of their God, the *great* concern of man, and seal the precept with our last expiring breath, these STARS, that even now enlighten half the world, shall shine a glorious constellation in this *western hemisphere*, 'till *stars* and suns shall shine no more, and all the kingdoms of *this* globe shall vanish like a scroll.

Source: John Warren (1753-1815). *An Oration, Delivered July 4th, 1783, at the Request of the Inhabitants of the Town of Boston; in Celebration of the Anniversary of American Independence.* Boston: John Gill, 1783, 5-10, 17-23, 25, 27-28, 30, 32.

139. Benjamin Rush
"Thoughts upon the Mode of Education Proper in a Republic" (1786)

The business of education has acquired a new complexion by the independence of our country. The form of government we have assumed, has created a new class of duties to every American. It becomes us, therefore, to examine our former habits upon this subject, and in laying the foundations for nurseries of wise and good men, to adapt our modes of teaching to the peculiar form of our government.

The first remark that I shall make upon this subject is, that an education in our own, is to be preferred to an education in a foreign country. The principle of patriotism stands in need of the reinforcement of *prejudice*, and it is well known that our strongest prejudices in favour of our country are formed in the first one and twenty years of our lives. The policy of the Lacedamonians[34] is well worthy of our imitation. When Antipater[35] de-

---

[33] A feeling of deep respect and reverence directed towards some person or thing.
[34] Spartans.

manded fifty of their children as hostages for the fulfillment of a distant engagement, those wise republicans refused to comply with his demand, but readily offered him double the number of their adult citizens, whose habits and prejudices could not be shaken by residing in a foreign country. Passing by, in this place, the advantages to the community from the early attachment of youth to the laws and constitution of their country, I shall only remark, that young men who have trodden the paths of science together, or have joined in the same sports, whether of swimming, scating, fishing, or hunting, generally feel, thro' life, such ties to each other, as add greatly to the obligations of mutual benevolence.

I conceive the education of our youth in this country to be peculiarly necessary in Pennsylvania, while our citizens are composed of the natives of so many different kingdoms in Europe. Our Schools of learning, by producing one general, and uniform system of education, will render the mass of the people more homogeneous, and thereby fit them more easily for uniform and peaceable government.

I proceed, in the next place, to enquire, what mode of education we shall adopt so as to secure to the state all the advantages that are to be derived from the proper instruction of youth; and here I beg leave to remark, that the only foundation for a useful education in a republic is to be laid in RELIGION. Without this, there can be no virtue, and without virtue there can be no liberty, and liberty is the object and life of all republican governments.

Such is my veneration for every religion that reveals the attributes of the Deity, or a future state of rewards and punishments, that I had rather see the opinions of Confucius or Mahomed inculcated upon our youth, than see them grow up wholly devoid of a system of religious principles. But the religion I mean to recommend in this place, is the religion of JESUS CHRIST. [...]

Next to the duty which young men owe to their Creator, I wish to see a SUPREME REGARD TO THEIR COUNTRY, inculcated upon them. When the Duke of Sully became prime minister to Henry the IVth of France, the first thing he did, he tells us, "Was to subdue and forget his own heart." The same duty is incumbent upon every citizen of a republic. Our country includes family, friends and property, and should be preferred to them all. Let our pupil be taught that he does not belong to himself, but that he is public property. Let him be taught to love his family, but let him be taught, at the same time, that he must forsake, and even forget them, when the welfare of his country requires it. He must watch for the state as if its liberties depended upon his vigilance alone, but he must do this in such a manner as not to defraud his creditors, or neglect his family. He must love private life, but he must decline no station, however public or responsable it may be, when called to it by the suffrages of his fellow-citizens. He must love popularity, but he must despise it when set in competition with the dictates of his judgement, or the real interest of his country. He must love character, and have a due sense of injuries, but he must be taught to appeal only to the laws of the state, to defend the one, and punish the other. He must love family honour, but must be taught that neither the rank nor antiquity of his ancestors can command respect, without personal merit. He must avoid neutrality in all questions that divide the state, but he must shun the rage, and acrimony[36] of party spirit. He must be taught to love his fellow creatures in every part of the world, but he must cherish with a more intense and peculiar affection, the citizens of Pennsylvania and of the United States. I do not wish to see our youth educated with a single

---

[35] Macedonian general 398?-319 BC.
[36] Bitterness of disposition or manner.

prejudice against any nation our country; but we impose a task upon human nature, repugnant alike to reason, revelation and the ordinary dimensions of the human heart, when we require him to embrace, with equal affection, the whole family of mankind. He must be taught to amass wealth, but it must be only to encrease his power of contributing to the wants and demands of the state. He must be indulged occasionally in amusements, but he must be taught that study and business should be his principal pursuits in life. Above all he must love life, and endeavour to acquire as many of its conveniences as possible by industry and œconomy, but he must be taught that this life "Is not his own," when the safety of his country requires it. These are practicable lessons, and the history of the commonwealths of Greece and Rome show, that human nature, without the aids of Christianity, has attained these degrees of perfection.

While we inculcate these republican duties upon our pupil, we must not neglect, at the same time, to inspire him with republican principles. He must be taught that there can be no durable liberty but in a republic, and that government, like all other sciences, is of a progressive nature. The chains which have bound this science in Europe are happily unloosed in America. *Here* it is open to investigation and improvement. While philosophy has protected us by its discoveries from a thousand natural evils, government has unhappily followed with an unequal pace. It would be to dishonour human genius only to name the many defects which still exist in the best systems of legislation. We daily see matter of a perishable nature rendered durable by certain chemical operations. In like manner, I conceive, that it is possible to analyze and combine power in such a manner as not only to encrease the happiness, but to promote the duration of republican forms of government far beyond the terms limited for them by history, or the common opinions of mankind.

To assist in rendering religious, moral and political instructions more effectual upon the minds of our youth, it will be necessary to subject their bodies to physical discipline. To obviate the inconveniences of their studious and sed[e]ntary[37] mode of life, they should live upon a temperate diet, consisting chiefly of broths, milk and vegetables. The black broth[38] of Sparta, and the barley broth of Scotland, have been alike celebrated for their beneficial effects upon the minds of young people. They should avoid tasting spirituous liquors. They should also be accustomed occasionally to work with their hands, in the intervals of study, and in the busy seasons of the year in the country. Moderate sleep, silence, occasional solitude, and cleanliness, should be inculcated upon them, and the utmost advantage should be taken of a proper direction of those great principles in human conduct, – sensibility, habit, imitation, and association.

[...] From the observations that have been made it is plain, that I consider it as possible to convert men into republican machines. This must be done, if we expect them to perform their parts properly, in the great machine of the government of the state. That republic is sophisticated with monarchy or aristocracy that does not revolve upon the wills of the people, and these must be fitted to each other by means of education before they can be made to produce regularity and unison in government.

Source: Benjamin Rush (1746-1813). *A Plan for the Establishment of Public Schools and the Diffusion of Knowledge in Pennsylvania; to Which Are Added Thoughts upon the Mode of Education, Proper in a Republic: Addressed to the Legislature and Citizens of the State.* Philadelphia: Thomas Dobson, 1786, 13-15, 20-24, 27.

---

[37] Not engaged in active business.
[38] Thin soup.

140. Joel Barlow
An Oration Delivered at the North Church in Hartford, at the Meeting of the Cincinnati, July 4th, 1787

Mr. PRESIDENT, Gentlemen of the Society,[39] And Fellow Citizens,
On the Anniversary of so great an event as the birth of the Empire in which we live, none will question the propriety of passing a few moments in contemplating the various objects suggested to the mind by the important occasion. But at the present period, while the blessings, claimed by the sword of victory and promised in the voice of peace, remain to be confirmed by our future exertions – while the nourishment, the growth, and even the existence of our empire depend upon the united efforts of an extensive and divided people – the duties of this day ascend from amusement and congratulation to a serious patriotic employment.

We are assembled, my friends, not to boast, but to realize – not to inflate our national vanity by a pompous relation of past achievements in the council or in the field; but, from a modest retrospect of the truly dignified part already acted by our countrymen, from an accurate view of our present situation, and from an anticipation of the scenes that remain to be unfolded – to discern and familiarize the duties that still await us, as citizens, as soldiers and as men. [...]

It would be wandering from the objects which ought to occupy our present attention,[40] again to recount the numerous acts of the British Parliament which compose that system of tyranny designed for the subjugation of America: Neither can we indulge in the detail of those memorable events which marked our various stages of resistance, from the glooms of unsuccessful supplication, to the splendor of victory and acknowledged sovereignty. The former were the theme of senatorial eloquence, producing miracles of union and exertion in every part of the continent, till we find them preserved for everlasting remembrance in that declaratory Act of Independence, which gave being to an empire and dignified the day we now commemorate; the latter are fresh in the memory of every person of the least information. It would be impertinence, if not a breach of delicacy, to attempt a recital of those glorious achievements, especially before an audience, part of whom have been distinguished actors in the scene, others the anxious and applauding spectators. To the faithful historian we resign the task; the historian, whom it is hoped the present age will deem it their duty as well as their interest, to furnish, encourage, and support.

Whatever praise is due for the task already performed, it is certain that much remains to be done. The revolution is but half completed. *Independence* and *Government* were the two objects contended for, and but one is yet obtained. To the glory of the present age

---

[39] The Society of the Cincinnati was founded by officers of the Continental Army in 1783. In 458 BC (according to tradition), Cincinnatus, who had been consul in 460 BC, was plowing his fields when messengers arrived to tell him he had been named dictator to defend Rome against the Aequi and the Volscians. He took up the supreme command, defeated Rome's enemies, and returned to his farm, all within 16 days. Further, he refused the honors that came with his military victories. George Washington was later called an American Cincinnatus because he too held his command only until the defeat of the British and, at a time when he could have chosen to exercise great political power, instead returned as soon as he could to cultivating his lands.
[40] Original footnote: "This Oration was preceded by the lecture of the Act of Independence; which, by an order of this State Society, is in future to make part of their public exercises at every annual meeting."

and the admiration of the future, our severance from the British empire was conducted upon principles as noble as they were new, and unprecedented in the history of human actions. Could the same generous principles, the same wisdom and unanimity be exerted in effecting the establishment of a permanent fœderal system, what an additional lustre would it pour upon the present age! a lustre hitherto unequalled; a display of magnanimity, for which mankind may never behold another opportunity.

Without an efficient government our Independence will cease to be a blessing. Shall that glow of patriotism and unshaken perseverance, which have been so long conspicuous in the American character, desert us at our utmost need? Shall we lose sight of our own happiness, because it has grown familiar by a near approach? Shall thy labours, O Washington, be bestowed in vain? Hast thou conducted us to independence and peace, and shall we not receive the blessings at thy hands? Where are the shades of our fallen friends? and what is their language on this occasion? *Warren, Montgomery, Mercer, Wooster, Scammel* and *Laurens*, all ye hosts of departed heroes! rich is the treasure you have lavished in the cause, and prevalent the price you have paid for our freedom. Shall the purchase be neglected? the fair inheritance lie without improvement, exposed to every daring invader? Forbid it, honour, forbid it, gratitude; and oh, may Heaven avert the impending evil. [...]

[...] Unite in a permanent fœderal government, put your commerce upon a respectable footing; your arts and manufactures, your population, your wealth and glory will increase: and when an hundred millions of people are comprised within your territory and made happy by your sway, then shall it be known that the hand of that monarch[41] assisted in planting the vine from which so great a harvest is produced. [...]

The present is justly considered an alarming crisis;[42] perhaps the most alarming that America ever saw. We have contended with the most powerful nation and subdued the bravest and best appointed armies; but now we have to contend with *ourselves*, and encounter passions and prejudices more powerful than armies and more dangerous to our peace. It is not for glory, it is for existence that we contend.

Much is expected from the Fœderal Convention[43] now sitting at Philadelphia; and it is a happy circumstance that so general a confidence from all parts of the country is centred in that respectable Body. Their former services as individuals command it, and our situation requires it. But although much is expected from them, yet more is demanded from ourselves.

The first great object is to convince the people of the importance of their present situation; for the majority of a great people, on a subject which they understand, will never act wrong. If ever there was a time, in any age or nation, when the fate of millions depended on the voice of one, it is the present period in these states. Every free citizen of the American Empire ought now to consider himself as the legislator of half mankind. When he views the amazing extent of territory, settled and to be settled under the operation of his laws – when, like a wise politician, he contemplates the population of future

---

[41] Louis XVI, King of France (r. 1774-1791). The reference to the vine that was planted in America establishes a typological parallel to Jesus Christ.

[42] Congress could pass resolutions and make recommendations, but it had no way of enforcing its orders. The weakness of the national government made the years from 1783 (Treaty of Paris) to 1789, according to American historians, the "Critical Period" of the Early Republic.

[43] The Constitution was written during the summer of 1787 at a convention of 55 delegates who met in Philadelphia, ostensibly to amend the Articles of Confederation, the country's first written constitution.

ages; the changes to be wrought by the possible progress of arts, in agriculture, commerce and manufactures; the increasing connection and intercourse of nations, and the effect of one rational political system upon the general happiness of mankind – his mind, dilated with the great idea, will realize a liberality of feeling which leads to a rectitude of conduct. He will see that the system to be established by his suffrage is calculated for the great benevolent purposes of extending peace, happiness and progressive improvement to a large proportion of his fellow creatures. As there is a probability that the system to be proposed by the Convention may answer this description, there is some reason to hope it will be viewed by the people with that candour and dispassionate respect which is due to the importance of the subject. [...]

The present is an age of philosophy; and America, the empire of reason. Here, neither the pageantry of courts nor the glooms of superstition have dazzled or beclouded the mind. Our duty calls us to act worthy of the age and the country which gave us birth. Though inexperience may have betrayed us into errors; yet these have not been fatal; and our own discernment will point us to their proper remedy.

However defective the present confederated system may appear; yet a due consideration of the circumstances under which it was framed, will teach us rather to admire its wisdom than to murmur at its faults. The same political abilities which were displayed in that institution, united with the experience we have had of its o[p]eration, will doubtless produce a system, which will stand the test of ages, in forming a powerful and happy people. [...]

Every possible encouragement for great and generous exertions, is now presented before us. Under the idea of a permanent and happy government, every point of view, in which the future situation of America can be placed, fills the mind with a peculiar dignity, and opens an unbounded field of thought. The natural resources of the country are inconceivably various and great; the enterprising genius of the people promises a most rapid improvement in all the arts that embellish human nature; the blessings of a rational government will invite emigrations from the rest of the world, and fill the empire with the worthiest and happiest of mankind; while the example of political wisdom and felicity here to be displayed will excite emulation through the kingdoms of the earth, and meliorate[44] the condition of the human race. [...]

Source: Joel Barlow (1754-1812). *An Oration, Delivered at the North Church in Hartford, at the Meeting of the Connecticut Society of the Cincinnati, July 4th, 1787. In Commemoration of the Independence of the United States.* Hartford: Hudson and Goodwin, 1787, 3-4, 7-13, 19-20.

---

[44] To make better; to improve.

141. Thomas Green Fessenden
"An Ode" (1798) [45]

Ye sons of Columbia, unite in the cause
Of liberty, justice, religion, and laws;
Should foes then invade us, to battle we'll hie,[46]
For the GOD OF OUR FATHERS will be our ally!
    Let Frenchmen advance,[47]
    And all Europe join France,
Designing our conquest and plunder;
    United and free
    For ever we'll be,
And our cannon shall tell them in thunder,
That foes to our freedom we'll ever defy,
Till the continent sinks, and the ocean is dry!

When Britain assail'd us, undaunted we stood,
Defended the land we had purchas'd with blood,
Our liberty won, and it shall be our boast,
If the old world united should menace our coast: –
    Should millions invade,
    In terror array'd,[48]
    Our liberties bid us surrender,
        Our country they'd find
        With bayonets lin'd,
And Washington here to defend her,
For foes to our freedom we'll ever defy,
Till the continent sinks, and the ocean is dry!

Should Buonapart' come with his sans culotte[49] band,
And a new sort of freedom we don't understand,

---

[45] Original footnote: "The above Ode was written, set to musick, and sung on a publick occasion on a public occasion in Rutland, Vermont, July, 1798. At that time the warship which afterwards sailed to Egypt under Bonaparte lay at Toulon: its destination was not known in America, but many supposed that it was intended to waft the blessings of *French liberty* to the United States."

[46] To hasten, speed.

[47] The poet refers to the anti-French sentiments that reached a climax in 1798, when the Alien and Sedition Acts were passed by the Federalist-controlled Congress, allegedly in response to the hostile actions of the French Revolutionary government on the seas and in the councils of diplomacy (see also XYZ Affair). The Alien and Sedition Acts, which were probably designed to destroy Thomas Jefferson's Republican party, did much to unify the Republican party and to secure its victory in the election of 1800. Most controversial was the Sedition Act, devised to silence Republican criticism of the Federalists. Its proscription of spoken or written criticism of the government, the Congress, or the President virtually nullified the First Amendment freedoms of speech and the press.

[48] Drawn up, prepared for battle.

[49] Napoleon Bonaparte (1769-1821), French general and later emperor of the French (1804-1814). Sans-culotte (French: "without knee breeches"), in the French Revolution, any of the poor and ill-equipped volunteers of the Revolutionary army; later, during the Reign of Terror, the term referred to the ultra-democrats of the Revolution.

And make us an offer to give us as much
As France has bestow'd on the Swiss and the Dutch,[50]
    His fraud and his force
    Will be futile of course;
We wish for no *Frenchified* Freedom:
    If folks beyond sea
    Are to bid us be free,
We'll send for them when we shall need 'em.
But sans culotte Frenchmen we'll ever defy,
Till the continent sinks, and the ocean is dry!

We're anxious that Peace may continue her reign,
We cherish the virtues which sport in her train;
Our hearts ever melt, when the fatherless sigh,
And we shiver at Horror's funeral cry!
    But still, though we prize
    That child of the skies,
We'll never like slaves be accosted.
    In a war of defence
    Our means are immense,
And we'll fight till our *all* is exhausted:
For foes to our freedom we'll ever defy,
Till the continent sinks, and the ocean is dry!

The EAGLE of FREEDOM with rapture behold,
Overshadow our land with his plumage of gold!
The flood-gates of glory are open on high,
And Warren and Mercer[51] descend from the sky!
    They come from above
    With a message of love,
To bid us be firm and decided;
    "At Liberty's call,
    "Unite one and all,
"For you conquer, unless you're divided.
"Unite, and the foes to your freedom defy,
"Till the continent sinks, and the ocean is dry!"

"Americans, seek no occasion for war;
"The rude deeds of rapine[52] still ever abhor:
"But if in defence of your rights you should arm,
"Let toils ne'er discourage, nor dangers alarm.

---

[50] In 1795, the Netherlands came under French domination, and in 1798, the French army invaded Switzerland and forced the cantons to accept the formation of the Helvetic Republic under French supervision.
[51] Joseph Warren (1741-1775), officer of the revolutionary army, killed in the Battle of Bunker Hill; Hugh Mercer (1725-1777), American general of the revolutionary Continental Army, mortally wounded in action at Princeton.
[52] The act of taking away by force the property of others; plunder, robbery.

"For foes to your peace
"Will ever increase,
"If freedom and fame you should barter,
"Let those rights be yours,
"While Nature endures,
"For OMNIPOTENCE gave you the charter!"
Then foes to our freedom we'll ever defy,
Till the continent sinks, and the ocean is dry!

Source: Thomas Green Fessenden, Esq. (1771-1837). "An Ode". *Original Poems*. Philadelphia: E. Bronson, 1806, 1-5.

142. Daniel Webster
An Oration, Pronounced at Hanover, New-Hampshire, the 4th Day of July, 1800

COUNTRYMEN, BRETHREN, AND FATHERS,

We are now assembled to celebrate an anniversary, ever to be held in dear remembrance by the sons of freedom. Nothing less than the birth of a nation, nothing less than the emancipation of three millions of people, from the degrading chains of foreign dominion, is the event we commemorate!

Twenty four years have this day elapsed, since United Columbia first raised the standard of Liberty, and echoed the shouts of Independence! [...]

As no nation on the globe can rival us in the rapidity of our growth, since the conclusion of the revolutionary war – so none, perhaps, ever endured greater hardships, and distresses, than the people of this country, previous to that period.

We behold a feeble band of colonists, engaged in the arduous undertaking of a new settlement, in the wilds of North America. Their civil liberty being mutilated, and the enjoyment of their religious sentiments denied them, in the land that gave them birth, they fled their country, they braved the dangers of the then almost unnavigated ocean, and sought, on the other side [of] the globe, an asylum from the iron grasp of tyranny, and the more intolerable scourge of ecclesiastical persecution. But gloomy, indeed, was their prospect, when [they] arrived on this side of the Atlantic. [...]

The pitiful tale of taxation now commences – the unhappy quarrel, which issued in the dismemberment of the British empire, has here its origin.

England, now triumphant over the united powers of France and Spain, is determined to reduce, to the condition of slaves, her American subjects.

We might now display the Legislatures of the several States, together with the general Congress, petitioning, praying, remonstrating; and, like dutiful subjects, humbly laying their grievances before the [British] throne. On the other hand, we could exhibit a British Parliament, assiduously devising means to subjugate America – disdaining our petitions, trampling on our rights, and menacingly telling us, in language not to be misunderstood. "Ye shall be slaves!" – We could mention the haughty, tyrannical, perfidious GAGE,[53] at the head of a standing army; we could show our brethren attacked and slaugh-

---

[53] Thomas Gage (1720-1787), British General, appointed Commander-in-Chief of the British Army in North America in 1763. Gage's troops suffered heavy casualties at Lexington, Concord and Bunker Hill.

tered at Lexington! our property plundered and destroyed at Concord! Recollection can still pain us, with the spiral flames of burning Charleston,[54] the agonizing groans of aged parents, the shrieks of widows, orphans and infants! [...]

But, haughty Albion,[55] thy reign shall soon be over, – thou shalt triumph no longer! thine empire already reels and totters! thy laurels even now begin to wither, and thy fame decays! Thou hast, at length, roused the indignation of an insulted people – thine oppressions they deem no longer tolerable!

The 4th day of July, 1776, is now arrived; and America, manfully springing from the torturing fangs of the British lion, now rises majestic in the pride of her sovereignty, and bids her Eagle elevate his wings! [...]

Thus, friends and citizens, did the kind hand of an over-ruling Providence conduct us, through toils, fatigues and dangers, to Independence and Peace. If piety be the rational exercise of the human soul, if religion be not a chimera, and if the vestiges of heavenly assistance are clearly traced in those events, which mark the annals of our nation, it becomes us, on this day, in consideration of the great things, which the LORD has done for us, to render the tribute of unfeigned thanks, to that GOD, who superintends the Universe, and holds aloft the scale, that weighs the destinies of nations. [...]

The natural superiority of America clearly indicates, that it was designed to be inhabited by a nobler race of men, possessing a superior form of government, superior patriotism, superior talents, and superior virtues. Let then the nations of the East vainly waste their strength in destroying each other. Let them aspire at conquest, and contend for dominion, till their continent is deluged in blood. But let none, however elated by victory, however proud of triumphs, ever presume to intrude on the neutral station assumed by our country. [...]

[...] Our ancestors bravely snatched expiring liberty from the grasp of Britain, whose touch is *poison;* shall we now consign it to France, whose embrace is *death?* We have seen our fathers, in the days of Columbia's trouble, assume the rough habiliments of war, and seek the hostile field. [...] Shall we, their descendants, now basely disgrace our lineage, and pusil[l]animously disclaim the legacy bequeathed us? Shall we pronounce the sad valediction to freedom, and immolate liberty on the altars our fathers have raise[d] to her? NO! – *The response of a nation is – "*NO!*" Let it be registered in the archives of Heaven!* – Ere the religion we profess, and the privileges we enjoy, are sacrificed at the shrines of despots and demagogues, let the pillars of creation tremble! let world be wrecked on world, and systems rush to ruin! – Let the sons of Europe be vassals; let her hosts of nations be a vast congregation of slaves; but let us, who are this day FREE, whose hearts are as yet unappalled, and whose right arms are yet nerved for war, assemble before the hallowed temple of Columbian Freedom, AND SWEAR TO THE GOD OF OUR FATHERS, TO PRESERVE IT SECURE, OR DIE AT ITS PORTALS!

Source: Daniel Webster(1782-1852). *An Oration, Pronounced at Hanover, New-Hampshire, the 4th Day of July, 1800: Being the Twenty-fourth Anniversary of American Independence.* Hanover, NH: Moses Davis, 1800, 3-8, 13-15.

---

[54] Lexington and Concord: towns in Eastern Massachusetts; Charleston: today Cambridge, Massachusetts.
[55] Great Britain.

143. Nathanael Emmons
"Sermon XI: God Never Forsakes His People: Annual Thanksgiving, November 27, 1800"

> For the Lord will not forsake his people for his great name's sake: because it hath pleased the Lord to make you his people. – 1 Samuel, 12: 22.

The children of Israel, having long experienced the evils of anarchy and confusion, earnestly requested Samuel to make them a king. Though this request was displeasing to God as well as to Samuel, yet God directed Samuel to anoint Saul to reign over his people.[56] [...] Samuel had a right to conclude from the perfection of the divine character, that God would, by a wise and consistent course of conduct, eventually answer the ends he proposed, in making the children of Israel his peculiar people. And the same mode of reasoning is still equally just and conclusive. As far as God has been pleased to make any nation his peculiar people, so far that people have reason to expect that he will not forsake them. Hence the spirit of the text suggests this general observation:

That since God has been pleased to make our nation his peculiar people, he will not forsake us.

In illustrating this subject, it is necessary to consider how God has made us his peculiar people, and what grounds we have to hope that he will not forsake us.

I. Let us consider how God has made our nation his peculiar people.

Here it may be proper to premise, that God has never taken us into a federal relation to himself, as he did the children of Israel. He made a public and mutual compact with them, in which he avouched them to be his people, and they avouched him to be their God. But though God never entered into such a national covenant with us or with our fathers, yet he has been pleased in various other ways to make us his peculiar people.

1. It hath pleased the Lord to separate us in a peculiar manner from other nations. It was by such a separation that he made the seed of Abraham his peculiar people. "I am the Lord your God, which have separated you from other people."[57] [...] Here we may discover a very great analogy between our separation and that of the Israelites. Were they taken from the midst of another nation? So were we. Were they planted in the midst of a barbarous and idolatrous people? So were we. Were they conducted to the place of their destination by extraordinary interpositions of Providence? So were we. Did they become a peculiar people by their peculiar separation from other nations? So did we. God's taking our fathers from their native country, and bringing them a thousand leagues across the mighty ocean to this then dreary wilderness, was practically setting them apart for himself, and making them his peculiar people.

2. It hath pleased the Lord to make us the objects of his peculiar care and protection. Thus he distinguished his ancient chosen people. [...] God displayed the wonders of his goodness to his people, not only while they were in Egypt, at the Red Sea, and in the wilderness, but all the while they remained in the land of promise. They were planted in the midst of the nations, and surrounded by enemies far and near. The Egyptians and

---

[56] 1 Sam. 8-10.
[57] Lev. 20.23-24: "And ye shall not walk in the manners of the nation, which I cast out before you: for they committed all these things, and therefore I abhorred them. But I have said unto you, Ye shall inherit their land, and I will give it unto you to possess it, a land that floweth with milk and honey: I am the Lord your God, which have separated you from other people."

Chaldeans[58] were their distant enemies, while the residue of the Canaanites remained "as pricks in their eyes and thorns in their sides."[59] But God graciously guarded them on every hand, by both a visible and invisible providence; and made it appear to the world that they were his peculiar people. [...] Though no proper miracles were wrought in favor of our fathers, yet God afforded them, as he did the Israelites, his peculiar presence and protection. He caused their enemies, at first, to flee before them; and afterwards, when they stood in perishing need of their help, he put it into their hearts to supply their wants. He sent, from time to time, the pestilence and the sword among the natives, by which they were gradually diminished, and effectually restrained from doing mischief. While, on the other hand, he caused our fathers, who were a few individuals, to spread far and wide, and multiply into a great and powerful people, and at length to become a free and independent nation, notwithstanding all attempts to destroy them. By such a series of signal interpositions in our favor, God has visibly owned us, and marked us for himself, in the view of surrounding nations. It must be added,

3. The Lord has been pleased to form us for his peculiar service, by making us, from the beginning, a religious people. The Israelites were more eminently the people of God on account of religion, than on any other account; yea, in that respect, they were the only people of God in the world. They were separated from the rest of mankind, for the great purpose of preserving and propagating the true religion, in opposition to the attempts of all other nations; to spread superstition and idolatry over the face of the earth. [...] Thus God formed his ancient peculiar people of religious characters and for a religious purpose. And did he not form our nation of similar characters, and for a similar purpose? Did not our fathers resemble the ancient patriarchs in sincere and fervent piety? Did they not leave their native country, and sacrifice their dearest temporal interests, for the sake of enjoying and promoting real religion in this dark corner of the earth? Did not the spirit and principles of religion govern them in their public as well as private transactions? Did they not make ample provision for maintaining the public worship of God among themselves? Did they not use all the means in their power to civilize and Christianize the native savages? Did they not lay broad and permanent foundations for the promotion of religion and the diffusion of Christian knowledge to the latest generations? In a word, was not our nation formed for religious purposes, founded on religious principles, and highly distinguished by religious advantages? And in this way did not God visibly set us apart as his own peculiar people? If we trace the uniform conduct of God towards us, from the day our forefathers landed on these inhospitable shores to the present moment, it will appear that he has done more to raise us up, to preserve and deliver us, to make us holy and happy, and to fit us for his service in building up his kingdom, than he has done for any other nation since the Christian era. And notwithstanding our present degeneracy in morals and religion, we even now appear in the eyes of all the world, as God's peculiar and favorite people. I proceed as proposed.

II. To show what ground we have to hope that God will not forsake us.

It appears from the preceding observations, that he has done a great deal to form us for himself. He separated the founders of our nation from their friends and from their country. He carried them through the dangers of the sea, and planted them here in a howling wilderness. He protected them amidst savage foes, and guarded them against foreign

---

[58] Chaldea is a land in southern Babylonia.
[59] Cf. Num. 33.55.

enemies. He granted them great and peculiar religious advantages. He enlarged their borders, increased their numbers, and caused them to grow up into a large and wealthy people. He carried them through a long and dangerous war, and finally made them a free, separate, independent nation. For almost two centuries he has been forming and owning us as his peculiar people. And does not this give us ground to hope that he will not forsake us? Can we suppose that he would spend so much time and employ so many means to make us his peculiar people, without some wise and weighty reasons? And whatever those reasons were, can we suppose that they will permit him to forsake us until he has completely answered his purposes? We may safely reason in the language of the text, "The Lord will not forsake us, for his great name's sake: because it hath pleased the Lord to make us his people."[60] Here, then, to give this argument its full force, I would observe,

1. God will not forsake us, because he loved and respected our fathers. His peculiar regard to them was one motive for making us his peculiar people. [...] They were men of extraordinary piety and devotion, and made religion their main business. They called upon God in season, and out of season, and presented ten thousand petitions to the throne of divine grace, for their nearest and remotest posterity. As the effectual, fervent prayers of such righteous men must have been pleasing to God, so they give us ground to hope that he will long remember our land, and not forsake the children of those whom he delighted to love.

2. We are encouraged to hope that God will not forsake us, because he loves the pious posterity of our pious ancestors. God often spared the whole Jewish nation for the sake of those pious individuals who remained heartily attached to his cause and his interest. [...] If God was pleased to spare his ancient people for the sake of eminent saints, why will he not spare our guilty nation for the sake of men of the same excellent character? Notwithstanding our great degeneracy, there are undoubtedly many thousands of sincere friends to God in our land, who are heartily engaged to maintain not only the form, but the power and spirit of religion. These are, at present, the ornaments of our churches and the defence of our country. And as long as a succession of these godly men shall remain, we have reason to hope that the Lord will spare us from national ruin.

3. We may confidently hope not to be forsaken by God, because he may still answer very important purposes, by preserving and treating us as his peculiar people. One end may be, to make it appear to the world that he is able to protect a nation whom he has set apart for himself, against their most powerful and subtle enemies. [...]

But there is another important end which God may answer, by continuing us his peculiar people: and that is, to maintain the true religion in the world, whilst it is visibly expiring among all other nations. God was pleased to preserve the Jews two thousand years, for the purpose of maintaining the true religion amidst the errors and corruptions which had overspread the world. During that long period of darkness, they were the only people on earth who retained the true worship of God, and safely preserved the sacred books of divine inspiration. Had they been destroyed before the Messiah came, the light of divine truth might have been totally extinguished. So, unless it please God to continue us his peculiar people, it seems that the light of the gospel and the means of religion may be, in a few years, entirely lost. Pagan idolatry and Mohammedan superstition have long excluded Christianity from Asia and Africa. Atheism, deism, and every species of infidelity are rapidly prevailing in Europe, and involving the most enlightened nations in all the

---

[60] 1 Sam. 12.22.

horrors of moral darkness. America, therefore, seems to be the only place where the church can live, and religion maintain its ground. Here the laws of the land, as well as the education and habits of the people, are in favor of Christianity. [...] This is certainly a very important end to be answered by our preservation. And as long as God can promote his own glory and the interests of his kingdom, by our instrumentality, we may safely conclude he will not give us up to national ruin. Or, to use the language of the text, we have good ground to hope "the Lord will not forsake us, for his great name's sake: because it hath pleased the Lord to make us his people."

Let me now apply this leading sentiment agreeably to the design of the day, and the present state of our religion and government.

1. If God will continue to own us as his peculiar people, then we may confide in his wisdom and goodness, to defeat the designs of those, who attempt to destroy our national peace and prosperity. We are greatly exposed to foes without and to foes within. The European nations are fiercely engaged in war, and seem determined to draw us into their fatal contentions. They have for years been using every political art and intrigue, to undermine our religion and government. And though their designs have been detected and opposed, yet they have succeeded so far as to poison our sentiments, to distract our councils, to injure our commerce, and to diminish the strength of the nation. These evils, great in themselves, are greatly enhanced by our present state of doubtful expectation, whether a professed infidel, or a professed Christian, will be raised to the first seat of our general government. But if the God of our fathers be our God, then we may justly expect, that he will in due time dissipate the dark clouds which are gathering over us, and prevent the ruin with which we are threatened. He can and will protect his own people against the united opposition of the whole world. He has the hearts, and tongues, and pens of our enemies in his power, and can either mediately or immediately counteract all their malignant effects. He can open our eyes to see the danger of civil and religious delusions, and cause us to pursue our true interests, in opposition to all foreign influence. In such a divine protector we may safely confide. But we have no ground to trust in ourselves; for abundant evidence has been exhibited in the course of a few years, that we are as liable to imbibe infidelity, and atheism, and to run into anarchy and confusion, as the nations of Europe. If God should forsake us, we should soon be destroyed by others, or destroy ourselves. But yet we have great encouragement to hope, that while he is making a full end of other nations, he will not make a full end of us, because he has been pleased to make us his people.

2. If God will not forsake us, then he will enlarge us, and make us an exceedingly great and flourishing nation. He made his ancient people extremely numerous, rich, and powerful. [...] And if God will not forsake our nation, but only treat us in time to come as he has done in times past, we shall soon rise superior to every other kingdom on earth in numbers, in wealth, in strength, and in every thing that human power and art can effect. If our present enterprising spirit continues to operate, and the smiles of Heaven continue to attend our vigorous exertions, we shall in a very short time have the possession and dominion of this whole western world. It seems to be the design of Providence to diminish other nations, and to increase and strengthen ours. The nations of Europe are destroying one another by millions year after year; and though they may cease hostilities for a season, yet there is no prospect of their establishing permanent peace. Their corrupt sentiments in religion and morals, and their disorganizing principles in politics, will naturally increase their discords and contentions, and gradually prepare them for final ruin.

One war after another will probably "gather them to the battle of that great day of God Almighty."[61] Hence there is great reason to believe that God is about to transfer the empire of the world from Europe to America, where he has planted his peculiar people. And should this be the design of Heaven, we shall undoubtedly continue to spread and increase until we become the most numerous and powerful nation on earth.

3. If God will not forsake us, but own us as his peculiar people, then it is to be expected that he will take effectual care to maintain the cause of religion among us. This will be necessary to promote our prosperity, and to prepare us to answer his chief design in making us his peculiar people. The cause of religion is now in a languishing state. The number is small who publicly appear on the Lord's side, and the number is still smaller who are warmly attached to the interests of his kingdom. The worship of God in public and in private is much neglected. The holy sabbath is openly abused and boldly profaned. The important doctrines of the gospel are greatly disrelished, disputed, and opposed. Atheism, deism, infidelity, and every species of moral corruption, are pouring in upon us from every quarter. All these causes are unitedly operating to extinguish the light of divine truth, and to throw us into more than pagan darkness. But if God means to acknowledge us as his peculiar people, he will maintain and revive his sinking cause among us. He treated his peculiar people of old in this manner. [...] He has raised up many pious rulers and faithful ministers among us, and often poured out his Spirit in great abundance. He has lately revived religion in one place and another, and made large additions to some of our churches. And there is reason to believe that he will continue to pour out his Spirit in still larger and larger effusions, until the latter-day glory shall commence in this western world. Notwithstanding, therefore, the present triumph of vice and infidelity, we may confidently hope that our churches will live, increase, and flourish, till the end of time. This God will do for us, for his great name's sake.

4. If God intends to own and build us up as his favorite people, then he has much for us to do, in carrying into execution his gracious designs. This is probably the last peculiar people which he means to form, and the last great empire which he means to erect, before the kingdoms of this world are absorbed in the kingdom of Christ. And if he intends to bring about these great events, he will undoubtedly make use of human exertions. Though in former ages he employed miracles to effect his purposes, yet he now carries on all his designs by the instrumentality of second causes. Hence we have no ground to expect to be made a great and happy people without our own labor and exertions. [...] The world is in arms and opposed to our national prosperity and existence. We must, therefore, like the Israelites, fight our way to empire, in opposition to the power, and policy, and disorganizing principles of the most formidable nations on earth. And it is much to be feared that while we have wars without, we shall have fightings within, and alternately experience the dreadful calamities of despotism, anarchy, and confusion. [...] It is to be expected that bolder attacks will be made upon our civil and religious privileges, by those who are bent upon banishing all religion and government from the earth, whenever they can get more power into their hands. And it is evident their power is at present increasing; and it will certainly continue to increase, unless the most wise and vigorous measures are pursued to restrain it. God is now loudly proclaiming that we have much to do to maintain his cause, and promote his designs, in opposition to his and our enemies. [...]

---

[61] Rev. 14.16.

The goodness of God to us his favorite people, demands our confidence as well as our gratitude. Since he has never forsaken us, but always appeared on our side, when men rose up against us, we ought to confide in his care and protection, in these perilous times. We may be assured, that he will not give us up to ruin, as long as his own glory requires our existence and prosperity. Though he may try us and chastise us for our deep declensions,[62] yet he will in due time interpose for our relief and deliverance. He seems to have permitted our enemies to push their schemes and disclose their designs too fast, on purpose to open our eyes to see the destructive nature of their vain philosophy, which threatens the subversion of our laws and religion. And their unhallowed zeal has actually alarmed not only the virtuous part of our nation, but even many who were inclining to the cause of infidelity. Those of this last description begin to believe and acknowledge that the principles of virtue and piety are essential to our political safety and happiness. It is easy to see that God may make use of civil and religious delusions, to establish the principles of true religion and good government. And it is our duty, at this day, to place an unshaken confidence in him, to bring light out of darkness, truth out of error, and order out of confusion. Let all ranks and classes of men feel their dependence on God, and place their ultimate dependence on his almighty protection. While all the powers of darkness are seeking their ruin, in God there is perfect safety. Our fathers trusted in him and were delivered. And the pious Psalmist exhorts every class of people to trust in God, with full confidence of his presence and protection, in the midst of national calamities. [...]

But faith without works is dead. Confidence in God, without proper exertions, is presumption. We shall incur his displeasure, if we hope for his peculiar favor without acting as his peculiar people. We have no ground to expect that God will afford us his peculiar assistance, unless we use all the means in our power to defend ourselves. And these we have great encouragement to use. The object to be attained is of vast magnitude; nothing less than the preservation of a nation, destined to be the ornament and admiration of the world, and the seat of virtue, piety, and happiness. Let us, therefore, take courage, and with united ardor and zeal, repel every weapon formed and pointed against us. If we would promote the great ends for which it hath pleased the Lord to raise us up and set us apart for himself, we must avoid all unnecessary intercourse and connections with those apostate and infidel nations who are aiming to corrupt and destroy us. We must feel and express a proper detestation of their religious and political delusions. We must guard the rising generation against their vain philosophy and destructive sentiments in morals, religion, and government. We must maintain a warm and persevering attachment to our own excellent religious and political institutions. We must be careful to fill our churches, our legislatures, our courts, and all our public and private schools, with men of sound principles in morals and religion. We must learn to distinguish good government from tyranny on the one hand, and from that liberty which is licentiousness, on the other. We must imbibe the spirit and follow the example of our pious ancestors, who were no less engaged to promote the purity and prosperity of the church, than the safety and happiness of the state. Our first and principal exertions are to be made in support of religion; which is the only basis that can support our free and efficient government, and which is the only thing that can properly denominate us the peculiar people of God.

---

[62] The process or state of sinking into a lower or inferior condition; gradual diminution, deterioration; decline.

And while we are sincerely engaged to promote his cause, we may sincerely and fervently pray that his blessing may attend our exertions. We have always found him a prayer-hearing God. For "what nation is there so great, who hath had God so nigh unto them, as the Lord our God has been in all things we have called upon him for?"[63] How often did our fathers fast and pray in the times of their distress! And how often did God hear and answer their requests! How often have their pious posterity imitated their pious example, and have found it not a vain thing to call upon God! Our late public deliverances have been evidently granted in answer to our public and united fastings and prayers. Let us now, therefore, carry all our own interests in subordination to the interests of Zion,[64] to the throne of divine grace, in the spirit and language of God's peculiar people. "Help us, O God of our salvation, for the glory of thy name; and deliver us, and purge away our sins, for thy name's sake. Wherefore should the heathen say, Where is their God? Let him be known among the heathen in our sight by the revenging of the blood of thy servants which is shed.– And render unto our neighbors sevenfold into their bosom their reproach wherewith they have reproached thee, O Lord. So we thy people and sheep of thy pasture will give thee thanks for ever: we will show forth thy praise to all generations."[65] Amen.

Source: Nathanael Emmons (1745-1840). "Sermon XI: God Never Forsakes His People." *The Works of Nathanael Emmons, D.D., Third Pastor of the Church in Franklin, Mass. With a Memoir of His Life*. 6 vols. Ed. Jacob Ide. Boston: Congregational Board, 1862, Vol. 5, 169-185.

144. Thomas Jefferson
"Inauguration Address – March 4, 1801"

Friends and Fellow Citizens: –

Called upon to undertake the duties of the first executive office of our country, I avail myself of the presence of that portion of my fellow citizens which is here assembled, to express my grateful thanks for the favor with which they have been pleased to look toward me, to declare a sincere consciousness that the task is above my talents, and that I approach it with those anxious and awful presentiments which the greatness of the charge and the weakness of my powers so justly inspire. A rising nation, spread over a wide and fruitful land, traversing all the seas with the rich productions of their industry, engaged in commerce with nations who feel power and forget right, advancing rapidly to destinies beyond the reach of mortal eye – when I contemplate these transcendent objects, and see the honor, the happiness, and the hopes of this beloved country committed to the issue and the auspices of this day, I shrink from the contemplation, and humble myself before the magnitude of the undertaking. Utterly indeed, should I despair, did not the presence of many whom I here see remind me, that in the other high authorities provided by our constitution, I shall find resources of wisdom, of virtue, and of zeal, on which to rely under all difficulties. To you, then, gentlemen, who are charged with the

---

[63] Deut. 4.7.
[64] In the Old Testament, the easternmost of the two hills of ancient Jerusalem. It was established by David as his royal capital. Although the name Zion is rare in the New Testament, it has been frequently used in Christian literature as a designation for the heavenly city or for the earthly city of Christian faith and fraternity.
[65] Ps. 79.9-10, 12-13.

sovereign functions of legislation, and to those associated with you, I look with encouragement for that guidance and support which may enable us to steer with safety the vessel in which we are all embarked amid the conflicting elements of a troubled world.

During the contest of opinion through which we have passed, the animation of discussion and of exertions has sometimes worn an aspect which might impose on strangers unused to think freely and to speak and to write what they think; but this being now decided by the voice of the nation, announced according to the rules of the constitution, all will, of course, arrange themselves under the will of the law, and unite in common efforts for the common good. All, too, will bear in mind this sacred principle, that though the will of the majority is in all cases to prevail, that will, to be rightful, must be reasonable; that the minority possess their equal rights, which equal laws must protect, and to violate which would be oppression. Let us, then, fellow citizens, unite with one heart and one mind. Let us restore to social intercourse that harmony and affection without which liberty and even life itself are but dreary things. And let us reflect that having banished from our land that religious intolerance under which mankind so long bled and suffered, we have yet gained little if we countenance a political intolerance as despotic, as wicked, and capable of as bitter and bloody persecutions. During the throes and convulsions of the ancient world, during the agonizing spasms of infuriated man, seeking through blood and slaughter his long-lost liberty, it was not wonderful that the agitation of the billows should reach even this distant and peaceful shore; that this should be more felt and feared by some and less by others; that this should divide opinions as to measures of safety. But every difference of opinion is not a difference of principle. We have called by different names brethren of the same principle. We are all republicans – we are federalists. If there be any among us who would wish to dissolve this Union or to change its republican form, let them stand undisturbed as monuments of the safety with which error of opinion may be tolerated where reason is left free to combat it. I know, indeed, that some honest men fear that a republican government cannot be strong; that this government is not strong enough. But would the honest patriot, in the full tide of successful experiment, abandon a government which has so far kept us free and firm, on the theoretic and visionary fear that this government, the world's best hope, may by possibility want energy to preserve itself? I trust not. I believe this, on the contrary, the strongest government on earth. I believe it is the only one where every man, at the call of the laws, would fly to the standard of the law, and would meet invasions of the public order as his own personal concern. Sometimes it is said that man cannot be trusted with the government of himself. Can he, then, be trusted with the government of others? Or have we found angels in the forms of kings to govern him? Let history answer this question.

Let us, then, with courage and confidence pursue our own federal and republican principles, our attachment to our union and representative government. Kindly separated by nature and a wide ocean from the exterminating havoc of one quarter of the globe; too high-minded to endure the degradations of the others; possessing a chosen country, with room enough for our descendants to the hundredth and thousandth generation; entertaining a due sense of our equal right to the use of our own faculties, to the acquisitions of our industry, to honor and confidence from our fellow citizens, resulting not from birth but from our actions and their sense of them; enlightened by a benign religion, professed, indeed, and practiced in various forms, yet all of them including honesty, truth, temperance, gratitude, and the love of man; acknowledging and adoring an overruling Providence, which by all its dispensations proves that it delights in the happiness of man here and his greater happiness hereafter; with all these blessings, what more is necessary to make us a happy and prosperous people? Still one thing more, fellow citizens – a wise and frugal government, which shall restrain men from injuring one another, which shall leave them otherwise free to regulate their own pursuits of industry and improvement, and shall not take from the mouth of labor the bread it has earned. This is the sum of good government, and this is necessary to close the circle of our felicities.

About to enter, fellow citizens, on the exercise of duties which comprehend everything dear and valuable to you, it is proper that you should understand what I deem the essential principles of our government, and consequently those which ought to shape its administration. I will compress them within the narrowest compass they will bear, stating the general principle, but not all its limitations. Equal and exact justice to all men, of whatever state or persuasion, religious or political; peace, commerce, and honest friendship, with all nations – entangling alliances with none; [...] freedom of religion; freedom of the press; freedom of person under the protection of the *habeas corpus*; and trial by juries impartially selected – these principles form the bright constellation which has gone before us, and guided our steps through an age of revolution and reformation. The wisdom of our sages and the blood of our heroes have been devoted to their attainment. They should be the creed of our political faith – the text of civil instruction – the touchstone by which to try the services of those we trust; and should we wander from them in moments of error or alarm, let us hasten to retrace our steps and to regain the road which alone leads to peace, liberty, and safety.

I repair, then, fellow citizens, to the post you have assigned me. With experience enough in subordinate offices to have seen the difficulties of this, the greatest of all, I have learned to expect that it will rarely fall to the lot of imperfect man to retire from this station with the reputation and the favor which bring him into it. Without pretensions to that high confidence reposed in our first and great revolutionary character, whose preëminent services had entitled him to the first place in his country's love, and destined for him the fairest page in the volume of faithful history, I ask so much confidence only as may give firmness and effect to the legal administration of your affairs. I shall often go wrong through defect of judgment. When right, I shall often be thought wrong by those whose positions will not command a view of the whole ground. I ask your indulgence for my own errors, which will never be intentional; and your support against the errors of others, who may condemn what they would not if seen in all its parts. The approbation implied by your suffrage is a consolation to me for the past; and my future solicitude will be to retain the good opinion of those who have bestowed it in advance, to conciliate that of others by doing them all the good in my power, and to be instrumental to the happiness and freedom of all.

Relying, then, on the patronage of your good will, I advance with obedience to the work, ready to retire from it whenever you become sensible how much better choice it is in your power to make. And may that Infinite Power which rules the destinies of the universe, lead our councils to what is best, and give them a favorable issue for your peace and prosperity.

Source: Thomas Jefferson (1743-1826). "Inauguration Address – March 4, 1801." *The Writings of Thomas Jefferson: Being His Autobiography, Correspondence, Reports, Messages, Addresses, and Other Writings, Official and Private*. 9 vols. Ed. H.A. Washington. New York: J.C. Riker/Washington, D.C.: Taylor & Maury, 1856, Vol. 8, 1-5.

145. *The Altar of Gallic Despotism* (1800)

Source: *The Providential Detection*. Broadside 1800. Courtesy Library Company of Philadelphia.

146. *Mad Tom in a Rage* (1802)

Source: *Mad Tom in a Rage*. Federalist cartoon, 1802 [showing Thomas Jefferson and the Devil in their attempt at bringing down the pillar of the federal government erected by George Washington and John Adams]. Courtesy Huntington Library. The texts in the balloons read: "Pull away. Pull away my Son, don't fear. I'll give you all my assistance." "Oh! I fear it is stronger rooted then I expected but with the assistance of my Old Friend & a little more Brandy I will bring it down."

147. Thomas Green Fessenden
"Almighty Power: An Ode"[66] (1806)

Almighty Power! – The One Supreme!
    Our souls inspire, attune our lays
With hearts as solemn as our theme,
    To sing hosannas to thy praise!
Then, while we swell the sacred song,
    And bid the pealing anthem rise,
May seraphim the strain prolong,
    And hymns of glory fill the skies.
Thy word omnific form'd this earth,
    Ere time began revolving years –
Thy fiat gave to nature birth,
    And tuned to harmony the spheres.
When stern oppression's iron hand,
    Our pious fathers forced to roam,
And o'er the wild wave seek the land
    Where freedom rears her hallow'd dome –
When tempests howl'd, and o'er the main,
    Pale horror rear'd his haggard form;
Thou didst the fragile bark sustain
    To stem the fury of the storm!
[When savage hordes, from wilds immense,
    Raised the shrill war-whoops frantic yell,
Thine arm made bare in our defence,
    Dispersed the gloomy hosts of hell!][67]
Thou bad'st the wilderness disclose
    The varied sweets of vernal bloom –
The desert blossom'd like the rose,
    And breathed Arabia's rich perfume!
Look down from heaven's empyreal height,
    And gild with smiles this happy day;
Send us some chosen Son of Light
    Our feet to guide in wisdom's way.
The sons of faction strike with awe,
    And hush the din of party rage,
That Liberty, secured by Law,
    May realize a golden age.
On those thy choicest blessings shower
    To whom the cares of State are given;

---

[66] This ode was written to the music of an anthem, previously composed for other words, by Oliver Holden, Esq. Charlestown, Mass., a gentleman eminent for his musical talents, and sung during divine service, at the anniversary of Vermont General Election.
[67] This stanza was included in an early version of the poem that was reprinted in *Specimens of American Poetry*. Ed. Samuel Kettell. 3 vols. Boston: Goodrich & Co., 1829, Vol. 2, 117-118.

> May Justice wield the sword of power,
> Till Earth's the miniature of Heaven!

Source: Thomas Green Fessenden, Esq. (1771-1837). "Almighty Power: An Ode." *Original Poems*. Philadelphia: E. Bronson, 1806, 8-10.

148. John Howard Payne
"Ode: For the Thirty-First Anniversary of American Independence" (1807)

> Written as a College Exercise.
>
> When erst our Sires their sails unfurl'd,
>   To brave the trackless sea,
> They boldly sought an unknown world,
>   Determin'd to be free!
> They saw their homes recede afar,
>   The pale blue hills diverge,
> And, Liberty their guiding star,
>   They plough'd the swelling surge!
>
> No splendid hope their wand'rings cheer'd;
>   No lust of wealth beguiled; –
> They left the towers that Plenty rear'd
>   To seek the desert wild;
> The climes where proud luxuriance shone
>   Exchang'd for forests drear;
> The splendor of a Tyrant's throne
>   For honest Freedom here!
>
> Though hungry wolves the nightly prowl
>   Around their log-hut took;
> Though savages with hideous howl
>   Their wild-wood shelter shook;
> Though tomahawks around them glared, –
>   To Fear could such hearts yield?
> No! GOD, for whom they danger dared,
>   In danger was their shield!
>
> When giant Power, with blood-stain'd crest,
>   Here grasp'd his gory lance,
> And dared the warriors of the West
>   Embattled to advance, –
> Our young COLUMBIA sprang, alone
>   (In God her only trust),
> And humbled, with a sling and stone,
>   This monster to the dust!

Thus nobly rose our greater Rome,
   Bright daughter of the skies –
Of Liberty the hallow'd home,
   Whose turrets proudly rise, –
Whose sails now whiten every sea,
   On every wave unfurl'd;
Form'd to be happy, great, and free,
   The Eden of the world!

Shall we, the sons of valiant Sires,
   Such glories tamely stain?
Shall these rich vales, these splendid spires,
   E'er brook a Monarch's reign?
No! If the Despot's iron hand
   Must here a sceptre wave,
Raz'd be those glories from the land,
   And be the land our grave!

Source: John Howard Payne (1791-1852). "Ode for the Thirty-First Anniversary of American Independence." *John Howard Payne, Dramatist, Poet, Actor, and Author of Home, Sweet Home! His Life and Writings*. Ed. Gabriel Harrison. Rev. ed. Philadelphia: J.B. Lippincott, 1885, 303-304.

149. John Quincy Adams
An Oration Delivered at Plymouth, December 22, 1802. At the Anniversary Commemoration of the First Landing of Our Ancestors at That Place

Among the sentiments of most powerful operation upon the human heart, and most highly honorable to the human character, are those of veneration for our forefathers, and of love for our posterity. They form the connecting links between the selfish and the social passions. By the fundamental principle of christianity the happiness of the individual is interwoven by innumerable and imperceptible ties with that of his cotemporaries: by the power of filial reverence and parental affection, individual existence is extended beyond the limits of individual life, and the happiness of every age is chained in mutual dependence upon that of every other. Respect for his ancestors excites in the breast of man, interest in their history, attachment to their characters, concern for their errors, involuntary pride in their virtues. Love for his posterity spurs him to exertion for their support, stimulates him to virtue for their example, and fills him with the tenderest solicitude for their welfare. [...]

The revolutions of time furnish no previous example of a nation, shooting up to maturity and expanding into greatness with the rapidity which has characterized the growth of the American people. In the luxuriance of youth and in the vigor of manhood it is pleasing and instructive to look backwards upon the helpless days of infancy: but in the continual and essential changes of a growing subject, the transactions of that early period would be soon obliterated from the memory, but for some periodical call of attention to aid the silent records of the historian. Such celebrations arouse and gratify the kindliest emotions of the bosom. They are faithful pledges of the respect we bear to the memory of our ancestors and of the tenderness with which we cherish the rising generation. They introduce the sages and heroes of ages past to the notice and emulation of succeeding times: they are at once testimonials of our gratitude, and schools of virtue to our children.

These sentiments are wise – they are honorable – they are virtuous – their cultivation is not merely innocent pleasure, it is incumbent duty. Obedient to their dictates, you my fellow-citizens have instituted and paid frequent observance to this annual solemnity. And what event of weightier intrinsic importance or of more extensive consequences was ever selected for this honorary distinction?

In reverting to the period of their origin, other nations have generally been compelled to plunge into the chaos of impenetrable antiquity, or to trace a lawless ancestry into the caverns of ravishers and robbers. It is your peculiar privilege to commemorate in this birth-day of your nation, an event ascertained in its minutest details: an event of which the principal actors are known to you familiarly as if belonging to your own age: an event of a magnitude before which Imagination shrinks at the imperfection of her powers. It is your further happiness to behold in those eminent characters who were most conspicuous in accomplishing the settlement of your country, men upon whose virtues you can dwell with honest exultation. [...] Theirs was the gentle temper of christian kindness – the rigorous observance of reciprocal justice – the unconquerable soul of conscious integrity. Worldly Fame has been parsimonious[68] of her favors to the memory of those generous champions. [...]

[...] Let it be then our present occupation to [...] examine with reiterated care and minute attention, the characters of those men who gave the first impulse to a new series of events in the history of the world. – To applaud and emulate those qualities of their minds which we shall find deserving of our admiration. – To recognize with candour those features which forbid approbation or even require censure, and finally, to lay alike their frailties and their perfections to our own hearts either as warning or as example.

Of the various European settlements upon this continent which have finally merged in one independent nation, the first establishments were made at various times, by several nations and under the influence of different motives. In many instances the convictions of religious obligation formed one and a powerful inducement of the adventurers; but in none, excepting the settlement at Plymouth, did they constitute the sole and exclusive actuating cause. Worldly interest and commercial speculation entered largely into the views of other settlers: but the commands of conscience were the only stimulus to the emigrants from Leyden. [...]

[...] Venerated shades of our forefathers! No! ye were indeed not ordinary men! That country which had ejected you so cruelly from her bosom, you still delighted to contemplate in the character of an affectionate and beloved mother. The sacred bond which knit you together was indissoluble while you lived – and oh! may it be to your descend[a]nts the example and the pledge of harmony to the latest period of time! The difficulties and dangers which so often had defeated attempts of similar establishments were unable to subdue souls tempered like yours. You heard the rigid interdictions – you saw the menacing forms of toil and danger, forbidding your access to this land of promise: but you heard without dismay – you saw and disdained retreat. Firm and undaunted in the confidence of that sacred bond – Conscious of the purity, and convinced of the importance of your motives, you put your trust in the protecting shield of Providence, and smiled defi-

---

[68] Careful in the use of money or resources.

ance at the combining terrors of human malice and of elemental strife. These, in the accomplishment of your undertaking, you were summoned to encounter in their most hideous forms: these you met with that fortitude, and combated with that perseverance which you had promised in their anticipation: these you completely vanquished in establishing the foundations of New-England, and the day which we now commemorate is the perpetual memorial of your triumph. [...]

No European settlement ever formed upon this continent has been more distinguished for undeviating kindness and equity towards the savages. There are indeed moralists, who have questioned the right of the Europeans to intrude upon the possessions of the aboriginals in any case, and under any limitations whatsoever. But have they maturely considered the whole subject? The Indian right of possession itself stands with regard to the greatest part of the country, upon a questionable foundation. Their cultivated fields; their constructed habitations; a space of ample sufficiency for their subsistence, and whatever they had annexed to themselves by personal labor, was undoubtedly by the laws of nature theirs. But what is the right of a huntsman to the forest of a thousand miles over which he has accidentally ranged in quest of prey? Shall the liberal bounties of Providence to the race of man be monopolized by one of ten thousand for whom they were created? Shall the exuberant bosom of the common mother, amply adequate to the nourishment of millions, be claimed exclusively by a few hundreds of her offspring? Shall the lordly savage not only disdain the virtues and enjoyments of civilization himself, but shall he controul the civilization of a world? Shall he forbid the wilderness to blossom like the rose? Shall he forbid the oaks of the forest to fall before the axe of industry, and rise again, transformed into the habitations of ease and elegance? Shall he doom an immense region of the globe to perpetual desolation, and to hear the howlings of the tyger and the wolf, silence for ever the voice of human gladness? Shall the fields and the vallies, which a beneficent God has formed to teem with the life of innumerable multitudes, be condemned to everlasting barrenness? Shall the mighty rivers poured out by the hands of nature, as channels of communication between numerous nations, roll their waters in sullen silence and eternal solitude to the deep? Have hundreds of commodious harbours, a thousand leagues of coast, and a boundless ocean been spread in the front of this land, and shall every purpose of utility to which they could apply be prohibited by the tenant of the woods? No, generous philanthropists! Heaven has not been thus inconsistent in the works of its hands! Heaven has not thus placed at irreconcileable strife, its moral laws with its physical creation! The Pilgrims of Plymouth obtained their right of possession to the territory on which they settled by titles as fair and unequivocal as any human property can be held. By their voluntary association they recognized their allegiance to the government of Britain; and in process of time received whatever powers and authorities could be conferred upon them by a Charter from their Sovereign. The spot on which they fixed had belonged to an Indian tribe, totally extirpated by that devouring pestilence which had swept the country, shortly before their arrival. The territory thus free from all exclusive possession, they might have taken by the natural right of occupancy. Desirous however of giving ample satisfaction to every pretence of prior right, by formal and solemn conventions with the chiefs of the neighboring tribes, they acquired the further security of a purchase. At their hands the children of the desert had no cause of complaint. On the great day of retribution, what thousands, what millions of the American race will appear at the bar of judgment to arraign their European invading conquerors! Let us humbly hope that the fathers of the Plymouth Colony will then appear in the whiteness of innocence. Let us indulge the belief that they will not only be free from all accusation of injustice to these unfortunate sons of nature, but that the testimonials of their acts of kindness and benevolence towards them will plead the cause of their virtues as they are now authenticated by the records of history upon earth.

Religious discord has lost her sting: the cumbrous weapons of theological warfare are antiquated: the field of politics supplies the alchymists of our times, with materials of more fatal explosion, and the butchers of mankind no longer travel to another world for instruments of cruelty and destruction. Our age is too enlightened to contend upon topics, which concern only the interests of eternity; and men who hold in proper contempt all controversies about trifles, except such as inflame their own passions, have made it a common-place censure against your ancestors, that their zeal was enkindled by subjects of trivial importance; and that however aggrieved by the intolerance of others, they were alike intolerant themselves. Against these objections, your candid judgment will not require an unqualified justification; but your respect and gratitude for the founders of the state may boldly claim an ample apology. The original grounds of their separation from the church of England, were not objects of a magnitude to dissolve the bonds of communion – much less those of charity, between christian bretheren of the same essential principles. Some of them however were not inconsiderable, and numerous inducements concurred to give them an extraordinary interest in their eyes. [...] Viewing their religious liberties here, as held only upon sufferance, yet bound to them by all the ties of conviction, and by all their sufferings for them, could they forbear to look upon every dissenter among themselves with a jealous eye? Within two years after their landing they beheld a rival settlement[69] attempted in their immediate neighbourhood; and not long after the laws of self preservation compelled them to break up a nest of revellers,[70] who boasted of protection from the mother country, and who had recurred to the easy but pernicious resource of feeding their wanton idleness by furnishing the savages with the means, the skill and the instruments of European destruction. Toleration in that instance would have been self-murder, and many other examples might be alleged in which their necessary measures of self-defence have been exaggerated into cruelty, and their most indispens[a]ble precautions distorted into persecution. Yet shall we not pretend that they were exempt from the common laws of mortality, or entirely free from all the errors of their age. Their zeal might sometimes be too ardent, but it was always sincere. At this day religious indulgence is one of our clearest duties, because it is one of our undisputed rights. While we rejoice that the principles of genuine christianity have so far triumphed over the prejudices of a former generation, let us fervently hope for the day when it will prove equally victorious over the malignant passions of our own.

[...] Two centuries have not yet elapsed since the first European foot touched the soil which now constitutes the American union – Two centuries more and our numbers must exceed those of Europe herself. The destinies of this empire, as they appear in prospect before us, disdain the powers of human calculation. Yet, as the original founder of the Roman State is said once to have lifted upon his shoulders the fame and fortunes of all his posterity, so let us never forget that the glory and greatness of all our descendants is in our hands. Preserve in all their purity, refine if possible from all their alloy,[71] those

---

[69] Original footnote: "*Weston's* Plantation at Wessagusset."
[70] Original footnote: "*Morton*, and his party at Mount Wollaston."
[71] A mixture with a base metal, something that lowers value or purity.

virtues which we this day commemorate as the ornament of our forefathers – Adhere to them with inflexible resolution, as to the horns of the altar; instill them with unwearied perseverance into the minds of your children; bind your souls and theirs to the national union as the chords of life are centred in the heart, and you shall soar with rapid and steady wing to the summit of human glory. Nearly a century ago, one of those rare minds[72] to whom it is given to discern future greatness in its seminal principles, upon contemplating the situation of this continent, pronounced in a vein of poetic inspiration,

"Westward the Star of empire takes its way."

Let us all unite in ardent supplications to the founder of nations and the builder of worlds, that what then was prophecy may continue unfolding into history – that the dearest hopes of the human race may not be extinguished in disappointment, and that the last may prove the noblest empire of time.

Source: John Quincy Adams (1767-1848), *An Oration Delivered at Plymouth, December 22, 1802. At the Anniversary Commemoration of the First Landing of Our Ancestors at That Place*. Boston: Russell and Cutler, 1802, 5-12, 15-16, 22-26, 28-31.

---

[72] Original footnote: "Bishop *Berkeley*."

150. Benjamin Tanner
America Guided by Wisdom (1815)

Source: Benjamin Tanner (1775-1848). *America Guided by Wisdom: An Allegorical Representation of the United States Denoting Their Independence and Prosperity* (engraving after a drawing by John J. Barrralet, 1815). Courtesy Library of Congress.

151. Hugh Swinton Legaré
An Oration, Delivered on the Fourth of July, 1823

CICERO begins a celebrated oration by congratulating himself upon the felicity of his subject [...]. For the occasion required him to dwell upon the virtues and achievments of the great POMPEY[73] – a man, who had been from his earliest youth, identified with the glory of his country [...] and under whose auspices, "victory flew with her eagles" from Lusitania[74] to Caucasus and the Euphrates. But what would not the genius of the Roman orator, who found so much scope for the amplifications of his unrivalled eloquence, in the events of a single life, and the glory of a few campaigns, have made of a subject – so interesting in itself – so peculiarly affecting, and so dear to his auditors – so fertile, so various, so inspiring – as that to which he who now addresses you will have been indebted, for whatever of interest, or of attention it may be his good fortune to awaken? What were the exploits of a single individual, to the efforts of a whole people – heated with all the enthusiasm of a mighty contest, and rushing into the battles of Liberty, under the impulses of a patriotism, the most heroic and self-devoting? What were the victories of POMPEY – to the united ach[ie]vements of our Washingtons and Montgomeries and Greenes – our Franklins and Jeffersons and Adams' and La[ur]ens'[75] – of the Senate of Sages, whose wisdom conducted – of the band of warriors, whose valour accomplished – of the "noble army of martyrs" whose blood, sealed and consecrated, the Revolution of '76? What were the events of a few campaigns – however brilliant and successful – [...] to an era that has fixed forever the destinies of a whole quarter of the globe, with the numbers without number that are soon to inhabit it, and has already had, as it will probably continue to have, a visible influence upon the condition of society in all the rest? Nay – shall I be accused of extravagance, if going still further I ask, what is there even in the most illustrious series of victories and conquests, that can justly be considered as affording to a mind that dares to make a philosophic estimate of human affairs, a nobler and more interesting subject of contemplation and discourse, than the causes which led to the foundation of this mighty empire – than the wonderful and almost incredible history of what it has since done and is already grown to – than the scene of unmingled prosperity and happiness that is opening and spreading all around us – than the prospect as dazzling as it is vast, that lies before us – the uncircumscribed career of aggrandizement and improvement which we are beginning to run under such happy auspices and with the advantage of having *started* at a point where it were well for the species had it been the lot of many nations even to have *ended* theirs.

It is true, we shall not boast to day that the pomp of triumph has three hundred times, ascended the steep of our capitol – or that the national temple upon its brow, blazes in the spoils of a thousand cities. True: we do not send forth our prætors[76] to plunder and

---

[73] Roman General (106-48 BC), the rival of Julius Caesar. Cf. Marcus Tullius Cicero (106-43 BC): "De imperio Cn. Pompei" (66 BC).
[74] Lusitania: Roman province on the Iberian Peninsula.
[75] George Washington (1732-1799), 1st president of the United States (1789-1797); Richard Montgomery (1738-1775), American Revolutionary general; Nathanael Greene (1742-1786), American Revolutionary general; Benjamin Franklin (1706-1790), American statesman, scientist, and writer; Thomas Jefferson (1743-1826), 3rd President of the United States (1801-1809); John Adams (1735-1826), 2nd President of the United States (1797-1801); John Laurens (1754-1782), American Revolutionary hero.
[76] In ancient Rome originally consuls, later magistrates (from c. 366 BC).

devastate, the most fertile and beautiful portions of the earth, in order that a haughty aristocracy may be enriched with booty, or a worthless populace be supplied with bread [...]. *Our* triumphs are the triumphs of *reason* – of happiness – of human nature. Our rejoicings are greeted with the most cordial sympathy of the cosmopolite and the philanthropist: and the good and the wise all round the globe give us back the echo of our acclamations. It is the singular fortune – or I should rather say – it is the proud distinction of Americans – it is what we are now met to return thanks for and to exult in – that in the race of moral improvement, which society has been every where running for some centuries past, we have outstript every competitor and have carried our institutions in the sober certainty of waking bliss, to a higher pitch of perfection than ever warmed the dreams of enthusiasm or the speculations of the theorist. It is that a whole continent has been set apart as if it were holy ground, for the cultivation of pure truth – for the pursuit of happiness upon rational principles, and in the way that is most agreeable to nature – for the developement of all the sensibilities, and capacities, and powers, of the human mind, without any artificial restraint or bias, in the broad day-light of modern science and political liberty. [...]

It has been usual on this occasion – as nothing certainly, can be more appropriate and natural – to expatiate upon the events of the revolutionary contest, and to honour in a suitable strain of panegyric,[77] such of the founders of the Republic as were supposed to have rendered it the most important services, at a crisis so full of peril and glory. But as these topics, however interesting in themselves, and eminently well fitted for the purposes of popular declamation, are become so trite that it would be difficult by any art of composition, to bestow upon them the graces of novelty, I have chosen rather to exhibit some of the *general features* – the great *leading characteristics* – by which, I conceive that memorable event to be distinguished from all others of a similar kind, that are recorded in the annals of empire. [...]

[... It was such heroes and tried champions of religious liberty], together with the unfortunate, the persecuted, the adventurous, the bold, the aspiring of all climes and conditions, congregated and confounded in one vast asylum, and exercised, by the hardships incident to the colonization of a new country, with a sort of Spartan discipline – that laid the foundations of those flourishing commonwealths, whose first united efforts are the subject of this commemoration. Is it wonderful that a nation composed of such elements and accustomed, too, to go on from one reform of abuses to another (for it is very important to observe, that the whole history of the colonies is a history of successive revolutions in their municipal government and administration, and it is only by a figure of speech that we confine that term exclusively to the declaration of independence) should have shown themselves, at once, so sensitive and so determined, in a contest in which their rights were so seriously concerned? [...]

But *another* most fortunate and striking peculiarity of the Revolution we are celebrating is, that it occurred in a NEW WORLD.

The importance that ought to be attached to this circumstance will be obvious to every one who will reflect, for a moment, upon the miracles which are exhibiting in the settlement of this country and the increase of its population. Behold how the pomœrium[78] of the republic advances in the wilderness of the West! See how empires are starting up

---

[77] A formal expression of praise.
[78] Sacred boundary of the ancient city of Rome.

into being, in periods of time, shorter even than the interval between infancy and manhood in the span allotted to the individuals that compose them! Contemplate the peaceful triumphs of industry – the rapid progress of cultivation – the diffusion of knowledge – the growth of populous cities, with all the arts that embellish life, and soften while they exalt the character of man – and think of the countless multitudes that are springing up to inherit these blessings! The three millions by whom our independence was achieved less than half a century ago, are already grown to *ten*, which in the course of another half century will have swelled up to *fifty*; and so on, with a continually accelerated progress, until, at no distant day, the language of MILTON[79] shall be spoken from shore to shore, over the vastest portion of this earth's surface, that was ever inhabited by a race worthy of speaking a language consecrated to Liberty. [...]

It is owing, then, to these circumstances that we find ourselves in a situation so novel and peculiar – so entirely unlike any of the antiquated and corrupt systems of the old world – so peaceful, so prosperous, so full of high hope, and unparalleled progression, and triumphant success. It looks almost like a special providence, that this continent was not revealed to mankind, until Europe was highly enlightened. It was then peopled not by her outcasts (as the first settlers have been sometimes called) but by men who were in more respects than one, the elect of the earth – circumstances favoured them in their new abode – every germ of excellence and improvement was fully developed and expanded – all the vices and redundances and defects produced, by accidental circumstances, in the institutions of older countries, were corrected and removed – the human race began a new career in a new universe, realizing the celebrated and prophetic lines of VIRGIL'S Pollio –

> Novus ab integro sœclorum nascitur ordo, &c.[80]

or, to borrow a most noble passage from one of the prose compositions of the first of poets and the first of *men* – the language in which MILTON himself has uttered a vision, inspired by his own holy zeal for social improvement, and the liberties of mankind – "methinks I see in my mind – a noble and puissant nation, rousing herself like a strong man after sleep, and shaking her invincible locks – methinks I see her as an eagle, mewing her mighty youth and kindling her undazzled eyes at the full mid-day beam, purging and unscaling her long abused sight at the fountain itself of heavenly radiance – while the whole noise of timorous and flocking birds, with those also that love the twilight, flutter about amazed at what she means."[81]

Such was that memorable epoch in the history of man, the Declaration of American Independence – such were the triumphs of the heroes and sages of '76 – such were the principles upon which they acted – such was the inheritance they bequeathed to us – such the example they set to the world. [... M]any ages of glory and freedom are before us – many nations shall learn, from our example, how to be free and great. The fortunes of the species, are thus, in some degree, identified with those of THE REPUBLIC – and if our experiment fail, there is no hope for man on this side of the grave. [...]

Source: Hugh S. Legaré (1797-1843). *An Oration, Delivered on the Fourth of July, 1823; before the '76 Association*. Charleston, SC: A.E. Miller, 1823, 5-9, 14-17, 20-21, 29.

---

[79] John Milton (1608-1674), English poet.
[80] Originally: "Magnus ab integro seclorum nascitur ordo" (Virgil's Eclogue IV,5): "The great series of ages begins anew."
[81] John Milton, *Areopagitica*, a treatise attacking the re-establishment of censorship of printed works in 1643.

152. John Quincy Adams
"Inaugural Address – March 4, 1825"

In compliance with an usage coeval with the existence of our Federal Constitution, and sanctioned by the example of my predecessors in the career upon which I am about to enter, I appear, my fellow-citizens, in your presence and in that of Heaven to bind myself by the solemnities of religious obligation to the faithful performance of the duties allotted to me in the station to which I have been called.

In unfolding to my countrymen the principles by which I shall be governed in the fulfillment of those duties my first resort will be to that Constitution which I shall swear to the best of my ability to preserve, protect, and defend. That revered instrument enumerates the powers and prescribes the duties of the Executive Magistrate, and in its first words declares the purposes to which these and the whole action of the Government instituted by it should be invariably and sacredly devoted – to form a more perfect union, establish justice, insure domestic tranquillity, provide for the common defense, promote the general welfare, and secure the blessings of liberty to the people of this Union in their successive generations. Since the adoption of this social compact one of these generations has passed away. It is the work of our forefathers. Administered by some of the most eminent men who contributed to its formation, through a most eventful period in the annals of the world, and through all the vicissitudes of peace and war incidental to the condition of associated man, it has not disappointed the hopes and aspirations of those illustrious benefactors of their age and nation. It has promoted the lasting welfare of that country so dear to us all; it has to an extent far beyond the ordinary lot of humanity secured the freedom and happiness of this people. We now receive it as a precious inheritance from those to whom we are indebted for its establishment, doubly bound by the examples which they have left us and by the blessings which we have enjoyed as the fruits of their labors to transmit the same unimpaired to the succeeding generation. [...]

Since [the 1770s] a population of four millions has multiplied to twelve. A territory bounded by the Mississippi has been extended from sea to sea. New States have been admitted to the Union in numbers nearly equal to those of the first Confederation. Treaties of peace, amity, and commerce have been concluded with the principal dominions of the earth. The people of other nations, inhabitants of regions acquired not by conquest, but by compact, have been united with us in the participation of our rights and duties, of our burdens and blessings. The forest has fallen by the ax of our woodsmen; the soil has been made to teem by the tillage of our farmers; our commerce has whitened every ocean. The dominion of man over physical nature has been extended by the invention of our artists. Liberty and law have marched hand in hand. All the purposes of human association have been accomplished as effectively as under any other government on the globe [...].

Such is the unexaggerated picture of our condition under a Constitution founded upon the republican principle of equal rights. To admit that this picture has its shades is but to say that it is still the condition of men upon earth. From evil – physical, moral, and political – it is not our claim to be exempt. We have suffered sometimes by the visitation of Heaven through disease; often by the wrongs and injustice of other nations, even to the extremities of war; and, lastly, by dissensions among ourselves – dissensions perhaps inseparable from the enjoyment of freedom, but which have more than once appeared to threaten the dissolution of the Union, and with it the overthrow of all the enjoyments of our present lot and all our earthly hopes of the future. The causes of these dissensions have been various, founded upon differences of speculation in the theory of republican government; upon conflicting views of policy in our relations with foreign nations; upon jealousies of partial and sectional interests, aggravated by prejudices and prepossessions which strangers to each other are ever apt to entertain.

It is a source of gratification and of encouragement to me to observe that the great result of this experiment upon the theory of human rights has at the close of that generation by which it was formed been crowned with success equal to the most sanguine expectations of its founders. Union, justice, tranquillity, the common defense, the general welfare, and the blessings of liberty – all have been promoted by the Government under which we have lived. Standing at this point of time, looking back to that generation which has gone by and forward to that which is advancing, we may at once indulge in grateful exultation and in cheering hope. From the experience of the past we derive instructive lessons for the future. Of the two great political parties which have divided the opinions and feelings of our country, the candid and the just will now admit that both have contributed splendid talents, spotless integrity, ardent patriotism, and disinterested sacrifices to the formation and administration of this Government, and that both have required a liberal indulgence for a portion of human infirmity and error. The revolutionary wars of Europe, commencing precisely at the moment when the Government of the United States first went into operation under this Constitution, excited a collision of sentiments and of sympathies which kindled all the passions and embittered the conflict of parties till the nation was involved in war and the Union was shaken to its center. This time of trial embraced a period of five and twenty years, during which the policy of the Union in its relations with Europe constituted the principal basis of our political divisions and the most arduous part of the action of our Federal Government. With the catastrophe in which the wars of the French Revolution terminated, and our own subsequent peace with Great Britain, this baneful weed of party strife was uprooted. From that time no difference of principle, connected either with the theory of government or with our intercourse with foreign nations, has existed or been called forth in force sufficient to sustain a continued combination of parties or to give more than wholesome animation to public sentiment or legislative debate. Our political creed is, without a dissenting voice that can be heard, that the will of the people is the source and the happiness of the people the end of all legitimate government upon earth. [...]

The collisions of party spirit which originate in speculative opinions or in different views of administrative policy are in their nature transitory. Those which are founded on geographical divisions, adverse interests of soil, climate, and modes of domestic life are more permanent, and therefore, perhaps, more dangerous. It is this which gives inestimable value to the character of our Government, at once federal and national. It holds out to us a perpetual admonition to preserve alike and with equal anxiety the rights of each individual State in its own government and the rights of the whole nation in that of the Union. [...] To respect the rights of the State governments is the inviolable duty of that of the Union; the government of every State will feel its own obligation to respect and preserve the rights of the whole. [...] The harmony of the nation is promoted and the whole Union is knit together by the sentiments of mutual respect, the habits of social intercourse, and the ties of personal friendship formed between the representatives of its several parts in the performance of their service at this metropolis. [...]

Fellow-citizens, you [...] have heard the exposition of the principles which will direct me in the fulfillment of the high and solemn trust imposed upon me in this station. Less possessed of your confidence in advance than any of my predecessors, I am deeply conscious of the prospect that I shall stand more and oftener in need of your indulgence. Intentions upright and pure, a heart devoted to the welfare of our country, and the unceasing application of all the faculties allotted to me to her service are all the pledges that I can give for the faithful performance of the arduous duties I am to undertake. To the guidance of the legislative councils, to the assistance of the executive and subordinate departments, to the friendly co-operation of the respective State governments, to the candid and liberal support of the people so far as it may be deserved by honest industry and zeal, I shall look for whatever success may attend my public service; and knowing that "except the Lord keep the city the watchman waketh but in vain,"[82] with fervent supplications for His favor, to His overruling providence I commit with humble but fearless confidence my own fate and the future destinies of my country.

Source: John Quincy Adams (1767-1848). "Inaugural Address – March 4, 1825." *The Selected Writings of John and John Quincy Adams.* Ed. Adrienne Koch and William Peden. New York: Knopf, 1946, 353-360.

153. James Gates Percival
"Ode. For the Fiftieth Anniversary of Independence, July 4, 1826"

Bring to this high and holy rite
A spirit worthy of our sires –
Still may their zeal, a guiding light,
Inform us with its noblest fires –
    This the day that saw them rise
    Bright, in glory, to the skies.

Then came they forth, a nation new,
To kindle and to warn a world;
Then high to heaven their eagle flew;
Defiance on their foe they hurled.
    Britons dared not call them slaves –
    Freedom flourished on their graves.

Be round us now, a sacred band;
Assist us, at the shrine ye raised;
Go fourth to animate our land,
Bright as at first your valour blazed.
    Fathers – Heroes – you we call;
    May your spirit grace us all.

---

[82] Cf. Ps. 127.1.

Look down from that sublime abode,
   Where now ye sit in high repose;
Fair are the battle fields ye trode;
   No more the tide of slaughter flows.
      Welcome, Peace – the boon is due,
      Full and glorious, all to you.

A few, an aged few remain,
   Your brethren in the war of death;
Their presence – be it not in vain –
   It stirs us with a quickening breath.
      Let us emulate our sires –
      Let us cherish long their fires.

O! gladly beats the veteran's heart
   To hail this holiest Jubilee;
Theirs was the noblest, proudest part,
   The toils that set a nation free.
      Now those generous toils are done;
      Liberty and peace are won.

The flame that warmed and waked their souls,
   Burns like a beacon on our hills;
Through all our favoured land it rolls;
   Bright is the heart it fires and fills.
      Still the watch-word sounds – be free:
      Still 'tis Death or Liberty.

Source: James Gates Percival (1795-1856). "Inaugural Address – March 4, 1825." James Gates Percival. *Clio* [No. III]. New York: G. and C. Carvill, 1827, 40-41.

EXPANSIONISM

In his novel *Moby-Dick*, published at the height of American expansionism in 1851, Herman Melville has his narrator Ishmael explain to his readers a principle of the whaling code, the concept of "Fast-Fish" and "Loose-Fish." What begins as a rendering of a professional consensus – "A Fast-Fish belongs to the party fast to it," and "A Loose-Fish is fair game for anybody who can soonest catch it" – then develops into a philosophical speculation about the precise meaning of "fast" and "loose": Is a whale still a Loose-Fish, for example, if a party has stuck a waif into it but subsequently abandoned it? Is it therefore fair game for anybody who happens to find it? And how is this whaling law applicable to the world at large: "What was America in 1492 but a Loose-Fish, in which Columbus struck the Spanish standard by way of waifing it for his royal master and mistress? What was Poland to the Czar? What Greece to the Turk? What India to England? What at last will Mexico be to the United States? All Loose-Fish."[1] Here as elsewhere in his "expansive" novel, Melville alludes to the political rhetoric and practice used during the period of American expansion, viewing it within a larger world-encompassing process of the imperial acquisition of new territories.

As a period, expansion extends throughout the nineteenth century, with a strong emphasis on the decades between 1830 (the era of the Indian Removal) and 1900 (with the recent completion of the 'imperial' Spanish-American War). But as the documents collected in this volume suggest, it is important to view expansion not merely as a period in American history but to recognize it as a particular philosophy of history as well. As an ideology, expansionism can be said to have been introduced to New England by the Puritans in its form of providentialism, a strongly felt mission of establishing in America the groundwork for a protestant model state (see sections "Providential Readings of American History" and "Early Conceptualizations of America," esp. doc. 17). Providentialism became reinforced and secularized by the rhetoric of the Founding Fathers and the early nationalist poets (Freneau, Dwight, Barlow), who regarded America as the culmination of a historical development reaching back to antiquity and who cast the notion of the westward course of empire (*translatio imperii*) into epic form (for a fusion of both strands, see, e.g., doc. 154, William Linn). The nineteenth century saw the partial realization of Thomas Jefferson's notion of the United States as an "empire for liberty" which would overspread the whole western hemisphere and eventually reach beyond the North American continent.

Historically, the period of continental growth covered by the documents in this section begins with the Louisiana Purchase of 1803. By way of this contract with France, the United States acquired for the sum of 15,000,000 US Dollars an area that extends from today's Montana to Louisiana and from Colorado to Minnesota. Practically over night the territory of the United States was increased by 140 per cent. After the withdrawal of France from continental America, the defeat of the British during the War of 1812 removed the only other major contender for territorial possessions in the northern part of the western hemisphere. The Indian Removal of the Jacksonian administration, which culminated in the so-called Trail of Tears – the mass-removal of the Cherokee to lands beyond the Mississippi – opened up all lands east of that river for settlement (see docs. 162-163). In spite of its sentimentalist justifications (Jackson), the event caused quite

---

[1] Herman Melville, *Moby-Dick*. Ed. Harrison Hayford and Hershel Parker. New York: Norton, 1967, 333-334.

some outrage both within the United States and in Europe, and forced American politicians like Lewis Cass to formulate long and circuitous explanations (doc. 161). The major remaining territorial acquisitions of the mid-nineteenth century consisted of the annexation of Texas under the presidency of James Polk in 1845 (see docs. 166-168, 171-172), the almost simultaneous reception of the Oregon territory from Britain by contract in 1846 (docs. 164-165), and the reception of the vast tract of land that fell to the United States as a result of the Mexican War of 1846-48 (today's California, Arizona, New Mexico, Utah and Nevada). Finally, Alaska was purchased from Russia in 1867, Hawaii annexed in 1895, and Puerto Rico won from Spain as a result of the Spanish-American War of 1898. By the end of the nineteenth century, then, the northern part of the American continent had come into full possession of the United States.

Rhetorically, this process was underpinned by a number of 'narratives', most of which can be traced back to earlier periods and mythical models. The predominant argument used in the political rhetoric represented here is the argument of history, of the "translation of empire," of the classical antecedents as models of present-day action. Historical determinism fused with the argument of "nature" – both as a philosophical principle on which the erection of the new nation was justified against the "unnatural" tyranny of Europe and as a geographical principle (see doc. 160, Thoreau). This fusion becomes apparent in the excerpt from Jedidiah Morse (doc. 154), who argues that the "God of nature" cannot have intended to leave such vast possessions in the hands of a potentate 4000 miles away. Successive acquisitions were frequently rationalized with the argument of the natural layout of the continent, which demanded that the whole northern part be subject to a unified political system. The same idea is contained in the Monroe Doctrine (1823) which held that Europe should attend to the affairs of the old world and leave the control of the American continent to the newly independent United States.

Next to the secular arguments based on history and nature – arguments that were reproduced, aestheticized, and rationalized, in the discourses of literary, historiographical and scientific romanticism – expansion continued to find justification in the notion of divine providence (e.g. doc. 180, "Editor's Table"), which by mid-century united with proto-Darwinistic accounts of the natural development of the human races to form the powerful ideologeme of "Manifest Destiny" (doc. 171, O'Sullivan 1845; cf. docs. 172-184). As is perhaps best illustrated by the excerpt from Thomas Hart Benton (doc. 177), race and the hierarchy of races became an important element in both the debates about slavery and about its expansion westward. With every new state's admission into the union, the debate about the equilibrium between free states and slave states flared up anew (see section "Slavery"). Other documents betray the influence of scientific racism on the political discourse about Indians and Mexicans. While Native Americans, including the so-called Five Civilized Tribes, were seen to be immutably frozen in the economic stage of the hunter and therefore doomed to extinction (see doc. 161, Cass), Mexicans were regarded as a 'degenerate' race due to their 'amalgamated' racial composition. As a mixed race, Mexicans were seen as fated to be overrun by the racially superior Anglo-Saxons, whose "blood" had already begun to be spilled on Mexican soil, calling out for retaliation (doc. 178 "The Destiny of the Country" and, for a continuation of the "blood" argument, doc. 184, Fiske). Next to the interest of introducing democracy to Mesoamerica, either by conquest or, as in the case of Texas, by admitting Mexican states into the union on the grounds of their settlers' request or consent (doc. 175, "The Popular Movement"), the United States was also interested in controlling the construction of a commercial route through the isthmus of Central America – either a railroad or a canal through Panama or Nicaragua – to facilitate the growing trade with Asia.

Some documents remind us that the arguments in favor of expansion, in spite of the popular appeal of the Manifest Destiny rhetoric, also excited critique and contradiction. The *Punch* cartoon "Land of Liberty" of 1847 (doc. 173) contrasts Americans' aggressive behaviour toward Africans and Mexicans with the principles of the Founding Fathers, here used by Uncle Sam as a footstool. Already in 1837, the abolitionist and social reformer William E. Channing opposed the ideology of Manifest Destiny and the annexation of Texas, arguing in favor of territorial "restraint" and comparing the present "career of acquisition and conquest" with the activities of "the late conqueror of Europe," Napoleon Bonaparte, who, Channing reminds his countrymen, was consigned by his "destiny" to "a lonely rock in the ocean" (doc. 167). And although the narrator of Herman Melville's novel *White-Jacket* (1850) announces himself as an advocate of expansion, Melville's next novel, *Moby-Dick*, can be seen as an extensive critique of America's imperial activities – a novel that anticipated, in the figure of the megalomaniac captain Ahab and in the image of the sinking Pequod, a gloomy outcome of expansionist enthusiasm.

Especially toward the end of the nineteenth-century, the Pacific Ocean gained importance in the public discourse of expansion. In his poem "Passage to India" (doc. 181), Walt Whitman celebrates the completion in 1869 of the two most important commercial links on a global scale, the Suez Canal and the transcontinental railroad. Whitman's poem reminds us that ever since the times of Jefferson and even Columbus, the ultimate aim of expansion was to find a navigable route to the markets of China. Hawaii, annexed in 1895, figured as an important entrepôt on that route. The American attack against the Philippines, as part of the Spanish-American War of 1898, may also be seen in this context. With that war, sparked by Cuba's rebellion against the colonial power of Spain, the expansionist century reaches its end. In spite of America's assistance to Cuba, the end of the war left one of America's most daring designs since the 1850s, possession of Cuba, unfulfilled (with the significant exception of temporary territorial rights to Guantánamo Bay).

In a famous speech, delivered at the World's Columbian Exposition at Chicago in 1893 and later published as "The Significance of the Frontier in American History" (doc. 185), Frederick Jackson Turner declared the frontier as "closed" while at the same time emphasizing its great mythical power in the forging of an American character and of American values such as democracy, individualism, inquisitiveness, inventiveness, and nervous restlessness, together with an inborn capacity of regenerating these character traits out of a continuous contest with the primitive forces of the wilderness. As the events of 1898 suggest, the closing of the continental frontier, encapsulated in the massacre of Wounded Knee of 1890 which demarcates the end of the Indian Wars, is not synonymous with the end of expansionism. In his essay "The Frontier Gone at Last" (doc. 187), the writer Frank Norris notes the persistence of the "energy" and the "desire" to move on, but he now sees trade as the primary field of American expansionist activities. With the perceptiveness of the wordsmith, Norris recognizes the militaristic semantics in the language of commerce, embedded in such terms as "commercial invasion," "trade war," the "capture of business," and "seized opportunities" (cf. section "Gilded Age"). As other writers before him, Norris evokes, in the middle of the materialistic "Gilded Age," the *humanistic* principles of expansion frequently suppressed by the ruling logic of material aggrandizement: the "true patriotism" that is to be found in the "brotherhood of man" and the true world empire of universal "humanity."

Gesa Mackenthun

154. Jedidiah Morse
The American Geography (1789)

[...] It is well known that empire has been travelling from east to west. Probably her last and broadest seat will be America. Here the sciences and the arts of civilized life are to receive their highest improvement. Here civil and religious liberty are to flourish, unchecked by the cruel hand of civil or ecclesiastical tyranny. Here Genius, aided by all the improvements of former ages, is to be exerted in humanizing mankind – in expanding and [e]nriching their minds with religious and philosophical knowledge, and in planning and executing a form of government, which shall involve all the excellencies of former governments, with as few of their defects as is consistent with the imperfection of human affairs, and which shall be calculated to protect and unite, in a manner consistent with the natural rights of mankind, the largest empire that ever existed. Elevated with these prospects, which are not merely the visions of fancy, we cannot but anticipate the period, as not far distant, when the AMERICAN EMPIRE will comprehend millions of souls, west of the Missis[s]ippi. Judging upon probable grounds, the Missis[s]ippi was never designed as the western boundary of the American empire. The God of nature never intended that some of the best part of his earth should be inhabited by the subjects of a monarch, 4000 miles from them. And may we not venture to predict, that, when the rights of mankind shall be more fully known, and the knowledge of them is fast increasing both in Europe and America, the power of European potentates will be confined to Europe, and their present American dominions, become, like the United States, free, sovereign and independent empires.

Source: Jedidiah Morse (1761-1826). *The American Geography*; or, *A View of the Present Situation of the United States of America*. Elizabethtown: Shepard Kollock, 1789, 469.

155. William Linn
The Blessings of America: A Sermon, Preached in the Middle Dutch Church, on the Fourth July, 1791

THE BLESSINGS OF AMERICA.
PSALM xvi. 6.
THE LINES ARE FALLEN UNTO ME IN PLEASANT PLACES; YEA, I HAVE A GOODLY HERITAGE.

In these words the Psalmist celebrates the agreeable and advantageous situation in which he was placed by Divine Providence. It was such as administered to his earthly comfort, and tended to promote his eternal welfare.

The like manner of expression may, with propriety, be used by every American; and it affords, on this auspicious day, a suitable and profitable subject for our meditation. [...]

Without incurring the charge of local prejudices, illiberal aspersions of others, or unreasonable partiality to ourselves, we may say, that our country is highly favored of God; that the *lines*, which measure our inheritance, *are fallen in pleasant places*; *yea*, that we *have a goodly heritage*. This will appear when we consider the natural advantages which we enjoy; the constitution of our civil government; and our religious privileges. Let us take a cursory view of each of these; and then attend to some reflections which the subject, together with the occasion, may inspire.

First, The natural advantages of our country are many and great. The territory is extensive, the soil luxuriant, the climates and productions various. We possess in abundance every thing necessary for our support, comfort and strength. [...]

In the diversity of the advantages which the States enjoy there is a resemblance to the division of the land of Canaan among the tribes of Israel. [...] He, whose *the sea is*, and whose *hands formed the dry land*, hath here lavished his bounty, and, as if on purpose, reserved the best for the latest discovery; he hath united, in this one, all the excellencies of the other parts of the earth.

Though much still remains to be done, yet the improvement of these advantages has been, for the time, uncommonly rapid. Less than two centuries ago, what was this now pleasant country? A dismal wilderness; the habitation of wild beasts, and of savage men. Where now the populous city lifts its spires, the solitary wigwam stood; where commerce spreads its sails, was seen the bark canoe; and where the sound of industry is heard, and all the arts of civilized life flourish, indolence, rudeness, and ignorance, held a gloomy reign. If our country has, so suddenly, risen into eminence, what may be expected when time has given it maturity, rendered its population complete, and called forth all its exertions? Then will it be rich, powerful, and happy. Then will *her wilderness* become *like Eden, and her desert like the garden of the Lord; joy and gladness shall be found therein, thanksgiving, and the voice of melody.*[2]

As we are not left to depend upon other countries for our necessaries and comforts, so our being removed at so great a distance from them, is no small advantage. We have thus, less temptation to invade, and are less liable to be invaded: we are in less danger of being infected with foreign vices, and involved in intrigues and wars. Happily, indeed, that desire of conquest, and love of domination, which have so long actuated the kingdoms of the world, and made man a scourge to man, do not actuate our nation. Separated, by Providence, from the continual jealousies, and bloody dissensions of the old world, our endeavour is, to cultivate every useful art, to enjoy in peace, the blessings which Heaven hath bestowed, and to extend them to all within our reach. This is a more noble ambition than Romans ever knew; a more just glory than to enlarge our dominion, or seek to build our advancement on the degradation of others.

It is cause of regret at this day, that the sword which has been sheathed, is now drawn against some of the Indian tribes. Who does not ardently wish, what peace may be speedily restored; that the natives of this land, instead of being extirpated, may exchange the hatchet for the book of divine knowledge; and that we may be brought to rejoice together as children of the same Almighty Parent, and partakers of the same common nature! Though it be ordered, in the course of events, that we possess their land, yet we owe them justice and charity; we owe them our attempts to recover them from abasement, that so they may enjoy with us the desirable inheritance.

In short, when we consider the manner in which this new world has been opened to us, its first settlement, the growing number of its inhabitants, the great advantages afforded, the prospects still in view, with every circumstance, may we not address the supreme Ruler of the universe in these beautiful words of the Psalmist? *Thou hast brought a vine out of Egypt; thou hast cast out the heathen, and planted it. Thou preparest room before it, and didst cause it to take deep root, and it filled the land. The hills were covered with the shadow of it, and the boughs thereof were like the goodly cedars. She sent out her boughs unto*

---

[2] Original footnote: "*Isaiah* 51.3."

*the sea, and her branches unto the river.*³

But all these natural advantages would be in vain, were we deprived of liberty. [...]

Religious freedom banished from every other corner of the earth has erected her standard in these States, and kindly invites the oppressed from all quarters to repair hither. [...] Here is an asylum for you, our brethren of the old world, whose lives are embittered by the cruel impositions of men; the fruit of whose labours go to support lazy priests and luxurious princes; who, though you rise early and late take rest, obtain only a scanty subsistence for yourselves and families. Forsake your hard task-masters. Refuse to dig an ungrateful soil which will not yield you bread. Haste you to the fertile plains of America. Fill her new, and as yet, uninhabited territory. She opens wide her arms to embrace millions, and waits to crown all the industrious and virtuous with plenty and happiness.⁴ [...]

Having now shown, that the words of the Psalmist equally express our own privileges, and are an acknowledgment highly proper from each of us, let us reflect more particularly,

First, On the distinguishing goodness of God in giving us this fair inheritance, and in defending it against those who sought unjustly to deprive us. *The earth is the Lord's, and the fulness thereof; the world, and they that dwell therein.*⁵ Of whom is it, that we inhabit this land rather than another? Of whom, that we are surrounded with so many blessings? Of whom, that we enjoy civil and religious liberty? Surely it is of the Lord, and he is entitled to all the praise. [...] It was the Lord who conducted to this place the original settlers, supported them under all their difficulties, *cast out the heathen before them, and divided them an inheritance by line, and made them to dwell in their tents.*⁶

[...] Of whom is it, that to day we commemorate our existence as a nation, and rejoice in the prospect of growing prosperity? Surely these are the doings of the Lord, whose interpositions in our favor were so numerous and remarkable, that they can never be forgotten. [...]

What must have been our condition, had our enemies succeeded? [...] The fruitful field would soon have returned to a wilderness, the nerves of industry and improvement been withered, and a languid spiritless temper pervaded the inhabitants. We would have been labourers in a vineyard not our own, and though we had borne the heat and burden of the day, a foreign and unjust lord, if he rewarded us with a penny, would have given us with it, frowns and ill-usage. [...]

May we not indulge the pleasing thought, that the time is not far distant, when tyranny every where shall be destroyed; when mankind shall be the slaves of monsters and idiots no more, but recover the true dignity of their nature! The cause of Liberty is continually gathering strength. The advocates of despotic rule must fail. [...]

And now, while we act on this first stage of our existence, may the Lord *ordain peace for us!* May we never hear the drum, the trumpet, and the clang of arms any more in battle; but may peace, leading in her train religion, knowledge, and liberty, forever dwell with us! [...]

Source: William Linn (1752-1808). *The Blessings of America. A Sermon, Preached in the Middle Dutch Church, on the Fourth July, 1791, Being the Anniversary of the Independence of America: At the Request of the Tammany Society, or Columbian Order.* New York: Thomas Greenleaf, 1791, 7-14, 20-21, 23-27, 33, 36.

---

³ Original footnote: "*Psalm,* lxxx. 8-11."
⁴ Original footnote: "*Besides the number of inhabitants which the old States can receive, and indeed, are necessary for their proper cultivation, the* WESTERN TERRITORY *alone, is vastly extensive. It is computed to contain 220.000.000 acres of land.* [...]"
⁵ Original footnote: "*Psalm* xxiv. 1."
⁶ Original footnote: "*Psalm* lxxviii. 55."

156. Charles Paine, Esq.
An Oration, Pronounced July 4, 1801

National sentiment, although frequently the result of circumstances, is yet the subject of education. [...] It merits cultivation; for its errors, though fatal, are involuntary. In all popular governments it is also the principal instrument by which the administration acquires energy, and one of the great sanctions by which law strengthens its authority. In moments of political hazard, created by foreign aggression, with confidence we resort to its honest zeal, to rally the phalanx of the passions, and to subsidize the pride of man in the defence of his injured country. But in seasons of civil serenity, though we may suspect their plausible treachery, the tone of national temper is no longer to be raised by appeals to the popular sensibility. It is then our duty to convince, not to inflame. Surrounded by circumstances of so peculiar a nature, the return of this auspicious anniversary, while it inspires our enthusiasm and revives our gratitude, arrests us amid this war of sentiment, invites us to reflection, and leads us back to principle. It points us to a time, when we were "all brethren and all Americans," in truth and in honour, without being seduced into the affinity by the necromancy of words.

Americans! to this period let us return for a moment; and while we trace back our footsteps to the goal from which we have started, we will cast a veil over the images of horror, which cro[w]d on our retrospect, and mark with fidelity our aberrations from the path of our fathers.

The "feelings, manners, and principles," leading to that great national epoch, which we are now assembled to commemorate, have annually been the theme of fervid orisons[7] and heartfelt gratulations. What subject can be more animating, what more useful to an assembly of enlightened freemen? Animating, because it inspires us with a veneration of that unimpeachable virtue, that magnanimous constancy, and that undaunted courage, which originated the settlement, which protected the progress, which asserted the independence of America. Useful, because it teaches us those principles, upon which are founded our national dignity and happiness, and without which we can neither efficiently support nor duly estimate them.

What then were those feelings, what those manners, what those principles, which gave birth to this auspicious era? [...]

Driven by ecclesiastical oppression from the land of their nativity, where lay inhersed the relics of their departed ancestors, our venerable forefathers committed themselves to the ocean and to GOD, in search of some secluded residence in this then howling wilderness, where they and their posterity might enjoy those civil and religious immunities, which they had long and unsuccessfully struggled to obtain on the shores of Britain. Liberty, their cloud by day and pillar of fire by night, directed them to this her chosen seat. America was already destined in the councils of Heaven to be a great and mighty empire. This vast continent, fertile and salubrious, which had for ages remained unvisited but by the necessitous foot of the savage, would probably at this day have been scarcely known even on the map of the world, had not its wilds been peopled by persecution and cultivated by banishment. But it had been reserved as the consecrated spot, on which should be erected the temple of liberty, when ecclesiastical bigotry and civil despotism had rendered the old world untenantable by her pure spirit. In that inveterate oppression,

---

[7] Prayers, speeches.

which exiled our ancestors from the abodes of civilized man; in that relentless vengeance, which pursued them even into these inhospitable forests; in that fortitude and patience, which supported them amid the dangers and the hardships, which harassed and encompassed their infant settlement; we behold the finger of Providence, pointing to the rising greatness of this western world. But in this operation of second causes, the blind calculations of human foresight were baffled and bewildered; and even the philosophy of later ages has been astonished at the effect. From this example the oppressors of mankind might have learned, that the correct and steady virtue of principle acquires new strength from the pressure of opposition which surrounds it, and enriches its triumph by the spoils of those efforts, which are employed to defeat it. [...]

[...] *It was decreed, that the tyranny of Britain should produce the freedom of America.* The parliamentary assumption of a right to bind us in all cases whatsoever,[8] and the abrogation of the charter of Massachusetts,[9] extinguished the last obligation of our allegiance, and with it destroyed the only tie of bootless servitude. The spirit of freedom flashed indignant through the continent; the manacles of oppression were burst asunder; America arose from the cradle of colonial infancy, and assumed the dignity of national manhood [...].

The horrors of the revolutionary conflict will ever be remembered by Americans as the price of their independence. What hardships did ye not endure; what miseries did ye not suffer in this unequal contest? Unequal, I say, because it was a contest between the hirelings of despotism on the one part, and the virtuous cultivators of the soil on the other. [...]

The American revolution, unparalleled in the history of nations, for the moderation with which it was conducted, and the momentous importance of its object, was merely defensive. It was not the mad purpose "of tearing the world from its poles and commencing a new era for the human race," but a deliberate plan of adherence to their ancient charter of rights, and of opposition to the attempted impositions of Britain. Compelled by the mighty interest of such motives and views, the assembled Patriots of America declared, that the arbitrary conduct of the mother country had dissolved her authority over the Colonies, and that the United States were, and of right ought to be, a Free, Sovereign, and Independent, Nation. [...]

But, Americans! having foiled the attempts of our foes, we have now to guard against ourselves. We have destroyed the viperous insect of foreign perfidy, whose cancerous tooth had blighted the foliage of our glory; we have now to cauterize[10] the wide spreading roots of domestic faction, which have nourished their rank vegetation on the strength of our soil. Escaped by great mastery and exertion from the sweeping tide of the ingulphing cataract, we render thanks to Heaven, that we have not now to toil against the headlong precipitation of the torrent; but little shall we have gained by this mighty preservation, if we have not learned from trembling experience to correct the course of our navigation.

What is the boasted strength of empires? Where are now the mighty republics of antiquity? They are all levelled with the dust, and can now be traced only by their ruins, which remain as monuments to posterity of that forgetfulness of principles, in which they have met their fall. Nations, like individuals, when arrived at the maturity of their greatness, easily forget the means by which they have obtained their eminence. Affluence, the fruit of industry, brings with it luxury, the bane of morality; and even learning, the source of liberty, has for its companions sophistry and faction. [...]

---

[8] Reference to the Declamatory Act, 1766.
[9] April 15, 1774.
[10] To burn with a hot iron or a caustic.

Americans! We possess a country, extensive in its domains, happy in its situation, fertile in its resources, and still richer in its prospects and its promises. [...] Can we appreciate these inestimable privileges; can we contemplate these ripening glories of our country, and not remember whence they have arisen? Shall we riot in luxury, in philosophy, and faction, and forget the heroes and the patriots, who projected and completed our independence [...]? Shall the Gothic hand of an infidel philosophy extinguish those luminaries of learning and religion, which irradiate our land? Shall Vandal faction overrun our liberties by the inroads of barbarism? [...] Should the common fate of republics be the destiny of America, and her name be added to the catalogue of fallen nations; amid the ruins of her greatness, the passing traveller would read inscribed on the monument which should [e]nclose the ashes of that venerable man, *Ingratitude, thou bane of republics?* [...]

[...] The liberty, of which we boast, consists in the security of our lives, our persons, and our property, in a modified restriction of individual will harmonizing with a public and equal right to do whatever experience has declared to be compatible with social order or the voice of legislative authority has pronounced to be lawful. This liberty is not the fantastic creature of an imagination, distempered by visionary schemes of happiness; but it is the product of cool, deliberate reason, operating upon the past miseries of mankind, and grown wise by the folly of ages. This, Americans, is the liberty, for which your Statesmen have toiled, and your Heroes have bled! Will you barter it for the wild projects of dreaming philosophers and moonstruck politicians? Will you abandon those sound principles, sanctioned by experience, those industrious habits and pure morals, the rock, on which are built your nation's freedom, strength, and greatness? No, my fellow citizens! Here is our country, here are our father's sepulchres, these are our liberties. While we enjoy and are grateful, let us remember and be wise. While with filial wonder and festive admiration we gather around the altars of our country, to devote and to consecrate this day of empire to national glory, let us celebrate and hallow it as a day of recurrence to national principles. [...]

Source: Charles Paine, Esq. (1775-1810). *An Oration, Pronounced July 4, 1801, at the Request of the Inhabitants of the Town of Boston, in Commemoration of the Anniversary of American Independence.* Boston: Manning & Loring, 1801, 5-11, 17-20, 22-23.

157. Samuel Woodworth
"Columbia, the Pride of the World" (1820s)

OH, there is a region, a realm in the West,
  To Tyranny's shackles unknown,
A country with union and liberty blest,
  That fairest of lands is our own.
Where commerce has opened her richest of marts,
  Where freedom's bright flag is unfurled,
The garden of science, the seat of the arts,
  Columbia, the pride of the world.

The rays of her glory have lighted the earth,
  While Tyranny's minions, dismayed,

Acknowledged her prowess, admitted her worth,
    And shrunk at the flash of her blade.
For conquest or plunder she never contends,
    For freedom, her flag is unfurled;
And foemen in battle, in peace are thy friends,
    Columbia, the pride of the world.

Her clime is a refuge for all the oppressed,
    Whom tyranny urges to roam;
And every exile we greet as a guest,
    Soon feels like a brother at home.
Then hail to our country, the land of our birth,
    Where freedom's bright flag is unfurled;
The rays of whose glory have lighted the earth,
    Columbia, the pride of the world.

Source: Samuel Woodworth (1784-1842). "Columbia, the Pride of the World" *The Poetical Works.* 2 vols. Ed. Frederick A. Woodworth. New York: Scribner, 1861, Vol. 2, 112-113.

158. *California: The Cornucopia of the World* (1883)

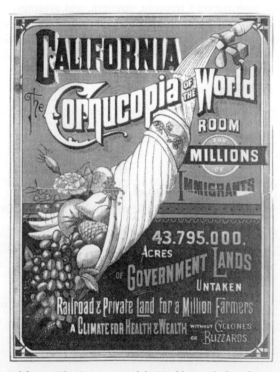

Source: *California: The Cornucopia of the World.* Broadside Advertisement of the Southern Pacific Railroad, 1883. Courtesy New York Historical Society.

159. *Missouri Is Free!* (1880s)

Source: Hannibal & St. Joseph Railroad Advertisement. Courtesy Missouri Historical Society.

160. Henry David Thoreau "Walking" (1862)

[...] Eastward I go only by force; but westward I go free. Thither no business leads me. It is hard for me to believe that I shall find fair landscapes or sufficient wildness and freedom behind the eastern horizon. I am not excited by the prospect of a walk thither; but I believe that the forest which I see in the western horizon stretches uninterruptedly towards the setting sun, and that there are no towns nor cities in it of enough consequence to disturb me. Let me live where I will, on this side is the city, on that the wilderness, and ever I am leaving the city more and more, and withdrawing into the wilderness. I should not lay so much stress on this fact, if I did not believe that something like this is the prevailing tendency of my countrymen. I must walk toward Oregon, and not toward Europe. And that way the nation is moving, and I may say that mankind progresses from east to west. [...]

We go eastward to realize history and study the works of art and literature, retracing the steps of the race; we go westward as into the future, with a spirit of enterprise and adventure. The Atlantic is a Lethean[11] stream, in our passage over which we have had an opportunity to forget the Old World and its institutions. If we do not succeed this time, there is perhaps

---

[11] Lethe: A river in Hades, the water of which produced forgetfulness of the past in those who drank it.

one more chance for the race left before it arrives on the banks of the Styx; and that is in the Lethe of the Pacific, which is three times as wide. [...]

Every sunset which I witness inspires me with the desire to go to a West as distant and as fair as that into which the sun goes down. He appears to migrate westward daily, and tempt us to follow him. He is the Great Western Pioneer whom the nations follow. We dream all night of those mountain-ridges in the horizon, though they may be of vapor only, which were last gilded by his rays. The island of Atlantis, and the islands and gardens of the Hesperides,[12] a sort of terrestrial paradise, appear to have been the Great West of the ancients, enveloped in mystery and poetry. Who has not seen in imagination, when looking into the sunset sky, the gardens of the Hesperides, and the foundation of all those fables? [...]

To Americans I hardly need to say, –

> "Westward the star of empire takes its way."

As a true patriot, I should be ashamed to think that Adam in paradise was more favorably situated on the whole than the backwoodsman in this country. [...]

The West of which I speak is but another name for the Wild; and what I have been preparing to say is, that in Wildness is the preservation of the world.

Source: Henry David Thoreau (1817-1862). "Walking." *The Atlantic Monthly* 9.56 (June 1862), 662-665.

161. Lewis Cass
"Remarks on the Policy and Practice of the United States in Their Treatment of the Indians" (1827)

ART. V. – *Indian Treaties, and Laws and Regulations relating to Indian Affairs; to which is added an Appendix, containing the Proceedings of the Old Congress, and other important State Papers in relation to Indian Affairs. Compiled and published under Orders of the Department of War.* 8vo. pp. 529. 1826. Washington. Way & Gideon.

We have placed the title of this work at the head of the present article, not only because it is a valuable compilation, judiciously executed, but because it contains many important documents, exhibiting the general policy of our government in its intercourse with the Indians. The true character of this policy has not been well understood, even in this country, and abroad it has too often furnished the motive or the pretext for grave accusation and virulent invective. This subject we now propose to examine, and in connexion with it briefly to review the conduct of the two rival nations, whose general measures in peace and war had produced the most permanent effects upon the manners, and morals, and condition of the Indians, previously to the existence of the American government. The operation of the British policy has been so much more extensive and durable than that of the French, that in the observations which we shall submit to our readers, this relative importance will be kept in view.

---

[12] In Greek mythology maidens who guarded the tree bearing golden apples.

The peace of 1763[13] terminated the long contest between the French and British, for superiority upon the North American continent. During its continuance, which exceeded a century, the Iroquois were in the English interest, and the other tribes in the French. [...] The great contending parties availed themselves of the passions and wants of the Indians to harass their enemies, and employed them without scruple, wherever their services were useful; and each was more successful in arraigning the conduct of its rival, than in defending its own, for this atrocious practice, equally repugnant to their duty, as civilized and as christian nations.

We feel no disposition to look back upon the revolting scenes of these times gone by. The Indians were employed with a full knowledge of their habits and propensities; and many a traditionary story, as well as the more permanent memorials of history, has brought down to us, even through successive generations, afflicting details of these enormities. The cupidity of the savages was stimulated by pecuniary rewards, and human scalps, as proofs of death, were bought and sold in christian markets.[14] [...]

In this general retrospect, it has been no part of our object to excite feelings which time has happily allayed. For ourselves, we were willing, that the story of these enormities should be forgotten. The losses and sufferings were our country's, and we had little reason to expect, that any attack upon its character and conduct, from the party which inflicted the injury, would render a public examination of these facts necessary. But so it is; imposing charges have gone forth to the world against us, and our relations with our aboriginal neighbors have furnished the occasion for accusations, which have been preferred in no measured terms. The subject has been frequently discussed in the British journals, and always in a tone of reproof and severity; but it was reserved for the sixtyfirst number of the London Quarterly Review, formally to arraign and censure the United States, in an article, not less reprehensible for its temper and sentiments, than false in its statements and conclusions. Its whole scope can be fully understood only by an examination; but its tone and spirit may be estimated from a few quotations.

"If the mode of warfare of the Indians was ferocious, that of the enemy with whom we had to contend [the Americans] was equally so." p. 102.

"However it may be attempted to preserve appearances by fraudulent and compulsory purchases of land, and declarations of benevolent intentions towards their injured possessors, it has always been the boast of American policy, that *'the Indians shall be made to vanish before civilization, as the snow melts before the sunbeam.'*" [The words printed in italics, are marked in the original as a quotation, and the idea is thus conveyed, that this ferocious sentiment is an acknowledged maxim of the American government. Let the place be pointed out, where this sentence is to be found, in a connexion to justify the inference obviously deducible from it, and we shall then have reason not to believe it a fabrication.] "How far," continues this journal, "the practice has been assimilated to the design, may be gathered from the butchery by the Kentuckians, of Indian families in cold

---

[13] The Treaty of Paris ended the French and Indian War that had been waged between the two major colonial powers, Britain and France, on the North American continent from 1754 through 1763. The terms of the treaty made Britain the world's leading colonial empire.

[14] Original footnote: "In the year 1754, the war assumed a very serious aspect, and the French government, in order to stimulate the savages to cruel and merciless depredations, provided a large premium for the scalp of every Anglo-American, which the Indians should produce. This open cruelty was not retaliated by the English government upon the French inhabitants of Canada, but a bounty was offered of £100 on the scalp of the Indians [...]."

blood, after their surprise at Tippacanoe on the Wabash;[15] from massacres committed by General Harrison's troops in their attacks on the Indian settlements in the autumn of 1812; from the murder, after the affair at the Moravian Town, of squaws and children, who received no more mercy, than did the wounded warriors;[16] and from the more recent and authorized horrors of General Jackson's Seminole war."[17] p. 108.

"We affirm without fear of contradiction or of error, that there is not to be found, on the face of the globe, a race of men, so utterly abandoned to vice and crime – so devoid of all fear of God and regard towards man, as the outsetlers of Kentucky, Ohio, and the other back states." p. 94. [...]

This article has gone forth to Christendom, and as yet uncontradicted. The whole discussion is in this temper, and specific charges are urged against us, with all due formality, evincing equal disregard of courtesy and truth. And shall our countrymen sit still, with folded arms, while the civilized world are believing, and judging, and condemning, deceived, as they well may be, by such bold assumptions, and by the imposing particulars of time, place, and circumstance, with which the statements are surrounded? And this, too, because all must be bland and courteous in literary discussions? We confess that we have no part in such frigid philosophy. Vainly shall we look back with pride, or forward with hope, or around us with congratulation, if we do not cherish a sacred regard for national character, and an unshaken determination to maintain and defend it against the detractions of malevolence, and the attacks of unprincipled illiberality. [...]

By peculiar circumstances we have been led to a knowledge of many of the occurrences, which form the groundwork of the charges, in the article to which we have referred, and we are persuaded that a correct relation of them will redeem our country from the imputations with which it has been assailed. Our Indian relations have frequently furnished, either directly or indirectly, the pretence for these misrepresentations; and "we think it due to the" world, which may "have been deceived, to state the real merits of the case, and to refute, as we trust we shall be able to do, these slanders, which in our opinion have been suffered to remain too long unanswered [... These slanders] we shall proceed to meet and confute."

The tenure, by which the primitive inhabitants of this continent held their land, is a question of metaphysical speculation, rather than one of practical right. All will agree, that they were entitled to as much as would supply them with subsistence, in the mode to which they were accustomed. And there will probably be an assent, little less general, to the proposition, that whatever was not thus wanted and employed might be appropriated by others to their own use. The new race of men, who landed upon these shores, found that their predecessors had affixed few distinctive marks of property in the forests where they roamed. There were none of those permanent improvements, which elsewhere by universal assent become the evidence and the security of individual appropriation. From

---

[15] Reference to the massacre of Native Americans by Governor Harrison's troops in 1811. In 1808, Tecumseh, a Shawnee chief, and his brother had founded a community on the Wabash River in Indiana, unifying Natives from various tribes of the region into their own state, separate from the United States. Alarmed by Tecumseh's success, Governor Harrison decided to advance against the Natives. On November 7, 1811, after repelling a provoked Indian attack, Harrison's troops destroyed Tippecanoe.
[16] Reference to a massacre of peaceful Moravian Indians on March 8, 1782, by militiamen from Pennsylvania who sought to avenge an Indian raid that was perpetrated, however, by Natives from a tribe in the neighborhood.
[17] During the First Seminole War (1817-1818) Major General Andrew Jackson was dispatched with an army of more than 3,000 soldiers to Florida to punish the Seminole Indians for saving runaway slaves from persecution. Jackson liquidated several native settlements.

Hudson's Bay to Cape Horn, the various nations of Europe have formed settlements, and have gradually by force or purchase reduced the aboriginal inhabitants to a state of vassalage, or driven them into the interior. European sovereigns have divided this immense country, by their charters or their treaties, into many colonies and provinces, and have assumed a general jurisdiction over them, without the slightest regard to the primitive occupants. [...]

Almost all the country, now composing the Atlantic portion of the United States, was thus acquired by England. Our colonial records contain the history of many of these negotiations and purchases, but time has swept away almost every vestige of the consideration paid to the Indians. Since the establishment of their independence, the United States have adopted the system of acquiring the aboriginal title by peaceable purchase, but they have adopted it with an important change, consolatory to all, who look with sympathy upon this falling race. The plan of *permanent annuities*[18] guaranties to the Indians a never failing resource against want, and its beneficial effects are apparent in the improved condition of the Wyandots, the Shawnese, and the Miamies. But one instance in the history of the United States can be found, where they have acquired any title to the unappropriated country by force; and that was at the termination of the wanton and unprovoked hostilities of the Creeks, originating probably in foreign influence, but prosecuted in a spirit of atrocious cruelty, not often displayed, even in Indian warfare. Peace, without exemplary chastisement, would have been but an invitation to new aggressions.

The condition of our primitive people, is a moral phenomenon, perhaps without a parallel in the whole history of man. During two centuries, they have been in contact with a civilized people. They have seen our improvements, and felt our superiority. They have relinquished their bows, and arrows, and skins, and flint knives, and stone tomahawks, and have adopted our arms and ammunition, our cloths, and many of our instruments of iron and steel. But in their own moral qualities, if they have not receded, they certainly have not advanced. A principle of progressive improvement seems almost inherent in human nature. Communities of men, as well as individuals, are stimulated by a desire to meliorate their condition. There is nothing stationary around us. We are all striving in the career of life to acquire riches, or honor, or power, or some other object, whose possession is to realize the day dreams of our imaginations; and the aggregate of these efforts constitutes the advance of society.

But there is little of all this in the constitution of our savages. Like the bear, and deer, and buffalo of his own forests, an Indian lives as his father lived, and dies as his father died. He never attempts to imitate the arts of his civilized neighbors. His life passes away in a succession of listless indolence, and of vigorous exertion to provide for his animal wants, or to gratify his baleful passions. He never looks around him, with a spirit of emulation, to compare his situation with that of others, and to resolve on improving it. In a season of abundance, he never provides for a season of scarcity. Want never teaches him to be provident, nor misery to be industrious. This fatuity is not the result of ignorance. Efforts, however ill directed, have not been wanting to teach and reclaim him. But he is perhaps destined to disappear with the forests, which have afforded him food and clothing, and whose existence seems essential to his own.

Under such circumstances, what ignorance, or folly, or morbid jealousy of our national progress does it not argue, to expect that our civilized border would become sta-

---

[18] The grant of an annual sum of money, for a term of years or for life.

tionary, and some of the fairest portions of the globe be abandoned to hopeless sterility. That a few naked wandering barbarians should stay the march of cultivation and improvement, and hold in a state of perpetual unproductiveness, immense regions formed by Providence to support millions of human beings? And has England furnished us with any example of such a system of self denial, or rather of canting[19] weakness? We will not inquire in India, for there no barbarians, strictly speaking, are found. But the Australasian continent is now a British province, acquired and settled within the memory of the present generation. And where are its aboriginal inhabitants? [...]

Source: Lewis Cass (1782-1866). "Indian Treaties, and Laws and Regulations Relating to Indian Affairs [...]." *North American Review* 24.55 (April 1827), 365-366, 387-392.

162. Andrew Jackson
"Second Annual Message, December 6, 1830"

[...] It gives me pleasure to announce to Congress that the benevolent policy of the Government, steadily pursued for nearly thirty years, in relation to the removal of the Indians beyond the white settlements is approaching to a happy consummation. Two important tribes have accepted the provision made for their removal at the last session of Congress, and it is believed that their example will induce the remaining tribes also to seek the same obvious advantages.

The consequences of a speedy removal will be important to the United States, to individual States, and to the Indians themselves. The pecuniary advantages which it promises to the Government are the least of its recommendations. It puts an end to all possible danger of collision between the authorities of the General and State Governments on account of the Indians. It will place a dense and civilized population in large tracts of country now occupied by a few savage hunters. By opening the whole territory between Tennessee on the north and Louisiana on the south to the settlement of the whites it will incalculably strengthen the southwestern frontier and render the adjacent States strong enough to repel future invasions without remote aid. It will relieve the whole State of Mississippi and the western part of Alabama of Indian occupancy, and enable those States to advance rapidly in population, wealth, and power. It will separate the Indians from immediate contact with settlements of whites; free them from the power of the States; enable them to pursue happiness in their own way and under their own rude institutions; will retard the progress of decay, which is lessening their numbers, and perhaps cause them gradually, under the protection of the Government and through the influence of good counsels, to cast off their savage habits and become an interesting, civilized, and Christian community. These consequences, some of them so certain and the rest so probable, make the complete execution of the plan sanctioned by Congress at their last session an object of much solicitude.

Toward the aborigines of the country no one can indulge a more friendly feeling than myself, or would go further in attempting to reclaim them from their wandering habits and make them a happy, prosperous people. I have endeavored to impress upon them my own solemn convictions of the duties and powers of the General Government in relation

---

[19] Here: in a state of decline; slanting, sloping.

to the State authorities. For the justice of the laws passed by the States within the scope of their reserved powers they are not responsible to this Government. As individuals we may entertain and express our opinions of their acts, but as a Government we have as little right to control them as we have to prescribe laws for other nations.

With a full understanding of the subject, the Choctaw and the Chickasaw tribes have with great unanimity determined to avail themselves of the liberal offers presented by the act of Congress, and have agreed to remove beyond the Mississippi River. Treaties have been made with them, which in due season will be submitted for consideration. In negotiating these treaties they were made to understand their true condition, and they have preferred maintaining their independence in the Western forests to submitting to the laws of the States in which they now reside. These treaties, being probably the last which will ever be made with them, are characterized by great liberality on the part of the Government. They give the Indians a liberal sum in consideration of their removal, and comfortable subsistence on their arrival at their new homes. If it be their real interest to maintain a separate existence, they will there be at liberty to do so without the inconveniences and vexations to which they would unavoidably have been subject in Alabama and Mississippi.

Humanity has often wept over the fate of the aborigines of this country, and Philanthropy has been long busily employed in devising means to avert it, but its progress has never for a moment been arrested, and one by one have many powerful tribes disappeared from the earth. To follow to the tomb the last of his race and to tread on the graves of extinct nations excite melancholy reflections. But true philanthropy reconciles the mind to these vicissitudes as it does to the extinction of one generation to make room for another. In the monuments and fortresses of an unknown people, spread over the extensive regions of the West, we behold the memorials of a once powerful race, which was exterminated or has disappeared to make room for the existing savage tribes. Nor is there anything in this which, upon a comprehensive view of the general interests of the human race, is to be regretted. Philanthropy could not wish to see this continent restored to the condition in which it was found by our forefathers. What good man would prefer a country covered with forests and ranged by a few thousand savages to our extensive Republic, studded with cities, towns, and prosperous farms, embellished with all the improvements which art can devise or industry execute, occupied by more than 12,000,000 happy people, and filled with all the blessings of liberty, civilization, and religion?

The present policy of the Government is but a continuation of the same progressive change by a milder process. The tribes which occupied the countries now constituting the Eastern States were annihilated or have melted away to make room for the whites. The waves of population and civilization are rolling to the westward, and we now propose to acquire the countries occupied by the red men of the South and West by a fair exchange, and, at the expense of the United States, to send them to a land where their existence may be prolonged and perhaps made perpetual. Doubtless it will be painful to leave the graves of their fathers; but what do they more than our ancestors did or than our children are now doing? To better their condition in an unknown land our forefathers left all that was dear in earthly objects. Our children by thousands yearly leave the land of their birth to seek new homes in distant regions. Does Humanity weep at these painful separations from everything, animate and inanimate, with which the young heart has become entwined? Far from it. It is rather a source of joy that our country affords scope where our young population may range unconstrained in body or in mind, developing the power and faculties of man in their highest perfection. These remove hundreds and almost thousands of miles at their own expense, purchase the lands they occupy, and support themselves at their new homes from the moment of their arrival. Can it be cruel in this Government when, by events which it can not control, the Indian is made discontented in his ancient home to purchase his lands, to give him a new and extensive territory, to pay the expense of his removal, and support him a year in his new abode? How many thousands of our own people would gladly embrace the opportunity of removing to the West on such conditions! If the offers made to the Indians were extended to them, they would be hailed with gratitude and joy.

And is it supposed that the wandering savage has a stronger attachment to his home than the settled, civilized Christian? Is it more afflicting to him to leave the graves of his fathers than it is to our brothers and children? Rightly considered, the policy of the General Government toward the red man is not only liberal, but generous. He is unwilling to submit to the laws of the States and mingle with their population. To save him from this alternative, or perhaps utter annihilation, the General Government kindly offers him a new home, and proposes to pay the whole expense of his removal and settlement. [...]

It is, therefore, a duty which this Government owes to the new States to extinguish as soon as possible the Indian title to all lands which Congress themselves have included within their limits. When this is done the duties of the General Government in relation to the States and the Indians within their limits are at an end. The Indians may leave the State or not, as they choose. The purchase of their lands does not alter in the least their personal relations with the State government. No act of the General Government has ever been deemed necessary to give the States jurisdiction over the persons of the Indians. That they possess by virtue of their sovereign power within their own limits in as full a manner before as after the purchase of the Indian lands; nor can this Government add to or diminish it.

May we not hope, therefore, that all good citizens, and none more zealously than those who think the Indians oppressed by subjection to the laws of the States, will unite in attempting to open the eyes of those children of the forest to their true condition, and by a speedy removal to relieve them from all the evils, real or imaginary, present or prospective, with which they may be supposed to be threatened. [...]

Source: Andrew Jackson (1767-1845). "Second Annual Message." *A Compilation of the Messages and Papers of the Presidents. Prepared under the Direction of the Joint Committee on Printing, of the House and Senate, Pursuant to an Act of the Fifty-Second Congress of the United States.* 20 vols. New York: Bureau of National Literature, 1897, Vol. 3, 1082-1086.

163. John Marshall
"Cherokee Nation v. Georgia" (1831)

MARSHALL, C. J.[20] This bill is brought by the Cherokee nation,[21] praying an injunction to restrain the state of Georgia from the execution of certain laws of that state, which, as is alleged, go directly to annihilate the Cherokee as a political society, and to seize for the use of Georgia, the lands of the nation which have been assured to them by the United States, in solemn treaties repeatedly made and still in force.

If courts were permitted to indulge their sympathies, a case better calculated to excite them can scarcely be imagined. A people, once numerous, powerful, and truly independent, found by our ancestors in the quiet and uncontrolled possession of an ample domain, gradually sinking beneath our superior policy, our arts and our arms, have yielded their lands, by successive treaties, each of which contains a solemn guarantee of the residue, until they retain no more of their formerly extensive territory than is deemed necessary to their comfortable subsistence. To preserve this remnant, the present application is made.

Before we can look into the merits of the case, a preliminary inquiry presents itself. Has this court jurisdiction of the cause? The third article of the constitution describes the extent of the judicial power. The second section closes an enumeration of the cases to which it is extended, with "controversies between a state or citizens thereof, and foreign states, citizens or subjects." A subsequent clause of the same section gives the supreme court original jurisdiction in all cases in which a state shall be a party. The party defendant may then unquestionably be sued in this court. May the plaintiff sue in it? Is the Cherokee nation a foreign state, in the sense in which that term is used in the constitution? The counsel for the plaintiffs have maintained the affirmative of this proposition with great earnestness and ability. So much of the argument as was intended to prove the character of the Cherokees as a state, as a distinct political society, separated from others, capable of managing its own affairs and governing itself, has, in the opinion of a majority of the judges, been completely successful. They have been uniformly treated as a state, from the settlement of our country. The numerous treaties made with them by the United States, recognize them as a people capable of maintaining the relations of peace and war, of being responsible in their political character for any violation of their engagements, or for any aggression committed on the citizens of the United States, by any individual of their community. Laws have been enacted in the spirit of these treaties. The acts of our government plainly recognize the Cherokee nation as a state, and the courts are bound by those acts. [...]

[...] The Indian territory is admitted to compose a part of the United States. In all our maps, geographical treaties, histories and laws, it is so considered. In all our intercourse with foreign nations, in our commercial regulations, in any attempt at intercourse between Indians and foreign nations, they are considered as within the jurisdictional limits of the United States, subject to many of those restraints which are imposed upon our own citizens. They acknowledge themselves, in their treaties, to be under the protection of the United States; they admit that the United States shall have the sole and exclusive

---

[20] Chief Justice of the United States, 1801-1835.
[21] In 1827 the Cherokee Indians, occupying extensive tracts of land in northwestern Georgia, declared themselves an independent nation. In response, the legislature of Georgia claimed ownership of all Cherokee territory, maintained that Georgian laws extended over the Cherokees and annulled all Indian claims. The Cherokee nation appealed to the Supreme Court for an injunction to prevent the execution of these laws.

right of regulating the trade with them, and managing all their affairs as they think proper [...]. Though the Indians are acknowledged to have an unquestionable, and heretofore unquestioned, right to the lands they occupy, until that right shall be extinguished by a voluntary cession to our government; yet it may well be doubted, whether those tribes which reside within the acknowledged boundaries of the United States can, with accuracy, be denominated foreign nations. They may, more correctly, perhaps, be denominated domestic dependent nations. They occupy a territory to which we assert a title independent of their will, which must take effect in point of possession, when their right of possession ceases. Meanwhile, they are in a state of pupilage; their relation to the United States resembles that of a ward to his guardian. They look to our government for protection; rely upon its kindness and its power; appeal to it for relief to their wants; and address the president as their great father. They and their country are considered by foreign nations, as well as by ourselves, as being so completely under the sovereignty and dominion of the United States, that any attempt to acquire their lands, or to form a political connection with them would be considered by all as an invasion of our territory and an act of hostility. These considerations go far to support the opinion, that the framers of our constitution had not the Indian tribes in view, when they opened the courts of the Union to controversies between a state or the citizens thereof and foreign states.

In considering this subject, the habits and usages of the Indians, in their intercourse with their white neighbors, ought not to be entirely disregarded. At the time the constitution was framed, the idea of appealing to an American court of justice for an assertion of right or a redress of wrong, had perhaps never entered the mind of an Indian or of his tribe. Their appeal was to the tomahawk, or to the government. This was well understood by the statesmen who framed the constitution of the United States, and might furnish some reason for omitting to enumerate them among the parties who might sue in the courts of the Union. [...]

A serious additional objection exists to the jurisdiction of the court. Is the matter of the bill the proper subject for judicial inquiry and decision? It seeks to restrain a state from the forcible exercise of legislative power over a neighboring people, asserting their independence; their right to which the state denies. On several of the matters alleged in the bill, for example, on the laws making it criminal to exercise the usual powers of self-government in their own country, by the Cherokee nation, this court cannot interpose; at least, in the form in which those matters are presented.

That part of the bill which respects the land occupied by the Indians, and prays the aid of the court to protect their possession, may be more doubtful. The mere question of right might, perhaps, be decided by this court, in a proper case, with proper parties. But the court is asked to do more than decide on the title. The bill requires us to control the legislature of Georgia, and to restrain the exertion of its physical force. The propriety of such an interposition by the court may be well questioned; it savors too much of the exercise of political power, to be within the proper province of the judicial department. But the opinion on the point respecting parties makes it unnecessary to decide this question.

If it be true, that the Cherokee nation have rights, this is not the tribunal in which those rights are to be asserted. If it be true, that wrongs have been inflicted, and that still greater are to be apprehended, this is not the tribunal which can redress the past or prevent the future. The motion for an injunction is denied.

Source: John Marshall (1755-1835). "Cherokee Nation v. Georgia." *Documents of American History*. Ed. Henry Steele Commager. New York: Appleton-Century-Crofts, [7]1963, 255-258.

164. Anonymous
"Oregon Territory" (1832)

We had thought that no part of the world presented a fairer field to enterprise and industry, than that portion of North-America which lies east of the Mississippi and south of the great lakes. We have good laws, and well administered; commerce and agriculture flourish, and honest labor is sure of its reward. We had thought that in New-England, especially, sickness and unavoidable accidents were the only causes for fear. Here education is more encouraged than any where else. The helpless poor, even those whom vice has rendered so, are not suffered to starve. All this is well; very well; but it seems we can do better. At least, so say, and perhaps think, the projectors of the intended expedition to the mouth of Columbia river.

A gentleman, for whose talents and ambition his native land does not afford sufficient scope, has been employing his leisure in devising schemes to better the condition of his fellow countrymen. His studies have not been in vain: if his plans should prove practicable, nations yet to be will bless him as their father and benefactor. In a word, he has issued advertisements, inviting the good people of New-England to leave their homes, their connections, and the comforts of civilized society, and follow him across the continent to the shores of the Pacific. When we heard of this scheme, our first impression respecting the morals of its originator was by no means favorable. His noble confidence in his abilities as a governor and a guide, over territories he had never seen, to a country in which he had never been, appeared extremely like impudence. We observed, too, that while his public programma spoke of the natural advantages of Oregon, and of two hundred acres of land which he intended to bestow on each emigrant, it said nothing of the sum said emigrant was to deposite in his hands previous to the commencement of the journey. But when we considered the hardships and dangers which he, as well as those he may delude, must undergo; when we thought of the risk he has run, and still runs, of being sent to the insane hospital; when we reflected on his certain disappointment, and the ridicule he will incur by it, we were constrained to believe that disinterested benevolence was his motive.

We are informed that this excellent person has now a list of the names of many hundreds who receive his dreams as oracles. Were our prisons to be emptied on the shores of the Pacific, the benefit to the United States would be undeniable, whether the convicts perished on the way or not. Even then a wrong would be done to the natives of Oregon. But we are informed that the persons who intend to leave us, and to lead their wives and children to misery, if not to destruction, are husbandmen, mechanics, and other respectable members of society. Such persons should not be lightly lost, and we write in the hope that they will read and pause.

The proceedings of our projector have been so involved in mystery, that it is impossible to speak minutely of his intentions. We understand, however, that his followers are to assemble at St. Louis as early next spring as possible, and thence proceed to cross the Rocky Mountains, somewhere near the sources of the river Platte.[22] The expedition is to go by land, but farther our informant saith not.

---

[22] Longest river of Nebraska.

Whether half the Oregon emigrants will ever reach St Louis is at least doubtful. Do they seek a fine country on the Oregon river? They will pass through a much finer, even allowing the tales on which they rely to be true, whether they go by the Ohio or the lakes. They will find as healthy a climate as is in the world, and a soil that yields eighty bushels to the acre. They will pass through lands of which they may buy two hundred acres for less than the farther expenses of their journey. They will pass through a kindred people, from whose society they will derive as much advantage, to say the least, as they could from the Clatsops and Chopunnish of Oregon. In short, they will see the state of things they expect to bring about at the end of a long and perilous journey, and after several years of strenuous exertion, already established, without trouble on their part. If they pass the Mississippi they will injure the reputation of New-England for sagacity.

Those who reach St. Louis will find there many who have been to Oregon and found no temptation to remain there. These will treat their undertaking with the scorn it deserves; and if they go farther it will be in spite of good advice. [...]

We will suppose that a considerable number persist and proceed onward. They may, possibly, charter a steamboat to take them to the mouth of the Platte, but no farther, for that stream is not navigable for steamboats, unless during freshets.[23] We take it for granted that women and children cannot perform so long a journey on foot, and that the baggage, household furniture, implements of husbandry, &c. cannot be conveyed on pack horses. Wheel-carriages will, therefore, be necessary, and animals to draw them.

So large a caravan must necessarily proceed slowly, especially as it will be encumbered with so many helpless persons. [...]

[...] At the above mentioned rate of traveling they would reach the dividing ridge about the last of September; that is, supposing they met no accident, hindrance, or delay. But there are many obstacles to their progress, against all of which they may, and some of which they must, be obliged to contend.

They cannot take provisions with them for more than a few days, and must, therefore, depend on their guns for support. The only game the country affords in abundance are buffaloes, and of these there are enough, and more than enough, in some seasons. [...] The Indians live on them, it is true; but they follow them in their travels as closely as the wolves, and if the herd enters the country of a hostile tribe, they endure the horrors of starvation. Very many of the buffalo-hunting savages perish every year of literal famine. There is ever either great abundance or extreme want. If the Indians suffer, how will the emigrants, who are not hunters, provide for themselves? [...]

The country through which the expedition must pass is precisely in the track of all the war parties that travel over the space between the Missouri and the Rocky Mountains. It is the abiding place and the battle ground of fifty warlike tribes. We grant that there is not an individual among them all who will not receive a stranger kindly in his wigwam, and give him to eat of the best; but neither is there an individual among them who will not cut that stranger's throat, for the value of his gun-flint, if he meets him alone in the prairie. Besides, it is their rule, when they undertake a warlike enterprise, not to bear the sword in vain, and if they happen to be unsuccessful, or defeated, wo[e] to him who crosses their path. We could adduce a hundred instances of American citizens who have been put to death for no other cause than having accidentally fallen in the way of an unsuccessful war-party. Was not the last caravan that went from St. Louis to Santa Fe re-

---

[23] A flood or overflowing of a river caused by heavy rains or melted snow.

peatedly assailed, and only preserved from destruction by a strong armed party of United States troops? Those traders gave no offence to the savages, unless passing through their country be considered such.

Allowing that the travelers can save their persons from the attacks of Ietans, Pawnees, Pawnee Loups, Pawnee Republicans, Appaches, Comanches, Arrapahoes, Shoshonees, Rickarees, Konzas, Crows, Blackfeet, and fifty more predatory hordes, whose very names are abominations, can they save their horses? Do they know that all the buffalo-hunting Indians are the most expert horse-thieves in the world? Do they know that they make their proficiency in horse-stealing, their boast and pride? that they consider the appropriation of a horse a very virtuous and praiseworthy action; little less glorious than the slaughter of a white man? Do they know that a horse is absolutely necessary to a buffalo-hunter's existence, and is, therefore, the greatest temptation that can be put in his way? Do they know that their path is directly in the track of the no less barbarous than brave Blackfeet, who, when Captain Lewis[24] killed two of their tribe (in an attempt to steal his horses) made a vow never to spare an American, and have religiously kept it ever since? Do they know that all the Indians of that region justly hold the very name of an American in abhorrence? Perhaps, if we give them the reason for this hatred, they will believe us the more readily. [...]

We can see no advantage in Oregon which the emigrant may not secure in the state of Maine. The sea washes the shores of both. The soil is good in both. There are fisheries pertaining to both. If the climate of Oregon is milder, it is not proved that it is better. There is waste land in both. There is plenty of timber in both. Maine has these advantages. Her inhabitants are under the protection of the laws. They are numerous enough to protect each other. They have free communication with every part of the world. There is no art or science of which she does not possess at least the rudiments. All that can be done in Oregon, within a hundred years, is already done in Maine. Above all, she has no Indians to root out with fire and sword, fraudulent treaties, or oppressive enactments.

That a party of young, brave, hardy men may cross the continent to the mouth of the Columbia, we know; but that a large body of the inhabitants of New-England, wholly unacquainted with Indian life, and encumbered with baggage and their families, can do so, we hold impossible. We think we have proved that it is so. Our facts cannot be disputed, and the inference is as clear as a geometrical demonstration. We do not know that the prime mover of the folly we have exposed is actuated by any evil motive; we do not believe it. We look upon him as an unfortunate man, who, deluded himself, is deluding others, and conceive it our duty to warn those who are about to follow him on the road to ruin. To conclude, we advise those who have been so unfortunate as to embark in this enterprise to erase their names from the list as soon as possible. If they cannot retrieve the money they may have advanced, let them consider it better lost, than followed to Oregon, and be thankful that they have so escaped.

W.J.S.

Source: Anonymous [W.J.S.]. "Oregon Territory." *The New-England Magazine* 2 (January-June 1832). Boston: J.T. and E. Buckingham, 123-127, 132.

---

[24] U.S. explorer with whom William Clark led the first overland expedition to the Pacific Northwest (1804-1806).

165. Lansford Warren Hastings
The Emigrants' Guide to Oregon and California (1845)

[...] I can not but believe, that the time is not distant, when those wild forests, trackless plains, untrodden valleys, and the unbounded ocean, will present one grand scene, of continuous improvements, universal enterprise, and unparalleled commerce: when those vast forests, shall have disappeared, before the hardy pioneer; those extensive plains, shall abound with innumerable herds, of domestic animals; those fertile valleys, shall groan under the immense weight of their abundant products: when those numerous rivers, shall team with countless steam-boats, steam-ships, ships, barques and brigs; when the entire country, will be everywhere intersected, with turnpike roads, rail-roads and canals; and when, all the vastly numerous, and rich resources, of that now, almost unknown region, will be fully and advantageously developed. To complete this picture, we may fancy to ourselves, a Boston, a New York, a Philadelphia and a Baltimore, growing up in a day, as it were, both in Oregon and California; crowded with a vast population, and affording all the enjoyments and luxuries, of civilized life. And to this we may add, numerous churches, magnificent edifices, spacious colleges, and stupendous monuments and observatories, all of Grecian architecture, rearing their majestic heads, high in the ærial region, amid those towering pyramids of perpetual snow, looking down upon all the busy, bustling scenes, of tumultuous civilization, amid the eternal verdure of perennial spring. And in fine, we are also led to contemplate the time, as fast approaching, when the supreme darkness of ignorance, superstition, and despotism, which now, so entirely pervade many portions of those remote regions, will have fled forever, before the march of civilization, and the blazing light, of civil and religious liberty; when genuine *republicanism*, and unsophisticated *democracy*, shall be reared up, and tower aloft, even upon the now wild shores, of the great Pacific; where they shall forever stand forth, as enduring monuments, to the increasing wisdom of *man*, and the infinite kindness and protection, of an all-wise, and over-ruling *Providence*.

Source: Lansford Warren Hastings (1819-ca. 1870). *The Emigrants' Guide, to Oregon and California, Containing Scenes and Incidents of a Party of Oregon Emigrants; a Description of Oregon; Scenes and Incidents of a Party of California Emigrants; and a Description of California; with a Description of the Different Routes to Those Countries; and All Necessary Information Relative to the Equipment, Supplies, and the Method of Traveling.* Cincinnati, OH: George Conclin, 1845, 151-152.

166. *Unanimous Declaration of Independence, by the Delegates of the People of Texas* (1836)

When a government has ceased to protect the lives, liberty, and property of the people, from whom its legitimate powers are derived, and for the advancement of whose happiness it was instituted; and so far from being a guarantee for their inestimable and inalienable rights, becomes an instrument in the hands of evil rulers for their oppression. When the Federal Republican Constitution of their country, which they have sworn to support, no longer has a substantial existence, and the whole nature of their government has been forcibly changed, without their consent, from a restricted Federative Republic, composed of Sovereign States, to a consolidated Central Military despotism, in which every interest is disregarded but that of the army and the priesthood, both the eternal enemies of civil liberty, the ever ready minions of power, and the usual instruments of tyrants. When, long after the spirit of the constitution has departed, moderation is at length so far lost by those in power, that even the semblance of freedom is removed, and the forms themselves of the constitution discontinued, and so far from their petitions and remonstrances being regarded, the agents who bear them are thrown into dungeons, and mercenary armies sent forth to force a new government upon them at the point of the bayonet.

When, in consequence of such acts of malfeasance and abduction on the part of the government, anarchy prevails and civil society is dissolved into its original elements, in such a crisis, the first law of nature, the right of self preservation, the inherent and inalienable right of the people to appeal to first principles, and take their political affairs into their own hands in extreme cases, enjoins it as a right towards themselves and a sacred obligation to their posterity to abolish such government, and create another in its ste[a]d, calculated to rescue them from impending dangers, and to secure their welfare and happiness.

Nations, as well as individuals, are amenable for their acts to the public opinion of mankind. A statement of a part of our grievances is therefore submitted to an impartial world, in justification of the hazardous but unavoidable step now taken, of severing our political connection with the Mexican people, and assuming an independent attitude among the nations of the earth.

The Mexican Government, by its colonization laws, invited and induced the Anglo American population of Texas to colonize its wilderness under the pledged faith of a written constitution, that they should continue to enjoy that constitutional liberty and republican government to which they had been habituated in the land of their birth, the United States of America. [...]

It has suffered the military commandants, stationed among us, to exercise arbitrary acts of oppression and tyranny, thus trampling upon the most sacred rights of the citizen, and rendering the military superior to the civil power. [...]

It denies us the right of worshipping the Almighty according to the dictates of our own conscience, by the support of a National Religion, calculated to promote the temporal interest of its human functionaries, rather than the glory of the true and living God.

It has demanded us to deliver up our arms, which are essential to our defence – the rightful property of freemen – and formidable only to tyrannical governments.

It has invaded our country both by sea and by land, with the intent to lay waste our territory, and drive us from our homes; and has now a large mercenary army advancing, to carry on against us a war of extermination.

It has, through its emissaries, incited the merciless savage, with the tomahawk and scalping knife, to massacre the inhabitants of our defenceless frontiers.

It has been, during the whole time of our connection with it, the contemptible sport and victim of successive military revolutions, and hath continually exhibited every characteristic of a weak, corrupt, and tyrannical government.

These, and other grievances, were patiently borne by the people of Texas, until they reached that point at which forbearance ceases to be a virtue. We then took up arms in defence of the National Constitution. We appealed to our Mexican brethren for assistance: our appeal has been made in vain, though months have elapsed, no sympathetic response has yet been heard from the interior. We are therefore forced to the melancholy conclusion, that the Mexican people have acquiesced in the destruction of their liberty, and the substitution therefor[e] of a military government; that they are unfit to be free, and incapable of self government.

The necessity of self preservation, therefore, now decrees our eternal political separation.

We, therefore, the del[e]gates, with plenary powers, of the people of Texas, in solemn convention assembled, appealing to a candid world for the necessities of our condition, do hereby resolve and DECLARE, *that our political connection with the Mexican nation has forever ended, and that the people of Texas, do now constitute a* FREE, SOVEREIGN, *and* INDEPENDENT REPUBLIC, *and are fully invested with all the rights and attributes which properly belong to independent nations; and, conscious of the rectitude of our intentions, we fearlessly and confidently commit the issue to the decision of the supreme Arbiter of the destinies of nations.*

[Signatures]

Source: *Unanimous Declaration of Independence, by the Delegates of the People of Texas, in General Convention, at the Town of Washington, on the Second Day of March 1836.* http://www.tsl.state.tx.us/treasures/images/republic/declar.jpg (access date: June 15, 2005).

167. William E. Channing
"A Letter to the Hon. Henry Clay, on the Annexation of Texas to the United States" (1837)

[...] II. Having unfolded the argument against the annexation of Texas from the criminality of the revolt, I proceed to a second very solemn consideration, namely, that by this act our country will enter on a career of encroachment, war, and crime, and will merit and incur the punishment and woe of aggravated wrong-doing. The seizure of Texas will not stand alone. It will darken our future history. It will be linked by an iron necessity to long-continued deeds of rapine and blood. Ages may not see the catastrophe of the tragedy, the first scene of which we are so ready to enact. It is strange that nations should be so much more rash than individuals; and this, in the face of experience, which has been teaching, from the beginning of society, that, of all precipitate and criminal deeds, those perpetrated by nations are the most fruitful of misery.

Did this county know itself, or were it disposed to profit by self-knowledge, it would feel the necessity of laying an immediate curb on its passion for extended territory. It would not trust itself to new acquisitions. It would shrink from the temptation to conquest. We are a restless people, prone to encroachment, impatient of the ordinary laws of progress, less anxious to consolidate and perfect than to extend our institutions, more ambitious of spreading ourselves over a wide space than of diffusing beauty and fruitfulness over a narrower field. We boast of our rapid growth, forgetting that, throughout nature, noble growths are slow. Our people throw themselves beyond the bounds of civilization, and expose themselves to relapses into a semi-barbarous state, under the impulse of wild imagination, and for the name of great possessions. [...]

It is full time, that we should lay on ourselves serious, resolute restraint. Possessed of a domain, vast enough for the growth of ages, it is time for us to stop in the career of acquisition and conquest. Already endangered by our greatness, we cannot advance without imminent peril to our institutions, union, prosperity, virtue, and peace. [...]

[...] It is sometimes said, that nations are swayed by laws, as unfailing as those which govern matter; that they have their destinies; that their character and position carry them forward irresistibly to their goal; [... that] the Indians have melted before the white man, and the mixed, degraded race of Mexico must melt before the Anglo-Saxon. Away with this vile sophistry! There is no necessity for crime. There is no Fate to justify rapacious nations, any more than to justify gamblers and robbers, in plunder. We boast of the progress of society, and this progress consists in the substitution of reason and moral principle for the sway of brute force. It is true, that more civilized must always exert a great power over less civilized communities in their neighbourhood. But it may and should be a power to enlighten and improve, not to crush and destroy. We talk of accomplishing our destiny. So did the late conqueror of Europe;[25] and destiny consigned him to a lonely rock in the ocean, the prey of an ambition which destroyed no peace but his own. [...]

Source: William E. Channing (1780-1842). "A Letter to the Hon. Henry Clay, on the Annexation of Texas to the United States [1837]." *The Works of William E. Channing*. 6 vols. Boston: James Munroe, 1847, Vol. 2, 204-206, 210.

168. *Anti-Texas Meeting at Faneuil Hall!* (1838)

Friends of Freedom!

A proposition has been made, and will soon come up for consideration in the United States Senate, to annex Texas to the Union. This territory has been wrested from Mexico by violence and fraud. Such is the character of the leaders in this enterprise that the country has been aptly termed "that valley of rascals." It is large enough to make nine or ten States as large as Massachusetts. It was, under Mexico, a free territory. The freebooters have made it a slave territory. The design is to annex it, with its load of infamy and oppression, to the Union. The immediate result may be a war with Mexico – the ultimate result *will be* some 18 or 20 more slaveholders in the Senate of the United States, a still larger number in the House of Representatives, and the balance of power in the hands of the South! And if, when in a minority in Congress, slaveholders browbeat the North, demand the passage of gag laws,[26] trample on the Right of Petition, and threaten, in defiance of the General Government, to hang every man, caught at the South, who dares to speak against their "domestic institutions,"[27] what limits shall be set to their intolerant demands and high handed usurpations, when they are in the majority?

All opposed to this scheme, of whatever sect or party, are invited to attend the meeting at the Old Cradle of Liberty,[28] to-morrow, (Thursday Jan. 25), at 10 o'clock, A.M., at which time addresses are expected from several able speakers.

Bostonians! Friends of Freedom!! Let your voices be heard in loud remonstrance against this scheme, fraught with such ruin to yourselves and such infamy to your country. January 24, 1838

Source: Library of Congress – http://memory.loc.gov/ammem/rbpehtml/rbpebibTitles09.html (access date: June 15, 2005).

---

[25] Napoleon.
[26] A law or regulation that prohibits public discussion of a particular matter.
[27] A euphemistic term refering to the 'institution' of slavery.
[28] Faneuil Hall, in downtown Boston.

169. John L. O'Sullivan
"The Great Nation of Futurity" (1839)

The American people having derived their origin from many other nations, and the Declaration of National Independence being entirely based on the great principle of human equality, these facts demonstrate at once our disconnected position as regards any other nation; that we have, in reality, but little connection with the past history of any of them, and still less with all antiquity, its glories, or its crimes. On the contrary, our national birth was the beginning of a new history, the formation and progress of an untried political system, which separates us from the past and connects us with the future only; and so far as regards the entire development of the natural rights of man, in moral, political, and national life, we may confidently assume that our country is destined to be *the great nation* of futurity.

It is so destined, because the principle upon which a nation is organized fixes its destiny, and that of equality is perfect, is universal. It presides in all the operations of the physical world, and it is also the conscious law of the soul – the self-evident dictate of morality, which accurately defines the duty of man to man, and consequently man's rights as man. Besides, the truthful annals of any nation furnish abundant evidence, that its happiness, its greatness, its duration, were always proportionate to the democratic equality in its system of government. [...]

What friend of human liberty, civilization, and refinement, can cast his view over the past history of the monarchies and aristocracies of antiquity, and not deplore that they ever existed? What philanthropist[29] can contemplate the oppressions, the cruelties, and injustice inflicted by them on the masses of mankind, and not turn with moral horror from the retrospect?

America is destined for better deeds. It is our unparalleled glory that we have no reminiscences of battle fields, but in defence of humanity, of the oppressed of all nations, of the rights of conscience, the rights of personal enfranchisement.[30] Our annals describe no scenes of horrid carnage, where men were led on by hundreds of thousands to slay one another, dupes[31] and victims to emperors, kings, nobles, demons in the human form called heroes. We have had patriots to defend our homes, our liberties, but no aspirants to crowns or thrones; nor have the American people ever suffered themselves to be led on by wicked ambition to depopulate the land, to spread desolation far and wide, that a human being might be placed on a seat of supremacy.

We have no interest in the scenes of antiquity, only as lessons of avoidance of nearly all their examples. The expansive future is our arena, and for our history. We are entering on its untrodden space, with the truths of God in our minds, beneficent objects in our hearts, and with a clear conscience unsullied[32] by the past. We are the nation of human progress, and who will, what can, set limits to our onward march? Providence is with us, and no earthly power can. We point to the everlasting truth on the first page of our national declaration, and we proclaim to the millions of other lands, that "the gates of hell" – the powers of aristocracy and monarchy – "shall not prevail against it."

---

[29] One who loves mankind.
[30] The rights of citizenship, especially the right to vote.
[31] A victim of deception.
[32] Unstained, spotless.

The far-reaching, the boundless future will be the era of American greatness. In its magnificent domain of space and time, the nation of many nations is destined to manifest to mankind the excellence of divine principles; to establish on earth the noblest temple ever dedicated to the worship of the Most High – the Sacred and the True. Its floor shall be a hemisphere – its roof the firmament of the star-studded heavens, and its congregation an Union of many Republics, comprising hundreds of happy millions, calling, owning no man master, but governed by God's natural and moral law of equality, the law of brotherhood – of "peace and good will amongst men." [...]

Yes, we are the nation of progress, of individual freedom, of universal enfranchisement. Equality of rights is the cynosure[33] of our union of States, the grand exemplar of the correlative equality of individuals; and while truth sheds its effulgence, we cannot retrograde, without dissolving the one and subverting the other. We must onward to the fulfilment of our mission – to the entire development of the principle of our organization – freedom of conscience, freedom of person, freedom of trade and business pursuits, universality of freedom and equality. This is our high destiny, and in nature's eternal, inevitable decree of cause and effect we must accomplish it. All this will be our future history, to establish on earth the moral dignity and salvation of man – the immutable truth and beneficence of God. For this blessed mission to the nations of the world, which are shut out from the life-giving light of truth, has America been chosen; and her high example shall smite unto death the tyranny of kings, hierarchs, and oligarchs, and carry the glad tidings of peace and good will where myriads now endure an existence scarcely more enviable than that of beasts of the field. Who, then, can doubt that our country is destined to be *the great nation* of futurity?

Source: John L. O'Sullivan (1813-1895?). "The Great Nation of Futurity." *The United States Magazine, and Democratic Review* 6.23 (November 1839), 426-427, 429-430.

170. Robert Charles Winthrop
"Address [Delivered before the New England Society]" (1839)

[...] Gentlemen of the New England Society and Fellow Citizens of New York, of this wonderful rise and progress of our Country, from the merely nominal and embryo existence which it had acquired at the dawn of the 17th Century, to the mature growth, the substantial prosperity, the independent greatness and National grandeur in which it is now beheld, we this day commemorate a main, original spring. The 22d of December, 1620, was not the mere birthday of a Town or a Colony.[34] [...]

Yes, the event which occurred two hundred and nineteen years ago yesterday, was of wider import than the confines of New Plymouth. The area of New England, greater than that of Old England, has yet proved far too contracted to comprehend all its influences. They have been coëxtensive with our country. They have pervaded our Continent. [...]

Inconceivable Fortune! Unimaginable Destiny! Inscrutable Providence! Are these the details of an event from which such all-important, all-pervading influences were to flow? Were these the means, and these the men, through which not New Plymouth only was to

---

[33] An object that serves as a focal point of attention and admiration.
[34] Reference to the founding of Plymouth Plantation in 1620.

be planted, not New England only to be founded, not our whole Country only to be formed and moulded, but the whole Hemisphere to be shaped and the whole world shaken? [...]

[...] I see something more than mere fortunate accidents or extraordinary coincidences in the whole discovery and colonization of our Country – in the age at which these events took place, in the People by whom they were effected, and more especially in the circumstances by which they were attended, and may my tongue cleave to the roof of my mouth if ever I am ashamed to say so!

When I reflect that this entire Hemisphere of ours remained so long in a condition of primeval barbarism – that the very existence of its vast Continents was so long concealed from the knowledge of civilized man – that these colossal mountains so long lifted their summits to the sky and cast their shadows across the earth – that these gigantic rivers so long poured their mighty, matchless waters to the sea – that these magnificent forests so long waved their unrivalled foliage to the winds, and these luxuriant fields and prairies so long spread out their virgin sods before the sun – without a single intelligent human being to enjoy, to admire, or even to behold them – when I reflect to what heights of civilization, ambition and power so many of the Nations of the Old World were successively advanced, reaching a perfection in some branches of art and of science which has destined their very ruins to be the wonder, the delight, the study and the models of mankind for ever, and pushing their Commerce and their Conquests over sea and shore with an energy so seemingly indomitable and illimitable, and yet that these seas and these shores, reserved for other Argonauts[35] than those of Greece and other Eagles than those of Rome, were protected alike from the reach of their arts and their arms, from their rage for glory and their lust for spoils – when I reflect that all the varieties of roaming tribes which, up to the period of the events of which I speak, had found their way nobody knows when or from whence, to this Northern Continent at least, were so mysteriously endowed with a nature, not merely to make no progress in improvement and settlement of themselves, but even to resist and defy every influence which could be brought to bear upon them by others, except such as tended to their own extirpation and overthrow – how they shrank at the approach of the civilized settler, melting away as they retired, and marking the trail of their retreat, I had almost said, by the scent of their own graves – or, if some stragglers of a race less barbarous, at some uncertain epoch, were brought unknowingly upon our shores, that, instead of stamping the Rock upon which they landed with the unequivocal foot-prints of the Fathers of a mighty Nation, they only scratched upon its surface a few illegible characters, to puzzle the future antiquary to decide whether they were of Scandinavian or of Carthaginian, of Runic or of Punic origin, and to prove only this distinctly – that their authors were not destined to be the settlers, or even the discoverers, in any true sense of that term, of the Country upon which they had thus prematurely stumbled – when I reflect upon the momentous changes in the institutions of society and in the instruments of human power, which were crowded within the period which was ultimately signalized by this discovery and this settlement – *the press*, by its magic enginery, breaking down every barrier and annihilating every monopoly in the paths of knowledge, and proclaiming all men equal in the arts of peace – [...] *the Bible*, rescued from its unknown tongues, its unauthorized interpretations and its unworthy perversions, opened at length in its original simplicity and purity to the world, and prov-

---

[35] Members of Jason's crew who sailed on the *Argo* in search of the Golden Fleece.

ing that all men were born equal in the eye of God – when I see learning reviving from its lethargy of centuries, religion reässerting its native majesty, and liberty – liberty itself – thus armed and thus attended, starting up anew to its long suspended career, and exclaiming, as it were, in the confidence of its new instruments and its new auxiliaries – "Give me now a place to stand upon – a place free from the interference of established power, a place free from the embarrassment of ancient abuses, a place free from the paralyzing influence of a jealous and overbearing prerogative – *give me but a place to stand upon and I will move the world*"[36] – I cannot consider it, I cannot call it, a mere fortunate coincidence, that then, at that very instant, the veil of waters was lifted up, that place revealed, and the world moved! [...]

Source: Robert Charles Winthrop (1809-1894). "Address [Delivered before the New England Society, December 23, 1839]." *The New England Society Orations*. 2 vols. Ed. Cephas Brainerd and Eveline Warner Brainerd. New York: Century, 1901, Vol. 1, 219-220, 227-228, 240-242.

171. John L. O'Sullivan "Annexation" (1845)

It is time now for opposition to the Annexation of Texas to cease [...]. It is time for the common duty of Patriotism to the Country to succeed; – or if this claim will not be recognized, it is at least time for common sense to acquiesce with decent grace in the inevitable and the irrevocable.

Texas is now ours. [...] Her star and her stripe may already be said to have taken their place in the glorious blazon of our common nationality; and the sweep of our eagle's wing already includes within its circuit the wide extent of her fair and fertile land. She is no longer to us a mere geographical space – a certain combination of coast, plain, mountain, valley, forest and stream. She is no longer to us a mere country on the map. She comes within the dear and sacred designation of Our Country; [...] and that which is at once a sentiment and a virtue, Patriotism, already begins to thrill for her too within the national heart. It is time then that all should cease to treat her as alien, and even adverse [...].

Why, were other reasoning wanting, in favor of now elevating this question of the reception of Texas into the Union, out of the lower region of our past party dissensions, up to its proper level of a high and broad nationality, it surely is to be found, found abundantly, in the manner in which other nations have undertaken to intrude themselves into it, between us and the proper parties to the case, in a spirit of hostile interference against us, for the avowed object of thwarting our policy and hampering our power, limiting our greatness and checking the fulfilment of our manifest destiny to overspread the continent allotted by Providence for the free development of our yearly multiplying millions. This we have seen done by England, our old rival and enemy; and by France, strangely coupled with her against us [...].

It is wholly untrue, and unjust to ourselves, the pretence that the Annexation has been a measure of spoliation, unrightful and unrighteous – of military conquest under forms of peace and law – of territorial aggrandizement at the expense of justice due by a double sanctity to the weak. This view of the question is wholly unfounded [...].

---

[36] Quote ascribed to Archimedes (290-212 BC).

Nor is there any just foundation for the charge that Annexation is a great pro-slavery measure – calculated to increase and perpetuate that institution. Slavery had nothing to do with it. Opinions were and are greatly divided, both at the North and South, as to the influence to be exerted by it on Slavery and the Slave States. [...]

[...] The country which was the subject of Annexation in this case, from its geographical position and relations, happens to be [...] a slave country. But a similar process might have taken place in proximity to a different section of our Union; and indeed there is a great deal of Annexation yet to take place, within the life of the present generation, along the whole line of our northern border. Texas has been absorbed into the Union in the inevitable fulfilment of the general law which is rolling our population westward; the connexion of which with that ratio of growth in population which is destined within a hundred years to swell our numbers to the enormous population of *two hundred and fifty millions* (if not more), is too evident to leave us in doubt of the manifest design of Providence in regard to the occupation of this continent. It was disintegrated from Mexico in the natural course of events, by a process perfectly legitimate on its own part, blameless on ours; and in which all the censures due to wrong, perfidy and folly, rest on Mexico alone. And possessed as it was by a population which was in truth but a colonial detachment from our own, and which was still bound by myriad ties of the very heart-strings to its old relations, domestic and political, their incorporation into the Union was not only inevitable, but the most natural, right and proper thing in the world [...].

California will, probably, next fall away from the loose adhesion which, in such a country of Mexico, holds a remote province in a slight equivocal kind of dependence on the metropolis. Imbecile and distracted, Mexico never can exert any real governmental authority over such a country. [...] The Anglo-Saxon foot is already on its borders. Already the advance guard of the irresistible army of Anglo-Saxon emigration has begun to pour down upon it, armed with the plough and the rifle, and marking its trail with schools and colleges, courts and representative halls, mills and meeting-houses. A population will soon be in actual occupation of California, over which it will be idle for Mexico to dream of dominion. They will necessarily become independent. All this without agency of our government, without responsibility of our people – in the natural flow of events, the spontaneous working of principles, and the adaptation of the tendencies and wants of the human race to the elemental circumstances in the midst of which they find themselves placed. And they will have a right to independence – to self-government – to the possession of the homes conquered from the wilderness of their own labors and dangers, sufferings and sacrifices – a better and a truer right than the artificial title of sovereignty in Mexico, a thousand miles distant, inheriting from Spain a title good only against those who have none better. Their right to independence will be the natural right of self-government belonging to any community strong enough to maintain it [...].

Source: John L. O'Sullivan (1813-1895?). "Annexation." *The United States Magazine, and Democratic Review* 17.85 (July/August 1845), 5-9.

172. James K. Polk
"Inaugural Address" (1845)

FELLOW-CITIZENS: Without solicitation on my part, I have been chosen by the free and voluntary suffrages of my countrymen to the most honorable and most responsible office on earth. I am deeply impressed with gratitude for the confidence reposed in me. Honored with this distinguished consideration at an earlier period of life than any of my predecessors, I can not disguise the diffidence with which I am about to enter on the discharge of my official duties.

If the more aged and experienced men who have filled the office of President of the United States even in the infancy of the Republic distrusted their ability to discharge the duties of that exalted station, what ought not to be the apprehensions of one so much younger and less endowed now that our domain extends from ocean to ocean, that our people have so greatly increased in numbers, and at a time when so great diversity of opinion prevails in regard to the principles and policy which should characterize the administration of our Government? Well may the boldest fear and the wisest tremble when incurring responsibilities on which may depend our country's peace and prosperity, and in some degree the hopes and happiness of the whole human family.

In assuming responsibilities so vast I fervently invoke the aid of that Almighty Ruler of the Universe in whose hands are the destinies of nations and of men to guard this Heaven-favored land against the mischiefs which without His guidance might arise from an unwise public policy. With a firm reliance upon the wisdom of Omnipotence to sustain and direct me in the path of duty which I am appointed to pursue, I stand in the presence of this assembled multitude of my countrymen to take upon myself the solemn obligation "to the best of my ability to preserve, protect, and defend the Constitution of the United States."

A concise enumeration of the principles which will guide me in the administrative policy of the Government is not only in accordance with the examples set me by all my predecessors, but is eminently befitting the occasion. [...]

The inestimable value of our Federal Union is felt and acknowledged by all. By this system of united and confederated States our people are permitted collectively and individually to seek their own happiness in their own way, and the consequences have been most auspicious. Since the Union was formed the number of the States has increased from thirteen to twenty-eight; two of these have taken their position as members of the Confederacy within the last week. Our population has increased from three to twenty millions. New communities and States are seeking protection under its ægis, and multitudes from the Old World are flocking to our shores to participate in its blessings. Beneath its benign sway peace and prosperity prevail. Freed from the burdens and miseries of war, our trade and intercourse have extended throughout the world. Mind, no longer tasked in devising means to accomplish or resist schemes of ambition, usurpation, or conquest, is devoting itself to man's true interests in developing his faculties and powers and the capacity of nature to minister to his enjoyments. Genius is free to announce its inventions and discoveries, and the hand is free to accomplish whatever the head conceives not incompatible with the rights of a fellow-being. All distinctions of birth or of rank have been abolished. All citizens, whether native or adopted, are placed upon terms of precise equality. All are entitled to equal rights and equal protection. No union exists between church and state, and perfect freedom of opinion is guaranteed to all sects and creeds.

These are some of the blessings secured to our happy land by our Federal Union. To perpetuate them it is our sacred duty to preserve it. Who shall assign limits to the achievements of free minds and free hands under the protection of this glorious Union? No treason to mankind since the organization of society would be equal in atrocity to that of him who would lift his hand to destroy it. He would overthrow the noblest structure of human wisdom, which protects himself and his fellow man. He would stop the progress of free government and involve his country either in anarchy or despotism. He would extinguish the fire of liberty, which warms and animates the hearts of happy millions and invites all the nations of the earth to imitate our example. If he say that error and wrong are committed in the administration of the Government, let him remember that nothing human can be perfect, and that under no other system of government revealed by Heaven or devised by man has reason been allowed so free and broad a scope to combat error. Has the sword of despots proved to be a safer or surer instrument of reform in government than enlightened reason? Does he expect to find among the ruins of this Union a happier abode for our swarming millions than they now have under it? Every lover of his country must shudder at the thought of the possibility of its dissolution, and will be ready to adopt the patriotic sentiment, "Our Federal Union – it must be preserved." To preserve it the compromises which alone enabled our fathers to form a common constitution for the government and protection of so many States and distinct communities, of such diversified habits, interests, and domestic institutions, must be sacredly and religiously observed. Any attempt to disturb or destroy these compromises, being terms of the compact of union, can lead to none other than the most ruinous and disastrous consequences.

It is a source of deep regret that in some sections of our country misguided persons have occasionally indulged in schemes and agitations whose object is the destruction of domestic institutions existing in other sections – institutions which existed at the adoption of the Constitution and were recognized and protected by it. All must see that if it were possible for them to be successful in attaining their object the dissolution of the Union and the consequent destruction of our happy form of government must speedily follow. [...]

The Republic of Texas has made known her desire to come into our Union, to form a part of our Confederacy and enjoy with us the blessings of liberty secured and guaranteed by our Constitution. Texas was once a part of our country – was unwisely ceded away to a foreign power – is now independent, and possesses an undoubted right to dispose of a part or the whole of her territory and to merge her sovereignty as a separate and independent state in ours. I congratulate my country that by an act of the late Congress of the United States the assent of this Government has been given to the reunion, and it only remains for the two countries to agree upon the terms to consummate an object so important to both.

I regard the question of annexation as belonging exclusively to the United States and Texas. They are independent powers competent to contract, and foreign nations have no right to interfere with them or to take exceptions to their reunion. Foreign powers do not seem to appreciate the true character of our Government. Our Union is a confederation of independent States, whose policy is peace with each other and all the world. To enlarge its limits is to extend the dominions of peace over additional territories and increasing millions. The world has nothing to fear from military ambition in our Government. While the Chief Magistrate and the popular branch of Congress are elected for short terms by the suffrages of those millions who must in their own persons bear all the burdens and miseries of war, our Government can not be otherwise than pacific. Foreign powers should therefore look on the annexation of Texas to the United States not as the conquest of a nation seeking to extend her dominions by arms and violence, but as the peaceful acquisition of a territory once her own, by adding another member to our confederation, with the consent of that member, thereby diminishing the chances of war and opening to them new and ever-increasing markets for their products.

To Texas the reunion is important, because the strong protecting arm of our Government would be extended over her, and the vast resources of her fertile soil and genial climate would be speedily developed, while the safety of New Orleans and of our whole southwestern frontier against hostile aggression, as well as the interests of the whole Union, would be promoted by it.

In the earlier stages of our national existence the opinion prevailed with some that our system of confederated States could not operate successfully over an extended territory, and serious objections have at different times been made to the enlargement of our boundaries. These objections were earnestly urged when we acquired Louisiana. Experience has shown that they were not well founded. The title of numerous Indian tribes to vast tracts of country has been extinguished; new States have been admitted into the Union; new Territories have been created and our jurisdiction and laws extended over them. As our population has expanded, the Union has been cemented and strengthened. As our boundaries have been enlarged and our agricultural population has been spread over a large surface, our federative system has acquired additional strength and security. It may well be doubted whether it would not be in greater danger of overthrow if our present population were confined to the comparatively narrow limits of the original thirteen States than it is now that they are sparsely settled over a more expanded territory. It is confidently believed that our system may be safely extended to the utmost bounds of our territorial limits, and that as it shall be extended the bonds of our Union, so far from being weakened, will become stronger.

None can fail to see the danger to our safety and future peace if Texas remains an independent state or becomes an ally or dependency of some foreign nation more powerful than herself. Is there one among our citizens who would not prefer perpetual peace with Texas to occasional wars, which so often occur between bordering independent nations? Is there one who would not prefer free intercourse with her to high duties on all our products and manufactures which enter her ports or cross her frontiers? Is there one who would not prefer an unrestricted communication with her citizens to the frontier obstructions which must occur if she remains out of the Union? Whatever is good or evil in the local institutions of Texas will remain her own whether annexed to the United States or not. None of the present States will be responsible for them any more than they are for the local institutions of each other. They have confederated together for certain specified objects. Upon the same principle that they would refuse to form a perpetual union with Texas because of her local institutions our forefathers would have been prevented from forming our present Union. Perceiving no valid objection to the measure and many reasons for its adoption vitally affecting the peace, the safety, and the prosperity of both countries, I shall on the broad principle which formed the basis and produced the adoption of our Constitution, and not in any narrow spirit of sectional policy, endeavor by all constitutional, honorable, and appropriate means to consummate the expressed will of the people and Government of the United States by the reannexation of Texas to our Union at the earliest practicable period.

Nor will it become in a less degree my duty to assert and maintain by all constitutional means the right of the United States to that portion of our territory which lies beyond the Rocky Mountains. Our title to the country of the Oregon is "clear and unquestionable," and already are our people preparing to perfect that title by occupying it with their wives and children. But eighty years ago our population was confined on the west by the ridge of the Alleghanies.[37]

---

[37] In the period of the revolution the frontier crossed the Alleghanies into Kentucky and Tennessee.

Within that period – within the lifetime, I might say, of some of my hearers – our people, increasing to many millions, have filled the eastern valley of the Mississippi, adventurously ascended the Missouri to its headsprings, and are already engaged in establishing the blessings of self-government in valleys of which the rivers flow to the Pacific. The world beholds the peaceful triumphs of the industry of our emigrants. To us belongs the duty of protecting them adequately wherever they may be upon our soil. The jurisdiction of our laws and the benefits of our republican institutions should be extended over them in the distant regions which they have selected for their homes. The increasing facilities of intercourse will easily bring the States, of which the formation in that part of our territory can not be long delayed, within the sphere of our federative Union. In the meantime every obligation imposed by treaty or conventional stipulations should be sacredly respected. [...]

Although in our country the Chief Magistrate must almost of necessity be chosen by a party and stand pledged to its principles and measures, yet in his official action he should not be the President of a part only, but of the whole people of the United States. While he executes the laws with an impartial hand, shrinks from no proper responsibility, and faithfully carries out in the executive department of the Government the principles and policy of those who have chosen him, he should not be unmindful that our fellow-citizens who have differed with him in opinion are entitled to the full and free exercise of their opinions and judgments, and that the rights of all are entitled to respect and regard.

Confidently relying upon the aid and assistance of the coordinate departments of the Government in conducting our public affairs, I enter upon the discharge of the high duties which have been assigned me by the people, again humbly supplicating that Divine Being who has watched over and protected our beloved country from its infancy to the present hour to continue His gracious benedictions upon us, that we may continue to be a prosperous and happy people.   MARCH 4. 1845.

Source: James K. Polk (1795-1849). "Inaugural Address." *A Compilation of the Messages and Papers of the Presidents: Prepared under the Direction of the Joint Committee on Printing, of the House and Senate, Pursuant to an Act of the Fifty-Second Congress of the United States*. 20 vols. New York: Bureau of National Literature, 1897, Vol. 5, 2223-2227, 2229-2232.

173. "Land of Liberty" (1847)

Source: "Land of Liberty." *Punch* 1847. Courtesy Library of Congress.

174. William Gilpin
"Manifest Destiny" (1846)

THERE has been a radical misapprehension in the popular mind as to the true character of the *"Great Plains of America,"* as complete as that which pervaded Europe respecting the Atlantic Ocean during the whole historic period prior to COLUMBUS. These PLAINS are not *deserts*, but the opposite, and are the cardinal basis of the future empire of commerce and industry now erecting itself upon the North American Continent.

They are calcareous,[38] and form the PASTORAL GARDEN of the world. [...]

It is not for me, in this season of gathering splendor, to speak *tamely* upon a subject of such intense and engrossing novelty and interest. I may properly here quote the concluding sentences of a report which I was required to make on the 2d of March, 1846, *to the United States Senate*, at that time brimful of illustrious statesmen. What I said then and there, in the first dawning twilight of our glory, I will now repeat:

"The calm, wise man sets himself to study aright and understand clearly the deep designs of Providence – to scan the great volume of nature – to fathom, if possible, the will of the Creator, and to receive with respect what may be revealed to him.

"Two centuries have rolled over our race upon this continent. From nothing we have become 20,000,000. From nothing we are grown to be in agriculture, in commerce, in civilization, and in natural strength, the first among nations existing or in history. So much is our *destiny* – so far, up to this time – *transacted*, accomplished, certain, and not to be disputed. From this threshold we read the future.

"The *untransacted* destiny of the American people is to subdue the continent – to rush over this vast field to the Pacific Ocean – to animate the many hundred millions of its people, and to cheer them upward – to set the principle of self-government at work – to agitate these herculean masses – to establish a new order in human affairs – to set free the enslaved – to regenerate superannuated[39] nations – to change darkness into light – to stir up the sleep of a hundred centuries – to teach old nations a new civilization – to confirm the destiny of the human race – to carry the career of mankind to its culminating point – to cause stagnant people to be re-born – to perfect science – to emblazon history with the conquest of peace – to shed a new and resplendent glory upon mankind – to unite the world in one social family – to dissolve the spell of tyranny and exalt charity – to absolve the curse that weighs down humanity, and to shed blessings round the world!

"*Divine task! immortal mission!* Let us tread fast and joyfully the open trail before us! Let every American heart open wide for patriotism to glow undimmed, and confide with religious faith in the sublime and prodigious destiny of his well-loved country."

Source: William Gilpin (1814-1894). *Mission of the North American People, Geographical, Social, and Political*. Philadelphia: J.B. Lippincott, 1873, 71 (Chapter VII: "Pastoral America"), 124 (Chapter XII: The North American Mission – Continued").

---

[38] Composed of or containing lime or lime-stone.
[39] Incapacitated by age; old and infirm.

175. Anonymous
"The Popular Movement" (1845)

From the time that the Pilgrim Fathers landed on these shores to the present moment, the older settlements have been constantly throwing off a hardy, restless and lawless pioneer population, which has kept in advance, subduing the wilderness and preparing the way for more orderly settlers who tread rapidly upon their footsteps. It is but a short time since Western Massachusetts, Connecticut and Rhode Island, although now proverbially the land of "steady habits" and good morals, presented a population no ways superior socially to that of Texas at the present day. As their numbers increased, law and order obtained control, and those unable to bear constraint sought new homes. Those latter have rolled forward in advance of civilization, like the surf on an advancing wave, indicative of its resistless approach. This is the natural, unchangeable effect of our position upon this continent, and it must continue until the waves of the Pacific have hemmed in and restrained the onward movement.

To say that the settlement of a fertile and unappropriated soil by right of individual purchase is the aggression of a government is absurd. Equally ridiculous is it to suppose that when a band of hardy settlers have reclaimed the wilderness, multiplied in numbers, built up a community and organized a government, that they have not the right to claim the confederation of that society of States from the bosom of which they emanated. An inalienable right of man is to institute for themselves that form of government which suits them best, and to change it when they please. On this continent communities grow up mostly by immigration from the United States. Such communities therefore inevitably establish the same form of government which they left behind and *demand* of them that they *come* into the Union. Mexico is a government professedly of the people. If that people choose to change its form they have the right to do so. They have already done so with the approbation of the world. If therefore Mexico, in whole or in part, becomes so settled by the Anglo-Saxon race that they have a majority and decide to alter the system to that of the United States model, and ask for admittance into the Union, the same inalienable right will exist and who will deny it?

Source: Anonymous (Editorial). "The Popular Movement." *New York Morning News* (May 24, 1845); quoted in Frederick Merk. *Manifest Destiny and Mission in American History: A Reinterpretation*. New York: Knopf, 1970, 22-23.

176. John L. O'Sullivan
"The True Title" (1845)

Away, away with all these cobweb tissues of rights of discovery, exploration, settlement, contiguity, etc. [... The American claim] is by the right of our manifest destiny to overspread and to possess the whole of the continent which Providence has given us for the development of the great experiment of liberty and federative self government entrusted to us. It is a right such as that of the tree to the space of air and earth suitable for the full expansion of its principle and destiny of growth – such as that of the stream to the channel required for the still accumulating volume of its flow. It is in our future far more than in our past, or in the past history of Spanish exploration or French colonial rights, that our True Title is to be found. [...] Oregon can never be to [England] or for her, any thing but a mere hunting ground for furs and peltries. [...] Nor can she ever colonize it with any sort of transplanted population of her own. It is far too remote and too ungenial for any such purpose. [...] In our hands [...] it must fast fill in with a population destined to establish within the life of the existing generation, a noble young empire of the Pacific, vying in all the elements of greatness with that already overspreading the Atlantic and the great Mississippi valley.

Source: John L. O'Sullivan (1813-1895?). "The True Title." *New York Morning News* (December 27, 1845); quoted in Frederick Merk. *Manifest Destiny and Mission in American History: A Reinterpretation*. New York: Knopf, 1970, 31-32.

177. Thomas Hart Benton
Speech on the Oregon Question (1846)

[...] Since the dispersion of man upon earth, I know of no human event, past or present, which promises a greater, and more beneficent change upon earth than the arrival of the van[40] of the Caucasian race (the Celtic-Anglo-Saxon division) upon the border of the sea which washes the shore of the eastern Asia.[41] The Mongolian, or Yellow race, is there, four hundred millions in number, spreading almost to Europe; a race once the foremost of the human family in the arts of civilization, but torpid and stationary for thousands of years. It is a race far above the Ethiopian, or Black – above the Malay, or Brown, (if we must admit five races) – and above the American Indian, or Red: it is a race far above all these, but still, far below the White; and, like all the rest, must receive an impression from the superior race whenever they come in contact. It would seem that the White race alone received the divine command, to subdue and replenish the earth! for it is the only race that has obeyed it – the only one that hunts out new and distant lands, and even a New World, to subdue and replenish. Starting from western Asia, taking Europe for their field, and the sun for their guide, and leaving the Mongolians behind, they arrived, after many ages, on the shores of the Atlantic, which they lit up with the lights of science and religion, and adorned with the useful and the elegant arts. Three and a half centuries ago, this race, in obedience to the great command, arrived in the New World, and found new lands to subdue and replenish. For a long time it was confined to the border of the new field,[42] (I now mean the Celtic-Anglo-Saxon division;) and even fourscore years ago the philosophic Burke was considered a rash man because he said the English colonists would top the Alleganies,[43] and d[e]scend into the valley of the Mississippi, and occupy without parchment if the Crown refused to make grants of land. What was considered a rash declaration eighty years ago, is old history, in our young country, at this day. Thirty years ago I said the same thing of the Rocky Mountains and the Columbia: it was ridiculed then: it is becoming history to-day. [...] The van of the Caucasian race now top the

---

[40] The foremost portion of, or the foremost position in, a company or train of persons moving.
[41] The implication is that by arriving in the Oregon Territory, the white settlers have reached the Pacific which 'connects' America to Asia. Similar ideas were voiced later by Walt Whitman in "Passage to India."
[42] I.e., the colonies bordering the Atlantic Ocean.
[43] Mountain range forming the western part of the Appalachian Mountains.

Rocky Mountains, and spread down to the shores of the Pacific. In a few years a great population will grow up there, luminous with the accumulated lights of European and American civilization. Their presence in such a position cannot be without its influence upon eastern Asia. The sun of civilization must shine across the sea: socially and commercially, the van of the Caucasians, and the rear of the Mongolians, must intermix. They must talk together, and trade together, and marry together. Commerce is a great civilizer – social intercourse as great – and marriage greater. The White and Yellow races can marry together, as well as eat and trade together. Moral and intellectual superiority will do the rest: the White race will take the ascendant, elevating what is susceptible of improvement – wearing out what is not. The Red race has disappeared from the Atlantic coast: the tribes that resisted civilization, met extinction. This is a cause of lamentation with many. For my part, I cannot murmur at what seems to be the effect of divine law. I cannot repine that this Capitol has replaced the wigwam – this Christian people, replaced the savages – white matrons, the red squaws – and that such men as Washington, Franklin, and Jefferson, have taken the place of Powhattan, Opechonecanough,[44] and other red men, howsoever respectable they may have been as savages. Civilization, or extinction, has been the fate of all people who have found themselves in the track of the advancing Whites, and civilization, always the preference of the Whites, has been pressed as an object, while extinction has followed as a consequence of its resistance. The Black and the Red races have often felt their ameliorating influence. The Yellow race, next to themselves in the scale of mental and moral excellence, and in the beauty of form, once their superiors in the useful and elegant arts, and in learning, and still respectable though stationary; this race cannot fail to receive a new impulse from the approach of the Whites, improved so much since so many ages ago they left the western borders of Asia. The apparition of the van of the Caucasian race, rising upon them in the east after having left them on the west, and after having completed the circumnavigation of the globe, must wake up and reanimate the torpid body of old Asia. Our position and policy will I commend us to their hospitable reception: political considerations will aid the action of social and commercial influences. Pressed upon by the great Powers of Europe – the same that press upon us – they must in our approach see the advent of friends, not of foes – of benefactors, not of invaders. The moral and intellectual superiority of the White race will do the rest: and thus, the youngest people, and the newest land, will become the reviver and the regenerator of the oldest.

It is in this point of view, and as acting upon the social, political, and religious condition of Asia, and giving a new point of departure to her ancient civilization, that I look upon the settlement of the Columbia river by the van of the Caucasian race as the most momentous human event in the history of man since his dispersion over the face of the earth.

These are the values of the Columbia river and its valley – these the advantages of its settlement by us. They are great and grand, beneficial to ourselves, and to the human race, and amply sufficient to justify the United States in vindicating their title to the country, and maintaining its possession at all hazards. [...]

Source: Thomas Hart Benton (1782-1858). *Speech of Mr. Benton, of Missouri on the Oregon Question Delivered in the Senate of the United States, May 22, 25, & 28, 1846.* Fairfield, WA: Ye Galleon Press, 1998, 66-68.

---

[44] Indian chiefs.

178. Anonymous
"The Destiny of the Country" (1847)

Notwithstanding the proverbial pride of Americans, few have yet attained any due sense of the magnificence of their country and the splendor of their national destiny. Indeed, the ridiculous vanity with which foreign tourists justly charge us, gathering their testimony from Fourth of July orations, or from patriotic resolutions passed at public meetings, is ascribable to the absence of that noble pride which a more intelligent and considerate acquaintance with our position among the nations of the earth would inspire. There is more to sober than to intoxicate, to awe than to addle, in a true estimate of ourselves and our country. Our vanity springs from the contemplation of what we have done, or what we are, and is often based upon comparisons which nothing but our own ignorance renders possible or flattering. We glory in the wars we have waged with the most powerful nation on the face of the earth, and confound the victory which a broad ocean, separating us from our foe, and a territory unconquerable chiefly in its extent, gave us, with our own valor and general superiority. The rapid growth of our population seems to us a merit of our own. Every providential advantage in our position we appropriate as the result of our own intentions and labors. We attribute our institutions wholly to the sagacity[45] of our Fathers, and the maintenance of them to the wisdom of their Sons. Our national importance seems to us to have been wrought out by our own right arms. And there is a very amusing feeling throughout the nation, that Americans are a different order of beings from others; that one American soldier is at least equal to four Mexicans, three French or two Englishmen; a vanity which, in common with other and worse weaknesses, has involved us in the present war, and lately came near plunging us into a war with Great Britain. Ours is the only nation that resents criticism of its literature, politics or manners as a crime. [...] Few of our own countrymen who have not been abroad, have as yet taken a comprehensive view of our circumstances, or have "risen to the height of that great argument" which conducts our people to their sublime destiny. It is rare for any American to look back upon his native shores from the cliffs of Albion[46] or the peaks of the Alps, without perceiving that he has left behind him the land of promise; that he has been ignorantly dwelling in the most favored region on God's earth, among institutions compared with which any others are intolerable, and where alone the hopes of humanity have an unclouded horizon, or the progress of the race an open field.

There is no nation on the face of the earth or in the records of history, if we except the Jews, whose origin, circumstances and progress have been so purely providential as ours; none which owes so little to itself and so much to the Ruler of its destiny. It is impossible not to trace in its brief but wonderful career the unfolding of a plan too vast, and requiring too much antecedent calculation and extraordinary concurrence of events, to be ascribed to any other than infinite wisdom. The concealment of this whole continent in the mysterious remoteness of the ocean during so many centuries, while our race were trying the many necessary experiments of civilization in the old world; its discovery at the precise period when the social and political theories and policies of Europe had evidently exhausted themselves, and when other and most potent instruments of civilization destined to revolutionize the whole order of society – the mariner's compass and the

---
[45] Soundness of judgment; intelligence.
[46] England.

printing press – were just coming into use; the peculiar complexion of events in England which decided the character and views of the colonists who shaped the political destinies of this country; all indicate a consummate and glorious plan involving the interest not of a nation, but of the race. And this is the peculiarity of our existence; that unlike any other, the people are not one nation among the other nations of the earth, but a people made up of all nations, the heirs of the united blood and experience of all, equally regarded by all as their own child, to whom the hopes of the race are intrusted, and who is sent to seek and to push the fortunes of the family in a new and fresh field of enterprise. "The new world" is a phrase which from familiarity has lost its emphasis. But it contains in it an idea of the most pregnant and momentous character. "The new world," was to the nations of decrepit, exhausted Europe – its soil full of the roots of social and political prejudices fatal to the culture of human rights – a new heavens and a new earth wherein dwelleth righteousness. It was a *new world*, a world as new as if the race had been translated to another planet, where man might begin over again the experiment of civil society with the benefit of a long experience, and without the obstacle of conventional or traditionary associations and customs. This new world properly belonged to the race and not to any portion of it. It was a world, not a country; a continent, not an island, a peninsula, or a region which a river or a chain of mountains could bound. It owed its being to the united efforts of the greatest powers on earth. Spain discovered it, France explored it, England gave it language and laws; and every nation has sent rivers to its blood to run in the great stream which now bears the most precious hopes of the race on its bosom. [... Into] the soil of America has trickled drop by drop the blood of every European nation. Commingled inseparably, the divided children of the old world are the united family of the new. For the first time the chief narrations of the earth are blended in a common fate, in which their individuality is wholly lost. American blood is neither English nor Irish, nor French, nor Spanish, nor German, nor Swiss. But it is all these in large proportions of each, and every day the purely Anglo-Saxon stock is losing its predominancy. We rejoice that England so far prevailed over the early fortunes of the new world, as to give its language, its religion and its laws and customs to those colonies before which all the rest have succumbed or must finally bend. But we rejoice also that the new world has been open to the emigration of all lands, and that it now shelters in its bosom the representatives of every European soil. Nay, we firmly believe that the Anglo-Saxon stock is to be greatly improved by intermixture with other races, and that it is a providential purpose that it should here be brought into contact and become ultimately merged in a new race compounded of the richness of every olden people. But at any rate, be it for better or worse, the new world was not destined to be a mere extension of British rule, or Saxon blood, or of the characteristic customs and prejudices of any one people. It was to be the home of delegates from the race. And here we have indeed a new world, inhabited by a new race. And this astonishing heterogeneousness of races, perfectly blended into one, is one of the most interesting and peculiar features in our condition, as it is one of the marks of the universal or general interest which appertains to our destiny.

Consider in the next place, in connection with our political institutions, providential origin and circumstances, the grandeur both in extent and features of the territory inherited by this new race. Let us place ourselves at the Capitol, and from the balcony overhanging that commanding height survey the land. The landscape within reach of the outward eye is magnificent and infinitely suggestive to the visionary orb within. The broad river, the ample plain, the distant mountains, the unfinished, wide-spread city well represent and characterize the country and the people to which they belong. No spot tells like this the whole story of our recent origin, our incredible or unexampled progress, our magnificent and half-realized hopes. [...]

[... T]his vast area with natural divisions to indicate it as the home of many nations, is, by the Providence of God, one country, speaking one language, rejoicing in one common Constitution, honoring the same great national names, celebrating the same great national events. It is one nation. And it is a free nation. It possesses an ideal form of government, the dream of ancient heroes no longer a vision of the night; the prophetic visionary song of poets become the prosaic language of matter-of-fact-men. It is without hereditary rulers, without a legalized aristocracy. It is self-governed. It is a land of equal rights. It is a stable republic.

And what a marvelous and providential history has it had! The hemisphere itself has been discovered only three and a half centuries, less than one-fifth of the period which has elapsed since the origin of Christianity. Two centuries only have passed since our territory was reached by two distant bands of colonists, one led by the spirit of chivalrous adventure and commercial enterprise, the other by the love of religious liberty and political freedom; but both from the land of Hampden and Pym.[47] But three-score and ten years – the life of one man – have sped, since this people, a handful of men, breaking loose from the most powerful nation on the face of the globe at the peril of everything held dear, proclaimed its independence, and after maintaining two wars with the parent country, the Queen of the Seas, is now become the third power on the earth, with a population little short of twenty millions, with resources of manufactures and agriculture which render it substantially independent of foreign commerce in war, although able and glad to compete with the commerce of the world in peace.

It is in no indulgence of national vanity that we repeat this history, whatever the appearances may be. There are stains enough upon our skirts to humble the pride of any patriotic American, stains that look darker here than anywhere else. But whatever our wrongs or follies or ill deserts, no lover of his race, no friend of Christianity, no one who waits upon God's providence and believes in a divine government, can fail to see that the great Ruler of events has shaped the natural features, the general history and the political institutions of our country, into a wonderful theatre of mercy and love, and fitted it for a great display of his power; nor can we hesitate to announce the preparation here for a glorious and unexampled triumph of the principles of justice, humanity and religion. Could [...] the three great bands that under Providence have made us what we are, the Discoverers, the Pilgrim Fathers, and the Revolutionary heroes, be gathered with us on this noble gallery and stretch their eyes where ours go over the land as it is and into the open secret of the Future as it must be, would not he who came expressly to erect the cross on heathen soil and to gain new victories for Christ, and the Puritans who sought religious liberty in the wilderness, and the patriots who fought for religious and political freedom – the discoverers, the settlers, and the founders of our country – unite in declaring this the land of promise and themselves men of destiny [...]? Would they not see, and should not we see, something more than the well-being of a particular people; something too momentous and solemn for national exultation, in the history and prospects of this our country? Aye. Their thoughts would be of the prospects of the human race thus opening before them. More understandingly than we, would they call this the *new* world;

---

[47] Here: England

the world beginning over again, with the riches, the experience, the literature, the morality and religion of the old world – but on a virgin soil, sustaining free institutions and enjoying perfect toleration – with a people covering a quarter of the globe, speaking one language, bound together by common interests, professing one common religion – yet in the dew of youth, but already full of wealth, health, power and prosperity! [...]

There is a growing feeling that the interests of the New World, and the prospects of humanity on this continent are largely dependent upon the preservation of the union of the United States. And in nothing has the Providence over us been more strikingly illustrated than in the unexpected bonds of stability which have disclosed themselves in the history of events. If the rapidity of our growth, the increase of our territory, the early and fierce agitation of the most exciting questions had been foreseen, it certainly would not have been credited that the Union of these States would have continued beyond a half century! The bare spread of territory would have been considered a sufficient cause of separation, to say nothing of the difference of interests and the apparent independence of each great section of the country of every other. But what an astonishing and inextricable mutual dependence has revealed itself, till this time increasing with the increase of causes of dissociation or severance; the centripetal ever counteracting the centrifugal forces, and in the very nick of time asserting new energy, until we are almost forced to believe the integrity of the Union a providential decree! [...]

There is, probably, no subject which has jeopardized the union of these States so much as slavery. But the principal danger was at the outset of the discussion. The firmness and constitutional fidelity which the North and West have shown in regard to that institution have quieted the apprehensions of the South. It has become perfectly plain, that no intention exists, anywhere in this country, to violate the chartered rights of the South. The policy agreed to by the North and West, is one in which the South itself concurs, if we may judge the matter by the course of their Coryphæus, Mr. Calhoun,[48] viz. to abide the compromises of the Constitution. Every indication exists, that abolition excitement has reached its head, and is exploding in every kind of extravagance and ultraism, until the calm and wise heads and hearts of the country are utterly alienated from all cooperation with it. Soon the economic view of the question, is to become the absorbing one, and the moment Southern intelligence takes *this* question into its own hands, healthier and more dispassionate views will be entertained on the subject at large, and the bands of union among the States will, we are persuaded, be drawn closer than ever. Every one must see that the cotton, sugar, and tobacco staples are every day losing their relative and preponderating importance among the exports of the country. [...] From these general and various considerations, we infer that disunion is not likely to proceed from the discussion of slavery, or from conflict of interests. To industrial change, bringing about a great community of labor and production, do we confidently look for the gradual dissipation of all sectional prejudices, in every part of the Union, and the growth in their stead of a lasting community of interest and regard.

[...] At this time greater apprehensions are doubtless felt for the permanency of the Union, from the spirit of conquest which seems to have seized our government, than from all other causes. The annexation of Texas seemed to be a disturbance of the mutual dependence of the parts of the country on each other. But, hating the extension it gave to

---

[48] John Caldwell Calhoun (1782-1850), vice-president of the United States (1825-1832) who maintained that the states had the right to nullify federal legislation.

slavery it did not really add a centrifugal territory to the Union, seeing that its connection with and dependence upon us, is much more direct and natural than with Mexico, from which it is divided by deserts and mountains. [...] It is calculated, we believe, that the advance of the tide of population upon the Western frontier is at the rate of seventeen miles annually. It becomes a simple calculation, how soon, at this rate, we shall reach the Pacific ocean. And long before that time our cup must run over in the southern direction. That Mexico will ultimately fall a political prey, not to force, but to a superior population, insensibly oozing[49] into her territories, changing her customs, and out-living, out-trading, exterminating her weaker blood, we regard with as much certainty, as we do the final extinction of the Indian races, to which the mass of the Mexican population seem very little superior; and we have no reason to doubt that this country will not have doubled its three centuries of existence, before South America will speak the English tongue and submit to the civilization, laws and religion of the Anglo-Saxon race. We, as a great civilized and Christian nation, have only to use all endeavors to have this tide of population regular and peaceful in its course – with no violence, or spirit of conquest; its sure progress we cannot help. [...]

Source: Anonymous. "The Destiny of Our Country." *The American Review: A Whig Journal of Politics, Literature, Art and Science* 5 (March 1847), 231-236, 238-239.

179. Herman Melville
White-Jacket, or, the World in a Man-of-War (1850)

[...] The world has arrived at a period which renders it the part of Wisdom to pay homage to the prospective precedents of the Future in preference to those of the Past. The Past is dead, and has no resurrection; but the Future is endowed with such a life, that it lives to us even in anticipation. The Past is, in many things, the foe of mankind; the Future is, in all things, our friend. In the Past is no hope; the Future is both hope and fruition. The Past is the text-book of tyrants; the Future the Bible of the Free. Those who are solely governed by the Past stand like Lot's wife, crystallized in the act of looking backward,[50] and forever incapable of looking before. [...]

But in many things we Americans are driven to a rejection of the maxims of the Past, seeing that, ere long, the van of the nations must, of right, belong to ourselves. There are occasions when it is for America to make precedents and not to obey them. We should, if possible, prove a teacher to posterity, instead of being the pupil of by-gone generations. More shall come after us than have gone before; the world is not yet middle-aged.

Escaped from the house of bondage, Israel of old did not follow after the ways of the Egyptians. To her was given an express dispensation; to her were given new things under the sun. And we Americans are the peculiar, chosen people – the Israel of our time; we bear the ark[51] of the liberties of the world. Seventy years ago we escaped from thrall; and, besides our first birth-right – embracing one continent of earth – God has given to us, for a future inheritance, the broad domains of the political pagans, that shall yet come and lie

---

[49] Seeping, passing slowly through small openings.
[50] Lot's wife was turned into a pillar of salt when she looked back as she and her husband fled from Sodom.
[51] The chest containing the Ten Commandments written on stone tablets, carried by the Hebrews during their desert wanderings.

down under the shade of our ark, without bloody hands being lifted. God has predestinated, mankind expects, great things from our race; and great things we feel in our souls. The rest of the nations must soon be in our rear. We are the pioneers of the world; the advance-guard, sent on through the wilderness of untried things, to break a new path in the New World that is ours. In our youth is our strength; in our inexperience, our wisdom. At a period when other nations have but lisped, our deep voice is heard afar. Long enough have we been skeptics with regard to ourselves, and doubted whether, indeed, the political Messiah had come. But he has come in *us*, if we would but give utterance to his promptings. And let us always remember that with ourselves, almost for the first time in the history of earth, national selfishness is unbounded philanthropy; for we can not do a good to America but we give alms to the world.

Source: Herman Melville (1819-1891). *White-Jacket, or, The World in a Man-of-War*. New York: Harper & Brothers, 1850, 150-151 [Chapter 36].

180. Anonymous
"Providence in American History" (1858)

Human society is a wonderful testimony to the omnipotence and the omnipresence of God. It is a standing miracle, demonstrating a wisdom above all comprehension, a watchfulness infinite in tenderness of spirit and variety of action. Each individual man presents some features that, however marred and defaced by sin, remind us of the glorious Creator. Amidst all the defilement of depravity we recognize God's image, and of what a magnificent estate is it the impressive remnant! In how many strange and startling forms does it authenticate itself! Now it is a light shining through a man's memory and falling upon the past innocence of childhood; then a light penetrating the future and opening a luminous vista to the throne of judgment; to-day in a tone, to-morrow in a look; here in the clasp of a hand, and there in the glance of an adoring eye; this image vindicates for every one a holier birth-place than earth, and a nobler destiny than time. But when we turn from man to society the wonder increases. To see such discordant elements harmonized – the lion and the lamb even now lying down together – the demon and the angel reposing in the same pavilion or walking abroad in company – opposite tastes, habits, natures fraternizing in peaceful companionship – how the mystery repeats itself anew every day, and wraps itself in thicker folds the more that our proud intellects seek to understand it! If the individual man has his counterpart in the planet on which he dwells, society affects us like the universe. The spectacle of millions of people, all cared for and sustained by the beneficent Hand, impresses a thoughtful mind in a manner similar to the scenery of the starry heavens.

A nation is a splendid object for a reflecting intellect to contemplate. Here are thousands of human beings, with their diversified forms of life; here are all kinds of industry; here are want and plenty, starvation and luxury, ignorance and learning, crime and virtue; here are heaven and hell in spirit and practice; and all dwelling side by side, all cemented into marvelous unity, and holding together as if one common soul had transformed them into one common mass. It is folly to attribute this to institutions of government. The institutions are only the outward symbol of the inward union. All the statesmanship of the world, unaided by other and mightier forces, could never organize the relations of two persons, or establish a foundation on which they could stand together. It is by God's act – partly in the original laws of our nature, and partly by the constant agency of His Providence – that this amazing complexity of character, interest, life is upheld. In our vanity we talk of the security of life and property, the stability of our institutions; but there are always thousands of volcanoes ready to burst forth and deluge the land with their streams of fire. A daily revolution would be no wonder. The wonder is that it does not happen. Happen it would if we had no higher protection than the mere jurisprudence and police of nations. How true it is that, *"except the Lord keep the city, the watchmen waketh but in vain!"* [...]

Happily for the American mind the sentiment of an overruling Providence is reverently cherished. [...] We believe that the deepest feeling of the American heart springs from a conviction that Providence has presided over the colonization and progress of this country. [...]

The capacity for progress that this sentiment awakens puts man in possession of all the means necessary to establish his sovereignty over matter and to build up the fabric of civilization. It has given us our best institutions, and, above all, created a spirit in our country that has signalized itself in education, philanthropy, and patriotism. The nature of this principle is such that it does not exhibit itself in formal modes of thought, nor fulfill its designs through preconceived plans. It is no adept in language; and not seldom when strongest in feeling it is weakest in logic. To trace its agency it is not necessary to consider it as deliberately entering on measures that forethought has suggested to be essential to the attainment of its end. For it is instinctive rather than argumentative, and by a higher form of mind than legislative ability ascertains what is proper and expedient for the accomplishment of its object. Often when least known it is most felt; and not until men, looking back to its results as incorporated into the structure of society, study its bearings are they prepared to read the seal of a divine hand on it. Indeed, it is impossible for us to see how this great sentiment could operate in man otherwise than through his unconsciousness. If his eyes were not holden how easily they might be dazzled! Man glories in the intellect that designs, in the hand that constructs, and, absorbed in his selfish aims, robs God of the praise of wisdom and power. The wonder-working spirit is, therefore, hidden from him; and although it is present in his sense of duty, in lofty and impassioned impulse, in the glow of inspiration, yet he obeys it by force of sympathy and not on the ground of knowledge – follows its mysterious guidance and sees not whither it is going, so that when the decree is fulfilled he is more astonished than his contemporaries at the manner in which it has been done. [...]

[...] Nothing, perhaps, in connection with this sentiment in the American mind, is more striking than the intense conviction that we are performing a work for the world. We say, intense conviction. No other language expresses the fact. The feeling of the popular heart – that trustworthy instinct so much more reliable than the popular judgement – always associates the institutions of our country with the progress of humanity in foreign lands. How the leaven is to work, how the influence is to be communicated, the intellect of the masses does not perceive. Nor can our statesmen see the mode in which it is to be done. But the impression is all the stronger for the obscurity in which it is involved. The very mystery that hangs about it is an intimation of its divine origin. [...]

If, however, the sense of Providence in national affairs is primarily due to the moral spirit which Christianity awakens in the heart, it is important to remember that this spirit, acting through the intellect, reads the manifestations of God in the outward world, and discerns His going forth in the events of the age. It is sense above the bodily senses, and higher than the understanding. Yet it disdains not to use these its humbler instruments, and by so using renders them the fitter for even their earthly offices. Providence is, indeed, a mystery, but it is also a fact. It is necessarily infinite, but it makes its appeal to a finite comprehension. In it there is always something to be known – a truth to be distinctly apprehended, an order to be observed and scrutinized, a movement to be traced out with satisfying clearness. Providence educates the intellect as well as the conscience, the reason no less than faith. A theory of Providence that rejected the natural would be as defective as one ignoring the supernatural; for each idea has its place, each throws light on the other, each is necessary to a perfect system. It is this that saves us, on the one hand, from superstition and enthusiasm, while guarding us, on the other hand, from measuring the ways of God by the dim and narrow perceptions of unaided judgment. The workings of Providence, therefore, if our minds are not blinded, will disclose themselves to us; for it is the essence of Providence to distinguish itself from ordinary phenomena, to separate itself from the common course of events, or to clothe these events in such aspects as to render them more significant than otherwise they would appear. Holding fast to this principle as our guide, we hope to be able, in the further discussion of this topic, to point out certain peculiarities in our national career that illustrate the doctrine of God's providence. [...]

Every thing connected with our position, history, progress, points out the United States of America as the land of the future. The physical features of our continent, presenting such marked contrasts of the Eastern Hemisphere, indicate a form of civilization that could not exist elsewhere on the globe. It is strikingly adapted not only to greatness of empire, but to that peculiar form of greatness which seems to be reserved for our inheritance. [...] Taken in whole, it is a wonderful provision for the intelligence, sagacity, energy, restlessness, and indomitable will of such a race as the Anglo-Saxon – a race that masters physical nature without being mastered by it – a race in which the intensest home-feelings combine with a love of enterprise, adventure, and colonization – a race that fears nothing, claims everything within reach, enjoys the future more than the present, and believes in a destiny of incomparable and immeasurable grandeur. Without the least extravagance it may be said that there never was such a character – such elements of activity, foresight, sovereignty – acting on a theatre so broad, so ample, so wonderful. It is the only country that holds out any general prospect to humanity – that offers ideas, sentiments, hopes for general diffusion – that has an educative power for the world in its principles and institutions. Where else is there a nationality more distinct, more self-defining and self-projecting, yet, withal, so open, free, and cordial in the strength and breadth of its receptiveness – so absorbing, but retaining all its vigorous and unyielding individuality? Where else are there such forces of conservatism and progress always acting and interacting? Where else is to-day a new birth out of yesterday and to-morrow, a picture for the imagination to paint from fresh materials? This, then, is the grand idea of the country, viz.: THE FUTURE. According to that idea, every thing, hitherto has been shaped. Where men have come in conflict with it and resisted its sway they have been set aside. Where measures have interfered with its mighty potency they have been swept away. [...]

Source: Anonymous [Alfred H. Guernsey (1824-1902)]. "Editor's Table." *Harper's New Monthly Magazine* 17.101 (October 1858), 694-695, 697, 699.

181. Walt Whitman
"Passage to India" (1871)

1

Singing my days,
Singing the great achievements of the present,
Singing the strong light works of engineers,
Our modern wonders, (the antique ponderous Seven outvied,)[52]
In the Old World the east the Suez canal,[53]
The New by its mighty railroad spann'd,
The seas inlaid with eloquent, gentle wires,
Yet first to sound, and ever sound, the cry with thee O soul,
The Past! the Past! the Past!

The Past – the dark unfathom'd retrospect!
The teeming gulf – the sleepers and the shadows!
The past – the infinite greatness of the past!
For what is the present after all but a growth out of the past?
(As a projectile form'd, impell'd, passing a certain line, still keeps on,
So the present, utterly form'd, impell'd by the past.) [...]

2

[...] Passage to India!
Lo, soul, seest thou not God's purpose from the first?
The earth to be spann'd, connected by network,
The races, neighbors, to marry and be given in marriage,
The oceans to be cross'd, the distant brought near,
The lands to be welded together. [...]

3

Passage to India!
Lo soul for thee of tableaus twain,
I see in one the Suez canal initiated, open'd, [...]
In one again, different, (yet thine, all thine, O soul, the same,)
I see over my own continent the Pacific railroad surmounting every barrier; [...]
Bridging the three or four thousand miles of land travel,
Tying the Eastern to the Western sea,
The road between Europe and Asia. [...]

4

Passage to India! [...]
Along all history, down the slopes,
As a rivulet running, sinking now, and now again to the surface rising,
A ceaseless thought, a varied train – lo, soul, to thee, thy sight, they rise,
The plans, the voyages again, the expeditions;

---

[52] The seven wonders of the world.
[53] Opened 1869.

Again Vasco de Gama sails forth,
Again the knowledge gain'd, the mariner's compass,
Lands found and nations born, thou born America,
For purpose vast, man's long probation fill'd,
Thou rondure of the world[54] at last accomplish'd.

5

O vast Rondure, swimming in space,
Cover'd all over with visible power and beauty,
Alternate light and day and the teeming spiritual darkness,
Unspeakable high processions of sun and moon and countless stars above,
Below, the manifold grass and waters, animals, mountains, trees,
With inscrutable purpose, some hidden prophetic intention,
Now first it seems my thought begins to span thee.

Down from the gardens of Asia descending radiating,
Adam and Eve appear, then their myriad progeny after them,
Wandering, yearning, curious, with restless explorations,
With questionings, baffled, formless, feverish, with never-happy hearts,
With that sad incessant refrain, *Wherefore unsatisfied soul?* and *Whither O mocking life?* [...]

6

Year at whose wide-flung door I sing!
Year of the purpose accomplish'd!
Year of the marriage of continents, climates and oceans!
(No mere Doge of Venice now, wedding the Adriatic,)
I see O year in you the vast terraqueous globe given, and giving all,
Europe to Asia, Africa join'd, and they to the New World,
The lands, geographies, dancing before you, holding a festival garland,
As brides and bridegrooms hand in hand.

Passage to India!
Cooling airs from Caucasus far, soothing cradle of man,
The river Euphrates flowing, the past lit up again.

Lo soul, the retrospect brought forward,
The old, most populous, wealthiest of earth's lands,
The streams of the Indus and the Ganges and their many affluents,
(I my shores of America walking to-day behold, resuming all,) [...].

Source: Walt Whitman (1819-1892). "Passage to India." *Leaves of Grass: Authoritative Text*. Ed. Sculley Bradley and Harold W. Blodgett. New York: Norton, 1973, 411-416.

---

[54] Roundness; here: circumnavigation.

182. John Gast
"American Progress" (1872/1874)

Frontispiece: *Crofutt's Trans-Continental Tourist Guide* (1874)

American Progress. – This beautiful picture, which will be found opposite the title page, is purely national in design, and represents the United States' portion of the American Continent; the beauty and variety, from the Atlantic to the Pacific Ocean, illustrating at a glance the grand drama of Progress in the civilization, settlement, and history of this country.

In the foreground, the central and principal figure, a beautiful and charming female, is floating westward through the air, bearing on her forehead the "Star of Empire." She has left the cities of the east far behind, crossed the Alleghanies and the "Father of Waters," and still her course is westward. In her right hand she carries a book – common school – the emblem of education and the testimonial of our national enlightenment, while with the left hand she unfolds and stretches the slender wires of the telegraph, that are to flash intelligence throughout the land. On the right of the picture, is a city, steamships, manufactories, schools and churches, over which beams of light are streaming and filling the air – indicative of civilization. The general tone of the picture on the left, declares darkness, waste and confusion. From the city proceed the three great continental lines of railway, passing the frontier settler's rude cabin and tending toward the Western Ocean. Next to these are the transportation wagons, overland stage, hunters, gold-seekers, pony-express, the pioneer emigrant and the war-dance of the "noble red man." Fleeing from

"Progress," and toward the blue waters of the Pacific, which shows itself on the left of the picture, beyond the snow-capped summits of the Sierra Nevadas, are the Indians, buffalo, wild horses, bears, and other game, moving westward – ever westward. The Indians with their squaws, papooses,[55] and "pony-lodges," turn their despairing faces toward the setting sun, as they flee from the presence of the wondrous vision. The "Star" is *too much for them.*

What American man, woman or child, does not feel a heart-throb of exultation as they think of the glorious achievements of PROGRESS since the landing of the Pilgrim Fathers, on stanch old Plymouth Rock!

This picture was the design of the author of the TOURIST – is NATIONAL,[56] and illustrates in the most artistic manner all the gigantic results of American brains and hands, which have caused the mighty wilderness to blossom like the rose!

Source: George A. Crofutt (?). "Annex No. 1: American Progress." *Crofutt's New Overland Tourist and Pacific Coast Guide: Containing a Condensed and Authentic Description of over One Thousand Two Hundred Cities, Towns, Villages, Stations, Government Fort and Camps, Mountains, Lakes, Rivers, Sulphur, Soda and Hot Springs [...] to Tell You What Is Worth Seeing – Where to See It – Where to Go – How to Go – and Whom to Stop With While Passing over the Union, Central and Southern Pacific Railroads, Their Branches and Connections, by Rail, Water and Stage [...] through Nebraska, Wyoming, Colorado, Utah, Montana, Idaho, Nevada, California and Arizona.* 2 vols. Chicago: The Overland Publishing Company, 1878-1879, Vol. 1, 300 [Annex explaining the 'meaning' of the frontispiece to the Guide].

---

[55] In Algonquian Indian language: infant or young child.
[56] Later editions point out that each subscriber to Crofutt's Western World will receive a colored print of Gast's "American Progress" for *free*, pointing out that there is no "home, from the miner's humble cabin to the stately marble mansion of the capitalist, that can afford to be without this GREAT National picture."

183. Fanny F. Palmer
Across the Continent (1868)

Source: Fanny F. [Frances Flora] Palmer (1812-1876). *Across the Continent – Westward the Course of Empire Takes Its Way* (Lithograph). New York: Currier & Ives, 1868.

184. John Fiske
"Manifest Destiny" (1885)

[... The] work which the English race began when it colonized North America is destined to go on until every land on the earth's surface that is not already the seat of an old civilization shall become English in its language, in its religion, in its political habits and traditions, and to a predominant extent in the blood of its people. The day is at hand when four-fifths of the human race will trace its pedigree to English forefathers, as four-fifths of the white people in the United States trace their pedigree to-day. The race thus spread over both hemispheres, and from the rising to the setting sun, will not fail to keep that sovereignty of the sea and that commercial supremacy which it began to acquire when England first stretched its arm across the Atlantic to the shores of Virginia and Massachusetts. The language spoken by these great communities will not be sundered into dialects like the language of the ancient Romans, but perpetual intercommunication and the universal habit of reading and writing will preserve its integrity, and the world's business will be transacted by English-speaking people to so great an extent that whatever language any man may have learned in his infancy, he will find it necessary sooner or later to learn to express his thoughts in English. And in this way it is by no means improbable that, as Jacob Grimm[57] long since predicted, the language of Shakespeare will ultimately become the language of mankind.

In view of these considerations as to the stupendous future of the English race, does it not seem very probable that in due course of time Europe, which has learned some valuable lessons from America already, will find it worth while to adopt the lesson of federalism in order to do away with the chances of useless warfare which remain so long as its different states own no allegiance to any common authority? [...]

[...] Is it too much to hope that by-and-by we may similarly put public warfare under the ban? I think not. Already in America, as we have seen, it has become customary to deal with questions between States just as we would deal with questions between individuals. This we have seen to be the real purport of American federalism. To have established such a system over one great continent is to have made a very good beginning toward establishing it over the world. To establish such a system in Europe will no doubt be difficult, for here we have to deal with an immense complication of prejudices, intensified by linguistic and ethnological differences. Nevertheless the pacific pressure exerted upon Europe by America is becoming so great that it will doubtless before long overcome all these obstacles. I refer to the industrial competition between the Old and the New World, which has become so conspicuous within the last ten years. [...] I believe, the industrial development of the English race outside of Europe will by-and-by enforce federalism upon Europe. I do not ignore the difficulties that grow out of differences in language, race, and creed; but we have seen how Switzerland has long since triumphantly surmounted such difficulties on a small scale. To surmount them on a great scale will soon be the political problem of Europe, and it is America which has set the example and indicated the method.

Thus we may foresee in general how, by the gradual concentration of physical power into the hands of the most pacific communities, we may finally succeed in rendering

---

[57] Jacob Ludwig Karl Grimm (1785-1863), German linguist and prolific writer, not only of fairytales, but also of linguistic treaties and compilations of German legends and poems.

warfare illegal all over the globe. As this process goes on, it may, after many more ages of political experience, become apparent that there is really no reason, in the nature of things, why the whole of mankind should not constitute politically one huge federation, each little group managing its local affairs in entire independence, but relegating all questions of international interest to the decision of one central tribunal supported by the public opinion of the entire human race. I believe that the time will come when such a state of things will exist upon the earth, when it will be possible [...] to speak of the United States as stretching from pole to pole, or with Tennyson to celebrate the "parliament of man and the federation of the world."[58] Indeed, only when such a state of things has begun to be realized can civilization, as sharply demarcated from barbarism, be said to have fairly begun. Only then can the world be said to have become truly Christian. Many ages of toil and doubt and perplexity will no doubt pass by before such a desideratum is reached. Meanwhile it is pleasant to feel that the dispassionate contemplation of great masses of historical facts goes far toward confirming our faith in this ultimate triumph of good over evil. Our survey began with pictures of horrid slaughter and desolation; it ends with the picture of a world covered with cheerful homesteads, blessed with a Sabbath of perpetual peace.

Source: John Fiske (1842-1901). "Manifest Destiny." *Harper's New Monthly Magazine* 70.418 (March 1885), 588-590.

185. Frederick Jackson Turner
"The Significance of the Frontier in American History" (1893)[59]

In a recent bulletin of the Superintendent of the Census for 1890 appear these significant words: "Up to and including 1880 the country had a frontier of settlement, but at present the unsettled area has been so broken into by isolated bodies of settlement that there can hardly be said to be a frontier line. In the discussion of its extent, its westward movement, etc., it can not, therefore, any longer have a place in the census reports." This brief official statement marks the closing of a great historic movement. Up to our own day American history has been in a large degree the history of the colonization of the Great West. The existence of an area of free land, its continuous recession, and the advance of American settlement westward, explain American development.

Behind institutions, behind constitutional forms and modifications, lie the vital forces that call these organs into life and shape them to meet changing conditions. The peculiarity of American institutions is the fact that they have been compelled to adapt themselves to the changes of an expanding people – to the changes involved in crossing a continent, in winning a wilderness, and in developing at each area of this progress out of the primitive economic and political conditions of the frontier into the complexity of city life. Said Calhoun in 1817, "We are great, and rapidly – I was about to say fearfully – growing!"[60] So saying, he touched the distinguishing feature of American life. All peoples show de-

---

[58] Reference to "Locksley Hall," a visionary poem written by Alfred Lord Tennyson in 1842, in which the poet expressed his belief that Great Britain had a moral obligation to consolidate the world under British rule.
[59] Original footnote: "A paper read at the meeting of the American Historical Association in Chicago, July 12, 1893. [...]"
[60] Original footnote: "Abridgment of Debates of Congress, V, 706."

velopment; the germ theory of politics has been sufficiently emphasized. In the case of most nations, however, the development has occurred in a limited area; and if the nation has expanded, it has met other growing peoples whom it has conquered. But in the case of the United States we have a different phenomenon. Limiting our attention to the Atlantic coast, we have the familiar phenomenon of the evolution of institutions in a limited area, such as the rise of representative government; the differentiation of simple colonial governments into complex organs; the progress from primitive industrial society, without division of labor, up to manufacturing civilization. But we have in addition to this a recurrence of the process of evolution in each western area reached in the process of expansion. Thus American development has exhibited not merely advance along a single line, but a return to primitive conditions on a continually advancing frontier line, and a new development for that area. American social development has been continually beginning over again on the frontier. This perennial rebirth, this fluidity of American life, this expansion westward with its new opportunities, its continuous touch with the simplicity of primitive society, furnish the forces dominating American character. The true point of view in the history of this nation is not the Atlantic coast, it is the Great West. Even the slavery struggle, which is made so exclusive an object of attention [...], occupies its important place in American history because of its relation to westward expansion.

In this advance, the frontier is the outer edge of the wave – the meeting point between savagery and civilization. Much has been written, about the frontier from the point of view of border warfare and the chase, but as a field for the serious study of the economist and the historian it has been neglected.

The American frontier is sharply distinguished from the European frontier – a fortified boundary line running through dense populations. The most significant thing about the American frontier is, that it lies at the hither edge of free land. In the census reports it is treated as the margin of that settlement which has a density of two or more to the square mile. The term is an elastic one, and for our purposes does not need sharp definition. We shall consider the whole frontier belt, including the Indian country and the outer margin of the "settled area" of the census reports. This paper will make no attempt to treat the subject exhaustively; its aim is simply to call attention to the frontier as a fertile field for investigation, and to suggest some of the problems which arise in connection with it.

In the settlement of America we have to observe how European life entered the continent, and how America modified and developed that life and reacted on Europe. Our early history is the study of European germs developing in an American environment. Too exclusive attention has been paid by institutional students to the Germanic origins, too little to the American factors. The frontier is the line of most rapid and effective Americanization. The wilderness masters the colonist. It finds him a European in dress, industries, tools, modes of travel, and thought. It takes him from the railroad car and puts him in the birch canoe. It strips off the garments of civilization and arrays him in the hunting shirt and the moccasin. It puts him in the log cabin of the Cherokee and Iroquois and runs an Indian palisade around him. Before long he has gone to planting Indian corn and plowing with a sharp stick; he shouts the war cry and takes the scalp in orthodox Indian fashion. In short, at the frontier the environment is at first too strong for the man. He must accept the conditions which it furnishes, or perish, and so he fits himself into the Indian clearings and follows the Indian trails. Little by little he transforms the wilderness, but the outcome is not the old Europe, not simply the development of Germanic germs, any more than the first phenomenon was a case of reversion to the Germanic mark. The fact is, that here is a new product that is American. At first, the frontier was the Atlantic coast. It was the frontier of Europe in a very real sense. Moving westward, the frontier became more and more American. As successive terminal moraines result from successive glaciations, so each frontier leaves its traces behind it, and when it becomes a settled area the region still partakes of the frontier characteristics. Thus the advance of the frontier has meant a steady movement away from the influence of Europe, a steady growth of independence on American lines. And to study this advance, the men who grew up under these conditions, and the political, economic, and social results of it, is to study the really American part of our history.

In the course of the seventeenth century the frontier was advanced up the Atlantic river courses, just beyond the "fall line," and the tidewater region became the settled area. In the first half of the eighteenth century another advance occurred. Traders followed the Delaware and Shawnese Indians to the Ohio as early as the end of the first quarter of the century. [...] When the first census was taken in 1790, the continuous settled area was bounded by a line which ran near the coast of Maine, and included New England except a portion of Vermont and New Hampshire, New York along the Hudson and up the Mohawk about Schenectady, eastern and southern Pennsylvania, Virginia well across the Shenandoah Valley, and the Carolinas and eastern Georgia [...]. The "West," as a self-conscious section, began to evolve. [...]

In the middle of this century the line indicated by the present eastern boundary of Indian Territory, Nebraska, and Kansas marked the frontier of the Indian country. Minnesota and Wisconsin still exhibited frontier conditions, but the distinctive frontier of the period is found in California, where the gold discoveries had sent a sudden tide of adventurous miners, and in Oregon, and the settlements in Utah. [...]

[...] In these successive frontiers we find natural boundary lines which have served to mark and to affect the characteristics of the frontiers [...]. Each was won by series of Indian wars. [...]

The Atlantic frontier was compounded of fisherman, fur-trader, miner, cattle-raiser, and farmer. Excepting the fisherman, each type of industry was on the march toward the West, impelled by an irresistible attraction. [...]

Why was it that the Indian trader passed so rapidly across the continent? What effects followed from the trader's frontier? The trade was coeval with American discovery. [...] The records of the various New England colonies show how steadily exploration was carried into the wilderness by this trade. What is true for New England is, as would be expected, even plainer for the rest of the colonies. All along the coast from Maine to Georgia the Indian trade opened up the river courses. [...] The trading frontier, while steadily undermining Indian power by making the tribes ultimately dependent on the whites, yet, through its sale of guns, gave to the Indian increased power of resistance to the farming frontier. French colonization was dominated by its trading frontier; English colonization by its farming frontier. There was an antagonism between the two frontiers as between the two nations. [...]

And yet, in spite of this opposition of the interests of the trader and the farmer, the Indian trade pioneered the way for civilization. The buffalo trail became the Indian trail, and this became the trader's "trace;" the trails widened into roads, and the roads into turnpikes, and these in turn were transformed into railroads. [...] The trading posts reached by these trails were on the sites of Indian villages which had been placed in positions suggested by nature; and these trading posts, situated so as to command the water systems of the country, have grown into such cities as Albany, Pittsburgh, Detroit, Chicago, St. Louis, Council Bluffs, and Kansas City. Thus civilization in America has followed the arteries made by geology, pouring an ever richer tide through them, until at last the slender paths of aboriginal intercourse have been broadened and interwoven into the complex mazes of modern commercial lines; the wilderness has been interpenetrated by lines of civilization growing ever more numerous. It is like the steady growth of a complex nervous system for the originally simple, inert continent. If one would understand why we are to-day one nation, rather than a collection of isolated states, he must study this economic and social consolidation of the country. [...]

Omitting those of the pioneer farmers who move from the love of adventure, the advance of the more steady farmer is easy to understand. Obviously the immigrant was attracted by the cheap lands of the frontier, and even the native farmer felt their influence strongly. Year by year the farmers who lived on soil whose returns were diminished by unrotated crops were offered the virgin soil of the frontier at nominal prices. Their growing families demanded more lands, and these were dear. The competition of the unexhausted, cheap, and easily tilled prairie lands compelled the farmer either to go west and continue the exhaustion of the soil on a new frontier, or to adopt intensive culture. [...] Thus the demand for land and the love of wilderness freedom drew the frontier ever onward.

Having now roughly outlined the various kinds of frontiers, and their modes of advance, chiefly from the point of view of the frontier itself, we may next inquire what were the influences on the East and on the Old World. [...]

First, we note that the frontier promoted the formation of a composite nationality for the American people. The coast was preponderantly English, but the later tides of continental immigration flowed across to the free lands. This was the case from the early colonial days. The Scotch-Irish and the Palatine Germans, or "Pennsylvania Dutch," furnished the dominant element in the stock of the colonial frontier. With these peoples were also the freed indented servants, or redemptioners, who at the expiration of their time of service passed to the frontier. [...]

The legislation which most developed the powers of the national government, and played the largest part in its activity, was conditioned on the frontier. [...]

It was this nationalizing tendency of the West that transformed the democracy of Jefferson into the national republicanism of Monroe and the democracy of Andrew Jackson.[61] [...] Nothing works for nationalism like intercourse within the nation. Mobility of population is death to localism, and the Western frontier worked irresistibly in unsettling population. [...]

But the most important effect of the frontier has been in the promotion of democracy here and in Europe. As has been indicated, the frontier is productive of individualism. Complex society is precipitated by the wilderness into a kind of primitive organization based on the family. The tendency is anti-social. It produces antipathy to control, and particularly to any direct control. The tax-gatherer is viewed as a representative of oppression. [... The] frontier conditions prevalent in the colonies are important factors in the explanation of the American Revolution, where individual liberty was sometimes

---

[61] James Monroe (1758-1831), 5th president of the US (1817-1825); Andrew Jackson (1767-1845), 7th president of the US (1829-1837).

confused with absence of all effective government. The same conditions aid in explaining the difficulty of instituting a strong government in the period of the confederacy. The frontier individualism has from the beginning promoted democracy.

The frontier States that came into the Union in the first quarter of a century of its existence came in with democratic suffrage provisions, and had reactive effects of the highest importance upon the older States whose peoples were being attracted there. An extension of the franchise became essential. It was *western* New York that forced an extension of suffrage in the constitutional convention of that State in 1821; and it was *western* Virginia that compelled the tide-water region to put a more liberal suffrage provision in the constitution framed in 1830, and to give to the frontier region a more nearly proportionate representation with the tide-water aristocracy. The rise of democracy as an effective force in the nation came in with western preponderance under Jackson and William Henry Harrison, and it meant the triumph of the frontier – with all of its good and with all of its evil elements. [...]

From the conditions of frontier life came intellectual traits of profound importance. The works of travelers along each frontier from colonial days onward describe certain common traits, and these traits have, while softening down, still persisted as survivals in the place of their origin, even when a higher social organization succeeded. The result is that to the frontier the American intellect owes its striking characteristics. That coarseness and strength combined with acuteness and inquisitiveness; that practical, inventive turn of mind, quick to find expedients; that masterful grasp of material things, lacking in the artistic but powerful to effect great ends; that restless, nervous energy; that dominant individualism, working for good and for evil, and withal that buoyancy and exuberance which comes with freedom – these are traits of the frontier, or traits called out elsewhere because of the existence of the frontier. Since the days when the fleet of Columbus sailed into the waters of the New World, America has been another name for opportunity, and the people of the United States have taken their tone from the incessant expansion which has not only been open but has even been forced upon them. He would be a rash prophet who should assert that the expansive character of American life has now entirely ceased. Movement has been its dominant fact, and, unless this training has no effect upon a people, the American energy will continually demand a wider field for its exercise. But never again will such gifts of free land offer themselves. For a moment, at the frontier, the bonds of custom are broken and unrestraint is triumphant. There is not *tabula rasa*. The stubborn American environment is there with its imperious summons to accept its conditions; the inherited ways of doing things are also there; and yet, in spite of environment, and in spite of custom, each frontier did indeed furnish a new field of opportunity, a gate of escape from the bondage of the past; and freshness, and confidence, and scorn of older society, impatience of its restraints and its ideas, and indifference to its lessons, have accompanied the frontier. What the Mediterranean Sea was to the Greeks, breaking the bond of custom, offering new experiences, calling out new institutions and activities, that, and more, the ever retreating frontier has been to the United States directly, and to the nations of Europe more remotely. And now, four centuries from the discovery of America, at the end of a hundred years of life under the Constitution, the frontier has gone, and with its going has closed the first period of American history.

Source: Frederick Jackson Turner (1861-1932). "The Significance of the Frontier in American History." Reprinted as Chapter I in: *The Frontier in American History*. New York: Henry Holt & Co., 1953, 1-6, 8-9, 12-15, 21-22, 24, 29-31, 37-38.

186. Frederick Jackson Turner
"The West and American Ideals" (1914)

[...] The appeal of the undiscovered is strong in America. For three centuries the fundamental process in its history was the westward movement, the discovery and occupation of the vast free spaces of the continent. We are the first generation of Americans who can look back upon that era as a historic movement now coming to its end. Other generations have been so much a part of it that they could hardly comprehend its significance. To them it seemed inevitable. The free land and the natural resources seemed practically inexhaustible. Nor were they aware of the fact that their most fundamental traits, their institutions, even their ideals were shaped by this interaction between the wilderness and themselves.

American democracy was born of no theorist's dream; it was not carried in the *Sarah Constant* to Virginia, nor in the *Mayflower* to Plymouth. It came out of the American forest, and it gained new strength each time it touched a new frontier. Not the constitution, but free land and an abundance of natural resources open to a fit people, made the democratic type of society in America for three centuries while it occupied its empire. [...]

When the backwoodsmen crossed the Alleghanies they put between themselves and the Atlantic Coast a barrier which seemed to separate them from a region already too much like the Europe they had left, and as they followed the courses of the rivers that flowed to the Mississippi, they called themselves "Men of the Western Waters," and their new home in the Mississippi Valley was the "Western World." Here, by the thirties, Jacksonian democracy flourished, strong in the faith of the intrinsic excellence of the common man, in his right to make his own place in the world, and in his capacity to share in government. [...]

Side by side with this westward marching army of individualistic liberty-loving democratic backwoodsmen, went a more northern stream of pioneers, who cherished similar ideas, but added to them the desire to create new industrial centers, to build up factories, to build railroads, and to develop the country by founding cities and extending prosperity. [...]

Both of these Western groups, Whigs and Democrats alike, had one common ideal: the desire to leave their children a better heritage than they themselves had received, and both were fired with devotion to the ideal of creating in this New World a home more worthy of mankind. Both were ready to break with the past, to boldly strike out new lines of social endeavor, and both believed in American expansion. [...]

First of all, there was the ideal of discovery, the courageous determination to break new paths, indifference to the dogma that because an institution or a condition exists, it must remain. All American experience has gone to the making of the spirit of innovation; it is in the blood and will not be repressed.

Then, there was the ideal of democracy, the ideal of a free self-directing people, responsive to leadership in the forming of programs and their execution, but insistent that the procedure should be that of free choice, not of compulsion.

But there was also the ideal of individualism. This democratic society was not a disciplined army, where all must keep step and where the collective interests destroyed individual will and work. Rather it was a mobile mass of freely circulating atoms, each seeking its own place and finding play for its own powers and for its own original initiative.

We cannot lay too much stress upon this point, for it was at the very heart of the whole American movement. The world was to be made a better world by the example of a democracy in which there was freedom of the individual, in which there was the vitality and mobility productive of originality and variety.

Bearing in mind the far-reaching influence of the disappearance of unlimited resources open to all men for the taking, and considering the recoil of the common man when he saw the outcome of the competitive struggle for these resources as the supply came to its end over most of the nation, we can understand the reaction against individualism and in favor of drastic assertion of the powers of government. Legislation is taking the place of the free lands as the means of preserving the ideal of democracy. But at the same time it is endangering the other pioneer ideal of creative and competitive individualism. Both were essential and constituted what was best in America's contribution to history and to progress. Both must be preserved if the nation would be true to its past, and would fulfil its highest destiny. [...]

Source: Frederick Jackson Turner (1861-1932). "The West and American Ideals: Commencement Address, University of Washington, June 17, 1914." Reprinted as Chapter XI in: *The Frontier in American History*. New York: Henry Holt & Co., 1953, 293, 302-304, 306-307.

187. Frank Norris
"The Frontier Gone at Last" (1902)

Suddenly we have found that there is no longer any Frontier. Until the day when the first United States marine landed in China we had always imagined that out yonder somewhere in the West was the border land where civilization disintegrated and merged into the untamed. Our skirmish line was there, our posts that scouted and scrimmaged with the wilderness, a thousand miles in advance of the steady march of civilization.

And the Frontier has become so much an integral part of our conception of things that it will be long before we shall all understand that it is gone. We liked the Frontier; it was romance, the place of the poetry of the Great March, the firing line where there was action and fighting, and where men held each other's lives in the crook of the forefinger. Those who had gone out came back with tremendous tales, and those that stayed behind made up other and even more tremendous tales. [...]

Then for centuries we halted and the van closed up with the firing line and we filled all England and all Europe with our clamor because for a while we seemed to have gone as far Westward as it was possible; and the checked energy of the race reacted upon itself, rebounded as it were, and back we went to the Eastward again – crusading, girding at the Mohammedan, conquering his cities, breaking into his fortresses with mangonel,[62] siege engine and catapult – just as the boy shut indoors finds his scope circumscribed and fills the whole place with the racket of his activity.

But always, if you will recall it, we had a curious feeling that we had not reached the ultimate West even yet, that there was still a Frontier. Always that strange sixth sense turned our heads toward the sunset; and all through the Middle Ages we were peeking

---

[62] A military device – consisting of a lever arm held and released under tension in a wooden frame – formerly used for hurling missiles (esp. incendiaries) against an enemy's position.

and prying at the Western horizon, trying to reach it, to run it down, and the queer tales about Vineland and that storm-driven Viking's ship would not down. [...]

[...] At last they forced the Frontier over the Sierra Nevada down to the edge of the Pacific. And here it would have been supposed that the Great March would have halted again as it did before the Atlantic, that here at last the Frontier ended.

But on the first of May, eighteen hundred and ninety-eight, a gun was fired in the Bay of Manila,[63] still further Westward, and in response the skirmish-line crossed the Pacific, still pushing the Frontier before it. Then came a cry for help from Legation Street in Peking and as the first boat bearing its contingent of American marines took ground on the Asian shore,[64] the Frontier – at last after so many centuries, after so many marches, after so much fighting, so much spilled blood, so much spent treasure, dwindled down and vanished; for the Anglo-Saxon in his course of empire had circled the globe and had brought the new civilization to the old civilization, had reached the starting point of history, the place from which the migrations began. So soon as the marines landed there was no longer any West, and the equation of the horizon, the problem of the centuries for the Anglo-Saxon was solved. [...]

Today we are the same race, with the same impulse, the same power and, because there is no longer a Frontier to absorb our overplus of energy, because there is no longer a wilderness to conquer and because we still must march, still must conquer, we remember the old days when our ancestors before us found the outlet for their activity checked and, rebounding, turned their faces Eastward, and went down to invade the Old World. So we. No sooner have we found that our path to the Westward has ended than, reacting Eastward, we are at the Old World again, marching against it, invading it, devoting our overplus of energy to its subjugation.

But though we are the same race, with the same impulses, the same blood-instincts as the old Frisian marsh people, we are now come into a changed time and the great word of our century is no longer War but Trade.

Or if you choose it is only a different word for the same race-characteristic. The desire for conquest – say what you will – was as big in the breast of the most fervid of the Crusaders as it is this very day in the most peacefully-disposed of American manufacturers. [...]

Competition and conquest are words easily interchangeable, and the whole spirit of our present commercial crusade to the Eastward betrays itself in the fact that we cannot speak of it but in terms borrowed from the glossary of the warrior. It is a commercial "invasion," a trade "war," a "threatened attack" on the part of America; business is "captured," opportunities are "seized," certain industries are "killed," certain former monopolies are "wrested away." [...]

So perhaps we have not lost the Frontier after all. A new phrase, reversing that of Berkeley's, is appropriate to the effect that "Eastward the course of commerce takes its

---

[63] Reference to the naval battle between the Americans and Spanish, May 1, 1898, off Cavité, in the Bay of Manila.

[64] In 1899 the anti-foreign activities of the so-called Boxers – a Chinese secret society known as the *I Ho Ch'uan* (Righteous Harmonious Fists) that propagated the expulsion of all 'foreign devils' from China – culminated in the killing of a British missionary and finally led Western governments to call for troops to protect the legations at Peking. Four hundred and thirty Sailors and Marines (including fifty-six Americans from USS *Oregon* and USS *Newark*) arrived at the legations in May and June 1900, but eventually some 20,000 soldiers were called after the Boxers began attacking foreign property in Peking. After fighting two major battles against huge Chinese forces, the "China Relief Expedition" reached the foreign legations at Peking on August 14, 1900.

way,"[65] and we must look for the lost battle-line not toward the sunset, but toward the East. And so rapid has been the retrograde movement that we must go far to find it, that scattered firing-line, where the little skirmishes are heralding the approach of the Great March. We must already go further afield than England. The main body, even to the reserves, are intrenched there long since, and even continental Europe is to the rear of the skirmishers. [...]

And so goes the great movement, Westward, then Eastward, forward and then back. The motion of the natural forces, the elemental energies, somehow appear to be thus alternative – action first, then reaction. [...]

Will it not go on, this epic of civilization, this destiny of the races, until at last and at the ultimate end of all, we who now arrogantly boast ourselves as Americans, supreme in conquest, whether of battle-ship or of bridge-building, may realize that the true patriotism is the brotherhood of man and know the whole world is our nation and simple humanity our countrymen?

Source: Frank Norris (1870-1902). "The Frontier Gone at Last: How Our Race Pushed It Westward around the World and Now Moves Eastward Again – The Broader Conception of Patriotism as the Age of Conquest Ends." *World's Work* (February 1902), 1728-1731.

---

[65] Cf. doc. 21 in this collection.

TRANSCENDENTALISM

American Transcendentalism first emerged during the 1830s with the literary, religious, and philosophical activities of loosely connected groups of New England intellectuals based in greater Boston. The late-nineteenth-century search for genuine American literature privileged the more literary aspects of the movement in a way that continues to shape our perception of it today. It encourages us, in fact, to picture transcendentalism as a series of concentric circles that centers on the essayistic and poetic work of Ralph Waldo Emerson, widens towards Henry David Thoreau's nature writings and Margaret Fuller's aesthetic and social criticism, and gradually fades into the peripheries of the movement's political, religious, and aesthetic satellites (among others, the socialist visionary Orestes Brownson, the educator Amos Bronson Alcott, the theologian Theodore Parker, the Fourierist reformer George Ripley, the politician-historian George Bancroft, and the "minor" poets Jones Very, C.P. Cranch, and W.E. Channing). The downside of this construction is that it retrospectively relegates a substantial part of transcendentalist discourse to the literary background – as if the significance of the movement lay mostly in providing a context for the so-called "American Renaissance," whose authors have been considered to derive their literary brilliance from the skeptical engagement with (Nathaniel Hawthorne, Herman Melville) or the sensuous radicalization of (Walt Whitman) Emersonian insights. That said, it is nonetheless hard to resist the viewpoint that the most intriguing formulations of American transcendentalism can be found in Emerson's treatise on *Nature* (1836), his *Essays* (1841 and 1844), Thoreau's *Walden* (1854), and Whitman's *Leaves of Grass* (1855).

Strictly speaking, transcendentalists must be considered late romantics, but they sit uneasily with the generic categories of European literary history. Like the slightly older "American Wordsworth" William Cullen Bryant or the "American Scott" James Fenimore Cooper, they negotiate the epistemological, political, and aesthetic discourse associated with European romantic schools. But their most productive phase (roughly between 1830s and 1860s) covers the post-romantic period characterized by positive science, biological evolutionism, and (in Europe) literary realism. This discontinuity is complicated by the continued (if partial) cultural authority, in the US, of pre-romantic discourse. Mid-nineteenth-century transcendentalist writers face an increasingly dynamic literary field and a literary public that reads two generations of European romantics (from Goethe to Keats) simultaneously with the great Victorians (from Carlyle to Dickens) and such neoclassical fixtures as Swift, Pope, and Dr. Johnson.

The contours of the transcendentalist school can be more clearly defined by its philosophical, theological, and socio-political visions. No single defining feature brings American transcendentalism as close to the previous generation of European romantics than its creative appropriation of the critical and speculative philosophies indicated in the movement's label. The late-eighteenth-century transcendental turn begins with Kant's *Critique of Pure Reason* (1781), which can be summarized as the attempt to base the theories of knowledge (epistemology) and practical reason (morality and ethics) on principles internal to the human mind, severing it from its traditional foundations (in empirical reality, human sentiment, or utility). This implies that the most direct route to moral truth lies in the "pure" judgments of innate reason, purged of the fickle impulses of senses and feeling and the calculation of consequences. But Kant's epistemology also leads the romantic vocabulary of inwardness to a distinctly unromantic punch line: it holds that because experience is based on mere appearances, the reality behind appearances ("the thing in itself") cannot be known to our senses, so that our grasp of reality will be restricted to the *internal* conditions of knowledge and experience. We can investigate the mental filters (*a priori* categories) with which the human mind fashions the spatial, temporal, and causal parameters of experience and synthesizes them into ideas about coherent existence, such as "God," "World," or "Soul." But we will have to surrender the hope that these ideas can ever be grounded in actual reality. One could simplify a complex reception history by saying that romantic thinkers admired Kant's turn to interiority but resisted his radical skepticism. In their creative misreadings, the concept of "pure reason" changes from a subjective mode of structuring experience to an innate organ for intuiting spiritual knowledge (analogous to the Quaker metaphor of an "inner light"). This change begins with the speculative idealism of the Schlegel brothers and Schelling's *Naturphilosophie*, and it arrives in Boston with a distinctly religious spin through the mediation of (among others) Coleridge's *Aids to Reflection* and Victor Cousin's Hegelian lectures on the history of philosophy (doc. 194). In the course of this conceptual reconfiguration, Kant's dichotomy of pure reason vs. understanding was reinterpreted in terms of a neoplatonic natural theology that posited a mystical correspondence between material nature and the realm of spiritual existence (docs. 188-192, 195-196, 200). Transcendental Reason was considered an "organic" faculty through which sensitive artist types who immersed themselves in the primal beauties of natural environments could reach levels of introspection that revealed mystical (i.e. pre-conceptual) experiences of capital-N Nature (variously labeled "the Infinite," "the Absolute," "Oversoul," "World Spirit," etc.). The faculty of understanding was downgraded to the level of a "mechanical" perception and "cold" conceptual analysis of the world's tangible surfaces, which made it the preferred mental faculty of dry dogmatists, empirical scientists, neoclassical poets, and aristocratic despots.

The impact of neoplatonism and idealism on New England intellectuals must be viewed in the context of their deep religious preoccupations (most transcendentalists were, or had been at one point in their lives, practicing clergy). The gradual disintegration of Calvinism during the early Republic coincided with a shift towards liberalism, individualism, and inwardness in religious theory and practice. The so-called "Second Great Awakening" destabilized traditional church hierarchies with a burst of religious enthusiasm that "burned over" rural New England, while the theological centers in Yale, Harvard, and Princeton challenged the Calvinist dualism of an angry God and a fallen humanity. By the early 1800s, the Boston area was under the influence of the Unitarian belief in man's intrinsic divinity (his "Likeness to God"). Unitarianism was an upper-class creed whose proponents disapproved of the emotionalism of lower-class revivalisms and attempted to combine religion with the premises of eighteenth-century science. But it also had a Rousseauist impulse that encouraged its more liberal theologians (such as William Ellery Channing) to locate the divine in nature rather than in formal dogma, and spiritual revelation in imaginative insight rather than in theological speculation (doc. 193). Most transcendentalist intellectuals of Emerson's generation began as liberal Unitarians attempting to convince their more conservative peers (doc. 197) of Channing's teachings – until during the 1830s these attempts propelled them beyond Unitarianism altogether. The transcendentalists' dissent was mainly directed at the Unitarian belief in miracles and adherence to empiricist or sensualist science. They accused their teachers of being too half-hearted to dispense with Calvinist supernaturalism and too cold-hearted to appreciate the importance of intuitive religious feeling over against intellectual rationalization. The theological rift became most apparent when Emerson argued, in his controversial Divinity School Address of 1838 (doc. 199), that the historical Jesus was a great poet-prophet who had seen the mysteries of soul (rather than the Son of God who had worked miracles). The implication was that Christ's teachings were to be understood, not as eternal truths, but as poetic renditions of divine Nature that should not be ossified into dogmatic beliefs and institutionalized rites but extended and injected with fresh visions by inspired poets of present-day America. Emerson's argument shows how transcendentalist positions mediate contemporary theology with the romantic vocabularies of inwardness, expressive individualism, and poetic inspiration. It resulted in a nature religion that considered the sublime US landscapes as privileged sites for the gaining of personal self-reliance and national identity (docs. 198, 201, 203).

The transcendentalists shared the interest in social improvement characteristic of early nineteenth-century intellectual culture, an interest that was furthered by the centrality of "perfectionist" millennialism in contemporary American religious discourse. Based on the belief that the Second Coming of Christ (and hence the salvation of the world) would be preceded by a thousand-year period of earthly harmony and peace, millennialism stimulated American visions of a utopian Christian society in which religious inspiration encourages social and educational reform (doc. 205) and economic and political advancement, as preconditions of the approaching rule of Christ on Earth. Transcendentalist intellectuals did not literally expect the Lord to return in person, but their conviction that spiritual regeneration requires a major reorganization of social structure carries a millennialist signature. This socioreligious approach to human perfectibility led them to propose communitarian visions of democratic progress (doc. 202), and it may partly explain the openness with which the deeply religious transcendentalist visionaries treated, not only the Christian socialism of Henri de Saint-Simon, but also the radically secular utopias of European social materialists such as Frances Wright, Robert Owen (doc. 206), and Charles Fourier. The influence of this tradition can be seen in Brownson's "The Laboring Classes" (doc. 204), which proceeds from Carlyle's critique of British *laissez faire* capitalism to a proto-Marxist indictment of the property-holding American merchant class. The more practical effects of social utopianism can be seen in the series of short-lived community experiments in the US modeled on Owenite and Fourierist examples. Owen was as notorious for his declared atheism as he was famous for the successful welfare programs with which his community project New Lanark in Great Britain had fought industrial pauperism (although his attempt to repeat his success in 1825 in New Harmony, Indiana, was a financial failure). Fourier developed an influential model of "phalanxes," autonomous communities in which precisely 1620 souls would live and work under natural conditions, independent of government interference, sustained by an economically self-sufficient arts-and-crafts agrarianism. Fourier's vision arrived in the US under the label "associationism," and its promise to overcome the alienating effects of industrial specialization inspired a number of Fourierist experiments, most of them of moderate scale and limited duration. The best known transcendentalist venture (and indeed apart from Alcott's "Fruitlands" debacle in 1844 virtually the only one) is the Brook Farm community founded by George Ripley in 1841, and continued by Albert Brisbane as a small-scale Fourierist phalanx until 1847 (docs. 207-209). All leading transcendentalists were interested in the outcome of this project, but many doubted the use of communitarian attempts for spiritual regeneration. Thoreau's famous retreat to a cabin at Walden Pond (1845-47) can be considered symbolic of the pervasive belief among Emersonian intellectuals that the route to social utopia led through the solitary effort of individualist self-culture (doc. 200).

Günter Leypoldt

188. Rembrandt Peale
"The Beauties of Creation" (1800)

Mark the beauties of Creation,
    Mark the harmony that reigns!
Each, supported in its station,
    Age to age unchang'd remains.

Water, earth, and air surrounding,
    Teem with life in every mode;
Foodful plants and herbs abounding,
    Fossils in their dark abode.

Flitting thro' the yielding heaven,
    Hark! the warblers of the grove!
Deck'd in plumage richly given,
    All their souls attun'd to Love.

Food and raiment, use and pleasure,
    Each, attend the bestial train;
Seas pour forth their finny treasure;
    Earth its fruits and plenteous grain.

Flutt'ring gay from flower to flower,
    See the vivid insect stray –
Changeful form! within the hour,
    Winged, bursting into day.

These, ten thousand times repeated
    Fill Creation's boundless plan;
Mark the finger that created
    Each, in proper place, as man.

Let us then, the whole surveying,
    Guide the moral to our heart –
Let us, Nature's voice obeying,
    Live in bliss and bliss impart.

Source: Rembrandt Peale (1778-1860). "The Beauties of Creation." Charles Wilson Peale (1741-1827). *Discourse Introductory to a Course of Lectures on the Science of Nature. With Original Music, Composed for, and Sung on, the Occasion: Delivered in the Hall of the University of Pennsylvania, Nov. 8, 1800*. Philadelphia: Francis and Robert Bailey, 1800, 6-7 [The score of "The Beauties of Creation" at the end of the volume identifies Rembrandt Peale as the author of the lyrics which were set to music by John J. Hawkins in November 1800].

189. Ralph Waldo Emerson
"The Rhodora: On Being Asked, Whence Is the Flower?" (1834/1839)

In May, when sea-winds pierced our solitudes,
I found the fresh Rhodora in the woods,
Spreading its leafless blooms in a damp nook,
To please the desert and the sluggish brook.
The purple petals, fallen in the pool,
Made the black water with their beauty gay;
Here might the red-bird come his plumes to cool,
And court the flower that cheapens his array.
Rhodora! if the sages ask thee why
This charm is wasted on the earth and sky,
Tell them, dear, that if eyes were made for seeing,
Then Beauty is its own excuse for being:
Why thou wert there, O rival of the rose!
I never thought to ask, I never knew:
But, in my simple ignorance, suppose
The self-same Power that brought me there brought you.

Source: Ralph Waldo Emerson (1803-1882). "The Rhodora: On Being Asked, Whence Is the Flower." *Poems*. Boston and New York: Houghton Mifflin/Riverside Press, 1918, 37-38.

190. Ralph Waldo Emerson
"Two Rivers" (1856/1858)

Thy summer voice, Musketaquit,[1]
Repeats the music of the rain;
But sweeter rivers pulsing flit
Through thee, as thou through Concord Plain.

Thou in thy narrow banks art pent:
The stream I love unbounded goes
Through flood and sea and firmament;
Through light, through life, it forward flows.

I see the inundation sweet,
I hear the spending of the stream
Through years, through men, through Nature fleet,
Through love and thought, through power and dream.

Musketaquit, a goblin strong,
Of shard and flint makes jewels gay;

---

[1] Indian name of Concord river, meaning the river of meadows.

> They lose their grief who hear his song,
> And where he winds is the day of day.
>
> So forth and brighter fares my stream, —
> Who drink it shall not thirst again;
> No darkness stains its equal gleam,
> And ages drop in it like rain.

Source: Ralph Waldo Emerson (1803-1882). "Two Rivers." *Poems*. Boston and New York: Houghton Mifflin/Riverside Press, 1918, 248.

191. Christopher Pearse Cranch "Correspondences" (1841)

> All things in Nature are beautiful types to the soul that will read them;
>   Nothing exists upon earth, but for unspeakable ends.
> Every object that speaks to the senses was meant for the spirit:
>   Nature is but a scroll, – God's hand-writing thereon.
> Ages ago, when man was pure, ere the flood overwhelmed him,
>   While in the image of God every soul yet lived,
> Everything stood as a letter or word of a language familiar,
>   Telling of truths which *now* only the angels can read.
> Lost to man was the key of those sacred hieroglyphics, –
>   Stolen away by sin, – till with Jesus restored.
> Now with infinite pains we here and there spell out a letter;
>   Now and then will the sense feebly shine through the dark.
> When we perceive the light which breaks through the visible symbol,
>   What exultation is ours! *we* the discovery have made!
> Yet is the meaning the same as when Adam lived sinless in Eden,
>   Only long-hidden it slept and now again is restored.
> Man unconsciously uses figures of speech every moment,
>   Little dreaming the cause why to such terms he is prone, –
> Little dreaming that everything has its own correspondence
>   Folded within it of old, as in the body the soul.
> Gleams of the mystery fall on us still, though much is forgotten,
>   And through our commonest speech illumines the path of our thoughts.
> Thus does the lordly sun shine out a type of the Godhead;
>   Wisdom and Love the beams that stream on a darkened world.
> Thus do the sparkling waters flow, giving joy to the desert,
>   And the great Fountain of Life opens itself to the thirst.
> Thus does the word of God distil like the rain and the dew-drops,
>   Thus does the warm wind breathe like to the Spirit of God,
> And the green grass and the flowers are signs of the regeneration.
>
>   O thou Spirit of Truth! visit our minds once more!
> Give us to read, in letters of light, the language celestial,

Written all over the earth, – written all over the sky:
Thus may we bring our hearts at length to know our Creator,
Seeing in all things around types of the Infinite Mind.

Source: Christopher Pearce Cranch (1813-1892). "Correspondences." *The Dial: A Magazine for Literature, Philosophy, and Religion* 1.3 (January 1841), 381.

192. Sampson Reed
Observations on the Growth of the Mind (1826)

Nothing is a more common subject of remark than the changed condition of the world. There is a more extensive intercourse of thought, and a more powerful action of mind upon mind, than formerly. The good and the wise of all nations are brought nearer together, and begin to exert a power, which, though yet feeble as infancy, is felt throughout the globe. Public opinion, that helm which directs the progress of events by which the world is guided to its ultimate destination, has received a new direction. The mind has attained an upward and onward look, and is shaking off the errors and prejudices of the past. The structure of the feudal ages, the ornament of the desert, has been exposed to the light of heaven; and continues to be gazed at for its ugliness, as it ceases to be admired for its antiquity. The world is deriving vigor, not from that which is gone by, but from that which is coming; not from the unhealthy moisture of the evening, but from the nameless influences of the morning. The loud call on the past to instruct us, as it falls on the rock of ages, comes back in echo from the future. Both mankind, and the laws and principles by which they are governed, seem about to be redeemed from slavery. The moral and intellectual character of man has undergone, and is undergoing, a change; and as this is effected, it must change the aspect of all things, as when the position-point is altered from which a landscape is viewed. [...]

There prevails a most erroneous sentiment, that the mind is originally vacant, and requires only to be filled up; and there is reason to believe, that this opinion is most intimately connected with false conceptions of time. The mind is originally a most delicate germ, whose husk[2] is the body; planted in this world, that the light and heat of heaven may fall upon it with a gentle radiance, and call forth its energies. The process of learning is not by synthesis, or analysis. It is the most perfect illustration of both. As subjects are presented to the operation of the mind, they are decomposed and reorganized in a manner peculiar to itself, and not easily explained.

[...] The mind must grow, not from external accretion,[3] but from an internal principle. Much may be done by others in aid of its development; but in all that is done, it should not be forgotten, that even from its earliest infancy, it possesses a character and a principle of freedom, which *should be* respected, and *cannot* be destroyed. Its peculiar propensities[4] may be discerned, and proper nutriment and culture supplied; but the infant plant, not less than the aged tree, must be permitted, with its own organs of absorption, to separate that which is peculiarly adapted to itself; otherwise it will be cast off as a foreign substance, or produce nothing but rottenness and deformity.

---

[2] The outside or external part of an object usually used in the depreciatory sense of a mere worthless exterior.
[3] The process of growth by external addition.
[4] Dispositions, tendencies.

[...] The body and the mind should grow together, and form the sound and perfect man, whose understanding may be almost measured by his stature. The mind will see itself in what it loves and is able to accomplish. Its own works will be its mirror; and when it is present in the natural world, feeling the same spirit which gives life to every object by which it is surrounded, in its very union with nature it will catch a glimpse of itself, like that of pristine beauty united with innocence, at her own native fountain.

[...] The natural world was precisely and perfectly adapted to invigorate and strengthen the intellectual and moral man. [...] It was intended to draw forth and mature the latent energies of the soul; to impart to them its own verdure[5] and freshness; to initiate them into its own mysteries; and by its silent and humble dependence on its Creator, to leave on them, when it is withdrawn by death, the full impression of his likeness. [...]

It is [...] the continual endeavor of Providence, that the natural sciences should be the spontaneous production of the human mind. To these should certainly be added, poetry and music; for when we study the works of God as we should, we cannot disregard that inherent beauty and harmony in which these arts originate. [...]

It belongs to the true poet to feel this spirit, and to be governed by it; to be raised above the senses; to live and breathe in the inward efforts of things; to feel the power of creation, even before he sees the effect; to witness the innocence and smiles of nature's infancy, not by extending the imagination back to chaos, but by raising the soul to nature's origin. The true poetic spirit, so far from misleading any, is the strongest bulwark against deception. It is the soul of science. Without it, the latter is a cheerless, heartless study, distrusting even the presence and power of Him to whom it owes its existence. Of all the poetry which exists, that only possesses the seal of immortality, which presents the image of God which is stamped on nature. Could the poetry which now prevails be viewed from the future, when all partialities and antipathies shall have passed away, and things are left to rest on their own foundations; [...] we might catch a glimpse of the rudiments of this divine art, amid the weight of extraneous matter by which it is now protected, and which it is destined to throw off. The imagination will be refined into a chaste and sober view of unveiled nature. It will be confined within the bounds of reality. It will no longer lead the way to insanity and madness, by transcending the works of creation, and, as it were, wandering where God has no power to protect it; but finding a resting-place in every created object, it will enter into it and explore its hidden treasures, the relation in which it stands to mind, and reveal the love it bears to its Creator. [...]

There is a language, not of words, but of things. When this language shall have been made apparent, that which is human will have answered its end; and being as it were resolved into its original elements, will lose itself in nature. [...] If we did but understand [nature's] language, what could our words add to its meaning? It is because we are unwilling to hear, that we find it necessary to say so much; and we drown the voice of nature with the discordant jargon of ten thousand dialects. Let a man's language be confined to the expression of that which actually belongs to his own mind; and let him respect the smallest blade which grows, and permit it to speak for itself. Then may there be poetry, which may not be written perhaps, but which may be felt as a part of our being. Everything which surrounds us is full of the utterance of one word, completely expressive of its nature. This word is its name; for God, even now, could we but see it, is creating all things, and giving a name to every work of his love, in its perfect adaptation to that

---

[5] Green color characteristic of flourishing vegetation.

for which it is designed. But man has abused his power, and has become insensible to the real character of the brute creation; still more so to that of inanimate nature, because, in his selfishness, he is disposed to reduce them to slavery. Therefore he is deaf. We find the animal world either in a state of savage wildness, or enslaved submission. [...]

Reason is beginning to learn the necessity of simply tracing the relations which exist between created things, and of not even touching what it examines, lest it disturb the arrangement in the cabinet of creation – and as, in the progress of moral improvement, the imagination (which is called the creative power of man) shall coincide with the actively creative will of God, reason will be clothed with eloquence, as nature is with verdure. [...]

Source: Sampson Reed (1800-1880). *Observations on the Growth of the Mind: With Remarks on Some Other Subjects*. Boston: Clapp, 1838, 1-2, 22, 31-33, 36-37, 40, 43-44, 46-47, 74 [first printed 1826].

193. William Ellery Channing: "Likeness to God" (1828)

[...] I begin with observing, what all indeed will understand, that the likeness to God, of which I propose to speak, belongs to man's higher or spiritual nature. It has its foundation in the original and essential capacities of the mind. In proportion as these are unfolded by right and vigorous exertion, it is extended and brightened. In proportion as these lie dormant, it is obscured. In proportion as they are perverted and overpowered by the appetites and passions, it is blotted out. In truth, moral evil, if unresisted and habitual, may so blight and lay waste these capacities, that the image of God in man may seem to be wholly destroyed. [...]

It is plain, too, that likeness to God is the true and only preparation for the enjoyment of the universe. In proportion as we approach and resemble the mind of God, we are brought into harmony with the creation; for, in that proportion, we possess the principles from which the universe sprung; we carry within ourselves the perfections, of which its beauty, magnificence, order, benevolent adaptations, and boundless purposes, are the results and manifestations. God unfolds himself in his works to a kindred mind. It is possible, that the brevity of these hints may expose to the charge of mysticism, what seems to me the calmest and clearest truth. I think, however, that every reflecting man will feel, that likeness to God must be a principle of sympathy or accordance with his creation; for the creation is a birth and shining forth of the Divine Mind, a work through which his spirit breathes. In proportion as we receive this spirit, we possess within ourselves the explanation of what we see. We discern more and more of God in every thing, from the frail flower to the everlasting stars. Even in evil, that dark cloud which hangs over the creation, we discern rays of light and hope, and gradually come to see, in suffering and temptation, proofs and instruments of the sublimest purposes of Wisdom and Love. [...]

That man has a kindred nature with God, and may bear most important and ennobling relations to him, seems to me to be established by a striking proof. This proof you will understand, by considering, for a moment, how we obtain our ideas of God. Whence come the conceptions which we include under that august name? Whence do we derive our knowledge of the attributes and perfections which constitute the Supreme Being? I answer, we derive them from our own souls. The divine attributes are first developed in ourselves, and thence transferred to our Creator. The idea of God, sublime and awful as it is, is the idea of our own spiritual nature, purified and enlarged to infinity. In ourselves are the elements of the Divinity. God, then, does not sustain a figurative resemblance to man. It is the resemblance of a parent to a child, the likeness of a kindred nature. [...]

God is another name for human intelligence raised above all error and imperfection, and extended to all possible truth. [...]

I am aware, that it may be objected to these views, that we receive our idea of God from the universe, from his works, and not so exclusively from our own souls. The universe, I know, is full of God. The heavens and earth declare his glory. In other words, the effects and signs of power, wisdom, and goodness, are apparent through the whole creation. But apparent to what? Not to the outward eye; not to the acutest organs of sense; but to a kindred mind, which interprets the universe by itself. It is only through that energy of thought, by which we adapt various and complicated means to distant ends, and give harmony and a common bearing to multiplied exertions, that we understand the creative intelligence which has established the order, dependencies, and harmony of nature. We see God around us, because he dwells within us. It is by a kindred wisdom, that we discern his wisdom in his works. The brute, with an eye as piercing as ours, looks on the universe; and the page, which to us is radiant with characters of greatness and goodness, is to him a blank. In truth, the beauty and glory of God's works, are revealed to the mind by a light beaming from itself. We discern the impress of God's attributes in the universe, by accordance of nature, and enjoy them through sympathy. [...]

[...] I would offer another answer to this objection, that God's infinity places him beyond the resemblance and approach of man. I affirm, and trust that I do not speak too strongly, that there are traces of infinity in the human mind; and that, in this very respect, it bears a likeness to God. The very conception of infinity, is the mark of a nature to which no limit can be prescribed. This thought, indeed, comes to us, not so much from abroad, as from our own souls. We ascribe this attribute to God, because we possess capacities and wants, which only an unbounded being can fill, and because we are conscious of a tendency in spiritual faculties to unlimited expansion. We believe in the Divine infinity, through something congenial with it in our own breasts. [...] We see [...] the tendency of the soul to the infinite, in more familiar and ordinary forms. Take, for example, the delight which we find in the vast scenes of nature, in prospects which spread around us without limits, in the immensity of the heavens and the ocean, and especially in the rush and roar of mighty winds, waves, and torrents, when, amidst our deep awe, a power within seems to respond to the omnipotence around us. The same principle is seen in the delight ministered to us by works of fiction or of imaginative art, in which our own nature is set before us in more than human beauty and power. In truth, the soul is always bursting its limits. It thirsts continually for wider knowledge. It rushes forward to untried happiness. It has deep wants, which nothing limited can appease. Its true element and end is an unbounded good. Thus, God's infinity has its image in the soul; and through the soul, much more than through the universe, we arrive at this conception of the Deity. [...]

The greatest use which I would make of the principles laid down in this discourse, is to derive from them just and clear views of the nature of religion. What then, is religion? I answer; it is not the adoration of a God with whom we have no common properties; of a distinct, foreign, separate being; but of an all-communicating Parent. [...] The conviction of this near and ennobling relation of God to the soul, and of his great purposes towards it, belongs to the very essence of true religion [...].

[...] Religion only ennobles us, in as far as it reveals to us the tender and intimate connexion of God with his creatures, and teaches us to see in the very greatness which might give alarm, the source of great and glorious communications to the human soul. [...]

To complete my views of this topic, I beg to add an important caution. I have said that the great work of religion is, to conform ourselves to God, or to unfold the divine likeness within us. Let none infer from this language, that I place religion in unnatural effort, in straining after excitements which do not belong to the present state, or in any thing separate from the clear and simple duties of life. I exhort you to no extravagance. I reverence human nature too much to do it violence. I see too much divinity in its ordinary operations, to urge on it a forced and vehement virtue. To grow in the likeness of God, we need not cease to be men. This likeness does not consist in extraordinary or miraculous gifts, in supernatural additions to the soul, or in any thing foreign to our original constitution; but in our essential faculties, unfolded by vigorous and conscientious exertion in the ordinary circumstances assigned by God. To resemble our Creator, we need not fly from society, and entrance ourselves in lonely contemplation and prayer. Such processes might give a feverish strength to one class of emotions, but would result in disproportion, distortion, and sickliness of mind. Our proper work is to approach God by the free and natural unfolding of our highest powers, of understanding, conscience, love, and the moral will. [...]

Source: William Ellery Channing (1780-1842). "Likeness to God." *The Works of William E. Channing*. 6 vols. Boston: James Munroe & Co., 1847, Vol. 3, 228, 230, 233-238, 240-244.

194. Orestes A. Brownson
"Cousin's Philosophy" (1836)

WHOEVER would see the American people as remarkable for their philosophy as they are for their industry, enterprise, and political freedom, must be gratified that these works have already attracted considerable attention among us, and are beginning to exert no little influence on our philosophical speculations. [...] We are, in fact, turning our attention to matters of deeper interest, than those which relate merely to the physical well-being of humanity. We are beginning to perceive that Providence, in the peculiar circumstances in which it has placed us, in the free institutions it has given us, has made it our duty to bring out the ideal man, and to prove, by a practical demonstration, what the human race may be, when and where it has free scope for the full and harmonious developement of all its faculties. In proportion as we perceive and comprehend this duty, we cannot fail to inquire for a sound philosophy, one which will enumerate and characterize all the faculties of the human soul, and determine the proper order and most efficient means of their developement.

[...] Religion subsists among us, and always will, for it has its seat in the human heart; but to a great extent it has lost its hold upon the understanding. Men are no longer satisfied with the arguments by which it has heretofore been defended; the old forms, in which it has been clothed, fail to meet the new wants which time and events have developed, and there is everywhere, in a greater or less degree, a tendency to doubt, unbelief, indifference, infidelity. We have outgrown tradition, and authority no longer seems to us a valid argument. We demand conviction. We do not, as in the middle ages, go to religion to prove our philosophy, but to our philosophy to prove our religion. [...]

[...] Everybody knows, that our religion and our philosophy are at war. We are religious only at the expense of our logic. This accounts for the fact, that, on the one hand, we disclaim logic, unchurch philosophy, and pronounce it a dangerous thing to reason; while, on the other, we reject religion, declaim against the clergy, and represent it exceedingly foolish to believe. This opposition cannot be concealed. It is found not only in the same community, but to a great extent in the same individual. The result cannot be doubtful. Philosophy will gain the victory. [... The] desire to philosophize, to account to ourselves for what we believe, cannot be suppressed. Instead, then, of quarrelling with this state of things, instead of denouncing the religious as do professed free inquirers, or the philosophizers, as is the case with too many of the friends of religion, we should reëxamine our philosophy, and inquire if there be not a philosophy true to human nature, and able to explain and verify, instead of destroying, the religious belief of mankind? We evidently need such a philosophy; such a philosophy we believe there is, and we know of no works so well fitted to assist us in finding it, as those of M. Cousin.[6] [...]

M. Cousin calls the system of philosophy which he and his friends profess and advocate, ECLECTICISM; because it recognises the leading principles of all the great schools into which the philosophical world has been divided, and attempts to mould them into one grand whole, which shall include them all, and yet be itself unlike any of them. [...]

[...] When we recognise only material existences [as sensualist philosophy does], thought itself becomes materialized [...]. All our notions of God, of the soul, of the Beautiful, the Right, inasmuch as they are not copies of outward material objects, which are observed alike by the senses, are illusions, mere fantasies, no more to be trusted than the dreams which disturb our nightly slumbers; religion withers into a mere form, hardens into a petrifaction, or entirely disappears; or, at least, can be retained only as an inconsequence or as an instrument; morality freezes into selfishness; pleasure and pain become the synonymes of right and wrong; and that alone which gives pleasure, – not to the soul but to the senses, – can be dignified with the name of *good*; the soul, having no longer any employment, takes its departure, and the man sinks in the animal, recognising and laboring only for animal wants. [...]

M. Cousin recognises in the consciousness three classes of phenomena, which result from the great elementary faculties which comprehend and explain all the rest. These faculties are Sensibility, Activity, and Reason. They are never found isolated one from another. Yet they are essentially distinct, and a scrupulous analysis distinguishes them in the complex phenomena of intellectual life without dividing them. To sensibility belong all the internal phenomena, which are derived from sensation, through our senses, from the external world; to the activity belong those, which we are conscious that we ourselves produce; and under the head of reason must be arranged all our ideas of the Absolute, the Supersensible, and all the internal facts which are purely intellectual, which we know we do not produce, and which cannot be derived through sensation from external nature. The activity is developed only by sensation. Activity and sensibility can generate no idea without the reason; and without sensibility and activity the reason would have no office. [...]

The Sensualist school admits and studies with great success the facts of the sensibility; but overlooking those of the activity and the reason, or not making a sufficient account of them, it mutilates the soul, and becomes false in its inductions. The Scotch school avoids this error; it distinguishes between the reason and sensibility, but without much scientific precision. The Kantian school has done it with more care and accuracy; it has also described with great clearness and precision the laws of the reason, but it has not

---

[6] Victor Cousin (1792-1867), French philosopher, appropriated European transcendentalist philosophy.

discerned with sufficient exactness the distinction between the reason and the activity. This deficiency has ruined the school. The activity is personal. *We* are in the activity; that alone is our *self*. To confound the reason with the activity, as Kant and his followers do, is to make the reason personal, and to deprive it of all but a subjective authority; that is, to make it of no authority except in relation to the individual in whom it is developed. To deprive the reason of all but a subjective authority, to allow it no validity out of the sphere of our own personality, is to deprive it of all legitimate authority, and to place philosophy on the route to a new and original skepticism. If the reason have no authority out of the sphere of the personality, out of the individual consciousness in which its phenomena appear, it can reveal to us no existences which lie beyond ourselves. Such may be the laws of our nature, that we cannot help believing that we are, that there is an external world, and God; but our belief can repose on no scientific basis. There is nothing to assure us, that it is not a mere illusion; nothing can demonstrate to us, that any thing really exists to respond to it. All certainty resolves itself into a mere personal affection. To this conclusion all are driven who assert the subjectivity of the reason. [...]

To avoid this extravagance, we must distinguish between the reason and the activity, and show that, though intimately connected, they are nevertheless fundamentally distinct. The reason, though appearing in us, is not our *self*. It is independent of us, and in no sense subject to our personality. If it depended on our personality, or if it constituted our personality, we could control its conceptions, prescribe its laws, and compel it to speak according to our pleasure. [...] Who does not feel, who does not know, that the truth is not his, – is nobody's, but independent of everybody? If, then, we are conscious that the conceptions of the reason are not ours, that the truths it reveals are not our truths, are not truths which are in any sense dependent on us, we must admit that the reason is independent of us, and, though appearing in us, is not ours, is not our *self*. [...]

[...] Now, what is it that *knows*? What is that inward light we call consciousness, which has these apperceptions in which we confide, which knows in any degree, – which knows at all? Is it not the reason?

The reason, once established in its true nature and independence, becomes a legitimate authority for whatever it reveals. A true analysis of it shows, that, instead of being imprisoned in the consciousness and compelled to turn for ever within the sphere of the subjective, it extends far beyond, and attains to beings as well as to phenomena. It reveals to us God and the world on precisely the same authority as our own existence, or the slightest modification of it. [...]

If this analysis of a fact of consciousness be accurate, we are authorized to say that no fact of consciousness is possible without the conception of our own existence, the existence of the world, and that of God. The ideas, of ourselves as a free personality, of nature, and of God as the substance, the cause, of both us and nature, constitute a single fact of the consciousness, are its inseparable elements, and without them consciousness is impossible. [...]

It should be remarked, that we do not *infer* the Absolute from the relative, the Infinite from the finite, God from nature and humanity. The Absolute is no logical creation, no production of reasoning. It could not be deduced from the relative. [...] But no man can say that a thing is finite without having at the same time the conception of the infinite; or that a thing is infinite without at the same time conceiving the finite. [...]

But if the absolute logically precedes the relative, and if the conceptions of the infinite, the finite, and their relation be indispensable conditions of all reasoning, it follows of course that our belief in God, in nature, in our own existence, is the result of no reasoning. When we first turned our minds inward in the act of reflection, we found that belief. We had it, and every man has it, from the first dawn of the intellect. It does not proceed then from reflection; and, as reflection is the only intellectual act in which we have any agency, it follows that it does not exist in consequence of any thing we have willed or done. It is prior to *our* action, and independent of it. Whence then its origin? It must be a primitive, spontaneous belief, the result of the spontaneity of the reason. The reason sees by its own light, is itself active; and, being in relation with the objective and the absolute, it can and does of itself reveal to the consciousness God and the world, giving by its own vigor the belief in question. The reason, being in its nature independent, and in its spontaneity acting independently of us, and though developing itself in us, is a good and legitimate witness for what lies beyond us, and exists independent of us. [...]

[...] The reason can reveal nothing which it has not in itself. If it reveal the absolute, it must itself be absolute. If absolute, it must be the Being of beings, God himself. The elements of the reason are then the elements of God. An analysis of the reason gives, as its elements, the ideas of the infinite, the finite, and their relation as cause and effect. Then these ideas are the elements of all thought, of thought in itself, of God. [...]

But God can manifest only what is in himself. He is thought, intelligence itself. Consequently there is in creation nothing but thought, intelligence. In nature, as in humanity, the supreme Reason is manifested, and there, where we had fancied all was dead and without thought, we are now enabled to see all living and essentially intellectual. There is no dead matter, there are no fatal causes; nature is thought, and God is its personality. This enables us to see God in nature, in a new and striking sense [...]. Well may we study nature, for, as a whole and in the minutest of its parts, it is a manifestation of the Infinite, the Absolute, the Everlasting, the Perfect, the universal Reason, – God. It should be loved, should be reverenced, not merely as a piece of mechanism, but as a glorious shining out of the Infinite and the Perfect. [...]

This is not Pantheism. Pantheism considers the universe as God; but this presents God as the cause, and the universe as the effect. God is as inseparable from the universe as the cause is inseparable from the effect [...]. The universe is his intention. It is what he wills, and he is in it, the substance of his volition; it is what he speaks, and he is in it, as a man is in his words; but he is distinct from it, by all the distinction there is between the energy that wills, and that which is willed, between him who speaks, and the words he utters. [...]

[...] The reason is God; it appears in us, therefore God appears in us. The light of reason, the light by which we see and know all that we do see and know, is truly the light of God. The voice of the spontaneous reason is the voice of God; those who speak by its authority, speak by the authority of God, and what they utter is a real revelation. [...] He in whom the spontaneous reason was more active than in his fellow beings, had a closer communion with God, could better interpret him than they, and was rightly termed the inspired, for he was inspired; – not indeed in a sense different from the rest of mankind, but in a different, a special, degree. [...]

Although there can be nothing in philosophy which is not in humanity, there may be much in humanity which is not in philosophy. A philosophy which does not embrace the whole of human nature is false [...]. Every sound philosopher, then, must be an Eclectic. [...]

Each of these schools [sensualism, idealism, skepticism, mysticism] has a truth, and embraces and explains a certain number of the phenomena of our nature; but neither embraces and explains them all. [...] A philosophy then, which embraces and explains the principles of these four schools is proved by history to be the true philosophy. [...]

We must be eclectics, excluding no element of humanity, but accepting and melting all into one vast system, which will be a true representative of humanity so far as it as yet developed. We must take broad and liberal views, expect truth and find it in all schools, in all creeds, in all ages, and in all countries. The great mission of our age is to unite the infinite and the finite. Union, harmony, whence proceed peace and love, are the points to be aimed at. We of the nineteenth century appear in the world as mediators. In philosophy, theology, government, art, industry, we are to conciliate hostile feelings, and harmonize conflicting principles and interests. We must bind together the past and the future, reconcile progress and immobility, by preserving what is good and studying to advance, that is, by meliorating instead of destroying; enable philosophy and theology to walk together in peace and love, by yielding to theology the authority of the spontaneous reason, – inspiration, – and vindicating for philosophy the absolute freedom of reflection.

Such is the very imperfect outline of M. Cousin's philosophy. [...]

Source: Orestes A. Brownson (1803-1876). "Cousin's Philosophy." *The Christian Examiner and General Review* 21.1 (September 1836), 33-35, 37-38, 40-45, 49-51, 54-56, 58-61.

195. George Ripley
Discourses on the Philosophy of Religion (1836)

Discourse II: On Faith in the Invisible

[...] The universe, with its varied beauty and splendor, is spread forth in our presence, it addresses every faculty and excites every feeling, we behold its vast and complicated changes with reverence and awe, and it is not surprising that we should regard it as clothed with original and independent reality. But, in truth, the things which are seen were not made of things which do appear. The material universe is the expression of an Invisible Wisdom and Power. It has its origin in the will of the Infinite, who has made it what it is, endowed it with all its properties, impressed it with all its tendencies, assigned it all its laws, and by whose energy it is ever constantly sustained. The creation in itself, without reference to the Almighty Spirit from which it sprung, is formless and without order – a mass of chaotic objects, of whose uses we are ignorant, and whose destiny we cannot imagine. It is only when its visible glory leads our minds to its unseen Author, and we regard it as a manifestation of Divine Wisdom, that we can truly comprehend its character and designs. To the eye of sense, what does the external creation present? Much less than we are generally apt to suppose. [...] Merely the different arrangements of matter, the various degrees and directions in which the light falls on the object admired, and the change of position with regard to space. This is all that is seen. The rest is felt. The forms are addressed to the eye, but the perception of beauty is in the soul. And the highest degree of this is perceived, when the outward creation suggests the wisdom of the Creator. Without that, it is comparatively blank and cold and lifeless. It is his existence which furnishes the ground for the existence of that, and connected with Him, as the Primal Fountain of Being, it derives all the reality which it possesses, from his Sovereign Will. How unwise, then, to confine our attention merely to the outward form, and to forget the inward spirit, which it represents! How unworthy of the character of a man, to be so occupied with the mere outside, the dry husk and shell of matter, as to lose sight of the Infinite and Divine Energy, from which it draws the reality of its being.

The things that are seen, moreover, are dependent, in a great measure, upon our own souls. We have another instance, here, of the relation between the visible and the invisible, and the subjection of the former to the latter. It is often said, I am aware, that the soul is dependent for its character and growth, on the external forms of matter, with which it is connected, and that it is greatly influenced by them is a fact, which no observer of human nature can deny; but it is no less true, that the outward universe is to a great degree, dependent upon our souls for its character and influence, and that by changes in our inward condition, a corresponding change is produced in the objects with which we are surrounded. It is from the cast and disposition of our souls, that external nature derives its hues and conformation. Place two men of different character, in the same outward scenes, how different is the effect which takes place. To one, perhaps, whose heart is tuned to the praises of his Maker, every thing suggests the presence of Divine Wisdom and Love. The voice of God is heard in the rushings of the wind and the whisperings of the breeze, in the roar of the thunder and the fall of the rain; his hand is visible in the glories of the midnight sky and the splendor of the opening morn, in the fierce majesty and might of winter, and in the greenness and beauty of the returning spring; every object is an image of the goodness of God; every sound, a call for his adoration; every spot a hallowed temple for his praise. But to the heart of the other, no such feelings are suggested. He looks coldly on, amid the fair scene of things, in which he is placed. No emotions of admiration or of gratitude penetrate his soul. No sound comes to him from the depths of nature, answering to an accordant sound within the depths of his own heart. He views all that is before him, with a spirit of calculation or a spirit of indifference. Yet he sees precisely the same objects with his companion. The same outward universe is unfolded to his view. The same material sights meet his eye; the same material sounds touch his ear; the same forms and colors and motions, are addressed to his senses. But is it in fact, the same world that is beheld in the two cases? In one, it is a living image, speaking forth the glory of God; in the other, a mute and dead mass of material forms. Whence is this difference? Whence, but from the souls of the two spectators? It is upon the inward condition that the outward reality depends. The visible universe is to us what our invisible souls choose to make it. Here, then, we have a reason for looking at the things which are unseen – for making them the chief object of our attention. In so doing, we become conversant with the primal source of reality. We ascend to the original fountain of Being, from which the streams that flow forth receive their properties and their direction. [...]

Discourse III: The Divine Elements of Human Nature

[...] Let us see if there is any thing in the nature of man, which may enable him to become a partaker of the divine nature – any capacities, which may be the germ of qualities in his character, similar to those which we reverence in the character of God.

I. When we examine the nature which we possess, we perceive at once, that it has a power of a remarkable character, which seems to bear some resemblance to one of the divine attributes – the power of perceiving truth. Man has a faculty, which enables him not merely to count, to weigh, and to measure, to estimate probabilities and to draw inferences from visible facts, but to ascertain and determine certain principles of original truth. [...] There are certain points on which the judgment of all men is alike – certain propositions, which every one would pronounce true, certain others which all would declare false. We are compelled to this by the nature of our Reason. It is not subject to the control of our will. We cannot say, that we choose to have two and two appear equal to five, and therefore they are so in the sight of Reason; but this faculty exercises its own judgment, announces its own decisions, enforces its own authority, from which there is no appeal. Does not this show, that Reason though within us is not created by us; though belonging to human nature, originates in a higher nature; though shining in the mind of man, is an emanation from the mind of God? Is not the faculty of reason similar to the wisdom of God? As he has the power of perceiving the pure and absolute truth on all subjects, has he not endowed man with the similar power of perceiving truth, on a limited number of subjects? In this respect, then, I believe that the nature of man has powers by which he may become a partaker of the divine nature – may exhibit qualities of a similar character to those which we reverence in God.

II. Again, man has the faculty of recognising moral distinctions. Of two courses of conduct that are presented to his choice, he is able to say that one is Right and that the other is Wrong. He perceives not merely what would be for his advantage, his interest, what will gratify his passions, or promote the happiness of society, but he sees that certain actions, though they might gratify his selfish inclinations, are forbidden by the law of Duty, and he feels an inward obligation to obey that law. Man does not obtain this knowledge through the medium of any of his senses. It is not the result of that part of his nature which calculates and compares. It is not subject to his own will. [...] A voice within speaks, which he cannot but hear, and tells him the character of the action which he is about to perform. It is common to call this voice within us, this conscience which speaks out its clear behests, whether we will hear or whether we will forbear, the voice of God – and is there not a truth of deep significance in the expression? Is not conscience in the human soul, a quality similar to that attribute of God, which makes him the righteous judge of all the earth? [...]

III. Again, man has the power of disinterested Love. [...] It is felt by the philanthropist, who is ready, at the expense of his tears and his blood, to alleviate the miseries of the human race. It is felt by the friend, who would willingly renounce his own life in behalf of his friend. It is felt by the parent, who knows that the happiness of his children [is] dearer to him than his own, and who would give up every thing himself to confer it upon them. It is felt by every good man, who has so devoted himself to a righteous cause, that he regards his own interests as but chaff and dust, compared with the promotion of the cause which he has at heart. And this love is the very essence of the Divine character. God is Love, and whoso dwelleth in Love, dwelleth in God and God in him. It is not of Earth, but of Heaven. It is the great attribute which binds the Almighty to the heart of Man. The more we possess of this quality, the more we resemble God. The germ of it, which exists in our hearts, is the foundation for our growing likeness to the Creator, and when it is fully developed within us, we have become partakers of the Divine Nature.

IV. Once more, man has the power of conceiving of a perfection higher than he has ever reached. Not only so. He can make this perfection a distinct object of pursuit. He has faculties which the present can never satisfy. After he has done his best, he feels how much better it might have been done. He can always form a conception of a higher model, than any which he can actually realize. And his nature impels him to follow this ideal standard – not to rest content in imperfection – to forget the things that are behind – and to press forward to higher attainments, to diviner excellence. [...] And this power, belonging to the human soul, is another element, by which man may become partaker of the divine nature. It is the germ of resemblance to God. It is intended to lead us on from strength to strength, from glory, to glory, in an ever-growing likeness to the Infinite Source of Beauty, and Goodness and Love.

Consider then, my friends, these four principles of human nature, the power of perceiving Truth – of recognising moral distinctions – of exercising disinterested love – and of aspiring after illimitable perfection, and tell me, if we were not made to become partakers of the Divine Nature? Does not the soul of Man bear the impress of God? Are we not created to exhibit the Image of our Maker in its divine purity and splendor? And if such be our destiny, how solemn is our responsibility! –

Source: George Ripley (1802-1880). *Discourses on the Philosophy of Religion, Addressed to the Doubters Who Wish to Believe*. Boston: James Munroe, 1836, 22-25, 34-40.

196. Ralph Waldo Emerson
Nature (1836)

INTRODUCTION.

Our age is retrospective. It builds the sepulchres of the fathers. It writes biographies, histories, and criticism. The foregoing generations beheld God and nature face to face; we, through their eyes. Why should not we also enjoy an original relation to the universe? Why should not we have a poetry and philosophy of insight and not of tradition, and a religion by revelation to us, and not the history of theirs? Embosomed for a season in nature, whose floods of life stream around and through us, and invite us by the powers they supply, to action proportioned to nature, why should we grope among the dry bones of the past, or put the living generation into masquerade out of its faded wardrobe? The sun shines to-day also. [...]

Philosophically considered, the universe is composed of Nature and the Soul. Strictly speaking, therefore, all that is separate from us, all which Philosophy distinguishes as the NOT ME, that is, both nature and art, all other men and my own body, must be ranked under this name, NATURE. In enumerating the values of nature and casting up their sum, I shall use the word in both senses; – in its common and in its philosophical import. In inquiries so general as our present one, the inaccuracy is not material; no confusion of thought will occur. *Nature*, in the common sense, refers to essences unchanged by man; space, the air, the river, the leaf. *Art* is applied to the mixture of his will with the same things, as in a house, a canal, a statue, a picture. But his operations taken together are so insignificant, a little chipping, baking, patching, and washing, that in an impression so grand as that of the world on the human mind, they do not vary the result.

NATURE.
CHAPTER I.

To go into solitude, a man needs to retire as much from his chamber as from society. I am not solitary whilst I read and write, though nobody is with me. But if a man would be alone, let him look at the stars. The rays that come from those heavenly worlds, will separate between him and vulgar things. One might think the atmosphere was made transparent with this design, to give man, in the heavenly bodies, the perpetual presence of the sublime. Seen in the streets of cities, how great they are! If the stars should appear one night in a thousand years, how would men believe and adore; and preserve for many generations the remembrance of the city of God which had been shown! But every night come out these preachers of beauty, and light the universe with their admonishing smile.

The stars awaken a certain reverence, because though always present, they are inaccessible; but all natural objects make a kindred impression, when the mind is open to their influence. Nature never wears a mean appearance. Neither does the wisest man extort all her secret, and lose his curiosity by finding out all her perfection. Nature never became a toy to a wise spirit. The flowers, the animals, the mountains, reflected all the wisdom of his best hour, as much as they had delighted the simplicity of his childhood. [...]

To speak truly, few adult persons can see nature. Most persons do not see the sun. At least they have a very superficial seeing. The sun illuminates only the eye of the man, but shines into the eye and the heart of the child. The lover of nature is he whose inward and outward senses are still truly adjusted to each other; who has retained the spirit of infancy even into the era of manhood. His intercourse with heaven and earth, becomes part of his daily food. In the presence of nature, a wild delight runs through the man, in spite of real sorrows. [...] Crossing a bare common, in snow puddles, at twilight, under a clouded sky, without having in my thoughts any occurrence of special good fortune, I have enjoyed a perfect exhilaration. Almost I fear to think how glad I am. In the woods too, a man casts off his years, as the snake his slough, and at what period soever of life, is always a child. In the woods, is perpetual youth. Within these plantations of God, a decorum and sanctity reign, a perennial festival is dressed, and the guest sees not how he should tire of them in a thousand years. In the woods, we return to reason and faith. There I feel that nothing can befal me in life, – no disgrace, no calamity, (leaving me my eyes,) which nature cannot repair. Standing on the bare ground, – my head bathed by the blithe air, and uplifted into infinite space, – all mean egotism vanishes. I become a transparent eye-ball. I am nothing. I see all. The currents of the Universal Being circulate through me; I am part or particle of God. The name of the nearest friend sounds then foreign and accidental. To be brothers, to be acquaintances, – master or servant, is then a trifle and a disturbance. I am the lover of uncontained and immortal beauty. In the wilderness, I find something more dear and connate than in streets or villages. In the tranquil landscape, and especially in the distant line of the horizon, man beholds somewhat as beautiful as his own nature. [...]

CHAPTER VII.

SPIRIT.

[...] And all the uses of nature admit of being summed in one, which yields the activity of man an infinite scope. Through all its kingdoms, to the suburbs and outskirts of things, it is faithful to the cause whence it had its origin. It always speaks of Spirit. It suggests the absolute. It is a perpetual effect. It is a great shadow pointing always to the sun behind us. [...]

Of that ineffable essence which we call Spirit, he that thinks most, will say least. We can foresee God in the coarse and, as it were, distant phenomena of matter; but when we try to define and describe himself, both language and thought desert us, and we are as helpless as fools and savages. That essence refuses to be recorded in propositions, but when man has worshipped him intellectually, the noblest ministry of nature is to stand as the apparition of God. It is the great organ through which the universal spirit speaks to the individual, and strives to lead back the individual to it. [...]

But when, following the invisible steps of thought, we come to inquire, Whence is matter? and Whereto? many truths arise to us out of the recesses of consciousness. We learn that the highest is present to the soul of man, that the dread universal essence, which is not wisdom, or love, or beauty, or power, but all in one, and each entirely, is that for which all things exist, and that by which they are; that spirit creates; that behind nature, throughout nature, spirit is present; that spirit is one and not compound; that spirit does not act upon us from without, that is, in space and time, but spiritually, or through ourselves. Therefore, that spirit, that is, the Supreme Being, does not build up nature around us, but puts it forth through us, as the life of the tree puts forth new branches and leaves through the pores of the old. As a plant upon the earth, so a man rests upon the bosom of God; he is nourished by unfailing fountains, and draws, at his need, inexhaustible power. Who can set bounds to the possibilities of man? Once inspire the infinite, by being admitted to behold the absolute natures of justice and truth, and we learn that man has access to the entire mind of the Creator, is himself the creator in the finite. This view [...] animates me to create my own world through the purification of my soul.

The world proceeds from the same spirit as the body of man. It is a remoter and inferior incarnation of God, a projection of God in the unconscious. But it differs from the body in one important respect. It is not, like that, now subjected to the human will. Its serene order is inviolable by us. It is therefore, to us, the present expositor[7] of the divine mind. It is a fixed point whereby we may measure our departure. As we degenerate, the contrast between us and our house is more evident. We are as much strangers in nature, as we are aliens from God. [...]

Source: Ralph Waldo Emerson (1803-1882). *Nature*. Boston: James Munroe & Co., 1836, 5, 7-13, 76-77, 79-81.

197. Francis Bowen
"Transcendentalism" (1837)

[...] Within a short period, a new school of philosophy has appeared, the adherents of which have dignified it with the title of Transcendentalism. In its essential features, it is a revival of the Old Platonic school. It rejects the aid of observation, and will not trust to experiment. The Baconian[8] mode of discovery is regarded as obsolete; induction is a slow and tedious process, and the results are uncertain and imperfect. General truths are to be attained without the previous examination of particulars, and by the aid of a higher power than the understanding. "The hand-lamp of logic" is to be broken, for the truths which are *felt* are more satisfactory and certain than those which are *proved*. The sphere of intuition is enlarged, and made to comprehend not only mathematical axioms, but the most abstruse and elevated propositions respecting the being and destiny of man. Pure intelligence usurps the place of humble research. Hidden meanings, glimpses of spiritual and everlasting truth are found, where former observers sought only for natural facts. The observation of sensible phenomena can lead only to the discovery of insulated, partial, and relative laws; but the consideration of the same phenomena, in a typical point of view, may lead us to infinite and absolute truth, – to a knowledge of the reality of things. [...]

---

[7] One who sets forth the meaning of a passage, word, etc.; an interpreter of dreams, etc.
[8] Francis Bacon (1561-1626), lawyer, philosopher, and lord chancellor of England (1618–1621), who held that knowledge of nature must derive from observation, not from abstract reasoning.

[...] The writers of whom we speak, openly avow their preference of such indistinct modes of reflection, and justify loose and rambling speculations, mystical forms of expression, and the utterance of truths that are but half perceived, on the same principle, it would seem, that influences the gambler, who expects by a number of random casts to obtain at last the desired combination. [...]

The distinguishing trait of Transcendental philosophy, is the appeal which it makes from the authority of reason and argument to that of passion and feeling. [...] In one sense, the heart is wiser than the head; the child is the teacher of the man. A process of reasoning, which leads to a false result, is a mere logical puzzle, and so far from establishing that result, it only demonstrates the weakness of the reasoning faculty, that cannot discover the mistake, which, through the medium of a higher power, we know must exist. The foundations of moral and religious truth are like the axioms on which the mathematician grounds his argument; if, either directly or by necessary inference, conclusions are found to be at variance with these first principles, they are at once rejected as being demonstrably absurd.

But some bounds must be set to the application of views like these. [...]

The aim of the Transcendentalists is high. They profess to look not only beyond facts, but without the aid of facts, to principles. What is this but Plato's doctrine of innate, eternal, and immutable ideas, on the consideration of which all science is founded? [...] Again, they are busy in the inquiry (to adopt their own phraseology,) after the Real and the Absolute, as distinguished from the Apparent. Not to repeat the same doubt as to their success, we may at least request them to beware lest they strip Truth of its relation to Humanity, and thus deprive it of its usefulness. Granted that we are imprisoned in matter, why beat against the bars in a fruitless attempt to escape, when a little labor might convert the prison to a palace, or at least render the confinement more endurable. The frame of mind which longs after the forbidden fruit of knowledge in subjects placed beyond the reach of the human faculties, as it is surely indicative of a noble temperament, may also, under peculiar circumstances, conduce to the happiness of the individual. But if too much indulged, there is danger lest it waste its energies in mystic and unprofitable dreams, and despondency result from frequent failures, till at last, disappointment darkens into despair. [...]

Source: F.B. [Francis Bowen (1811-1890)]. "Transcendentalism" [Review Article of *Nature*. Boston: James Munroe & Co., 1836]. *The Christian Examiner and General Review* 21.3 (January 1837), 377, 380, 383-385.

198. Ralph Waldo Emerson
"The American Scholar" (1837)

Mr. President and Gentlemen:

I greet you on the recommencement of our literary year. Our anniversary is one of hope, and, perhaps, not enough of labor. We do not meet for games of strength or skill, for the recitation of histories, tragedies, and odes, like the ancient Greeks; for parliaments of love and poesy, like the Troubadours; nor for the advancement of science, like our contemporaries in the British and European capitals. Thus far, our holiday has been simply a friendly sign of the survival of the love of letters amongst a people too busy to give to letters any more. As such it is precious as the sign of an indestructible instinct. Perhaps the time is already come when it ought to be, and will be, something else; when the sluggard intellect of this continent will look from under its iron lids and fill the postponed expectation of the world with something better than the exertions of mechanical skill. Our day of dependence, our long apprenticeship to the learning of other lands, draws to a close. The millions that around us are rushing into life, cannot always be fed on the sere[9] remains of foreign harvests. Events, actions arise, that must be sung, that will sing themselves. Who can doubt that poetry will revive and lead in a new age, as the star in the constellation Harp,[10] which now flames in our zenith, astronomers announce, shall one day be the pole-star for a thousand years?

In this hope I accept the topic which not only usage but the nature of our association seem to prescribe to this day, – the AMERICAN SCHOLAR. Year by year we come up hither to read one more chapter of his biography. Let us inquire what light new days and events have thrown on his character and his hopes.

It is one of those fables which out of an unknown antiquity convey an unlooked-for wisdom, that the gods, in the beginning, divided Man into men, that he might be more helpful to himself; just as the hand was divided into fingers, the better to answer its end.

The old fable covers a doctrine ever new and sublime; that there is One Man, – present to all particular men only partially, or through one faculty; and that you must take the whole society to find the whole man. Man is not a farmer, or a professor, or an engineer, but he is all. Man is priest, and scholar, and statesman, and producer, and soldier. In the *divided* or social state these functions are parcelled out to individuals, each of whom aims to do his stint of the joint work, whilst each other performs his. [...]

In this distribution of functions the scholar is the delegated intellect. In the right state he is *Man Thinking*. In the degenerate state, when the victim of society, he tends to become a mere thinker, or still worse, the parrot of other men's thinking.

[... Let us consider Man Thinking] in reference to the main influences he receives.

I. The first in time and the first in importance of the influences upon the mind is that of nature. Every day, the sun; and, after sunset, Night and her stars. Ever the winds blow; ever the grass grows. Every day, men and women, conversing – beholding and beholden. The scholar is he of all men whom this spectacle most engages. He must settle its value in his mind. What is nature to him? There is never a beginning, there is never an end, to the inexplicable continuity of this web of God, but always circular power returning into itself. Therein it resembles his own spirit, whose beginning, whose ending, he never can

---

[9] Dry, withered.
[10] Brightest star in the northern constellation Lyra and fourth brightest in the night sky.

find, – so entire, so boundless. Far too as her splendors shine, system on system shooting like rays, upward, downward, without centre, without circumference, – in the mass and in the particle, Nature hastens to render account of herself to the mind. [...]

[...] Yet when this spiritual light shall have revealed the law of more earthly natures, – when he has learned to worship the soul, and to see that the natural philosophy that now is, is only the first gropings of its gigantic hand, he shall look forward to an ever expanding knowledge as to a becoming creator. He shall see that nature is the opposite of the soul, answering to it part for part. One is seal and one is print. Its beauty is the beauty of his own mind. Its laws are the laws of his own mind. Nature then becomes to him the measure of his attainments. So much of nature as he is ignorant of, so much of his own mind does he not yet possess. And, in fine, the ancient precept, "Know thyself," and the modern precept, "Study nature," become at last one maxim.[11]

II. The next great influence into the spirit of the scholar is the mind of the Past, – in whatever form, whether of literature, of art, of institutions, that mind is inscribed. Books are the best type of the influence of the past, and perhaps we shall get at the truth, – learn the amount of this influence more conveniently, – by considering their value alone. [...]

Yet hence arises a grave mischief. [... The] book becomes noxious: the guide is a tyrant. [...]

Undoubtedly there is a right way of reading so it be sternly subordinated. Man Thinking must not be subdued by his instruments. Books are for the scholar's idle times. When he can read God directly, the hour is too precious to be wasted in other men's transcripts of their readings. But when the intervals of darkness come, as come they must, – when the sun is hid and the stars withdraw their shining, – we repair to the lamps which were kindled by their ray, to guide our steps to the East again, where the dawn is. [...]

The world, – this shadow of the soul, or *other me*, – lies wide around. Its attractions are the keys which unlock my thoughts and make me acquainted with myself. [...]

[...] Help must come from the bosom alone. The scholar is that man who must take up into himself all the ability of the time, all the contributions of the past, all the hopes of the future. He must be an university of knowledges. If there be one lesson more than another which should pierce his ear, it is, The world is nothing, the man is all; in yourself is the law of all nature, and you know not yet how a globule of sap ascends; in yourself slumbers the whole of Reason; it is for you to know all; it is for you to dare all. Mr. President and Gentlemen, this confidence in the unsearched might of man belongs, by all motives, by all prophecy, by all preparation, to the American Scholar. We have listened too long to the courtly muses of Europe. [...] A nation of men will for the first time exist, because each believes himself inspired by the Divine Soul which also inspires all men.

Source: Ralph Waldo Emerson (1803-1882). "The American Scholar: An Oration Delivered before the Phi Beta Kappa Society, at Cambridge, August 31, 1837." *Nature: Addresses and Lectures*. Centenary Edition of *The Complete Works of Ralph Waldo Emerson*. 14 vols. Boston and New York: Houghton Mifflin Company/The Riverside Press Cambridge, 1918, Vol. 1, 81-89, 91, 95, 113-115.

---

[11] Synthesis of the paradigms of ancient philosophy (Socrates, Oracle of Delphi) and Enlightenment Philosophy (Newton etc.).

199. Ralph Waldo Emerson
"Divinity School Address" (1838)

In this refulgent summer, it has been a luxury to draw the breath of life. The grass grows, the buds burst, the meadow is spotted with fire and gold in the tint of flowers. The air is full of birds, and sweet with the breath of the pine, the balm-of-Gilead,[12] and the new hay. Night brings no gloom to the heart with its welcome shade. Through the transparent darkness the stars pour their almost spiritual rays. Man under them seems a young child, and his huge globe a toy. The cool night bathes the world as with a river, and prepares his eyes again for the crimson dawn. The mystery of nature was never displayed more happily. The corn and the wine have been freely dealt to all creatures, and the never-broken silence with which the old bounty goes forward has not yielded yet one word of explanation. One is constrained to respect the perfection of this world in which our senses converse. How wide; how rich; what invitation from every property it gives to every faculty of man! [...]

But when the mind opens and reveals the laws which traverse the universe and make things what they are, then shrinks the great world at once into a mere illustration and fable of this mind. What am I? and What is? asks the human spirit with a curiosity new-kindled, but never to be quenched. Behold these outrunning laws, which our imperfect apprehension can see tend this way and that, but not come full circle. Behold these infinite relations, so like, so unlike; many, yet one. I would study, I would know, I would admire forever. These works of thought have been the entertainments of the human spirit in all ages.

A more secret, sweet, and overpowering beauty appears to man when his heart and mind open to the sentiment of virtue. Then he is instructed in what is above him. He learns that his being is without bound; that to the good, to the perfect, he is born, low as he now lies in evil and weakness. That which he venerates is still his own, though he has not realized it yet. [...]

The intuition of the moral sentiment is an insight of the perfection of the laws of the soul. These laws execute themselves. They are out of time, out of space, and not subject to circumstance. [...]

These facts have always suggested to man the sublime creed that the world is not the product of manifold power, but of one will, of one mind; and that one mind is everywhere active, in each ray of the star, in each wavelet of the pool; and whatever opposes that will is everywhere balked and baffled, because things are made so, and not otherwise. Good is positive. Evil is merely privative, not absolute [...]. All evil is so much death or nonentity. Benevolence is absolute and real. So much benevolence as a man hath, so much life hath he. For all things proceed out of this same spirit, which is differently named love, justice, temperance, in its different applications [...]. All things proceed out of this spirit, and all things conspire with it. [...]

The perception of this law of laws awakens in the mind a sentiment which we call the religious sentiment, and which makes our highest happiness. Wonderful is its power to charm and to command. It is a mountain air. It is the embalmer of the world. [...]

This sentiment is divine and deifying. It is the beatitude of man. It makes him illimitable. Through it, the soul first knows itself. It corrects the capital mistake of the infant man, who seeks to be great by following the great, and hopes to derive advantages *from*

---

[12] The area of Gilead was rich in spices and aromatic gums that provided balm, which was exported to Egypt and Tyre; cf. "Go up to Gilead and take balm," Jer. 46.11.

another, – by showing the fountain of all good to be in himself, and that he, equally with every man, is an inlet into the deeps of Reason. When he says, "I ought;" when love warms him; when he chooses, warned from on high, the good and great deed; then, deep melodies wander through his soul from Supreme Wisdom. – Then he can worship, and be enlarged by his worship; for he can never go behind this sentiment. In the sublimest flights of the soul, rectitude is never surmounted, love is never outgrown. [...]

Meantime, whilst the doors of the temple stand open, night and day, before every man, and the oracles of this truth cease never, it is guarded by one stern condition; this, namely; it is an intuition. It cannot be received at second hand. Truly speaking, it is not instruction, but provocation, that I can receive from another soul. What he announces, I must find true in me, or reject [...].

Jesus Christ belonged to the true race of prophets. He saw with open eye the mystery of the soul. Drawn by its severe harmony, ravished with its beauty, he lived in it, and had his being there. Alone in all history he estimated the greatness of man. One man was true to what is in you and me. He saw that God incarnates himself in man, and evermore goes forth anew to take possession of his World. He said, in this jubilee of sublime emotion, 'I am divine. Through me, God acts; through me, speaks. Would you see God, see me; or see thee, when thou also thinkest as I now think.' But what a distortion did his doctrine and memory suffer in the same, in the next, and the following ages! [...]

1. In this point of view we become sensible of the first defect of historical Christianity. Historical Christianity has fallen into the error that corrupts all attempts to communicate religion. [...]

2. The second defect of the traditionary and limited way of using the mind of Christ is a consequence of the first; this, namely; that the Moral Nature, that Law of laws whose revelations introduce greatness – yea, God himself – into the open soul, is not explored as the fountain of the established teaching in society. Men have come to speak of the revelation as somewhat long ago given and done, as if God were dead. [...]

It is very certain that it is the effect of conversation with the beauty of the soul, to beget a desire and need to impart to others the same knowledge and love. [...]

The man enamored of this excellency becomes its priest or poet. [...]

And now, my brothers, you will ask, What in these desponding days can be done by us? The remedy is already declared in the ground of our complaint of the Church. We have contrasted the Church with the Soul. In the soul then let the redemption be sought. [...] The stationariness of religion; the assumption that the age of inspiration is past, that the Bible is closed; the fear of degrading the character of Jesus by representing him as a man; – indicate with sufficient clearness the falsehood of our theology. It is the office of a true teacher to show us that God is, not was; that He speaketh, not spake. [...]

Let me admonish you, first of all, to go alone; to refuse the good models, even those which are sacred in the imagination of men, and dare to love God without mediator or veil. [...]

Yourself a newborn bard of the Holy Ghost, cast behind you all conformity, and acquaint men at first hand with Deity. Look to it first and only, that fashion, custom, authority, pleasure, and money, are nothing to you, – are not bandages over your eyes, that you cannot see, – but live with the privilege of the immeasurable mind. [...]

Source: Ralph Waldo Emerson (1803-1882). "An Address Delivered before the Senior Class in Divinity College, Cambridge, Sunday Evening, July 15, 1838." *Nature: Addresses and Lectures*. Centenary Edition of *The Complete Works of Ralph Waldo Emerson*. 14 vols. Boston and New York: Houghton Mifflin Company/The Riverside Press Cambridge, 1918, Vol. 1, 119-126, 128, 130, 134, 143-146.

200. Henry David Thoreau
Walden (1854)

Economy

When I wrote the following pages, or rather the bulk of them, I lived alone, in the woods, a mile from any neighbor, in a house which I had built myself, on the shore of Walden Pond, in Concord, Massachusetts, and earned my living by the labor of my hands only. I lived there two years and two months. At present I am a sojourner in civilized life again. [...]

Most men, even in this comparatively free country, through mere ignorance and mistake, are so occupied with the factitious cares and superfluously coarse labors of life that its finer fruits cannot be plucked by them. [...]

Where I Lived, and What I Lived For

[...] I went to the woods because I wished to live deliberately, to front only the essential facts of life, and see if I could not learn what it had to teach, and not, when I came to die, discover that I had not lived. I did not wish to live what was not life, living is so dear; nor did I wish to practise resignation, unless it was quite necessary. I wanted to live deep and suck out all the marrow of life, to live so sturdily and Spartan-like as to put to rout all that was not life, to cut a broad swath and shave close, to drive life into a corner, and reduce it to its lowest terms, and, if it proved to be mean, why then to get the whole and genuine meanness of it, and publish its meanness to the world; or if it were sublime, to know it by experience, and be able to give a true account of it in my next excursion. For most men, it appears to me, are in a strange uncertainty about it, whether it is of the devil or of God, and have *somewhat hastily* concluded that it is the chief end of man here to "glorify God and enjoy him forever."

Still we live meanly, like ants; though the fable tells us that we were long ago changed into men; like pygmies we fight with cranes; it is error upon error, and clout upon clout, and our best virtue has for its occasion a superfluous and evitable wretchedness. Our life is frittered away by detail. An honest man has hardly need to count more than his ten fingers, or in extreme cases he may add his ten toes, and lump the rest. Simplicity, simplicity, simplicity! I say, let your affairs be as two or three, and not a hundred or a thousand; instead of a million count half a dozen, and keep your accounts on your thumb nail. [...]

Why should we live with such hurry and waste of life? We are determined to be starved before we are hungry. Men say that a stitch in time saves nine, and so they take a thousand stitches to-day to save nine to-morrow. [...]

[...] Men esteem truth remote, in the outskirts of the system, behind the farthest star, before Adam and after the last man. In eternity there is indeed something true and sublime. But all these times and places and occasions are now and here. God himself culminates in the present moment, and will never be more divine in the lapse of all the ages. And we are enabled to apprehend at all what is sublime and noble only by the perpetual instilling and drenching of the reality which surrounds us. The universe constantly and obediently answers to our conceptions; whether we travel fast or slow, the track is laid for us. Let us spend our lives in conceiving then. The poet or the artist never yet had so fair and noble a design but some of his posterity at least could accomplish it. [...]

Time is but the stream I go a-fishing in. I drink at it; but while I drink I see the sandy bottom and detect how shallow it is. Its thin current slides away, but eternity remains. I would drink deeper; fish in the sky, whose bottom is pebbly with stars. I cannot count one. I know not the first letter of the alphabet. I have always been regretting that I was not as wise as the day I was born. The intellect is a cleaver; it discerns and rifts its way into the secret of things. I do not wish to be any more busy with my hands than is necessary. My head is hands and feet. I feel all my best faculties concentrated in it. My instinct tells me that my head is an organ for burrowing, as some creatures use their snout and fore-paws, and with it I would mine and burrow my way through these hills. I think that the richest vein is somewhere hereabouts; so by the divining rod and thin rising vapors I judge; and here I will begin to mine. [...]

Solitude

This is a delicious evening, when the whole body is one sense, and imbibes delight through every pore. I go and come with a strange liberty in Nature, a part of herself. As I walk along the stony shore of the pond in my shirt sleeves, though it is cool as well as cloudy and windy, and I see nothing special to attract me, all the elements are unusually congenial to me. [...]

Yet I experienced sometimes that the most sweet and tender, the most innocent and encouraging society may be found in any natural object, even for the poor misanthrope and most melancholy man. There can be no very black melancholy to him who lives in the midst of Nature and has his senses still. There was never yet such a storm but it was Æolian music[13] to a healthy and innocent ear. Nothing can rightly compel a simple and brave man to a vulgar sadness. While I enjoy the friendship of the seasons I trust that nothing can make life a burden to me. [...] To be alone was something unpleasant. But I was at the same time conscious of a slight insanity in my mood, and seemed to foresee my recovery. In the midst of a gentle rain while these thoughts prevailed, I was suddenly sensible of such sweet and beneficent society in Nature, in the very pattering of the drops, and in every sound and sight around my house, an infinite and unaccountable friendliness all at once like an atmosphere sustaining me, as made the fancied advantages of human neighborhood insignificant, and I have never thought of them since. Every little pine needle expanded and swelled with sympathy and befriended me. I was so distinctly made aware of the presence of something kindred to me, even in scenes which we are accustomed to call wild and dreary, and also that the nearest of blood to me and humanest was not a person nor a villager, that I thought no place could ever be strange to me again. [...]

Brute Neighbors

[...] I was witness to events of a less peaceful character. One day when I went out to my wood-pile, or rather my pile of stumps, I observed two large ants, the one red, the other much larger, nearly half an inch long, and black, fiercely contending with one another. Having once got hold they never let go, but struggled and wrestled and rolled on the chips incessantly. Looking farther, I was surprised to find that the chips were covered with such combatants, that it was not a *duellum*, but a *bellum*, a war between two races of ants, the red always pitted against the black, and frequently two red ones to one black. The legions of these Myrmidons covered all the hills and vales in my wood-yard, and the

---

[13] The Aeolian Harp – named for Aeolus, Greek keeper of the winds – was commonly placed in the open air so that the wind could cause it to produce sounds.

ground was already strewn with the dead and dying, both red and black. It was the only battle which I have ever witnessed, the only battle-field I ever trod while the battle was raging; internecine war; the red republicans on the one hand, and the black imperialists on the other. On every side they were engaged in deadly combat, yet without any noise that I could hear, and human soldiers never fought so resolutely. I watched a couple that were fast locked in each other's embraces, in a little sunny valley amid the chips, now at noon-day prepared to fight till the sun went down, or life went out. The smaller red champion had fastened himself like a vice to his adversary's front, and through all the tumblings on that field never for an instant ceased to gnaw at one of his feelers near the root, having already caused the other to go by the board; while the stronger black one dashed him from side to side, and, as I saw on looking nearer, had already divested him of several of his members. They fought with more pertinacity than bull-dogs. Neither manifested the least disposition to retreat. It was evident that their battle-cry was Conquer or die. In the mean while there came along a single red ant on the hillside of this valley, evidently full of excitement, who either had despatched his foe, or had not yet taken part in the battle; probably the latter, for he had lost none of his limbs; whose mother had charged him to return with his shield or upon it. Or perchance he was some Achilles, who had nourished his wrath apart, and had now come to avenge or rescue his Patroclus.[14] He saw this unequal combat from afar, – for the blacks were nearly twice the size of the red, – he drew near with rapid pace till he stood on his guard within half an inch of the combatants; then, watching his opportunity, he sprang upon the black warrior, and commenced his operations near the root of his right fore-leg, leaving the foe to select among his own members; and so there were three united for life, as if a new kind of attraction had been invented which put all other locks and cements to shame. I should not have wondered by this time to find that they had their respective musical bands stationed on some eminent chip, and playing their national airs the while, to excite the slow and cheer the dying combatants. I was myself excited somewhat even as if they had been men. The more you think of it, the less the difference. And certainly there is not the fight recorded in Concord history, at least, if in the history of America, that will bear a moment's comparison with this, whether for the numbers engaged in it, or for the patriotism and heroism displayed. For numbers and for carnage it was an Austerlitz or Dresden.[15] Concord Fight! Two killed on the patriots' side, and Luther Blanchard wounded! Why here every ant was a Buttrick, – "Fire! for God's sake fire!" – and thousands shared the fate of Davis and Hosmer.[16] There was not one hireling there. I have no doubt that it was a principle they fought for, as much as our ancestors, and not to avoid a three-penny tax on their tea; and the results of this battle will be as important and memorable to those whom it concerns as those of the battle of Bunker Hill,[17] at least.

I took up the chip on which the three I have particularly described were struggling, carried it into my house, and placed it under a tumbler on my window-sill, in order to see the issue. Holding a microscope[18] to the first-mentioned red ant, I saw that, though he was assiduously gnawing at the near fore-leg of his enemy, having severed his remaining

---

[14] In the Trojan War, the Greeks would have perished, had not Achilles decided to return to the battle to revenge the death of his friend Patroclus.
[15] Important battles of the Napoleonic Wars.
[16] Participants in the Battle of Concord on April 19, 1775.
[17] The Battle of Bunker Hill, which was fought near Boston on June 16, 1775, was one of the earliest major battles in the American Revolution; the Americans were defeated.
[18] Here: magnifying glass.

feeler, his own breast was all torn away, exposing what vitals he had there to the jaws of the black warrior, whose breast-plate was apparently too thick for him to pierce; and the dark carbuncles of the sufferer's eyes shone with ferocity such as war only could excite. They struggled half an hour longer under the tumbler, and when I looked again the black soldier had severed the heads of his foes from their bodies, and the still living heads were hanging on either side of him like ghastly trophies at his saddle-bow, still apparently as firmly fastened as ever, and he was endeavoring with feeble struggles, being without feelers and with only the remnant of a leg, and I know not how many other wounds, to divest himself of them; which at length, after half an hour more, he accomplished. I raised the glass, and he went off over the window-sill in that crippled state. Whether he finally survived that combat, and spent the remainder of his days in some Hotel des Invalides,[19] I do not know; but I thought that his industry would not be worth much thereafter. I never learned which party was victorious, nor the cause of the war; but I felt for the rest of that day as if I had had my feelings excited and harrowed by witnessing the struggle, the ferocity and carnage, of a human battle before my door. [...]

Spring

[...] At length the sun's rays have attained the right angle, and warm winds blow up mist and rain and melt the snow banks, and the sun dispersing the mist smiles on a checkered landscape of russet and white smoking with incense, through which the traveller picks his way from islet to islet, cheered by the music of a thousand tinkling rills and rivulets whose veins are filled with the blood of winter which they are bearing off.

Few phenomena gave me more delight than to observe the forms which thawing sand and clay assume in flowing down the sides of a deep cut on the railroad through which I passed on my way to the village, a phenomenon not very common on so large a scale, though the number of freshly exposed banks of the right material must have been greatly multiplied since railroads were invented. The material was sand of every degree of fineness and of various rich colors, commonly mixed with a little clay. When the frost comes out in the spring, and even in a thawing day in the winter, the sand begins to flow down the slopes like lava, sometimes bursting out through the snow and overflowing it where no sand was to be seen before. Innumerable little streams overlap and interlace one with another, exhibiting a sort of hybrid product, which obeys half way the law of currents, and half way that of vegetation. As it flows it takes the forms of sappy leaves or vines, making heaps of pulpy sprays a foot or more in depth, and resembling, as you look down on them, the laciniated lobed and imbricated[20] thalluses of some lichens; or you are reminded of coral, of leopards' paws or birds' feet, of brains or lungs or bowels, and excrements of all kinds. It is a truly *grotesque* vegetation, whose forms and color we see imitated in bronze, a sort of architectural foliage more ancient and typical than acanthus, chiccory, ivy, vine, or any vegetable leaves; destined perhaps, under some circumstances, to become a puzzle to future geologists. [...]

The whole bank, which is from twenty to forty feet high, is sometimes overlaid with a mass of this kind of foliage, or sandy rupture, for a quarter of a mile on one or both sides, the produce of one spring day. What makes this sand foliage remarkable is its springing into existence thus suddenly. When I see on the one side the inert bank, – for the sun

---

[19] Old soldiers' home in Paris.
[20] Lapped over, deeply and irregularly lobed.

acts on one side first, – and on the other this luxuriant foliage, the creation of an hour, I am affected as if in a peculiar sense I stood in the laboratory of the Artist who made the world and me, – had come to where he was still at work, sporting on this bank, and with excess of energy strewing his fresh designs about. I feel as if I were nearer to the vitals of the globe, for this sandy overflow is something such a foliaceous mass as the vitals of the animal body. You find thus in the very sands an anticipation of the vegetable leaf. No wonder that the earth expresses itself outwardly in leaves, it so labors with the idea inwardly. The atoms have already learned this law, and are pregnant by it. The overhanging leaf sees here its prototype. [...]

Thus it seemed that this one hillside illustrated the principle of all the operations of Nature. The Maker of this earth but patented a leaf. What Champollion[21] will decipher this hieroglyphic for us, that we may turn over a new leaf at last? This phenomenon is more exhilarating to me than the luxuriance and fertility of vineyards. [...]

[...] We can never have enough of Nature. We must be refreshed by the sight of inexhaustible vigor, vast and Titanic features, the sea-coast with its wrecks, the wilderness with its living and its decaying trees, the thunder cloud, and the rain which lasts three weeks and produces freshets. We need to witness our own limits transgressed, and some life pasturing freely where we never wander. We are cheered when we observe the vulture feeding on the carrion which disgusts and disheartens us and deriving health and strength from the repast. There was a dead horse in the hollow by the path to my house, which compelled me sometimes to go out of my way, especially in the night when the air was heavy, but the assurance it gave me of the strong appetite and inviolable health of Nature was my compensation for this. I love to see that Nature is so rife with life that myriads can be afforded to be sacrificed and suffered to prey on one another; that tender organizations can be so serenely squashed out of existence like pulp, – tadpoles which herons gobble up, and tortoises and toads run over in the road; and that sometimes it has rained flesh and blood! With the liability to accident, we must see how little account is to be made of it. The impression made on a wise man is that of universal innocence. Poison is not poisonous after all, nor are any wounds fatal. Compassion is a very untenable ground. It must be expeditious. Its pleadings will not bear to be stereotyped. [...]

Conclusion

[...] I learned this, at least, by my experiment; that if one advances confidently in the direction of his dreams, and endeavors to live the life which he has imagined, he will meet with a success unexpected in common hours. He will put some things behind, will pass an invisible boundary; new, universal, and more liberal laws will begin to establish themselves around and within him; or the old laws be expanded, and interpreted in his favor in a more liberal sense, and he will live with the license of a higher order of beings. In proportion as he simplifies his life, the laws of the universe will appear less complex, and solitude will not be solitude, nor poverty poverty, nor weakness weakness. If you have built castles in the air, your work need not be lost; that is where they should be. Now put the foundations under them. [...]

However mean your life is, meet it and live it; do not shun it and call it hard names. It is not so bad as you are. It looks poorest when you are richest. The fault-finder will find

---

[21] Jean François Champollion (1790-1832), French archaeologist whose deciphering of the inscription on the Rosetta Stone fueled interest in Egyptology.

faults even in paradise. Love your life, poor as it is. You may perhaps have some pleasant, thrilling, glorious hours, even in a poor-house. The setting sun is reflected from the windows of the alms-house as brightly as from the rich man's abode; the snow melts before its door as early in the spring. I do not see but a quiet mind may live as contentedly there, and have as cheering thoughts, as in a palace. [...]

The life in us is like the water in the river. It may rise this year higher than man has ever known it, and flood the parched uplands; even this may be the eventful year, which will drown out all our muskrats. It was not always dry land where we dwell. I see far inland the banks which the stream anciently washed, before science began to record its freshets. Every one has heard the story which has gone the rounds of New England, of a strong and beautiful bug which came out of the dry leaf of an old table of apple-tree wood, which had stood in a farmer's kitchen for sixty years, first in Connecticut, and afterward in Massachusetts, – from an egg deposited in the living tree many years earlier still, as appeared by counting the annual layers beyond it; which was heard gnawing out for several weeks, hatched perchance by the heat of an urn. Who does not feel his faith in a resurrection and immortality strengthened by hearing of this? Who knows what beautiful and winged life, whose egg has been buried for ages under many concentric layers of woodenness in the dead dry life of society, deposited at first in the alburnum[22] of the green and living tree, which has been gradually converted into the semblance of its well-seasoned tomb, – heard perchance gnawing out now for years by the astonished family of man, as they sat round the festive board, – may unexpectedly come forth from amidst society's most trivial and handselled furniture, to enjoy its perfect summer life at last!

I do not say that John or Jonathan[23] will realize all this; but such is the character of that morrow which mere lapse of time can never make to dawn. The light which puts out our eyes is darkness to us. Only that day dawns to which we are awake. There is more day to dawn. The sun is but a morning star.

THE END

Source: Henry David Thoreau (1817-1862). *Walden*. Ed. J. Lyndon Shanley. Princeton, NJ: Princeton University Press, 1971, 3, 6, 81, 90-91, 93, 96-98, 129, 131-132, 223, 228-231, 299, 304-306, 308, 318, 320, 323-324, 328, 332-333.

201. Margaret Fuller
Summer on the Lakes, in 1843

CHAPTER I.

Niagara, June 10, 1843.

[...] Before [leaving Niagara Falls], I think I really saw the full wonder of the scene. After awhile it so drew me into itself as to inspire an undefined dread, such as I never knew before, such as may be felt when death is about to usher us into a new existence. The perpetual trampling of the waters seized my senses. I felt that no other sound, however near, could be heard, and would start and look behind me for a foe. I realized the identity of that mood of nature in which these waters were poured down with such absorbing force, with that in which the Indian was shaped on the same soil. For continually

---

[22] The soft part of wood between the bark and heart-wood of a tree.
[23] Everyman.

upon my mind came, unsought and unwelcome, images, such as never haunted it before, of naked savages stealing behind me with uplifted tomahawks; again and again this illusion recurred, and even after I had thought it over, and tried to shake it off, I could not help starting and looking behind me. [...]

Chapter III.

In the afternoon of this day we reached the Rock river,[24] in whose neighborhood we proposed to make some stay, and crossed at Dixon's ferry.

This beautiful stream flows full and wide over a bed of rocks, traversing a distance of near two hundred miles, to reach the Mississippi. Great part of the country along its banks is the finest region of Illinois, and the scene of some of the latest romance of Indian warfare. To these beautiful regions Black Hawk[25] returned with his band "to pass the summer," when he drew upon himself the warfare in which he was finally vanquished. No wonder he could not resist the longing, unwise though its indulgence might be, to return in summer to this home of beauty. [...]

There was a peculiar charm in coming here, where the choice of location, and the unobtrusive good taste of all the arrangements, showed such intelligent appreciation of the spirit of the scene, after seeing so many dwellings of the new settlers, which showed plainly that they had no thought beyond satisfying the grossest material wants. Sometimes they looked attractive, the little brown houses, the natural architecture of the country, in the edge of the timber. But almost always when you came near, the slovenliness of the dwelling and the rude way in which objects around it were treated, when so little care would have presented a charming whole, were very repulsive. Seeing the traces of the Indians, who chose the most beautiful sites for their dwellings, and whose habits do not break in on that aspect of nature under which they were born, we feel as if they were the rightful lords of a beauty they forbore to deform. But most of these settlers do not see it at all; it breathes, it speaks in vain to those who are rushing into its sphere. Their progress is Gothic, not Roman,[26] and their mode of cultivation will, in the course of twenty, perhaps ten, years, obliterate the natural expression of the country.

This is inevitable, fatal; we must not complain, but look forward to a good result. Still, in travelling through this country, I could not but be struck with the force of a symbol. Wherever the hog comes, the rattlesnake disappears; the omnivorous traveller, safe in its stupidity, willingly and easily makes a meal of the most dangerous of reptiles, and one whom the Indian looks on with a mystic awe. Even so the white settler pursues the Indian, and is victor in the chase. But I shall say more upon the subject by-and-by. [...]

The aspect of this country was to me enchanting, beyond any I have ever seen, from its fullness of expression, its bold and impassioned sweetness. Here the flood of emotion has passed over and marked everywhere its course by a smile. The fragments of rock touch it with a wildness and liberality which give just the needed relief. I should never be tired here, though I have elsewhere seen country of more secret and alluring charms, better calculated to stimulate and suggest. Here the eye and heart are filled.

---

[24] River in the north central United States, rising in eastern Wisconsin, and joining the Mississippi at Rock Island, IL.
[25] Indian name Ma-ka-tai-me-she-kia-kiak (1767-1838). Chief of a faction of Sauk and Fox Indians. He led an effort to reclaim traditional Sauk lands from white appropriation.
[26] The Goths conquered Rome and tried to destroy its civilization; Easterners coming west would do the same.

How happy the Indians must have been here! It is not long since they were driven away, and the ground, above and below, is full of their traces.

"The earth is full of men."

You have only to turn up the sod to find arrowheads and Indian pottery. On an island, belonging to our host, and nearly opposite his house, they loved to stay, and, no doubt, enjoyed its lavish beauty as much as the myriad wild pigeons that now haunt its flower-filled shades. Here are still the marks of their tomahawks, the troughs in which they prepared their corn, their caches.

A little way down the river is the site of an ancient Indian village, with its regularly arranged mounds. As usual, they had chosen with the finest taste. It was one of those soft shadowy afternoons when we went there, when nature seems ready to weep, not from grief, but from an overfull heart. Two prattling, lovely little girls, and an African boy, with glittering eye and ready grin, made our party gay; but all were still as we entered their little inlet and trod those flowery paths. They may blacken Indian life as they will, talk of its dirt, its brutality, I will ever believe that the men who chose that dwelling-place were able to feel emotions of noble happiness as they returned to it, and so were the women that received them. Neither were the children sad or dull, who lived so familiarly with the deer and the birds, and swam that clear wave in the shadow of the Seven Sisters.[27] The whole scene suggested to me a Greek splendor, a Greek sweetness, and I can believe that an Indian brave, accustomed to ramble in such paths, and be bathed by such sunbeams, might be mistaken for Apollo [...].

Here a man need not take a small slice from the landscape, and fence it in from the obtrusions of an uncongenial neighbor, and there cut down his fancies to miniature improvements which a chicken could run over in ten minutes. He may have water and wood and land enough, to dread no incursions on his prospect from some chance Vandal that may enter his neighborhood. He need not painfully economise and manage how he may use it all; he can afford to leave some of it wild, and to carry out his own plans without obliterating those of nature.

Here, whole families might live together, if they would. The sons might return from their pilgrimages to settle near the parent hearth; the daughters might find room near their mother. Those painful separations, which already desecrate and desolate the Atlantic coast, are not enforced here by the stern need of seeking bread; and where they are voluntary, it is no matter. To me, too, used to the feelings which haunt a society of struggling men, it was delightful to look upon a scene where nature still wore her motherly smile and seemed to promise room not only for those favored or cursed with the qualities best adapting for the strifes of competition, but for the delicate, the thoughtful, even the indolent or eccentric. She did not say, Fight or starve; nor even, Work or cease to exist; but, merely showing that the apple was a finer fruit than the wild crab, gave both room to grow in the garden.

A pleasant society is formed of the families who live along the banks of this stream upon farms. They are from various parts of the world, and have much to communicate to one another. Many have cultivated minds and refined manners, all a varied experience, while they have in common the interests of a new country and a new life. [...]

The great drawback upon the lives of these settlers, at present, is the unfitness of the women for their new lot. It has generally been the choice of the men, and the women fol-

---

[27] The Seven Hills of Rome.

low, as women will, doing their best for affection's sake, but too often in heart-sickness and weariness. Beside it frequently not being a choice or conviction of their own minds that it is best to be here, their part is the hardest, and they are least fitted for it. The men can find assistance in field labor, and recreation with the gun and fishing-rod. Their bodily strength is greater, and enables them to bear and enjoy both these forms of life.

The women can rarely find any aid in domestic labor. All its various and careful tasks must often be performed, sick or well, by the mother and daughters, to whom a city education has imparted neither the strength nor skill now demanded. [...]

[...] Their culture has too generally been that given to women to make them "the ornaments of society." They can dance, but not draw; talk French, but know nothing of the language of flowers; neither in childhood were allowed to cultivate them, lest they should tan their complexions. Accustomed to the pavement of Broadway, they dare not tread the wildwood paths for fear of rattlesnakes!

Seeing much of this joylessness, and inaptitude, both of body and mind, for a lot which would be full of blessings for those prepared for it, we could not but look with deep interest on the little girls, and hope they would grow up with the strength of body, dexterity, simple tastes, and resources that would fit them to enjoy and refine the western farmer's life.

But they have a great deal to war with in the habits of thought acquired by their mothers from their own early life. Everywhere the fatal spirit of imitation, of reference to European standards, penetrates, and threatens to blight whatever of original growth might adorn the soil.

If the little girls grow up strong, resolute, able to exert their faculties, their mothers mourn over their want of fashionable delicacy. Are they gay, enterprising, ready to fly about in the various ways that teach them so much, these ladies lament that "they cannot go to school, where they might learn to be quiet." They lament the want of "education" for their daughters, as if the thousand needs which call out their young energies, and the language of nature around, yielded no education.

Their grand ambition for their children, is to send them to school in some eastern city, the measure most likely to make them useless and unhappy at home. [...]

To a girl really skilled to make home beautiful and comfortable, with bodily strength to enjoy plenty of exercise, the woods, the streams, a few studies, music, and the sincere and familiar intercourse, far more easily to be met here than elsewhere, would afford happiness enough. Her eyes would not grow dim, nor her cheeks sunken, in the absence of parties, morning visits, and milliner's shops. [...]

CHAPTER VI.
MACKINAW.

Late at night we reached this island,[28] so famous for its beauty, and to which I proposed a visit of some length. It was the last week in August, when a large representation from the Chippewa and Ottowa tribes are here to receive their annual payments from the American government. As their habits make travelling easy and inexpensive to them, neither being obliged to wait for steamboats, or write to see whether hotels are full, they come hither by thousands, and those thousands in families, secure of accommodation on

---

[28] Mackinac Island. An island of North Michigan in the Straits of Mackinac, a passage connecting Lake Huron and Lake Michigan between the Upper and Lower peninsulas.

the beach, and food from the lake, to make a long holiday out of the occasion. There were near two thousand encamped on the island already, and more arriving every day. [...]

I had reason to expect a room to myself at the hotel, but found none, and was obliged to take up my rest in the common parlor and eating-room, a circumstance which ensured my being an early riser.

With the first rosy streak, I was out among my Indian neighbors, whose lodges honeycombed the beautiful beach, that curved away in long, fair outline on either side the house. They were already on the alert, the children creeping out from beneath the blanket door of the lodge; the women pounding corn in their rude mortars, the young men playing on their pipes. [...]

Mackinaw has been fully described by able pens, and I can only add my tribute to the exceeding beauty of the spot and its position. [...]

[...] The first afternoon I was there, looking down from a near height, I felt that I never wished to see a more fascinating picture. It was an hour of the deepest serenity; bright blue and gold, rich shadows. Every moment the sunlight fell more mellow. The Indians were grouped and scattered among the lodges; the women preparing food, in the kettle or frying-pan, over the many small fires; the children, half-naked, wild as little goblins, were playing both in and out of the water. Here and there lounged a young girl, with a baby at her back, whose bright eyes glanced, as if born into a world of courage and of joy, instead of ignominious servitude and slow decay. Some girls were cutting wood, a little way from me, talking and laughing, in the low musical tone, so charming in the Indian women. Many bark canoes were upturned upon the beach, and, by that light, of almost the same amber as the lodges. Others, coming in, their square sails set, and with almost arrowy speed, though heavily laden with dusky forms, and all the apparatus of their house-hold. Here and there a sail-boat glided by, with a different, but scarce less pleasing motion.

It was a scene of ideal loveliness, and these wild forms adorned it, as looking so at home in it. All seemed happy, and they were happy that day, for they had no firewater to madden them, as it was Sunday, and the shops were shut. [...]

Notwithstanding the homage paid to women, and the consequence allowed her in some cases, it is impossible to look upon the Indian women, without feeling that they *do* occupy a lower place than women among the nations of European civilization. The habits of drudgery expressed in their form and gesture, the soft and wild but melancholy expression of their eye, reminded me of the tribe mentioned by Mackenzie,[29] where the women destroy their female children, whenever they have a good opportunity; and of the eloquent reproaches addressed by the Paraguay woman to her mother, that she had not, in the same way, saved her from the anguish and weariness of her lot.

More weariness than anguish, no doubt, falls to the lot of most of these women. They inherit submission, and the minds of the generality accommodate themselves more or less to any posture. Perhaps they suffer less than their white sisters, who have more aspiration and refinement, with little power of self-sustenance. But their place is certainly lower, and their share of the human inheritance less. [...]

I have spoken of the hatred felt by the white man for the Indian: with white women it seems to amount to disgust, to loathing. How I could endure the dirt, the peculiar smell of the Indians, and their dwellings, was a great marvel in the eyes of my lady acquaint-

---

[29] Sir Alexander Mackenzie (1755-1820), British-born Canadian explorer who navigated the Mackenzie River (1789).

ance; indeed, I wonder why they did not quite give me up, as they certainly looked on me with great distaste for it. "Get you gone, you Indian dog," was the felt, if not the breathed, expression towards the hapless owners of the soil. All their claims, all their sorrows quite forgot, in abhorrence of their dirt, their tawny skins, and the vices the whites have taught them. [...]

Whether the Indian could, by any efforts of love and intelligence from the white man, have been civilized and made a valuable ingredient in the new state, I will not say; but this we are sure of; the French Catholics, at least, did not harm them, nor disturb their minds merely to corrupt them. The French they loved. But the stern Presbyterian, with his dogmas and his task-work, the city circle and the college, with their niggard concessions and unfeeling stare, have never tried the experiment. It has not been tried. Our people and our government have sinned alike against the first-born of the soil, and if they are the fated agents of a new era, they have done nothing – have invoked no god to keep them sinless while they do the hest of fate.

Worst of all, when they invoke the holy power only to mask their iniquity; when the felon trader, who, all the week, has been besotting and degrading the Indian with rum mixed with red pepper, and damaged tobacco, kneels with him on Sunday before a common altar, to tell the rosary which recalls the thought of him crucified for love of suffering men, and to listen to sermons in praise of "purity" !!

My savage friends, cries the old fat priest, you must, above all things, aim at *purity*.

Oh, my heart swelled when I saw them in a Christian church. Better their own dog-feasts and bloody rites than such mockery of that other faith. [...]

"You say," said the Indian of the South to the missionary, "that Christianity is pleasing to God. How can that be? – Those men at Savannah[30] are Christians."

Yes! slave-drivers and Indian traders are called Christians, and the Indian is to be deemed less like the Son of Mary than they! Wonderful is the deceit of man's heart! [...]

The Indian is steady to that simple creed, which forms the basis of all this mythology; that there is a God, and a life beyond this; a right and wrong which each man can see, betwixt which each man should choose; that good brings with it its reward and vice its punishment. Their moral code, if not refined as that of civilized nations, is clear and noble in the stress laid upon truth and fidelity. And all unprejudiced observers bear testimony that the Indians, until broken from their old anchorage by intercourse with the whites, who offer them, instead, a religion of which they furnish neither interpretation nor example, were singularly virtuous, if virtue be allowed to consist in a man's acting up to his own ideas of right. [...]

I have not wished to write sentimentally about the Indians, however moved by the thought of their wrongs and speedy extinction. I know that the Europeans who took possession of this country, felt themselves justified by their superior civilization and religious ideas. Had they been truly civilized or Christianized, the conflicts which sprang from the collision of the two races, might have been avoided; but this cannot be expected in movements made by masses of men. The mass has never yet been humanized, though the age may develop a human thought. [...]

Source: Margaret Fuller (1810-1850). *Summer on the Lakes, in 1843*. Boston: C.C. Little and James Brown/New York: C.S. Francis, 1844, 43, 46-47, 52-53, 59-63, 169-171, 173-174, 179, 183-185, 208, 234.

---

[30] Savannah was the colonial government seat in southeastern Georgia, and capital of Georgia until 1786.

202. Anonymous [George Bancroft]
"On the Progress of Civilization" (1838)

The material world does not change in its masses or in its powers. The stars shine with no more lustre,[31] than when they first sang together in the glory of their birth. The flowers that gemmed the fields and the forests, before America was discovered, now bloom around us in their season. The sun that shone on Homer still shines on us in unchanging lustre. The bow that beamed on the patriarch still glitters in the clouds. Nature is the same. For her no new powers are generated; no new capacities are discovered. The earth turns on its axis, and perfects its revolutions, and renews its seasons, without increase or advancement.

Does the same passive destiny attach to the inhabitants of the earth? Is there for us no increase of capacity; no gathering of intellectual riches? Are the expectations of social improvement a delusion; and the hopes of philanthropy but a dream? Or is there an advancement of the human condition? Can there be progress in the human race? [...]

I. [...] The capacity of the human race for improvement is connected with the universal diffusion of the gifts of mind.

The five senses do not constitute the whole inventory of our sources of knowledge. They are the organs by which thought connects itself with the external universe; but the power of thought is not merged in the exercise of its instruments. We have functions which connect us with heaven, as well as organs which set us in relation with earth. We have not merely the senses opening to us the external world, but an internal moral sense, which places us in connexion with the world of intelligence and the decrees of God.

It is the possession of this higher faculty which renders advancement possible. There is *a spirit in man*: not in the privileged few; not in those of us only who by the favor of Providence have been nursed in public schools: IT IS IN MAN: it is the attribute of the race. The spirit, which is the guide to truth, is the gracious gift to each member of the human family; not one is disfranchised;[32] not one is cut off from the heavenly inheritance.

Reason exists within every breast. I mean not that faculty which deduces inferences from the experience of the senses, but that higher faculty, which from the infinite treasures of its own consciousness, originates truth, and assents to it by the force of intuitive evidence; that faculty which raises us beyond the control of time and space, and gives us faith in things eternal and invisible. [...]

If it be true, that the gifts of mind and heart are universally diffused, if the sentiment of truth, justice, love, and beauty exists in every one, then it follows, as a necessary consequence, that the common judgment in politics, morals, character, and taste is the highest authority on earth, and the nearest possible approach to an infallible decision. This inference I dare not avoid; and if from the consideration of individual powers we turn to the action of the human mind in masses, we shall still retain our good hopes for the race. [...]

The same confidence may exist in the capacity of the human race for political advancement. The absence of the prejudices of the old world leaves us here the opportunity of consulting independent truth; and man is left to apply the instinct of freedom to every social relation and public interest. We have approached so near to nature, that we can hear her gentlest whispers; we have made Humanity our lawgiver and our oracle; and, therefore, principles, which in Europe the wisest receive with distrust, are here the common property

---

[31] Brilliancy, luminous splendor.
[32] Excluded from a privilege or right.

of the public mind. [...] Freedom of mind, freedom of the seas, freedom of industry, each great truth is firmly grasped; and whenever a great purpose has been held up, or a useful reform proposed, the national mind has calmly, steadily, and irresistibly pursued its aim.

II. A devotion to the cause of mind is therefore a devotion to the cause of Humanity, and assures its progress.

Every great object, connected with the benevolent exertions of the day, has reference to the culture of mind. The moral and intellectual powers are alone become the common inheritance; and every victory in the cause of Humanity is due to the progress of moral and intellectual culture. For this the envoys of religion cross seas, and visit remotest isles; for this the press in its freedom teems with the productions of maturest thought; for this the philanthropist plans new schemes of education; for this halls in every city and village are open to the public instruct[o]r. Not that we view with indifference the glorious efforts of material industry; the vast means of internal intercourse; the accumulations of thrifty labor; the varied results of concentrated action. But even here it is mind that achieves the triumph, and that exults in expectation. [...]

III. [...] The irresistible tendency of the human race is to advancement. Absolute power has never succeeded in suppressing a single truth. An idea once generated may find its admission into every living breast and live there. Like God it becomes immortal and omnipresent. The tendency of the species is upward, irresistibly upward. The individual is often lost; Providence never disowns the race. The individual is often corrupt; Humanity is redeemed. No principle, once promulgated,[33] has ever been forgotten. No "timely tramp" of a despot's foot ever trod out one idea. The world cannot retrograde;[34] the dark ages cannot return. Dynasties perish; cities are buried; nations have been victims to error, or martyrs for right; Humanity has always been on the advance; its soul has always been gaining maturity and power.

Yes, truth is immortal; it cannot be destroyed; it is invincible, it cannot long be resisted. Not every great principle has yet been generated; but when once developed, it lives without end, in the safe custody of the race. States may pass away; every just principle of legislation which has been once established will endure without end. [...]

No truth can perish; no truth can pass away. Succeeding generations transmit to each other the undying flame. Thus the progress of the race is firm and sure. Wherever moral truth has started into being, Humanity claims and guards the bequest.[35] Each generation gathers together the imperishable children of the past, and increases them by new sons of light, alike radiant with immortality.

Source: Anonymous [George Bancroft (1800-1891)]. "On the Progress of Civilization, or Reasons Why the Natural Association of Men of Letters Is with the Democracy." *The Boston Quarterly Review* 1 (October 1838), 389-391, 395, 400-401, 406-407.

---

[33] To make known by public declaration, to proclaim.
[34] Move backward.
[35] Legacy.

203. Ralph Waldo Emerson
"The Young American" (1844)

[...] Columbus alleged as a reason for seeking a continent in the West, that the harmony of nature required a great tract of land in the western hemisphere, to balance the known extent of land in the eastern; and it now appears that we must estimate the native values of this broad region to redress the balance of our own judgments, and appreciate the advantages opened to the human race in this country which is our fortunate home. The land is the appointed remedy for whatever is false and fantastic in our culture. The continent we inhabit is to be physic and food for our mind, as well as our body.[...]

The habit of living in the presence of these invitations of natural wealth is not inoperative; and this habit, combined with the moral sentiment which, in the recent years, has interrogated every institution, usage, and law, has naturally given a strong direction to the wishes and aims of active young men, to withdraw from cities and cultivate the soil. [...]

We cannot look on the freedom of this country, in connexion with its youth, without a presentiment that here shall laws and institutions exist on some scale of proportion to the majesty of nature. To men legislating for the area betwixt the two oceans, betwixt the snows and the tropics, somewhat of the gravity of nature will infuse itself into the code. A heterogeneous population crowding on all ships from all corners of the world to the great gates of North America, namely Boston, New York, and New Orleans, and thence proceeding inward to the prairie and the mountains, and quickly contributing their private thought to the public opinion, their toll to the treasury, and their vote to the election, it cannot be doubted that the legislation of this country should become more catholic[36] and cosmopolitan than that of any other. It seems so easy for America to inspire and express the most expansive and humane spirit; new-born, free, healthful, strong, the land of the laborer, of the democrat, of the philanthropist, of the believer, of the saint, she should speak for the human race. It is the country of the Future. [...]

Gentlemen, there is a sublime and friendly Destiny by which the human race is guided, – the race never dying, the individual never spared, – to results affecting masses and ages. Men are narrow and selfish, but the Genius or Destiny is not narrow, but beneficent. It is not discovered in their calculated and voluntary activity, but in what befalls, with or without their design. [...]

I call upon you, young men, to obey your heart and be the nobility of this land. In every age of the world there has been a leading nation, one of a more generous sentiment, whose eminent citizens were willing to stand for the interests of general justice and humanity, at the risk of being called, by the men of the moment, chimerical and fantastic. Which should be that nation but these States? Which should lead that movement, if not New England? Who should lead the leaders, but the Young American?

Source: Ralph Waldo Emerson (1803-1882). "The Young American: A Lecture Read before the Mercantile Library Association, Boston, February 7, 1844." Centenary Edition of *The Complete Works of Ralph Waldo Emerson*. 14 vols. Boston and New York: Houghton Mifflin Company/The Riverside Press Cambridge, 1918, Vol. 1, 365-366, 370-371, 387-388.

---

[36] Common, prevalent (obsolete), of universal human interest or use.

204. Anonymous [Orestes A. Brownson] "The Laboring Classes" (1840)

[...] No one can observe the signs of the times with much care, without perceiving that a crisis as to the relation of wealth and labor is approaching. It is useless to shut our eyes to the fact, and like the ostrich fancy ourselves secure because we have so concealed our heads that we see not the danger. We or our children will have to meet this crisis. The old war between the King and the Barons is well nigh ended, and so is that between the Barons and the Merchants and Manufacturers, – landed capital and commercial capital. The business man has become the peer of my Lord. And now commences the new struggle between the operative and his employer, between wealth and labor. Every day does this struggle extend further and wax[37] stronger and fiercer; what or when the end will be God only knows.

[...] All over the world this fact stares us in the face, the workingman is poor and depressed, while a large portion of the non-workingmen, in the sense we now use the term, are wealthy. It may be laid down as a general rule, with but few exceptions, that men are rewarded in an inverse ratio to the amount of actual service they perform. Under every government on earth the largest salaries are annexed to those offices, which demand of their incumbents[38] the least amount of actual labor either mental or manual. And this is in perfect harmony with the whole system of repartition[39] of the fruits of industry, which obtains in every department of society. Now here is the system which prevails, and here is its result. The whole class of simple laborers are poor, and in general unable to procure anything beyond the bare necessaries of life. [...]

Now, what is the prospect of those who fall under the operation of this system? We ask, is there a reasonable chance that any considerable portion of the present generation of laborers, shall ever become owners of a sufficient portion of the funds of production, to be able to sustain themselves by laboring on their own capital, that is, as independent laborers? We need not ask this question, for everybody knows there is not. Well, is the condition of a laborer at wages the best that the great mass of the working people ought to be able to aspire to? Is it a condition, – nay can it be made a condition, – with which a man should be satisfied; in which he should be contented to live and die?

In our own country this condition has existed under its most favorable aspects, and has been made as good as it can be. It has reached all the excellence of which it is susceptible. It is now not improving but growing worse. The actual condition of the workingman to-day, viewed in all its bearings, is not so good as it was fifty years ago. [...]

Now the great work for this age and the coming, is to raise up the laborer, and to realize in our own social arrangements and in the actual condition of all men, that equality between man and man, which God has established between the rights of one and those of another. In other words, our business is to emancipate the proletaries, as the past has emancipated the slaves. This is our work. There must be no class of our fellow men doomed to toil through life as mere workmen at wages. [... T]he evil we speak of is inherent in all our social arrangements, and cannot be cured without a radical change of those arrangements. Could we convert all men to Christianity in both theory and practice, as held by the most enlightened sect of Christians among us, the evils of the social state would remain untouched.

---

[37] To increase gradually.
[38] The holder of an office.
[39] Distribution, allotment.

[...] For our part we are disposed to seek the cause of the inequality of conditions of which we speak, in religion, and to charge it to the priesthood. [...]

Through awe of the gods, through fear of divine displeasure, and dread of the unforeseen chastisements that displeasure may inflict, [...] the priests are able to reduce the people to the most wretched subjection, and to keep them there; at least for a time.

[...] Why not abolish the priestly office? Why continue to sustain what the whole history of man condemns as the greatest of all obstacles to intellectual and social progress? [...]

The next step in this work of elevating the working classes will be to resuscitate[40] the Christianity of Christ. [...]

According to the Christianity of Christ no man can enter the kingdom of God, who does not labor with all zeal and diligence to establish the kingdom of God on the earth [...]. No man can be a Christian who does not labor to reform society, to mould it according to the will of God and the nature of man; so that free scope shall be given to every man to unfold himself in all beauty and power, and to grow up into the stature of a perfect man in Christ Jesus. [...]

Having, by breaking down the power of the priesthood and the Christianity of the priests, obtained an open field and freedom for our operations, and by preaching the true Gospel of Jesus, directed all minds to the great social reform needed, and quickened in all souls the moral power to live for it or to die for it; our next resort must be to government, to legislative enactments. Government is instituted to be the agent of society, or more properly the organ through which society may perform its legitimate functions. [...]

But what shall government do? Its first doing must be an *un*doing. There has been thus far quite too much government, as well as government of the wrong kind. The first act of government we want, is a still further limitation of itself. It must begin by circumscribing within narrower limits its powers. And then it must proceed to repeal all laws which bear against the laboring classes, and then to enact such laws as are necessary to enable them to maintain their equality. We have no faith in those systems of elevating the working classes, which propose to elevate them without calling in the aid of the government. We must have government, and legislation expressly directed to this end.

But again what legislation do we want so far as this country is concerned? We want first the legislation which shall free the government, whether State or Federal, from the control of the Banks. The Banks represent the interest of the employer, and therefore of necessity interests adverse to those of the employed; that is, they represent the interests of the business community in opposition to the laboring community. [...]

Following the destruction of the Banks, must come that of all monopolies, of all PRIVILEGE. There are many of these. We cannot specify them all; we therefore select only one, the greatest of them all, the privilege which some have of being born rich while others are born poor. It will be seen at once that we allude to the hereditary descent of property, an anomaly in our American system, which must be removed, or the system itself will be destroyed. [...] We only say now, that as we have abolished hereditary monarchy and hereditary nobility, we must complete the work by abolishing hereditary property.[41] A man shall have all he honestly acquires, so long as he himself belongs to the

---

[40] To revive, renew, restore.
[41] Original footnote: "I am aware that I broach in this place a delicate subject, though I by no means advance a novel doctrine. [...]. I cannot be supposed to be ignorant of the startling nature of the proposition I have made, nor can I, if I regard myself of the least note in the commonwealth, expect to be able to put forth such propositions, and go scathless. Because I advance singular doctrines, it is not necessary to

world in which he acquires it. But his power over his property must cease with his life, and his property must then become the property of the state, to be disposed of by some equitable[42] law for the use of the generation which takes his place. [...]

Source: Anonymous [Orestes A. Brownson (1803-1876)]. "The Laboring Classes" [Review Article of "*Chartism*, by Thomas Carlyle. Boston: C.C. Little & James Brown, 1840]." *The Boston Quarterly Review* 3 (July 1840), 366-368, 371-373, 375, 378, 381, 386, 388-389, 391-394.

205. Amos Bronson Alcott
The Doctrine and Discipline of Human Culture (1836)

Idea of Education.

[...] Human Culture is the art of revealing to a man the true Idea of his Being – his endowments – his possessions – and of fitting him to use these for the growth, renewal, and perfection of his Spirit. It is the art of completing a man. It includes all those influences, and disciplines, by which his faculties are unfolded and perfected. It is that agency which takes the helpless and pleading Infant from the hands of its Creator; and, apprehending its entire nature, tempts it forth [...] and thus molds it at last into the Image of a Perfect Man [...]. It seeks to realize in the Soul the Image of the Creator. – Its end is a perfect man. Its aim, through every stage of influence and discipline, is self-renewal. [...]

Idea of Genius.

For Genius is but the free and harmonious play of all the faculties of a human being. It is a Man possessing his Idea and working with it. It is the Whole Man – the central Will – working worthily, subordinating all else to itself; and reaching its end by the simplest and readiest means. It is human nature rising superior to things and events, and transfiguring these into the image of its own Spiritual Ideal. It is the Spirit working in its own way, through its own organs and instruments, and on its own materials. It is the Inspiration of all the faculties of a Man by a life conformed to his Idea. It is not indebted to others for its manifestation. It draws its life from within. It is self-subsistent. It feeds on Holiness; lives in the open vision of Truth; enrobes itself in the light of Beauty; and bathes its powers in the fount of Temperance. It aspires after the Perfect. It loves Freedom. It dwells in Unity. All men have it, yet it does not appear in all men. It is obscured by ignorance; quenched by evil; discipline does not reach it; nor opportunity cherish it. Yet there it is – an original, indestructible element of every spirit; and sooner or later, in this corporeal, or in the spiritual era – at some period of the Soul's development – it shall be tempted forth, and assert its claims in the life of the Spirit. It is the province of education to wake it, and discipline it into the perfection which is its end, and for which it ever thirsts. Yet Genius alone can wake it. Genius alone inspire it. It comes not at the incantation of mere talent. It respects itself. It is strange to all save its kind. It shrinks from vulgar gaze, and lives in its own world. None but the eye of Genius can discern it, and it obeys the call of none else.

---

suppose that I am ignorant of public opinion, or that I need to be informed as to the manner in which my doctrines are likely to be received. I have made the proposition, which I have, deliberately, with what I regard a tolerably clear view its essential bearings, and after having meditated it, and been satisfied of its soundness, for many years. I make it then with my eyes open, if the reader please, "with malice pretense." I am then entitled to no favor, and I ask as I expect none."
[42] Unbiased, impartial, candid.

Wane of Genius.

Yet among us Genius is at its wane. Human Nature appears shorn of her beams. We estimate man too low to hope for bright manifestations. And our views create the imperfection that mocks us. We have neither great men, nor good institutions. Genius visits us but seldom. The results of our culture are slender. Thirsting for life and light, Genius is blessed with neither. It cannot free itself from the incumbrance[43] that it inherits. The Idea of a Man does not shine upon it from any external Image. Such Corporeal Types[44] it seeks in vain. It cries for instruction, and none satisfies its wants. There is little genius in our schoolrooms. Those who enter yearly upon the stage of life, bearing the impress of our choicest culture, and most watchful discipline, are often unworthy specimens of our nature. Holiness attends not their steps. Genius adorns not their brow. Many a parent among us – having lavished upon his child his best affections, and spared no pains which money and solicitude could supply, to command the best influences within his reach – sees him return, destitute of that high principle, and those simple aims, that alone ennoble human nature, and satisfy the parental heart. Or, should the child return with his young simplicity and truth, yet how unarmed is his intellect with the quiver of genius, to achieve a worthy name, and bless his race. The Soul is spilt out in lust; buried in appetite; or wasted in vulgar toils; and retreats, at last, ignobly from the scene of life's temptations; despoiled of its innocence; bereft of its hopes, and sets in the dark night of disquietude, lost to the race.

Genius alone Inspires.

[...] To nurse the young spirit as it puts forth its pinions in the fair and hopeful morning of life, it must be placed under the kindly and sympathising agency of Genius – heaven-inspired and hallowed – or there is no certainty that its aspirations will not die away in the routine of formal tuition, or spend themselves in the animal propensities that coexist with it. Teachers must be men of genius. They must be men inspired. The Divine Idea of a Man must have been unfolded from their being, and be a living presence. Philosophers, and Sages, and Seers, – the only real men – must come as of old, to the holy vocation of unfolding human nature. Socrates, and Plato, and the Diviner Jesus, must be raised up to us, to breathe their wisdom and will into the genius of our era, to recast our institutions, remould our manners, and regenerate our men. Philosophy and Religion, descending from the regions of cloudy speculation, must thus become denizens of our common earth, known among us as friends, and uttering their saving truths through the mouths of our little ones. Thus shall our being be unfolded. Thus the Idea of a man be reinstated in our consciousness. Thus Jesus be honored among us. And thus shall Man grow up, as the tree of the primeval woods, luxuriant, vigorous – armed at all points, to brave the winds and the storms of the finite and the mutable – bearing his Fruit in due season.

Idea of Inspiration.

To fulfil its end, Instruction must be an Inspiration. The true Teacher, like Jesus, must inspire in order to unfold. He must know that instruction is something more than mere impression on the understanding. He must feel it to be a kindling influence; that, in himself alone, is the quickening, informing energy; that the life and growth of his charge preëxist in him. He is to hallow and refine as he tempts forth the soul. He is to inform

---

[43] Troubles, burdens, impediments.
[44] Material, of the nature of the animal body as opposed to the spirit.

the understanding, by chastening the appetites, allaying the passions, softening the affections, vivifying the imagination, illuminating the reason, giving pliancy and force to the will; for a true understanding is the issue of these powers, working freely and in harmony with the Genius of the soul, conformed to the law of Duty. He is to put all the springs of Being in motion. And to do this, he must be the personation and exampler of what he would unfold in his charge. Wisdom, Truth, Holiness, must have preëxistence in him, or they will not appear in his pupils. These influence alone in the concrete. They must be made flesh and blood in him, to reappear to the senses, and reproduce their like. – And thus shall his Genius subordinate all to its own force. Thus shall all be constrained to yield to its influence; and this too, without violating any Law, spiritual, intellectual, corporeal – but in obedience to the highest Agency, co-working with God. Under the melting force of his Genius, thus employed, Mind shall become fluid, and he shall mould it into Types of Heavenly Beauty. His agency is that of mind leaping to meet mind; not of force acting on opposing force. The Soul is touched by the live coal of his lips. A kindling influence goes forth to inspire; making the mind think; the heart feel; the pulse throb with his own. He arouses every faculty. He awakens the Godlike. He images the fair and full features of a Man. And thus doth he drive at will the drowsy Brute, that the Eternal hath yoked to the chariot of Life, to urge man across the Finite! [...]

Means of Reform.

Our plans of influence, to be successful, must become more practical. We must be more faithful. We must deal less in abstractions; depend less on precepts and rules. We must fit the soul for duty by the practice of duty. We must watch and enforce. Like unsleeping Providence, we must accompany the young into the scenes of temptation and trial, and aid them in the needful hour. Duty must sally forth an attending Presence into the work-day world, and organize to itself a living body. It must learn the art of uses. It must incorporate itself with Nature. To its sentiments we must give a Heart. Its Ideas we must arm with Hands. For it ever longs to become flesh and blood. The Son of God delights to take the Son of Man as a co-mate, and to bring flesh and blood even to the very gates of the Spiritual Kingdom. It would make the word Flesh, that it shall be seen and handled and felt.

Source: Amos Bronson Alcott (1799-1888). *The Doctrine and Discipline of Human Culture*. Boston: James Munroe & Co., 1836, 3-4, 13-15, 17-22.

206. Robert Owen
First Discourse on a New System of Society (1825)

The subject which I shall now endeavour to explain is, without exception, the most important that can be presented to the human mind; and, if I have been enabled to take a right view of it, then are changes at hand greater than all the changes which have hitherto occurred in the affairs of mankind. [...]

It is, therefore, no light duty that is about to devolve on those who are to direct the affairs of this extensive Empire. For the time is come when they will have to decide, whether ignorance and poverty, and disunion and counteraction, and deception and imbecility, shall continue to inflict their miseries upon its subjects; or whether affluence and intelligence, and union and good feeling, and the most open sincerity in all things, shall change the condition of this population, and give continually increasing prosperity to all the states, and secure happiness to every individual within them. And this is but a part, and a small part, of the responsibility with which they cannot avoid being invested: for it is not merely the ten or twelve millions who are now in these states who will be injured or essentially benefitted by their decisions, but their neighbours in the Canadas, in the West Indies, and over the whole continent of South America, will be almost immediately affected by the measures that shall be adopted here. Nor will their responsibility be limited within this new Western world; the influence of their proceedings will speedily operate most powerfully upon the Governments and people of the old world.

[...] Therefore, the rulers of these states, in coming to a decision on this subject, will have to decide upon the destinies of the human race, both in this and in future generations. [...]

The reflections which I am enabled to make upon the facts which the history of our race presented to me, led me to conclude that the great object intended to be attained, by the various institutions of every age and country, was, or ought to be, to secure happiness for the greatest number of human beings. That this object could be obtained only, first, by a proper training and education from birth, of the physical and mental powers of *each* individual; second, by arrangements to enable *each* individual to procure in the best manner at all times, a full supply of those things which are necessary and the most beneficial for human nature; and third, that *all* individuals should be so united and combined in a social system, as to give to each the greatest benefit from society.

These are, *surely*, the great objects of human existence: yet the facts conveyed to us by history, and the experience of the present, assure us that no arrangements have been formed – that no institutions exist, even to this hour, competent to produce these results. For, is it not a fact, that, at this moment, ignorance, poverty, and disunion, pervade the earth? Are not these evils severely felt in those countries esteemed the most civilized? Do they not now abound in those nations in which the arts and sciences and general knowledge, and wealth and political power, have made the most rapid and extensive progress? Then, permit me to ask, Why have these plain and simple, yet most important objects, not been attained? Why has so little real progress been made in the road to substantial happiness? My reading and reflection induced me to conclude, that man continued degraded, and poor, and miserable, because he was forced, by the prejudices of past times, to remain ignorant of his own nature, and, in consequence, that he had formed institutions not in unison, but in opposition to it – and thence proceeded the conflict between a supposed duty and his nature. [...]

It seemed to me that a government founded on justice, kindness, and sincerity as soon as the world could be induced to admit of sincerity, in its transactions, would be one more suited to human nature, and much more likely to improve the condition of any people. To enable me to ascertain the truth or error of these suppositions, at the age of eighteen I commenced a series of experiments upon a limited population.

At that period circumstances occurred which placed five hundred persons – men, women, and children – under my management; and from that time to this, I have had from 500 to 2,500, the present number, under my immediate direction.

Without any regard to the previous character of these people, I determined to govern them upon principles of strict justice and impartial kindness. [...]

My desire now is to introduce into these States, and through them to the world at large, a new social system, formed in practice of an entire new combination of circumstances, all of them having a direct moral, intellectual, and beneficial tendency, fully adequate to effect the most important improvements throughout society. This system has been solely derived from the facts relative to our common nature [...].

In this new social arrangement, a much more perfect system of liberty and equality will be introduced than has yet any where existed, or been deemed attainable in practice. Within it there will be no privileged thoughts or belief; every one will be at full liberty to express the genuine impressions which the circumstances around them have made on their minds as well as their own undisguised reflections thereon, and then no motive will exist for deception or insincerity of any kind.

Every one will be instructed in the outline of all the real knowledge which experience has yet discovered. This will be effected on a plan in unison with our nature, and by which the equality of the mental faculties will be rendered more perfect, and by which all will be elevated much above what any can attain under the existing despotism of mind; and by these arrangements the general intellect of society will be enabled to make greater advances in a year, than it has been hitherto allowed to attain in a century. The innumerable and incalculable evils and absurdities which have arisen from the inequality of wealth, will be effectually overcome and avoided throughout all the future. By arrangements, as simple and desirable as they will be beneficial for every one, all will possess, at all times, a full supply of the best of every thing for human nature, as far as present experience on these matters can direct our knowledge.

The degrading and pernicious practices in which we are now trained, of buying cheap and selling dear, will be rendered wholly unnecessary: for, so long as this principle shall govern the transactions of men, nothing really great or noble can be expected from mankind.

The whole trading system is one of deception; one by which each engaged in it is necessarily trained to endeavour to obtain advantages over others, and in which the interest of all is opposed to each, and in consequence, not one can attain the advantages that, under another and a better system might be, with far less labour, and without risk, secured in perpetuity to all. [...]

In the new system, union and co-operation will supersede individual interest, and the universal counteraction of each other's objects; and, by the change, the powers of one man will obtain for him the advantages of many, and all will become as rich as they will desire. [...]

Under this system, real wealth will be too easily obtained in perpetuity and full security to be much longer valued as it now is by society, for the distinctions which it makes between the poor and rich. For, when the new arrangements shall be regularly organized and completed, a few hours daily, of healthy and desirable employment, chiefly applied to direct modern mechanical and other scientific improvements, will be amply sufficient to create a full supply, at all times, of the best of every thing for every one, and then all things will be valued according to their intrinsic worth, will be used beneficially, and nothing will be wasted or abused. [...]

Well knowing the great extent of these advantages, my wish now is to give them, in the shortest time, to the greatest number of my fellow creatures, and that the change from the present erroneous practices should be effected, if possible, without injury to a human being. [...]

Source: Robert Owen (1771-1858). *First Discourse on a New System of Society [As Delivered in the Hall of Representatives, at Washington, in the Presence of the President of the United States, the President Elect, Heads of Departments, Members of Congress, etc., on the 25th of February, 1825]*. Manchester: Heywood, 1825, 3-6, 11-13.

207. George Ripley
"Letter to Ralph Waldo Emerson" (1840)

BOSTON, *November* 9, 1840.

MY DEAR SIR, – Our conversation in Concord was of such a general nature, that I do not feel as if you were in complete possession of the idea of the Association[45] which I wish to see established. As we have now a prospect of carrying it into effect, at an early period, I wish to submit the plan more distinctly to your judgment, that you may decide whether it is one that can have the benefit of your aid and coöperation.

Our objects, as you know, are to insure a more natural union between intellectual and manual labor than now exists; to combine the thinker and the worker, as far as possible, in the same individual; to guarantee the highest mental freedom, by providing all with labor, adapted to their tastes and talents, and securing to them the fruits of their industry; to do away the necessity of menial services, by opening the benefits of education and the profits of labor to all; and thus to prepare a society of liberal, intelligent, and cultivated persons, whose relations with each other would permit a more simple and wholesome life, than can be led amidst the pressure of our competitive institutions.

To accomplish these objects, we propose to take a small tract of land, which, under skillful husbandry, uniting the garden and the farm, will be adequate to the subsistence of the families; and to connect with this a school or college, in which the most complete instruction shall be given, from the first rudiments to the highest culture. Our farm would be a place for improving the race of men that lived on it; thought would preside over the operations of labor, and labor would contribute to the expansion of thought; we should have industry without drudgery, and true equality without its vulgarity.

An offer has been made to us of a beautiful estate, on very reasonable terms, on the borders of Newton, West Roxbury, and Dedham. [...]

The step now to be taken at once is the procuring of funds for the necessary capital. [...]

I can imagine no plan which is suited to carry into effect so many divine ideas as this. If wisely executed, it will be a light over this country and this age. If not the sunrise, it will be the morning star. As a practical man, I see clearly that we must have some such arrangement, or all changes less radical will be nugatory.[46] I believe in the divinity of labor; I wish to "harvest my flesh and blood from the land;" but to do this, I must either be insulated and work to disadvantage, or avail myself of the services of hirelings, who are not of my order, and whom I can scarce make friends; for I must have another to drive the plough, which I hold. I cannot empty a cask of lime upon my grass alone. I wish to see a society of educated friends, working, thinking, and living together, with no strife, except that of each to contribute the most to the benefit of all.

---

[45] Reference to the Brook Farm Association.
[46] Worthless.

Personally, my tastes and habits would lead me in another direction. I have a passion for being independent of the world, and of every man in it. [...] But I feel bound to sacrifice this private feeling, in the hope of a great social good. [...]

Source: George Ripley (1802-1880). "Letter from George Ripley to Ralph Waldo Emerson (1840)." *George Ripley*. Ed. Octavius Brooks Frothingham. Boston: Houghton, Mifflin & Co./New York: Riverside Press, 1882, 307-311 [Appendix].

208. [George Ripley] "Advertisement" and "Introductory Notice" for the *Harbinger* (1845)

THE HARBINGER,
DEVOTED TO SOCIAL AND POLITICAL PROGRESS,

Published simultaneously at New York and Boston, by the Brook Farm Phalanx.

"All things, at the present day, stand provided and prepared, and await the light."

Under this title it is proposed to publish a weekly newspaper, for the examination and discussion of the great questions in social science, politics, literature, and the arts, which command the attention of all believers in the progress and elevation of humanity.

In politics, the Harbinger will be democratic in its principles and tendencies; cherishing the deepest interest in the advancement and happiness of the masses; warring against all exclusive privilege in legislation, political arrangements, and social customs; and striving with the zeal of earnest conviction, to promote the triumph of the high democratic faith, which it is the chief mission of the nineteenth century to realize in society. [...] With tolerance for all opinions, we have no patience with hypocrisy and pretence; least of all, with that specious fraud, which would make a glorious principle the apology for personal ends. It will therefore be a leading object of the Harbinger to strip the disguise from the prevailing parties, to show them in their true light, to give them due honor, to tender them our grateful reverence whenever we see them true to a noble principle; but at all times, and on every occasion, to expose false professions, to hold up hollow-heartedness and duplicity to just indignation, to warn the people against the demagogue who would cajole them by honeyed flatteries, no less than against the devotee of mammon who would make them his slaves.

The Harbinger will be devoted to the cause of a radical, organic social reform as essential to the highest development of man's nature, to the production of those elevated and beautiful forms of character of which he is capable, and to the diffusion of happiness, excellence, and universal harmony upon the earth. The principles of universal unity as taught by Charles Fourier,[47] in their application to society, we believe, are at the foundation of all genuine social progress; and it will ever be our aim, to discuss and defend these principles, without any sectarian bigotry, and in the catholic and comprehensive spirit of their great discoverer. While we bow to no man as an authoritative, infallible master, we revere the genius of Fourier too highly, not to accept, with joyful welcome, the light which he has shed on the most intricate problems of human destiny. The social reform, of whose advent the signs are every where visible, comprehends all others; and in laboring

---

[47] (François Marie) Charles Fourier (1772-1837), French social reformer who propounded the reorganization of society into phalanxes.

for its speedy accomplishment, we are conscious that we are devoting our best ability to the removal of oppression and injustice among men, to the complete emancipation of the enslaved, to the promotion of genuine temperance, and to the elevation of the toiling and down-trodden masses to the inborn rights of humanity. [...]

INTRODUCTORY NOTICE.

In meeting our friends, for the first time, in the columns of the Harbinger, we wish to take them by the hand with cheerful greetings, to express the earnest hope that our intercourse may be as fruitful of good, as it will be frank and sincere, and that we to-day may commence a communion of spirit, which shall mutually aid us in our progress towards the truth and beauty, the possession of which is the ultimate destiny of man. We address ourselves to the aspiring and free minded youth of our country; to those whom long experience has taught the emptiness of past attainments and inspired with a better hope; to those who cherish a living faith in the advancement of humanity, whose inner life consists not in doubting, questioning, and denying, but in believing; who, resolute to cast off conventional errors and prejudices, are hungering and thirsting for positive truth; and who, with reliance on the fulfilment of the prophetic voice in the heart of man, and on the Universal Providence of God, look forward to an order of society founded on the divine principles of justice and love, to a future age of happiness, harmony, and of great glory to be realized on earth.

We have attained, in our own minds, to firm and clear convictions, in regard to the problem of human destiny; we believe that principles are now in operation, which will produce as great a change on the face of society, as that which caused beauty and order to arise from the chaos of the primitive creation by the movings of the divine Spirit; and to impart these convictions and principles to the hearts of our readers, will be our leading purpose in the columns of this paper. [...]

With a deep reverence for the Past, we shall strive so to use its transmitted treasures, as to lay in the Present, the foundation of a better Future. Our motto is, the elevation of the whole human race, in mind, morals, and manners, and the means, which in our view are alone adapted to the accomplishment of this end, are not violent outbreaks and revolutionary agitations, but orderly and progressive reform.

In Politics, it will be our object to present fair discussions of the measures of political parties, taking the principles of Justice to all men as our standard of judgment. By sympathy and conviction we are entirely democratic; our faith in democracy is hardly inferior to our faith in humanity; but by democracy we do not understand a slavish adherence to "regular nominations," nor that malignant mobocracy[48] which would reduce to its own meanness all who aspire to nobler ends than itself, but that benevolent, exalting, and refining creed, which holds that the great object of government, should be to secure the blessings of Liberty, Intelligence, and Good Order, to the whole people. We believe in the Rights of Man, – best summed up in the right to a perfect development of his whole nature, physical, intellectual, and moral, – and shall oppose partial or class legislation, as inconsistent with the fundamental principles of Republican Institutions. [...]

The interests of Social Reform, will be considered as paramount to all others, in whatever is admitted into the pages of the Harbinger. We shall suffer no attachment to literature, no taste for abstract discussion, no love of purely intellectual theories, to seduce us

---

[48] Rule of the common people, mob.

from our devotion to the cause of the oppressed, the down-trodden, the insulted and injured masses of our fellow men. Every pulsation of our being vibrates in sympathy with the wrongs of the toiling millions, and every wise effort for their speedy enfranchisement will find in us resolute and indomitable advocates. If any imagine from the literary tone of the preceding remarks, that we are indifferent to the radical movement for the benefit of the masses, which is the crowning glory of the nineteenth century, they will soon discover their egregious mistake. To that movement, consecrated by religious principle, sustained by an awful sense of justice, and cheered by the brightest hopes of future good, all our powers, talents, and attainments are devoted. We look for an audience among the refined and educated circles, to which the character of our paper will win its way; but we shall also be read by the swart and sweaty artizan; the laborer will find in us another champion; and many hearts, struggling with the secret hope which no weight of care and toil can entirely suppress, will pour on us their benedictions as we labor for the equal rights of All.

We engage in our enterprise, then, with faith in our cause, with friendship for our readers, with an exulting hope for Humanity, and with a deep conviction which long years of experience have confirmed, that every sincere endeavor for a universal end will not fail to receive a blessing from all that is greatest and holiest in the universe. In the words of the illustrious Swedenborg,[49] which we have selected for the motto of the Harbinger, "all things, at the present day, stand provided and prepared, and await the light. The ship is in the harbor; the sails are swelling; the east wind blows; let us weigh anchor, and put forth to sea."

Source: Anonymous [George Ripley] (1802-1880). "Advertisement" and "Introductory Notice," *The Harbinger Devoted to Social and Political Progress* 1/1 (14 June 1845), 16, 8-10.

209. Ralph Waldo Emerson
"Historic Notes of Life and Letters in New England" (1883)

BROOK FARM

The West Roxbury Association was formed in 1841, by a society of members, men and women, who bought a farm in West Roxbury, of about two hundred acres, and took possession of the place in April. Mr. George Ripley was the President, and I think Mr. Charles Dana (afterwards well known as one of the editors of the New York Tribune) was the Secretary. [...]

It was a noble and generous movement in the projectors, to try an experiment of better living. They had the feeling that our ways of living were too conventional and expensive, not allowing each to do what he had a talent for, and not permitting men to combine cultivation of mind and heart with a reasonable amount of daily labor. At the same time, it was an attempt to lift others with themselves, and to share the advantages they should attain, with others now deprived of them.

There was no doubt great variety of character and purpose in the members of the community. It consisted in the main of young people, – few of middle age, and none old. Those who inspired and organized it were of course persons impatient of the routine, the

---

[49] Emanuel Swedenborg (1688-1772), Swedish scientist and theologian whose visions and writings inspired his followers to establish the Church of the New Jerusalem.

uniformity, perhaps they would say the squalid contentment of society around them, which was so timid and skeptical of any progress. One would say then that impulse was the rule in the society, without centripetal balance; perhaps it would not be severe to say, intellectual sans-culottism,[50] an impatience of the formal, routinary character of our educational, religious, social and economical life in Massachusetts. Yet there was immense hope in these young people. There was nobleness; there were self-sacrificing victims who compensated for the levity and rashness of their companions. The young people lived a great deal in a short time, and came forth some of them perhaps with shattered constitutions. [...]

The Founders of Brook Farm should have this praise, that they made what all people try to make, an agreeable place to live in. All comers, even the most fastidious, found it the pleasantest of residences. It is certain that freedom from household routine, variety of character and talent, variety of work, variety of means of thought and instruction, art, music, poetry, reading, masquerade, did not permit sluggishness or despondency; broke up routine. There is agreement in the testimony that it was, to most of the associates, education; to many, the most important period of their life [...]. It was a perpetual picnic, a French Revolution in small, an Age of Reason in a patty-pan.[51] [...]

In Brook Farm was this peculiarity, that there was no head. In every family is the father; in every factory, a foreman; in a shop, a master; in a boat, the skipper; but in this Farm, no authority; each was master or mistress of his or her actions; happy, hapless anarchists. [...]

The society at Brook Farm existed, I think, about six or seven years, and then broke up, the Farm was sold, and I believe all the partners came out with pecuniary loss. Some of them had spent on it the accumulations of years. I suppose they all, at the moment, regarded it as a failure. I do not think they can so regard it now, but probably as an important chapter in their experience which has been of lifelong value. What knowledge of themselves and of each other, what various practical wisdom, what personal power, what studies of character, what accumulated culture many of the members owed to it! [...]

Source: Ralph Waldo Emerson (1803-1882). "Historic Notes of Life and Letters in New England." *Atlantic Monthly* (October 1883). *The Complete Works of Ralph Waldo Emerson*. 14 vols. Ed. E. W. Emerson. Boston: Houghton Mifflin Company, 1904, Vol. 10, 359-361, 364, 367-369.

---

[50] Revolutionary spirit; of republican character.
[51] Small pan.

WOMEN'S ROLES IN AMERICAN SOCIETY

While man "plunges into the turmoil and bustle of an active, selfish world [...] to encounter innumerable difficulties, hardships and labors" (doc. 224), "Home! – [is woman's...] shrine, / Around which all her heart-strings twine! / There, loved and loving – safe from fear, / Lies ever woman's noblest sphere!" (doc. 228). The idea of such fundamentally different gender roles as they are described here dominated American culture far into the twentieth century and is, in fact, latently present still today. From the time when gender became an issue in colonial America to the late nineteenth century, gender debates revolved around a rather consistent set of issues. Among these were a gender-specific education, the segregation of the sexes into two social spheres as well as the question whether gender binaries originated in nature, biology and religion, or whether gender was subject to social custom and historical change. Over the centuries, these issues were discussed, interpreted, and modified according to three different major paradigms of femininity concepts, which were each predominant in different phases: while the "republican mother" was the leading ideal of patriotic womanliness in the 1760s through the 1820s, the modest "true woman" was the crown of gender idealism for most of the nineteenth century; the rather independent "new woman," however, could only gradually gain ground after the Civil War. The texts in this section illustrate these three paradigms as well as the controversies about them. It may be rewarding to read them *en bloc* (docs. 211-223, 224-241, 243-247), since they enter into an intertextual dialogue among themselves and thus comment on as well as qualify one another (e.g. docs. 242 and 243). Some of them are canonized cornerstones of the nineteenth-century gender debate, such as the "Declaration of Sentiments" (doc. 237), while others stand for a legion of rather commonplace contributions to the ongoing controversy about 'proper' gender roles.

The categories of the "republican mother," the "true woman," and the "new woman" were only prototypes not always occurring in their pure form in public and literary discourse. In fact, most of the time, they were much contested. Furthermore, the various paradigms did not simply succeed and replace each other, but they often existed side by side or intermingled and overlapped. Some of the selected authors helped to construct and support the respective prevalent gender ideology of their own time. Others modified the dominant line of argumentation only to secure small niches for women within the established cultural order where they could act freely. Others again openly attacked the dominant gender hierarchy. No matter, however, whether the different texts employed affirmative or subversive strategies, the reader should always keep in mind that none of the authors could simply step outside their cultural frames of mind – criticism was possible only from within the system.

Throughout the centuries, women employed varying arguments to demand from men autonomy, respect, social and political rights, as well as access to higher education. A few claimed that there was no difference at all between the sexes. They based their demand for equal rights on the equality of "all men" guaranteed by nature and the Constitution. While most men and many women claimed that women were by nature morally superior to men and should, therefore, not mingle with the morally corrupted world, others insisted that it was for her moral purity that woman should enjoy legal independence and enter the public realm to purify it. Other supporters of the idea of an "essential" difference between the sexes argued that women, as the potent guardians of the family in the private realm, were the fitting complements to men, who fought for their families' survival in the public sphere; here, women were considered 'different but equal' to men and they should, as men's equals, have the same autonomy and independence as their husbands. Over the centuries these different lines of argumentation were repeatedly revived and adjusted to new contexts or the aims of those who used them in the ongoing gender debate. A closer look at the texts may help us to understand the developments and the complexity of this controversy.

In the seventeenth century, "Men can doe best, and Women know it well" (doc. 211). The puritan woman's role was clearly defined as man's "help-meet," humbly submitting to her father's or her husband's ruling and guidance – just as man submitted to God's. Personal ambitions were considered sinful in both sexes as long as they did not aim at religious refinement. Later, from the time of the Early Republic through the 1820s, however, the "female patriot" (doc. 213) was assigned a crucial function in the national project: as first educator of her children, the "republican mother" used her influence upon the next generation of citizens (and on future mothers) to secure the survival of the young American republic and to "thus keep our country virtuous" (doc. 220).

As documents 211 to 223 demonstrate, the consequences of this idea were discussed very controversially: Should women be allowed to play a politically active role? Did the idea of the *natural* equality of *all* men necessarily imply their *legal* equality in all parts of American society, including the field of intellect and education? The young republic's answer was "no" – and women continued to be denied the status of legal citizens and female suffrage. Instead, they were put off by means of republican rhetoric: women's supposedly humanizing, purifying, and ennobling influence on the moral disposition of the men (i.e. citizens) and children (i.e. future citizens) in their restricted domestic sphere was glorified as the greatest moral and political power to hold in American society: "While you thus keep our country virtuous, you maintain its independence and ensure its prosperity" (doc. 220). Many women, and a few men, picked up this line of argumentation in order to advance their struggle for women's higher education. They argued that a better education qualified women not only intellectually for their crucial function as educators of future citizens but it also fortified them morally against degenerate influences which seemed to constantly threaten women's and, consequently, the young republic's innocence and virtue (cf. docs. 216, 217, 220, 223).

During the first half of the nineteenth century, women's indirect political influence remained unquestioned, but the focus in their lives gradually narrowed onto the small circle of their families. As documents 224-241 illustrate, from the 1830s through most of the century, home was glorified as a haven to which man could retreat from his fight for survival in a hostile, materialistic and corrupted world. At home, the "true woman" lovingly used her ennobling, refining, and healing influence to turn the family, a microcosm of society, into a stronghold against moral decay and social disorder. Men's and women's supposedly inherent and opposite features seemed to naturally assign them these opposite functions and cultural fields in society (cf. doc. 224). Middle-class ideology of "true womanhood" thus divided society along the gender line into two separate spheres – i.e. the 'masculine' public and the 'feminine' private realm. However, it was, in fact, only the women who were restricted to a single sphere while to men all regions of American public *and* private life were open.

Although the "cult of true womanhood" seemed to exalt women on a pedestal, not all of them considered their inferior position to men, their being restricted to passiveness in their homes, as well as their moral "reign" in the family a privilege, but rather another form of slavery. They criticized that the right to individuality was ignored whenever women's characteristics and purpose in life were determined solely by their sex. Their fight for political and legal rights, therefore, continued and culminated in the Seneca Falls convention in 1848, when they declared after the role-model of the *Declaration of Independence* that "all men and women are created equal" (doc. 237, cf. docs. 238 and 239). In order to justify the idea of the equality of the sexes, these early feminists referred to republican and humanistic principles such as the inalienability of human rights (cf. doc. 233). Moreover, they declared the fundamental equality of men and women to be either a God-given or a natural order. Elaborate lists of female heroines throughout world history were to illustrate women's potency beyond motherhood (cf. doc. 229). Yet, whenever women demanded more intellectual and personal freedom for themselves, they were put off by the old argument of their supposedly moral superiority and the warning not to lose their femininity by leaving their 'proper sphere' and usurping man's position.

It was not before well after the Civil War that the more liberal gender concept of the 'new woman' gradually gained ground in American middle-class society. The (usually unmarried) new woman boldly entered institutions of higher education as well as 'male' professions, she managed her own business and she claimed autonomy over her own life, mind, body, and property. The ideology of 'separate spheres' as well as that of man's superiority over woman was then openly criticized as based on historical and, therefore, changeable conventions, which had too long been silently accepted by women. Since most 'new women' were unmarried (yet), the 'sacred duties of wife and mother' seemed to remain untouched. The 'new women's' many critics, however, continued to claim that these "monstrous" females "were all unsexing [them]selves" (doc. 242). When such criticism implied that the 'new women' tried to imitate and replace men, this was a gross oversimplification of the highly complex cultural strategies women with a feminist agenda employed here. In fact, in lieu of simple imitation, 'new women' tried to appropriate and integrate liberties and privileges which had been reserved to men into a modified concept of womanhood.

Although men seemed to be the main obstacle to women's autonomy, the biggest barrier to overcome was, in fact, in people's minds, both male and female. The patriarchal and dualistic gender ideology, which kept women in a dependent position, was so deeply internalized by everybody involved that it took almost 250 years to break this vicious circle and gradually denaturalize these ideas. Even then, the new gender concept did not find a majority in American middle-class society; in fact, the process of unmasking the supposedly 'God-given' or 'natural gender' system as a cultural construct still continues today.

Isabell Klaiber

210. Anne Bradstreet

An Epitaph on My Dear and Ever Honoured Mother Mrs. Dorothy Dudley, Who Deceased Decemb. 27. 1643. and of Her Age, 61 (1643)

Here lyes,
A Worthy Matron of unspotted life,
A loving Mother and obedient wife,
A friendly Neighbor, pitiful to poor,
Whom oft she fed, and clothed with her store;
To Servants wisely aweful, but yet kind,
And as they did, so they reward did find:
A true Instructer of her Family,
The which she ordered with dexterity.
The publick meetings ever did frequent,
And in her Closet constant hours she spent;
Religious in all her words and wayes,
Preparing still for death, till end of dayes:
Of all her Children, Children, liv'ed to see,
Then dying, left blessed memory.

Source: Anne Bradstreet (1612-1672). *The Works of Anne Bradstreet in Prose and Verse.* Ed. John Harvard Ellis. Gloucester, MA: Smith, 1962, 369.

211. Anne Bradstreet
"The Prologue" (1650)

1.

TO sing of Wars, of Captaines, and of Kings,
Of Cities founded, Common-wealths begun,
For my mean[1] Pen, are too superiour things,
And how they all, or each, their dates have run:
Let Poets, and Historians set these forth,
My obscure Verse, shal not so dim their worth.

2.

But when my wondring eyes, and envious heart,
Great *Bartas*[2] sugar'd lines do but read o're;
Foole,[3] I doe grudge,[4] the Muses did not part

---

[1] Humble.
[2] Guillaume du Bartas (1544-1590), French writer much admired by the Puritans; author of *The Divine Weeks*, an epic poem translated by Joshua Sylvester, recounting the great moments in Christian history.
[3] Like a fool.
[4] To complain.

'Twixt him and me, that over-fluent store;
A *Bartas* can, doe what a *Bartas* wil,
But simple I, according to my skill.

3.
From School-boyes tongue, no Rhethorick we expect,
Nor yet a sweet Consort, from broken strings,
Nor perfect beauty, where's a maine defect,
My foolish, broken, blemish'd Muse so sings;
And this to mend, alas, no Art is able,
'Cause Nature made it so irreparable.

4.
Nor can I, like that fluent sweet tongu'd *Greek*[5]
Who lisp'd at first, speake afterwards more plaine
By Art, he gladly found what he did seeke,
A full requitall of his striving paine:
Art can doe much, but this maxime's most sure,
A weake or wounded braine admits no cure.

5.
I am obnoxious to each carping tongue,
Who sayes, my hand a needle better fits,
A Poets Pen, all scorne, I should thus wrong;
For such despight they cast on female wits:
If what I doe prove well, it wo'nt advance,
They'l say its stolne, or else, it was by chance.

6.
But sure the antick *Greeks* were far more milde,
Else of our Sex, why feigned they those nine,
And poesy made, *Calliope's*[6] owne childe,
So 'mongst the rest, they plac'd the Arts divine:
But this weake knot they will full soone untye,
The *Greeks* did nought, but play the foole and lye.

7.
Let *Greeks* be *Greeks*, and Women what they are,
Men have precedency, and still excell,
It is but vaine, unjustly to wage war,
Men can doe best, and Women know it well;
Preheminence in each, and all is yours,
Yet grant some small acknowledgement of ours.

---

[5] The Greek orator Demosthenes (c. 384-322 BC) conquered a speech defect.
[6] Muse of epic poetry.

8.
And oh, ye high flown quils,[7] that soare the skies,
And ever with your prey, still catch your praise,
If e're you daigne these lowly lines, your eyes
Give wholsome Parsley wreath, I ask no Bayes:[8]
This meane and unrefined stuffe of mine,
Will make your glistering gold but more to shine.

Source: Anne Bradstreet (1612-1672). "The Prologue." *The Tenth Muse Lately Sprung up in America: Or Severall Poems, Compiled with Great Variety of Wit and Learning, Full of Delight*. London: Stephen Bowtell, 1650, 3-4.

212. John Winthrop
Journal (1645)

[*April* 13.] Mr. Hopkins, the governor of Hartford upon Connecticut, came to Boston, and brought his wife with him, (a godly young woman, and of special parts,) who was fallen into a sad infirmity, the loss of her understanding and reason, which had been growing upon her divers years, by occasion of her giving herself wholly to reading and writing, and had written many books. Her husband, being very loving and tender of her, was loath to grieve her; but he saw his error, when it was too late. For if she had attended her household affairs, and such things as belong to women, and not gone out of her way and calling to meddle in such things as are proper for men, whose minds are stronger, etc., she had kept her wits, and might have improved them usefully and honorably in the place God had set her. He brought her to Boston, and left her with her brother, one Mr. Yale, a merchant, to try what means might be had here for her. But no help could be had.

Source: John Winthrop (1588-1649). *Winthrop's Journal "History of New England," 1630-1649*. Ed. James Kendall Hosmer. 2 vols. New York: Charles Scribner's Sons, 1908, Vol. 2, 225.

---

[7] Quill: A writing pen made from the shaft of a feather.
[8] Bay-tree or Bay Laurel; here: garlands of laurel, used to crown the head of a poet.

213. Milcah Martha [Hill] Moore
"The Female Patriots: Address'd to the Daughters of Liberty in America"
(1768)

Since the Men from a Party, or fear of a Frown,
Are kept by a Sugar-Plumb, quietly down.
Supinely asleep, & depriv'd of their Sight
Are strip'd of their Freedom, & rob'd of their Right.
If the Sons (so degenerate) the Blessing despise,
Let the Daughters of Liberty, nobly arise,
And tho' we've no Voice, but a negative here.
The use of the Taxables, let us forebear,
(Then Merchants import till yr. Stores are all full
May the Buyers be few & yr. Traffick be dull.)
Stand firmly resolved & bid Grenville[9] to see
That rather than Freedom, we'll part with our Tea
And well as we love the dear Draught when a dry,
As American Patriot,– our Taste we deny,
Sylvania's, gay Meadows, can richly afford,
To pamper our Fancy, or furnish our Board,
And Paper sufficient (at home) still we have,
To assure the Wise-acre, we will not sign Slave.
When this Homespun shall fail, to remonstrate our Grief
We can speak with the Tongue or scratch on a Leaf.
  Refuse all their Colours, tho richest of Dye,
The juice of a Berry – our Paint can supply,
To humour our Fancy – & as for our Houses,
They'll do without painting as well as our Spouses,
While to keep out the Cold of a keen winter Morn
We can screen the Northwest, with a well polish'd Horn,
And trust me a Woman by honest Invention
Might give this State Doctor a Dose of Prevention.
Join mutual in this, & but small as it seems
We may Jostle a Grenville & puzzle his Schemes
But a motive more worthy our patriot Pen,
Thus acting – we point out their Duty to Men,
And should the bound Pensioners, tell us to hush
We can throw back the Satire by biding them blush.

Source: Milcah Martha [Hill] Moore (1740-1829). "The Female Patriots: Address'd to the Daughters of Liberty in America." *Milcah Martha Moore's Book: A Commonplace Book from Revolutionary America*. Eds. Catherine La Courreye Blecki and Karin A. Wulf. University Park, PA: Pennsylvania State University Press, 1997, 172-173.

---

[9] George Grenville (1712-1770), English statesman whose tax policy in the American colonies (e.g., the Revenue Act of 1764 and the Stamp Act of 1765) became one of the causes of the American Revolution.

214. Anonymous
"Impromptu, on Reading an Essay on Education" (1773)

Yes, Women, if they dar'd, would nobly soar,
And every Art and Science would explore;
Though weak their Sex, their Notions are refin'd,
And e'er would prove a Blessing to Mankind.
If they our free-born Minds would not enslave,
No other Boon[10] of Heaven they need to crave;
But while our Minds in Fetters[11] are enchain'd,
On it rely your Hearts will e'er be pain'd:
While Dissipation[12] fondly we pursue,
Believe we small Regard can have for you.
Be it your Task our Intellects to aid,
And you with tenfold Interest shall be paid;
Improve our Morals, us to Honour guide,
And teach us Vice from Virtue to divide,
And, far as our weak Geniusses can go,
Let us each useful Theme of Learning know:
'Tis then, and then alone, you'll surely prove
There is no Blessing like conjugal Love.
Thus form'd, the humble Friend you'll find, for Life,
The faithful Comforter, and loving Wife.
Should Sickness come, she will attend you still,
And ever be obedient to your Will.
Should Cares attend (as who from Cares are free)
A faithful Counsellor she'll prove to thee;
Though every Friend thy Sufferings should desert,
In her thou'lt find a true and honest Heart,
Who all thy Woes will cheerfully partake,
And suffer all for thy beloved Sake.
Be generous then, and us to Knowledge lead,
And Happiness to you will sure succeed;
Then sacred Hymen[13] shall in Triumph reign,
And all be proud to wear his pleasing Chain.

Source: Anonymous [By a Lady]. "Poets Corner: Impromptu, on Reading an Essay on Education." *Virginia Gazette* (February 11, 1773), 4.

---

[10] Favor, gift freely or graciously bestowed.
[11] A chain for the feet of a human being or animal.
[12] Distraction of the mental faculties or energies from concentration on serious subjects.
[13] In Greek and Roman mythology the god of marriage; represented as a young man carrying a torch and a veil.

215. Abigail Adams
"Letter to John Adams" (1776)

Braintree, 31 March, 1776.

[...] I long to hear that you have declared an independency. And, by the way, in the new code of laws which I suppose it will be necessary for you to make, I desire you would remember the ladies and be more generous and favorable to them than your ancestors. Do not put such unlimited power into the hands of the husbands. Remember, all men would be tyrants if they could. If particular care and attention is not paid to the ladies, we are determined to foment a rebellion, and will not hold ourselves bound by any laws in which we have no voice or representation.

That your sex are naturally tyrannical is a truth so thoroughly established as to admit of no dispute; but such of you as wish to be happy willingly give up the harsh title of master for the more tender and endearing one of friend. Why, then, not put it out of the power of the vicious and the lawless to use us with cruelty and indignity with impunity? Men of sense in all ages abhor those customs which treat us only as the vassals of your sex; regard us then as beings placed by Providence under your protection, and in imitation of the Supreme Being make use of that power only for our happiness.

Source: Abigail Adams (1744-1818). "Letter March 31, 1776." *Familiar Letters of John Adams and His Wife Abigail Adams, during the Revolution*: With a Memoir of Mrs. Adams. Ed. Charles Francis Adams. Boston: Houghton, Mifflin & Co., 1875, 149-150.

216. Benjamin Rush
Thoughts upon Female Education (1787)

GENTLEMEN,

I HAVE yielded with diffidence to the solicitations of the Principal of the Academy, in undertaking to express my regard for the prosperity of this Seminary of Learning, by submitting to your candor a few Thoughts upon Female Education.

The first remark that I shall make upon this subject, is, that female education should be accommodated to the state of society, manners, and government of the country, in which it is conducted.

This remark leads me at once to add, that the education of young ladies, in this country, should be conducted upon principles very different from what it is in Great-Britain, and in some respects different from what it was when we were part of a monarchical empire.

There are several circumstances in the situation, employments, and duties of women in America, which require a peculiar mode of education.

I. The early marriages of our women, by contracting the time allowed for education, renders it necessary to contract its plan, and to confine it chiefly to the more useful branches of literature.

II. The state of property, in America, renders it necessary for the greatest part of our citizens to employ themselves, in different occupations, for the advancement of their fortunes. This cannot be done without the assistance of the female members of the community. They must be the stewards, and guardians of their husbands' property. That education, therefore, will be most proper for our women, which teaches them to discharge the duties of those offices with the most success and reputation.

III. From the numerous avocations to which a professional life exposes gentlemen in America from their families, a principal share of the instruction of children naturally devolves upon the women. It becomes us therefore to prepare them, by a suitable education, for the discharge of this most important duty of mothers.

IV. The equal share that every citizen has in the liberty, and the possible share he may have in the government of our country, make it necessary that our ladies should be qualified to a certain degree, by a peculiar and suitable education, to concur in instructing their sons in the principles of liberty and government. [...]

The branches of literature most essential for a young lady in this country, appear to be,

I. A knowledge of the English language. She should not only read, but speak and spell it correctly. And to enable her to do this, she should be taught the English grammar, and be frequently examined in applying its rules in common conversation.

II. Pleasure and interest conspire to make the writing of a fair and legible hand, a necessary branch of female education. For this purpose she should be taught not only to shape every letter properly, but to pay the strictest regard to points and capitals.[14]

[...] I know of few things more rude or illiberal, than to obtrude a letter upon a person of rank or business, which cannot be easily read. [...]

III. Some knowledge of figures and bookkeeping is absolutely necessary to qualify a young lady for the duties which await her in this country. There are certain occupations in which she may assist her husband with this knowledge; and should she survive him, and agreeably to the custom of our country be the executrix of his will, she cannot fail of deriving immense advantages from it.

IV. An acquaintance with geography and some instruction in chronology will enable a young lady to read history, biography, and travels, with advantage; and thereby qualify her not only for a general intercourse with the world, but to be an agreeable companion for a sensible man. To these branches of knowledge may be added, in some instances, a general acquaintance with the first principles of astronomy, and natural philosophy, particularly with such parts of them as are calculated to prevent superstition, by explaining the causes, or obviating[15] the effects of natural evil.

V. Vocal music should never be neglected, in the education of a young lady, in this country. Besides preparing her to join in that part of public worship which consists in psalmody, it will enable her to soothe the cares of domestic life. The distress and vexation of a husband – the noise of a nursery, and, even, the sorrows that will sometimes intrude into her own bosom, may all be relieved by a song, where sound and sentiment unite to act upon the mind. [...]

VI. DANCING is by no means an improper branch of education for an American lady. It promotes health, and renders the figure and motions of the body easy and agreeable. [...]

VII. The attention of our young ladies should be directed, as soon as they are prepared for it, to the reading of history – travels – poetry – and moral essays. These studies are accommodated, in a peculiar manner, to the present state of society in America, and

---

[14] Original footnote: "The present mode of writing among persons of taste is to use a capital letter only for the first word of a sentence, and for names of persons, places and months, and for the first word of every line in poetry. The words should be so shaped that a strait line may be drawn between two lines, without touching the extremities of the words in either of them."

[15] To prevent or avoid by anticipatory measures.

when a relish is excited for them, in early life, they subdue that passion for reading novels, which so generally prevails among the fair sex. I cannot dismiss this species of writing and reading without observing, that the subjects of novels are by no means accommodated to our present manners. They hold up *life*, it is true, but it is not as yet *life* in America. Our passions have not as yet "overstepped the modesty of nature," nor are they "torn to tatters,"[16] to use the expressions of the poet, by extravagant love, jealousy, ambition, or revenge. As yet the intrigues of a British novel are as foreign to our manners as the refinements of Asiatick vice. Let it not be said, that the tales of distress, which fill modern novels, have a tendency to soften the female heart into acts of humanity. The fact is the reverse of this. The abortive sympathy which is excited by the recital of imaginary distress, blunts the heart to that which is real; and, hence, we sometimes see instances of young ladies, who weep away a whole forenoon over the criminal sorrows of a fictitious Charlotte or Werter,[17] turning with disdain at two o'clock from the sight of a beggar, who solicits in feeble accents or signs, a small portion only, of the crumbs which fall from their fathers' tables.

VIII. It will be necessary to connect all these branches of education with regular instruction in the Christian religion. For this purpose the principles of the different sects of Christians should be taught and explained, and our pupils should early be furnished with some of the most simple arguments in favour of the truth of Christianity.[18] [...]

Rousseau has asserted that the great secret of education consists in "wasting the time of children profitably."[19] There is some truth in this observation. I believe that we often impair their health, and weaken their capacities, by imposing studies upon them, which are not proportioned to their years. But this objection does not apply to religious instruction. There are certain simple propositions in the Christian religion, that are suited in a peculiar manner, to the infant state of reason and moral sensibility. [...] The female breast is the natural soil of Christianity; and while our women are taught to believe its doctrines, and obey its precepts, the wit of Voltaire,[20] and the stile of Bolingbroke,[21] will never be able to destroy its influence upon our citizens. [...] Christianity exerts the most friendly influence upon science, as well as upon the morals and manners of mankind. Whether this be occasioned by the unity of truth, and the mutual assistance which truths upon different subjects afford each other, or whether the faculties of the mind be sharpened and corrected by embracing the truths of revelation, and thereby prepared to investigate and perceive truths upon other subjects, I will not determine, but it is certain that the greatest discoveries in science have been made by Christian philosophers, and that there is the most knowledge in those countries where there is the most Christianity. [...]

It should not surprise us that British customs, with respect to female education, have been transplanted into our American schools and families. We see marks of the same incongruity, of time and place, in many other things. [...] We behold our ladies panting in a heat of ninety degrees, under a hat and cushion, which were calculated for the temperature of a British summer. We behold our citizens condemned and punished by a criminal

---

[16] An irregularly torn piece or scrap of cloth, a rag.
[17] Reference to the two lovers in Johann Wolfgang von Goethe's *Die Leiden des jungen Werthers* (1774).
[18] Original footnote: "Baron Haller's letters to his daughter on the truths of the Christian religion, and Dr. Beatie's 'evidences of the Christian religion briefly and plainly stated,' are excellent little tracts, and well adapted for this purpose."
[19] Jean Jacques Rousseau (1712-1778), *Emile ou de l'éducation* (1762).
[20] Francois-Marie Voltaire (1694-1778), French philosopher and skeptic.
[21] Henry St. John, 1st Viscount Bolingbroke (1678-1751), statesman and philosopher.

law, which was copied from a country where maturity in corruption renders publick executions a part of the amusements of the nation. It is high time to awake from this servility – to study our own character – to examine the age of our country – and to adopt manners in every thing, that shall be accommodated to our state of society, and to the forms of our government. In particular it is incumbent upon us to make ornamental accomplishments yield to principles and knowledge, in the education of our women. [...]

I am not enthusiastical upon the subject of education. In the ordinary course of human affairs, we shall probably too soon follow the footsteps of the nations of Europe in manners and vices. The first marks we shall perceive of our declension, will appear among our women. Their idleness, ignorance and profligacy will be the harbingers of our ruin. Then will the character and performance of a buffoon on the theatre, be the subject of more conversation and praise, than the patriot or the minister of the gospel; – then will our language and pronunciation be enfeebled and corrupted by a flood of French and Italian words; – then will the history of romantick amours, be preferred to the immortal writings of Addison, Hawkesworth and Johnson;[22] – then will our churches be neglected, and the name of the Supreme Being never be called upon, but in profane exclamations; – then will our Sundays be appropriated, only to feasts and concerts; – and then will begin all that train of domestick and political calamities – But, I forbear. The prospect is so painful, that I cannot help, silently, imploring the great Arbiter of human affairs, to interpose his almighty goodness, and to deliver us from these evils, that, at least one spot of the earth may be reserved as a monument of the effects of good education, in order to shew in some degree, what our species was, before the fall, and what it shall be, after its restoration. [...] I cannot dismiss the subject of female education without remarking, that the city of Philadelphia first saw a number of gentlemen associated for the purpose of directing the education of young ladies. By means of this plan, the power of teachers is regulated and restrained, and the objects of education are extended. By the separation of the sexes in the unformed state of their manners, female delicacy is cherished and preserved. Here the young ladies may enjoy all the literary advantages of a boarding school, and at the same time live under the protection of their parents.[23] Here emulation may be excited without jealousy, – ambition without envy, – and competition without strife. [...]

[...] I know that the elevation of the female mind, by means of moral, physical and religious truth, is considered by some men as unfriendly to the domestic character of a woman. But this is the prejudice of little minds, and springs from the same spirit which opposes the general diffusion of knowledge among the citizens of our republics. If men believe that ignorance is favourable to the government of the female sex, they are certainly deceived; for a weak and ignorant woman will always be governed with the greatest difficulty. I have sometimes been led to ascribe the invention of ridiculous and expensive fashions in female dress, entirely to the gentlemen,[24] in order to divert the ladies from improving their minds, and thereby to secure a more arbitrary and unlimited authority over them. It will be in your power, LADIES, to correct the mistakes and practice of our

---

[22] Joseph Addison (1672-1719); John Hawkesworth (1715?–1773), Samuel Johnson (1709-1784); English writers.
[23] Original footnote: "'Unnatural confinement makes a young woman embrace with avidity every pleasure when she is set free. To relish domestick life one must be acquainted with it; for it is in the house of her parents a young woman acquires the relish.' Lord Kaims's thoughts upon education, and the culture of the heart."
[24] Original footnote: "The very expensive prints of female dresses which are published annually in France, are invented and executed wholly by GENTLEMEN."

sex upon these subjects, by demonstrating, that the female temper can only be governed by reason, and that the cultivation of reason in women, is alike friendly to the order of nature, and to private as well as publick happiness.

Source: Benjamin Rush (1745-1813). *Thoughts upon Female Education Accommodated to the Present State of Society, Manners, and Government in the United States of America: Addressed to the Visitors of the Young Ladies' Academy in Philadelphia, 28 July, 1787, at the Close of the Quarterly Examination.* Philadelphia: Prichard & Hall, 1787, 5-13, 18-24.

217. Judith Sargent Murray
"Desultory Thoughts upon the Utility of Encouraging a Degree of Self-Complacency, Especially in Female Bosoms" (1784)

>Self estimation, kept within due bounds,
>However oddly the assertion sounds,
>May, of the fairest efforts be the root,
>May yield the embow'ring[25] shade – the mellow fruit;
>May stimulate to most exalted deeds,
>Direct the soul where blooming honor leads;
>May give her there, to act a noble part,
>To virtuous pleasures yield the willing heart.
>Self-estimation will debasement shun,
>And, in the path of wisdom, joy to run;
>An unbecoming act in fears to do,
>And still, its exaltation keeps in view.
>   [...]
>Ne'er taught to "rev'rence self," or to aspire;
>Our bosoms never caught ambition's fire;
>An indolence of virtue still prevail'd,
>Nor the sweet gale of praise was e'er inhal'd;
>Rous'd by a new stimulus, no kindling glow,
>No soothing emulations gentle flow,
>We judg'd that nature, not to us inclin'd,
>In narrow bounds our progress had confin'd,
>And, that our forms, to say the very best,
>Only, not frightful, were by all confest.

I think, to teach young minds to aspire, ought to be the ground work of education: many a laudable achievement is lost, from a persuasion that our efforts are unequal to the arduous attainment. Ambition is a noble principle, which properly directed, may be productive of the most valuable consequences. It is amazing to what heights the mind by exertion may tow'r: I would, therefore, have my pupils believe, that every thing in the compass of mortality, was placed within their grasp, and that, the avidity of application, the intenseness of study, were only requisite to endow them with every external grace, and

---

[25] Sheltering in a bower-like retreat.

mental accomplishment. Thus I should impel them to progress on, if I could not lead them to the heights I would wish them to attain. It is too common with parents to expatiate[26] in their hearing, upon all the foibles[27] of their children, and to let their virtues pass, in appearance, unregarded: this they do, least they should, (were they to commend) swell their little hearts to pride, and implant in their tender minds, undue conceptions of their own importance. Those, for example, who have the care of a beautiful female, they assiduously guard every avenue, they arrest the stream of due admiration, and endeavour to divest her of all idea of the bounties of nature: what is the consequence? She grows up, and of course mixes with those who are less interested: strangers will be sincere; she encounters the tongue of the flatterer, he will exaggerate, she finds herself possessed of accomplishments which have been studiously concealed from her, she throws the reins upon the neck of fancy, and gives every encomiast[28] full credit for his most extravagant eulogy. [...] Now, I should be solicitous that my daughter should possess for me the fondest love, as well as that respect which gives birth to duty; in order to promote this wish of my soul, from my lips she should be accustomed to hear the most pleasing truths, and, as in the course of my instructions, I should doubtless find myself but too often impelled to wound the delicacy of youthful sensibility. I would therefore, be careful to avail myself of this exuberating balance: I would, from the early dawn of reason, address her as a rational being; hence, I apprehend, the most valuable consequences would result in some such language as this, she might from time to time be accosted. A pleasing form is undoubtedly advantageous. Nature, my dear, hath furnished you with an agreeable person, your glass, was I to be silent, would inform you that you are pretty, your appearance will sufficiently recommend you to a stranger, the flatterer will give a more than mortal finishing to every feature; but, it must be your part, my sweet girl, to render yourself worthy respect from higher motives: you must learn "to reverence yourself," that is, your intellectual exist[e]nce; you must join my efforts, in endeavouring to adorn your mind, for, it is from the proper furnishing of that, you will become indeed a valuable person, you will, as I said, give birth to the most favorable impressions at first sight: but, how mortifying should this be all, if, upon a more extensive knowledge you should be discovered to possess no one mental charm, to be fit only at best, to be hung up as a pleasing picture among the paintings of some spacious hall. [...] Now, then, my best Love, is the time for you to lay in such a fund of useful knowledge, as shall continue, and augment every kind sentiment in regard to you, as shall set you above the snares of the artful betrayer.

Thus, that sweet form, shall serve as a polished casket, which will contain a most beautiful gem, highly finished, and calculated for advantage, as well as ornament. Was she, I say, habituated thus to reflect, she would be taught to aspire; she would learn to estimate every accomplishment, according to its proper value; [...] her young mind would not be enervated or intoxicated, by a delicious surprise, she would possess her soul in serenity, and by that means, rise superior to the deep laid schemes which, too commonly, encompass the steps to beauty. [...]

[...] I would early impress under proper regulations, a reverence of self; I would endeavour to rear to worth, and a consciousness thereof: I would be solicitous to inspire the glow of virtue, with that elevation of soul, that dignity, which is ever attendant upon

---

[26] To enlarge, magnify (here: praise, glory).
[27] Weakness of character.
[28] A praiser, flatterer.

self-approbation, arising from the genuine source of innate rectitude. I must be excused for thus insisting upon my hypothesis, as I am, from observation, persuaded, that many have suffered materially all their life long, from a depression of soul, early inculcated, in compliance to a false maxim, which hath supposed pride would thereby be eradicated. I know there is a contrary extreme, and I would, in almost all cases, prefer the happy medium. However, if these fugitive hints may induce some abler pen to improve thereon, the exemplification will give pleasure to the heart of

          CONSTANTIA.   October 22, 1784.

Source: Judith Sargent Murray (1751-1820). "Desultory Thoughts upon the Utility of Encouraging a Degree of Self-Complacency, Especially in Female Bosoms." *The Gentleman and Lady's Town and Country Magazine: Or, Repository of Instruction and Entertainment* (October 1784), 251-253.

218. Judith Sargent Murray
"On the Equality of the Sexes" (1790)

That minds are not alike, full well I know,
This truth each day's experience will show;
To heights surprising some great spirits soar,
With inborn strength mysterious depths explore;
Their eager gaze surveys the path of light,
Confest it stood to Newton's piercing sight.
 Deep science, like a bashful maid retires,
And but the *ardent* breast her worth inspires;
By perseverance the coy fair is won.
And Genius, led by Study, wears the crown.
 But some there are who wish not to improve,
Who never can the path of knowledge love,
Whose souls almost with the dull body one,
With anxious care each mental pleasure shun;
 Weak is the level'd, enervated mind,
And but while here to vegetate design'd.
The torpid spirit mingling with its clod,
Can scarcely boast its origin from God;
Stupidly dull – they move progressing on –
 They eat, and drink, and all their work is done.
While others, emulous[29] of sweet applause,
Industrious seek for each event a cause,
Tracing the hidden springs whence knowledge flows,
 Which nature all in beauteous order shows.
Yet cannot I their sentiments imbibe,[30]
Who this distinction to the sex ascribe,
As if a woman's form must needs enrol,

---

[29] Greedy (of praise or power).
[30] To instill sth. into (the mind).

> A weak, a servile, an inferiour soul;
> And that the guise of man must still proclaim,
> Greatness of mind, and him, to be the same:
> Yet as the hours revolve fair proofs arise,
> Which the bright wreath of growing fame supplies;
> And in past times some men have *sunk* so *low*,
> That female records nothing *less* can show.
> But imbecility is still confin'd,
> And by the lordly sex to us consign'd;
> They rob us of the power t' improve,
> And then declare we only trifles love;
> Yet haste the era, when the world shall know,
> That such distinctions only dwell below;
> The soul unfetter'd, to no sex confin'd,
> Was for the abodes of cloudless day design'd.
>   Mean time we emulate their manly fires,
> Though erudition all their thoughts inspires,
> Yet nature with *equality* imparts,
> And *noble passions*, swell e'en *female hearts*.

Is it upon mature consideration we adopt the idea, that nature is thus partial in her distributions? Is it indeed a fact, that she hath yielded to one half of the human species so unquestionable a mental superiority? I know that to both sexes elevated understandings, and the reverse, are common. But, suffer me to ask, in what the minds of females are so notoriously deficient, or unequal. May not the intellectual powers be ranged under these four heads – imagination, reason, memory and judgment. The province of imagination hath long since been surrendered up to us, and we have been crowned undoubted sovereigns of the regions of fancy. Invention is perhaps the most arduous effort of the mind; this branch of imagination hath been particularly ceded to us, and we have been time out of mind invested with that creative faculty. Observe the variety of fashions (here I bar the contemptuous smile) which distinguish and adorn the female world; how continually are they changing, insomuch that they almost render the wise man's assertion problematical, and we are ready to say, *there is something new under the sun*. Now what a playfulness, what an exuberance of fancy, what strength of inventi[v]e imagination, doth this continual variation discover? Again, it hath been observed, that if the turpitude of the conduct of our sex, hath been ever so enormous, so extremely ready are we, that the very first thought presents us with an apology, so plausible, as to produce our actions even in an amiable light. Another instance of our creative powers, is our talent for slander; how ingenious are we at inventive scandal? what a formidable story can we in a moment fabricate merely from the force of a prolifick imagination? how many reputations, in the fertile brain of a female, have been utterly despoiled? how industrious are we at improving a hint? suspicion how easily do we convert into conviction, and conviction, embellished by the power of eloquence, stalks abroad to the surprise and confusion of unsuspecting innocence. Perhaps it will be asked if I furnish these facts as instances of excellency in our sex. Certainly not; but as proofs of a creative faculty, of a lively imagination. Assuredly great activity of mind is thereby discovered, and was this activity properly directed, what beneficial effects would follow. Is the needle and kitchen sufficient to employ the operations of a soul thus organized? I should conceive not. Nay, it is a truth that those very departments leave the intelligent principle vacant, and at liberty for speculation. Are we deficient in reason? we can only reason from what we know, and if an opportunity of acquiring knowledge hath been denied us, the inferiority of our sex cannot fairly be deduced from thence. [...] "But our judgment is not so strong – we do not distinguish so well." – Yet it may be questioned, from what doth this superiority, in this determining faculty of the soul, proceed. May we not trace its source in the difference of education, and continued advantages? Will it be said that the judgment of a male of two years old, is more sage than that of a female's of the same age? I believe the reverse is generally observed to be true. But from that period what partiality! how is the one exalted, and the other depressed, by the contrary modes of education which are adopted! the one is taught to aspire, and the other is early confined and limitted. As their years increase, the sister must be wholly domesticated, while the brother is led by the hand through all the flowery paths of science. Grant that their minds are by nature equal, yet who shall wonder at the *apparent* superiority, if indeed custom becomes *second nature*; nay if it taketh place of nature, and that it doth the experience of each day will evince. At length arrived at womanhood, the uncultivated fair one feels a void, which the employments allotted her are by no means capable of filling. What can she do? to books she may not apply; or if she doth, *to those only of the novel kind*, lest she merit the appellation of a *learned lady*; and what ideas have been affixed to this term, the observation of many can testify. Fashion, scandal, and sometimes what is still more reprehensible, are then called in to her relief; and who can say to what lengths the liberties she takes may proceed. Meantime she herself is most unhappy; she feels the want of a cultivated mind. Is she single, she in vain seeks to fill up time from sexual employments or amusements. Is she united to a person whose soul nature made equal to her own, education hath set him so far above her, that in those entertainments which are productive of such rational felicity, she is not qualified to accompany him. She experiences a mortifying consciousness of inferiority, which embitters every enjoyment. Doth the person to whom her adverse fate hath consigned her, possess a mind incapable of improvement, she is equally wretched, in being so closely connected with an individual whom she cannot but despise. Now, was she permitted the same instructors as her brother, (with an eye however to their particular departments) for the employment of a rational mind an ample field would be opened. In astronomy she might catch a glimpse of the immensity of the Deity, and thence she would form amazing conceptions of the august and supreme Intelligence. In geography she would admire Jehovah in the midst of his benevolence; thus adapting this globe to the various wants and amusements of its inhabitants. In natural philosophy she would adore the infinite majesty of heaven, clothed in condescension; and as she traversed the reptile world, she would hail the goodness of a creating God. A mind, thus filled, would have little room for the trifles with which our sex are, with too much justice, accused of amusing themselves, and they would thus be rendered fit companions for those, who should one day wear them as their crown. [...] Should it [...] be vociferated, "Your domestick employments are sufficient" – I would calmly ask, is it reasonable, that a candidate for immortality, for the joys of heaven, an intelligent being, who is to spend an eternity in contemplating the works of Deity, should at present be so degraded, as to be allowed no other ideas, than those which are suggested by the mechanism of a pudding, or the sewing the seams of a garment? Pity that all such censurers of female improvement do not go one step further, and deny their future existence; to be consistent they surely ought.

Yes, ye lordly, ye haughty sex, our souls are by nature *equal* to yours; the same breath of God animates, enlivens, and invigorates us; and that we are not fallen lower than yourselves, let those witness who have greatly towered above the various discouragements by which they have been so heavily oppressed; and though I am unacquainted with the list of celebrated characters on either side, yet from the observations I have made in the contracted circle in which I have moved, I dare confidently believe, that from the commencement of time to the present day, there hath been as many females, as males, who, by the *mere force of natural powers*, have merited the crown of applause; who, *thus unassisted*, have seized the wreath of fame. I know there are those who assert, that as the animal powers of the one sex are superiour, of course their mental faculties must also be stronger; thus attributing strength of mind to the transient organization of this earth born tenement. But if this reasoning is just, man must be content to yield the palm to many of the brute creation, since by not a few of his brethren of the field, he is far surpassed in bodily strength. Moreover, was this argument admitted, it would prove too much, for ocular demonstration evinceth, that there are many robust masculine ladies, and effeminate gentlemen. [...] Besides, were we to grant that animal strength proved anything, taking into consideration the accustomed impartiality of nature, we should be induced to imagine, that she had invested the female mind with superiour strength as an equivalent for the bodily powers of man. But waiving this however palpable advantage, for equality only, we wish to contend.

[...] We must be constantly upon our guard; prudence and discretion must be our characteristicks; and we must rise superior to, and obtain a complete victory over those who have been long adding to the native strength of their minds, by an unremitted study of men and books, and who have, moreover, conceived from the loose characters which they have been portrayed in the extensive variety of their reading, a most contemptible opinion of the sex. Thus unequal, we are, notwithstanding, forced to the combat, and the infamy which is consequent upon the smallest deviation in our conduct, proclaims the high idea which was formed of our native strength; and thus, indirectly at least, is the preference acknowledged to be our due. And if we are allowed an equality of acquirement, let serious studies equally employ our minds, and we will bid our souls arise to equal strength. We will meet upon even ground, the despot man; we will rush with alacrity to the combat, and, crowned by success, we shall then answer the exalted expectations which are formed. [...] O ye arbiters of our fate! we confess that the superiority is indubitably yours; you are by nature formed for our protectors; we pretend not to vie with you in bodily strength; upon this point we will never contend for victory. Shield us then, we beseech you, from external evils, and in return *we* will transact *your* domestick affairs. Yes, *your*, for are you not equally interested in those matters with ourselves? Is not the elegancy of neatness as agreeable to your sight as to ours; is not the well favoured viand[31] equally delightful to your taste; and doth not your sense of hearing suffer as much, from the discordant sounds prevalent in an ill regulated family, produced by the voices of children and many *et ceteras?*

CONSTANTIA.

Source: Judith Sargent Murray (1751-1820). "On the Equality of the Sexes." *The Massachusetts Magazine* (March 1790), 132-134; (April 1790), 223-224.

---

[31] Articles of food, provisions.

219. Anonymous
"On Female Education" (1794)

By a young Lady, a Student in a Seminary in Beekman-Street, New-York.

WHEN I allow myself a few moments of reflection, to consider the world, and the infinite number of reasonable creatures that inhabit it, I am struck with amazement to observe the material difference in the education of the sexes: Whilst the male are rising and shining in all the branches of literature, fitting to be useful members of civil society, an honour to their parents and a blessing to the world, the poor females are excluded in some obscure corner, contented with the admiration and flattery of the gentlemen, (even the most despicable of all flatterers) who praise only their beauty, elevate their vanity, and glory in their ignorance. But since we have the same natural abilities as themselves, why should we not have the same opportunity of polishing and displaying them by the principles of an independent and virtuous education; and like them establish our rights, and trample on the despised flattery of those who wish to keep us in the base chains of ignorance? Even to this day I fear there is too many of my sex, who, from a wrong education, have retained those principles, that beauty is their only accomplishment, and consequently neglect all the most necessary qualifications, without which life would not be worth enjoying. If we consider a female without education, she must be compared to a vapour which appears but for a moment, and then vanisheth away; or to the gay morning flower, which puts forth its painted leaves, stands trembling for a while, and then expires. Whereas, a lady of education will appear more and more pleasing the longer you are acquainted with her; you will feel a certain pleasure in her company you know not how to account for, a desire for her wellfare, and a wish for her happiness; and when the rosy down of beauty[32] is expiring on her cheek, she looses not her excellence; but on the contrary, never appears so amiable as now, when the wrinkles of age grace her forehead, and wisdom and experience crown her with dignity, and now she is preparing for a speedy exit to the world of spirits, which she performs with the greatest cheerfulness and content, and yields her breath, with that resignation, becoming the noblest sentiments she exprest in every action of her life. Oh! learning, thou art one of the greatest blessings mankind can enjoy: for the want of thee, the great, and the virtuous of my sex have lain buried in obscurity, which, with thy aid, might have raised their heads like the lofty cedar of the forest, and had an opportunity of ranking themselves with the renowned in every age, of becoming an ornament to society, and a pattern to their sex. Neither can I conceive that learning was intended merely for the improvement of one sex, but by its true attendants, humanity, affability, and unbounded friendship, to add happiness to the whole race of mankind; for it hath been remarked by the wise in every age, that those who have been the most learned, have been the most happy: and not only that, but health, wealth, victory, and honour, are all attendants, to that noble qualification, which, next to virtue, is truly capable of raising one soul above another. It adds content to solitude, pleasure to retirement, and fills a public station with all those amiable qualities, which distinguish true merit in the person possessed of it.

There is one reason why I think learning more necessary for our sex than the other: that is, because we lead a more solitary life, and must, unavoidably, sometimes fall into melancholy and dejection, if not supported by a good education, which would enable us

---

[32] The first feathering of young birds, here: metaphorically first appearance of s.th.

to pass those pensive hours in contemplation and writing, which would not only be an amusement to us, but a benefit to our sex; and by our wise, virtuous and pious examples, improve society, sweeten adversity, and soften all the cares of life. But at the present day learning seems diffusing itself through the dark corners of the earth, and like the bright morning sun, displays a thousand unseen beauties, which, without light, would have been lost in oblivion. And since the Americans have bravely established their liberties, (notwithstanding the vain efforts of tyranny) we hope their modesty will keep them from exercising that despotism over us, which they so openly despised in their master. But for their sovereignty over us in the former ages, they are more excuseable, as I am sensible it was through ignorance; for whilst in a state of slavery what else could be expected? But now, when learning has enlarged their ideas, and improved their minds, may that base selfishness of soul be entirely excluded from the society of free men; and now, may they wish to see the fair sex on an equal footing with themselves, enjoying all the blessings of freedom. Then should we see them extolled for the beauties of their minds instead of their persons, and then would mankind enjoy that happiness which was first intended for the happy pair in Paradise. G.U.

> Source: Anonymous [A Young Lady, a Student in a Seminary in Beekman-Street, New-York]. "On Female Education." *New York Magazine or Literary Repository* (September 1794), 569-570.

220. Anonymous
"Female Influence" (1795)

FEMALE influence, no doubt, has its origin in the institution of Infinite Wisdom: "It is not good that the man should be alone; I will make him an help meet for him."[33] The social intercourse between the sexes commences very early in life; it increases with rapidity as they advance towards maturity, and continues undiminished throughout the single state. In its progressive stages the influence of the fair operates with growing efficacy. Hence, if their minds be duly cultivated, the consequences will be highly beneficial to society. "To form the manners of men," says a celebrated preacher, "various causes contribute; but nothing, I apprehend, so much as the turn of the women with whom they converse. Those who are most conversant with women of virtue and understanding will be always found the most amiable characters, other circumstances being supposed alike: their principles will have nothing ferocious or forbidding: their affections will be chaste and soothing at the same instant. In their case, the gentleman, the man of worth, the christian, will all melt insensibly and sweetly into one another. How agreeable the composition!"[34] Man, formed for society, is ever desirous of pleasing those with whom he is conversant; and never is this desire more manifest, than when a young man associates with the young of the other sex. So circumstanced, he will constantly endeavour to be and to do whatever he sees most acceptable to his acquaintances of that sex. If he observes them to turn with disgust from the strained language of adulation, to discountenance every species of light and silly behaviour, and decidedly to prefer a manly deportment to the apish grimaces of a fop; if he perceives that the most distant appearance of vice and

---

[33] Gen. 3.18-25.
[34] Original footnote: "Dr. Fordyce."

loose principles would render him peculiarly disagreeable to them, he will from that moment earnestly aim at such a manner of life, as he has every reason to believe they will approve. His assiduous endeavours will quickly form settled habits, and his character, due allowance being made for the difference of sex, will finally be assimilated to theirs. Thus he will arrive at that real merit which always commands the respect, and that amiableness of manners which ensures the esteem of the valuable part of both sexes.

This general intercourse is succeeded by one more particular, subsisting between persons cautiously selected, whose characters have been more clearly ascertained; and in such small circles are commonly found the candidates for a young lady's hand in matrimony. Her future happiness, it may be for the term of a long life, being then in agitation, will not her most vigilant prudence be excited; and will she not act most circumspectly in the discrimination and estimation of characters? For it is presumed no man will be permitted to enjoy the privilege of intimacy, whose character would appear to disqualify him for becoming her husband. If this be the case, the pretensions of libertines and coxcombs[35] are at once defeated; and, while they merit these disgraceful appellations, they suffer a penal exclusion from the sweetest pleasures of society. – Hence, if vice and dissipation be not too deeply rooted; if they be not entirely deaf to the calls of honour and of generous pleasure; they will zealously endeavour to reform their lives, and improve their understandings, that they may have some chance of obtaining female approbation. The effects resulting from this conduct of the ladies must be especially beneficial to the younger part of our sex, whose characters are not yet formed; whose minds are in some measure a blank, on which the salutary influence of the fair may make the most conspicuous impression. The possession of real merit being the sole terms of admission into female society, every one will ardently strive to act and converse rationally, and to regulate his behaviour by the strictest rules of virtue; and this not more from a sense of the improvement and pleasure to be derived from female conversation, than from the desire of recommending himself to some accomplished fair one for life. Let young men be convinced, that virtue and understanding are chiefly prized by the fair sex, that alone will be a sufficient incitement to them to seek for these endowments, and upon these only will they value themselves. [...]

The social intercourse with the fair sex, whether general or particular, is desired by the hopeful part of ours, from the most powerful incentives; incentives, founded equally in reason and in nature. When either business or study necessarily gives way to relaxation, how pleasurable, how profitable is it to step into the polite drawing-room, or the happier domesticated parlour, where the conversation of an accomplished fair circle equally delights and improves; where native innocence prompts the cheering smile; where wit without a sting, without a stain, flows artless along, or simple heart-moving melody pours forth enchanting strains; where the heaven-born virtues reign, the mental graces diffuse benignity and joy around, and all the little distinctions of personal attraction are lost in the more unfading beauties of the soul? [...] A well informed mind, a gentle, modest disposition, an uniform rectitude of conduct, and an unaffected goodness of heart, united in the fair, must be perfectly irresistible. They must effectually tend to humanize, purify, and ennoble the mind of man; to give it an energy, elasticity, and vigour, adequate to the most dignified undertaking. "Were virtue," said an ancient philosopher, "to put on a visible shape, and appear amongst men, what ardent desires would she enkindle?" But

---

[35] A foolish, conceited, showy person, a fop.

surely she does put on the most charming of all visible shapes, when the looks, the words, the actions of a lovely intelligent woman, are habitually exerted in her cause. Then operates the combined charm; then is displayed the captivating influence which never fails of disengaging the men from every debasing, every destructive pursuit, and ordaining them to be honourable and useful members of society.

But there is one period in which the fair are possessed of power literally unlimited. Love and courtship, it is universally allowed, invest a lady with more authority than in any other situation falls to the lot of human beings. She can mould the taste, the manners, and the conduct of her admirers, according to her pleasure. She can, even to a great degree, change their tempers and dispositions, and superinduce habits entirely new. She can influence them to a sacred regard for truth, honour, candour, and a manly sincerity in their intercourse with her sex. [...] What passion has ever wrought such wonders as that of love? "Honourable love," says the excellent preacher above-mentioned, "that great preservative of purity; that powerful softener of the fiercest spirit; that mighty improver of the rudest carriage; that all subduing, yet all exalting principle of the human breast; which humbles the proud, and bends the stubborn, yet fills with lofty conceptions, and animates with a fortitude that nothing can conquer! What shall I say more? which converts the savage into a man, and lifts the man into a hero!" By the judicious management of this noble passion, a passion with which the truly accomplished of the fair sex never fail of inspiring the men, what almost miraculous reformation may be brought about? In this, the beneficial power of the sex exceeds conception.

Let us now observe the lovely object moving in a higher sphere: let us consider her in the relation of a wife. In this situation, her influence, far from suffering diminution, is in many respects enlarged. On her the husband's fortune in a great measure depends; by her his fate is determined. As treasurer of his family, her œconomy makes his income doubly productive. From the continued practice of frugality, she enjoys the heavenly delights arising from benevolence and charity, generously distributing part of her prudent savings among the children of indigence. And who, let me ask, can be a constant witness of such displays of the spirit of christianity, without becoming a better man? Her gentle manners alleviate her husband's cares, sooth to peace his anxious mind, and blunt the stings of misfortune to which frail mortality is necessarily exposed. By the sympathetic effusions of a feeling heart, by the sweet accents flowing from a persuasive tongue, she restrains his imperious passions, and obliterates every gloomy, doleful impression. It rests with her, not only to confirm those virtuous habits which he has already acquired, but also to excite his perseverance in the paths of rectitude. By continually attracting him towards home, she prevents many of the greatest evils that befall mankind. Let a man discern that his own house contains not only his most faithful friend, but likewise a most agreeable and rational companion, and he will never unnecessarily leave that seat of felicity, or when obliged to leave it will hasten his return. This domestic propensity will serve as a never-failing antidote against the most dangerous temptations to vice. Rarely do we see, in the married state, a man whose affections tend remarkably towards home, who is not at the same time possessed of a large portion of happiness and virtue. Rarely do we see a family reduced to misery and ruin, whose misfortunes have not originated from the husband's inclination to roving, and aversion to home.

The cares, the studies, the desires of a virtuous woman are all undoubtedly concentered in her husband, and her attention pre-eminently engaged by her family affairs. Yet by this very circumstance is her influence greatly heightened and extended. All her words and actions, sanctioned by reason, appear to the world so disinterested; their propriety so demonstrable, from the situation of her own family, that she is regarded as a conducting angel by all around her. [...]

But let us contemplate the amiable woman shining with more brilliant lustre in the exalted situation of a mother! Here, the ideas of tenderness, of magnanimity, of every thing interesting to the social and the civil state, crowd together upon the astonished mind. The concerns of thousands yet unborn, their temporal, even their eternal interests, are to a great degree dependant upon the conduct of a mother. In proportion as she is worthy or unworthy, will those take a happy or an unhappy direction.

That the education of children is an affair of infinite importance, is beyond dispute. [...] Let us contemplate the mother distributing the mental nourishment to the fond smiling circle, by means proportionate to their different powers of reception, watching the gradual openings of their minds, and studying their various turns of temper: – See, under her cultivating hand, reason assuming the reins of government, and knowledge increasing gradually to her beloved pupils. The buds of intelligence begin to shoot in one; in another, they expand; in a third, they are in full blossom. She encourages, she manages, she checks; conducting by easy gradations the growing faculties of the soul, to heaven and eternity. Religion, fairest offspring of the skies, smiles suspicious on her endeavours; the Genius of Liberty hovers triumphant over the glorious scene; Fame, with her golden trump, spreads wide the well-earned honours of the fair [...].

It is well known, that among the Romans, the men were frequently trained to the greatest and most heroic actions, by the cares and management of the matrons. It would be needless to single out from among the number, Cornelia,[36] to whom the eloquent, the brave, the patriotic Gracchi[37] were indebted for their glory. To this remarkable care of the Roman mothers, we are doubtless to attribute the many illustrious characters, which at various times ennobled and supported that wonderful republic. [...] These great endowments being possessed by the women, what can equal the cultivating hand of a mother, in laying a foundation in the mind of a youth, whereon to raise the noblest superstructure? in impressing habits that will ripen into excellence; that will inspire him when grown up with magnanimity, and enable him to acquire true renown; that will conduct him invariably in the paths of undisguised honour, of truth, of virtue and religion; that will make him the stay and support of his aged parents, the boast of his country, and the glory of humanity?

But the education of sons, however important, constitutes but part of the benefit accruing to society from a worthy mother: that of daughters is of still greater moment. In this case, her utmost exertions are indispensibly necessary, and when properly and seasonably conducted, never fail of proving effectual. The education of daughters is the province, I had almost said of the mother alone. She can embellish and enrich their minds with a thousand elegancies, and in a thousand ways, which nothing but her own good sense and accomplishments could ever suggest. By a proper attention to this province, she not only diffuses more widely her benign influence over the present generation, but also to future ages; whilst in every succeeding period, it will increase in a rapid progression. Her precepts and her example instruct the rising fair; ambition, and an innate sense of propriety, prompt them to follow her footsteps, and to imitate her blessed character in the various grades of virgin, wife, and mother. [...]

---

[36] A highly cultured mother of the late 2nd century BC.
[37] Gaius Sempronius Gracchus; Roman reformer of the late 2nd century BC.

Thus it has been attempted to shew, that the fair sex give a decisive bent to the manners and morals of men. And for the truth of this we appeal to the history of all nations; we appeal to the experience of all ages; we appeal to reason itself. Reason says it cannot be otherwise. In what an exalted rank in the scale of existence has the God of nature placed the lovely sex? How important their conduct towards promoting the dignity and happiness of man? What a spring is this to the noblest ambition that can ever fire the breasts of mortals? An ambition founded in the broad eternal basis of virtue? Yes, ye fair, the reformation of a world is in your power. By employing those faculties with which a good providence has endowed you, you may be the instruments of inestimable blessings to society even at a very early age; by exerting your auspicious influence over your sex, you may, in a great measure, banish vice and folly from the earth. [...] Prophanity, libertinism, gaming, prodigality, and a long train of crimes and follies which vilify the manly character, would fall into disrepute, and soon be consigned over to merited contempt and odium. They would more effectually sink under the united efforts of the female sex, than ever they were known to do under the operation of the best laws and sagest maxims produced by the collected wisdom of the world. Virtue and vice, wisdom and folly, are apparently dependent, under providence, upon the female smile; and never does the female smile diffuse such a captivating charm, never does it strike with such irresistible power, as when it beams with a portion of the divine effulgence on the side of reason and religion. By its influence on our hearts, we are inspired with the noblest sentiments; the faculties of the soul become vigorous and active; and we press forward with ardour to the acquisition of every thing great and excellent.

Reflect on the result of your efforts. Contemplate the rising glory of confederated America. Consider that your exertions can best secure, increase, and perpetuate it. The solidity and stability of the liberties of your country rest with you; since Liberty is never sure, 'till Virtue reigns triumphant. Your country therefore demands, the felicity of unborn myriads demands, that you exercise all your power and influence in this cause. Nor shall these demands be made in vain. Already may we see the lovely daughters of Columbia asserting the importance and the honour of their sex. "Let us not," say they, "let us not passively rest satisfied with the esteem even of the worthy, since it is active virtue alone, that can produce real glory to ourselves and usefulness to our fellow-creatures. Let us assiduously employ our influence over the men, in promoting their happiness and the best interests of society. Let us exert our combined efforts, to restore the dignity of human nature, which has been infamously violated, and which a torrent of folly and wickedness threatens totally to destroy."

Begin then, ye fair! your efforts are now seasonable. Many virtues are yet conspicuous in our country. The refinements of fashion have not yet silenced the voice of reason, nor banished the vestiges of nature. But the tempest is gathering. The deluge of vice and luxury, which has well nigh overwhelmed Europe, is pouring in upon us through different channels. How honourable would it be for you to stop its progress, to save, to aggrandize your country! Already we behold it an asylum for the oppressed of every nation! Whether they have been driven from their native lands by the tyranny of one, of the few, or of the many, amongst us they find a peaceful and happy retreat. It rests with you to make this retreat doubly peaceful, doubly happy, by banishing from it those crimes and corruptions, which have never yet failed of giving rise to tyranny, or anarchy. While you thus keep our country virtuous, you maintain its independence and ensure its prosperity. Let the brilliancy of the undertaking animate your fortitude. Let the blessings to be derived from its prosecution inflame your ardour. Let the conscious pleasures arising from such a conduct prompt you to assiduity and constancy in your endeavours. In the midst of such occupations and successes, you will enjoy a happiness unalloyed[38] and unalterable; a happiness which will not expire with your fair earthly forms; which will pass the narrow boundaries of time and sense, and accompany you when sister spirits shall hail you partakers of a GLORIOUS IMMORTALITY.

Source: Anonymous. "Female Influence: Being the Substance of an Oration Delivered at the Annual Commencement of Columbia College, May 6, 1795." *New York Magazine or Literary Repository* (May 1795), 297-305.

221. Emma Willard
A Plan for Female Education (1819)

ADDRESS, &c.

THE object of this Address, is to convince the public, that a reform, with respect to female education, is necessary; that it cannot be effected by individual exertion, but that it requires the aid of the legislature: and further, by shewing the justice, the policy, and the magnanimity of such an undertaking, to persuade that body, to endow a seminary for females, as the commencement of such reformation. [...]

If the improvement of the American female character, and that alone, could be effected by public liberality, employed in giving better means of instruction; such improvement of one half of society, and that half, which barbarous and despotic nations have ever degraded, would of itself be an object, worthy of the most liberal government on earth; but if the female character be raised, it must inevitably raise that of the other sex: and thus does the plan proposed, offer, as the object of legislative bounty, to elevate the whole character of the community.

As evidence, that this statement does not exaggerate the female influence in society, our sex need but be considered, in the single relation of mothers. In this character, we have the charge of the whole mass of individuals, who are to compose the succeeding generation; during that period of youth, when the pliant mind takes any direction, to which it is steadily guided by a forming hand. How important a power is given by this charge! yet, little do too many of my sex know how, either to appreciate or improve it. Unprovided with the means of acquiring that knowledge, which flows liberally to the other sex – having our time of education devoted to frivolous acquirements, how should we understand the nature of the mind, so as to be aware of the importance of those early impressions, which we make upon the minds of our children? – or how should we be able to form enlarged and correct views, either of the character, to which we ought to mould them, or of the means most proper to form them aright? [...]

It is the duty of a government, to do all in its power to promote the present and future prosperity of the nation, over which it is placed. This prosperity will depend on the character of its citizens. The characters of these will be formed by their mothers; and it is through the mothers, that the government can control the characters of its future citizens, to form them such as will ensure their country's prosperity. If this is the case, then

---

[38] Not mixed with a baser metal, not debased.

it is the duty of our present legislators to begin now, to form the characters of the next generation, by controling that of the females, who are to be their mothers, while it is yet with them a season of improvement. [...]

BENEFITS OF FEMALE SEMINARIES.

In inquiring, concerning the benefits of the plan proposed, I shall proceed upon the supposition, that female seminaries will be patronized throughout our country.

Nor is this altogether a visionary supposition. If one seminary should be well organized, its advantages would be found so great, that others would soon be instituted; and, that sufficient patronage can be found to put one in operation, may be presumed from its reasonableness, and from the public opinion, with regard to the present mode of female education. [...]

It is believed, that such institutions, would tend to prolong, or perpetuate our excellent government.

An opinion too generally prevails, that our present form of government, though good, cannot be permanent. Other republics have failed, and the historian and philosopher have told us, that nations are like individuals; that, at their birth, they receive the seeds of their decline and dissolution. Here deceived by a false analogy, we receive an apt illustration of particular facts, for a general truth. The existence of nations, cannot, in strictness, be compared with the duration of animate life; for by the operation of physical causes, this, after a certain length of time, must cease: but the existence of nations, is prolonged by the succession of one generation to another, and there is no physical cause, to prevent this succession's going on, in a peaceable manner, under a good government, till the end of time. We must then look to other causes, than necessity, for the decline and fall of former republics. If we could discover these causes, and seasonably prevent their operation, then might our latest posterity enjoy the same happy government, with which we are blessed; or if but in part, then might the triumph of tyranny, be delayed, and a few more generations be free.

Permit me then to ask the enlightened politician of my country, whether amidst his researches for these causes, he cannot discover one, in the neglect, which free governments, in common with others, have shown, to whatever regarded the formation of the female character.

In those great republics, which have fallen of themselves, the loss of republican manners and virtues, has been the invariable precursor, of their loss of the republican form of government. But is it not in the power of our sex, to give society its tone, both as to manners and morals? And if such is the extent of female influence, it is wonderful, that republics have failed, when they calmly suffered that influence, to become enlisted in favour of luxuries and follies, wholly incompatible with the existence of freedom?

It may be said, that the depravation of morals and manners, can be traced to the introduction of wealth, as its cause. But wealth will be introduced; even the iron laws of Lycurgus[39] could not prevent it. Let us then inquire, if means may not be devised, to prevent its bringing with it the destruction of public virtue. May not these means be found in education? – in implanting, in early youth, habits, that may counteract the temptations, to which, through the influence of wealth, mature age will be exposed? and in giving strength and expansion to the mind, that it may comprehend, and prize those principles,

---

[39] Lycurgus (9th century BC), a Spartan lawmaker, considered the founder of the Spartan constitution.

which teach the rigid performance of duty? Education, it may be said, has been tried as a preservative of national purity. But was it applied to every exposed part of the body politic? For if any part has been left within the pestilential atmosphere of wealth, without this preservative, then that part becoming corrupted, would communicate the contagion to the whole; and if so, then has the experiment, whether education may not preserve public virtue, never yet been fairly tried. Such a part has been left in all former experiments. Females have been exposed to the contagion of wealth without the preservative of a good education; and they constitute that part of the body politic, least endowed by nature to resist, most to communicate it. Nay, not merely have they been left without the defence of a good education, but their corruption has been accelerated by a bad one. The character of women of rank and wealth has been, and in the old governments of Europe now is, all that this statement would lead us to expect. Not content with doing nothing to promote their country's welfare, like pampered children, they revel in its prosperity, and scatter it to the winds, with a wanton profusion: and still worse, – they empoison its source, by diffusing a contempt for useful labour. To court pleasure their business, – within her temple, in defiance of the laws of God and man, they have erected the idol fashion; and upon her altar, they sacrifice, with shameless rites, whatever is sacred to virtue or religion. Not the strongest ties of nature, – not even maternal love can restrain them! Like the worshipper of Moloch,[40] the mother while yet yearning over the new born babe, tears it from the bosom, which God has swelled with nutrition for its support, and casts it remorseless from her, the victim of her unhallowed devotion!

But while, with an anguished heart, I thus depict the crimes of my sex, let not the other stand by and smile. Reason declares, that you are guiltier than we. You are our natural guardians, – our brothers, – our fathers, and our rulers. You know that our ductile minds, readily take the impressions of education. Why then have you neglected our education? Why have you looked with lethargic indifference, on circumstances ruinous to the formation of our characters, which you might have controlled? [...]

The inquiry, to which these remarks have conducted us is this – What is offered by the plan of female education, here proposed, which may teach, or preserve, among females of wealthy families, that purity of manners, which is allowed, to be so essential to national prosperity, and so necessary, to the existence of a republican government.

1. Females, by having their understandings cultivated, their reasoning powers developed and strengthened, may be expected to act more from the dictates of reason, and less from those of fashion and caprice.

2. With minds thus strengthened they would be taught systems of morality, enforced by the sanctions of religion; and they might be expected to acquire juster and more enlarged views of their duty, and stronger and higher motives to its performance.

3. This plan of education, offers all that can be done to preserve female youth from a contempt of useful labour. The pupils would become accustomed to it, in conjunction with the high objects of literature, and the elegant pursuits of the fine arts; and it is to be hoped, that both from habit and association, they might in future life, regard it as respectable.

To this it may be added, that if housewifery could be raised to a regular art, and taught upon philosophical principles, it would become a higher and more interesting occupation; and ladies of fortune, like wealthy agriculturalists, might find, that to regulate their business, was an agreeable employment.

---

[40] In the Bible, the god of the Ammonites and Phoenicians to whom children were sacrificed.

4. The pupils might be expected to acquire a taste for moral and intellectual pleasures, which would buoy them above a passion for show and parade, and which would make them seek to gratify the natural love of superiority, by endeavouring to excel others in intrinsic merit, rather than in the extrinsic frivolities of dress, furniture, and equipage.

5. By being enlightened in moral philosophy, and in that, which teaches the operations of the mind, females would be enabled to perceive the nature and extent, of that influence, which they possess over their children, and the obligation, which this lays them under, to watch the formation of their characters with unceasing vigilance, to become their instructors, to devise plans for their improvement, to weed out the vices from their minds, and to implant and foster the virtues. And surely, there is that in the maternal bosom, which, when its pleadings shall be aided by education, will overcome the seductions of wealth and fashion, and will lead the mother, to seek her happiness in communing with her children, and promoting their welfare, rather than in a heartless intercourse, with the votaries of pleasure: especially, when with an expanded mind, she extends her views to futurity, and sees her care to her offspring rewarded by peace of conscience, the blessings of her family, the prosperity of her country, and finally with everlasting happiness to herself and them. [...]

In calling on my patriotic countrymen, to effect so noble an object, the consideration of national glory, should not be overlooked. Ages have rolled away; – barbarians have trodden the weaker sex beneath their feet; – tyrants have robbed us of the present light of heaven, and fain would take its future. Nations, calling themselves polite, have made us the fancied idols of a ridiculous worship, and we have repaid them with ruin for their folly. But where is that wise and heroic country, which has considered, that our rights are sacred, though we cannot defend them? that tho' a weaker, we are an essential part of the body politic, whose corruption or improvement must affect the whole? and which, having thus considered, has sought to give us by education, that rank in the scale of being, to which our importance entitles us? History shows not that country. It shows many, whose legislatures have sought to improve their various vegetable productions, and their breeds of useful brutes; but none, whose public councils have made it an object of their deliberations, to improve the character of their women. Yet though history lifts not her finger to such an one, anticipation does. She points to a nation, which, having thrown off the shackles of authority and precedent, shrinks not from schemes of improvement, because other nations have never attempted them; but which, in its pride of independence, would rather lead than follow, in the march of human improvement: a nation, wise and magnanimous to plan, enterprising to undertake, and rich in resources to execute. Does not every American exult that this country is his own? And who knows how great and good a race of men, may yet arise from the forming hand of mothers, enlightened by the bounty of that beloved country, – to defend her liberties, – to plan her future improvement, – and to raise her to unparalleled glory?

Source: Emma Willard (1787-1870). *An Address to the Public; Particularly to the Members of the Legislature of New-York, Proposing a Plan for Improving Female Education*. Middlebury, VT: J.W. Copeland, 1819, 3-6, 25-26, 49-60.

222. *Keep within Your Compass* (c. 1785-1805)

Source: *Keep Within Compass* (c. 1785-1805). Courtesy Henry Francis du Pont Winterthur Museum. [Inscriptions (top to bottom): "How blest the Maid whose bosom no headstrong passion knows, / Her days in Joy she Passes, her nights in soft repose." "KEEP WITHIN COMPASS AND YOU SHALL BE SURE TO AVOID MANY TROUBLES WHICH OTHERS ENDURE." "A Virtuous Woman is a Crown to her Husband." "ENTER NOT INTO THE WAY OF THE WICKED, AND GO NOT IN THE PATH OF EVIL MEN."]

223. Catharine E. Beecher
Suggestions Respecting Improvements in Education (1829)

[... A] defect in education has arisen from the fact, that teachers have depended too much upon *authority*, and too little upon *the affections*, in guiding the objects of their care. It is not uncommon to see teachers in their intercourse with pupils, feeling it *necessary*, to maintain a dignity and reserve, which keeps their scholars at such a distance as prevents all assimilation of feeling and interest.

[... O]ften times teachers are so oppressed with care and responsibility, and their efforts are so constantly needed in discharging other duties, that it is *impossible* to seek a frequent and familiar intercourse with their pupils. Yet still it is believed, that if teachers generally would make this a *definite object* of attention and effort, more than double the influence could be exerted over the minds of their charge; for the *wishes* of a beloved teacher, have unspeakably more influence, than the *authority* of one who is always beheld only at a respectful distance.

For these and other reasons, it seems of great importance that the formation of the female character should be committed to the female hand. It will be long, if ever, before the female mind can boast of the accurate knowledge, the sound judgment, and ready discrimination which the other sex may claim. But if the mind is to be guided chiefly by means of the affections; if the regulation of the disposition, the manners, the social habits and the moral feelings, are to be regarded before the mere acquisition of knowledge, is not *woman* best fitted to accomplish these important objects[?] Beside this, in order to secure the correction and formation of intellectual and moral character which is deemed so important, it is necessary that a degree of familiarity of intercourse, at all times and places, an intimate knowledge of feelings, affections, and weaknesses be sought by a teacher, which is not practicable or proper for one of the other sex to attain.

It may be said, and said truly, that women are not prepared by *sufficient knowledge* to become teachers in many branches. But they *can be prepared*, and where they are not so well qualified as one of the other sex, they so often excel in patience and persevering interest, as to more than counter-balance the deficiency.

The writer cannot but believe, that all female institutions, for these and *many other reasons* ought to be conducted exclusively by females, *so soon as suitable teachers of their own sex can be prepared*. [...]

Woman has been but little aware of the high incitements that should stimulate to the cultivation of her noblest powers. The world is no longer to be governed by *physical* force, but by *the influence which mind exerts over mind*. How are the great springs of action in the political world put in motion? Often by the secret workings of *a single mind*, that in retirement plans its schemes, and comes forth to execute them only by presenting motives of prejudice, passion, self-interest or pride to operate on other minds.

[...] Here then is the only lawful field for the ambition of our sex. Woman in all her relations is bound to "honour and obey" those on whom she depends for protection and support, nor does the truly feminine mind desire to exceed this limitation of Heaven. But where the dictates of authority may never controul, the voice of reason and affection, may ever convince and persuade; and while others govern by motives that mankind are ashamed to own, the dominion of woman may be based on influence that the heart is proud to acknowledge.

And if it is indeed the truth, that reason and conscience guide to the only path of happiness, and if affection will gain a hold on these powerful principles which can be attained no other way, what high and holy motives are presented to woman for cultivating her noblest powers. The developement of the reasoning faculties, the fa[s]cinations of a purified imagination, the charms of a cultivated taste, the quick perceptions of an active mind, the power of exhibiting truth and reason, by perspicuous,[41] and animated conversation and writing, all these can be employed by woman as much as by man. And with these attainable facilities for gaining influence, woman has already received from the hand of her Maker those warm affections and quick susceptibilities, which can most surely gain the empire of the heart.

Woman has never wakened to her highest destinies and holiest hopes. She has yet to learn the purifying and blessed influence she may gain and maintain over the intellect and affections of the human mind. Though she may not teach from the portico, nor thunder from the forum, in her secret retirements she may form and send forth the sages that shall govern and renovate the world. Though she may not gird herself for bloody conflict, nor sound the trumpet of war, she may enwrap herself in the panoply[42] of Heaven, and send the thrill of benevolence through a thousand youthful hearts. Though she may not enter the lists in legal collision, nor sharpen her intellect amid the passions and conflicts of men, she may teach the law of kindness, and hush up the discords and conflicts of life. Though she may not be cloathed as the ambassador of Heaven, nor minister at the altar of God; as a secret angel of mercy she may teach its will, and cause to ascend the humble, but most accepted sacrifice. [...]

Source: Catharine E. Beecher (1800-1878). *Suggestions Respecting Improvements in Education, Presented to the Trustees of the Hartford Female Seminary, and Published at their Request.* Hartford: Packard & Butler, 1829, 49-54.

224. Thomas R. Dew
"Dissertation: On the Characteristic Differences between the Sexes, and on the Position and Influence of Woman in Society" (1835)

Relative Position of the Sexes in Society.

The relative position of the sexes in the social and political world, may certainly be looked upon as the result of organization. The greater physical strength of man, enables him to occupy the foreground in the picture. He leaves the domestic scenes; he plunges into the turmoil and bustle of an active, selfish world; in his journey through life, he has to encounter innumerable difficulties, hardships and labors which constantly beset him. His mind must be nerved against them. Hence courage and boldness are his attributes. It is his province, undismayed, to stand against the rude shocks of the world; to meet with a lion's heart, the dangers which threaten him. He is the shield of woman, destined by nature to guard and protect her. Her inferior strength and sedentary habits confine her within the domestic circle; she is kept aloof from the bustle and storm of active life; she is not familiarized to the out of door dangers and hardships of a cold and scuffling world:

---

[41] Clear in statement or expression.
[42] Any splendid enveloping array, protective armor.

timidity and modesty are her attributes. In the great strife which is constantly going forward around her, there are powers engaged which her inferior physical strength prevents her from encountering. She must rely upon the strength of others; man must be engaged in her cause. How is he to be drawn over to her side? Not by menace – not by force; for weakness cannot, by such means, be expected to triumph over might. No! It must be by conformity to that character which circumstances demand for the sphere in which she moves; by the exhibition of those qualities which delight and fascinate – which are calculated to win over to her side the proud lord of creation, and to make him an humble suppliant at her shrine. Grace, modesty and loveliness are the charms which constitute her power. By these, she creates the magic spell that subdues to her will the more mighty physical powers by which she is surrounded. Her attributes are rather of a passive than active character. Her power is more emblematical of that of divinity: it subdues without an effort, and almost creates by mere volition; – whilst man must wind his way through the difficult and intricate mazes of philosophy; with pain and toil, tracing effects to their causes, and unravelling the deep mysteries of nature – storing his mind with useful knowledge, and exercising, training and perfecting his intellectual powers, whilst he cultivates his strength and hardens and matures his courage; all with a view of enabling him to assert his rights, and exercise a greater sway over those around him. Woman we behold dependant and weak; but out of that very weakness and dependance springs an irresistible power. She may pursue her studies too – not however with a view of triumphing in the senate chamber – not with a view to forensic display – not with a view of leading armies to combat, or of enabling her to bring into more formidable action the physical power which nature has conferred on her. No! It is but the better to perfect all those feminine graces, all those fascinating attributes, which render her the centre of attraction, and which delight and charm all those who breathe the atmosphere in which she moves [...].

Source: Thomas R. Dew (1802-1846). "Dissertation: On the Characteristic Differences between the Sexes, and on the Position and Influence of Woman in Society." *Southern Literary Messenger*, Vol. 1.9 (May 1835), 495-496.

225. Jonathan F. Stearns
Female Influence and the True Christian Mode of Its Exercise (1837)

[...] The influence of woman in forming the character of her relatives, gentle and unobserved as it is, is one which can never be adequately appreciated, till the great day of revelation shall disclose the secret springs of human action and feeling. We all know, by experience, what a charm there is in the word HOME, and how powerful are the influences of domestic life upon the character. It is the province of woman to make home, *whatever it is*. If she makes that delightful and salutary – the abode of order and purity, though she may never herself step beyond the threshold, she may yet send forth from her humble dwelling, a power that will be felt round the globe. She may at least save some souls that are dear to her from disgrace and punishment, present some precious ornaments to her country and the church, and polish some jewels, to shine brightly in the Saviour's crown. [...]

But the influence of woman is not limited to the domestic circle. *Society* is her empire, which she governs almost at will. Its nameless charms and accomplishments are chiefly the fruit of her cultivation. She is the arbitress of taste and of manners. It is her province to *adorn* social life, to throw a *charm* over the intercourse of the world, and thus to cement the bond of human fellowship, by making it lovely and attractive, pure and improving. [...]

Now to form the character of society, and give it a healthy tone, woman not only contributes, but is, as it were, the mainspring. The order and decency, the courtesy and mutual respect, which prevail in all civilized society, and distinguish it from the barbarous state, are mainly the result of her influence. Remove this, and these would soon disappear. Cherish this, and increase it, let it be *fully developed* and *rightly directed*, and scarcely one vice and evil habit would find a place in the community. This, if *any thing earthly*, must purify society, and fit it to subserve the great ends of its formation.

The cause of benevolence is peculiarly indebted to the agency of woman. She is fitted by nature to cheer the afflicted, elevate the depressed, minister to the wants of the feeble and diseased, and lighten the burden of human misery, in all its varieties and trying forms. God has endowed her with qualities peculiarly adapted to these offices; and the history of benevolence will testify how well she has fulfilled her trust. The friendless orphan blesses her. The homeless sailor, the wandering exile, the child of affliction, and even the penitent outcast, find in her a patroness and friend.

But the highest merit of all is yet to be mentioned. *Religion* seems almost to have been entrusted by its author to her particular custody. [...] It is the standing sneer of the infidel, and his last resort when arguments fail, that the religion of Christ is chiefly prevalent among women, and chiefly indebted to them for its spread. [...]

[...] When we consider what woman was in classic Greece, and what she still is, in barbarous and savage lands, darkened and degraded, without knowledge, without influence, without honor, the mere drudge of society, or still worse, the miserable slave of sensual passion; and contrast with this dark picture, the happier scenes which christianity presents, where she stands forth in her true dignity, as the *companion* and *equal* of man, his helper on earth, and co-heir of immortal felicity, we cannot wonder that *she* should exhibit peculiar attachment to a faith which has bestowed upon her such blessings. [...]

Much dispute has arisen in modern times in regard to the comparative intellectual ability of the sexes. On the one hand it has been confidently maintained, that God and nature have established a *perfect equality*; and that it is only the circumstances of habit and education which have occasioned the difference which we see. On the other, it has been asserted as confidently, that man is, by the very structure of his mind, immensely the superior, and that no change of circumstances and advantages could ever, as a general thing, render it otherwise.

Now the whole debate, as it seems to me, proceeds from a mistake. The truth is, there is a natural *difference*, in the mental as well as physical constitution of the two classes – a difference which implies not *inferiority* on the one part, but only *adaptation to a different sphere*. Cultivate as highly as you will the mind of a female, and you do not deprive it of its distinguishing peculiarities. On the other hand, deprive man of his advantages, keep him in ignorance and intellectual depression, and you make him a kind of *brute beast*, but you do not approximate his character to the character of a woman. [...]

[...] I am confident no virtuous and delicate female, who rightly appreciates the design of her being, and desires to sustain her own influence and that of her sex, and fulfil the high destiny for which she is formed, would desire to abate one jot or tittle[43] from the

---

[43] A small stroke or point in writing or printing, e.g. the dot over the letter "i;" often in the phrase "jot or tittle": a very little part, or amount.

seeming restrictions imposed upon her conduct in these and the like passages. They are designed, not to *degrade*, but to *elevate* her character, – not to cramp, but to afford a *salutary* freedom, and give a useful direction to the energies of the feminine mind. [...]

[...] Let her lay aside delicacy, and her influence over our sex is gone; all the benefits she is now so peculiarly fitted to confer on the church and the world are sacrificed, and her own honor and safety exposed to the greatest danger.

And for what object should she make such sacrifices? That she may do good more extensively? Then she sadly mistakes her vocation. But why then? That she may see her name blazoned[44] on the rolls of fame, and hear the shouts of delighted assemblies, applauding her eloquence? That she may place her own sex on a fancied equality with men, obtain the satisfaction of calling herself *independent*, and occupy a station in life which she can never adorn? For *this* would she sacrifice the almost magic power, which, in her own proper sphere, she now wields over the destinies of the world? Surely *such privileges*, obtained at *such cost*, are unworthy of a wise and virtuous woman's ambition. [...]

That there are ladies who are capable of public debate, who could make their voices heard from end to end of the church and the senate house, – that there are those who might bear a favorable comparison with others as eloquent orators, and who might speak to better edification than most of those on whom the office has hitherto devolved, I am not disposed to deny. The question is not in regard to *ability*, but to *decency*, to order, to christian *propriety*. [...]

My hearers must pardon me for speaking thus explicitly. The advocates of such principles and measures have, in times past, been confined principally to the ranks of unbelievers, whom no pious and respectable female would desire to encourage. But when popular female writers, and women professing godliness, begin to take the same ground, it is time for the pulpit as well as the press to speak plainly. I verily believe, that should the practice I have censured become *prevalent*, and the consequent change in the treatment of females, already anticipated by some of its advocates, take place in the community, the influence of ladies, now so important to the cause of philanthropy and piety, would very speedily be crushed, and religion, morality and good order, suffer a wound from which they would not soon nor easily recover. [...]

On you, ladies, depends, in a most important degree, the destiny of our country. In this day of disorder and turmoil, when the foundations of the great deep seem fast breaking up, and the flood of desolation threatening to roll over the whole face of society, it peculiarly devolves upon you to say what shall be the result. Yours it is to determine, whether the beautiful order of society [...] shall continue as it has been, to be the source of blessings to the world; or whether, despising all forms and distinctions, all boundaries and rules, society shall break up and become a chaos of disjointed and unsightly elements. Yours it is to decide, under God, whether we shall be a nation of refined and high minded christians, or whether, rejecting the civilities of life, and throwing off the restraints of morality and piety, we shall become a fierce race of semi-barbarians, before whom neither order, nor honor, nor chastity can stand.

And be assured, ladies, if the hedges and borders of the social garden should be broken up, the lovely vine, which now twines itself so gracefully upon the trellis, and bears such rich clusters, will be the first to fall and be trodden under foot. [...]

---

[44] To depict or paint according to the rules of heraldry.

Source: Jonathan F. Stearns (1808-1889). *Female Influence and the True Christian Mode of Its Exercise: A Discourse Delivered in the First Presbyterian Church in Newburyport, July 30, 1837*. Newburyport: John G. Tilton, 1837, 8-14, 17-20, 23-24.

226. Lydia Sigourney
Letters to Mothers (1838)

My Friend, if in becoming a mother, you have reached the climax of your happiness, you have also taken a higher place in the scale of being. A most important part is allotted you, in the economy of the great human family. Look at the gradations of your way onward, – your doll, your playmates, your lessons, – perhaps to decorate a beautiful person, – to study the art of pleasing, – to exult in your own attractions, – to feed on adulation, – to wear the garland of love; – and then to introduce into existence a being never to die; – and to feel your highest, holiest energies enlisted to fit it for this world and the next.

No longer will you now live for self, – no longer be noteless and unrecorded, passing away without name or memorial among the people. [...] In bequeathing your own likeness to the world, you will naturally be anxious to array it in that beauty of virtue, which fades not at the touch of time. What a scope for your exertions, to render your representative, an honour to its parentage, and a blessing to its country.

You have gained an increase of power. The influence which is most truly valuable, is that of mind over mind. How entire and perfect is this dominion, over the unformed character of your infant. Write what you will, upon the printless tablet, with your wand of love. [...]

What an appeal to mothers! What an acknowledgement of the dignity of their office! The aid of the "weaker vessel," is now invoked by legislation and sages. It has been discovered that there are signs of disease in the body politick, which can be best allayed, by the subordination taught in families, and through her agency to whom is committed the "moulding of the whole mass of mind in its first formation." [...]

It seems now to be conceded, that the vital interests of our country, may be aided by the zeal of mothers. Exposed as it is, to the influx of untutored foreigners, often unfit for its institutions, or adverse to their spirit, it seems to have been made a repository for the waste and refuse of other nations. To neutralize this mass, to rule its fermentations, to prevent it from becoming a lava-stream in the garden of liberty, and to purify it for those channels where the life-blood of the nation circulates, is a work of power and peril. The force of public opinion, or the terror of law, must hold in check these elements of danger, until Education can restore them to order and beauty. Insubordination is becoming a prominent feature in some of our principal cities. Obedience in families, respect to magistrates, and love of country, should therefore be inculcated with increased energy, by those who have earliest access to the mind. A barrier to the torrent of corruption, and a guard over the strong holds of knowledge and of virtue, may be placed by the mother, as she watches over her cradled son. Let her come forth with vigour and vigilance, at the call of her country, not like Boadicea[45] in her chariot, but like the mother of Washington,

---

[45] Boadicea, or Boudicca meaning Victorious, was Queen of the Iceni tribe of East Anglia. She led a bloody rebellion in 60 AD against the Romans, but was eventually defeated by the Romans, and rather than be humiliated by them, she poisoned herself.

feeling that the first lesson to every incipient ruler should be, *"how to obey."* The degree of her diligence in preparing her children to be good subjects of a just government, will be the true measure of her patriotism. While she labours to pour a pure and heavenly spirit into the hearts that open around her, she knows not but she may be appointed to rear some future statesman, for her nation's helm, or priest for the temple of Jehovah.

Source: L. H. [Lydia Howard] Sigourney (1791-1865). *Letters to Mothers.* Hartford, CT: Hudson & Skinner, 1838), 9-10, 12-15.

227. Heman Humphrey
Domestic Education (1840)

[...] Families, are so many divinely instituted and independent communities, upon the well ordering of which, the most momentous interests of the church and the state, of time and eternity are suspended. The relation between parents and children, and the obligations growing out of it, are elementary and fundamental. They lie at the foundation of all virtue, of all social happiness, and of all good government. Were some great convulsion suddenly to subvert the political institutions of a state, without breaking up its families, those institutions might, under the same or modified forms, soon be re-established; but let the sacred ties of husband and wife, parent and child, brother and sister, once be severed; let these elements of social order be driven asunder and scattered, and it would be impossible, out of such materials, ever to reconstruct any tolerable form of civil government. It would be like dissolving the attraction of cohesion in every substance upon the face of the earth. What human power and skill could ever, after that, build a city, or even erect the humblest human habitation?

Every family is a little state, or empire within itself, bound together by the most endearing attractions, and governed by its patriarchal head, with whose prerogative no power on earth has a right to interfere. Nations may change their forms of government at pleasure, and may enjoy a high degree of prosperity under different constitutions; and perhaps the time will never come, when any *one* form will be adapted to the circumstances of all mankind. But in the family organization there is but one model, for all times and all places. It is just the same now, as it was in the beginning, and it is impossible to alter it, without marring its beauty, and directly contravening the wisdom and benevolence of the Creator. It is at once the simplest, the safest and the most efficient organization that can be conceived of. Like everything else, it may be perverted to bad purposes; but it is a divine model, and must not be altered.

Every father is the constituted head and ruler of his household. God has made him the supreme earthly legislator over his children, accountable, of course, to Himself, for the manner in which he executes his trust; but amenable to no other power, except in the most extreme cases of neglect, or abuse. The will of the parent is the law to which the child is bound in all cases to submit, unless it plainly contravenes the law of God. Children are brought into existence and placed in families, not to follow their own wayward inclinations, but to look up to their parents for guidance; not to teach, but to be taught; not to govern but to be governed. [...]

[...] Children must be prepared to reverence the majesty of the laws, and to yield a prompt obedience to the civil magistrate, by habitual subjection to their parents. If they are not governed in the family, they will be restive under all the wholesome and necessary restraints of after life; and the freer the form of government is, in any state, the more necessary is it that parents should fit their children "to lead quiet and peaceable lives in all godliness and honesty" under it, by a proper course of domestic training. We cannot, in this country, hope to preserve and hand down our free and glorious institutions in any other way. To remain free, the mass of the people must be virtuous and enlightened; and to this end, domestic education, including all suitable restraints and discipline, must engage the earnest attention of heads of families throughout the land. It has been said a thousand times, that the practicability of maintaining a highly republican form of government has been *tried* and is *settled* in the United States, however it may have failed everywhere else. I wish it were so: but I am afraid the question is settled, so far *only* as we have gone. What the future may disclose, who can certainly tell? It is yet a grand desideratum, whether we have religion and virtue and intelligence enough to sustain our blessed institutions. The danger is, that our liberties will degenerate into licentiousness, and that the growing laxity of family government in this country will hasten on the fearful crisis. There is, if I am not deceived, a reaction in our unparalleled political freedom, upon our domestic relations. It is more difficult than it was, half, or even a quarter of a century ago, for parents to "command their household after them." Our children hear so much about liberty and equality, and are so often told how glorious it is to be "born free and equal," that it is hard work to make them understand for what good reason their liberties are abridged in the family; and I have no doubt this accounts, in multitudes of instances, for the reluctance with which they submit to parental authority. The boy wants to be "his own man," long before his wisdom teeth are cut; and the danger lies in conceding the point to him under the notion, that our fathers were quite too rigid and that a more indulgent domestic policy, corresponding with the "spirit of the age," is better. This may be the way to make *rulers* enough for a hundred republics; but not to make a single good *subject.* I repeat, therefore, that if it is important to secure a prompt obedience to the wholesome laws of the state, then is family government indispensably necessary, and the father who takes no care to control his own sons, is not himself a patriot, if he is a good citizen.

Moreover, without family government there will be very little *self-government* in any community. If you do not restrain the waywardness of your child, in its early developments, and thus assist him to get the mastery of it while yet the conquest is comparatively easy, it will be in vain for you to expect him ever to gain that self-control which is so essential to his happiness and safety. [...]

Source: Heman Humphrey (1779-1861). *Domestic Education.* Amherst, MA: J.S. & C. Adams, 1840, 15-16, 22-23.

228. Lewis Jacob Cist
"Original. Woman's Sphere" (1845)

Inscribed to Miss A. B.

"She filled her woman's sphere on earth."

"Her woman's sphere!" – and tell us, thou
To whom our hearts in reverence bow –
    Thou who so well dost fill it here –
Say how could nobler sphere be given
This side the white-robed choirs of heaven,
    Than, rightly filled, is "woman's sphere?"
Where lieth woman's sphere? – Not there,
Where strife and fierce contentions are;
Not in the bloody battle-field,
With sword and helmet, lance and shield;
Not in the wild and angry crowd,
Mid threat'nings high, and clamors loud;
Not in the halls of rude debate
And legislation, is *her* seat;
Nor yet in scenes of weak display –
Of vanity, with its array
Of pride and selfishness – not *here*,
Lieth *true-hearted* "Woman's Sphere!"

What then *is* "woman's sphere?" – The sweet
    And quiet precincts of her home;
Home! – where the blest affections meet,
    Where strife and hatred may not come!
Home! – sweetest word in mother-tongue,
Long since in verse undying sung!
Home! – of her holiest hopes the shrine,
Around which all her heart-strings twine!
There, loved and loving – safe from fear,
Lies ever woman's noblest sphere!
There hers it is a power to wield,
To which the warrior's lance and shield,
Helmet and sword, are powerless –
The god-like gift to save and bless!
To save – the erring from his sin,
And back to paths of virtue win;
To bless – in every stage of life,
As Mother – Daughter – Sister – Wife!

As Mother! – Sweet and holy tie,
First known, best loved in infancy! –
From her our vital breath we draw,

Her gentle looks our infant law;
Her love our refuge in alarm;
Her watchful care our shield from harm;
Her lessons the first precepts given
To form for earth and fit for heaven;
Her love – unselfish, ever known
To seek our interest, not her own–
Through all this changing scene extends:
With life begun – with death but ends!

AS DAUGHTER! – 'Tis upon her laid
To be the aged mother's aid;
In one, the varied ties to blend
Of child, companion, helper, friend;
Repay in thousand gentle ways,
The love that crowned her childish days;
From thousand cares of age to save,
And smooth life's pathway to the grave:
And Heaven's benignest gifts are shed
Ever on such a daughter's head!

AS SISTER! – He who doth not prove
    Her kindness, cannot know its worth!
How all unselfish that pure love
    That in a sister's heart hath birth!
Playmate! companion up from youth!
    Gentle and sympathizing friend!
Whose lips like hers, with faithful truth,
    So well can kind persuasion blend?
Thou who hast such – that long on earth
    She may be spared thee, kneel and pray!
Such too had I – nor knew her worth,
    Till she was called from earth away!
A pious sister! who can tell
    How oft to her it may be given,
To save a brother's feet from hell –
    To lead his wandering steps to heaven!

But more than all 'tis hers, as WIFE!
    To wield her mightiest influence still;
To check and temper manhood's strife,
    And mold his purpose to her will:
For where is he who does not feel
That he could easier burst through steel,
Than wound that fond and faithful heart,
Of his *own more than self*, a part –
Or spurn the gentle thraldom known
To seek *his* happiness alone!

> O! woman hath, in every phase,
> Controlling influence o'er our ways;
> But chief, as man's companion high,
> 'Tis hers to guide his destiny:
> And from that day our parents erst
>   Were driven from Eden's blissful shade –
> When both had fall'n – yet woman *first*,
>   Man by *her* weakness then betrayed –
> All potent still, for good or ill,
> Hath been the force of woman's will;
> And mightier, with each added year,
> Grows WOMAN'S POWER, in WOMAN'S SPHERE!

Source: Lewis Jacob Cist (1818-1885). "Original. Woman's Sphere." *The Ladies' Repository, and Gatherings of the West* 5 (April 1845), 104.

229. Anonymous
"Influence of Woman. – Past and Present" (1840)

IT has ever been acknowledged by the reflecting and the wise, that the power possessed and wielded by woman, is great, and to be used or abused for the good or evil of mankind. States revolutionized, cities burnt, kings dethroned, empires overthrown, unite to prove it true. In the page of history her name is indellibly written, whether it be for superiority in virtue or crime; whether it be for the admiration or detestation of a world! There it is stamped – let us deeply ponder upon it! Numberless are the examples in the lessons of the past, which, in tones of fearful warning, speak to the hearts of all – "Beware!"

On the other hand, we may be strengthened in the exercise of every virtue, by the contemplation of those beautiful traits of character, those high heroic actions of the buried past, which, amid the surrounding gloom, with an undying, unwavering brilliancy, "burns throughout all Time."

A Nero was formed by the pernicious counsels of woman; an Antony lost the world by the persuasive arts and beauty of a Cleopatra. A woman stepped forth in the hour of her country's peril, breathed hope in the hearts of despairing warriors, and led them forth to conquer. Victory perched upon her banners, and the Maid of Orleans[46] received the crown of martyrdom! And who could have caused the desolation of the fatal night of blood,[47] when the guardian genius of France slumbered; when the alarm rang in the midnight air, and the shrieks of the living were mingled with the agonizing groans of the dying, "piercing the dull ear of night?" Who, but woman, base, unprincipled, ambitious woman? Who, but a Catharine de Medici, could thus have played upon the passions of a weak son, and caused him to shed the blood of thousands of Huguenots, to gratify her love of power? Another form rises before me, but how unlike the former. Isabella of

---

[46] Jeanne d'Arc, national heroine of France.
[47] The Massacre of St. Bartholomew's Day (August 24/25, 1572). Massacre of French Huguenots (Protestants) in Paris plotted by Catharine de Medici and carried out by Roman Catholic nobles.

Castile,[48] I hail thee! Patroness and friend of the great "world-finder,"[49] thy name ever be honored! The influence of thy friendship shall be felt, 'till the world is not. The maiden monarch of England,[50] too, though arbitrary and severe in her government, and her fame stained with a dark spot which can never be effaced, yet gave an impulse to commerce and industry, which is still felt throughout the world. *She* showed what woman can do when possessed of power to sway the destinies of a mighty people! [...]

[...] That age is past – its ideas, prejudices, feelings with it "in the deep ocean buried." Now intellect, genius, assert their independence, and here, again, woman, Proteus-like, assumes a new form of influence. Splendid have been the creations of her mind. Released from the arbitrary fetters which had, for ages, bound it, the wing of Genius soars in power Omnipotent. Need we point to a Siddons, a Baillie, a More, an Edgeworth,[51] names which dare compare with the noblest of man's, in their respective walks? These, and hundreds of others exercise a vast amount of influence over the present age, which will be carried far into the future. Education has, indeed, done wonders for the sex. But religion has done still more; it has taught them to look beyond this life, which is but preparatory to another; as a state of probation, where we are all placed to aid one another with counsel and comfort. And it is in this, woman should find the proper exercise of her faculties. Far retired from the busy highways of Ambition, she should wander in the shady, green lanes of domestic life. It should be hers to cheer the drooping head of Sickness, and pour balm into the bosom of the wretched. To seek out the abodes of Poverty, and cheer their inmates with aid, advice and sympathy. To welcome to the quiet hearth, the partner of her joys and sorrows, when worn and weary with the world's conflict; to rear her offsprings in the fear of God, and love of every thing good and holy. These are duties which every woman of the present day is bound to perform. Unseen, unfelt, she extends her influence far and wide. She is forming the future patriot, statesman, or enemy of his country; more than this, she is sowing the seeds of virtue or vice, which will fit him for Heaven, or for eternal misery. Noble, sublime, is the task of the American mother – see that it be well performed.

Mother of Washington! would thy name could be sounded with a trumpet's voice throughout the land! Would that the women of our beloved country emulated thy virtues and glorious example, to rear their children as "wisely and as well." Then would Columbia be indeed the land of heroes, not such as the old world saw, "basely trampling" on the sacred rights of humanity, but a race born to bless – to humanize the world!

Source: Anonymous, "Influence of Woman. – Past and Present." *The Ladies' Companion, a Monthly Magazine; Devoted to Literature and the Fine Arts* 13 (September 1840), 245f.

---

[48] Isabella I, Queen of Castile (1474–1504) and of Aragon (1479–1504), ruling the two kingdoms jointly from 1479 with her husband, Ferdinand II of Aragon.
[49] Christopher Columbus.
[50] Elizabeth I, Queen of England (1558-1603).
[51] Sarah Siddons (1755-1831), one of the greatest English tragic actresses; Lady Grizel Baillie (1665-1746), Scottish poetess; Hannah More (1745-1833), British writer; Maria Edgeworth (1767-1849), Anglo-Irish writer.

230. Anonymous
"Pastoral Letter of the Massachusetts Congregationalist Clergy" (1837)

PASTORAL LETTER.
The General Association of Massachusetts to the churches under their care.

[...] III. We invite your attention to the dangers which at present seem to threaten the female character, with wide spread and permanent injury.

The appropriate duties and influence of women are clearly stated in the New Testament. Those duties and that influence are unobtrusive and private, but the sources of mighty power. When the mild, dependant, softening influence of woman upon the sternness of man's opinions is fully exercised, society feels the effects of it in a thousand forms. The power of woman is in her dependence, flowing from the consciousness of that weakness which God has given her for her protection, and which keeps her in those departments of life that form the character of individuals and of the nation. There are social influences which females use in promoting piety and the great objects of Christian benevolence which we cannot too highly commend. We appreciate the unostentatious prayers and efforts of woman in advancing the cause of religion at home and abroad; in Sabbath schools; in leading religious inquirers to the pastors for instruction; [...] and in all such associated effort as becomes the modesty of her sex; and earnestly hope that she may abound more and more in these labors of piety and love.

But when she assumes the place and tone of man as a public reformer, our care and protection of her seem unnecessary; we put ourselves in self-defence against her; she yields the power which God has given her for protection, and her character becomes unnatural. If the vine, whose strength and beauty is to lean upon the trellis work[52] and half conceal its clusters, thinks to assume the independence and the overshading nature of the elm, it will not only cease to bear fruit, but fall in shame and dishonor into the dust. We cannot, therefore, but regret the mistaken conduct of those who encourage females to bear an obtrusive and ostentatious part in measures of reform, and countenance any of that sex who so far forget themselves as to itinerate in the character of public lecturers and teachers. – We especially deplore the intimate acquaintance and promiscuous conversation of females with regard to things 'which ought not to be named;' by which that modesty and delicacy which is the charm of domestic life, and which constitutes the true influence of woman in society is consumed, and the way opened, as we apprehend, for degeneracy and ruin. We say these things, not to discourage proper influences against sin, but to secure such reformation as we believe is Scriptural, and will be permanent. [...]

Source: Anonymous. "Pastoral Letter." *The Liberator* 7 (August 11, 1837), 1.

---

[52] Wood or metal work consisting of light cross-bars.

231. Sarah Moore Grimké
"Province of Woman: The Pastoral Letter" (1837)

Haverhill, 7th Mo.

DEAR FRIEND, – When I last addressed thee, I had not seen the Pastoral Letter of the General Association. It has since fallen into my hands, and is, I think, so extraordinary a document, that when the minds of men and women become emancipated from the thraldom of superstition, and 'traditions of men,' it will be recurred to with as much astonishment as the opinions of Cotton Mather and other distinguished men of his day, on the subject of witchcraft [...].

But to the [Pastoral] letter: it says, 'we invite your attention to the dangers which at present seem to threaten the FEMALE CHARACTER with wide-spread and permanent injury.' I rejoice that they have called the attention of my sex to this subject, because I believe if woman investigates it, she will soon discover that danger is impending, though from a totally different source from that which the Association apprehends, – danger from those who, having long held the reins of *usurped* authority, are unwilling to permit us to fill that sphere which God created us to move in, and who have entered into league to crush the immortal mind of woman. I rejoice, because I am persuaded that the rights of woman, like the rights of slaves, need only be examined, to be understood and asserted, even by some of those who are now endeavoring to smother the irrepressible desire for mental and spiritual freedom which glows in the breast of many who hardly dare to speak their sentiments.

'The appropriate duties and influence of woman are clearly stated in the New Testament. Those duties are unobtrusive and private, but the sources of *mighty power*. When the mild, *dependent*, softening influence of woman upon the sternness of man's opinions, is fully exercised, society feels the effects of it in a thousand ways.' No one can desire more earnestly than I do, that woman may move exactly in the sphere which her Creator has assigned her; and I believe her having been displaced from that sphere, has introduced confusion into the world. It is therefore of vast importance to herself, and to all the rational creation, that she should ascertain what are her duties and her privileges as a responsible and immortal being. The New Testament has been referred to, and I am willing to abide by its decisions, and must enter my protest against the false translations of some passages by the MEN who did that work, and against the perverted interpretation by the MEN who undertook to write commentaries thereon. I am inclined to think, when we are admitted to the honor of studying Greek and Hebrew, we shall produce some various readings of the Bible, a little different from those we now have.

I find the Lord Jesus defining the duties of his followers in his sermon on the Mount, laying down grand principles by which they should be governed, without any reference to sect or condition: – 'Ye are the light of the world. A city that is set on a hill cannot be hid. Neither do men light a candle and put it under a bushel, but on a candlestick, and it giveth light unto all that are in the house. Let your light so shine before men, that they may see your good works, and glorify your Father which is in heaven.'[53] I follow him through all his precepts, and find him giving the same directions to women as to men, never even referring to the distinction now so strenuously insisted upon between mascu-

---

[53] Matt. 5.14-16.

line and feminine virtues: this is one of the anti-christian 'traditions of men' which are taught instead of the 'commandments of God.' Men and women were CREATED EQUAL: they are both moral and accountable beings, and whatever is right for man to do, is right for woman to do.

But the influence of woman, says the Association, is to be private and unobtrusive; her light is not to shine before man like that of her brethren; but she is passively to let the lords of the creation, as they call themselves, put the bushel over it, lest peradventure it might appear that the world has been benefitted by the rays of her candle. Then her quenched light is of more use than if it were set on the candlestick: – 'Her influence is the source of mighty power.' This has ever been the language of man since he laid aside the whip as a means to keep woman in subjection. He spares her body, but the war he has waged against her mind, her heart, and her soul, has been no less destructive to her as a moral being. How monstrous is the doctrine that woman is to be dependent on man! Where in all the sacred scriptures is this taught? But, alas, she has too well learned the lesson which he has labored to teach her. She has surrendered her dearest RIGHTS, and been satisfied with the privileges which man has assumed to grant her; whilst he has amused her with the show of power, and absorbed all the reality into himself. He has adorned the creature, whom God gave him as a companion, with baubles and gewgaws, turned her attention to personal attractions, offered incense to her vanity, and made her the instrument of his selfish gratification, a plaything to please his eye, and amuse his hours of leisure. – 'Rule by obedience, and by submission sway,' or in other words, study to be a hypocrite, pretend to submit, but gain your point, has been the code of household morality which woman has been taught. The poet has sung in sickly strains the loveliness of woman's dependence upon man, and now we find it re-echoed by those who profess to teach the religion of the Bible. God says, 'Cease ye from man whose breath is in his nostrils, for wherein is he to be accounted of?'[54] Man says, depend upon me. God says, 'He will teach us of his ways.'[55] Man says, believe it not; I am to be your teacher. This doctrine of dependence upon man is utterly at variance with the doctrine of the Bible. In that book I find nothing like the softness of woman, nor the sternness of man; both are equally commanded to bring forth the fruits of the Spirit – Love, meekness, gentleness.

But we are told, 'the power of woman is in her dependence, flowing from a consciousness of that weakness which God has given her for her protection.' If physical weakness is alluded to, I cheerfully concede the superiority; if brute force is what my brethren are claiming, I am willing to let them have all the honor they desire: but if they mean to intimate that mental or moral weakness belongs to woman more than to man, I utterly disclaim the charge; our powers of mind have been crushed, as far as man could do it, our sense of morality has been impaired by his interpretation of our duties, but no where does God say that he made any distinction between us as moral and intelligent beings. [...]

Source: Sarah Moore Grimké (1792-1873). "Province of Woman: The Pastoral Letter." *The Liberator* 7 (October 6, 1837), 1.

---

[54] Isa. 2.22.
[55] Isa. 2.3; Mic. 4.2.

232. Sarah Moore Grimké
"Letter IV: Social Intercourse of the Sexes" (1837)

Andover, 7th Mo. 27th, 1837.

MY DEAR FRIEND, – Before I proceed with the account of that oppression which woman has suffered in every age and country from her *protector*, man, permit me to offer for your consideration, some views relative to the social intercourse of the sexes. Nearly the whole of this intercourse is, in my apprehension, derogatory to man and woman, as moral and intellectual beings. We approach each other, and mingle with each other, under the constant pressure of a feeling that we are of different sexes; and, instead of regarding each other only in the light of immortal creatures, the mind is fettered by the idea which is early and industriously infused into it, that we must never forget the distinction between male and female. Hence our intercourse, instead of being elevated and refined, is generally calculated to excite and keep alive the lowest propensities of our nature. Nothing, I believe, has tended more to destroy the true dignity of woman, than the fact that she is approached by man in the character of a female. The idea that she is sought as an intelligent and heaven-born creature, whose society will cheer, refine and elevate her companion, and that she will receive the same blessings she confers, is rarely held up to her view. On the contrary, man almost always addresses himself to the weakness of woman. By flattery, by an appeal to her passions, he seeks access to her heart; and when he has gained her affections, he uses her as the instrument of his pleasure – the minister of his temporal comfort. He furnishes himself with a housekeeper, whose chief business is in the kitchen, or the nursery. And whilst he goes abroad and enjoys the means of improvement afforded by collision of intellect with cultivated minds, his wife is condemned to draw nearly all her instruction from books, if she has time to peruse them; and if not, from her meditations, whilst engaged in those domestic duties, which are necessary for the comfort of her lord and master.

Surely no one who contemplates, with the eye of a Christian philosopher, the design of God in the creation of woman, can believe that she is now fulfilling that design. The literal translation of the word 'help-meet'[56] is a helper like unto himself; it is so rendered in the Septuagint,[57] and manifestly signifies a companion. Now I believe it will be impossible for woman to fill the station assigned her by God, until her brethren mingle with her as an equal, as a moral being; and lose, in the dignity of her immortal nature, and in the fact of her bearing like himself the image and superscription of her God, the idea of her being a female. [...] Man has inflicted an unspeakable injury upon woman, by holding up to her view her animal nature, and placing in the back ground her moral and intellectual being. Woman has inflicted an injury upon herself by submitting to be thus regarded; and she is now called upon to rise from the station where *man*, not God, has placed her, and claim those sacred and inalienable rights, as a moral and responsible being, with which her Creator has invested her. [...]

Source: Sarah Moore Grimké (1792-1873). "Letter IV: Social Intercourse of the Sexes." *The Liberator* 8 (January 12, 1838), 8.

---

[56] Cf. Gen. 2.18.
[57] Earliest extant Greek translation of the Old Testament from the original Hebrew, dating from the 3rd and 2nd centuries BC.

233. Angelina Emily Grimké
Letters to Catherine E. Beecher (1837)

LETTER XI.
THE SPHERE OF WOMAN AND MAN AS MORAL BEINGS THE SAME.

BROOKLINE, Mass. 8th *month*, 28th, 1837.

DEAR FRIEND: I come now to that part of thy book, which is, of all others, the most important to the women of this country; thy 'general views in relation to the place woman is appointed to fill by the dispensations of heaven.' I shall quote paragraphs from thy book, offer my objections to them, and then throw before thee my own views.

Thou sayest, 'Heaven has appointed to one sex the *superior*, and to the other the *subordinate* station, and this without any reference to the character or conduct of either.' This is an assertion without proof. Thou further sayest, that 'it was designed that the mode of gaining influence and exercising power should be *altogether different and peculiar*.' Does the Bible teach this? 'Peace on earth, and good will to men, is the character of all the rights and privileges, the influence and the power of *woman*.' Indeed! Did our Holy Redeemer preach the doctrines of *peace to our sex* only? [...] If so, I should come to a very different conclusion from the one at which thou hast arrived: I should suppose that *woman was the superior*, and *man the subordinate being*, inasmuch as moral power is immeasurably superior to 'physical force.' [...]

Thou sayest, 'the moment woman begins to feel the promptings of ambition, or the thirst for power, her ægis of defence is gone.' Can man, then, retain his ægis when he indulges these guilty passions? Is it woman only who suffers this loss?

'All the generous promptings of chivalry, all the poetry of romantic gallantry, depend upon woman's retaining her place as *dependent* and *defenceless*, and making no claims, and maintaining no rights, but what are the gifts of honor, rectitude and love.'

I cannot refrain from pronouncing this sentiment as beneath the dignity of any woman who names the name of Christ. No woman, who understands her dignity as a moral, intellectual, and accountable being, cares aught for any attention or any protection, vouchsafed by 'the promptings of chivalry, and the poetry of romantic gallantry'? Such a one loathes such littleness, and turns with disgust from all such silly insipidities. Her noble nature is insulted by such paltry, sickening adulation, and she will not stoop to drink the foul waters of so turbid a stream. If all this sinful foolery is to be withdrawn from our sex, with all my heart I say, *the sooner the better*. Yea, I say more, no woman who lives up to the true glory of her womanhood, will ever be treated with such *practical contempt*. Every man, when in the presence of true moral greatness, 'will find an influence thrown around him,' which will utterly forbid the exercise of 'the poetry of romantic gallantry.' [...]

'A woman may seek the aid of co-operation and combination among her own sex, to assist her in her appropriate offices of piety, charity,' &c. *Appropriate* offices! Ah! here is the great difficulty. What are they? Who can point them out? Who has ever attempted to draw a line of separation between the duties of men and women, as *moral* beings, without committing the grossest inconsistencies on the one hand, or running into the most arrant absurdities or the other?

'Whatever, in any measure, throws a woman into the attitude of a combatant, either for herself or others – whatever binds her in a party conflict – whatever obliges her in any way to exert coercive influences, throws her out of her appropriate sphere.' If, by a *combatant*, thou meanest one who 'drives by *physical force*,' then I say, *man* has no more right to appear as *such* a combatant than woman; for all the pacific precepts of the gospel were given to *him*, as well as to her. If, by a *party conflict*, thou meanest a struggle for power, either civil or ecclesiastical, a thirst for the praise and the honor of man, why, then I would ask, is this the proper sphere of *any* moral, accountable being, man or woman? If, by *coercive influences*, thou meanest the use of force or of fear, such as slaveholders and warriors employ, then, I repeat, that *man* has no more right to exert these than *woman*. All such influences are repudiated by the precepts and examples of Christ, and his apostles; so that, after all, this appropriate sphere of woman is *just as appropriate to man*. These 'general principles are correct,' if thou wilt only permit them to be of *general application*. [...]

[...] The right of petition is the only political right that women have: why not let them exercise it whenever they are aggrieved? Our fathers waged a bloody conflict with England, because *they* were taxed without being represented. This is just what unmarried women of property now are. *They* were not willing to be governed by laws which *they* had no voice in making; but this is the way in which women are governed in this Republic. If, then, *we* are taxed without being represented, and governed by laws *we* have no voice in framing, then, surely, we ought to be permitted at least to remonstrate against 'every political measure that may tend to injure and oppress our sex in various parts of the nation, and under the various public measures that may hereafter be enforced.' Why not? Art thou afraid to trust the women of this country with discretionary power as to petitioning? Is there not sound principle and common sense enough among them, to regulate the exercise of this right? I believe they will always use it wisely. I am not afraid to trust my sisters – not I. [...]

LETTER XII.
HUMAN RIGHTS NOT FOUNDED ON SEX.
EAST BOYLSTON, Mass. 10th mo. 2^{d}, 1837.

DEAR FRIEND: [...]
The investigation of the rights of the slave has led me to a better understanding of my own. I have found the Anti-Slavery cause to be the high school of morals in our land – the school in which *human rights* are more fully investigated, and better understood and taught, than in any other. Here a great fundamental principle is uplifted and illuminated, and from this central light, rays innumerable stream all around. Human beings have *rights*, because they are *moral* beings: the rights of *all* men grow out of their moral nature; and as all men have the same moral nature, they have essentially the same rights. These rights may be wrested from the slave, but they cannot be alienated: his title to himself is as perfect *now*, as is that of Lyman Beecher: it is stamped on his moral being, and is, like it, imperishable. Now if rights are founded in the nature of our moral being, then the *mere circumstance of sex* does not give to man higher rights and responsibilities, than to woman. To suppose that it does, would be to deny the self-evident truth, that the 'physical constitution is the mere instrument of the moral nature.' To suppose that it does, would be to break up utterly the relations, of the two natures, and to reverse their functions, exalting the animal nature into a monarch, and humbling the moral into a slave; making the former a proprietor, and the latter its property. When human beings are regarded as *moral* beings, *sex*, instead of being enthroned upon the summit, administering

upon rights and responsibilities, sinks into insignificance and nothingness. My doctrine then is, that whatever it is morally right for man to do, it is morally right for woman to do. Our duties originate, not from difference of sex, but from the diversity of our relations in life, the various gifts and talents committed to our care, and the different eras in which we live.

This regulation of duty by the mere circumstance of sex, rather than by the fundamental principle of moral being, has led to all that multifarious train of evils flowing out of the anti-christian doctrine of masculine and feminine virtues. By this doctrine, man has been converted into the warrior, and clothed with sternness, and those other kindred qualities, which in common estimation belong to his character as a *man*; whilst woman has been taught to lean upon an arm of flesh, to sit as a doll arrayed in 'gold, and pearls, and costly array,'[58] to be admired for her personal charms, and caressed and humored like a spoiled child, or converted into a mere drudge to suit the convenience of her lord and master. [...] This principle has given to man a charter for the exercise of tyranny and selfishness, pride and arrogance, lust and brutal violence. It has robbed woman of essential rights, the right to think and speak and act on all great moral questions, just as men think and speak and act; the right to share their responsibilities, perils and toils; the right to fulfil the great end of her being, as a moral, intellectual and immortal creature, and of glorifying God in her body and her spirit which are His. Hitherto, instead of being a help meet to man, in the highest, noblest sense of the term, as a companion, a co-worker, an equal; she has been a mere appendage of his being, an instrument of his convenience and pleasure, the pretty toy with which he wiled away his leisure moments, or the pet animal whom he humored into playfulness and submission. Woman, instead of being regarded as the equal of man, has uniformly been looked down upon as his inferior, a mere gift to fill up the measure of his happiness. In 'the poetry of romantic gallantry,' it is true, she has been called 'the last *best* gift of God to man;'[59] but I believe I speak forth the words of truth and soberness when I affirm, that woman never was given to man. She was created, like him, in the image of God, and crowned with glory and honor; created only a little lower than the angels, – not, as is almost universally assumed, a little lower than man; on her brow, as well as on his, was placed the 'diadem of beauty,'[60] and in her hand the sceptre of universal dominion. [...]

Thou sayest, 'an ignorant, a narrow-minded, or a stupid woman, cannot feel nor understand the rationality, the propriety, or the beauty of this relation' – i.e. subordination to man. Now, verily, it does appear to me, that nothing but a narrow-minded view of the subject of human rights and responsibilities can induce any one to believe in *this subordination to a fallible* being. Sure I am, that the signs of the times clearly indicate a vast and rapid change in public sentiment, on this subject. Sure I am that she is not to be, as she has been, '*a mere second-hand agent*' in the regeneration of a fallen world, but the acknowledged equal and co-worker with man in this glorious work. Not that 'she will carry her measures by tormenting when she cannot please, or by petulant complaints or obtrusive interference, in matters which are out of her sphere, and which she cannot comprehend.' But just in proportion as her moral and intellectual capacities become enlarged, she will rise higher and higher in the scale of creation, until she reaches that elevation prepared for her by her Maker, and upon whose summit she was originally stationed, only 'a

---

[58] 1 Tim. 2.9.
[59] John Milton, *Paradise Lost*, Book 5
[60] Isa. 28.5

little lower than the angels.'⁶¹ Then will it be seen that nothing which concerns the well-being of mankind is either beyond her sphere, or above her comprehension: *Then* will it be seen 'that America will be distinguished above all other nations for well educated women, and for the influence they will exert on the general interests of society.' [...]

Source: Angelina Emily Grimké (1805-1879). *Letters to Catherine E. Beecher, in Reply to an Essay on Slavery and Abolitionism, Addressed to A.E. Grimké.* Boston: I. Knapp, 1838, 103-104, 106-109, 112, 114-117, 120-121.

234. Anonymous
"Woman" (1841)

There have been no topics, for the last two years, more generally talked of than woman, and "the sphere of woman." In society, everywhere, we hear the same oft-repeated things said upon them by those who have little perception of the difficulties of the subject; and even the clergy have frequently flattered "the feebler sex," by proclaiming to them from the pulpit what lovely things they may become, if they will only be good, quiet, and gentle, attend exclusively to their domestic duties, and the cultivation of religious feelings, which the other sex very kindly relinquish to them as their inheritance. Such preaching is very popular!

Blessed indeed would that man be, who could penetrate the difficulties of this subject, and tell the world faithfully and beautifully what new thing he has discovered about it, or what old truth he has brought to light. The poet's lovely vision of an etherial being, hovering half seen above him, in his hour of occupation, and gliding gently into his retirement, sometimes a guardian angel, sometimes an unobtrusive companion, wrapt in a silvery veil of mildest radiance, his idealized Eve or Ophelia, is an exquisite picture for the eye; the sweet verse in which he tells us of her, most witching music to the ear; but she is not woman, she is only the spiritualized image of that tender class of women he loves the best, – one whom no true woman could or would become; and if the poet could ever be unkind, we should deem him most so when he reproves the sex, planted as it is in the midst of wearing cares and perplexities, for its departure from this high, beatified ideal of his, to which he loves to give the name of woman. Woman may be soothed by his sweet numbers, but she cannot be helped by his counsels, for he knows her not as she is and must be. All adjusting of the whole sex to a sphere is vain, for no two persons naturally have the same. Character, intellect creates the sphere of each. What is individual and peculiar to each determines it. We hear a great deal everywhere of the religious duties of women. That heaven has placed man and woman in different positions, given them different starting points, (for what is the whole of life, with its varied temporal relations, but a starting point,) there can be no doubt; but religion belongs to them as beings, not as male and female. The true teacher addresses the same language to both. Christ did so, and this separation is ruinous to the highest improvement of both. Difference of position surely does not imply different qualities of head and heart, for the same qualities, as we see every day, are demanded in a variety of positions, the variety merely giving them a different direction.

As we hear a great deal in society, and from the pulpit, of the religious duties of women, so do we hear a great deal of the contemplative life they lead, or ought to lead. It

---
⁶¹ Cf. Ps. 8.5; Heb. 2.7-9.

seems an unknown, or at least an unacknowledged fact, that in the spot where man throws aside his heavy responsibilities, his couch of rest is often prepared by his faithful wife, at the sacrifice of all her quiet contemplation and leisure. She is pursued into her most sacred sanctuaries by petty anxieties, haunting her loneliest hours, by temptations taking her by surprise, by cares so harassing, that the most powerful talents and the most abundant intellectual and moral resources are scarce sufficient to give her strength to ward them off. If there is a being exposed to turmoil and indurating[62] care, it is woman, in the retirement of her own home; and if she makes peace and warmth there, it is not by her sweet religious sensibility, her gentle benevolence, her balmy tenderness, but by a strength and energy as great and untiring as leads man to battle, or supports him in the strife of the political arena, though these sturdier qualities unfold often, both in man and woman, in an atmosphere of exquisite refinement and sensibility. [...]

In our present state of society woman possesses not; she is under possession. A dependant, except in extreme hours of peril or moral conflict, when each is left to the mercy of the unfriendly elements alone, for in every mental or physical crisis of life the Infinite has willed each soul to be alone, nothing interposing between it and himself. At times, when most a being needs protection, none but the highest can protect. Man may soothe, but he cannot shelter from, or avert the storm, however solemnly he may promise it to himself or others in the bright hours. When most needed he is most impotent.

Woman is educated with the tacit understanding, that she is only half a being, and an appendage. First, she is so to her parents, whose opinions, perhaps prejudices, are engrafted into her before she knows what an opinion is. Thus provided she enters life, and society seizes her; her faculties of observation are sharpened, often become fearfully acute, though in some sort discriminating, and are ever after so occupied with observing that she never penetrates. In the common course of events she is selected as the life-companion of some one of the other sex; because selected, she fixes her affections upon him, and hardly ventures to exercise upon him even her powers of observation. Then he creates for her a home, which should be constructed by their mutual taste and efforts. She finds him not what she expected; she is disappointed and becomes captious, complaining of woman's lot, or discouraged and crushed by it. She thinks him perfect, adopts his prejudices, adds them to her early stock, and ever defends them with his arguments; where she differs from him in taste and habits, she believes herself in the wrong and him in the right, and spends life in conforming to him, instead of moulding herself to her own ideal. Thus she loses her individuality, and never gains his respect. Her life is usually bustle and hurry, or barren order, dreary decorum and method, without vitality. Her children perhaps love her, but she is only the upper nurse; the father, the oracle. His wish is law, hers only the unavailing sigh uttered in secret. She looks out into life, finds nothing there but confusion, and congratulates herself that it is man's business, not hers, to look through it all, and find stern principle seated tranquilly at the centre of things. Is this woman's destiny? Is she to be the only adventurer, who pursues her course through life aimless, tossed upon the waves of circumstance, intoxicated by joy, panic-struck by misfortune, or stupidly receptive of it? Is she neither to soar to heaven like the lark, nor bend her way, led by an unerring guide, to climes congenial to her nature? Is she always to flutter and flutter, and at last drop into the wave? Man would not have it so, for he reveres the gently firm. Man does not ridicule nor expose to suffering the woman who

---

[62] Something that hardens or makes hard.

aspires, he wishes not for blind reverence, but intelligent affection; not for supremacy, but to be understood; not for obedience, but companionship; it is the weak and ignorant of her own sex who brand her, but the enigma still remains unsolved, why are so many of the sex allowed to remain weak and frivolous?

The minor cares of life thronging[63] the path of woman, demand as much reflection and clear-sightedness, and involve as much responsibility, as those of man. Why is she not encouraged to think and penetrate through externals to principles? She should be seen, after the first dreamlike years of unconscious childhood are passed, meekly and reverently questioning and encouraged to question the opinions of others, calmly contemplating beauty in all its forms, studying the harmony of life, as well as of outward nature, deciding nothing, learning all things, gradually forming her own ideal, which, like that represented in the sculptured figures of the old Persian sovereigns, should cheeringly and protectingly hover over her. Society would attract her, and then gracefully mingling in it, she should still be herself, and there find her relaxation, not her home. She should feel that our highest hours are always our lonely ones, and that nothing is good that does not prepare us for these. Beautiful and graceful forms should come before her as revelations of divine beauty, but no charm of outward grace should tempt her to recede one hair's breadth from her uncompromising demand for the noblest nature in her chosen companion, guided in her demands by what she finds within herself, seeking an answering note to her own inner melody, but not sweetly lulling herself into the belief that she has found in him the full-toned harmony of the celestial choirs. If her demand is satisfied, let her not lean, but attend on him as a watchful friend. Her own individuality should be as precious to her as his love. Let her see that the best our most sympathising friend can do for us is, to throw a genial atmosphere around us, and strew our path with golden opportunities; but our path can never be another's, and we must always walk alone. Let no drudgery degrade her high vocation of creator of a happy home. Household order must prevail, but let her ennoble it by detecting its relation to that law which keeps the planets in their course. Every new relation and every new scene should be a new page in the book of the mysteries of life, reverently and lovingly perused, but if folded down, never to be read again, it must be regarded as only the introduction to a brighter one. The faults of those she loves should never be veiled by her affection, but placed in their true relation to character, by the deep insight with which she penetrates beneath them. With high heroic courage, she should measure the strength of suffering before it comes, that she may not meet it unprepared. Her life-plan should be stern, but not unyielding. Her hours, precious treasures lent to her, carefully to be protected from vulgar intrusion, but which women are constantly scattering around them, like small coin, to be picked up by every needy wayfarer. Thought should be her atmosphere; books her food; friends her occasional solace. Prosperity will not dazzle her, for her own spirit is always brighter than its sunshine, and if the deepest sorrow visits her, it will only come to lift her to a higher region, where, with all of life far beneath her, she may sit regally apart till the end.

Is this the ideal of a perfect woman, and if so, how does it differ from a perfect man?

W. N.

Source: Anonymous [W.N. =Sophia Ripley]. "Woman." *The Dial: A Magazine for Literature, Philosophy, and Religion* 1.3 (January 1841), 362-366.

---

[63] Assembling in large numbers.

235. Margaret Fuller
Woman in the Nineteenth Century (1844)

Preface

The following essay is a reproduction, modified and expanded, of an article published in "The Dial, Boston, July, 1843," under the title of "The Great Lawsuit. – Man *versus* Men; Woman *versus* Women." [...]

Objections having been made to the former title, as not sufficiently easy to be understood, the present has been substituted as expressive of the main purpose of the essay; though, by myself, the other is preferred, partly for the reason others do not like it, – that is, that it requires some thought to see what it means, and might thus prepare the reader to meet me on my own ground. Besides, it offers a larger scope, and is, in that way, more just to my desire. I meant by that title to intimate the fact that, while it is the destiny of Man, in the course of the ages, to ascertain and fulfil the law of his being, so that his life shall be seen, as a whole, to be that of an angel or messenger, the action of prejudices and passions which attend, in the day, the growth of the individual, is continually obstructing the holy work that is to make the earth a part of heaven. By Man I mean both man and woman; these are the two halves of one thought. I lay no especial stress on the welfare of either. I believe that the development of the one cannot be effected without that of the other. My highest wish is that this truth should be distinctly and rationally apprehended, and the conditions of life and freedom recognized as the same for the daughters and the sons of time; twin exponents of a divine thought.

I solicit a sincere and patient attention from those who open the following pages at all. I solicit of women that they will lay it to heart to ascertain what is for them the liberty of law. It is for this, and not for any, the largest, extension of partial privileges that I seek. I ask them, if interested by these suggestions, to search their own experience and intuitions for better, and fill up with fit materials and trenches that hedge them in. From men I ask a noble and earnest attention to anything that can be offered on this great and still obscure subject, such as I have met from many with whom I stand in private relations.

And may truth, unpolluted by prejudice, vanity or selfishness, be granted daily more and more as the due inheritance, and only valuable conquest for us all!

November, 1844.

[...] It may well be an Anti-Slavery party that pleads for Woman, if we consider merely that she does not hold property on equal terms with men; so that, if a husband dies without making a will, the wife, instead of taking at once his place as head of the family, inherits only a part of his fortune, often brought him by herself, as if she were a child, or ward only, not an equal partner.

We will not speak of the innumerable instances in which profligate and idle men live upon the earnings of industrious wives; or if the wives leave them, and take with them the children, to perform the double duty of mother and father, follow from place to place, and threaten to rob them of the children, if deprived of the rights of a husband, as they call them, planting themselves in their poor lodgings, frightening them into paying tribute by taking from them the children, running into debt at the expense of these otherwise so overtasked helots.[64] Such instances count up by scores within my own memory.

---

[64] Serf in ancient Sparta.

I have seen the husband who had stained himself by a long course of low vice, till his wife was wearied from her heroic forgiveness, by finding that his treachery made it useless, and that if she would provide bread for herself and her children, she must be separate from his ill fame [...]. I have known these men steal their children, whom they knew they had no means to maintain, take them into dissolute company, expose them to bodily danger, to frighten the poor woman, to whom, it seems, the fact that she alone had borne the pangs of their birth, and nourished their infancy, does not give an equal right to them. I do believe that this mode of kidnapping – and it is frequent enough in all classes of society – will be by the next age viewed as it is by Heaven now, and that the man who avails himself of the shelter of men's laws to steal from a mother her own children, or arrogate any superior right in them, save that of superior virtue, will bear the stigma he deserves, in common with him who steals grown men from their mother-land, their hopes, and their homes.

I said, we will not speak of this now; yet I *have* spoken, for the subject makes me feel too much. I could give instances that would startle the most vulgar and callous; but I will not, for the public opinion of their own sex is already against such men, and where cases of extreme tyranny are made known, there is private action in the wife's favor. But she ought not to need this, nor, I think, can she long. Men must soon see that as, on their own ground, Woman is the weaker party, she ought to have legal protection, which would make such oppression impossible. But I would not deal with "atrocious instances," except in the way of illustration, neither demand from men a partial redress in some one matter, but go to the root of the whole. If principles could be established, particulars would adjust themselves aright. Ascertain the true destiny of Woman; give her legitimate hopes, and a standard within herself; marriage and all other relations would by degrees be harmonized with these.

But to return to the historical progress of this matter. Knowing that there exists in the minds of men a tone of feeling toward women as toward slaves, such as is expressed in the common phrase, "Tell that to women and children;" that the infinite soul can only work through them in already ascertained limits; that the gift of reason, Man's highest prerogative, is allotted to them in much lower degree; that they must be kept from mischief and melancholy by being constantly engaged in active labor, which is to be furnished and directed by those better able to think, &c. &c, – we need not multiply instances, for who can review the experience of last week without recalling words which imply, whether in jest or earnest, these views, or views like these, – knowing this, can we wonder that many reformers think that measures are not likely to be taken in behalf of women, unless their wishes could be publicly represented by women?

"That can never be necessary," cry the other side. "All men are privately influenced by women; each has his wife, sister, or female friends, and is too much biased by these relations to fail of representing their interests; and, if this is not enough, let them propose and enforce their wishes with the pen. The beauty of home would be destroyed, the delicacy of the sex be violated, the dignity of halls of legislation degraded, by an attempt to introduce them there. Such duties are inconsistent with those of a mother;" and then we have ludicrous pictures of ladies in hysterics at the polls, and senate-chambers filled with cradles.

But if, in reply, we admit as truth that Woman seems destined by nature rather for the inner circle, we must add that the arrangements of civilized life have not been, as yet, such as to secure it to her. Her circle, if the duller, is not the quieter. If kept from "excitement," she is not from drudgery. Not only the Indian squaw carries the burdens of the camp, but [...] the washerwoman stands at her tub, and carries home her work at all seasons, and in all states of health. Those who think the physical circumstances of Woman would make a part in the affairs of national government unsuitable, are by no means those who think it impossible for the negresses to endure field-work, even during pregnancy, or for sempstresses to go through their killing labors. [...]

Under these circumstances, without attaching importance, in themselves, to the changes demanded by the champions of Woman, we hail them as signs of the times. We would have every arbitrary barrier thrown down. We would have every path laid open to Woman as freely as to Man. Were this done, and a slight temporary fermentation allowed to subside, we should see crystallizations more pure and of more various beauty. We believe the divine energy would pervade nature to a degree unknown in the history of former ages, and that no discordant collision, but a ravishing harmony of the spheres, would ensue.

Yet, then and only then will mankind be ripe for this, when inward and outward freedom for Woman as much as for Man shall be acknowledged as a *right*, not yielded as a concession. As the friend of the negro assumes that one man cannot by right hold another in bondage, so should the friend of Woman assume that Man cannot by right lay even well-meant restrictions on Woman. If the negro be a soul, if the woman be a soul, apparelled in flesh, to one Master only are they accountable. There is but one law for souls, and if there is to be an interpreter of it, he must come not as man, or son of man, but as son of God.

Were thought and feeling once so far elevated that Man should esteem himself the brother and friend, but nowise the lord and tutor, of Woman, – were he really bound with her in equal worship, – arrangements as to function and employment would be of no consequence. What Woman needs is not as a woman to act or rule, but as a nature to grow, as an intellect to discern, as a soul to live freely and unimpeded, to unfold such powers as were given her when we left our common home. If fewer talents were given her, yet if allowed the free and full employment of these, so that she may render back to the giver his own with usury,[65] she will not complain; nay, I dare to say she will bless and rejoice in her earthly birth-place, her earthly lot. Let us consider what obstructions impede this good era, and what signs give reason to hope that it draws near. [...]

There are two aspects of Woman's nature, represented by the ancients as Muse and Minerva.[66] It is the former to which the writer in the Pathfinder[67] looks. It is the latter which Wordsworth has in mind, when he says,

> "With a placid brow,
> Which woman ne'er should forfeit, keep thy vow."[68]

The especial genius of Woman I believe to be electrical in movement, intuitive in function, spiritual in tendency. She excels not so easily in classification, or recreation, as in an instinctive seizure of causes, and a simple breathing out of what she receives, that has the singleness of life, rather than the selecting and energizing of art.

---

[65] The practice of lending money at an exorbitant rate of interest.
[66] Fuller uses the muses to represent woman's artistic nature. Minerva, the Roman goddess of wisdom and handicrafts, is usually portrayed in armor thus representing intellectual strength.
[67] A New York newspaper in which two articles under the title "Femality" had previously been published.
[68] Slightly altered from *Liberty: Sequel to the Preceding* (1835) by the English poet William Wordsworth.

More native is it to her to be the living model of the artist than to set apart from herself any one form in objective reality; more native to inspire and receive the poem, than to create it. In so far as soul is in her completely developed, all soul is the same; but in so far as it is modified in her as Woman, it flows, it breathes, it sings, rather than deposits soil, or finishes work; and that which is especially feminine flushes, in blossom, the face of earth, and pervades, like air and water, all this seeming solid globe, daily renewing and purifying its life. Such may be the especially feminine element spoken of as Femality. But it is no more the order of nature that it should be incarnated pure in any form, than that the masculine energy should exist unmingled with it in any form.

Male and female represent the two sides of the great radical dualism. But, in fact, they are perpetually passing into one another. Fluid hardens to solid, solid rushes to fluid. There is no wholly masculine man, no purely feminine woman.

History jeers at the attempts of physiologists to bind great original laws by the forms which flow from them. They make a rule; they say from observation what can and cannot be. In vain! Nature provides exceptions to every rule. She sends women to battle, and sets Hercules spinning; she enables women to bear immense burdens, cold, and frost; she enables the man, who feels maternal love, to nourish his infant like a mother. [...]

Man partakes of the feminine in the Apollo, Woman of the masculine as Minerva.

What I mean by the Muse is that unimpeded clearness of the intuitive powers, which a perfectly truthful adherence to every admonition of the higher instincts would bring to a finely organized human being. It may appear as prophecy or as poesy. [...]

Let us be wise, and not impede the soul. Let her work as she will. Let us have one creative energy, one incessant revelation. Let it take what form it will, and let us not bind it by the past to man or woman, black or white. Jove sprang from Rhea, Pallas from Jove.[69] So let it be.

If it has been the tendency of these remarks to call Woman rather to the Minerva side, – if I, unlike the more generous writer, have spoken from society no less than the soul, – let it be pardoned! It is love that has caused this, – love for many incarcerated souls, that might be freed, could the idea of religious self-dependence be established in them, could the weakening habit of dependence on others be broken up.

Proclus[70] teaches that every life has, in its sphere, a totality or wholeness of the animating powers of the other spheres; having only, as its own characteristic, a predominance of some one power. Thus Jupiter comprises, within himself, the other twelve powers, which stand thus: The first triad is *demiurgic or fabricative*, that is, Jupiter, Neptune, Vulcan; the second, *defensive*, Vesta, Minerva, Mars; the third, *vivific*, Ceres, Juno, Diana; and the fourth, Mercury, Venus, Apollo, *elevating and harmonic*. In the sphere of Jupiter, energy is predominant – with Venus, beauty; but each comprehends and apprehends all the others. [...]

Every relation, every gradation of nature is incalculably precious, but only to the soul which is poised upon itself, and to whom no loss, no change, can bring dull discord, for it is in harmony with the central soul.

If any individual live too much in relations, so that he becomes a stranger to the resources of his own nature, he falls, after a while, into a distraction, or imbecility, from which he can only be cured by a time of isolation, which gives the renovating fountains

---

[69] The chief Roman god Jupiter or Jove was the son of Rhea. The goddess Pallas Athene, the Greek goddess of wisdom, sprang fully armored from his head.
[70] Greek philosopher (c. 485-410 BC).

time to rise up. With a society it is the same. Many minds, deprived of the traditional or instinctive means of passing a cheerful existence, must find help in self-impulse, or perish. It is therefore that, while any elevation, in the view of union, is to be hailed with joy, we shall not decline celibacy as the great fact of the time. It is one from which no vow, no arrangement, can at present save a thinking mind. For now the rowers are pausing on their oars; they wait a change before they can pull together. All tends to illustrate the thought of a wise cotemporary. Union is only possible to those who are units. To be fit for relations in time, souls, whether of Man or Woman, must be able to do without them in the spirit.

It is therefore that I would have Woman lay aside all thought, such as she habitually cherishes, of being taught and led by men. I would have her, like the Indian girl, dedicate herself to the Sun, the Sun of Truth, and go nowhere if his beams did not make clear the path. I would have her free from compromise, from complaisance, from helplessness, because I would have her good enough and strong enough to love one and all beings, from the fulness, not the poverty of being. [...]

Man is a being of two-fold relations, to nature beneath, and intelligence above him. The earth is his school, if not his birth-place; God his object; life and thought his means of interpreting nature, and aspiring to God.

Only a fraction of this purpose is accomplished in the life of any one man. Its entire accomplishment is to be hoped only from the sum of the lives of men, or Man considered as a whole.

As this whole has one soul and one body, any injury or obstruction to a part, or to the meanest member, affects the whole. Man can never be perfectly happy or virtuous, till all men are so.

To address Man wisely, you must not forget that his life is partly animal, subject to the same laws with Nature.

But you cannot address him wisely unless you consider him still more as soul, and appreciate the conditions and destiny of soul.

The growth of Man is two-fold, masculine and feminine.

So far as these two methods can be distinguished, they are so as

> Energy and Harmony;
> Power and Beauty;
> Intellect and Love;

or by some such rude classification; for we have not language primitive and pure enough to express such ideas with precision.

These two sides are supposed to be expressed in Man and Woman, that is, as the more and less, for the faculties have not been given pure to either, but only in preponderance. There are also exceptions in great number, such as men of far more beauty than power, and the reverse. But, as a general rule, it seems to have been the intention to give a preponderance on the one side, that is called masculine, and on the other, one that is called feminine.

There cannot be a doubt that, if these two developments were in perfect harmony, they would correspond to and fulfil one another, like hemispheres, or the tenor and bass in music.

But there is no perfect harmony in human nature; and the two parts answer one another only now and then; or, if there be a persistent consonance, it can only be traced at long intervals, instead of discoursing an obvious melody. [...]

Source: Margaret Fuller (1810-1850). *Woman in the Nineteenth Century* [1844]. In: *Woman in the Nineteenth Century and Kindred Papers Relating to the Sphere, Condition and Duties of Woman. By Margaret*

Fuller Ossoli. Ed. Arthur B. Fuller. Boston: John P. Jewett & Company, 1855, 13-14, 31-35, 37-38, 115-120, 168-170.

236. Mrs. E. Little
"What Are the Rights of Woman?" (1847)

"The rights of woman" – what are they?
The right to labor and to pray,
The right to watch while others sleep,
The right o'er others' woes to weep;
The right to succour in distress,
The right, while others curse, to bless;
The right to love whom others scorn,
The right to comfort all that mourn;
The right to shed new joy on earth,
The right to feel the soul's high worth,
The right to lead that soul to God,
Along the path her Savior trod –
The path of meekness and of love,
The path of patience under wrong,
The path in which the weak grow strong.
Such woman's rights, and God will bless
And crown their champions with success.

Source: "Declaration of Sentiments and Resolutions." *Ladies' Wreath: A Magazine Devoted to Literature, Industry and Religion* 2 (Aug. 1847), 133.

237. *Declaration of Sentiments and Resolutions, Seneca Falls Convention* (1848)

DECLARATION OF SENTIMENTS.

When, in the course of human events, it becomes necessary for one portion of the family of man to assume among the people of the earth a position different from that which they have hitherto occupied, but one to which the laws of nature and of nature's God entitle them, a decent respect to the opinions of mankind requires that they should declare the causes that impel them to such a course.

We hold these truths to be self-evident: that all men and women are created equal; that they are endowed by their Creator with certain inalienable rights; that among these are life, liberty, and the pursuit of happiness; that to secure these rights governments are instituted, deriving their just powers from the consent of the governed. Whenever any form of government becomes destructive of these ends, it is the right of those who suffer from it to refuse allegiance to it, and to insist upon the institution of a new government, laying its foundation on such principles, and organizing its powers in such form, as to them shall seem most likely to effect their safety and happiness. Prudence, indeed, will dictate that governments long established should not be changed for light and transient causes; and accordingly all experience hath shown that mankind are more disposed to suffer, while evils are sufferable, than to right themselves by abolishing the forms to which they were accustomed. But when a long train of abuses and usurpations, pursuing invariably the same object evinces a design to reduce them under absolute despotism, it is their duty to throw off such government, and to provide new guards for their future security. Such has been the patient sufferance of the women under this government, and such is now the necessity which constrains them to demand the equal station to which they are entitled.

The history of mankind is a history of repeated injuries and usurpations on the part of man toward woman, having in direct object the establishment of an absolute tyranny over her. To prove this, let facts be submitted to a candid world.

He has never permitted her to exercise her inalienable right to the elective franchise.

He has compelled her to submit to laws, in the formation of which she had no voice.

He has withheld from her rights which are given to the most ignorant and degraded men – both natives and foreigners.

Having deprived her of this first right of a citizen, the elective franchise, thereby leaving her without representation in the halls of legislation, he has oppressed her on all sides.

He has made her, if married, in the eye of the law, civilly dead.

He has taken from her all right in property, even to the wages she earns.

He has made her, morally, an irresponsible being, as she can commit many crimes with impunity, provided they be done in the presence of her husband. In the covenant of marriage, she is compelled to promise obedience to her husband, he becoming, to all intents and purposes, her master – the law giving him power to deprive her of her liberty, and to administer chastisement.

He has so framed the laws of divorce, as to what shall be the proper causes, and in case of separation, to whom the guardianship of the children shall be given, as to be wholly regardless of the happiness of women – the law, in all cases, going upon a false supposition of the supremacy of man, and giving all power into his hands.

After depriving her of all rights as a married woman, if single, and the owner of property, he has taxed her to support a government which recognizes her only when her property can be made profitable to it.

He has monopolized nearly all the profitable employments, and from those she is permitted to follow, she receives but a scanty remuneration. He closes against her all the avenues to wealth and distinction which he considers most honorable to himself. As a teacher of theology, medicine, or law, she is not known.

He has denied her the facilities for obtaining a thorough education, all colleges being closed against her.

He allows her in Church, as well as State, but a subordinate position, claiming Apostolic authority for her exclusion from the ministry, and, with some exceptions, from any public participation in the affairs of the Church.

He has created a false public sentiment by giving to the world a different code of morals for men and women, by which moral delinquencies which exclude women from society, are not only tolerated, but deemed of little account in man.

He has usurped the prerogative of Jehovah himself, claiming it as his right to assign for her a sphere of action, when that belongs to her conscience and to her God.

He has endeavored, in every way that he could, to destroy her confidence in her own powers, to lessen her self-respect, and to make her willing to lead a dependent and abject life.

Now, in view of this entire disfranchisement of one-half the people of this country, their social and religious degradation – in view of the unjust laws above mentioned, and because women do feel themselves aggrieved, oppressed, and fraudulently deprived of their most sacred rights, we insist that they have immediate admission to all the rights and privileges which belong to them as citizens of the United States.

In entering upon the great work before us, we anticipate no small amount of misconception, misrepresentation, and ridicule; but we shall use every instrumentality within our power to effect our object. We shall employ agents, circulate tracts, petition the State and National legislatures, and endeavor to enlist the pulpit and the press in our behalf. We hope this Convention will be followed by a series of Conventions embracing every part of the country.

The following resolutions were discussed by Lucretia Mott, Thomas and Mary Ann McClintock, Amy Post, Catharine A. F. Stebbins, and others, and were adopted:

WHEREAS, The great precept of nature is conceded to be, that "man shall pursue his own true and substantial happiness." Blackstone[71] in his Commentaries remarks, that this law of Nature being coeval[72] with mankind, and dictated by God himself, is of course superior in obligation to any other. It is binding over all the globe, in all countries and at all times; no human laws are of any validity if contrary to this, and such of them as are valid, derive all their force, and all their validity, and all their authority, mediately and immediately, from this original; therefore,

Resolved, That such laws as conflict, in any way, with the true and substantial happiness of woman, are contrary to the great precept of nature and of no validity, for this is "superior in obligation to any other."

Resolved, That all laws which prevent woman from occupying such a station in society as her conscience shall dictate, or which place her in a position inferior to that of man, are contrary to the great precept of nature, and therefore of no force or authority.

Resolved, That woman is man's equal – was intended to be so by the Creator, and the highest good of the race demands that she should be recognized as such.

Resolved, That the women of this country ought to be enlightened in regard to the laws under which they live, that they may no longer publish their degradation by declaring themselves satisfied with their present position, nor their ignorance, by asserting that they have all the rights they want.

Resolved, That inasmuch as man, while claiming for himself intellectual superiority, does accord to woman moral superiority, it is pre-eminently his duty to encourage her to speak and teach, as she has an opportunity, in all religious assemblies.

Resolved, That the same amount of virtue, delicacy, and refinement of behavior that is required of woman in the social state, should also be required of man, and the same transgressions should be visited with equal severity on both man and woman.

Resolved, That the objection of indelicacy and impropriety, which is so often brought against woman when she addresses a public audience, comes with a very ill-grace from those who encourage, by their attendance, her appearance on the stage, in the concert, or in feats of the circus.

---

[71] William Blackstone (1723-1780), English jurist.
[72] Of the same age, equally old.

Resolved, That woman has too long rested satisfied in the circumscribed limits which corrupt customs and a perverted application of the Scriptures have marked out for her, and that it is time she should move in the enlarged sphere which her great Creator has assigned her.

Resolved, That it is the duty of the women of this country to secure to themselves their sacred right to the elective franchise.

Resolved, That the equality of human rights results necessarily from the fact of the identity of the race in capabilities and responsibilities.

Resolved, therefore, That, being invested by the Creator with the same capabilities, and the same consciousness of responsibility for their exercise, it is demonstrably the right and duty of woman, equally with man, to promote every righteous cause by every righteous means; and especially in regard to the great subjects of morals and religion, it is self-evidently her right to participate with her brother in teaching them, both in private and in public, by writing and by speaking, by any instrumentalities proper to be used, and in any assemblies proper to be held; and this being a self-evident truth growing out of the divinely implanted principles of human nature, any custom or authority adverse to it, whether modern or wearing the hoary[73] sanction of antiquity, is to be regarded as a self-evident falsehood, and at war with mankind. [...]

Resolved, That the speedy success of our cause depends upon the zealous and untiring efforts of both men and women, for the overthrow of the monopoly of the pulpit, and for the securing to woman an equal participation with men in the various trades, professions, and commerce. [...]

Source: "Declaration of Sentiments and Resolutions." *History of Woman Suffrage*. 6 vols. Eds. Elizabeth Cady Stanton, Susan B. Anthony, and Matilda Joslyn Gage. Vol. 1. New York: Fowler & Wells, 1881, 70-73.

238. Theodore Parker
A Sermon of the Public Function of Woman (1853)

Psalm 144: 12. – "That our daughters may be as corner-stones."

Last Sunday I spoke of the Domestic Function of Woman, what she may do for the higher development of the human race at home. To-day, I ask your attention to a sermon of the Ideal Public Function of Woman, and the Economy thereof, in the higher development of the Human Race.

The domestic function of woman, as a housekeeper, wife and mother, does not exhaust her powers. Woman's function, like charity, begins at home; then, like charity, goes everywhere. To make one half of the human race consume all their energies in the functions of housekeeper, wife and mother, is a monstrous waste of the most precious material that God ever made. [...]

By nature, woman has the same political rights that man has, – to vote, to hold office, to make and administer laws. These she has as a matter of right. The strong hand and the great head of man keep her down; nothing more. In America, in Christendom, woman has no political rights, is not a citizen in full; she has no voice in making or administering

---

[73] Ancient, venerable from age, time-honoured.

the laws, none in electing the rulers or administrators thereof. She can hold no office, – cannot be committee of a primary school, overseer of the poor, or guardian to a public lamp-post. But any man, with conscience enough to keep out of jail, mind enough to escape the poor-house, and body enough to drop his ballot into the box, he is a voter. He may have no character – even no money; – that is no matter – he is male. The noblest woman has no voice in the state. Men make laws, disposing of her property, her person, her children; still she must bear it, "with a patient shrug."

Looking at it as a matter of pure right and pure science, I know no reason why woman should not be a voter, or hold office, or make and administer laws. I do not see how I can shut myself into political privileges and shut woman out, and do both in the name of unalienable right. Certainly, every woman has a natural right to have her property represented in the general representation of property, and her person represented in the general representation of persons.

Looking at it as a matter of expediency, see some facts. Suppose woman had a share in the municipal regulation of Boston, and there were as many alderwomen as aldermen, as many common-council women as common-council men, do you believe that, in defiance of the law of Massachusetts, the city government, last spring, would have licensed every two hundred and forty-fourth person of the population of the city to sell intoxicating drink? would have made every thirty-fifth voter a rumseller? I do not. [...]

Do you believe that the women of Boston, in 1851, would have spent three or four thousand dollars to kidnap a poor man, and have taken all the chains which belonged to the city and put them round the court-house, and have drilled three hundred men, armed with bludgeons and cutlasses, to steal a man and carry him back to slavery?[74] I do not. Do you think, if the women had had the control, "fifteen hundred men of property and standing" would have volunteered to take a poor man, kidnapped in Boston, and conduct him out of the state, with fire and sword? I believe no such thing. [...]

If women had a voice in the affairs of Massachusetts, do you think they would ever have made laws so that a lazy husband could devour all the substance of his active wife – spite of her wish; so that a drunken husband could command her bodily presence in his loathly house; and when an infamous man was divorced from his wife, that he could keep all the children? I confess I do not.

If the affairs of the nation had been under woman's joint control, I doubt that we should have butchered the Indians with such exterminating savagery, that, in fifty years, we should have spent seven hundreds of millions of dollars for war, and now, in time of peace, send twenty annual millions more to the same waste. I doubt that we should have spread slavery into nine new states, and made it national. I think the Fugitive Slave Bill would never have been an act. Woman has some respect for the natural law of God.

I know men say woman cannot manage the great affairs of a nation. Very well. Government is political economy – national housekeeping. Does any respectable woman keep house so badly as the United States? with so much bribery, so much corruption, so much quarreling in the domestic councils?

But government is also political morality, it is national ethics. Is there any worthy woman who rules her household as wickedly as the nations are ruled? who hires bullies to

---

[74] Reference to the Fugitive Slave Law, the most controversial measure of the Compromise of 1850, which installed federal commissioners with authority to issue warrants, gather posses, and force citizens to help catch runaway slaves under penalty of a fine or imprisonment. Accused runaways could be sent to the South on the basis of a supposed owner's affidavit.

fight for her? Is there any woman who treats one sixth part of her household as if they were cattle and not creatures of God, as if they were things and not persons? I know of none such. In government as housekeeping, or government as morality, I think man makes a very poor appearance, when he says woman could not do as well as he has done and is doing.

I doubt that women will ever, as a general thing, take the same interest as men in political affairs, or find therein an abiding satisfaction. But that is for women themselves to determine, not for men.

In order to attain the end, – the development of man in body and spirit, – human institutions must represent all parts of human nature, both the masculine and the feminine element. For the well-being of the human race, we need the joint action of man and woman, in the family, the community, the church and the state. A family without the presence of woman – with no mother, no wife, no sister, no womankind – is a sad thing. I think a community without woman's equal social action, a church without her equal ecclesiastical action, and a state without her equal political action, is almost as bad – very much what a house would be without a mother, wife, sister or friend.

You see what prevails in the Christian civilization of the nineteenth century; it is Force – force of body, force of brain. There is little justice, little philanthropy, little piety. Selfishness preponderates everywhere in Christendom – individual, domestic, social, ecclesiastical, national selfishness. It is preached as gospel and enacted as law. It is thought good political economy for a strong people to devour the weak nations; – for "Christian" England and America to plunder the "heathen" and annex their land; for a strong class to oppress and ruin the feeble class; for the capitalists of England to pauperize the poor white laborer, for the capitalists of America to enslave the poorer black laborer; for a strong man to oppress the weak men; for the sharper to buy labor too cheap, and sell its product too dear, and so grow rich by making many poor. Hence, nation is arrayed against nation, class against class, man against man. Nay, it is commonly taught that mankind is arrayed against God, and God against man; that the world is a universal discord; that there is no solidarity of man with man, of man with God. I fear we shall never get far beyond this theory and this practice, until woman has her natural rights as the equal of man, and takes her natural place in regulating the affairs of the family, the community, the church and the state.

It seems to me God has treasured up a reserved power in the nature of woman to correct many of those evils which are Christendom's disgrace to-day. [...]

Hitherto, with woman, circumstances have hindered the development of intellectual power, in all its forms. She has not knowledge, has not ideas or practical skill to equal the force of man. But circumstances have favored the development of pure and lofty emotion in advance of man. She has moral feeling, affectional feeling, religious feeling, far in advance of man; her moral, affectional and religious intuitions are deeper and more trustworthy than his. Here she is eminent, as he is in knowledge, in ideas, in administrative skill.

I think man will always lead in affairs of intellect, – of reason, imagination, understanding, – he has the bigger brain; but that woman will always lead in affairs of emotion, – moral, affectional, religious, – she has the better heart, the truer intuition of the right, the lovely, the holy. The literature of women in this century is juster, more philanthropic, more religious, than that of men. [...]

Well, we want the excellence of man and woman both united; intellectual power, knowledge, great ideas – in literature, philosophy, theology, ethics – and practical skill;

but we want something better – the moral, affectional, religious intuition, to put justice into ethics, love into theology, piety into science and letters. Everywhere in the family, the community, the church and the state, we want the masculine and feminine element coöperating and conjoined. Woman is to correct man's taste, mend his morals, excite his affections, inspire his religious faculties. Man is to quicken her intellect, to help her will, translate her sentiments to ideas, and enact them into righteous laws. Man's moral action, at best, is only a sort of general human providence, aiming at the welfare of a part, and satisfied with achieving the "greatest good of the greatest number." Woman's moral action is more like a special human providence, acting without general rules, but caring for each particular case. We need both of these, the general and the special, to make a total human providence. [...]

To every woman let me say, – Respect your nature as a human being, your nature as a woman; then respect your rights, then remember your duty to possess, to use, to develop and to enjoy every faculty which God has given you, each in its normal way.

And to men let me say, – Respect, with the profoundest reverence respect the mother that bore you, the sisters who bless you, the woman that you love, the woman that you marry. As you seek to possess your own manly rights, seek also, by that great arm, by that powerful brain, seek to vindicate her rights as woman, as your own as man. Then we may see better things in the church, better things in the state, in the community, in the home. Then the green shall show what buds it hid, the buds shall blossom, the flowers bear fruit, and the blessing of God be on us all.

Source: Theodore Parker (1810-1860). *A Sermon of the Public Function of Woman, Preached at the Music Hall, March 27, 1853.* Boston: Robert F. Wallcut, 1853, 1, 17-20, 22-24.

239. Lucy Stone
"The Marriage of Lucy Stone under Protest" (1855)

MARRIAGE OF LUCY STONE UNDER PROTEST.

It was my privilege to celebrate May day by officiating at a wedding in a farm-house among the hills of West Brookfield. The bridegroom was a man of tried worth, a leader in the Western Anti-Slavery Movement; and the bride was one whose fair name is known throughout the nation; one whose rare intellectual qualities are excelled by the private beauty of her heart and life.

I never perform the marriage ceremony without a renewed sense of the iniquity of our present system of laws in respect to marriage; a system by which "man and wife are one, and that one is the husband." It was with my hearty concurrence, therefore, that the following protest was read and signed, as a part of the nuptial ceremony; and I send it to you, that others may be induced to do likewise.

Rev. THOMAS WENTWORTH HIGGINSON.

PROTEST.

While acknowledging our mutual affection by publicly assuming the relationship of husband and wife, yet in justice to ourselves and a great principle, we deem it a duty to declare that this act on our part implies no sanction of, nor promise of voluntary obedience to such of the present laws of marriage, as refuse to recognize the wife as an independent, rational being, while they confer upon the husband an injurious and unnatural superiority, investing him with legal powers which no honorable man would exercise, and which no man should posses. We protest especially against the laws which give to the husband:

1. The custody of the wife's person.
2. The exclusive control and guardianship of their children.
3. The sole ownership of her personal, and use of her real estate, unless previously settled upon her, or placed in the hands of trustees, as in the case of minors, lunatics, and idiots.
4. The absolute right to the product of her industry.
5. Also against laws which give to the widower so much larger and more permanent an interest in the property of his deceased wife, than they give to the widow in that of the deceased husband.
6. Finally, against the whole system by which "the legal existence of the wife is suspended during marriage," so that in most States, she neither has a legal part in the choice of her residence, nor can she make a will, nor sue or be sued in her own name, nor inherit property.

We believe that personal independence and equal human rights can never be forfeited, except for crime; that marriage should be an equal and permanent partnership, and so recognized by law; that until it is so recognized, married partners should provide against the radical injustice of present laws, by every means in their power.

We believe that where domestic difficulties arise, no appeal should be made to legal tribunals under existing laws, but that all difficulties should be submitted to the equitable adjustment of arbitrators mutually chosen.

Thus reverencing law, we enter our protest against rules and customs which are unworthy of the name, since they violate justice, the essence of law.

(Signed),   HENRY B. BLACKWELL,
Worcester Spy, 1855.   LUCY STONE.

Source: Lucy Stone (1818-1893). "The Marriage of Lucy Stone under Protest." *History of Woman Suffrage*. 6 vols. Eds. Elizabeth Cady Stanton, Susan B. Anthony and Matilda Joslyn Gage. Vol. 1. New York: Fowler & Wells, 1881, 260-261.

240. *Age of Iron: Man as He Expects to Be* (1869)

Source: Nathaniel Currier (1813-1888) and James Merritt Ives (1824-1895). *Age of Iron: Man as He Expects to Be.* New York, 1869.

241. Catharine E. Beecher and Harriet Beecher Stowe "The Christian Family" (1869)

I. THE CHRISTIAN FAMILY.

It is the aim of this volume to elevate both the honor and the remuneration of all employments that sustain the many difficult and varied duties of the family state, and thus to render each department of woman's profession as much desired and respected as are the most honored professions of men.

What, then, is the end designed by the family state which Jesus Christ came into this world to secure?

It is to provide for the training of our race to the highest possible intelligence, virtue, and happiness, by means of the self-sacrificing labors of the wise and good, and this with chief reference to a future immortal existence.

The distinctive feature of the family is self-sacrificing labor of the stronger and wiser members to raise the weaker and more ignorant to equal advantages. The father undergoes toil and self-denial to provide a home, and then the mother becomes a self-sacrificing laborer to train its inmates. The useless, troublesome infant is served in the humblest offices; while both parents unite in training it to an equality with themselves in every advantage. Soon the older children become helpers to raise the younger to a level with their own. When any are sick, those who are well become self-sacrificing ministers. When the parents are old and useless, the children become their self-sacrificing servants.

Thus the discipline of the family state is one of daily self-devotion of the stronger and wiser to elevate and support the weaker members. Nothing could be more contrary to its first principles than for the older and more capable children to combine to secure to themselves the highest advantages, enforcing the drudgeries on the younger, at the sacrifice of their equal culture.

Jesus Christ came to teach the fatherhood of God and consequent brotherhood of man. He came as the "first-born Son" of God and the Elder Brother of man, to teach by example the self-sacrifice by which the great family of man is to be raised to equality of advantages as children of God. For this end, he "humbled himself" from the highest to the lowest place. He chose for his birthplace the most despised village; for his parents the lowest in rank; for his trade, to labor with his hands as a carpenter, being "subject to his parents" thirty years. And, what is very significant, his trade was that which prepares the family home, as if he would teach that the great duty of man is labor – to provide for and train weak and ignorant creatures. Jesus Christ worked with his hands nearly thirty years, and preached less than three. And he taught that his kingdom is exactly opposite to that of the world, where all are striving for the highest positions. "Whoso will be great shall be your minister, and whoso will be chiefest shall be servant of all."[75]

The family state then, is the aptest earthly illustration of the heavenly kingdom, and in it woman is its chief minister. Her great mission is self-denial, in training its members to self-sacrificing labors for the ignorant and weak: if not her own children, then the neglected children of her Father in heaven. She is to rear all under her care to lay up treasures, not on earth, but in heaven. All the pleasures of this life end here; but those who train immortal minds are to reap the fruit of their labor through eternal ages.

To man is appointed the out-door labor – to till the earth, dig the mines, toil in the foundries, traverse the ocean, transport merchandise, labor in manufactories, construct houses, conduct civil, municipal, and state affairs, and all the heavy work, which, most of the day, excludes him from the comforts of a home. But the great stimulus to all these toils, implanted in the heart of every true man, is the desire for a home of his own, and the hopes of paternity. Every man who truly lives for immortality responds to the beatitude, "Children are a heritage from the Lord: blessed is the man that hath his quiver full of them!"[76] The more a father and mother live under the influence of that "immortality which Christ hath brought to light," the more is the blessedness of rearing a family understood and appreciated. Every child trained aright is to dwell forever in exalted bliss with those that gave it life and trained it for heaven.

The blessed privileges of the family state are not confined to those who rear children of their own. Any woman who can earn a livelihood, as every woman should be trained to do, can take a properly qualified female associate, and institute a family of her own, receiving to its heavenly influences the orphan, the sick, the homeless, and the sinful, and by motherly devotion train them to follow the self-denying example of Christ, in educating his earthly children for true happiness in this life and for his eternal home. [...]

---

[75] Mark 10.43-44.
[76] Ps. 127.4-5.

Source: Catharine Esther Beecher (1800-1878) and Harriet Beecher Stowe (1811-1896). "The Christian Family." *The American Woman's Home (or, Principles of Domestic Science; Being a Guide to the Formation and Maintenance of Economical, Healthful, Beautiful and Christian Homes)*. Ed. Nicole Tonkovich. Hartford, CT: Harriet Beecher Stowe Center, and New Brunswick, NJ: Rutgers University Press, 2002, 23-25.

242. Sarah Grand
"The New Aspect of the Woman Question" (1894)

IT is amusing as well as interesting to note the pause which the new aspect of the woman question has given to the Bawling Brothers[77] who have hitherto tried to howl down every attempt on the part of our sex to make the world a pleasanter place to live in. That woman should ape man and desire to change places with him was conceivable to him as he stood on the hearth-rug in his lord-and-master-monarch-of-all-I-survey attitude, well inflated with his own conceit; but that she should be content to develop the good material which she finds in herself and be only dissatisfied with the poor quality of that which is being offered to her in man, her mate, must appear to him to be a thing as monstrous as it is unaccountable. "If women don't want to be men, what do they want?" asked the Bawling Brotherhood when the first misgiving of the truth flashed upon them; and then, to reassure themselves, they pointed to a certain sort of woman in proof of the contention that we were all unsexing ourselves.

It would be as rational for us now to declare that men generally are Bawling Brothers or to adopt the hasty conclusion which makes all men out to be fiends on the one hand and all women fools on the other. We have our Shrieking Sisterhood, as the counterpart of the Bawling Brotherhood. The latter consists of two sorts of men. First of all is he who is satisfied with the cow-kind of woman as being most convenient; it is the threat of any strike among his domestic cattle for more consideration that irritates him into loud and angry protests. The other sort of Bawling Brother is he who is under the influence of the scum of our sex, who knows nothing better than women of that class in and out of society, preys upon them or ruins himself for them, takes his whole tone from them, and judges us all by them. Both the cow-woman and the scum-woman are well within range of the comprehension of the Bawling Brotherhood, but the new woman is a little above him, and he never even thought of looking up to where she has been sitting apart in silent contemplation all these years, thinking and thinking, until at last she solved the problem and proclaimed for herself what was wrong with Home-is-the-Woman's-Sphere, and prescribed the remedy. [...]

We must look upon man's mistakes, however, with some leniency, because we are not blameless in the matter ourselves. We have allowed him to arrange the whole social system and manage or mismanage it all these ages without ever seriously examining his work with a view to considering whether his abilities and his motives were sufficiently good to qualify him for the task. We have listened without a smile to his preachments, about our place in life and all we are good for [...]. We have allowed him to exact all things of us, and have been content to accept the little he grudgingly gave us in return. We have

---

[77] Sarah Grand obviously coined this term in response to the derogative term "Shrieking Sisterhood" that Eliza Lynn Linton, a British journalist, had created much earlier in order to attack women who demanded suffrage and admission to the workplace (cf. "The Shrieking Sisterhood," *Saturday Review*, March 12, 1870).

meekly bowed our heads when he called us bad names instead of demanding proofs of the superiority which alone would give him a right to do so. [...] Man deprived us of all proper education, and then jeered at us because we had no knowledge. He narrowed our outlook on life so that our view of it should be all distorted, and then declared that our mistaken impression of it proved us to be senseless creatures. He cramped our minds so that there was no room for reason in them, and then made merry at our want of logic. Our divine intuition was not to be controlled by him, but he did his best to damage it by sneering at it as an inferior feminine method of arriving at conclusions; and finally, after having had his own way until he lost his head completely, he set himself up as a sort of a god and required us to worship him, and, to our eternal shame be it said, we did so. The truth has all along been in us, but we have cared more for man than for truth, and so the whole human race has suffered. We have failed of our effect by neglecting our duty here, and have deserved much of the obloquy that was cast upon us. All that is over now, however, and while on the one hand man has shrunk to his true proportions in our estimation, we, on the other, have been expanding to our own; and now we come confidently forward to maintain, not that this or that was "intended," but that there are in ourselves, in both sexes, possibilities hitherto suppressed or abused, which, when properly developed, will supply to either what is lacking in the other.

The man of the future will be better, while the woman will be stronger and wiser. To bring this about is the whole aim and object of the present struggle, and with the discovery of the means lies the solution of the Woman Question. Man, having no conception of himself as imperfect from the woman's point of view, will find this difficult to understand, but we know his weakness, and will be patient with him, and help him with his lesson. It is the woman's place and pride and pleasure to teach the child, and man morally is in his infancy. There have been times when there was a doubt as to whether he was to be raised or woman was to be lowered, but we have turned that corner at last; and now woman holds out a strong hand to the child-man, and insists, but with infinite tenderness and pity, upon helping him up.

He must be taught consistency. There are ideals for him which it is to be presumed that he tacitly agrees to accept when he keeps up an expensive establishment to teach them: let him live up to them. [...]

But with all his assumption man does not make the most of himself. He has had every advantage of training to increase his insight, for instance, but yet we find him, even at this time of day, unable to perceive that woman has a certain amount of self-respect and practical good sense [...].

[...] O man! man! you are a very funny fellow now we know you! But take care. The standard of your pleasure and convenience has already ceased to be our conscience. On one point, however, you may reassure yourself. True womanliness is not in danger, and the sacred duties of wife and mother will be all the more honorably performed when women have a reasonable hope of becoming wives and mothers of *men*. But there is the difficulty. The trouble is not because women are mannish, but because men grow ever more effeminate. Manliness is at a premium now because there is so little of it, and we are accused of aping men in order to conceal the side from which the contrast should evidently be drawn. Man in his manners becomes more and more wanting until we seem to be near the time when there will be nothing left of him but the old Adam, who said, "It wasn't me." [...]

Source: Sarah Grand (1854-1943). "The New Aspect of the Woman Question [by Sarah Grand, Author of 'The Heavenly Twins']." *The North American Review* 158 (March 1894), 270-275.

243. Ouida
"The New Woman" (1894)

It can scarcely be disputed, I think, that in the English language there are conspicuous at the present moment two words which designate two unmitigated bores: The Workingman and the Woman. The Workingman and the Woman, the New Woman, be it remembered, meet us at every page of literature written in the English tongue; and each is convinced that on its own especial W hangs the future of the world. Both he and she want to have their values artificially raised and rated, and a status given to them by favor in lieu of desert. In an age in which persistent clamor is generally crowned by success they have both obtained considerable attention; is it offensive to say much more of it than either deserves? [...]

There is something deliciously comical in the idea, thus suggested, that man has only been allowed to "manage or mismanage" the world because woman has graciously refrained from preventing his doing so. But the comic side of this pompous and solemn assertion does not for a moment offer itself to the New Woman sitting aloof and aloft in her solitary meditation on the superiority of her sex. For the New Woman there is no such thing as a joke. She has listened without a smile to her enemy's "preachments"; she has "endured poignant misery for his sins," she has "meekly bowed her head" when he called her bad names; and she has never asked for "any proof of the superiority" which could alone have given him a right to use such naughty expressions. The truth has all along been in the possession of woman; but strange and sad perversity of taste! she has "cared more for man than for truth, and so the whole human race has suffered!"

"All that is over, however," we are told, and "while on the one hand man has shrunk to his true proportions" she has, all the time of this shrinkage, been herself expanding, and has in a word come to "fancy herself" extremely. So that he has no longer the slightest chance of imposing upon her by his game-cock[78] airs.

Man, "having no conception of himself as imperfect," will find this difficult to understand at first; but the New Woman "knows his weakness," and will "help him with his lesson." "*Man morally is in his infancy.*" There have been times when there was a doubt as to whether he was to be raised to her level, or woman to be lowered to his, but we "have turned that corner at last and now woman holds out a strong hand to the child-man and insists upon helping him up." The child-man [...] must have his tottering baby steps guided by the New Woman, and he must be taught to live up to his ideals. To live up to an ideal, whether our own or somebody else's, is a painful process; but man must be made to do it. For, oddly enough, we are assured that despite "all his assumption he does not make the best of himself," which is not wonderful if he be still only in his infancy; and he has the incredible stupidity to be blind to the fact that "woman has self-respect and good sense," and that "she does not in the least intend to sacrifice the privileges she enjoys on the chance of obtaining others." [...]

Woman, whether new or old, has immense fields of culture untilled, immense areas of influence wholly neglected. She does almost nothing with the resources she possesses, because her whole energy is concentrated on desiring and demanding those she has not. [...] Her influence on children might be so great that through them she would practically rule the future of the world; but she delegates her influence to the vile school boards if

---

[78] A cock bred and trained for fighting.

she be poor, and if she be rich to governesses and tutors; nor does she in ninety-nine cases out of a hundred ever attempt to educate or control herself into fitness for the personal exercise of such influence. [...]

The immense area which lies open to her in private life is almost entirely uncultivated, yet she wants to be admitted into public life. Public life is already overcrowded, verbose, incompetent, fussy, and foolish enough without the addition of her in her sealskin coat with the dead humming bird on her hat. Woman in public life would exaggerate the failings of men, and would not have even their few excellencies. Their legislation would be, as that of men is too often, the offspring of panic or prejudice; and she would not put on the drag of common-sense as man frequently does in public assemblies. There would be little to hope from her humanity, nothing from her liberality; for when she is frightened she is more ferocious than he, and when she has power more merciless. [...]

The error of the New Woman (as of many an old one) lies in speaking of women as the victims of men, and entirely ignoring the frequency with which men are the victims of women. In nine cases out of ten the first to corrupt the youth is the woman. In nine cases out of ten also she becomes corrupt herself because she likes it.

It is all very well to say that prostitutes were at the beginning of their career victims of seduction; but it is not probable and it is not provable. Love of drink and of finery, and a dislike to work, are the more likely motives and origin. It never seems to occur to the accusers of man that women are just as vicious and as lazy as he is in nine cases out of ten, and need no invitation from him to become so.

A worse prostitution than that of the streets, *i.e.*, that of loveless marriages of convenience, are brought about by women, not by men. In such unions the man always gives much more than he gains, and the woman in almost every instance is persuaded or driven into it by women – her mother, her sisters, her acquaintances. It is rarely that the father interferes to bring about such a marriage.

In even what is called a well-assorted marriage, the man is frequently sacrificed to the woman. [...]

[...E]very word, whether written or spoken, which urges the woman to antagonism against the man, every word which is written or spoken to try and make of her a hybrid, self-contained, opponent of men, makes a rift in the lute to which the world looks for its sweetest music.

The New Woman reminds me of an agriculturist who, discarding a fine farm of his own, and leaving it to nettles, stones, thistles, and wire-worms, should spend his whole time in demanding neighboring fields which are not his. The New Woman will not even look at the extent of ground indisputably her own, which she leaves unweeded and untilled.

Not to speak of the entire guidance of childhood, which is certainly already chiefly in the hands of woman (and of which her use does not do her much honor), so long as she goes to see one of her own sex dancing in a lion's den, the lions being meanwhile terrorized by a male brute; so long as she wears dead birds as millinery and dead seals as coats; so long as she goes to races, steeplechases,[79] coursing and pigeon matches; so long as she "walks with the guns"; [...] so long as she makes no attempt to interest herself in her servants, in her animals, in the poor slaves of her tradespeople; so long as she shows herself as she does at present without scruple at every brutal and debasing spectacle which is

---

[79] A horse-race across country or on a made course with fences and other obstacles. Formerly, a race having a church steeple in view as goal.

considered fashionable; so long as she understands nothing of the beauty of meditation, of solitude, of Nature; so long as she is utterly incapable of keeping her sons out of the shambles of modern sport, and lifting her daughters above the pestilent miasma[80] of modern society – so long as she does not, can not, or will not either do, or cause to do, any of these things, she has no possible title or capacity to demand the place or the privilege of man.   OUIDA.

Source: Ouida, pseudonym for Louisa de la Ramé (1839-1908). "The New Woman." *The North American Review* 158 (May 1894), 610-615, 618-619.

244. Max O'Rell
"Petticoat Government" (1896)

WITH COMMENTS BY MRS. H. P. SPOFFORD AND MRS. MARGARET BOTTOME, PRESIDENT OF THE INTERNATIONAL ORDER OF KING'S DAUGHTERS AND SONS.

I.

I LOATHE the domination of woman, but I ever crave for her influence, and I believe that any man of refinement and thinking, that any lover and admirer of woman, will echo this sentiment.

I know of one country only where the government by woman was given a real trial, and that is New Zealand. The law was passed and the experiment was made. The law had to be repealed after six months. The government had taken such a tyrannical form that that loveliest of spots on the earth was on the eve of a revolution, of a desperate struggle for liberty.

Things were pretty badly managed in a small Ohio city when I was visiting it four years ago. The following year women put up their names as candidates for the City Council in every ward and were all returned. They did manage the city. The following year the experiment had been made, and not one woman was returned again.

The American men are so busy, so long absent from home, that many of their womankind have to find out a way of using the leisure time left at their disposal, with results that are not always altogether satisfactory. Some devote that time to literature, to the improvement of their brilliant native intellect; some spend it in frivolities; some indulge in all the fads of Anglo-Saxon life.

The women of good society in America are what they are everywhere else, satisfied with their lot which consists in being the adored goddesses of refined households; but there exists in this country, among the middle – perhaps what I should call in European parlance, lower-middle – classes, restless, bumptious, ever poking-their-noses-everywhere women who are slowly, but surely and safely, transforming this great land of liberty into a land of petty, fussy tyranny, and trying, often with complete success, to impose on the community fads of every shape and form.

If there is one country in the world where the women appear, in the eyes of the foreign visitor, to enjoy all manner of privileges and to have the men in leading strings, that country is America. You would imagine, therefore, that America should be the last country where the "new woman" was to be found airing her grievances. Yet she is flourishing

---

[80] Noxious vapour rising from putrescent organic matter which pollutes the atmosphere.

throughout the length and breadth of this huge continent. She is petted by her husband, the most devoted and hard-working of husbands in the world; she is literally covered with precious stones by him. [...] She is the superior of her husband in education, and almost in every respect. She is surrounded by the most numerous and delicate attentions. Yet she is not satisfied.

The Anglo-Saxon "new woman" is the most ridiculous production of modern times and destined to be the most ghastly failure of the century. She is *par excellence* the woman with a grievance, and self-labelled the greatest nuisance of modern society. The new woman wants to retain all the privileges of her sex and secure, besides, all those of man. She wants to be a man and to remain a woman. She will fail to become a man, but she may succeed in ceasing to be a woman.

And, now, where is that "new woman" to be found? Put together a hundred women, intelligent and of good society; take out the beautiful ones, then take out the married ones who are loved by their husbands and their children, and kindly seek the "new woman" among what is left – ugly women, old maids, and disappointed wives.

Woman has no grievance against man. Her only grievance should be, I admit, against Nature, which made her different from man; with duties different, physically and otherwise, almost always to her disadvantage. The world exists and marches on through love. I pity from the bottom of my heart the good woman who is not to know the whispers of love of a good husband or the caresses of little children, but I am not prepared to see life become a burden for her sake.

There is no possibility of denying or ignoring the fact. The purpose, the *raison d'être*, of woman is to be a mother, as the *raison d'être* of a fruit tree is to bear fruit. And woe to the next generations; for everybody knows that *only* the children of quiet and reposed women are healthy and intelligent.

The woman question will only be solved by the partnership in life of man and wife, as it exists in France, where, thank God! the "new woman" is unknown; by the equality of the sexes, but each with different, well-defined duties to perform.

The "new woman" is not to be found outside of Great Britain, where woman is her husband's inferior, and of the United States, where she is his superior.

The woman who devotes a good deal of her time to the management of public affairs is a woman who is not required to devote much of it to private ones.

Show me a woman of forty!

Look on this picture: eyes bright, beaming with joy and happiness, complexion clear, rosy, plump, not a wrinkle, mouth smiling. See her lips bearing the imprint of holy kisses, and her neck the mark of her little children's arms. She has no grievance. Ask her to join the "new woman" army. "No, thanks," she will say with a smile of pity, "the old style is good enough for me."

And on this: thin, sallow complexion, eyes without lustre, wrinkled, mouth sulky, haughty, the disgust of life written on every feature. That woman will join the ranks of every organization which aims at taking the cup of love away from the lips of every happy being. [...]

Source: Max O'Rell (1848-1903). "Petticoat Government." *The North American Review*, 163 (July 1896), 101-103.

245. Rebecca L. Leeke
"The New Lady" (1896)

The misuse of the word "lady" has driven it into the background, and the abuse of the word "woman" has pushed it too far to the front. The word "lady" has come to be regarded as a weakling, and the class of humanity which it represents has shrunk into insignificance before the pretentious claims of the new woman. But the old-time lady has not gone away to stay; she has merely stepped aside to avoid being run over by the wheel of the new woman, and will reappear when the dust has settled. The word "lady" suggests nobility of origin, or, at least, nobility of character. Both the title and its possessor were once regarded with reverent respect. A renewal of the popularity of the title would awaken a revival of the sentiment which the title evoked, and the time for a reaction in its favor is at hand.

This is a time of wild agitation concerning the portion of power that belongs to woman, as well as of wild conjecture concerning the limits of the sphere within which her power is to be exerted. Her interpretation of her sphere and of her privileges distinguishes the woman of the new school from the lady of the old. The woman of the new school claims rights that are separate from the rights of man, and opposed to his; the lady of the old school claimed no rights that were in conflict with the rights of man, and in defense of her own rights she desired the protection that is due to her sex from men. She gratefully accepted the chivalrous courtesy that has been shown to her in all ages until now. That she does not receive it to the same extent now is the fault of the advanced woman, who scorns it, who is ambitious to direct the affairs of state, and who, in order to gratify that ambition, is willing to forego to some extent the usual courtesies which women have hitherto expected and received.

As a result of her advancement, her more unassuming sisters are obliged to witness a marked decline in politeness to women as women. The lady deplores the dawn of such a day, and is looking for a better day, which she may reasonably hope is coming through the very education which the advanced woman is perverting to her own ends.

In times past the lady has been able to influence the affairs of men because she has not attempted to direct their affairs; in the future she can maintain her power only by being as well educated as men are, "by knowing the things that men know as well as men know them," and by using her knowledge to supplement man's work in the world, not to usurp it. When the elements of the present agitation shape themselves into a new type of womanhood, the characteristics of the lady will be stamped upon the composite, which will differ in its essential features from the type anticipated by the present theories of the coming woman. If the new type is the lady of Ruskin's portrayal, "enduringly, incorruptibly good, instinctively wise," her education must make her so. "She must know sciences to be accurate, mathematics to be logical, history to be sympathetic, and languages to be hospitable." "She must have the same kind of education for social service that man has for business and for professional service,"[81] and then she must use it to accomplish her own purposes, not his. The new type will not be the mere housewife: the

---

[81] Quotes from John Ruskin's essay "Of Queen's Gardens" (published in *Sesame and Lilies*, 1865). This essay eloquently portrays the conservative ideal of Victorian womanhood and urges women to abandon trivial feminine pursuits in order to act as a moral force in society.

breadwinner she may be, but not the imitator of man, nor the woman who is ambitious to usurp his rights. She will be loyal to her womanhood, and as proud to retain the title "lady" as women once were to assume it.

Sculpture has realized the ideal in art – "to assemble into a whole the characteristics of different individuals, excluding the unseemly." Photography has interpreted the ideal in the composite picture. So the new education will produce the new lady, the type of everything that is strong and sensible and intellectual and noble and pure in womanhood. In her broader sphere she will be the lady of the old school revised and improved.

Source: Rebecca L. Leeke. "The New Lady." *The Century* 51.3 (Jan. 1896), 476-477.

246. John Paul MacCorrie
"The War of the Sexes" (1896)

The alarmist is again abroad. This time he is at once exceedingly disturbed and exceedingly amusing. He is, of course, as usual, distressingly solicitous for the welfare of the commonwealth. He will save society at any cost; and so, always keenly alive to its present dangers and necessities, he feels called upon to lift a warning voice against the formidable ebullitions[82] of the "New Woman."

To be sure, he hastens to assure us that the threatening cloud is as yet but very small, perhaps not larger than a man's thumb-nail – but still unquestionably portentous of evil; it is, in fact, quite alarming. For all great tempests have just such beginnings, we are told; and who can say what the event will be when that little cloud grows up to be a great large thunderstorm, and its winds have lashed the surface of society into angry foam, while its lightnings, announcing the "supremacy of woman," flash out all over the land? [...]

The chief aim of the New Woman, in so far as she can be accused of having any definite purpose in view, is, we believe, the equality of sex. From certain points of observation this is surely a laudable ambition. Before God, for example, all rational beings are equal. There is no distinction between sex and sex in view of unity of origin and destiny. In the participation of eternal reward or punishment they are one. Again, there is no intrinsic reason why the intellectual capacities of woman should not equal, and in some instances even outstrip, those of her sterner brothers; although the distinction is sometimes made that the one is more quick and the other more judicious; the former remarkable for delicacy of association, while the latter is characterized by stronger power of attention. And advancing still further, we would aver that in its own proper sphere the female sex is not only equal but often decidedly the superior of the male. But, unfortunately, none of this forms the basis of contention. The New Woman lays claim not only to what we have herein gladly granted her, but, over and above that, she would fain step out of the natural modesty of her sex and strive to become man's equal in his special and peculiar province, his rival in the struggle for what at best are but doubtful honors.

A DECLARATION OF WAR.

She tells us, "there is no intellectual, social, or professional advancement for woman except as she asserts her independence of man and arrays herself against him as the en-

---

[82] A state of agitation in a liquid resembling that produced by boiling heat.

emy of her sex." That "marriage under the existing conditions is unmitigated slavery." That the barriers begotten of masculine selfishness and conceit, "excluding woman from the more serious avocations of life, must be abolished." [...]

She will "no longer receive her religious creeds from men, but will construct her own on a new and improved basis."

She must be actively represented in the government of the state.

In short, every right and liberty enjoyed by men, whether political, moral or religious, must be forthwith and univocally extended to women.[83] [...]

DISTORTION OF THE ARGUMENT FROM SCRIPTURE.

[...] "According to the Christian idea the husband and wife are two in one flesh. They are united by an intimate and mutual love in God, and should edify each other in peace, in fidelity, and mutual support. The husband is the head of the wife, whom he should love, esteem, and protect. The wife is, within the circle of her duties, at the side of the man, not subject to him as the child is subject to its father or as the slave to the master; but as the mother, side-by-side with the father, having, no less than he, sacred and imprescriptible rights. But as in every company or corporation it is necessary that some hold superior rank and authority that order and peace may prevail, so in that association of man and woman called marriage, in which the parties are bound one to the other, there must be a superior while each according to rank has necessities, duties, and rights. [...]"

These are the doctrines which have stricken the bonds of heathen servitude from the trampled neck of woman and raised her to that lofty eminence which she now enjoys in the presence of the Church of Christ. The next step above and beyond that point is social disorder pure and simple. [...]

WOMAN'S TRUE DUTY AND PRIVILEGES.

We contend, and we regret not without some opposition, that in the home and family are concentrated woman's first and highest "rights." [...]

Say what we will, woman was created to be a wife and a mother; that is, after a special religious calling to the service of God, her highest destiny. To that destiny all her instincts are fashioned and directed; for it she has been endowed with transcendent virtues of endurance, patience, generous sympathies, and indomitable perseverance.

To her belongs the special function of moulding the youthful mind, of scattering the seeds of virtue, love, reverence, and obedience among her children, that her sons may become upright and loving husbands, and her daughters modest and affectionate wives, tender and judicious mothers, careful and prudent housekeepers. This the best of men can never do, for the office demands the sympathetic touch with children, the strong maternal instinct which is peculiar to the female heart. And the instant woman neglects that duty, for the exercise of other occupations, howsoever virtuous, in the sight of all reflecting men and women she is false to the first and most sacred principle of her existence – her life is a shameful lie. For women were not intended by the Creator to be men; they are needed not for that which men can do as well as they, but for that which man cannot accomplish.

Given, then, the faithful performance of this the grandest and most ennobling of woman's work, unwavering fidelity and devotion to the home, a responsibility sacred and

---

[83] Original footnote: "See reports of conventions at Washington and elsewhere."

above all things else, there are surely none more willing and anxious than we to accord to her every legitimate right which is hers, every liberty that can in any way contribute to the sum of her personal happiness. And here we must content ourselves with a few words on what to us seems the most timely and important of these – woman's undeniable right to a high and liberal education. [...]

MISTAKEN TENDENCY OF EDUCATION.

It is to be deeply regretted that our system of female education inclines rather to present accomplishment than to a solid discipline and training of the mind along the more serious avenues of thought. There is a tendency to embellish the heyday of youth, that of its nature needs little to enhance it, and leaves the remainder of life without taste or relish. Music is, indeed, a beautiful accomplishment that diffuses its charms to others. Painting is alike generous and extends its pleasure to many. A woman who can sing well may move and win the hearts of many friends by the exercise of her talent; but these things after all constitute but a short-lived blaze which presently goes out. A woman of accomplishments may entertain for an hour with great brilliancy; but a woman of ideas is an abiding source of exhilaration and joy. [...]

What is really needed are resources that will endure as long as life endures, habits of mind that will render adversity and sickness tolerable, and solitude, if not a pleasure, at least not unbearable; a mental training that will ease the cares of maternity, render age venerable, and death less terrible.

In this we would not have the lighter graces neglected, but we would wish them subordinated to, or shall we rather say harmonized with, a solid intellectual instruction, a moral and religious culture. And, therefore, instead of having a woman's understanding go out in paint, or dissolve away in musical vibrations, it should be primarily directed to that deeper knowledge that diffuses equally over a whole existence, better loved as it is longer felt.

In conclusion it must be fairly confessed that women have suffered many wrongs through the selfishness and tyranny of men. But it must be admitted, on the other hand, that men have borne their share of sorrow also from the follies and caprices of women. There is much wrong on both sides, some necessary, a great deal needless. Neither men nor women are as good as they might or should be.

And since the present advocates of woman's rights insist that in intellect woman is man's equal, while in will power his superior, it is hardly fair to charge him alone with all that is wrong or painful in her condition. Much of it, we fear, can be traced to her own execution, and we dare to maintain that the solution of the question is to be found, not so much in a direct attempt at even a relative equalizing of forces as in the reverence which should be borne by woman to her own sex. [...]

Source: John Paul MacCorrie, "The War of the Sexes." *Catholic World* 63/377 (August 1896), 605-606, 611-612, 614-617.

247. "New Woman" (1915)

Source: "The New Woman" [Ivory Soap advertisement]. Proctor & Gamble Co., 1915. *The Century*.

SLAVERY

American slavery emerged in the context of the first European attempts at colonization in the New World and, as a system of forced labor, contributed to the economic network of the triangular trade prevalent in the seventeenth and eighteenth centuries. Slavery found its way into the British colonies in North America at a very early date. Already in 1619, the first African indentured servants arrived in Jamestown. Since the alternative sources of unfree labor in the young colonies – enslaved Native Americans and indentured servants from Europe – proved ineffective or ran dry by the end of the seventeenth century, African slavery provided the labor necessary especially on Southern plantations growing tobacco, sugar, and rice for the European markets. By mid-century, colonial American courts had recognized Africans as chattel, the personal property of their owners, and had proclaimed that the status of the mother would determine the future status of her children, thus rendering the importation of African slaves a lucrative business. Reflecting on the dreadful Middle Passage in her poetry, Phillis Wheatley, a slave girl who was bought by a Boston merchant and who is credited with being the first African American to publish a book, seemingly accepts the notion that the slave trade resulted in the conversion of pagans to Christianity. At the same time, she inscribes a subversive critique of slavery in her poem "On Being Brought from Africa to America" (doc. 249). Commenting on the negative moral and political consequences of slavery, Virginian planter William Byrd expresses his apprehensions about importing increasing numbers of slaves to the American colonies in a 1736 letter to an English correspondent (doc. 250). He is not only concerned with the public safety of the colonists, but also cautions against the moral degeneration of the settlers. Despite the importance of the slave trade to the British economy, he suggests that Parliament "put an end to this unchristian traffick of making merchandize of our fellow creatures." The American Quaker John Woolman shared Byrd's perception of slavery as a transatlantic economic system and as a threat to the political and moral constitution of the colonies. As a traveling minister, he urged his fellow Friends to emancipate their slaves and thus quit their involvement in an injustice that was irreconcilable with Christianity and possibly the well-being of an emerging American society (cf. doc. 252).

Beginning with the American Revolution, the question of slavery and the slave trade turned into a genuinely American debate. While the proportion of slaves in the colonial population grew steadily in the South (40 to 50 percent in most parts at the end of the eighteenth century), the system of slavery remained less significant in the North. On the eve of the Revolution, the slave population consisted of half a million slaves and would grow to four million by the 1860s, despite the fact that the importation of slaves was outlawed in the United States in 1808. The slave population augmented due to natural reproduction and became more and more African American in nature. The debate on the future of slavery became ever more significant after the invention of the cotton gin in 1793, which made the growth of cotton increasingly profitable and perpetuated the institution of slavery. The letters of the Frenchman St. John De Crèvecœur's persona of an American farmer depict America not only as a place of opportunity for Europeans, but also illustrate "the horrors of slavery" prevalent in the young republic (doc. 253). While Thomas Jefferson's *Notes on the State of Virginia* (doc. 251) can similarly be read as a condemnation of slavery, he provides at the same time a statement of racism not singular in Enlightenment philosophy by stating his belief in black people's inferiority "in the endowments both of body and mind." As the author of the Declaration of Independence was known to be a slaveholder himself, Jefferson was harshly criticized for failing to live up to the ideals of human rights, especially liberty and equality, as put forth in the Declaration.

Southerners propagated various justifications for maintaining the status quo and for extending slavery into the western territories. In their eyes, slavery was a "necessary evil" in an economic sense and indispensable for a region referred to as the "cotton kingdom." The owners of slaves even pronounced the institution a "positive good" for the slaves and claimed that slaves, as members of the extended family, were better off under a paternalistic system than they would be on their own (cf. docs. 260, 261). Such arguments were rooted in the firm belief in the racial inferiority of black people and were employed to supplement the biblical interpretation that traced the emergence of black slavery to the curse of Ham by Noah in the Old Testament. The circulation of proslavery arguments in the South increased especially after David Walker published his *Appeal to the Coloured Citizens of the World* in 1829 (doc. 255) where he called upon black people to unite and prove the supporters of the ideology of black inferiority wrong. A free black, Walker appropriated the 1776 patriots' language of violent resistance to a tyrannical order in his pamphlet and his writing was subsequently blamed by Southerners to be an incendiary piece of propaganda giving rise to slave revolts like that of Nat Turner in 1831. From a Southern point of view, however, the benevolent treatment of slaves by the slaveholders provided for their well-being and happiness in the first place. The South Carolinian Senator John C. Calhoun, for example, proclaimed in 1837 that "[n]ever before has the black race [...] attained a condition so civilized and so improved, not only physically, but morally and intellectually" and that "the relation now existing in the slave-holding States between [black and white people], is, instead of an evil, a good – a positive good" (doc. 260). Later apologists, for instance George Fitzhugh in *Sociology for the South*, extended the argument to include a direct comparison between workers in the Northern capitalist system and Southern slaves, declaring slavery by far the more humane system (doc. 264, cf. also docs. 270 and 271).

Northern white Americans challenged slave owners who viewed themselves as kind patriarchs and questioned the institution per se. From the late 1770s, all northern states had worked toward the gradual abolition of slavery, a process that was completed by the early years of the new century and produced a considerable free black population. However, not all Northerners were abolitionists; indeed, early antislavery sentiment was rather moderate among the white population in the North and comprised models embracing the gradual emancipation of the slaves in the South, often in connection with the colonization of black people in Africa (cf. doc. 254). Jefferson in his *Notes on the State of Virginia* had already anticipated this political movement when he argued for the African Americans' removal, and therefore the separation of the races, in the case of their emancipation. Even though the founding of the American Colonization Society in 1816 marked the beginning of a widespread political movement to end slavery, most free blacks rejected the idea of leaving the United States and going 'back' to Africa.

Black abolitionists insisted on the immediate emancipation of slaves from an early stage of the antislavery campaign, while white opponents of slavery embraced immediatism only from the 1830s. Gradualism and colonization began to be widely rejected at the same time that the Southern discourse in favor of the "peculiar institution" grew more determined and as gradualist and colonizationist approaches were exposed as half-hearted measures whose promotion rested principally on racist assumptions. White abolitionist William Lloyd Garrison, the publisher of the weekly magazine *The Liberator* (1831-1865), stands like no other figure for the immediate abolition of slavery in the United States. Immediatism, with its strategies of moral suasion and nonviolence, replaced gradual and colonization solutions to the question of slavery and was institutionalized in 1833 when the American Anti-Slavery Society was established. These early abolitionist ideas primarily drew from two sources, from Revolutionary and from Christian (evangelical) thought. Christian abolitionists such as George B. Cheever and Albert Barnes (cf. docs. 257 and 258) rejected the institution of slavery on the grounds of its immorality, and one female abolitionist, Angelina Grimké, appealed specifically to her southern "sisters" to get involved in the campaign to end slavery and to employ unlawful means if necessary (doc. 259). Grimké denounced slavery as sin and demanded that women fulfill their duty as Christians by joining the struggle.

Starting in the 1840s, the abolitionist movement split into competing factions over the question of which means should be employed to achieve the common goal. While some put their hopes into politics, Garrison, a stark supporter of nonviolent approaches to the immediate end of slavery (cf. docs. 266 and 267), continued to perceive the fight against slavery as a primarily religious and moral question. He consequently rejected the Constitution as a proslavery document and refused to get involved in political parties and elections. However, Garrison's creed of nonviolence and nonresistance was met with opposition within abolitionist circles even before a new Fugitive Slave Law came into effect in 1850 and further escalated the national debate on slavery. The black antislavery activist and Presbyterian minister Henry Highland Garnet whose manifesto for active violent resistance was published together with Walker's *Appeal* (and with the financial help of John Brown, the white man who would later fail in his raid on Harper's Ferry) provides one such example. In his 1843 "Address to the Slaves" (doc. 265) Garnet argues that slaves had a moral obligation to attempt to break free from slavery and that they should "rather die than live on as slaves." Even though Frederick Douglass, at this point the most eminent black abolitionist, denounced Garnet's position, Douglass, too, would later turn more militant and break with Garrison over the question of voting and the Constitution which Douglass viewed as a "glorious liberty document." In his most famous speech on the meaning of the Fourth of July for African Americans (doc. 268), Douglass continues the tradition of invoking the ideals of the American Revolution, claiming that its achievements, especially freedom and justice, are not valid for African Americans and that the celebration of independence is thus meaningless for them. A multifaceted movement, abolitionism began to lose its original significance as the political realities of the sectional conflict that had arisen between the Northern and the Southern states pointed toward a resolution through civil war. The passing of the Thirteenth Amendment in 1865 ultimately pronounced the official end of slavery, certainly without, for the time being, securing full civil rights for the freedmen.

Melanie Fritsch

248. To Be Sold (1769)

CHARLESTOWN, *April* 27, 1769.

TO BE SOLD,

On WEDNESDAY *the Tenth Day of* MAY *next*,

A CHOICE CARGO OF

Two Hundred & Fifty

NEGROES:

A RRIVED in the Ship COUNTESS of SUSSEX, THOMAS DAVIES, Mafter, directly from GAMBIA, by

JOHN CHAPMAN, & Co.

₊ *THIS is the Veffel that had the Small-Pox on Board at the Time of her Arrival the* 31ſt *of March laſt : Every neceſſary Precaution hath ſince been taken to cleanſe both Ship and Cargo thoroughly, ſo that thoſe who may be inclined to purchaſe need not be under the leaſt Apprehenſion of Danger from Infection.*

The NEGROES *are allowed to be the likelieſt Parcel that have been imported this Seaſon.*

Source: *To Be Sold*. Charleston, April 27, 1769. Courtesy Library of Congress.

249. Phillis Wheatley
"On Being Brought from Africa to America" (1786)

'Twas mercy brought me from my *Pagan* land,
Taught my benighted soul to understand
That there's a God, that there's a *Saviour* too:
Once I redemption neither sought nor knew,
Some view our sable race with scornful eye,
"Their colour is a diabolic die."
Remember, *Christians, Negroes*, black as *Cain*,
May be refin'd, and join th' angelic train.

Source: Phillis Wheatley (1753-1784). "On Being Brought from Africa to America." *Poems on Various Subjects, Religious and Moral, by Phillis Wheatley, Negro servant to Mr. John Wheatley, of Boston, in New England*. Philadelphia: Joseph Crukshank, 1786, 13 [first published London, 1773].

250. William Byrd II
"Letter to John Perceval, Earl of Egmont (1736)"

My Lord   Virginia, the 12th of July, 1736

[...] Your Lordships opinion concerning rum & Negros is certainly very just, and your excludeing both of them from your colony of Georgia will be very happy; tho' with respect to rum, the saints of New England I fear will find out some trick to evade your Act of Parliament. They have a great dexterity at palliating a perjury so well as to leave no tast[e] of it in the mouth, nor can any people like them slip through a penal statute. They will give some other name to their rum, which they may safely do, because it go[e]s by that of kill-devil in this country from its banefull qualitys. A watchfull eye must be kept on these foul traders or all the precautions of the trustees will be vain.

I wish my Lord we coud be blesst with the same prohibitions. They import so many Negros hither, that I fear this colony will some time or other be confirmd by the name of New Guinea. I am sensible of many bad consequences of multiplying these Ethiopians amongst us. They blow up the pride, & ruin the industry of our white people, who seing a rank of poor creatures below them, detest work for fear it shoud make them look like slaves. Then that poverty which will ever attend upon idleness, disposes them as much to pilfer, as it dos the Portuguese, who account it much more like a gentleman to steal, than to dirty their hands with labour of any kind.

Another unhappy effect of many Negros, is, the necessity of being severe. Numbers make them insolent, & then foul means must do, what fair will not. We have however nothing like the inhumanity here, that is practiced in the islands, & God forbid we ever shoud. But these base tempers require to be rid with a tort rein, or they will be apt to throw their rider. Yet even this is terrible to a good naturd man, who must submit to be either a fool or a fury. And this will be more our unhappy case, the more Negros are increast amongst us.

But these private mischeifs are nothing if compard to the publick danger. We have already at least 10,000 men of these descendants of Ham fit to bear arms, & their numbers increase every day as well by birth as importation. And in case there shoud arise a man of desperate courage amongst us, exasperated by a desperate fortune, he might with more advantage than Cataline, kindle a sevile war. Such a man might be dreadfully mischeivous before any opposition coud be formed against him, and tinge our rivers as wide as they are with blood. Besides the calamitys which woud be brought upon us by such an attempt, it woud cost our mother country many a fair million to make us as profitable as we are at present.

It were therefore worth the consideration of a British Parliament, my Lord, to put an end to this unchristian traffick of makeing merchandize of our fellow creatures. At least the farther importation of them into our colonys shoud be prohibited lest they prove as troublesome & dangerous every where, as they have been lately in Jamaica, where besides a vast expence of mony, they have cost the lives of many of His Majestys subjects. We have mountains in Virginia too, to which they may retire as safely, and do as much mischeif as they do in Jamaica. All these matters duly considerd, I wonder the legislature will indulge a few ravenous traders to the danger of the publick safety, and such traders as woud freely sell their fathers, their elder brothers, & even the wives of their bosomes, if they coud black their faces & get any thing by them. [...]

Source: William Byrd II (1674-1744). "Letter to John Perceval, Earl of Egmont" (July 12, 1736). *The Correspondence of the Three William Birds of Westover, Virginia, 1684-1776*. Ed. Marion Tinling. Vol. 2. Charlottesville, VA: The University Press of Virginia, 1977, 487-488.

251. Thomas Jefferson
Notes on the State of Virginia (1788)

QUERY XIV.

[...] It will probably be asked, Why not retain and incorporate the blacks into the state, and thus save the expense of supplying, by importation of white settlers, the vacancies they will leave? Deep rooted prejudices entertained by the whites; ten thousand recollections, by the blacks, of the injuries they have sustained; new provocations; the real distinctions which nature has made; and many other circumstances, will divide us into parties, and produce convulsions which will probably never end but in the extermination of the one or the other race. – To these objections, which are political, may be added others, which are physical and moral. The first difference which strikes us is that of colour. – Whether the black of the negro resides in the reticular membrane[1] between the skin and scarf-skin,[2] or in the scarf-skin itself; whether it proceeds from the colour of the blood, the colour of the bile, or from that of some other secretion, the difference is fixed in nature, and is as real as if its seat and cause were better known to us. And is this difference of no importance? Is it not the foundation of a greater or less share of beauty in the two races? Are not the fine mixtures of red and white, the expressions of every passion by greater or less suffusions of colour in the one, preferable to that eternal monotony, which reigns in the countenances, that immovable veil of black which covers all the emotions of the other race? Add to these, flowing hair, a more elegant symmetry of form, their own judgment in favour of the whites, declared by their preference of them, as uniformly as is the preference of the Oranootan[3] for the black women over those of his own species. The circumstance of superior beauty is thought worthy attention in the propagation of our horses, dogs, and other domestic animals; why not in that of man? Besides those of colour, figure, and hair, there are other physical distinctions proving a difference of race. They have less hair on the face and body. They secrete less by the kidnies, and more by the glands of the skin, which gives them a very strong and disagreeable odour. This greater degree of transpiration renders them more tolerant of heat, and less so of cold, than the whites. Perhaps too a difference of structure in the pulmonary apparatus, which a late ingenious[4] experimentalist has discovered to be the principal regulator of animal heat, may have disabled them from extricating, in the act of inspiration, so much of that fluid from the outer air, or obliged them in expiration, to part with more of it. They seem to require less sleep. A black after hard labour through the day, will be induced by the slightest amusements to sit up till midnight, or later, though knowing he must be out with the first dawn of the morning. They are at least as brave, and more adventuresome. But this may perhaps proceed from a want of fore-thought, which prevents their seeing a danger till it be present. When present, they do not go through it with more coolness or steadiness than the whites. They are more ardent after their female: but love seems with them to be more an eager desire, than a tender delicate mixture of sentiment and sensation. Their griefs are transient. Those numberless afflictions, which render it doubtful whether heaven has given life to us in mercy or in wrath, are less felt, and sooner forgotten with them. In general, their existence appears to participate

---
[1] Membrane resembling a net in appearance or construction; consisting of closely interwoven fibres.
[2] The outer layer of the skin.
[3] Orangutan.
[4] Original footnote: "Crawford."

more of sensation than reflection. To this must be ascribed their disposition to sleep when abstracted from their diversions, and unemployed in labour. An animal whose body is at rest, and who does not reflect, must be disposed to sleep of course. Comparing them by their faculties of memory, reason, and imagination, it appears to me that in memory they are equal to the whites; in reason much inferior, as I think one could scarcely be found capable of tracing and comprehending the investigations of Euclid;[5] and that in imagination they are dull, tasteless, and anomalous. It would be unfair to follow them to Africa for this investigation. We will consider them here, on the same stage with the whites, and where the facts are not apocryphal on which a judgment is to be formed. It will be right to make great allowances for the difference of condition, of education, of conversation, of the sphere in which they move. Many millions of them have been brought to, and born in America. Most of them indeed have been confined to tillage,[6] to their own homes, and their own society: yet many have been so situated, that they might have availed themselves of the conversation of their masters; many have been brought up to the handicraft arts, from that circumstance have always been associated with the whites. Some have been liberally educated, and all have lived in countries where the arts and sciences are cultivated to a considerable degree, and have had before their eyes samples of the best works from abroad. The Indians, with no advantages of this kind, will often carve figures on their pipes not destitute of design and merit. They will crayon out an animal, a plant, or a country, so as to prove the existence of a germ in their minds which only wants cultivation. They astonish you with strokes of the most sublime oratory; such as prove their reason and sentiment strong, their imagination glowing and elevated. But never yet could I find that a black had uttered a thought above the level of plain narration; never see even an elementary trait of painting or sculpture. In music they are more generally gifted than the whites with accurate ears for tune and time [...]. Whether they will be equal to the composition of a more extensive run of melody, or of complicated harmony, is yet to be proved. Misery is often the parent of the most affecting touches in poetry. – Among the blacks is misery enough, God knows, but no poetry. Love is the peculiar œstrum[7] of the poet. Their love is ardent, but it kindles the senses only, not the imagination. Religion indeed has produced a Phyllis Whately;[8] but it could not produce a poet. The compositions published under her name are below the dignity of criticism. [...] The improvement of the blacks in body and mind, in the first instance of their mixture with the whites, has been observed by every one, and proves that their inferiority is not the effect merely of their condition of life. [...] Whether further observation will or will not verify the conjecture, that nature has been less bountiful to them in the endowments of the head, I believe that in those of the heart she will be found to have done them justice. That disposition to theft with which they have been branded, must be ascribed to their situation, and not to any depravity of the moral sense. The man, in whose favour no laws of property exist, probably feels himself less bound to respect those made in favour of others. When arguing for ourselves, we lay it down as a fundamental, that laws, to be just, must give a reciprocation of right: that, without this, they are mere arbitrary rules of conduct, founded in force, and not in conscience: and it is a problem which I give to the master to solve, whether the religious precepts against the

---

[5] Greek mathematician of the 3rd century BC.
[6] The act or art of tilling or cultivating land.
[7] A parasite, gadfly; here: *fig.* something that incites or stings a person into activity; a vehement impulse.
[8] Reference to Phillis Wheatley (1753-1784), African-American poet.

violation of property were not framed for him as well as his slave? And whether the slave may not as justifiably take a little from one, who has taken all from him, as he may slay one who would slay him? That a change in the relations in which a man is placed should change his ideas of moral right and wrong, is neither new, nor peculiar to the colour of the blacks. [...]

[...] Notwithstanding these considerations which must weaken their respect for the laws of property, we find among them numerous instances of the most rigid integrity, and as many as among their better instructed masters, of benevolence, gratitude and unshaken fidelity. – The opinion, that they are inferior in the faculties of reason and imagination, must be hazarded with great diffidence. To justify a general conclusion, requires many observations, even where the subject may be submitted to the anatomical knife, to optical glasses, to analysis by fire, or by solvents. How much more then where it is a faculty, not a substance, we are examining; where it eludes the research of all the senses; where the conditions of its existence are various and variously combined; where the effects of those which are present or absent bid defiance to calculation; let me add too, as a circumstance of great tenderness, where our conclusion would degrade a whole race of men from the rank in the scale of beings which their Creator may perhaps have given them. To our reproach it must be said, that though for a century and a half we have had under our eyes the races of black and of red men, they have never yet been viewed by us as subjects of natural history. I advance it therefore as a suspicion only, that the blacks, whether originally a distinct race, or made distinct by time and circumstances, are inferior to the whites in the endowments both of body and mind. It is not against experience to suppose, that different species of the same genus, or varieties of the same species, may possess different qualifications. Will not a lover of natural history then, one who views the gradations in all the races of animals with the eye of philosophy, excuse an effort to keep those in the department of man as distinct as nature has formed them? This unfortunate difference of colour, and perhaps of faculty, is a powerful obstacle to the emancipation of these people. Many of their advocates, while they wish to vindicate the liberty of human nature, are anxious also to preserve its dignity and beauty. Some of these, embarrassed by the question 'What further is to be done with them?' join themselves in opposition with those who are actuated by sordid avarice only. Among the Romans emancipation required but one effort. The slave, when made free, might mix with, without staining the blood of his master. But with us a second is necessary, unknown to history. When freed, he is to be removed beyond the reach of mixture. [...]

Query XVIII.

[...] There must doubtless be an unhappy influence on the manners of our people produced by the existence of slavery among us. The whole commerce between master and slave is a perpetual exercise of the most boisterous passions, the most unremitting despotism on the one part, and degrading submissions on the other. Our children see this, and learn to imitate it; for man is an imitative animal. This quality is the germ of all education in him. From his cradle to his grave he is learning to do what he sees others do. If a parent could find no motive either in his philanthropy or his self-love, for restraining the intemperance of passion towards his slave, it should always be a sufficient one that his child is present. But generally it is not sufficient. The parent storms, the child looks on, catches the lineaments of wrath, puts on the same airs in the circle of smaller slaves, gives a loose to his worst of passions, and thus nursed, educated, and daily exercised in tyranny, cannot but be stamped by it with odious peculiarities. The man must be a prodigy[9] who can retain his manners and morals undepraved by such circumstances. And with what execration should the statesman be loaded, who permitting one half the citizens thus to trample on the rights of the other, transforms those into despots, and these into enemies, destroys the morals of the one part, and the amor patriæ[10] of the other. For if a slave can have a country in this world, it must be any other in preference to that in which he is born to live and labour for another: in which he must lock up the faculties of his nature, contribute as far as depends on his individual endeavours to the evanishment[11] of the human race, or entail his own miserable condition on the endless generations proceeding from him. With the morals of the people, their industry also is destroyed. For in a warm climate, no man will labour for himself who can make another labour for him. This is so true, that of the proprietors of slaves a very small proportion indeed are ever seen to labour. And can the liberties of a nation be thought secure when we have removed their only firm basis, a conviction in the minds of the people that these liberties are of the gift of God? That they are not to be violated but with his wrath? Indeed I tremble for my country when I reflect that God is just: that his justice cannot sleep for ever: that considering numbers, nature and natural means only, a revolution of the wheel of fortune, an exchange of situation, is among possible events: that it may become probable by supernatural interference! The Almighty has no attribute which can take side with us in such a contest. – But it is impossible to be temperate and to pursue this subject through the various considerations of policy, of morals, of history natural and civil. We must be contented to hope they will force their way into every one's mind. I think a change already perceptible, since the origin of the present revolution. The spirit of the master is abating, that of the slave rising from the dust, his condition mollifying, the way I hope preparing, under the auspices[12] of heaven, for a total emancipation, and that this is disposed, in the order of events, to be with the consent of the masters, rather than by their extirpation.[13] [...]

Source: Thomas Jefferson (1743-1826). *Notes on the State of Virginia.* Philadelphia: Prichard and Hall, 1788, 147-154, 172-174.

252. John Woolman
Considerations on Keeping Negroes (1762)

[...] Placing on Men the ignominious Title SLAVE, dressing them in uncomely Garments, keeping them to servile Labour, in which they are often dirty, tends gradually to fix a Notion in the Mind, that they are a Sort of People below us in Nature, and leads us to consider them as such in all our Conclusions about them. And, moreover, a Person which in our Esteem is mean and contemptible, if their Language or Behaviour toward us is unseemly or disrespectful, it excites Wrath more powerfully than the like Conduct in one we accounted our Equal or Superior; and where this happens to be the Case, it disqualifies for candid Judgment; for it is unfit for a Person to sit as Judge in a Case where his own personal Resentments are stirred up; and, as Members of Society in a well framed

---

[9] Anything that causes wonder or surprise.
[10] Love of one's country.
[11] Disappearance.
[12] Any divine or prophetic token, premonition; *esp.* indication of a happy future.
[13] The action of rooting up trees or weeds; total destruction.

Government, we are mutually dependant. Present Interest incites to Duty, and makes each Man attentive to the Convenience of others; but he whose Will is a Law to others, and can enforce Obedience by Punishment; he whose Wants are supplied without feeling any Obligation to make equal Returns to his Benefactor, his irregular Appetites find an open Field for Motion, and he is in Danger of growing hard, and inattentive to their Convenience who labour for his Support; and so loses that Disposition, in which alone Men are fit to govern.

The *English* Government hath been commended by candid Foreigners for the Disuse of Racks and Tortures, so much practiced in some States; but this multiplying Slaves now leads to it; for where People exact hard Labour of others, without a suitable Reward, and are resolved to continue in that Way, Severity to such who oppose them becomes the Consequence; and several *Negroe* Criminals, among the *English* in *America*, have been executed in a lingering, painful Way, very terrifying to others.

It is a happy Case to set out right, and persevere in the same Way: A wrong Beginning leads into many Difficulties; for to support one Evil, another becomes customary; two produces more; and the further Men proceed in this Way, the greater their Dangers, their Doubts and Fears; and the more painful and perplexing are their Circumstances; so that such who are true Friends to the real and lasting Interest of our Country, and candidly consider the Tendency of Things, cannot but feel some Concern on this Account.

There is that Superiority in Men over the Brute Creatures, and some of them so manifestly dependant on Men for a Living, that for them to serve us in Moderation, so far as relates to the right Use of Things, looks consonant to the Design of our Creator.

There is nothing in their Frame, nothing relative to the propagating their Species, which argues the contrary; but in Men there is. The Frame of Mens Bodies, and the Disposition of their Minds are different; some, who are tough and strong, and their Minds active, chuse Ways of Life requiring much Labour to support them; others are soon weary; and though Use makes Labour more tolerable, yet some are less apt for Toil than others, and their Minds less sprightly. These latter labouring for their Subsistance, commonly chuse a Life easy to support, being content with a little. When they are weary they may rest, take the most advantageous Part of the Day for Labour; and in all Cases proportion one Thing to another, that their Bodies be not oppressed.

Now, while each is at Liberty, the latter may be as happy, and live as comfortably as the former; but where Men of the first Sort have the latter under absolute Command, not considering the Odds in Strength and Firmness, do, sometimes, in their eager Pursuit, lay on Burthens grievous to be borne; by Degrees grow rigorous, and, aspiring to Greatness, they increase Oppression, and the true Order of kind Providence is subverted. [...]

Seed sown with the Tears of a confined oppressed People, Harvest cut down by an overborne discontented Reaper, makes Bread less sweet to the Taste of an honest Man, than that which is the Produce, or just Reward of such voluntary Action, which is one proper Part of the Business of human Creatures.

Again, the weak State of the human Species, in bearing and bringing forth their Young, and the helpless Condition of their Young beyond that of other Creatures, clearly shew that *Perfect Goodness* designs a tender Care and Regard should be exercised toward them; and that no imperfect, arbitrary Power should prevent the cordial Effects of that Sympathy, which is, in the Minds of well-met Pairs, to each other, and toward their Offspring.

In our Species the mutual Ties of Affection are more rational and durable than in others below us; the Care and Labour of raising our Offspring much greater. The Satisfaction arising to us in their innocent Company, and in their Advances from one rational Improvement to another, is considerable, when two are thus joined, and their Affections sincere; it however happens among Slaves, that they are often situated in different Places; and their seeing each other depends on the Will of Men, liable to human Passions, and a Byas in Judgment; who, with Views of Self-interest, may keep them apart more than is right. Being absent from each other, and often with other Company, there is a Danger of their Affections being alienated, Jealousies arising, the Happiness otherwise resulting from their Offspring frustrated, and the Comforts of Marriage destroyed. – These Things being considered closely, as happening to a near Friend, will appear to be hard and painful.

He who reverently observes that Goodness manifested by our Gracious Creator toward the various Species of Beings in this World, will see, that in our Frame and Constitution is clearly shewn that innocent Men, capable to manage for themselves, were not intended to be Slaves.

A person lately travelling amongst the *Negroes* near *Senegal*, hath this Remark; "Which Way soever I turned my Eyes on this pleasant Spot, I beheld a perfect Image of pure Nature; an agreeable Solitude, bounded on every Side by charming Landskips, the rural Situation of Cottages in the Midst of Trees. The Ease and Indolence of the *Negroes* reclined under the Shade of their spreading Foliage; the Simplicity of their Dress and Manners; the Whole revived in my Mind the Idea of our first Parents, and I seemed to contemplate the World in its primitive State." *M. Adanson*, Page 55. [...]

Through the Force of long Custom, it appears needful to speak in Relation to Colour. – Suppose a white Child, born of Parents of the meanest Sort, who died and left him an Infant, falls into the Hands of a Person who endeavours to keep him a Slave, some Men would account him an unjust Man in doing so, who yet appear easy while many Black People, of honest Lives, and good Abilities, are enslaved, in a Manner more shocking than the Case here supposed. This is owing chiefly to the Idea of Slavery being connected with the Black Colour, and Liberty with the White: – And where false Ideas are twisted into our Minds, it is with Difficulty we get fairly disentangled.

A traveller, in cloudy Weather, misseth his Way, makes many Turns while he is lost; still forms in his Mind the Bearing and Situation of Places, and though the Ideas are wrong, they fix as fast as if they were right. Finding how Things are, we see our Mistake; yet the Force of Reason, with repeated Observations on Places and Things, do not soon remove those false Notions, so fastened upon us, but it will seem in the Imagination as if the annual Course of the Sun was altered; and though, by Recollection, we are assured it is not, yet those Ideas do not suddenly leave us.

Selfishness being indulged, clouds the Understanding; and where selfish Men, for a long Time, proceed on their Way, without Opposition, the Deceiveableness of Unrighteousness gets so rooted in their Intellects, that a candid Examination of Things relating to Self-interest is prevented; and in this Circumstance, some who would not agree to make a Slave of a Person whose Colour is like their own, appear easy in making Slaves of others of a different Colour, though their Understandings and Morals are equal to the Generality of Men of their own Colour.

The Colour of a Man avails nothing, in Matters of Right and Equity. [...]

Whence is it that Men, who believe in a righteous Omnipotent Being, to whom all Nations stand equally related, and are equally accountable, remain so easy in it; but for that the Ideas of *Negroes* and Slaves are so interwoven in the Mind, that they do not discuss this Matter with that Candour and Freedom of Thought, which the Case justly calls for? [...]

Source: John Woolman (1720-1772). *Considerations on Keeping Negroes: Recommended to the Professors of Christianity, of Every Denomination. Part Second*. Philadelphia: B. Franklin and D. Hall, 1762, 24-31.

253. St. John De Crèvecœur
Letters from an American Farmer (1782)

Letter IX

[...] While all is joy, festivity, and happiness in Charles-Town, would you imagine that scenes of misery overspread in the country? Their ears by habit are become deaf, their hearts are hardened; they neither see, hear, nor feel for the woes of their poor slaves, from whose painful labours all their wealth proceeds. Here the horrors of slavery, the hardship of incessant toils, are unseen; and no one thinks with compassion of those showers of sweat and of tears which from the bodies of Africans, daily drop, and moisten the ground they till. The cracks of the whip urging these miserable beings to excessive labour, are far too distant from the gay Capital to be heard. The chosen race eat, drink, and live happy, while the unfortunate one grubs up the ground, raises indigo, or husks the rice; exposed to a sun full as scorching as their native one; without the support of good food, without the cordials of any che[e]ring liquor. This great contrast has often afforded me subjects of the most afflicting meditation. On the one side, behold a people enjoying all that life affords most bewitching and pleasurable, without labour, without fatigue, hardly subjected to the trouble of wishing. With gold, dug from Peruvian mountains, they order vessels to the coasts of Guinea; by virtue of that gold, wars, murders, and devastations are committed in some harmless, peaceable African neighbourhood, where dwelt innocent people, who even knew not but that all men were black. The daughter torn from her weeping mother, the child from the wretched parents, the wife from the loving husband; whole families swept away and brought through storms and tempests to this rich metropolis! There, arranged like horses at a fair, they are branded like cattle, and then driven to toil, to starve, and to languish for a few years on the different plantations of these citizens. And for whom must they work? For persons they know not, and who have no other power over them than that of violence; no other right than what this accursed metal has given them! Strange order of things! Oh, Nature, where art thou? – Are not these blacks thy children as well as we? On the other side, nothing is to be seen but the most diffusive misery and wretchedness, unrelieved even in thought or wish! Day after day they drudge on without any prospect of ever reaping for themselves; they are obliged to devote their lives, their limbs, their will, and every vital exertion to swell the wealth of masters; who look not upon them with half the kindness and affection with which they consider their dogs and horses. Kindness and affection are not the portion of those who till the earth, who carry the burdens, who convert the logs into useful boards. This reward, simple and natural as one would conceive it, would border on humanity; and planters must have none of it!

If negroes are permitted to become fathers, this fatal indulgence only tends to increase their misery: the poor companions of their scanty pleasures are likewise the companions of their labours; and when at some critical seasons they could wish to see them relieved, with tears in their eyes they behold them perhaps doubly oppressed, obliged to bear the burden of nature – a fatal present – as well as that of unabated tasks. How many have I seen cursing the irresistible propensity, and regretting, that by having tasted of those harmless joys, they had become the authors of double misery to their wives. Like their masters, they are not permitted to partake of those ineffable sensations with which nature inspires the hearts of fathers and mothers; they must repel them all, and become callous and passive. This unnatural state often occasions the most acute, the most pungent of their afflictions; they have no time, like us, tenderly to rear their helpless offspring, to nurse them on their knees, to enjoy the delight of being parents. Their paternal fondness is embittered by considering, that if their children live, they must live to be slaves like themselves; no time is allowed them to exercise their pious office, the mothers must fasten them on their backs, and, with this double load, follow their husbands in the fields, where they too often hear no other sound than that of the voice or whip of the task-master, and the cries of their infants, broiling in the sun. These unfortunate creatures cry and weep like their parents, without a possibility of relief; the very instinct of the brute, so laudable, so irresistible, runs counter here to their master's interest; and to that god, all the laws of nature must give way. Thus planters get rich; so raw, so unexperienced am I in this mode of life, that were I to be possessed of a plantation, and my slaves treated as in general they are here, never could I rest in peace; my sleep would be perpetually disturbed by a retrospect of the frauds committed in Africa, in order to entrap them; frauds surpassing in enormity every thing which a common mind can possibly conceive. I should be thinking of the barbarous treatment they meet with on ship-board; of their anguish, of the despair necessarily inspired by their situation, when torn from their friends and relations; when delivered into the hands of a people differently coloured, whom they cannot understand; carried in a strange machine over an ever agitated element, which they had never seen before; and finally delivered over to the severities of the whippers, and the excessive labours of the field. Can it be possible that the force of custom should ever make me deaf to all these reflections, and as insensible to the injustice of that trade, and to their miseries, as the rich inhabitants of this town seem to be? What then is man; this being who boasts so much of the excellence and dignity of his nature, among that variety of unscrutable mysteries, of unsolvable problems, with which he is surrounded? The reason why man has been thus created, is not the least astonishing! It is said, I know that they are much happier here than in the West-Indies; because land being cheaper upon this continent than in those islands, the fields allowed them to raise their subsistence from, are in general more extensive. The only possible chance of any alleviation depends on the humour of the planters, who, bred in the midst of slaves, learn from the example of their parents to despise them; and seldom conceive either from religion or philosophy, any ideas that tend to make their fate less calamitous; except some strong native tenderness of heart, some rays of philanthropy, overcome the obduracy contracted by habit.

 I have not resided here long enough to become insensible of pain for the objects which I every day behold. In the choice of my friends and acquaintance, I always endeavour to find out those whose dispositions are somewhat congenial with my own. We have slaves likewise in our northern provinces; I hope the time draws near when they will be all emancipated: but how different their lot, how different their situation, in every possible respect! They enjoy as much liberty as their masters, they are as well clad, and as well fed; in health and sickness they are tenderly taken care of; they live under the same roof, and are, truly speaking, a part of our families. Many of them are taught to read and write, and are well instructed in the principles of religion; they are the companions of our labours, and treated as such; they enjoy many perquisites,[14] many established holidays, and are not obliged to work more than white people. They marry where inclination leads them; visit their wives every week; are as decently clad as the common people; they are indulged in educating, cherishing, and chastising their children, who are taught subordination to them as to their lawful parents: in short, they participate in many of the benefits of our society, without being obliged to bear any of its burthens. They are fat, healthy, and hearty, and far from repining at their fate; they think themselves happier than many of the lower class whites: they share with their masters the wheat and meat provision they help to raise; many of those whom the good Quakers have emancipated, have received that great benefit with tears of regret, and have never quitted, though free, their former masters and benefactors.

But is it really true, as I have heard it asserted here, that those blacks are incapable of feeling the spurs of emulation, and the che[e]rful sound of encouragement? By no means; there are a thousand proofs existing of their gratitude and fidelity: those hearts in which such noble dispositions can grow, are then like ours, they are susceptible of every generous sentiment, of every useful motive of action; they are capable of receiving lights, of imbibing ideas that would greatly alleviate the weight of their miseries. But what methods have in general been made use of to obtain so desirable an end? None; the day in which they arrive and are sold, is the first of their labours; labours, which from that hour admit of no respite; for though indulged by law with relaxation on Sundays, they are obliged to employ that time which is intended for rest, to till their little plantations. What can be expected from wretches in such circumstances? Forced from their native country, cruelly treated when on board, and not less so on the plantations to which they are driven; is there any thing in this treatment but what must kindle all the passions, sow the seeds of inveterate resentment, and nourish a wish of perpetual revenge? They are left to the irresistible effects of those strong and natural propensities; the blows they receive are they conducive to extinguish them, or to win their affections? They are neither soothed by the hopes that their slavery will ever terminate but with their lives; or yet encouraged by the goodness of their food, or the mildness of their treatment. The very hopes held out to mankind by religion, that consolatory system, so useful to the miserable, are never presented to them; neither moral nor physical means are made use of to soften their chains; they are left in their original and untutored state; that very state where in the natural propensities of revenge and warm passions, are so soon kindled. Cheered by no one single motive that can impel the will, or excite their efforts; nothing but terrors and punishments are presented to them; death is denounced if they run away; horrid delaceration[15] if they speak with their native freedom; perpetually awed by the terrible cracks of whips, or by the fear of capital punishments, while even those punishments often fail of their purpose.

A clergyman settled a few years ago at George-Town, and feeling as I do now, warmly recommended to the planters, from the pulpit, a relaxation of severity; he introduced the benignity of Christianity, and pathetically made use of the admirable precepts of that system to melt the hearts of his congregation into a greater degree of compassion toward their slaves than had been hitherto customary; "Sir (said one of his hearers) we pay you a genteel salary to read to us the prayers of the liturgy, and to explain to us such parts of the Gospel as the rule of the church directs; but we do not want you to teach us what we

---

[14] Property acquired otherwise than by inheritance.
[15] The action of tearing parts of the body asunder.

are to do with our blacks." The clergyman found it prudent to with-hold any farther admonition. Whence this astonishing right, or rather this barbarous custom, for most certainly we have no kind of right beyond that of force? We are told, it is true, that slavery cannot be so repugnant to human nature as we at first imagine, because it has been practised in all ages, and in all nations: the Lacedemonians[16] themselves, those great assertors of liberty, conquered the Helotes[17] with the design of making them their slaves; the Romans, whom we consider as our masters in civil and military policy, lived in the exercise of the most horrid oppression; they conquered to plunder and to enslave. What a hideous aspect the face of the earth must then have exhibited! Provinces, towns, districts, often depopulated; their inhabitants driven to Rome, the greatest market in the world, and there sold by thousands! The Roman dominions were tilled by the hands of unfortunate people, who had once been, like their victors free, rich, and possessed of every benefit society can confer; until they became subject to the cruel right of war, and to lawless force. Is there then no superintending power who conducts the moral operations of the world, as well as the physical? The same sublime hand which guides the planets round the sun with so much exactness, which preserves the arrangement of the whole with such exalted wisdom and paternal care, and prevents the vast system from falling into confusion; doth it abandon mankind to all the errors, the follies, and the miseries, which their most frantic rage, and their most dangerous vices and passions can produce?

The history of the earth! doth it present any thing but crimes of the most heinous nature, committed from one end of the world to the other? We observe avarice, rapine, and murder, equally prevailing in all parts. History perpetually tells us, of millions of people abandoned to the caprice of the maddest princes, and of whole nations devoted to the blind fury of tyrants. Countries destroyed; nations alternately buried in ruins by other nations; some parts of the world beautifully cultivated, returned again to the pristine state; the fruits of ages of industry, the toil of thousands in a short time destroyed by a few! If one corner breathes in peace for a few years, it is, in turn subjected, torne, and levelled; one would almost believe the principles of action in man, considered as the first agent of this planet, to be poisoned in their most essential parts. We certainly are not that class of beings which we vainly think ourselves to be; man an animal of prey, seems to have rapine and the love of bloodshed implanted in his heart; nay, to hold it the most honourable occupation in society: we never speak of a hero of mathematics, a hero of knowledge of humanity; no, this illustrious appellation is reserved for the most successful butchers of the world. If Nature has given us a fruitful soil to inhabit, she has refused us such inclinations and propensities as would afford us the full enjoyment of it. Extensive as the surface of this planet is, not one half of it is yet cultivated, not half replenished; she created man, and placed him either in the woods or plains, and provided him with passions which must for ever oppose his happiness; every thing is submitted to the power of the strongest; men, like the elements, are always at war [...].

[...] Almost every where, liberty so natural to mankind, is refused, or rather enjoyed but by their tyrants; the word slave, is the appellation of every rank, who adore as a divinity, a being worse than themselves; subject to every caprice, and to every lawless rage which unrestrained power can give. Tears are shed, perpetual groans are heard, where only the accents of peace, alacrity, and gratitude should resound. There the very delirium of tyranny tramples on the best gifts of nature, and sports with the fate, the happiness,

---

[16] Spartans.
[17] State-owned serfs of the ancient Spartans.

the lives of millions: there the extreme fertility of the ground always indicates the extreme misery of the inhabitants!

Every where one part of the human species are taught the art of shedding the blood of the other; of setting fire to their dwellings; of levelling the works of their industry: half of the existence of nations regularly employed in destroying other nations. What little political felicity is to be met with here and there, has cost oceans of blood to purchase; as if good was never to be the portion of unhappy man. Republics, kingdoms, monarchies, founded either on fraud or successful violence, increase by pursuing the steps of the same policy, until they are destroyed in their turn, either by the influence of their own crimes, or by more successful but equally criminal enemies.

If from this general review of human nature, we descend to the examination of what is called civilized society; there the combination of every natural and artificial want, makes us pay very dear for what little share of political felicity we enjoy. It is a strange heterogeneous assemblage of vices and virtues, and of a variety of other principles, for ever at war, for ever jarring,[18] for ever producing some dangerous, some distressing extreme. Where do you conceive then that nature intended we should be happy? Would you prefer the state of men in the woods, to that of men in a more improved situation? Evil preponderates in both; in the first they often eat each other for want of food, and in the other they often starve each other for want of room. For my part, I think the vices and miseries to be found in the latter, exceed those of the former; in which real evil is more scarce, more supportable, and less enormous. Yet we wish to see the earth peopled; to accomplish the happiness of kingdoms, which is said to consist in numbers. Gracious God! to what end is the introduction of so many beings into a mode of existence in which they must grope amidst as many errors, commit as many crimes, and meet with as many diseases, wants, and sufferings!

The following scene will I hope account for these melancholy reflections, and apologize for the gloomy thoughts with which I have filled this letter: my mind is, and always has been, oppressed since I became a witness to it. I was not long since invited to dine with a planter who lived three miles from ——, where he then resided. In order to avoid the heat of the sun, I resolved to go on foot, sheltered in a small path, leading through a pleasant wood. I was leisurely travelling along, attentively examining some peculiar plants which I had collected, when all at once I felt the air strongly agitated; though the day was perfectly calm and sultry. I immediately cast my eyes toward the cleared ground, from which I was but a small distance, in order to see whether it was not occasioned by a sudden shower; when at that instant a sound resembling a deep rough voice, uttered, as I thought, a few inarticulate monosyllables. Alarmed and surprised, I precipitately[19] looked all round, when I perceived at about six rods[20] distance something resembling a cage, suspended to the limbs of a tree; all the branches of which appeared covered with large birds of prey, fluttering about, and anxiously endeavouring to perch on the cage. Actuated by an involuntary motion of my hands, more than by any design of my mind, I fired at them; they all flew to a short distance, with a most hideous noise: when, horrid to think and painful to repeat, I perceived a negro, suspended in the cage, and left there to expire! I shudder when I recollect that the birds had already picked out his eyes, his cheekbones were bare; his arms had been attacked in several places, and his body seemed

---

[18] Coming into conflict, clashing
[19] With a sudden rush, in great haste.
[20] Rod: measure of length, equal 16.5 feet; 6 rods = approximately 30 meters.

covered with a multitude of wounds. From the edges of the hollow sockets and from the lacerations with which he was disfigured, the blood slowly dropped, and tinged the ground beneath. No sooner were the birds flown, than swarms of insects covered the whole body of this unfortunate wretch, eager to feed on his mangled flesh and to drink his blood. I found myself suddenly arrested by the power of affright and terror; my nerves were convulsed; I trembled, I stood motionless, involuntarily contemplating the fate of this negro, in all its dismal latitude. The living spectre, though deprived of his eyes, could still distinctly hear, and in his uncouth dialect begged me to give him some water to allay his thirst. Humanity herself would have recoiled back with horror; she would have balanced whether to lessen such reliefless distress, or mercifully with one blow to end this dreadful scene of agonizing torture! Had I had a ball in my gun, I certainly should have despatched him; but finding myself unable to perform so kind an office, I sought, though trembling, to relieve him as well as I could. A shell ready fixed to a pole, which had been used by some negroes, presented itself to me; filled it with water, and with trembling hands I guided it to the quivering lips of the wretched sufferer. Urged by the irresistible power of thirst, he endeavoured to meet it, as he instinctively guessed its approach by the noise it made in passing through the bars of the cage. "Tankè, you whitè man, tankè you, putè somè poyson and givè me." How long have you been hanging there? I asked him. "Two days, and me no die; the birds, the birds; aaah me!" Oppressed with the reflections which this shocking spectacle afforded me, I mustered strength enough to walk away, and soon reached the house at which I intended to dine. There I heard that the reason for this slave being thus punished, was on account of his having killed the overseer of the plantation. They told me that the laws of self-preservation rendered such executions necessary; and supported the doctrine of slavery with the arguments generally made use of to justify the practice; with the repetition of which I shall not trouble you at present.

Adieu.

Source: J. Hector St. John de Crèvecœur (1735-1813). "Letter IX. Description of Charles-Town; Thoughts on Slavery; On Physical Evil; A Melancholy Scene." *Letters from an American Farmer. Reprinted from the Original Edition. With a Prefatory Note by W.P. Trent.* New York: Fox, Duffield & Company, 1904, 225-236, 240-245.

254. *Documents of the American Colonization Society* (1816/1817)

Extracts from the Speech of Mr. Clay,[21] *(on taking the chair.)*

"That class of the mixt population of our country was peculiarly situated. They neither enjoyed the immunities of freemen, nor were they subject to the incapacities of slaves, but partook in some degree of the qualities of both. From their condition, and the unconquerable prejudices resulting from their colour, they never could amalgamate[22] with the free whites of this country. It was desirable, therefore, as it respected them, and the residue of the population of the country, to drain them off. Various schemes of colonization had been thought of, and a part of our own continent, it was supposed by some, might furnish a suitable establishment for them. But for his part, Mr. C. said, he had a

---

[21] Henry Clay (1777-1852), American statesman and orator who served in both the House of Representatives and the U.S. Senate.
[22] Here: To unite together (classes, races, etc.) so as to form a homogeneous or harmonious whole.

decided preference for some part of the coast of Africa. There ample provision might be made for the colony itself, and it might be rendered instrumental to the introduction, into that extensive quarter of the globe, of the arts, civilization and christianity. There was a peculiar, a moral fitness in restoring them to the land of their fathers. And if, instead of the evils and sufferings which we had been the innocent cause of inflicting upon the inhabitants of Africa, we can transmit to her the blessing of our arts, our civilization, and our religion, may we not hope that America will extinguish a great portion of that moral debt which she has contracted to that unfortunate continent? Can there be a nobler cause than that which, whilst it proposes, &c. contemplates the spreading of the arts of civilized life, and the possible redemption from ignorance and barbarism of a benighted quarter of the globe?

It was proper and necessary distinctly to state, that he understood it constituted no part of the object of this meeting to touch or agitate in the slightest degree, a delicate question connected with another portion of the coloured population of our country. It was not proposed to deliberate upon, or consider at all, any question of emancipation, or that was connected with the abolition of slavery. It was upon that condition alone, he was sure, that many gentlemen from the south and the west, whom he saw present, had attended, or could be expected to co-operate. It was upon that condition, only, that he had himself attended."

Extracts from the speech of Elias B. Caldwell,[23] Esq. of the District of Columbia:
"The more you improve the condition of these people, the more you cultivate their minds, the more miserable you make them in their present state. You give them a higher relish for those privileges which they can never attain, and turn what we intend for a blessing into a curse. No, if they must remain in their present situation, keep them in the lowest state of degradation and ignorance. The nearer you bring them to the condition of brutes, the better chance do you give them of possessing their apathy. Surely, Americans ought to be the last people on earth, to advocate such slavish doctrines, to cry peace and contentment to those who are deprived of the privileges of civil liberty. They who have so largely partaken of its blessings – who know so well how to estimate its value, ought to be among the foremost to extend it to others."

These sentiments [...] clash diametrically with those which I had previously advanced [...] on the subject of extending mental cultivation to the African race in this country. And notwithstanding I have no inclination to retract the sentiments which I have heretofore had occasion to express, concerning the practical benevolence and ardent zeal of Mr. Caldwell in the cause of religion and human happiness; yet, it is out of my power to unite with him in his opinion, of the utility of subjecting *men* of any colour, or any situation whatever, to *"the lowest state of degradation and ignorance,"* and, as near as possible, *"to the condition of brutes."* Right education and knowledge, should teach the legitimate slave fortitude, and the advantages of submission, duty, and fidelity; and should elevate the free man of whatever colour, above the unhallowed crime of despising himself for its having been ordained this or that tint, or for its being obnoxious to those who have been created with a different colour, or with none at all. [...]

Mr. Caldwell, having considered the various positions in which it had been respectively proposed to establish the colony, and expressing his preference of Africa, enlarged

---

[23] Elias B. Caldwell (1756-1834), Secretary of the Colonization Society.

upon the greater importance of selecting that quarter of the globe, "in the belief and hope of thereby introducing civilization and the christian religion, &c." correspondent to the sentiments of Mr. Clay. "The great movements (said he) and mighty efforts in the moral and religions world, seem to indicate some great design of Providence on the eve of accomplishment. The unexampled and astonishing success attending the various and numerous plans which have been devised and which are now in operation in different parts of the world, and the union and harmony with which christians of different denominations unite in promoting these plans, clearly indicate a Divine Hand in their direction. Nay, sir, the subject on which we are now deliberating has been brought to public view, nearly about the same time in different parts of our country. In New Jersey, New York, Indiana, Tennessee, Virginia, and perhaps other places not known to me, the public attention seems to have been awakened, as from slumber, to this subject." [...]

Extracts from the Speech of Mr. Wright.[24]

"Mr. Robert Wright (of Md.) said he could not withhold his approbation of a measure, that had for its object the amelioration of the lot of any portion of the human race, particularly of the free people of colour, whose degraded state robs them of the happiness of selfgovernment, so dear to the American people. And, said he, as I discover the most delicate regard to the rights of property, I shall with great pleasure lend my aid to restore this unfortunate people to the enjoyment of their liberty, but I fear gentlemen are too sanguine in their expectation, that they would be willing to abandon the land of their nativity, so dear to man. However, I have no indisposition to give them that election by furnishing all the means contemplated by the honourable and benevolent propositions submitted to our consideration.

Nothing would have a stronger tendency to effect the contemplated relief of the free people of colour, than some efficient laws to secure the restoration of those not entitled to liberty, to their masters, whose rights ought to be protected by law, and who, without such law, would be certainly sacrificed by the transportation of the free blacks with whom they would most certainly mix for that purpose. However, I feel no hesitation in saying, I should be happy to see some plan for the gradual abolition of slavery, that would prepare the rising generation for that state, and remunerate the master out of the funds of the nation, amply abundant for that purpose, without being felt by the people of America." [...]

I will conclude for the present, with a transcript of the proceedings of a meeting of the free coloured people at Richmond, (Virg.) which have come to hand (through the "Freeman's Journal,") just in time for insertion, before this work is dismissed from the press. – They are similar to those of a similar meeting at Georgetown several weeks ago:

RICHMOND, Jan. 28.
MEETING OF FREE PEOPLE OF COLOUR.

At a meeting of a respectable portion of the Free People of Colour, of the city of Richmond, on Friday, the 24th of January, 1817, [... the] following Preamble and Resolution was read, unanimously adopted, and ordered to be printed:

Whereas, A Society has been formed at the seat of Government, for the purpose of "colonizing (with their own consent,) the Free People of Colour of the United States;" therefore, we the Free People of Colour of the city of Richmond, have thought it advise-

---

[24] Robert Wright (1765?-1826; Democratic-Republican), governor of Maryland (1806-1809), strong supporter of the founding of the Colonization Society.

able to assemble together, under the sanction of authority, for the purpose of making a public expression of our sentiments on a question in which we are so deeply interested: we perfectly agree with the Society, that it is not only proper, but would ultimately tend to the benefit and advantage of a great portion of our suffering fellow-creatures, to be colonized: but while we thus express our entire approbation of a measure, laudable in its purposes and beneficent in its designs, it may not be improper in us to say, we prefer being colonized in the most remote corner of the land of our nativity, to being exiled to a foreign country.

And whereas, The President and Board of Managers of the said Society, have been pleased to leave it to the entire discretion of Congress to provide a suitable place for carrying their laudable intentions into effect –

Be it therefore resolved, That we respectfully submit to the wisdom of Congress, whether it would not be an act of charity to grant us a small portion of their territory, either on the Missouri river, or any place that may seem to them most conducive to the public good, and our future welfare; subject, however, to such rules and regulations as the government of the United States may think proper to adopt.

W. BOWLER, *Chairman*, etc.

Source: Jesse Torrey, Jr. (c. 1787-c. 1834). *A Portraiture of Domestic Slavery in the United States: With Reflections on the Practicability of Restoring the Moral Rights of the Slave, without Impairing the Legal Privileges of the Possessor; and a Project of a Colonial Asylum for Free Persons of Colour: Including Memoirs of Facts on the Interior Traffic in Slaves, and on Kidnapping*. Philadelphia: J. Bioren, 1817, 85-89, 93-94.

255. David Walker
David Walker's Appeal to the Colored Citizens of the World (1829)

PREAMBLE.

My dearly beloved Brethren and Fellow Citizens –
Having travelled over a considerable portion of these United States, and having in the course of my travels taken the most accurate observations of things as they exist – the result of my observations has warranted the full and unshakened conviction, that we, (coloured people of these United States) are, the most degraded, wretched, and abject set of beings, that ever lived since the world began, and I pray God, that none like us ever may live again until time shall be no more. They tell us of the Israelites in Egypt, the Helots in Sparta,[25] and of the Roman Slaves, which last, were made up from almost every nation under heaven, whose sufferings under those ancient and heathen nations, were, in comparison with ours, under this enlightened and Christian nation, no more than a cypher – or in other words, those heathen nations of antiquity, had but little more among them than the name and form of slavery; while wretchedness and endless miseries were reserved, apparently in a phial,[26] to be poured out upon our fathers, ourselves, and our children by Christian Americans.

These positions, I shall endeavour, by the help of the Lord, to demonstrate in the course of this appeal, to the satisfaction of the most incredulous mind – and may God

---

[25] State-owned serfs of the ancient Spartans.
[26] A vessel for holding liquids, usually a small glass bottle for liquid medicine.

Almighty, who is the father of our Lord Jesus Christ, open your hearts to understand and believe the truth.

The causes my brethren, which produce our wretchedness and miseries, are so very numerous and aggravating, that I believe the pen only of a Josephus[27] or a Plutarch,[28] can well enumerate and explain them. Upon subjects, then, of such incomprehensible magnitude, so impenetrable, and so notorious, I shall be obliged to omit a large class of, and content myself with giving you an exposition of a few of those, which do indeed rage to such an alarming pitch, that they cannot but be a perpetual source of terror and dismay to every reflecting mind.

I am fully aware, in making this appeal to my much afflicted and suffering brethren, that I shall not only be assailed by those whose greatest earthly desires are, to keep us in abject ignorance and wretchedness, and who are of the firm conviction that heaven has designed us and our children, to be slaves and beasts of burden to them and their children. – I say, I do not only expect to be held up to the public as an ignorant, impudent and restless disturber of the public peace, by such avaricious creatures, as well as a mover of insubordination – and perhaps put in prison or to death, for giving a superficial exposition of our miseries, and exposing tyrants. But I am persuaded, that many of my brethren, particularly those who are ignorantly in league with slave-holders or tyrants, who acquire their daily bread by the blood and sweat of their more ignorant brethren – and not a few of those too, who are too ignorant to see an inch beyond their noses, will rise up and call me cursed – Yea, the jealous ones among us will perhaps use more abject subtlety, by affirming that this work is not worth perusing; that we are well situated, and there is no use in trying to better our condition, for we cannot. – I will ask one question here – Can our condition be any worse? Can it be more mean and abject? If there are any changes, will they not be for the better, though they may appear for the worst at first? Can they get us any lower? Where can they get us? They are afraid to treat us worse; for they know well the day they do it they are gone. But against all accusations, which may or can be preferred against me, I appeal to heaven for my motive in writing – who knows that my object is, if possible to awaken in the breasts of my afflicted, degraded and slumbering brethren, a spirit of enquiry and investigation respecting our miseries and wretchedness in this *Republican land of Liberty*!!!!!

The sources from which our miseries are derived, and on which I shall comment, I shall not combine in one, but shall put them under distinct heads and expose them in their turn; in doing which, keeping truth on my side, and not departing from the strictest rules of morality, I shall endeavour to penetrate, search out, and lay them open for your inspection. If you cannot or will not profit by them, I shall have done *my* duty, to you, my country and my God.

And as the inhuman system of slavery, is the source from which most of our miseries proceed, I shall begin with that curse to nations; which has spread terror and devastation through so many nations of antiquity, and which is raging to such a pitch at the present day, in Spain and in Portugal. It had one tug in England, in France, and in the United States of America, yet the inhabitants thereof, do not learn wisdom, and erase it entirely from their dwellings and from all with whom they have to do. The fact is, the labour of slaves comes so cheap to the avaricious usurpers, and is of such great utility to the country where it exists, that those who are actuated only by sordid avarice, overlook the evils,

---

[27] Flavius Josephus (37-100 AD), Jewish priest, scholar, and historian.
[28] Greek biographer (46?-120? AD)

which will as sure as the Lord lives, follow after the good. In fact, they are so happy to keep in ignorance and degradation, and to receive the homage and the labour of the slaves, they forget that God rules in the armies of heaven and among the inhabitants of the earth, having his ears continually open to the cries, tears and groans of his oppressed people. And being a just and holy Being will at one day appear fully in behalf of the oppressed, and arrest the progress of the avaricious oppressors; for although the destruction of the oppressors God may not effect by the oppressed, yet the Lord our God will bring other destructions upon them – for not unfrequently will he cause them to rise up one against another, to be split, divided, and to oppress each other, and sometimes to open hostilities with sword in hand. Some may ask what is the matter with this united and happy people? Some say it is the cause of political usurpers, tyrants, oppressors, &c. But has not the Lord an oppressed and suffering people among them? Does the Lord condescend to hear their cries and see their tears in consequence of oppression? Will he let the oppressors rest comfortably and happy always? Will he not cause the very children of the oppressors to rise up against them, and oftimes put them to death? God works in many ways his wonders to perform.

I will not here speak of the destructions which the Lord brought upon Egypt, in consequence of the oppression and consequent groans of the oppressed – of the hundreds and thousands of Egyptians whom God hurled into the Red Sea for afflicting his people in their land [...].

All persons who are acquainted with history, and particularly the Bible, who are not blinded by the God of this world, and are not actuated by an avaricious spirit – who are able to lay aside prejudice long enough to view candidly and impartially, things as they were, are, and probably will be – who are willing to admit that God made man to serve Him alone, and that man should have no other Lord or Lords but Himself – that God Almighty is the sole proprietor or master of the whole human family, and will not on any consideration, admit of a colleague, being unwilling to divide his glory with another. – And who can dispense with prejudice long enough to admit that we are *men*, notwithstanding our impromient noses and woolly heads, and believe that we feel for our fathers, mothers, wives and children, as well as they do for theirs. – I say, all who are permitted to see and believe these things, can easily recognize the judgements of God among the Spaniards. Though others may lay the cause of the fierceness with which they cut each other's throats, to some other circumstance, yet they who believe that God is a God of justice, will believe that SLAVERY is the principle *cause*. [...]

Will any peace be given unto them? Their destruction may indeed be procrastinated awhile, but can it continue long, while they are oppressing the Lord's people? Has he not the hearts of all men in his hand? Will he suffer one part of his creatures to go on oppressing and treating another like brutes, always, with impunity? And yet, these avaricious wretches are calling for *Peace*!!!! I declare, it does appear to me, as though some nations think God is asleep, or that he made the Africans for nothing else but to dig their mines and work their farms, or they cannot believe history, sacred or profane. I ask every man who has a heart, and is blessed with the privilege of believing – Is not God a God of justice to all his creatures? Do you say he is? Then if he gives peace and tranquility to tyrants, and permits them to keep our fathers, our mothers, ourselves and our children in eternal ignorance and wretchedness, would he be to us a God of justice? I ask O ye Christians! who hold us and our children in the most abject ignorance and degradation, that ever a people were afflicted with since the world began – I say if God gives you peace and tranquility, and suffers you thus to go on afflicting us, and our children, who have never given you the least provocation – would he be to us a God of justice? If you will allow that we are men, who feel for each other, does not the blood of our fathers and of us their children, cry aloud to the Lord of Sabaoth[29] against you, for the cruelties with which you have, and do continue to afflict us. But it is time for me to close my remarks on the suburbs, just to enter more fully into the interior of this system of cruelty and oppression.

ARTICLE 1.
OUR WRETCHEDNESS IN CONSEQUENCE OF SLAVERY.

My beloved brethren: – The Indians of North and of South America – the Greeks – the Irish, subjected under the king of Great Britain – the Jews, that ancient people of the Lord – the inhabitants of the Islands of the Sea – in fine, all the inhabitants of the Earth, (except, however the sons of Africa) are called men, and of course are, and ought to be free. – But we, (coloured people) and our children are *brutes*, and of course are, and ought to be *slaves* to the American people and their children, forever – to dig their mines and work their farms; and thus go on enriching them, from one generation to another with our *blood* and our *tears*!!!!!!

I promised in a preceding page, to demonstrate to the satisfaction of the most incredulous, that we, (coloured people of these United States of America) are the most wretched, degraded and abject set of beings that ever lived since the world began. – And that the white Americans having reduced us to the wretched state of slavery treat us in that condition more cruel (they being an enlightened and Christian People,) than any Heathen Nation did any People whom it had reduced to our condition. These affirmations are so well confirmed in the minds of all unprejudiced men, who have taken the trouble to read Histories, that they need no elucidation from me, but to put them beyond all doubt; I refer you in the first place to the children of Jacob, or of Israel in Egypt, under Pharoah and his people. – Some of my Brethren do not know who Pharoah and the Egyptians were – I know it to be a fact, that some of them take the Egyptians to have been a gang of Devils, not knowing any better, and that they (Egyptians) having got possess[i]on of the Lord's people, treated them nearly as cruel as Christian Americans do us at the present day. [...]

Now, I appeal to Heaven and to Earth, and particularly to the American People themselves, who cease not to declare that our condition is not hard and that we are, comparatively, satisfied to rest in wretchedness and misery, under them and their children. [...]

I ask those people who treat us so *well*, Oh! I ask them, where is the most barren spot of land which they have given unto us? Israel had the most fertile land in all Egypt. Need I mention the very notorious fact, that I have known a poor man of colour, who laboured night and day, to acquire a little money, and having acquired it, he vested it in a small piece of land, and got him a house erected thereon, and having paid for the whole he moved his family into it, where he was suffered to remain but nine months when he was cheated out of his property by a white man, and driven out of door. And is not this the case generally? Can a man of colour buy a piece of land and keep it peaceably? Will not some white man try to get it from him, even if it is in a mud hole? I need not comment any farther on a subject which all, both black and white will readily admit. But I most, really, observe that in this very city, when a man of colour dies, if he owned any real estate it most generally falls into the hands of some white person – the wife and children

---

[29] Hebrew word: 'armies', 'hosts'.

of the deceased may weep and lament if they please, but the estate will be kept snug enough by its white possessor.

But to prove farther that the condition of the Israelites was better under the Egyptians than ours is under the whites. I call upon the professing Christians, I call upon the Philanthropist, I call upon the very tyrant himself, to show me a page of history, either sacred or profane, on which a verse can be found which maintains, that the Egyptians heaped the insupportable insult upon the children of Israel, by telling them that they were not of the human family. Can the whites deny this charge? Have they not, after having reduced us to the deplorable condition of slaves, under their feet, held us up, as descending originally from the tribes of Monkies, or Orang-Outangs? O! my God! I appeal to ev[e]ry man of feeling – is not this insupportable? Is it not heaping the most gross insult upon our miseries, because they have got us under their feet, and we cannot help ourselves? O! pity us we pray thee, Lord Jesus, Master. – Has Mr. Jefferson declared to the world, that we are inferiour to the whites, both in the endowments of our bodies and of minds? It is indeed surprising, that a man of such great learning, combined with such excellent natural parts, should speak so of a set of men in chains. [...]

I saw a paragraph, a few years since, in a South Carolina paper which, speaking of the barbarity of the Turks, it said "The Turks are the most barbarous people in the world – they treat the Greeks more like brutes than human beings." And in the same paper was an advertisement, which said: "Eight well built Virginia and Maryland Negro fellows, and 4 wenches, will positively be sold, this day, to the highest bidder!" And what astonished me still more, was, to see in this same *humane* paper!! the cuts of three men, with clubs and budgets on their backs, and an advertisement, offering a considerable sum of money for their apprehension, and delivery. [...]

I have been for years troubling the pages of historians, to find out what our fathers have done to the Americans, to merit such condign[30] punishment as they have inflicted on them, and do contrive to inflict on us their children. But must aver, that my researches have hitherto, been to no effect. I have therefore, come to the immovable conclusion, that they (Americans) have, and do continue to punish us for nothing else, but for enriching them and their country. For I cannot conceive of anything else. Nor will I ever believe otherwise, until the Lord shall convince me. [...]

Are we men? – I ask you, O! my brethren, are we men? Did our creator make us to be slaves to dust and ashes like ourselves? Are they not dying worms as well as we? Have they not to make their appearance before the tribunal of heaven, to answer for the deeds done in the body, as well as we? – Have we any other master but Jesus Christ, alone? Is he not their master as well as ours? What right then, have we to obey and call any other master but himself? How we could be so submissive to a gang of men, whom we cannot tell whether they are as good as ourselves, or not, I never could conceive. However, this is shut up with the Lord, and we cannot precisely tell – but I declare, we judge men by their works.

The whites have always been an unjust, jealous, unmerciful, avaricious and blood-thirsty set of beings, always seeking after power and authority. – We view them all over the Confederacy of Greece, where they were first known to be any thing, (in consequence of education) we see them there, cutting each other's throats – trying to subject each other to wretchedness and misery – to effect which, they used all kinds of deceitful, unfair, and

---

[30] Deserving, appropriate.

unmerciful means. – We view them next in Rome, where the spirit of tyranny and deceit raged still higher. We view them in Gaul, Spain and in Britain – in fine we view them all over Europe, together with what were scattered about in Asia and Africa, as heathens, and we see them acting more like devils than accountable men. But some may ask, did not the blacks of Africa, and the Mullattoes of Asia go on in the same way, as did the whites of Europe. I answer, No – They never were half so avaricious, deceitful and unmerciful as the whites, according to their knowledge.

But we will leave the whites or Europeans as heathens, and take a view of them as christians, in which capacity we see them as cruel, if not more so, than ever. In fact, take them as a body, they are ten times more cruel, avaricious and unmerciful than ever they were; for while they were heathens, they were bad enough, it is true, but it is positively a fact, that they were not quite so audacious as to go and take vessel loads of men, women and children, and in cold blood, and through devilishness, – throw them into the sea, and murder them in all kind of ways. While they were heathens, they were too ignorant for such barbarity. But being Christians, enlightened and sensible, they are completely prepared for such hellish cruelties. Now suppose God were to give them more sense, what would they do? If it were possible would they not dethrone Jehovah and seat themselves up on his throne? I therefore, in the name and fear of the Lord God of heaven and of earth, divested of prejudice either on the side of my colour or that of the whites, advance my suspicion of them, whether they are as good by nature as we are or not. Their actions, since they were known as a people, have been the reverse, I do indeed suspect them, but this as I before observed is shut up with the Lord, we cannot exactly tell, it will be proved in succeeding generations. The whites have had the essence of the gospel as it was preached by my master and his apostles – the Ethiopians have not, who are to have it in its meridian splendor – the Lord will give it to them, to their satisfaction. I hope and pray my God, that they will make good use of it, that it may be well with them.

Source: David Walker(1785-1830). *David Walker's Appeal in Four Articles; Together with a Preamble, to the Colored Citizens of the World, but in Particular and Very Expressly to Those in the United States of America. Written in Boston, State of Massachusetts, September 28, 1829.* Boston: David Walker, 1829, 3-15, 18-19.

256. William Lloyd Garrison "Truisms" (1831)

1. All men are born equal, and entitled to protection, excepting those whose skins are black and hair woolly; or, to prevent mistake, excepting Africans, and their descendants.

2. If white men are ignorant and depraved, they ought freely to receive the benefits of education; but if black men are in this condition, common sense dictates that they should be held in bondage, and never instructed.

3. He who steals a sheep, or buys one of a thief, deserves severe punishment. He who steals a negro, or buys him of a kidnapper, is blameless. Why? [...]

4. The color of the skin determines whether a man has a soul or not. If white, he has an immortal essence; if black, he is altogether beastly. Mulattoes, however, derive no benefit from this rule.

5. The blacks ought to be held in fetters, because they are too stupid to take care of themselves; at least, we are not so stupid as to suffer them to make the experiment.

6. To kidnap children on the coast of Africa is a horrid crime, deservedly punishable with death; but he who steals them, in this country, as soon as they are born, performs not merely an innocent but a praiseworthy act.

7. In Africa, a man who buys or sells another, is a monster of hell. In America, he is an heir of heaven.

8. A man has a right to heap unbounded execration upon the foreign slave trade, and the abettors thereof; but if he utter a sentiment derogatory to the domestic traffic, or to those who assist in the transportation of victims, he is to be imprisoned for publishing a libel, and sentenced to pay a fine of not less than one thousand dollars.

9. He who calls American slaveholders *tyrants*, is a fool, a fanatic, or a madman; but if he apologise for monarchical governments, or an hereditary aristocracy, set him down as a tory, and a traitor to his country.

10. There is not the least danger of a rebellion among the slaves; and even if they should revolt *en masse*, what could they do? Their united physical force would be utterly contemptible.

11. None but fanatics or idiots desire immediate abolition. If the slaves were liberated at once, our throats would be cut, and our houses pillaged and burnt!

12. Our slaves must [not] be educated for freedom. Our slaves must never learn the alphabet, because knowledge would teach them to throw off their yoke. [...]

15. A white man, who kills a tyrant, is a hero, and deserves a monument. If a slave kill his master, he is a murderer, and deserves to be burnt.

16. The slaves are kept in bondage *for their own good*. Liberty is a curse to the free people of color – their condition is worse than that of the slaves! Yet it would be very wicked to bind them with fetters for *their* good!

17. The slaves are contented and happy. If sometimes they are so ungrateful or deluded as to abscond, it is pure philanthropy that induces their masters to offer a handsome reward for their detection.

18. Blacks have no intellect. The laws, at the south, which forbid their instruction, were not enacted because it was supposed these brutes had brains, or for the sake of compliment, but are owing simply to an itch for superfluous legislation.

19. Slaves are held as property. It is the acme of humanity and justice, therefore, in the laws, to recognise them also as moral agents, and punish them in the most aggravated manner, if they perpetrate a crime; though they cannot read, and have neither seen nor known the laws! [...]

24. The Africans are our slaves – not because we like to oppress, or to make money unjustly – but because Noah's curse must be fulfilled, and the scriptures obeyed.

Source: William Lloyd Garrison (1805-1879). "Truisms." *The Liberator* 1.2 (January 8, 1831), 5.

257. George B. Cheever
God's Hand in America (1841)

We cannot conceal from ourselves, nor would we wish to do it, that the responsibilities of every kind resting upon this country are mightier than those which belong to any other nation in the world. Especially is this the case with the religious responsibilities of a Christian church which God has so remarkably blessed. If we redeem them, it will be glorious for us and glorious for the world. It is good for us, on this mount of vision, commanding on all sides an immense moral view, to call to mind our multiplied responsibilities, and see what sublime motives animate us onward. We stand upon a lofty and imposing situation. We are compassed about by a great cloud of witnesses, being made a spectacle, not only to the world, but to an innumerable company of angels and the spirits of the just made perfect. It may be no dream of the imagination, but an undoubted reality, that higher orders of intelligences are watching our movements with intense interest, and that Paul, and Peter, and John, and all the beloved apostles of our Saviour, and all who have since trod in their footsteps, and through toil and pain and death inherited the promises, are looking down upon us, and waiting, I had almost said with painful anxiety, the result of this mighty experiment. It seems as if Heaven had placed our country in this situation to try us; to see whether we would faithfully use the incalculable power in our hands for speeding forward the world's regeneration, and if not, how many accumulated blessings we could waste and reject.

In contemplating the picture of our happiness in a course of national piety, and in making such an enumeration of our national talents for a wide moral influence, we are not to forget that it is only through a probation of severe and holy discipline, that we can hope to arrive at the attainment of such glory. Nor must we for a moment let the remembrance pass from our minds, that it is "not by might, nor by power, BUT BY MY SPIRIT, SAITH THE LORD OF HOSTS," that the great work is to be accomplished. We may have had the noblest and most pious ancestry on earth; we may possess the freest institutions, the strongest physical power, the most inexhaustible wealth, the highest foreign influence and reputation; we may enjoy the most universal diffusion of knowledge; and what is more than all, the Spirit of God may be poured out upon us for a time in accumulated revivals of religion; and yet we may turn every one of our vast capabilities to ruin, except God keep us humble, and preserve in us a spirit of deep contrition and dependance on him.

Besides, there is another and a widely different view of our whole subject. There is a gloomier prospect in the probabilities of our country's future destiny. There is at least one dark spot in our moral and political horizon. Yet we cannot suffer ourselves to believe that God will permit, with the growth of our nation in populousness and power, the continuance of the enormous evil of SLAVERY, the indulgence of that great sin, which would inevitably prove the destruction of all our hopes of usefulness and glory. If he should do this, and give us over, like his ancient people, to our own heart's lusts then we should indeed become a signal and terrible example of God's holy indignation. Then, in the prophetic language of Milton,[31] and with allusion to our past extraordinary history, "as if God were weary of protecting us, *we shall be seen to have passed through the fire, that we might perish in the smoke.*" For we cannot ourselves remain free, and yet persist in imposing bondage on others. "And it usually happens," (that great writer profoundly

---
[31] John Milton (1608-1674).

remarks in his Second Defence of the People of England,) "by the appointment, and as it were retributive justice of the Deity, that that people which cannot govern themselves, and moderate their passions, but voluntarily crouch under the slavery of their lusts, should be delivered up to the sway of those whom they abhor, and made to submit to an involuntary servitude." But if after all our lofty privileges and excitements to glory, we do deny God, and turn from following his pleasure, to follow our own depravity, and fill up the measure of our iniquities, then our fall and punishment must be a second Jewish tragedy on a wider and more awful scale, and all the curses written in the book of the law[32] cannot but descend upon us. [...]

Though this be all hypothetical and visionary, yet we do not know that there is any thing in the record of prophecy to conflict with the supposition or the possibility of such an additional scene in the great instructive drama, which God is permitting to be played in this world, and which he will suffer to be played out without interruption. At any rate, however far the designs of God's providence may seem manifested and in process of execution in regard to ourselves, and however important the instrumentality of a nation and a church so trained and disciplined might appear in the midst of a world so depraved and degraded, it becomes us to remember that as God out of the stones in the streets of Jerusalem could have raised up children unto Abraham, so he can now just as easily accomplish his purposes and his prophecies without our aid.

George B. Cheever (1807-1890). "Chapter IX: Interest and Grandeur of the Divine Experiment with Us as a People. – Conditions of Success. – Causes at Work to Disturb and Thwart It." *God's Hand in America*. New York: M.W. Dodd / London: Wiley & Putnam, 1841, 139-144, 148.

258. Albert Barnes
An Inquiry into the Scriptural View of Slavery (1846)

The Principles Laid Down

[... The] Christian religion teaches that "God hath made of one blood all the nations of men for to dwell on all the face of the earth," (Acts xvii. 26,) and that as the children of the common Father they are regarded as equal. All the right which one human being has ever been supposed to have over another, in virtue of any superiority in rank, complexion, or blood, is evidently contrary to this doctrine of the Bible in regard to the origin and equality of the human race. The *common nature* which man has, is not affected, in any respect, by the colour of his hair or his skin, by the difference of his stature, by national physiognomy, or by any ethnographical distinctions in the form of the skull. This common nature, as distinct from the brute creation, remains the same under every external appearance, and every form of intellectual and moral development. A man may be wiser or less wise than I am; he may have more or less property; he may have a more richly endowed, or an inferior mental capacity, but this does not affect our common nature. He is in every respect, notwithstanding our difference in these things, as completely a human being as myself; and he stands in precisely the same relations towards the Creator and Father of all. He, like myself, has an immortal soul, and is placed in a state of probation, as a candidate for everlasting happiness or everlasting wo[e]. He has an intel-

---
[32] Reference to the Mosaic laws.

lect capable of an endless progression in knowledge; and God has given him the right to improve it to the utmost. He is endowed with a conscience, which, like his immortal intellect, for ever constitutes an impassable line between him and the inferior races of the animal creation. In virtue of this endowment, it is his right and privilege to seek to know the will of God, and to act always with reference to the future state on which he is soon to enter. He is a sinner, and, as such, is placed in substantially the same circumstances with all others before God, in reference to the rewards of heaven or the pains of hell. It was with reference to this *common nature* that redemption was provided. It was our common nature which the Son of God assumed when he became incarnate, and, *in* that assumption, and in all his sufferings for man, he regarded the race as having such a common nature. He was not a *Jew*, except by the accident of his birth; but he was a *man*, and in his human frame there was as distinct a relation to the African and the Malay, as there was to the Caucasian. The blood that flowed in his veins, and that was shed on the cross for human redemption, was the blood of a human being – a descendant of Adam – and had as much reference, when it warmed his heart with benevolence, and when it was shed on the cross, to a descendant of Ham as to the posterity of Japheth or Shem. Every human being has a right to feel that when the Son of God became incarnate he took *his* nature upon him, and to regard him as the representative of that common humanity. It is on the basis of that common nature that the gospel is commanded to be preached to 'every creature,' and any one human being has a right to consider that gospel as addressed to him with as specific an intention as to any other human being whatever. [...]

If these views are correct, then all the reliance which the system of slavery has ever been thought to derive from the supposed fact that one class of human beings is essentially inferior to another, is a false reliance. At all events, such views will find no support in the Bible, and they must be left to be maintained by those who recognise the Christian Scriptures as of no authority. A man acting on the views laid down in the Bible on this subject, would never *make* a slave; a man acting on these views would not long *retain* a slave: and Christianity, by laying down this doctrine of the essential equality of the race, has stated a doctrine which *must* sooner or later emancipate every human being from bondage. [...]

And can any man believe, that it was the design of God to sanction such a system, or that it is in accordance with the principles of the New Testament, and is to be perpetuated for the good of society? Can it be believed, that God meant to put the authority to regulate entirely the manner in which he should be worshipped, into the hands of any man? The whole chivalry of the South would be in arms, if an attempt were made, from any quarter, to impose on them the same restrictions in regard to the worship of God which the laws make necessary respecting the slaves; and there is not on earth a class of men that would be more ready to shed their last drop of blood in opposition to such an attempt, and in defense of the very principles which are set at naught by their own laws respecting three millions of human beings – as free, by nature, to worship God in the manner which they prefer, as themselves.

Slavery interferes with the rights of *property*. If any principle is clear, not only from reason, but from the Bible, it is, that a man has a right to the avails of his own labour. This is founded on the right which he has to *himself*, and of course to all that he himself can honestly earn. If any portion of this is taken away by taxes for the support of government, it is not on the principle that another *man*, though at the head of the government and ruling over him, has any right to it, but it is, that he himself is *represented* in that government; and that it is, to all practical purposes, an appropriation by himself, of his own property, to make himself, his family, and the remainder of his property more secure. It is not taken *from* him; it is committed *by* him to others, to be employed in his own service, and in the protection which he receives there is a full equivalent for all that is rendered to the government. He is still regarded as the lawful owner, and as having a right to all the avails of his own industry, until it is thus surrendered to other hands.

This right, while it enters into all our notions of liberty, and while the denial of it led to all the sacrifices which secured American Independence, is abundantly recognised in the Bible. An attempt to prove it is scarcely necessary; but the following passages show what are the current statements of the Scriptures on the subject: "Wherefore I perceive that there is nothing better than that a man should rejoice in his own works; for that is his portion: for who shall bring him to see what shall be after him." Eccl. iii. 22. "Behold that which I have seen: it is good and comely for one to eat and to drink, and to enjoy the good of all his labour that he taketh under the sun all the days of his life, which God giveth him: for that is his portion." Eccl. v. 18. "Behold the hire of the labourers who have reaped down your fields, which is of you kept back by fraud, crieth; and the cries of them which have reaped are entered into the ears of the Lord of Sabaoth." James v. 4. "Thou shalt not defraud thy neighbour, neither rob him; the wages of him that is hired shall not abide with thee all night until the morning." Lev. xix. 13. "Rob not the poor because he is poor; neither oppress the afflicted in the gate: for the Lord will plead their cause, and spoil the soul of those that spoiled them." Prov. xxii. 22, 23. "For I the Lord love judgment, I hate robbery for burnt-offering." Isa. lxi. 8. "The people of the land have used oppression, and exercised robbery, and have vexed the poor and needy; yea they have oppressed the stranger wrongfully. And I sought for a man among them that should make up the hedge, and stand in the gap before me in the land, that I should not destroy it: but I found none. Therefore have I poured out mine indignation upon them; I have consumed them with the fire of my wrath; their own way have I recompensed upon their heads, saith the Lord God." Ezek. xxii. 29-31. "Wo[e] unto him that buildeth his house by unrighteousness, and his chambers by wrong; *that useth his neighbour's service without wages, and giveth him not for his work.*" Jer. xxii. 13.

Now it is unnecessary to attempt to prove, that this essential principle of the right of property is wholly at variance with slavery as it exists in this land, and indeed with all proper notions of its nature, wherever it exists. It is a fundamental doctrine in the idea of slavery, that the slave can be the legal owner of no property; can have no right to the avails of his own labour. [...]

Now, if the principles of the Bible on the subject of property are permanent principles, it is clear that the system of slavery is not in accordance with the word of God, and that it is not the intention of Christianity to perpetuate the system in the world. The fair application of these principles would soon bring the system to an end. Can it be believed that the New Testament sanctions the power of making void the marriage relation; of abrogating the authority of parents; of nullifying the command which requires children to obey their parents; of interfering with the right which every man has to worship God according to his own views of duty and truth; and of appropriating to ourselves entirely the avails of the labour of another man? Whatever may be the abstract views which any man may defend on the subject of human rights, yet no one can seriously maintain – I know not that any one has ever attempted to maintain – that these things are sanctioned by the New Testament. And yet, they are *essential* to the system. Slavery, in the proper sense of the term, never has existed without some or all of these things; it never can. [...]

Source: Albert Barnes (1798-1870). *An Inquiry into the Scriptural View of Slavery*. Philadelphia: Parry & McMillan, 1857, 344-346, 351-354 [first published 1846].

259. Angelina Emily Grimké "Appeal to the Christian Women of the South" (1836)

[...] Now the Bible is my ultimate appeal in all matters of faith and practice, and it is to *this test* I am anxious to bring the subject at issue between us. Let us then begin with Adam and examine the charter of privileges which was given to him. "Have dominion over the fish of the sea, and over the fowl of the air, and over every living thing that moveth upon the earth."[33] In the eighth Psalm we have a still fuller description of this charter which through Adam was given to all mankind. "Thou madest him to have dominion over the works of thy hands; thou hast put all things under his feet. All sheep and oxen, yea, and the beasts of the field, the fowl of the air, the fish of the sea, and whatsoever passeth through the paths of the seas." And after the flood when this charter of human rights was renewed, we find *no additional* power vested in man. "And the fear of you and the dread of you shall be upon every beast of the earth, and every fowl of the air, and upon all that moveth upon the earth, and upon all the fishes of the sea, into your hand are they delivered."[34] In this charter, although the different kinds of *irrational* beings are so particularly enumerated, and supreme dominion over *all of them* is granted, yet *man* is *never* vested with this dominion *over his fellow man*; he was never told that any of the human species were put *under his feet*; it was only *all things*, and man, who was created in the image of his Maker, *never* can properly be termed a *thing*, though the laws of Slave States do call him "a chattel personal;" *Man* then, I assert *never* was put *under the feet of man*, by that first charter of human rights which was given by God, to the Fathers of the Antediluvian and Postdiluvian[35] worlds, therefore this doctrine of equality is based on the Bible.

But it may be argued, that in the very chapter of Genesis from which I have last quoted, will be found the curse pronounced upon Canaan, by which his posterity was consigned to servitude under his brothers Shem and Japheth.[36] I know this prophecy was uttered, and was most fearfully and wonderfully fulfilled, through the immediate descendants of Canaan, i.e. the Canaanites, and I do not know but it has been through all the children of Ham, but I do know that prophecy does *not* tell us what *ought to be*, but what actually does take place, ages after it has been delivered, and that if we justify America for enslaving the children of Africa, we must also justify Egypt for reducing the children of Israel to bondage, for the latter was foretold as explicitly as the former. I am well aware that prophecy has often been urged as an excuse for Slavery, but be not deceived, the fulfilment of prophecy will *not cover one sin* in the awful day of account. Hear what our Saviour says on this subject; "it most needs be that offences come, but *woe unto that man through whom they come*."[37] [...]

---

[33] Gen. 1.28.
[34] Gen. 9.2.
[35] Belonging to the world before resp. after the deluge; existing before resp. after the Flood.
[36] Reference here is to Gen. 9.18 and 9.22, where Ham appears as the father of Canaan. In Noah's prediction (9.25-27) Canaan is cursed to be "a servant of servants" to his brothers Shem and Japheth.
[37] Matt. 18.7.

Shall I ask you now my friends, to draw the *parallel* between Jewish *servitude* and American *slavery*? No! For there is *no likeness* in the two systems; I ask you rather to mark the contrast. The laws of Moses *protected servants* in their *rights* as *men and women*, guarded them from oppression and defended them from wrong. The Code Noir[38] of the South *robs the slave of all his rights* as a *man*, reduces him to a chattel personal, and defends the *master* in the exercise of the most unnatural and unwarantable power over his slave. They each bear the impress of the hand which formed them. The attributes of justice and mercy are shadowed out in the Hebrew code; those of injustice and cruelty, in the Code Noir of America. Truly it was wise in the slaveholders of the South to declare their slaves to be "chattels personal;" for before they could be robbed of wages, wives, children, and friends, it was absolutely necessary to deny they were human beings. It is wise in them, to keep them in abject ignorance, for the strong man armed must be bound before we can spoil his house – the powerful intellect of man must be bound down with the iron chains of nescience before we can rob him of his rights as a man; we must reduce him to a *thing* before we can claim the right to set our feet upon his neck, because it was only *all things* which were originally *put under the feet of man* by the Almighty and Beneficent Father of all, who has declared himself to be *no respecter* of persons, whether red, white or black.

But some have even said that Jesus Christ did not condemn slavery. To this I reply that our Holy Redeemer lived and preached among the Jews only. The laws which Moses had enacted fifteen hundred years previous to his appearance among them, had never been annulled, and these laws *protected* every servant in Palestine. [...] If then He did not condemn Jewish temporary servitude, this does not prove that he would not have condemned such a monstrous system as that of AMERICAN *slavery*, if that had existed among them. But did not Jesus condemn slavery? Let us examine some of his precepts. "*Whatsoever* ye would that men should do to you, do *ye even so to them*,"[39] Let every slaveholder apply these queries to his own heart; Am *I* willing to be a slave – Am *I* willing to see *my* husband the slave of another – Am *I* willing to see my mother a slave, or my father, my *white* sister or my *white* brother? If *not*, then in holding others as slaves, I am doing what I would *not* wish to be done to me or any relative I have; and thus have I broken this golden rule which was given *me* to walk by.

But some slaveholders have said, "we were never in bondage to any man," and therefore the yoke of bondage would be insufferable to us, but slaves are accustomed to it, their backs are fitted to the burden. Well, I am willing to admit that you who have lived in freedom would find slavery even more oppressive than the poor slave does, but then you may try this question in another form – Am I willing to reduce *my little child* to slavery? You know that *if it is brought up a slave*, it will never know any contrast between freedom and bondage its back will become fitted to the burden just as the negro child's does – *not by nature* – but by daily, violent pressure, in the same way that the head of the Indian child becomes flattened by the boards in which it is bound. It has been justly remarked that "*God never made a slave*," he made man upright; his back was *not* made to

---

[38] Black Code; the Code Noir initially took shape in Louis XIV's edict of 1685, which established the main lines for the policing of slavery in the French Colonies. For the most part, the code concentrated on defining the condition of slavery (passing the condition through the mother not the father) and establishing harsh controls over the conduct of those enslaved. Slaves had virtually no rights, though the code did enjoin masters to take care of the sick and old.

[39] Matt. 7.12.

carry burdens as the slave of another, nor his neck to wear a yoke, and the *man* must be crushed within him, before *his* back can be *fitted* to the burden of perpetual slavery; and that his back is *not* fitted to it, is manifest by the insurrections that so often disturb the peace and security of slaveholding countries. Who ever heard of a rebellion of the beasts of the field; and why not? simply because *they* were all placed *under the feet of man*, into whose hand they were delivered; it was originally designed that they should serve him, therefore their necks have been formed for the yoke, and their backs for the burden; but *not so with man*, intellectual, immortal man! I appeal to you, my friends, as mothers; Are you willing to enslave *your* children? You start back with horror and indignation at such a question. But why, if slavery is *no wrong* to those upon whom it is imposed? [...]

[...] It is manifest to every reflecting mind, that slavery must be abolished; the era in which we live, and the light which is overspreading the whole world on this subject, clearly show that the time cannot be distant when it will be done. Now there are only two ways in which it can be effected, by moral power or physical force, and it is for *you* to choose which of these you prefer. Slavery always has, and always will produce insurrections wherever it exists, because it is a violation of the natural order of things, and no human power can much longer perpetuate it. The opposers of abolitionists fully believe this; one of them remarked to me not long since, there is no doubt there will be a most terrible overturning at the South in a few years, such cruelty and wrong, must be visited with Divine vengeance soon. Abolitionists believe, too, that this must inevitably be the case if you do not repent, and they are not willing to leave you to perish without entreating you, to save yourselves from destruction; well may they say with the apostle, "am I then your enemy because I tell you the truth," and warn you to flee from impending judgments.

[... My] object has been to arouse *you*, as the wives and mothers, the daughters and sisters, of the South, to a sense of your duty as *women*, and as Christian women, on that great subject, which has already shaken our country, from the St. Lawrence and the lakes, to the Gulf of Mexico, and from the Mississippi to the shores of the Atlantic; *and will continue mightily to shake it*, until the polluted temple of slavery fall and crumble into ruin. I would say unto each one of you, "what meanest thou, O sleeper! arise and call upon thy God, if so be that God will think upon us that we perish not." Perceive you not that dark cloud of vengeance which hangs over our boasting Republic? Saw you not the lightnings of Heaven's wrath, in the flame which leaped from the Indian's torch to the roof of yonder dwelling, and lighted with its horrid glare the darkness of midnight? Heard you not the thunders of Divine anger, as the distant roar of the cannon came rolling onward, from the Texian country, where Protestant American Rebels are fighting with Mexican Republicans – for what? For the re-establishment of *slavery*; yes! of American slavery in the bosom of a Catholic Republic, where that system of robbery, violence, and wrong, had been legally abolished for twelve years. Yes! citizens of the United States, after plundering Mexico of her land, are now engaged in deadly conflict, for the privilege of fastening chains, and collars, and manacles – upon whom? upon the subjects of some foreign prince? No! upon native born American Republican citizens, although the fathers of these very men declared to the whole world, while struggling to free themselves from the three penny taxes of an English king, that they believed it to be a *self-evident* truth that *all men* were created equal, and had an *unalienable right to liberty*. [...]

Source: Angelina Emily Grimké (1805-1879). "Appeal to the Christian Women of the South." *The Anti-Slavery Examiner* 1.2 (September 1836), 3, 12-13, 24-25.

260. John C. Calhoun
"Slavery a Positive Good" (1837)

[...] As widely as this incendiary spirit [of Northern abolitionism] has spread, it has not yet infected this body [i.e. Congress], or the great mass of the intelligent and business portion of the North; but unless it be speedily stopped, it will spread and work upwards till it brings the two great sections of the Union into deadly conflict. [...]

Standing at the point of time at which we have now arrived, it will not be more difficult to trace the course of future events now than it was then. Those who imagine that the [abolitionist] spirit now abroad in the North, will die away of itself without a [shock] or convulsion, have formed a very inadequate conception of its real character; it will continue to rise and spread, unless prompt and efficient measures, to stay its progress, be adopted. Already it has taken possession of the pulpit, of the schools, and to a considerable extent of the press; those great instruments by which the mind of the rising generation will be formed.

However sound the great body of the non-slaveholding States are at present, in the course of a few years they will be succeeded by those who will have been taught to hate the people and institutions of nearly one half of this Union, with a hatred more deadly than one hostile nation ever entertained towards another. It is easy to see the end. By the necessary course of events, if left to themselves, we must become, finally, two people[s]. It is impossible under the deadly hatred which must spring up between the two great sections, if the present causes are permitted to operate unchecked, that we should continue under the same political system. The conflicting elements would burst the Union asunder as powerful as are the links which hold it together. Abolition and the Union cannot co-exist. As the friend of the Union I openly proclaim it, and the sooner it is known the better. The former may now be controlled, but in a short time it will be beyond the power of man to arrest the course of events. We of the South will not, can not surrender our institutions. To maintain the existing relations between the two races, inhabiting that section of the Union, is indispensable to the peace and happiness of both. It cannot be subverted without drenching the country in blood, and extirpating one or the other of the races. [...] But let me not be understood as admitting even by implication that the existing relations between the two races in the slave-holding States is an evil – far otherwise; I hold it to be a good, as it has thus far proved itself to be to both, and will continue to prove so if not disturbed by the fell[40] spirit of abolition. I appeal to facts. Never before has the black race of Central Africa, from the dawn of history to the present day, attained a condition so civilized and so improved, not only physically, but morally and intellectually. [...]

In the mean time, the white or European race has not degenerated. It has kept pace with its brethren in other sections of the Union where slavery does not exist. It is odious to make comparison; but I appeal to all sides whether the South is not equal in virtue, intelligence, patriotism, courage, disinterestedness, and all the high qualities which adorn our nature. [...]

But I take higher ground. I hold that in the present state of civilization, where two races of different origin, and distinguished by color, and other physical differences, as well as intellectual, are brought together, the relation now existing in the slave-holding

---

[40] Fierce, lethal, destructive, inhumanly cruel.

States between the two, is, instead of an evil, a good – a positive good. I feel myself called upon to speak freely upon the subject where the honor and interests of those I represent are involved. I hold then, that there never has yet existed a wealthy and civilized society in which one portion of the community did not, in point of fact, live on the labor of the other. Broad and general as is this assertion, it is fully borne out by history. This is not the proper occasion, but if it were, it would not be difficult to trace the various devices by which the wealth of all civilized communities has been so unequally divided, and to show by what means so small a share has been allotted to those by whose labor it was produced, and so large a share given to the non-producing classes. The devices are almost innumerable, from the brute force and gross superstition of ancient times, to the subtle and artful fiscal contrivances of modern. I might well challenge a comparison between them and the more direct, simple, and patriarchal mode by which the labor of the African race is among us commanded by the European. I may say with truth, that in few countries so much is left to the share of the laborer, and so little exacted from him, or where there is more kind attention to him in sickness or infirmities of age. Compare his condition with the tenants of the poor houses in the most civilized portions of Europe – look at the sick, and the old and infirm slave, on one hand, in the midst of his family and friends, under the kind superintending care of his master and mistress, and compare it with the forlorn and wretched condition of the pauper in the poor house. But I will not dwell on this aspect of the question; I turn to the political; and here I fearlessly assert that the existing relation between the two races in the South, against which these blind fanatics are waging war, forms the most solid and durable foundation on which to rear free and stable political institutions. It is useless to disguise the fact. There is and always has been in an advanced stage of wealth and civilization, a conflict between labor and capital. The condition of society in the South exempts us from the disorders and dangers resulting from this conflict; and which explains why it is that the political condition of the slave-holding States has been so much more stable and quiet than those of the North. [...]

Surrounded as the slave-holding States are with such imminent perils, I rejoice to think that our means of defence are ample, if we shall prove to have the intelligence and spirit to see and apply them before it is too late. All we want is concert,[41] to lay aside all party differences, and unite with zeal and energy in repelling approaching dangers. Let there be concert of action, and we shall find ample means of security without resorting to secession or disunion. I speak with full knowledge and a thorough examination of the subject, and for one see my way clearly. [...] I dare not hope that any thing I can say will arouse the South to a due sense of danger; I fear it is beyond the power of mortal voice to awaken it in time from the fatal security into which it has fallen.

Source: John C. Calhoun (1782-1850). "Slavery a Positive Good" (Speech given in the Senate February 6, 1837). *The Papers of John C. Calhoun*. 28 vols. Vol. 13: *1835-1837*. Ed. Clyde N. Wilson. Columbia, SC: University of South Carolina Press, 1980, 393-397.

---

[41] Basic agreement in purpose, feeling, or action.

261. Matthew Estes
A Defence of Negro Slavery as It Exists in the United States (1846)

There is less beauty in the general form and outline of the Negro than in that of the white man. He has a flat, ugly foot; evidently designed, like the foot of the camel, to tread upon the sands of the great tropical deserts. There is, in all the works of God, a harmony and adaption of the parts to each other, which evince the highest possible degree of wisdom and goodness. The Negro has a black, thick skin, which emits a disagreeable odor; thick, woolly hair; a large mouth; ugly features; thick lips; a small calf to his leg, situated near the knee; a projecting shin bone. In a word, there is in the whole outline of the Negro, much less of symmetry and beauty than in that of the white man. [...]

But the Negro has other physical peculiarities which fit him for the situation that he occupies on this continent, and which I shall now proceed to mention.

Every one has observed at the inner corner of the eye of fowls, a semi-lunar[42] membrane, which moves with great rapidity over the eye, when exposed to the solar rays. This has been called by naturalists, the *nictillating* membrane.[43] It is designed to direct the course of the tears, and to protect the eye from the intense rays of the sun. In the eye of the white man, this membrane is very small, and seems only to direct the tears into a *sac* situated behind and below a small prominence at the inner *canthus*[44] of the eye. In the Negro, this membrane is greatly expanded; and serves, in addition to the purpose of directing the tears, as in the white man, to protect the eye, as in the case of fowls, from the effects of the solar rays.

This membrane serves as a protection to the Negro against the effects of the hardships, necessarily incident to the condition of Slavery.

"The Master," says Dr. CARTWRIGHT, of Natchez,[45] "may forget or neglect to provide his Slaves with a covering for the head, to shield the eyes from the brilliancy of the sun, while laboring in the fields. Such neglect would greatly increase the irksomeness of labor, under a tropical sun, if GOD, in his goodness, had not provided the race of Canaan,[46] whom he has doomed to Slavery, with the above-mentioned anatomical contrivance, or membranous wing, to protect the eyes against the brightness of the solar rays."

The difference between the Negro and the white man extends even to the intimate structure of their organs. The brain proper – that is, the *cerebrum* – in the Negro, is about ten per cent smaller than it is in the white man: and in texture it is coarser, more watery and flabby. When put into a dish it sinks loosely down, instead of standing firm and erect, as in the case of the higher orders of white men. The head of Lord Byron was small; and was, in consequence, said to contradict one of the fundamental principles of phrenology,[47] viz: "that size, *ceteris paribus*, is a measure of power;" but after the death of

---

[42] Half-moon-shaped.
[43] A whitish or translucent membrane that forms an inner eyelid in birds, reptiles, and some mammals to keep the eye moist and protect it from dust.
[44] The corner of the eye, where the two lids meet.
[45] Samuel A. Cartwright (1793-1863), physician in Natchez, Mississippi and a professor of diseases of the Negro in the Medical Department of the University of Louisiana.
[46] Reference to the African Americans. The term treats African Americans as decendants of Ham's son Canaan. In Gen. 9.18 and 9.22, Ham appears as the father of Canaan and in Noah's prediction (9.25-27) Canaan is cursed to be "a servant of servants" to his brothers Shem and Japheth.
[47] Theory originated by Franz Josef Gall (1758-1828) and Johann Caspar Spurzheim (1776-1823) that the mental powers of the individual consist of separate faculties located in a definite region of the surface of

his lordship, his brain was taken out and weighed – and to the astonishment of all, was found heavier than most brains of the largest size. [...] Now the same difference that exists between the brain of Lord Byron, and those of ordinary individuals, exists between the white and black races of men. The power of Byron lay in the density of his brain; and the mental superiority of the white over the black face, is owing to the superior size and density of the brain.

Whatever may be said of phrenology in all its details, one position I consider established beyond controversy, viz: "that the brain is the seat of mind." This principle being true, it follows that the efficiency and power of the mind must depend on the efficiency and power of the brain. The inferiority of the Negro is thus clearly manifest.

But the difference between the white and black races does not end here; there is a considerable difference even in the bones. This extends not only to the general outline, but to their intimate structure. In general outline, the bones of the white man are much more elegant, smooth and symmetrical; all the protuberances[48] are rounder, smoother, and the angles less abrupt than those of the Negro. The bones of the Negro are of a more dingy color, more spongy in structure, and coarser grained, than those of the white man. Among the higher orders of the white race, the bones have almost the appearance of ivory. [...]

The reader will please call to mind a fact already mentioned, viz: that the constitution of the Negro peculiarly fits him for a hot climate: that in such a climate he is in his proper element, whilst the white man, on the contrary, is adapted to a more northern climate, and cannot bear extensive exposure at the South, without great risk of injury to his constitution. It must be admitted as a fact, then, that without Negro labor, the larger and more fertile portion of the South would be left uncultivated. I take it for granted that the Negroes must be in a state of Slavery; for if it were otherwise, free black labor could never be commanded to the extent necessary to cultivate the soil as at present. The history of the world contains abundant proof that people in the condition of our blacks will never labor to any extent, unless driven to it by necessity or by authority: hence so long as we have such a boundless extent of unsettled country, we could not reasonably expect the Negroes to labor unless they were driven to it by the authority of the Master. The institution of Slavery, then, is the source of vast benefits to the country; destroy it, and you ruin Southern agriculture, with all the numberless blessings that flow from it. But for the sake of perspicuity,[49] I will use a little system:

1st. *Slave Labor improves the Health of the Country.* – In every country – in every southern country in particular, there are extensive sources of disease, as ponds, marshes, &c. New-Orleans, Charleston, and other Southern towns and cities, are built upon marshes, which have been filled up by Slave labor. Our Southern climate being unfriendly to the constitution of the white man, he could never be induced voluntarily to undertake the removal of such sources of disease. The Negro, on the contrary, can perform such labor without the slightest injury to his constitution. In Spain, Italy, Mexico, and in some of the South-American Republics, where Negro Slavery does not exist, the causes of disease have accumulated to an extent which renders the climate in the highest degree unfriendly to the constitution of the white man. Negro Slavery, as we have it here, under the guidance of intelligent white men, would make those now desolate countries blossom as the

---

the brain. They regarded the size or development of the brain and the external conformation of the cranium as an index to the development of particular faculties.
[48] The protruding, knoblike parts of a bone.
[49] Clearness of statement.

rose. Sources of disease would be removed and man would soon regain his true position in the scale of being.

2d. The cotton, tobacco, rice, and sugar of the South, all the products of Slave labor, constitute the basis of much of the wealth of this country, North and South, and also of Europe. Destroy the production of cotton at the South, and you will almost ruin Europe and America; for all other portions of the world, it has been ascertained, could not supply the demand for this article. [...]

But I have not as yet enumerated any of the advantages of Slavery:

3d. *Slavery adds security and strength to the South, in a Military point* of view. – I am aware that the South, in case of war, is considered the most vulnerable part of the Union. This conclusion has resulted from a belief that our Slaves, like the down-trodden masses of England and other countries, would avail themselves of the first opportunity to throw off the yoke of Slavery: and hence it has been inferred by the less informed of our opponents, that our Slaves would be ready to join any foe that might invade our shores. Acting on this impression, the attempt has been several times made to stir up insurrection among our Slaves. [...] During the long period of seventy years, in which various attempts have been made to stimulate the Slaves to insurrection, there has never been any serious disturbance among them. A few disturbances have occurred in particular neighborhoods, in which a few white persons have been killed, but they have all been easily suppressed and peace restored. There is not a country under Heaven, where as few domestic disturbances have occurred within the same period, as in the Slave States of this Union. [...]

4th. *Slavery will tend to preserve the purity of our Republican Institutions.* – I agree with Mr. MCDUFFIE,[50] that "Slavery is the corner stone of our republican edifice." In a republican government like ours, the right of suffrage must extend to all freemen who have reached the age of twenty-one years; at least, such is the case in most of the States of this Union. Such being the fact, the nonslaveholding States must have a larger proportionate number of unenlightened voters than the Slaveholding States. The reason of this is very obvious: it is this: the great body of those who perform the drudgery of society at the South, are Slaves; and in consequence, are excluded from the ballot-box – whilst at the North, the whole mass, though but little superior to our blacks, many of them, enjoy the right of suffrage. I do not wish to be understood as intimating that all labor is incompatible with mental culture – far otherwise – for some of the most intelligent men in our land are laborers. [...] I need not be reminded that occasionally, men engaged in the severest toil, excel in mental improvement: there are exceptions to all rules, but exceptions constitute no objection to the rule itself. I should be pleased to see a larger number of those engaged in severe toil, engaged in the laudable effort to improve their minds; but this cannot be expected to the fullest extent, until we have made still further advance in labor-saving machinery. [...]

Source: Matthew Estes (?). A *Defence* of *Negro Slavery as It Exists in the United States.* Montgomery: Press of the *Alabama Journal*, 1846, 63, 65-68, 154-156, 162-164, 168-170.

---

[50] George McDuffie (1788-1851), Governor of South Carolina from 1834-1836.

262. *Am I Not a Man and a Brother?* (late 1830s)

THE NEGROES COMPLAINT

Forc'd from home and all its pleasures,
Africa's coast I left forlorn;
To increase a stranger's treasures,
O'er the raging billows borne.
Men from England* bought and sold me,
Paid my price in paltry gold;
But though slave they have enroll'd me,
Minds are never to be sold.

Still in thought as free as ever –
What are England's rights (I ask).
Me from my delights to sever,
Me to torture, me to task?
Fleecy locks and black complexion
Cannot forfeit Nature's claim;
Skins may differ, but affection,
Dwells in White and Black the same.

Why did all-creating Nature
Make the Plant for which we toil,
Sighs must fan it, tears must water,
Sweat of ours must dress the soil.
Think, ye masters iron-hearted,
Lolling at your jovial boards,
Think how many backs have smarted
For the sweets your Cane affords.

Is there, as ye sometimes tell us –
Is there ONE who reigns on high?
Has He bid you buy and sell us –
Speaking from his throne, the sky?

Ask HIM if your knotted scourges,
Matches, blood-extorting screws,
Are the means that duty urges
Agents of his will to use?

Hark! He answers! – Wild tornadoes
Strewing yonder sea with wrecks,
Wasting towns, plantations, meadows,
Are the voice with which He speaks.
He, foreseeing what vexation,
Afric's sons would undergo,
Fixed their tyrants' habitation
Where his whirlwind answers – "No!"

By our blood in Afric wasted,
Ere our necks receiv'd the chain –
By the miseries which we tasted,
Crossing in your barks the main –
By our sufferings, since ye brought us
To the man-degrading mart,
All sustain'd by patience, taught us
Only by a broken heart;

Deem our nation brutes no longer,
Till some reason ye shall find
Worthier to regard, and stronger
Than the *color* of our kind!
Slaves of gold! whose sordid dealings
Tarnish all your boasted powers,
Prove that *ye* have human feelings,
Ere ye proudly question ours.

He that stealeth a man and selleth him, or if he be found in his hand, he shall be put to death. Exodus xxi.16
* England had 800,000 Slaves, and she has made them FREE. America has 2,225,000! – and she HOLDS THEM FAST!!!

Source: *Am I Not a Man and a Brother?* Broadside of a widely circulated woodcut – here with William Cowper's (1731-1800) "The Negroes Complaint" (1788) –, which was sold at the American Anti-Slavery Office, 143, Nassau Street, New York. Courtesy New York Public Library. The woodcut of the supplicant slave was originally adopted as the seal of the Abolition Society of England. There also exists a similar broadside with John Greenleaf Whittier's poem "Our Countrymen in Chains."

263. *Caution!! Colored People of Boston* (1851)

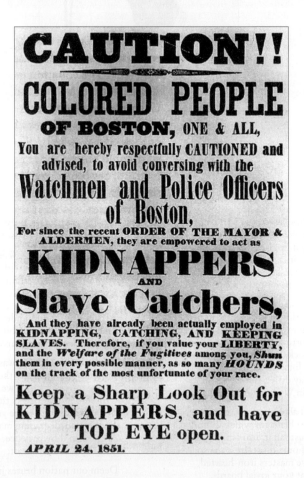

Source: Notice posted in Boston in 1851 by abolitionist Theodore Parker in response to the Fugitive Slave Law. Courtesy Boston Public Library.

264. George Fitzhugh
"Negro Slavery" (1854)

We have already stated that we should not attempt to introduce any new theories of government and of society, but merely try to justify old ones, so far as we could deduce such theories from ancient and almost universal practices. Now it has been the practice in all countries and in all ages, in some degree, to accommodate the amount and character of government control to the wants, intelligence, and moral capacities of the nations or individuals to be governed. A highly moral and intellectual people, like the free citizens of ancient Athens, are best governed by a democracy. For a less moral and intellectual one, a limited and constitutional monarchy will answer. For a people either very ignorant or very wicked, nothing short of military despotism will suffice. So among individuals, the most moral and well-informed members of society require no other government than law. They are capable of reading and understanding the law, and have sufficient self-control and virtuous disposition to obey it. Children cannot be governed by mere law; first, because they do not understand it, and secondly, because they are so much under the influence of impulse, passion and appetite, that they want sufficient self-control to be deterred or governed by the distant and doubtful penalties of the law. They must be constantly controlled by parents or guardians, whose will and orders shall stand in the place of law for them. Very wicked men must be put into penitentiaries; lunatics into asylums, and the most wild of them into straight jackets, just as the most wicked of the sane are manacled with irons; and idiots must have committees to govern and take care of them. Now, it is clear the Athenian democracy would not suit a negro nation, nor will the government of mere law suffice for the individual negro. He is but a grown up child, and must be governed as a child, not as a lunatic or criminal. The master occupies towards him the place of parent or guardian. We shall not dwell on this view, for no one will differ with us who thinks as we do of the negro's capacity, and we might argue till dooms-day, in vain, with those who have a high opinion of the negro's moral and intellectual capacity.

Secondly. The negro is improvident; will not lay up in summer for the wants of winter; will not accumulate in youth for the exigencies of age. He would become an insufferable burden to society. Society has the right to prevent this, and can only do so by subjecting him to domestic slavery.

In the last place, the negro race is inferior to the white race, and living in their midst, they would be far outstripped or outwitted in the chase of free competition. Gradual but certain extermination would be their fate. We presume the maddest abolitionist does not think the negro's providence of habits and money-making capacity at all to compare to those of the whites. This defect of character would alone justify enslaving him, if he is to remain here. In Africa or the West Indies, he would become idolatrous, savage and cannibal, or be devoured by savages and cannibals. At the North he would freeze or starve.

We would remind those who deprecate and sympathize with negro slavery, that his slavery here relieves him from a far more cruel slavery in Africa, or from idolatry and cannibalism, and every brutal vice and crime that can disgrace humanity; and that it christianizes, protects, supports and civilizes him; that it governs him far better than free laborers at the North are governed. There, wife-murder has become a mere holiday pastime; and where so many wives are murdered, almost all must be brutally treated. Nay, more: men who kill their wives or treat them brutally, must be ready for all kinds of crime, and the calendar of crime at the North proves the inference to be correct. Negroes never kill their wives. If it be objected that legally they have no wives, then we reply, that in an experience of more than forty years, we never yet heard of a negro man killing a negro woman. Our negroes are not only better off as to physical comfort than free laborers, but their moral condition is better.

But abolish negro slavery, and how much of slavery still remains. Soldiers and sailors in Europe enlist for life; here, for five years. Are they not slaves who have not only sold their liberties, but their lives also? And they are worse treated than domestic slaves. No domestic affection and self-interest extend their ægis over them. No kind mistress, like a guardian angel, provides for them in health, tends them in sickness, and soothes their dying pillow. [...] Wives and apprentices are slaves; not in theory only, but often in fact. Children are slaves to their parents, guardians and teachers. Imprisoned culprits are slaves. Lunatics and idiots are slaves also. Three-fourths of free society are slaves, no better treated, when their wants and capacities are estimated, than negro slaves. The masters in free society, or slave society, if they perform properly their duties, have more cares and less liberty than the slaves themselves. "In the sweat of thy face shalt thou earn thy bread!" made all men slaves, and such all *good men* continue to be.

Negro slavery would be changed immediately to some form of peonage, serfdom or villienage, if the negroes were sufficiently intelligent and provident to manage a farm. No one would have the labor and trouble of management, if his negroes would pay in hires and rents one-half what free tenants pay in rent in Europe. Every negro in the South would be soon liberated, if he would take liberty on the terms that white tenants hold it. The fact that he cannot enjoy liberty on such terms, seems conclusive that he is only fit to be a slave. [...]

Would the abolitionists approve of a system of society that set white children free, and remitted them at the age of fourteen, males and females, to all the rights, both as to person and property, which belong to adults? Would it be criminal or praiseworthy to do so? Criminal, of course. Now, are the average of negroes equal in information, in native intelligence, in prudence or providence, to well-informed white children of fourteen? We who have lived with them for forty years, think not. The competition of the world would be too much for the children. They would be cheated out of their property and debased in their morals. Yet they would meet every where with sympathizing friends of their own color, ready to aid, advise and assist them. The negro would be exposed to the same competition and greater temptations, with no greater ability to contend with them, with these additional difficulties. He would be welcome nowhere; meet with thousands of enemies and no friends. If he went North, the white laborers would kick him and cuff him, and drive him out of employment. If he went to Africa, the savages would cook him and eat him. If he went to the West Indies, they would not let him in, or if they did, they would soon make of him a savage and idolater. [...]

For four thousand years [the negro] has had opportunities of becoming civilized. Like the wild horse, he must be caught, tamed and domesticated. When his subjugation ceases he again runs wild, like the cattle on the Pampas of the South, or the horses on the prairies of the West. His condition in the West Indies proves this. [...]

We need never have white slaves in the South, because we have black ones. Our citizens, like those of Rome and Athens, are a privileged class. We should train and educate them to deserve the privileges and to perform the duties which society confers on them. Instead, by a low demagoguism depressing their self-respect by discourses on the equality of man, we had better excite their pride by reminding them that they do not fulfil the menial offices which white men do in other countries. Society does not feel the burden of providing for the few helpless paupers in the South. And we should recollect that here we have but half the people to educate, for half are negroes; whilst at the North they profess to educate all. It is in our power to spike this last gun of the abolitionists. We should educate all the poor. The abolitionists say that it is one of the necessary consequences of slavery that the poor are neglected. It was not so in Athens, and in Rome, and should not be so in the South. If we had less trade with and less dependence on the North, all our poor might be profitably and honorably employed in trades, professions and manufactures. Then we should have a rich and denser population. Yet we but marshal her in the way that she was going. The South is already aware of the necessity of a new policy, and has begun to act on it. Every day more and more is done for education, the mechanic arts, manufactures and internal improvements. We will soon be independent of the North. [...]

We abhor the doctrine of the "Types of Mankind;" first, because it is at war with scripture, which teaches us that the whole human race is descended from a common parentage; and, secondly, because it encourages and incites brutal masters to treat negroes, not as weak, ignorant and dependent brethren, but as wicked beasts, without the pale of humanity. The Southerner is the negro's friend, his only friend. Let no intermeddling abolitionist, no refined philosophy, dissolve this friendship.

Source: George Fitzhugh (1806-1881). "Negro Slavery." *Sociology for the South, or the Failure of Free Society*. Richmond, VA: A. Morris, 1854, 82-86, 88-89, 93-95.

265. Henry Highland Garnet
"Address to the Slaves of the United States of America" (1843)

BRETHREN AND FELLOW CITIZENS:

Your brethren of the north, east, and west have been accustomed to meet together in National Conventions, to sympathize with each other, and to weep over your unhappy condition. In these meetings we have addressed all classes of the free, but we have never until this time, sent a word of consolation and advice to you. We have been contented in sitting still and mourning over your sorrows, earnestly hoping that before this day, your sacred liberties would have been restored. But, we have hoped in vain. Years have rolled on, and tens of thousands have been borne on streams of blood, and tears, to the shores of eternity. While you have been oppressed, we have also been partakers with you; nor can we be free while you are enslaved. We therefore, write to you as being bound with you.

Many of you are bound to us, not only by the ties of a common humanity, but we are connected by the more tender relations of parents, wives, husbands, children, brothers, and sisters, and friends. As such we most affectionately address you.

Slavery has fixed a deep gulf between you and us, and while it shuts out from you the relief and consolation which your friends would willingly render, it afflicts and persecutes you with a fierceness which we might not expect to see in the fiends of hell. But still the Almighty Father of Mercies has left to us a glimmering ray of hope, which shines out like a lone star in a cloudy sky. Mankind are becoming wiser and better – the oppressor's power is fading and you, every day, are becoming better informed, and more numerous.

Your grievances, brethren, are many. We shall not attempt, in this short address, to present to the world, all the dark catalogue of this nation's sins, which have been committed upon an innocent people. Nor is it indeed, necessary, for you feel them from day to day, and all the civilized world look upon them with amazement.

Two hundred and twenty-seven years ago, the first of our injured race were brought to the shores of America. They came not with glad spirits to select their homes in the New World. They came not with their own consent, to find an unmolested enjoyment of the blessings of this fruitful soil. The first dealings they had with men calling themselves Christians, exhibited to them the worst features of corrupt and sordid hearts; and convinced them that no cruelty is too great, no villainy and no robbery too abhorrent for even enlightened men to perform, when influenced by avarice, and lust. Neither did they come flying upon the wings of Liberty, to a land of freedom. But, they came with broken hearts, from their beloved native land, and were doomed to unrequited toil, and deep degradation. Nor did the evil of their bondage end at their emancipation by death. Succeeding generations inherited their chains, and millions have come from eternity into time, and have returned again to the world of spirits, cursed, and ruined by American Slavery.

The propagators of the system, or their immediate ancestors very soon discovered its growing evil, and its tremendous wickedness, and secret promises were made to destroy it. The gross inconsistency of a people holding slaves, who had themselves "ferried o'er the wave," for freedom's sake, was too apparent to be entirely overlooked. The voice of Freedom cried, "emancipate your Slaves." Humanity supplicated with tears, for the deliverance of the children of Africa. Wisdom urged her solemn plea. The bleeding captive plead his innocence, and pointed to Christianity who stood weeping at the cross. Jehovah frowned upon the nefarious institution, and thunderbolts, red with vengeance, struggled to leap forth to blast the guilty wretches who maintained it. But all was vain. Slavery had stretched its dark wings of death over the land, the Church stood silently by – the priests prophesied falsely, and the people loved to have it so. Its throne is established, and now it reigns triumphantly.

Nearly three millions of your fellow citizens, are prohibited by law, and public opinion, (which in this country is stronger than law), from reading the Book of Life. Your intellect has been destroyed as much as possible, and every ray of light they have attempted to shut out from your minds. The oppressors themselves have become involved in the ruin. They have become weak, sensual, and rapacious. They have cursed you – they have cursed themselves – they have cursed the earth which they have trod. [...]

The colonists threw the blame upon England. They said that the mother country entailed the evil upon them, and that they would rid themselves of it if they could. The world thought they were sincere, and the philanthropic pitied them. But time soon tested their sincerity. In a few years, the colonists grew strong, and severed themselves from the British Government. Their Independence was declared, and they took their station among the sovereign powers of the earth. The declaration was a glorious document. Sages admired it, and the patriotic of every nation reverenced the Godlike sentiments which it contained. When the power of Government returned to their hands, did they emancipate the slaves? No; they rather added new links to our chains. Were they ignorant of the principles of Liberty? Certainly they were not. The sentiments of their revolutionary orators fell in burning eloquence upon their hearts, and with one voice they cried, LIBERTY OR DEATH. O, what a sentence was that! It ran from soul to soul like electric fire, and nerved the arm of thousands to fight in the holy cause of Freedom. Among the diversity of opinions that are entertained in regard to physical resistance, there are but a few found to gainsay that stern declaration. We are among those who do not.

SLAVERY! How much misery is comprehended in that single word. What mind is there that does not shrink from its direful effects? Unless the image of God is obliterated from the soul, all men cherish the love of Liberty. The nice discerning political economist does not regard the sacred right, more than the untutored African who roams in the wilds of Congo. Nor has the one more right to the full enjoyment of his freedom than the other. In every man's mind the good seeds of liberty are planted, and he who brings his fellow down so low, as to make him contented with a condition of slavery, commits the highest crime against God and man. Brethren, your oppressors aim to do this. They endeavor to make you as much like brutes as possible. When they have blinded the eyes of your mind – when they have embittered the sweet waters of life – when they have shut out the light which shines from the word of God – then, and not till then, has American slavery done its perfect work.

TO SUCH DEGRADATION IT IS SINFUL IN THE EXTREME FOR YOU TO MAKE VOLUNTARY SUBMISSION. The divine commandments, you are in duty bound to reverence, and obey. If you do not obey them, you will surely meet with the displeasure of the Almighty. He requires you to love him supremely, and your neighbor as yourself – to keep the Sabbath day holy – to search the Scriptures – and bring up your children with respect for his laws, and to worship no other God but him. But slavery sets all these at nought, and hurls defiance in the face of Jehovah. The forlorn condition in which you are placed, does not destroy your moral obligation to God. You are not certain of Heaven, because you suffer yourselves to remain in a state of slavery, where you cannot obey the commandments of the Sovereign of the universe. If the ignorance of slavery is a passport to heaven, then it is a blessing, and no curse, and you should rather desire its perpetuity than its abolition. God will not receive slavery, nor ignorance, nor any other state of mind, for love, and obedience to him. Your condition does not absolve you from your moral obligation. The diabolical injustice by which your liberties are cloven down, NEITHER GOD, NOR ANGELS, OR JUST MEN, COMMAND YOU TO SUFFER FOR A SINGLE MOMENT. THEREFORE IT IS YOUR SOLEMN AND IMPERATIVE DUTY TO USE EVERY MEANS, BOTH MORAL, INTELLECTUAL, AND PHYSICAL, THAT PROMISES SUCCESS. If a band of heathen men should attempt to enslave a race of Christians, and to place their children under the influence of some false religion, surely, heaven would frown upon the men who would not resist such aggression, even to death. If, on the other hand, a band of Christians should attempt to enslave a race of heathen men, and to entail slavery upon them, and to keep them in heathenism in the midst of Christianity, the God of heaven would smile upon every effort which the injured might make to disenthral themselves. [...]

Brethren, the time has come when you must act for yourselves. It is an old and true saying that, "if hereditary bondmen would be free, they must themselves strike the blow." You can plead your own cause, and do the work of emancipation better than any others. The nations of the world are moving in the great cause of universal freedom, and some of them at least, will, ere long, do you justice. The combined powers of Europe have placed their broad seal of disapprobation upon the African slave trade. But in the slave holding parts of the United States, the trade is as brisk as ever. They buy and sell you as though you were brute beasts. [...] Look around you, and behold the bosoms of your loving wives, heaving with untold agonies! Hear the cries of your poor children! Remember the stripes your fathers bore. Think of the torture and disgrace of your noble mothers.

Think of your wretched sisters, loving virtue and purity, as they are driven into concubinage, and are exposed to the unbridled lusts of incarnate devils. Think of the undying glory that hangs around the ancient name of Africa: – and forget not that you are native-born American citizens, and as such, you are justly entitled to all the rights that are granted to the freest. Think how many tears you have poured out upon the soil which you have cultivated with unrequited toil, and enriched with your blood; and then go to your lordly enslavers, and tell them plainly, that YOU ARE DETERMINED TO BE FREE. Appeal to their sense of justice, and tell them that they have no more right to oppress you, than you have to enslave them. Entreat them to remove the grievous burdens which they have imposed upon you, and to remunerate you for your labor. Promise them renewed diligence in the cultivation of the soil, if they will render to you an equivalent for your services. Point them to the increase of happiness and prosperity in the British West Indies since the act of Emancipation. Tell them in language which they cannot misunderstand, of the exceeding sinfulness of slavery, and of a future judgment, and of the righteous retributions of an indignant God. Inform them that all you desire, is FREEDOM, and that nothing else will suffice. Do this, and for ever after cease to toil for the heartless tyrants, who give you no other reward but stripes and abuse. If they then commence the work of death, they, and not you, will be responsible for the consequences. You had far better all die – *die immediately*, than live slaves, and entail your wretchedness upon your posterity. If you would be free in this generation, here is your only hope. However much you and all of us may desire it, there is not much hope of Redemption without the shedding of blood. If you must bleed, let it all come at once – rather, *die freemen, than live to be slaves*. It is impossible, like the children of Israel, to make a grand Exodus from the land of bondage. [...]

Fellow-men! patient sufferers! behold your dearest rights crushed to the earth! See your sons murdered, and your wives, mothers, and sisters, doomed to prostitution! In the name of the merciful God! and by all that life is worth, let it no longer be a debatable question, whether it is better to choose LIBERTY or DEATH! [...]

We do not advise you to attempt a revolution with the sword, because it would be INEXPEDIENT. Your numbers are too small, and moreover the rising spirit of the age, and the spirit of the gospel, are opposed to war and bloodshed. But from this moment cease to labor for tyrants who will not remunerate you. Let every slave throughout the land do this, and the days of slavery are numbered. You cannot be more oppressed than you have been – you cannot suffer greater cruelties than you have already. RATHER DIE FREEMEN THAN LIVE TO BE SLAVES. Remember that you are THREE MILLIONS!

It is in your power so to torment the God-cursed slaveholders, that they will be glad to let you go free. If the scale was turned, and black men were the masters, and white men the slaves, every destructive agent and element would be employed to lay the oppressor low. Danger and death would hang over their heads day and night. Yes, the tyrants would meet with plagues more terrible than those of Pharaoh. But you are a patient people. You act as though you were made for the special use of these devils. You act as though your daughters were born to pamper the lusts of your masters and overseers. And worse than all, you tamely submit, while your lords tear your wives from your embraces, and defile them before your eyes. In the name of God we ask, are you men? Where is the blood of your fathers? Has it all run out of your veins? Awake, awake; millions of voices are calling you! Your dead fathers speak to you from their graves. Heaven, as with a voice of thunder, calls on you to arise from the dust.

Let your motto be RESISTANCE! RESISTANCE! RESISTANCE! – No oppressed people have ever secured their liberty without resistance. What kind of resistance you had better make, you must decide by the circumstances that surround you, and according to the suggestion of expediency. Brethren, adieu. Trust in the living God. Labor for the peace of the human race, and remember that you are three millions.

Source: Henry Highland Garnet (1815-1882). "An Address to the Slaves of the United States of America (Rejected by the National Convention, 1843)." *Walker's Appeal, with a Brief Sketch of His Life. By Henry Highland Garnet. And also Garnet's Address to the Slaves of the United States of America.* New York: J.H. Tobitt, 1848, 90-96.

266. William Lloyd Garrison
"Universal Emancipation" (1831)

Though distant be the hour, yet come it must –
    Oh! hasten it, *in mercy*, righteous Heaven!
When Afric's sons, uprising from the dust,
    Shall stand erect – their galling fetters riven;[51]
    When from his throne Oppression shall be driven,
An exiled monster, powerless through all time;
    When freedom – glorious freedom, shall be given
To every race, complexion, caste, and clime,
And nature's sable hue shall cease to be a crime!

Wo[52] if it come with storm, and blood, and fire,
    When midnight darkness veils the earth and sky!
Wo to the innocent babe – the guilty sire –
    Mother and daughter – friends of kindred tie!
    Stranger and citizen alike shall die!
Red-handed Slaughter his revenge shall feed,
    And Havoc yell his ominous death-cry,
    And wild Despair in vain for mercy plead –
While hell itself shall shrink, and sicken at the deed!

Thou who avengest blood! long-suffering Lord!
    My guilty country from destruction save!
Let Justice sheathe his sharp and terrible sword,
    And Mercy rescue, e'en as from the grave!
    O, for the sake of those who firmly brave
The lust of power – the tyranny of law
    To bring redemption to the perishing slave
Fearless, though few – Thy presence ne'er withdraw,
But quench the kindling flames of hot, rebellious war!

---

[51] Split, torn asunder.
[52] Archaic form of woe: sorrow, grief; exclamation of grief or lamentation.

And ye – sad victims of base avarice!
    Hunted like beasts – and trodden like the earth;
Bought and sold daily, at a paltry[53] price –
    The scorn of tyrants, and of fools the mirth –
    Your souls debased from their immortal birth!
Bear meekly – as ye've borne – your cruel woes;
    Ease follows pain – light, darkness – plenty, dearth:[54]
So time shall give you freedom and repose,
And high exalt your heads above your bitter foes!

Not by the sword shall your deliverance be;
    Not by the shedding of your masters' blood;
Not by rebellion – or foul treachery,
    Upspringing suddenly, like swelling flood:
    Revenge and rapine[55] ne'er did bring forth good.
GOD'S *time is best!* – nor will it long delay:
    Even now your barren cause begins to bud,
And glorious shall the fruit be! – Watch and pray,
For, lo! the kindling dawn, that ushers in the day!

Source: William Lloyd Garrison (1805-1879). "Universal Emancipation." *The Liberator* 1.1 (January 1, 1831), 2.

267. William Lloyd Garrison
"Address to the Slaves of the United States" (1843)

[...] Take courage! Be filled with hope and comfort! Your redemption draws nigh, for the Lord is mightily at work in your behalf. Is it not frequently the darkest before daybreak? The word has gone forth that you shall be delivered from your chains, and it has not been spoken in vain.

Although you have many enemies, yet you have also many friends – warm, faithful, sympathizing, devoted friends – who will never abandon your cause; who are pledged to do all in their power to break your chains; who are laboring to effect your emancipation without delay, in a peaceable manner, without the shedding of blood; who regard you as brethren and countrymen, and fear not the frowns or threats of your masters. They call themselves abolitionists. They have already suffered much, in various parts of the country, for rebuking those who keep you in slavery – for demanding your immediate liberation – for revealing to the people the horrors of your situation – for boldly opposing a corrupt public sentiment, by which you are kept in the great southern prison-house of bondage. Some of them have been beaten with stripes; others have been stripped, and covered with tar and feathers; others have had their property taken from them, and burnt in the streets; others have had large rewards offered by your masters for their seizure; others have been cast into jails and penitentiaries; others have been mobbed and lynched

---

[53] Insignificant, contemptible.
[54] A condition in which food is scarce; time of scarcity with its accompanying privations such as famine.
[55] Plunder, robbery.

with great violence; others have lost their reputation, and been ruined in their business; others have lost their lives. All these, and many other outrages of an equally grievous kind, they have suffered for your sakes, and because they are your friends. [...] They are scattering all over the land their newspapers, books, pamphlets, tracts, and other publications, to hold up to infamy the conduct of your oppressors, and to awaken sympathy in your behalf. They are continually holding anti-slavery meetings in all parts of the free States, to tell the people the story of your wrongs. Wonderful has been the change effected in public feeling, under God, through their instrumentality. Do not fear that they will grow weary in your service. They are confident of success, in the end. They know that the Lord Almighty is with them – that truth, justice, right, are with them – that you are with them. They know, too, that your masters are cowardly and weak, through conscious wrong-doing, and already begin to falter in their course. Lift up your heads, O ye despairing slaves! Yet a little while, and your chains shall snap asunder, and you shall be tortured and plundered no more! Then, fathers and mothers, your children shall be yours, to bring them up in the nurture and admonition of the Lord. Then, husbands and wives, now torn from each other's arms, you shall be reunited in the flesh, and man shall no longer dare to put asunder those whom God has joined together. Then, brothers and sisters, you shall be sold to the remorseless slave speculator no more, but dwell together in unity. 'God hasten that joyful day!' is now the daily prayer of millions.

The weapons with which the abolitionists seek to effect your deliverance are not bowie knives, pistols, swords, guns, or any other deadly implements. They consist of appeals, warnings, rebukes, arguments and facts, addressed to the understandings, consciences and hearts of the people. Many of your friends believe that not even those who are oppressed, whether their skins are white or black, can shed the blood of their oppressors in accordance with the will of God; while many others believe that it is right for the oppressed to rise and take their liberty by violence, if they can secure it in no other manner; but they, in common with all your friends, believe that every attempt at insurrection would be attended with disaster and defeat, on your part, because you are not strong enough to contend with the military power of the nation; consequently, their advice to you is, to be patient, long-suffering, and submissive, yet awhile longer – trusting that, by the blessing of the Most High on their labors, you will yet be emancipated without shedding a drop of your masters' blood, or losing a drop of your own.

The abolitionists of the North are the only true and unyielding friends on whom you can rely. They will never deceive nor betray you. They have made your cause their own, and they mean to be true to themselves and to you, whatever may be the consequence. They are continually increasing in number, in influence, in enterprise and determination; and, judging from the success which has already attended their measures, they anticipate that, in a comparatively short period, the entire North will receive you with open arms, and give you shelter and protection, as fast as you escape from the South. We, who now address you, are united with them in spirit and design. We glory in the name of abolitionists, for it signifies friendship for all who are pining in servitude. We advise you to seize every opportunity to escape from your masters, and, fixing your eyes on the North star, travel on until you reach a land of liberty. You are not the property of your masters. God never made one human being to be owned by another. Your right to be free, at any moment, is undeniable; and it is your duty, whenever you can, peaceably to escape from the plantations on which you are confined, and assert your manhood. [...]

Source: William Lloyd Garrison (1805-1879). "Address to the Slaves of the United States." *The Liberator* 13.22 (June 2, 1843), 89.

268. Frederick Douglass
What to the Slave Is the Fourth of July?
An Address Delivered in Rochester, New York, on 5 July 1852

Mr. President, Friends and Fellow Citizens: He who could address this audience without a quailing[56] sensation, has stronger nerves than I have. I do not remember ever to have appeared as a speaker before any assembly more shrinkingly, nor with greater distrust of my ability, than I do this day. A feeling has crept over me, quite unfavorable to the exercise of my limited powers of speech. The task before me is one which requires much previous thought and study for its proper performance. I know that apologies of this sort are generally considered flat and unmeaning. I trust, however, that mine will not be so considered. Should I seem at ease, my appearance would much misrepresent me. The little experience I have had in addressing public meetings, in country school houses, avails me nothing on the present occasion.

The papers and placards say, that I am to deliver a 4th [of] July oration. This certainly sounds large, and out of the common way, for me. It is true that I have often had the privilege to speak in this beautiful Hall, and to address many who now honor me with their presence. But neither their familiar faces, nor the perfect gage I think I have of Corinthian Hall, seems to free me from embarrassment.

The fact is, ladies and gentlemen, the distance between this platform and the slave plantation, from which I escaped, is considerable – and the difficulties to be overcome in getting from the latter to the former, are by no means slight. That I am here to-day is, to me, a matter of astonishment as well as of gratitude. You will not, therefore, be surprised, if in what I have to say, I evince no elaborate preparation, nor grace my speech with any high sounding exordium.[57] With little experience and with less learning, I have been able to throw my thoughts hastily and imperfectly together; and trusting to your patient and generous indulgence, I will proceed to lay them before you.

This, for the purpose of this celebration, is the 4th of July. It is the birthday of your National Independence, and of your political freedom. This, to you, is what the Passover was to the emancipated people of God. It carries your minds back to the day, and to the act of your great deliverance; and to the signs, and to the wonders, associated with that act, and that day. This celebration also marks the beginning of another year of your national life; and reminds you that the Republic of America is now 76 years old. I am glad, fellow-citizens, that your nation is so young. Seventy-six years, though a good old age for a man, is but a mere speck in the life of a nation. Three score years and ten is the allotted time for individual men;[58] but nations number their years by thousands. According to this fact, you are, even now, only in the beginning of your national career, still lingering in the period of childhood. I repeat, I am glad this is so. There is hope in the thought, and hope is much needed, under the dark clouds which lower above the

---

[56] Losing hope or courage.
[57] Introductory part of a speech.
[58] Ps. 90.10.

horizon. The eye of the reformer is met with angry flashes, portending disastrous times; but his heart may well beat lighter at the thought that America is young, and that she is still in the impressible stage of her existence. May he not hope that high lessons of wisdom, of justice and of truth, will yet give direction to her destiny? Were the nation older, the patriot's heart might be sadder, and the reformer's brow heavier. Its future might be shrouded in gloom, and the hope of its prophets go out in sorrow. There is consolation in the thought that America is young. Great streams are not easily turned from channels, worn deep in the course of ages. They may sometimes rise in quiet and stately majesty, and inundate the land, refreshing and fertilizing the earth with their mysterious properties. They may also rise in wrath and fury, and bear away, on their angry waves, the accumulated wealth of years of toil and hardship. They, however, gradually flow back to the same old channel, and flow on as serenely as ever. But, while the river may not be turned aside, it may dry up, and leave nothing behind but the withered branch, and the unsightly rock, to howl in the abyss-sweeping wind, the sad tale of departed glory. As with rivers so with nations.

Fellow-citizens, I shall not presume to dwell at length on the associations that cluster about this day. The simple story of it is that, 76 years ago, the people of this country were British subjects. The style and title of your "sovereign people" (in which you now glory) was not then born. You were under the British Crown. Your fathers esteemed the English Government as the home government; and England as the fatherland. This home government, you know, although a considerable distance from your home, did, in the exercise of its parental prerogatives, impose upon its colonial children, such restraints, burdens and limitations, as, in its mature judgement, it deemed wise, right and proper.

But, your fathers, who had not adopted the fashionable idea of this day, of the infallibility of government, and the absolute character of its acts, presumed to differ from the home government in respect to the wisdom and the justice of some of those burdens and restraints. They went so far in their excitement as to pronounce the measures of government unjust, unreasonable, and oppressive, and altogether such as ought not to be quietly submitted to. [...]

[...] But, with that blindness which seems to be the unvarying characteristic of tyrants, since Pharoah and his hosts were drowned in the Red Sea, the British Government persisted in the exactions complained of.

The madness of this course, we believe, is admitted now, even by England; but we fear the lesson is wholly lost on our present rulers.

Oppression makes a wise man mad. Your fathers were wise men, and if they did not go mad, they became restive under this treatment. They felt themselves the victims of grievous wrongs, wholly incurable in their colonial capacity. With brave men there is always a remedy for oppression. Just here, the idea of a total separation of the colonies from the crown was born! It was a startling idea, much more so, than we, at this distance of time, regard it. The timid and the prudent (as has been intimated) of that day, were, of course, shocked and alarmed by it. [...]

Their opposition to the then dangerous thought was earnest and powerful; but, amid all their terror and affrighted vociferations[59] against it, the alarming and revolutionary idea moved on, and the country with it. [...]

---

[59] Utterance of loud outcries or shouts.

Citizens, your fathers [...] succeeded; and to-day you reap the fruits of their success. The freedom gained is yours; and you, therefore, may properly celebrate this anniversary. The 4th of July is the first great fact in your nation's history – the very ring-bolt in the chain of your yet undeveloped destiny.

Pride and patriotism, not less than gratitude, prompt you to celebrate and to hold it in perpetual remembrance. I have said that the Declaration of Independence is the RING-BOLT to the chain of your nation's destiny; so, indeed, I regard it. The principles contained in that instrument are saving principles. Stand by those principles, be true to them on all occasions, in all places, against all foes, and at whatever cost.

From the round top of your ship of state, dark and threatening clouds may be seen. Heavy billows, like mountains in the distance, disclose to the leeward huge forms of flinty rocks! That *bolt* drawn, that *chain* broken, and all is lost. *Cling to this day – cling to it*, and to its principles, with the grasp of a storm-tossed mariner to a spar at midnight. [...]

Fellow Citizens, I am not wanting in respect for the fathers of this republic. The signers of the Declaration of Independence were brave men. They were great men too – great enough to give fame to a great age. It does not often happen to a nation to raise, at one time, such a number of truly great men. The point from which I am compelled to view them is not, certainly, the most favorable; and yet I cannot contemplate their great deeds with less than admiration. They were statesmen, patriots and heroes, and for the good they did, and the principles they contended for, I will unite with you to honor their memory.

They loved their country better than their own private interests; and, though this is not the highest form of human excellence, all will concede that it is a rare virtue, and that when it is exhibited, it ought to command respect. He who will, intelligently, lay down his life for his country, is a man whom it is not in human nature to despise. Your fathers staked their lives, their fortunes, and their sacred honor, on the cause of their country. In their admiration of liberty, they lost sight of all other interests.

They were peace men; but they preferred revolution to peaceful submission to bondage. They were quiet men; but they did not shrink from agitating against oppression. They showed forbearance; but that they knew its limits. They believed in order; but not in the order of tyranny. With them, nothing was "*settled*" that was not right. With them, justice, liberty and humanity were "*final;*" not slavery and oppression. [...]

Friends and citizens, I need not enter further into the causes which led to this anniversary. Many of you understand them better than I do. You could instruct me in regard to them. That is a branch of knowledge in which you feel, perhaps, a much deeper interest than your speaker. [...]

I leave, therefore, the great deeds of your fathers to other gentlemen whose claim to have been regularly descended will be less likely to be disputed than mine!

The Present.

My business, if I have any here to-day, is with the present. The accepted time with God and his cause is the ever-living now.

"Trust no future, however pleasant,
Let the dead past bury its dead;

> Act, act in the living present,
> Heart within, and God overhead."⁶⁰

We have to do with the past only as we can make it useful to the present and to the future. To all inspiring motives, to noble deeds which can be gained from the past, we are welcome. But now is the time, the important time. Your fathers have lived, died, and have done their work, and have done much of it well. You live and must die, and you must do your work. You have no right to enjoy a child's share in the labor of your fathers, unless your children are to be blest by your labors. You have no right to wear out and waste the hard-earned fame of your fathers to cover your indolence. [...]

Fellow-citizens, pardon me, allow me to ask, why am I called upon to speak here to-day? What have I, or those I represent, to do with your national independence? Are the great principles of political freedom and of natural justice, embodied in that Declaration of Independence, extended to us? and am I, therefore, called upon to bring our humble offering to the national altar, and to confess the benefits and express devout gratitude for the blessings resulting from your independence to us?

Would to God, both for your sakes and ours, that an affirmative answer could be truthfully returned to these questions! Then would my task be light, and my burden easy and delightful. For *who* is there so cold, that a nation's sympathy could not warm him? Who so obdurate and dead to the claims of gratitude, that would not thankfully acknowledge such priceless benefits? Who so stolid and selfish, that would not give his voice to swell the hallelujahs of a nation's jubilee, when the chains of servitude had been torn from his limbs? I am not that man. In a case like that, the dumb might eloquently speak, and the "lame man leap as an hart."

But, such is not the state of the case. I say it with a sad sense of the disparity between us. I am not included within the pale⁶¹ of this glorious anniversary! Your high independence only reveals the immeasurable distance between us. The blessings in which you, this day, rejoice, are not enjoyed in common. The rich inheritance of justice, liberty, prosperity and independence, bequeathed by your fathers, is shared by you, not by me. The sunlight that brought life and healing to you, has brought stripes and death to me. This Fourth [of] July is *yours*, not *mine*. *You* may rejoice, *I* must mourn. To drag a man in fetters into the grand illuminated temple of liberty, and call upon him to join you in joyous anthems, were inhuman mockery and sacrilegious irony. Do you mean, citizens, to mock me, by asking me to speak to-day? If so, there is a parallel to your conduct. And let me warn you that it is dangerous to copy the example of a nation whose crimes, towering up to heaven, were thrown down by the breath of the Almighty, burying that nation in irrecoverable ruin! I can to-day take up the plaintive lament of a peeled and woe-smitten people!

"By the rivers of Babylon, there we sat down. Yea! we wept when we remembered Zion. We hanged our harps upon the willows in the midst thereof. For there, they that carried us away captive, required of us a song; and they who wasted us required of us mirth, saying, Sing us one of the songs of Zion. How can we sing the Lord's song in a strange land? If I forget thee, O Jerusalem, let my right hand forget her cunning. If I do not remember thee, let my tongue cleave to the roof of my mouth."⁶²

---

⁶⁰ The stanza quoted is from Henry Wadsworth Longfellow's "A Psalm of Life." *Poems*, 22.
⁶¹ Sphere of activity or influence; domain, field.
⁶² Ps. 137.1-6.

Fellow-citizens; above your national, tumultuous joy, I hear the mournful wail of millions! whose chains, heavy and grievous yesterday, are, to-day, rendered more intolerable by the jubilee shouts that reach them. If I do forget, if I do not faithfully remember those bleeding children of sorrow this day, "may my right hand forget her cunning, and may my tongue cleave to the roof of my mouth!" To forget them, to pass lightly over their wrongs, and to chime in with the popular theme, would be treason most scandalous and shocking, and would make me a reproach before God and the world. My subject, then fellow-citizens, is AMERICAN SLAVERY. I shall see, this day, and its popular characteristics, from the slave's point of view. Standing, there, identified with the American bondman, making his wrongs mine, I do not hesitate to declare, with all my soul, that the character and conduct of this nation never looked blacker to me than on this 4th of July! Whether we turn to the declarations of the past, or to the professions of the present, the conduct of the nation seems equally hideous and revolting. America is false to the past, false to the present, and solemnly binds herself to be false to the future. Standing with God and the crushed and bleeding slave on this occasion, I will, in the name of humanity which is outraged, in the name of liberty which is fettered, in the name of the constitution and the Bible, which are disregarded and trampled upon, dare to call in question and to denounce, with all the emphasis I can command, everything that serves to perpetuate slavery – the great sin and shame of America! "I will not equivocate; I will not excuse";[63] I will use the severest language I can command; and yet not one word shall escape me that any man, whose judgement is not blinded by prejudice, or who is not at heart a slaveholder, shall not confess to be right and just. [...]

At a time like this, scorching irony, not convincing argument, is needed. O! had I the ability, and could I reach the nation's ear, I would, to-day, pour out a fiery stream of biting ridicule, blasting reproach, withering sarcasm, and stern rebuke. For it is not light that is needed, but fire; it is not the gentle shower, but thunder. We need the storm, the whirlwind, and the earthquake. The feeling of the nation must be quickened; the conscience of the nation must be roused; the propriety of the nation must be startled; the hypocrisy of the nation must be exposed; and its crimes against God and man must be proclaimed and denounced.

What, to the American slave, is your 4th of July? I answer: a day that reveals to him, more than all other days in the year, the gross injustice and cruelty to which he is the constant victim. To him, your celebration is a sham; your boasted liberty, an unholy license; your national greatness, swelling vanity; your sounds of rejoicing are empty and heartless; your denunciations of tyrants, brass fronted impudence; your shouts of liberty and equality, hollow mockery; your prayers and hymns, your sermons and thanksgivings, with all your religious parade, and solemnity, are, to him, mere bombast, fraud, deception, impiety, and hypocrisy – a thin veil to cover up crimes which would disgrace a nation of savages. There is not a nation on the earth guilty of practices, more shocking and bloody, than are the people of these United States, at this very hour.

Go where you may, search where you will, roam through all the monarchies and despotisms of the old world, travel through South America, search out every abuse, and when you have found the last, lay your facts by the side of the everyday practices of this

---

[63] Douglass quotes from the first issue of the *Liberator*, in which William Lloyd Garrison promised, "I am earnest – I will not equivocate – I will not excuse – I will not retreat a single inch – and *I will be heard.*" *The Liberator* 1 January 1831; John L. Thomas, *The Liberator: William Lloyd Garrison* (Boston, 1963), 128.

nation, and you will say with me, that, for revolting barbarity and shameless hypocrisy, America reigns without a rival. [...]

RELIGION IN ENGLAND AND RELIGION IN AMERICA.

[...] Americans! your republican politics, not less than your republican religion, are flagrantly inconsistent. You boast of your love of liberty, your superior civilization, and your pure Christianity, while the whole political power of the nation (as embodied in the two great political parties), is solemnly pledged to support and perpetuate the enslavement of three millions of your countrymen. You hurl your anathemas at the crowned headed tyrants of Russia and Austria, and pride yourselves on your Democratic institutions, while you yourselves consent to be the mere *tools* and *bodyguards* of the tyrants of Virginia and Carolina. [...] You declare, before the world, and are understood by the world to declare, that you *"hold these truths to be self evident, that all men are created equal; and are endowed by their Creator with certain inalienable rights; and that, among these are, life, liberty, and the pursuit of happiness;"*[64] and yet, you hold securely, in a bondage which, according to your own Thomas Jefferson, *"is worse than ages of that which your fathers rose in rebellion to oppose,"*[65] *a seventh part* of the inhabitants of your country.

Fellow-citizens! I will not enlarge further on your national inconsistencies. The existence of slavery in this country brands your republicanism as a sham, your humanity as a base pretence, and your Christianity as a lie. It destroys your moral power abroad; it corrupts your politicians at home. It saps the foundation of religion; it makes your name a hissing, and a by-word to a mocking earth. It is the antagonistic force in your government, the only thing that seriously disturbs and endangers your *Union*. It fetters your progress; it is the enemy of improvement, the deadly foe of education; it fosters pride; it breeds insolence; it promotes vice; it shelters crime; it is a curse to the earth that supports it; and yet, you cling to it, as if it were the sheet anchor of all your hopes. Oh! be warned! be warned! a horrible reptile is coiled up in your nation's bosom; the venomous creature is nursing at the tender breast of your youthful republic; *for the love of God, tear away*, and fling from you the hideous monster, and *let the weight of twenty millions crush and destroy it forever!*

THE CONSTITUTION.

[...] Allow me to say, in conclusion, notwithstanding the dark picture I have this day presented of the state of the nation, I do not despair of this country. There are forces in operation, which must inevitably work the downfall of slavery. *"The arm of the Lord is not shortened,"*[66] and the doom of slavery is certain. I, therefore, leave off where I began, with *hope*. While drawing encouragement from the Declaration of Independence, the great principles it contains, and the genius of American Institutions, my spirit is also cheered by the obvious tendencies of the age. [...]

---

[64] Douglass quotes the American Declaration of Independence.
[65] Writing to Jean Nicholas Démeunier on 26 June 1786, Thomas Jefferson observed: "What a stupendous, what an incomprehensible machine is man! Who can endure toil, famine, stripes, imprisonment or death itself in vindication of his own liberty, and the next moment be deaf to all those motives whose power supported him thro' his trial, and inflict on his fellow men a bondage, one hour of which is fraught with more misery than ages of that which he rose in rebellion to oppose." Thomas Jefferson. *Papers*. Ed. Julian B. Boyd. 31 vols. Vol. 10: *22 June to 31 December 1786*. Princeton: Princeton University Press, 1954, 63.
[66] Douglass paraphrases Isa. 59.1: "Behold, the Lord's hand is not shortened, that it cannot save; neither his ear heavy, that it cannot hear [...]."

[...] The Celestial Empire, the mystery of ages, is being solved. The fiat of the Almighty, "*Let there be Light*,"[67] has not yet spent its force. No abuse, no outrage whether in taste, sport or avarice, can now hide itself from the all-pervading light. [...] In the fervent aspirations of William Lloyd Garrison, I say, and let every heart join in saying it:

> God speed the year of jubilee
> The wide world o'er!
> When from their galling chains set free,
> Th' oppress'd shall vilely bend the knee,
> And wear the yoke of tyranny
> Like brutes no more.
> That year will come, and freedom's reign,
> To man his plundered rights again
> Restore.
>
> God speed the day when human blood
> Shall cease to flow!
> In every clime be understood,
> The claims of human brotherhood,
> And each return for evil, good,
> Not blow for blow;
> That day will come all feuds to end,
> And change into a faithful friend
> Each foe.
>
> God speed the hour, the glorious hour,
> When none on earth
> Shall exercise a lordly power,
> Nor in a tyrant's presence cower;
> But all to manhood's stature tower,
> By equal birth!
> THAT HOUR WILL COME, to each, to all,
> And from his prison-house, the thrall
> Go forth.
>
> Until that year, day, hour, arrive,
> With head, and heart, and hand I'll strive,
> To break the rod, and rend the gyve,[68]
> The spoiler of his prey deprive –
> So witness Heaven!
> And never from my chosen post,
> Whate'er the peril or the cost,
> Be driven.[69]

Source: Frederick Douglass (1817-1895). "What to the Slave is the Fourth of July? An Address Delivered in Rochester, New York, on 5 July 1852." *The Frederick Douglass Papers*. 5 vols. Ed. John W. Blassingame. Series 1: *Speeches, Debates, and Interviews*, Vol. 2: *1847-1854*. New Haven and London: Yale University Press, 1982, 359-369, 371, 381-384, 386-388.

---

[67] Gen. 1.3.
[68] A shackle, esp. for the leg; a fetter.
[69] William Lloyd Garrison, "The Triumph of Freedom," in *Liberator*, 10 January 1845.

269. William Lloyd Garrison
No Compromise with Slavery (1854)

[...] I. I am a believer in that portion of the Declaration of American Independence in which it is set forth, as among self-evident truths, "that all men are created equal; that they are endowed by their Creator with certain inalienable rights; that among these are life, liberty, and the pursuit of happiness." Hence, I am an abolitionist. Hence, I cannot but regard oppression in every form – and most of all, that which turns a man into a thing – with indignation and abhorrence. Not to cherish these feelings would be recreancy to principle. They who desire me to be dumb on the subject of Slavery, unless I will open my mouth in its defence, ask me to give the lie to my professions, to degrade my manhood, and to stain my soul. I will not be a liar, a poltroon, or a hypocrite, to accommodate any party, to gratify any sect, to escape any odium or peril, to save any interest, to preserve any institution, or to promote any object. Convince me that one man may rightfully make another man his slave, and I will no longer subscribe to the Declaration of Independence. Convince me that liberty is not the inalienable birthright of every human being, of whatever complexion or clime, and I will give that instrument to the consuming fire. I do not know how to espouse freedom and slavery together. I do not know how to worship God and Mammon at the same time. If other men choose to go upon all-fours, I choose to stand erect, as God designed every man to stand. If, practically falsifying its heaven-attested principles, this nation denounces me for refusing to imitate its example, then, adhering all the more tenaciously to those principles, I will not cease to rebuke it for its guilty inconsistency. Numerically, the contest may be an unequal one, for the time being; but the Author of liberty and the Source of justice, the adorable God, is more than multitudinous, and he will defend the right. My crime is, that I will not go with the multitude to do evil. My singularity is, that when I say that Freedom is of God, and Slavery is of the devil, I mean just what I say. My fanaticism is, that I insist on the American people abolishing Slavery, or ceasing to prate of the rights of man. [...]

II. Notwithstanding the lessons taught us by Pilgrim Fathers and Revolutionary Sires, at Plymouth Rock, on Bunker Hill, at Lexington, Concord and Yorktown; notwithstanding our Fourth of July celebrations, and ostentatious displays of patriotism: in what European nation is personal liberty held in such contempt as in our own? Where are there such unbelievers in the natural equality and freedom of mankind? Our slaves outnumber the entire population of the country at the time of our revolutionary struggle. In vain do they clank their chains, and fill the air with their shrieks, and make their supplications for mercy. In vain are their sufferings portrayed, their wrongs rehearsed, their rights defended. [...] For one rebuke of the man-stealer, a thousand denunciations of the Abolitionists are heard. For one press that bears a faithful testimony against Slavery, a score are ready to be prostituted to its service. For one pulpit that is not "recreant to its trust," there are ten that openly defend slaveholding as compatible with Christianity, and scores that are dumb. For one church that excludes the human enslaver from its communion table, multitudes extend to him the right hand of religious fellowship. [...]

[...] I have expressed the belief that, so lost to all self-respect and all ideas of justice have we become by the corrupting presence of Slavery, in no European nation is personal liberty held at such a discount, as a matter of principle, as in our own. See how clearly this is demonstrated. The reasons adduced among us in justi[fi]cation of slaveholding, and therefore against personal liberty, are multitudinous. I will enumerate only a dozen of these: 1. "The victims are black." 2. "The slaves belong to an inferior race." 3. "Many of them have been fairly purchased." 4. "Others have been honestly inherited." 5. "Their emancipation would impoverish their owners." 6. "They are better off as slaves than they would be as freemen." 7. "They could not take care of themselves if set free." 8. "Their simultaneous liberation would be attended with great danger." 9. "Any interference in their behalf will excite the ill-will of the South, and thus seriously affect Northern trade and commerce." 10. "The Union can be preserved only by letting Slavery alone, and that is of paramount importance." 11. "Slavery is a lawful and constitutional system, and therefore not a crime." 12. "Slavery is sanctioned by the Bible; the Bible is the word of God; therefore God sanctions Slavery, and the Abolitionists are wise above what is written."

Here, then, are twelve reasons which popularly urged in all parts of the country, as conclusive against the right of a man to himself. If they are valid, in any instance, what becomes of the Declaration of Independence? [...]

III. The Abolitionism which I advocate is as absolute as the law of God, and as unyielding as His throne. It admits of no compromise. Every slave is a stolen man; every slaveholder is a man-stealer. By no precedent, no example, no law, no compact, no purchase, no bequest, no inheritance, no combination of circumstances, is slaveholding right or justifiable. While a slave remains in his fetters, the land must have no rest. Whatever sanctions his doom must be pronounced accursed. The law that makes him a chattel is to be trampled under foot; the compact that is formed at his expense, and cemented with his blood, is null and void; the church that consents to his enslavement is horribly atheistical; the religion that receives to its communion the enslaver is the embodiment of all criminality. Such, at least, is the verdict of my own soul, on the supposition that I am to be the slave; that my wife is to be sold from me for the vilest purposes; that my children are to be torn from my arms, and disposed of to the highest bidder, like sheep in the market. And who am I but a man? What right have I to be free, that another man cannot prove himself to possess by nature? Who or what are my wife and children, that they should not be herded with four-footed beasts, as well as others thus sacredly related? [...]

[...] If the slaves are not men; if they do not possess human instincts, passions, faculties and powers; if they are below accountability, and devoid of reason; if for them there is no hope of immortality, no God, no heaven, no hell; if, in short, they are, what the Slave Code declares them to be, rightly "deemed, sold, taken, reputed and adjudged in law to be chattels personal in the hands of their owners and possessors, and their executors, administrators and assigns, to all intents, constructions, and purposes whatsoever;" then, undeniably, I am mad, and can no longer discriminate between a man and a beast. But, in that case, away with the horrible incongruity of giving them oral instruction, of teaching them the catechism, of recognizing them as suitably qualified to be members of Christian churches, of extending to them the ordinance of baptism, and admitting them to the communion table, and enumerating many of them as belonging to the household of faith! Let them be no more included in our religious sympathies or denominational statistics than are the dogs in our streets, the swine in our pens, or the utensils in our dwellings. It is right to own, to buy, to sell, to inherit, to breed, and to control them, in the most absolute sense. All constitutions and laws which forbid their possession ought to be so far modified or repealed as to concede the right.

But, if they are men; if they are to run the same career of immortality with ourselves; if the same law of God is over them as over all others; if they have souls to be saved or lost; if Jesus included them among those for whom he laid down his life; if Christ is within many of them "the hope of glory;" then, when I claim for them all that we claim for ourselves, because we are created in the image of God, I am guilty of no extravagance, but am bound, by every principle of honour, by all the claims of human nature, by obedience to Almighty God, to "remember them that are in bonds as bound with them," and to demand their immediate and unconditional emancipation. [...]

These are solemn times. It is not a struggle for national salvation; for the nation, as such, seems doomed beyond recovery. The reason why the South rules, and the North falls prostrate in servile terror, is simply this: With the South, the preservation of Slavery is paramount to all other considerations – above party success, denominational unity, pecuniary interest, legal integrity, and constitutional obligation. With the North, the preservation of the Union is placed above all other things – above honour, justice, freedom, integrity of soul, the Decalogue and the Golden Rule – the Infinite God himself. All these she is ready to discard for the Union. Her devotion to it is the latest and the most terrible form of idolatry. She has given to the Slave Power a *carte blanche*, to be filled as it may dictate – and if, at any time, she grows restive under the yoke, and shrinks back aghast at the new atrocity contemplated, it is only necessary for that Power to crack the whip of Disunion over her head, as it has done again and again, and she will cower and obey like a plantation slave – for has she not sworn that she will sacrifice everything in heaven and on earth, rather than the Union?

What then is to be done? Friends of the slave, the question is not whether by our efforts we can abolish Slavery, speedily or remotely – for duty is ours, the result is with God; but whether we will go with the multitude to do evil, sell our birthright for a mess of pottage, cease to cry aloud and spare not, and remain in Babylon when the command of God is "Come out of her, my people, that ye be not partakers of her sins, and that ye receive not of her plagues."[70] Let us stand in our lot, "and having done all, to stand." At least, a remnant shall be saved. Living or dying, defeated or victorious, be it ours to exclaim, "No compromise with Slavery! Liberty for each, for all, forever! Man above all institutions! The supremacy of God over the whole earth!"

Source: William Lloyd Garrison (1805-1879). *No Compromise with Slavery: An Address Delivered in the Broadway Tabernacle, New York, February 14, 1854.* New York: American Anti-Slavery Society, 1854, 5-10, 14-15, 17-18, 34-36.

---

[70] Rev. 18.4.

270. Black and White Slaves: England (c. 1841)

Source: E.W.C. [Edward Williams Clay] (1799-1857). *Black and White Slaves*. New York: A. Donnelly, lithograph with watercolor, c. 1841. Courtesy Library of Congress. Inscription on plate II "England": "Oh heaven! in this boasted land of freedom to be starving for want of employment! No relief from the purse of proud aristocracy whose bloated fortunes have been made by our blood and toil! Come pack off to the work houses! That's the only fit asylum for you!"

271. *Black and White Slaves: America* (c. 1841)

Source: E.W.C. [Edward Williams Clay] (1799-1857). *Black and White Slaves*. New York: A. Donnelly, lithograph with watercolor, c. 1841. Courtesy Library of Congress. Inscription on plate I "America": "God bless you massa! you feed and clothe us. When we are sick you nurse us and when too old to work you provide for us. These poor creatures are a sacred legacy from my ancestors and while a dollar is left me, nothing shall be spared to increase their comfort and happiness."

272. William J. Grayson
The Hireling and the Slave (1855)

How small the choice, from cradle to the grave,
Between the lot of Hireling and of Slave!
To each alike applies the stern decree,
That man shall labour; whether bond or free,
For all that toil, the recompense we claim –
Food, fire, a home and clothing – is the same.
[...]
   Taught by the Master's efforts, by his care,
Fed, clothed, protected many a patient year,
From trivial numbers now to millions grown,
With all the Whiteman's useful arts their own,
Industrious, docile, skilled in wood and field,
To guide the plough, the sturdy axe to wield,
The Negroes schooled by Slavery embrace
The highest portion of the Negro race;
And none the savage native will compare,
Of barbarous Guinea, with its offspring here.
   If bound to daily labour while he lives,
His is the daily bread that labour gives;
Guarded from want, from beggary secure,
He never feels what Hireling crowds endure,
Nor knows, like them, in hopeless want to crave,
For wife and child, the comforts of the slave,
Or the sad thought that, when about to die,
He leaves them to the world's cold charity,
And sees them slowly seek the poor-house door –
The last, vile, hated refuge of the poor.
[...]
   And yet the Master's lighter rule ensures
More order than the sternest code secures;
No mobs of factious workmen gather here,
No strikes we dread, no lawless riots fear;
[...]
Seditious schemes in bloody tumults end,
Parsons incite, and Senators defend,
But not where Slaves their easy labours ply,
Safe from the snare, beneath a Master's eye;
In useful tasks engaged, employed their time,
Untempted by the demagogue to crime,
Secure they toil, uncursed their peaceful life,
With labour's hungry broils and wasteful strife.[1]

---

[1] The late Preston strike lost to the parties – masters and workmen – over two million dollars and ended where it had begun.

No want to goad, no faction to deplore,
The Slaves escape the perils of the poor.

Source: William J. Grayson (1788-1863). *The Hireling and the Slave*. Charleston, SC: John Russell, 1855, 43, 46, 48-49.

273. Theodore Parker
"Letter to Francis Jackson" (1859)

TO FRANCIS JACKSON.   Rome, Nov. 24, 1859.

MY DEAR FRIEND, –

America is rich in able men, in skilful writers, in ready and accomplished speakers. But few men dare treat public affairs with reference to the great principles of justice and the American Democracy; nay, few with reference to any remote future, or even with a comprehensive survey of the present. Our public writers ask what effect will this opinion have on the Democratic party, or the Republican party? how will it affect the Presidential election? what will the great State of Pennsylvania, or Ohio, or New York say to it? This is very unfortunate for us all, especially when the people have to deal practically, and that speedily, with a question concerning the very existence of Democratic institutions in America; for it is not to be denied that we must give up DEMOCRACY if we keep SLAVERY, or give up SLAVERY if we keep DEMOCRACY.

I greatly deplore this state of things. Our able men fail to perform their natural function, to give valuable instruction and advice to the people; and at the same time they debase and degrade themselves. The hurrahs and the offices they get are poor compensation for falseness to their own consciences.

In my best estate, I do not pretend to much political wisdom, and still less now while sick; but I wish yet to set down a few thoughts [...]. They are, at least, the result of long meditation on the subject; besides, they are not at all new nor peculiar to me, but are a part of the public knowledge of all enlightened men.

1. A MAN HELD AGAINST HIS WILL AS A SLAVE HAS A NATURAL RIGHT TO KILL EVERY ONE WHO SEEKS TO PREVENT HIS ENJOYMENT OF LIBERTY. This has long been recognized as a self-evident proposition, coming so directly from the primitive instincts of human nature, that it neither required proofs nor admitted them.

2. IT MAY BE A NATURAL DUTY OF THE SLAVE TO DEVELOPE THIS NATURAL RIGHT IN A PRACTICAL MANNER, AND ACTUALLY KILL ALL THOSE WHO SEEK TO PREVENT HIS ENJOYMENT OF LIBERTY. For if he continue patiently in bondage – First, he entails the foulest of curses on his children; and, second, he encourages other men to commit the crime against nature which he allows his own master to commit. It is my duty to preserve my own body from starvation. If I fail thereof through sloth, I not only die, but incur the contempt and loathing of my acquaintances while I live. It is not less my duty to do all that is in my power to preserve my body and soul from slavery; and if I submit to that through cowardice, I not only become a bondman and suffer what thraldom inflicts, but I incur also the contempt and loathing of my acquaintance. Why do freemen scorn and despise a slave? Because they think his condition is a sign of his cowardice, and believe that he ought to prefer death to bondage. The Southerners hold the Africans in great

contempt, though mothers of their children. Why? Simply because the Africans are slaves; that is, because the Africans fail to perform the natural duty of securing freedom by killing their oppressors.

3. THE FREEMAN HAS A NATURAL RIGHT TO HELP THE SLAVES RECOVER THEIR LIBERTY, AND IN THAT ENTERPRISE TO DO FOR THEM ALL WHICH THEY HAVE A RIGHT TO DO FOR THEMSELVES.

This statement, I think, requires no argument or illustration.

4. IT MAY BE A NATURAL DUTY FOR THE FREEMAN TO HELP THE SLAVES TO THE ENJOYMENT OF THEIR LIBERTY, AND AS MEANS TO THAT END, TO AID THEM IN KILLING ALL SUCH AS OPPOSE THEIR NATURAL FREEDOM.

If you were attacked by a wolf, I should not only have a *right* to aid you in getting rid of that enemy, but it would be my DUTY to help you in proportion to my power. If it were a MURDERER, and not a wolf, who attacked you, the duty would be still the same. Suppose it is not a murderer who would kill you, but a KIDNAPPER who would enslave, does that make it less my duty to help you out of the hands of your enemy? Suppose he is not a kidnapper who would make you a bondman, but a SLAVEHOLDER who would keep you one, does that remove my obligation to help you?

5. THE PERFORMANCE OF THIS DUTY IS TO BE CONTROLLED BY THE FREEMAN'S POWER AND OPPORTUNITY TO HELP THE SLAVES. [...]

These five maxims have a direct application to America at this day, and the people of the Free States have a certain dim perception thereof, which, fortunately, is becoming clearer every year.

Thus, the people of Massachusetts *feel* that they ought to protect the fugitive slaves who come into our State. [...]

Of course, I was not astonished to hear that an attempt had been made to free the slaves in a certain part of Virginia, nor should I be astonished if another "insurrection" or "rebellion" took place in the State of —, or a third in —, or a fourth in —. Such things are to be expected; for they do not depend merely on the private will of men like Capt. Brown[2] and his associates, but on the great general causes which move all human kind to hate Wrong and love Right. Such "insurrections" will continue as long as Slavery lasts, and will increase, both in frequency and in power just as the people become intelligent and moral. Virginia may hang John Brown and all that family, but she cannot hang the HUMAN RACE; and until that is done noble men will rejoice in the motto of that once magnanimous State – "*Sic semper Tyrannis!*"[3] "Let such be the end of every oppressor."

[...] A few years ago it did not seem difficult first to check Slavery, and then to end it without any bloodshed. I think this cannot be done now, nor ever in the future. All the great charters of HUMANITY have been writ in blood. I once hoped that of American Democracy would be engrossed in less costly ink; but it is plain, now, that our pilgrimage

---

[2] Pursuing his mission of abolishing slavery, John Brown, a fervid abolitionist, led 21 men on a raid of the federal arsenal at Harper's Ferry, Virginia, on October 16, 1859. His plan to arm slaves with the weapons he and his men seized from the arsenal was thwarted, however, by local farmers, militiamen, and troops led by Robert E. Lee, and within 36 hours of the attack, most of Brown's men had been killed or captured. Brown himself was captured, tried, and convicted of treason, and hanged on December 2, 1859.

[3] Latin: "Thus always to tyrants." The phrase is attributed to Brutus at the assassination of Julius Ceasar; it now is the state motto of Virginia. This motto also appears at the lower edge of the great seal of Virginia which features the Roman goddess Virtus standing over a defeated tyrannical opponent. Virtus represents the virtues of heroism, righteousness, freedom, and valor.

must lead through a Red Sea, wherein many a Pharaoh will go under and perish.[4] Alas! that we are not wise enough to be just, or just enough to be wise, and so gain much at small cost!

Look, now, at a few notorious facts:

I. There are four million slaves in the United States violently withheld from their natural right to life, liberty, and the pursuit of happiness. [...]

There are men in all the Northern States who feel the obligation which citizenship imposes on them – the duty to help those slaves. Hence arose the ANTI-SLAVERY SOCIETY, which seeks simply to excite the white people to perform their natural duty to their dark fellow-countrymen. Hence comes CAPT. BROWN'S EXPEDITION – an attempt to help his countrymen enjoy their natural right to life, liberty, and the pursuit of happiness.

He sought by violence what the Anti-Slavery Society works for with other weapons. The two agree in the end, and differ only in the means. Men like Capt. Brown will be continually rising up among the white people of the Free States, attempting to do their *natural duty* to their black countrymen – that is, help them to freedom. [...]

II. But it is not merely white men who will fight for the liberty of Americans; the negroes will take their defence into their own hands, especially if they can find white men to lead them. No doubt, the African race is greatly inferior to the Caucasian[5] in general intellectual power, and also in that instinct for Liberty which is so strong in the Teutonic family, and just now obvious in the Anglo-Saxons of Britain and America; besides, the African race have but little desire for vengeance – the lowest form of the love of justice. [...]

But *there is a limit even to the negro's forbearance.* [...]

[...] And, one day, even the sluggish African will wake up under the three-fold stimulus of the Fourth of July cannon, the whip of the slaveholder, and the sting of his heartless mockery. Then, if "oppression maketh wise men mad," what do you think it will do to African slaves, who are familiar with scenes of violence, and all manner of cruelty? Still more: if the negroes have not general power of mind, or instinctive love of liberty, equal to the whites, they are much our superiors in *power of cunning*, and in *contempt for death* – rather formidable qualities in a servile war. There already have been several risings of slaves in this century; they spread fear and consternation. The future will be more terrible. [...]

Now, Slavery is a wickedness so vast and so old, so rich and so respectable, supported by the State, the Press, the Market, and the Church, that all those agencies are needed to oppose it with – those, and many more which I cannot speak of now. You and I prefer the peaceful method; but I, at least, shall welcome the violent if no other accomplish the end. So will the great mass of thoughtful and good men at the North; else why do we honor the Heroes of the Revolution, and build them monuments all over our blessed New England? [...]

Brown will die, I think, like a martyr, and also like a saint. His noble demeanor, his unflinching bravery, his gentleness, his calm, religious trust in God, and his words of truth and soberness, cannot fail to make a profound impression on the hearts of Northern men; yes, and on Southern men. [...] I think there have been few spirits more pure and devoted than John Brown's, and none that gave up their breath in a nobler cause. Let the American State hang his body, and the American Church damn his soul; still, the blessing of such as are ready to perish will fall on him, and the universal justice of the Infinitely

---

[4] Reference to the exodus of the Israelites from Egypt.
[5] The term Caucasian race is used almost exclusively in North America to mean 'white.'

Perfect God will take him welcome home. The road to heaven is as short from the gallows as from the throne; perhaps, also, as easy.

[...] God bless you and yours, and comfort you!

Ever affectionately yours,

THEODORE PARKER.

Source: Theodore Parker (1810-1860). "John Brown and the Philosophy of Freedom." *Life and Correspondence of Theodore Parker, Minister of the Twenty-Eighth Congregational Society, Boston*. 2 vols. Ed. John Weiss. New York: Appleton, 1864, Vol. 2, 170-175, 177-178.

CIVIL WAR & RECONSTRUCTION

As the rift between North and South steadily increased after the middle of the nineteenth century, issues of states' rights and the debate about the future of slavery brought the United States to the brink of civil war in 1861. After four years of military conflict, Reconstruction efforts sought to establish a new political, social, and economic order. Although most Reconstruction measures proved abortive, the Civil War and Reconstruction eras came to demarcate the transformation of the United States into a modern society. The victorious conclusion of the war against Mexico in 1848, which resulted in the annexation of new territories in the Southwest, rekindled sectional conflicts rooted in the revolutionary period and in the Early Republic. The accelerated pace of westward expansion led to fierce debates over the admittance of new states as free or slaveholding members of the union and threatened to tip the fragile political balance between North and South in Congress.

Despite the aggravation of sectional conflict and the repeated threats of secession in the South, leading political figures such as the Northern senator Daniel Webster sustained the hope of a legal compromise on the basis of the federal constitution to reconcile the two sections of the nation. Speaking at the time of the complex process of legislation which resulted in the Compromise of 1850, Webster not only calls for the preservation of the Union but also warns against the calamitous consequences of secession (doc. 274). Although the Compromise of 1850 resolved many of the legal issues involved in the debate over the extension of slavery into the western territories and the admission of new states into the Union, some of its provisions – such as the Fugitive Slave Law which extended the power of federal authorities to deport actual and suspected runaway slaves to the South – ignited new conflicts between the sections. Eventually, the growing alienation between the two sections climaxed in the split of political parties and religious denominations into northern and southern branches, and finally, in the collapse of the national party system. The rise of the Republican Party in the North during the second half of the 1850s already signaled the impossibility to resolve the antagonism through political compromise. However, the conflict was not confined to the political sphere, but also led to violent clashes between the supporters of pro- and anti-slavery positions.

After Abraham Lincoln's victory in the presidential election of 1860, political debates in the North were primarily concerned with the threat of secession and the possibilities of preserving the Union. However, discussions about the interpretation of the constitution and Southern arguments for secession temporarily overshadowed the question of slavery prior to the outbreak of the Civil War. Led by South Carolina, the first state to pass an ordinance of secession in December 1860, the majority of slave-holding states seceded from the Union and moved toward the creation of the Confederate States of America. In an address of the convention in South Carolina to other slave-holding states, the champions of Southern independence justified secession in arguing that the federal constitution was a failed experiment and that Northern infringements of the constitution violated the achievements and the spirit of the American Revolution (doc. 275). In a similar vein, Jefferson Davis, the President of the Confederacy, employs the rhetoric of the Declaration of Independence to justify secession in his inaugural address when he invokes the "American idea" that it is the right of the people to "alter or abolish governments whenever they become destructive of the end for which they were established" (doc. 276). Lincoln, in his first inaugural address, replies to these charges and refutes the Southern recourse to the Declaration of Independence (doc. 277). He upholds the federal constitution and rejects the Southern re-appropriation of the Declaration asserting that his administration would not interfere with the fundamental rights and liberties of Southerners – including the institution of slavery in those territories where it already existed. Strongly contesting the right of an individual state to secede from the Union, Lincoln proclaims the perpetual character of the Constitution and the federal government, and gives priority to the preservation of the Union over the abolition of slavery.

While the Confederacy fought for its political independence and for the continuation of slavery, public opinion in the North gradually embraced measures to abolish slavery on the federal level. Although Lincoln had initially declared to fight the war for the perpetuation of the Union, he presented his first plans to issue an Emancipation Proclamation to his cabinet in July 1862 and made them public in September (doc. 278). Intended as a military measure to cripple the South's war economy, the Proclamation provided for the liberation of all "slaves within any State or designated part of a State, the people whereof shall then be in rebellion against the United States" on January 1, 1863, and, among other things, the enlistment of free African Americans into military service for the Union. The direct impact of the Proclamation on the situation of the slaves in the South remained marginal, but generated further support for the war effort from Northern abolitionists and supporters of the Republican Party. In effect, however, the Proclamation had made the abolition of slavery an official war aim and shaped debates over the re-admission of the Confederate States into the Union and the future status of African Americans in a post-war society.

In his second inaugural address, Lincoln put the issue of slavery at the core of his religious interpretation of the Civil War (doc. 280). Invoking the possibility of national reconciliation, Lincoln avoided the pugnacious rhetoric of many of his contemporaries. Assassinated shortly after the Confederate surrender in April 1865, Lincoln had not developed a detailed program for the political reconstruction of the nation and his reconciliatory plans met the resistance of supporters of a harsher treatment of the vanquished South. Nor had Lincoln intended radical measures to improve the situation of the freedmen in the South except the extension of suffrage to a select group of African Americans.

In the two years after the Civil War, the political agenda for Reconstruction was set by Andrew Johnson, whose presidency witnessed the abolition of slavery in the Thirteenth Amendment. However, his policies also resulted in a return to power of the antebellum Southern elite and in a continuation of economic inequality through the implementation of Black Codes in most Southern states. As the eminent spokesperson of his race, the black abolitionist Frederick Douglass led the campaign for the "enfranchisement of the black man" and attempted to adopt the abolitionist discourse to the struggle for political equality in the post-war years (doc. 281). In Congress, Northern Republicans began to define the national policies of Reconstruction against the President and toward the goal of transforming Southern society through federal legislation. Under the influence of the Radical Republicans, Congress established the Freedmen's Bureau, a federal agency intended to provide aid and relief in the transformation of Southern states from slavery to freedom, and passed the first Civil Rights Act which extended national citizenship to everyone born within the United States and defined equal rights for all citizens regardless of race. The enfranchisement of black citizens led, however, to many forms of new discrimination as, for instance, the pamphlets used during the gubernatorial campaign in Pennsylvania in 1866 amply illustrate (cf. docs. 283 and 284). During the period of Congressional Reconstruction after 1867, Congress adopted the Fourteenth Amendment which codified the right to "equal protection of the law" for all citizens, including former slaves, and which was intended to coerce the South into cooperating in the Reconstruction effort. The Fifteenth Amendment made it illegal for states to deprive anyone of the right to vote "on account of race, color, or previous condition of servitude." All these measures were ultimately geared toward establishing a republic whose powerful federal government benevolently guaranteed political equality for all citizens.

In the South, opposition to emancipation and Congressional Reconstruction did not prevent the establishment of Republican state governments that also included African American representatives and officials. These governments often derived their electoral majorities from a solid support by newly enfranchised African Americans. While Republican governments sought a speedy modernization of Southern society, opposition to allegedly treacherous Southerners, termed scalawags, and the stereotypical northern profiteers, referred to as carpetbaggers, soon turned violent throughout the South. The secret organization of the Ku Klux Klan effectually waged a terrorist campaign against Reconstruction policies and – though finally suppressed by the federal government – contributed to the overthrow of most Republican state governments. The climate of racial violence continued to pervade the South after the withdrawal of federal troops and after the termination of Reconstruction in the wake of the 1876 presidential elections.

American visual culture produced a vivid pictorial discourse reflecting the political developments of the Reconstruction years. While images of an idyllic life on Southern plantations persisted throughout the nineteenth century, cartoonists like Thomas Nast sided with the politics of the Radical Republicans and attacked Southern obstruction to Congressional Reconstruction (cf. doc. 282). However, satirical comments, for instance on the political participation of African Americans in Southern legislatures, indicate a waning support for Reconstruction in the North during the early 1870s. At the same time, the resurgent Democratic Party began to attack Congressional policies on the grounds of a white supremacist platform.

Despite the short-lived and ambivalent achievements of the Reconstruction era, Frederick Douglass sustained the vision of a peaceful interracial society in his comments on the heritage of slavery and on the pervasiveness of American racism (doc. 287). In his famous Atlanta Compromise speech (doc. 289), Booker T. Washington, principal of the black industrial Tuskegee Institute, criticized the political participation of African Americans in the post-war years as misguided efforts to ameliorate the situation of the freedmen. Instead, he suggested that African Americans accept the separation of the races and concentrate on economic improvement to assure the "mutual progress" of the New South.

Frank Obenland

274. Daniel Webster
"The Constitution and the Union Speech" (1850)

Mr. President, – I wish to speak to-day, not as a Massachusetts man, nor as a Northern man, but as an American, and a member of the Senate of the United States. It is fortunate that there is a Senate of the United States; a body not yet moved from its propriety, not lost to a just sense of its own dignity and its own high responsibilities, and a body to which the country looks, with confidence, for wise, moderate, patriotic, and healing counsels. It is not to be denied that we live in the midst of strong agitations, and are surrounded by very considerable dangers to our institutions and government. The imprisoned winds are let loose. The East, the North, and the stormy South combine to throw the whole sea into commotion, to toss its billows to the skies, and disclose its profoundest depths. I do not affect to regard myself, Mr. President, as holding, or as fit to hold, the helm in this combat with the political elements; but I have a duty to perform, and I mean to perform it with fidelity, not without a sense of existing dangers, but not without hope. I have a part to act, not for my own security or safety, for I am looking out for no fragment upon which to float away from the wreck, if wreck there must be, but for the good of the whole, and the preservation of all; and there is that which will keep me to my duty during this struggle, whether the sun and the stars shall appear, or shall not appear for many days. I speak to-day for the preservation of the Union. "Hear me for my cause." I speak to-day, out of a solicitous and anxious heart for the restoration to the country of that quiet and that harmony which make the blessings of this Union so rich, and so dear to us all. [...]

We all know, Sir, that slavery has existed in the world from time immemorial. There was slavery, in the earliest periods of history, among the Oriental nations. There was slavery among the Jews; the theocratic government of that people issued no injunction against it. There was slavery among the Greeks; and the ingenious philosophy of the Greeks found, or sought to find, a justification for it exactly upon the grounds which have been assumed for such a justification in this country; that is, a natural and original difference among the races of mankind, and the inferiority of the black or colored race to the white. The Greeks justified their system of slavery upon that idea, precisely. They held the African and some of the Asiatic tribes to be inferior to the white race; but they did not show, I think, by any close process of logic, that, if this were true, the more intelligent and the stronger had therefore a right to subjugate the weaker.

The more manly philosophy and jurisprudence of the Romans placed the justification of slavery on entirely different grounds. The Roman jurists, from the first and down to the fall of the empire, admitted that slavery was against the natural law, by which, as they maintained, all men, of whatsoever clime, color, or capacity, were equal; but they justified slavery, first, upon the ground and authority of the law of nations, arguing, and arguing truly, that at that day the conventional law of nations admitted that captives in war, whose lives, according to the notions of the times, were at the absolute disposal of the captors, might, in exchange for exemption from death, be made slaves for life, and that such servitude might descend to their posterity. [...] At the introduction of Christianity, the Roman world was full of slaves, and I suppose there is to be found no injunction against the relation between man and man in the teachings of the Gospel of Jesus Christ or of any of his Apostles. The object of the instruction imparted to mankind by the founder of Christianity was to touch the heart, purify the soul, and improve the lives of individual men. That object went directly to the first fountain of all the political and social relations of the human race, as well as of all true religious feeling, the individual heart and mind of man. [...]

Sir, wherever there is a substantive good to be done, wherever there is a foot of land to be prevented from becoming slave territory, I am ready to assert the principle of the exclusion of slavery. I am pledged to it from the year 1837; I have been pledged to it again and again; and I will perform those pledges; but I will not do a thing unnecessarily that wounds the feelings of others, or that does discredit to my own understanding. [...]

[...] Secession! Peaceable secession! Sir, your eyes and mine are never destined to see that miracle. The dismemberment of this vast country without convulsion! The breaking up of the fountains of the great deep without ruffing the surface! Who is so foolish, I beg every body's pardon, as to expect to see any such thing? Sir, he who sees these States, now revolving in harmony around a common centre, and expects to see them quit their places and fly off without convulsion, may look the next hour to see the heavenly bodies rush from their spheres, and jostle against each other in the realms of space, without causing the wreck of the universe. There can be no such thing as a peaceable secession. Peaceable secession is an utter impossibility. Is the great Constitution under which we live, covering this whole country, is it to be thawed and melted away by secession, as the snows on the mountain melt under the influence of a vernal sun, disappear almost unobserved, and run off? No, Sir! No, Sir! I will not state what might produce the disruption of the Union; but, Sir, I see as plainly as I see the sun in heaven what that disruption itself must produce; I see that it must produce war, and such a war as I will not describe, *in its twofold character*. [...]

And now, Mr. President, instead of speaking of the possibility or utility of secession, instead of dwelling in those caverns of darkness, instead of groping with those ideas so full of all that is horrid and horrible, let us come out into the light of day; let us enjoy the fresh air of Liberty and Union; let us cherish those hopes which belong to us; let us devote ourselves to those great objects that are fit for our consideration and our action; let us raise our conceptions to the magnitude and the importance of the duties that devolve upon us; let our comprehension be as broad as the country for which we act, our aspirations as high as its certain destiny; let us not be pigmies in a case that calls for men. Never did there devolve on any generation of men higher trusts than now devolve upon us, for the preservation of this Constitution and the harmony and peace of all who are destined to live under it. Let us make our generation one of the strongest and brightest links in that golden chain which is destined, I fondly believe, to grapple the people of all the States to this Constitution for ages to come. We have a great, popular, constitutional government, guarded by law and by judicature, and defended by the affections of the whole people. No monarchical throne presses these States together, no iron chain of military power encircles them; they live and stand under a government popular in its form, representative in its character, founded upon principles of equality, and so constructed, we hope, as to last for ever. In all its history it has been beneficent; it has trodden down no man's liberty; it has crushed no State. Its daily respiration is liberty and patriotism; its yet youthful veins are full of enterprise, courage, and honorable love of glory and renown. Large before, the country has now, by recent events[1] become vastly

---

[1] Reference to the Annexation of Texas and to the Mexican-American War.

larger. This republic now extends, with a vast breadth, across the whole continent. The two great seas of the world wash the one and the other shore. We realize, on a mighty scale, the beautiful description of the ornamental border of the buckler[2] of Achilles: –

> "Now, the broad shield complete, the artist crowned
> With his last hand, and poured the ocean round;
> In living silver seemed the waves to roll,
> And beat the buckler's verge, and bound the whole."[3]

Source: Daniel Webster (1782-1852). "The Constitution and the Union, March 7, 1850." *The Papers of Daniel Webster. Speeches and Formal Writings*. 20 vols. Vol. 19 (Series 4, Vol. 2): *1834-1852*. Ed. Charles M. Wiltse. Hanover, NH, and London: University Press of New England, 1988, 515-516, 519-520, 539, 546-547, 550-551.

275. The Address of the People of South Carolina, Assembled in Convention, to the People of the Slaveholding States of the United States (1860)

It is seventy-three years, since the Union between the United States was made by the Constitution of the United States. During this time, their advance in wealth, prosperity and power, has been with scarcely a parallel in the history of the world. The great object of their Union, was defence against external aggressions; which object is now attained, from their mere progress in power. Thirty-one millions of people, with a commerce and navigation which explore every sea, and with agricultural productions which are necessary to every civilized people, command the friendship of the world. But unfortunately, our internal peace has not grown with our external prosperity. Discontent and contention have moved in the bosom of the Confederacy, for the last thirty-five years. During this time, South Carolina has twice called her people together in solemn Convention, to take into consideration, the aggressions and unconstitutional wrongs, perpetrated by the people of the North on the people of the South. These wrongs, were submitted to by the people of the South, under the hope and expectation, that they would be final. But such hope and expectation, have proved to be vain. Instead of producing forbearance, our acquiescence has only instigated to new forms of aggressions and outrage; and South Carolina, having again assembled her people in Convention, has this day dissolved her connexion with the States, constituting the United States.

The one great evil, from which all other evils have flowed, is the overthrow of the Constitution of the United States. The Government of the United States, is no longer the Government of Confederated Republics, but of a consolidated Democracy. It is no longer a free Government, but a Despotism. It is, in fact, such a Government as Great Britain attempted to set over our Fathers; and which was resisted and defeated by a seven years' struggle for independence.

The Revolution of 1776, turned upon one great principle, self-government, – and self-taxation, the criterion of self-government. Where the interests of two people united together under one Government, are different, each must have the power to protect its interests by the organization of the Government, or they cannot be free. [...]

---

[2] A small round shield.
[3] Alexander Pope (transl.): Homer, *Illiad* (1816), Book 18, ll. 701-704.

The Southern States, now stand exactly in the same position towards the Northern States, that the Colonies did towards Great Britain. The Northern States, having the majority in Congress, claim the same power of omnipotence in legislation as the British parliament. "The General Welfare," is the only limit to the legislation of either; and the majority in Congress, as in the British parliament, are the sole judges of the expediency of the legislation, this "General Welfare" requires. Thus, the Government of the United States has become a consolidated Government; and the people of the Southern States, are compelled to meet the very despotism, their fathers threw off in the Revolution of 1776. [...]

No man can for a moment believe, that our ancestors intended to establish over their posterity, exactly the same sort of Government they had overthrown. The great object of the Constitution of the United States, in its internal operation, was, doubtless, to secure the great end of the Revolution – a limited free Government – a Government limited to those matters only, which were general and common to all portions of the United States. All sectional or local interests, were to be left to the States. By no other arrangement, would they obtain free Government, by a Constitution common to so vast a Confederacy. Yet by gradual and steady encroachments on the part of the people of the North, and acquiescence on the part of the South, the limitations in the Constitution have been swept away; and the Government of the United States has become consolidated, with a claim of limitless powers in its operations. [...]

The Constitution of the United States, was an experiment. The experiment consisted, in uniting under one Government, peoples living in different climates, and having different pursuits and institutions. It matters not, how carefully the limitations of such a Government be laid down in the Constitution, – its success must at least depend, upon the good faith of the parties to the constitutional compact, in enforcing them. [...] The Constitution of the United States, irrespective of the interposition of the States, rested on the assumption, that power would yield to faith, – that integrity would be stronger than interest; and that thus, the limitations of the Constitution would be observed. The experiment, has been fairly made. The Southern States, from the commencement of the Government, have striven to keep it, within the orbit prescribed by the Constitution. The experiment, has failed. [... The] General Government must necessarily be a despotism, because all sectional or local interests must ever be represented by a minority in the councils of the General Government – having no power to protect itself against the rule of the majority. The majority, constituted from those who do not represent these sectional or local interests, will control and govern them. A free people, cannot submit to such a Government. [...]

[...] The repeated efforts made by South Carolina, in a wise conservatism, to arrest the progress of the General Government in its fatal progress to consolidation, have been unsupported, and she has been denounced as faithless to the obligations of the Constitution, by the very men and States, who were destroying it by their usurpations. It is now too late, to reform or restore the Government of the United States. All confidence in the North, is lost by the South. The faithlessness of the North for a half century, has opened a gulf of separation between the North and the South which no promises nor engagements can fill.

It cannot be believed, that our ancestors would have assented to any Union whatever with the people of the North, if the feelings and opinions now existing amongst them, had existed when the Constitution was framed. [...] Time and the progress of things, have totally altered the relations between the Northern and Southern States, since the Union was established. That identity of feelings, interests and institutions, which once existed, is gone. They are now divided, between agricultural – and manufacturing, and commercial States;

between slaveholding, and non-slaveholding States. Their institutions and industrial pursuits, have made them, totally different peoples. That Equality in the Government between the two sections of the Union which once existed, no longer exists. We but imitate the policy of our fathers in dissolving a union with non-slaveholding confederates, and seeking a confederation with slaveholding States. [...]

Citizens of the slaveholding States of the United States! Circumstances beyond our control, have placed us in the van of the great controversy between the Northern and Southern States. We would have preferred, that other States should have assumed the position we now occupy. Independent ourselves, we disclaim any design or desire, to lead the counsels of the other Southern States. Providence has cast our lot together, by extending over us an identity of pursuits, interests and institutions. [...] You have loved the Union, in whose service your great statesmen have labored, and your great soldiers have fought and conquered – not for the material benefits it conferred, but with the faith of a generous and devoted chivalry. You have long lingered in hope over the shattered remains of a broken Constitution. Compromise after compromise, formed by your concessions, has been trampled under foot, by your Northern confederates. All fraternity of feeling between the North and the South is lost, or has been converted into hate; and we, of the South, are at last driven together, by the stern destiny which controls the existence of nations. Your bitter experience, of the faithlessness and rapacity of your Northern confederates, may have been necessary, to evolve those great principles of free government, upon which the liberties of the world depend, and to prepare you for the grand mission of vindicating and re-establishing them. [...] All we demand of other peoples is, to be let alone, to work out our own high destinies. United together, and we must be the most independent, as we are among the most important, of the nations of the world. United together, and we require no other instrument to conquer peace, than our beneficent productions. United together, and we must be a great, free and prosperous people, whose renown must spread throughout the civilized world, and pass down, we trust, to the remotest ages. We ask you to join us, in forming a Confederacy of Slaveholding States.

Source: *The Address of the People of South Carolina, Assembled in Convention, to the People of the Slaveholding States of the United States* [December 25, 1860]. Charleston, SC: Evans & Cogswell, 1860, 3-5; 7-12; 14-16.

276. Jefferson Davis
"First Inaugural Address, February 18, 1861"

Gentlemen of the Congress of the Confederate States of America, Friends and Fellow-Citizens:

Called to the difficult and responsible station of Chief Executive of the Provisional Government which you have instituted, I approach the discharge of the duties assigned to me with an humble distrust of my abilities, but with a sustaining confidence in the wisdom of those who are to guide and to aid me in the administration of public affairs, and an abiding faith in the virtue and patriotism of the people.

Looking forward to the speedy establishment of a permanent government to take the place of this, and which by its greater moral and physical power will be better able to combat with the many difficulties which arise from the conflicting interests of separate nations, I enter upon the duties of the office to which I have been chosen with the hope that the beginning of our career as a Confederacy may not be obstructed by hostile opposition to our enjoyment of the separate existence and independence which we have asserted, and, with the blessing of Providence, intend to maintain. Our present condition, achieved in a manner unprecedented in the history of nations, illustrates the American idea that governments rest upon the consent of the governed, and that it is the right of the people to alter or abolish governments whenever they become destructive of the ends for which they were established.

The declared purpose of the compact of Union from which we have withdrawn was "to establish justice, insure domestic tranquillity, provide for the common defense, promote the general welfare, and secure the blessings of liberty to ourselves and our posterity;" and when, in the judgment of the sovereign States now composing this Confederacy, it had been perverted from the purposes for which it was ordained, and had ceased to answer the ends for which it was established, a peaceful appeal to the ballot-box declared that so far as they were concerned, the government created by that compact should cease to exist. In this they merely asserted a right which the Declaration of Independence of 1776 had defined to be inalienable; of the time and occasion for its exercise, they, as sovereigns, were the final judges, each for itself. The impartial and enlightened verdict of mankind will vindicate the rectitude of our conduct, and He who knows the hearts of men will judge of the sincerity with which we labored to preserve the Government of our fathers in its spirit. [...]

Sustained by the consciousness that the transition from the former Union to the present Confederacy has not proceeded from a disregard on our part of just obligations, or any failure to perform every constitutional duty, moved by no interest or passion to invade the rights of others, anxious to cultivate peace and commerce with all nations, if we may not hope to avoid war, we may at least expect that posterity will acquit us of having needlessly engaged in it. Doubly justified by the absence of wrong on our part, and by wanton aggression on the part of others, there can be no cause to doubt that the courage and patriotism of the people of the Confederate States will be found equal to any measures of defense which honor and security may require.

An agricultural people, whose chief interest is the export of a commodity required in every manufacturing country, our true policy is peace, and the freest trade which our necessities will permit. It is alike our interest, and that of all those to whom we would sell and from whom we would buy, that there should be the fewest practicable restrictions upon the interchange of commodities. There can be but little rivalry between ours and any manufacturing or navigating community, such as the Northeastern States of the American Union. It must follow, therefore, that a mutual interest would invite good will and kind offices. If, however, passion or the lust of dominion should cloud the judgment or inflame the ambition of those States, we must prepare to meet the emergency and to maintain, by the final arbitrament of the sword, the position which we have assumed among the nations of the earth. We have entered upon the career of independence, and it must be inflexibly pursued. Through many years of controversy with our late associates, the Northern States, we have vainly endeavored to secure tranquillity, and to obtain respect for the rights to which we were entitled. As a necessity, not a choice, we have resorted to the remedy of separation; and henceforth our energies must be directed to the conduct of our own affairs, and the perpetuity of the Confederacy which we have formed. If a just perception of mutual interest shall permit us peaceably to pursue our separate political career, my most earnest desire will have been fulfilled. But, if this be denied to us, and the integrity of our territory and jurisdiction be assailed, it will but remain for us, with firm resolve, to appeal to arms and invoke the blessings of Providence on a just cause. [...]

It is joyous, in the midst of perilous times, to look around upon a people united in heart, where one purpose of high resolve animates and actuates the whole – where the sacrifices to be made are not weighed in the balance against honor and right and liberty and equality. Obstacles may retard, they cannot long prevent the progress of a movement sanctified by its justice, and sustained by a virtuous people. Reverently let us invoke the God of our fathers to guide and protect us in our efforts to perpetuate the principles which, by his blessing, they were able to vindicate, establish and transmit to their posterity, and with a continuance of His favor, ever gratefully acknowledged, we may hopefully look forward to success, to peace, and to prosperity.

Source: Jefferson Davis (1808-1889). "First Inaugural Address, February 18, 1861."*The Papers of Jefferson Davis*. 11 vols. Ed. Lynda Lasswell Crist and Mary Seaton Dix. Vol. 7: *1861*. Baton Rouge and London: Louisiana State University Press, 1992, 46-48, 50.

277. Abraham Lincoln
"First Inaugural Address, Monday, March 4, 1861"

Fellow citizens of the United States:

In compliance with a custom as old as the government itself, I appear before you to address you briefly, and to take, in your presence, the oath prescribed by the Constitution of the United States, to be taken by the President "before he enters on the execution of this office."

I do not consider it necessary, at present, for me to discuss those matters of administration about which there is no special anxiety, or excitement.

Apprehension seems to exist among the people of the Southern States, that by the accession of a Republican Administration, their property, and their peace, and personal security, are to be endangered. There has never been any reasonable cause for such apprehension. Indeed, the most ample evidence to the contrary has all the while existed, and been open to their inspection. It is found in nearly all the published speeches of him who now addresses you. I do but quote from one of those speeches when I declare that "I have no purpose, directly or indirectly, to interfere with the institution of slavery in the States where it exists. I believe I have no lawful right to do so, and I have no inclination to do so." Those who nominated and elected me did so with full knowledge that I had made this, and many similar declarations, and had never recanted them. And more than this, they placed in the platform, for my acceptance, and as a law to themselves, and to me, the clear and emphatic resolution which I now read:

"*Resolved*, That the maintenance inviolate of the rights of the States, and especially the right of each State to order and control its own domestic institutions according to its own judgment exclusively, is essential to that balance of power on which the perfection and endurance of our political fabric depend; and we denounce the lawless invasion by armed force of the soil of any State or Territory, no matter what pretext, as among the gravest of crimes." [...]

There is much controversy about the delivering up of fugitives from service or labor. The clause I now read is as plainly written in the Constitution as any other of its provisions:

"No person held to service or labor in one State, under the laws thereof, escaping into another, shall, in consequence of any law or regulation therein, be discharged from such service or labor, but shall be delivered up on claim of the party to whom such service or labor may be due."

It is scarcely questioned that this provision was intended by those who made it, for the reclaiming of what we call fugitive slaves; and the intention of the law-giver is the law. All members of Congress swear their support to the whole Constitution – to this provision as much as to any other. [...]

It is seventy-two years since the first inauguration of a President under our national Constitution. During that period fifteen different and greatly distinguished citizens, have, in succession, administered the executive branch of the government. They have conducted it through many perils; and, generally, with great success. Yet, with all this scope of precedent, I now enter upon the same task for the brief constitutional term of four years, under great and peculiar difficulty. A disruption of the Federal Union heretofore only menaced, is now formidably attempted.

I hold, that in contemplation of universal law, and of the Constitution, the Union of these States is perpetual. Perpetuity is implied, if not expressed, in the fundamental law of all national governments. It is safe to assert that no government proper, ever had a provision in its organic law for its own termination. Continue to execute all the express provisions of our national Constitution, and the Union will endure forever – it being impossible to destroy it, except by some action not provided for in the instrument itself.

Again, if the United States be not a government proper, but an association of States in the nature of contract merely, can it, as a contract, be peaceably unmade, by less than all the parties who made it? One party to a contract may violate it – break it, so to speak; but does it not require all to lawfully rescind it?

Descending from these general principles, we find the proposition that, in legal contemplation, the Union is perpetual, confirmed by the history of the Union itself. The Union is much older than the Constitution. It was formed in fact, by the Articles of Association in 1774. It was matured and continued by the Declaration of Independence in 1776. It was further matured and the faith of all the then thirteen States expressly plighted and engaged that it should be perpetual, by the Articles of Confederation in 1778. And finally, in 1787, one of the declared objects for ordaining and establishing the Constitution, was *to form a more perfect union.*"

But if destruction of the Union, by one, or by a part only, of the States, be lawfully possible, the Union is *less* perfect than before the Constitution, having lost the vital element of perpetuity.

It follows from these views that no State, upon its own mere motion, can lawfully get out of the Union – that *resolves* and *ordinances* to that effect are legally void; and that acts of violence, within any State or States, against the authority of the United States, are insurrectionary or revolutionary, according to circumstances.

I therefore consider that, in view of the Constitution and the laws, the Union is unbroken; and, to the extent of my ability, I shall take care, as the Constitution itself expressly enjoins upon me, that the laws of the Union be faithfully executed in all the States. Doing this I deem to be only a simple duty on my part; and I shall perform it, so far as practicable, unless my rightful masters, the American people, shall withhold the requisite means, or, in some authoritative manner, direct the contrary. I trust this will not be regarded as a menace, but only as the declared purpose of the Union that it *will* constitutionally defend, and maintain itself.

In doing this there needs to be no bloodshed or violence; and there shall be none, unless it be forced upon the national authority. The power confided to me, will be used to hold, occupy, and possess the property, and places belonging to the government, and to collect the duties and imposts; but beyond what may be necessary for these objects, there will be no invasion – no using of force against, or among the people anywhere. [...]

The course here indicated will be followed, unless current events, and experience, shall show a modification, or change, to be proper; and in every case and exigency, my best discretion will be exercised, according to circumstances actually existing, and with a view and a hope of a peaceful solution of the national troubles, and the restoration of fraternal sympathies and affections.

That there are persons in one section, or another who seek to destroy the Union at all events, and are glad of any pretext to do it, I will neither affirm nor deny; but if there be such, I need address no word to them. To those, however, who really love the Union, may I not speak?

Before entering upon so grave a matter as the destruction of our national fabric, with all its benefits, its memories, and its hopes, would it not be wise to ascertain precisely why we do it? Will you hazard so desperate a step, while there is any possibility that any portion of the ills you fly from, have no real existence? Will you, while the certain ills you fly to, are greater than all the real ones you fly from? Will you risk the commission of so fearful a mistake? [...]

One section of our country believes slavery is *right*, and ought to be extended, while the other believes it is *wrong*, and ought not to be extended. This is the only substantial dispute. The fugitive slave clause of the Constitution, and the law for the suppression of the foreign slave trade, are each as well enforced, perhaps, as any law can ever be in a community where the moral sense of the people imperfectly supports the law itself. The great body of the people abide by the dry legal obligation in both cases, and a few break over in each. This, I think, cannot be perfectly cured; and it would be worse in both cases *after* the separation of the sections, than before. The foreign slave trade, now imperfectly suppressed, would be ultimately revived without restriction, in one section; while fugitive slaves, now only partially surrendered, would not be surrendered at all, by the other.

Physically speaking, we cannot separate. We cannot remove our respective sections from each other, nor build an impassable wall between them. A husband and wife may be divorced, and go out of the presence, and beyond the reach of each other; but the different parts of our country cannot do this. They cannot but remain face to face; and intercourse, either amicable or hostile, must continue between them. Is it possible then to make that intercourse more advantageous, or more satisfactory, *after* separation than *before*? Can aliens make treaties easier than friends can make laws? Can treaties be more faithfully enforced between aliens, than laws can among friends? Suppose you go to war, you cannot fight always; and when, after much loss on both sides, and no gain on either, you cease fighting, the identical old questions, as to terms of intercourse, are again upon you.

This country, with its institutions, belongs to the people who inhabit it. Whenever they shall grow weary of the existing government, they can exercise their *constitutional* right of amending it, or their *revolutionary* right to dismember, or overthrow it. I can not be ignorant of the fact that many worthy, and patriotic citizens are desirous of having the national constitution amended. While I make no recommendation of amendments, I fully recognize the rightful authority of the people over the whole subject, to be exercised in either of the modes prescribed in the instrument itself [...].

The Chief Magistrate derives all his authority from the people, and they have conferred none upon him to fix terms for the separation of the States. The people themselves can do this also if they choose; but the executive, as such, has nothing to do with it. His duty is to administer the present government, as it came to his hands, and to transmit it, unimpaired by him, to his successor.

Why should there not be a patient confidence in the ultimate justice of the people? Is there any better, or equal hope, in the world? In our present differences, is either party without faith of being in the right? If the Almighty Ruler of nations, with his eternal truth and justice, be on your side of the North, or on yours of the South, that truth, and that justice, will surely prevail, by the judgment of this great tribunal, the American people.

By the frame of the government under which we live, this same people have wisely given their public servants but little power for mischief; and have, with equal wisdom, provided for the return of that little to their own hands at very short intervals.

While the people retain their virtue, and vigilance, no administration, by any extreme of wickedness or folly, can very seriously injure the government, in the short space of four years.

My countrymen, one and all, think calmly and *well*, upon this whole subject. Nothing valuable can be lost by taking time. If there be an object to *hurry* any of you, in hot haste, to a step which you would never take *deliberately*, that object will be frustrated by taking time; but no good object can be frustrated by it. Such of you as are now dissatisfied, still have the old Constitution unimpaired, and, on the sensitive point, the laws of your own framing under it; while the new administration will have no immediate power, if it would, to change either. If it were admitted that you who are dissatisfied, hold the right side in the dispute, there still is no single good reason for precipitate action. Intelligence, patriotism, Christianity, and a firm reliance on Him, who has never yet forsaken this favored land, are still competent to adjust, in the best way, all our present difficulty.

In *your* hands, my dissatisfied fellow countrymen, and not in *mine*, is the momentous issue of civil war. The government will not assail *you*. You can have no conflict, without being yourselves the aggressors. *You* have no oath registered in Heaven to destroy the government, while *I* shall have the most solemn one to "preserve, protect, and defend" it.

I am loth to close. We are not enemies, but friends. We must not be enemies. Though passion may have strained, it must not break our bonds of affection. The mystic chords of memory, stretching from every battle-field, and patriot grave, to every living heart and hearthstone, all over this broad land, will yet swell the chorus of the Union, when again touched, as surely they will be, by the better angels of our nature.

Source: Abraham Lincoln (1809-1865). "First Inaugural Address, Monday, March 4, 1861." *The Collected Works of Abraham Lincoln*. 9 vols. Ed. Roy P. Basler et al. Vol. 4: *1860-1861*. New Brunswick, NJ: Rutgers University Press, 1953, 262-271.

278. Abraham Lincoln
Emancipation Proclamation January 1, 1863

A Proclamation.

Whereas, on the twenty-second day of September, in the year of our Lord one thousand eight hundred and sixty-two, a proclamation was issued by the President of the United States, containing, among other things, the following, to wit:

"That on the first day of January, in the year of our Lord one thousand eight hundred and sixty-three, all persons held as slaves within any State or designated part of a State, the people whereof shall then be in rebellion against the United States, shall be then, thenceforward, and forever free; and the Executive Government of the United States, including the military and naval authority thereof, will recognize and maintain the freedom of such persons, and will do no act or acts to repress such persons, or any of them, in any efforts they may make for their actual freedom."

"That the Executive will, on the first day of January aforesaid, by proclamation, designate the States and parts of States, if any, in which the people thereof, respectively, shall then be in rebellion against the United States; and the fact that any State, or the people thereof, shall on that day be, in good faith, represented in the Congress of the United States by members chosen thereto at elections wherein a majority of the qualified voters of such State shall have participated, shall, in the absence of strong countervailing testimony, be deemed conclusive evidence that such State, and the people thereof, are not then in rebellion against the United States."

Now, therefore I, Abraham Lincoln, President of the United States, by virtue of the power in me vested as Commander-in-Chief, of the Army and Navy of the United States in time of actual armed rebellion against the authority and government of the United States, and as a fit and necessary war measure for suppressing said rebellion, do, on this first day of January, in the year of our Lord one thousand eight hundred and sixty-three, and in accordance with my purpose so to do publicly proclaimed for the full period of one hundred days, from the day first above mentioned, order and designate as the States and parts of States wherein the people thereof respectively, are this day in rebellion against the United States, the following, to wit:

Arkansas, Texas, Louisiana, [...] Mississippi, Alabama, Florida, Georgia, South Carolina, North Carolina, and Virginia, [...] and which excepted parts, are for the present, left precisely as if this proclamation were not issued.

And by virtue of the power, and for the purpose aforesaid, I do order and declare that all persons held as slaves within said designated States, and parts of States, are, and henceforward shall be free; and that the Executive government of the United States, including the military and naval authorities thereof, will recognize and maintain the freedom of said persons.

And I hereby enjoin upon the people so declared to be free to abstain from all violence, unless in necessary self-defence; and I recommend to them that, in all cases when allowed, they labor faithfully for reasonable wages.

And I further declare and make known, that such persons of suitable condition, will be received into the armed service of the United States to garrison forts, positions, stations, and other places, and to man vessels of all sorts in said service.

And upon this act, sincerely believed to be an act of justice, warranted by the Constitution, upon military necessity, I invoke the considerate judgment of mankind, and the gracious favor of Almighty God.

In witness whereof, I have hereunto set my hand and caused the seal of the United States to be affixed.

Done at the City of Washington, this first day of January, in the year of our Lord one thousand eight hundred and sixty three, and of the Independence of the United States of America the eighty-seventh.

By the President: Abraham Lincoln William H. Seward, Secretary of State.

Source: Abraham Lincoln (1809-1865). "Emancipation Proclamation January 1, 1863." http://www.archives.gov/exhibit_hall/featured_documents/emancipation_proclamation/transcript.html (access date July 30, 2005).

279. "The Promise of the Declaration of Independence Fulfilled" (1870)

Source: "The Promise of the Declaration of Independence Fulfilled." *Frank Leslie's Illustrated Newspaper*, March 19, 1870 [commemorating the 15th Amendment to the Constitution]. Courtesy Library of Congress.

280. Abraham Lincoln
"Second Inaugural Address, Saturday, March 4, 1865"

[Fellow Countrymen:]

At this second appearing to take the oath of the presidential office, there is less occasion for an extended address than there was at the first. Then a statement, somewhat in detail, of a course to be pursued, seemed fitting and proper. Now, at the expiration of four years, during which public declarations have been constantly called forth on every point and phase of the great contest which still absorbs the attention, and engrosses the ene[rg]ies of the nation, little that is new could be presented. The progress of our arms, upon which all else chiefly depends, is as well known to the public as to myself; and it is, I trust, reasonably satisfactory and encouraging to all. With high hope for the future, no prediction in regard to it is ventured.

On the occasion corresponding to this four years ago, all thoughts were anxiously directed to an impending civil-war. All dreaded it – all sought to avert it. While the inaugural address was being delivered from this place, devoted altogether to *saving* the Union without war, insurgent agents were in the city seeking to *destroy* it without war – seeking to dissol[v]e the Union, and divide effects, by negotiation. Both parties deprecated war; but one of them would *make* war rather than let the nation survive; and the other would *accept* war rather than let it perish. And the war came.

One eighth of the whole population were colored slaves, not distributed generally over the Union, but localized in the Southern part of it. These slaves constituted a peculiar and powerful interest. All knew that this interest was, somehow, the cause of the war. To strengthen, perpetuate, and extend this interest was the object for which the insurgents would rend the Union, even by war; while the government claimed no right to do more than to restrict the territorial enlargement of it. Neither party expected for the war, the magnitude, or the duration, which it has already attained. Neither anticipated that the *cause* of the conflict might cease with, or even before, the conflict itself should cease. Each looked for an easier triumph, and a result less fundamental and astounding. Both read the same Bible, and pray to the same God; and each invokes His aid against the other. It may seem strange that any men should dare to ask a just God's assistance in wringing their bread from the sweat of other men's faces; but let us judge not that we be not judged. The prayers of both could not be answered; that of neither has been answered fully. The Almighty has His own purposes. "Woe unto the world because of offences! for it must needs be that offences come; but woe to that man by whom the offence cometh!"[4] If we shall suppose that American Slavery is one of those offences which, in the providence of God, must needs come, but which, having continued through His appointed time, He now wills to remove, and that He gives to both North and South, this terrible war, as the woe due to those by whom the offence came, shall we discern therein any departure from those divine attributes which the believers in a Living God always ascribe to Him? Fondly do we hope – fervently do we pray – that this mighty scourge of war may speedily pass away. Yet, if God wills that it continue, until all the wealth piled by the bond-man's two hundred and fifty years of unrequited toil shall be sunk, and until every drop of blood drawn with the lash, shall be paid by another drawn with the sword, as was said

---

[4] Matt. 18.7.

three thousand years ago, so still it must be said "the judgments of the Lord, are true and righteous altogether."[5]

With malice toward none; with charity for all; with firmness in the right, as God gives us to see the right, let us strive on to finish the work we are in; to bind up the nation's wounds; to care for him who shall have borne the battle, and for his widow, and his orphan – to do all which may achieve and cherish a just, and lasting peace, among ourselves, and with all nations.

A. LINCOLN

Source: Abraham Lincoln (1809-1865). "Second Inaugural Address, Saturday, March 4, 1865." *The Collected Works of Abraham Lincoln*. 9 vols. Ed. Roy P. Basler et al. Vol. 8: *1864-1865*. New Brunswick, NJ: Rutgers University Press, 1953, 332-333.

281. Frederick Douglass "What the Black Man Wants" (1865)

I have had but one idea for the last three years to present to the American people, and the phraseology in which I clothe it is the old abolition phraseology. I am for the "immediate, unconditional, and universal" enfranchisement of the black man, in every State in the Union. (Loud applause.) Without this, his liberty is a mockery; without this, you might as well almost retain the old name of slavery for his condition; for, in fact, if he is not the slave of the individual master, he is the slave of society, and holds his liberty as a privilege, not as a right. He is at the mercy of the mob, and has no means of protecting himself.

It may be objected, however, that this pressing of the negroes' right to suffrage is premature. Let us have slavery abolished, it may be said, let us have labor organized, and then, in the natural course of events, the right of suffrage will be extended to the negro. I do not agree with this. The constitution of the human mind is such, that if it once disregards the conviction forced upon it by a revelation of truth, it requires the exercise of a higher power to produce the same conviction afterwards. The American people are now in tears. The Shenandoah[6] has run blood – the best blood of the North. All around Richmond the blood of New England and of the North has been shed – of your sons, your brothers and your fathers. We all feel, in the existence of this rebellion, that judgments terrible, wide-spread, far-reaching, overwhelming, are abroad in the land; and we feel, in view of these judgments, just now, a disposition to learn righteousness. This is the hour. Our streets are in mourning, tears are falling at every fireside, and under the chastisement of this rebellion we have almost come up to the point of conceding this great, this all-important right of suffrage. I fear that if we fail to do it now, if Abolitionists fail to press it now, we may not see, for centuries to come, the same disposition that exists at this moment. (Applause.) Hence, I say, now is the time to press this right.

It may be asked, "Why do you want it? Some men have got along very well without it. Women have not this right." Shall we justify one wrong by another? That is a sufficient answer. Shall we at this moment justify the deprivation of the negro of the right to vote because some one else is deprived of that privilege? I hold that women as well as men

---

[5] Ps. 19.
[6] River in northern Virginia.

have the right to vote (applause), and my heart and voice go with the movement to extend suffrage to woman. But that question rests upon another basis than that on which our right rests. We may be asked, I say, why we want it. I will tell you why we want it. We want it because it is our *right*, first of all. (Applause.) No class of men can, without insulting their own nature, be content with any deprivation of their rights. We want it, again, as a means for educating our race. Men are so constituted that they derive their conviction of their own possibilities largely from the estimate formed of them by others. If nothing is expected of a people, that people will find it difficult to contradict that expectation. By depriving us of suffrage, you affirm our incapacity to form an intelligent judgment respecting public men and public measures; you declare before the world that we are unfit to exercise the elective franchise, and by this means lead us to undervalue ourselves, to put a low estimate upon ourselves, and to feel that we have no possibilities like other men. [...]

I know that we are inferior to you in some things – virtually inferior. We walk about you like dwarfs among giants. Our heads are scarcely seen above the great sea of humanity. The Germans are superior to us; the Irish are superior to us; the Yankees are superior to us (laughter); they can do what we cannot, that is, what we have not hitherto been allowed to do. But, while I make this admission, I utterly deny that we are originally, or naturally, or practically, or in any way, or in any important sense, inferior to anybody on this globe. (Loud applause.) This charge of inferiority is an old dodge. It has been made available for oppression on many occasions. It is only about six centuries since the blue-eyed and fair-haired Anglo-Saxons were considered inferior by the haughty Normans, who once trampled upon them. [...]

The story of our inferiority is an old dodge, as I have said; for wherever men oppress their fellows, wherever they enslave them, they will endeavor to find the needed apology for such enslavement and oppression in the character of the people oppressed and enslaved. When we wanted, a few years ago, a slice of Mexico, it was hinted that the Mexicans were an inferior race, that the old Castilian blood had become so weak that it would scarcely run down hill, and that Mexico needed the long, strong and beneficent arm of the Anglo-Saxon care extended over it. We said that it was necessary to its salvation, and a part of the "manifest destiny" of this Republic, to extend our arm over that dilapidated government. So, too, when Russia wanted to take possession of a part of the Ottoman Empire, the Turks were "an inferior race." So, too, when England wants to set the heel of her power more firmly in the quivering heart of old Ireland, the Celts are "an inferior race." So, too, the negro, when he is to be robbed of any right which is justly his, is "an inferior man." It is said that we are ignorant; I admit it. But if we know enough to be hung, we know enough to vote. If the negro knows enough to pay taxes to support the Government, he knows enough to vote – taxation and representation should go together. If he knows enough to shoulder a musket and fight for the flag, fight for the Government, he knows enough to vote. If he knows as much when he is sober as an Irishman knows when drunk, he knows enough to vote, on good American principles. (Laughter and applause.)

But I was saying that you needed a counterpoise in the persons of the slaves to the enmity that would exist at the South after the rebellion is put down. I hold that the American people are bound, not only in self-defence, to extend this right to the freedmen of the South, but they are bound by their love of country, and by all their regard for the future safety of those Southern States to do this – to do it as a measure essential to the preservation of peace there. But I will not dwell upon this. I put it to the American sense of honor. The honor of a nation is an important thing. It is said in the Scriptures, "What doth it profit a man if he gain the whole world, and lose his own soul!"[7] It may be said also, what doth it profit a nation if it gain the whole world, but lose its honor? I hold that the American Government has taken upon itself a solemn obligation of honor to see that this war, let it be long or let it be short, let it cost much, or let it cost little, – that this war shall not cease until every freedman at the South has the right to vote. (Applause.) It has bound itself to do it. [...]

I ask my friends who are apologizing for not insisting upon this right, where can the black man look in this country for the assertion of this right if he may not look to the Massachusetts Anti-Slavery Society? Where under the whole heavens can he look for sympathy in asserting this right if he may not look to this platform? Have you lifted us up to a certain height to see that we are men, and then are any disposed to leave us there, without seeing that we are put in possession of all our rights? We look naturally to this platform for the assertion of all our rights, and for this one especially. I understand the anti-slavery societies of this country to be based on two principles – first, the freedom of the blacks of this country; and, second, the elevation of them. Let me not be misunderstood here. I am not asking for sympathy at the hands of Abolitionists, sympathy at the hands of any. [...] I have had but one answer from the beginning. Do nothing with us! Your doing with us has already played the mischief with us. Do nothing with us! If the apples will not remain on the tree of their own strength, if they are worm-eaten at the core, if they are early ripe and disposed to fall, let them fall! I am not for tying or fastening them on the tree in any way, except by nature's plan, and if they will not stay there let them fall. And if the negro cannot stand on his own legs, let him fall also. All I ask is, give him a chance to stand on his own legs! Let him alone! If you see him on his way to school, let him alone, – don't disturb him! If you see him going to the dinner table at a hotel, let him go! If you see him going to the ballot-box, let him alone! – don't disturb him! (Applause.) If you see him going into a workshop, just let him alone, – your interference is doing him a positive injury. [...] If you will only untie his hands, and give him a chance, I think he will live. He will work as readily for himself as the white man. A great many delusions have been swept away by this war. One was, that the negro would not work; he has proved his ability to work. Another was, that the negro would not fight; that he possessed only the most sheepish attributes of humanity; was a perfect lamb, or an "Uncle Tom;" disposed to take off his coat whenever required, fold his hands, and be whipped by any body who wanted to whip him; – but the war has proved that there is a great deal of human nature in the negro, and that he will fight, as Mr. Quincy,[8] our President, said, in earlier days than these, "when there is a reasonable probability of his whipping anybody." (Laughter and applause.)

Source: Frederick Douglass (1818?-1895). "What the Black Man Wants: An Address Delivered in Boston, Massachusetts, on 26 January 1865." *The Frederick Douglass Papers*. 5 vols. Ed. John W. Blassingame. Series 1: *Speeches, Debates, and Interviews*. Vol. 4: *1864-80*. New Haven and London: Yale University Press, 1991, 62-63, 65-69.

---

[7] Mark 8.36 (slight misquote).
[8] Edmund Quincy (1808-1877) joined the abolitionists in reaction to the murder of Elijah Lovejoy in 1837. Quincy served the Massachusetts Anti-Slavery Society for many years.

282. Thomas Nast
"He Wants a Change, Too" (1876)

Source: Thomas Nast (1840-1902). "He Wants a Change, Too." *Harper's Weekly*, October 28, 1876. Courtesy Library of Congress.

283. *The Freedman's Bureau!* (1866)

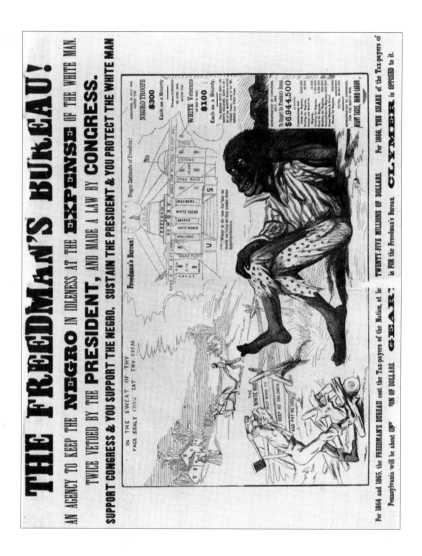

Source: *The Freedman's Bureau! An Agency to Keep the Negro in Idleness at the Expense of the White Man* (Democratic broadside from Pennsylvania congressional campaign, 1866). Courtesy Library of Congress. The Freedman's Capitol bears the following inscriptions (top to bottom): "Freedom and No Work," "Goods to Eat and Drink," "Uncle Sam Will have to Keep me," the Capitol's walls and pillars represent "Candy, Rum, Gin, Whiskey, Sugar Plums, Indolence, White Women, Apathy, White Sugar, Idleness, Fish Balls, Games, Stews, Pies"; below the Capitol's steps one reads: "Whar is de use for me to work as long as dey make dese appropriations." The left part of the broadside bears the following inscriptions: "In the Sweat of Thy Face Shalt Thou Eat Thy Food" and "The White Man Must Work to Keep His Children and Pay His Taxes."

284. *The Two Platforms* (1866)

Source: *The Two Platforms*. [Poster attacking Radical Republican exponents of black suffrage issued during the 1866 Pennsylvania gubernatorial race.] Courtesy Library of Congress.

285. "The Great Labor Question from a Southern Point of View" (1865)

Source: "The Great Labor Question from a Southern Point of View." *Harper's Weekly Journal of Civilization*, IX.448 (July 29, 1865), 1. [Text in the ballon: "My boy, we've toiled and taken care of you long enough. Now you've got to work!"]. Courtesy Library of Congress.

286. Thomas Nast
"Colored Rule in a Reconstructed (?) State" (1874)

Source: Thomas Nast (1840-1902): "Colored Rule in a Reconstructed (?) State." *Harper's Weekly Journal of Civilization*, 18.898 (March 14, 1874), 1. [Text below: "(The Members Call Each Other Thieves, Liars, Rascals, and Cowards.) COLUMBIA. 'You are Aping the lowest Whites. If you disgrace your Race in this way you had better take Back Seats.'"] Courtesy Library of Congress.

287. Frederick Douglass
"The Future of the Colored Race" (1886)

It is quite impossible, at this early date, to say with any decided emphasis what the future of the colored people will be. Speculations of that kind, thus far, have only reflected the mental bias and education of the many who have essayed to solve the problem.

We all know what the negro has been as a slave. In this relation we have his experience of two hundred and fifty years before us, and can easily know the character and qualities he has developed and exhibited during this long and severe ordeal. In his new relation to his environments, we see him only in the twilight of twenty years of semi-freedom; for he has scarcely been free long enough to outgrow the marks of the lash on his back and the fetters on his limbs. He stands before us, to-day, physically, a maimed and mutilated man. His mother was lashed to agony before the birth of her babe, and the bitter anguish of the mother is seen in the countenance of her offspring. Slavery has twisted his limbs, shattered his feet, deformed his body and distorted his features. He remains black, but no longer comely. Sleeping on the dirt floor of the slave cabin in infancy, cold on one side and warm on the other, a forced circulation of blood on the one side and chilled and retarded circulation on the other, it has come to pass that he has not the vertical bearing of a perfect man. His lack of symmetry, caused by no fault of his own, creates a resistance to his progress which cannot well be overestimated, and should be taken into account, when measuring his speed in the new race of life upon which he has now entered. As I have often said before, we should not measure the negro from the heights which the white race has attained, but from the depths from which he has come. [...]

Laying aside all prejudice in favor of or against race, looking at the negro as politically and socially related to the American people generally, and measuring the forces arrayed against him, I do not see how he can survive and flourish in this country as a distinct and separate race, nor do I see how he can be removed from the country either by annihilation or expatriation. [...]

My strongest conviction as to the future of the negro therefore is, that he will not be expatriated nor annihilated, nor will he forever remain a separate and distinct race from the people around him, but that he will be absorbed, assimilated, and will only appear finally, as the Phœnicians now appear on the shores of the Shannon,[9] in the features of a blended race. I cannot give at length my reasons for this conclusion, and perhaps the reader may think that the wish is father to the thought, and may in his wrath denounce my conclusion as utterly impossible. To such I would say, tarry a little, and look at the facts. Two hundred years ago there were two distinct and separate streams of human life running through this country. They stood at opposite extremes of ethnological classification: all black on the one side, all white on the other. Now, between these two extremes, an intermediate race has arisen, which is neither white nor black, neither Caucasian nor Ethiopian, and this intermediate race is constantly increasing. [...]

---

[9] Shannon: river in North-central Ireland. Douglass implies that the Irish are descendants of the Phoenicians. This theory has been prominent since the 18th century when scholars began to document 'the Phoenician origin' of Western (especially Celtic) civilization. Historians have given the Phoenicians most of the credit for this emigration from Palestine to Europe. In 1772, General Charles Vallancey, a leading Irish scholar of the day, published, for instance, his famous *Essay on the Antiquity of the Irish Language, Being a Collation of the Irish with the Punic (Hebrew) Language*.

Of course this result will not be reached by any hurried or forced processes. It will not arise out of any theory of the wisdom of such blending of the two races. If it comes at all, it will come without shock or noise or violence of any kind, and only in the fullness of time, and it will be so adjusted to surrounding conditions as hardly to be observed. I would not be understood as advocating intermarriage between the two races. I am not a propagandist, but a prophet. I do not say that what I say *should* come to pass, but what I think is likely to come to pass, and what is inevitable. While I would not be understood as advocating the desirability of such a result, I would not be understood as deprecating it. Races and varieties of the human family appear and disappear, but humanity remains and will remain forever. [...]

Source: Frederick Douglass (1818?-1895). "The Future of the Colored Race." *The North American Review* 142 (May 1886), 437-339.

288. E. Malcolm Argyle
"Report from Arkansas" (1892)

There is much uneasiness and unrest all over this State among our people, owing to the fact that the [black] people (our race variety) all over the State are being lynched upon the slightest provocation; some being strung up to telegraph poles, others burnt at the stake and still others being shot like dogs. In the last 30 days there have been not less than eight colored persons lynched in this State. At Texarkana a few days ago, a man was burnt at the stake. In Pine Bluff a few days later two men were strung up and shot [...]. At Varner, George Harris was taken from jail and shot for killing a white man, for poisoning his domestic happiness. At Wilmar, a boy was induced to confess to the commission of an outrage, upon promise of his liberty, and when he had confessed, he was strung up and shot. Over in Toneoke County, a whole family consisting of husband, wife and child were shot down like dogs. Verily the situation is alarming in the extreme.

At this writing 500 people are hovering upon wharves in Pine Bluff, awaiting the steamers to take them up the Arkansas River to Oklahoma. [...] What is the outcome of all this? It is evident that the white people of the South have no further use for the Negro. He is being worse treated now, than at any other time, since the [Confederate] surrender. The white press of the South seems to be subsidized by this lawless element, the white pulpits seem to condone lynching. [...] The Northern press seems to care little about the condition of the Negroes [in the] South. The pulpits of the North are passive. Will not some who are not in danger of their lives, speak out against the tyrannical South [...] speak out against these lynchings and mob violence? For God's sake, say or do something, for our condition is precarious in the extreme.

Source: E. Malcolm Argyle (?). "Report from Arkansas." *Christian Recorder*. March 24, 1892. Repr. in: *A Documentary History of the Negro People in the United States*. 2 vols. Ed. Herbert Aptheker. Vol. 2: *From the Reconstruction Era to 1910*. Secaucus, NJ: Citadel, 1972, 793.

289. Booker T. Washington
"The Atlanta Exposition Address" (1895)

MR. PRESIDENT AND GENTLEMEN OF THE BOARD OF DIRECTORS AND CITIZENS.

One-third of the population of the South is of the Negro race. No enterprise seeking the material, civil, or moral welfare of this section can disregard this element of our population and reach the highest success. I but convey to you, Mr. President and Directors, the sentiment of the masses of my race when I say that in no way have the value and manhood of the American Negro been more fittingly and generously recognized than by the managers of this magnificent Exposition at every stage of its progress. It is a recognition that will do more to cement the friendship of the two races than any occurrence since the dawn of our freedom.

Not only this, but the opportunity here afforded will awaken among us a new era of industrial progress. Ignorant and inexperienced, it is not strange that in the first years of our new life we began at the top instead of at the bottom; that a seat in Congress or the state legislature was more sought than real estate or industrial skill; that the political convention of stump speaking had more attractions than starting a dairy farm or truck garden.

A ship lost at sea for many days suddenly sighted a friendly vessel. From the mast of the unfortunate vessel was seen a signal, "Water, water; we die of thirst!" The answer from the friendly vessel at once came back, "Cast down your bucket where you are." A second time the signal, "Water, water; send us water!" ran up from the distressed vessel, and was answered, "Cast down your bucket where you are." And a third and fourth signal for water was answered, "Cast down your bucket where you are." The captain of the distressed vessel, at last heeding the injunction, cast down his bucket, and it came up full of fresh, sparkling water from the mouth of the Amazon River. To those of my race who depend on bettering their condition in a foreign land or who underestimate the importance of cultivating friendly relations with the Southern white man, who is their next-door neighbour, I would say: "Cast down your bucket where you are" – cast it down in making friends in every manly way of the people of all races by whom we are surrounded.

Cast it down in agriculture, mechanics, in commerce, in domestic service, and in the professions. And in this connection it is well to bear in mind that whatever other sins the South may be called to bear, when it comes to business, pure and simple, it is in the South that the Negro is given a man's chance in the commercial world, and in nothing is this Exposition more eloquent than in emphasizing this chance. Our greatest danger is that in the great leap from slavery to freedom we may overlook the fact that the masses of us are to live by the productions of our hands, and fail to keep in mind that we shall prosper in proportion as we learn to dignify and glorify common labour and put brains and skill into the common occupations of life; shall prosper in proportion as we learn to draw the line between the superficial and the substantial, the ornamental gewgaws[10] of life and the useful. No race can prosper till it learns that there is as much dignity in tilling a field as in writing a poem. It is at the bottom of life we must begin, and not at the top. Nor should we permit our grievances to overshadow our opportunities.

To those of the white race who look to the incoming of those of foreign birth and strange tongue and habits for the prosperity of the South, were I permitted I would re-

---

[10] A pretty thing of little value, trifle.

peat what I say to my own race, "Cast down your bucket where you are." Cast it down among the eight millions of Negroes whose habits you know, whose fidelity and love you have tested in days when to have proved treacherous meant the ruin of your firesides. Cast down your bucket among these people who have, without strikes and labour wars, tilled your fields, cleared your forests, built your railroads and cities, and brought forth treasures from the bowels of the earth, and helped make possible this magnificent representation of the progress of the South. Casting down your bucket among my people, helping and encouraging them as you are doing on these grounds, and to education of head, hand, and heart, you will find that they will buy your surplus land, make blossom the waste places in your fields, and run your factories. While doing this, you can be sure in the future, as in the past, that you and your families will be surrounded by the most patient, faithful, law-abiding, and unresentful people that the world has seen. As we have proved our loyalty to you in the past, in nursing your children, watching by the sickbed of your mothers and fathers, and often following them with tear-dimmed eyes to their graves, so in the future, in our humble way, we shall stand by you with a devotion that no foreigner can approach, ready to lay down our lives, if need be, in defence of yours, interlacing our industrial, commercial, civil, and religions life with yours in a way that shall make the interests of both races one. In all things that are purely social we can be as separate as the fingers, yet one as the hand in all things essential to mutual progress.

There is no defence or security for any of us except in the highest intelligence and development of all. If anywhere there are efforts tending to curtail the fullest growth of the Negro, let these efforts be turned into stimulating, encouraging, and making him the most useful and intelligent citizen. Effort or means so invested will pay a thousand per cent interest. These efforts will be twice blessed – "blessing him that gives and him that takes."[11]

There is no escape through law of man or God from the inevitable: –

> The laws of changeless justice bind
>   Oppressor with oppressed;
> And close as sin and suffering joined
>   We march to fate abreast.[12]

Nearly sixteen millions of hands will aid you in pulling the load upward, or they will pull against you the load downward. We shall constitute one-third and more of the ignorance and crime of the South, or one-third its intelligence and progress; we shall contribute one-third to the business and industrial prosperity of the South, or we shall prove a veritable body of death, stagnating, depressing, retarding every effort to advance the body politic. [...]

The wisest among my race understand that the agitation of questions of social equality is the extremest folly, and that progress in the enjoyment of all the privileges that will come to us must be the result of severe and constant struggle rather than of artificial forcing. No race that has anything to contribute to the markets of the world is long in any degree ostracized. It is important and right that all privileges of the law be ours, but it is vastly more important that we be prepared for the exercises of these privileges. The opportunity to earn a dollar in a factory just now is worth infinitely more than the opportunity to spend a dollar in an opera-house.

---

[11] Cf. William Shakespeare, *The Merchant of Venice*, Act IV, scene 1, ll. 1667-70: "The quality of mercy is not strain'd; / It droppeth as the genle rain from heaven / Upon the place beneath. It is twice blest: / It blesseth him that gives and him that takes."
[12] Cf. John Greenleaf Whittier, "Song of the Negro Boatman."

In conclusion, may I repeat that nothing in thirty years has given us more hope and encouragement, and drawn us so near to you of the white race, as this opportunity offered by the Exposition; and here bending, as it were, over the altar that represents the results of the struggles of your race and mine, both starting practically empty-handed three decades ago, I pledge that in your effort to work out the great and intricate problem which God has laid at the doors of the South, you shall have at all times the patient, sympathetic help of my race; only let this be constantly in mind, that, while from representations in these buildings of the product of field, of forest, of mine, of factory, letters, and art, much good will come, yet far above and beyond material benefits will be that higher good, that, let us pray God, will come, in a blotting out of sectional differences and racial animosities and suspicions, in a determination to administer absolute justice, in a willing obedience among all classes to the mandates of law. This, th[en], coupled with our material prosperity, will bring into our beloved South a new heaven and a new earth.

Source: Booker T. Washington (1856-1915). "The Atlanta Exposition Address." *Up From Slavery: An Autobiography*. New York: Doubleday, Page & Co., 1901, 218-225.

290. *The Dogwood Tree* (1908)

SCENE IN SABINE COUNTY, TEXAS, JUNE 15, 1908.

The Dogwood Tree.

This is only the branch of the Dogwood tree;
 An emblem of WHITE SUPREMACY.
A lesson once taught in the Pioneer's school,
 That this is a land of WHITE MAN'S RULE.
The Red Man once in an early day,
 Was told by the Whites to mend his way.
The negro, now, by eternal grace,
 Must learn to stay in the negro's place.
In the Sunny South, the Land of the Free,
 Let the WHITE SUPREME forever be.
Let this a warning to all negroes be,
 Or they'll suffer the fate of the DOGWOOD TREE.

Copyrighted — Pub. by Harkrider Drug Co., Center, Tex.

Source: *The Dogwood Tree.* US Postcard: Scene in Sabine County, Texas, June 15, 1908.

Gilded Age: Problems at Home and Abroad

In 1967 historian Robert Wiebe coined the phrase "the search for order" as a descriptor for the period in United States history from 1877 to 1921. This time is commonly known by two names, each one representing a distinct yet interconnected era. The first, known as the "Gilded Age," refers to the period from the end of Reconstruction in 1877 to the beginning of Theodore Roosevelt's presidency in 1901. The second beginning in 1901, is commonly referred to as the "Progressive era," and concludes in 1921 with the return of the Republicans, under Warren G. Harding, to the White House. Despite the chronological division in 1901, Wiebe's thesis serves as a unifying principle in this crucial period of the nation's history. During this time America underwent fundamental transformations both at home and abroad. Leading the rather long list of these transformations is the United State's transition from a hemispheric to a world power, as well as its rise to the world's foremost industrial and economic nation – a process completed when the European powers exhausted themselves in the Great War.

The forces of change – unleashed in America during this time – left the nation grasping for order amidst the ever quickening pace of modernity. In essence, the upheavals faced by Americans in the Gilded Age resulted in the reforms of the Progressive era and, to a large extent, the birth of the modern United States. The search for order would not be an easy quest as Americans faced both external and internal pressures that contested the desire to achieve an order that was based upon traditional American values of democracy, freedom, progress and nationalism. This antagonism during the Gilded Age led to a fundamental question of how to promote change and progress while still maintaining a firm grasp on the core beliefs and ideals upon which the nation was founded (doc. 291)? At the height of the Progressive era, the transition from Jeffersonian idealism and agrarianism culminated in a Wilsonian vision for a new world order that changed this fundamental question to: How can one promote change and progress throughout the world while simultaneously maintaining a firm grasp on traditional beliefs and ideals at home? By 1921 change had come with a price and also with responsibilities not envisioned by the people of the United States and their government in 1877.

With a victory over Spain in 1898, America faced the deep political and moral dilemma of whether or not a democracy can or should possess an empire. A nation that at one time was merely concerned with remaining a single country and expanding across a continent, now found itself responsible for the lives of people outside the continental boundaries of the United States. That same nation, which at one time viewed sea power as simply a way to defend the coastline, now sought to develop a two-ocean navy and the means to quickly combine those fleets in times of war. The birth of a global empire in the Gilded Age fostered the building of the Panama Canal in the Progressive era to accomplish, in part, just such a task.

At home a number of factors threatened to alter the course of everyday life. In 1893 Frederick Jackson Turner announced the end of the frontier as the era of continental expansion drew to a close (doc. 185). The "frontier myth" was central to the American ethos both before and during the Gilded Age. Expanding that frontier in a new direction was part of the legacy left for the Progressive era and beyond (docs. 187, 317).

During the late nineteenth century the very foundation of national identity began to shift (doc. 312). Large scale immigration after the Civil War slowly began to tip the balance away from the predominantly homogeneous Anglo-Saxon nation of the mid-nineteenth century to a more heterogeneous one by the second decade of the twentieth century. Beginning in the 1880s Congress engaged in an ongoing debate over immigration restriction (the primary target of which were non-European ethnic groups; docs. 311-313, 315-316), a battle which still continues to this day.

From 1877-1901 Jeffersonian agrarianism squared off against an increasingly aggressive capitalism (docs. 300, 304-305, 307-309) as rural America grudgingly gave way to an urban industrial nation. The culmination of this "contest" was the election of 1896, a race which (in combination with the election of 1912) gave rise to modern perceptions of what it means to be a Democrat and what it means to be a Republican. The president elect, William McKinley, symbolized the ascendancy of big business as the dominant force in American life. The losing candidate, William Jennings Bryan, reflected an age relegated to the past. In effect, populist idealism mirrored what many had come to view as the quaintness of the Jeffersonian vision of a nation dominated by agrarian interests and yeoman farmers. Ironically, American populism survived because many of the ideals of the Populist Party would bear fruit. These ideals included the reforms of the Progressive era and the manifestation of Franklin Roosevelt's New Deal of the 1930s.

The rapid growth of American cities during the Gilded Age, stimulated to a great degree by immigration and industrialization, resulted in challenges for both the public and private sectors. American cities of the late nineteenth century struggled with the need for safe and affordable housing, the assimilation of immigrants, proper sanitation and hygiene, including the need for clean water, increasing urban sprawl, and rising rates of crime (docs. 294-297). Compounding these many problems was the fact that most American cities of the time were administered by ineffectual and often corrupt governments.

Finally there was industrialization itself, which threatened to rock the very foundations of the Republic. The last three decades of the nineteenth century witnessed some of the most violent clashes between labor and management in the nation's history. Events such as the Great Railroad Strike, the Haymarket Strike, the Homestead Strike (Pennsylvania), and the Pullman Strike (Chicago) represented attempts on the part of workers to claim a share of the prosperity which they had helped to create (doc. 301). The conflict was also an ideological one for many workers who saw in the political philosophies of socialism and anarchism (docs. 302-304, 306-307, 309) a means of achieving goals not possible to attain within the existing framework of democratic capitalism. In its battle against these "foreign" ideologies, management sought to enlist local, state and federal governments in an attempt to stop what it promoted as a dangerous threat to the American way of life.

This chapter includes texts which represent just some of the forces of change which were set free during the Gilded Age. The emphasis is placed on social unrest in its many manifestations, immigration, urbanization, competing political ideologies, and overseas expansion, with the connecting theme being some of the problems faced by the United States both at home and abroad.

Henry Grady's "The New South" (doc. 293) is a blueprint for the South as it grappled not only with the question of race, but also with the need for the South to develop its own domestic economy and infrastructure. Jacob Riis, in his classic *How the Other Half Lives* (doc. 297), brings to light the struggles and challenges faced by an immigrant community which is both welcomed and loathed by the "native" population. The excerpt from Henry George's *Progress and Poverty* (doc. 298) emphasizes the cost associated with the idea of continued progress. This theme is reinforced in the piece by Andrew Carnegie entitled *Wealth* (doc. 308). For Carnegie, an individual accorded with wealth is merely a caretaker of that prosperity for the overall good of society. The viewpoint of labor is detailed in *The Constitution of the Knights of Labor* (doc. 302) as well as the "Pittsburgh Manifesto" ("To the Workingmen of America," doc. 303) and John Most's *The Beast of Property* (doc. 304). The first document provides specific goals for organized labor, while the last two documents provide an alternative vision to the existing capitalist system. The question of empire and imperialism is addressed by Carl Schurz in his piece "Manifest Destiny" (doc. 317, cf. also 318-320). For Schurz, expansion overseas could potentially erode the American character and with it the very moral and political institutions upon which the nation was founded.

The chapter concludes with two documents, Theodore Roosevelt's "Annual Message to Congress, December 6, 1904" and his *New Nationalism* (docs. 321-322). These selections, although not from the Gilded Age, are significant representations of the foreign and domestic policy responses to many of the challenges faced by the United States in its quest for "a search for order."

Charles T. Johnson

291. William M. Evarts
"Oration" (1876)

[...] Now, after a century of growth, of trial, of experience, of observation, and of demonstration, we are met, on the spot and on the date of the great Declaration, to compare our age with that of our fathers, our structure with their foundation, our intervening history and present condition with their faith and prophecy. That "respect to the opinion of mankind," in attention to which our statesmen framed the Declaration of Independence, we, too, acknowledge as a sentiment most fit to influence us in our commemorative gratulations to-day. [...]

Who can recount in an hour what has been done in a century on so wide a field and in all its multitudinous aspects? Yet I may not avoid insisting upon some decisive lineaments of the material, social, and political development of our country which the record of the hundred years displays, and thus present to "the opinion of mankind," for its generous judgment, our nation as it is to-day, – our land, our people, and our laws.

And, first, we notice the wide territory to which we have steadily pushed on our limits. Lines of climate mark our boundaries north and south, and two oceans east and west. The space between, speaking by and large, covers the whole temperate zone of the continent, and in area measures near tenfold the possessions of the thirteen colonies; the natural features, the climate, the productions, the influences of the outward world, are all implied in the immensity of this domain, for they embrace all that the goodness and the power of God have planned for so large a share of the habitable globe. The steps of the successive acquisitions, the impulses which assisted, and the motives which retarded the expansion of our territory; the play of the competing elements in our civilization and their incessant struggle each to outrun the other; the irrepressible conflict thus nursed in the bosom of the State; the lesson in humility and patience, "in charity for all and malice toward none," which the study of the manifest designs of Providence so plainly teach us, – these may well detain us for a moment's illustration.

And this calls attention to that ingredient in the population of this country which came, not from the culminated pride of Europe, but from the abject despondency of Africa. A race discriminated from all the converging streams of immigration which I have named by ineffaceable distinctions of nature; which was brought hither by a forced migration and into slavery, while all others came by choice and for greater liberty; a race unrepresented in the Congress which issued the Declaration of Independence, but now, in the persons of four million of our countrymen raised, by the power of the great truths then declared, as it were from the dead, and rejoicing in one country and the same constituted liberties with ourselves. [...] The immense social and political forces which the existence of slavery in this country, and the invincible repugnance to it of the vital principles of our State, together, generated, have had their play upon the passions and the interests of this people, have formed the basis of parties, divided sects, agitated and invigorated the popular mind, inspired the eloquence, inflamed the zeal, informed the understandings, and fired the hearts of three generations. At last the dread debate escaped all bounds of reason, and the nation in arms solved, by the appeal of war, what was too hard for civil wisdom. With our territory unmutilated, our Constitution uncorrupted, a united people, in the last years of the century, crowns with new glory the immortal truths of the Declaration of Independence by the emancipation of a race.

I find, then, in the method and the results of the century's progress of the nation in this amplification of its domain, sure promise of the duration of the body politic, whose growth to these vast proportions has, as yet, but laid out the ground-plan of the structure. For I find the vital forces of the free society and the people's government, here founded, have by their own vigor made this a natural growth. Strength and symmetry have knit together the great frame as its bulk increased, and the spirit of the nation animates the whole:

– "totamque, infusa per artus,
Mens agitat molem, et magno se corpore miscet."[1]

We turn now from the survey of this vast territory, which the closing century has consolidated and confirmed as the ample home for a nation, to exhibit the greatness in numbers, the spirit, the character, the port and mien of the people that dwell in this secure habitation. That in these years our population has steadily advanced, till it counts forty millions, instead of three millions, bears witness, not to be disparaged[2] or gainsaid,[3] to the general congruity of our social and civil institutions with the happiness and prosperity of man. But if we consider further the variety and magnitude of foreign elements to which we have been hospitable, and their ready fusion with the earlier stocks, we have new evidence of strength and vivid force in our population, which we may not refuse to admire. The disposition and capacity thus shown give warrant of a powerful society. [...]

[...] The "breed and disposition" of a people, in regard of courage, public spirit, and patriotism, are, however, the test of the working of their institutions, which the world most values, and upon which the public safety most depends. [... Through] the period whose years we count to-day, the greatest lesson of all is the preponderance of public over private, of social over selfish, tendencies and purposes in the whole body of the people, and the persistent fidelity to the genius and spirit of popular institutions, of the educated classes, the liberal professions, and the great men of the country. These qualities transfuse and blend the hues and virtues of the manifold rays of advanced civilization into a sunlight of public spirit and fervid patriotism, which warms and irradiates the life of the nation. Excess of publicity as the animating spirit and stimulus of society more probably than its lack will excite our solicitudes in the future. Even the public discontents take on this color, and the mind and heart of the whole people ache with anxieties and throb with griefs which have no meaner scope than the honor and the safety of the nation. [...]

He who doubts needs but to look around to find all things full of the original spirit and testifying to its wisdom and strength. We have taken no steps backward, nor have we needed to seek other paths in our progress than those in which our feet were planted at the beginning. [...]

[...] We cannot then hesitate to declare that the original principles of equal society and popular government still inspire the laws, live in the habits of the people, and animate their purposes and their hopes. These principles have not lost their spring or elasticity. They have sufficed for all the methods of government in the past; we feel no fear for their adequacy in the future. [...]

[...] The spirit of the nation is at the highest, – its triumph over the inborn, inbred perils of the Constitution has chased away all fears, justified all hopes, and with universal

---

[1] *Aeneid*, Book VI, l. 726f.: " – and mind, permeating the members, moves the whole mass and mingles with its mighty frame."
[2] To dishonour, discredit.
[3] To contradict, deny.

joy we greet this day. We have not proved unworthy of a great ancestry; we have had the virtue to uphold what they so wisely, so firmly, established. With these proud possessions of the past, with powers matured, with principles settled, with habits formed, the nation passes as it were from preparatory growth to responsible development of character and the steady performance of duty. What labors await it, what trials shall attend it, what triumphs for human nature, what glory for itself, are prepared for this people in the coming century, we may not assume to foretell. "One generation passeth away, and another generation cometh; but the earth abideth forever,"[4] and we reverently hope that these our constituted liberties shall be maintained to the unending line of our posterity, and so long as the earth itself shall endure.

In the great procession of nations, in the great march of humanity, we hold our place. Peace is our duty, peace is our policy. In its arts, its labors, and its victories, then, we find scope for all our energies, rewards for all our ambitions, renown enough for all our love of fame. In the august presence of so many nations, which, by their representatives, have done us the honor to be witnesses of our commemorative joy and gratulation, and in sight of the collective evidences of the greatness of their own civilization with which they grace our celebration, we may well confess how much we fall short, how much we have to make up, in the emulative competitions of the times. Yet, even in this presence, and with a just deference to the age, the power, the greatness of the other nations of the earth, we do not fear to appeal to the opinion of mankind whether, as we point to our land, our people, and our laws, the contemplation should not inspire us with a lover's enthusiasm for our country.

Source: William M. Evarts (1818-1901). "Oration" (Centennial Ceremonies, 4 July 1876). United States Centennial Commission, *International Exhibition*, 1876. 11 vols.. Vol. 2: *Reports of the President, Secretary, and Executive Committee*. Washington, D.C., 1880, 67-73, 75-76.

---

[4] Eccles. 1.4.

292. Frank Leslie's Illustrated Historical Register of the Centennial Exposition (1876)

Source: *Frank Leslie's Illustrated Historical Register of the Centennial Exposition 1876* (Cover). Courtesy Library of Congress.

293. Henry W. Grady
"The New South" (1886)

"There was a South of slavery and secession – that South is dead. There is a South of union and freedom – that South, thank God, is living, breathing, growing every hour." These words, delivered from the immortal lips of Benjamin H. Hill,[5] at Tammany Hall,[6] in 1866, true then and truer now, I shall make my text to-night.

Mr. President and Gentlemen: Let me express to you my appreciation of the kindness by which I am permitted to address you. [...]

Pardon me one word, Mr. President, spoken for the sole purpose of getting into the volumes that go out annually freighted with the rich eloquence of your speakers – the fact that the Cavalier as well as the Puritan, was on the continent in its early days, and that he was "up and able to be about." [...]

[...] But both Puritan and Cavalier were lost in the storm of the first Revolution, and the American citizen, supplanting both and stronger than either, took possession of the republic bought by their common blood and fashioned to wisdom, and charged himself with teaching men government and establishing the voice of the people as the voice of God.

My friends, Dr. Talmage[7] has told you that the typical American has yet to come. Let me tell you that he has already come. Great types, like valuable plants, are slow to flower and fruit. But from the union of these colonists, Puritans and Cavaliers, from the straightening of their purposes and the crossing of their blood, slow perfecting through a century, came he who stands as the first typical American, the first who comprehended within himself all the strength and gentleness, all the majesty and grace of this republic – Abraham Lincoln.[8] He was the sum of Puritan and Cavalier, for in his ardent nature were fused the virtues of both, and in the depths of his great soul the faults of both were lost. He was greater than Puritan, greater than Cavalier, in that he was American, and that in his honest form were first gathered the vast and thrilling forces of his ideal government – charging it with such tremendous meaning and elevating it above human suffering that martyrdom, though infamously aimed, came as a fitting crown to a life consecrated from the cradle to human liberty. Let us, each cherishing the traditions and honoring his fathers, build with reverent hands to the type of this simple but sublime life, in which all types are honored, and in our common glory as Americans there will be plenty and to spare for your forefathers and for mine.

Dr. Talmage has drawn for you, with a master's hand, the picture of your returning armies. He has told you how, in the pomp and circumstance of war, they came back to you, marching with proud and victorious tread, reading their glory in a nation's eyes! Will you bear with me while I tell you of another army that sought its home at the close of the late war – an army that marched home in defeat and not in victory – in pathos and not in splendor, but in glory that equaled yours, and to hearts as loving as ever welcomed heroes home!

---

[5] Politician from the state of Georgia.
[6] The Tammany Society was founded in New York City in 1789 by William Mooney, a Revolutionary War veteran. It drew its name from a respected Delaware chief, Tammend, who had reportedly befriended William Penn. The Society, sometimes called the Columbian Order, was originally a patriotic and charitable organization.
[7] Thomas Talmage de Witt (1832-1902), editor of the New York religious weekly *The Christian at Work*.
[8] Abraham Lincoln (1809-1865), 16th president of the US.

Let me picture to you the footsore Confederate soldier [...]. Think of him as ragged, half-starved, heavy-hearted, enfeebled by want and wounds, having fought to exhaustion, he surrenders his gun, wrings the hands of his comrades in silence, and lifting his tear-stained and pallid face for the last time to the graves that dot old Virginia hills, pulls his gray cap over his brow and begins the slow and painful journey.

What does he find [...] when [...] he reaches the home he left so prosperous and beautiful? He finds his house in ruins, his farm devastated, his slaves free, his stock killed, his barns empty, his trade destroyed, his money worthless, his social system, feudal in its magnificence, swept away; his people without law or legal status; his comrades slain, and the burdens of others heavy on his shoulders. Crushed by defeat, his very traditions are gone. Without money, credit, employment, material, or training; and beside all this, confronted with the gravest problem that ever met human intelligence – the establishment of a status for the vast body of his liberated slaves.

What does he do – this hero in gray with a heart of gold? Does he sit down in sullenness and despair? Not for a day. Surely God, who had stripped him of his prosperity, inspired him in his adversity. As ruin was never before so overwhelming, never was restoration swifter. [...]

But what is the sum of our work? We have found out that in the summing up the free negro counts more than he did as a slave. We have planted the schoolhouse on the hilltop and made it free to white and black. We have sowed towns and cities in the place of theories, and put business above politics. [...]

[...] Above all, we know that we have achieved in these "piping times of peace" a fuller independence for the South than that which our fathers sought to win in the forum by their eloquence or compel in the field by their swords.

It is a rare privilege, sir, to have had part, however humble, in this work. Never was nobler duty confided to human hands than the uplifting and upbuilding of the prostrate and bleeding South – misguided, perhaps, but beautiful in her suffering, and honest, brave, and generous always. In the record of her social, industrial, and political illustration we await with confidence the verdict of the world.

But what of the negro? Have we solved the problem he presents or progressed in honor and equity toward solution? Let the record speak to the point. No section shows a more prosperous laboring population than the negroes of the South, none in fuller sympathy with the employing and land-owning class. He shares our school fund, has the fullest protection of our laws and the friendship of our people. Self-interest, as well as honor, demand that he should have this. Our future, our very existence depend upon our working out this problem in full and exact justice. We understand that when Lincoln signed the emancipation proclamation, your victory was assured, for he then committed you to the cause of human liberty, against which the arms of man cannot prevail – while those of our statesmen who trusted to make slavery the cornerstone of the Confederacy doomed us to defeat as far as they could, committing us to a cause that reason could not defend or the sword maintain in sight of advancing civilization.

[...] We fought hard enough to know that we were whipped, and in perfect frankness accept as final the arbitrament of the sword to which we had appealed. The South found her jewel in the toad's head of defeat. The shackles that had held her in narrow limitations fell forever when the shackles of the negro slave were broken. Under the old regime the negroes were slaves to the South; the South was a slave to the system. [...]

The old South rested everything on slavery and agriculture, unconscious that these could neither give nor maintain healthy growth. The new South presents a perfect democracy, the oligarchs leading in the popular movement – a social system compact and closely knitted, less splendid on the surface, but stronger at the core – a hundred farms for every plantation, fifty homes for every palace – and a diversified industry that meets the complex needs of this complex age.

The new South is enamored of her new work. Her soul is stirred with the breath of a new life. The light of a grander day is falling fair on her face. She is thrilling with the consciousness of growing power and prosperity. As she stands upright, full-statured and equal among the people of the earth, breathing the keen air and looking out upon the expanded horizon, she understands that her emancipation came because through the inscrutable wisdom of God her honest purpose was crossed and her brave armies were beaten.

This is said in no spirit of time-serving or apology. The South has nothing for which to apologize. She believes that the late struggle between the States was war and not rebellion; revolution and not conspiracy, and that her convictions were as honest as yours. I should be unjust to the dauntless spirit of the South and to my own convictions if I did not make this plain in this presence. The South has nothing to take back.

[...] I am glad that the omniscient God held the balance of battle in His Almighty hand and that human slavery was swept forever from American soil – that the American Union was saved from the wreck of war.

This message, Mr. President, comes to you from consecrated ground. Every foot of soil about the city in which I live is sacred as a battle-ground of the republic. Every hill that invests it is hallowed to you by the blood of your brothers who died for your victory, and doubly hallowed to us by the blood of those who died hopeless, but undaunted, in defeat – sacred soil to all of us – rich with memories that make us purer and stronger and better – silent but staunch witnesses in its red desolation of the matchless valor of American hearts and the deathless glory of American arms – speaking an eloquent witness in its white peace and prosperity to the indissoluble union of American States and the imperishable brotherhood of the American people.

Now, what answer has New England to this message? Will she permit the prejudice of war to remain in the hearts of the conquerors, when it has died in the hearts of the conquered? Will she transmit this prejudice to the next generation, that in their hearts which never felt the generous ardor of conflict it may perpetuate itself? Will she withhold, save in strained courtesy, the hand which straight from his soldier's heart Grant offered to Lee at Appomattox?[9] Will she make the vision of a restored and happy people, which gathered above the couch of your dying captain, filling his heart with grace, touching his lips with praise, and glorifying his path to the grave – will she make this vision on which the last sigh of his expiring soul breathed a benediction, a cheat and a delusion?

If she does, the South, never abject in asking for comradeship, must accept with dignity its refusal; but if she does not refuse to accept in frankness and sincerity this message of good will and friendship, then will the prophecy of Webster,[10] delivered in this very society forty years ago amid tremendous applause, become true, be verified in its fullest sense, when he said: "Standing hand to hand and clasping hands, we should remain

---

[9] Confederate General Robert E. Lee (1807-1870) surrendered to Union General Ulysses S. Grant (1822-1885) at Appomattox courthouse in April 9, 1865, thus ending the Civil War.
[10] Daniel Webster (1782-1852), American legislator, warned against Southern secession.

united as we have been for sixty years, citizens of the same country, members of the same government, united, all united now and united forever." There have been difficulties, contentions, and controversies, but I tell you that in my judgment,

> "Those opened eyes,
> Which like the meteors of a troubled heaven,
> All of one nature, of one substance bred,
> Did lately meet in th' intestine shock,
> Shall now, in mutual well beseeming ranks,
> March all one way."

Source: Henry W. Grady (1850-1889). "The New South [December 21, 1886]." *The New South and Other Addresses*. Ed. Edna Henry Lee Turpin. New York: Charles E. Merrill, 1904, 23, 25, 27-30, 32-34, 37-42.

294. Charles L. Brace
The Dangerous Classes of New York (1872/1880)

CHAPTER II.
THE PROLETAIRES OF NEW YORK.

New York is a much younger city than its European rivals; and with perhaps one-third the population of London, yet it presents varieties of life among the "masses" quite as picturesque, and elements of population even more dangerous. The throng of different nationalities in the American city gives a peculiarly variegated air to the life beneath the surface, and the enormous over-crowding in portions of the poor quarters intensifies the evils, peculiar to large towns, to a degree seen only in a few districts in such cities as London and Liverpool.

The *mass* of poverty and wretchedness is, of course, far greater in the English capital. There are classes with inherited pauperism and crime more deeply stamped in them, in London or Glasgow, than we ever behold in New York; but certain small districts can be found in our metropolis with the unhappy fame of containing more human beings packed to the square yard, and stained with more acts of blood and riot, within a given period, than is true of any other equal space of earth in the civilized world.

There are houses, well known to sanitary boards and the police, where Fever has taken a perennial lease, and will obey no legal summons to quit; where Cholera – if a single germ-seed of it float anywhere in American atmosphere – at once ripens a black harvest; where Murder has stained every floor of its gloomy stories, and Vice skulks[11] or riots from one year's end to the other. Such houses are never reformed. The only hope for them is in the march of street improvements, which will utterly sweep them away.

It is often urged that the breaking-up of these "dens"[12] and "fever-nests" only scatters the pestilence and moral disease, but does not put an end to them.

The objection is more apparent than real. The abolishing of one of these centres of crime and poverty is somewhat like withdrawing the virus from one diseased limb and diffusing it through an otherwise healthy body. It seems to lose its intensity. The diffusion weakens. Above all, it is less likely to become hereditary.

---

[11] Company of people in hiding, evading work.
[12] Secret lurking-place of thieves.

One of the remarkable and hopeful things about New York, to a close observer of its "dangerous classes," is, as I shall show in a future chapter, that they do not tend to become fixed and inherited, as in European cities.

But, though the crime and pauperism of New York are not so deeply stamped in the blood of the population, they are even more dangerous. The intensity of the American temperament is felt in every fibre of these children of poverty and vice. Their crimes have the unrestrained and sanguinary character of a race accustomed to overcome all obstacles. They rifle a bank, where English thieves pick a pocket; they murder, where European *prolétaires* cudgel or fight with fists; in a riot, they begin what seems about to be the sacking of a city, where English rioters would merely batter policemen, or smash lamps. The "dangerous classes" of New York are mainly American-born, but the children of Irish and German immigrants. They are as ignorant as London flash-men[13] or costermongers.[14] They are far more brutal than the peasantry from whom they descend, and they are much banded together, in associations, such as "Dead Rabbit,"[15] "Plug-ugly,"[16] and various target companies. They are our *enfants perdus*, grown up to young manhood. The murder of an unoffending old man [...] is nothing to them. They are ready for any offense or crime, however degraded or bloody. New York has never experienced the full effect of the nurture of these youthful ruffians as she will one day. They showed their hand only slightly in the riots during the war. At present, they are like the athletes and gladiators of the Roman demagogues. They are the "roughs" who sustain the ward politicians, and frighten honest voters. [...]

We shall speak more particularly of the causes of crime in future chapters, but we may say in brief, that the young ruffians of New York are the products of accident, ignorance, and vice. Among a million people, such as compose the population of this city and its suburbs, there will always be a great number of misfortunes; fathers die, and leave their children unprovided for; parents drink, and abuse their little ones, and they float away on the currents of the street; step-mothers or step-fathers drive out, by neglect and ill-treatment, their sons from home. Thousands are the children of poor foreigners, who have permitted them to grow up without school, education, or religion. All the neglect and bad education and evil example of a poor class tend to form others, who, as they mature, swell the ranks of ruffians and criminals. So, at length, a great multitude of ignorant, untrained, passionate, irreligious boys and young men are formed, who become the "dangerous class" of our city. [...]

THE DANGERS.

It has been common, since the recent terrible Communistic outbreak in Paris, to assume that France alone is exposed to such horrors; but, in the judgment of one who has been familiar with our "dangerous classes" for twenty years, there are just the same explosive social elements beneath the surface of New York as of Paris.

There are thousands on thousands in New York who have no assignable home, and "flit" from attic to attic, and cellar to cellar; there are other thousands more or less connected with criminal enterprises; and still other tens of thousands, poor, hard-pressed,

---

[13] Companion of thieves.
[14] A man who sells fruit, vegetables, etc. in the street from a barrow.
[15] Applied contemptuously to a person, thief.
[16] A city ruffian or rowdy. More widely, a man of violence.

and depending for daily bread on the day's earnings, swarming in tenement-houses, who behold the gilded rewards of toil all about them, but are never permitted to touch them.

All these great masses of destitute, miserable, and criminal persons believe that for ages the rich have had all the good things of life, while to them have been left the evil things. Capital to them is the tyrant.

Let but Law lift its hand from them for a season, or let the civilizing influences of American life fail to reach them, and, if the opportunity offered, we should see an explosion from this class which might leave this city in ashes and blood.

To those incredulous of this, we would recall the scenes in our streets during the riots in 1863, when, for a short period, the guardians of good order – the local militia – had been withdrawn for national purposes, and when the ignorant masses were excited by dread of the draft.

[...] No one doubted then, or during the Orange riot of 1871,[17] the existence of "dangerous classes" in New York. And yet the separate members of these riotous and ruffianly masses are simply neglected and street-wandering children who have come to early manhood.

The true preventive of social catastrophes like these, are just such Christian reformatory and educational movements as we are about to describe.

Of the number of the distinctively homeless and vagrant youth in New York, it is difficult to speak with precision. We should be inclined to estimate it, after long observation, as fluctuating each year between 20,000 and 30,000.[18] But to these, as they mature, must be added, in the composition of the dangerous classes, all those who are professionally criminal, and who have homes and lodging-places. And again to these, portions of that vast and ignorant[19] multitude, who, in prosperous times, just keep their heads above water, who are pressed down by poverty or misfortune, and who look with envy and greed at the signs of wealth and luxury all around them, while they themselves have nothing but hardship, penury, and unceasing drudgery.

Source: Charles Loring Brace (1826-1890). *The Dangerous Classes of New York and Twenty Years' Work among Them*. New York: Wynkoop & Hallenbeck, ³1880, 25-31

295. Edward Crapsey
"Prostitution" (1872)

Take the lowest type first, and find it in the middle of any night by merely sauntering through Broadway from Grand to Fourteenth street, or again from Twenty-third to Thirtieth street, or in some of the side streets. The type is the night-walker, and gradations of the class are almost as numerous as its representatives. To meet the worst, Greene, Wooster, Houston, Bleecker, or Amity streets must be traversed. There was a time, and it is not long past, when only the Fourth Ward could show the prowling prostitute in her most abject degradation, but it is not necessary now to get lost in the tortuous

---

[17] Orange riot in New York, July 12, 1871, following a Catholic attack on the Protestant march.
[18] Original footnote: "The homeless children who come each year under the charitable efforts afterwards to be described amount to some 12.000."
[19] Original footnote: "It should be remembered that there are in this city over 60.000 persons above ten years of age who cannot write their names."

mazes of the old town, to find the most repulsive phases of female frailty. The Eighth Ward has taken the place of the Fourth, and the stranger need only turn three hundred feet out of Broadway anywhere between Grand and Amity streets, to encounter the most startling evidence of the possibility of total depravity.

To see the worst, stand for the hour before midnight on the corner of Houston and Greene streets. In that time a hundred women apparently will pass, but the close observer will notice that each woman passes the spot on an average of about twice, so that in fact there are not more than fifty of them. This frequency of appearance leads to the supposition that they do not go far, which is the fact. Each set of prostitutes has its metes and bounds laid down by an unwritten code of its own enactment, which is rarely violated. The set now under consideration travels Houston, Bleecker, Wooster, and Greene streets, with occasional forays upon Broadway, which is the common property of all. But these poor fallen creatures rarely go there to put themselves in fruitless competition with more attractive sin. They are poorly dressed, have nothing of beauty in form or face, and are always uncouth or brazenly vulgar in manner. They are miserably poor, herding in garrets or cellars, and are driven by their necessities to accost every stranger they meet with what the silly law of New York calls "Soliciting for the purpose of prostitution." When a woman offers to sell her body to a man she never saw before, for fifty cents, she has fallen low indeed, and this offer will be made at least a dozen times within the hour to any observer at the spot mentioned, whose appearance does not absolutely forbid advances.

Next stand for the same period at Amity and Greene streets. As many women will pass, and in about the same ratio as to reappearances. They are a shade better in appearance as to dress, and some of them have the faint remnants of former personal beauty. They are vulgar yet, but are a vast improvement on the set first seen. All of them will so look at you as to invite advances, but only about one in five will speak first. When they do, it is merely to say "Good evening" or "How are you, my dear," instead of a direct invitation to go home with them, which is the first greeting of the other set. These Amity street women are, as a rule, better housed and fed than the first set, as they live in the houses bordering their tramping-ground, which are all well built and finished. Some of the women have attained to, or more correctly speaking, have not fallen below the prosperity of occupying a room in one of these houses alone, and none of them have more than one female room-mate. Instead of the rough pine furniture of Houston street, the rooms here are given an almost decent appearance by imitation oak, or else are filled up with those strainings for respectable adornments known as "cottage furniture." Another decided proof of better condition is the absence of the cooking stove, for these girls either board with the "Madam" or obtain their food at restaurants. This class, which is thus better housed, better dressed, better behaved, has the middle rank, and contains the majority of all women plying their vocation in the public streets. [...]

In all the great cities of the United States, so far as my personal observation extends – and I have been in all of them – the walking of the streets after nightfall by prostitutes has become an alarming evil; but New York is entitled, I am afraid, to preëminence in this respect. Not only is the city first in the number of its street-walkers, but nowhere else has the class become so degraded. I have hinted something of the profanity and obscenity of the women who can be found after midnight in any of the side streets, but it is not possible to describe in detail the scenes which will be forced upon the observer any night in Houston, Bleecker, Amity, and Fourth streets, as well as in the lower Bowery, Chatham street, and some other eastside thoroughfares. Singly, in couples, or groups, these girls, many of whom are mere children and very few of whom have scarcely passed maturity, plunge along the sidewalks, accosting every man they meet, or, stopping at the street corners, annoy all passers until they are driven away by the police. Many of them are under the influence of liquor, and not a night passes but some of these degraded creatures are carried into the station-houses helplessly or furiously drunk. Until within the past two years I never saw any of these women drinking in public bar-rooms, but now it has become so common that it has ceased to be remarked; it is true there are few of the saloons which will serve them, but there is always one on each route of the tramps which will sell to any one, and here these poor painted wrecks of womanhood can be seen standing at the bar, drinking vile liquors until they have won the beatitude of stupefaction, or until they reel out into the streets indecently drunk. If the unconsciousness of inebriety is ever a blessing, it is such in the case of these lost women, as it permits them for the time to forget what they are and must be always. Often suffering for the necessaries of life, burdened almost without exception with "lovers" who despoil them of the pittance they receive for moral and physical death, harassed by the police, shunned by their more prosperous sisters in sin, corroded morally and physically with the leprosy of their vice, no class needs so much of pity, none has less of it, and none is so little aware that it needs commiseration. Calloused[20] by crime which is unnatural and bestializing, the street-walkers have forgotten that they were ever undefiled and lost all desire to be other than they are. Numbering about two thousand, constantly infesting the public thoroughfares, inoculated and inoculating with loathsome diseases, they are the great danger and shame of civilization found in all cities, but here more numerous, more dangerous and more shameful than anywhere else on the continent.

It has not been from any wish to pander to a morbid desire for the repulsive that I have set this type of prostitution in the foreground. Palpable facts cannot be ignored, and a vice that is thus obtruded upon every passer through the public streets cannot be too soon or too fully described; but having presented the facts in such plain terms that they cannot be misunderstood, I gladly take leave of this lowest type of metropolitan prostitution. It is hardly more agreeable to speak of the next grade, which is found in the lowest of what are known as "parlor houses." The chief difference between the inmates and the street-walkers is that the former do not cruise the streets to entice strangers to their dens. If this is a comparative virtue it is the only one these women can boast, as they are fully as bestial in every other respect as their sisters of the pave. The houses in which they live and ply their infamous vocation are always unmistakable even to the novice. In Greene and Wooster streets several blocks are almost wholly taken up by such houses, but others but little less open and degraded can be found in many other quarters of the city. In many of these houses there is a public bar; in all of them the orgies are indecent to such a degree that they cannot be described. Next above these dens are houses a shade more sufferable, which attempt to hide their infamy behind cigar stores or some other kind of shop, and are filled with women who do not shock at the first glance. Above these again are houses which really have parlors, and in which the women make a pretence to decency in their demeanor while in public. After these come the grand saloons where the evil is painted in the most alluring colors. The houses are of the largest and stateliest, the furniture the most elegant, the inmates beautiful, accomplished, captivating in dress and manner, who, with woman's only priceless jewel, would adorn any circle. It

---

[20] Made unfeeling, emotionally hardened.

is difficult to persuade one who has no personal knowledge of the matter, that, taken into the parlors of one of these houses and meeting the inmates without a previous intimation of the character of the place, he would believe himself in a pure, refined home. Yet such is the fact. Such houses as these can be found in every desirable neighborhood, and no man can be sure that he has not one of the sepulchres next door. [...]

[...] Woman is naturally chaste, and if those who have fallen can be induced to tell the cause, it will be found that at least six in every ten are forced by sheer necessity to become confirmed prostitutes. I do not mean to say that they will plead this as the cause of the first lapse from virtue, as nine cases out of ten of them will charge that to their betrayal by men whom they loved. But after that first lapse, and after their desertion by these men, they claim they had no choice between their way of life and death from starvation. The story is told by types of every class of prostitutes, from the adroit adventuress who lays her snares in the great hotels, to the poor drunken creature who tramps the streets [...].

[...] As I look upon it in the light of many facts which are of such character that they cannot be hinted at, much less mentioned, the chief danger that threatens the city from the social evil does not come from the street-walkers, nor the inmates of public houses of prostitution. These are women known to be unchaste, who are without home ties and without influence except to a very limited extent. On the contrary, those women who are unsuspected prostitutes occupy and defile the holiest positions of domestic life, and there is no limit to the evil which their crime produces. And this form of the plague is more deplorable because it is one which no law can cure, although it might be mitigated to some extent by statutory remedies. [...]

Source: Edward Crapsey (?). "Prostitution." *The Nether Side of New York; or, The Vice, Crime and Poverty of the Great Metropolis*. New York: Sheldon & Co., 1872, 138-139, 142-145.

296. Josiah Strong
"Perils. – The City" (1885)

The city is the nerve center of our civilization. It is also the storm center. The fact, therefore, that it is growing much more rapidly than the whole population is full of significance. In 1790 one-thirtieth of the population of the United States lived in cities of 8,000 inhabitants and over; [...] in 1840, one-twelfth; [...] and in 1880, 22.5 per cent., or nearly one-fourth.[21] From 1790 to 1880 the whole population increased twelve fold, the urban population eighty-six fold. [...]

The city has become a serious menace to our civilization, because in it, excepting Mormonism, each of the dangers we have discussed is enhanced, and all are focalized. It has a peculiar attraction for the immigrant. Our fifty principal cities contain 39.3 per cent. of our entire German population, and 45.8 per cent. of the Irish. Our ten larger cities contain only nine per cent. of the entire population, but 23 per cent. of the foreign. While a little less than one-third of the population of the United States is foreign by birth or parentage, sixty-two per cent. of the population of Cincinnati are foreign, eighty-three per cent. of Cleveland, sixty-three per cent. of Boston, eighty-eight per cent. of New York, and ninety-one per cent. of Chicago.[22]

---

[21] Original footnote: "Compendium of the Tenth Census, Part 1., pp. xxx and 8."

[22] Original footnote: "The Compendium of the Tenth Census gives the number of persons, foreign-born,

Because our cities are so largely foreign, Romanism[23] finds in them its chief strength.

For the same reason the saloon, together with the intemperance and the liquor power which it represents, is multiplied in the city. East of the Mississippi there was, in 1880, one saloon to every 438 of the population; in Boston, one to every 329; in Cleveland, one to every 192; in Chicago, one to every 179; in New York, one to every 171; in Cincinnati, one to every 124. Of course the demoralizing and pauperizing power of the saloons and their debauching influence in politics increase with their numerical strength.

It is the city where wealth is massed; and here are the tangible evidences of it piled many stories high. Here the sway of Mammon is widest, and his worship the most constant and eager. Here are luxuries gathered – everything that dazzles the eye, or tempts the appetite; here is the most extravagant expenditure. Here, also, is the *congestion* of wealth the severest. Dives[24] and Lazarus[25] are brought face to face; here, in sharp contrast, are the *ennui*[26] of surfeit and the desperation of starvation. The rich are richer, and the poor are poorer, in the city than elsewhere; and, as a rule, the greater the city, the greater are the riches of the rich and the poverty of the poor. Not only does the proportion of the poor increase with the growth of the city, but their condition becomes more wretched. [...] Is it strange that such conditions arouse a blind and bitter hatred of our social system?

Socialism not only centers in the city, but is almost confined to it; and the materials of its growth are multiplied with the growth of the city. Here is heaped the social dynamite; here roughs, gamblers, thieves, robbers, lawless and desperate men of all sorts, congregate; men who are ready on any pretext to raise riots for the purpose of destruction and plunder; here gather foreigners and wage-workers; here skepticism and irreligion abound; here inequality is the greatest and most obvious, and the contrast between opulence and penury the most striking; here is suffering the sorest. As the greatest wickedness in the world is to be found not among the cannibals of some far off coast, but in Christian lands where the light of truth is diffused and rejected, so the utmost depth of wretchedness exists not among savages, who have few wants, but in great cities, where, in the presence of plenty and of every luxury men starve. Let a man become the owner of a home, and he is much less susceptible to socialistic propagandism. But real estate is so high in the city that it is almost impossible for a wage-worker to become a householder. [...] Let us remember that those seventy thousand voters represent a population of two hundred and eighty thousand, or fifty-six thousand families, not one of which has property to the value of two hundred and fifty dollars. [...] Said a New York Supreme Judge, not long since: "There is a large class – I was about to say a majority – of the population of New York and Brooklyn, who just live, and to whom the rearing of two or more children means inevitably a boy for the penitentiary, and a girl for the brothel."[27] Under such conditions smolder the volcanic fires of a deep discontent.

We have seen how the dangerous elements of our civilization are each multiplied and all concentered in the city. Do we find there the conservative forces of society equally numer-

---

in each of the fifty principal cities, but does not give the native-born population of foreign parentage. We are enabled to compute it, however, by knowing that the total number of foreigners and their children of the first generation is, according to the Census, 2.24 times larger than the total number of foreign-born."

[23] Roman Catholicism.
[24] Latin word for 'rich (man)', occurring in Luke 16.
[25] A leper; a beggar.
[26] Feeling of mental weariness and dissatisfaction.
[27] Original footnote: "Henry George's 'Social Problems,' p. 98."

ous and strong? Here are the tainted spots in the body-politic; where is the salt? In 1880 there was in the United States one Evangelical church organization to every 516 of the population. In Boston there is one church to every 1,600 of the population; in Chicago, one to 2,081; in New York, one to 2,468; in St. Louis, one to 2,800. The city, where the forces of evil are massed, and where the need of Christian influence is peculiarly great, is from one-third to one-fifth as well supplied with churches as the nation at large. And church accommodations in the city are growing more inadequate every year. [...]

If moral and religious influences are peculiarly weak at the point where our social explosives are gathered, what of city government? Are its strength and purity so exceptional as to insure the effective control of these dangerous elements? In the light of notorious facts, the question sounds satirical. It is commonly said in Europe, and sometimes acknowledged here, that the government of large cities in the United States is a failure. [...]

As a rule, our largest cities are the worst governed. It is natural, therefore, to infer that, as our cities grow larger and more dangerous, the government will become more corrupt, and control will pass more completely into the hands of those who themselves most need to be controlled. If we would appreciate the significance of these facts and tendencies, we must bear in mind that the disproportionate growth of the city is undoubtedly to continue, and the number of great cities to be largely increased. [...] This strong tendency toward the city is the result chiefly of manufacturers and railway communication, and their influence will, of course, continue. If the growth of the city in the United States has been so rapid during this century, while many millions of acres were being settled, what may be expected when the settlement of the West has been completed? The rapid rise in the value of lands will stimulate yet more the growth of the city; for the man of small means will be unable to command a farm, and the town will become his only alternative. When the public lands are all taken, immigration, though it will be considerably restricted thereby, will continue, and will crowd the cities more and more. [...] Thus is our civilization multiplying and focalizing the elements of anarchy and destruction. [...]

These dangerous elements are now working, and will continue to work, incalculable harm and loss – moral, intellectual, social, pecuniary. But the supreme peril, which will certainly come, eventually, and must probably be faced by multitudes now living, will arise, when, the conditions having been fully prepared, some great industrial or other crisis precipitates an open struggle between the destructive and the conservative elements of society. [...] When such a commercial crisis has closed factories by the ten thousand, and wage-workers have been thrown out of employment by the million; when the public lands, which hitherto at such times have afforded relief, are all exhausted; when our urban population has been multiplied several fold, and our Cincinnatis have become Chicagos, our Chicagos New Yorks, and our New Yorks Londons; when class antipathies are deepened; when socialistic organizations, armed and drilled, are in every city, and the ignorant and vicious power of crowded populations has fully found itself; when the corruption of city governments is grown apace; when crops fail, or some gigantic "corner" doubles the price of bread; with starvation in the home; with idle workmen gathered, sullen and desperate, in the saloons; with unprotected wealth at hand; with the tremendous forces of chemistry within easy reach; then, with *the opportunity, the means, the fit agents, the motive, the temptation to destroy, all brought into evil conjunction*, THEN will come the real test of our institutions, then will appear whether we are capable of self-government.

Source: Josiah Strong (?). "Perils. – The City." *Our Country: Its Possible Future and Its Present Crisis.* New York: Baker and Taylor, 1885, 128-130, 132-138, 142-144.

297. Jacob A. Riis
How the Other Half Lives (1890)

Chapter XIV: The Common Herd

[...] In the dull content of life bred on the tenement-house dead level there is little to redeem it, or to calm apprehension for a society that has nothing better to offer its toilers; while the patient efforts of the lives finally attuned to it to render the situation tolerable, and the very success of these efforts, serve only to bring out in stronger contrast the general gloom of the picture by showing how much farther they might have gone with half a chance. Go into any of the "respectable" tenement neighborhoods – the fact that there are not more than two saloons on the corner, nor over three or four in the block will serve as a fair guide – where live the great body of hard-working Irish and German immigrants and their descendants, who accept naturally the conditions of tenement life, because for them there is nothing else in New York; be with and among its people until you understand their ways, their aims, and the quality of their ambitions, and unless you can content yourself with the scriptural promise that the poor we shall have always with us, or with the menagerie view that, if fed, they have no cause of complaint, you shall come away agreeing with me that, humanly speaking, life there does not seem worth the living. Take at random one of these uptown tenement blocks, not of the worst nor yet of the most prosperous kind, within hail of what the newspapers would call a "fine residential section." These houses were built since the last cholera scare made people willing to listen to reason. The block is not like the one over on the East Side in which I actually lost my way once. There were thirty or forty rear houses in the heart of it, three or four on every lot, set at all sorts of angles, with odd, winding passages, or no passage at all, only "runways" for the thieves and toughs of the neighborhood. These yards are clear. There is air there, and it is about all there is. The view between brick walls outside is that of a stony street; inside, of rows of unpainted board fences, a bewildering maze of clothes-posts and lines; underfoot, a desert of brown, hard-baked soil from which every blade of grass, every stray weed, every speck of green, has been trodden out, as must inevitably be every gentle thought and aspiration above the mere wants of the body in those whose moral natures such home surroundings are to nourish. In self-defence, you know, all life eventually accommodates itself to its environment, and human life is no exception. [...]

Why complete the sketch? It is drearily familiar already. Such as it is, it is the frame in which are set days, weeks, months, and years of unceasing toil, just able to fill the mouth and clothe the back. Such as it is, it is the world, and all of it, to which these weary workers return nightly to feed heart and brain after wearing out the body at the bench, or in the shop. To it come the young with their restless yearnings, perhaps to pass on the threshold one of the daughters of sin, driven to the tenement by the police when they raided her den, sallying forth in silks and fine attire after her day of idleness. These in their coarse garments – girls with the love of youth for beautiful things, with this hard life before them – who shall save them from the tempter? Down in the street the saloon, always bright and gay, gathering to itself all the cheer of the block, beckons the boys. In many such blocks the census-taker found two thousand men, women, and children, and over, who called them home.

The picture is faithful enough to stand for its class wherever along both rivers the Irish brogue[28] is heard. As already said, the Celt falls most readily victim to tenement influences since shanty-town and its original free-soilers[29] have become things of the past. If he be thrifty and shrewd his progress thenceforward is along the plane of the tenement, on which he soon assumes to manage without improving things. The German has an advantage over his Celtic neighbor in his strong love for flowers, which not all the tenements on the East Side have power to smother. His garden goes with him wherever he goes. Not that it represents any high moral principle in the man; rather perhaps the capacity for it. He turns his saloon into a shrubbery as soon as his back-yard. But wherever he puts it in a tenement block it does the work of a dozen police clubs. In proportion as it spreads the neighborhood takes on a more orderly character. As the green dies out of the landscape and increases in political importance, the police find more to do. Where it disappears altogether from sight, lapsing into a mere sentiment, police-beats are shortened and the force patrols double at night. Neither the man nor the sentiment is wholly responsible for this. It is the tenement unadorned that is. [...]

Life in the tenements in July and August spells death to an army of little ones whom the doctor's skill is powerless to save. When the white badge of mourning flutters from every second door, sleepless mothers walk the streets in the gray of the early dawn, trying to stir a cooling breeze to fan the brow of the sick baby. There is no sadder sight than this patient devotion striving against fearfully hopeless odds. Fifty "summer doctors," especially trained to this work, are then sent into the tenements by the Board of Health, with free advice and medicine for the poor. Devoted women follow in their track with care and nursing for the sick. Fresh-air excursions run daily out of New York on land and water; but despite all efforts the grave-diggers in Calvary[30] work over-time, and little coffins are stacked mountain-high on the deck of the Charity Commissioners' boat when it makes its semi-weekly trips to the city cemetery.

Under the most favorable circumstances, an epidemic, which the well-to-do can afford to make light of as a thing to be got over or avoided by reasonable care, is excessively fatal among the children of the poor, by reason of the practical impossibility of isolating the patient in a tenement. The measles, ordinarily a harmless disease, furnishes a familiar example. Tread it ever so lightly on the avenues, in the tenements it kills right and left. Such an epidemic ravaged three crowded blocks in Elizabeth Street on the heels of the grippe last winter, and, when it had spent its fury, the death-maps in the Bureau of Vital Statistics looked as if a black hand had been laid across those blocks, over-shadowing in part the contiguous tenements in Mott Street, and with the thumb covering a particularly packed settlement of half a dozen houses in Mulberry Street. The track of the epidemic through these teeming barracks was as clearly defined as the track of a tornado through a forest district. There were houses in which as many as eight little children had died in five months. The records showed that respiratory diseases, the common heritage of the grippe and the measles, had caused death in most cases, discovering the trouble to be, next to the inability to check the contagion in those crowds, in the poverty of the parents and the wretched home conditions that made proper care of the sick impossible. [...]

Perhaps of all the disheartening experiences of those who have devoted lives of unselfish thought and effort, and their number is not so small as often supposed, to the lifting

---

[28] A strongly-marked dialectal pronunciation or accent.
[29] A free man who lives on his 'own soil;' also a politician in favor of free soil and opposed to slavery.
[30] Cemetery in Queens.

of this great load, the indifference of those they would help is the most puzzling. They will not be helped. Dragged by main force out of their misery, they slip back again on the first opportunity, seemingly content only in the old rut. The explanation was supplied by two women of my acquaintance in an Elizabeth Street tenement, whom the city missionaries had taken from their wretched hovel and provided with work and a decent home somewhere in New Jersey. In three weeks they were back, saying that they preferred their dark rear room to the stumps out in the country. But to me the oldest, the mother, who had struggled along with her daughter making cloaks at half a dollar apiece, twelve long years since the daughter's husband was killed in a street accident and the city took the children, made the bitter confession: "We do get so kind o' downhearted living this way, that we have to be where something is going on, or we just can't stand it." And there was sadder pathos to me in her words than in the whole long story of their struggle with poverty; for unconsciously she voiced the sufferings of thousands, misjudged by a happier world, deemed vicious because they are human and unfortunate. [...]

Source: Jacob August Riis (1849-1914). *How the Other Half Lives. Studies Among the Tenements of New York. With Illustrations Chiefly from Photographs Taken by the Author*. New York, Charles Scribner's Sons, 1890, 159, 162-167, 174-175.

298. Henry George
Progress and Poverty (1879)

The Problem

The present century has been marked by a prodigious increase in wealth-producing power. The utilization of steam and electricity, the introduction of improved processes and labor-saving machinery, the greater subdivision and grander scale of production, the wonderful facilitation of exchanges, have multiplied enormously the effectiveness of labor.

At the beginning of this marvelous era it was natural to expect, and it was expected, that labor-saving inventions would lighten the toil and improve the condition of the laborer; that the enormous increase in the power of producing wealth would make real poverty a thing of the past. [...]

And out of these bounteous material conditions he would have seen arising, as necessary sequences, moral conditions realizing the golden age of which mankind has always dreamed. Youth no longer stunted and starved; age no longer harried by avarice; the child at play with the tiger; the man with the muck-rake drinking in the glory of the stars! Foul things fled, fierce things tame; discord turned to harmony! For how could there be greed where all had enough? How could the vice, the crime, the ignorance, the brutality, that spring from poverty and the fear of poverty, exist where poverty had vanished? Who should crouch where all were freemen; who oppress where all were peers?

More or less vague or clear, these have been the hopes, these the dreams born of the improvements which give this wonderful century its preëminence. They have sunk so deeply into the popular mind as to radically change the currents of thought, to recast creeds and displace the most fundamental conceptions. [...]

It is true that disappointment has followed disappointment, and that discovery upon discovery, and invention after invention, have neither lessened the toil of those who most need respite, nor brought plenty to the poor. But there have been so many things to which it seemed this failure could be laid, that up to our time the new faith has hardly weakened. We have better appreciated the difficulties to be overcome; but not the less trusted that the tendency of the times was to overcome them. [...]

This association of poverty with progress is the great enigma of our times. It is the central fact from which spring industrial, social, and political difficulties that perplex the world, and with which statesmanship and philanthropy and education grapple in vain. From it come the clouds that overhang the future of the most progressive and self-reliant nations. It is the riddle which the Sphinx of Fate puts to our civilization, and which not to answer is to be destroyed. So long as all the increased wealth which modern progress brings goes but to build up great fortunes, to increase luxury and make sharper the contrast between the House of Have and the House of Want, progress is not real and cannot be permanent. [...]

The Current Theory of Human Progress – Its Insufficiency

[...] The prevailing belief now is, that the progress of civilization is a development or evolution, in the course of which man's powers are increased and his qualities improved by the operation of causes similar to those which are relied upon as explaining the genesis of species – viz., the survival of the fittest and the hereditary transmission of acquired qualities. [...]

[...] But this I take to be the current view of civilization: That it is the result of forces [...] which slowly change the character, and improve and elevate the powers of man; [...] and that this improvement tends to go on increasingly, to a higher and higher civilization. [...]

But [...] the moment that this theory of progression, which seems so natural to us amid an advancing civilization, looks around the world, it comes against an enormous fact – the fixed, petrified civilizations. [... How], upon the theory that human progress is the result of general and continuous causes, shall we account for the civilizations that have progressed so far and then stopped? [...] If progress be the result of fixed laws, inevitable and eternal, which impel men forward, how shall we account for this? [...]

[...] It is not merely that men have gone so far on the path of progress and then stopped; it is that men have gone far on the path of progress and then gone back. It is not merely an isolated case that thus confronts the theory – *it is the universal rule*. Every civilization that the world has yet seen has had its period of vigorous growth, of arrest and stagnation; its decline and fall. Of all the civilizations that have arisen and flourished, there remain to-day but those that have been arrested, and our own, which is not yet as old as were the pyramids when Abraham looked upon them – while behind the pyramids were twenty centuries of recorded history.

That our own civilization has a broader base, is of a more advanced type, moves quicker and soars higher than any preceding civilization is undoubtedly true; but in these respects it is hardly more in advance of the Greco-Roman civilization than that was in advance of Asiatic civilization; and if it were, that would prove nothing as to its permanence and future advance, unless it be shown that it is superior in those things which caused the ultimate failure of its predecessors. [...]

In truth, nothing could be further from explaining the facts of universal history than this theory that civilization is the result of a course of natural selection which operates to improve and elevate the powers of man. That civilization has arisen at different times in different places and has progressed at different rates, is not inconsistent with this theory;

[...] but that progress [...] has nowhere been continuous, but has everywhere been brought to a stand or retrogression, *is* absolutely inconsistent. [...]

How Modern Civilization May Decline

[...] The conditions of social progress, as we have traced the law, are association and equality. The general tendency of modern development, since the time when we can first discern the gleams of civilization in the darkness which followed the fall of the Western Empire, has been towards political and legal equality – to the abolition of slavery; to the abrogation of status; to the sweeping away of hereditary privileges; to the substitution of parliamentary for arbitrary government; to the right of private judgment in matters of religion; to the more equal security in person and property of high and low, weak and strong; to the greater freedom of movement and occupation, of speech and of the press. The history of modern civilization is the history of advances in this direction – of the struggles and triumphs of personal, political, and religious freedom. And the general law is shown by the fact that just as this tendency has asserted itself civilization has advanced, while just as it has been repressed or forced back civilization has been checked. [...]

Where there is anything like an equal distribution of wealth [...] the more democratic the government the better it will be; but where there is gross inequality in the distribution of wealth, the more democratic the government the worse it will be; for, while rotten democracy may not in itself be worse than rotten autocracy, its effects upon national character will be worse. [...]

[... T]he very foundations of society are being sapped before our eyes, while we ask, *how* it is possible that such a civilization as this, with its railroads, and daily newspapers, and electric telegraphs, should ever be destroyed? While literature breathes but the belief that we have been, are, and for the future must be, leaving the savage state further and further behind us, there are indications that we are actually turning back again towards barbarism. [...]

Whence shall come the new barbarians? Go through the squalid[31] quarters of great cities, and you may see, even now, their gathering hordes! How shall learning perish? Men will cease to read, and books will kindle fires and be turned into cartridges! [...]

And how the retrogression of civilization, following a period of advance, may be so gradual as to attract no attention at the time; nay, how that decline must necessarily, by the great majority of men, be mistaken for advance, is easily seen. [...]

[... T]he tendency to inequality, which is the necessary result of material progress where land is monopolized, cannot go much further without carrying our civilization into that downward path which is so easy to enter and so hard to abandon. Everywhere the increasing intensity of the struggle to live, the increasing necessity for straining every nerve to prevent being thrown down and trodden under foot in the scramble for wealth, is draining the forces which gain and maintain improvements. [...]

[...] When the tide turns in bay or river from flood to ebb, it is not all at once; but here it still runs on, though there it has begun to recede. When the sun passes the meridian, it can only be told by the way the short shadows fall; for the heat of the day yet increases. But as sure as the turning tide must soon run full ebb; as sure as the declining sun must bring darkness, so sure is it, that though knowledge yet increases and invention marches on, and new states are being settled, and cities still expand, civilization has begun to wane when, in

---

[31] Foul and repulsive by the presence of slime, mud, etc., and the absence of all cultivation or care.

proportion to population, we must build more and more prisons, more and more almshouses, more and more insane asylums. It is not from top to bottom that societies die; it is from bottom to top. [...]

[...] There is a vague but general feeling of disappointment; an increased bitterness among the working classes; a widespread feeling of unrest and brooding revolution. If this were accompanied by a definite idea of how relief is to be obtained, it would be a hopeful sign; but it is not. Though the schoolmaster has been abroad some time, the general power of tracing effect to cause does not seem a whit improved. [...] What change may come, no mortal man can tell, but that some great change *must* come, thoughtful men begin to feel. The civilized world is trembling on the verge of a great movement. Either it must be a leap upward, which will open the way to advances yet undreamed of, or it must be a plunge downward, which will carry us back toward barbarism.

The Central Truth

[... T]he truth to which we were led in the politico-economic branch of our inquiry, is [...] clearly apparent in the rise and fall of nations and the growth and decay of civilizations, [...] it accords with those deep-seated recognitions of relation and sequence that we denominate moral perceptions. [...]

This truth involves both a menace and a promise. It shows that the evils arising from the unjust and unequal distribution of wealth [...] are not incidents of progress, but tendencies which must bring progress to a halt; that they will not cure themselves, but, on the contrary, must, unless their cause is removed, grow greater and greater, until they sweep us back into barbarism by the road every previous civilization has trod. But it also shows that these evils are not imposed by natural laws; that they spring solely from social mal-adjustments which ignore natural laws, and that in removing their cause we shall be giving an enormous impetus to progress. [...]

[...] In permitting the monopolization of the natural opportunities which nature freely offers to all, we have ignored the fundamental law of justice [...]. But by sweeping away this injustice and asserting the rights of all men to natural opportunities, we shall conform ourselves to the law – we shall remove the great cause of unnatural inequality in the distribution of wealth and power; we shall abolish poverty; tame the ruthless passions of greed; dry up the springs of vice and misery; light in dark places the lamp of knowledge; give new vigor to invention and a fresh impulse to discovery; substitute political strength for political weakness; and make tyranny and anarchy impossible.

The reform I have proposed accords with all that is politically, socially, or morally desirable. It has the qualities of a true reform, for it will make all other reforms easier. What is it but the carrying out in letter and spirit of the truth enunciated in the Declaration of Independence – the "self-evident" truth that is the heart and soul of the Declaration – "*That all men are created equal; that they are endowed by their Creator with certain unalienable rights; that among them are life, liberty, and the pursuit of happiness!*"

These rights are denied when the equal right to land – on which and by which men alone can live – is denied. Equality of political rights will not compensate for the denial of the equal right to the bounty of nature. Political liberty, when the equal right to land is denied, becomes, as population increases and invention goes on, merely the liberty to compete for employment at starvation wages. [...]

We honor Liberty in name and in form. We set up her statues and sound her praises. But we have not fully trusted her. And with our growth so grow her demands. She will have no half service! [...]

We speak of Liberty as one thing, and virtue, wealth, knowledge, invention, national strength and national independence as other things. But, of all these, Liberty is the source, the mother, the necessary condition. She is to virtue what light is to color; to wealth what sunshine is to grain; to knowledge what eyes are to sight. She is the genius of invention, the brawn of national strength, the spirit of national independence. Where Liberty rises, there virtue grows, wealth increases, knowledge expands, invention multiplies human powers [...]. Where Liberty sinks, there virtue fades, wealth diminishes, knowledge is forgotten, invention ceases, and empires once mighty in arms and arts become a helpless prey to freer barbarians!

Only in broken gleams and partial light has the sun of Liberty yet beamed among men, but all progress hath she called forth. [...]

In our time, as in times before, creep on the insidious forces that, producing inequality, destroy Liberty. On the horizon the clouds begin to lower. Liberty calls to us again. We must follow her further; we must trust her fully. Either we must wholly accept her or she will not stay. It is not enough that men should vote; it is not enough that they should be theoretically equal before the law. They must have liberty to avail themselves of the opportunities and means of life; they must stand on equal terms with reference to the bounty of nature. Either this, or Liberty withdraws her light! Either this, or darkness comes on, and the very forces that progress has evolved turn to powers that work destruction. This is the universal law. This is the lesson of the centuries. Unless its foundations be laid in justice the social structure cannot stand.

Our primary social adjustment is a denial of justice. In allowing one man to own the land on which and from which other men must live, we have made them his bondsmen in a degree which increases as material progress goes on. This is the subtle alchemy that in ways they do not realize is extracting from the masses in every civilized country the fruits of their weary toil; that is instituting a harder and more hopeless slavery in place of that which has been destroyed and is bringing political despotism out of political freedom, and must soon transmute democratic institutions into anarchy.

It is this that turns the blessings of material progress into a curse. It is this that crowds human beings into noisome cellars and squalid tenement houses; that fills prisons and brothels; that goads men with want and consumes them with greed; that robs women of the grace and beauty of perfect womanhood; that takes from little children the joy and innocence of life's morning. [...]

In the very centers of our civilization to-day are want and suffering enough to make sick at heart whoever does not close his eyes and steel his nerves. Dare we turn to the Creator and ask Him to relieve it? Supposing the prayer were heard, and at the behest with which the universe sprang into being there should glow in the sun a greater power; new virtue fill the air; fresh vigor the soil; that for every blade of grass that now grows two should spring up, and the seed that now increases fifty fold should increase a hundred fold! Would poverty be abated or want relieved? Manifestly no! Whatever benefit would accrue would be but temporary. The new powers streaming through the material universe could only be utilized through land. And land, being private property, the classes that now monopolize the bounty of the Creator would monopolize all the new bounty. Land owners would alone be benefitted. Rents would increase, but wages would still tend to the starvation point! [...]

Can it be that the gifts of the Creator may be thus misappropriated with impunity? Is it a light thing that labor should be robbed of its earnings while greed rolls in wealth – that the many should want while the few are surfeited? Turn to history, and on every page may be read the lesson that such wrong never goes unpunished; that the Nemesis[32] that follows injustice never falters nor sleeps! Look around to-day. Can this state of things continue? May we even say, "After us the deluge!" Nay; the pillars of the state are trembling even now, and the very foundations of society begin to quiver with pent-up forces that glow underneath. The struggle that must either revivify, or convulse in ruin, is near at hand, if it be not already begun.

The fiat[33] has gone forth! With steam and electricity, and the new powers born of progress, forces have entered the world that will either compel us to a higher plane or overwhelm us, as nation after nation, as civilization after civilization, have been overwhelmed before. [...] Between democratic ideas and the aristocratic adjustments of society there is an irreconcilable conflict. [...] We cannot go on permitting men to vote and forcing them to tramp. We cannot go on educating boys and girls in our public schools and then refusing them the right to earn an honest living. We cannot go on prating of the inalienable rights of man and then denying the inalienable right to the bounty of the Creator. [...]

But if, while there is yet time, we turn to Justice and obey her, if we trust Liberty and follow her, the dangers that now threaten must disappear, the forces that now menace will turn to agencies of elevation. Think of the powers now wasted; of the infinite fields of knowledge yet to be explored; of the possibilities of which the wondrous inventions of this century give us but a hint. With want destroyed; with greed changed to noble passions; with the fraternity that is born of equality taking the place of the jealousy and fear that now array men against each other; with mental power loosed by conditions that give to the humblest comfort and leisure; and who shall measure the hights to which our civilization may soar? Words fail the thought! It is the Golden Age of which poets have sung and high-raised seers have told in metaphor! It is the glorious vision which has always haunted man with gleams of fitful splendor. It is what he saw whose eyes at Patmos were closed in a trance.[34] It is the culmination of Christianity – the City of God on earth, with its walls of jasper and its gates of pearl! It is the reign of the Prince of Peace!

Source: Henry George (1839-1897). *Progress and Poverty: An Inquiry into the Cause of Industrial Depressions, and of Increase of Want with Increase of Wealth. The Remedy*. New York: H. George & Co., 1879, 3-5, 9, 427, 429-430, 432-433, 435-436, 475-476, 478, 481, 484-496.

---

[32] In classical mythology the goddess of retribution or vengeance. Nemesis reverses excessive good fortune and punishes wrongdoing; hence any agent of retribution.
[33] An authoritative pronouncement, decree, or order. With reference to "fiat lux" (let there be light) Gen. 1.3: A command having for its object the creation of something.
[34] Reference to the Revelation of St. John.

299. William Graham Sumner
"The Challenge of Facts" (c. 1878-1882)

Socialism is no new thing. In one form or another it is to be found throughout all history. It arises from an observation of certain harsh facts in the lot of man on earth, the concrete expression of which is poverty and misery. These facts challenge us. It is folly to try to shut our eyes to them. We have first to notice what they are, and then to face them squarely.

Man is born under the necessity of sustaining the existence he has received by an onerous struggle against nature, both to win what is essential to his life and to ward off what is prejudicial to it. He is born under a burden and a necessity. Nature holds what is essential to him, but she offers nothing gratuitously. He may win for his use what she holds, if he can. Only the most meager and inadequate supply for human needs can be obtained directly from nature. There are trees which may be used for fuel and for dwellings, but labor is required to fit them for this use. There are ores in the ground, but labor is necessary to get out the metals and make tools or weapons. For any real satisfaction, labor is necessary to fit the products of nature for human use. In this struggle every individual is under the pressure of the necessities for food, clothing, shelter, fuel, and every individual brings with him more or less energy for the conflict necessary to supply his needs. The relation, therefore, between each man's needs and each man's energy, or "individualism," is the first fact of human life. [...]

So far as I have yet spoken, we have before us the struggle of man with nature, but the social problems, strictly speaking, arise at the next step. Each man carries on the struggle to win his support for himself, but there are others by his side engaged in the same struggle. If the stores of nature were unlimited, or if the last unit of the supply she offers could be won as easily as the first, there would be no social problem. If a square mile of land could support an indefinite number of human beings, or if it cost only twice as much labor to get forty bushels of wheat from an acre as to get twenty, we should have no social problem. If a square mile of land could support millions, no one would ever emigrate and there would be no trade or commerce. [...]

The constant tendency of population to outstrip the means of subsistence is the force which has distributed population over the world, and produced all advance in civilization. To this day the two means of escape for an overpopulated country are emigration and an advance in the arts. The former wins more land for the same people; the latter makes the same land support more persons. If, however, either of these means opens a chance for an increase of population, it is evident that the advantage so won may be speedily exhausted if the increase takes place. The social difficulty has only undergone a temporary amelioration, and when the conditions of pressure and competition are renewed, misery and poverty reappear. The victims of them are those who have inherited disease and depraved appetites, or have been brought up in vice and ignorance, or have themselves yielded to vice, extravagance, idleness, and imprudence. In the last analysis, therefore, we come back to vice, in its original and hereditary forms, as the correlative of misery and poverty.

The condition for the complete and regular action of the force of competition is liberty. Liberty means the security given to each man that, if he employs his energies to sustain the struggle on behalf of himself and those he cares for, he shall dispose of the product exclusively as he chooses. [...]

Private property, also, which we have seen to be a feature of society organized in accordance with the natural conditions of the struggle for existence produces inequalities between men. The struggle for existence is aimed against nature. It is from her niggardly hand that we have to wrest the satisfactions for our needs, but our fellow-men are our competitors for the meager supply. Competition, therefore, is a law of nature. Nature is entirely neutral; she submits to him who most energetically and resolutely assails her. She grants her rewards to the fittest, therefore, without regard to other considerations of any kind. If, then, there be liberty, men get from her just in proportion to their works, and their having and enjoying are just in proportion to their being and their doing. Such is the system of nature. If we do not like it, and if we try to amend it, there is only one way in which we can do it. We can take from the better and give to the worse. We can deflect the penalties of those who have done ill and throw them on those who have done better. We can take the rewards from those who have done better and give them to those who have done worse. We shall thus lessen the inequalities. We shall favor the survival of the unfittest, and we shall accomplish this by destroying liberty. Let it be understood that we cannot go outside of this alternative: liberty, inequality, survival of the fittest; not-liberty, equality, survival of the unfittest. The former carries society forward and favors all its best members; the latter carries society downwards and favors all its worst members. [...]

What we mean by liberty is civil liberty, or liberty under law; and this means the guarantees of law that a man shall not be interfered with while using his own powers for his own welfare. It is, therefore, a civil and political status; and that nation has the freest institutions in which the guarantees of peace for the laborer and security for the capitalist are the highest. Liberty, therefore, does not by any means do away with the struggle for existence. We might as well try to do away with the need of eating, for that would, in effect, be the same thing. What civil liberty does is to turn the competition of man with man from violence and brute force into an industrial competition under which men vie with one another for the acquisition of material goods by industry, energy, skill, frugality, prudence, temperance, and other industrial virtues. Under this changed order of things the inequalities are not done away with. Nature still grants her rewards of having and enjoying, according to our being and doing, but it is now the man of the highest training and not the man of the heaviest fist who gains the highest reward. It is impossible that the man with capital and the man without capital should be equal. To affirm that they are equal would be to say that a man who has no tool can get as much food out of the ground as the man who has a spade or a plough [...].

It follows from what we have observed that it is the utmost folly to denounce capital. To do so is to undermine civilization, for capital is the first requisite of every social gain, educational, ecclesiastical, political, æsthetic, or other. [...]

We have now before us the facts of human life out of which the social problem springs. These facts are in many respects hard and stern. It is by strenuous exertion only that each one of us can sustain himself against the destructive forces and the ever recurring needs of life; and the higher the degree to which we seek to carry our development the greater is the proportionate cost of every step. For help in the struggle we can only look back to those in the previous generation who are responsible for our existence. In the competition of life the son of wise and prudent ancestors has immense advantages over the son of vicious and imprudent ones. The man who has capital possesses immeasurable advantages for the struggle of life over him who has none. The more we break down privileges of class, or industry, and establish liberty, the greater will be the inequalities and the more exclusively will the vicious bear the penalties. Poverty and misery will exist in society just so long as vice exists in human nature.

I now go on to notice some modes of trying to deal with this problem. There is a modern philosophy which has never been taught systematically, but which has won the faith of vast masses of people in the modern civilized world. For want of a better name it may be called the sentimental philosophy. It has colored all modern ideas and institutions in politics, religion, education, charity, and industry, and is widely taught in popular literature, novels, and poetry, and in the pulpit. The first proposition of this sentimental philosophy is that nothing is true which is disagreeable. If, therefore, any facts of observation show that life is grim or hard, the sentimental philosophy steps over such facts with a genial platitude, a consoling commonplace, or a gratifying dogma. The effect is to spread an easy optimism, under the influence of which people spare themselves labor and trouble, reflection and forethought, pains and caution – all of which are hard things, and to admit the necessity for which would be to admit that the world is not all made smooth and easy, for us to pass through it surrounded by love, music, and flowers.

Under this philosophy, "progress" has been represented as a steadily increasing and unmixed good; as if the good steadily encroached on the evil without involving any new and other forms of evil; and as if we could plan great steps in progress in our academies and lyceums, and then realize them by resolution. [...] Assuming, therefore, that we can solve all these problems and eradicate all these evils by expending our ingenuity upon them, of course we cannot hasten too soon to do it.

A social philosophy, consonant with this, has also been taught for a century. It could not fail to be popular, for it teaches that ignorance is as good as knowledge, vulgarity as good as refinement, shiftlessness as good as painstaking, shirking as good as faithful striving, poverty as good as wealth, filth as good as cleanliness – in short, that quality goes for nothing in the measurement of men, but only numbers. Culture, knowledge, refinement, skill, and taste cost labor, but we have been taught that they have only individual, not social value, and that socially they are rather drawbacks than otherwise. In public life we are taught to admire roughness, illiteracy, and rowdyism. The ignorant, idle, and shiftless have been taught that they are "the people," that the generalities inculcated at the same time about the dignity, wisdom, and virtue of "the people" are true of them, that they have nothing to learn to be wise, but that, as they stand, they possess a kind of infallibility, and that to their "opinion" the wise must bow. It is not cause for wonder if whole sections of these classes have begun to use the powers and wisdom attributed to them for their interests, as they construe them, and to trample on all the excellence which marks civilization as an obsolete superstition.

Another development of the same philosophy is the doctrine that men come into the world endowed with "natural rights," or as joint inheritors of the "rights of man," which have been "declared" times without number during the last century. [...] The notion of natural rights is destitute of sense, but it is captivating, and it is the more available on account of its vagueness. It lends itself to the most vicious kind of social dogmatism, for if a man has natural rights, then the reasoning is clear up to the finished socialistic doctrine that a man has a natural right to whatever he needs, and that the measure of his claims is the wishes which he wants fulfilled. [...]

The origin of socialism, which is the extreme development of the sentimental philosophy, lies in the undisputed facts which I described at the outset. The socialist regards this misery as the fault of society. He thinks that we can organize society as we like and that an organization can be devised in which poverty and misery shall disappear. He goes further even than this. He assumes that men have artificially organized society as it now exists. Hence if anything is disagreeable or hard in the present state of society it follows, on that view, that the task of organizing society has been imperfectly and badly performed, and that it needs to be done over again. These are the assumptions with which the socialist starts, and many socialists seem also to believe that if they can destroy belief in an Almighty God who is supposed to have made the world such as it is, they will then have overthrown the belief that there is a fixed order in human nature and human life which man can scarcely alter at all, and, if at all, only infinitesimally.

The truth is that the social order is fixed by laws of nature precisely analogous to those of the physical order. The most that man can do is by ignorance and self-conceit to mar the operation of social laws. The evils of society are to a great extent the result of the dogmatism and self-interest of statesmen, philosophers, and ecclesiastics who in past time have done just what the socialists now want to do. Instead of studying the natural laws of the social order, they assumed that they could organize society as they chose, they made up their minds what kind of a society they wanted to make, and they planned their little measures for the ends they had resolved upon. It will take centuries of scientific study of the facts of nature to eliminate from human society the mischievous institutions and traditions which the said statesmen, philosophers, and ecclesiastics have introduced into it. Let us not, however, even then delude ourselves with any impossible hopes. The hardships of life would not be eliminated if the laws of nature acted directly and without interference. The task of right living forever changes its form, but let us not imagine that that task will ever reach a final solution or that any race of men on this earth can ever be emancipated from the necessity of industry, prudence, continence, and temperance if they are to pass their lives prosperously. [...]

The progress which men have made in developing the possibilities of human existence has never been made by jumps and strides. It has never resulted from the schemes of philosophers and reformers. It has never been guided through a set program by the wisdom of any sages, statesmen, or philanthropists. The progress which has been made has been won in minute stages by men who had a definite task before them, and who have dealt with it in detail, as it presented itself, without referring to general principles, or attempting to bring it into logical relations to an *a priori* system. In most cases the agents are unknown and cannot be found. New and better arrangements have grown up imperceptibly by the natural effort of all to make the best of actual circumstances. In this way, no doubt, the new problems arising in our modern society must be solved or must solve themselves. The chief safeguard and hope of such a development is in the sound instincts and strong sense of the people, which, although it may not reason closely, can reject instinctively. If there are laws – and there certainly are such – which permit the acquisition of property without industry, by cunning, force, gambling, swindling, favoritism, or corruption, such laws transfer property from those who have earned it to those who have not. Such laws contain the radical vice of socialism. They demand correction and offer an open field for reform because reform would lie in the direction of greater purity and security of the right of property. Whatever assails that right, or goes in the direction of making it still more uncertain whether the industrious man can dispose of the fruits of his industry for his own interests exclusively, tends directly towards violence, bloodshed, poverty, and misery. If any large section of modern society should rise against the rest for the purpose of attempting any such spoliation,[35] either by violence or through the

---

[35] The action of plundering, pillaging; seizure of property by violent means.

forms of law, it would destroy civilization as it was destroyed by the irruption of the barbarians into the Roman Empire. [...]

Source: William Graham Sumner (1840-1910). "The Challenge of Facts." *Essays of William Graham Sumner*. Ed. Albert Galloway Keller and Maurice R. Davie. New Haven: Yale University Press, 1934, 87, 92-93, 95-97, 100-104, 106-108, 120-121.

300. James W. Buel
"The Rich" (1882)

The wealth of New York is enormous, so great in fact that she is recognized as the financial center of America, to which nearly all business pays tribute. And yet, as a manufacturing city, Gotham is hardly half so important as Pittsburg or St. Louis, and the tax yielding wealth of Boston is much greater. But several advantages have combined to make her the chief commercial entrepot, and money gravitates to her financial institutions, and is held there by a magnetic force. Wall street controls the stock market and New York's rich magnates hold our railroads and shipping by a firm grip. It is a trite but well proved adage that "money is the root of all evil," and while we may all be striving for some of the root, yet its evils are too apparent in the great Metropolis for us to neglect the lesson which its acquisition teaches. [...]

Those who are most familiar with the other millionaires of New York have no hesitancy in declaring that these monied princes are infinitely less happy than are the honest laborers, whose daily duties are a constant striving for only limited comforts. There is much reason to confirm this truth. [William H.] Vanderbilt[36] betrays a lack of confidence in his own abilities, and it is said he is the victim of a singular delusion – that he may some day become a pauper. To guard against such an impossible event, he has purchased government bonds to the amount of $65,000,000, which he has deposited in the United States treasury. [...]

Of the rich men [...] nearly all have acquired their wealth by inheritance, and are therefore incapable of appreciating their fortunes; they can only live like other men, by eating, and but little money suffices for nature's wants; large investments create anxiety, for with so much wealth in active employment some of their enterprises are languishing while others are profitable; the consolation which the latter may bring is therefore destroyed by the former, and no point is reached where contentment is in full fruition.

But the absence of happiness is more noticeable in the homes of these favored sons of Mammon. Wealth is like blasted fruit if it is not made the means for display, and society only rears its superstructure on a gilded foundation. The rich of New York, speaking always in general terms, are slaves to society, which places them in a straight-jacket of punctilious mannerisms. The parlors and drawing-rooms, though filled with antique bric-a-brac,[37] elegant paintings and the rarest productions of sculptor genius, are animated by senseless conversation, betraying a want of intellectual training. There is scarcely such a thing as domestic privacy – those moments when man and wife may survey the fields of love together and watch the full, round honeymoon as it blazes out upon a sky bejeweled

---

[36] William Henry Vanderbilt (1821-1885), son of Cornelius Vanderbilt; succeeded his father as president of the New York Central Railroad and augmented the family fortune.
[37] Old curiosities, knick-knacks, antiquarian odds-and-ends.

with laughing stars of affection. Under social separation all the sentiment of conjugal devotion and that holy relation becomes pulseless, leaving only bonds of convenience and a mummified love holding them together. Is it strange, under such circumstances, that the rich man's home becomes little less than a sepulchre for young hearts' ambitions, with dead leaves of myrtle entwining Love's sarcophagus?

Life, to the wives and daughters of millionaires, is a problem only in the opportunities they may find for destroying its *ennui*;[38] surfeited with idle vaporings from fawning associates, stupefied by excesses and enervated by a variety of dissipations, existence not infrequently becomes a burden grievous in its oppressiveness.

The abstinence observed during Lent is a blessing only too brief for many women, and the saturnalia which follows wastes the nerve force and vitality that has accumulated. There is no cessation, for if a lady holds membership in an exclusive circle of wealth she must be a part of the social gatherings, *soirees, bal-masques*, weddings, funerals, receptions, dinner parties, private theatricals, fencing practice among sturdy belles, and the endless category of society pastimes. If exhausted nature becomes painfully felt, there is wine to warm the sluggish blood, cosmetics for blanching cheeks and *pastilles* for ageing furrows. [...]

The permissibilities of New York society not only promote discord and alienation, but are equally efficacious in making drunkards, male and female. The rich of to-day may become the poor of to-morrow; speculation runs through the city like an infectious fever, and all classes become victims. A poor man may invest a few spare dollars in stocks and if fortune should place him on the breast of an incoming tide he may gather a harvest of wealth at high-water mark absolutely bewildering. Suddenly accumulated riches become a passport for his family to enter the gay circle of fashion, though ignorance and boorishness be his only inherent characteristics. It is quite sufficient to be rich, regardless of personal qualities or the means employed. A metamorphosis so radical often disconcerts the ephemerally[39] rich and causes them to plunge into excesses which they would have considered abhorrent before their acquisition. Circumstances are the very reverse, when the rich take a tumble under a pressure of bad investments. Fifth avenue princes very often doff[40] their ermine[41] out of deference to adverse fortune, and become street-car drivers, with philosophical if not stoical cheerfulness. Society is therefore a melange of shocking composition, full of idiosyncrasies, if not monstrosities.

Around the festal board of assembled fashionables the cup that cheers makes graceful circuit, nor stops short of the borders of inebriety.[42] Many young men, old ere of age, besotted and degraded in their adolescence, with the slavery of intemperance full upon them, can see through the mists of their reeling brains a vision of some bright-eyed girl with a cup of wine in her jewelled fingers pleading for a social bumper, – forging the first chains which bind the soul to appetite and make them votaries of vice. [...]

"All is vanity," sayeth the preacher, and this clerical aphorism has many illustrations in the ways of the wealthy that prove its truthfulness.

Source: James W. Buel (1849-1920). "The Rich." *Metropolitan Life Unveiled; or the Mysteries and Miseries of America's Great Cities, Embracing New York, Washington City, San Francisco, Salt Lake City, and New Orleans*. St. Louis: Historical Publishing, 1882, 93-96, 101-104, 106.

---

[38] The feeling of mental weariness and dissatisfaction produced by lack of occupation.
[39] Short-lived, transitory.
[40] To put off or take off clothing; to take off or raise a hat by way of a salutation or token of respect.
[41] The fur of the ermine. Here: garments made of this fur.
[42] Drunkenness, intoxication, chiefly applied to habitual drunkenness.

301. Thure de Thulstrup: "The Anarchist Riot in Chicago" (1886)

Source: Thure de Thulstrup (1848-1930). "The Anarchist Riot in Chicago – A Dynamite Bomb Exploding among the Police" [wood engraving]. *Harper's Weekly* 30 (May 15, 1886), 312-313. Courtesy Library of Congress.

302. *Constitution of the Knights of Labor* (1878)

Preamble

The recent alarming development and aggression of aggregated wealth, which, unless checked, will inevitably lead to the pauperization and hopeless degradation of the toiling masses, render it imperative, if we desire to enjoy the blessings of life, that a check should be placed upon its power and upon unjust accumulation, and a system adopted which will secure to the laborer the fruits of his toil; and as this much-desired object can only be accomplished by the thorough unification of labor, and the united efforts of those who obey the divine injunction that "In the sweat of thy brow shalt thou eat bread," we have formed the * * * * * with a view of securing the organization and direction, by co-operative effort, of the power of the industrial classes; and we submit to the world the object sought to be accomplished by our organization, calling upon all who believe in securing "the greatest good to the greatest number" to aid and assist us: –

I. To bring within the folds of organization every department of productive industry, making knowledge a standpoint for action, and industrial and moral worth, not wealth, the true standard of individual and national greatness.

II. To secure to the toilers a proper share of the wealth that they create; more of the leisure that rightfully belongs to them; more societary advantages; more of the benefits, privileges, and emoluments of the world; in a word, all those rights and privileges necessary to make them capable of enjoying, appreciating, defending, and perpetuating the blessings of good government.

III. To arrive at the true condition of the producing masses in their educational, moral and financial condition, by demanding from the various governments the establishment of bureaus of Labor Statistics.

IV. The establishment of co-operative institutions, productive and distributive.

V. The reserving of the public lands – the heritage of the people – for the actual settler; not another acre for railroads or speculators.

VI. The abrogation[43] of all laws that do not bear equally upon capital and labor, the removal of unjust technicalities, delays and discriminations in the administration of justice, and the adopting of measures providing for the health and safety of those engaged in mining, manufacturing, or building pursuits.

VII. The enactment of laws to compel chartered corporations to pay their employe[e]s weekly, in full, for labor performed during the preceding week, in the lawful money of the country.

VIII. The enactment of laws giving mechanics and laborers a first lien[44] on their work for their full wages.

IX. The abolishment of the contract system on national, State and municipal work.

X. The substitution of arbitration for strikes, whenever and wherever employers and employe[e]s are willing to meet on equitable grounds.

XI. The prohibition of the employment of children in workshops, mines, and factories before attaining their fourteenth year.

XII. To abolish the system of letting out by contract the labor of convicts in our prisons and reformatory institutions.

XIII. To secure for both sexes equal pay for equal work.

XIV. The reduction of the hours of labor to eight per day, so that the laborers may have more time for social enjoyment and intellectual improvement, and be enabled to reap the advantages conferred by the labor-saving machinery which their brains have created.

XV. To prevail upon governments to establish a purely national circulating medium, based upon the faith and resources of the nation, and issued directly to the people, without the intervention of any system of banking corporations, which money shall be a legal tender in payment of all debts, public or private.

Source: "Preamble." *Constitution of the Knights of Labor* [Adopted Jan. 1, 1878]. *Documents of American History.* Ed. Henry Steele Commager. 2 vols. New York: Appleton – Century – Crofts, 1963, Vol. 1, 546-547.

303. "To the Workingmen of America" (1883)[45]

FELLOW-WORKMEN: – The Declaration of Independence says:

"... But when a long train of abuses and usurpations, pursuing invariably the same object, evinces a design to reduce them (the people) under absolute Despotism, it is their right, it is their duty to throw off such government and provide new guards for their future security."

---

[43] Abolishment by authority.
[44] Right to take or sell the property of a debtor as security or payment for a debt.
[45] The so-called "Pittsburgh Manifesto" of the International Working Peoples' Association was drafted by a committee consisting of Victor Drury (a refugee from the Paris Commune,) Johann Most, Albert Parsons, Joseph Reifgraber (Editor of *Die Parole*, St. Louis) and August Spies. It was adopted by the Pittsburgh Congress of the International Working Peoples' Association on October 16, 1883.

This thought of Thomas Jefferson was the justification for armed resistance by our forefathers, which gave birth to our Republic, and do not the necessities of our present time compel us to reassert their declaration?

Fellow-Workmen, we ask you to give us your attention for a few moments. We ask you candidly to read the following manifesto issued in your behalf; in the behalf of your wives and children; in behalf of humanity and progress.

Our present society is founded on the exploitation of the propertyless classes by the propertied. This exploitation is such that the propertied (capitalists) buy the working force body and soul of the propertyless, for the price of the mere costs of existence (wages), and take for themselves, i.e. steal the amount of new values (products) which exceeds this price, whereby wages are made to represent the necessities instead of the earnings of the wage-laborer.

As the non-possessing classes are forced by their poverty to offer for sale to the propertied their working forces, and as our present production on a grand scale enforces technical development with immense rapidity, so that by the application of an always decreasing number of human working forces, an always increasing amount of products is created; so does the supply of working forces increase constantly, while the demand therefore decreases. This is the reason why the workers compete more and more intensely in selling themselves, causing their wages to sink, or at least on the average, never raising them above the margin necessary for keeping intact their working ability.

Whilst by this process the propertyless are entirely debarred from entering the ranks of the propertied even by the most strenuous exertions, the propertied, by means of the ever-increasing plundering of the working class, are becoming richer day by day, without in any way being themselves productive.

If now and then one of the propertyless class become rich, it is not by their own labor but from opportunities which they have to speculate upon, and absorb the labor-product of others.

With the accumulation of individual wealth, the greed and power of the propertied grows. They use all the means for competing among themselves for the robbery of the people. In this struggle generally the less-propertied (middle-class) are overcome, while the great capitalists par excellence swell their wealth enormously, concentrate entire branches of production as well as trade, and inter-communication, into their hands, and develop into monopolists. The increase of products, accompanied by simultaneous decrease of the average income of the working mass of the people, leads to so-called "business" and "commercial" crises, when the misery of the wage-workers is forced to the extreme. [...]

The increasing eradication of working forces from the productive process, annually increases the percentage of the propertyless population, which becomes pauperized and is driven to "crime," vagabondage, prostitution, suicide, starvation, and general depravity. This system is unjust, insane and murderous. It is therefore necessary to totally destroy it with and by all means, and with the greatest energy on the part of every one who suffers by it and who does not want to be made culpable for its continued existence by his inactivity.

Agitation for the purpose of organization; organization for the purpose of rebellion. In these few words the ways are marked which the workers must take if they want to be rid of their chains, as the economic condition is the same in all countries of so-called "civilization," as the governments of all Monarchies and Republics work hand in hand for the purpose of opposing all movements of the thinking part of the workers, as finally the victory in the decisive combat of the proletarians against their oppressors can only be gained by the simultaneous struggle along the whole line of the bourgeois (capitalistic) society, so therefore the international fraternity of peoples as expressed in the International Working People's Association presents itself a self-evident necessity.

True order should take its place. This can only be achieved when all implements of labor, the soil and other premises of production, in short, capital produced by labor, is changed into societary property. Only by this pre-supposition is destroyed every possibility of the future spoliation[46] of man by man. Only by common, undivided capital can all be enabled to enjoy in their fullness the fruits of the common toil. Only by the impossibility of accumulating individual (private) capital can every one be compelled to work who makes a demand to live.

This order of things allows production to regulate itself according to the demand of the whole people, so that nobody need work more than a few hours a day, and that all nevertheless can satisfy their needs. Hereby time and opportunity are given for opening to the people the way to the highest possible civilization; the privileges of higher intelligence fall with the privileges of wealth, and birth. To the achievement of such a system the political organizations of the capitalistic classes – be they Monarchies or Republics – form the barriers. These political structures (States), which are completely in the hands of the propertied, have no other purpose than the upholding of the present disorder of exploitation.

All laws are directed against the working people. In so far as the opposite appears to be the case, they serve on one hand to blind the worker, while on the other they are simply evaded. Even the school serves only the purpose of furnishing the offspring of the wealthy with those qualities necessary to uphold their class domination. The children of the poor get scarcely a formal elementary training, and this, too, is mainly directed to such branches as tend to producing prejudices, arrogance and servility; in short, want of sense. The Church finally seeks to make complete idiots out of the mass and to make them forego the paradise on earth by promising a fictitious heaven. The capitalistic Press, on the other hand, takes care of the confusion of spirits in public life. All these institutions, far from aiding in the education of the masses, have for their object the keeping in ignorance of the people. They are all in the pay and under the direction of the capitalistic classes. The workers can therefore expect no help from any capitalistic party in their struggle against the existing system. They must achieve their liberation by their own efforts. As in former times a privileged class never surrendered its tyranny, neither can it be expected that the capitalists of this age will give up their rulership without being forced to do it. [...]

We could show by scores of illustrations that all attempts in the past to reform this monstrous system by peaceable means, such as the ballot, have been futile, and all such efforts in the future must necessarily be so, for the following reasons:

The political institutions of our time are the agencies of the propertied class; their mission is the upholding of the privileges of their masters; any reform in your own behalf would curtail these privileges. To this they will not and cannot consent, for it would be suicidal to themselves.

That they will not resign their privileges voluntarily we know, that they will not make any concessions to us we likewise know. Since we must then rely upon the kindness of our masters for whatever redress we have, and knowing that from them no good may be

---

[46] Spoilure, the act of plundering or despoiling.

expected, there remains but one recourse – force! Our forefathers have not only told us that against despots force is justifiable, because it is the only means, but they themselves have set the immemorial example.

By force our ancestors liberated themselves from political oppression, by force their children will have to liberate themselves from economic bondage. "It is, therefore, your right, it is your duty," says Jefferson, "to arm!"

What we would achieve is, therefore, plainly and simply:

First. – Destruction of the existing class rule, by all means, i.e. by energetic, relentless, revolutionary and international action.

Second. – Establishment of a free society based upon co-operative organization of production.

Third. – Free exchange of equivalent products by and between the productive organizations without commerce and profit-mongery.

Fourth. – Organization of education on a secular, scientific and equal basis for both sexes.

Fifth. – Equal rights for all without distinction to sex or race.

Sixth. – Regulation of all public affairs by free contracts between the autonomous (independent) communes and associations, resting on a federalistic basis.

Whoever agrees with this ideal let him grasp our outstretched brother hands! Proletarians of all countries, unite!

Fellow workingmen, all we need for the achievement of this great end is ORGANIZATION and UNITY.

There exists now no great obstacle to that unity. The work of peaceful education and revolutionary conspiracy well can and ought to run in parallel lines.

The day has come for solidarity. Join our ranks. Let the drum beat defiantly the roll of battle. Workmen of all lands, unite! [You] have nothing to lose, but your chains; you have a world to win!

Tremble! Oppressors of the world! Not far beyond your purblind sight there dawn the scarlet and sable lights of the Judgment day!

Source: "To the Workingmen of America." *The Alarm* (November 1, 1884), 14-22.

304. John Most
The Beast of Property (1884)

"Among the beasts of prey, man is certainly the worst." This expression, very commonly made now a days, is only relatively true. Not man as such, but man in connection with wealth is a beast of prey. The richer a man, the greater his greed for more. We may call such monster the *beast of property*; it now rules the world, makes mankind miserable, and gains in cruelty and voracity with the progress of our so called *civilization*. This monster we will in the following characterize and recommend to extermination. Look about ye! In every so-called *civilized* country there are among every 100 men about 95 more, or less destitute and about five money-bags.

It is unnecessary to trace all the sneaking ways by which the latter have gained their possessions. The fact that they own ALL, while the others exist, or rather vegetate merely, admits of no doubt, that these few have grown rich at the cost of the many. Either by direct brute force, by cunning, or by fraud, this horde has from time to time seized the soil with all its wealth. The laws of inheritance and entail, and the changing of hands, have lent a *venerable* color to this robbery, and consequently mystified and erased the true character of such actions. For this reason the *beast of property* is not yet fully recognized, but is, on the contrary, worshiped with a holy awe.

And yet, all who do not belong to this class are its victims. Every offspring of a non-possessor (poor man) finds every nook and corner of the earth occupied at his entrance into the world. There is nothing which is *lordless*. Without labor nothing is produced; and in order to labor, there are required not only ability and will, but also room to work, tools, raw materials and means of sustenance. The poor man must, by force of necessity, apply to those who possess these things in plenty. And, behold! the rich give him permission to continue his existence. But in return for this he must divest himself of his skill and power. These qualities henceforth his pretended *saviours* use for themselves. They place him under the yoke of labor – they force him to the utmost of his mental and physical abilities to produce new treasures, which, however, he is not entitled to own. [...]

To perpetuate this state of affairs is the only aim of the *prominent* classes. Though not always united among themselves – one seeking to gain advantage over the other by tricks of trade, cunning in speculation and divers machinations of competition – yet in opposition to the proletariat they stand in one united hostile phalanx. [...]

When the workers combine in order to obtain better wages, shorte[r] hours of labor, or similar advantages, the money-bags immediately decry it as *conspiracy*, which must be prevented.

When the workers organize politically, it is denounced as resistance to the *divine* order of things, which must be nullified by laws of exception or discrimination.

Should the people finally contemplate rebellion, an unceasing howl of rage raised by the *gold tigers* will be heard throughout the world – they pant for massacres and their thirst for blood is insatiable. The life of the poor is valued as nothing by the rich. [...]

[...] The greed for wealth is closely associated with the greed for power. Wealth is not only a generator of more wealth, it is also a political power. Under the present capitalistic system venality is an all-pervading vice. It is as a rule a mere matter of price which will buy over those who may be of service either by speech or silence, by the pen or by the press, by acts of violence or any other means, to the *beast of property*, which by its golden dictates is the absolute, almighty divinity. [...]

In America the place of the monarchs is filled by the monopolists. Should monopolism in the alleged *free* United States of America develop at the rate it has in the last quarter of a century, there will remain free from monopolization only daylight and air. Five hundred million acres of land in the United States, about six times the area of Great Britain and Ireland, have been divided within a generation among the railroad companies and the great landlords of Europeo-aristocratic origin. Within a few decades Vanderbilt alone amassed $200,000,000; several dozen of his competitors in robbery bid fair to outdo him. San Francisco was settled hardly thirty years ago, to-day it harbors eighty-five millionaires! All the wealth of this great republic, although established but a century, its mines, its coal-fields, its oil-wells, etc., etc., has been *taken* from the people and are the property of a handful of daring adventurers and cunning schemers.

The *sovereignty of the people* falls prostrate into the dust before the influence of these money kings, railroad magnates, coal barons and factory lords. These fellows carry the whole United States in their pockets, and that, which is vaunted as untrammeled legislation and free ballot, is a farce, a delusion and a snare. [...]

Let those who labor to live understand, that this monster cannot be tamed, nor be made harmless or useful to man; let them learn to know, that there is but one means of safety: unrelenting, pitiless, thorough war of extermination! [...]

[...] Whoever has recognized the villainy of the present conditions, is in duty bound to raise his voice, in order to expose them, and thereby open the eyes of the people. Only avoid to reach this result by super-scientific reflections. Let us leave this to those well-meaning scientists, who in this manner tear the mask of humanity from the *better class* and disclose the hideous countenance of the beast of prey. The language of and to the proletariat must be clear and forcible.

Whoever thus uses speech will be accused of inciting disturbance by the governing rabble; he will be bitterly hated and persecuted. This shows, that the only possible and practical enlightenment must be of an inciting nature. Then let us incite! [...]

The revolution of the proletariat – the war of the poor against the rich, is the only way from oppression to deliverance!

But, some interpose, revolutions can not be made! Certainly not, but they can be prepared for by directing the people's attention to the fact, that such events are imminent, and calling upon them to be ready for all emergencies.

Capitalistic development, of which many theorists assert, that it must proceed to the total extinction of the middle class, before the conditions favorable to a social revolution are at hand, has reached such a point of perfection, that its farther progress is almost impossible. [...]

Everything, therefore, is ripe for Communism; it is only necessary to remove its interested inveterate enemies, the capitalists and their abettors. During these crises the people will become sufficiently prepared for the struggle. Everything will then depend on the presence of a well trained revolutionary nucleus at all points, which is fit and able to crystalize around itself the masses of the people, driven to rebellion by misery and want of work, and which can then apply the mighty forces so formed to the destruction of all existing hostile institutions.

Therefore organize and enlarge everywhere the Socialistic revolutionary party, before it be too late! The victory of the people over its tyrants and vampires will then be certain. [...]

The former (present) system will be abolished in the most rapid and thorough manner [...]. The case standing thus: – If the people do not crush them, they will crush the people, drown the revolution in the blood of the best, and rivet the chains of slavery more firmly than ever. Kill or be killed is the alternative. Therefore massacres of the people's enemies must be instituted. All free communities enter into an offensive and defensive alliance during the continuance of the combat. The revolutionary communes must incite rebellion in the adjacent districts. The war can not terminate until the enemy (the *beast of property*) has been pursued to its last lurking place, and totally destroyed. [...]

Source: John [Johann Joseph] Most (1846-1906). *The Beast of Property*. New Haven: International Workingmen's Association, Group New Haven, ²1884, 3-5, 7, 9-13.

305. "The Commercial Vampire" (1898)

Source: Leon Barritt (1852-1938). "The Commercial Vampire." *Vim* (July 20, 1898). Courtesy Library of Congress.

306. August Spies
"Speech at Haymarket Trial" (1886)

Your Honor: In addressing this court I speak as the representative of one class to the representative of another. I will begin with the words uttered five hundred years ago on a similar occasion, by the Venetian Doge Faheri, who, addressing the court, said: *"My defense is your accusation; the causes of my alleged crime your history!"* I have been indicted on a charge of murder, as an accomplice or accessory. Upon this indictment I have been convicted. There was no evidence produced by the State to show or even indicate that I had any knowledge of the man who threw the bomb, or that I myself had anything to do with the throwing of the missile, unless, of course, you weigh the testimony of the accomplices of the State's attorney and Bonfield,[47] the testimony of Thompson and Gilmer, by the price they were paid for it. If there was no evidence to show that I was legally responsible for the deed, then my conviction and the execution of the sentence is nothing less than willful, malicious, and deliberate murder, as foul a murder as may be found in the annals of religious, political, or any other sort of persecution. There have been many judicial murders committed where the representatives of the State were acting in good faith, believing their victims to be guilty of the charge accused of. In this case the representatives of the State cannot shield themselves with a similar excuse. For they themselves have fabricated most of the testimony which was used as a pretense to convict us; to convict us by a jury picked out to convict! Before this court, and before the public,

---

[47] Captain John Bonfield, Malvern M. Thompson, Harry L. Gilmer testified in the court case.

which is supposed to be the State, I charge the State's attorney and Bonfield with the heinous conspiracy to commit murder. [...]

The contemplated murder of eight men, whose only crime is that they have dared to speak the truth, may open the eyes of these suffering millions; may wake them up. Indeed, I have noticed that our conviction has worked miracles in this direction already. The class that clamors for our lives, the good, devout Christians, have attempted in every way, through their newspapers and otherwise, to conceal the true and only issue in this case. By simply designating the defendants as Anarchists, and picturing them as a newly discovered tribe or species of cannibals, and by inventing shocking and horrifying stories of dark conspiracies said to be planned by them – these good Christians zealously sought to keep the naked fact from the working people and other righteous parties, namely: That on the evening of May 4, two hundred armed men, under the command of a notorious ruffian, attacked a meeting of peaceable citizens! With what intention? With the intention of murdering them, or as many of them as they could. I refer to the testimony given by two of our witnesses. The wage workers of this city began to object to being fleeced too much – they began to say some very true things, but they were highly disagreeable to our Patrician class; they put forth – well, some very modest demands. They thought eight hours hard toil a day for scarcely two hours' pay was enough. This "lawless rabble" had to be silenced! The only way to silence them was to frighten them, and murder those whom they looked up to as their leaders. Yes, these "foreign dogs" had to be taught a lesson, so that they might never again interfere with the high-handed exploitation of their benevolent and Christian masters. [...] If I had thrown that bomb, or had caused it to be thrown, or had known of it, I would not hesitate a moment to say so. It is true that a number of lives were lost – many were wounded. But hundreds of lives were thereby saved! But for that bomb, there would have been a hundred widows and hundreds of orphans where now there are a few. These facts have been carefully suppressed, and we were accused and convicted of conspiracy by the real conspirators and their agents. This, your honor, is one reason why sentence should not be passed by a court of justice – if that name has any significance at all.

[...] As to the destruction of society which we have been accused of seeking, sounds this not like one of Aesop's fables – like the cunning of the fox? We, who have jeopardized our lives to save society from the fiend – the fiend who has grasped her by the throat; who sucks her life-blood, who devours her children – we, who would heal her bleeding wounds, who would free her from the fetters you have wrought around her; from the misery you have brought upon her – we her enemies!! Honorable judge, the demons of hell will join in the laughter this irony provokes!

"We have preached dynamite!" Yes, we have predicted from the lessons history teaches, that the ruling classes of today would no more listen to the voice of reason than their predecessors; that they would attempt by brute force to stay the wheels of progress. Is it a lie, or was it the truth we told? Are not the large industries of this once free country already conducted under the surveillance of the police, the detectives, the military and the sheriffs – and is this return to militancy not developing from day to day? American sovereigns – think of it – working like galley convicts under military guards! We have predicted this, and predict that soon these conditions will grow unbearable. What then? The mandate of the feudal lords of our time is slavery, starvation, and death! This has been their program for years. We have said to the toilers, that science had penetrated the mystery of nature [...] dynamite! If this declaration is synonymous with murder, why not charge those with the crime to whom we owe the invention?

To charge us with an attempt to overthrow the present system on or about May 4, by force, and then establish Anarchy, is too absurd a statement, I think, even for a political office holder to make. [...]

[...] But, if you think that by hanging us you can stamp out the labor movement – the movement from which the downtrodden millions, the millions who toil and live in want and misery, the wage slaves, expect salvation – if this is your opinion, then hang us! Here you will tread upon a spark, but here, and there, and behind you, and in front of you, and everywhere, flames will blaze up. It is a subterranean fire. You cannot put it out. The ground is on fire upon which you stand. [...]

You, gentlemen, are the revolutionists! You rebel against the effects of social conditions which have tossed you, by the fair hand of Fortune, into a magnificent paradise. Without inquiring, you imagine that no one else has a right in that place. You insist that you are the chosen ones, the sole proprietors. The forces that tossed you into the paradise, the industrial forces, are still at work. They are growing more active and intense from day to day. Their tendency is to elevate all mankind to the same level, to have all humanity share in the paradise you now monopolize. You, in your blindness, think you can stop the tidal wave of civilization and human emancipation by placing a few policemen, a few gatling guns,[48] and some regiments of militia on the shore – you think you can frighten the rising waves back into the unfathomable depths, whence they have arisen, by erecting a few gallows in the perspective. You, who oppose the natural course of things, you are the real revolutionists. You and you alone are the conspirators and destructionists!

[...] Socialism is a constructive and not a destructive science. While capitalism expropriates the masses for the benefit of the privileged class; while capitalism is that school of economics which teaches how one can live upon the labor (i.e., property) of others; Socialism teaches how all may possess property, and further teaches that every man must work honestly for his own living [...]. Under capitalism the great inventions of the past, far from being a blessing for mankind, have been turned into a curse! Under Socialism the prophecy of the Greek poet, Antiporas,[49] would be fulfilled, who, at the invention of the first water mill, exclaimed: "This is the emancipator of male and female slaves" [...].

Socialism teaches that the machines, the means of transportation and communication are the result of the combined efforts of society, past and present, and that they are therefore rightfully the indivisible property of society, just the same as the soil and the mines and all natural gifts should be. This declaration implies that those who have appropriated this wealth wrongfully, though lawfully, shall be expropriated by society. The expropriation of the masses by the monopolists has reached such a degree that the expropriation of the expropriators has become an imperative necessity, an act of social self-preservation. Society will reclaim its own, even though you erect a gibbet on every street corner. And Anarchism, this terrible "ism," deduces that under a co-operative organization of society, under economic equality and individual independence, the State – the political State – will pass into barbaric antiquity. And we will be where all are free, where there are no longer masters and servants, where intellect stands for brute force; there will no longer be any use for the policemen and militia to preserve the so-called "peace and order" – the order that the Russian general spoke of when he telegraphed to the Czar after he had massacred half of Warsaw, "Peace reigns in Warsaw!"

---

[48] Machine guns.
[49] Greek poet who lived at the time of Cicero.

Anarchism does not mean bloodshed; does not mean robbery, arson, etc. These monstrosities are, on the contrary, the characteristic features of capitalism. Anarchism means peace and tranquillity to all. [...]

[...] You have no good law. Your decision, your verdict, our conviction is nothing but an arbitrary will of this lawless court. It is true there is no precedent in jurisprudence in this case! It is true we have called upon the people to arm themselves. It is true that we told them time and again that the great day of change was coming. It was not our desire to have bloodshed. We are not beasts. We would not be Socialists if we were beasts. It is because of our sensitiveness that we have gone into this movement for the emancipation of the oppressed and suffering. It is true we have called upon the people to arm and prepare for the stormy times before us.

This seems to be the ground upon which the verdict is to be sustained. "But when a long train of abuses and usurpations pursuing invariably the same object evinces a design to reduce the people under absolute despotism, it is their right, it is their duty to throw off such government and provide new guards for their future safety." This is a quotation from the Declaration of Independence. Have we broken any laws by showing to the people how these abuses, that have occurred for the last twenty years, are invariably pursuing one object, viz. to establish an oligarchy in this country so strong and powerful and monstrous as never before has existed in any country? [...]

Source: August Spies (1855-1887). "Address of August Spies." *Famous Speeches of the Eight Chicago Anarchists*. Ed. Lucy Parsons. New York: Arno Press & New York Times, 1969, 11-12, 14-17, 21-22, 24.

307. "The Bosses of the Senate" (1889)

Source: Joseph Keppler (1838-1894). "The Bosses of the Senate." *Puck* (January 23, 1889). Courtesy Library of Congress.

308. Andrew Carnegie
"Wealth" (1889)

The problem of our age is the proper administration of wealth, so that the ties of brotherhood may still bind together the rich and poor in harmonious relationship. The conditions of human life have not only been changed, but revolutionized, within the past few hundred years. In former days there was little difference between the dwelling, dress, food, and environment of the chief and those of his retainers. The Indians are to-day where civilized man then was. When visiting the Sioux, I was led to the wigwam of the chief. It was just like the others in external appearance, and even within the difference was trifling between it and those of the poorest of his braves. The contrast between the palace of the millionaire and the cottage of the laborer with us to-day measures the change which has come with civilization.

This change, however, is not to be deplored, but welcomed as highly beneficial. It is well, nay, essential for the progress of the race, that the houses of some should be homes for all that is highest and best in literature and the arts, and for all the refinements of civilization, rather than that none should be so. Much better this great irregularity than universal squalor.[50] Without wealth there can be no Mæcenas.[51] The "good old times" were not good old times. Neither master nor servant was as well situated then as to-day. A relapse to old conditions would be disastrous to both – not the least so to him who serves – and would sweep away civilization with it. But whether the change be for good or ill, it is upon us, beyond our power to alter, and therefore to be accepted and made the best of. It is a waste of time to criticise the inevitable. [...]

The price we pay for this salutary change is, no doubt, great. We assemble thousands of operatives in the factory, in the mine, and in the counting-house, of whom the employer can know little or nothing, and to whom the employer is little better than a myth. [...] Under the law of competition, the employer of thousands is forced into the strictest economies, among which the rates paid to labor figure prominently, and often there is friction between the employer and the employed, between capital and labor, between rich and poor. Human society loses homogeneity.

The price which society pays for the law of competition, like the price it pays for cheap comforts and luxuries, is also great; but the advantages of this law are also greater still, for it is to this law that we owe our wonderful material development, which brings improved conditions in its train. But, whether the law be benign or not, we must say of it, as we say of the change in the conditions of men to which we have referred: It is here; we cannot evade it; no substitutes for it have been found; and while the law may be sometimes hard for the individual, it is best for the race, because it insures the survival of the fittest in every department. We accept and welcome, therefore, as conditions to which we must accommodate ourselves, great inequality of environment, the concentration of business, industrial and commercial, in the hands of a few, and the law of competition between these, as being not only beneficial, but essential for the future progress of the race. Having accepted these, it follows that there must be great scope for the exercise of special ability in the merchant and in the manufacturer who has to conduct affairs upon a great scale. [...] It is a law, as certain as any of the others named, that men possessed of

---

[50] The state of being morally squalid, i.e., of lacking intellectual sensitivity.
[51] A patron, esp. one generous to artists; after Gaius Maecenas (70-8 BC).

this peculiar talent for affairs, under the free play of economic forces, must, of necessity, soon be in receipt of more revenue than can be judiciously expended upon themselves; and this law is as beneficial for the race as the others.

Objections to the foundations upon which society is based are not in order, because the condition of the race is better with these than it has been with any others which have been tried. Of the effect of any new substitutes proposed we cannot be sure. The Socialist or Anarchist who seeks to overturn present conditions is to be regarded as attacking the foundation upon which civilization itself rests, for civilization took its start from the day that the capable, industrious workman said to his incompetent and lazy fellow, "If thou dost not sow, thou shalt not reap," and thus ended primitive Communism by separating the drones from the bees. One who studies this subject will soon be brought face to face with the conclusion that upon the sacredness of property civilization itself depends [...].

We start, then, with a condition of affairs under which the best interests of the race are promoted, but which inevitably gives wealth to the few. Thus far, accepting conditions as they exist, the situation can be surveyed and pronounced good. The question then arises, – and, if the foregoing be correct, it is the only question with which we have to deal, – What is the proper mode of administering wealth after the laws upon which civilization is founded have thrown it into the hands of the few? And it is of this great question that I believe I offer the true solution. It will be understood that *fortunes* are here spoken of, not moderate sums saved by many years of effort, the returns from which are required for the comfortable maintenance and education of families. This is not *wealth*, but only *competence*, which it should be the aim of all to acquire.

There are but three modes in which surplus wealth can be disposed of. It can be left to the families of the decedents; or it can be bequeathed for public purposes; or, finally, it can be administered during their lives by its possessors. Under the first and second modes most of the wealth of the world that has reached the few has hitherto been applied. Let us in turn consider each of these modes. The first is the most injudicious. In monarchical countries, the estates and the greatest portion of the wealth are left to the first son, that the vanity of the parent may be gratified by the thought that his name and title are to descend to succeeding generations unimpaired. The condition of this class in Europe to-day teaches the futility of such hopes or ambitions. [...] Under republican institutions the division of property among the children is much fairer, but the question which forces itself upon thoughtful men in all lands is: Why should men leave great fortunes to their children? If this is done from affection, is it not misguided affection? Observation teaches that, generally speaking, it is not well for the children that they should be so burdened. Neither is it well for the state. Beyond providing for the wife and daughters moderate sources of income, and very moderate allowances indeed, if any, for the sons, men may well hesitate, for it is no longer questionable that great sums bequeathed oftener work more for the injury than for the good of the recipients. Wise men will soon conclude that, for the best interests of the members of their families and of the state, such bequests are an improper use of their means.

It is not suggested that men who have failed to educate their sons to earn a livelihood shall cast them adrift in poverty. If any man has seen fit to rear his sons with a view to their living idle lives, or, what is highly commendable, has instilled in them the sentiment that they are in a position to labor for public ends without reference to pecuniary considerations, then, of course, the duty of the parent is to see that such are provided for *in moderation*. [...]

As to the second mode, that of leaving wealth at death for public uses, it may be said that this is only a means for the disposal of wealth, provided a man is content to wait until he is dead before it becomes of much good in the world. Knowledge of the results of legacies bequeathed is not calculated to inspire the brightest hopes of much posthumous good being accomplished. The cases are not few in which the real object sought by the testator is not attained, nor are they few in which his real wishes are thwarted. [...]

The growing disposition to tax more and more heavily large estates left at death is a cheering indication of the growth of a salutary change in public opinion. [...] Men who continue hoarding great sums all their lives, the proper use of which for public ends would work good to the community, should be made to feel that the community, in the form of the state, cannot thus be deprived of its proper share. By taxing estates heavily at death the state marks its condemnation of the selfish millionaire's unworthy life.

It is desirable that nations should go much further in this direction. [...] This policy would work powerfully to induce the rich man to attend to the administration of wealth during his life, which is the end that society should always have in view, as being that by far most fruitful for the people. Nor need it be feared that this policy would sap the root of enterprise and render men less anxious to accumulate, for to the class whose ambition it is to leave great fortunes and be talked about after their death, it will attract even more attention, and, indeed, be a somewhat nobler ambition to have enormous sums paid over to the state from their fortunes.

There remains, then, only one mode of using great fortunes; but in this we have the true antidote for the temporary unequal distribution of wealth, the reconciliation of the rich and the poor – a reign of harmony – another ideal, differing, indeed, from that of the Communist in requiring only the further evolution of existing conditions, not the total overthrow of our civilization. It is founded upon the present most intense individualism, and the race is prepared to put it in practice by degrees whenever it pleases. Under its sway we shall have an ideal state, in which the surplus wealth of the few will become, in the best sense, the property of the many, because administered for the common good, and this wealth, passing through the hands of the few, can be made a much more potent force for the elevation of our race than if it had been distributed in small sums to the people themselves. Even the poorest can be made to see this, and to agree that great sums gathered by some of their fellow-citizens and spent for public purposes, from which the masses reap the principal benefit, are more valuable to them than if scattered among them through the course of many years in trifling amounts. [...]

This, then, is held to be the duty of the man of Wealth: First, to set an example of modest, unostentatious living, shunning display or extravagance; to provide moderately for the legitimate wants of those dependent upon him; and after doing so to consider all surplus revenues which come to him simply as trust funds, which he is called upon to administer, and strictly bound as a matter of duty to administer in the manner which, in his judgment, is best calculated to produce the most beneficial results for the community – the man of wealth thus becoming the mere agent and trustee for his poorer brethren, bringing to their service his superior wisdom, experience, and ability to administer, doing for them better than they would or could do for themselves. [...]

The best uses to which surplus wealth can be put have already been indicated. Those who would administer wisely must, indeed, be wise, for one of the serious obstacles to the improvement of our race is indiscriminate charity. It were better for mankind that the millions of the rich were thrown into the sea than so spent as to encourage the slothful,[52] the drunken, the unworthy. Of every thousand dollars spent in so called charity to-day, it is probable that $950 is unwisely spent; so spent, indeed, as to produce the very evils which it proposes to mitigate[53] or cure. A well-known writer of philosophic books admitted the other day that he had given a quarter of a dollar to a man who approached him as he was coming to visit the house of his friend. He knew nothing of the habits of this beggar; knew not the use that would be made of this money, although he had every reason to suspect that it would be spent improperly. This man professed to be a disciple of Herbert Spencer;[54] yet the quarter-dollar given that night will probably work more injury than all the money which its thoughtless donor will ever be able to give in true charity will do good. He only gratified his own feelings, saved himself from annoyance, – and this was probably one of the most selfish and very worst actions of his life, for in all respects he is most worthy.

In bestowing charity, the main consideration should be to help those who will help themselves; to provide part of the means by which those who desire to improve may do so; to give those who desire to rise the aids by which they may rise; to assist, but rarely or never to do all. Neither the individual nor the race is improved by alms-giving. Those worthy of assistance, except in rare cases, seldom require assistance. The really valuable men of the race never do, except in cases of accident or sudden change. [...]

Thus is the problem of Rich and Poor to be solved. The laws of accumulation will be left free; the laws of distribution free. Individualism will continue, but the millionaire will be but a trustee for the poor; intrusted for a season with a great part of the increased wealth of the community, but administering it for the community far better than it could or would have done for itself. The best minds will thus have reached a stage in the development of the race in which it is clearly seen that there is no mode of disposing of surplus wealth creditable to thoughtful and earnest men into whose hands it flows save by using it year by year for the general good. This day already dawns. But a little while, and although, without incurring the pity of their fellows, men may die sharers in great business enterprises from which their capital cannot be or has not been withdrawn, and is left chiefly at death for public uses, yet the man who dies leaving behind him millions of available wealth, which was his to administer during life, will pass away "unwept, unhonored, and unsung," no matter to what uses he leaves the dross which he cannot take with him. Of such as these the public verdict will then be: "The man who dies thus rich dies disgraced."

Such, in my opinion, is the true Gospel concerning Wealth, obedience to which is destined some day to solve the problem of the Rich and the Poor, and to bring "Peace on earth, among men Good-Will." ANDREW CARNEGIE.

Andrew Carnegie (1835-1919). "Wealth." *North American Review* 148.391 (June 1889), 653-664.

---

[52] Full of sloth; indolent, lazy, sluggish.
[53] To alleviate or give relief from pain, suffering, or trouble.
[54] British philosopher (1820-1903), who applied the theory of evolution to ethics and social life.

309. Mary Elizabeth Lease
"Monopoly Is the Master" (1890)

[...] This is a nation of inconsistencies. The Puritans fleeing from oppression became in turn oppressors. We fought England for our liberty and put chains on four millions of blacks. We wiped out slavery and by our tariff laws and national banks began a system of white wage slavery worse than the first. Wall Street owns the country. It is no longer a government of the people, by the people and for the people, but a government of Wall Street, by Wall Street and for Wall Street. The great common people of this country are slaves, and monopoly is the master. The West and South are bound and prostrate before the manufacturing East. Money rules, and our Vice President is a London banker. Our laws are the output of a system which clothes rascals in robes and honesty in rags. The parties lie to us and the political speakers mislead us. [...] Then the politicians said we suffered from over-production. Over-production, when 10,000 little children, so statistics tell us, starve to death every year in the United States, and over 100,000 shop-girls in New York are forced to sell their virtue for the bread their niggardly wages deny them. [...] We will stand by our homes and stay by our fireside by force if necessary, and we will not pay our debts to the loan-shark companies until the Government pays its debts to us. The people are at bay, let the blood-hounds of money who have dogged us thus far beware.

Source: Mary Elizabeth Lease (1850-1933). "Monopoly Is the Master" [1890]. William E. Connelley. *History of Kansas: State and People*. Vol. 2. Chicago and New York: American Historical Society, 1928, 1167.

310. T. McCants Stewart
"Popular Discontent" (1891)

Our ancestors have bequeathed unto us a discontent against certain existing conditions that is growing and spreading like a cloud over this and other lands. It is in the air. Its ominous signs confront us on every hand. It is not local, not transient, not spasmodic, not riotous or disorderly. It is the steady evolution of a great principle, the growth of a great germinal idea, the intelligent protest of a progressive generation, the awakening of nations to the doctrine of human rights. It is a many-millioned cry for justice. That cry is heard across the trampled centuries. It has caught up the voices of the wronged and the oppressed. It swells with the heavings of humanity. It grows and gathers as it comes nearer. [...]

[...] Discontent is dissatisfaction with existing conditions; but whether it be a virtue or an evil depends largely, if not entirely, upon the form in which it manifests itself. A discontent that simply mutters, that exhausts itself in complaints, that carries a knife but no salve, no bandage, that bewails dolefully existing conditions as evil, but suggests no remedial measures and formulates no improvements, is detestable. It is the brand upon the brow of the skulking mutterers that stigmatizes them as possessed of an ulcerous disease which is at best but a compound of the very worst passions – latent pride, disguised envy, malignant hatred. This form of discontent has been the bane[55] of the human race. It threw our archangels out of heaven. It has cursed the world from its earliest existence. It has added nothing to the sum of human endeavor. It is destructive, not constructive [...]. It holds nothing sacred. It respects no rights. It would ruthlessly tear down the family altar,

---

[55] Cause of destruction, deadly poison.

close the Bible, shut up the church, destroy the foundations of government, hold high carnival upon the fragments of the Temple of Justice, and having done all this sit and scream like a flock of unseemly satyrs among grand old immortal ruins. [...]

But there is another form of discontent with existing conditions which is part and parcel of the unfolding plan of the universe itself, and as such it is divine – a discontent that does not mutter, but that protests, agitates, presents remedies and persists until sooner or later it reforms. It is not simply iconoclastic. It is architectural. It constructs. It builds. It develops. It is the pioneer of destiny. [...]

Discontent with existing conditions is a fundamental law of growth in the universe and runs all the way through it from the bottom to the top. It turns the wheel of the globe. It paints the seasons. It lifts the bud and opens the blossom. [...]

[...] All the great inventions that have blessed mankind grew out of a chafing discontent at oppressive conditions. We gaze with wonder at the greatest triumph of engineering skill to be seen anywhere in the world. It hangs over a river and unites two great cities. It is the New York and Brooklyn Bridge. Thousands of tons of iron and steel suspended in the air are held firmly in their place by great cables, held so firmly that the bridge, in its power to stand the ravages of time and the corroding teeth of the elements, is like the everlasting hills which are the work of an Almighty hand. [...]

The history of the world shows that progress follows upon the heels of discontent. Its absence marks the Dark Ages, when the human intellect became enfeebled, religion declined, public and private morals were corrupted, the people were indifferent to popular liberty, and life was cheap. [...]

Periods of discontent there have been, culminating occasions when great leaders sprang out, signal displays of courage, character and eloquence; but, after all, the real working cause is a principle that is never decorated by occasion, but that works steadily on, growing stronger and stronger, and producing all those great results which take place from time to time upon the earth. Whatever has been done in this world has been done by men, struggling, suffering, toiling men – men who, dissatisfied with their condition, rose out of it into a higher one. But often they have had to wade through seas of blood with the lighted torch of despair in their hands, as in the French Revolution. It is for this reason that I beg you to note the discontent that is abroad in our land to-day, and to consider some of the causes of it.

The distribution, not the centralization of power, the health, comfort, occupation and general well-being of the many rather than the few, the co-operation of all men for the interests of each other – this is the great question that is forcing itself more and more seriously at every step into the thoughts of men at this moment. There are many just grounds for this growing discontent. Corporations hold the great trunk lines of transit, as bloated spiders sit in the dark recesses of their webs; cover the life-products of the land and speculate in necessary vital foods that should come directly to the people; tax the masses outrageously in their homes and grind their employees in the mill of starvation wages [...].

The condition of the colored man in the South is a discontented one. Emancipation which made him a citizen, instead of a mere chattel, is fraught necessarily with serious embarrassments to both races dwelling in the Southland. The masses of the colored people are poor and ignorant, but they are aspiring. They find themselves face to face with the problem of hewing their own way to a self-supporting, self-respecting manhood and to an independent citizenship. The emancipation of the race from the trammels[56] of slavery

---

[56] Something that restricts free movement, confinement.

will take time, and those who are responsible for our condition should encourage and help us in our struggles toward a new life. [...]

But there is a problem that is wider than this, and that, in a sense, includes this – it is the problem of industrial slavery. Sixty millions of people in this land cry out in the struggle for existence against oppression. Discontent is brewing into the ferment of aggression. A great people is awakening to the consciousness of its strength; and when it bursts its chains, woe be unto those by whom offenses come! Let us be distinctly understood. We do not overlook the fact that the workingman is to blame for a part of his poverty. Intemperance and the saloon rob him of much of the money that on Saturday night should pass into the pocket of his family. [...] That workingman who saves his money, works steadily, turns his back on the saloon and his face toward God and family, even among discouraging and hard conditions will be apt to prosper.

And yet the masses have just grounds for discontent. We suffer, for example, from oppressive taxation, both local and governmental. [...]

But, connected and correlated with this matter of taxation, there is a deeper source of discontent. It grows out of the antagonisms existing between capital and labor. The tendency of our civilization seems to be toward the creation of a moneyed oligarchy. The standard of measurement in these days is not so much character, is not so much learning – it is wealth. Old Moneybags rules the world and dictates in society, in church, in state. Newly erected palaces rise amidst old dilapidated huts. The rich get richer, and the poor get poorer. The production rather than the distribution of wealth seems to be the product of our industrial machinery. The laboring masses cry for bread while their masters revel in luxury.

To change these extremes of wealth and poverty, to more equitably distribute the profits of toil, is the problem of to-day. Capital, it is true, is an invaluable stimulant of labor, but labor produces capital. One is a natural possession, being co-equal and co-existent with the muscle and the blood. Capital is artificial, being the creature of labor, the surplus not necessary to existence, that which is not needed for sustenance, and which, therefore, may be used to stimulate labor. Labor is superior to capital [...].

There is certainly great cause for discontent, and rich men and poor men alike should thoughtfully ponder the situation before the dark cloud which hangs over our national sky break in torrents of destruction! One thing is sure. The poor are beginning to loudly contend that the evils of our economic condition must be speedily remedied, and that they must be protected in their inalienable rights against the encroachments of soulless monopolies. [... The] well-being and interests of the many, instead of the selfish rapacity of the few, should be the great corner stone of this commonwealth.

I have great hope for the future, because just as nations in the settlement of disputes are turning from war to arbitration, and just as the universal tendency is toward personal liberty, so there are abroad in this land and throughout the world influences which will result in the complete emancipation of labor from the trammels of a past civilization – influences that are rapidly turning away both labor and capital from the brutal force of feudal ages to the calm reason of this enlightened century and the sweet spirit of Christianity. And I rejoice because this is so, because upon this soil dedicated to liberty, consecrated to equal and exact justice among men, there is at least the prospect of a solution of the economic difficulties which have perplexed men in all ages, and which have been sources of discontent in all periods of the world. The peoples of the earth are watching us. Thirsty eyes drink in the vision. [...]

Ladies and gentlemen: If this fight is to be won by us it must be won by our own hands. [...] If the trampled people of this country are to rebuke a tyranny worse than that of the throne, they must do it for themselves. [...]

[...] Let them insist upon equal and exact justice for every man everywhere in this broad land. Let them inquire what is the chief end of human life. Let them learn wisdom. Let them seek to know what are their inalienable rights in every respect and in every direction; and then let them combine and stand together until they enjoy those rights to the fullest extent. [...]

The toiling masses in their struggle against the unsympathetic classes appeal to you, ye men and women of Boston, to be true to your historic past, and to lead them on to the certain victory and complete triumph that awaits them. For the time surely cometh, when, before all the assembled galleries of earth and heaven, the people, taking back the sovereignty of authority and power, shall rise, and, laying hold of the pillars of the Temple of Injustice, they will pull it down and bury forever in its ruins the arrogant usurpers of human rights, with their stolen scepter of authority and their stolen crown of power.

Source: Thomas McCants Stewart (1854?-1923). "Popular Discontent: A Lecture Delivered in Tremont Temple, Boston, Mass., January 2, 1891, for the Benefit of the Wendell Phillips' Hall Association." *African Methodist Episcopal Church Review* 7.4 (April 1891), 357-359, 362-363, 365-366, 368-372.

311. Frederick Saunders / Thomas Bangs Thorpe
The Progress and Prospects of America (1855)

[...] Demagogues enunciate a monstrous proposition in asserting this republic to be one of composite races. It is not. The Republic of the United States is Anglo-Saxon in all its bearings: other peoples may arrive, but they must be gradually absorbed, and, in process of time, become amalgamated with, and lost among, the predominant race. Ethnology and history both assert this fact, and the senseless opponents of it are merely perpetuating the evils of *caste*, in pandering to the prejudices of various nationalities. It is the province and duty of the patriot to discountenance such endeavors. [...]

[...] The foreign voters, who are proved to be *ignorant* and in every way *incompetent*, are admitted to the enjoyment of the electoral franchise.

We, who never knew what a blind and passive obedience to law is, can form no adequate idea of the recklessness and delirium which seize hold of so many foreign immigrants the moment they put foot upon our shores. We admit that some of them are men of intellectual culture, while it will not be denied that too many are persons of the most degraded character, and destitute even of the most meager attainments. The ignorance, however, from which Americans experience the greatest cause for distrust, is that which relates to the nature and spirit of republican institutions. These they do not seem either able or inclined to comprehend. They scout all ideas of obedience, because they claim that here they are free. Liberty and lawlessness are with them one and the same thing. Hitherto, they have never borne any intelligent relation to the existence or execution of law, but have occupied the places of unreflecting persons, accustomed, in passive silence, to bear the burdens with which they were weighed down. Coming to a country like America, and hearing the most exaggerated and extravagant stories of its ample freedom for all men, without a thought of their responsibility to the nation sustaining the fabric of this glorious freedom, they conclude that here the field of license lies open, and that any sort of restraint is powerless and illegal against unbounded indulgence. [...]

[...] The danger to be apprehended from carelessness in this particular, has been foreseen by our best men. The following extract from the writings of Thomas Jefferson, one of the wisest and most farseeing of the great men who have influenced the politics of our country, fully sustains the views here taken of the essential significance of naturalization laws, and of the dangers to our country, from laxity in making or administering them. He says: "But are there no inconveniences to be thrown into the scale against the advantages expected from a multiplication of numbers by the importation of foreigners? It is for the happiness of those united in society to harmonize as much as possible in matters, which they must of necessity transact together. Civil government being the sole object of forming societies, its administration must be conducted by common consent. Every species of government has its specific principles. Ours, perhaps, are more peculiar than those of any other in the universe. It is a composition of the freest principles in the English Constitution, with others derived from natural reason. To these nothing can be more opposed than the maxims of absolute monarchies. Yet from such we are to expect the greatest number of emigrants. They will bring with them the principles of the governments they leave, imbibed in their early youth; or, if able to throw them off, it will be in exchange for an unbounded licentiousness, passing, as is usual, from one extreme to the other. It would be a miracle were they to stop precisely at the point of temperate liberty. These principles, with their language, they will transmit to their children. In proportion to their numbers, they will share with us the legislation. They will infuse into it their spirit, warp and bias its directions, and render it a heterogeneous, incoherent, distracted mass."[57]

Have not these predictions been fulfilled? Have we not already amongst us an Irish nationality, a German nationality, a French nationality, a Dutch nationality, an Italian nationality? Has not our legislation already been "warped and biased" by their influence? Have they not already, to a great extent, "infused their spirit" into it, and are they not trying to make the infusion stronger? [...]

[...] The prospect of future immigration, however, demands some consideration. There seems to be no reason why the exodus from Europe to America should not yet grow and continue. Even if the remainder of the Irish population should stay at home, there are millions and millions on the Continent who will complete the yearly number of immigrants. So far as material interests are concerned, greater and greater inducements are offered by the increasing wealth, enlarged capacity, and demand for labor within our own country. We have abundance of room and of riches. Such inducements have already operated upon so many of the overcrowded and poverty-stricken European nations, that it is quite certain that they will continue to operate. And on the other side of the Atlantic there are not wanting impulses to co-operate with the attractions here. The future of the European nations is stormy and dark. Revolutionary principles are seething under the apparently smooth surface of her political aspect, and before long, despotism, anarchy, and liberty will be struggling together; wars and rebellions exert their disorganizing and unhappy influence, and increasing crowds will flee from the home misery to the foreign peace upon our territory. [...]

[...] Upon our fortunes rests the destiny of the world. Our success and our example are making all peoples restive; our moral strength is more powerful than fleets, more dreaded by tyrants than unnumbered men in arms. We are to conquer, but not by the sword. We are

---

[57] Thomas Jefferson, *Notes on the State of Virginia* (1788), Query 8 on the number of Virginia's inhabitants.

to subjugate, but not by violence. All nations are to come under the sway of our principles, but never are they to pass under any yoke. All is to be freedom and light, and the eye is to see as clearly as at the noonday. Whatever is done, will be done in the direction of a single purpose: and that is, the *emancipation of our race*. We are not working for mere wealth; nor position; nor social consideration; but while laboring for all these, we are insensibly helping on the great cause, and solving the grand problem of a world's freedom.

America – not even yet thinly populated – is the battle-field where the contest is waged between the armies of freedom and tyranny. Every sign points to this imposing fact. Here the last great onset must be made by the phalanxes of darkness, bigotry, illiberality, and bondages of all descriptions; and, under God, if Americans are but true to themselves and their principles, here will occur a glorious victory for freedom and truth – a victory having the regeneration of man for its object, and the happiness of the universe for its result.

[...] It is too important a truth for any of us to overlook, that the American Republic is the home of Liberty, and the final hope of the world. Through the efficacy of her example and her teachings, must redemption finally come. We hold the treasure in our own keeping; we are the trustees of a possession that is to enrich mankind. On our soil dwells that living spirit, which is, in time, to overthrow error, tear away the deceits of usurpation, deprive tyranny of its power, and everywhere animate the human soul with the belief that freedom was coeval with its birth.

Source: Frederick Saunders (1807-1902) and Thomas Bangs Thorpe (1815-1878). *The Progress and Prospects of America* [1855]. Quoted in: *Major Problems in American Immigration and Ethnic History: Documents and Essays*. Ed. Jon Gjerde. Boston and New York: Houghton Mifflin, 1998, 141-144.

312. Thomas Nast
"Uncle Sam's Thanksgiving Dinner" (1869)

Source: Thomas Nast (1840-1902). "Uncle Sam's Thanksgiving Dinner." *Harper's Weekly* 13 (November 20, 1869), 746.

313. *Chinese Exclusion Act* (1882)

Preamble.
Whereas, in the opinion of the Government of the United States the coming of Chinese laborers to this country endangers the good order of certain localities within the territory thereof: Therefore,

Be it enacted, That from and after the expiration of ninety days next after the passage of this act, and until the expiration of ten years next after the passage of this act, the coming of Chinese laborers to the United States be [...] suspended; and during such suspension it shall not be lawful for any Chinese laborer to come, or, having so come after the expiration of said ninety days, to remain within the United States.

SEC. 2. That the master of any vessel who shall knowingly bring within the United States on such vessel, and land or permit to be landed, any Chinese laborer, from any foreign port of place, shall be deemed guilty of a misdemeanor, and on conviction thereof shall be punished by a fine of not more than five hundred dollars for each and every such Chinese laborer so brought, and may be also imprisoned for a term not exceeding one year.

SEC. 3. That the two foregoing sections shall not apply to Chinese laborers who were in the United States on the seventeenth day of November, eighteen hundred and eighty [...].

SEC. 12. That no Chinese person shall be permitted to enter the United States by land without producing to the proper officer of customs the certificate in this act required of Chinese persons seeking to land from a vessel. And any Chinese person found unlawfully within the United States shall be caused to be removed therefrom to the country from whence he came, by direction of the President of the United States, and at the cost of the United States, after being brought before some justice, judge, or commissioner of a court of the United States and found to be one not lawfully entitled to be or remain in the United States. [...]

Source: *An Act to Execute Certain Treaty Stipulations Relating to Chinese* (Forty-Seventh Congress. Session I. 1882 – Chapter 126). *Documents of American History.* Ed. Henry Steele Commager. 2 vols. New York: Appleton – Century – Crofts, ⁷1963, Vol. 1, 560-561.

314. Emma Lazarus
"The New Colossus" (1883)

Not like the brazen giant of Greek fame,
With conquering limbs astride from land to land,
Here at our sea-washed, sunset gates shall stand
A mighty woman, with a torch, whose flame
Is the imprisoned lightning, and her name
Mother of Exiles. From her beacon-hand
Glows world-wide welcome; her mild eyes command
The air-bridged harbor that twin-cities frame.

"Keep, ancient lands, your storied pomp!" cries she,
With silent lips. "Give me your tired, your poor,
Your huddled masses, yearning to breathe free;

The wretched refuse of your teeming shore –
Send these, the homeless, tempest-tost to me –
I lift my lamp beside the golden door!"

Source: Emma Lazarus (1849-1887). "The New Colossus." *Catalogue of the Pedestal Fund Art Loan Exhibition at the National Academy of Design, 23rd Street and Fourth Avenue.* New York: The Academy, 1883, n.p.

315. Josiah Strong
"Perils – Immigration" (1885)

Political optimism is one of the vices of the American people. There is a popular faith that "God takes care of children, fools, and the United States." We deem ourselves a chosen people, and incline to the belief that the Almighty stands pledged to our prosperity. Probably not one in a hundred of our population has ever questioned the security of our future. Such optimism is as senseless as pessimism is faithless. The one is as foolish as the other is wicked.

Thoughtful men see perils on our national horizon. [...] America, as the land of promise to all the world, is the destination of the most remarkable migration of which we have any record. During the last four years we have suffered a peaceful invasion by an army more than twice as vast as the estimated number of Goths and Vandals that swept over Southern Europe and overwhelmed Rome. During the ninety years preceding 1880, ten million foreigners made their homes in the United States, and three-quarters of them came during the last third of that period. Not only are they coming in great numbers, but in numbers rapidly increasing. [...]

In view of the fact that Europe is able to send us nearly nine times as many immigrants during the next thirty years as during the thirty years past, without any diminution of her population, and in view of all the powerful influences co-operating to stimulate the movement, is it not reasonable to conclude that we have seen only the advance guard of the mighty army which is moving upon us?

The Tenth Census gives our total foreign-born population as 6,679,943; but we must not forget their children of the first generation, who, as we shall see, present a more serious problem than their parents, the immigrants. [...] And if the proportion of foreign-born to native-born of foreign parentage continues the same, our foreign population in 1900 will be 43,000,000. So immense a foreign element must have a profound influence on our national life and character. [...]

Consider briefly the moral and political influence of immigration. 1. Influence on morals. Let me hasten to recognize the high worth of many of our citizens of foreign birth, not a few of whom are eminent in the pulpit and in all the learned professions. Many come to us in full sympathy with our free institutions, and desiring to aid us in promoting a Christian civilization. But no one knows better than these same intelligent and Christian foreigners that they do not represent the mass of immigrants. The typical immigrant is a European peasant, whose horizon has been narrow, whose moral and religious training has been meager or false, and whose ideas of life are low. Not a few belong to the pauper and criminal classes. [...] Moreover, immigration is demoralizing. No man is held upright simply by the strength of his own roots; his branches interlock with those of other men, and thus society is formed, with all its laws and customs and force of public opinion. [...]

All this strength the emigrant leaves behind him. He is isolated in a strange land, perhaps doubly so by reason of a strange speech. He is transplanted from a forest to an open prairie, where, before he is rooted, he is smitten with the blasts of temptation.

We have a good deal of piety in our churches that will not bear transportation. [...] Very many church-members, when they go west, seem to think they have left their Christian obligations with their church-membership in the East. And a considerable element of our American-born population are apparently under the impression that the Ten Commandments are not binding west of the Missouri. Is it strange, then, that those who come from other lands, whose old associations are all broken and whose reputations are left behind, should sink to a lower moral level? Across the sea they suffered many restraints which are here removed. Better wages afford larger means of self-indulgence; often the back is not strong enough to bear prosperity, and liberty too often lapses into license. Our population of foreign extraction is sadly conspicuous in our criminal records. This element constituted in 1870 twenty per cent. of the population of New England, and furnished seventy-five per cent. of the crime. That is, it was twelve times as much disposed to crime as the native stock. The hoodlums and roughs of our cities are, most of them, American-born of foreign parentage. [...]

Moreover, immigration not only furnishes the greater portion of our criminals, it is also seriously affecting the morals of the native population. It is disease and not health which is contagious. Most foreigners bring with them continental ideas of the Sabbath, and the result is sadly manifest in all our cities, where it is being transformed from a holy day into a holiday. But by far the most effective instrumentality for debauching popular morals is the liquor traffic, and this is chiefly carried on by foreigners.

2. We can only glance at the political aspects of immigration. As we have already seen, it is immigration which has fed fat the liquor power; and there is a liquor vote. Immigration furnishes most of the victims of Mormonism; and there is a Mormon vote. Immigration is the strength of the Catholic church; and there is a Catholic vote. Immigration is the mother and nurse of American socialism; and there is to be a socialist vote. Immigration tends strongly to the cities, and gives to them their political complexion. And there is no more serious menace to our civilization than our rabble-ruled cities. [...]

Many American citizens are not Americanized. It is as unfortunate as it is natural, that foreigners in this country should cherish their own language and peculiar customs, and carry their nationality, as a distinct factor, into our politics. [...] A mass of men but little acquainted with our institutions, who will act in concert and who are controlled largely by their appetites and prejudices, constitute a very paradise for demagogues.

We have seen that immigration is detrimental to popular morals. It has a like influence upon popular intelligence, for the percentage of illiteracy among the foreign-born population is thirty-eight per cent. greater than among the native-born whites. Thus immigration complicates our moral and political problems by swelling our dangerous classes. And as immigration is to increase much more rapidly than the population, we may infer that the dangerous classes are to increase more rapidly than hitherto.[58] It goes without saying, that there is a dead-line of ignorance and vice in every republic, and when it is touched by the average citizen, free institutions perish; for intelligence and virtue are as essential to the life of a republic as are brain and heart to the life of a man. [...]

---

[58] Original footnote: "From 1870 to 1880 the population increased 30.06 per cent. During the same period the number of criminals increased 82.33 per cent."

Source: Josiah Strong (1847-1916). "Perils – Immigration." *Our Country: Its Possible Future and Its Present Crisis*. New York: Baker and Taylor, 1885, 30, 39-44.

316. *The Magic Washer – The Chinese Must Go* (c. 1886)

Source: *The Magic Washer – The Chinese Must Go.* (c. 1886). Courtesy Library of Congress.

317. Carl Schurz
"Manifest Destiny" (1893)

Whenever there is a project on foot to annex foreign territory to this republic the cry of "manifest destiny" is raised to produce the impression that all opposition to such a project is a struggle against fate. Forty years ago this cry had a peculiar significance. The slave-holders saw in the rapid growth of the free States a menace to the existence of slavery. In order to strengthen themselves in Congress they needed more slave States, and looked therefore to the acquisition of foreign territory on which slavery existed – in the first place, the island of Cuba. Thus to the pro-slavery man "manifest destiny" meant an increase of the number of slave States by annexation. There was still another force behind the demand for territorial expansion. It consisted in the youthful optimism at that time still inspiring the minds of many Americans with the idea that this republic, being charged with the mission of bearing the banner of freedom over the whole civilized world, could transform any country, inhabited by any kind of population, into something like itself simply by extending over it the magic charm of its political institutions. [...]

The civil war weakened the demand for territorial expansion in two ways. With the abolition of slavery the powerful interest which had stood behind the annexation policy disappeared forever. [...] The troubles and perplexities left behind by the civil war sobered the minds of the most sanguine. A healthy scepticism took the place of youthful over-confidence. It stimulated earnest inquiry into existing conditions, and brought forth a strong feeling among our people that we should rather make sure of what we had, and improve it, than throw our energies into fanciful foreign ventures. [...]

The recent attempt made by President Harrison to precipitate the Hawaiian Islands into our Union[59] has again stirred up the public interest in the matter of territorial expansion, and called forth the cry of "manifest destiny" once more. [...]

The new "manifest-destiny" precept means, in point of principle, not merely the incorporation in the United States of territory contiguous to our borders, but rather the acquisition of such territory, far and near, as may be useful in enlarging our commercial advantages, and in securing to our navy facilities desirable for the operations of a great naval power. Aside from the partisan declaimers whose interest in the matter is only that of political effect, this policy finds favor with several not numerically strong but very demonstrative classes of people – Americans who have business ventures in foreign lands, or who wish to embark in such; citizens of an ardent national ambition who think that the conservative traditions of our foreign policy are out of date, and that it is time for the United States to take an active part and to assert their power in the international politics of the world, and to this end to avail themselves of every chance for territorial aggrandizement; and lastly, what may be called the navy interest – officers of the navy and others taking especial pride in the development of our naval force, many of whom advocate a large increase of our war-fleet to support a vigorous foreign policy, and a vigorous foreign policy to give congenial occupation and to secure further increase to our war-fleet. These forces we find bent upon exciting the ambition of the American people whenever a chance for the acquisition of foreign territory heaves in sight. [...]

---

[59] At the end of his administration, Benjamin Harrison (1833-1901), 23rd President of the US (1889-1893), submitted to the Senate a treaty to annex Hawaii. This treaty was never signed, however, as President Cleveland, his successor, withdrew it. Hawaii did not become a state until 1959.

The patriotic ardor of those who would urge this republic into the course of indiscriminate territorial aggrandizement to make it the greatest of the great powers of the world deserves more serious consideration. To see his country powerful and respected among the nations of the earth, and to secure to it all those advantages to which its character and position entitle it, is the natural desire of every American. In this sentiment we are all agreed. There may, however, be grave differences of opinion, as to how this end can be most surely, most completely, and most worthily attained. This is not a mere matter of patriotic sentiment, but a problem of statesmanship. No conscientious citizen will think a moment of incorporating a single square mile of foreign soil in this Union without most earnestly considering how it will be likely to affect our social and political condition at home as well as our relations with the world abroad. [...]

If the people of Canada should some day express a desire to be incorporated in this Union, there would, as to the character of the country and of the people, be no reasonable doubt of the fitness, or even the desirability, of the association. Their country has those attributes of soil and climate which are most apt to stimulate and keep steadily at work all the energies of human nature. The people are substantially of the same stock as ours, and akin to us in their traditions, their notions of law and morals, their interests and habits of life. They are accustomed to the peaceable and orderly practices of self-government. They would mingle and become one with our people without difficulty. The new States brought by them into the Union would soon be hardly distinguishable from the old in any point of importance. Their accession would make our national household larger, but it would not seriously change its character. It might take place – and, in fact, it should take place only in that way – as a result of a feeling common to both sides that the two countries and peoples naturally belong together in their sympathies as well as their interests. Nor would the union of the two countries excite among us any ambition of further aggrandizement in the same direction, for the acquisition of the Canadian Dominion would give to the United States the whole of the northern part of the continent.

Very unlike would be the situation produced by the acquisition of territory to the south of us. In the first place, it would spring from motives of a different kind – not the feeling of naturally belonging together, but the desire on our part to gain certain commercial advantages; to get possession of the resources of other countries, and by exploiting them to increase our wealth; to occupy certain strategical positions which in case of war might be of importance, and so on. It is evident that if we once are fairly started in the annexation policy for such purposes, the appetite will grow with the eating. There will always be more commercial advantages to be gained, the riches of more countries to be made our own, more strategical positions to be occupied to protect those already in our hands. Not only a taste for more, but interest, the logic of the situation, would push us on and on.

The consequences which inevitably would follow the acquisition of Cuba, which is especially alluring to the annexationist, may serve as an example. Cuba, so they tell us, possesses rich natural resources worth having. It is in the hands of a European power that may, under certain circumstances, become hostile to us. It is only a few miles from the coast of Florida. It "threatens" that coast. It "commands" also the Gulf of Mexico, with the mouths of the Mississippi and the Caribbean Sea. Its population is discontented; it wishes to cut loose from Spain and join us. If we do not take Cuba "some other power will take it." That power may be hostile. Let us take it ourselves. What then? Santo Domingo is only a few miles distant from Cuba; also a country of rich resources; other powers several times tried to get it; if in the hands of a hostile power it would "threaten" Cuba; it also "commands" the Caribbean Sea; the Dominican Republic, occupying the larger part of the island, offered to join us once, and will wish to do so again; to acquire the Haitian Republic we shall have to fight; it will cost men and money, but we can easily beat the negroes. We must have Santo Domingo. Puerto Rico will come as a matter of course with Cuba. [...]

Imagine now fifteen or twenty, or even more, States inhabited by a people so utterly different from ours in origin, in customs and habits, in traditions, language, morals, impulses, ways of thinking – in almost everything that constitutes social and political life – and these people remaining under the climatic influences which in a great measure have made them what they are, and render an essential change of their character impossible – imagine a large number of such States to form part of this Union, and through dozens of Senators and scores of Representatives in Congress, and millions of votes in our Presidential elections, to participate in making our laws, in filling the executive places of our government, and in impressing themselves upon the spirit of our political life. The mere statement of the case is sufficient to show that the incorporation of the American tropics in our national system would essentially transform the constituency of our government, and be fraught with incalculable dangers to the vitality of our democratic institutions. Many of our fellow-citizens are greatly disturbed by the immigration into this country of a few hundred thousand Italians, Slavs, and Hungarians. But if these few hundred thousand cause apprehension as to the future of the republic, although under the inspiring influence of active American life in our bracing climate the descendants of the most ignorant of them in the second or third generation are likely to be Americanized to the point of being hardly distinguishable from other Americans in the same social sphere, what should we fear from the admission to full political fellowship of many millions of the inhabitants of the tropics whom under the influence of their climatic condition the process of true Americanization can never reach? [...]

The fate of the American people is in their own wisdom and will. If they devote their energies to the development of what they possess within their present limits, and look for territorial expansion only to the north, where some day a kindred people may freely elect to cast their lot with this republic, their "manifest destiny" will be the preservation of the exceptional and invaluable advantages they now enjoy, and the growth on a congenial soil of a vigorous nationality in freedom, prosperity, and power. If they yield to the allurements of the tropics and embark in a career of indiscriminate aggrandizement, their "manifest destiny" points with equal certainty to a total abandonment of their conservative traditions of policy, to a rapid deterioration in the character of the people and their political institutions, and to a future of turbulence, demoralization, and final decay.

Source: Carl Schurz (1829-1906). "Manifest Destiny." *Harper's New Monthly Magazine* 87.521 (October 1893). 737-740, 742, 746.

318. Josiah Strong
"The Anglo-Saxon and the World's Future" (1885)

[...] It seems to me that God, with infinite wisdom and skill, is training the Anglo-Saxon race for an hour sure to come in the world's future. Heretofore there has always been in the history of the world a comparatively unoccupied land westward, into which the crowded countries of the East have poured their surplus populations. But the widening waves of migration, which millenniums ago rolled east and west from the valley of the Euphrates, meet to-day on our Pacific coast. There are no more new worlds. The unoccupied arable lands of the earth are limited, and will soon be taken. The time is coming when the pressure of population on the means of subsistence will be felt here as it is now felt in Europe and Asia. Then will the world enter upon a new stage of its history – *the final competition of races, for which the Anglo-Saxon is being schooled*. Long before the thousand millions are here, the mighty *centrifugal* tendency, inherent in this stock and strengthened in the United States, will assert itself. Then this race of unequaled energy, with all the majesty of numbers and the might of wealth behind it – the representative, let us hope, of the largest liberty, the purest Christianity, the highest civilization – having developed peculiarly aggressive traits calculated to impress its institutions upon mankind, will spread itself over the earth. If I read not amiss, this powerful race will move down upon Mexico, down upon Central and South America, out upon the islands of the sea, over upon Africa and beyond. And can any one doubt that the result of this competition of races will be the "survival of the fittest"? "Any people," says Dr. Bushnell,[60] "that is physiologically advanced in culture, though it be only in a degree beyond another which is mingled with it on strictly equal terms, is sure to live down and finally live out its inferior. Nothing can save the inferior race but a ready and pliant[61] assimilation. Whether the feebler and more abject races are going to be regenerated and raised up, is already very much of a question. What if it should be God's plan to people the world with better and finer material? Certain it is, whatever expectations we may indulge, that there is a tremendous overbearing surge of power in the Christian nations, which, if the others are not speedily raised to some vastly higher capacity, will inevitably submerge and bury them forever. These great populations of Christendom – what are they doing, but throwing out their colonies on every side, and populating themselves, if I may so speak, into the possession of all countries and climes?" To this result no war of extermination is needful; the contest is not one of arms, but of vitality and of civilization. "At the present day," says Mr. Darwin, "civilized nations are everywhere supplanting barbarous nations, excepting where the climate opposes a deadly barrier; and they succeed mainly, though not exclusively, through their arts, which are the products of the intellect?" Thus the Finns were supplanted by the Aryan races in Europe and Asia, the Tartars by the Russians, and thus the aborigines of North America, Australia and New Zealand are now disappearing before the all-conquering Anglo-Saxons. It would seem as if these inferior tribes were only precursors of a superior race [...]. [...] Every civilization has its destructive and preservative elements. The Anglo-Saxon race would speedily decay but for the salt of Christianity. Bring savages into contact with our civilization, and its destructive

---

[60] Horace Bushnell (1802-1876), called for Christianity to make ample use of the "dawning" scientific age created by Charles Darwin's (1809-1882) *Origin of Species* (1859).
[61] Compliant; accommodating.

forces become operative at once, while years are necessary to render effective the saving influences of Christian instruction. Moreover, the pioneer wave of our civilization carries with it more scum than salt. Where there is one missionary, there are hundreds of miners or traders or adventurers ready to debauch the native. Whether the extinction of inferior races before the advancing Anglo-Saxon seems to the reader sad or otherwise, it certainly appears probable. I know of nothing except climatic conditions to prevent this race from populating Africa as it has peopled North America. And those portions of Africa which are unfavorable to Anglo-Saxon life are less extensive than was once supposed. The Dutch Boers, after two centuries of life there, are as hardy as any race on earth. The Anglo-Saxon has established himself in climates totally diverse – Canada, South Africa, and India – and, through several generations, has preserved his essential race characteristics. He is not, of course, superior to climatic influences; but, even in warm climates, he is likely to retain his aggressive vigor long enough to supplant races already enfeebled. Thus, in what Dr. Bushnell calls "the out-populating power of the Christian stock," may be found God's final and complete solution of the dark problem of heathenism among many inferior peoples.

[...] Thus, while on this continent God is training the Anglo-Saxon race for its mission, a complemental work has been in progress in the great world beyond. God has two hands. Not only is he preparing in our civilization the die with which to stamp the nations, but, by what Southey[62] called the "timing of Providence," he is preparing mankind to receive our impress. [...]

Source: Josiah Strong (1847-1916). "The Anglo-Saxon and the World's Future." *Our Country: Its Possible Future and Its Present Crisis*. New York: Baker & Taylor, 1885, 174-178.

319. Albert Beveridge
"The March of the Flag" (1898)

It is a noble land that God has given us; a land that can feed and clothe the world; a land whose coastlines would inclose half the countries of Europe; a land set like a sentinel between the two imperial oceans of the globe, a greater England with a nobler destiny.

It is a mighty people that He has planted on this soil; a people sprung from the most masterful blood of history; a people perpetually revitalized by the virile, man-producing working-folk of all the earth; a people imperial by virtue of their power, by right of their institutions, by authority of their Heaven-directed purposes – the propagandists and not the misers of liberty.

It is a glorious history our God has bestowed upon His chosen people; a history heroic with faith in our mission and our future; a history of statesmen who flung the boundaries of the Republic out into unexplored lands and savage wilderness; a history of soldiers who carried the flag across blazing deserts and through the ranks of hostile mountains, even to the gates of sunset; a history of a multiplying people who overran a continent in half a century; a history of prophets who saw the consequences of evils inherited from the past and of martyrs who died to save us from them; a history divinely logical, in the process of whose tremendous reasoning we find ourselves to-day.

---

[62] Robert Southey (1774-1843), British writer.

Therefore, in this campaign, the question is larger than a party question. It is an American question. It is a world question. Shall the American people continue their march toward the commercial supremacy of the world? Shall free institutions broaden their blessed reign as the children of liberty wax in strength, until the empire of our principles is established over the hearts of all mankind?

Have we no mission to perform, no duty to discharge to our fellow-man? Has God endowed us with gifts beyond our deserts and marked us as the people of His peculiar favor, merely to rot in our own selfishness, as men and nations must, who take cowardice for their companion and self for their deity – as China has, as India has, as Egypt has?

Shall we be as the man who had one talent and hid it, or as he who had ten talents and used them until they grew to riches? And shall we reap the reward that waits on our discharge of our high duty; shall we occupy new markets for what our farmers raise, our factories make, our merchants sell – aye, and, please God, new markets for what our ships shall carry?

Hawaii is ours; Porto Rico is to be ours; at the prayer of her people Cuba finally will be ours; in the islands of the East, even to the gates of Asia, coaling stations are to be ours at the very least; the flag of a liberal government is to float over the Philippines, and may it be the banner that Taylor unfurled in Texas and Fremont carried to the coast.[63]

The Opposition tells us that we ought not to govern a people without their consent. I answer, The rule of liberty that all just government derives its authority from the consent of the governed, applies only to those who are capable of self-government. We govern the Indians without their consent, we govern our territories without their consent, we govern our children without their consent. How do they know that our government would be without their consent? Would not the people of the Philippines prefer the just, humane, civilizing government of this Republic to the savage, bloody rule of pillage and extortion from which we have rescued them?

And, regardless of this formula of words made only for enlightened, self-governing people, do we owe no duty to the world? Shall we turn these peoples back to the reeking hands from which we have taken them? Shall we abandon them, with Germany, England, Japan, hungering for them? [...]

Will you say by your vote that American ability to govern has decayed; that a century's experience in self-rule has failed of a result? Will you affirm by your vote that you are an infidel to American power and practical sense? [...] Will you remember that we do but what our fathers did – we but pitch the tents of liberty farther westward, farther southward – we only continue the march of the flag?

The march of the flag! In 1789 the flag of the Republic waved over 4,000,000 souls in thirteen states, and their savage territory which stretched to the Mississippi, to Canada, to the Floridas. The timid minds of that day said that no new territory was needed, and, for the hour, they were right. But Jefferson, through whose intellect the centuries marched; Jefferson, who dreamed of Cuba as an American state; Jefferson, the first Imperialist of the Republic – Jefferson acquired that imperial territory which swept from the Mississippi to the mountains, from Texas to the British possessions, and the march of the flag began!

The infidels to the gospel of liberty raved, but the flag swept on! The title to that noble land out of which Oregon, Washington, Idaho and Montana[64] have been carved was

---

[63] References to Zachary Taylor (1784-1850), 12th President of the US (1849-1850), who became a national hero during the Mexican War, also called "Old Rough and Ready," as well as to John Charles Frémont (1813-1890), American soldier and politician who explored the American West.
[64] These states were admitted to the US in 1859 (Oregon), 1889 (Washington and Montana), 1890 (Idaho).

uncertain; Jefferson, strict constructionist of constitutional power though he was, obeyed the Anglo-Saxon impulse within him, whose watchword then and whose watchword throughout the world to-day is, "Forward!": another empire was added to the Republic, and the march of the flag went on!

Those who deny the power of free institutions to expand urged every argument, and more, that we hear, to-day; but the people's judgment approved the command of their blood, and the march of the flag went on!

A screen of land from New Orleans to Florida shut us from the Gulf, and over this and the Everglade Peninsula waved the saffron flag of Spain; Andrew Jackson seized both, the American people stood at his back, and, under Monroe, the Floridas came under the dominion of the Republic, and the march of the flag went on! The Cassandras prophesied every prophecy of despair we hear, to-day, but the march of the flag went on!

Then Texas responded to the bugle calls of liberty, and the march of the flag went on! And, at last, we waged war with Mexico, and the flag swept over the southwest, over peerless California, past the Gate of Gold to Oregon on the north, and from ocean to ocean its folds of glory blazed.

And, now, obeying the same voice that Jefferson heard and obeyed, that Jackson heard and obeyed, that Monroe heard and obeyed, [...] our President to-day plants the flag over the islands of the seas, outposts of commerce, citadels of national security, and the march of the flag goes on!

Distance and oceans are no arguments. The fact that all the territory our fathers bought and seized is contiguous,[65] is no argument. In 1819 Florida was farther from New York than Porto Rico is from Chicago to-day; Texas, farther from Washington in 1845 than Hawaii is from Boston in 1898; California, more inaccessible in 1847 than the Philippines are now. Gibraltar is farther from London than Havana is from Washington; Melbourne is farther from Liverpool than Manila is from San Francisco.

The ocean does not separate us from lands of our duty and desire – the oceans join us, rivers never to be dredged, canals never to be repaired. Steam joins us; electricity joins us – the very elements are in league with our destiny. Cuba not contiguous! Porto Rico not contiguous! Hawaii and the Philippines not contiguous! The oceans make them contiguous. And our navy will make them contiguous.

But the Opposition is right – there is a difference. We did not need the western Mississippi Valley when we acquired it, nor Florida, nor Texas, nor California, nor the royal provinces of the far northwest. We had no emigrants to people this imperial wilderness, no money to develop it, even no highways to cover it. No trade awaited us in its savage fastnesses. Our productions were not greater than our trade. There was not one reason for the land-lust of our statesmen from Jefferson to Grant,[66] other than the prophet and the Saxon within them. But, to-day, we are raising more than we can consume, making more than we can use. Therefore we must find new markets for our produce.

And so, while we did not need the territory taken during the past century at the time it was acquired, we do need what we have taken in 1898, and we need it now. The resources and the commerce of these immensely rich dominions will be increased as much as American energy is greater than Spanish sloth. In Cuba, alone, there are 15,000,000 acres of forest unacquainted with the ax, exhaustless mines of iron, priceless deposits of

---

[65] Touching, in actual contact, next in space.
[66] Ulysses Simpson Grant (1822-1885), 18th President of the US (1869-1877) and a Civil War general.

manganese, millions of dollars' worth of which we must buy, to-day, from the Black Sea districts. There are millions of acres yet unexplored.

The resources of Porto Rico have only been trifled with. The riches of the Philippines have hardly been touched by the finger-tips of modern methods. [...]

The commercial supremacy of the Republic means that this Nation is to be the sovereign factor in the peace of the world. For the conflicts of the future are to be conflicts of trade – struggles for markets – commercial wars for existence. And the golden rule of peace is impregnability of position and invincibility of preparedness. So, we see England, the greatest strategist of history, plant her flag and her cannon on Gibraltar, at Quebec, in the Bermudas, at Vancouver, everywhere. [...]

There are so many real things to be done – canals to be dug, railways to be laid, forests to be felled, cities to be built, fields to be tilled, markets to be won, ships to be launched, peoples to be saved, civilization to be proclaimed and the flag of liberty flung to the eager air of every sea. Is this an hour to waste upon triflers with nature's laws? Is this a season to give our destiny over to word-mongers and prosperity-wreckers? No! It is an hour to remember our duty to our homes. It is a moment to realize the opportunities fate has opened to us. And so it is an hour for us to stand by the Government.

Wonderfully has God guided us. Yonder at Bunker Hill and Yorktown[67] His providence was above us. At New Orleans and on ensanguined seas His hand sustained us. Abraham Lincoln was His minister and His was the altar of freedom the Nation's soldiers set up on a hundred battle-fields. His power directed Dewey[68] in the East and delivered the Spanish fleet into our hands, as He delivered the elder Armada into the hands of our English sires two centuries ago. The American people can not use a dishonest medium of exchange; it is ours to set the world its example of right and honor. We can not fly from our world duties; it is ours to execute the purpose of a fate that has driven us to be greater than our small intentions. We can not retreat from any soil where Providence has unfurled our banner; it is ours to save that soil for liberty and civilization.

Source: Albert Jeremiah Beveridge (1862-1927). "The March of the Flag" [1898]. *The Meaning of the Times, and Other Speeches*. Indianapolis: Bobbs-Merrill, 1908, 47-54, 56-57.

320. William Jennings Bryan "Imperialism" (1900)

Mr. Chairman and Members of the Notification Committee:

I shall, at an early day, and in a more formal manner, accept the nomination which you tender, and I shall at that time discuss the various questions covered by the Democratic platform. It may not be out of place, however, to submit a few observations at this time upon the general character of the contest before us and upon the question which is declared to be of paramount importance in this campaign.

When I say that the contest of 1900 is a contest between Democracy on the one hand and plutocracy on the other I do not mean to say that all our opponents have deliberately

---

[67] Reference to famous battles of the Revolutionary War.
[68] Admiral George Dewey (1837-1917), defeated the Spanish fleet in Manila Bay on May 1, 1898.

chosen to give to organized wealth a predominating influence in the affairs of the Government, but I do assert that on the important issues of the day the Republican party is dominated by those influences which constantly tend to substitute the worship of mammon for the protection of the rights of man. [...]

Even now we are beginning to see the paralyzing influence of imperialism. Heretofore this nation has been prompt to express its sympathy with those who were fighting for civil liberty. While our sphere of activity has been limited to the Western Hemisphere, our sympathies have not been bounded by the seas. We have felt it due to ourselves and to the world, as well as to those who were struggling for the right to govern themselves, to proclaim the interest which our people have, from the date of their own independence, felt in every contest between human rights and arbitrary power. [...]

Our opponents, conscious of the weakness of their cause, seek to confuse imperialism with expansion, and have even dared to claim Jefferson as a supporter of their policy. Jefferson spoke so freely and used language with such precision that no one can be ignorant of his views. On one occasion he declared: "If there be one principle more deeply rooted than any other in the mind of every American, it is that we should have nothing to do with conquest."[69] And again he said: "Conquest is not in our principles; it is inconsistent with our government."[70]

The forcible annexation of territory to be governed by arbitrary power differs as much from the acquisition of territory to be built up into states as a monarchy differs from a democracy. The Democratic party does not oppose expansion when expansion enlarges the area of the Republic and incorporates land which can be settled by American citizens, or adds to our population people who are willing to become citizens and are capable of discharging their duties as such.

The acquisition of the Louisiana territory, Florida, Texas and other tracts which have been secured from time to time enlarged the Republic and the Constitution followed the flag into the new territory. It is now proposed to seize upon distant territory already more densely populated than our own country and to force upon the people a government for which there is no warrant in our Constitution or our laws. [...]

What is our title to the Philippine Islands? Do we hold them by treaty or by conquest? Did we buy them or did we take them? [...]

We could extinguish Spain's title by treaty, but if we hold title we must hold it by some method consistent with our ideas of government. When we made allies of the Filipinos and armed them to fight against Spain, we disputed Spain's title. If we buy Spain's title we are not innocent purchasers.

There can be no doubt that we accepted and utilized the services of the Filipinos, and that when we did so we had full knowledge that they were fighting for their own independence, and I submit that history furnishes no example of turpitude[71] baser than ours if we now substitute our yoke for the Spanish yoke. [...]

When our opponents are unable to defend their position by argument they fall back upon the assertion that it is destiny, and insist that we must submit to it, no matter how much it violates our moral precepts and our principles of government. This is a compla-

---

[69] Quotes in "Jefferson to William Short, 1791," cf. *The Writings of Thomas Jefferson*. Ed. Paul Leicester Ford. New York: Putnam, 1892, Vol. 5, 364.
[70] Jefferson, "Instructions to William Carmichael, 1790," cf. *The Writings of Thomas Jefferson*. Ed. Paul Leicester Ford. New York: Putnam, 1892, Vol. 5, 230.
[71] Baseness, depravity, wickedness.

cent philosophy. It obliterates the distinction between right and wrong and makes individuals and nations the helpless victims of circumstance.

Destiny is the subterfuge of the invertebrate, who, lacking the courage to oppose error, seeks some plausible excuse for supporting it. [...]

I can conceive of a national destiny surpassing the glories of the present and the past – a destiny which meets the responsibilities of today and measures up to the possibilities of the future. Behold a republic, resting securely upon the foundation stones quarried by revolutionary patriots from the mountain of eternal truth – a republic applying in practice and proclaiming to the world the self-evident proposition that all men are created equal; that they are endowed with inalienable rights; that governments are instituted among men to secure these rights, and that governments derive their just powers from the consent of the governed. Behold a republic in which civil and religious liberty stimulate all to earnest endeavor and in which the law restrains every hand uplifted for a neighbor's injury – a republic in which every citizen is a sovereign, but in which no one cares to wear a crown. Behold a republic standing erect while empires all around are bowed beneath the weight of their own armaments – a republic whose flag is loved while other flags are only feared. Behold a republic increasing in population, in wealth, in strength, and in influence, solving the problems of civilization and hastening the coming of an universal brotherhood – a republic which shakes thrones and dissolves aristocracies by its silent example and gives light and inspiration to those who sit in darkness. Behold a republic gradually but surely becoming a supreme moral factor in the world's progress and the accepted arbiter of the world's disputes – a republic whose history, like the path of the just, "is as the shining light that shineth more and more unto the perfect day."[72]

Source: William Jennings Bryan (1860-1925). "Imperialism; Being the Speech of Hon. William Jennings Bryan in Response to the Committee Appointed to Notify Him of His Nomination to the Presidency of the United States, Delivered at Indianapolis, August 8, 1900." William Jennings Bryan. *Bryan on Imperialism; Speeches, Newspaper Articles and Interviews*. Chicago: Bentley & Co., 1900, 69, 74-76, 80, 90-92.

321. Theodore Roosevelt "Fourth Annual Message, December 6, 1904"

[Policy Toward Other Nations of the Western Hemisphere][73]

[...] It is not true that the United States feels any land hunger or entertains any projects as regards the other nations of the Western Hemisphere save such as are for their welfare. All that this country desires is to see the neighboring countries stable, orderly, and prosperous. Any country whose people conduct themselves well can count upon our hearty friendship. If a nation shows that it knows how to act with reasonable efficiency and decency in social and political matters, if it keeps order and pays its obligations, it need fear no interference from the United States. Chronic wrongdoing, or an impotence which results in a general loosening of the ties of civilized society, may in America, as elsewhere, ultimately require intervention by some civilized nation, and in the Western Hemisphere the adher-

---

[72] Prov. 4.18-19.
[73] The passage quoted here is often referred to as Roosevelt's Corollary to the Monroe Doctrine (1823), which defined the U.S. policy of opposition to outside political interference in the Americas.

ence of the United States to the Monroe Doctrine may force the United States, however reluctantly, in flagrant cases of such wrongdoing or impotence, to the exercise of an international police power. If every country washed by the Caribbean Sea would show the progress in stable and just civilization which with the aid of the Platt amendment[74] Cuba has shown since our troops left the island, and which so many of the republics in both Americas are constantly and brilliantly showing, all question of interference by this Nation with their affairs would be at an end. Our interests and those of our southern neighbors are in reality identical. They have great natural riches, and if within their borders the reign of law and justice obtains, prosperity is sure to come to them. While they thus obey the primary laws of civilized society they may rest assured that they will be treated by us in a spirit of cordial and helpful sympathy. We would interfere with them only in the last resort, and then only if it became evident that their inability or unwillingness to do justice at home and abroad had violated the rights of the United States or had invited foreign aggression to the detriment of the entire body of American nations. It is a mere truism to say that every nation, whether in America or anywhere else, which desires to maintain its freedom, its independence, must ultimately realize that the right of such independence can not be separated from the responsibility of making good use of it.

In asserting the Monroe Doctrine, in taking such steps as we have taken in regard to Cuba, Venezuela, and Panama, and in endeavoring to circumscribe the theater of war in the Far East, and to secure the open door in China, we have acted in our own interest as well as in the interest of humanity at large. There are, however, cases in which, while our own interests are not greatly involved, strong appeal is made to our sympathies. Ordinarily it is very much wiser and more useful for us to concern ourselves with striving for our own moral and material betterment here at home than to concern ourselves with trying to better the condition of things in other nations. We have plenty of sins of our own to war against, and under ordinary circumstances we can do more for the general uplifting of humanity by striving with heart and soul to put a stop to civic corruption, to brutal lawlessness and violent race prejudices here at home than by passing resolutions about wrongdoing elsewhere. Nevertheless there are occasional crimes committed on so vast a scale and of such peculiar horror as to make us doubt whether it is not our manifest duty to endeavor at least to show our disapproval of the deed and our sympathy with those who have suffered by it. The cases must be extreme in which such a course is justifiable. There must be no effort made to remove the mote from our brother's eye if we refuse to remove the beam from our own. But in extreme cases action may be justifiable and proper. What form the action shall take must depend upon the circumstances of the case; that is, upon the degree of the atrocity and upon our power to remedy it. The cases in which we could interfere by force of arms as we interfered to put a stop to intolerable conditions in Cuba are necessarily very few. [...]

Source: Theodore Roosevelt (1858-1919). "Fourth Annual Message, December 6, 1904." *A Compilation of the Messages and Papers of the Presidents, Prepared under the Direction of the Joint Committee on Printing, of the House and Senate, Pursuant to an Act of the Fifty-Second Congress of the United States.* 20 vols. New York: Bureau of National Literature, 1917, Vol. 16, 6923-6924.

---

[74] The Platt Amendments are part of the U.S. treaty with Cuba of May 22, 1903, in which the U.S. modified their former policy of non-intervention in the sovereignty of the government of the Island of Cuba (cf. the so-called Teller Amendment of the Resolutions of April 19, 1898). In Article III of the Platt Amendment the Government of Cuba "consents that the United States may exercise the right to intervene for the preservation of Cuban independence, the maintenance of a government adequate for the protection of life, property, and individual liberty [...]."

322. Theodore Roosevelt
The New Nationalism (1910)

We come here to-day to commemorate one of the epoch-making events of the long struggle for the rights of man – the long struggle for the uplift of humanity. Our country – this great republic – means nothing unless it means the triumph of a real democracy, the triumph of popular government, and, in the long run, of an economic system under which each man shall be guaranteed the opportunity to show the best that there is in him. That is why the history of America is now the central feature of the history of the world; for the world has set its face hopefully toward our democracy; and, O my fellow citizens, each one of you carries on your shoulders not only the burden of doing well for the sake of your own country, but the burden of doing well and of seeing that this nation does well for the sake of mankind.

There have been two great crises in our country's history: first, when it was formed, and then, again, when it was it was perpetuated; and, in the second of these great crises – in the time of stress and strain which culminated in the Civil War, on the outcome of which depended the justification of what had been done earlier, you men of the Grand Army, you men who fought through the Civil War, not only did you justify your generation, not only did you render life worth living for our generation, but you justified the wisdom of Washington and Washington's colleagues. [...]

[...] I care for the great deeds of the past chiefly as spurs to drive us onward in the present. I speak of the men of the past partly that they may be honored by our praise of them, but more that they may serve as examples for the future.

It was a heroic struggle; and, as is inevitable with all such struggles, it had also a dark and terrible side. Very much was done of good, and much also of evil; and, as was inevitable in such a period of revolution, often the same man did both good and evil. For our great good fortune as a nation, we, the people of the United States as a whole, can now afford to forget the evil, or, at least, to remember it without bitterness, and to fix our eyes with pride only on the good that was accomplished. Even in ordinary times there are very few of us who do not see the problems of life as through a glass, darkly; and when the glass is clouded by the murk of furious popular passion, the vision of the best and the bravest is dimmed. Looking back, we are all of us now able to do justice to the valor and the disinterestedness and the love of the right, as to each it was given to see the right, shown both by the men of the North and the men of the South in that contest which was finally decided by the attitude of the West. We can admire the heroic valor, the sincerity, the self-devotion shown alike by the men who wore the blue and the men who wore the gray;[75] and our sadness that such men should have had to fight one another is tempered by the glad knowledge that ever hereafter their descendants shall be found fighting side by side, struggling in peace as well as in war for the uplift of their common country, all alike resolute to raise to the highest pitch of honor and usefulness the nation to which they all belong. As for the veterans of the Grand Army of the Republic,[76] they deserve honor and recognition such as is paid to no other citizens of the republic; for to them the republic owes its all; for to them it owes its very existence. It is because of what you and

---

[75] Reference to the two contending Civil War armies, the army of the Union (blue) and of the Southern Confederation (gray).
[76] The Grand Army of the Republic or GAR was formed shortly after the Civil War by Benjamin F. Stephenson. It was the largest organization of Union veterans of the Civil War.

your comrades did in the dark years that we of to-day walk, each of us, head erect, and proud that we belong, not to one of a dozen little squabbling[77] contemptible commonwealths, but to the mightiest nation upon which the sun shines.

I do not speak of this struggle of the past merely from the historic standpoint. Our interest is primarily in the application to-day of the lessons taught by the contest of half a century ago. It is of little use for us to pay lip loyalty to the mighty men of the past unless we sincerely endeavor to apply to the problems of the present precisely the qualities which in other crises enabled the men of that day to meet those crises. It is half melancholy and half amusing to see the way in which well-meaning people gather to do honor to the men who, in company with John Brown,[78] and under the lead of Abraham Lincoln, faced and solved the great problems of the nineteenth century, while, at the same time, these same good people nervously shrink from, frantically denounce, those who are trying to meet the problems of the twentieth century in the spirit which was accountable for the successful resolution of the problems of Lincoln's time.

Of that generation of men to whom we owe so much, the man to whom we owe most, is of course, Lincoln. Part of our debt to him is because he forecast our present struggle and saw the way out. He said: –

> I hold that while man exists it is his duty to improve not only his own condition, but to assist in ameliorating mankind.

And again: –

> Labor is prior to, and independent of, capital. Capital is only the fruit of labor, and could never have existed if labor had not first existed. Labor is the superior of capital, and deserves much the higher consideration.

If that remark was original with me, I should be even more strongly denounced as a communist agitator than I shall be anyhow. It is Lincoln's. I am only quoting it; and that is one side; that is the side the capitalist should hear. Now, let the workingman hear his side.

> Capital has its rights, which are as worthy of protection as any other rights. ... Nor should this lead to a war upon the owners of property. Property is the fruit of labor; ... property is desirable; is a positive good in the world.

And then comes a thoroughly Lincolnlike sentence: –

> Let not him who is houseless pull down the house of another, but let him work diligently and build one for himself, thus by example assuring that his own shall be safe from violence when built.

It seems to me that, in these words, Lincoln took substantially the attitude that we ought to take; he showed the proper sense of proportion in his relative estimates of capital and labor, of human rights and property rights. Above all, in this speech, as in many others, he taught a lesson in wise kindliness and charity; an indispensable lesson to us of to-day. But this wise kindliness and charity never weakened his arm or numbed his heart. We cannot afford weakly to blind ourselves to the actual conflict which faces us to-day. The issue is joined, and we must fight or fail.

In every wise struggle for human betterment one of the main objects, and often the only object, has been to achieve in large measure equality of opportunity. In the struggle for this great end, nations rise from barbarism to civilization, and through it people press

---

[77] Quarrelling or wrangling.
[78] John Brown (1800-1859), American abolitionist who captured the US arsenal at Harper's Ferry as part of an effort to liberate Southern slaves.

forward from one stage of enlightenment to the next. One of the chief factors in progress is the destruction of special privilege. The essence of any struggle for healthy liberty has always been, and must always be, to take from some one man or class of men the right to enjoy power, or wealth, or position, or immunity, which has not been earned by service to his or their fellows. That is what you fought for in the Civil War, and that is what we strive for now. [...]

Practical equality of opportunity for all citizens, when we achieve it, will have two great results. First, every man will have a fair chance to make of himself all that in him lies; to reach the highest point to which his capacities, unassisted by special privilege of his own and unhampered by the special privilege of others, can carry him, and to get for himself and his family substantially what he has earned. Second, equality of opportunity means that the commonwealth will get from every citizen the highest service of which he is capable. No man who carries the burden of the special privileges of another can give to the commonwealth that service to which it is fairly entitled.

I stand for the square deal. But when I say that I am for the square deal, I mean not merely that I stand for fair play under the present rules of the game, but that I stand for having those rules changed so as to work for a more substantial equality of opportunity and of reward for equally good service. One word of warning, which, I think, is hardly necessary in Kansas. When I say I want a square deal for the poor man, I do not mean that I want a square deal for the man who remains poor because he has not got the energy to work for himself. If a man who has had a chance will not make good, then he has got to quit. And you men of the Grand Army, you want justice for the brave man who fought, and punishment for the coward who shirked his work. Is not that so?

Now, this means that our government, national and state, must be freed from the sinister influence or control of special interests. Exactly as the special interests of cotton and slavery threatened our political integrity before the Civil War, so now the great special business interests too often control and corrupt the men and methods of government for their own profit. We must drive the special interests out of politics. [...]

The true friend of property, the true conservative, is he who insists that property shall be the servant and not the master of the commonwealth; who insists that the creature of man's making shall be the servant and not the master of the man who made it. The citizens of the United States must effectively control the mighty commercial forces which they have themselves called into being. [...]

Nothing is more true than that excess of every kind is followed by reaction; a fact which should be pondered by reformer and reactionary alike. We are face to face with new conceptions of the relations of property to human welfare, chiefly because certain advocates of the rights of property as against the rights of men have been pushing their claims too far. The man who wrongly holds that every human right is secondary to his profit must now give way to the advocate of human welfare, who rightly maintains that every man holds his property subject to the general right of the community to regulate its use to whatever degree the public welfare may require it.

But I think we may go still further. The right to regulate the use of wealth in the public interest is universally admitted. Let us admit also the right to regulate the terms and conditions of labor, which is the chief element of wealth, directly in the interest of the common good. The fundamental thing to do for every man is to give him a chance to reach a place in which he will make the greatest possible contribution to the public welfare. Understand what I say there. Give him a chance, not push him up if he will not be pushed. Help any man who stumbles; if he lies down, it is a poor job to try to carry him; but if he is a worthy man, try your best to see that he gets a chance to show the worth that is in him. No man can be a good citizen unless he has a wage more than sufficient to cover the bare cost of living, and hours of labor short enough so that after his day's work is done he will have time and energy to bear his share in the management of the community, to help in carrying the general load. We keep countless men from being good citizens by the conditions of life with which we surround them. We need comprehensive workmen's compensation acts, both state and national laws to regulate child labor and work for women, and, especially, we need in our common schools not merely education in book learning, but also practical training for daily life and work. We need to enforce better sanitary conditions for our workers and to extend the use of safety appliances for our workers in industry and commerce, both within and between the states. Also, friends, in the interest of the workingman himself we need to set our faces like flint against mob violence just as against corporate greed; against violence and injustice and lawlessness by wage workers just as much as against lawless cunning and greed and selfish arrogance of employers. If I could ask but one thing of my fellow countrymen, my request would be that, whenever they go in for reform, they remember the two sides, and that they always exact justice from one side as much as from the other. I have small use for the public servant who can always see and denounce the corruption of the capitalist, but who cannot persuade himself, especially before election, to say a word about lawless mob violence. And I have equally small use for the man, be he a judge on the bench, or editor of a great paper, or wealthy and influential private citizen, who can see clearly enough and denounce the lawlessness of mob violence, but whose eyes are closed so that he is blind when the question is one of corruption in business on a gigantic scale. Also remember what I said about excess in reformer and reactionary alike. If the reactionary man, who thinks of nothing but the rights of property, could have his way, he would bring about a revolution; and one of my chief fears in connection with progress comes because I do not want to see our people, for lack of proper leadership, compelled to follow men whose intentions are excellent, but whose eyes are a little too wild to make it really safe to trust them. Here in Kansas there is one paper which habitually denounces me as the tool of Wall Street, and at the same time frantically repudiates the statement that I am a Socialist on the ground that that is an unwarranted slander of the Socialists. [...]

The object of government is the welfare of the people. The material progress and prosperity of a nation are desirable chiefly so far as they lead to the moral and material welfare of all good citizens. Just in proportion as the average man and woman are honest, capable of sound judgment and high ideals, active in public affairs, – but, first of all, sound in their home life, and the father and mother of healthy children whom they bring up well, – just so far, and no farther, we may count our civilization a success. [...] We must have the right kind of character – character that makes a man, first of all, a good man in the home, a good father, a good husband – that makes a man a good neighbor. You must have that, and, then, in addition, you must have the kind of law and the kind of administration of the law which will give to those qualities in the private citizen the best possible chance for development. The prime problem of our nation is to get the right type of good citizenship, and, to get it, we must have progress, and our public men must be genuinely progressive.

Source: Theodore Roosevelt (1858-1919). *The New Nationalism* [Speech at Osawatomie 31 August, 1910; with an introduction by Ernest Hamlin Abbott]. New York: Outlook, 1910, 3-13, 23-26, 31, 33.

ABBREVIATIONS

Old Testament

1 Chron.	1 Chronicles
2 Chron.	2 Chronicles
Dan.	Daniel
Deut.	Deuteronomy
Eccles.	Ecclesiastes
Exod.	Exodus
Ezek.	Ezekiel
Gen.	Genesis
Hab.	Habakkuk
Hag.	Haggai
Hos.	Hosea
Isa.	Isaiah
Jer.	Jeremiah
Jon.	Jonah
Josh.	Joshua
Judg.	Judges
Lev.	Leviticus
Mal.	Malachi
Mic.	Micah
Neh.	Nehemiah
Num.	Numbers
Obad.	Obadiah
Prov.	Proverbs
Ps.	Psalms
1 Sam.	1 Samuel
2 Sam.	2 Samuel

New Testament

Col.	Colossians
1 Cor.	1 Corinthians
2 Cor.	2 Corinthians
Eph.	Ephesians
Gal.	Galatians
Heb.	Hebrews
Jas.	James
Matt.	Matthew
1 Pet.	1 Peter
Rev.	Revelation (=Apocalypse)
Rom.	Romans
1 Thess.	1 Thessalonians
2 Thess.	2 Thessalonians
1 Tim.	1 Timothy
2 Tim.	2 Timothy

INDEX

Adams, Abigail
"Letter to John Adams" 483
Adams, John Quincy
"Inaugural Address" 354-356
Oration Delivered at Plymouth, An 345-349
Adams, Samuel
"Rights of Colonists, The" 279-280
Address of the People of South Carolina 624-626
Alcott, Amos Bronson
Doctrine and Discipline of Human Culture 464-466
Am I Not a Man and a Brother? 591-592
Anon.
"Female Influence" 494-499
"Influence of Woman" 514-515
"Letter to Mrs. Bradford" 556-557
"On Female Education" 493-494
"On Reading an Essay on Education" 482
"Oregon Territory" 379-381
"Pastoral Letter of the Massachusetts Congregationalist Clergy" 516
"Providence in American History" 405-407
"The Destiny of the Country" 400-404
"The Popular Movement" 397
"Woman" 523-525
Anti-Texas Meeting at Faneuil Hall! 385
Argyle, E. Malcolm
"Report from Arkansas" 644
Aspasio
"Anniversary Ode, for July 4, 1789" 315-316

Bancroft, George
"On the Progress of Civilization" 459-460
Barlow, Joel
Oration Delivered July 4, 1787, An 325-327
Vision of Columbus, The 255-257
Barnes, Albert
Inquiry into the Scriptural View of Slavery, An 580-583
Beecher, Catharine E.
"Christian Family, The" 539-541
Improvements in Education 504-505
Benezet, Anthony
Thoughts on the Nature of War 277-278
Benton, Thomas Hart
Speech on the Oregon Question 398-399

Berkeley, George
"On the Prospect of Planting Arts and Learning in America" 32
Beveridge, Albert
"March of the Flag, The" 710-713
Bowen, Francis
"Transcendentalism" 442-443
Brace, Charles L.
Dangerous Classes of New York, The 659-661
Bradford, William
"Of Boston in New-England" 116-117
"Of Plymouth Plantation" 49-50, 109-115
"Word to New-Eingland, A" 118
Bradstreet, Anne
"Epitaph" 478
"Flesh and the Spirit, The" 70-72
"Prologue, The" 478-480
"To My Dear Children" 77-79
Brownson, Orestes A.
"Cousin's Philosophy" 433-437
"Laboring Classes, The" 462-464
Bryan, William Jennings
"Imperialism" 713-715
Buel, James W.
"Rich, The" 679-680
Byrd II, William
"Letter to John Perceval, Earl of Egmont" 557

Calhoun, John C.
"Slavery a Positive Good" 586-587
Carleill, Christopher
"Concerning a Voyage" 19-20
Carnegie, Andrew
"Wealth" 692-695
Cass, Lewis
"Policy and Practice of the United States in Their Treatment of the Indians, The" 370-374
Channing, William Ellery
"Letter on the Annexation of Texas, A" 384-385
"Likeness to God" 431-433
Chauncy, Charles
Enthusiasm Described and Cautioned Against 228-232
Cheever, George B.
God's Hand in America 579-580
Chinese Exclusion Act 702
Cist, Lewis Jacob
"Woman's Sphere" 512-514

Cole, Nathan
  "Spiritual Travels of Nathan Cole, The" 221-223
Columbus, Christopher
  Journal of the First Voyage to America 9-10
Constitution of the Knights of Labor 681-682
Cotton, John
  Churches Resurrection, The 163-164
  Exposition upon the Thirteenth Chapter of the Revelation, An 166-168
  Gods Promise to His Plantation 25-27
Cranch, Christopher Pearse
  "Correspondences" 428-429
Crapsey, Edward
  "Prostitution" 661-664
Crèvecœur, St. John De
  Letters from an American Farmer 564-569
Cushman, Robert
  "On the Lawfulnesse of Removing out of England into the Parts of America" 27-29

Davis, Jefferson
  "First Inaugural Address" 626-628
Declaration of Sentiments, Seneca Falls Convention 531-534
Dew, Thomas R.
  "Characteristic Differences between the Sexes" 505-506
Dickinson, John
  New Song, A 275-276
Documents of the American Colonization Society 569-572
Douglass, Frederick
  "Future of the Colored Race, The" 643-644
  "What the Black Man Wants" 635-637
  What to the Slave Is the Fourth of July? 602-608
Drayton, Michael
  "To the Virginian Voyage" 20-21
Duché, Jacob
  "American Vine, The" 294-296
Dwight, Timothy
  America 190-191

Edwards, Jonathan
  "Account of His Conversion, An" 217-221
  Faithful Narrative, A 216-217
  Present Revival of Religion in New-England, The 184-185
  Sinners in the Hands of an Angry God 211-216
Emerson, Ralph Waldo
  "American Scholar, The" 444-445
  "Divinity School Address" 446-447
  "Life and Letters in New England" 472-473
  Nature 440-442
  "*Rhodora, The*" 461
  "Two Rivers" 427-428
  "Young American, The" 461
Emmons, Nathanael
  "God Never Forsakes His People" 332-338
Estes, Matthew
  Defence of Negro Slavery, A 588-590
Evarts, William M.
  "Oration" 652-654
Exhortation to Young and Old to Be Cautious of Small Crime 99

Fern, Fanny
  "Chapter on Literary Women, A" 536-537
Fessenden, Thomas Green
  "Almighty Power: An Ode" 343-344
  "Ode Sung July 4, 1798" 328-330
Fiske, John
  "Manifest Destiny" 413-414
Fitzhugh, George
  "Negro Slavery" 593-595
Franklin, Benjamin
  Autobiography, The 240-252
  "Letter to Ezra Stiles" 236
  "Rules by Which a Great Empire May Be Reduced to a Small One" 281-282
  "Way to Wealth, The" 237-239
Freneau, Philip
  "Indian Convert, The" 58-59
  "On the Emigration to America and Peopling the Western Country" 201-202
  On the Rising Glory of America 186-190
  "On the Universality of the God of Nature" 236-237
Fuller, Margaret
  Summer on the Lakes 453-458
  Women in the 19th Century 526-531

Garnet, Henry Highland
  "Address to the Slaves of the United States of America" 595-599
Garrison, William Lloyd
  "Address to the Slaves of the United States" 600-602
  No Compromise with Slavery 609-611
  "Truisms" 577-578
  "Universal Emancipation" 599-600
George, Henry
  Progress and Poverty 699-674
Gilpin, William
  "Manifest Destiny" 396
Goodwin, George
  Automachia, or The Self-Conflict of a Christian 67-69
Grady, Henry W.
  "New South, The" 656-659

Grand, Sarah
  "New Aspect of the Woman Question, The" 541-542
Grayson, William J.
  Hireling and the Slave, The 614-615
Grimké, Angelina Emily
  Appeal to the Christian Women of the South 583-585
  Letters to Catherine E. Beecher 520-523
Grimké, Sarah Moore
  "Province of Woman" 517-518
  "Social Intercourse of the Sexes" 519

Hakluyt the Younger, Richard
  "On Westerne Discoveries" 10-12
Hancock, John
  Oration, An 284-286
Hariot, Thomas
  Briefe and True Report 16-18
Hastings, Lansford W.
  Emigrants' Guide to Oregon and California 382
Hawthorne, Nathaniel
  Scarlet Letter, The 93-94
Hayes, Edward
  "Concerning a Voyage" 19-20
  "Report of the Voyage and Successe Thereof, A" 12-14
Higginson, Francis
  New-Englands Plantation 29-30
Higginson, John
  Cause of God and His People in New-England, The 135-136
Hooker, Thomas
  Application of Redemption, The 79-81
Hopkins, Samuel
  Treatise on the Millennium, A 195-199
Humphrey, Heman
  Domestic Education 510-511
Humphreys, David
  Future Glory of the United States of America, The 202-204

Illustrations see below, page 728
Irving, Washington
  "Philip of Pokanoket" 59-62, 93

Jackson, Andrew
  "Second Annual Message" 374-376
Jefferson, Thomas
  Declaration of Independence, The 303-304
  "Inauguration Address" 338-340
  Notes on the State of Virginia 558-561
  Summary View of the Rights of British America, A 288-290

Las Casas, Bartholomew de
  "Destruction of the Indes" 41-43
Lazarus, Emma
  "New Colossus, The" 702
Lease, Mary Elizabeth
  "Monopoly Is the Master" 696
Leeke, Rebecca L.
  "New Lady, The" 547-548
Legaré, Hugh Swinton
  Oration, Delivered on the Fourth of July, 1823, An 351-353
Lincoln, Abraham
  Emancipation Proclamation 632-633
  "First Inaugural Address" 628-631
  "Second Inaugural Address" 634-635
Linn, William
  Blessings of America, The 362-364
Little, E., Mrs.
  "What Are the Rights of Woman?" 531
Locke, John
  Essay on Civil Government, An 262-264

MacCorrie, John Paul
  "War of the Sexes, The" 548-550
Mandeville, John
  Mandeville's Travels 36
Marshall, John
  "Cherokee Nation v. Georgia" 377-378
Mather, Cotton
  Bonifacius 252-253
  Christian in His Personal Calling, A 94-97
  "Confession of Faith, A" 81-87
  "General Introduction," *Magnalia Christi Americana* 147-150
  "Letter to John Richards" 150-152
  "Life of Sir William Phips, The" 155-158
  "Life of the Renowned John Eliot, The" 52-55
  "Nehemias Americanus: Life of John Winthrop" 123-127
  "Troubles of the Churches of New-England" 55-58
  "Venisti tandem? Or Discoveries of America" 182-183
Mather, Increase
  Cases of Conscience Concerning Evil Spirits 152-155
  Day of Trouble is Near, The 170-174
  Doctrine of Divine Providence, The 140-141
  Mystery of Israel's Salvation, The 168-169
Mather, Samuel
  Figures or Types of the Old Testament, The 87-89

Mayhew, Jonathan
Discourse Concerning Unlimited Submission and Non-Resistance to the Higher Powers, A 264-268
Mede, Joseph
"Coniecture Concerning *Gog* and *Magog*, A" 164-166
Melville, Herman
White-Jacket 404-405
Montaigne, Michel Eyquem de
"Of the Caniballes" 38-40
Moore, Milcah Martha [Hill]
"Female Patriots, The" 481
Morse, Jedidiah
American Geography 362
Most, John
Beast of Property, They 685-687
Murray, Judith Sargent
"On the Equality of the Sexes" 489-492
"Thoughts upon Self-Complacency" 487-489

Norris, Frank
"Frontier Gone at Last, The" 420-422
Noyes, Nicholas
New-Englands Duty 178-182

O'Rell, Max
"Petticoat Government" 545-546
O'Sullivan, John L.
"Annexation" 389-390
"Great Nation of Futurity, The" 386-387
"True Title, The" 397-398
Oakes, Urian
Soveraign Efficacy of Divine Providence, The 138-140
Otis, James
Rights of the British Colonies Asserted and Proved, The 268-270
Ouida
"New Woman, The" 543-545
Owen, Robert
First Discourse on a New System of Society 466-469

Pain, Philip
Daily Meditations 69-70
Paine, Charles
Oration, Pronounced July 4, 1801, An 365-367
Paine, Thomas
Common Sense 298-303
"Of the Religion of Deism" 234-236
"Predestination" 233
Parker, Theodore
"Letter to Francis Jackson" 615-618

Sermon of the Public Function of Woman, A 534-537
Payne, John Howard
"Ode on American Independence" 344-346
Peale, Rembrandt
"Beauties of Creation, The" 426
Peckham, Sir George
True Reporte of the Late Discoveries, A 14-16
Percival, James Gates
Ode. For the 50th Anniversary of Independence, July 4, 1826" 356-357
Philoleutherus
Constitutional Courant, The 270-271
Philo Patriæ
Constitutional Courant, The 272-274
Polk, James K.
"Inaugural Address" 391-394
Pond, John[?]
"Letter to William Pond March 15, 1630/1" 115-116
"Preamble to the Massachusetts Articles of War" 293-294
"Proclamation by the Great and General Court of the Colony of Massachusetts Bay, January 23, 1776" 297-298

Ramsay, David
"On the Advantages of American Independence" 306-308
Reed, Sampson
Observations on the Growth of the Mind 429-431
Resolutions of the Stamp Act Congress, October 19, 1765 274-275
Richards, George
"Anniversary Ode on American Independence" 199-200
Riis, Jacob A.
How the Other Half Lives 667-669
Ripley, George
"Advertisement" and "Introductory Notice" 470-472
Discourses on the Philosophy of Religion 437-440
"Letter to Ralph Waldo Emerson" 469-470
Roosevelt, Theodore
"Fourth Annual Message" 715-716
New Nationalism, The 717-720
Rowlandson, Mary
Soveraignty & Goodness of God, The 50-52, 142-147
Rush, Benjamin
"Thoughts upon Education Proper in a Republic" 322-324
Thoughts upon Female Education 483-487

Saunders, Frederick
Progress and Prospects of America, The 700-701
Schurz, Carl
"Manifest Destiny" 706-708
Sewall, Samuel
Little before Break-a-Day, A 31-32
Phænomena Quædam Apocalyptica 175-178
Shepard, Thomas
"Autobiography, The" 74-77
Sherwood, Samuel
Church's Flight into the Wilderness, The 191-195
Sigourney, Lydia
Letters to Mothers 509-510
Smith, John
Description of New England, A 23-24
Spies, August
"Speech at Haymarket Trial" 688-691
Stearns, Jonathan F.
Female Influence 506-509
Stewart, T. McCants
"Popular Discontent" 697-699
Stone, Lucy
"Marriage of Lucy Stone Under Protest, The" 537-538
Stowe, Harriet Beecher
"Christian Family, The" 539-540
Strong, Josiah
"Anglo-Saxon and the World's Future, The" 709-710
"Perils – Immigration" 703-705
"Perils – The City" 664-666
Sumner, William Graham
"Challenge of Facts, The" 675-679

Taylor, Edward
"Meditation 26" 73-74
Tennent, Gilbert
Solemn Warning to the Secure World, A 210
Thoreau, Henry David
Walden 448-453
"Walking" 369-370
Thorpe, T. Banks
Progress and Prospects of America, The 699-701
Tillam, Thomas
"Uppon the First Sight of New-England" 30-31
"To the Workingmen of America" 682-685
Trollope, Frances
Domestic Manners of the Americans 225-227

Turner, Frederick Jackson
"Significance of the Frontier, The" 414-418
"West and American Ideals, The" 419-420
Twain, Mark
"Late Benjamin Franklin, The" 254

Unanimous Declaration of Independence, by the Delegates of the People of Texas 382-384

Vespucci, Amerigo
Letter to Piero Soderini 36-37

Walker, David
Appeal to the Coloured Citizens of the World 572-577
Warren, John
Oration, Delivered July 4th, 1783, An 318-322
Washington, Booker T.
"Atlanta Exposition Address" 645-647
Webster, Daniel
"Constitution and the Union Speech" 622-624
Oration, Pronounced the 4th Day of July, 1800, An 330-331
Wheatley, Phillis
"On Being Brought from Africa to America" 556
Whitaker, Alexander
Good Newes from Virginia 21-23
Whitman, Walt
"Passage to India" 408-409
Wigglesworth, Michael
"God's Controversy with New-England" 128-136
Willard, Emma
Plan for Female Education, A 499-502
Williams, Samuel
Discourse on the Love of Our Country 290-293
Winthrop, John
"Modell of Christian Charity, A" 118-121
Journal 480
"Speech on Liberty" 122-123
Winthrop, Robert Charles
"New England Society Address" 387-389
Wiswall, Ichabod
Judicious Observation of That Dreadful Comet, A 90-92
Witherspoon, John
Dominion of Providence over the Passions of Men 304-306

Woodworth, Samuel
    "Columbia, the Pride of the World" 367-368
Woolman, John
    Considerations on Keeping Negroes 561-564

Illustrations

Altar of Gallic Despotism 341
"America Triumphant – Britannia in Distress" 309
Age of Iron: Man as He Expects to Be 539
Apianus, Petrus
    "Charta Cosmographica" 6

Barralet, John James
    Apotheosis of Washington 317
Black and White Slaves: England 612
Black and White Slaves: America 613
Blazing Stars, Messengers of God's Wrath 89
"Bosses of the Senate" 691
Bostonians Paying the Excise-man 287
Bünting, Heinrich
    "Die gantze Welt in ein Kleberblat" 8

California: Cornucopia of the World 368
Caution!! Colored People of Boston 592
"Commercial Vampire" 687

Dogwood Tree 648

"Earth Must Burn / and Christ Return, The" 205

Franklin, Benjamin
    "Join or Die" 268
    Magna Britannia: Her Colonies Reduc'd 278
Freedman's Bureau! 639
Froschauer, Johann
    Dise figur anzaigt uns das volck und insel 37

Galle, Philippe
    "America" 45
Gast, John
    "American Progress" 410
"Great Labor Question from a Southern Point of View" 641

Hoeye, François van den
    "America" 18
Hulsius, Levinus
    Kurtze Wunderbare Beschreibung 46

Keep within Your Compass 503

Ladder of Fortune 100
"Land of Liberty" 395
Leslie's Illustrated Historical Register of the Centennial Exposition 655

Mad Tom in Rage 342
Magic Washer – The Chinese Must Go 705
Massachusetts Spy, The 279
Missouri Is Free 369

Nast, Thomas
    "Colored Rule in a Reconstructed (?) State" 642
    "He Wants a Change, Too" 638
    "Uncle Sam's Thanksgiving Dinner" 701
New-England Primer 98
"New Woman" 551

Ortelius, Abraham
    "Theatrum Orbis Terrarum" 7

Palmer, Fanny F.
    Across the Continent 412
Passe the Elder, Crispijn van de
    "America" 47
"Promise of the Declaration of Independence Fulfilled" 633

Raleigh, Walter
    History of the World 108
Revere, Paul
    Able Doctor, The 288
    Bloody Massacre in Boston, The 283
Rider, Alexander
    Camp Meeting 224

Sadeler the Elder, Jan
    "America" 44
Schedel, Hartmann
    Buch der Chroniken 4
Straet, Jan van der
    "Discovery of America" 48

Tanner, Benjamin
    America Guided by Wisdom 350
Thulstrup, Thure de
    "Anarchist Riot in Chicago, The" 681
To Be Sold 556
Tree of Life – The Christian 101
Two Platforms 640
"Typus Cosmographicus Universalis" 5

"Wheel of Fortune" 107
"While Commerce Spreads Her Canvas O'er the Main" 314